Handbook of Personality at Work

Personality has emerged as a key factor when trying to understand why people think, feel, and behave the way they do at work. Recent research has linked personality to important aspects of work such as job performance, employee attitudes, leadership, teamwork, stress, and turnover. This handbook brings together into a single volume the diverse areas of work psychology where personality constructs have been applied and investigated, providing expert review and analysis based on the latest advances in the field.

Neil D. Christiansen, Ph.D., is a professor of psychology at Central Michigan University where he teaches courses in personnel psychology, personality psychology, and structural equation modeling. His research interests focus on advancing our understanding of the relationship between personality and work behavior.

Robert P. Tett, Ph.D., is an associate professor of industrial/organizational psychology and director of the I/O program at the University of Tulsa where he teaches courses in I/O psychology, personnel selection, leadership, and statistics. His research interests lie primarily in personality testing in work settings and in managerial and leadership competence.

Series in Applied Psychology

Jeanette N. Cleveland, Colorado State University
Kevin R. Murphy, Landy Litigation and Colorado State University

Series Editors

Edwin A. Fleishman, Founding series editor (1987–2010)

Winfred Arthur, Jr., Eric Day, Winston Bennett, Jr., and Antoinette Portrey
Individual and Team Skill Decay: The Science and Implications for Practice

Gregory Bedny and David Meister
The Russian Theory of Activity: Current Applications to Design and Learning

Winston Bennett, David Woehr, and Charles Lance
Performance Measurement: Current Perspectives and Future Challenges

Michael T. Brannick, Eduardo Salas, and Carolyn Prince
Team Performance Assessment and Measurement: Theory, Research, and Applications

Neil D. Christiansen and Robert P. Tett
Handbook of Personality at Work

Jeanette N. Cleveland, Margaret Stockdale, and Kevin R. Murphy
Women and Men in Organizations: Sex and Gender Issues at Work

Aaron Cohen
Multiple Commitments in the Workplace: An Integrative Approach

Russell Cropanzano
Justice in the Workplace: Approaching Fairness in Human Resource Management, Volume 1

Russell Cropanzano
Justice in the Workplace: From Theory to Practice, Volume 2

David V. Day, Stephen Zaccaro, and Stanley M. Halpin
Leader Development for Transforming Organizations: Growing Leaders for Tomorrow's Teams and Organizations

Stewart I. Donaldson, Mihaly Csikszentmihalyi, and Jeanne Nakamura
Applied Positive Psychology: Improving Everyday Life, Health, Schools, Work, and Safety

James E. Driskell and Eduardo Salas
Stress and Human Performance

Sidney A. Fine and Steven F. Cronshaw
Functional Job Analysis: A Foundation for Human Resources Management

Sidney A. Fine and Maury Getkate
Benchmark Tasks for Job Analysis: A Guide for Functional Job Analysis (FJA) Scales

J. Kevin Ford, Steve W. J. Kozlowski, Kurt Kraiger, Eduardo Salas, and Mark S. Teachout
Improving Training Effectiveness in Work Organizations

Jerald Greenberg
Insidious Workplace Behavior

Jerald Greenberg
Organizational Behavior: The State of the Science, Second Edition

Edwin Hollander
Inclusive Leadership: The Essential Leader–Follower Relationship

Ann Hergatt Huffman and Stephanie R. Klein
Green Organizations: Driving Change with I-O Psychology

Jack Kitaeff
Handbook of Police Psychology

Uwe E. Kleinbeck, Hans-Henning Quast, Henk Thierry, and Hartmut Häcker
Work Motivation

Laura L. Koppes
Historical Perspectives in Industrial and Organizational Psychology

Ellen Kossek and Susan Lambert
Work and Life Integration: Organizational, Cultural, and Individual Perspectives

Martin I. Kurke and Ellen M. Scrivner
Police Psychology into the 21st Century

Joel Lefkowitz
Ethics and Values in Industrial and Organizational Psychology

Manuel London
How People Evaluate Others in Organizations

Manuel London
Job Feedback: Giving, Seeking, and Using Feedback for Performance Improvement, Second Edition

Manuel London
Leadership Development: Paths to Self-Insight and Professional Growth

Robert F. Morrison and Jerome Adams
Contemporary Career Development Issues

Michael D. Mumford
Pathways to Outstanding Leadership: A Comparative Analysis of Charismatic, Ideological, and Pragmatic Leaders

Michael D. Mumford, Garnett Stokes, and William A. Owens
Patterns of Life History: The Ecology of Human Individuality

Kevin Murphy
A Critique of Emotional Intelligence: What Are the Problems and How Can They Be Fixed?

Kevin R. Murphy
Validity Generalization: A Critical Review

Kevin R. Murphy and Frank E. Saal
Psychology in Organizations: Integrating Science and Practice

Susan E. Murphy and Rebecca J. Reichard
Early Development and Leadership: Building the Next Generation of Leaders

Susan E. Murphy and Ronald E. Riggio
The Future of Leadership Development

Margaret A. Neal and Leslie Brett Hammer
Working Couples Caring for Children and Aging Parents: Effects on Work and Well-Being

Robert E. Ployhart, Benjamin Schneider, and Neal Schmitt
Staffing Organizations: Contemporary Practice and Theory, Third Edition

Steven A.Y. Poelmans
Work and Family: An International Research Perspective

Erich P. Prien, Jeffery S. Schippmann, and Kristin O. Prien
Individual Assessment: As Practiced in Industry and Consulting

Robert D. Pritchard, Sallie J. Weaver, and Elissa L. Ashwood
Evidence-Based Productivity Improvement: A Practical Guide to the Productivity Measurement and Enhancement System

Ned Rosen
Teamwork and the Bottom Line: Groups Make a Difference

Eduardo Salas, Stephen M. Fiore, and Michael P. Letsky
Theories of Team Cognition: Cross-Disciplinary Perspectives

Heinz Schuler, James L. Farr, and Mike Smith
Personnel Selection and Assessment: Individual and Organizational Perspectives

John W. Senders and Neville P. Moray
Human Error: Cause, Prediction, and Reduction

Lynn Shore, Jacqueline Coyle-Shapiro, and Lois E. Tetrick
The Employee–Organization Relationship: Applications for the 21st Century

Kenneth S. Shultz and Gary A. Adams
Aging and Work in the 21st Century

Frank J. Smith
Organizational Surveys: The Diagnosis and Betterment of Organizations Through Their Members

Dianna Stone and Eugene F. Stone-Romero
The Influence of Culture on Human Resource Processes and Practices

Kecia M. Thomas
Diversity Resistance in Organizations

George C. Thornton III and Rose Mueller-Hanson
Developing Organizational Simulations: A Guide for Practitioners and Students

George C. Thornton III and Deborah Rupp
Assessment Centers in Human Resource Management: Strategies for Prediction, Diagnosis, and Development

Yoav Vardi and Ely Weitz
Misbehavior in Organizations: Theory, Research, and Management

Patricia Voydanoff
Work, Family, and Community

Mo Wang, Deborah A. Olson, and Kenneth S. Shultz
Mid and Late Career Issues: An Integrative Perspective

Mark A. Wilson, Winston Bennett, Shanan G. Gibson, and George M. Alliger
The Handbook of Work Analysis: Methods, Systems, Applications and Science of Work Measurement in Organizations

Handbook of Personality at Work

Edited by
Neil D. Christiansen
Robert P. Tett

Routledge
Taylor & Francis Group
LONDON AND NEW YORK

First published 2013 by Routledge

2 Park Square, Milton Park, Abingdon, Oxfordshire OX14 4RN
52 Vanderbilt Avenue, New York, NY 10017

Routledge is an imprint of the Taylor & Francis Group, an informa business

First issued in paperback 2019

Library of Congress Cataloging-in-Publication Data
A catalog record has been requested.

ISBN: 978-1-84872-942-1 (hbk)
ISBN: 978-0-367-86624-2 (pbk)

Typeset in Bembo
by Book Now Ltd, London

Contents

List of Tables

List of Figures

Series Foreword

Jeanette N. Cleveland
Colorado State University

Kevin R. Murphy
Landy Litigation and Colorado State University

Series Editors

The goal of the Applied Psychology Series is to create books that exemplify the use of scientific research, theory, and findings to help solve real problems in organizations and society. Christiansen and Tett's *Handbook of Personality at Work* sits solidly within this tradition for concern with both solid science and real-world relevance.

The study of personality and its relationships with work has a long and checkered history. In the 1970s and 1980s, it was accepted wisdom that the study of personality had little to offer for understanding behavior in the workplace. Starting in the early 1990s, a series of influential meta-analyses reestablished interest in this area of research. In recent years, the pendulum seems to be swinging back toward a stance of skepticism. Christiansen and Tett have done a masterful job pulling together leading researchers in the field and documenting the current state of research and theory in the area of personality in the workplace.

The first section of this book reviews current theory and thinking in the area of personality. It addresses advances in the conceptualization of what personality means, how work situations activate personality traits and the complex relationships between personality and performance. The second section of this book represents a wide-ranging review of personality assessment, covering topics ranging from personality testing to assessment centers, from faking to understanding competing perspectives on the personality traits individuals exhibit. The third section covers the applications of personality research, measures, and theory in the workplace. Topics covered range from legal issues to validation studies, and it includes coverage of the relationship between personality and stress, job performance, and team behavior. The final section of this volume lays out challenges for the future and the way research and theory in this vital area is rising to those challenges.

The *Handbook of Personality at Work* meets a very important set of needs, documenting what has been done in this area, how theory relates to practice, how measures work or fail to work, and how organizations can use information about the personalities of job applicants and incumbents to improve their efficiency and viability in a complex and evolving workplace. We are extremely happy to add the *Handbook of Personality at Work* to the Applied Psychology Series.

Foreword

Paul R. Sackett

One of the first papers I tried to publish in the beginning of my career in the late 1970s dealt in part with paper-and-pencil tests of a personality attribute labeled "honesty." Reviewers were skeptical, with one noting that it was well known that personality characteristics were ineffective as predictors of behavior at work. That skepticism toward personality was widespread at the time, due to critiques within the field of Industrial and Organizational Psychology (e.g., Guion & Gottier's [1965] oft-cited conclusion that "it is difficult . . . to advocate, with a clear conscience, the use of personality measures in most situations as a basis for making employment decisions about people" [p. 160]) and external to the field (e.g., strong advocacy from social psychologists such as Walter Mischel [1968] of the role situational factors in driving behavior).

Fortunately for me, the paper was eventually accepted for publication (Sackett & Decker, 1979). But papers on the topic were uncommon. I pulled old issues of *The Industrial–Organizational Psychologist* (TIP) off my bookshelf and reviewed the program from the annual convention for the years 1977–1979. The program averaged one presentation on a personality-related topic per year. In contrast, the online searchable program for the 2012 Society for Industrial and Organizational Psychology conference lists 84 matches for the search term "personality." While the conference is much bigger today than it was in the 1970s, this nonetheless reflects a dramatic change of emphasis.

Several factors contributed to the resurgence of interest in the study of personality in organizational settings. First, marked advances were made in the person versus situation debate, with convergence on a person-by-situational interaction approach. Of course, the situation matters (even the most talkative are generally quiet during the Sunday sermon), but a key research finding is that when one aggregates over multiple opportunities to observe behavior, stable patterns of behavior emerge, and the influence of personality characteristics becomes apparent. Second, the emergence of the Five-Factor Model (i.e., Big Five) of personality replaced the abundance of personality trait labels with a common vocabulary. Third, the development of meta-analytic methods for cumulating research findings across studies aided in organizing what we know about relationships between personality and a wide variety of work behaviors.

These last two factors proved a perfect complement. Seemingly diverse studies using test-specific trait labels could be reorganized in the Big Five framework and integrated using meta-analytic techniques. The watershed moment was the Barrick and Mount (1991) meta-analysis of Big Five–job performance relationships. It is by a large margin the most cited paper ever published in *Personnel Psychology*.

This handbook is a splendid manifestation of the resurgence of interest in the study of personality in organizational settings over the last two decades. It examines the role of personality in a wide range of workplace topics, including selection, training, vocational choice, job attitudes, teamwork, leadership, and occupational stress. It offers thoughtful treatments of issues such as the value of focusing on personality as one's inner sense of self (identity) versus personality as seen by others (reputation), the reliance on differing sources of information (e.g., self-report, other-report, behavior sampling), and the role of faking. It presents a range of theoretical perspectives on personality. I have enjoyed the opportunity to immerse myself in this broad and rich set of chapters and trust you will as well.

References

Barrick, M. R., & Mount, M. K. (1991). The Big Five personality dimensions and job performance: A meta-analysis. *Personnel Psychology, 44*, 1–26.

Guion, R. M., & Gottier, R. F. (1965). Validity of personality measures in personnel selection. *Personnel Psychology, 18*, 135–164.

Mischel, W. (1968). *Personality and assessment*. Hoboken, NJ: John Wiley & Sons.

Sackett, P. R., & Decker, P. J. (1979). The detection of deception in the employment context: A review and critical analysis. *Personnel Psychology, 32*, 487–506.

Preface

Personality has emerged as a key factor when trying to understand why people think, feel, and behave the way they do at work. Research has linked personality to many important aspects of work, including job performance, employee attitudes, stress, training, motivation, leadership, and teamwork. This handbook brings together into a single volume the diverse areas of work psychology where personality constructs have been applied and investigated, providing expert review and analysis based on the latest advances in the field.

The role of personality in understanding work behavior has entered a renaissance of renewed discovery and theoretical advancement. Beyond simply supporting the use of personality tests in organizations, recent research offers clues to substantial gains that can be realized from using personality to explain valued criteria. To take advantage of such predictive potential, a better understanding is needed of the conditions in the workplace where personality will be an important determinant of behavior, as well as the associated processes involving an array of dispositional, situational, motivational, attitudinal, and ability-based constructs. In light of such complexities and the growing appreciation for personality in work settings, the time is ripe to take stock of what is known and consider where future research is likely to yield the highest dividends.

This handbook is divided into three main sections, followed by a few critical concluding chapters. The main sections are (1) Foundations and Theoretical Perspectives, (2) Assessment of Personality at Work, and (3) Applications of Personality to the Psychology of Work. Embedded in each of the primary chapters is a "Practitioner's Window," highlighting the most salient contributions toward the practice of Industrial–Organizational Psychology. Taken together, the chapters offer clear foundations for programmatic research, theory development, and evidence-based practice based on the role of personality at work. In addition to being a useful reference for researchers and practitioners, this volume is well suited as a text for graduate-level courses in applied psychology and human resource management.

Acknowledgments

Thanks to my family, students, colleagues, and friends who have supported my "hobby research" over the years. A special thank you to all of my teachers and professors, without whom I would not be half the person that I am today and this handbook might not exist. I am indebted to Andrew Speer for his editorial assistance that went above and beyond the call of duty. Finally, I am grateful to my wife for her unwavering belief in me even in tough times; she is just awesome like that.

– Neil D. Christiansen

A lot of people assisted in bringing this book to fruition. Especially helpful were the 16 graduate students in my Spring 2012 course on Personality at Work, who, working in pairs, debated the pros and cons of 23 of this handbook's chapters (sometimes with the chapter authors in attendance). Their astute (and sometimes fearless) observations helped formulate my guidance to authors in revising their chapters. The 16 students are, in alphabetical order, Mack Ayer, Cameron Brown, Laura Browne, Andre Cooks, Jonathan Davis, Alex Jackson, Drew Kropff, Satin Martin, Brian Miller, Lu Najselova, Courtney Nelson, Katie Packell, Kelsey Parker, Jacob Romaine, Dan Simonet, and Ben Walser. I will always remember that class and especially the professionalism and objectivity shown by those students in making good chapters better. I must also thank my family for tolerating missed evenings and weekends at home to allow time for me to work on this project and for grounding my otherwise largely academic existence.

– Robert P. Tett

About the Editors

Neil D. Christiansen, Ph.D., is a professor of psychology at Central Michigan University where he teaches courses in personnel psychology, personality psychology, and structural equation modeling. He received his Ph.D. in social and organizational psychology in 1997 from Northern Illinois University. His research interests focus on advancing our understanding of the relationship between personality and work behavior. His research has concentrated on issues involving the assessment of personality in the workplace (including the validity of personality tests, applicant faking of personality inventories, and alternative methods of assessing personality), the interaction of personality and work situations as determinants of work behavior, and the accuracy of personality judgments made in organizations. He has published his research in journals such as *Journal of Applied Psychology*, *Personnel Psychology*, *Journal of Organizational Behavior*, *Human Performance*, *International Journal of Selection and Assessment*, *Educational and Psychological Measurement*, and *Journal of Applied Social Psychology*. Outside of work, he invests his time as the father of two sons, by playing and developing board games, and by throwing the occasional round of disc golf.

Robert P. Tett, Ph.D., is an associate professor of industrial/organizational psychology and director of the I/O program at the University of Tulsa where he teaches courses in I/O psychology, personnel selection, leadership, and statistics. He received his Ph.D. in industrial/organizational psychology in 1995 from the University of Western Ontario under the mentorship of Doug Jackson. His research interests lie primarily in personality testing in work settings and in managerial and leadership competence. More specific areas of interest include conditions affecting personality trait expression and its value in work settings, the use of general versus narrow personality measures, and the nature and measurement of self-reported emotional intelligence and its outcomes. He has published in peer-reviewed outlets including *Journal of Applied Psychology*, *Journal of Organizational Behavior*, *Personnel Psychology*, *Human Performance*, *Journal of Personality*, *Personality and Social Psychology Bulletin*, and *Personality and Individual Differences*. He is a devoted father of three, dabbles at the piano, and plays ice hockey whenever he can find the time.

About the Contributors

Neil Anderson is a professor of HRM at Brunel University Business School, London, United Kingdom. His research interests include recruitment and selection, applicant reactions in selection, innovation and creativity in organizations, and the science–practice divide in HRM. His work has appeared in several top-tier journals including *Academy of Management Journal, Journal of Applied Psychology, Personnel Psychology, Journal of Organizational Behavior*, and the *International Journal of Selection and Assessment*. He has coedited a number of handbooks including the *Handbook of Industrial, Work and Organizational Psychology* (Sage) and the *Handbook of Selection* (Wiley). He is currently the director of the Research, Work and Organization Research Centre, at Brunel Business School. He is a fellow of the APA, SIOP, BPS, and IAAP, and an academic fellow of the CIPD in the United Kingdom.

David Bartram is a chief psychologist for SHL Group, Ltd. Prior to his position with SHL, he was dean of the Faculty of Science and the Environment, and professor of psychology in the Department of Psychology at the University of Hull. He is a fellow of the British Psychological Society (BPS) and of the International Association of Applied Psychology (IAAP) and past president of IAAP Division 2 (Assessment and Evaluation). He is president-elect of the International Test Commission, Convenor of the European Federation of Psychologists' Association's Board of Assessment and a past Chair of the BPS's Committee on Test Standards. He was appointed honorary professor in occupational psychology and measurement at the University of Nottingham in 2007 and Professor Extraordinarius in the Department of Human Resource Management at the University of Pretoria in 2010. In 2004, he received the BPS Award for Distinguished Contribution to Professional Psychology. He has published widely in the area of psychological testing both in scientific research articles and in relation to professional issues.

Tanner Bateman is a senior project associate for Virginia Tech's Youth Science Cooperative Outreach Agreement in which he manages assessment and evaluation for a catalog of Army-sponsored STEM outreach initiatives. He received his B.S. in psychology from Colorado State University and has received his M.S. in industrial/organizational psychology at Virginia Tech where he is currently a Ph.D. candidate. His research focus is on individual differences in motivation including construct validity, predictive validity, and measurement. He has also presented several research pieces at the annual Society for Industrial and Organizational Psychology conference. He has presented research at several national conferences for educational research and has published assessment research in the international *Assessment and Evaluation in Higher Education* journal. His current job involves work that focuses on assessment creation, educational outcomes assessment, and program evaluation.

Gerhard Blickle is a professor of work and organizational psychology at the University of Bonn, Germany. He received his Ph.D. in psychology in 1993 from the University of Heidelberg. He served as editor and coeditor of two leading German journals in psychology and currently serves on the board of Psychology of the German Research Foundation—the national research funding agency. His research focuses on the assessment of job performance and personality in the workplace, mentoring, and politics in organizations. He has published in peer-reviewed journals such as the *Journal of Vocational Behavior, Applied Psychology: An International Review, European Journal of Personality, Journal of Language and Social Psychology, European Journal of Psychological Assessment, European Journal of Work & Organizational Psychology, Personality and Individual Differences, Journal of Managerial Psychology, International Journal of Selection and Assessment*, and *Journal of Applied Social Psychology*.

Walter C. Borman received his Ph.D. in industrial/organizational psychology from the University of California (Berkeley). He is currently chief scientist of Personnel Decisions Research Institutes and is professor of industrial–organizational psychology at the University of South Florida. He is a fellow of the Society for Industrial and Organizational Psychology. He has written more than 350 books, book chapters, journal articles, and conference papers. He has also served on the editorial boards of several journals in the I/O field, including the *Journal of Applied Psychology, Personnel Psychology*, and the *International Journal of Selection and Assessment*. He is currently editor of *Human Performance*. Finally, he was the recipient of the Society for Industrial and Organizational Psychology's Distinguished Scientific Contributions Award for 2003; the M. Scott Myers Award for Applied Research in the Workplace for 2000, 2002, 2004, and 2010; and the American Psychological Foundation's Gold Medal Award for Life Achievement in the Application of Psychology in 2011.

Nathan A. Bowling is a professor of psychology at Wright State University in Dayton, Ohio, where he teaches courses on organizational psychology, personality, and job attitudes. He received his Ph.D. in industrial and organizational psychology in 2005 from Central Michigan University. His research has focused on job satisfaction, counterproductive work behavior, and occupational stress and has appeared in a number of top scholarly journals, including the *Journal of Applied Psychology, Journal of Occupational and Organizational Psychology, Human Performance, International Journal of Selection and Assessment*, and *Journal of Vocational Behavior*. He has received funding from the Society for Industrial and Organizational Psychology (SIOP) Foundation, and he currently serves on the editorial boards of several journals, including *Journal of Organizational Behavior* and *Journal of Business and Psychology*.

Cameron Brown is a doctoral student of the I/O Graduate Program at the University of Tulsa. He received a bachelor's degree from Southern Utah University, with a major in psychology and a minor in business management. His research interests include personality, motivation, and selection. He recently married his sweetheart, Chelsea, and he enjoys the outdoors, canyoneering, and rock climbing.

Bradley J. Brummel is an assistant professor of industrial/organizational psychology at the University of Tulsa where he teaches courses in I/O psychology, psychological testing, training, and job attitudes. He received his Ph.D. in industrial/organizational psychology in 2008 from the University of Illinois at Urbana-Champaign. His research interests include the effectiveness of simulations and role-plays in training, the structure and incremental validity of job attitudes including employee engagement, and personality in the workplace. He has published in peer-reviewed outlets including *Journal of Management, Personnel Psychology, Journal of Applied Social Psychology, Military Psychology*, and *Science and Engineering Ethics*.

Gary N. Burns is an assistant professor in the human factors and industrial/organizational psychology program at Wright State University and is the director of the Workplace Personality Project Laboratory at Wright State. He received his Ph.D. in industrial and organizational psychology from Central Michigan University in 2006. His published work primarily focuses on the measurement of personality and understanding the connections between personality, decision making, and behavior. Current research projects focus on understanding how information in resumes is related to the employer's perceptions of applicants and how the presence of sexual orientation information can influence personality judgments. His applied work focuses on the development and revision of performance appraisal systems in organizational settings.

Michael C. Campion is a Ph.D. student in business administration at the Darla Moore School of Business, University of South Carolina. He received his undergraduate degree in business administration from Krannert School of Business, Purdue University. Currently, his primary interests are in staffing and employee development as they relate to individual differences in motivation and behavior.

Tiffani R. Chen is a doctoral student of industrial/organizational psychology at George Mason University, where she also teaches courses in organizational behavior at George Mason's School of Management. She received her B.A. in psychology in 2006 from Princeton University, where she wrote her undergraduate thesis on language acquisition and cognition. Her research focuses on understanding shared leadership development on teams and multiteam systems and improving communication and collaboration across geographically dispersed teams. She also studies the unique challenges faced by teleworkers. She has published her research in various academic journals, such as the *Journal of Management*, and has presented at numerous conferences. She has also worked on multiple grants funded through organizations like the Army Research Institute and the National Science Foundation.

Brian S. Connelly is an assistant professor in the Department of Management at University of Toronto Scarborough and the Rotman School of Management. He teaches courses in human resources, organizational behavior, and research methods. He received his Ph.D. in industrial and organizational psychology from the University of Minnesota. His research examines how organizations can best use personality measures to solve workplace challenges, particularly in employee selection and development. In current and on-going research, he has used personality ratings from others (e.g., one's peers, friends, or family) to study the limitations of self-knowledge, how first impressions are formed, the way people "fake" personality measures, and the structure of personality. He has published his research in journals such as *Psychological Bulletin, American Psychologist, Journal of Applied Psychology, Journal of Personality and Social Psychology, Journal of Personality*, and the *International Journal of Selection and Assessment.*

Jeffrey S. Conway is a doctoral candidate at the University of South Florida (USF). Prior to attending USF, he worked on his master's degree in IO psychology at Indiana University-Purdue University Indianapolis (IUPUI). His research interests primarily concern selection and assessment with a specific focus on individual differences and personality. He has presented several papers at the annual meeting for the Society for Industrial/Organizational Psychology (SIOP).

Filip De Fruyt obtained a degree in psychology, a degree in biomedical sciences, and a Ph.D. in psychology. He was appointed as full professor in differential psychology and personality assessment at Ghent University in Belgium and is currently the director of Teaching Affairs of the Faculty of Psychology and Educational Sciences at Ghent University. He is also teaching in the Executive Master Class in Human Resources Management of the Vlerick Leuven Gent Management School. His research expands a broad domain including adaptive and maladaptive traits, their structure and development, cross-cultural manifestations of personality, and applied personality psychology. He is president-elect of the European Association of Personality Psychology (EAPP). He served as associate editor of the *European Journal of Personality* from 2000 to 2004 and is still consulting editor of the *European Journal of Personality*, the *International Journal of Selection and Assessment*, the *Review* *of Work and Organizational Psychology*, and the *Journal of Personality and Social Psychology* (section Personality Processes and Individual Differences). He has (co-)authored more than 100 papers in a broad range of leading international academic journals including *Assessment, Clinical Psychology Review, Development and Psychopathology, European Journal of Personality, Journal of Affective Disorders, Journal of Applied Psychology, Journal of Personality, Journal of Personality Disorders, Journal of Personality and Social Psychology, Journal of Abnormal Psychology, Journal of Vocational Behavior, Personnel Psychology, Psychological Assessment, Psychology and Aging*, and *Science*. He is consulted by national and international profit and nonprofit organizations for advice and training with respect to personnel selection, development, and staffing problems.

Paige J. Deckert is a Ph.D. candidate at Penn State University. She has publications on the measurement of performance appraisal and the assessment of adverse impact in personnel selection, and she has presented on subjects such as adverse impact as a function of educational attainment, and the use of Facebook in personnel selection. Beyond personnel selection and performance appraisal, her research interests also include trust in the workplace.

John J. Donovan is an associate professor of management in the College of Business Administration at Rider University, as well as the chair of the Management Department and the director of the Executive MBA program. He received his Ph.D. in industrial/organizational psychology in 1998 from the University at Albany. His research interests focus on understanding the processes underlying work motivation, as well as the role of personality in determining employee behavior. His research on factors that influence goal establishment and revision and the validity of personality testing for employee selection has been published in journals such as *Journal of Applied Psychology, Human Performance, Educational and Psychological Measurement*, and *Journal of Applied Social Psychology*. He also serves on the editorial board for *Journal of Business and Psychology, Human Performance*, and *Journal of Organizational Behavior*.

James E. Driskell has over 20 years' experience in behavioral science R&D, serving in the academic, government, and private sectors. He is a fellow of the American Psychological Association, serves on the editorial board of *Human Factors*, and is Contributing Editor of the *Journal of Applied Psychology*. He received his Ph.D. from the University of South Carolina in 1981. He has served as principal investigator on research projects for the Department of Homeland Security, National Science Foundation, Office of Naval Research, Defense Intelligence Agency, National Institutes of Health, NASA, Army Research Institute, FAA, Naval Research Laboratory, and other organizations. His primary research interests are in the areas of deception, group dynamics, human performance under stress, and training and simulation. He has published his research in outlets such as the *Journal of Applied Psychology, American Psychologist, Human Factors, Journal of Experimental Social Psychology, Military Psychology, Small Group Research, Journal of Occupational Health Psychology*, and *Group Dynamics*.

Christopher T. Frost is a consultant at Shaker Consulting Group in Beachwood, Ohio. At Shaker, he assists organizations in generating content to be included in innovative online selection systems. These systems are also designed to serve as a realistic job preview for job candidates. He received his master's degree in industrial and organizational psychology from Central Michigan University in 2011. He has also instructed multiple undergraduate statistics/research methods courses during his time at Central Michigan University and received an award for teaching excellence in 2012. He is currently working on completing his dissertation with his mentor Neil Christiansen. For his dissertation project, he is attempting to develop an automated scoring process to predict interview performance as well as applicant personality-based online interviews response content. His primary research interests are in personality testing, applicant faking, interviews, automated scoring processes, work stress, and competition in the workplace.

Adrian Furnham was educated at the London School of Economics where he obtained a distinction in an M.Sc. Econ. and at Oxford University where he completed a doctorate (D.Phil.) in 1981. He has subsequently earned D.Sc. (1991) and D.Litt. (1995) degrees. Previously a lecturer in psychology at Pembroke College, Oxford, he has been a professor of psychology at University College London since 1992. He has lectured widely abroad and held scholarships and visiting professorships at, amongst others, the University of New South Wales, the University of the West Indies, the University of Hong Kong, and the University of KwaZulu-Natal. He has also been a visiting professor of management at Henley Management College. He has recently been made adjunct professor of management at the Norwegian School of Management (2009).

He has written over 1,000 scientific papers and 70 books. Many have been translated into foreign languages including Chinese, French, German, Italian, Japanese, Korean, Polish, Portuguese, and Spanish. He is a fellow of the British Psychological Society and is among the most productive psychologists in the world. He is on the editorial board of a number of international journals, as well as the past elected president of the *International Society for the Study of Individual Differences*. He is also a founder director of Applied Behavioural Research Associates (ABRA), a psychological consultancy. He has been a consultant to over 30 major international companies, with particular interests in top team development, management change performance management systems, psychometric testing, and leadership derailment. He speaks regularly at academic and business conferences and is noted for his motivational speaking.

He is also a newspaper columnist previously at the *Financial Times*, now at the *Sunday Times*. He wrote regularly for the *Daily Telegraph* and is a regular contributor to national and international radio and television stations including the BBC, CNN, and ITV. More details can be found in the latest *Who's Who*. Since 2007, he has been nominated by *HR Magazine* as one of the 20 Most Influential People in HR. He was nominated to the seventh most influential thinker in 2011. He speaks regularly at academic, business, and training conferences around the world, being well known as approachable, well informed, and entertaining. He also runs in-house workshops for various blue-chip companies. Like Noel Coward, he believes work is more fun than fun and considers himself to be a well-adjusted workaholic. He rides a bicycle to work (as he has always done) very early in the morning and does not have a mobile phone. He enjoys writing popular articles, traveling to exotic countries, consulting on real-life problems, arguing at dinner parties, and going to the theater. He hopes never to retire.

Jennifer M. George is the Mary Gibbs Jones Professor of management and professor of psychology in the Jesse H. Jones Graduate School of Business at Rice University. She is the director of the Ph.D. program and area coordinator of the Organizational Behavior Group in the Jones School. She received her Ph.D. in management and organizational behavior from New York University. Her research interests include the role of affect, mood, and emotion in the workplace, nonconscious processes, personality influences, groups and teams, creativity, prosocial behavior, customer service, values, work–life linkages, and stress and well-being. She has published her research in peer-reviewed journals including the *Academy of Management Journal, Academy of Management Review, Journal of Applied Psychology, Psychological Bulletin, Organizational Behavior and Human Decision Processes, Journal of Personality and Social Psychology*, and the *Journal of Management*. She serves on the editorial review boards for *Administrative Science Quarterly, Journal of Applied Psychology, Academy of Management Journal, Academy of Management Review, Organizational Behavior and Human Decision Processes, Organization Science*, and the *Journal of Management*.

Richard D. Goffin is a professor of industrial–organizational psychology at the University of Western Ontario. Previous appointments include Northern Illinois University, the Canadian Public Service Commission, and Revenue Canada. He has conducted research and consulted in the areas of performance appraisal/management, personnel selection, personality assessment, job/work analysis, test-taking anxiety and attitudes, and quantitative methods. He has authored/coauthored articles appearing in numerous journals, including *Journal of Applied Psychology, Personnel Psychology, Perspectives on Psychological Science, Organizational Research Methods, Leadership Quarterly, Organizational Behavior and Human Decision Processes, Journal of Personality and Social Psychology, Human Resource Management Review, Journal of Occupational and Organizational Psychology, Journal of Organizational Behavior, Human Performance, Human Resource Management, International Journal of Selection and Assessment, Personality and Individual Differences*, and *Multivariate Behavioral Research*.

Richard L. Griffith is a professor in the industrial–organizational psychology program at the Florida Institute of Technology, and the director of the Institute for Cross-Cultural Management. He received his doctoral degree in I/O psychology from the University of Akron in 1997. He is an expert in testing and personality assessment. He has served as an associate editor of *Human Performance* and edited the recent special edition, *Uncovering the Nature of Applicant Faking Behavior: A Presentation of Theoretical Perspectives*. He is the author of over 75 publications, presentations, and book chapters in the area of selection and is the coeditor of the book *A Closer Examination of Applicant Faking Behavior*. His work has been featured in *Time* magazine and *The Wall Street Journal*.

Fred Guest is an I/O psychologist and managing director of TTS—Top Talent Solutions. His most recent position was that of head of Professional Services with SHL South Africa. As practitioner he assisted a range of companies in the manufacturing, financial, and service industries in the design of competency frameworks for integrated talent management systems, the development of recruitment and selection strategies, as well as the implementation of Internet-based competency and occupational assessment practices. Working with executives and senior management teams, he implemented projects in Southern Africa, Egypt, Europe, Singapore, and Australia. He is a past president of the Society of Industrial and Organisational Psychology of South Africa (SIOPSA) and was awarded honorary membership of the Society for his contribution to I/O psychology in South Africa in 2008.

Jo-Ida C. Hansen is a professor in the Department of Psychology and adjunct professor with the Department of Human Resources and Industrial Relations at the University of Minnesota. She directs the Center for Interest Measurement Research and the Counseling Psychology Program. Her research interests focus broadly on vocational psychology and career development and more specifically on vocational and leisure interests and their assessment; she is the author of the Hansen Leisure Interest Questionnaire. She is a member of the AERA/APA/NCME Joint Committee to Revise the Educational and Psychological Testing Standards, past president of Division 17 (Society of Counseling Psychology) of the American Psychological Association (APA), and past editor of the *Journal of Counseling Psychology*. She is a fellow of APA, the American Psychological Society, and the American Counseling Association. Her awards include the Leona Tyler Award for Research and Professional Service, the E. K. Strong, Jr. Gold Medal for her work in interest measurement, and the Society for Vocational Psychology Distinguished Achievement Award.

Eric D. Heggestad is an associate professor of psychology and organizational science at the University of North Carolina at Charlotte and is the director of the Industrial and Organizational Psychology Masters Degree Program there. He received his Ph.D. and M.A. degrees from the University of Minnesota and his B.A. in psychology from St. Olaf College in Northfield, MN. He has over 25 publications addressing issues such as personality and cognitive ability testing for pre-employment screening, personality-oriented job analysis, person–job fit, and the assessment of social skills. He is an associate editor of the *Journal of Business and Psychology* and serves on the editorial board of *Journal of Applied Psychology*. He has also served on the executive committee for the Society of Industrial and Organizational Psychology.

Brian J. Hoffman is an associate professor of psychology at the University of Georgia. He received his doctorate from the University of Tennessee in 2006. His research focuses on criterion development, leadership assessment, and the application of management principles to sports settings. He was the coeditor of *The Psychology of Assessment Centers*, and his peer-reviewed research has appeared in journals such as *Psychological Bulletin*, *Journal of Applied Psychology*, *Personnel Psychology*, and *Academy of Management Journal*.

Robert Hogan is president of Hogan Assessment Systems and an international authority on personality assessment, leadership, and organizational effectiveness. He was McFarlin Professor and chair of the Department of Psychology at the University of Tulsa for 14 years. Prior to that, he was a professor of psychology and social relations at the Johns Hopkins University. He has received a number of research and teaching awards and is the editor of the *Handbook of Personality Psychology* and the author of the Hogan Personality Inventory. He received his Ph.D. from the University of California, Berkeley, specializing in personality assessment.

He is the author of more than 300 journal articles, chapters, and books. He is widely credited with demonstrating how careful attention to personality factors can influence organizational effectiveness in a variety of areas—ranging from organizational climate and leadership to selection and effective team performance. He is a fellow of the American Psychological Association and the Society for Industrial/Organizational Psychology.

Leaetta Hough is founder and president of the Dunnette Group, Ltd., past president of SIOP, and past president of the Federation of Associations in Behavioral and Brain Sciences, a coalition of 22 scientific societies. She received her Ph.D. from the University of Minnesota in 1981 and is a fellow of APS, APA, and APA's Divisions 5 (Evaluation, Measurement, and Statistics) and 14 (SIOP). She has specialized in personnel selection and measurement of personality and hard-to-measure behavior. She has developed hundreds of valid and defensible assessment measures, many of which are innovative, nontraditional assessment strategies that have shown excellent validity, with minimal, if any, adverse impact against protected groups. She has published dozens of articles in refereed journals, book chapters, and reviews. Noteworthy has been her role as coeditor of the four-volume *Handbook of Industrial & Organizational Psychology*. Three of her articles have been reprinted in a book consisting of the seminal I-O publications of the last 100 years. Her work has helped shape the science and practice of I-O psychology.

Jason L. Huang is an assistant professor of psychology at Wayne State University where he teaches courses in industrial/organizational psychology, statistics, and psychological measurement. He received his Ph.D. in organizational psychology in 2012 from Michigan State University. His research interest focuses on individuals' adaptation to their work experience. More specific areas of interest include personality's influence on adaptability at work, training processes and subsequent transfer of trained knowledge and skills to novel contexts and tasks, and cultural influences on individual-level work phenomena. He has published his research in peer-reviewed outlets such as *Personnel Psychology*, *Journal of Management*, and *Journal of Business and Psychology*.

Samuel T. Hunter is an assistant professor of industrial and organizational psychology at Pennsylvania State University. He received his Ph.D. from the University of Oklahoma in 2007. His two primary areas of research focus are leadership and innovation management, with a particular focus on understanding the varying influences of individual differences (e.g., personality) across contextual factors in the workplace. Author of more than 50 papers, books, and book chapters, he has published in outlets such as the *Journal of Applied Psychology, The Leadership Quarterly, Human Resource Management Review*, and the *Journal of Business and Psychology*. He currently serves on the editorial board for *The Leadership Quarterly* and the *Journal of Creative Behavior*.

Steve M. Jex is currently a professor of industrial/organizational psychology at Bowling Green State University. He has also held faculty positions at Central Michigan University and the University of Wisconsin Oshkosh. He received his Ph.D. in industrial/organizational psychology from the University of South Florida and has spent most of his post-doctoral career conducting research on occupational stress. His research has appeared in a number of scholarly journals including *Journal of Applied Psychology, Journal of Organizational Behavior, Journal of Occupational Health Psychology, Journal of Applied Social Psychology*, and *Work & Stress*. He is the author of two books: *Stress and Job Performance: Theory, Research, and Implications for Managerial Practice* and *Organizational Psychology: A Scientist–Practitioner Approach*.

Jeff W. Johnson is a principal research scientist at PDRI, where he has directed many applied organizational research projects for a variety of government and private sector clients. He received his Ph.D. in industrial and organizational psychology from the University of Minnesota in 1994. His primary research interests are in the areas of personnel selection, performance measurement, research methods, and statistics. His personality research has focused on developing and testing models of the process by which personality characteristics and other constructs influence job performance. His research has been published in academic journals such as *Journal of Applied Psychology, Personnel Psychology*, and *Multivariate Behavioral Research*. He is a past associate editor of *Personnel Psychology* and is on the editorial boards of *Human Performance* and *Industrial and Organizational Psychology: Perspectives on Science and Practice*. He is a SIOP fellow and was awarded SIOP's M. Scott Myers Award for Applied Research in the Workplace in 2012.

John A. Kostek received his master's degree in industrial/organizational psychology in 2012 from Bowling Green State University under the mentorship of Scott Highhouse. He studied personality measurement, individual assessment and selection, judgment and decision making, and the history of I/O psychology. His research focused on advancing the understanding of how individual differences can influence the decisions made by organizations (e.g., hiring, promoting) as well as the decisions made by people within organizations (e.g., how many hours to work, when to retire).

Kurt Kraiger is a professor of psychology and chair of the Department of Psychology at Colorado State University where he teaches courses in industrial psychology, individual differences, training, leadership, and multivariate statistics. He received his Ph.D. in industrial/organizational psychology in 1983 from the Ohio State University. He is a noted expert on training and training evaluation, having edited two books and published or presented over 130 papers on training and related topics. He is also actively engaged in research on learning in ill-structured environments (e.g., computer-based training and through mentoring programs). He has published in peer-reviewed outlets including *Psychological Bulletin, Psychological Science in the Public Interest, Journal of Applied Psychology, Personnel Psychology, Human Performance*, and *Industrial and Organizational Psychology: Perspectives on Science and Practice*.

Filip Lievens is currently a professor at the Department of Personnel Management and Work and Organizational Psychology of Ghent University, Belgium. He is the author of over 100 articles in the areas of organizational attractiveness, high-stakes testing, and selection including assessment centers, situational judgment tests, and web-based assessment. He has also given over 200 presentations, workshops, and invited keynote presentations across all continents (Europe, USA, Asia, Africa, and Australia). He serves on the editorial board of both *Journal of Applied Psychology* and *Personnel Psychology* and was a past book review editor of the *International Journal of Selection and Assessment*. He has received several awards. He was the first European winner of the Distinguished Early Career Award of the Society for Industrial and Organizational Psychology (2006) and the first industrial and organizational psychologist to be laureate of the Royal Flemish Academy of Sciences and Arts (2008).

Lynn A. McFarland is a professor in the Management Department in the Darla Moore School of Business at the University of South Carolina. She received her Ph.D. from Michigan State University in 2000. Her research is in the areas of staffing, social influence in organizations, and workplace diversity. She has published in several leading management journals such as the *Journal of Applied Psychology*, *Personnel Psychology*, and *Journal of Management* and has presented over 50 papers at national conferences. She is also the president and cofounder of Human Capital Solutions, Inc., an HR consulting firm specializing in staffing and performance management. The company was founded in 2004 and serves clients from both the private and the public sectors.

Silvia Moscoso is a professor of work psychology at the University of Santiago de Compostela (Spain) where she teaches courses in work psychology, organizational behavior, and personnel selection. She received her Ph.D. in work psychology in 1999 from the University of Santiago de Compostela. She has authored over 30 journal articles and book chapters on topics related to personnel selection and work psychology. She was a visiting scholar at Brunel University. Currently, she is the associate editor of the *Journal of Work and Organizational Psychology*. She has published her research in journals such as *Journal of Applied Psychology*, *Personnel Psychology*, *International Journal of Selection and Assessment*, *European Journal of Work and Organizational Psychology*, *Journal of Business and Psychology*, and *European Journal of Personality*.

Kevin R. Murphy is a consulting expert at Lamorinda Consulting LLC and an affiliate member of the Department of Psychology at Colorado State University. He has served as editor of *Journal of Applied Psychology* and is the current editor of *Industrial and Organizational Psychology: Perspectives on Science and Practice*. He is the author of 11 books and over 160 papers and chapters in areas ranging from psychometrics to gender in the workplace. He has served as chair of the Department of Defense Advisory Committee on Personnel Testing and as a member of four National Academies of Science Committees. His current research focuses on the validation process.

Anupama Narayan is an assistant professor of industrial/organizational psychology at the University of Tulsa where she teaches courses in work groups and teams, organizational psychology, and social psychology. She received her Ph.D. in industrial/organizational psychology in 2008 from Wright State University. Her research interests lie primarily in individual and team effectiveness, motivation and personality, and training and development. More specific areas of interest include self-regulated learning in collaborative environments, individual and team goal setting, and creativity in dyadic interactions. She has published in peer-reviewed outlets including *International Journal of Training and Development*, *Journal of Applied Behavioral Sciences*, and *Journal of Applied Social Psychology*.

Christopher D. Nye is an assistant professor of psychology at Bowling Green State University. He received his Ph.D. in industrial and organizational psychology from the University of Illinois at Urbana-Champaign in 2011. His research interests include personnel selection and assessment, the role of personality at work, organizational research methods, and workplace deviance. He has published a number of scholarly articles and/or chapters on these topics, and his work has appeared in journals such as *Perspectives on Psychological Science*, *Journal of Applied Psychology*, *Journal of Management*, *Organizational Research Methods*, *Journal of Research in Personality*, and the *International Journal of Selection and Assessment*. He has received awards for his research from the Society of Industrial and Organizational Psychology, the College Board, and the International Personnel Assessment Council. He has also been a senior consortium research fellow for the U.S. Army Research Institute for the Behavioral and Social Sciences.

Jisoo Ock is a graduate student in industrial/organizational psychology at Rice University. He received his B.A. from the University of Minnesota in 2008. His research interest is in quantitative methods in organizational psychology research, including examining the practical impacts that psychometric characteristics (e.g., reliability, factor structure) of the psychological measurements have on effectiveness and fairness of the personnel selection applications (e.g., utility, legal defensibility, measurement equivalence). He currently serves as assistant editor of the *Journal of Business and Psychology*.

Thomas A. O'Neill is an assistant professor of psychology at the University of Calgary, Canada. He graduated from the University of Western Ontario where he completed his M.Sc. and Ph.D. in organizational psychology. His research involves personality, teams, virtual work, methods, and performance ratings. He is the director of the individual and team performance laboratory, and he is the current communications coordinator on the executive committee of the Canadian Society for Industrial and Organizational Psychology. His research has been funded by the Social Sciences and Humanities Research Council of Canada and the Society for Industrial and Organizational Psychology.

Fred L. Oswald is a professor in industrial/organizational psychology at Rice University. His research, statistical, consulting, and legal expertise and experience focuses on personnel selection systems and psychological measurement in organizational, military, and educational settings (e.g., the U.S. Navy, College Board, American Association of Medical Schools), as reflected in his large-scale grants in addition to 50 peer-reviewed papers, 15 book chapters, and 100+ presentations. His recent personality research has addressed computerized adaptive personality testing, the statistical equivalence of personality measures between gender and racial/ethnic groups, and the strategies and implications for shortening the length of personality tests. He currently serves as an associate editor of both the *Journal of Management* and the *Journal of Business and Psychology*. He serves on the editorial boards for several major organizational research journals, including *Journal of Applied Psychology*, *International Journal of Selection and Assessment*, *Journal of Management*, *Military Psychology*, and *Organizational Research Methods*. He is a fellow of the Society for Industrial and Organizational Psychology (SIOP) and a member of the international Society for Research Synthesis Methods (SRSM). He received his Ph.D. in psychology in 1999 from the University of Minnesota.

Sampo V. Paunonen is a professor in the Department of Psychology at the University of Western Ontario, where he received his Ph.D. in 1984. His research interests include person perception, personality assessment, and personnel selection. He also has interests in multivariate methods, such as factor analysis, and in psychometric theory. He has published extensively in leading psychology journals and has served on the editorial boards of the *Journal of Personality* and *Journal of Personality and Social Psychology*.

Robert E. Ployhart is the Bank of America Professor of Business Administration at the Darla Moore School of Business, University of South Carolina. He received his Ph.D. from Michigan State

University. His primary interests include human capital, staffing, recruitment, and advanced statistical methods.

Matthew S. Prewett is an assistant professor of psychology at Central Michigan University where he teaches courses in personnel psychology, team performance, technology in I/O psychology, hierarchical linear modeling, and undergraduate statistics. He received his Ph.D. in industrial/organizational psychology in 2009 from the University of South Florida. His research has concentrated on issues involving the staffing and composition of work teams, including the effects of different approaches to measuring personality at a team level, the relationship between team personality and work-related criteria, and the relationship between personality traits and the acceptance of negative feedback. His other work includes the evaluation of new technologies and training programs designed to improve human performance. He has published in *Human Performance, The Oxford Handbook of Organizational Well-Being, Journal of Applied Social Psychology, Computers in Human Behavior*, and the *Journal of Medical Education.*

Jennifer M. Ragsdale is an assistant professor of industrial/organizational psychology at the University of Tulsa where she teaches courses in personnel psychology, research methods, and psychology of advertising. She received her Ph.D. in industrial/organizational psychology in 2011 from Central Michigan University. Her research interests lie primarily in occupational stress and personality assessment in the workplace. More specific areas of interest include the assessment of traits and motive dispositions from work narratives and the role of individual differences in the occupational stress and recovery processes. She has published her research in the *International Journal of Stress Management.*

John A. Rahael is an entrepreneur and a talent management consultant. While building his business and finishing up his doctoral degree at Central Michigan University, he works with leaders as they develop their companies, their teams, and themselves. He has taught courses in personnel and organizational psychology, personality psychology, and introduction to statistics. His research interests lie primarily in personality assessment, motivation, leadership assessment, and development. His current areas of focus include assessing individuals' intrinsic motives and passions, leadership and inspiration, and exploring the training design features and trainer behaviors that lead to the greatest development outcomes. He has presented several studies at the Annual Conference of the Society for Industrial and Organizational Psychology. This will be his first publication.

Patrick H. Raymark is a professor of psychology and chair of the Psychology Department at Clemson University where he teaches courses in personnel selection, leadership, and performance appraisal. He received his Ph.D. in industrial-organizational psychology in 1993 from Bowling Green State University. Much of his research has focused on the relative usefulness of various personnel selection constructs (e.g., personality, integrity) and methods of assessment (e.g., interviews). More specific areas of interest include patterns of faking behavior on personality tests, impression management behaviors within the selection interview, as well as the development of job analysis techniques designed to uncover the personality demands of different jobs. He has published in peer-reviewed outlets including *Journal of Applied Psychology, Personnel Psychology, Journal of Management, Organizational Behavior and Human Decision Processes, Human Performance*, and the *Journal of Personality.*

James H. Reynierse is an experimental psychologist with a Ph.D. from Michigan State University (1964). He was a postdoctoral fellow at Indiana University (psychology) and later a postdoctoral senior scientist fellow at the University of Edinburgh (zoology). After a 10-year research and teaching career at the University of Nebraska-Lincoln and Hope College, he left academia as a full professor for the business world, where he remained for 26 years—first in human resource management and later in management consulting. He retired in 2000 but continued his research and writing. His research has focused on differences between entrepreneurs and levels of management, theoretical issues related to psychological type and the MBTI instrument, business values, and management of organizational change strategies. He is the author of the management classic, "Ten Commandments for CEOs Seeking Organizational Change" (*Business Horizons*). He was editor and on the editorial board of *Human Resource Planning* and on the editorial board of the *Journal of Psychological Type* from 1994.

Brent W. Roberts is a professor of psychology in the Department of Psychology at the University of Illinois, in the Social-Personality-Organizational Division. He received his Ph.D. in personality psychology from University of California, Berkeley in 1994 and worked at the University of Tulsa until 1999 when he joined the faculty at the University of Illinois. He received the J. S. Tanaka Dissertation Award for methodological and substantive contributions to the field of personality psychology in 1995. He was awarded the prize for the most important paper published in the *Journal of Research in Personality* in 2000. Most recently he received the Diener Mid-Career award in Personality Psychology from the Foundation for Personality and Social Psychology and the Theodore Millon Mid-Career award in Personality Psychology from the American Psychological Foundation, and was appointed as a Richard and Margaret Romano Professorial Scholar at the University of Illinois. He has served as the associate editor for the *Journal of Research in Personality* and as a member-at-large and executive officer for the Association for Research in Personality, and serves on the editorial board of the *Journal of Personality and Social Psychology*, *International Journal of Selection and Assessment*, *Personality and Social Psychology Review*, and *Perspectives on Psychological Science*.

Chet Robie is a professor in organizational behavior/human resource management in the School of Business at Wilfrid Laurier University in Ontario, Canada. His current research, funded by the Social Sciences and Humanities Research Council of Canada, addresses noncognitive testing and cross-cultural measurement issues. He has published in such peer-reviewed journals as *Journal of Applied Psychology*, *Personnel Psychology*, *Organizational Research Methods*, and the *International Journal of Selection and Assessment*. He is currently a member of the editorial boards of *Human Performance* and the *Journal of Business and Psychology*. He is also currently a member of the Professional Advisory Board for SkillSurvey, Inc., a firm that specializes in web-based reference checking. His undergraduate education was at Towson University. He also received his master's degree in experimental psychology from Towson University. He received his Ph.D. in industrial/organizational psychology from Bowling Green State University.

Mitchell Rothstein is the director of the DAN Management and Organizational Studies Program in the Faculty of Social Science at the University of Western Ontario. Prior to this position, he was a professor of organizational behavior at the Richard Ivey School of Business from 1988 to 2008, and prior to that, he spent 6 years as a management consultant. He obtained his Ph.D. in 1983 in industrial and organizational psychology and has published extensively in the areas of personnel selection, the use of interpersonal networks in leadership and career development, expatriate adjustment to international assignments, and the integration of skilled immigrants to the Canadian economy. In 2010, he published a book called *Self-Management and Leadership Development*. A chapter he cowrote in this book, on the topic of resiliency in leadership, is now the focus of his current research interests, with a number of new projects under development. He has consulted for a wide variety of private and public sector organizations regarding personnel selection practices, performance evaluation systems, executive team building, leadership development, and various organizational development programs.

Ann Marie Ryan is a professor of organizational psychology at Michigan State University. Her major research interests involve improving the quality and fairness of employee selection methods, and topics related to diversity and justice in the workplace. In addition to publishing extensively in these areas, she regularly consults with organizations on improving assessment processes. She is a past president of the Society of Industrial and Organizational Psychology, past editor of the journal *Personnel Psychology*, and current associate editor of *American Psychologist*. She has a long record of professional service on association committees, National Academy of Science panels, and the Defense Advisory Committee on Military Testing.

Paul R. Sackett is the Beverly and Richard Fink Distinguished Professor of psychology and liberal arts at the University of Minnesota. He received his Ph.D. in industrial and organizational psychology at the Ohio State University in 1979. His research interests revolve around various aspects of testing and assessment in workplace, educational, and military settings. He has served as editor of two journals: *Industrial and Organizational Psychology: Perspectives on Science and Practice* and *Personnel Psychology*. He has served as president of the Society for Industrial and Organizational Psychology, as cochair of the committee producing the *Standards for Educational and Psychological Testing*, as a member of the National Research Council's Board on Testing and Assessment, as chair of APA's Committee on Psychological Tests and Assessments, and as chair of APA's Board of Scientific Affairs.

Eduardo Salas is University Trustee Chair and Pegasus Professor of psychology at the University of Central Florida (UCF). He also holds an appointment as program director for Human Systems Integration Research Department at UCF's Institute for Simulation & Training. Previously, he was a Senior Research Psychologist and Head of the Training Technology Development Branch of NAVAIR-Orlando for 15 years. During this period, he served as a principal investigator for numerous R&D programs focusing on teamwork, team training, simulation-based training, decision-making under stress, learning methodologies, and performance assessment. He has coauthored over 350 journal articles and book chapters and has coedited over 20 books. He is currently the president of SIOP and Series Editor of the Organizational Frontier Book Series. He is a fellow of the American Psychological Association (SIOP and Divisions 19, 21, and 49), the Human Factors and Ergonomics Society, and the Association for Psychological Science. He received his Ph.D. degree (1984) in industrial and organizational psychology from Old Dominion University.

Jesús F. Salgado is a professor of psychology at the University of Santiago de Compostela, Spain, where he teaches courses in personnel selection, organizational behavior, and meta-analysis. He received his Ph.D. in social psychology in 1983 from the University of Santiago de Compostela. He has authored over 100 journal articles and book chapters on topics relating to personnel selection, personality and organizational behavior, and performance. He was editor of the *International Journal of Selection and Assessment* from 2002 to 2006 and has served on ten editorial boards. He has also been a visiting fellow at Goldsmiths College, University of London. He has published his research in journals such as *Journal of Applied Psychology*, *Personnel Psychology*, *Academy of Management Journal*, *Journal of Organizational Behavior*, *Journal of Occupational and Organizational Psychology*, *Human Performance*, *International Journal of Selection and Assessment*, *European Journal of Personality*, *European Journal of Work and Organizational Psychology*, *Applied Psychology: An International Review*, and *Journal of Business and Psychology*, among others. He is a fellow of the Society for Industrial and Organizational Psychology (SIOP).

Gerard Saucier is a professor of psychology at the University of Oregon. He has been on the Oregon faculty since 1997, after prior appointments at Eastern Illinois University and California State University (San Bernardino). He obtained his Ph.D. in 1991 from the University of Oregon. His major areas of interest are the generalizable structure and optimal assessment of personality attributes and of beliefs and values. Author of some 60 articles and chapters on these subjects, he received the

Cattell Award in 1999 from the Society of Multivariate Experimental Psychology and is past associate editor for the *Journal of Research in Personality* and for the *Journal of Personality and Social Psychology*. His work has been published in these journals as well as *Psychological Assessment*, *Journal of Personality*, and *Perspectives on Psychological Science*.

Mark J. Schmit is the vice president of Research for the Society for Human Resource Management (SHRM). In this capacity, he leads the association's research activities. He has more than 25 years' experience in the field of human resources and has also been an academic, applied researcher, HR generalist, and internal and external consultant to both public and private organizations. He has developed recruitment, selection, promotion, performance management, and organizational effectiveness/development tools and systems for numerous organizations. He earned a Ph.D. in industrial and organizational psychology from Bowling Green State University in 1994. He has published more than 25 professional journal articles and book chapters and delivered more than 50 presentations at professional meetings on HR and Industrial/Organizational Psychology topics. He is a fellow in both the Society for Industrial and Organizational Psychology and the American Psychological Association. He is also certified as a senior professional in human resources (SPHR).

Robert J. Schneider is president of Research & Assessment Solutions, Ltd., and spent most of his career at Personnel Decisions Research Institutes, Inc. He has conducted large-scale research for public sector, private sector, and military clients. He currently develops and validates assessments, assesses novel constructs, and formulates and evaluates theoretical models both to advance the field and to facilitate solution of important client problems. He has authored or coauthored over 100 technical reports, publications, and conference papers. One of his senior-authored publications has been reprinted in a collection of readings on individual differences, and he was a coawardee of the M. Scott Myers Award for Applied Research in the Workplace in 2010. His primary interests and expertise are in personnel selection; personality theory, research, and assessment; social competence and related constructs; and multimedia assessment approaches. He received his Ph.D. in industrial/organizational psychology from the University of Minnesota in 1992.

Megan N. Shaw is a talent assessment program manager at Amazon. She has worked as a survey analyst for 3 years and a personnel research psychologist for 5 years as an external and internal consultant for private and public sectors. She received her master's degree in I/O psychology from George Mason University and is currently a doctoral candidate at the George Washington University. Her primary research interests are focused on understanding response distortions on self-report measures and developing implicit measures to reduce motivated responding. Her areas of expertise include assessment design and validation, ranging from work simulations and personality assessments to job knowledge and reasoning tests for personnel selection, assignment/placement, and promotion.

Mindy K. Shoss is an assistant professor of psychology at Saint Louis University where she teaches courses in personality, occupational health psychology, and employee training and development. She received her B.A. degree in psychology and economics from Washington University in Saint Louis and her Ph.D. in industrial/organizational psychology from the University of Houston. Her research interests involve personality, employee stress and coping, adaptive performance, and counterproductive work behaviors. Her research has appeared in outlets including the *Journal of Applied Psychology*, *Organizational Behavior and Human Decision Processes*, *Journal of Occupational Health Psychology*, and *Journal of Organizational Behavior*.

Brian P. Siers is an assistant professor of psychology at Roosevelt University where he teaches courses in personnel psychology. He received his Ph.D. in industrial and organizational psychology from Central Michigan University. His research interests are focused on the use of implicit measures in organizational contexts and the use of personality measures for selection purposes. In addition, he regularly works with organizations all over the globe to improve their HRM processes. His research has been published in journals including *Applied Psychology: An International Review*, *International Journal of Selection and Assessment*, and the *Journal of Organizational Behavior Management*.

Daniel V. Simonet is a Ph.D. candidate in the I/O psychology program at the University of Tulsa where he teaches introduction to industrial/organizational psychology and theories of personality. He is currently working under the mentorship of Dr. Robert Tett on his dissertation examining the dyadic-level effects of emotional intelligence under integrative and competitive bargaining situations. His research interests include the nature of dysfunctional and incompetent leadership, the social bases of psychological empowerment, the role of emotional intelligence in interpersonal functioning, team compositional effects of personality, and the role of situations in understanding the linkage between personality and performance. He has published in peer-reviewed outlets including *Human Performance* and *Violence and Victims* and has presented at national and regional conferences. In his free time, he enjoys running 5 km and marathons, participating in cross-fit, playing the piano, and exploring Oklahoma with his significant other.

Andrew B. Speer, M.A., is a doctoral candidate of Industrial and Organizational Psychology at Central Michigan University. Andrew has taught courses in research methods and advertising and has engaged in a wide variety of applied consulting. He has several research manuscripts currently under review or accepted for publication, with his focus being primarily in the realm of personnel selection and personality. Recently, Andrew accepted a consultant position at SHL, Minneapolis.

Amber Gayle Thalmayer is a Ph.D. candidate in psychology at the University of Oregon. Her dissertation research—"Personality attributes in clinical presentation and treatment"—applies knowledge of personality psychology to psychological treatment seeking to improve efficacy and efficiency.

Other research interests include personality assessment and cultural psychology. She has won several graduate student awards, including the Betty Foster McCue Scholarship for work related to human performance and development. Her work has been published in *Psychological Assessment*.

Chad H. Van Iddekinge is the Synovus Associate Professor of management at the Florida State University. He received his Ph.D. in industrial–organizational psychology from Clemson University. His research focuses on how organizations make staffing decisions and how those decisions affect job applicants and the quality and diversity of a firm's workforce. His work has helped advance knowledge in areas such as the construct validity of selection interviews, the consequences of applicant retesting, and effects of staffing procedures on unit-level outcomes. His research has been published in journals such as *Academy of Management*, *Human Performance*, *Journal of Applied Psychology*, *Journal of Management*, and *Personnel Psychology*. Currently, he is an associate editor for *Personnel Psychology* and serves on the editorial board of *Journal of Applied Psychology*.

Nicholas L. Vasilopoulos is the chief of Personnel Assessment Research and Development at the National Security Agency. He received his Ph.D. in applied psychology from Stevens Institute of Technology. He has over 15 years of experience developing, validating, and implementing assessments for use in employee selection and promotion. In addition to his applied experience, he was a tenured faculty member in the Industrial and Organizational Psychology Doctoral program at the George Washington University in Washington, DC, serving as the program director for 3 years. He maintains an active research program that focuses on the development of innovative methods to assess personality in applied settings. He has coauthored over 75 publications and conference presentations, including articles in professional journals such as the *Journal of Applied Psychology, Journal of Personality, Journal of Occupational and Organizational Psychology, International Journal of Selection and Assessment, Human Performance,* and *Personnel Psychology.*

Benjamin Walser is a Ph.D. student in the industrial/organizational psychology program at the University of Tulsa under Dr. Robert P. Tett. He received his M.A. in counseling psychology in 2010 from the University of Central Oklahoma. His research interests include leadership, executive coaching, personnel selection, and the workplace experience of individuals on the autism spectrum. In what free time he has, he enjoys movies, running, playing the piano, reading, and occasional podcasting.

Bart Wille is a Ph.D. candidate at the Department of Developmental, Personality, and Social Psychology of Ghent University. His research interests include personality assessment, personality development, career development, and the longitudinal predictive validity of traits for work and career outcomes. His Ph.D. research specifically focuses on the dynamic and reciprocal relations between traits and vocational experiences across the first 15 years of the professional career. He has published in peer-reviewed journals including *Journal of Vocational Behavior* and *Applied Psychology: An International Review*. Furthermore, he is also involved in undergraduate and graduate teaching programs on the assessment of personality traits (adaptive and maladaptive) in various populations (children, adolescents, and adults) and across settings (clinical, personnel selection, and career counseling).

Christina L. Wilson is an adjunct faculty member at the University of Colorado Denver in both the Business School and the Psychology Department, where she teaches courses in industrial and organizational psychology, organizational behavior, human resource management, theories of personality, and social psychology. She received her master's degree in industrial and organizational psychology from Colorado State University, where she is currently an advanced Ph.D. candidate. She has extensive experience developing, delivering, and evaluating training in a variety of field settings. This experience includes development and delivery of content for courses in a police academy based on State-required curriculum, delivering classroom and on-the-job training to working police officers, and development, delivery, and evaluation of safety training for workers in the plumbing and pipefitting industries. She has completed more than a dozen presentations at national conferences and is currently completing a dissertation that focuses on aspects of personality relevant to the workplace. Her research interests include safety and security; training, and implicit attitudes.

L. A. Witt is a fellow of the APA, APS, and SIOP. He is a professor of psychology, professor of management, and director of the Ph.D. program in I/O psychology at the University of Houston.

Stephen J. Zaccaro is a professor of psychology at George Mason University, Fairfax, Virginia. He received his Ph.D. from the University of Connecticut in 1981. He is also an experienced leadership development consultant. He has written over 120 journal articles, book chapters, and technical reports on group dynamics, team performance, leadership, and work attitudes. He has authored a book titled *The Nature of Executive Leadership: A Conceptual and Empirical Analysis of Success* (2001) and coedited four other books: *Occupational Stress and Organizational Effectiveness* (1987), *The Nature of Organizational Leadership: Understanding the Performance Imperatives Confronting Today's Leaders* (2001), *Leader Development for Transforming Organizations* (2004), and *Multiteam Systems: An Organization Form for Dynamic and Complex Environments* (2012). He has directed funded projects in the areas of multiteam systems, team performance, leader–team interfaces, leadership training and development, leader adaptability, executive leadership, and executive coaching. He serves on the editorial board of *The Leadership Quarterly*, and he is an associate editor for *Journal of Business and Psychology* and

Military Psychology. He is a fellow of the Association for Psychological Science and of the American Psychological Association, Divisions 14 (Society for Industrial and Organizational Psychology) and 19 (Military Psychology).

Michael J. Zickar is a professor of psychology and department chair at Bowling Green State University. He received a Ph.D. in industrial–organizational psychology from the University of Illinois at Urbana-Champaign. He has research interests in the areas of personality measurement, item response theory, and the history of applied psychology, and he is the author of articles published in such journals as the *Journal of Applied Psychology*, *Organizational Behavior and Human Decision Processes*, *Applied Psychological Measurement*, and the *Journal of Vocational Behavior*. He is on the editorial boards of the *Journal of Management* and *Journal of Business and Psychology*. He serves on the Executive Board of the Society for Industrial–Organizational Psychology, where he is also a fellow.

1

The Long and Winding Road

An Introduction to the *Handbook of Personality at Work*

Neil D. Christiansen and Robert P. Tett

No matter where or what, there are makers, takers, and fakers.

Robert Heinlein

Personality surrounds us at work. Of course, personality is inherently psychological and therefore cannot be directly observed, but the effects are everywhere. A morning training session goes smoothly, but in the afternoon, the negative disposition of one individual sours the experience for the trainer and trainees alike. A manager tries to decide whether the self-esteem of her struggling direct report would be able to handle more forceful encouragement or if a pep talk would be a better tactic. A service representative gets encouraged by coworkers to apply for an open position in management because they believe he would be a "natural leader." Laypeople and applied psychologists now agree that personality plays an important role in understanding work behavior, and there is a shared awareness that people differ—sometimes greatly—in how they respond to situations encountered in the workplace.

Agreement on the importance of personality constructs at work is a relatively recent development, and research progress has been anything but smooth over the years. Schneider (2007) reviewed the evolution of the study of personality at work and noted extended periods of skepticism preceding this consensus. Issues related to measurement, research design, and the lack of an organizing framework for traits obscured cumulative inferences about the importance of personality in the workplace (Tett, Jackson, & Rothstein, 1991). Moreover, personality psychology as a field of inquiry was troubled at times (e.g., Adelson, 1969; Carlson, 1971), adding challenges to the effort to apply personality research to the psychology of work. Despite these setbacks, the industry of personality assessment continued to thrive over the decades, and this was no less true in organizations where assessment results were commonly used to help identify desirable job applicants and develop existing employees (Hale, 1982).

The disconnect between what research scientists alleged about the inutility of personality constructs in work settings and what laypeople, consultants, and business leaders believed persisted until the late 1980s and early 1990s. During this period, events converged to convince the last bastion of skeptics to abandon their nihilistic position. Primary research studies using improved personality tests and better criterion measures were published and demonstrated trait scores could predict work behavior (e.g., Day & Silverman, 1989; Hough, Eaton, Dunnette, Kamp, & McCloy, 1990). At the same time, meta-analytic methods of aggregating research results had matured, permitting quantitative reviews of the literature to confirm that personality tests can be used to predict valued outcomes. For example, personality traits showed substantive relationships with leadership emergence (Lord, De Vader, & Alliger, 1986) and job performance (Barrick & Mount, 1991; Tett et al., 1991). In the decade following this watershed period, the psychological research community more generally found this evidence compelling (Hogan & Roberts, 2001; Hough, 2001).

By the mid-1990s, the landscape had been transformed from what it was just a few years earlier. There was an explosion in the number of studies published using personality constructs to explain different aspects of work attitudes, work behavior, and job performance. Research investigated advantages of expanding the criterion domain of job performance when using personality traits as predictors to include citizenship (Organ & Ryan, 1995) and counterproductive work behavior (Collins & Schmidt, 1993). Disagreements emerged as to the relative merits of measuring broad versus narrow trait constructs (Ones & Viswesvaran, 1996; Paunonen, Rothstein, & Jackson, 1999) and whether applicant faking was a serious problem (Christiansen, Goffin, Johnston, & Rothstein, 1994; Ones, Viswesvaran, & Reiss, 1996). Some studies examined personality variables as moderators of relationships, such as between stressors and strains (Moyle, 1995); others posited various mediators of relationships between personality and work outcomes (e.g., Fritzsche, McIntire, & Yost, 2002; Judge, Bono, & Locke, 2000). With a straightened road toward scientific progress, personality and work emerged as a vigorous research area that continues to run its course with no end in sight. From here on out, it would appear to be full speed ahead.

The purpose of this handbook is to bring together into a single volume the diverse areas of work psychology where personality constructs have been applied and investigated. Over the past two decades alone, an enormous amount of research has been done across these areas, and it would be a daunting task for anyone to stay abreast of all of it in the primary literature. The chapters herein provide expert review and analysis of the key topics relating to personality in work settings, offering clear foundations for programmatic research, theory development, and evidence-based guidance to practitioners. Before offering an outline of this handbook's structure, we introduce a general discussion of what personality is and our reasons for compiling this book.

What Is Personality?

Although there are many definitions of personality, there are some common features. Funder (2010) identifies those commonalities by defining personality as the individual's characteristic patterns of thought, emotion, and behavior, together with the psychological mechanisms behind those patterns. There are two other important concepts often associated with personality. First, personality is thought to drive and direct behavior. As a cause of people's actions, it is intrinsically motivational in nature. Second, it is involved in determining how people react to situations. The idea that personality is involved in differences in adaptation to the environment was an important aspect of the earliest theories of personality psychologists, including Kurt Lewin (1952), Gordon Allport (1937), and Henry Murray (1939). Thus, the impact of personality on behavior has always been construed to be an interaction between the person and the situation.

The study of personality therefore involves attempts to explain and predict behavior by trying to determine "why" people do things in context. For many, this makes it the core of psychological inquiry. Hall and Lindzey (1957), in characterizing the perspective of Henry Murray, said, "Personality is the essence of a human being" (p. 9). In *Explorations in Personality*, Murray (1939) had argued that all psychology was really the study of personality; it is just some approaches settle for taking different kinds of snapshots in time and location rather than viewing the whole. It is beyond a doubt that personality psychology is what the average person thinks of first when asked what a psychologist is most likely to study (McAdams, 1997).

Why Study Personality at Work?

By this point in the introduction, the answer to this question may be obvious to the reader. One way to appreciate the question is to try to envision a field that attempted to develop explanations and interventions with regard to what people do at work *without* the idea of personality. Individual differences in ability and experience would still come into play but very little could be said of interests, preferences, or temperament. Motivation might be discussed in terms of general principles (e.g., goal setting) that apply to all of us, but dealing with individual differences in motivation would quickly prove restrictive and incomplete without taking account of constructs closely related to personality, such as self-concept, needs, and reward preferences. Without personality, a host of questions would defy satisfactory resolution. Why do people who tend to be late showing up for work also have a propensity to be absent more often? Why are some workers excited by learning new software that could make their work easier but others are apprehensive? Why is it that the individuals who are dissatisfied at their present jobs are also likely to have been dissatisfied with their previous jobs? Questions such as these are grist for the mill of efforts to explain people in the workplace, and answers to such questions can be found in this volume.

Although integral to understanding why employees think, feel, and act as they do at work, applying personality theory and research in this context involves a host of challenges due to the complexity of how personality functions. Personality cannot be understood to develop, find expression, or be measured without consideration of many difficult issues that may operate at multiple levels. Here are a few sources of complexity demanding attention when dealing with personality.

Personality Is Multidimensional

Discovery of the Five-Factor Model (FFM; e.g., Tupes & Christal, 1961) has contributed greatly to the advance of personality psychology from a trait perspective, perhaps no more so than in work settings. Although offering a valuable organizing framework for dealing with diverse traits, the FFM falls toward the tip of the taxonomic iceberg of personality trait content. Beneath the surface of this highly popular Openness to Experience, Conscientiousness, Extraversion, Agreeableness, Neuroticism (OCEAN) model lie layers of more specific traits that, although interrelated within broader clusters, are *not* interchangeable. Assertive workers, for example, tend to be sociable and sensation seeking. Sometimes assertiveness is the critical factor needed to explain job success and the other narrow traits (if relevant at all) are secondary; in other circumstances, the reverse might hold true. Complicating this, important personality constructs such as locus of control have been shown to lie outside the FFM entirely, but these traits can explain important work behavior beyond those dimensions (Hattrup, O'Connell, & Labrador, 2005). The multidimensionality of personality is an important complexity to be reckoned with when using personality variables in research and practice.

Trait-by-Trait Interactions

Personality in work settings is most often studied in terms of single traits as predictors of a given criterion. If multiple traits are considered, their contributions are almost always identified as additive and compensatory. Such single-trait applications are important, but personality affords the possibility of additional depth due to trait-by-trait interactions. If you ask people, for example, whether it is okay to have a boss who is dominant (i.e., is comfortable telling others what to do), most will say "yes." But many quickly change their answer if you add that the dominant boss also tends to be argumentative (versus supportive), volatile (versus emotionally stable), or unyielding (versus open-minded). Thus, whether dominance has a positive or negative effect on leadership may depend on the leader's standing on other traits. Multiplicative trait interactions, and configural profiles more broadly, can be critical in determining personality-based fit to a given situation. Long valued by those involved in clinical personality assessment, researchers have only recently begun to explore these complexities in the psychology of work (e.g., Witt, 2002; Witt, Burke, Barrick, & Mount, 2002).

Personality Measurement Is Challenging

We draw inferences about personality by what we see people do and by what they say about themselves. Personality assessment, whether by direct observation or self-report, is in itself very complex and invites error and uncertainty. Some traits are easier to see, some are more likely to evoke exaggerated self-descriptions, some people are better observers, some methods yield better validity, and so on. Entire literatures are devoted to person perception, response biases, and measurement methods intended to improve the validity of personality-based inferences. Personality research and its applications depend critically on measurement, and so part of the complexity in dealing with personality in general comes from dealing with complexities in its measurement.

Personality as an Explanatory Construct

At the simplest level, personality traits are brief and convenient descriptions of an individual's behavioral tendencies. When we say someone is extraverted, for example, we are suggesting that we have seen that person behaving in an outgoing manner, positively engaging others, possibly with dominant tendencies, and gladly accepting (if not seeking) to be the center of attention. We are not only describing what we have seen that person do in the past, we are also projecting what we expect him or her to do in future, at least under similar conditions. The descriptive economy of personality traits is sufficient to warrant central focus on traits in the psychology of individual differences. But traits also have close motivational ties to needs, values, goals, interests, self-concept, and related constructs. The way that traits relate to motivation, whether as need satisfaction or in relation to other variables such as interests or preferences, invites consideration of the psychological processes beyond a merely descriptive function. For the researcher interested in the psychology of work, personality offers a challenging and engaging target of investigation. To the practitioner in this area, it demands careful theoretical consideration for the full predictive potential of personality to be realized.

Personality and Situations

As noted above, situations are key in any consideration of personality, serving many roles. First, they shape the way genes serving personality are expressed. Second, they affect personality development, especially in the early years of life, in tandem with experience. Third, they are the primary source of stimuli bringing certain traits into action and not others. This is critical in work settings where we seek to identify the specific traits that underlie behavior, performance, and satisfaction in particular jobs, groups, and organizations. Fourth, they provide the context in which behavior is interpreted as trait expression. Providing detailed instructions can be helpful to novices but overbearing to the highly skilled. Situations also assist with inferences about which trait has been expressed by similar behaviors with different psychological meaning; in one context interrupting someone may involve the trait of rudeness, but in another, it could be a manifestation of impulsivity. Fifth, personality can lead individuals to seek out or even create situations where a need is fulfilled or certain behavioral tendencies are valued and rewarded. One cannot speak meaningfully about personality and behavior without invoking situations in one or more ways, and considering all the connections between traits and situations is a challenging undertaking.

Situations Are Highly Differentiated

Few terms in psychology are as broad, encompassing, and potentially confusing as "situation." Countless concepts fall within this general class of variables. Consider the following: task demands, job type, reward contingency, coworker attributes, group norms, team size, leadership style, organizational culture, and economic climate. Each of these terms captures taxonomies of more specific situational factors potentially relevant to the expression and evaluation of personality. The sheer number of such "situational" variables is humbling and the possibilities for interactions among them in their effects on personality processes can be daunting.

The Value of a Trait Depends on Context

Individual traits tend to have a default value as positive or negative. Averaging across situations, people typically prefer that those around them fall at one pole of a trait rather than the other pole. However, certain situations can accentuate, attenuate, or even override a trait's default value. We may generally favor being around extraverts who tend to be engaging and display positive emotions, but there are times when we seek more quiet, reserved, and contemplative company because extraverts may be distracting when deadlines encroach. Along the same vein, many tasks are performed better by workers who are dependable, meticulous, and rule oriented. However, some tasks demand flexibility and creativity. In these instances, timeliness, attention to detail, and rule following are sacrificed when success demands more open-minded performance. Evidence abounds for situational specificity in the strength and direction of personality–performance relationships (cf. Tett & Christiansen, 2007), and it is only by recognizing that situations vary in the demands placed on relevant traits that we can begin to make sense of, and exploit, such complexity involving personality at work.

In light of these factors that point toward complication and convolution (e.g., multidimensionality, potential for interactions between traits, challenges entailed in measurement, motivational and process implications, along with the many different ways situations are involved), one faces a monumental task in trying to piece them all together into a cohesive whole when considering the role of personality. This book attempts the more modest objective of highlighting these complexities as they intersect with the research and practice of applying personality psychology to the workplace.

Structure of *Handbook of Personality at Work*

The chapters in this handbook address the issues noted above and many other recent developments in theory and research findings that have changed how industrial–organizational (I-O) psychologists think about the potential of personality constructs. This handbook is divided into three sections, the chapters of which focus on a specific topic as follows:

- Section I: Foundations and Theoretical Perspectives
- Section II: Assessment of Personality at Work
- Section III: Applications of Personality to the Psychology of Work

Embedded in each of the primary chapters, the authors have included a "Practitioner's Window," highlighting the most salient contributions toward the practice of I-O psychology. Taken together, these represent the take-home messages for those applied psychologists who seek to incorporate research findings into their practice.

The seven chapters in Section I focus on the conceptual underpinnings that serve as the building blocks for the assessment and application of personality. It has been argued that there are two types of knowledge that applied psychologists must attempt to integrate: "theory knowledge" that explains things and "practical knowledge" that involves how things get done (Sandelands, 1990). Both of these key areas of knowledge rest upon a common foundation in terms of the assumptions about what personality is and how personality constructs operate in causing work behavior. Although it is possible to develop interventions without theory, they would look quite different and would be less useful than those that are theory driven (Craig, 1996). It is in this context that we are reminded of the often-repeated words of Kurt Lewin (1952): "There is nothing so practical as a good theory" (p. 6). It is a testament to the progress in this area to note that 20 years ago very little of the foundations for this section would have existed. Although much more is needed in terms of personality theory specific to the psychology of work, important inroads have been made and these chapters review and continue this progress.

The second section deals specifically with how personality constructs can be assessed in order to generate scores to be used for examining relationships and making decisions about people. It begins with a historical perspective on personality testing, foreshadowing later chapters by noting the early and continued use of methods of assessment that go beyond personality inventories. The majority of the remaining chapters in this section focus on specific issues related to the use of personality tests in organizations, including reviews of the psychometric characteristics of 10 popular commercial inventories, methods of determining that traits are relevant to a job, effects of applicant faking, applicants' reactions to personality tests, trade-offs involved in assessing constructs at different levels of breadth, challenges in assessing personality across cultures, use of personality types, and configural approaches to personality. The five chapters ending the section all involve the use of other methods of personality assessment, namely, use of selection interviews, situational judgment tests, observer judgments, assessment centers, and content coding of written and verbal material. Personality is not a simple phenomenon and the chapters on assessment highlight the complexity involved in the measurement of multidimensional constructs that can be expressed in very different ways.

The third section on applications draws together a range of topics related to how personality constructs are utilized in the research and practice based on the study of how people behave at work. The initial chapters take on practical issues such as legal aspects of the use of personality tests in the workplace, implications of personality for training programs, and use of personality test results in talent management programs. The focus of the remaining chapters in this section shifts to reviews of how personality has been incorporated into the most important research areas in the psychology of work, including prediction of contextual (citizenship and counterproductive work behavior) and traditional job performance, vocational behavior, mood and emotions, work stress, job attitudes, teams, and leadership. This section concludes with a chapter on how personality can change and develop as a result of work experience. As a whole, the chapters in this section underscore the impact of personality across an array of subject matter at the core of I-O psychology.

The concluding chapters present three perspectives on the current state of the study of personality at work. In the first concluding chapter, a renowned personality psychologist takes stock of how research is conducted and has progressed when personality constructs are applied to work. This is followed by musings of one of the leading researchers to have applied those constructs to work settings. The volume closes with some thoughts from one of the editors, aimed at carrying forward select themes identified in earlier chapters. These concluding chapters provide a clear message: Although progress in the study of personality at work has been extraordinary, the road goes ever on.

References

Adelson, J. (1969). Personality. *Annual Review of Psychology, 20*, 136–252.

Allport, G. W. (1937). *Personality: A psychological interpretation.* New York: Holt, Rinehart & Winston.

Barrick, M. R., & Mount, M. K. (1991). The big five personality dimensions and job performance: A meta-analysis. *Personnel Psychology, 44*, 1–26.

Carlson, R. (1971). Where is the person in personality research? *Psychological Bulletin, 75*, 203–219.
Christiansen, N. D., Goffin, R. D., Johnston, N. G., & Rothstein, M. R. (1994). Correcting the 16PF for faking: Effects on the criterion-related validity and individual hiring decisions. *Personnel Psychology, 47*, 847–860.
Collins, J. M., & Schmidt, F. L. (1993). Personality, integrity, and white collar crime: A construct validity study. *Personnel Psychology, 46*, 295–311.
Craig, R. T. (1996). Practical theory: A reply to Sandelands. *Journal for the Theory of Social Behaviour, 26*, 65–79.
Day, D.V., & Silverman, S. B. (1989). Personality and job performance: Evidence of incremental validity. *Personnel Psychology, 42*, 25–36.
Fritzsche, B. A., McIntire, S. A., & Yost, A. P. (2002). Holland type as a moderator of personality-performance predictions. *Journal of Vocational Behavior, 60*, 422–436.
Funder, D. C. (2010). *The personality puzzle* (5th ed.). New York: W. W. Norton.
Hale, M. (1982). History of employment testing. In A. Wigdor & W. Garner (Eds.), *Ability testing: Uses, consequences, and controversies* (pp. 3–38). Washington, DC: National Academy Press.
Hall, C. S., & Lindzey, G. (1957). *Theories of personality*. New York: John Wiley & Sons.
Hattrup, K., O'Connell, M. S., & Labrador, J. R. (2005). Incremental validity of locus of control after controlling for cognitive ability and conscientiousness. *Journal of Business and Psychology, 19*, 461–481.
Hogan, R., & Roberts, B. W. (2001). Personality and I/O psychology. In B. W. Roberts & R. T. Hogan (Eds.), *Personality psychology in the workplace* (pp. 3–18). Washington, DC: American Psychological Association.
Hough, L. M. (2001). I/Owes its advance to personality. In B. W. Roberts & R. Hogan (Eds.), *Personality psychology in the workplace* (pp. 19–44). Washington, DC: American Psychological Association.
Hough, L. M., Eaton, N. R., Dunnette, M. D., Kamp, J. D., & McCloy, R. A. (1990). Criterion-related validities of personality constructs and the effect of response distortion on those validities. *Journal of Applied Psychology, 75*, 581–595.
Judge, T. A., Bono, J. E., & Locke, E. A. (2000). Personality and job satisfaction: The mediating role of job characteristics. *Journal of Applied Psychology, 85*, 237–249.
Lewin, K. (1952). *Field theory in social science: Selected theoretical papers by Kurt Lewin*. London: Tavistock.
Lord, R. G., De Vader, C. L., & Alliger, G. M. (1986). A meta-analysis of the relation between personality traits and leadership perceptions: An application of validity generalization procedures. *Journal of Applied Psychology, 71*, 402–410.
McAdams, D. P. (1997). A conceptual history of personality psychology. In R. Hogan, J. Johnson, & S. Briggs (Eds.), *Handbook of personality psychology* (pp. 3–39). San Diego, CA: Academic Press.
Moyle, P. (1995). The role of negative affectivity in the stress process: Tests of alternative models. *Journal of Organizational Behavior, 16*, 647–668.
Murray, H. A. (1939). *Explorations in personality*. New York: Oxford University Press.
Ones, D. S., & Viswesvaran, C. (1996). Bandwidth-fidelity dilemma in personality measurement for personnel selection. *Journal of Organizational Behavior, 17*, 609–626.
Ones, D. S., Viswesvaran, C., & Reiss, A. D. (1996). Role of social desirability in personality testing for personnel selection: The red herring. *Journal of Applied Psychology, 81*, 660–679.
Organ, D. W., & Ryan, K. (1995). A meta-analytic review of attitudinal and dispositional predictors of organizational citizenship behavior. *Personnel Psychology, 48*, 775–802.
Paunonen, S.V., Rothstein, M. G., & Jackson, D. N. (1999). Narrow reasoning about the use of broad personality measures for personnel selection. *Journal of Organizational Behavior, 20*, 389–405.
Sandelands, L. E. (1990). What is so practical about theory? Lewin revisited. *Journal for the Theory of Social Behaviour, 20*, 357–379.
Schneider, B. (2007). Evolution of the study and practice of personality at work. *Human Resource Management, 46*, 583–610.
Tett, R. P., & Christiansen, N. D. (2007). Personality tests at the crossroads: A reply to Morgeson, Campion, Dipboye, Hollenbeck, Murphy, and Schmitt. *Personnel Psychology, 60*, 267–293.
Tett, R. P., Jackson, D. N., & Rothstein, M. (1991). Meta-analysis of personality–job performance relationships. *Personnel Psychology, 47*, 157–172.
Tupes, E. C., & Christal, R. E. (1961). Recurrent personality factors based on trait ratings. *Journal of Personality, 60*, 225–251.
Witt, L. (2002). The interactive effects of extraversion and conscientiousness on performance. *Journal of Management, 28*, 835–851. doi:10.1177/014920630202800607
Witt, L., Burke, L., Barrick, M., & Mount, M. (2002). The interactive effects of conscientiousness and agreeableness on job performance. *Journal of Applied Psychology, 87*, 164–169.

Section I

Foundations and Theoretical Perspectives

2

Theoretical and Empirical Structures of Personality

Implications for Measurement, Modeling, and Prediction

Fred L. Oswald, Leaetta Hough, and Jisoo Ock

Do theory and data support a single factor of personality? Do narrowly defined personality traits offer added conceptual and practical benefits over the Five-Factor Model (FFM)? Should we consider the six-factor HEXACO model or other taxonomic structures more seriously? What personality constructs are overlooked in a model/structure? The answers to these questions are important. In this chapter, we examine taxonomies of personality with a sensitivity to theory as well as how personality constructs are measured, modeled, and ultimately used to enhance our understanding of higher-level phenomena (e.g., organizational climate), mediators (e.g., goal-setting, reactions to feedback, and teamwork), and outcomes in organizations (e.g., turnover, job satisfaction, and individual and team-level performance). We also suggest directions for future research that builds upon this knowledge.

Defining Personality Traits

Personality traits are stable individual-difference constructs that reflect reliable and distinct habits, consistencies, or patterns in a person's thoughts, feelings, and behaviors over time and across situations. This definition serves as a heuristic because it can be parsed into a set of conceptual considerations and empirically testable propositions such as "How much stability exists in people, and how much must be shown before earning the status of a trait?" "How are thoughts and feelings best measured and inferred (e.g., self vs. other ratings; current vs. retrospective vs. prospective assessments)?" "What constitutes an accurate summary, and how does one know once it is obtained?"

Personality trait labels apply to a conceptual average or tendency of a person's thoughts, feelings, and behaviors across time and situations. Critics of personality traits disfavor labeling a person's tendencies across situational and cross-temporal consistencies (perhaps for fear of surrendering to stereotypes or determinism) and favor requiring highly complex situational contingencies—ones that compete against the principle of scientific parsimony, as they generally call upon complex models and greater empirical evidence to be supported. Modesty and self-discipline, for instance, imply that the person tends to manifest higher levels of these traits than other people across situations. It does not mean that the person does not exhibit moments of immodesty or impulsivity in some situations. Within-person variance may be important (Fleeson, 2001), but it is often correlated with the within-person mean, to the point where its unique variance may be reliable but may not add incremental validity over the mean (Baird, Le, & Lucas, 2006).

Information on personality traits can be very valuable in work settings. For example, when employers hire entry-level employees, they lack information about how the person might behave in work situations. Although "past performance predicts future performance," the resume may not document enough critical behavior or provide evidence of consistency of documented behavior.

General Definition of Taxonomies

The Big Five is the primary organizing structure relied upon when conducting and considering personality research in organizational settings. This chapter will also review other structures of personality that provide appealing alternatives, but before doing so, we take the opportunity to consider the following general question: What are the characteristics of a useful organizing taxonomy (or structure or framework) of personality? The answer, we think, is found by examining two sides of the personality coin. The "internal" side of the coin refines taxonomies by considering relatively internal measurement influences by (a) relating items to traits (e.g., a measurement model), (b) relating traits to one another (e.g., a multifactor measurement model or multitrait matrix), or (c) relating traits to higher-order latent traits. The "external" side of the coin refines taxonomies by considering relatively external influences by (a) taking method factors into account (e.g., measurement format and rating source), (b) relating traits to organizational outcomes, (c) relating traits to group differences, or (d) qualifying validity and/or group differences by moderators (e.g., trait × situation × time) and/or mediators (e.g., motivation and self-regulation).

A discussion of the merits of factors versus facets requires an awareness of a tension between personality theory and the use of personality variables in employment settings to which our research is intended to generalize. More specifically, practitioners often need to know whether or not a specific personality measure will be useful within the assessment system of a particular company, whereas researchers seek a broader and more theoretical understanding of the underlying nature, dimensionality, and relationships between latent personality constructs. Both sides of the research-practice coin are clearly necessary, as a theoretical understanding of personality constructs informs the development and practical use of measures. The present-day practice of applying meta-analysis to a wide array of personality measures in organizational research has been beneficial for interpreting our results in terms of theoretical constructs. Whether we have identified—or ever will identify—fundamental constructs (taxons) that form the structure of human personality may be less important than the extent to which we have consistent patterns of evidence for personality constructs predicting organizationally relevant constructs, thereby contributing meaningfully to practice as well as to our theoretical knowledge base.

We discuss below, in greater depth, the Five-Factor and HEXACO models. We also discuss the usefulness of personality facets, which, both theoretically and empirically, are one level more refined than the factors contained in these models (see Table 2.1). We then describe a nomological web-clustering approach that incorporates facets in a more flexible bottom-up manner that increases our understanding of the structure of personality as well as patterns of criterion-related validity.

Internal Structures

Correlation coefficients that reflect linear relationships between measures of personality traits, such as the Big Five, usually fall somewhere between 0 and 1, leaving room for researchers to debate (as they have) about whether personality traits should be usefully combined or remain usefully distinct. On the one hand, combining traits might serve to uphold the principle of Occam's Razor: Avoid complexity that does not justify its benefit over simplicity. In addition, any positive correlations that are observed might be higher at the latent level, once measurement reliability and range restriction effects are taken into account (Hunter & Schmidt, 2004). On the other hand, respecting each trait

Table 2.1 Comparing Factors Versus Facets

2 Factors	*Big Five (B5)/HEXACO (HX)*	*12 Facets*
Alpha/stability	Honesty/humility (HX)	Sincerity, greed avoidance
	Neuroticism (B5)	Volatility, withdrawal
	Emotionality (HX)	
	Conscientiousness (B5/HX)	Industriousness, orderliness
	Agreeableness (B5/HX)	Compassion, politeness
Beta/plasticity	Extraversion (B5)	Enthusiasm, assertiveness
	Surgency (HX)	
	Openness (B5/HX)	Intellect, artistic openness

Note: Alpha and beta factor labels come from Digman (1997); the stability and plasticity labels come from DeYoung (2006); the facet labels come from DeYoung, Quilty, and Peterson (2007); the Big Five and HEXACO labels are standard labels for these factor models. We recommend that greater research attention be paid to these facet-level constructs, not the broader constructs.

on its own, despite any positive correlation, gives the differential prediction and differential validity of traits a chance to manifest themselves.[1]

A General Factor of Personality?

Correlations between personality traits (the Big Five in particular) can be interpreted as evidence for the existence of higher-order factors. Digman (1997) offered evidence for the existence of two higher-order factors, one called *alpha*, which was related to socialization or fitting into group contexts (low neuroticism, high conscientiousness, and high agreeableness), and the other called *beta*, related to self-actualization or personal growth (high extraversion and high openness). These factors are aligned with two factors that DeYoung (2006) labeled as *stability* and *plasticity*, respectively, when investigating higher-order factors of the Big Five in multi-informant and multimeasure samples.

These two factors are themselves correlated, which some researchers have taken as evidence for a general factor of personality (GFP), a single higher-order dimension that is thought to range from adaptive (high standing on GFP) to maladaptive (low standing on GFP). Rushton et al. (2009) provided recent evidence for the GFP in terms of its heritability in multiple-informant and behavior genetic (twin) studies, as well as in terms of its robustness across different personality measures (Rushton & Irwing, 2011). Despite stability and replicability of the GFP, whether GFP is a useful and substantively interpretable construct or a methodological artifact is debatable. Donnellan, Hopwood, and Wright (2012) detected problems within the reported results of Rushton and Irwing (2009). Nor could they replicate the GFP in a large participant sample that was administered the *Multidimensional Personality Questionnaire* (MPQ). They could, however, replicate a three-factor structure that has received wide empirical support in the developmental, clinical, and personality literatures (i.e., positive emotionality, negative emotionality, and constraint).

The higher-order factor model is "wildly unparsimonious" (Ashton, Lee, Goldberg, & de Vries, 2009, p. 86), in that the correlation between the scales is often quite low, especially after rater-specific halo factors are accounted for (Anusic, Schimmack, Pinkus, & Lockwood, 2009; Chang, Connelly, & Geeza, 2012). Accounting for reverse-scored items within a scale can reduce the GFP even further (Revelle & Wilt, 2010). Some researchers have suggested, in addition, that correlations between personality factors largely stem from nonsubstantive response patterns (e.g., tendencies to respond to positively worded items versus negatively worded items) that artificially inflate the measured relationships (Chang et al., 2012).

In short, although there has been some evidence for a GFP, it has been quite weak, both in terms of GFP summarizing trait-relevant covariances (higher-order reliability) and in terms of predicting relevant outcomes (higher-order validity). Compared to psychometric *g*, the general factor for cognitive ability, personality traits such as the Big Five tend to show low correlations with one another. Moreover, traits are bipolar. Reverse-scoring a trait (e.g., scoring neuroticism as emotional stability) is arbitrary with respect to the nature of the structure of personality. Thus, GFP is ill-defined because its mix of positive and negative correlations is equally legitimate. In the cognitive ability domain, abilities such as math, verbal, and spatial tend to show high positive correlations with one another (positive manifold), and reverse-scoring a specific ability in the context of the others does not make sense (e.g., re-scoring math as "low math"). Whether the personality or cognitive ability domains are of interest, the multiple factors underlying GFP and *g*, respectively, are often important for improving both scientific understanding and empirical prediction involving personality and cognitive ability. However, there has been a much longer research history and stronger empirical case for the general factor for cognitive ability (*g*) summarizing a substantial amount of the correlations between specific factors (abilities), which then has also been found to predict important academic, employment, and life outcomes (Gottfredson, 1997). The GFP is not based on underlying unipolar factors with strong positive manifold; it does not capture much variance in the factors (even if that variance is reliable), and it therefore does not lead to practical levels of validity. In these three ways, GFP is radically different from *g*.

The Big Five

Since the 1990s, the FFM has enjoyed a renaissance in the development, evaluation, and use of personality measures in organizational research and is considered by many to be the strongest or most fundamental organizing structure of personality traits. The FFM emerged from a factor analysis of ratings of personality-descriptive adjectives selected from the dictionary. The *lexical hypothesis* was the driver behind this analysis, namely, the more important a personality trait was to human experience and functioning, the more those trait-relevant words would tend to recur in the dictionary, and thus the stronger empirical presence of that trait as a factor (Allport & Odbert, 1936; Goldberg, 1990, 1993; Tupes & Christal, 1961, 1992). Thus, the deepest historical basis of the FFM lies in the English lexicon that in turn reflects people's "folk" perceptions of personality. Only subsequently has the FFM been more strongly moored to human cultures, human biology, and human behavior (Tellegen, 1993; and see Hough & Schneider, 1996, for a history of the FFM).

Although the lexicon is the source of the FFM, over two decades of research have generally supported FFM trait stability across racial, gender, and cultural groups as well as over time (see McCrae & Costa, 2008, for a review of this research). Extraversion and emotional stability are found in virtually all factor-analytic studies, with conscientiousness being almost as consistently found. Openness to experience is usually the least replicable factor, perhaps because it contains diverse facets. For instance, openness to ideas has been shown to correlate more strongly with intelligence measures (Zimprich, Allemand, & Dellenbach, 2009) and with work-relevant criteria (Mussel, Winter, Gelléri, & Schuler, 2011) than do other facets of openness (e.g., openness to ideas, feelings, and actions).

Expanding personality constructs and content beyond the Big Five can lead to a more diverse set of personality constructs that might provide even greater insight into understanding and explaining work behavior, performance, and outcomes. Thus, assuming a broad structure of personality, such as the Big Five, has the benefit of organizing a wide array of confusing and redundant constructs, but treating broad factors as fundamental has the potential to stifle or misdirect the development of more sophisticated theory and research (Block, 1995).

Organizational researchers have begun to explore and refine the taxonomic structure of personality further. At the level of broad factor models, the HEXACO is the major contender to the FFM in the organizational research literature.

The HEXACO Model

The HEXACO model is both an acronym and a reference to six factors, where essentially (but not entirely), an honesty/humility factor is added to the FFM, providing greater breadth of measurement in the personality domain (Ashton & Lee, 2001). Similar to the FFM, the honesty/humility factor in the HEXACO model has been replicated in lexical research across multiple languages and cultures (e.g., Ashton et al., 2004). An initial concern about the HEXACO model was that the honesty/humility factor was contingent on culture and language in non-English-speaking countries. However, an analysis of 1,710 English adjectives also found empirical support for six factors instead of only the FFM (Ashton, Lee, & Goldberg, 2004). Thus, there is increasing support for the claim that a lexicon that is more inclusive than previous FFM lexical studies allows for considering a broader range of personal descriptors and therefore provides the potential (but no guarantee) for empirical support for a wider nomological net (Ashton & Lee, 2008; Lee & Ashton, 2008).

Honesty/humility does not merely broaden the factor structure of personality; it also enhances the prediction of workplace outcomes over the FFM, such as workplace delinquency (see Lee, Ashton, & de Vries, 2005, supporting this finding in a cross-cultural study). It is also noteworthy to contrast this sixth factor of honesty/humility with a sixth "ideal employee" factor that has been found in FFM data for job applicants—but not in nonapplicants (Schmit & Ryan, 1993). Whereas the HEXACO honesty/humility factor is distinct from the FFM and reflects *internal* virtues of sincerity and greed avoidance, the "ideal employee" factor seems to be a general method factor, where some job applicants are *externally* motivated to indicate to employers that they have a high-positive standing on all FFM traits.

Future Factor Model Research

Organizational research that makes use of personality measures will often examine the overall stability of the 5- or 6-model factors by use of exploratory factor analysis (Goldberg & Velicer, 2006). Modern statistical methods need to be brought to bear on these investigations of the stability and generalizability of factor structures of personality.

First, when the goal is not only to assess the fit of factor models to the data but also to do so across cultural, racial, or gender groups, the use of congruence coefficients (essentially correlations of corresponding factor loadings between groups; Bijnen, van der Net, & Poortinga, 1986) is antiquated and should be supplanted by modern measurement invariance techniques that test for equivalent loadings in a more formal manner (e.g., Cheung & Lau, 2012). Measurement invariance techniques test for model fit within groups as a prerequisite for appropriate comparisons between groups. Then, they impose a series of constrained models to find the appropriate level at which model equivalence holds (i.e., equal factor loadings across items, then equal item intercepts, and then possibly equal error variances; see A. D. Wu, Li, & Zumbo, 2007, for an accessible tutorial).

Second, exploratory factor analyses often yield loadings on the Big Five that are similar across samples yet also show fluctuation. This underlying fluctuation, along with item cross-loadings on unintended factors, is generally why more rigorous confirmatory factor analysis (CFA) models of personality have failed to meet the standards of model-fit criteria. One way to continue to use CFA in personality measurement is to compare fit statistics with those that have arisen from other efforts. Although model-fit statistics may not reach traditional benchmarks, they may reflect improvements over past attempts at model fit (Hopwood & Donnellan, 2010).

Another approach, exploratory structural equation modeling (ESEM; Asparouhov & Muthen, 2009), balances exploratory and confirmatory approaches. In ESEM, a CFA model is analyzed, but factor-loading rotations are allowed, and all factor loadings are estimated. This means that items with small cross-loadings do not need to be eliminated from the model to achieve good model fit. A related approach is similar to CFA but instead of setting factor-loading estimates to zero, factor loadings are relaxed to allow for small variation around zero (Bayesian model estimation allows for setting this type of constraint). Allowing for small cross-loadings to be estimated provides more accurate estimates of covariance or correlation between factors, assuming the model is not overfitting the data (Muthén & Asparouhov, 2012).

Personality Facets

It is important to note that the FFM and HEXACO are broad factor models that can organize the content and structure of many underlying facets. For example, the factor of conscientiousness contains both industriousness and orderliness facets, and the factor of extraversion contains both enthusiasm and assertiveness facets (DeYoung, Quilty, & Peterson, 2007). Factor-based measures are sometimes created by selecting items across a range of facets that happen to show the highest factor loadings on the corresponding personality factor. As a result, these may reflect some facets more than others, and there is no guarantee that the facets themselves are psychometrically reliable with enough representative items. To the extent that facets of FFM and HEXACO factors are not given enough attention to be measured reliably, they may be given a "bad rap" by not being given a fair psychometric chance to yield more useful information beyond the measures of broader personality factors. Thus, although FFM and HEXACO factors have shown themselves to be theoretically and practically useful, researchers and practitioners should not be lulled into thinking that factor-level personality represents the most comprehensive, fundamental, or the best that personality research can provide.

In various writings, we have maintained that broad personality factors are often too conceptually diverse or heterogeneous to advance our understanding of personality traits and prediction of behavior in the workplace much farther than we are today. Facets have the potential to provide a more substantive understanding of the importance of personality-driven criterion-related validity, and more research is needed at this level (see Hough, 1992; Hough & Oswald, 2000; Schneider, Hough, & Dunnette, 1996).

At least one study or meta-analysis involving facets underlying each of the FFM factors exists: extraversion (e.g., Moon, Hollenbeck, Marinova, & Humphrey, 2008), emotional stability (e.g., van Doorn & Lang, 2010), conscientiousness (e.g., MacCann, Duckworth, & Roberts, 2009; Roberts, Bogg, Walton, Chernyshenko, & Stark, 2004; Roberts, Chernyshenko, Stark, & Goldberg, 2005), agreeableness (e.g., Piedmont & Weinstein, 1993), and openness (e.g., Connelly, Ones, Davies, & Birkland, 2012; Mussel et al., 2011; Woo, Chernyshenko, Stark, & Conz, in press). Taken together, this body of research suggests that personality facets serve as a vital source for improving our understanding of the modeling and validity of personality traits.

It seems a bit surprising that the developers of FFM or HEXACO personality measures have discovered an equal number of narrower facet-level constructs for each factor (e.g., the NEO-PI-R contains exactly six facets for each factor; and the HEXACO-PI-R measure contains exactly four for each factor, with an Altruism vs. Antagonism scale loading on multiple factors). Less surprising is the fact that many important personality facets appear to reside outside FFM and HEXACO models. Hough and Furnham (2003) detail 21 such facets, such as rugged individualism (masculinity–femininity) and social insight. Surely, there are more facets such as these that may not fit into any broader factor model yet are relevant or even critical to understanding and predicting organizational behavior. A personality researcher or test developer may decide to ignore facets (narrower constructs) of personality entirely or decide to sample items across facets to develop reliable measures of broad factors, where the facets themselves are not reliably measured. These decisions, usually practical and not theoretical, may lead to obscuring our understanding of important constructs, processes, and patterns of validity at the facet level. More careful measurement and research are needed at the facet level before concluding that the broader factors are the level at which personality research in organizations should remain.

Facet-level constructs are very promising building blocks for both organizational theory and practice, and organizational research supports differential validity at the facet level that would not be discovered at the level of broader factors. Stewart (1999) found that, in the initial stages of a sales career, the conformity facet of conscientiousness (responsibility and rule-following) was relevant to attracting new clients, but as a salesperson gains experience, the achievement facet was more relevant. In examining the same two facets, Lepine, Colquitt, and Erez (2000) found that in a complex and changing task, those higher in conformity committed more errors, yet achievement was not predictive of errors. In other research also examining conformity and achievement, differential validity is found for predicting job performance and lawful behaviors (Hough, 1992; Roberts et al., 2005).

Recently, we provided an abundance of other examples for personality facets predicting organizationally relevant outcomes that would not have been discovered at the broader factor level. Rather than reviewing those once again, see Oswald and Hough (2010; also see Paunonen & Jackson, 2000). We add to that review by citing J. Wu and LeBreton (2011), whose extensive review departs from broad factor models of normal personality and ventures into constructs related to aberrant personality—narcissism, Machiavellianism, and psychopathy—and how measures of those constructs predicts counterproductive work behaviors in organizations (e.g., theft, drug use, and unsafe work behaviors).

As a general concluding point, validities for facet-level personality measurement versus a general factor are a matter that is subject to ongoing empirical testing. Neither "side" of this personality debate should dominate across all factors, samples, and settings; the nature of the criteria being measured and the quality of measurement are influential determinants of the results. The often-neglected benefits for facet-level measurement are real benefits, not functions of sampling variability or differential facet reliability that create a mirage of differential validity. Thus, we assert that the FFM, HEXACO, or other broad factor models are useful for organizing a range of facets, yet there remain important and measurable facets that coexist outside of these models.

Circumplex Models: Circular Arrangements of Factors or Facets

Circumplex models of personality stand as a complementary approach to factor models of personality in how constructs are represented. In circumplex models, the relationship between constructs can be visualized as a circle, where constructs near one another on the circle are positively correlated with one another, and constructs diametrically opposite to one another on the circle are minimally or negatively correlated. For example, extraversion and agreeableness are FFM factors in the interpersonal domain and can be represented as a circumplex (circle) defined by two axes that represent warmth (vs. coldness) and assertiveness (vs. submissiveness; see McCrae & Costa, 1989). Under the principle of simple structure, factor models might minimize or reject those variables that are defined by both axes and not just one (e.g., gregariousness), but circumplex models are somewhat less restrictive and can accommodate such variables gracefully in multivariate space. By viewing the circular arrangement of traits as an analytic solution, one quickly learns about convergent and discriminant relationships between personality traits that one may not gain as quickly from factor models. Thus, both circumplex models and factor models provide value in understanding the personality domain; they complement one another in understanding relationships between personality constructs. Circumplex modeling has been around for quite some time, with the term *circumplex* being introduced by Guttman (1954).

The example just provided is one circumplex that can be created using the FFM, but in fact 10 different possible circumplexes are derivable from all possible pairs of FFM factors. All of these circumplexes have been considered in the Abridged Big Five-Dimensional Circumplex (AB5C) taxonomy (Hofstee, de Raad, & Goldberg, 1992). Results support circumplex representations for these factor pairings that have received independent empirical support from data that include peer ratings (Johnson & Ostendorf, 1993). In short, we believe that there is a divide between the evidence in support of circumplex models, particularly in the interpersonal and emotional domains (Plutchik & Conte, 1997), and the application of these models in organizational research. Given the importance of interpersonal communication, teamwork, and emotional regulation in the workplace, the nature and value of circumplex models of personality deserve revisiting. Circumplexes may be a way to tie in the aforementioned family of personality facets that do not fall cleanly within factor models. Moreover, the validity of vocational interests has seen a recent resurgence in the organizational literature (e.g., Nye, Su, Rounds, & Drasgow, 2012; Van Iddekinge, Putka, & Campbell, 2011). Vocational interests are related to personality traits (Ackerman & Heggestad, 1997; Barrick, Mount, & Gupta, 2003; De Fruyt & Mervielde, 1999; Larson, Rottinghaus, & Borgen, 2002; McKay & Tokar, 2012) and are also very commonly represented by circumplex structures (e.g., Tracey & Rounds, 1996; for additional information on circumplex models, see Chapter 17, this volume).

External Influences on Personality Taxonomies

Structure and Utility of Personality Using "Other" Reports

The FFM is often assumed to be based on self-reports of personality, yet historically, it is actually based on "other" reports of personality: Tupes and Christal (1961), who are credited with the origin of the FFM, used peer ratings of personality in their research. Their research on the structure of personality was of interest to them because Tupes' earlier research (Tupes, 1957, 1959) and research by Kelly and Fiske (1951) indicated other-reports of personality predicted later performance. With recent research and interest in the validity of others' ratings of personality (Vazire & Carlson, 2011), personality research has come full circle; in terms of the rating source for personality data, we are back where we started (for full coverage of personality based on others' observations, see Chapter 20, this volume).

Norman (1963) also used peer ratings in his research that "yielded clear and consistent evidence for the existence of 5 relatively orthogonal, easily interpreted personality factors" (p. 574), especially in samples where the targets were well known to the raters. Interestingly, Norman's research program included development of self-report measures that were based on other-report measures that he used to study the structure of personality (Norman, 1963). More than 20 years later, McCrae, Costa, and Busch (1986) reported convergent and discriminant validity of FFM measures using both self-reports and other-reports (peer ratings, spouse ratings, and interviewer ratings for the latter). Morgeson et al.'s (2007) statement that ". . . personality constructs may have value for employee selection, but future research should focus on finding alternatives to self-report personality measures" (p. 683) reveals a lack of awareness of this aspect of the history of personality research. Practitioners and researchers have long been using other-reports of personality to predict work-related criteria, as are indicated by two recent published meta-analyses on the topic (i.e., Connelly & Ones, 2010; Oh, Wang, & Mount, 2011).[2]

Given that the structure of personality is the same for both self- and other-report measures, important research questions follow: Do other-reports of personality show incremental validity over self-reports for predicting work-related criteria? What factors moderate incremental validity? Clearly, the accuracy of other-reports and the extent they provide unique information relevant to the criterion are moderators. Another key moderator is whether a criterion is itself an other-report measure, because in that case, the criterion may be influenced (enhanced or contaminated) by others' perceptions of employee personality and related implicit perceptions of performance.

Funder's (1995) Realistic Accuracy Model posits a four-part process for forming accurate judgments about another person's personality. They are relevance, availability, detection, and utilization.

Relevance means that the environment must allow people to express their level of the trait in question. In other words, environmental cues must activate traits and not suppress them for personality to be relevant (Beaty, Cleveland, & Murphy, 2001; Tett & Burnett, 2003). *Availability* relates to relevance but means that the observer must have the opportunity to observe or perceive the target's trait expression. *Detection* refers to whether or not the observer can detect and perceive the trait in question, and *utilization* means the observer must be able to assemble the perceived trait information appropriately. Thus, accuracy of others' judgments about a target's personality requires signal expression and signal detection. Signal detection means that the trait in question must be meaningfully expressed in the target person's behaviors (relevance and availability), and signal detection means that the observers perceive and process the trait-relevant information with relatively low error (detection and utilization).

The accuracy of other-reports can be estimated by calculating interrater agreement between multiple other-reports; accuracy is also implied—but not guaranteed—by criterion-related validity (Funder & West, 1993). Using these metrics for accuracy, five meta-analyses, one by Connolly, Kavanagh, and Viswesvaran (2007), three by Connelly and Ones (2010), and one by Oh et al. (2011), offer persuasive evidence that other-reports provide more accurate reports of a person's personality than do self-reports.

Accuracy as Rater Consensus: Interrater Reliability Evidence

Meta-analytic observed other-report reliability estimates for the FFM factors are .43, .36, .33, .32, and .32, respectively, for a single observer with regard to extraversion, conscientiousness, emotional stability, openness, and agreeableness (Connelly & Ones, 2010). As one might expect (also see Funder, 1995; John & Robins, 1993), the reliability estimates were relatively higher for highly visible traits such as extraversion and conscientiousness than for other less-visible traits that tend to reflect internal psychological processes such as internal thoughts or feelings that are not directly accessible to others. Although these reliability estimates tend to be higher for ratings by multiple raters and by family or friends compared to ratings by coworkers. The correlation between different other-rating sources might be considered validity coefficients, to the extent that each rating source has access to different aspects of the person being rated. Given these complexities, other-reports of personality will benefit from research that identifies strategies and methods for increasing accuracy and separating reliability into the reliable variance that converges between raters versus the reliable variance unique to raters.

Accuracy as Self-Other Consensus: Self-Other Correlational Evidence

Two meta-analyses (Connolly et al., 2007; Connelly & Ones, 2010) examined self-other correlations of personality ratings, finding very similar values for the FFM variables. Both also found the highest observed self-other correlations for extraversion, .41 (Connelly & Ones, 2010) and .45 (Connolly et al., 2007), and the lowest observed self-other correlations for agreeableness, .29 (Connelly & Ones, 2010) and .30 (Connolly et al., 2007). Although neither meta-analysis produced evidence that traits moderate the relationship between self- and other-reports, both studies again provide some support for Funder's (1995) point of view that more visible traits are more accurately rated. Both meta-analyses did, however, conclude that familiarity with the target as indicated by level of acquaintanceship (Connolly et al., 2007) and interpersonal intimacy (Connelly & Ones, 2010) moderated the self-other relationship such that higher acquaintanceship led to higher convergence between self- and other-reports. Enough unique variance remains between the self versus other sources of personality assessment to leave room for differences in criterion-related validity, to be discussed next.

Criterion-Related Validity Evidence

Meta-analysis again provides persuasive evidence about the relative level of criterion-related validity of self- and other-reports: Other-reports tend to have greater validity than self-reports for predicting job performance, academic achievement, and first impressions. On average, criterion-related validities are approximately .10 higher for other-reports (single-rater) than self-reports (Connelly & Ones, 2010; Oh et al., 2011). The higher criterion-related validities have been attributed to others having a more accurate or "clearer lens" than the self (Connelly & Hülsheger, 2012).

Still higher criterion-related validities are possible from other-reports through the basic principles of reliability: If multiple others (multiple raters) provide ratings of a target individual (Oh et al., 2011), the resulting increase in interrater reliability can lead to increases in validity. Similarly, ensuring that other-reporters are familiar with the person in the organization being rated on personality may result in higher levels of criterion-related validity. This latter topic is underresearched, and we think worthy of further research attention.

There are at least three possible explanations for the higher criterion-related validities for other-reports. First, other ratings may not be as contaminated with error variance from idiosyncratic and systematic biases as are self-reports. However, given past evidence that clearly demonstrates the potential for subjective ratings to harbor systematic error, whether it is in personality ratings or in criterion ratings of performance (Murphy, Cleveland, Skattebo, & Kinney, 2004), more evidence that supports this point of view is needed. Second, according to R. Hogan (1996), personality measurement is about describing a person's reputation, which itself is defined by the perceptions of others. Thus, someone other than the target may be likely to be better equipped to provide information about the target's reputation.

Finally, frame-of-reference or situational contexts may have contributed to other-report validity findings. Self-reports likely incorporate perceptions of self across a variety of contexts, whereas others' perceptions about the target person are already more likely to be formed within the specific context in which the observer interacts with the target person. Thus, self-report measures that do not specify the relevant context may obscure the validity of the self-reported personality measures. Several studies demonstrate that context-specific self-report personality measures provide higher validity compared with general personality measures (e.g., Bing, Whanger, Davison, & VanHook, 2004; Bowling & Burns, 2010; Hunthausen, Truxillo, Bauer, & Hammer, 2003; Pace & Brannick, 2010; Schmit, Ryan, Stierwalt, & Powell, 1995; Shafer & Postlethwaite, 2012). The noted gain in validity for other-reports of personality in work settings may be capitalizing on this frame-of-reference effect.

Clearly, taxonomies of personality supported by the accuracy of other-reports can be compromised by motivated distortion, just as it can for self-reports. Thus, the possibility that others may be motivated to distort the personality ratings of the target should be considered, whether it is due to the organizational context or due to the personality characteristics of the other-raters themselves. Another consideration is how—just as other-reports have been found to be more accurate with greater knowledge of the target (e.g., longer duration of acquaintanceship and greater personal intimacy with the target person)—self-reports might be improved when the person possesses high levels of self-insight or self-knowledge. Thus, self-knowledge might moderate criterion-related validities of self-reports. Prior research evidence indicates that self-knowledge predicts work-related criteria, but it was not found to moderate criterion-related validities of other personality variables such as self-reported conscientiousness (Hough, Eaton, Dunnette, Kamp, & McCloy, 1990). Self-knowledge might be examined more closely in future research, however, to determine whether validity of self-reports can be better understood for reasons that bear similarity to the improved validity found in other-reports.

Hough's Nomological Web Clustering

The nomological web-clustering approach is another way to understand how external influences affect, and in part define, personality taxonomies. Under this approach, units within a cluster should demonstrate very high construct validity, including similar patterns of convergent and discriminant validity; clusters themselves should be empirically distinct from one another. Clusters are formed using a wide variety of information, making use of evidence such as correlational evidence between personality variables, criterion-related validities between personality variables and outcome variables, factor and component analyses, expert judgments, and different indices between subgroups of people on personality variables. Because of potentially diverse sources of information and diverse methods for analyzing and clustering information, nomological web clustering is as much an art as it is a science. It is intended to improve scientific understanding of the nature of personality traits and to reap practical benefits through understanding the usefulness of trait measures in organizations when predicting training or work performance, turnover, teamwork, or other critical organizational outcomes. Nomological web clustering is a working taxonomy that places the FFM, HEXACO, circumplexes, or independent traits within a broader context. Unlike personality taxonomies that seek to uncover stable and universal personality traits, nomological web clusters are *expected* to change as more research data are gathered to inform the clusters further.

The nomological web-clustering philosophy or approach is that personality variables or units that are clustered together should be similar, whether in terms of their relationships (correlations) with other individual-difference variables, their validities across multiple criteria, or their moderator (interaction) effects. When a cluster masks important differences between demographic subgroups, the cluster should be subdivided. For example, if men and women score similarly on extraversion but have different profiles on the sociability and dominance facets of extraversion (e.g., women scoring higher on the former), this serves as a signal that sociability and dominance should be considered within separate nomological web clusters. In other words, within a cluster, personality traits (or facets) in the same cluster should, ideally:

(a) Correlate similarly with other individual-difference variables;
(b) Correlate similarly with particular criteria;
(c) Interact similarly with other predictors;
(d) Correlate similarly with other individual-difference variables when demographic subgroup analyses are performed (i.e., no evidence of differential validity across demographic subgroups);
(e) Interact similarly with other variables when demographic subgroup analyses are performed; and
(f) Have similar patterns of mean score differences when subgroup analyses are performed.

These standards for convergent and discriminant validity required in the nomological web-clustering approach are stringent and, if met, produce highly construct-valid clusters of personality variables. It is an open system, similar to the periodic table in chemistry, in that new criteria for clustering can be added such as types of nonlinearity (Vasilopolous, Cucina, & Hunter, 2007) or types of intraindividual longitudinal processes implied by traits (Bauer, 2011; Kanfer & Ackerman, 2004; Yeo & Neal, 2008). Furthermore, clusters can emerge whenever accumulated evidence supports their integrity: Whereas in factor analysis, variables or units are dropped from further analysis if they do not account for enough variance in the data set, when units in the nomological web-clustering approach are not sufficiently similar to units in other clusters to warrant their inclusion in an existing cluster, a "loose" and provisional unit can exist on its own. The philosophy of bootstrapping, a series of successive approximations, serves to strengthen, refine, or otherwise alter the nomological web clusters of personality constructs.

Historical Roots

Although Hough and her colleagues continue to refine the nomological web-clustering approach, its historical roots lie in the research undertaken during the Army Research Institute's Project A of the 1980s. Project A was an ambitious, large-scale research project to expand the individual-difference constructs (predictor space) and work performance constructs (criterion space) and to understand the relationships between the two domains in a garrisoned army setting (for a thorough description of the project and many of its findings, see Campbell & Knapp, 2001, Hough et al., 1990, and the entire 1990 summer issue of *Personnel Psychology*, volume 43).

One of the first steps was a literature review to identify predictor constructs that might increment criterion-related validities over and above cognitive ability measures. The then-accepted wisdom in academic circles (early 1980s) was that personality variables explained very little variance in work-related criteria (see Barrick & Mount, 2005, for a cogent refutation). Nonetheless, personality variables were included in Project A; they were included in the pool of predictor domain variables to be measured, and Leaetta Hough was assigned responsibility for noncognitive variables—personality and interest variables. Hough was well trained for the challenge; her doctoral dissertation advisor was Auke Tellegen, a highly respected University of Minnesota personality theorist and researcher, and the University of Minnesota was well known for its emphasis on individual differences. Its graduates and professors, such as Harrison Gough, Stark Hathaway, John Holland, E. K. Strong, David Campbell, René Dawis, and Lloyd Lofquist, collectively had developed the *California Personality Inventory*, *Minnesota Multiphasic Personality Inventory*, *Holland Vocational Interest Inventory*, *Strong Vocational Interest Inventory*, the Theory of Work Adjustment, and other highly regarded individual-difference measures. She and her research team of John Kamp, another of Auke Tellegen's students, and Bruce Barge, an industrial–organizational (I-O) student of Marvin Dunnette, began to review the literature on personality, interests, their correlations with one another and with work-related criteria, and issues related to their development and use.

One of the then-innovative aspects of Project A was its construct-driven approach, as opposed to approaches that narrowly tie constructs to specific measures, resulting in data that confound them. It was the early 1980s, and the "noncognitive" team (Hough, Kamp, and Barge) needed to identify a set of personality constructs with which to operate. At the time, and as is true today, there was a plethora of personality variables and measures. Multiscale inventories were the most numerous of all published tests (Jackson & Paunonen, 1980), and at this time, there was no well-accepted taxonomy for myriad existing personality scales.

A variety of possible taxonomies existed. For example, Guilford (1975) provided evidence for 58 factors. Cattell, Eber, and Tatsuoka (1970) provided evidence for 24 primary factors. Tupes and Christal (1961) provided evidence for five basic factors that they labeled surgency (now called extraversion), agreeableness, dependability (now called conscientiousness), emotional stability, and culture (now called openness to experience). Norman (1963) confirmed the same set of five, and Goldberg (1981) embraced these same five factors for self-report measures of personality. R. T. Hogan (1982) reviewed and summarized much of the literature and proposed six factors—four of the five Tupes and Christal (1961) factors but the surgency factor was separated into two, ascendancy and sociability—a total of six factors. Hogan's thinking about the important conceptual differences between ascendancy and sociability persuaded the Project A noncognitive team to proceed with their review of the literature using an initial framework of six personality factors (note that this is different from the HEXACO model).

As described in Hough et al. (1990), the Project A noncognitive team tentatively clustered all 146 personality scales of 12 widely used, multiscale personality inventories into one of the six personality categories plus a "miscellaneous" category based on item content, available factor-analytic results, and to some degree a visual evaluation of correlational patterns. They then summarized hundreds of personality scale correlations, reassigning measures that appeared to be misfits within a cluster and then recalculating the mean correlations. They found a reasonable convergent-discriminant structure for the six clusters. More specifically, the observed within-cluster correlations ranged from .33 to .46, with a median of .40. The observed between-cluster correlations ranged from −.14 to .24, with a median of .06. A total of 29 of the 146 scales were assigned to the miscellaneous category.

The team then gathered dozens of criterion-related validity studies of personality scales that were conducted between 1960 and 1984. They summarized the validities of the measures within each cluster for predicting a variety of work-related criteria. They found dependability and emotional stability correlated with criteria at useful levels (e.g., observed validities in the .10s and .20s), and an examination of the validities of personality scales in the miscellaneous category revealed that some of the highest validities were for measures in that category. Upon closer examination, they found that three additional clusters could be identified—achievement, masculinity, and locus of control—and that the observed validities of these three personality clusters for some criterion constructs were in the .20s and .30s (see more detailed results reported in Hough et al., 1990). Masculinity and locus of control measures are compound variables, that is, heterogeneous variables consist of elements that are relatively independent (Hough & Schneider, 1996). Thus, seven reasonably homogeneous personality constructs or factors existed: ascendancy/surgency, affiliation, dependability, achievement, emotional stability/adjustment, agreeableness, and openness/intellectance.

Hough (1992) further developed the criterion-related database to include dozens more studies involving thousands more people, also adding several additional criterion constructs to the research base. Results confirmed that the validities of personality constructs, often obscured when the FFM was used to summarize validities, emerged when the seven clusters were used to summarize validities according to criterion construct; observed validities for some predictor–criterion construct combinations were in the .40s. She also examined validities within job type and found that achievement and dependability, clusters that in the FFM are merged to form a conscientiousness factor, correlate differently with job performance across job types. For example, achievement is an effective predictor of job performance for managers and executives but not for health-care workers, whereas dependability is an effective predictor of job performance for health-care workers but not for managers and executives. In the nomological web-clustering approach, these data argued for separate clusters.

During the 1990s, Hough continued to gather new data and search the literature for evidence of similarities and differences in relationships between facets of the FFM that would indicate that new, separate clusters were needed. The goal was to continue to identify clusters characterized by extensive evidence for construct validity.

In a head-to-head contest, pitting the criterion-related validities of the FFM against criterion-related validities of facet-level personality variables, Hough, Ones, and Viswesvaran (1998) conducted a large-scale meta-analysis of the criterion-related validities of personality variables—both FFM and facet-level variables—for predicting managerial performance constructs. Results supported the importance of distinguishing dominance, sociability/affiliation, and energy level within separate clusters; the FFM factor extraversion masked the utility of its facets for predicting managerial performance constructs. Similarly, the Big Five factor, conscientiousness, masked the differential validity of achievement and dependability for predicting managerial performance constructs (Hough, Ones, & Viswesvaran, 1998), corroborating the conclusions of Hough et al. (1990), Hough (1992), Jackson, Paunonen, Fraboni, and Goffin (1996), and Vinchur, Schippmann, Switzer, and Roth (1998).

Revisions, an Expanded Taxonomy, and More Evidence

The aforementioned collaboration led Hough and Ones (2001) to expand the set of construct-valid, facet-level clusters. They described their clustering process as follows:

> We reviewed existing taxonomies, scale definitions, and correlations between scales that were available in inventory manuals and published and unpublished sources. We independently

> classified each scale into one of the working taxons. When we disagreed about the placement of a scale in a taxon, we jointly reviewed the reference materials described above, discussing our reasons for classifying the scales as we had until we agreed upon the taxon to which it should be assigned.
>
> *Hough & Ones, 2001, p. 238*

Several researchers and meta-analytic studies have incorporated these taxons into their work. Not only Hough, Ones, and Viswesvaran meta-analysis made use of this structure but also Hough, Oswald, and Ployhart (2001) used it to identify different patterns of mean score differences between gender, ethnic, and age groups on personality variables. For example, they determined that male–female score differences were similar for personality scales grouped within the same cluster but that those differences were obscured when the clusters were incorporated into FFM factors. Similarly, mean score ethnic group differences between Whites and African Americans, for example, were similar for personality scales grouped within the same cluster, but the differences were obscured when the clusters were incorporated into FFM factors. Hough and Johnson (2013) also used the taxonomy to summarize meta-analyses of criterion-related validities of personality constructs for a wide variety of criterion outcomes and constructs. Other researchers, such as Dudley, Orvis, Lebiecki, and Cortina (2006) and Foldes, Duehr, and Ones (2008), have incorporated this structure into their research.

Conclusion

The review of nomological web clustering provides an appropriate conclusion to this chapter, because it integrates all the topics that have preceded it. Each time it is used, nomological web clustering has provided greater insights into the characteristics, relationships, and functioning of personality variables in the behavior of people in organizations and at work. It provides organizational researchers and practitioners with enhanced knowledge about applicant and employee personality by providing important specifics that follow the classic call by Cronbach and Meehl (1955) to test nomological networks in the ongoing process of determining construct validity. We earnestly hope that connecting our coverage of taxonomic considerations in this chapter to the history and nature of the nomological web-clustering approach will serve to improve future understanding, relevance, and application of personality constructs and measures that apply to individuals and, by extension, to the selection and training settings, task and team settings, and organizations in which they operate.

Practitioner's Window

- Personality traits are constructs that summarize reliable and distinct habits, consistencies, or patterns in a person's thoughts, feelings, and behavior over time and across situations.
- The Five-Factor Model (FFM) has historically served as a useful framework for organizing personality traits and their validity (particularly the validity of conscientiousness and extraversion traits); however, advancing our understanding of personality will require more expansive factor models (e.g., HEXACO), more flexible modeling (e.g., circumplexes)—and especially a greater focus on facets (narrower factors) as the fundamental building blocks of personality, drivers of more carefully developed workplace criteria, and contributors to higher criterion-related validities. General factors of personality (i.e., two or even one factor) have received continued research attention but are too broad to be of use in workplace applications.

- Personality ratings provided by external raters have demonstrated higher criterion-related validities than self-reports, especially when the external rater has greater familiarity with the person and/or the context being rated, especially when the context allows for personality-relevant behavior to be expressed (versus suppressed), and especially for traits that are more externally visible and accessible to the rater (e.g., sociability). Future research on the incremental validity of other-reports over self-reports is needed, as is research on the moderating effects of the characteristics of external raters (including their personality), the self-awareness of raters who rate themselves, and the potential for personality perceptions to contaminate external ratings on criterion measures.
- The nomological web-clustering approach operates in a bottom-up manner, as opposed to the factor model approach that is more top-down. The clustering approach seeks to maintain internal consistency and external distinctiveness of clusters on a wide range of features, including correlations between traits and other individual differences; criterion-related validities for personality traits; interactions between traits, other variables, and situations when predicting various outcomes; mean differences between groups across variables; and so on. Both the nature and number of the clusters and the members within the clusters are provisional as more data and more variables contribute to the nomological web. Nomological web clustering has served to improve our understanding of the nature of personality constructs and their potential to reap higher levels of validity and prediction for specific samples and contexts.

Notes

1 A .70 correlation, although strong by most standards, leaves more than 50% unique variance available for correlation with other variables (i.e., $.70^2 = 49\%$).

2 Incidentally, it is worth noting that neither meta-analysis included Kelly and Fiske's (1951) or Tupes' (1957, 1959) studies.

References

Ackerman, P.-L., & Heggestad, E. D. (1997). Intelligence, personality, and interests: Evidence for overlapping traits. *Psychological Bulletin, 121*, 219–245.

Allport, G. W., & Odbert, H. S. (1936). Trait names: A psycholexical study. *Psychological Monographs, 47*, 1–171.

Anusic, I., Schimmack, U., Pinkus, R. T., & Lockwood, P. (2009). The nature and structure of correlations among Big Five ratings: The halo-alpha-beta model. *Journal of Personality and Social Psychology, 97*, 1142–1156.

Ashton, M. C., & Lee, K. (2001). A theoretical basis for the major dimensions of personality. *European Journal of Personality, 15*, 327–353.

Ashton, M. C., & Lee, K. (2008). The prediction of Honesty-Humility-related criteria by the HEXACO and the Five-Factor models of personality. *Journal of Research in Personality, 42*, 1216–1228.

Ashton, M. C., Lee, K., & Goldberg, G. R. (2004). A hierarchical analysis of 1,071 English personality-descriptive adjectives. *Journal of Personality and Social Psychology, 87*, 707–721.

Ashton, M. C., Lee, K., Goldberg, L. R., & de Vries, R. E. (2009). Higher order factors of personality: Do they exist? *Personality and Social Psychology Review, 2*, 79–91.

Ashton, M. C., Lee, K., Perugini, M., Szarota, P., De Vries, R. E., Di Blas, L., & De Raad, B. (2004). A six-factor structure of personality-descriptive adjectives: Solutions from psycholexical studies in seven languages. *Journal of Personality and Social Psychology, 86*, 356–366.

Asparouhov, T., & Muthen, B. (2009). Exploratory structural equation modeling. *Structural Equation Modeling: A Multidisciplinary Journal, 16*, 397–438.

Baird, B. M., Le, K., & Lucas, R. E. (2006). On the nature of intraindividual personality variability: Reliability, validity, and associations with well-being. *Journal of Personality and Social Psychology, 90*, 512–527.

Barrick, M. R., & Mount, M. K. (2005). Yes, personality matters: Moving on to more important matters. *Human Performance, 18*, 359–372.

Barrick, M. R., Mount, M. K., & Gupta, R. (2003). Meta-analysis of the relationship between the five-factor model of personality and Holland's occupational types. *Personnel Psychology, 56*, 45–74.
Bauer, D. J. (2011). Evaluating individual differences in psychological processes. *Current Directions in Psychological Science, 20*, 115–118.
Beaty, J. C., Cleveland, J. N., & Murphy, K. R. (2001). The relation between personality and contextual performance in "strong" versus "weak" situations. *Human Performance, 14*, 125–148.
Bijnen, E. J., van der Net, T. Z., & Poortinga, Y. H. (1986). On cross-cultural comparative studies with the Eysenck Personality Questionnaire. *Journal of Cross-Cultural Psychology, 17*, 3–16.
Bing, M. N., Whanger, J. C., Davison, H. K., & VanHook, J. B. (2004). Incremental validity of the frame-of-reference effect in Personality Scale scores: A replication and extension. *Journal of Applied Psychology, 89*, 150–157.
Block, J. (1995). A contrarian view of the five-factor approach to personality description. *Psychological Methods, 117*, 187–215.
Bowling, N. A., & Burns, G. N. (2010). A comparison of work-specific and general personality measures as predictors of work and non-work criteria. *Personality and Individual Differences, 49*, 95–101.
Campbell, J. P., & Knapp, D. (2001). *Project A: Exploring the limits of performance improvement through personnel selection and classification.* Hillsdale, NJ: Erlbaum.
Cattell, R. B., Eber, H. W., & Tatsuoka, M. M. (1970). *Handbook for the sixteen personality factor questionnaire.* Champaign, IL: Institute for Personality and Ability Testing.
Chang, L., Connelly, B. S., & Geeza, A. A. (2012). Separating method factors and higher order traits of the Big Five: A meta-analytic multitrait-multimethod approach. *Journal of Personality and Social Psychology, 102*, 408–426.
Cheung, G. W., & Lau, R. S. (2012). A direct comparison approach for testing measurement invariance. *Organizational Research Methods, 15*, 167–198.
Connelly, B. S., & Hülsheger, U. R. (2012). A narrower scope or a clearer lens for personality? Examining sources of observers' advantages over self-reports for predicting performance. *Journal of Personality, 80*, 603–631.
Connelly, B. S., & Ones, D. S. (2010). An other perspective on personality: Meta-analytic integration of observers' accuracy and predictive validity. *Psychological Bulletin, 136*, 1092–1122.
Connelly, B. S., Ones, D. S., Davies, S. E., & Birkland, A. (2012). *Opening up openness: A theoretical sort following critical incidents methodology and meta-analytic investigation of the trait family measures.* Unpublished manuscript.
Connolly, J. J., Kavanagh, E. J., & Viswesvaran, C. (2007). The convergent validity between self and observer ratings of personality: A meta-analytic review. *International Journal of Selection and Assessment, 15*, 110–117.
Cronbach, L., & Meehl, P. (1955). Construct validity in psychological tests. *Psychological Bulletin, 52*, 281–302.
De Fruyt, F., & Mervielde, I. (1999). RIASEC types and Big Five traits as predictors of employment status and nature of employment. *Personnel Psychology, 52*, 701–727.
DeYoung, C. G. (2006). Higher-order factors of the Big Five in a multi-informant sample. *Journal of Personality and Social Psychology, 91*, 1138–1151.
DeYoung, C. G., Quilty, L. C., & Peterson, J. B. (2007). Between facets and domains: 10 aspects of the Big Five. *Journal of Personality and Social Psychology, 93*, 880–896.
Digman, J. M. (1997). Higher-order factors of the Big Five. *Journal of Personality and Social Psychology, 73*, 1246–1256.
Donnellan, M. B., Hopwood, C. J., & Wright, G. C. (2012). Reevaluating the evidence for the General Factor of Personality in the Multidimensional Personality Questionnaire: Concerns about Rushton and Irwing (2009). *Personality and Individual Differences, 52*, 285–289.
Dudley, N. M., Orvis, K. A., Lebiecki, J. E., & Cortina, J. M. (2006). A meta-analytic investigation of conscientiousness in the prediction of job performance: Examining the intercorrelations and the incremental validity of narrow traits. *Journal of Applied Psychology, 91*, 40–57.
Fleeson, W. (2001). Toward a structure- and process-integrated view of personality: Traits as density distributions of states. *Journal of Personality and Social Psychology, 80*, 1011–1027.
Foldes, H. J., Duehr, E. E., & Ones, D. S. (2008). Group differences in personality: Meta-analyses comparing five U.S. racial groups. *Personnel Psychology, 61*, 579–616.
Funder, D. C. (1995). On the accuracy of personality judgment: A realistic approach. *Psychological Review, 102*, 652–670.
Funder, D. C., & West, S. G. (1993). Consensus, self-other agreement, and accuracy in personality judgment: An introduction. *Journal of Personality, 61*, 457–476.
Goldberg, L. R. (1981). Language and individual differences: The search for universals in personality lexicons. In L. Wheeler (Ed.), *Personality and social psychology review* (Vol. 2, pp. 141–165). Beverly Hills, CA: Sage.
Goldberg, L. R. (1990). An alternative "description of personality": The Big Five factor structure. *Journal of Personality and Social Psychology, 59*, 1216–1229.

Goldberg, L. R. (1993). The structure of phenotypic personality traits. *American Psychologist, 48*, 26–34.
Goldberg, L. R., & Velicer, W. F. (2006). Principles of exploratory factor analysis. In S. Strack (Ed.), *Differentiating normal and abnormal personality* (2nd ed., pp. 209–237). New York: Springer.
Gottfredson, L. S. (1997). Why *g* matters: The complexity of everyday life. *Intelligence, 24*, 79–132.
Guilford, J. P. (1975). Factors and factors of personality. *Psychological Bulletin, 82*, 802–814.
Guttman, L. (1954). A new approach to factor analysis: The radex. In P. F. Lazarsfeld (Ed.), *Mathematical thinking in the social sciences* (pp. 258–348). Glencoe, IL: Free Press.
Hofstee, W. K., de Raad, B., & Goldberg, L. R. (1992). Integration of the Big Five and circumplex approaches to trait structure. *Journal of Personality and Social Psychology, 63*, 146–163.
Hogan, R. (1996). A socioanalytic perspective on the five-factor model. In J. S. Wiggins (Ed.), *The five-factor model of personality: Theoretical perspectives* (pp. 163–179). New York: Guilford.
Hogan, R. T. (1982). A socioanalytic theory of personality. In M. M. Page (Ed.), *1982 Nebraska symposium on motivation* (pp. 55–89). Lincoln: University of Nebraska Press.
Hopwood, C. J., & Donnellan, M. B. (2010). How should the internal structure of personality inventories be evaluated? *Personality and Social Psychology Review, 14*, 332–346.
Hough, L. M. (1992). The "Big Five" personality variables—Construct confusion: Description versus prediction. *Human Performance, 5*, 139–155.
Hough, L. M., Eaton, N. L., Dunnette, M. D., Kamp, J. D., & McCloy, R. A. (1990). Criterion-related validities of personality constructs and the effect of response distortion on those validities [Monograph]. *Journal of Applied Psychology, 75*, 581–595.
Hough, L. M., & Furnham, A. (2003). Importance and use of personality variables in work settings. In I. B. Weiner (Editor in Chief), W. Borman, D. Ilgen, & R. Klimoski (Vol. Eds.), *Comprehensive handbook of psychology: Industrial organizational psychology* (Vol. 12, pp. 131–169). New York: Wiley & Sons.
Hough, L. M., & Johnson, J. W. (2013). Use and importance of personality variables in work settings. In I. B. Weiner (Editor in Chief), N. Schmitt, & S. Highhouse (Vol. Eds.), *Handbook of psychology: Vol. 12. Industrial and organizational psychology* (pp. 211–243). New York: Wiley.
Hough, L. M., & Ones, D. S. (2001). The structure, measurement, validity, and use of personality variables in industrial, work, and organizational psychology. In N. Anderson, D. S. Ones, H. K. Sinangil, & C. Viswesvaran (Eds.), *Handbook of industrial, work & organizational psychology* (pp. 233–277). New York: Sage.
Hough, L. M., Ones, D. S., & Viswesvaran, C. (1998). Personality correlates of managerial performance constructs. In R. Page (Chair), *Personality determinants of managerial potential, performance, progression and ascendancy*. Symposium conducted at 13th Annual Conference of the Society for Industrial and Organizational Psychology, Dallas, TX.
Hough, L. M., & Oswald, F. L. (2000). Personnel selection: Looking toward the future – Remembering the past. *Annual Review of Psychology, 51*, 631–664.
Hough, L. M., Oswald, F. L., & Ployhart, R. E. (2001). Determinants, detection, and amelioration of adverse impact in personnel selection procedures: Issues, evidence, and lessons learned. *International Journal of Selection and Assessment, 9*, 152–194.
Hough, L. M., & Schneider, R. J. (1996). Personality traits, taxonomies, and applications in organizations. In K. Murphy (Ed.), *Individual differences and behavior in organizations* (pp. 31–88). San Francisco, CA: Jossey-Bass.
Hunter, J. E., & Schmidt, F. L. (2004). *Methods of meta-analysis: Correcting error and bias in research findings* (2nd ed.). Thousand Oaks, CA: Sage.
Hunthausen, J. M., Truxillo, D. M., Bauer, T. N., & Hammer, L. B. (2003). A field study of frame-of-reference effects on personality test validity. *Journal of Applied Psychology, 88*, 869–879.
Jackson, D. N., & Paunonen, S. V. (1980). Personality structure and assessment. *Annual Review of Psychology, 31*, 503–551.
Jackson, D. N., Paunonen, S. V., Fraboni, M., & Goffin, R. D. (1996). A five-factor versus six-factor model of personality structure. *Personality and Individual Differences, 20*, 33–45.
John, O. P., & Robins, R. W. (1993). Determinants of interjudge agreement on personality traits: The Big Five domains, observability, evaluativeness, and the unique perspective of the self. *Journal of Personality, 61*, 521–551.
Johnson, J. A., & Ostendorf, F. (1993). Clarification of the five-factor model with the Abridged Big Five Dimensional Circumplex. *Journal of Personality and Social Psychology, 65*, 563–576.
Kanfer, R., & Ackerman, P. (2004). Aging, adult development, and work motivation. *Academy of Management Review, 29*, 440–458.
Kelly, E. L., & Fiske, D. W. (1951). *The prediction of performance in clinical psychology.* Ann Arbor: University of Michigan Press.
Larson, L. M., Rottinghaus, P. J., & Borgen, F. H. (2002). Meta-analyses of big six interests and Big Five personality factors. *Journal of Vocational Behavior, 61*, 217–239.

Lee, K., & Ashton, M. C. (2008). The HEXACO personality factors in the indigenous personality lexicons of English and 11 other languages. *Journal of Personality, 76*, 1001–1053.
Lee, K., Ashton, M. C., & de Vries, R. E. (2005). Predicting workplace delinquency and integrity with the HEXACO and five-factor models of personality structure. *Human Performance, 18*, 179–197.
LePine, J. A., Colquitt, J. A., & Erez, A. (2000). Adaptability to changing task contexts: Effects of general cognitive ability, conscientiousness, and openness to experience. *Personnel Psychology, 53*, 563–593.
MacCann, C., Duckworth, A. L., & Roberts, R. D. (2009). Empirical identification of the major facets of conscientiousness. *Learning and Individual Differences, 19*, 451–458.
McCrae, R. R., & Costa, P. T. (1989). The structure of interpersonal traits: Wiggins's circumplex and the five factor model. *Journal of Personality and Social Psychology, 56*, 586–595.
McCrae, R. R., & Costa, P. T. (2008). The five-factor theory of personality. In O. P. John, R. W. Robins, & L. A. Pervin (Eds.), *Handbook of personality: Theory and research* (3rd ed., pp. 159–181). New York: Guilford.
McCrae, R. R., Costa, P. T., & Busch, C. M. (1986). Evaluating comprehensiveness in personality systems: The California Q-Set and the five-factor model. *Journal of Personality, 54*, 430–446.
McKay, D. A., & Tokar, D. M. (2012). The HEXACO and five-factor models of personality in relation to RIASEC vocational interests. *Journal of Vocational Behavior, 81*, 138–149.
Moon, H., Hollenbeck, J. R., Marinova, S., & Humphrey, S. E. (2008). Beneath the surface: Uncovering the relationship between extraversion and organizational citizenship behavior through a facet approach. *International Journal of Selection and Assessment, 16*, 143–154.
Morgeson, F. P., Campion, M. A., Dipboye, R. L., Hollenbeck, J. R., Murphy, K., & Schmitt, N. (2007). Reconsidering the use of personality tests in personnel selection contexts. *Personnel Psychology, 60*, 683–729.
Murphy, K. R., Cleveland, J. N., Skattebo, A. L., & Kinney, T. B. (2004). Raters who pursue different goals give different ratings. *Journal of Applied Psychology, 89*, 158–164.
Mussel, P., Winter, C., Gelléri, P., & Schuler, H. (2011). Explicating the openness to experience construct and its subdimensions and facets in a work setting. *International Journal of Selection and Assessment, 19*, 145–156.
Muthén, B., & Asparouhov, T. (2012). Bayesian SEM: A more flexible representation of psychological theory. *Psychological Methods, 17*, 313–335.
Norman, W. T. (1963). Toward an adequate taxonomy of personality attributes: Replicated factor structure in peer nomination personality ratings. *Journal of Abnormal and Social Psychology, 66*, 574–583.
Nye, C. D., Su, R., Rounds, J., & Drasgow, F. (2012). Vocational interests and performance: A quantitative summary of over 60 years of research. *Perspectives on Psychological Science, 7*, 384–403.
Oh, I., Wang, G., & Mount, M. K. (2011). Validity of observer ratings of the five-factor model of personality traits: A meta-analysis. *Journal of Applied Psychology, 96*, 762–773.
Oswald, F. L., & Hough, L. M. (2010). Personality and its assessment in organizations: Theoretical and empirical developments. In S. Zedeck (Ed.), *APA handbook of industrial and organizational psychology: Selecting and developing members for the organization* (Vol. 2, pp. 153–184). Washington, DC: American Psychological Association.
Pace, V. L., & Brannick, M. T. (2010). Improving prediction of work performance through frame-of-reference consistency: Empirical evidence using openness to experience. *International Journal of Selection and Assessment, 18*, 230–235.
Paunonen, S. V., & Jackson, D. N. (2000). What is beyond the Big Five? Plenty! *Journal of Personality, 68*, 821–835.
Piedmont, R. L., & Weinstein, H. P. (1993). A psychometric evaluation of the new NEO-PIR facet scales for agreeableness and conscientiousness. *Journal of Personality Assessment, 60*, 302–318.
Plutchik, R., & Conte, H. R. (Eds.) (1997). *Circumplex models of personality and emotions*. Washington, DC: American Psychological Association.
Revelle, W., & Wilt, J. (2010). A methodological critique of claims for a general factor of personality. In N. Waller (Chair), *Mapping the personality sphere*. Symposium conducted at the European Conference on Personality, Brno, Czech Republic.
Roberts, B. W., Bogg, T., Walton, K. E., Chernyshenko, O. S., & Stark, S. E. (2004). A lexical investigation of the lower-order structure of conscientiousness. *Journal of Research in Personality, 38*, 164–178.
Roberts, B. W., Chernyshenko, O. S., Stark, S. E., & Goldberg, L. R. (2005). The structure of conscientiousness: An empirical investigation based on seven major personality questionnaires. *Personnel Psychology, 58*, 103–139.
Rushton, J. P., Bons, T. A., Ando, J., Hur, Y.-M., Irwing, P., Vernon, P. A., & Barbaranelli, C. (2009). A general factor of personality from multi-trait multi-method data and cross-national twins. *Twin Research and Human Genetics, 12*, 356–365.
Rushton, J. P., & Irwing, P. (2009). A general factor of personality (GFP) from the Multidimensional Personality Questionnaire. *Personality and Individual Differences, 47*, 571–576.

Rushton, J. P., & Irwing, P. (2011). The general factor of personality: Normal and abnormal. In T. Chamorro-Premuzic, S. von Stumm, & A. Furnham (Eds.), *The Wiley-Blackwell handbook of individual differences* (pp. 132–161). London: Wiley-Blackwell.

Schmit, M. J., & Ryan, A. M. (1993). The Big Five in personnel selection: Factor structure in applicant and non-applicant populations. *Journal of Applied Psychology, 78*, 996–974.

Schmit, M. J., Ryan, A. M., Stierwalt, S. L., & Powell, S. L. (1995). Frame-of-reference effects on personality scores and criterion-related validity. *Journal of Applied Psychology, 80*, 607–620.

Schneider, R. J., Hough, L. M., & Dunnette, M. D. (1996). Broadsided by broad traits: How to sink science in five dimensions or less. *Journal of Organizational Behavior, 17*, 639–655.

Shafer, J. A., & Postlethwaite, B. E. (2012). A matter of context: A meta-analytic investigation of the relative validity of contextualized and noncontextualized personality measures. *Personnel Psychology, 65*, 445–494.

Stewart, G. (1999). Trait bandwidth and stages of job performance: Assessing differential effects for conscientiousness and its subtraits. *Journal of Applied Psychology, 84*, 959–968.

Tellegen, A. (1993). Folk concepts and psychological concepts of personality and personality disorder. *Psychological Inquiry, 4*, 122–130.

Tett, R. P., & Burnett, D. D. (2003). A personality trait-based interactionist model of job performance. *Journal of Applied Psychology, 88*, 500–517.

Tracey, T. J. G., & Rounds, J. (1996). The spherical representation of vocational interests. *Journal of Vocational Behavior, 48*, 3–41.

Tupes, E. C. (1957). *Relationship between behavior trait ratings by peers and later officer performance of USAF Officer Candidate School graduates* (Research Report AFPTRC-TN-57-125, ASTIA Document No. AD-134 257). San Antonio, TX: Air Force Personnel and Training Research Center.

Tupes, E. C. (1959). *Personality traits related to effectiveness of junior and senior Air Force officers* (Technical Note, WADC-TN-59-198). San Antonio, TX: Personnel Laboratory, Wright Air Development Center.

Tupes, E. C., & Christal, R. E. (1961). *Recurrent personality factors based on trait ratings* (USAF Technical Report No. 61-97). San Antonio, TX: U.S. Air Force.

Tupes, E. C., & Christal, R. E. (1992). Recurrent personality factors based on trait ratings. *Journal of Personality, 60*, 225–251.

van Doorn, R. R. A., & Lang, J. W. B. (2010). Performance differences explained by the neuroticism facets withdrawal and volatility, variations in task demand, and effort allocation. *Journal of Research in Personality, 44*, 446–452.

Van Iddekinge, C. H., Putka, D. J., & Campbell, J. P. (2011). Reconsidering vocational interests for personnel selection: The validity of an interest-based selection test in relation to job knowledge, job performance, and continuance intentions. *Journal of Applied Psychology, 96*, 13–33.

Vasilopolous, N. L., Cucina, J. M., & Hunter, A. E. (2007). Personality and training proficiency: Issues of bandwidth-fidelity and curvilinearity. *Journal of Occupational and Organizational Psychology, 80*, 109–131.

Vazire, S., & Carlson, E. N. (2011). Others sometimes know us better than we know ourselves. *Current Directions in Psychological Science, 20*, 104–108.

Vinchur, A. J., Schippmann, J. S., Switzer, F. S., & Roth, P. L. (1998). A meta-analytic review of predictors of job performance for salespeople. *Journal of Applied Psychology, 83*, 586–597.

Woo, S. E., Chernyshenko, O. S., Stark, S., & Conz, G. (in press). Validity of six openness facets in predicting work behaviors: A meta-analysis. *Journal of Personality Assessment.*

Wu, A. D., Li, Z., & Zumbo, B. D. (2007). Decoding the meaning of factorial invariance and updating the practice of multi-group confirmatory factor analysis: A demonstration with TIMSS data. *Practical Assessment, Research & Evaluation, 12*, 1–26.

Wu, J., & LeBreton, J. M. (2011). Reconsidering the dispositional basis of counterproductive work behavior: The role of aberrant personality. *Personnel Psychology, 64*, 593–626.

Yeo, G., & Neal, A. (2008). Subjective cognitive effort: A model of states, traits, and time. *Journal of Applied Psychology, 93*, 617–631.

Zimprich, D., Allemand, M., & Dellenbach, M. (2009). Openness to experience, fluid intelligence, and crystallized intelligence in middle-aged and old adults. *Journal of Research in Personality, 43*, 444–454.

3

Advancing Our Understanding of Processes in Personality–Performance Relationships

Jeff W. Johnson and Robert J. Schneider

When it comes to predicting behavior at work, personality measures have complex patterns of validity results. In contrast to the highly generalizable validities of cognitive ability tests (e.g., Hunter, 1986; Salgado et al., 2003; Schmidt, 2002; Schmidt & Hunter, 2004), personality measure validities tend to be situationally specific and are influenced by a number of factors (Hough & Oswald, 2008; Tett & Christiansen, 2007). Although job complexity seems to moderate the level of the validity coefficient (Hunter & Hunter, 1984), tests of general cognitive ability tend to predict performance at a useful level across all occupations (Schmidt, 2002). In contrast, personality measures show a great deal of variability in validity coefficients across studies, and this variability is not accounted for by sampling error (Tett & Christiansen, 2007).

Accounting for a substantial proportion of the variance in the criterion space requires theories and models that reflect the complexity of the determinants of job performance (Hough & Oswald, 2005). A number of personality–performance process models have been proposed in recent years, both for individual job performance and for counterproductive work behavior (CWB). The purpose of this chapter is to (a) discuss the properties of process models, (b) present a general model describing the many ways by which personality can influence work behavior, (c) review specific personality–performance process models and how they fit into the general model, and (d) suggest a strategy for refining theories and models in future research. The goal is to stimulate research on mediated models involving personality and performance to improve our understanding of how personality influences different aspects of job performance.

Theories and Models

Process models attempt to explain the relationship between an antecedent variable (e.g., a measure of dependability) and an outcome variable (e.g., supervisor ratings of decision-making performance). The term *model* is frequently used interchangeably with the term *theory*. The distinction between these two terms is not perfectly clear and we do not address this distinction in depth, but we do briefly discuss these terms because of their relevance to this chapter.

According to Meehl (1990), "a scientific theory is a set of statements in general form which are interconnected in the sense that they contain over-lapping terms that designate the constructs of the theory" (p. 109). This is the nomological network familiar to most psychologists (Cronbach & Meehl, 1955). The nodes of the net are the theoretical constructs and the strands of the net are postulates relating the constructs to one another. The empirical meaning of the constructs derives from their operational definitions as well as "upward seepage" from a subset of constructs that are operationally tied to the database. Campbell (1990b) offers a complementary definition of theory: "A collection of assertions, both verbal and symbolic, that identifies what variables are important for what reasons, specifies how they are interrelated and why, and identifies the conditions under which they should be related or not related" (p. 65).

While some definitions of the term "model" sound very much like definitions of "theory," we consider a model to be "a deliberately simplified theory" or a "structure . . . used to represent some other system" (Godfrey-Smith, 2003, p. 238). Models "provide the bridge between theories and empirical evidence" (Marewski & Olsson, 2009, p. 51). A theory could be represented by a model, but a model does not necessarily have to be considered a theory. One could propose a model that is not based on a theory (or is only partially based on a theory) and it could be thought of as a set of hypotheses. Because this chapter deals with process models, we generally refer to theories that can be represented by models, but when we refer to a model we do not necessarily consider it to be a theory.

Properties of Process Models

Researchers who develop process models generally hypothesize two types of variables in an attempt to explain these relationships: (a) mediating variables and (b) moderating variables. Most process models include both types of variables. *Mediation* occurs when a third variable explains the relationship between two other variables, providing a causal link (Edwards & Lambert, 2007). For example, motivation is often seen as mediating the relationship between personality and performance. Barrick, Stewart, and Piotrowski (2002) found that the motivational variables of accomplishment striving and status striving mediated the relationship between conscientiousness and job performance for sales representatives, and that status striving mediated the relationship between extraversion and job performance.

Full mediation occurs when the relationship between two variables is fully explained by a mediating variable. We often see partial mediation, where a variable has a direct effect on another variable in addition to an effect that is mediated by a third variable. For example, Mount, Ilies, and Johnson (2006) found that the relationship between agreeableness and self-rated CWB directed at individuals (CWB-I) was partially mediated by job satisfaction, but there was also a direct path from agreeableness to CWB-I. Partial mediation may be due to a variable having a true direct effect that is independent of the mediated effect, but in many cases the direct effect is probably an indirect effect through an unmeasured mediating variable. For example, Mount et al. suggested that the direct effect they found between agreeableness and CWB-I could be explained by the influence of communion striving or needs fulfillment motives.

A *moderating variable* is a variable that influences the relationship between two other variables, producing an interaction effect. For example, Blickle, Wendel, and Ferris (2010) found that political skill moderated the relationship between extraversion and sales performance. This relationship was positive for car salespeople who were high on political skill, but negative when salespeople were low on political skill. This analysis demonstrated that the relationship between extraversion and cars sold was much more complex than could be seen by simply examining the correlation between the variables ($r = -.36$).

Because mediation and moderation are often combined within a single model or theory, it is important to distinguish between moderated mediation and mediated moderation. Moderated mediation is relatively straightforward, and essentially coincides with the definition of a moderator variable. That is, *moderated mediation* occurs when a mediation effect depends on the level of a moderator variable (MacKinnon, Fairchild, & Fritz, 2007). For example, Ng, Ang, and Chan (2008) found that leadership self-efficacy mediated the relationships between three personality variables (neuroticism, extraversion, and conscientiousness) and leader effectiveness for leaders with low job demands but not for leaders with high job demands. In addition, the effects of neuroticism and conscientiousness on leader effectiveness were mediated by leadership self-efficacy for leaders with high job autonomy but not for leaders with low job autonomy.

Mediated moderation occurs when a variable mediates the relationship between an interaction effect and a dependent variable. In other words, the mediating variable explains how the interaction effect influences the dependent variable (MacKinnon et al., 2007). For example, Bond, Flaxman, and Bunce (2008) found that the effect of a work redesign intervention on mental health and absence rates was moderated by psychological flexibility. Perceived job control fully mediated this interaction effect on absence rates and partially mediated the interaction effect on mental health.

A General Personality Process Model

After reviewing many recent process models representing the relationship between personality and either individual job performance or CWB, Johnson and Hezlett (2008) determined that the models are generally consistent with each other, with each emphasizing different aspects of the personality–performance process. Johnson and Hezlett integrated these models into a general model that incorporates the major potential influences of personality on performance, with all variables representing broad construct domains. The purpose of the general model is to provide a guide for constructing models for predicting specific types of performance (e.g., leadership, sales, citizenship performance, and adaptive performance). The general model is intended to stimulate research to determine what elements of the model operate for specific types of performance. When researching a specific type of performance, the general model can be used to generate hypotheses about relationships between specific variables. The model can be evaluated through programmatic research that tests relationships between subsets of its variables.

A reconceptualization of Johnson and Hezlett's (2008) model is shown in Figure 3.1. Throughout this chapter, we refer to the model in Figure 3.1 as the "general model." Although the model is quite comprehensive, we claim neither that all possible variables that could influence performance are included, nor that all possible relationships are specified. We do, however, suggest that the general model represents the many different pathways through which personality can influence performance. To provide more detail, we also present more specific models highlighting relationships involving subsets of variables in the general model.

Based on an integration of models presented by Campbell (1990a) and Motowidlo, Borman, and Schmit (1997), Johnson (2003) proposed four direct determinants of performance: (a) knowledge, (b) skill, (c) motivation, and (d) work habits. Direct performance determinants are distinguished from indirect performance determinants, which can only influence performance via the direct determinants. Personality is an indirect determinant, along with variables such as abilities, education, experience, training, and management practices. In the general model, the most distal indirect performance determinants are work context and the individual-difference domains of personality, abilities, and experience. When applying the general model to a given performance component, specific variables from each broad predictor domain would be specified that are theoretically related to each of the more proximal determinants of that performance component. The specific variables should be drawn from previous research and theories focusing on the relevant portions of the general model. There is a rich empirical research literature documenting relationships between personality traits, abilities, and different aspects of the general model. Personality traits directly influence all other domains of the model, as well as moderating some relationships. Abilities have their strongest relationships with knowledge and skill, but may have weaker relationships with many other aspects of the model.

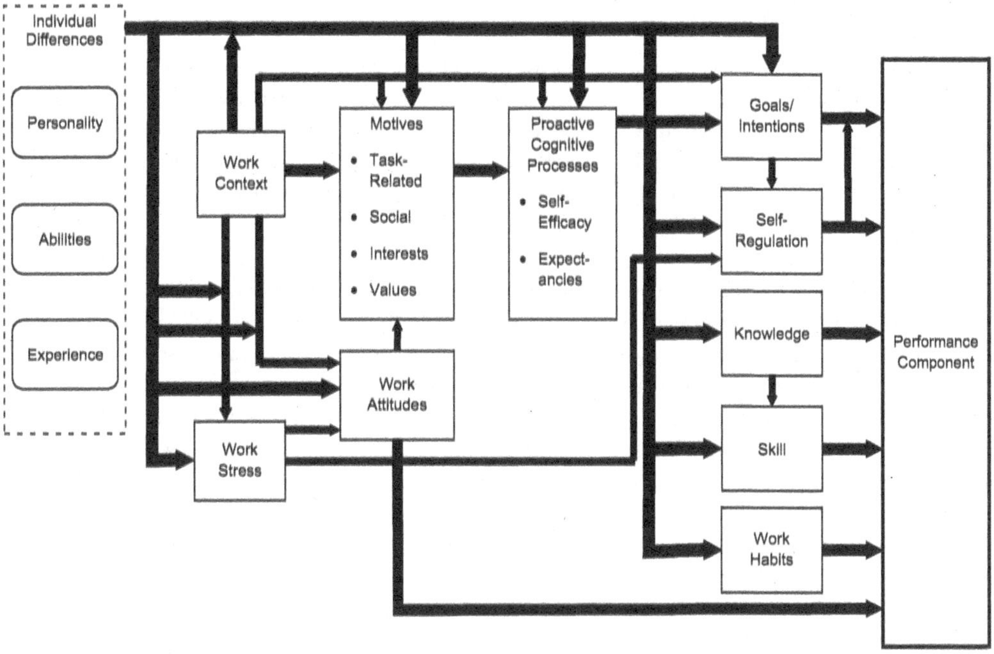

Figure 3.1 General Model of the Potential Influence of Personality Traits and Other Variables on Determinants of Performance.

Experience can be operationalized as either (a) amount of time on the job, or (b) number of times a task has been performed (Lance & Bennett, 2000). Experience has been shown to be a meaningful indirect determinant in process models of job performance, exerting its influence on performance through job knowledge, skill, and/or motivation (Johnson, Duehr, Hezlett, Muros, & Ferstl, 2008; Lance & Bennett, 2000; Schmidt, Hunter, & Outerbridge, 1986). Experience may also moderate the relationships between certain variables.

We use the term work context to refer to a wide variety of both work and organizational context variables, including Tett and Burnett's (2003) task, social, and organizational cues (i.e., demands, distracters, constraints, and releasers; see Chapter 5, this volume). Other examples of work context variables are supervision, procedural fairness, training, reward systems, autonomy, and stressors (Arad, Hanson, & Schneider, 1999; Strong, Jeanneret, McPhail, Blakely, & D'Egidio, 1999). Work context directly influences many aspects of the model in addition to moderating the relationship between individual differences and performance (Ones, Dilchert, Viswesvaran, & Judge, 2007).

The motivation component of the model is represented by several different kinds of variables. When describing motivational processes, Mitchell and Daniels (2003) distinguished between proactive cognitive processes (e.g., expectancies, self-efficacy, goal-setting) and on-line cognitive processes (e.g., self-regulation). Johnson (2003) added psychological motives (i.e., reasons for taking certain courses of action, such as values, interests, preferences, or attitudes) as a third component of motivation that mediates the relationship between personality and proactive cognitive processes. Johnson and Hezlett (2008) further expanded this component of motivation by (a) separating task-related motives from social motives (Barrick, Mitchell, & Stewart, 2003), and (b) separating work attitudes from other motives. Although an attitude can be a motive for performing a behavior, it can also have a direct effect on both task-related and social motives.

Attitudes and Motives

Figure 3.2 provides a more specific look at the attitudes and motives aspects of the general model. Task-related motives are similar to Barrick et al.'s (2003) accomplishment striving, which is a generalized intention to exert effort and work hard. This is determined jointly by personality (e.g., need for achievement), work context (e.g., task difficulty), experience, ability, and work attitudes. Social motives include communion striving and status striving, which mediate the relationship between accomplishment striving and performance (Barrick et al., 2003). In the general model, social motives mediate the relationship between task-related motives and intentions, but we also allow for a direct path from task-related motives to intentions. The relationship between task-related motives and social motives is moderated by personality and work context. For example, Barrick et al. predict that the path from accomplishment striving to status striving is moderated by extraversion and competitive demands in the situation. Social motives are determined primarily by personality, as well as by work context and work attitudes.

Perceived job characteristics, specific attitudes (e.g., supervisor support), and general attitudes (e.g., job satisfaction) are depicted in a single work attitudes construct domain. Personality has a direct influence on work attitudes (e.g., positive or negative affectivity may lead people to form more positive or negative perceptions of their environment). Personality and experience may moderate the relationship between work context and attitudes (e.g., a lack of feedback would likely be evaluated more negatively by someone lower on tolerance for ambiguity or someone with less experience). Although work attitudes can be a motive for action (e.g., commitment to the organization could be a reason for working late to complete a task), they can also have a direct effect on both task-related and social motives. For example, satisfaction with the work group may cause communion striving to be a more salient motive, whereas dissatisfaction with the work group may increase the salience of status striving so that the individual can get ahead of the rest of the members of the group. Work attitudes are directly related to expectancies, probably because employees who are more satisfied are more likely to see or have experienced the link between good performance and valued rewards (Johnson et al., 2008). Stress is

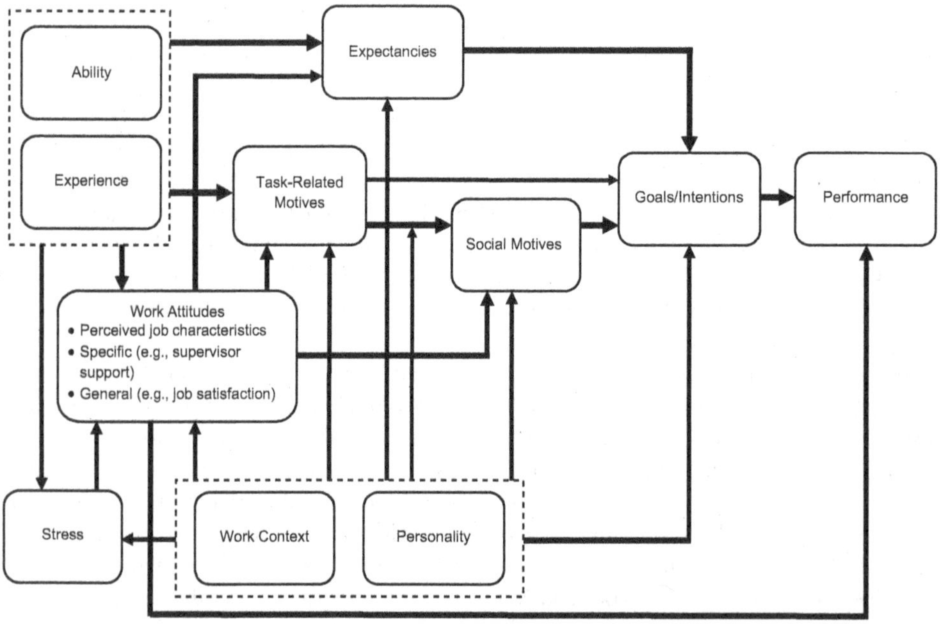

Figure 3.2 More Complete Description of the Attitudes and Motives Aspect of the General Model.

included as a direct influence on work attitudes, based on research showing that work stress mediated the relationship between personality and attitudes (Day, Bedeian, & Conte, 1998; Van den Berg & Feij, 2003). Work context, experience, and ability also influence the experience of stress.

Figure 3.2 also includes a direct path from work attitudes to performance, which we expect for citizenship performance dimensions (Johnson et al., 2008). Given that citizenship performance often involves behaviors that are not formally required and do not directly benefit the individual, it is not surprising that work attitudes can directly determine citizenship performance. If a person experiences job dissatisfaction, does not have an affective attachment to the organization, and does not share the values of the organization, he or she would be unlikely to engage in behaviors like participating in social activities, exceeding standards when carrying out assignments, or performing extra work without being asked.

Goals/Intentions

Cullen and Sackett (2003) incorporated the theory of reasoned action (TRA; Fishbein & Ajzen, 1975) into their model of the determinants of CWB. The TRA posits that intention to perform a behavior (the most proximal determinant of actually performing a behavior) is a function of (a) an individual's attitude toward the behavior, and (b) subjective norms about what relevant others think about the behavior. Similarly, Johnson and Hezlett (2008) incorporated Ajzen's (1985) theory of planned behavior (TPB) into their model. The TPB builds on the TRA by adding perceived behavioral control to attitudes and subjective norms as the determinants of intention formation. Figure 3.3 focuses on this aspect of the general model.

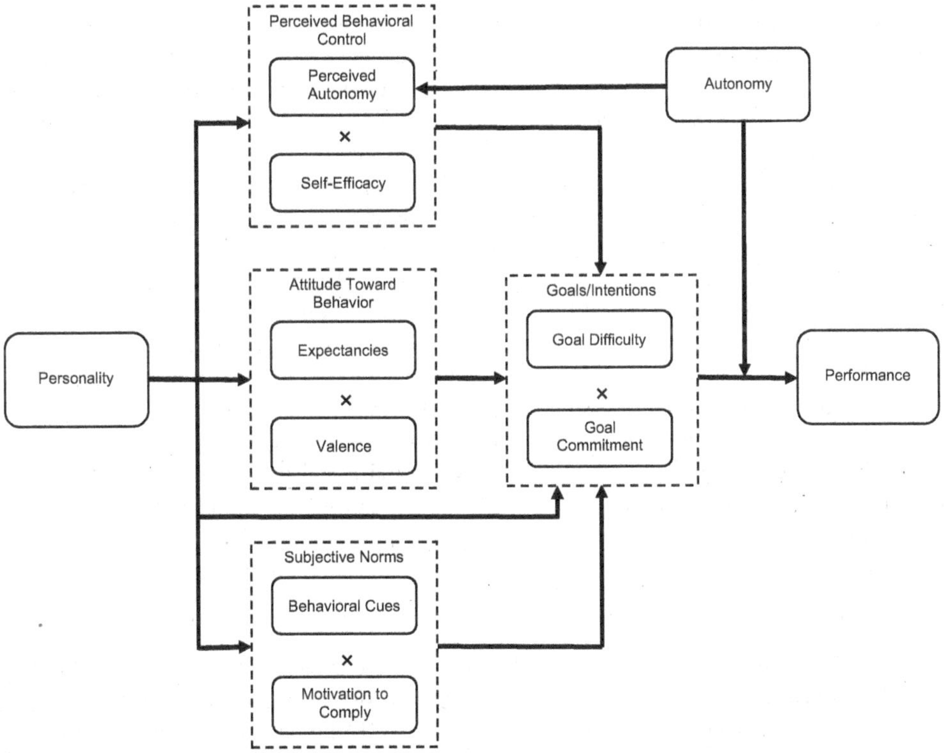

Figure 3.3 More Complete Description of the Goals/Intentions Aspect of the General Model.

The TPB overlaps considerably with concepts in motivation and personality theories. First, goal-setting theory is based on the idea that most behaviors are the result of consciously chosen goals and intentions (Mitchell & Daniels, 2003). Setting and being committed to a goal is very similar to forming an intention to engage in behavior aimed at goal attainment. Thus, the general model equates goal-setting with forming an intention, making this aspect of motivation a direct determinant of performance. In Figure 3.3, the goal-setting process is represented by the interaction between goal difficulty and goal commitment, because more difficult goals tend to produce higher performance (Wright, 1990) and goal commitment moderates this relationship (H. J. Klein, Wesson, Hollenbeck, & Alge, 1999).

Second, an attitude toward a behavior is a function of (a) the individual's beliefs about the consequences of performing the behavior, and (b) the desirability of those consequences (Fishbein & Ajzen, 1975). These components of an attitude are similar to the components of expectancy theories of motivation (i.e., expectancy, instrumentality, and valence; Mitchell & Daniels, 2003). Expectancy theories represent cognitive choices as Expectancy × Value (E × V), just as Fishbein and Ajzen (1975) represented the formation of an attitude. Thus, expectancies influence goals/intentions in the same way that attitudes influence intentions in the TPB, and we represent attitude toward a behavior as E × V in Figure 3.3.

Third, subjective norms are a combination of (a) a normative belief about whether others think the individual should perform the behavior, and (b) the individual's motivation to comply with what others think. According to trait activation theory, task, social, and organizational cues indicate what kind of behavior is valued positively and negatively in an organization (Tett & Burnett, 2003; Chapter 5, this volume). Individuals form normative beliefs about what others in the organization think they should do as the individual experiences trait-relevant cues and the value placed on certain behavior is communicated. Motivation to comply with what others think depends on the intrinsic and extrinsic satisfaction gained by engaging in certain behaviors. Individuals gain extrinsic satisfaction when rewarded for good performance, which happens when they express their traits in an environment that values such trait expression. Individuals also gain intrinsic satisfaction simply by expressing their traits, so motivation to comply will be especially high when features of tasks, people, and the organization provide opportunities for expressing one's traits.

Finally, perceived behavioral control refers to one's perception of the relative difficulty and volitional control associated with performing a behavior. We represent perceived behavioral control with the constructs of self-efficacy and perceived autonomy. Self-efficacy is the belief in one's own capabilities to successfully execute a course of action (Wood & Bandura, 1989). High self-efficacy should lead to a stronger perception that a behavior is under one's control (Ajzen, 2006). Autonomy is the extent to which the situation allows a person freedom to behave idiosyncratically (Barrick et al., 2003). The degree of autonomy in the situation has been found to moderate the relationship between personality and performance (e.g., Barrick & Mount, 1993; Beaty, Cleveland, & Murphy, 2001). Personality is more highly related to performance when people are free to perform their jobs in idiosyncratic ways. Thus, the amount of autonomy the individual perceives in a situation will contribute to the amount of perceived behavioral control, so the general model includes a direct path from autonomy to goals/intentions.

Self-Regulation

The final motivation component in the general model is self-regulation, which we define as the higher-level cognitive processes that (a) guide the allocation of attention, time, and effort across activities directed toward attaining a goal (Kanfer, 1990); and (b) protect an intention from being replaced by a competing action tendency before the intended action is completed (Kuhl, 1985). Figure 3.4 presents a specific model that focuses on self-regulation. Self-regulation partially mediates

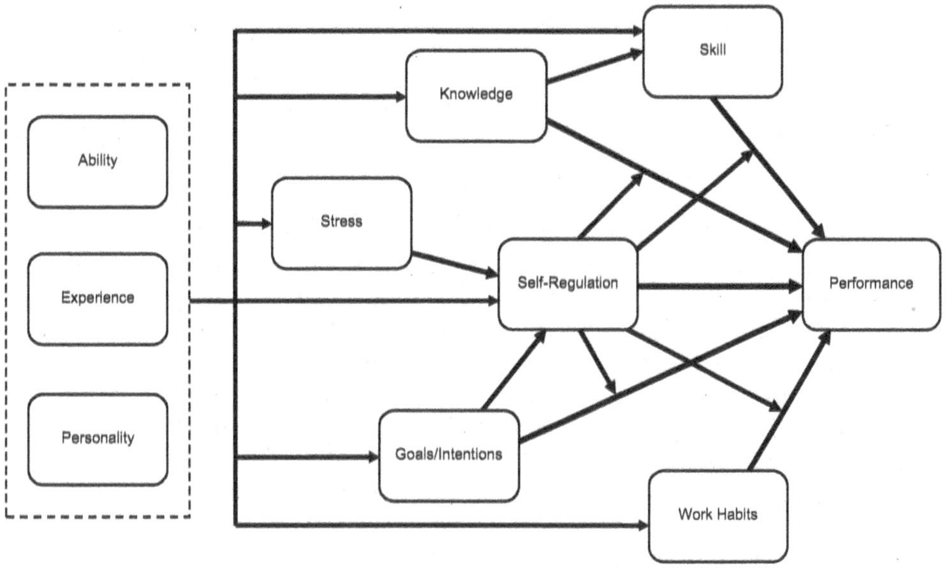

Figure 3.4 More Complete Description of the Self-Regulation Aspect of the General Model.

the relationship between goals/intentions and performance, because those who are more committed to a goal are likely to work harder at maintaining goal-directed action. Self-regulation also moderates relationships between performance and other direct determinants. Performance differences between two people with similar knowledge, skill, habits, and desire to perform could be explained by differing levels of ability to self-regulate. Work habits that detract from good performance can be overcome through self-regulatory strategies, so these habits will have less of an influence for people who are better at self-regulating. Self-regulation moderates the relationship between intentions and performance because this relationship is stronger the greater one's ability to protect the intention from competing action tendencies (Kuhl, 1985).

Self-regulatory ability is also expected to enable people to more effectively use their knowledge, skills, and abilities, especially in reaction to stress (Sinclair & Tucker, 2006). Self-regulation is related to both personality (Kanfer & Heggestad, 1997) and ability (Kanfer & Ackerman, 1989). Experience should also influence the acquisition of self-regulatory strategies because, as more situations are encountered in which self-regulation is necessary, effective strategies are learned and refined while ineffective strategies are dropped (Johnson et al., 2008).

Specific Personality Process Models

In this section, we briefly review some recent research on process models relating specific personality traits to specific types of performance, commenting on each model's implications for the general model. Space prohibits an exhaustive review, so we have chosen a few examples to illustrate how the general model can be applied in future research. Because the literature on moderators of personality–performance relationships is voluminous, we focus on process models featuring mediators.

Job Satisfaction as a Mediator

Ilies, Fulmer, Spitzmuller, and Johnson (2009) used a meta-analytic correlation matrix to test job satisfaction as a mediator of the relationship between personality (agreeableness and conscientiousness) and organizational citizenship behavior (OCB). OCB was split into OCB-I (behavior that benefits individuals) and OCB-O (behavior that benefits the organization). Both agreeableness and conscientiousness were directly related to job satisfaction, which was directly related to both OCB-I and OCB-O. In addition to the indirect effect through job satisfaction, agreeableness had a direct effect on OCB-I and conscientiousness had a direct effect on OCB-O (for more coverage on personality and citizenship behaviors, see Chapter 26, this volume).

The Ilies et al. (2009) model is very similar to a model tested by Mount et al. (2006) for predicting CWB from personality. Mount et al. distinguished between interpersonal CWBs (behaviors directed at individuals in the organization with the intent to produce emotional or physical discomfort or harm) and organizational CWBs (behaviors directed toward harming the interests of the organization). Mount et al. found that job satisfaction partially mediated the relationships between personality traits and CWB. Agreeableness had a direct effect on interpersonal CWB and an indirect effect on both types of CWB through job satisfaction. Conscientiousness had a direct path to organizational CWB, but the mediating effect through job satisfaction was weaker. Although not the same as CWB, OCB-I and OCB-O should be highly negatively correlated with interpersonal CWB and organizational CWB, respectively (for more coverage on personality and CWB, see Chapter 27, this volume).

Similar to these two studies, Johnson et al. (2008) found that agreeableness had an indirect effect on maintaining good working relationships (similar to OCB-I) through both job satisfaction and knowledge. In the organizational commitment (similar to OCB-O) model, conscientiousness had an indirect influence through job satisfaction and self-regulation.

Li, Liang, and Crant (2010) proposed leader-member exchange (LMX) as a mediator of the relationship between proactive personality (tendency to identify opportunities to change things and to act on those impulses) and both job satisfaction and OCB. LMX is the quality and depth of the relationship between employee and immediate supervisor, so this is a work context variable in the general model. LMX mediated both the proactive personality–job satisfaction relationship and the proactive personality–OCB relationship. This is consistent with the general model, which includes work context as a mediating variable between personality and work attitudes, which then are directly related to OCB. Li et al. did not test job satisfaction as a mediator between LMX and OCB, so this is a logical next step in this line of research.

Schneider and Johnson (2005) tested social knowledge and motivation to perform in a socially competent manner as mediators of the relationship between indirect performance determinants and social performance. There were three categories of indirect determinants: (a) social intelligence, (b) interpersonal personality traits, and (c) general cognitive ability (*g*). In a study of 160 Reserve Officers' Training Corps (ROTC) cadets, the mediating effect of social knowledge was found for three social performance dimensions: (a) effective supervision, (b) interpersonal sensitivity, and (c) social presence. Motivation was only a significant mediator when predicting effective supervision.

The measure of motivation focused primarily on the importance respondents placed on performing behaviors relevant to each performance dimension, placing it in the proactive cognitions category of motivation (Mitchell & Daniels, 2003). Johnson et al. (2008) found similar results to Schneider and Johnson (2005) for the broad social performance dimension of maintaining good working relationships. Knowledge mediated the relationship between personality and performance, but proactive cognitions (i.e., expectancies) was not a mediator. Rather, Johnson et al. found that general motives (job satisfaction, military values, and affective commitment) were directly related to citizenship performance dimensions such as maintaining good working relationships. Schneider and Johnson did not include a measure of work attitudes or other types of motives in their study. Had they included these types of variables, the expected mediating effect of motivation may have been found for all types of performance.

The results of Ilies et al. (2009) and Johnson et al. (2008), along with the negative results of Schneider and Johnson (2005), suggest that the primary motivation component through which personality influences OCB is motives such as work attitudes (see Chapter 32, this volume, for more coverage on personality and work attitudes). Ilies et al. did not include other components of motivation, but Johnson et al. included expectancies, goal commitment, and self-regulation. Job satisfaction makes sense as the primary motivational mediator because OCB is often a spontaneous behavior that does not require proactive cognitions such as goal-setting.

The next step in this line of research is to add other potential mediating variables to explain the direct effects of agreeableness and conscientiousness on OCB or CWB. For OCB-I, interpersonal knowledge mediates the relationship between personality and performance (Johnson et al., 2008; Schneider & Johnson, 2005). Whenever behavior involves interacting with other people, the effectiveness of that behavior depends on the individual's knowledge of what behaviors are effective in interpersonal situations and/or the individual's interpersonal skill at applying those behaviors, both of which are determined to some extent by personality. People are likely to form an intention to engage in CWB (Cullen & Sackett, 2003), so other motivational components besides job satisfaction are likely to mediate the relationship between personality and CWB. Another way of expanding these models is to add other personality variables that would be expected to influence hypothesized mediating variables.

Goal Orientation as a Mediator

Goal orientation refers to one's predisposition to set certain kinds of goals in achievement situations (Dweck, 1986). Lee, Sheldon, and Turban (2003) proposed a model of the process by which personality influences performance and satisfaction through goal orientation. In a study of 284 management students, Lee et al. demonstrated that three personality characteristics derived from self-determination theory (autonomy orientation, control orientation, and amotivated orientation) directly influenced goal orientation. Autonomy orientation influenced the choice of mastery goals, which focus on mastering a task, developing skills, and meeting personal standards of accomplishment. Performance–approach goals focus on displaying competence and earning positive evaluations from others. Performance–avoidance goals focus on avoiding failure. Amotivation orientation (also called impersonal orientation) influenced the choice of performance-avoiding goals and control orientation influenced the choice of both performance–approach goals and performance–avoidance goals.

People with a performance–approach orientation tended to set more difficult goals while people with a performance–avoidance orientation tended to set less difficult goals. Goal level was positively related to performance. All three types of goal orientation predicted mental focus, which is the degree to which one is able to concentrate and become absorbed in an activity, with performance–avoidance goals being negatively related to mental focus. Mental focus directly influenced both course enjoyment (i.e., satisfaction) and performance. Mastery goal orientation also had a direct influence on satisfaction.

Comparing Lee et al.'s (2003) model to the general model underscores the importance of understanding terminology, because at first glance the models appear to be somewhat contradictory. Lee et al. refer to different types of goal orientation as forms of self-regulation, which would suggest that self-regulation leads to goal-setting rather than the other way around. Our definition of self-regulation (higher-level cognitive processes that guide the allocation of attention, time, and effort across activities directed toward attaining a goal) is more like Lee et al.'s definition of mental focus, which is predicted by goal orientation. The different types of goal orientation are what we would consider task-related motives (see Figure 3.2). Therefore, the two models are really quite consistent, as personality influences task-related motives (goal orientation), which influence goals/intentions (goal level), which influence performance.

Both models also propose self-regulation (mental focus) as a direct determinant of performance, but they diverge in the relationship between self-regulation (mental focus) and goals/intentions (goal level). Lee et al. (2003) propose no relationship, whereas we propose that self-regulation both mediates and moderates the relationship between goals and performance. The mediating relationship is between goal commitment and performance (those who are more committed to a goal are likely to work harder at maintaining goal-directed action), however, and goal commitment was not measured by Lee et al. Future research on Lee et al.'s model could focus on examining the moderating effect of mental focus on the relationship between goal level and performance. It is important to note that the measure of mental focus was not a direct measure, but rather a measure of the extent to which students expected to be able to concentrate on studying for the upcoming exam. A more appropriate measure of self-regulation or mental focus would assess the extent to which students actually were able to concentrate on studying.

In a laboratory study, Hendricks and Payne (2007) studied goal orientation as a mediator of the relationship between personality and leadership effectiveness. Like Lee et al. (2003), personality predicted different types of goal orientation, which predicted different components of motivation. The motivation variables had direct effects on leader effectiveness.

The results of Lee et al. (2003) and Hendricks and Payne (2007) suggest possible changes to the general model. The concept of task-oriented motives was similar to Barrick et al.'s (2003) accomplishment striving construct, which is a generalized intention to exert effort and work hard. This concept could be expanded to include the different types of goal orientation. This change would also result in adding a direct path from task-oriented motives to self-regulation, as the type of goal orientation would be expected to influence the type of self-regulatory activities one engages in while maintaining goal-directed behavior.

Leadership

Chan and Drasgow (2001) introduced a construct called motivation to lead (MTL), which has antecedents of various personality traits, *g*, sociocultural values, past leadership experience, and leadership self-efficacy (LSE). They created a measure of MTL consisting of three factors (affective-identity MTL, noncalculative MTL, and social-normative MTL), based on Fishbein and Ajzen's (1975) determinants of behavior: (a) valences associated with an act, (b) beliefs about the outcomes associated with engaging in the behavior, and (c) social norms related to the behavior. As explained previously, valences and beliefs about outcomes are represented by expectancies and social norms are represented by concepts from trait activation theory in the general model (see Figure 3.3). Also consistent with Chan and Drasgow, the general model has experience as antecedent to both self-efficacy and expectancies.

Hendricks and Payne (2007) tested MTL and LSE as determinants of leader effectiveness, adding goal orientation to the Big Five as antecedents of these variables. Following a team manufacturing task in a laboratory setting, they found that affective-identity MTL and noncalculative MTL were significantly and positively related to team ratings of leader effectiveness beyond the Big Five and previous leader performance. Social-normative MTL was negatively related to leader effectiveness, contrary to expectations. They did not test MTL as a mediator of the relationship between LSE and leader effectiveness, but they did find evidence suggesting that LSE partially mediated the relationship between learning goal orientation (same as mastery goal orientation) and both affective-identity MTL and social-normative MTL.

Ng et al. (2008) tested LSE as a mediator of the relationship between personality (specifically, neuroticism, extraversion, and conscientiousness) and leader effectiveness. Ng et al. found that this mediating effect was moderated by job demands and job autonomy. For neuroticism, extraversion, and conscientiousness, the mediating effect was present for leaders with low job demands but not for leaders with high job demands. For neuroticism and conscientiousness, the mediating effect was present for leaders with high job autonomy but not for leaders with low job autonomy. This is not entirely inconsistent with the general model, because both job demands and autonomy are aspects of the work context that are recognized as potential moderators of the relationship between goals/intentions and performance (goals/intentions mediates the relationship between self-efficacy and performance in the general model). If this relationship is weak under conditions of low autonomy or high job demands, there could not be a mediating effect between personality and performance. Nevertheless, the general model could be amended to reflect the possibility of moderated mediation effects like this.

Van Iddekinge, Ferris, and Heffner (2009) developed their own model of leader performance and tested it in a sample of 471 noncommissioned officers in the U.S. Army. They proposed leadership knowledge, skills, and abilities (KSAs) as the most proximal determinant of leader performance. We consider ability to be an indirect determinant of performance and keep knowledge and skill separate as direct determinants. Examining the KSA measures Van Iddekinge et al. used, however, suggests that there was really no difference between leadership ability and leadership skill. They combined their measures into a single KSA variable to keep the model parsimonious, so there is little disagreement between the two models at this point.

Van Iddekinge et al. (2009) proposed cognitive ability, leadership experiences, and MTL as the determinants of leadership KSAs. The general model includes ability and experience but not motivation as determinants of knowledge and skill. Van Iddekinge et al. tested alternative models that allowed for (a) a direct effect of MTL on performance, and (b) both a direct effect and an indirect effect through leadership KSAs. The direct effect alternative model did not fit as well as the original model and the partial mediating effect alternative model was not significantly better than the original model. This result is limited to the type of motivation measured in this study, which was the affective-identity factor of Chan and Drasgow's (2001) measure. Affective-identity MTL is a measure of the affect associated with being a leader and does not measure the components of motivation we expect to directly determine performance (goal level, goal commitment, and self-regulation). It does make sense that those with a preference for leading would tend to seek out opportunities to gain knowledge and skill relevant to leading. This is consistent with Colquitt, LePine, and Noe's (2000) model of training motivation, in which personality influences self-efficacy and valence, which influence motivation to learn, which influences knowledge and skill acquisition. This suggests that the general model could be amended to include direct paths from expectancies to both knowledge and skill.

Another difference between the models is that Van Iddekinge et al. (2009) considered personality to influence leadership KSAs only through the mediating variables of leadership experiences and MTL, whereas we consider personality to be a direct influence on knowledge and skill and do not consider a mediating effect of experience. When testing alternative models, however, Van Iddekinge et al. found that the indirect effect of personality on performance was primarily through leader KSAs rather than through experience or MTL. In fact, the direct effect of personality (conscientiousness and extraversion) on performance was larger than the indirect effect. The direct effects likely influence performance through unmeasured motivational variables. Thus, Van Iddekinge et al.'s results were highly consistent with the general model.

The general model suggests many avenues for future research in explaining the relationship between personality and leadership effectiveness. None of the studies reviewed here included all components of motivation through which personality is expected to influence performance, so future research should focus on more fully explicating the motivation domain. Ng et al. (2008) used trait activation theory (Tett & Burnett, 2003) to formulate hypotheses on moderated mediation effects involving job demands and autonomy, and these effects would also be expected for motivation components other than self-efficacy. In addition, other mediators such as skill and knowledge could be tested for moderated mediation effects.

Burnout

The general model includes stress as a direct influence on work attitudes based on research showing that work stress mediated the relationship between personality and attitudes (Day et al., 1998; Van den Berg & Feij, 2003). We also included stress as a direct determinant of self-regulation, based on Sinclair and Tucker's (2006) model of individual differences in Soldier performance under stress, in which stress constrains the amount of motivational resources that can be allocated to performance. The relationship between stress and other variables in the model could be better understood by incorporating the construct of burnout. *Burnout* is an affective response to ongoing stress, resulting in the gradual depletion over time of an individual's energy. There are competing conceptualizations of the dimensions of burnout (e.g., Halbesleben & Bowler, 2007; Maslach, Schaufeli, & Leiter, 2001; Shirom, 2003), but all incorporate exhaustion as a core component. Exhaustion manifests as emotional exhaustion, physical fatigue, and cognitive weariness (Melamed, Shirom, Toker, Berliner, & Shapira, 2006). *Emotional exhaustion* involves feeling that one does not possess the energy to invest in work relationships, resulting in interpersonal withdrawal; *physical fatigue* refers to feeling tired and having little energy to carry out daily work tasks; and *cognitive weariness* refers to slowed cognition and reduced mental agility. Two other dimensions of burnout that have repeatedly emerged in factor-analytic work are (a) *depersonalization*, meaning that individuals are negative, cynical, or detached from coworkers/clients; and (b) a reduced sense of *personal accomplishment*—feelings that one's competence and productivity have declined.

Swider and Zimmerman (2010) studied burnout dimensions as mediators of the relationship between personality and job performance (in addition to turnover and absenteeism). They conducted a meta-analysis of the relationships between the Big Five and the burnout dimensions of emotional exhaustion, depersonalization, and personal accomplishment. They found that each Big Five personality trait had at least a moderate correlation with at least one burnout dimension, with neuroticism being highly related to all three. Based on this meta-analysis and others involving other relevant variables, Swider and Zimmerman constructed a meta-analytic correlation matrix to test alternative models of the process through which burnout influences different outcome variables. For job performance, support was found for a model in which job performance was directly influenced by personal accomplishment, which was negatively influenced by both emotional exhaustion and depersonalization. Emotional exhaustion also had an indirect effect on personal accomplishment through depersonalization. Adding these burnout dimensions to the general model would add another layer of understanding to how personality can potentially influence performance (for more coverage on personality and stress-related outcomes, see Chapter 31, this volume).

Strategy for Researching Personality–Performance Process Theories

In this section, we consider strategies for accelerating development of personality–performance theories (PPTs). In doing so, we consider (a) some general criteria for appraisal of scientific theories and models, (b) aspects of theories and models relevant to PPTs, (c) methods for facilitating the development of PPTs that are simultaneously rigorous and feasible, and (d) the relationship between PPTs and the dual needs of industrial/organizational (I/O) academics and professionals. We focus on building theories rather than models in this section because our ultimate goal is to create good theories with significant explanatory power.

Metatheory and PPTs

Metatheory refers to a theory of theories. For example, just as we have criteria to evaluate hypotheses specified by a theory, there are also criteria against which to evaluate theories themselves. "Good theories" have certain characteristics on which there is reasonable agreement (e.g., Campbell, 1990b; K. J. Klein & Zedeck, 2004; Meehl, 2002). These characteristics include (a) the ability to organize and simplify a set of previously unorganized and scattered facts and data (e.g., by providing a means by which archival and new data can be interpreted and coded as in a meta-analysis); (b) clearly defined constructs; (c) thoughtful propositions that describe clearly the nature of the relationship between constructs; (d) falsifiability; and (e) verisimilitude. This is not a comprehensive list, although all of these are important characteristics for PPTs. We include these because of their criticality for research progress, and discuss each in turn.

Ability to Organize and Simplify Facts and Data

Simonton (2006) observed the following:

> According to Kuhn (1970), the researchers in preparadigmatic disciplines are engaged in random fact gathering. Because no formal theoretical position separates wheat from chaff, all facts become equally important. Accordingly, findings gather helter-skelter, without rhyme or reason. In contrast, in highly paradigmatic disciplines scientists are engaged in "puzzle-solving" research that closely follows theoretical dictates, and thus the collective research effort is more strongly coordinated, and the results more cohesive and cumulative.
>
> *p. 105*

The first part of this quotation seems, to a large extent, to describe I/O personality research prior to the widespread acceptance of the Five-Factor Model (FFM) that coalesced in the early 1990s. Prior to FFM coalescence, I/O personality research was badly in need of a paradigm and was not progressing very efficiently, if at all. Indeed, in the face of Mischel's (1968) situationist critique of personality psychology, some began to wonder whether personality traits were worthy of investigation at all. One does not have to subscribe fully to the FFM to reach the conclusion that it has served as a useful organizing framework if nothing else, and has facilitated progress in I/O personality research, albeit somewhat crudely. By the early 1990s, the person-situation debate had essentially run its course (cf. Kenrick & Funder, 1988), and many appeared ready to accept the FFM taxonomy (cf. Barrick & Mount, 1991; Goldberg, 1990; McCrae & Costa, 1987; but see Block, 1995, and Hough, 1992).

At approximately the same time that acceptance of the FFM taxonomy was coalescing, Campbell (1990b) proposed a broad taxonomy of job performance dimensions and a model of the performance prediction problem. Campbell's job performance taxonomy and general model of performance prediction have been highly generative. Each of the process models reviewed in this chapter can trace their origins to Campbell's model. Indeed, the last 20 years have seen the emergence of a nascent paradigm in I/O personality research that has resulted in a cumulative research record that would have made a chapter such as this one unthinkable 20 years ago. Researchers now have a good sense of what variables to include in their PPT research and some sense of the nomological net making up PPTs.

Clear Definition of Constructs

Requiring clarity in the definitions of PPT constructs has slowed the field down because traits, performance constructs, and other PPT constructs are inherently inexact phenomena that are difficult to pin down. Meehl (1978) pointed out that constructs in fields such as ours are "open concepts," the operational indicators of which are not finite, are probabilistically related to their theoretical constructs, and usually have definitions that are partly derived from relationships with other constructs within the overall nomological network. He also noted that, as a result of refinement of measures and corresponding revision of construct definitions, psychological constructs are subject to psychometric drift over time, whereby the meaning of the construct changes.

There are two types of fallacies that are related to the openness of psychological constructs. The *jingle fallacy* occurs when the same name is given to two different constructs. The *jangle fallacy* occurs when different names or labels are given to the same construct (see Block, 1995, pp. 209–210, for a discussion of these fallacies in relation to the FFM). Construct openness, psychometric drift, and the jingle and jangle fallacies can slow our scientific progress by making meta-analytic findings more difficult to interpret and making the language we use to communicate findings ambiguous. Increasing scientific precision takes time and much effort, however, which can slow our ability to make progress in addressing research questions upon which having some type of taxonomy (such as the FFM) is important. One way of addressing this problem is to be as clear as possible in the text of original research reports regarding the definition of the constructs studied. Similarly, meta-analysts must be vigilant in their coding and cumulation of data, noting and mitigating to the extent possible any ambiguities.

Describing Clearly How and Why Constructs Are Linked

PPTs require clear specification of the nomological net that links constructs in the personality and job performance taxonomies. In particular, attention must be given to "explaining what construct leads to what, when, how, and why" (K. J. Klein & Zedeck, 2004, p. 932). Of course, this quotation describes a program of research that may take many years. This process is highly iterative; is both exploratory and confirmatory; and likely involves multiple samples, multiple methods, multiple points in time, and evaluation of many competing explanations. PPTs require specification of the functional form of the relationships (e.g., linear, quadratic, monotonically increasing or decreasing) as well as the direction of causal arrow(s) (bidirectionality should be specified if there is mutual influence). The approximate magnitude of expected relationship(s) between constructs, appropriately contextualized, should also be stated, most likely as an interval of effect sizes.

Boundary conditions (e.g., type of situation, organizational characteristics, population, job family, stage in the organizational socialization process, and career stage) should also be explicitly stated to the extent that they may be expected to affect the existence and/or magnitude of construct relationships. The role of time should be considered, when appropriate (George & Jones, 2000). Time may be thought of as a special type of boundary condition. For example, does one construct affect another construct instantaneously or only after a period of time has elapsed and certain critical events have transpired? In the case of bidirectionality, is the mutual influence between constructs one of increasing intensity in an upward or downward direction over time, such that some type of exponential relationship in three dimensions is required for an adequate description (e.g., spiraling)? As a general rule, more specific theories are better. Propositions should be stated clearly and specifically enough that they can be replicated by other researchers. The more knowledge that we gain, the more elaborate the propositions should become.

Mediation and moderation are particularly salient to PPTs, as they specify important aspects of the path from personality to performance. Mediation can be viewed as an explanation of causality and moderation can be viewed as a qualification of causality. Baron and Kenny (1986) specify a relatively straightforward sequence of multiple regressions to provide evidence for mediation. Caution should be exercised, however, so that looking for mediation does not become a routine exercise that can be reduced down to a series of steps. Understanding mediated relationships requires extensive knowledge of the process under study and a careful and thoughtful analysis of the data (Kenny, 2008). Mediation has an implicit assumption of causation in the mediation chain, but Baron and Kenny's technique does not permit causal inference by itself. Causal inference must be established using theory, randomized experimental studies, and qualitative methods

(MacKinnon et al., 2007). Longitudinal data also bolster causality evidence if temporal precedence can be established with respect to the variables in the mediation chain.

Falsifiability and Verisimilitude

We discuss the criteria of falsifiability and verisimilitude simultaneously because they are conceptually related. Karl Popper emphasized the importance of falsifiability of scientific theories. According to Popper, "insofar as a scientific statement speaks about reality, it must be falsifiable; and insofar as it is not falsifiable, it does not speak about reality" (Miller, 1985, p. 91). While one may prove a mathematical theorem (which does not relate to reality, but only furnishes tools to investigate reality), the truth of an empirical scientific theory can never be proven. Meehl (1978) focused attention on the importance of this idea for psychology. Falsification occurs if a theory predicts an outcome and the outcome is not observed in an experiment designed to test the theory. If this occurs, the theory is considered to be refuted by the logical syllogism known as *modus tollens* (i.e., if A, then B/not B/ therefore, not A).

Meehl (1978) noted that refutation by modus tollens is difficult due to auxiliary theories. *Auxiliary theories* are independently testable hypotheses, or conjunctions of hypotheses, relevant to the derivation of the theoretical outcome that can account for an apparent refutation by modus tollens (Miller, 1985). (Essentially, if A + C, then B/not B/therefore, not A + C; the conclusion of "not A" does not follow.) Examples of other factors that can account for an apparent refutation of the theory are (a) certain systematic factors not accounted for in the experiment; (b) flawed experimental instrumentation (e.g., tests); and/or (c) experimental conditions that were not the same (note the importance of clear and specific postulates, as described above, to mitigate this). As noted by Meehl (1990), refutation of a theory by modus tollens can only occur if the conjunction of auxiliary hypotheses and alternative explanations (sometimes referred to as the "protective belt" around the core theoretical postulates) can be ruled out.

Considered in this light, refutation may seem problematic. Given the complexities of PPTs and many other psychological theories, however, refutation probably should be a difficult proposition. For example, a high-potential theory should not be abandoned as a result of one negative result. We should keep the baby and discard the bathwater rather than the other way around. To this point, Popper's methodology of conjecture and refutation was enriched by the work of Lakatos (Meehl, 1990). Lakatosian methodology states that theories that have already accumulated a number of successes, defined as corroborating evidence of risky predictions, should be slower to be discarded than other theories. Lakatos also formulated the concept of a degenerating research program, which generally involves much *ad hoc* theorizing to address discorroborating evidence. By contrast, if exploration of a theory's protective belt is "content increasing, empirically successful, and in some sense inspired by the leading ideas of the theory (rather than alien elements pasted on), the research program is said to be progressive" (Meehl, 1990, pp. 111–112).

Constructing a crude index of a theory's track record requires a shift from falsification to *verisimilitude*, or the extent to which the theory approximates the phenomena that it seeks to address. Strong corroboration occurs when a theory predicts a point value within a confidence interval and succeeds. A less favorable, but still positive, appraisal occurs when a theory misses, but comes reasonably close. "Reasonably close" would be an interval, typically justified rationally. Risky predictions corroborated by evidence are key to the evaluation of the verisimilitude of a psychological theory and the growth of scientific knowledge. Riskiness can take a number of forms. Edwards and Berry (2010) note the desirability of increasing the precision of theoretical predictions and offer useful guidelines for making theories more precise. These include (a) setting upper and lower limits for prediction, based, for example, on the role of the constructs being related in the theory's nomological net; (b) making "non-nil predictions" that specify the range of values that would constitute support for a theory, with narrower ranges constituting riskier tests; (c) development of contingent predictions, such as those that incorporate moderator variables specifying boundary conditions; and (d) specifying the functional form relating constructs in a theory.

An especially important suggestion made by Edwards and Berry (2010) involves making comparative predictions (e.g., predicting that one effect will differ from another effect by an amount that falls within a specified range). A powerful form of comparative prediction was articulated by Platt (1964), who argued that the growth of scientific knowledge occurs through studies that permit "strong inference," which consists of the following steps: (1) devising alternative hypotheses; (2) devising a crucial experiment (or several of them) with alternative possible outcomes, each of which will exclude one or more of the hypotheses as nearly as possible; (3) carrying out the experiment so as to get a clean result; and (4) recycling the procedure, making subhypotheses or sequential hypotheses to refine the possibilities that remain.

Consistent with the foregoing, Greenwald, Pratkanis, Leippe, and Baumgardner (1986) argued that theoretical progress is enhanced by adopting a disconfirmatory methodology, including devising alternative hypotheses in addition to those that would corroborate a theory. Both Greenwald et al. and Nickerson (1998) noted the potential for confirmation bias to influence theory evaluation and inhibit theoretical progress. *Confirmation bias* is "the seeking or interpreting of evidence in ways that are partial to existing beliefs, expectations, or a hypothesis in hand" (Nickerson, 1998, p. 175). Greenwald (1980) linked the tendency toward confirmation rather than disconfirmation in theory evaluation to egocentricity, in that subjecting one's theory to possible disconfirmation is a threat to one's ego. Greenwald et al. (1986) suggested that one way around this dilemma is to adopt a problem-centered approach to scientific progress as opposed to a theory-centered approach, a suggestion echoed by Campbell (1990b).

A problem-centered approach would greatly benefit the broad research program involving illumination of processes linking personality to job performance, though certainly parts of that approach will involve development and rigorous empirical evaluation of both taxonomic theories and process theories linking both personality and performance taxonomies. Crucial tests, risky hypotheses, willingness to discard theories when a series of studies reveal clear signs of a degenerating research program, and coordinated focus on theories that studies suggest constitute progressive research programs will result in greater, and a more rapid path to, verisimilitude.

Theory Pruning

One of the challenges involved in providing an adequate explanation of the "black box" linking personality taxonomies to performance taxonomies is the large number of constructs and the number and potential complexity of the relationships linking those constructs. Building on much of the meta-theoretical literature cited and described above, Leavitt, Mitchell, and Peterson (2010) proposed a process that may yield a partial solution to this problem, which they refer to as *theory pruning*. Leavitt et al. defined theory pruning as "hypothesis specification in study design intended to bound and reduce theory" (p. 644). This approach is essentially an elaboration of the strong inference argument advanced by Platt (1964). To a large extent, it is an argument that methods for disconfirming and revising theories espoused by many others should be applied routinely. Leavitt et al.'s elaboration, however, is very useful in many respects. For example, the authors note that crucial tests pitting entire theories against other entire theories are very hard to do. Noting that that there is a continuum from theory pitting of the sort envisaged by Platt to testing parts of theories, Leavitt et al. provided a framework that specifies a number of ways in which studies can be conducted that can be used to evaluate an overall theory. They also suggested initial comparisons that should be made to establish the comparability of different theories prior to conducting a true crucial test. For example, are equivalently labeled constructs truly comparable, both with respect to content and structure? Is the timeframe for relationships between constructs comparable? Do the theories apply to the same population and context?

Short of a true crucial test, Leavitt et al. (2010) suggested several alternative hypotheses that can be advanced to evaluate parts of multiple theories. For example, when evaluating relationships between constructs specified in two theories, do the constructs from one theory explain additional variance? Do they explain the same variance using fewer terms and conditions (i.e., more parsimoniously)? Does one theory explain a greater range of distinguishable phenomena than another theory?

Leavitt et al. (2010) also specified a number of statistical tests associated with the various alternative hypotheses suggested in their framework. These tests include (a) including control variables in hierarchical regression and evaluating change in variance accounted for (this could, for example, justify inclusion of additional constructs or additional content in similarly named constructs in a given theory, and determine potential boundary conditions through use of covariates); (b) using a structural equation modeling (SEM) framework to test nested models (this could, for example, point to a more parsimonious explanation); (c) specifying range-based, directional, and meaningful null hypotheses (this could, for example, be used to corroborate a portion of one or more theories); (d) conducting meta-analyses to compare differences in cumulated effect size estimates, including theoretical approach as a categorical moderator (this could, for example, be used to conduct a quasi-crucial test of differences in explanatory power between two or more theories or theoretical approaches); (e) conducting a series of studies including multiple-criteria tests with multiple timeframes (this could, for example, be used to evaluate differences between two or more theories in stability and generalizability); and (f) conducting studies in which two theories predict mutually incompatible outcomes and determining which outcome is observed (this could be a full crucial test or a crucial test of some subset of the two comparable theories, depending on how much of the theories are evaluated).

Theory Pruning and SEM

SEM is commonly used to test theories about how a set of variables work together to explain some process (e.g., the personality–performance process). The typical approach is to evaluate a model against arbitrary benchmarks (e.g., χ^2, GFI, CFI, NFI, and RMSEA). A good fit against these benchmarks simply means the model is one of a large pool of plausible models, and says little about the verisimilitude of the theory the model is intended to represent. Vandenberg and Grelle (2009) discuss alternative model specification (AMS) within the context of covariance structure modeling and make many of the same points as others cited in this chapter relative to the need to shift from confirmation to disconfirmation. In addition, however, they show how SEM can be used in a manner consistent with this philosophy of how to do science in general and theory pruning in particular.

Vandenberg and Grelle (2009) emphasize that greater effort should be made to specify and test alternative models that are theoretically plausible prior to data collection. The greatest scientific value is realized when one of two or more competing models emerges as the strongest over several replications. They also note that evaluating an alternative model that specifies a mediating path without a priori theoretical plausibility and justification against a model that does not specify that path is not really putting a theory at risk. Specification of alternate models that include mediators or moderators of construct relationships specified by the focal structural model is required prior to data collection and analysis. Vandenberg and Grelle cite several examples of studies in which such a priori justification of mediators or moderators was done (e.g., Kinicki, Prussia, Wu, & McKee-Ryan, 2004).

Vandenberg and Grelle (2009) also addressed AMS separately for equivalent models, nested models, and nonnested models, noting differences in implications for pitting models against one another and inferring differences. The overarching theme, however, is that AMS should be based on theoretical plausibility and alternative models should be specified before data are collected and analyzed. Post hoc theorizing, while sometimes necessary, should be avoided.

Research Agenda

The general model of the personality–performance process and its submodels suggest a number of avenues for research. For example, research is necessary on specific performance dimensions to determine what elements of the model operate for different types of performance. Certain elements may be consistent across all types of performance, but many will depend on the performance dimension. Task performance dimensions seem most likely to be influenced by all elements of the model, while citizenship performance and CWB are likely to be determined by a simpler model (Johnson et al., 2008). It is necessary to determine to what extent a single model describes the performance prediction process for performance dimensions within the same broad category (e.g., different aspects of citizenship performance; cf. Ilies et al., 2009).

The general model can guide research on the relationships between specific personality traits and specific performance dimensions by helping identify theoretically relevant predictors for different criteria, which will be facilitated by the development of a nomological net linking personality variables to the various elements of the model. Meta-analyses have been conducted on personality predictors of work attitudes, proactive cognition aspects of motivation, and performance dimensions, but research linking personality to the other elements of the model is necessary to help identify likely personality predictors of specific performance dimensions.

Research is necessary to determine how the aspect of performance being studied moderates the relationship between personality and motivation. For example, certain personality traits may be highly related to motives, expectancies, self-efficacy, goal content, and goal commitment when the criterion is a dimension of citizenship performance, but have no relationship to these constructs when the criterion is a dimension of task performance. For example, Johnson et al. (2008) found that agreeableness was related to the components of motivation when predicting citizenship performance, but was not related to motivation when predicting task performance. The opposite relationship would be expected for achievement, although achievement is commonly used as a proxy for motivation for any kind of performance. Research should be directed at creating a taxonomy of personality predictors of motivation for different performance constructs that can be used to facilitate our understanding of how personality influences performance.

In this chapter, we demonstrated that most personality–performance process models are not inconsistent with each other. When these models differ, it is primarily because (a) a variable is included in one model but not another, or (b) there are definitional issues in that similar variables have different names or variables with the same name are defined differently. We recommend using the general model as a guide to what variables to include when reconciling different models or formulating new ones and for consistent construct definition. When two models suggest different explanations for observed phenomena, research should be designed to pit the competing models against each other. Hochwarter et al. (2006) is a good example of an investigation that was set up to determine which of two alternative theories better explained a relationship, in this case how understanding affects the relationship between politics perceptions and job performance. These authors designed a study that provided a fair test of the alternative explanations, and then constructively replicated the results in two additional samples.

Practitioner's Window

Although the study of the process through which personality influences performance may be considered basic research, having an understanding of this process has several potential applications for practitioners. For personnel selection purposes, the general model could be used to choose appropriate predictors for whatever criterion construct is of interest for a particular job. Because of the situational specificity of the validity of personality measures, it is difficult to determine which personality traits should be measured to predict performance in a given situation without having an understanding of the numerous pathways through which different personality traits can influence different types of performance.

The general model also adds significantly to our evolving understanding of the nature and antecedents of job performance. Practitioners can use this information to identify interventions that will have the greatest impact on areas of performance that are deficient in certain employees. For example, increasing citizenship performance behavior could be accomplished by focusing on increasing job satisfaction. The general model would also be effective in identifying training and/or development needs. Given a criterion construct on which an individual's performance is in need of improvement, this model can help to identify the determinants of performance on that construct. For example, an individual possessing adequate skill and knowledge may determine that he or she must learn new self-regulatory strategies to maintain goal-directed behavior. As process model research allows us to gain more knowledge of the complexity with which personality determines job performance, both theory and practice will benefit.

References

Ajzen, I. (1985). From intentions to actions: A theory of planned behavior. In J. Kuhl & J. Beckmänn (Eds.), *Action control: From cognitions to behavior* (pp. 11–39). New York: Springer-Verlag.

Ajzen, I. (2006). Perceived behavioral control, self-efficacy, locus of control, and the theory of planned behavior. *Journal of Applied Social Psychology, 32*, 665–683.

Arad, S., Hanson, M. A., & Schneider, R. J. (1999). Organizational context. In N. G. Peterson, M. D. Mumford, W. C. Borman, P. R. Jeanneret, & E. A. Fleishman (Eds.), *An occupational information system for the 21st century: The development of O*NET* (pp. 147–174). Washington, DC: American Psychological Association.

Baron, R. M., & Kenny, D. A. (1986). The moderator-mediator variable distinction in social psychological research: Conceptual, strategic, and statistical considerations. *Journal of Personality and Social Psychology, 51*, 1173–1182.

Barrick, M. R., Mitchell, T. R., & Stewart, G. L. (2003). Situational and motivational influences on trait–behavior relationships. In M. R. Barrick & A. M. Ryan (Eds.), *Personality and work: Reconsidering the role of personality in organizations* (pp. 60–82). San Francisco: Jossey-Bass.

Barrick, M. R., & Mount, M. K. (1991). The Big Five personality dimensions and job performance: A meta-analysis. *Personnel Psychology, 44*, 1–26.

Barrick, M. R., & Mount, M. K. (1993). Autonomy as a moderator of the relationships between the Big Five personality dimensions and job performance. *Journal of Applied Psychology, 78*, 111–118.

Barrick, M. R., Stewart, G. L., & Piotrowski, M. (2002). Personality and job performance: Test of the mediating effects of motivation among sales representatives. *Journal of Applied Psychology, 87*, 43–51.

Beaty, J. C., Cleveland, J. N., & Murphy, K. R. (2001). The relation between personality and contextual performance in "strong" versus "weak" situations. *Human Performance, 14*, 125–148.

Blickle, G., Wendel, S., & Ferris, G. R. (2010). Political skill as moderator of personality–job performance relationships in socioanalytic theory: Test of the getting ahead motive in automobile sales. *Journal of Vocational Behavior, 76*, 326–335.

Block, J. (1995). A contrarian view of the five-factor approach to personality description. *Psychological Bulletin, 117*, 187–215.

Bond, F. W., Flaxman, P. E., & Bunce, D. (2008). The influence of psychological flexibility on work redesign: Mediated moderation of a work reorganization intervention. *Journal of Applied Psychology, 93*, 645–654.

Campbell, J. P. (1990a). Modeling the performance prediction problem in industrial and organizational psychology. In M. D. Dunnette & L. M. Hough (Eds.), *Handbook of industrial and organizational psychology* (2nd ed., Vol. 1, pp. 687–732). Palo Alto, CA: Consulting Psychologists Press.

Campbell, J. P. (1990b). The role of theory in industrial and organizational psychology. In M. D. Dunnette & L. M. Hough (Eds.), *Handbook of industrial and organizational psychology* (2nd ed., Vol. 1, pp. 39–73). Palo Alto, CA: Consulting Psychologists Press.

Chan, K., & Drasgow, F. (2001). Toward a theory of individual differences and leadership: Understanding the motivation to lead. *Journal of Applied Psychology, 86*, 481–498.

Colquitt, J. A., LePine, J. A., & Noe, R. A. (2000). Toward an integrative theory of training motivation: A meta-analytic path analysis of 20 years of research. *Journal of Applied Psychology, 85*, 678–707.
Cronbach, L. J., & Meehl, P. E. (1955). Construct validity in psychological tests. *Psychological Bulletin, 52*, 281–302.
Cullen, M. J., & Sackett, P. R. (2003). Personality and counterproductive workplace behavior. In M. R. Barrick & A. M. Ryan (Eds.), *Personality and work: Reconsidering the role of personality in organizations* (pp. 150–182). San Francisco: Jossey-Bass.
Day, D. V., Bedeian, A. G., & Conte, J. M. (1998). Personality as predictor of work-related outcomes: Test of a mediated latent structure model. *Journal of Applied Social Psychology, 28*, 2068–2088.
Dweck, C. S. (1986). Motivational processes affecting learning. *American Psychologist, 41*, 1040–1048.
Edwards, J. R., & Berry, J. W. (2010). The presence of something or the absence of nothing: Increasing theoretical precision in management research. *Organizational Research Methods, 13*, 668–689.
Edwards, J. R., & Lambert, L. S. (2007). Methods for integrating moderation and mediation: A general analytical framework using moderated path analysis. *Psychological Methods, 12*, 1–22.
Fishbein, M., & Ajzen, I. (1975). *Belief, attitude, intention, and behavior: An introduction to theory and research*. Reading, MA: Addison-Wesley.
George, J. M., & Jones, G. R. (2000). The role of time in theory and theory building. *Journal of Management, 2*, 657–684.
Godfrey-Smith, P. (2003). *Theory and reality: An introduction to the philosophy of science*. Chicago: The University of Chicago Press.
Goldberg, L. R. (1990). An alternative "description of personality": The Big-Five factor structure. *Journal of Personality and Social Psychology, 59*, 1216–1229.
Greenwald, A. G. (1980). The totalitarian ego: Fabrication and revision of personal history. *American Psychologist, 3*, 603–618.
Greenwald, A. G., Pratkanis, A. R., Leippe, M. R., & Baumgardner, M. H. (1986). Under what conditions does theory obstruct research progress? *Psychological Review, 93*, 216–229.
Halbesleben, J. R. B., & Bowler, W. M. (2007). Emotional exhaustion and job performance: The mediating role of motivation. *Journal of Applied Psychology, 92*, 93–106.
Hendricks, J. W., & Payne, S. C. (2007). Beyond the Big Five: Leader goal orientation as a predictor of leadership effectiveness. *Human Performance, 20*, 317–343.
Hochwarter, W. A., Kolodinsky, R. W., Witt, L. A., Hall, A. T., Ferris, G. R., & Kacmar, M. K. (2006). Competing perspectives on the role of understanding in the politics perceptions–job performance relationship: A test of the "antidote" versus "distraction" hypotheses. In E. Vigoda-Gadot & A. Drory (Eds.), *Handbook of organizational politics* (pp. 271–285). Northampton, MA: Edward Elgar.
Hough, L. M. (1992). The "Big Five" personality variables—Construct confusion: Description versus prediction. *Human Performance, 5*, 139–155.
Hough, L. M., & Oswald, F. L. (2005). They're right, well ... mostly right: Research evidence and an agenda to rescue personality testing from 1960s insights. *Human Performance, 18*, 373–387.
Hough, L. M., & Oswald, F. L. (2008). Personality testing and industrial-organizational psychology: Reflections, progress, and prospects. *Industrial and Organizational Psychology: Perspectives on Science and Practice, 1*, 272–290.
Hunter, J. E. (1986). Cognitive ability, cognitive aptitudes, job knowledge, and job performance. *Journal of Vocational Behavior, 29*, 340–362.
Hunter, J. E., & Hunter, R. F. (1984). Validity and utility of alternative predictors of job performance. *Psychological Bulletin, 96*, 72–98.
Ilies, R., Fulmer, I. S., Spitzmuller, M., & Johnson, M. D. (2009). Personality and citizenship behavior: The mediating role of job satisfaction. *Journal of Applied Psychology, 94*, 945–959.
Johnson, J. W. (2003). Toward a better understanding of the relationship between personality and individual job performance. In M. R. Barrick & A. M. Ryan (Eds.), *Personality and work: Reconsidering the role of personality in organizations* (pp. 83–120). New York: Jossey-Bass.
Johnson, J. W., Duehr, E. E., Hezlett, S. A., Muros, J. P., & Ferstl, K. L. (2008). *Modeling the direct and indirect determinants of different types of individual job performance* (ARI Technical Report No. 1236). Arlington, VA: U.S. Army Research Institute for the Behavioral and Social Sciences.
Johnson, J. W., & Hezlett, S. A. (2008). Modeling the influence of personality on individuals at work: A review and research agenda. In S. Cartwright & C. L. Cooper (Eds.), *Oxford handbook of personnel psychology* (pp. 59–92). Oxford, UK: Oxford University Press.
Kanfer, R. (1990). Motivation theory and industrial and organizational psychology. In M. D. Dunnette & L. M. Hough (Eds.), *Handbook of industrial and organizational psychology* (2nd ed., Vol. 1, pp. 75–170). Palo Alto, CA: Consulting Psychologists Press.

Kanfer, R., & Ackerman, P. L. (1989). Motivation and cognitive abilities: An integrative/aptitude-treatment interaction approach to skill acquisition [Monograph]. *Journal of Applied Psychology, 74*, 657–690.
Kanfer, R., & Heggestad, E. D. (1997). Motivational traits and skills: A person-centered approach to work motivation. In L. L. Cummings & B. M. Staw (Eds.), *Research in organizational behavior* (Vol. 19, pp. 1–56). Greenwich, CT: JAI Press.
Kenny, D. A. (2008). Reflections on mediation. *Organizational Research Methods, 11*, 353–358.
Kenrick, D. T., & Funder, D. C. (1988). Profiting from controversy: Lessons from the person-situation debate. *American Psychologist, 43*, 23–34.
Kinicki, A. J., Prussia, G. E., Wu, B. J., & McKee-Ryan, F. M. (2004). A covariance structure analysis of employees' response to performance feedback. *Journal of Applied Psychology, 89*, 1057–1069.
Klein, H. J., Wesson, M. J., Hollenbeck, J. R., & Alge, B. J. (1999). Goal commitment and the goal-setting process: Conceptual clarification and empirical synthesis. *Journal of Applied Psychology, 84*, 885–896.
Klein, K. J., & Zedeck, S. (2004). Introduction to the special section on theoretical models and conceptual analyses: Theory in applied psychology: Lessons (re)learned. *Journal of Applied Psychology, 89*, 931–933.
Kuhl, J. (1985). Volitional mediators of cognition-behavior consistency: Self-regulatory processes and action vs. state orientation. In J. Kuhl & J. Beckmänn (Eds.), *Action control: From cognition to behavior* (pp. 101–128). New York: Springer-Verlag.
Kuhn, T. S. (1970). *The structure of scientific revolutions* (2nd ed.). Chicago, IL: The University of Chicago Press.
Lance, C. E., & Bennett, W. (2000). Replication and extension of models of supervisory job performance ratings. *Human Performance, 13*, 139–158.
Leavitt, K., Mitchell, T. R., & Peterson, J. (2010). Theory pruning: Strategies to reduce our dense theoretical landscape. *Organizational Research Methods, 13*, 644–667.
Lee, F. K., Sheldon, K. M., & Turban, D. B. (2003). Personality and the goal-striving process: The influence of achievement goal patterns, goal level, and mental focus on performance and enjoyment. *Journal of Applied Psychology, 88*, 256–265.
Li, N., Liang, J., & Crant, J. M. (2010). The role of proactive personality in job satisfaction and organizational citizenship behavior: A relational perspective. *Journal of Applied Psychology, 95*, 395–404.
MacKinnon, D. P., Fairchild, A. J., & Fritz, M. S. (2007). Mediation analysis. *Annual Review of Psychology, 58*, 593–614.
Marewski, J. N., & Olsson, H. (2009). Beyond the null ritual: Formal modeling of psychological processes. *Zeitschrift für Psychologie [Journal of Psychology], 217*, 49–60.
Maslach, C., Schaufeli, W. B., & Leiter, M. P. (2001). Job burnout. *Annual Review of Psychology, 52*, 397–422.
McCrae, R. R., & Costa, P. T. (1987). Validation of the five-factor model of personality across instruments and observers. *Journal of Personality and Social Psychology, 52*, 81–90.
Meehl, P. E. (1978). Theoretical risks and tabular asterisks: Sir Karl, Sir Ronald, and the slow progress of soft psychology. *Journal of Consulting and Clinical Psychology, 46*, 806–834.
Meehl, P. E. (1990). Appraising and amending theories: The strategy of Lakatosian defense and two principles that warrant it. *Psychological Inquiry, 1*, 108–141.
Meehl, P. E. (2002). Cliometric metatheory: II. Criteria scientists use in theory appraisal and why it is rational to do so. *Psychological Reports, 91*, 339–404.
Melamed, S., Shirom, A., Toker, S., Berliner, S., & Shapira, I. (2006). Burnout and risk of cardiovascular disease: Evidence, possible causal paths, and promising research directions. *Psychological Bulletin, 132*, 327–353.
Miller, D. (Ed.). (1985). *Popper selections*. Princeton, NJ: Princeton University Press.
Mischel, W. (1968). *Personality and assessment*. Hoboken, NJ: Wiley.
Mitchell, T. R., & Daniels, D. (2003). Motivation. In W. Borman, D. Ilgen, & R. Klimoski (Eds.), *Handbook of psychology: Industrial and organizational psychology* (Vol. 12, pp. 225–254). Hoboken, NJ: Wiley.
Motowidlo, S. J., Borman, W. C., & Schmit, M. J. (1997). A theory of individual differences in task and contextual performance. *Human Performance, 10*, 71–83.
Mount, M., Ilies, R., & Johnson, E. (2006). Relationship of personality traits and counterproductive work behaviors: The mediating effects of job satisfaction. *Personnel Psychology, 59*, 591–622.
Ng, K., Ang, S., & Chan, K. (2008). Personality and leader effectiveness: A moderated mediation model of leadership self-efficacy, job demands, and job autonomy. *Journal of Applied Psychology, 93*, 733–743.
Nickerson, R. S. (1998). Confirmation bias: A ubiquitous phenomenon in many guises. *Review of General Psychology, 2*, 175–220.
Ones, D. S., Dilchert, S., Viswesvaran, C., & Judge, T. A. (2007). In support of personality assessment in organizational settings. *Personnel Psychology, 60*, 995–1027.
Platt, J. R. (1964). Strong inference. *Science, 146*, 347–353.
Salgado, J. F., Anderson, N., Moscoso, S., Bertua, C., de Fruyt, F., & Rolland, J. P. (2003). A meta-analytic study of general mental ability validity for different occupations in the European community. *Journal of Applied Psychology, 88*, 1068–1081.

Schmidt, F. L. (2002). The role of general cognitive ability and job performance: Why there cannot be a debate. *Human Performance, 15*, 187–210.
Schmidt, F. L., & Hunter, J. E. (2004). General mental ability in the world of work: Occupational attainment and job performance. *Journal of Personality and Social Psychology, 86*, 162–173.
Schmidt, F. L., Hunter, J. E., & Outerbridge, A. N. (1986). Impact of job experience and ability on job knowledge, work sample performance, and supervisory ratings of job performance. *Journal of Applied Psychology, 71*, 432–439.
Schneider, R. J., & Johnson, J. W. (2005). *Direct and indirect predictors of social competence in United States Army junior commissioned officers* (ARI Technical Report No. 1131). Arlington, VA: U.S. Army Research Institute for the Behavioral and Social Sciences.
Shirom, A. (2003). Job-related burnout. In J. C. Quick & L. Tetrick (Eds.), *Handbook of occupational health psychology* (pp. 245–265). Washington, DC: American Psychological Association.
Simonton, D. K. (2006). Scientific status of disciplines, individuals, and ideas: Empirical analyses of the potential impact of theory. *Review of General Psychology, 10*, 98–112.
Sinclair, R. R., & Tucker, J. S. (2006). Stress-CARE: An integrated model of individual differences in soldier performance under stress. In T. W. Britt, C. A. Castro, & A. B. Adler (Eds.), *Military life: The psychology of serving in peace and combat: Military performance* (Vol. 1, pp. 202–231). Westport, CT: Praeger Security International.
Strong, M. H., Jeanneret, P. R., McPhail, S. M., Blakely, B. R., & D'Egidio, E. L. (1999). Work context: Taxonomy and measurement of the work environment. In N. G. Peterson, M. D. Mumford, W. C. Borman, P. R. Jeanneret, & E. A. Fleishman (Eds.), *An occupational information system for the 21st century: The development of O*NET* (pp. 127–146). Washington, DC: American Psychological Association.
Swider, B. W., & Zimmerman, R. D. (2010). Born to burnout: A meta-analytic path model of personality, job burnout, and work outcomes. *Journal of Vocational Behavior, 76*, 487–506.
Tett, R. P., & Burnett, D. B. (2003). A personality trait-based interactionist model of job performance. *Journal of Applied Psychology, 88*, 500–517.
Tett, R. P., & Christiansen, N. D. (2007). Personality tests at the crossroads: A response to Morgeson, Campion, Dipboye, Hollenbeck, Murphy, and Schmitt (2007). *Personnel Psychology, 60*, 967–993.
Van den Berg, P. T., & Feij, J. A. (2003). Complex relationships among personality traits, job characteristics, and work behaviors. *International Journal of Selection and Assessment, 11*, 326–339.
Vandenberg, R. J., & Grelle, D. M. (2009). Alternative model specifications in structural equation modeling: Facts, fictions, and truth. In C. E. Lance & R. J. Vandenberg (Eds.), *Statistical and methodological myths and urban legends: Doctrine, verity and fable in the organizational and social sciences* (pp. 165–191). New York: Routledge/Taylor & Francis Group.
Van Iddekinge, C. H., Ferris, G. R., & Heffner, T. S. (2009). Test of a multistage model of distal and proximal antecedents of leader performance. *Personnel Psychology, 62*, 463–495.
Wood, R., & Bandura, A. (1989). Social cognitive theory or organizational management. *Academy of Management Review, 14*, 361–384.
Wright, P. M. (1990). Operationalization of goal difficulty as a moderator of the goal difficulty–performance relationship. *Journal of Applied Psychology, 75*, 227–234.

4
Socioanalytic Theory

Robert Hogan and Gerhard Blickle

Concepts without percepts are empty; percepts without concepts are blind.

Immanuel Kant

Introduction

The foregoing quotation reflects the view that theories and facts must evolve together in order for knowledge to develop. Textbooks in industrial–organizational (I-O) psychology and organizational behavior (I-O-OB) focus on specific research topics (e.g., motivation and leadership), and offer few conceptual connections between them. But a common theme underlies every topic—the theme is people (or human nature)—human nature underlies all discussions of people at work in organizations. Because personality theory concerns the nature of human nature, it provides a conceptual basis for understanding organizational behavior and occupational performance. This chapter is organized into three sections. The first section summarizes our perspective on personality. The second section outlines our perspective on personality measurement. In the third section, we review the literature regarding the links between personality and occupational performance, personnel selection, and leadership. We close with a discussion of a dreary but unavoidable topic—faking.

Socioanalytic Theory

Like Sigmund Freud (1913), socioanalytic theory assumes that (1) evolutionary theory is important for understanding human nature, (2) people's responses to authority and leadership are pre-programmed, (3) people are largely unaware of the meaning of their actions, and (4) career success depends on gaining some self-awareness. Like G. H. Mead (1934), we assume that (1) the most important events in life occur during social interaction; (2) to take part in social interactions, we must have roles to play; (3) the roles we play shape how we think about ourselves; (4) people are largely unaware of how they play their roles; and (5) career success depends on becoming aware of how one plays one's organizational roles. Like Darwin (1971), we assume that (1) people evolved as group-living animals, (2) people need social acceptance and social status (because both confer reproductive advantages), (3) behaviors that are good for the group (altruism) will be good for the individuals in it,

(4) behaviors that are good for the individual (selfishness) are not often good for the group, and (5) organizational effectiveness is the appropriate standard for evaluating all organizational interventions, and the interventions usually involve trying to align individual and group interests.

In addition, anthropology and sociology point out that religion is a cultural universal, and history points out that religion is the most powerful force in human affairs. This leads us to assume that people have a need to believe in something bigger than themselves.

Defining Personality

Although I-O psychology rediscovered personality in the early 1990s, one searches that literature in vain for a definition. Typically, personality is defined implicitly in terms of the Five-Factor Model (FFM), but the FFM is a taxonomy of trait terms, not a theory of personality. Personality theory concerns (1) the important ways in which people are all alike (general laws) and (2) the important ways in which they differ (individual differences). Regarding general laws, the three universal features of human groups provide a clue: (1) People evolved as group-living animals—people always live in groups; (2) every group has a status hierarchy—the fundamental dynamic in every group is the individual search for power; and (3) every group has a religion—religion is a cultural universal. Based on this, we conclude that social behavior rests on three powerful and probably unconscious motives: (1) People need attention, acceptance, and approval and find any rejection stressful; (2) people need status and power, and find losing any status stressful; and (3) people need structure and meaning, and find any ambiguity and unpredictability in the environment stressful. We refer to these themes as the needs to get along, to get ahead, and to find meaning.

Regarding individual differences, people differ widely in the degree to which they need acceptance, power, and meaning. But more importantly, they differ widely in their ability to acquire these crucial resources. Finally, personality assessment concerns capturing individual differences in people's potential for getting along, getting ahead, and finding meaning.

The word personality is defined in two very different ways (MacKinnon, 1944; May, 1932). On the one hand, personality refers to the distinctive impression that a person makes on others—this is the observer's view of personality, about which six points should be noted. First, personality from the observer's view is the same thing as a person's reputation. Second, personality from the observer's view is easy to study using rating forms, Q sorts, or assessment center exercises. Third, the best predictor of future behavior is past behavior, and a person's reputation is a summary of his/her past behavior; therefore, a person's reputation is the best data source we have for predicting his/her future performance. Fourth, because the FFM is based on factor analytic studies of observer ratings, the FFM concerns the structure of reputation (cf. R. Hogan, 1996). Fifth, although most people attempt to control their reputations (Goffman, 1958), it is hard to do and people's reputations essentially belong to other people—who evaluate their behavior and create their reputations. Finally, a person's reputation is an index of his/her success at getting along and getting ahead.

The second definition of personality concerns the processes inside people that explain their actions and create their reputations. The most important of these internal processes is a person's identity—the actor's view of personality—about which five points should be noted. First, identity is very hard to study because to do so we must rely on other people's inherently unreliable reports about themselves. Second, social interaction is powerfully shaped by actors' identities. Our identities determine the interactions we are willing to enter, the roles we are willing to play, and how we play them (R. Hogan & Roberts, 1999). Third, identities are "personal narratives" that are adopted from role models in a person's culture—family, friends, characters in movies, novels, and TV. Fourth, we have neither an adequate taxonomy of identities nor a measurement base for specifying them. Finally, although personality research for the past 100 years has focused on identity, it has produced very few reliable generalizations; in contrast, the empirical literature associated with the study of reputation (e.g., the FFM) is substantial and replicable.

Reputation and identity serve different logical functions. We use reputation to *predict* what people are likely to do; we use identity to *explain* why they do it. It is also important to remember that, as observers, we rarely think about other people from their perspective—in terms of their goals and intentions (their identity)—in order to understand them; rather, we think about them from our perspective—in terms of traits, recurring consistencies in their behavior (their reputation)—in order to predict how they will behave.

Interaction

At a deep and often unconscious level, people are motivated to get along, get ahead, and find meaning, and they accomplish these goals during social interaction rather than private reflection. The most consequential interactions for adults take place at work while pursuing a career. Interactions depend on two components: (1) agendas ("Let's get together and talk about this issue"); and (2) roles ("I am the client and you are the sales person"). If there is no agenda, then the interaction lacks purpose; if there are no roles, then interaction will collapse because, outside of our roles, we have little to say to one another. In organizations, roles are defined by a person's job, and agendas are usually dictated by the needs of the organization—or its key players.

As Mead (1934) noted, interactions resemble little games; extending this analogy, one's career can be seen as a game of games, and some people are more successful at the game than others. These are the individual differences with which socioanalytic theory is concerned, and these differences are formally identical with job performance.

Social and occupational life consists of episodes (Motowidlo, Borman, & Schmit, 1997) or interaction sequences each of which has an agenda and associated roles. But people also have identities that influence the agendas they are willing to follow, the roles they are willing to play, and how they play them. When people enter any interaction at work, they will have some understanding of the agendas (corporate and personal) that underlie the interaction, the roles that the various participants will play, and how they will play them. Everyone has expectations regarding the agenda and the roles. These expectations, along with the individual members' roles and identities, powerfully determine individual performance during every interaction.

After every interaction, the participants evaluate the performance of the other members. These evaluations ultimately turn into performance appraisals. And on what do these evaluations depend? They primarily reflect the degree to which people are rewarding to deal with. Being rewarding involves (1) helping others advance their agendas, (2) being compliant and attentive, and (3) fitting with the culture of the group. Being rewarding may involve good performance, but more often it has to do with making another person look good; sometimes doing a good job has this effect.

Meanwhile, the constant subtext for these interactions is individual efforts to get along and get ahead, and there are huge differences in people's success in doing this, as evaluated by themselves and others. How can we predict and explain these individual differences, which are more or less related to successful job performance?

Social Skill and Impression Management

Normal people want to get along and get ahead but some people are better at it than others. What can be done for those who are struggling? People choose their identities in order to maximize their acceptance and status (and minimize their loss). Depending on their identities, they may want to be seen as smart, compliant, honest, creative, or perhaps as menacing and dangerous. Social skill concerns choosing a smart identity, and then translating it into convincing and effective social behavior; social skill allows people to achieve their interpersonal goals in the same way that hand–eye coordination facilitates their tennis game. Thus, social skill is the same as competent impression management—which involves controlling the impressions that others form of us—which concerns managing our reputations.

Argyle (1969) noted that social skill is demonstrated in the ability to control others by counseling, persuading, and suggesting rather than by ordering, criticizing, and coercing them. Personality and social skill are different in that personality (identity and reputation) is rather stable whereas social skills are, in principle, trainable. Moreover, good social skills can coexist with deeply flawed personalities—where flawed is defined in terms of insecurity, selfishness, strange and irrational goals, and a disposition toward treachery and deceit (Leary, 1995). People can improve their social skill and talent for impression management if: (1) they feel the need to improve; and (2) understand what needs to be improved (understand their reputation).

A Perspective on Personality Measurement

We have defined personality and described our preferred perspective on the subject. Now, we turn to personality measurement, because most of the empirical literature supporting socioanalytic theory involves measurement-based research. Our views on personality measurement are (1) consistent with our views on personality theory and (2) different from those of the mainstream. It might be useful to outline briefly how our views differ from the mainstream.

Most I-O/OB psychologists think about personality in terms of "trait theory," a viewpoint introduced by R. B. Cattell (1957), H. J. Eysenck (1960), and Allport (1961)—the modern "father" of trait theory—and supported by the FFM (Wiggins, 1996). But trait theory has some significant shortcomings as a model of personality. First, traits are defined as (1) "neuro-psychic entities" (structures in the brain) *and* (2) recurring patterns of behavior. This makes no sense—it is like comparing apples with Bruce Springsteen. Behavior patterns are real and can be observed and quantified—that is what the FFM is about. But the neuro-psychic structures assumed to underlie behavior are unknown; no doubt some day we will map the underlying neurological architecture of personality, but that day has yet to arrive.

In addition, trait theory is an intrapsychic model of personality—intrapsychic theories assume that what is important in life is going on inside a person's mind and other people are just "out there" as objects or distractions. In contrast, socioanalytic theory is an interpersonal model of personality—interpersonal theories assume that what is important in life takes place during social interaction, and that the contents of consciousness reflect the history of a person's social interactions. That is, how you think about yourself reflects how others have treated you, and that then impacts your future performance. For trait theory, social skill is just another (compound) trait. For interpersonal theory, social skill is crucial for career success; social skill involves being able to read other people's expectations and then acting appropriately vis-à-vis those expectations.

Next, think for a moment about the specifics of the assessment process. Alfred Binet (1903) developed his original test as a method for *predicting* academic performance. When Lewis Terman (Terman & Miles, 1912) translated Binet's items and called them the Stanford Binet, he thought he had created a method to *measure* intelligence. The historical movement was from an effort to predict outcomes to an effort to measure entities, and that is a radical change. The Minnesota Multiphasic Personality Inventory (MMPI; Hathaway & McKinley, 1951) and the California Psychological Inventory (CPI; Gough, 1957), both gold standard personality assessments, were designed to *predict* social behavior. The 16 Personality Factors (PF; Cattell, 1957) and the Neuroticism–Extraversion–Openness (NEO; Costa & McCrae, 1985) are designed to *measure* traits. The historical movement was from predicting outcomes to measuring traits. The intent of the assessment process shifted from predicting behavior to measuring entities.

Mainstream psychometrics is a version of Platonism—the meaning of scores on, for example, the NEO is defined by reference to entities that exist somewhere else. There are obtained scores—the score of an applicant—and then there are "true scores," hypothetical entities that exist in a nontemporal, nonspatial universe—and we understand obtained scores by referring them to true scores. This is precisely Platonic metaphysics. We prefer to use Wittgenstein (1945) to understand test scores. Wittgenstein was criticizing Platonism when he said the meaning of something was given by its use. Test scores mean what they predict, not what they refer to. That is, assessment has a job to do, and the job is to predict nontest performance.

Finally, what are people doing when they endorse items on a personality questionnaire? Trait theory says people are providing "self-reports." The hypothesis is that people compare the content of an item ("I read 10 books per year") with the content of their memory, then respond to the item accordingly. The problem is that memory is not like a videotape that can be replayed; rather, people invent their memories to be consistent with their "personal narratives," which means self-report theory cannot be true, in principle. In contrast, we think that, when people endorse items, they are providing "self-presentations"; they are using the items to tell other people how they want to be regarded. Item endorsements are self-presentations in the same way that answers to questions during an interview are self-presentations. Socioanalytic theory has the virtue of being able to account for its own data base—it leads to a consistent theory of item responses.

Personality and Job Performance

Observers use trait terms to describe and evaluate other people, and people's reputations are encoded in trait words. Trait words evaluate the potential contribution of a person to the success of the groups to which the person belongs—tribe, family, combat-unit, or work team. Trait terms are the units of reputation and they can be organized in terms of the FFM (Wiggins, 1996).

Socioanalytic theory argues that people evolved as group-living animals, and trait words are used to evaluate a person's potential contribution to his/her group (R. Hogan, 1996). The emotional stability dimension of the FFM concerns how well a person will perform under pressure and how volatile he or she is on a day-to-day basis. The extraversion dimension concerns leadership potential. The openness dimension concerns the degree to which a person can solve technical problems confronting the group. The agreeableness dimension concerns a person's contributions to group morale. The conscientiousness dimension concerns trustworthiness and integrity.

A large number of personality measures are now available that are based on the FFM. As noted above, these questionnaires are typically called *self-report measures*, and users assume that respondents report on their "true" thoughts, feelings, and behaviors. In contrast, we assume that item endorsements are self-presentations that reflect a person's identity (or personal narrative). People use items on personality questionnaires to express their desired reputation, because people are motivated to convince others to accept these idealized views. In addition, socioanalytic theory argues that self-presentations are not necessarily or even routinely conscious because, over time, self-presentation tends to become automatic role behavior.

Most measures of personality based on the FFM assume that the five factors are independent. However, Digman (1997) factor analyzed personality data from nine samples of children, adolescents, and adults and found, in every sample, two higher order factors. The first was defined by agreeableness, conscientiousness, and emotional stability. The second was defined by openness and extraversion. Digman (1997) interpreted the first factor as successful socialization—which parallels the basic getting along motive; he interpreted the second factor as personal growth and self-enhancement, which parallels the basic getting ahead motive. This suggests the operation of two broad, mainly unconscious motives: maintaining popularity and achieving status in groups.

Defining Job Performance

In the workplace, social behavior is structured by "situations," which researchers rarely define. Building on Argyle (1976), socioanalytic theory defines situations in terms of the required ingredients for social interaction: goals, rules, environmental settings, roles, and agendas (R. Hogan & Roberts, 1999). These ingredients are inputs from the external environment. Formal roles include supervisor, subordinate, peer, and so on. Informal roles may include friend, rival, newcomer, and so on. Agendas concern the purposes for an interaction. There are public and private agendas. Private agendas concern the personal pursuit of status and acceptance. Public agendas in the workplace can be classified in terms of the six Holland (1973) categories. People can get together and fix something (realistic theme), analyze something (investigative theme), create or design something (artistic theme), help someone (social theme), persuade and manipulate someone (enterprising theme), or regulate something (conventional theme). Individuals use these public agendas to advance their private agendas.

People's behavior is controlled simultaneously by their identities and situational factors. Their identities influence (1) the roles they are willing to play, (2) how they play them, (3) the agendas they are willing to follow, or (4) the agendas they try to avoid. A person's identity is related to the reputation he/she is trying to establish, especially at work.

People at work are judged to be rewarding depending on the degree to which they support the identity another person wants to project. Thus, a subordinate who complies with the requests of his/her supervisor, and respects her/his status, will be seen as rewarding because the subordinate helps the supervisor look good. Supervisors rarely think about subordinates in terms of the subordinate's goals, fears, and aspirations; rather, supervisors think about subordinates in terms of how rewarding they are to deal with—defined in terms of protecting, supporting, and enhancing the supervisor's identity. The same is true for peers at the workplace. The low degree of self-other agreement for personality trait ratings in the workplace (cf. Connelly & Ones, 2010) suggests that actors and observers think about one another in different terms; actors think about themselves in terms of their personal narratives (identities); observers evaluate them in terms of the degree to which they are good team players, good service providers, and so on. The more an actor protects, supports, and enhances an observer's identity, the better the actor is evaluated.

People exchange views on how rewarding others are to deal with and create reputations for those people in the workplace:

> Reputation is a perceptual identity formed from the collective perceptions of others, which is reflective of the complex combination of salient personal characteristics and accomplishments, demonstrated behavior, and intended images presented over some period of time as observed directly and/or reported from secondary sources, which reduces ambiguity about expected future behavior.
>
> *Zinko, Ferris, Blass, & Laird, 2007, p. 165*

Consequences of a positive reputation at work include: *elbow room*—more discretion to act; *power*—others will defer to one's judgment; *improved job performance*—more discretion and power makes it easier to get things done; enhanced *job performance ratings*; and *better compensation*. Other long-term consequences of a positive reputation include *career success* and *enhanced subjective well-being* (Zinko et al., 2007).

Our reputation-based view of job performance ratings is consistent with the findings of a general factor in ratings of job performance:

> Before assigning ratings, each rater forms an overall impression of the merits or standing of each rater. This overall impression in part overlaps the overall impressions of other raters and in part is

unique to that one rater. The part of the overall impression that is in common with other raters is not halo; that part is considered true variance.

Viswesvaran, Schmidt, & Ones, 2005, p. 109

Viswesvaran et al. (2005) found in a meta-analysis that, after controlling for random response error, transient error, leniency or stringency effects, and halo error, a general factor in job performance ratings accounted for 60% of the total variance in ratings for interpersonal competence, administrative competence, quality, productivity, effort, job knowledge, leadership, acceptance of authority, and communication competence.

Personality and Job Performance

Meta-analysis is a method for evaluating the relationships among psychometric constructs. In personnel psychology, a common version of meta-analysis is called validity generalization (Hunter & Schmidt, 2004). The correlation between personality scores and job performance criteria in any single study is taken as one data point, and that correlation is assumed to be attenuated by several statistical artifacts. To compensate, meta-analysis researchers collect as many studies as are available on the relationship between a construct (e.g., a personality dimension) and job performance. The correlations in these studies are combined and then corrected for statistical artifacts (e.g., sampling error depending on sample size, range restriction, and measurement error in the personality and job performance scores). Researchers believe that these corrected results provide the best estimate of the "true" relationship between the construct and the job performance criteria.

Barrick, Mount, and Judge (2001) synthesized 15 meta-analytic studies of the relationship between personality scale scores and overall job performance ratings provided by supervisors. They organized the various personality measures using the FFM. Scores on measures of conscientiousness and emotional stability generally predicted overall job performance, and scores for measures of extraversion, openness, and agreeableness did not generally predict overall job performance (see Table 4.1).

J. Hogan and Holland (2003) also used meta-analysis to evaluate the links between personality and job performance. However, in order to avoid the confusion caused by trying to combine results from different personality measures, they only used data based on the Hogan Personality Inventory (HPI; R. Hogan & Hogan, 1995). The HPI scale for emotional stability is called *Adjustment*. The HPI breaks extraversion into *Ambition* and *Sociability*. The HPI breaks openness into *Inquisitive*—which reflects creativity—and *Learning Approach*—which reflects academic achievement orientation. The HPI *Interpersonal Sensitivity* assesses (roughly) agreeableness, and the HPI *Prudence* scale assesses conscientiousness.

J. Hogan and Holland (2003) followed Campbell's (1990) recommendations and aligned predictors with criteria. Thus, rather than using ratings for overall job performance as a criterion, each scale was evaluated against content relevant criteria. For example, Adjustment was aligned with ratings for "*Manages people, crisis, and stress*," Ambition was aligned with ratings for "*Exhibits leadership*," Inquisitive with "*Seems market savvy*," Learning Approach with "*Possesses job knowledge*," Interpersonal Sensitivity with "*Exhibits capacity to compromise*," and Prudence with "*Stays organized*." J. Hogan and Holland (2003, p. 105) report that median correlations between the criterion ratings ranged from .47 to .72 with an average of .60. As previously noted, Viswesvaran et al. (2005, p. 116) found a mean correlation of r = .58 between criterion categories of supervisory ratings. These findings suggest a convergence between dimension-specific and generalized performance evaluations.

With the exception of HPI Sociability, *every* HPI scale positively predicted its appropriate performance dimension (cf. Table 4.1). The true-score estimates of the Ambition-performance,

Table 4.1 Personality and Job Performance: Summary of Meta-Analytic Results

FFM Dimension	*k*	*N*	r_{obs}	ρ
Emotional stability				
SR (Barrick, Mount, & Judge 2001)	224	38,817	.06	.12*
SR HPI—*Adjustment* (Hogan & Holland, 2003)	24	2,573	.25	.43*
OR (Connelly & Ones, 2010)	7	1,190	.14	.37*
Extraversion				
SR (Barrick et al., 2001)	222	39,432	.06	.12
SR HPI—*Ambition* (Hogan & Holland, 2003)	28	3,698	.20	.35*
OR (Connelly & Ones, 2010)	6	1,135	.08	.18*
Openness				
SR (Barrick et al., 2001)	143	23,225	.03	.05
SR HPI—*Inquisitive* (Hogan & Holland, 2003)	7	1,190	.20	.34*
SR HPI—*Learning Style* (Hogan & Holland, 2003)	9	1,366	.15	.25*
OR (Connelly & Ones, 2010)	6	1,135	.18	.45*
Agreeableness				
SR (Barrick et al., 2001)	206	36,210	.06	.13
SR HPI—*IP Sensitivity* (Hogan & Holland, 2003)	18	2,500	.18	.34*
OR (Connelly & Ones, 2010)	7	1,190	.13	.31*
Conscientiousness				
SR (Barrick et al., 2001)	239	48,100	.12	.23*
SR HPI—*Prudence* (Hogan & Holland, 2003)	26	3,379	.22	.36*
OR (Connelly & Ones, 2010)	7	1,190	.23	.55*

Notes: FFM: Five-Factor Model of Personality; *k*: number of samples; *N*: total sample size; r_{obs}: sample size corrected mean observed correlation; ρ: true-score validity, correcting for unreliability in the predictor and criterion and for range restriction; however, Connelly and Ones (2010, p. 1112) did not correct for range restrictions in the criteria; SR: self-ratings of personality items; OR: other-ratings of personality items; *90% credibility interval does not include zero (transportability; Kemery, Mossholder, & Ross, 1987).

Prudence-performance, and Learning Approach-performance relationships fell within the confidence intervals for these dimensions as reported by Barrick et al. (2001), suggesting the relationships were about the same size. However, the estimates of the Adjustment-performance, Inquisitive-performance, and Interpersonal Sensitivity-performance relationships fell outside of the confidence intervals for these dimensions as reported in the Barrick et al. (2001) study, indicating that these relationships were significantly higher in the study by J. Hogan and Holland (2003).

Connelly and Ones (2010) conducted a meta-analytic study of the links between observer ratings of actors' personalities (a measure of reputation) and rated job performance. The various personality rating instruments were classified according to the FFM (openness, conscientiousness, extraversion, agreeableness, and neuroticism). In essence, they aligned reputation assessments of personality with reputation assessments of overall job performance (see also Oh, Wang, & Mount, 2011). All reputation-ratings of the FFM-dimensions positively predicted overall job performance (cf. Table 4.1). Observer ratings for openness and conscientiousness had higher true-score correlations with overall rated job performance than scale scores for Inquisitive (HPI) and Prudence (HPI) with the specific performance criteria. In the cases of openness and Inquisitive, the confidence intervals were not overlapping, indicating that the correlation between observer ratings and overall performance was higher than the correlation between scale scores and specific performance.

We can now ask, how well does personality assessment predict job performance compared to other assessment procedures? Schmidt and Hunter (1998) document the validity of the best-known predictors of job performance. They report that general mental ability is the best single predictor of overall job performance (ρ = .51; for a more accurate estimate, see Schmidt, Shaffer, & Oh, 2008). Work sample tests (ρ = .54; for an alternative estimate, see Roth, Bobko, & McFarland, 2005) and structured employment interviews (ρ = .51) are the best procedure-predictors of job performance. However, observer ratings of conscientiousness slightly outperform these predictors (true-score correlations ρ = .55; for operational validity estimates, see Oh et al., 2011). Validity coefficients for other popular predictor procedures, such as reference checks (ρ = .26), biographical data measures (ρ = .35), assessment center performance (ρ = .37), unstructured employment interview (ρ = .38), and integrity tests (ρ = .41), are in the same range as validities for the HPI scales ($.25 \leq \rho \leq .43$). However, unlike work sample tests, personality measures do not require specific job knowledge, the standardization of the assessment process does not melt away like structured interviews (interview creep), personality measures are far more cost-effective than assessment centers, and personality measures show incremental validity when combined with measures of general mental ability (Schmidt & Hunter, 1998). In sum, well-constructed personality measures predict job performance as well as any other procedure, and, in fact, outperform most other predictors.

Social Skill

The key elements of socioanalytic theory are identity and reputation. Identity refers to how a person wants to be seen by others. Reputation refers to how other people perceive and evaluate that person. Identities reflect people's desired reputations or idealized self-narratives. Individuals behave so as to convince others that their idealized views are true. Some people are better at this than others—that is, their social behavior is more persuasive and effective. R. Hogan and Shelton (1998) suggest that the ability to translate one's identity into one's desired reputation is moderated by social skill. They defined social skill as competent impression management, which involves controlling the impressions that others form of oneself. Social skill translates identity into reputation.

An important facet of social skill is called empathy, the ability accurately to take the perspective of others (R. Hogan, 1969). Mills and Hogan (1978) found that the magnitude of the discrepancy between self- and other-ratings of personality traits correlated $r = -.87$ with a person's score on R. Hogan's (1969) empathy scale. This supports the claim that social skill mediates the congruence between identity and reputation. Successful impression management also depends on selecting the appropriate audience, apt timing, sensitivity to others' emotional cues, the correct language-style, and sending the appropriate nonverbal cues. Empirical research supports the idea that socially skilled individuals more quickly identify and attend to the emotional cues in others and choose appropriate facial expressions, hand gestures, body postures, voice textures, and other paralinguistic cues (Gangestad & Snyder, 2000; Momm, Blickle, & Liu, 2010).

The political skill construct (Ferris et al., 2005; Ferris et al., 2007) refers to social skill at the workplace. Social skill at the workplace combines social understanding with the ability to adjust behavior to the demands of situations in ways that inspire trust, confidence, and support, appear genuine, and effectively influence others. In three studies, Witt and Ferris (2003) demonstrated that the interaction of social skill and self-ratings of conscientiousness predicted supervisors' ratings of contextual and sales performance. Among employees with high social skill, self-ratings of conscientiousness positively predicted supervisory performance ratings. Blickle et al. (2008) found that the agreeableness by social skill interaction predicted job performance ratings by supervisors, peers, and subordinates. Among employees with high social skill, self-ratings of agreeableness positively predicted performance ratings by others. Meurs, Perrewé, and Ferris (2011) reported that social skill and self-ratings of sincerity (a facet of honesty–humility; Ashton & Lee, 2005) predicted supervisors' ratings of employee task performance; for employees with high social skill, self-ratings of sincerity predicted supervisors' ratings of task performance.

Blickle, Fröhlich, et al. (2011) gathered employees' self-ratings of their desires to get along and get ahead, and supervisors' ratings of overall job performance. For both the getting ahead by social skill and the getting along by social skill interaction, they found support for predictions derived from socioanalytic theory. Among employees with high social skill self-ratings, the motives to get ahead and to get along positively predicted supervisors' performance ratings.

Early career employees can use modesty as a self-presentation strategy: "*By slightly under stating one's positive characteristics one can manage one's image in an adroit fashion that increases liking, preserves high levels of perceived competence, and does no damage to attributions of honesty*" (Cialdini & De Nicholas, 1989, p. 626). Blickle, Diekmann, Schneider, Kalthöfer, and Summers (2012) found, in a predictive study over a 3-year period with 141 early career employees, that social skill positively moderated the relationship between employees' modesty self-presentations and career success (attained position and career satisfaction). For employees with high social skill, modesty self-presentation positively predicted higher attained position and career satisfaction after 3 years (see Figure 4.1).

We argued earlier that the more employees support the identities of their supervisors, the better they will be evaluated. However, success in the work environment depends not only on projecting images that influence raters, but also on behaving consistently across raters. Blickle, Ferris, et al. (2011) found, in a multi-source, multi-study investigation of job performance ratings, that employees with good social skills effectively enhanced their reputations among different supervisors and peers—they used their networking skills and appropriate influence tactics to create favorable images with others. Social skill consistently predicted job performance ratings across multiple assessors. Thus, in the workplace, social skill enables individuals to create a common, positive reputation across raters.

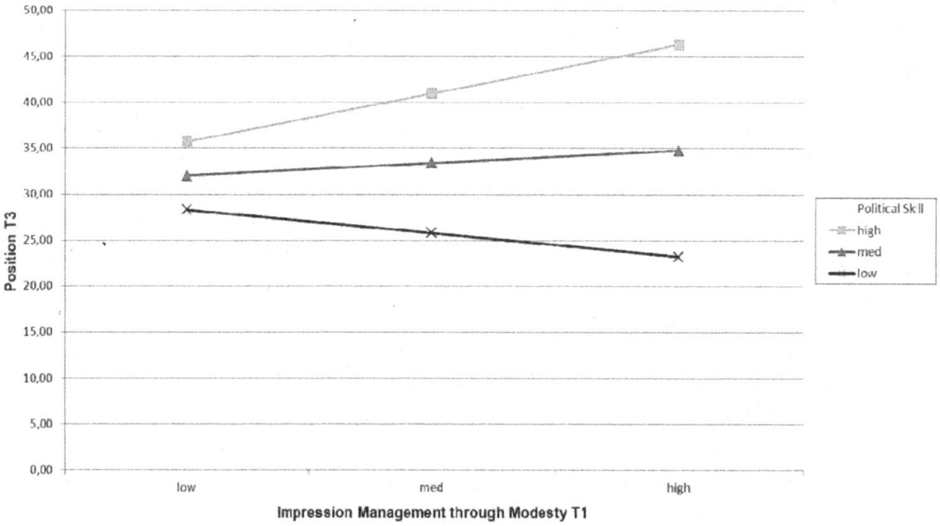

Figure 4.1 Interaction of Impression Management Through Modesty and Social Skill on Hierarchical Position (Blickle, Diekmann, Schneider, Kalthöfer, & Summers, 2012).

Notes: *N* = 141 early career employees; T1; wave one; T3: wave after 3 years. Social skill at the workplace was measured by the Political Skill Inventory (PSI; Ferris et al., 2005). Position: 0,00 = at the bottom of the organization, 50,00 = middle level of the organization.

Moderated Versus Unitary Self-Presentation

Socioanalytic theory assumes that people will be careful about their self-presentations during consequential interactions—that is, during employment interviews, public speeches, and conversations with superiors. However, when people are socializing with family and friends in casual circumstances, they can be more relaxed about how they present themselves (cf. Kaiser & Hogan, 2006)—they can afford to let down their "guard." Not surprisingly, people describe themselves differently when in family roles (e.g., daughter and son) than when in work roles (e.g., job applicant, coworker, and supervisor). Therefore, people's self-descriptions in casual or informal roles should not predict supervisors' ratings of their performance at work, but self-descriptions in work-related roles should (as usual) predict supervisory job performance ratings. Blickle, Momm, Schneider, Gansen, and Kramer (2009) tested this hypothesis in a sample of 192 job incumbents. The incumbents rated themselves on the dimensions of the FFM, and supervisors rated their task performance, leadership, and contextual performance. The researchers combined self-ratings of emotional stability, agreeableness, and conscientiousness into a single score reflecting the desire to get along, and combined the self-ratings for extraversion and openness into a single score reflecting the desire to get ahead. The participants were randomly assigned to two experimental groups. In the job application condition, participants were asked to describe themselves as if they were applying for an attractive job. In the family condition, participants were asked to respond as honestly as possible. In the job application condition, self-ratings for getting ahead predicted ratings for task performance and leadership ($r = .19, p < .05$) and self-ratings for getting along predicted ratings for contextual performance ($r = .18, p < .05$). Self-ratings in the family condition were uncorrelated with supervisors' ratings of job performance. The moral is clear: just being yourself is the path to career disaster.

To summarize, empirical findings strongly support the view that social skill moderates the relationship between people's desired identity (personal narrative) and their actual reputation in the workplace. Social skill explains between 2% and 6% of additional variance in job performance ratings. Social skill also predicts being perceived as both rewarding and consistent across rater interactions. Additionally, over time, employees with good social skills have better careers—providing they choose appropriate identities.

Personality and Career Success

Roberts, Kuncel, Shiner, Caspi, and Goldberg (2007) evaluated the links between personality and income, occupational prestige, and occupational stability, and concluded that ". . . personality traits predict all of the work-related outcomes"; and that ". . . the modal effect size of personality traits was comparable with the effect of childhood SES and IQ on similar outcomes" (p. 333). In the best of the studies that they review, Judge, Higgins, Thoresen, and Barrick (1999) compiled a sample of 354 people from longitudinal research conducted at the Institute for Human Development at UC Berkeley in the 1950s. In this sample, they found that personality and IQ assessed in childhood each correlated about .50 with occupational status in adulthood, and the multiple correlation was .64. Similarly, Sutin, Costa, Miech, and Eaton (2009), in a longitudinal sample of 731 adults, report that (low) neuroticism and (high) conscientiousness measured concurrently predicted income, and extraversion predicted increased salary across 10 years. Consistent with this, Viinikainen, Kokko, Pulkkinen, and Pehkonen (2010) report significant correlations between neuroticism and conscientiousness assessed at age 8 and salary and employability at age 42.

Personality and Leadership

Sociologists and historians often argue that leadership is the function of certain organizational and historical circumstances, but we prefer to think of leadership in terms of individual differences, where some people have more talent for leadership than others. Socioanalytic theory suggests that life is about getting along and getting ahead, some people will be better at the game of life than others, and they should arrive in positions of leadership. In principle, we should be able to identify them in advance.

To evaluate the links between personality and leadership, one needs scores for individual leaders on the FFM, and quantitative indices of performance in leadership roles (for more coverage of personality and leadership see Chapter 34, this volume). The more of this sort of data we can find, the better we can make the evaluation. In the best study yet published on this topic, Judge, Bono, Ilies, and Gerhardt (2002) aggregated the results of 222 correlations contained in 73 studies of personality and leadership performance. Their sample contained more than 25,000 managers from every level in organizations across every industry sector. They report that four of the five dimensions of the FFM were significantly correlated with leadership performance, with adjustment/ emotional stability as the best predictor (.33), and agreeableness/interpersonal sensitivity as the weakest predictor (.07). In this study, conscientiousness/prudence, extraversion, and openness each had significant correlations with leadership (.29, .27, and .21, respectively), and the multiple correlation between personality and leadership was .53. We also acknowledge that leadership is more a function of personality in some contexts than in others. Nonetheless, for people who believe in data, this study definitively seals the argument—personality predicts leadership performance across all organizational levels and industry sectors, and does so more powerfully than any known alternative.

Faking

The data are quite clear: well-constructed measures of personality predict occupational performance at every level of the status hierarchy, and do so as well or better than measures of cognitive ability. Because personality measures are blind to the gender and ethnicity of job applicants, personality assessment would seem to be an optimal method for personnel selection. However, despite the documented validity and the practical usefulness of personality measures for personnel selection, the conventional wisdom in I-O/OB psychology is that personality measures can be "faked" and this fact substantially impugns their utility (cf. Scott & Reynolds, 2010; Chapters 1, 13, 16, and 24; for more coverage of this issue, see Chapter 12, this volume).

Beginning with Kelly, Miles, and Terman (1936), an enormous and complex literature has developed on the faking issue—see Hough and Furnham (2003) for a thoughtful review. This literature leads to four generalizations. First, when instructed, *some* people can change their personality scores as compared with their scores when not so instructed. Second, the actual base rate of faking in the job application process is minimal. Third, faking seems not to affect criterion-related validity. And fourth, in the long history of faking research, there has rarely been a study that used a research design that was fully appropriate to the problem. The existing research consists of: (1) laboratory studies, artificial conditions, and student research participants; (2) between-subjects designs with no retest data to evaluate change; and (3) studies mixing real-world and artificial instructions to create honest versus faking conditions. What is needed is data from real job applicants, in a repeated measures design, where applicants have an incentive to improve their scores on the second occasion.

J. Hogan, Barrett, and Hogan (2007) conducted the appropriate study. A sample of 266,582 adults applied for a customer service job with a very large U.S. employer in the transportation industry. The selection battery included the HPI (R. Hogan & Hogan, 1995). A substantial percentage of the applicants were denied employment. Six months later, 5,266 persons from the original sample reapplied for the job and again completed the HPI. So a sample of 5,266 people completed the HPI at

T1, was denied employment, and then completed the HPI at T2. It seems reasonable to assume that these people were motivated to improve their scores at T2, so as to get the job. By comparing their scores at T1 with their scores at T2, we can evaluate the degree to which people change their scores by faking. The authors used a five-scale scoring key to be able to discuss the HPI results in terms of the standard FFM.

For the Emotional Stability scale, 3.1% of the applicants changed their scores in the negative direction (got worse) beyond the 95% confidence interval (CI); 4.3% changed their scores in the positive direction (got better) beyond the 95% CI. For the Extraversion scale, 5.4% changed their scores in the negative direction, and 5.2% changed their scores in the positive direction. For the Openness scale, 3% of the applicants changed their scores in the negative direction, while 3.6% changed their scores in the positive direction. For the Agreeableness scale, 3.3% of applicants changed their scores in the negative direction, and 1.7% changed their scores in the positive direction. For the Conscientiousness scale, 3.5% of the applicants changed their scores in the negative direction, and 3.2% changed their scores in the positive direction.

On average, across the five scales, 3.7% of the applicants' scores got worse, and 3.6% of their scores improved. Averaged across the five scales, the scores for 92.7% of the applicants stayed the same from T1 to T2. Of the 7.3% whose scores changed between T1 and T2, the scores were equally likely to go down or up. These data provide no evidence whatsoever for faking on the part of real job applicants, where faking means systematically improving one's score from T1 to T2. But even more interesting, it is possible to predict in advance whose scores will go down or up. Embedded in the HPI are short measures of Social Skill and Socially Desirable responding. The data showed quite clearly that across all five HPI dimensions, applicants with higher scores for Social Skill and Social Desirability tended to increase their scores at T2, whereas applicants with lower scores for Social Skill and Social Desirability tended to lower their scores across all five HPI dimensions at T2.

It is useful to review once more the two competing models of item response theory: (1) self-report theory and (2) impression management theory. Self-report theory is based on two assumptions. The first is that, prior to responding to an item, people play back their memory videotape to review what is true about them ("I read 10 books per year"). The second assumption is that when people endorse items, they try to provide factual accounts of how an item matches their memory tape. Faking involves providing inaccurate reports about the match between an item and the memory. There are two problems with this theory. First, memory researchers from Bartlett (1937) to the present argue that memories are not factual, they are self-serving reconstructions. Second, social communication is not typically about accurately reporting on the world; mostly communication is about controlling others (Dunbar, 2004). Self-report theory is inconsistent with modern memory research and modern thinking about the function of communication—both of which suggest that people construct their memories and use communication to project an image.

Consider the process of child rearing. Small children act in ways that reflect their real desires and urges. Socialization primarily involves training children to delay or hide their real desires and to behave in ways that are consistent with the norms of adult behavior. For self-report theory, socialization involves training children to fake. For impression management theory, socialization involves training children in the appropriate forms of self-expression. Items on well-constructed personality measures sample ordinary socialized adult behavior. Most adults know the rules of conduct and respond to the items in terms of social norms rather than in terms of their real desires. Criminals and other rebels respond in ways that are closer to their real desires—in ways that are consistent with their typical behavior. Our point is that it is nearly impossible to distinguish faking from socialized behavior, which means it is hard to know what it means to say that some people fake when they respond to items on a personality measure.

Socioanalytic theory interprets item responses in terms of impression management; people use the items on a personality measure to tell others how they want to be regarded. This, then, suggests an alternative way to understand faking in the assessment process:

> Deception is a conscious, deliberate deviation from typical forms of self-presentation, a deviation that acquaintances would describe as uncharacteristic behavior. This view of deception contrasts with the view that deception involves acting in a way that is inconsistent with a single "true self" hidden inside of us.
>
> *Johnson & Hogan, 2006, p. 211*

> When individuals try to act in deceptive ways in everyday life (e.g., introverts try to act like extraverts) their natural tendencies "leak through" and observers readily detect them . . . Only good actors can make atypical performances seem convincing . . .
>
> *Johnson & Hogan, 2006, pp. 210–211*

It is also worth noting that it is possible to test empirically the claims of self-report and impression management item response theory, and empirical research has not been kind to self-report theory. For example, self-report theory predicts that the scores of people with high scores on a measure of honesty will be more consistent than persons with low scores. Impression management theory predicts that the scores of persons with high scores for social skill will be more consistent than persons with low scores. Johnson and Hogan (2006) tested these predictions in three separate samples; they report overwhelming support for impression management theory and no support for self-report theory.

In a related study, Ones, Viswesvaran, and Reiss (1996), based on a large meta-analysis, report that tendencies to respond in a social desirable manner do not attenuate the criterion-related validity of personality scales—that is, socially desirable responding does not affect the links between personality measures and job performance. In addition, social desirability does not mediate the relationship between self-ratings of personality and job performance. In addition, scores on measures of social desirability do not predict job performance ratings. Socially desirable responding, a hypothesized form of distorting "self-reports," has no empirical consequences.

Finally, Johnson and Hogan (2006, pp. 220–222) report on a study using six unlikely virtue scales. Each scale corresponded to one of six scales on the HPI (R. Hogan, 1986). The following is an unlikely virtue item for the Inquisitive scale: "*In my own way, I am an intellectual giant*," and the following is for the Adjustment scale: "*I have no psychological problems whatsoever.*" Students completed the HPI and the unlikely virtue scales. In addition, two people who knew each student rated that student on the six HPI dimensions. Most students endorsed unlikely virtue items proportional to their scores on the HPI scales. Thus, each unlikely virtue scale was most highly correlated with its corresponding HPI scale and with the peer ratings for the same dimension. This implies that, although the students sometimes exaggerated by endorsing specific unlikely virtue items, their exaggerated self-presentations were consistent with their rated reputations. Thus, endorsing unlikely virtue items provides information that predicts job performance because the endorsements are consistent with the respondents' typical self-presentations; the exaggerations are deviations that acquaintances still describe as characteristic of the person.

The J. Hogan et al. (2007) study makes a simple claim. When people complete a well-validated personality measure as part of a job application, are denied employment, reapply later, and take the measure a second time, their scores will not change significantly. It is reasonable to assume that the applicants will try to improve their scores on the second occasion. The J. Hogan et al. (2007) data show that when (or if) they try, they are unable to improve their scores. The study shows that the faking issue is a red herring. R. Hogan, Hogan, and Roberts (1996) reviewed the faking literature and concluded that the data clearly show that faking does not adversely affect the validity of personality measures for employment decision (for an opposing viewpoint, see Tett & Christiansen, 2007). Hogan et al. also concluded that the critics of personality measurement will not be persuaded by data.

Summary and Conclusion

This chapter outlines the key issues associated with socioanalytic theory—a model of personality that attempts to combine the best insights of psychoanalysis, symbolic interactionism, and evolutionary psychology to analyze career success. In brief, we assume that, at a deep and perhaps unconscious level, people need social acceptance, status, and structure and meaning—because these resources enhance fitness and well-being. People primarily acquire these resources during social interaction over the course of their careers. The units of analysis for socioanalytic theory are identity, reputation, and social skill. Identity is the part a person wants to play in the game of life; reputation reflects that person's success in the game; social skill translates identity into reputation.

Personality assessment is the methodological base supporting socioanalytic theory. We briefly review the literature linking personality with occupational performance and conclude that the results are consistent with our major claims. We end with a brief review of the faking literature, which reveals faking to be a bogus issue, both logically and empirically. Whatever shortcomings socioanalytic theory may have as an account of occupational performance, it has logical and empirical advantages over trait theory.

Practitioner's Window

Socioanalytic theory assumes that the three big problems in life concern gaining social acceptance (or avoiding rejection), gaining status, power, and the control of resources (or avoiding losing them), and finding meaning and purpose for one's life. People pursue these resources (acceptance, status, and meaning) at work in the course of their careers. The model also assumes that there are individual differences in people's ability to do this, the differences primarily concern social skill, and the differences can be assessed or measured. The model has three obvious implications for practitioners.

- First, measures of social skill can be used for selection purposes, to predict supervisors' ratings of on-the-job performance. Supervisors prefer employees with better social skills over employees with better technical skills but poor social skills.
- Second, employability (the ability to find and retain employment) can be enhanced with social skill training.
- Third, employee engagement is a function of the degree to which employees find opportunities to gain acceptance, status, and meaning from their jobs. This means that managers should treat their subordinates with respect, evaluate them fairly, and provide them with credible accounts of how their work fits in with the larger goals of the organization. That managers do not do this routinely explains the high levels of employee alienation routinely discovered in climate surveys.

Acknowledgment

The authors would like to express their gratitude to the editors and In-Sue Oh for their thorough and insightful comments on a previous draft of this chapter.

References

Allport, G. W. (1961). *Pattern and growth in personality*. New York: Holt, Rinehart & Winston.
Argyle, M. (1969). *Social interaction*. Chicago: Aldine.
Argyle, M. (1976). *Personality and social behavior*. Oxford, UK: Blackwell.
Ashton, M. C., & Lee, K. (2005). Honesty-humility, the big five, and the five-factor model. *Journal of Personality, 73*, 1321–1353.
Barrick, M. R., Mount, M. K., & Judge, T. A. (2001). Personality and job performance at the beginning of the new millennium: What do we know and where do we go next? *International Journal of Selection and Assessment, 9*, 9–30.
Bartlett, F. A. (1937). *On remembering*. Cambridge, UK: Cambridge University Press.
Binet, A. (1903). *L'etude experimentale de l'intelligence*. Paris: Schleicher.
Blickle, G., Diekmann, C., Schneider, P. B., Kalthöfer, Y., & Summers, J. (2012). When modesty wins: Impression management through modesty, political skill, and career success; A two-study investigation. *European Journal of Work and Organizational Psychology, 21*, 899–922.
Blickle, G., Ferris, G. R., Munyon, T. P., Momm, T. E., Zettler, I., Schneider, P. B., & Buckley, M. R. (2011). A multi-source, multi-study investigation of job performance prediction by political skill. *Applied Psychology: An International Review, 60*, 449–474.
Blickle, G., Fröhlich, J., Ehlert, S., Pirner, K., Dietl, E., Hanes, T. J., & Ferris, G. R. (2011). Socioanalytic theory and work behavior: Roles of work values and political skill in job performance and promotability assessment. *Journal of Vocational Behavior, 78*, 136–148.
Blickle, G., Meurs, J. A., Zettler, I., Solga, J., Noethen, D., Kramer, J., & Ferris, G. R. (2008). Personality, political skill, and job performance. *Journal of Vocational Behavior, 72*, 377–387.
Blickle, G., Momm, T., Schneider, P. B., Gansen, D., & Kramer, J. (2009). Does acquisitive self-presentation in personality self-ratings enhance validity? Evidence from two experimental field studies. *International Journal of Selection and Assessment, 17*, 142–153.
Campbell, J. P. (1990). Modeling the performance prediction problem in industrial and organizational psychology. In M. D. Dunnette & L. M. Hough (Eds.), *Handbook of industrial and organizational psychology* (2nd ed., Vol. 1, pp. 39–74). Palo Alto, CA: Consulting Psychologists Press.
Cattell, R. B. (1957). *Personality and motivation structure and measurement*. Yonkers, NY: World Book.
Cialdini, R. B., & De Nicholas, M. E. (1989). Self-presentation by association. *Journal of Personality and Social Psychology, 57*, 626–631.
Connelly, B. S., & Ones, D. S. (2010). An other perspective on personality: Meta-analytic integration of observers' accuracy and predictive validity. *Psychological Bulletin, 136*, 1092–1122.
Costa, P. T., Jr., & McCrae, R. R. (1985). *The NEO Personality Inventory manual*. Odesssa, FL: PAR.
Darwin, C. (1971). *The descent of man*. Princeton, NY: Princeton University Press.
Digman, J. M. (1997). Higher-order factors of the big five. *Journal of Personality and Social Psychology, 73*, 1246–1256.
Dunbar, R. I. M. (2004). *Grooming, gossip, and the evolution of language*. London: Faber & Faber.
Eysenck, H. J. (1960). *The structure of human personality*. London: Methuen.
Ferris, G. R., Treadway, D. C., Kolodinsky, R. W., Hochwarter, W. A., Kacmar, C. J., Douglas, C., & Frink, D. D. (2005). Development and validation of the political skill inventory. *Journal of Management, 31*, 126–152.
Ferris, G. R., Treadway, D. C., Perrewe, P. L., Brouer, R. L., Douglas, C., & Lux, S. (2007). Political skill in organizations. *Journal of Management, 33*, 290–320.
Freud, S. (1913). *Totem und tabu*. Vienna: Heller.
Gangestad, S. W., & Snyder, M. (2000). Self-monitoring: Appraisal and reappraisal. *Psychological Bulletin, 126*, 530–555.
Goffman, E. (1958). *The presentation of self in everyday life*. New York: Anchor.
Gough, H. G. (1957). *The California Psychological Inventory manual*. Palo Alto, CA: Consulting Psychologists Press.
Hathaway, W. R., & McKinley, J. C. (1951). *The Minnesota Multiphasic Personality Inventory revised*. New York: Psychological Corporation.
Hogan, J., Barrett, P., & Hogan, R. (2007). Personality measurement, faking, and employment selection. *Journal of Applied Psychology, 92*, 1270–1285.
Hogan, J., & Holland, B. (2003). Using theory to evaluate personality and job-performance relations: A socioanalytic perspective. *Journal of Applied Psychology, 88*, 100–112.
Hogan, R. (1969). Development of an empathy scale. *Journal of Consulting and Clinical Psychology, 33*, 307–316.
Hogan, R. (1986). *The Hogan Personality Inventory: Manual*. Minneapolis, MN: National Computer Systems.

Hogan, R. (1996). A socioanalytic interpretation of the five-factor model. In J. Wiggins (Ed.), *The five-factor model of personality* (pp. 163–179). New York: Guilford.

Hogan, R., & Hogan, J. (1995). *The Hogan Personality Inventory manual* (2nd ed.). Tulsa, OK: Hogan Assessment Systems.

Hogan, R., Hogan, J., & Roberts, B. W. (1996). Personality measurement and employment decisions. *American Psychologist, 51*, 469–477.

Hogan, R., & Roberts, B. W. (1999). A socioanalytic perspective on person/environment interactions. In W. B. Walsh, K. H. Craik, & R. H. Price (Eds.), *New directions in person–environment psychology* (pp. 1–23). Mahwah, NJ: Erlbaum.

Hogan, R., & Shelton, D. (1998). A socioanalytic perspective on job performance. *Human Performance, 11*, 129–144.

Holland, J. L. (1973). *Making vocational choices: A theory of vocational personalities and work environments* (1st ed.). Odessa, FL: Psychological Assessment Resources.

Hough, L. M., & Furnham, A. (2003). Use of personality variables in work settings. In W. C. Borman, D. R. Ilgen, & R. J. Klimoski (Eds.), *Comprehensive handbook of psychology: Vol. 12. Industrial and organizational psychology* (pp. 131–161). New York: Wiley.

Hunter, J. E., & Schmidt, F. L. (2004). *Methods of meta-analysis.* Thousand Oaks, CA: Sage.

Johnson, J. A., & Hogan, R. (2006). A socioanalytic view of faking. In R. Griffith & H. M. Peterson (Eds.), *A closer examination of applicant faking* (pp. 207–229). Greenwich, CT: Information Age.

Judge, T. A., Bono, J. E., Ilies, R., & Gerhardt, M. (2002). Personality and leadership. *Journal of Applied Psychology, 87*, 765–780.

Judge, T. A., Higgins, C. A., Thoresen, C. J., & Barrick, M. R. (1999). The big five personality traits, general mental ability, and career success across the life span. *Personnel Psychology, 52*, 621–652.

Kaiser, R. B., & Hogan, R. (2006). The dark side of discretion. In R. Hooijberg, J. Hunt, J. Antonakis, K. Boal, & W. Macey (Eds.), *Monographs on leadership and management* (Vol. 4, pp. 177–197). London: Elsevier.

Kelly, E. L., Miles, C. C., & Terman, L. M. (1936). Ability to influence one's score on a typical paper-and-pencil test of personality. *Journal of Personality and Social Psychology, 4*, 206–215.

Kemery, E. R., Mosholder, K. W., & Ross, L. (1987). The power of the Schmidt and Hunter additive model of validity generalization. *Journal of Applied Psychology, 72*, 30–37.

Leary, M. R. (1995). *Self-presentation: Impression management and interpersonal behavior.* Boulder, CO: Westview.

MacKinnon, D. W. (1944). The structure of personality. In J. M. V. Hunt (Ed.), *Personality and the behavior disorders* (Vol. I, pp. 4–43). New York: Ronald Press.

May, M. A. (1932). The foundations of personality. In P. S. Achilles (Ed.), *Psychology at work* (pp. 81–101). New York: McGraw-Hill.

Mead, G. H. (1934). *Mind, self, & society*. Chicago: University of Chicago Press.

Meurs, J. A., Perrewé, P. L., & Ferris, G. R. (2011). Political skill as moderator of the trait sincerity—task performance relationship: A socioanalytic, narrow trait perspective. *Human Performance, 24*, 119–134.

Mills, C., & Hogan, R. (1978). A role theoretical interpretation of personality scale item responses. *Journal of Personality, 46*, 778–785.

Momm, T., Blickle, G., & Liu, Y. (2010). Political skill and emotional cue learning. *Personality and Individual Differences, 49*, 396–401.

Motowidlo, S. J., Borman, W. C., & Schmit, J. J. (1997). A theory of individual differences in task and contextual performance. *Human Performance, 10*, 71–83.

Oh, I., Wang, G., & Mount, M. K. (2011). Validity of observer ratings of the five-factor model of personality traits: A meta-analysis. *Journal of Applied Psychology, 96*, 762–773.

Ones, D. S., Viswesvaran, C., & Reiss, A. D. (1996). Role of social desirability in personality testing for personnel selection: The red herring. *Journal of Applied Psychology, 81*, 660–679.

Roberts, B. W., Kuncel, N. R., Shiner, R., Caspi, A., & Goldberg, L. R. (2007). The power of personality: The comparative validity of personality traits, socioeconomic status, and cognitive ability for predicting important life outcomes. *Perspectives on Psychological Science, 2*, 313–332.

Roth, P. L., Bobko, P., & McFarland, L. A. (2005). A meta-analysis of work sample test validity: Updating and integrating some classic literature. *Personnel Psychology, 58*, 1009–1037.

Schmidt, F. L., & Hunter, J. E. (1998). The validity and utility of selection methods in personnel psychology: Practical and theoretical implications of 85 years of research findings. *Psychological Bulletin, 124*, 437–454.

Schmidt, F. L., Shaffer, J. A., & Oh, I.-S. (2008). Increased accuracy for range restriction corrections: Implications for the role of personality and general mental ability in job and training performance. *Personnel Psychology, 61*, 827–868.

Scott, J. C., & Reynolds, D. H. (Eds.). (2010). *Handbook of workplace assessment.* San Francisco: Jossey-Bass.

Sutin, A. R., Costa, P. T., Jr., Miech, R., & Eaton, W. W. (2009). Personality and career success: Concurrent and longitudinal relations. *European Journal of Personality, 23*, 71–84.
Terman, L. M., & Miles, H. G. (1912). A tentative revision and extension of the Binet-Simon measuring scale of intelligence. *Journal of Educational Psychology, 3*, 277–289.
Tett, R. P., & Christiansen, N. D. (2007). Personality tests at the crossroads: A response to Morgeson, Campion, Dipboye, Hollenbeck, Murphy, and Schmitt (2007). *Personnel Psychology, 60*, 967–993.
Viinikainen, J., Kokko, K., Pulkkinen, L., & Pehkonen, J. (2010). Personality and labor market income: Evidence from longitudinal data. *Labour, 24*, 201–220.
Viswesvaran, C., Schmidt, F. L., & Ones, D. S. (2005). Is there a general factor in ratings of job performance? A meta-analytic framework for disentangling substantive and error influences. *Journal of Applied Psychology, 90*, 108–131.
Wiggins, J. S. (Ed.). (1996). *The five-factor model of personality*. New York: Guilford.
Witt, L. A., & Ferris, G. R. (2003). Social skill as moderator of the conscientiousness-performance relationship: Convergent results across four studies. *Journal of Applied Psychology, 88*, 809–820.
Wittgenstein, L. (1945). *Philosophische untersuchungen*. New York: Macmillan.
Zinko, R., Ferris, G. R., Blass, F. R., & Laird, M. D. (2007). Toward a theory of reputation in organizations. In J. J. Martocchio (Ed.), *Research in personnel and human resources management* (Vol. 26, pp. 163–204). Oxford, UK: Elsevier.

5

Trait Activation Theory

Applications, Developments, and Implications for Person–Workplace Fit

Robert P. Tett, Daniel V. Simonet, Benjamin Walser, and Cameron Brown

This chapter has four aims. First, we summarize how trait activation theory (TAT) has been used in the literature since its introduction (Tett & Burnett, 2003; Tett & Guterman, 2000), as a basis for tracking complexities in how personality plays out in the workplace and for identifying further applications. Second, we describe two developments of TAT, specifically (1) with respect to the role of work autonomy and situation strength and (2) in terms of performance feedback and associated extrinsic rewards. Third, we present a trait activation perspective on person–workplace fit, promoting special status for personality traits regarding fit. Finally, we identify recent studies of trait–situation interactions in the workplace to assess how well TAT, as an integrative framework, might account for observed effects (regardless of whether TAT is cited in those works). To begin, we describe TAT and the two articles that introduced it.

Overview of TAT

The principle of trait activation captures the basic notions that (1) personality traits are latent propensities to behave in certain ways, (2) traits are expressed as responses to trait-relevant situational cues (e.g., nurturance in responding to a call for help), and (3) intrinsic satisfaction is gained from expressing one's traits (much as eating satiates hunger). These ideas are rooted in interactional psychology, most notably the work of Murray (1938), who introduced the concept of situation "press" (cf. Tett & Guterman, 2000). Eysenck and Eysenck (1985) argued that "trait and situation form two sides of a coin that cannot be separated from each other" (p. 39), and Kenrick and Funder (1988) noted that "traits influence behavior only in relevant situations . . . Anxiety, for example, shows up only in situations that the person finds threatening" (p. 29). The basic principle of trait activation, then, is not new. TAT builds on that idea, however, in several ways, particularly in work settings. Five elaborations are depicted in the model offered by Tett and Burnett (2003). Others are offered independently of the figure. We start with the model represented here in Figure 5.1.

The main trait activation principle is evident in the top-right of Figure 5.1: Latent traits are expressed as work behavior in reaction to trait-relevant situational cues, yielding intrinsic reward as need satisfaction. The first elaboration, noted in the upper left, is articulation of three distinct sources or levels of trait-relevant cues. Task-level cues include all the day-to-day duties identifiable by job

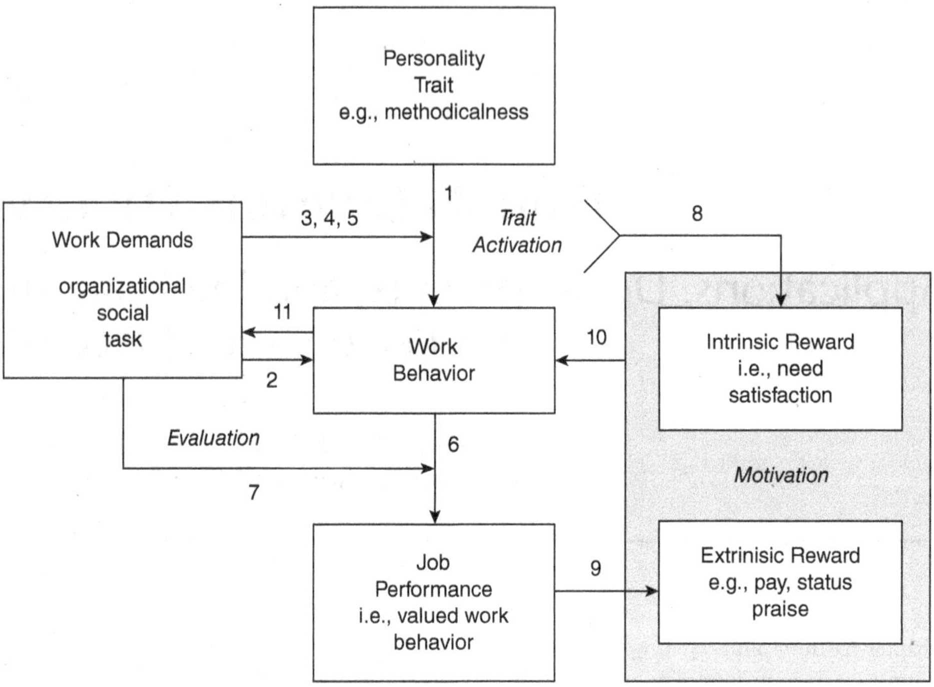

Figure 5.1 Tett and Burnett's (2003) Personality Trait-Based Model of Job Performance.

analysis (e.g., resolving customers' problems in customer service jobs), social-level cues arise from interacting with coworkers (e.g., in lunchroom encounters), and organization-level cues include organizational culture, climate, and policies (e.g., dress norms, flexible work schedules). The fact that trait-activating cues operate at multiple levels encourages a complex understanding of trait-based fit, in which cues operating at different levels combine and perhaps compete for the individual's attention as trait expression opportunities.

The second elaboration is the separation of trait-expressive behavior and (valued) job performance, critical for understanding how a given personality trait can be positively or negatively linked to job performance. Such bidirectionality in trait–performance relations is most evident in meta-analytic findings (cf. Tett & Christiansen, 2007; Tett, Jackson, Rothstein, & Reddon, 1999). Positive and negative correlations are considered to occur by the same process; what varies is the value placed on trait-expressive behavior. Sociability expressed in customer service, for example, might prompt a favorable evaluation, but it could undermine performance if expressed as idle banter that interferes with coworkers' productivity.

The third elaboration is recognition that the same situational cues that activate traits to produce trait-expressive behavior are also used to evaluate that behavior as performance. Thus, a customer's inquiry is both a cue for helpfulness and a target for evaluating customer service performance. The multiple levels of demand, in this light, can help frame biases in performance appraisal: For example, a customer service rep's task performance might be undervalued if the person providing the evaluation is put off by the rep's social-level behavior, expressing the same or different traits.

The fourth elaboration of the basic trait activation principle is incorporation of extrinsic rewards offered by others in reaction to the individual's evaluated performance. The intrinsic/extrinsic distinction aids in conceptualizing situation strength: consistent with Mischel (1968), a strong situation is one whose extrinsic consequential value in terms of rewards and punishments overpowers its intrinsic consequential value in terms of trait expression as need fulfillment. Trait-based behavioral variance will manifest only when extrinsic outcomes are not so strong as to lead everyone to behave the same way (this idea is refined later in the chapter in terms of work autonomy).

The last elaboration made evident in Figure 5.1 is that work behavior is both an effect and a cause of workplace demands. The direct situation–behavior link acknowledges, for example, that weddings can elevate sociability even in introverts, and funerals can suppress sociability even in extraverts. Furthermore, people naturally alter their situations so as to increase or decrease trait-relevant cues. A conscientious worker, for example, might enhance opportunities to express C by setting detailed goals (positive feedback loop), or restrict future C expression by diligently establishing computer-automated work routines (negative feedback loop).

The main upshot of TAT is that people should want to work where (1) job tasks, social interactions, and organizational culture and climate offer ample opportunities to express their traits (trait activation per se) and (2) trait-expressive behaviors are appreciated by those in a position to offer valued extrinsic rewards (evaluation). In short, people want to work where they are rewarded for being themselves. Implications for understanding person–workplace fit are discussed in a later section. Next, we turn to elaborations of the trait activation principle not evident in Figure 5.1.

Tett and Burnett (2003) offer a taxonomy of what might be called *functional trait-relevant situational features*, including demands, distracters, constraints, releasers, and facilitators. They are "functional" by the way they contribute to the trait activation process, cutting across trait content and levels of operation. Demands are trait-relevant cues, responses to which contribute positively to performance. Conversely, distracters are trait-relevant cues, responses to which contribute negatively to performance. A call from a client could present a demand for sociability, such that expressing that trait confers positive appraisals. A lunchroom gathering of coworkers, on the other hand, might serve as a distracter for sociability, whereby expressing sociability (as lively banter) interferes with task performance. Constraints limit cues for trait expression and releasers counteract constraints. If a bureaucratic culture constrains creativity, a committee assembled within that culture to plan a company picnic might offer cues to release it. Facilitators are uniquely multiplicative in that they magnify trait-relevant cues (e.g., demands) already present. An explicit call to "think outside the box," announced at the picnic-planning event, for example, could amplify creativity demands.

Key applications of the model include (1) an accounting of situational specificity of personality–outcome relationships evident in meta-analyses (cf. Tett & Christiansen, 2007) and, by extension, (2) personality-oriented job analysis (for coverage of personality-oriented work analysis [POWA] see Chapter 11, this volume). Further applications include (3) team-building, in which team members are selected not only for how well their traits promote teamwork in general and fit individualized role demands (e.g., leader) but also for how well a given member's traits complement those of other members as mutual trait activation (for coverage of personality and work teams see Chapter 33, this volume); (4) motivation, in which individual subordinates' traits guide use of customized reward contingencies (for coverage of individual differences in motivation see Chapter 6, this volume); and (5) cross-situational consistency (CSC), a definitive property of personality traits, which is expected under TAT only to the degree situations offer similar trait-relevant cues and valued outcomes.

The foregoing overview of TAT derives mostly from Tett and Burnett (2003). Key aspects of the theory were presented in an earlier empirical paper by Tett and Guterman (2000). The study's primary aims were to test the effects of situation trait relevance on trait–behavior relationships and CSC in trait-expressive behavior. After completing a self-report personality test, students were presented with 10 brief scenarios targeting each of five traits (risk-taking, complexity, empathy, sociability, and organization). Subjects were asked to indicate what they would do in each scenario, and intentions were scored per trait. For example, a risk-taking scenario described an opportunity to join friends planning a skydiving trip. Responses were scored from 1 = *avoids the jump*, through 3 = *neutral*, to 5 = *(tries to) go on the jump* (2 and 4 = *intermediate intentions*). The 50 scenarios were rated independently on trait relevance as a manipulation check and to capture variance in trait relevance across like-targeted (e.g., risk-taking) scenarios.

The impact of situation trait relevance on trait–behavior relations was assessed in two ways. First, self-report trait scores on each of the five traits were correlated with behavioral intentions averaged over like-targeted scenarios (e.g., self-report risk-taking correlated with mean intentions in the risk-taking scenarios as well as with mean intentions in the remaining four sets of scenarios). The expected trait relevance effect was observed: Correlations for matched trait–situation cases ranged from .16 to .46 (mean = .36) compared to those for unmatched cases, ranging from −.14 to .30 (mean absolute value = .08). Second, self-report trait scores were correlated with behavioral intentions in each of the 50 scenarios, and then those correlations were themselves correlated with situation trait relevance values, with $n = 10$ per targeted trait. The trait–intention correlations tended to be stronger in situations rated higher in trait relevance on targeted traits. For example, the second-order correlation for risk-taking was .66. Corresponding (matched) values for sociability, organization, and empathy were .61, .55, and .09, respectively. Correcting for range restriction in situation trait relevance (due to the scenarios explicitly targeting a given trait) yielded .84 (for risk-taking), .90, .68, and .24, respectively. The results for complexity were counter to prediction (−.23 and −.33 corrected), possibly owing to confusion on the part of the trait relevance judges between opportunity to express complexity and the "complicatedness" of the scenario description (i.e., an opportunity to express complexity can be worded simply or complexly).

The effect of situation trait relevance on CSC was assessed by (1) correlating each pair of behavioral intentions within situation blocks (e.g., risk-taking intention in each risk-taking scenario was correlated with risk-taking intention in each of the other risk-taking scenarios), and then (2) correlating the resulting 45 correlations, per trait, with an index of trait relevance similarity, taken as the square root of the product of two scenarios' trait relevance values. This "weighted similarity index" operates such that both scenarios in a given pair must have positive trait relevance in order for similarity to matter; similarity at the low end of trait relevance (close to 0) is moot as an expected effect on CSC. Results were generally supportive: CSC in risk-taking intentions correlated .55 with similarity in trait relevance (.79, correcting for range restriction). Values in the remaining cases ranged from .16 (.21) for organization to .35 (.35) for complexity.

All told, Tett and Guterman's findings support the idea that traits are expressed behaviorally to the degree the situation offers opportunities for their expression. They also show that situations can be distinguished reliably on trait relevance, even those targeting the same trait. Results raised further questions. For example, who makes the best judges of situation trait relevance? Are such judgments themselves related to judges' traits (e.g., do anxious people see the world as a stressful place)? Such questions promote a richer understanding of trait–situation linkages with the potential to improve predictions of trait-expressive behavior in the workplace and elsewhere.

Having described the two papers introducing TAT, we now consider how they have been cited in related literatures. Our aim here is to see what aspects of the theory have been found useful, offering possible direction for what might be clarified or otherwise encouraged in future research.

Summary of TAT Literature 2000–2011

We conducted our review by (1) identifying all published sources listed in PsycINFO that have cited either of the two main TAT papers and (2) mining each source for the degree and type of reliance on TAT in terms of focal topic areas (e.g., leadership, motivation) and applied TAT principles (e.g., situational specificity, bidirectionality). As of December 2011, the two initial papers had been cited in 189 articles and book chapters, 5 of which (book chapters and papers in foreign languages) were inaccessible.

Degree of Reliance on TAT by Year of Publication

Figure 5.2 shows the number of empirical versus conceptual/review articles citing the two noted papers by year. Overall, empirical papers outnumber conceptual papers by nearly 2 to 1 (66% vs. 34%). Figure 5.3 depicts citation frequencies by year and degree of reliance. TAT was a primary explicit focus in 23 cases (13%), served a secondary explicit (i.e., supporting) role in 88 cases (48%),

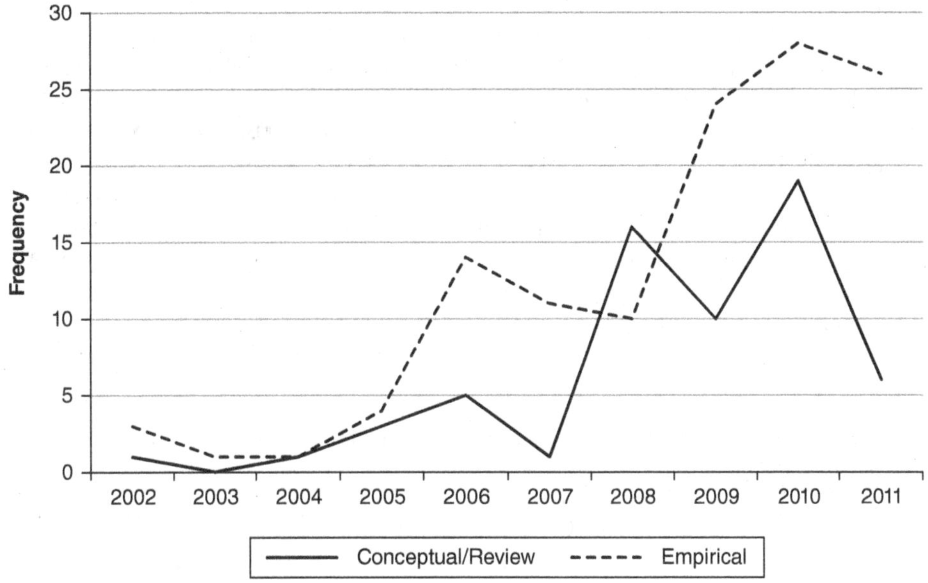

Figure 5.2 Frequency Counts of TAT Article Type by Year of Publication.

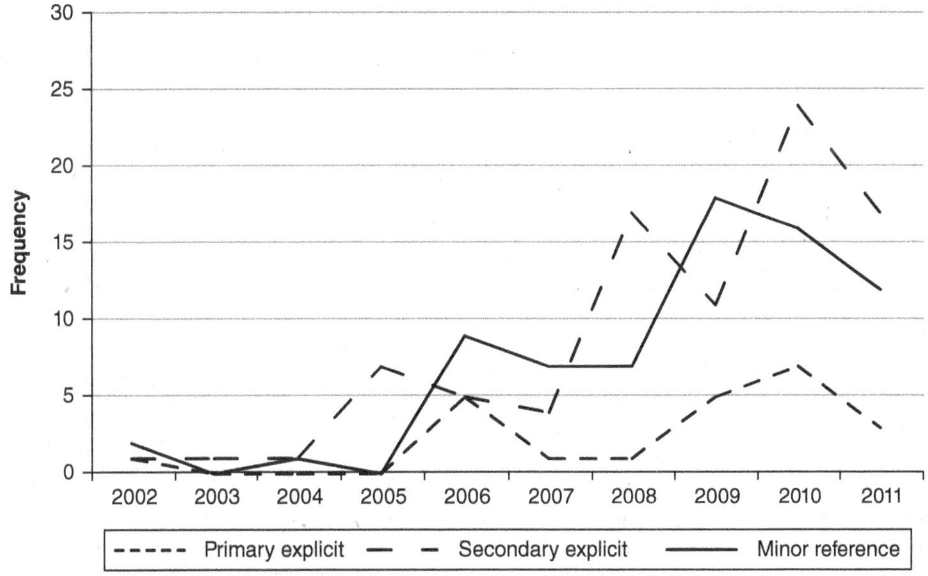

Figure 5.3 Frequency Counts of TAT Reliance by Year of Publication.

and was a minor referent (e.g., post hoc explanation or future research consideration) in 72 (39%). The predominance of secondary reliance on TAT may reflect the theory's interactional focus: Papers targeting a trait–criterion relationship often consider interactions as secondary.

TAT Applications by Criteria and General Content Areas

Table 5.1 presents frequencies of TAT citations by content areas crossed with conceptual/review versus empirical sources. The 72 sources citing TAT as a minor referent are excluded from this analysis.[1] Task performance has been the most common criterion considered with respect to TAT, followed by contextual performance, and counterproductive work behavior, a pattern paralleling that observed in the broader industrial/organizational (I/O) literature. Both task and contextual performance show a higher reference rate in empirical over conceptual/review papers ($\chi^2 = 4.00, p < .05$, and $\chi^2 = 8.00, p < .01$, respectively. Leadership has been a frequent target of TAT writings (18%), especially in empirical works ($\chi^2 = 7.20, p < .01$). Assessment (particularly assessment centers [ACs]), teams, motivation, management, work attitudes, affect, and culture/climate were targeted in 14%–7% of TAT applications, with culture/climate more often the focus of empirical inquiries ($\chi^2 = 5.44, p < .01$). All told, TAT has been applied in a relatively diverse array of I/O psychology content areas. It has seen further use in nonemployment domains (e.g., evolutionary psychology; Uher, 2011).

Table 5.1 Frequency Counts of TAT Citation by Assorted Content Dimensions in Primary Explicit and Secondary Explicit (i.e., Supporting Role) Sources

General/Specific Content Dimension	*Conceptual/Review (N = 42)*		*Empirical (N = 70)*		*Total (N = 112)*	
	f	%	*f*	%	*f*	%
Criteria						
Task performance	12	28.6*	24	34.3*	36	32.1
Contextual performance	3	7.1*	15	21.4*	18	16.1
Counterproductive work behavior	5	11.9	5	7.1	10	8.9
PO fit/career preference	1	2.4	6	8.6	7	6.3
Withdrawal (e.g., turnover)	2	4.8	2	2.9	4	3.6
Nonpersonality subject domains						
Leadership	4	9.5*	16	22.9*	20	17.9
Assessment	7	16.7	8	11.4	15	13.4
Teams	4	9.5	10	14.3	14	12.5
Motivation	4	9.5	9	12.9	13	11.6
Management	7	16.7	5	7.1	12	10.7
Attitudes	3	7.1	7	10.0	10	8.9
Affect	3	7.1	5	7.1	8	7.1
Culture/climate	1	2.4*	8	11.4*	9	8.0
KSA/competencies	0	0.0	3	4.3	3	2.7

Notes: TAT: trait activation theory; PO: person–organization; KSA: knowledge, skills, and abilities.

* Frequencies for conceptual/review and empirical sources are significantly different ($p < .05$).

Applications of TAT Principles

Situational Specificity

Not surprisingly, TAT has been most commonly used to support situational specificity of personality–work behavior relationships (59%). The rationales vary in detail, some simply suggesting that TAT might account for inconsistent personality–performance relationships (e.g., Jiang, Wang, & Zhou, 2009), others being more explicit (e.g., Chen, Kirkman, Kim, Farh, & Tangirala, 2010; Hochwarter, Witt, Treadway, & Ferris, 2006). Some consider situational specificity as it applies to particular trait–behavior linkages (e.g., Harris, Harvey, & Booth, 2010), whereas others apply it to broad reviews of the personality literature (e.g., Hough & Oswald, 2008). Growing appreciation for situational specificity in personality–work behavior relationships supports TAT as a model for explaining nonartifactual meta-analytic variance in personality–job performance linkages (Tett & Burnett, 2003; Tett & Christiansen, 2007).

Bidirectionality

Fourteen papers (8%) cited TAT with respect to a given personality trait correlating positively or negatively with performance depending on the situation. Judge, Piccolo, and Kosalka (2009), for example, argued that, in some situations, a leader's socially desirable traits can be counterproductive. Kacmar, Collins, Harris, and Judge (2009) showed that the relationship between core self-evaluations and performance is negative when the work environment is highly political, but positive otherwise. Verbeke, Dietz, and Verwaal (2011) suggested that traits needed to meet persuasive demands in sales jobs undermine good relations with others. Robert and Cheung (2010) found that conscientiousness predicts creative performance negatively, and Crawford, Shaver, and Goldsmith (2007) suggested that conscientiousness can be detrimental to attachment security. Moss, McFarland, Ngu, and Kijowska (2007) illustrated that, when resources are scarce, openness to experience is inversely related to normative commitment.

Growing evidence for bidirectionality of personality–work behavior relationships, both within and between jobs, confirms the need for interactionist theories, like TAT, that attempt to account for it. It also validates concerns with meta-analytic means of personality–criterion linkages that underestimate relationship strength due to cancellation of positive and negative population estimates (Tett et al., 1999).

CSC

The idea that behavioral consistency across situations, a definitive feature of personality traits, should be conditional on situation trait relevance was cited in 13 papers (7%). Eight of those works focused on ACs, which offer ideal conditions for studying CSC. In a direct test of TAT, Lievens, Chasteen, Day, and Christiansen (2006) found that dimensional convergence across exercises (i.e., CSC) was positively related to similarity in situation trait relevance. Haaland and Christiansen (2002) offered similar findings in terms of the trait activation potential of AC exercises. TAT thus offers insight into the resilient challenge of AC construct validity (Lievens, 2002; for coverage of personality and ACs, see Chapter 21, this volume). Van Mechelen (2009), on the other hand, cited trait relevance only briefly in a paper devoted entirely to CSC (in general). The importance of situation trait relevance in understanding CSC broadly remains to be seen.

Situation Strength/Autonomy

TAT was cited with respect to situation strength in 32 papers (17%). Particular points regarding situation strength ranged from textbook cases of restricted trait variance (e.g., Hough & Oswald,

2008) to more novel propositions. Lievens, Ones, and Dilchert (2009), for example, suggested that work situations tend to be stronger during honeymoon periods and so personality–performance linkages should strengthen as tenure lengthens. Huffcutt, Van Iddekinge, and Roth (2011) linked situation strength to interview structure, with implications for designing personality-based interviews; Kamdar and Van Dyne (2007) linked it to reciprocity norms triggered by social exchange processes; and Dierdorff and Surface (2007) linked it to clarity of performance demands, such that stronger/clearer situations, contrary to the typical argument, should yield *more* performance variance in peer evaluations. In their detailed review of situation strength, Meyer, Dalal, and Hermida (2010) called for deeper inquiry from a TAT perspective. We address this call in a later section.

Operational Levels

Of the three levels at which TAT is proposed to operate, the task level has been the most common target (37%), followed by the social/group level (24%), and the organizational level (11%). Twenty-one papers (19%) explicitly highlight the importance of considering trait processes at multiple levels (e.g., Robert & Cheung, 2010). Ng, Feldman, and Lam (2010) draw parallels to job attitude research, and Ng and Sorensen (2009) include the three levels in their work situation taxonomy. Farmer and Van Dyne (2010) found that role occupancy activates traits at all three levels, and Johnson and Hezlett (2008) include the three cue levels in their performance model. Minbashian, Wood, and Beckmann (2010) suggested that, whereas cues at the task and social levels vary across the workday, those at the organizational level remain relatively constant. Although researchers are tuning in to the idea that personality traits play out at multiple levels, comparisons across levels and joint effects remain largely untested.

Functional Taxonomy of Cue Types

Fifteen papers (8%) discuss situational effects on personality trait expression consistent with the functional taxonomy (i.e., demands, distracters, etc.). Three main themes emerge. First, papers vary markedly in their reliance on the taxonomy. Warr, Bartram, and Martin (2005) list all five terms but do not incorporate them further in any way. Robert and Cheung (2010), on the other hand, discuss constraints and demands in some detail. Second, the facilitator concept is commonly invoked but is not necessarily labeled as such. Gelfand, Leslie, and Fehr (2008) report that industry type might "amplify" cultural effects by increasing the salience of culture, consistent with the TAT facilitator concept. Farmer and Van Dyne (2010) also present results consistent with a facilitator hypothesis without using the facilitator term. Third, terms are used inconsistently. For instance, Bipp (2009) uses "constraints" to denote inhibiting motivation, whereas TAT defines the term with respect to limited availability of cues for personality expression. All told, the concepts included in the taxonomy are clearly identifiable in the TAT literature, particularly demands and facilitators. Yet, the taxonomy has not been adopted in any systematic fashion. We suggest that communication and accumulation of research findings (e.g., in meta-analysis) will advance more rapidly by shared reliance on a common situational taxonomy, whether from TAT or elsewhere.

Personality-Oriented Work Analysis

Eight papers (4%) cited TAT in the context of POWA. Recognizing that jobs are embedded in larger systems, job analytic papers (citing TAT) recommend greater consideration of the organizational context (Morgeson & Dierdorff, 2011) and team features (LePine, Buckman, Crawford, & Methotet, 2011). Despite empirical support for POWA (Kell, Rittmayer, Crook, & Motowidlo, 2010), many papers merely discuss the idea of a more sophisticated POWA (e.g., Murphy & Dzieweczynski, 2005; Shaffer, Harrison, Gregersen, Black, & Ferzandi, 2006). To date, little headway has been made on the development of multilevel POWA capturing multiple functional cues, offering potentially rich, untapped opportunities for future study (for more complete coverage of POWA, see Chapter 11, this volume).

Knowledge, Skills, and Abilities (KSAs) Activation

Tett and Burnett (2003) briefly discuss an ability-activation process paralleling that for personality. Seven papers (4%) applied TAT to abilities/skills. Hochwarter et al. (2006) reported that contextual cues can activate social skills. C. Anderson, Spataro, and Flynn (2008) found that the ability to influence decisions was activated in extraverts in situations requiring teamwork but in conscientious workers in less team-oriented situations. Blickle et al. (2009) considered how environmental cues activate social influence ability. Applications of TAT to KSAs, although limited to date, bring KSAs and personality under the same conceptual umbrella, supporting TAT as a unifying model for studying individual differences at work.

Intrinsic Motivation

Ten papers (5%) used TAT to discuss intrinsic motivation deriving from personality trait expression. Moss and Ngu (2006), for example, found that employees high on openness tend to be more satisfied when afforded greater variety in the workplace. Kacmar et al. (2009) showed that favorable situations are especially motivating to individuals high on core self-evaluations because they are predisposed to select and thrive in such environments. Jeng and Teng (2008) found that individuals are especially motivated to play games offering cues relevant to their personality traits. Fuller, Hester, and Cox (2010) found that managers can motivate employees with proactive personalities by providing cues to engage in untried work methods and problem-solving. Such applications support the intended purpose of TAT to invest personality traits with motivational force, beyond simply being descriptive summaries.

Extrinsic Motivation

Six articles (3%) cited TAT with respect to extrinsic motivation. TAT is relevant in two ways. First, extrinsic outcomes reinforce valued work behavior independently of trait effects, contributing to situation strength. In this light, Zhang and Peterson (2011) suggested that rewards and goal-setting might compensate for low motivation in workers low on core self-evaluations. Second, the motivational force of specific outcomes may depend on workers' outcome-relevant traits. Sung and Choi (2009) showed how extrinsic motivation activates workers' openness. Spurk and Abele (2011) found that career-advancement goals served as cues for conscientious individuals to pursue success and promotion opportunities. We expand on both roles of extrinsic motivation in TAT in later sections (for more coverage on individual differences in work motivation, see Chapter 6, this volume).

Team-Building

TAT was tied to team-building in eight works (4%). Peeters, Van Tuijl, Rutte, and Reymen (2006), for instance, found that conscientiousness contributes to satisfaction through team member similarity. Tett and Murphy (2002) showed that people prefer working with others offering cues for trait expression (e.g., low-autonomous people prefer dominant coworkers) and that such relationships are stronger under some conditions than others (e.g., working together vs. apart). Complexities in personality-based team staffing are echoed by LePine et al. (2011):

> [T]he research to date suggests that it is not enough to consider just measures of individual and team personality traits when using personality to predict performance. One must also consider situational factors such as the type of team that is being staffed, the nature of the task charged

> to the team, the level of autonomy given to the team, and the manner in which the individual members of the team will be rewarded. Without taking all of these variables into account, the use of personality measures to select individuals for teams will likely be ineffective.
>
> *p. 324*

TAT offers a framework for managing such complexities, prompting consideration of (1) the overall "teaminess" of individual members (e.g., high A, high C, low N), (2) matching members' traits to the team's particular task or type (e.g., production team, think tank), (3) matching members' traits to individual team member roles (e.g., leader, devil's advocate), and (4) matching members' traits to other members' traits, each member offering cues for others to respond in mutually beneficial ways. Team-building thus offers rich, untapped opportunities for testing TAT (for more coverage on personality and work teams, see Chapter 33, this volume).

Personality and Performance Appraisal

TAT was cited in connection to performance appraisal in four papers (2%). Lievens et al. (2006) highlight the role of trait activation potential (i.e., trait relevance) in judging performance in ACs, and Fleenor, Smither, Atwater, Braddy, and Sturm (2010) similarly use trait activation to explain the role of opportunity to observe. Netemeyer and Maxham (2007) suggest that customers rate their providers' performance relative to how well the latter have met customers' needs. This resembles Tett and Burnett's (2003) proposition that judges will tend to overrate a coworker's performance to the degree the coworker satisfies judges' needs (e.g., by offering them trait expression opportunities). Performance rating bias from a TAT perspective, however, has yet to be directly investigated.

Complex Interactions (e.g., Trait × Trait × Situation)

Eight papers (4%) drew from TAT to examine the joint operation of multiple factors involving a specific trait. For instance, Kim, Hon, and Lee (2010) showed that proactive personality is most strongly related to creative activities when the job requires creativity and employees receive supervisory support. Three-way interactions for personality have been extended to research on group negotiations (Mohammed, Rizzuto, Hiller, Newman, & Chen, 2008), interpersonal complementarity (Tett & Murphy, 2002), and stress management (Parker, Jimmieson, & Amiot, 2009). This stream of research strongly underscores the major impetus behind TAT: Personality processes at work are complex, and simplification to main effects risks underestimation of the potential value of personality tests under theoretically relevant conditions (cf. Morgeson et al., 2007; Tett & Christiansen, 2007; for more information on this issue, see Chapter 17, this volume).

Companion Theories

TAT was paired with other theories in 13 papers (7%). Hülsheger and Maier (2010) classified TAT as a congruency theory (e.g., complementary fit [Cable & Edwards, 2004] and trait-congruent affect [Moskowitz & Coté, 1995]), predicting that workers are more satisfied when their jobs and actions are trait-concordant. Compensatory theories, in contrast, predict that employees are more responsive to situations that compensate for low trait standing. Griffin, Parker, and Mason (2010) used TAT in conjunction with Mischel and Shoda's (1995) cognitive affective personality system (CAPS) theory, describing how situational features trigger affective and cognitive scripts. Sears and Hackett (2011) linked TAT to leader–member exchange (LMX) theory; Farmer and Van Dyne (2010), to identity salience in role theory; and Caldwell and Moberg (2007), to "trait centrality," predicting that those with a strong self-identity are less susceptible to situational effects. Tett and Murphy (2002) tied TAT to circumplex predictions bearing on communion (similarity) and agency (complementarity) as mutual trait activation in coworker preference; Tett and Simonet (2011) used TAT to develop a "multisaturation" model of response distortion; and Uher (2008, 2011) used TAT to elucidate individual behavioral phenotypes in evolutionary psychology. Connectivity to such diverse theories supports TAT as a theory catalyst and integrator.

Summary

Our review suggests that TAT is being used with increasing frequency to focus attention on important complexities involving personality at work (e.g., situational specificity, bidirectionality). By offering a relatively parsimonious integration of personality traits, job performance, and intrinsic and extrinsic motivation, all operating at multiple levels, the theory stands to guide further studies of personality at work aimed at refining use of personality tests in employment settings. We judge three applications to warrant especially close consideration going forward: (1) POWA sensitive to multilevel cues, bidirectionality, and trait specificity in light of functional situational features (e.g., demands, distracters); (2) team-building accounting for multilevel demands (e.g., team tasks, roles, norms, other members); and (3) integration of TAT with extant theories of workplace motivation, leadership, and person–environment (PE) fit. POWA and personality in teams are explicit targets of other chapters in this volume (Chapters 11 and 33, respectively). We offer some thoughts on personality-based fit later on. First, we present two significant developments of TAT.

Extensions of TAT

An expanded model of TAT is presented in Figure 5.4, with new paths numbered from 12 to 20. Two major extensions are the addition of work autonomy (upper middle) and differential outcome preference (bottom). Before discussing those additions in detail, we briefly note two relatively minor differences from the original model, presented in Figure 5.1.

At the top of Figure 5.4, KSAs are distinguished from traits in accordance with Tett and Burnett's (2003) parallel KSA-activation process (Path 12). A key difference, portrayed in Figure 5.4, is that KSAs do not confer intrinsic motivation when activated, whereas personality traits do. We show a correlation between KSAs and personality traits (Path 13) because we judge it likely that people will tend to develop skills that build on their natural tendencies (e.g., leadership skills built on E), and that some reverse-effects may occur as well (e.g., self-confidence instilled by leadership training). A second difference from Figure 5.1 is the addition of "others" on the left side, which is implicit in Tett and Burnett's original model. Specifying "others" clarifies their roles in evaluation (Path 14) and in offering differentially preferred outcomes (Path 17), discussed below.

Trait Activation, Work Autonomy, and Situation Strength

TAT posits that personality traits are expressed in response to trait-relevant cues. A general situational feature that has emerged with increasing relevance to trait expression is work autonomy, the extent to which a job allows discretion in what, how, when, and with whom work is undertaken (Breaugh, 1985; Grant, Fried, & Juillerat, 2011; Wall, Jackson, & Mullarkey, 1995). TAT variables relevant to work autonomy are work demands, distracters, and constraints. We later introduce a new class of cue, especially relevant to work autonomy, but we begin with demands.

A work demand is a cue for behavior that, if engaged, is valued positively by others; meeting a demand is judged as good performance, and not meeting a demand is judged as poor performance. Two broad types of demand bear consideration in discussing work autonomy. *Primary demands* concern major tasks, goals, and deliverables, whereas *secondary demands* concern how, when, where, and with whom primary demands are engaged. Primary demands are "primary" in the sense that they

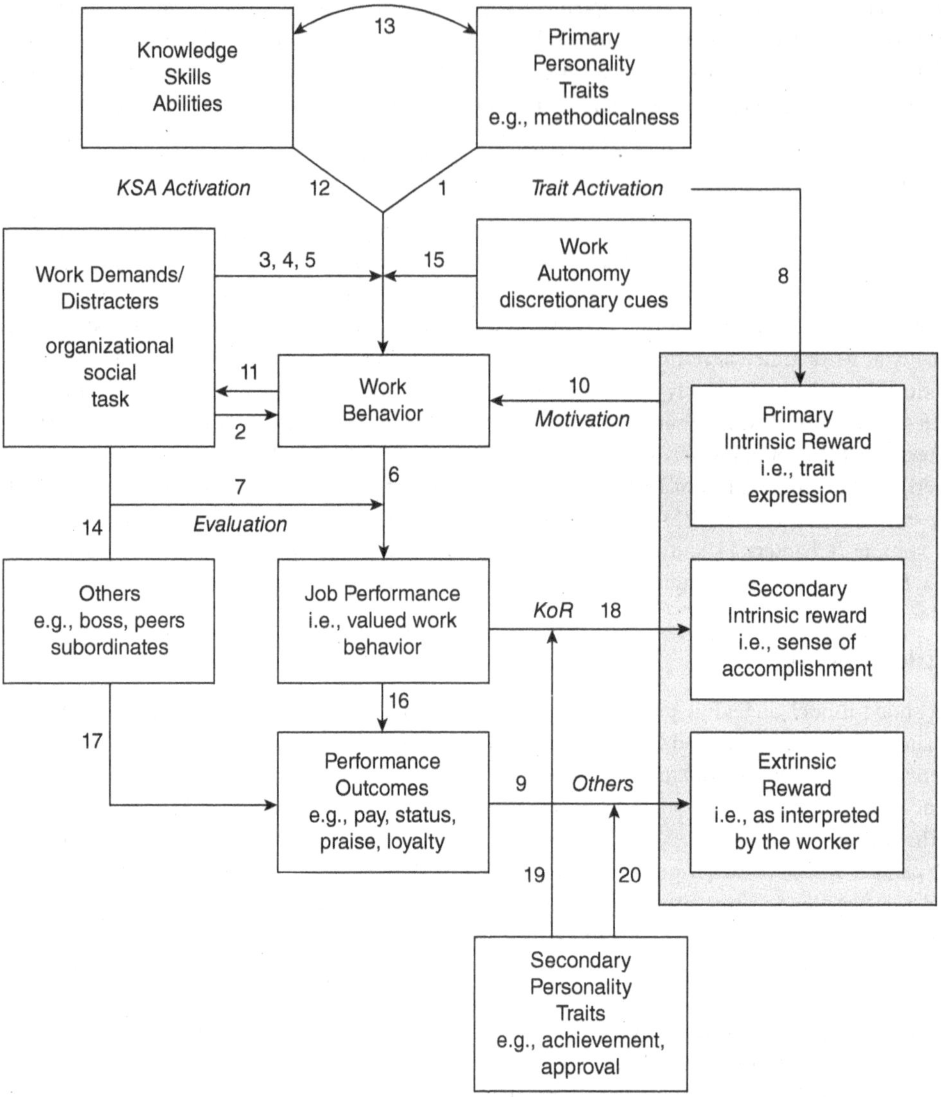

Workplace fit = (1) the expression of KSAs and primary personality traits in response to organizational, social, and task cues, yielding primary intrinsic reward, and (2) expression of secondary traits by (a) knowledge or results (KoR), yielding secondary intrinsic reward (e.g., as a sense of accomplishment), and (b) interpretation of performance outcomes distributed by others, yielding extrinsic reward.

Figure 5.4 Revised Trait Activation Model of Job Performance.

more clearly define the worker's role in the organization, for example, an "Accounts Manager" manages accounts and a "Mail Carrier" carries mail. Secondary demands are less definitive but may be critical; for example, deadlines are often important "when" demands, and requiring the boss' approval could be a vital "with whom" demand.

The primary/secondary distinction facilitates discussion of work autonomy because primary demands afford less autonomy than do secondary demands and treating them separately promotes reasoned discussion of the role of personality at work. The distinction formally recognizes that every job carries expectations offering workers very little wiggle room in whether and, in some cases, how they are met, whereas other aspects of the job allow considerable leeway. How personality plays out at work will depend on what aspects of work are being considered, particularly with respect to their status as primary versus secondary demands.

Distracters, like demands, are cues for behavior valued by others. The difference is that, whereas responding to a demand is valued positively, responding to a distracter is valued negatively (e.g., analysis paralysis when cues for diligence arise under short timelines). Workers will be judged as good performers to the degree they respond to demands and avoid responding to distracters.

Closely tied to demands and distracters are valued outcomes contingent on good versus poor performance. More important demands, of course, are tied to weightier outcomes. Meeting versus failing to meet primary demands could mean the difference between promotion and termination. Following versus ignoring a dress code, on the other hand (where dress is not a primary demand), could mean being accepted or shunned by coworkers; more extreme reactions are possible (e.g., reprimand for repeat offenses), but valued contributions in meeting primary demands might reasonably engender tolerance. Outcomes, to the degree they are expected and valued, determine the strength of work demands.

Whereas demands and distracters are types of cue, constraints restrict cues for trait expression. The availability of trait-relevant demands and distracters, thus, requires a lack of constraints.

In light of the abovementioned, a work situation is autonomous to the degree it (1) lacks constraints (i.e., offers cues to express a variety of traits) and (2) lacks work demands and distracters tied to weighty outcomes. A highly autonomous work situation is one in which cues for trait expression are plentiful, prompting diverse approaches to work, and what the worker chooses to do, and how, when, where, and with whom he or she chooses to do it, carry no expectations of positive or negative outcomes, including reactions from others. A low autonomy work situation, at the other extreme, is one in which trait-relevant cues are lacking, and/or meeting versus not meeting demands is expected to yield strongly desirable versus undesirable outcomes.

Notably, highly autonomous work situations are rare because, as noted above, jobs tend to be identified by primary demands, which tend to be weighty (e.g., treating the sick, in the case of a doctor). Moreover, most jobs carry secondary demands in the form of professional standards, organizational rules and policies, and local norms, collectively limiting options regarding how, when, where, and with whom the primary demands are engaged. Highly structured jobs (e.g., bank teller) offer very limited autonomy, as both primary and secondary demands in such cases are set out in considerable predetermined structure. Notwithstanding the various constraints on personality expression at work, secondary demands confer relative autonomy to conduct the job as the worker chooses.

Two important questions arise from this discussion. First, if autonomous work situations are defined by the absence of work demands/distracters, which are main trait (and KSA) activators, then how does trait activation work in autonomous situations? Second, considering demand strength in terms of the desirability of contingent outcomes raises the issue of situation strength: What exactly is "situation strength" in the context of work autonomy and trait activation? We address each of these questions, in turn.

Trait Activation in Autonomous Work Situations

Of the five functional situational features proposed by Tett and Burnett (2003), none clearly explains how traits (and KSAs) might come to be expressed in fully autonomous work situations. Demands prompt expression of relevant traits but restrict autonomy to the degree they are tied to weighty outcomes; distracters operate similarly with respect to outcomes. Constraints limit the availability of cues, releasers counteract constraints, and facilitators amplify the salience of cues already present. The latter three features can operate in autonomous situations, but on what sort of cue are they operating, if not demands and distracters? An additional situational feature is needed to capture opportunity for trait expression in truly autonomous situations.

Being free to choose what to do and/or how, when, where, and with whom to do it, with no direct ties to valued outcomes, may be considered in terms of *discretionary* cues, which, opposite to demands and distracters, are defined by the lack of connection to judged performance. Thus, such cues are "pure" trait activators in that responding to them yields intrinsic reward (as need satisfaction; Path 8) without the added extrinsic outcome (positive or negative) contingent on others' evaluations (Path 9).

There is a fundamental connection between demands and distracters, on the one hand, and discretionary cues, on the other. Demands and distracters vary in the strength of their associated outcomes: Few outcomes are so strong as to completely nullify work autonomy, and many, perhaps most, are closer to the weaker end of the outcome value continuum. As outcome value approaches zero, demands and distracters become increasingly discretionary. But demands and distracters are tied, via performance, to outcomes of nonzero value. To avoid contradiction, "discretionary" offers a distinct class of cue especially relevant to personality trait expression in autonomous work situations. The result is a continuum identified by discretionary cues at one pole and heavily weighted demands at the other. Points in between can be described equivocally in terms of relative discretion and/or outcome weight.

If discretionary cues are defined by the lack of connection to valued extrinsic outcomes, then of what relevance are they to understanding the role of personality in job performance, which is always tied to outcomes? The answer derives from both intrinsic motivation and the distinction between primary and secondary demands. Discretionary cues carry no direct performance implications, but they contribute to meeting primary demands by serving intrinsic motivation. A creative manager, for example, will be more engaged in meeting primary demands when the situation offers discretionary creativity cues. Creativity in this autonomous situation is neither encouraged nor discouraged by extrinsic outcomes; the key is that the *creative* manager will be motivated to keep the team successful (as a primary demand) if the how, when, where, and with whom issues permit creative engagement. A nurturant manager, by the same token, will be especially engaged in meeting primary demands when discretionary cues prompt supportive behavior. The following analogy is offered for clarification.

Three travelers are tasked with getting to a distant town by nightfall. Three successful routes are available: one by water, one over a mountain, and one on foot, around the mountain. It is irrelevant how each traveler gets to the town. However, one traveler is a seasoned mariner with a boat, one is an experienced and avid climber, and the third prefers a steady level walk. It is reasonable to expect each traveler to more eagerly undertake the journey if allowed to take the route best suited to his or her preferred mode of travel. By equal measure, each should be less eager if forced to travel by an ill-fitting route. Getting to the town by nightfall is clearly the primary demand, the optional routes are discretionary cues, and the preferred modes of travel represent each traveler's unique set of personality traits (and abilities/skills). Taking any route will meet the primary demand, but taking the individually preferred route has the advantage of driving demand fulfillment by intrinsic motivation.

Attaching an extrinsic outcome to the primary demand clarifies the role of autonomy. Consider that failing to reach the town by nightfall carries the credible promise of a long and painful execution (a la Vlad the Impaler). Now, all three travelers should be amply motivated to arrive by any route, with intrinsic motivation tied to route choice playing a diminished role in the process. Even here, though, would we not expect each traveler to take the more preferred route if offered the chance? Moreover, if forced to take an alternative path, might we expect them to feel even more anxious about their timely arrival? That is, might the severity of the outcome amplify the desire for choosing the best-fit route?

There are two lessons here. First, heavily weighted outcomes will prompt stronger efforts to meet primary demands, but discretion in meeting secondary demands, despite their lacking any direct connection to valued extrinsic outcomes (only the travelers themselves care which route they take), may nonetheless offer motivational potential relevant to efficacy, satisfaction, and, ultimately, the individual's performance. Organizations fostering autonomy tend to facilitate self-determined motivation, healthy development, and optimal functioning (Deci, Connell, & Ryan, 1989). By increasing workers' options, intrinsic motivation increases as employees internalize the purpose and interest in their work. From a trait activation perspective, individuals with a true sense of choice are likely to pursue their primary objectives consonant with their sense of self. Rogers and Dymond (1954) referred to this as freedom of expression: People are motivated to "be themselves" when presented the opportunity.

The second lesson is that strong (Vlad-inspired) outcomes, despite reducing or eliminating performance differences in meeting primary demands, may amplify the role of work autonomy in linking personality to satisfaction as need fulfillment in meeting secondary demands. If so, outcome severity (tied to primary demands) should moderate the impact of work autonomy (in undertaking secondary demands) on the personality trait–satisfaction relationship. As satisfaction is linked to turnover and other valued withdrawal criteria (e.g., Scott & Taylor, 1985; Tett & Meyer, 1993), work autonomy regarding secondary demands warrants especially close attention when the stakes in meeting primary demands are high.[2]

In summary, (1) purely autonomous work situations are those offering a variety of discretionary cues prompting trait expressions with no extrinsic outcomes; (2) work demands permit autonomy only to the degree their associated outcomes are weak; (3) primary demands, defining the given job, tend to carry heavier outcomes, affording less autonomy, than secondary demands, regarding how, when, where, and with whom primary demands are engaged; (4) to the degree a situation is autonomous, motivation derives more purely from intrinsic sources; and (5) strong outcomes tied to primary demands may restrict variance in whether those demands are met, but (6) they may accentuate discretionary pursuits in meeting secondary demands (i.e., workers tasked with important goals especially appreciate the freedom to achieve those goals as they see fit[3]). It follows that (7) trait activation is important to the degree extrinsic outcomes are weak, but (8) it can play a role even when extrinsic outcomes are heavily weighted, to the degree secondary demands afford discretion in how primary demands are met. This, in turn, suggests that (9) trait variance disconnected from performance variance when primary demands are heavily weighted may still be linked to satisfaction stemming from choices in dealing with secondary demands. In sum, autonomy in meeting secondary demands may be critical for work engagement driving the meeting of even heavily weighted primary demands. This secondary role for personality in work motivation seems a reasonable target for research.

TAT and Situation Strength

Organizational researchers have discussed situation strength in a variety of ways, not only in terms of work autonomy (Barrick & Mount, 1993; Cooper & Withey, 2009) but also in terms of structural ambiguity and consequence of error (Bowles, Babcock, & McGinn, 2005; Meyer et al., 2010). As noted in our literature review, TAT has been cited with reference to situation strength. Here, we respond to Meyer et al.'s call for developing a TAT perspective on situation strength by conceptually mapping the former to the latter. We begin by offering a brief review of two definitive takes on situation strength, one old, one new.

According to Mischel (1973),

> psychological "situations" and "treatments" are powerful to the degree that they lead all persons to construe the particular events the same way, induce uniform expectancies regarding the most appropriate response pattern, provide adequate incentives for the performance of that response pattern, and instill the skills necessary for its satisfactory construction and execution.
>
> *p. 276*

Meyer et al. (2010) further this conceptualization by summarizing the literature on how situation strength has been operationalized. They identified four distinct themes: (1) *clarity* is the extent to which work cues are available and easy to understand (e.g., explicit supervisory instructions), (2) *consistency* is the extent to which work cues from multiple sources are similar (e.g., agreement among coworkers driving strong work norms), (3) *constraints* are externally imposed limits to the individual's freedom of decision and action (e.g., formal company policies and procedures), and (4) *consequences* are important positive or negative outcomes tied to particular work behaviors. We consider TAT with respect to Meyer et al.'s themes first, before turning to Mischel's widely cited account.

Note that Meyer et al.'s first two themes deal with cue perception, and the latter two, with outcomes. "Constraints" (3) are essentially directions regarding what to do. In TAT terms, these are primary and/or secondary demands. (TAT "constraints" are different.) "Consequences" (4) are extrinsic outcomes in TAT. Constraints and consequences are inextricably linked because constraints, as demands, are strong only to the degree they are associated with weighty outcomes (rules never enforced are hardly constraining), and consequences operate only with respect to whether demands are met. These themes are distinguished in the literature (as per Meyer et al.'s review), despite their connection, because each offers tangible opportunities for variance. We should expect, nonetheless, that studies focusing on "constraints" (i.e., TAT demands) assume some weighty consequence, whereas those focusing on consequences assume (if not specify) associated demands. TAT thus maps onto Meyer et al.'s second two situation strength themes in terms of the connection between work demands and extrinsic outcomes, as described above.

Regarding Meyer et al.'s first two themes, dealing with cue perception, TAT offers several points of contact. (1) Trait-relevant cues must be perceived at some level of awareness to be acted upon as trait expression: Cue perception is thus largely assumed. (2) The TAT concept of "constraint" ties to cue perception, denoting situational features restricting cues for trait expression. (3) Situational features affecting cue clarity might include TAT facilitators, which amplify extant cues (e.g., the explicit call to "think outside the box" in picnic-planning). (4) Cue consistency invites consideration from the perspective of multiple levels, which, in TAT, include task, group, and organization. Consistency across levels has implications for fit and promotion opportunities. (5) Demand ambiguity, in TAT terms, may itself be a cue for creativity, curiosity, anxiety, and/or methodicalness (to resolve the ambiguity). Furthermore, TAT makes salient the parallel issue of outcome perception, and Murray (1938) proposed "beta" press to denote subjective interpretation of trait-relevant cues. TAT thus maps onto cue perception in several ways. More explicit articulation of the cognitive aspects of situation strength, nonetheless, may prove worthwhile. These are matters for ongoing consideration from a TAT perspective.

This brings us to Mischel's (1973) conditions for situation strength. That everyone construes strong situations the same way is closely related to cue clarity and consistency and, accordingly, to the TAT concepts of constraints, facilitators, multiple levels, ambiguity-relevant trait activation, and to Murray's "beta" press. "Uniform expectancies" connect well to primary and secondary demands (i.e., regarding what gets done, and how, when, etc.). "Adequate incentives" is closely tied to "weighty extrinsic outcomes" in TAT, and is arguably the most critical contributor to situation strength (nothing clarifies a cue or expectancy better than the promise of an extreme outcome; for example, "high stakes" situations). As to "instilling necessary skills," this sounds suspiciously close to trait relevance. Indeed, traits suited to meeting a given demand may be construed as "skills." "People skills," for example, may be little more than a productive combination of E, A, C, and low N, observed when corresponding demands converge (e.g., in customer service jobs). If so, Mischel's early reflections on situation strength may have anticipated Tett and Burnett's (2003) assertion that situation strength permits consideration only with respect to particular traits (i.e., as a radio's volume matters only when the radio is tuned to a given station).

Notably, all the concepts raised in mapping TAT to the outcome aspects of situation strength are contained in our discussion of work autonomy. The cue perception aspects are less fully integrated, but TAT does offer a few relevant concepts (e.g., facilitators). More importantly, because cue perception seems no less relevant to work autonomy than to situation strength, we suggest that work autonomy and situation strength are opposite ends of a single continuum, understood fundamentally in terms of work demands and the severity of associated outcomes. If so, TAT offers three points for discussion of situation strength.

First, situation strength regarding primary demands warrants distinction from SS regarding secondary demands. Most if not all jobs are stronger in the former sense than in the latter. Accordingly, traits can be expected to show stronger relationships with behavior expressed in meeting secondary demands than that in meeting primary demands. If task performance relates more closely to primary demands, and contextual performance to secondary demands (as "in-role" vs. "extra-role" behavior), current discussion may help explain why personality traits are better predictors of contextual than of task performance (Borman, Penner, Allen, & Motowidlo, 2001). Specifically, primary demands being tied to stronger outcomes limit the influence of personality traits on task performance relative to their influence on contextual performance in meeting discretionary secondary demands. Second, situation strength bears consideration in terms of constraints on cues for trait expression. A weak (i.e., autonomous) situation is one offering discretionary cues for a variety of traits; a strong situation offers opportunity to express very few, if any, traits. This may be subsumed under cue perception, but we expect that counting the number of traits with potential for activation in a given situation may add uniquely to consideration and measurement of situation strength. A third contribution of TAT to situation strength, noted above, is that ambiguity in secondary demands (i.e., low situation strength) itself offers cues for expressing relevant traits (e.g., methodicalness), perhaps all the more salient when primary demands are severe.

Differential Outcome Preference and Secondary Trait Activation

The second major development of TAT offered here is that how people react to performance and its outcomes will depend on their personality traits. Differential outcome preference has received surprisingly little attention in the literature. Two distinct processes involving personality traits can be identified. The first targets differential reactions to success and failure per se, and the second targets differential reactions to tangible performance outcomes controlled by others (e.g., pay, recognition). We address each process, in turn.

Differential Response to Knowledge of Results: Secondary Intrinsic Reward

Performance is centrally important to organizations. It also has psychological meaning to workers with respect to motivation. Knowledge of results (KoR) is a key mediator in goal-setting theory (e.g., Locke, 1968), and performance feedback is similarly identified in many models of work motivation (e.g., Frese & Zapf, 1994; Hackman & Oldham, 1980; Taylor, Fisher, & Ilgen, 1984). Few models, however, identify personality as a key motivational variable (Landy & Conte, 2007), and fewer still suggest that how feedback is received may depend on one's personality traits. Evidence regarding the latter is sparse but encouraging.

Baumeister and Tice (1985) reported that those with high self-esteem respond to success with heightened interest in the task and to humiliating failure with avoidance, whereas those with low self-esteem respond to success with trepidation and to failure with improved effort. Ilgen and Davis (2000) summarize the goal orientation literature as supporting the idea that negative feedback prompts more desirable positive effects in performers with a learning goal orientation than in those with a performance goal orientation. Hackman and Oldham's (1976) job characteristics theory posits KoR as mediating the effect of feedback on internal work motivation, job performance, job satisfaction, and withdrawal, with stronger linkages expected in those with the propensity to seek stimulating and challenging work (i.e., growth need strength [GNS]).

Lack of reliance on a coherent personality taxonomy impedes integration of research on differential responses to success and failure. The Five-Factor Model (FFM) offers untapped potential in this respect. Cursory review suggests that each of the five major dimensions may be relevant: N with respect to self-esteem, C and O to GNS (cf. de Jong, van der Velde, & Jansen, 2001), and all five to goal orientation (Zweig & Webster, 2004). Need for achievement (a facet of C) seems especially relevant in this context as achievement is defined as successful performance: Satisfying this need requires at least the expectation of positive feedback that work demands have been met. Accordingly, KoR should be especially influential in those high on achievement motivation.

Figure 5.4 presents personality traits as moderators (Path 19) of the effect of KoR/feedback on motivation (Path 18), resulting in secondary intrinsic reward to the degree trait needs are met. The reward is labeled "secondary" to distinguish it from primary intrinsic reward, deriving from trait expression in responding to work cues (Path 8). The distinction is based on timing. Which source of intrinsic reward is more important is a matter for research. For example, one might compare satisfaction resulting from trait expression opportunities (per se) with, versus without, performance feedback further differentiated as success versus failure. TAT would predict higher satisfaction in those offered opportunities to express their particular traits (as per primary intrinsic reward), and, independently, that performance feedback will be motivating (as secondary intrinsic reward) to the degree it meets the performer's particular needs (e.g., negative feedback motivating high-O participants more so than low-O participants). We highlight need for achievement yielding the secondary intrinsic reward of a sense of accomplishment (on receipt of positive feedback; see Sekaran & Wagner, 1980). The particular psychological state experienced as secondary reward on KoR will depend on the trait in interaction with feedback valence.

The lowermost box in the model, representing personality traits directly relevant to performance and its outcomes, is similarly identified as "secondary" in a temporal sense. The relative importance of primary and secondary traits in the expanded TAT model is a matter for research.

Differential Response to Performance Outcomes: Extrinsic Reward

Separately from how a worker responds to success or failure informed by KoR/performance feedback, differential reactions are also possible to tangible performance outcomes controlled by others. In the revised model, performance outcomes are shown to be contingent on judged performance (Path 16) and under others' distributional control (Path 17). Their impact as rewards (Path 9) is explicitly considered a function of secondary personality traits (Path 20). Paths 19 and 20 are separated to reflect the possibility that secondary traits activated in response to KoRs/feedback (Path 19) may be distinct from those activated in response to performance outcomes (Path 20).

Research on differential reactions to performance outcomes is scant. In a rare study, Furnham (2003) asked subjects to rate the motivational potential of various outcomes (e.g., pay, high-status job title, training), and then linked common themes to judges' personality traits. Incentives relating to time and benefits were valued by those low on C, O, and N, and high on A. In the case of C, Furnham reasoned that high-C individuals prefer equity over unconditional increases. Also, status-based incentives were especially valued by extraverts. Results are not discussed in trait activation terms, but the links seem plausible: Extraverts, for example, are especially motivated by enhanced status because it satisfies needs for dominance and exhibition, key facets of E.

The performance outcomes investigated by Furnham are a subset of those available as trait-relevant rewards in work settings. A distinct set can be identified as future trait-relevant demands, such as those entailed by promotion (e.g., increased supervisory responsibility, job complexity, and work autonomy). Each of these job features offers opportunities to express certain traits (e.g., dominance, achievement, openness to experience, independence, self-esteem), with trait expression contributing to performance. As noted earlier, Spurk and Abele (2011) found that high-C individuals pursue success and promotion opportunities as cues for career-advancement. Thus, TAT encourages consideration of a broad array of performance outcomes whose potential as rewards depends on workers' personality traits. It also captures a cyclical understanding of work motivation in which trait-based success or failure at Time 1 can determine the relevance of the same or different traits following promotion or demotion.

Transforming work psychology from black-box behaviorist traditions, Locke (1968) asserted that "any adequate theory of task motivation must take account of the individual's conscious goals and intentions," and that, "if goals or intentions are a necessary condition for most kinds of behavior, then incentives will affect behavior only through their effects on goals and intentions" (p. 161). Moving further away from behaviorist ideals, a trait activation approach to goal-setting theory would suggest that the goals workers set in pursuing performance outcomes will depend on their personality traits. Further research like that of Furnham (2003) and Spurk and Abele (2011) is needed to more fully explore the merits of differential trait-based responses to extrinsic performance outcomes, and the role of traits more specifically in goal-setting. The expanded TAT offers a potentially useful framework for such investigations.

Person–Workplace Fit From a Trait Activation Perspective

Few concepts are more central to I/O psychology than PE fit (Kristof-Brown & Guay, 2011; Saks & Ashforth, 1997; Schneider, 2001). As evidence, consider Figure 5.5: Fit is key to every major intervention targeting an organization's success through people. Changing the person to fit the job, for example, is the essence of training, and finding the (best) person to fit the existing work situation is the goal of selection. That fit permeates so much of I/O psychology, and human resource (HR) practice suggests that theories about fit should have broad applications. How TAT might contribute to understanding fit at work is the focus of this section of the chapter.[4]

PE fit at work is "the compatibility that occurs when individual and work environment characteristics are well matched" (Kristof-Brown, Zimmerman, & Johnson, 2005). An earlier definition, targeting fit between the person and the organization but readily generalized, articulates fit more specifically as "the compatibility between people and organizations that occurs when: (a) at least one entity provides what the other needs, or (b) they share similar fundamental characteristics, or (c) both" (p. 6; Kristof, 1996). Part (a) is called "complementary" fit, and part (b), "supplementary" fit (Muchinsky & Monahan, 1987). The former further divides into needs–supplies fit and demands–abilities fit (Kristof, 1996). All these forms can operate at multiple levels within the workplace, most commonly, the job (person–job [PJ] fit), group (person–group [PG] fit), and organization (person–organization [PO] fit).

The reader will note at least two points of contact with TAT as described above. First, both trait activation and fit are held to occur at the job, group, and organization levels. The overlap invites consideration of how TAT might contribute to understanding fit at multiple levels. We discuss this later in the chapter.

	Change . . .	Find . . .
. . . the person to fit the work setting	Training Motivation/ Leadership	Selection Promotion Team building
. . . the work setting to fit the person	Job design Organizational development	Placement Career counseling

Figure 5.5 Major HR/IO Initiatives as PE Fit Strategies.

The second point of contact is reference to "demands." In both frameworks, a demand is a situational cue, responses to which can be evaluated as good or poor performance. A critical difference, however, is that, in traditional fit theory, demands are paired with abilities; personality comes into play either in supplemental terms (e.g., an innovative person fitting an innovative organization) or in pairing needs with supplies. In trait activation terms, the needs–supplies connection is the basis for intrinsic motivation as need satisfaction. But trait activation, unlike traditional fit theory, also pairs work demands directly with traits as cues for trait expression and reference points for evaluation of that expression as performance.

The difference in the role of demands in the two frameworks speaks to the centrality of personality in understanding job performance and, more broadly, fit. The trait–demand link in TAT implies that performance may be as proximate to personality traits as to abilities. It also suggests that personality trait activation may contribute to fit with respect to both needs–supplies, feeding intrinsic motivation, and to traits–demands, feeding performance and, thereby, extrinsic motivation (and secondary intrinsic motivation, as per Figure 5.4). The housing of both types of complementary fit within a single construct class may be unique to personality. We develop this line of thinking, as follows.

Fit as Performance and Satisfaction

"Fit" is both a state and a process. As a state, it is the degree to which an individual's work behavior meets situational demands and/or the individual's psychological needs are met. The fit process describes how the fit state arises and how it changes. Fit regarding situational demands being met is closely tied to *performance* and fit regarding the individual's psychological needs being met is closely tied to *satisfaction*. Thus, we can speak of fit in terms of the performance state and process as well as the satisfaction state and process.

Both performance- and satisfaction-based fit operate at the task, social, and organizational levels. Task-level performance is what we normally think of as "job performance." Social-level and organization-level performances (of individuals), however, also merit consideration as the judged meeting of situational demands operating at those levels. Satisfaction is more widely understood in terms of multiple levels (e.g., work itself at the task level, coworkers and supervision at the social level, and promotion opportunities, arguably, at the organization level).

In addition to operating at multiple levels, each type of fit can be viewed from both the organization's and the worker's perspectives. Performance-based fit, however, is primarily the organization's concern, and satisfaction-based fit, the worker's (Kristof-Brown & Guay, 2011). Performance-based fit is what the organization strives to achieve through personnel selection, placement, promotion, training, job design, and leadership. In terms of process, it occurs when (1) the task, group, and/or organization present the individual with demands (prompting failure if left unmet); (2) the individual has relevant knowledge, skills, abilities, and traits (KSATs) to meet those demands; and (3) the individual is suitably motivated, either extrinsically or intrinsically, to engage those KSATs in meeting the demands.[5] Satisfaction-based fit is what workers strive to achieve through career choice, job search, training (e.g., being mentored), and promotion. It occurs when (1) the individual has psychological needs (prompting dissatisfaction if left unmet) and (2) those needs are met by engaging the task, group, and organization. In light of earlier discussion of work autonomy, the engagement can be driven not only by work demands involved in performance-based fit but also by discretionary cues (e.g., to be creative when creativity is not demanded by tasks, groups, or the organization).

Four points are worth noting here. First, performance-based fit carries no intrinsic motivational force, although knowledge of performance results (KoR) can interact with relevant motivational traits (e.g., need for achievement, as per secondary trait activation) and is typically tied to important extrinsic rewards (e.g., pay, continued employment, etc.), which may also interact with personality traits. Satisfaction-based fit, on the other hand, is inherently motivating: Being satisfied is its own reward.[6]

Second, performance-based fit is not necessary for satisfaction-based fit and vice versa: One can perform well without being satisfied (motivation deriving from extrinsic sources) or be satisfied without performing well (needs being met in ways not tied to work demands). Third, however, fit will be highest when performance-based fit and satisfaction-based fit are working together, that is, when employing one's KSATs meets work demands (as performance) while simultaneously fulfilling psychological needs (as satisfaction). The value of matching performance- and satisfaction-based fit is explicitly recognized in Dawis and Lofquist's (1984) Theory of Work Adjustment. The matching is ideal for the organization because, as work demands are being met, the performance is motivated intrinsically, augmenting extrinsic incentives. Happy workers tend to want to stay with the organization, and those with job-relevant KSATs are the ones the organization especially wants to keep. The combined fit is also ideal for the worker because the fulfillment of psychological needs entailed by meeting work demands is intrinsically rewarding, and good performance earns further extrinsic rewards. In short (and building on an earlier statement), people want to work where they are rewarded for being themselves, *and* organizations want people whose performance is self-motivating.

This leads to the fourth and more important point. Note that personality traits (Ts) operate differently from KSAs in that Ts are uniquely motivational. A trait whose expression helps meet a work demand to produce performance *simultaneously* yields satisfaction by its expression. KSAs are not directly tied to satisfaction, as they are not needs. Motivation for engaging KSAs must come from some other source, whether extrinsic (e.g., pay, job security) or intrinsic (e.g., needs for achievement, acceptance). Personality traits, therefore, have special status in fit theory: They are unique in contributing directly to both performance- and satisfaction-based fit. Identifying the KSAs needed for successful performance and then hiring people who have those KSAs will always be important in personnel selection. But hiring on the basis of personality traits has the advantage of gaining good workers (via demands–traits fit) who are also happy workers (via needs–supplies fit), which, as noted above, is good for both the organization and the individual.

Summary

The complexity of workplace fit with respect to its conceptualization, measurement, and application (Kristof-Brown & Guay, 2011) poses challenges for any theory that attempts to account for it. TAT is no exception. To date, however, the role of personality traits in fit theory has been relegated almost entirely to "other" in the knowledge, skills, abilities, and other (KSAO) taxonomy and/or to supplementary processes operating at the organizational level (e.g., attraction–selection–attrition [ASA] theory; Schneider, 1987). TAT promotes a more central position for personality traits operating at multiple levels with respect, in particular, to PJ, PG, and PO fit, and imbues them with special status deriving from their uniquely dual role in satisfaction- and performance-based fit. That fit is central to so many key I/O psychology and HR initiatives (see Figure 5.5) suggests that, to the degree personality traits contribute to fit, they should, in turn, contribute to understanding and designing those fit-based initiatives. Deeper discussions along those lines are warranted beyond the space afforded here.

Trait–Situation Interactions in the Workplace in Terms of TAT

Earlier, we summarized the literature for reliance on TAT as presented by Tett and Guterman (2000) and Tett and Burnett (2003). Here, we examine how well the theory, in its updated form, might serve to integrate trait–situation interaction research regardless of its reliance explicitly on TAT. Findings not readily accounted for by the framework could suggest the need for refinement or, potentially, entirely new theory. Furthermore, successful application of TAT as an organizing framework would support its use in future meta-analysis of trait–situation interaction effects in the workplace.

Published studies of trait–situation interactions in the workplace likely number in the hundreds.[7] To narrow our scope, we targeted only those articles listed in Google Scholar reporting "person–situation interaction" and "personality" that were available between January 2007 and June 2012 in either of three journals: *Journal of Applied Psychology*, *Personnel Psychology*, and *Journal of Organizational Behavior*. These three outlets were selected because of their notable impact on the field of I/O psychology, and the 5-year window was used simply because it yielded a manageable number of articles. Our selectivity of sources and time frame precludes any claim to representativeness of the literature in this area. It is, in effect, a convenience sample.

Our search yielded 34 articles, 19 of which were secondary reviews (e.g., meta-analyses) or did not examine personality traits or a trait–situation interaction. Summaries of the 15 relevant studies are offered in Table 5.2. Of particular interest are the descriptions of study results using TAT terminology. Several points bear discussion. First, regardless of whether or not TAT was cited as a foundation for the research, the theory offers a relatively parsimonious account of the observed interactions. How well it might apply to the entirety of trait–situation interaction research is a matter for more extensive inquiry. Second, all six situational cue types (demands, distracters, constraints, releasers, facilitators, and discretionary cues) are included in the summary. Demands and distracters are more prominent, consistent with their being linked more directly to valued trait expression (e.g., job performance). Third, all three levels of cue operation (task, social, organizational) are also represented. Interestingly, the organizational level is most often invoked. Possible reasons for this include the variables operating at that level (e.g., climate, culture, justice) being more theoretically generative, more easily studied (e.g., between independent organizations), and/or more appealing to journal readership. Cue type and level distributions in the broader trait–situation interaction literature are matters for future study.

Fourth, several studies (e.g., Ilies, Johnson, Judge, & Keeney, 2010; Yang & Diefendorff, 2009) report internal, non-behavioral outcomes (e.g., attitudes). TAT was developed explicitly as a job performance model, and so its relevance in explaining more internal, proximal criteria is less clear. Developments described above on how TAT can contribute to understanding fit may prove useful here, particularly with respect to satisfaction as need fulfillment. In one of the reviewed studies (Fletcher, Major, & Davis, 2007), competitiveness resulted in both high satisfaction and poor performance. In TAT terms, high satisfaction attends trait expression per se, whereas poor performance comes from others judging that trait expression negatively. Application of TAT to internal psychological criteria is a matter for continued theoretical development.

Fifth, situational variables in several studies (e.g., Inness, LeBlanc, & Barling, 2008; Kacmar et al., 2009) were operationalized as perceptions. TAT, in its current form, does not explicitly separate objective from subjective situations. Since Murray (1938) introduced the distinction between alpha and beta press, the role of situation perception in trait–situation interactions has been a worthy yet largely ignored target of research and theory advance. Especially interesting is how personality might affect situation perception. Finally, TAT helps to clarify multiple situational effects in some studies. For example, Oreg and Berson (2011) examined teachers' reactions to a planned organizational change. No baseline assessment was undertaken with which to test effects of the change; the impending change is essentially a "given."[8] By identifying the change as an implicit trait activator (a distracter in this case), TAT suggests that transformational leadership, a key independent variable, operates as a constraint on the expression of a negatively valued trait. Through such clarifications, TAT offers to advance understanding of the potentially nuanced and combinative roles situations play in personality trait expression at work.

In sum, our cursory review of recent studies of trait–situation interactions reveals considerable complexity in how personality is being applied in understanding both psychological (proximate) and behavioral (distal) workplace criteria as a function of situational variables. TAT, considered in terms of multiple cue types (e.g., demands, distracters) operating at multiple levels (task, social, organizational) with respect to both internal (need satisfaction) and external motivators (e.g., pay), provides

Table 5.2 Summary of Trait–Situation Interaction Effects in the Workplace From a TAT Perspective

Journal/Authors	*TAT Interpretation*	*N of T-S Interactional Hypotheses*	*% Hypotheses Supported*	*TAT Cited?*
Journal of Applied Psychology				
Anderson, Spataro, and Flynn (2008)	Team-oriented organizational culture activates E; solitary/technical organizational culture activates C; and trait expression in each case is judged positively, indicative of PO fit, leading to perceived influence. Team-oriented and solitary/technical cultures, operating at the organizational level, present *demands* for E and C, respectively.	2	100%	Yes
Aryee, Chen, Sun, and Debrah (2007)	Perceived interactional injustice activates authoritarian leadership style (as a trait), and trait expression as abusive supervision is judged negatively. Conditions leading to perceived interactional injustice, which likely operate at the organizational level, are *distracters* for authoritarian leadership style.	1	100%	No
Dimotakis, Conlon, and Ilies (2012)	Negotiation situations activate A, and expression of high A is judged positively in integrative negotiations and negatively in distributive negotiations. Integrative negotiations offer *demands* for high A and distributive negotiations offer *demands* for low A; negotiations offer mostly social-level cues, but can be conceived as operating at the task level where negotiation is an assigned task.	1	100%	Yes
Grizzle, Zablah, Brown, Mowen, and Lee (2009)	CO climate activates and/or magnifies existing opportunities for customer orientation (as a trait) to be expressed in positively valued ways, including unit profitability. CO climate, operating at the organizational level, offers *demands* and/or *facilitators* for customer orientation.	2	50%	No
Inness, LeBlanc, and Barling (2008)	Perceived organizational sanctions limit the outward expression of negatively valued trait anger and aggression. Operating at the organizational level, sanctions create a strong situation by eliminating *discretionary cues* for trait expression.	10	30%	No
Kacmar, Collins, Harris, and Judge (2009)	Perceived organizational politics and supervisory competence (via reciprocity) interact with CSE in their effects on rated performance. High perceived politics, operating at the organizational level, serves as a *constraint* for CSE, and supervisory competence, operating at the social level, presents a *demand* for CSE.	2	100%	Yes
Krings and Facchin (2009)	Perceived injustice activates low A and high hostility, and trait expression as sexual harassment is judged negatively. Conditions operating at the organizational level, leading to perceived injustice, are *distracters* for low A and high hostility.	6	33%	No
Yeo, Loft, Xiao, and Kiewitz (2009)	Level of task complexity functions as either a *demand* or *distracter* for PAO, and simple tasks bring out the best in people high on PAO and complex tasks bring out the worst.	4	25%	No

(Continued)

Table 5.2 (Continued)

Journal/Authors	*TAT Interpretation*	*N of T-S Interactional Hypotheses*	*% Hypotheses Supported*	*TAT Cited?*
Personnel Psychology				
Liu, Wang, Zhan, and Shi (2009)	Work stress activates N; trait expression, in the form of alcohol consumption on the job, is judged negatively; and work stressors, operating at the task, social, or organizational level, function as *distracters* for N.	2	100%	No
Oreg and Berson (2011)	Large-scale organizational change activates teachers' DRC, which is negatively valued; organizational change, thus, serves as a *distracter* for DRC (untested); and transformational leadership, operating at the social level, *constrains* DRC, thereby reducing the correlation between DRC and intentions to resist change.	1	100%	No
Yang and Diefendorff (2009)	SIJ activates trait NA, leading to daily negative emotions; such emotions can be judged negatively if expressed as counterproductive work behavior; and SIJ, thus, is a social-level *distracter* for NA.	3	33%	No
Journal of Organizational Behavior				
M. H. Anderson (2007)	Social network characteristics (e.g., number of personal contacts) interact with NC in predicting information gathering, and where information gathering is a task-level *demand* (implicit in this study), social network characteristics aid in meeting that demand, and, as such, may be interpreted as *releasers* (i.e., lack of social connections would *constrain* information gathering).	2	50%	No
Fletcher, Major, and Davis (2007)	Competitive climate activates trait competitiveness, and trait expression is intrinsically rewarding (i.e., higher satisfaction, higher commitment) yet judged negatively for performance. Competitive climate, operating at the social and organizational levels, serves as both a *distracter* and intrinsic motivator for trait competitiveness.	10	30%	No
Ilies, Johnson, Judge, and Keeney (2010)	Interpersonal conflict activates A, resulting in greater state negative affect. Interpersonal conflict episodes function as *distracters*, operating at the social level, with an internal state (i.e., state NA) as the outcome variable rather than valued behavior (e.g., performance).	1	100%	No
Schmidt, Ogunfowora, and Bourdage (2012)	Extraverted teams activate individual E, yielding higher CWB; groups high on CGE activate individual C, yielding lower CWB; conscientious groups and groups higher on CGE activate individual C, yielding higher performance; high E teams are a *distracter* for individual E, low CGE groups are a *distracter* for low individual C, and high C and high CGE teams are *demands* for individual C; and all situational effects are operating at the *social* level.	6	58%	Yes

Notes: TAT: trait activation theory; PO: person–organization; T-S: trait–situation; CO: customer-oriented; CSE: core self-evaluations; PAO: performance-approach orientation; DRC: dispositional resistance to change; SIJ: supervisor interpersonal injustice; NC: need for cognition; NA: negative affectivity; CWB: counterproductive work behavior; CGE: core group evaluation.

a potentially useful framework for organizing and integrating such interactionist research, including that undertaken without explicit reference to TAT. Our summary serves as impetus for more thorough quantitative review.

Conclusions

TAT was borne of the need to understand key complexities involving personality at work, including, most importantly, situational specificity and bidirectionality of trait–performance relationships evident in relevant meta-analyses, and motivational implications of personality traits. Our focused review suggests that TAT frames useful discussion of those and related issues, toward furthering reliance on personality traits in fitting people with jobs. We strongly urge TAT-based research on POWA, team-building, and integrative motivational theory. The proposed developments of TAT, regarding (1) work autonomy/situation strength and (2) differential reactions to performance feedback and outcomes, are intended to better capture the complex realities of how personality plays out in work settings. TAT further clarifies that personality traits offer untapped potential for understanding PE fit at work. Finally, the theory shows potential to serve as a framework for integrating past research on trait–situation interactions in the workplace, encouraging systematic investigation into the relative importance of different types of situational variable in trait–outcome relations. The full extent of our intended contributions awaits further conceptual and empirical inquiry. We hope our chapter stimulates such work toward realizing the fuller potential of personality assessment in work settings.

Practitioner's Window

Trait activation theory (TAT) holds that workers will better fit their work environments when their tasks, coworkers, and organizational culture offer opportunities for them to express their traits in ways others judge as valuable. In brief, *people want to work where they are rewarded for being themselves and organizations want people whose performance is self-motivating.* TAT encourages several applications of personality traits aimed at improving organizational success. Key examples include the following.

1. Knowing the job is the first step in selecting good workers. Personality-oriented work analysis targeting trait demands and distracters at the task, social, and organizational levels should improve efficiency in recruitment, hiring, and succession/promotion.
2. Motivation is rarely one-size-fits-all. Managers and leaders can better motivate their workers as individuals by offering them rewards suited to their traits; for example, extraverts should work harder than introverts to be employee of the month. Workers can also be motivated individually by assigning them tasks, coworkers, and department cultures demanding traits (and KSAs) those workers possess, and by constraining trait-relevant distracters (e.g., sociability at the water cooler).
3. Teams will be more productive and cohesive when composed of individuals high on "teaminess" (e.g., dependability, likeability) who are further suited, by their traits, to meet primary team goals (e.g., compete vs. cooperate with other groups), engage particular roles within the team (e.g., leader, devil's advocate), and work well together as teammates via mutual trait activation: Teams should be built such that members' traits naturally bring out the best in other members.
4. Training and developmental feedback, regarding both content and mode of delivery (e.g., preferred learning style), will be more effective when customized to individuals' personality traits (e.g., extraverts prefer hands-on learning).

5. Performance appraisal bias may be reduced, yielding more valid assessment, when raters are trained to avoid being influenced by job-irrelevant factors affecting ratees' likeability (i.e., just because the rater does not get along with the ratee does not mean the ratee is a poor performer).
6. All else being equal, organizations that adopt TAT-driven strategies can expect their workforce to be happier in what they do, with whom they do it, and the organization as a whole, yielding higher productivity and loyalty and lower withdrawal (e.g., turnover) and counterproductive work behavior.

Notes

1 Content areas in these cases were judged tangential to trait activation theory (TAT) and, accordingly, as less indicative of its influence.
2 No pun intended.
3 Including those who would prefer being told what to do, as an expression of dependence.
4 Fit at work is a complex topic both conceptually and in terms of measurement (cf. Kristof-Brown & Guay, 2011). What follows addresses key aspects of fit theory; more complete mapping awaits deeper considerations than can be given here.
5 This rendering of performance exactly parallels that of Blumberg and Pringle (1982), in which performance is the three-way product of opportunity, ability, and motivation ($P = O \times A \times M$). See also Tett and Simonet (2011).
6 This is why satisfaction-based fit is described above as occurring under two conditions (a and b) relative to three for performance-based fit; condition c, bearing on motivation, is not a condition for satisfaction-based fit because it is intrinsic to it. Extrinsic motivation may contribute to satisfaction (e.g., satisfaction with pay), but it is ancillary.
7 It is difficult to determine the exact number due to variability in searchable terms used to describe such research.
8 This is not a criticism of the noted studies.

References

Anderson, C., Spataro, S., & Flynn, F. (2008). Personality and organizational culture as determinants of influence. *Journal of Applied Psychology, 93*, 702–710.

Anderson, M. H. (2007). Social networks and the cognitive motivation to realize network opportunities: A study of managers' information gathering behaviors. *Journal of Organizational Behavior, 29*, 51–78.

Aryee, S., Chen, Z. X., Sun, L., & Debrah, Y. A. (2007). Antecedents and outcomes of abusive supervision: Test of a trickle-down model. *Journal of Applied Psychology, 92*, 191–201.

Barrick, M. R., & Mount, M. K. (1993). Autonomy as a moderator of the relationships between the Big Five personality dimensions and job performance. *Journal of Applied Psychology, 78*, 111–118.

Baumeister, R. F., & Tice, D. M. (1985). Toward a theory of situational structure. *Environment & Behavior, 17*, 147–192.

Bipp, T. (2009). Linking personality to work motivation and performance: Individual differences effects. In M. Wosnitza, S. A. Karabenick, A. Efklides, & P. Nenninger (Eds.), *Contemporary motivation research: From global to local perspectives* (pp. 167–184). Ashland, OH: Hogrefe & Huber.

Blickle, G., Kramer, J., Zettler, I., Momm, T., Summers, J., Munyon, T., . . . Ferris, G. R. (2009). Job demands as a moderator of the political skill–job performance relationship. *The Career Development International, 14*, 333–350.

Blumberg, M., & Pringle, C. D. (1982). The missing opportunity in organizational research: Some implications for a theory of work performance. *Academy of Management Review, 7*, 560–569.

Borman, W. C., Penner, L. A., Allen, T. D., & Motowidlo, S. J. (2001). Personality predictors of citizenship performance. *International Journal of Selection and Assessment, 9*, 52–69.

Bowles, H., Babcock, L., & McGinn, K. L. (2005). Constraints and triggers: Situational mechanics of gender in negotiation. *Journal of Personality and Social Psychology, 89*, 951–965.

Breaugh, J. A. (1985). The measurement of work autonomy. *Human Relations, 38*, 551–570.

Cable, D. M., & Edwards, J. R. (2004). Complementary and supplementary fit: A theoretical and empirical integration. *Journal of Applied Psychology, 89*, 822–834.

Caldwell, D., & Moberg, D. (2007). An exploratory investigation of the effect of ethical culture in activating moral imagination. *Journal of Business Ethics, 73*, 193–204.

Chen, G., Kirkman, B. L., Kim, K., Farh, C. C., & Tangirala, S. (2010). When does cross-cultural motivation enhance expatriate effectiveness? A multilevel investigation of the moderating roles of subsidiary support and cultural distance. *Academy of Management Journal, 53*, 1110–1130.

Cooper, W., & Withey, M. (2009). The strong situation hypothesis. *Personality and Social Psychology Review, 13*, 62–72.

Crawford, T., Shaver, P., & Goldsmith, H. (2007). How affect regulation moderates the association between anxious attachment and neuroticism. *Attachment and Human Development, 9*, 95–109.

Dawis, R. V., & Lofquist, L. H. (1984). *A psychological theory of work adjustment*. Minneapolis, MN: University of Minnesota Press.

Deci, E. L., Connell, J. P., & Ryan, R. M. (1989). Self-determination in a work organization. *Journal of Applied Psychology, 74*, 580–590.

de Jong, R. D., van der Velde, M. G., & Jansen, P. W. (2001). Openness to experience and growth need strength as moderators between job characteristics and satisfaction. *International Journal of Selection and Assessment, 9*, 350–356.

Dierdorff, E., & Surface, E. (2007). Placing peer ratings in context: Systematic influences beyond ratee performance. *Personnel Psychology, 60*, 93–126.

Dimotakis, N., Conlon, D. E., & Ilies, R. (2012). The mind and heart (literally) of the negotiator: Personality and contextual determinants of experiential reactions and economic outcomes in negotiation. *Journal of Applied Psychology, 97*, 183–193.

Eysenck, H., & Eysenck, M. W. (1985). *Personality and individual differences: A natural science approach*. New York, NY: Plenum Press.

Farmer, S., & Van Dyne, L. (2010). The idealized self and the situated self as predictors of employee work behaviors. *Journal of Applied Psychology, 95*, 503–516.

Fleenor, J. W., Smither, J. W., Atwater, L. E., Braddy, P. W., & Sturm, R. E. (2010). Self–other rating agreement in leadership: A review. *The Leadership Quarterly, 21*, 1005–1034.

Fletcher, T. D., Major, D. A., & Davis, D. D. (2007). The interactive relationship of competitiveness with workplace attitudes, stress, and performance. *Journal of Organizational Behavior, 29*, 899–922.

Frese, M., & Zapf, D. (1994). Action as the core of work psychology: A German approach. In H. C. Triandis, M. D. Dunnette, & L. M. Hough (Eds.), *Handbook of industrial and organizational psychology* (Vol. 4, pp. 271–340). Palo Alto, CA: Consulting Psychologists Press.

Fuller, J. R., Hester, K., & Cox, S. S. (2010). Proactive personality and job performance: Exploring job autonomy as a moderator. *Journal of Managerial Issues, 22*, 35–51.

Furnham, A. (2003). Personality, individual differences and incentive schemes. *North American Journal of Psychology, 5*, 325–334.

Gelfand, M., Leslie, L., & Fehr, R. (2008). To prosper, organizational psychology should . . . adopt a global perspective. *Journal of Organizational Behavior, 29*, 493–517.

Grant, A. M., Fried, Y., & Juillerat, T. (2011). Work matters: Job design in classic and contemporary perspectives. In S. Zedeck (Ed.), *APA handbook of industrial and organizational psychology, Vol. 1: Building and developing the organization* (pp. 417–453). Washington, DC: American Psychological Association.

Griffin, M., Parker, S., & Mason, C. (2010). Leader vision and the development of adaptive and proactive performance: A longitudinal study. *Journal of Applied Psychology, 95*, 174–182.

Grizzle, J. W., Zablah, A. R., Brown, T. J., Mowen, J. C., & Lee, J. M. (2009). Employee customer orientation in context: How the environment moderates the influence of customer orientation on performance outcomes. *Journal of Applied Psychology, 94*, 1227–1242.

Haaland, S., & Christiansen, N. D. (2002). Implications of trait-activation theory for evaluating the construct validity of assessment center ratings. *Personnel Psychology, 55*, 137–163.

Hackman, J. R., & Oldham, G. R. (1976). Motivation through the design of work: Test of a theory. *Organizational Behavior and Human Performance, 16*, 250–279.

Hackman, J. R., & Oldham, G. R. (1980). *Work redesign*. Reading, MA: Addison-Wesley.

Harris, K., Harvey, P., & Booth, S. L. (2010). Who abuses their coworkers? An examination of personality and situational variables. *The Journal of Social Psychology, 150*, 608–627.

Hochwarter, W., Witt, L., Treadway, D., & Ferris, G. (2006). The interaction of social skill and organizational support on job performance. *Journal of Applied Psychology, 91*, 482–489.

Hough, L. M., & Oswald, F. L. (2008). Personality testing and industrial–organizational psychology: Reflections, progress, and prospects. *Industrial and Organizational Psychology: Perspectives on Science and Practice, 1*, 272–290.

Huffcutt, A. I., Van Iddekinge, C. H., & Roth, P. L. (2011). Understanding applicant behavior in employment interviews: A theoretical model of interviewee performance. *Human Resource Management Review, 21*, 353–367.

Hülsheger, U. R., & Maier, G.W. (2010). The careless or the conscientious: Who profits most from goal progress? *Journal of Vocational Behavior, 77*, 246–254.
Ilgen, D. R., & Davis, C. A. (2000). Bearing bad news: Reactions to negative performance feedback. *Applied Psychology: An International Review, 49*, 550–565.
Ilies, R., Johnson, M. D., Judge, T. A., & Keeney, J. (2010). A within-individual study of interpersonal conflict as a work stressor: Dispositional and situational moderators. *Journal of Organizational Behavior, 32*, 44–64.
Inness, M., LeBlanc, M. M., & Barling, J. (2008). Psychosocial predictors of supervisor-, peer-, subordinate-, and service-provider-targeted aggression. *Journal of Applied Psychology, 93*, 1401–1411.
Jeng, S., & Teng, C. (2008). Personality and motivations for playing online games. *Social Behavior and Personality, 36*, 1053–1060.
Jiang, C., Wang, D., & Zhou, F. (2009). Personality traits and job performance in local government organizations in China. *Social Behavior and Personality, 37*, 451–458.
Johnson, J. W., & Hezlett, S. A. (2008). Modeling the influence of personality on individuals at work: A review and research agenda. In S. Cartwright & C. L. Cooper (Eds.), *Oxford handbook of personnel psychology* (pp. 59–92). Oxford, UK: Oxford University Press.
Judge, T., Piccolo, R., & Kosalka, T. (2009). The bright and dark sides of leader traits: A review and theoretical extension of the leader trait paradigm. *The Leadership Quarterly, 20*, 855–875.
Kacmar, K., Collins, B., Harris, K., & Judge, T. (2009). Core self-evaluations and job performance: The role of the perceived work environment. *Journal of Applied Psychology, 94*, 1572–1580.
Kamdar, D., & Van Dyne, L. (2007). The joint effects of personality and workplace social exchange relationships in predicting task performance and citizenship performance. *Journal of Applied Psychology, 92*, 1286–1298.
Kell, H. J., Rittmayer, A. D., Crook, A. E., & Motowidlo, S. J. (2010). Situational content moderates the association between the big five personality traits and behavioral effectiveness. *Human Performance, 23*, 213–228.
Kenrick, D. T., & Funder, D. C. (1988). Profiting from controversy: Lessons from the person–situation debate. *American Psychologist, 43*, 23–34.
Kim, T., Hon, A., & Lee, D. (2010). Proactive personality and employee creativity: The effects of job creativity requirement and supervisor support for creativity. *Creativity Research Journal, 22*, 37–45.
Krings, F., & Facchin, S. (2009). Organizational justice and men's likelihood to sexually harass: The moderating role of sexism and personality. *Journal of Applied Psychology, 94*, 501–510.
Kristof, A. L. (1996). Person–organization fit: An integrative review of its conceptualizations, measurement, and implications. *Personnel Psychology, 49*, 1–49.
Kristof-Brown, A. L., & Guay, R. P. (2011). Person–environment fit. In S. Zedeck (Eds.), *APA handbook of industrial and organizational psychology, Vol. 3: Maintaining, expanding, and contracting the organization* (pp. 3–50). Washington, DC: American Psychological Association.
Kristof-Brown, A. L., Zimmerman, R. D., & Johnson, E. C. (2005). Consequences of individual's fit at work: A meta-analysis of person–job, person–organization, person–group, and person–supervisor fit. *Personnel Psychology, 58*, 281–342.
Landy, F. J., & Conte, J. M. (2007). *Work in the 21st century: An introduction to industrial and organizational psychology* (2nd ed.). Malden, MA: Blackwell.
LePine, J. A., Buckman, B. R., Crawford, E. R., & Methot, J. R. (2011). A review of research on personality in teams: Accounting for pathways spanning levels of theory and analysis. *Human Resource Management Review, 21*, 311–330.
Lievens, F. (2002). Trying to understand the different pieces of the construct validity puzzle of assessment centers: An examination of assessor and assessee effects. *Journal of Applied Psychology, 87*, 675–686.
Lievens, F., Chasteen, C. S., Day, E., & Christiansen, N. D. (2006). Large-scale investigation of the role of trait activation theory for understanding assessment center convergent and discriminant validity. *Journal of Applied Psychology, 91*, 247–258.
Lievens, F., Ones, D., & Dilchert, S. (2009). Personality scale validities increase throughout medical school. *Journal of Applied Psychology, 94*, 1514–1535.
Liu, S., Wang, M., Zhan, Y., & Shi, J. (2009). Daily work stress and alcohol use: Testing the cross-level moderation effects of neuroticism and job involvement. *Personnel Psychology, 62*, 57–88.
Locke, E. A. (1968). Toward a theory of task motivation and incentives. *Organizational Behavior and Human Performance, 3*, 157–189.
Meyer, R., Dalal, R., & Hermida, R. (2010). A review and synthesis of situational strength in the organizational sciences. *Journal of Management, 36*, 121–140.
Minbashian, A., Wood, R., & Beckmann, N. (2010). Task-contingent conscientiousness as a unit of personality at work. *Journal of Applied Psychology, 95*, 793–806.
Mischel, W. (1968). *Personality and assessment.* Hoboken, NJ: John Wiley & Sons.

Mischel, W. (1973). Toward a cognitive social learning reconceptualization of personality. *Psychological Review, 80*, 252–283.
Mischel, W., & Shoda, Y. (1995). A cognitive-affective system theory of personality: Reconceptualizing situations, dispositions, dynamics, and invariance in personality structure. *Psychological Review, 102*, 246–268.
Mohammed, S., Rizzuto, T., Hiller, N., Newman, D., & Chen, T. (2008). Individual differences and group negotiation: The role of polychronicity, dominance, and decision rule. *Negotiation and Conflict Management Research, 1*, 282–307.
Morgeson, F. P., Campion, M. A., Dipboye, R. L., Hollenbeck, J. R., Murphy, K., & Schmitt, N. (2007). Are we getting fooled again? Coming to terms with limitations in the use of personality tests for personnel selection. *Personnel Psychology, 60*, 1029–1049.
Morgeson, F. P., & Dierdorff, E. C. (2011). Work analysis: From technique to theory. In S. Zedeck (Eds.), *APA handbook of industrial and organizational psychology, Vol. 2: Selecting and developing members for the organization* (pp. 3–41). Washington, DC: American Psychological Association.
Moskowitz, D. S., & Coté, S. (1995). Do interpersonal traits predict affect? A comparison of three models. *Journal of Personality and Social Psychology, 69*, 915–924.
Moss, S. A., McFarland, J., Ngu, S., & Kijowska, A. (2007). Maintaining an open mind to closed individuals: The effect of leadership style and resource availability on the association between openness to experience and organizational commitment. *Journal of Research in Personality, 41*, 259–275.
Moss, S. A., & Ngu, S. (2006). The relationship between personality and leadership preferences. *Current Research in Social Psychology, 11*, 70–91. Retrieved from PsycINFO database.
Muchinsky, P. M., & Monahan, C. J. (1987). What is person–environment congruence? Supplementary versus complementary models of fit. *Journal of Vocational Behavior, 31*, 268–277.
Murphy, K., & Dzieweczynski, J. (2005). Why don't measures of broad dimensions of personality perform better as predictors of job performance? *Human Performance, 18*, 343–357.
Murray, H. (1938). *Explorations in personality*. New York, NY: Oxford University Press.
Netemeyer, R. G., & Maxham, J. G. (2007). Employee versus supervisor ratings of performance in the retail customer service sector: Differences in predictive validity for customer outcomes. *Journal of Retailing, 83*, 131–145.
Ng, T. W. H., Feldman, D. C., & Lam, S. S. (2010). Psychological contract breaches, organizational commitment, and innovation-related behaviors: A latent growth modeling approach. *Journal of Applied Psychology, 95*, 744–751.
Ng, T. W. H., & Sorensen, K. L. (2009). Dispositional affectivity and work-related outcomes: A meta-analysis. *Journal of Applied Social Psychology, 39*, 1255–1287.
Oreg, S., & Berson, Y. (2011). Leadership and employees' reactions to change: The role of leaders' personal attributes and transformational leadership style. *Personnel Psychology, 64*, 627–659.
Parker, S., Jimmieson, N., & Amiot, C. (2009). The stress-buffering effects of control on task satisfaction and perceived goal attainment: An experimental study of the moderating influence of desire for control. *Applied Psychology: An International Review, 58*, 622–652.
Peeters, M. A., Van Tuijl, H. F., Rutte, C. G., & Reymen, I. M. (2006). Personality and team performance: A meta-analysis. *European Journal of Personality, 20*, 377–396.
Robert, C., & Cheung, Y. (2010). An examination of the relationship between conscientiousness and group performance on a creative task. *Journal of Research in Personality, 44*, 222–231.
Rogers, C., & Dymond, R. (Ed.). (1954). *Psychotherapy and personality change*. Chicago: University of Chicago Press.
Saks, A. M., & Ashforth, B. E. (1997). Organizational socialization: Making sense of the past and present as a prologue for the future. *Journal of Vocational Behavior, 51*, 234–279.
Schmidt, J., Ogunfowora, B., & Bourdage, J. S. (2012). No person is an island: The effects of group characteristics on individual trait expression. *Journal of Organizational Behavior, 33*, 865–1030.
Schneider, B. (1987). The people make the place. *Personnel Psychology, 40*, 437–453.
Schneider, B. (2001). Fits about fit. *Applied Psychology: An International Review, 50*, 141–152.
Scott, K., & Taylor, G. (1985). An examination of conflicting findings on the relationship between job satisfaction and absenteeism: A meta-analysis. *Academy of Management Journal, 28*, 599–612.
Sears, G. J., & Hackett, R. D. (2011). The influence of role definition and affect in LMX: A process perspective on the personality–LMX relationship. *Journal of Occupational and Organizational Psychology, 84*, 544–564.
Sekaran, U., & Wagner, F. R. (1980). Sense of competence: A cross-cultural analysis for managerial application. *Group & Organization Studies, 5*, 340–352.
Shaffer, M. A., Harrison, D. A., Gregersen, H., Black, J., & Ferzandi, L. A. (2006). You can take it with you: Individual differences and expatriate effectiveness. *Journal of Applied Psychology, 91*, 109–125.
Spurk, D., & Abele, A. E. (2011). Who earns more and why? A multiple mediation model from personality to salary. *Journal of Business and Psychology, 26*, 87–103.

Sung, S., & Choi, J. (2009). Do big five personality factors affect individual creativity? The moderating role of extrinsic motivation. *Social Behavior and Personality, 37*, 941–956. Retrieved from PsycINFO database.

Taylor, M. S., Fisher, C. D., & Ilgen, D. R. (1984). Individuals' reactions to performance feedback in organizations: A control theory perspective. In K. M. Rowland & G. R. Ferris (Eds.), *Research in personnel and human resources management* (Vol. 2, pp. 161–187). Greenwich, CT: JAI Press.

Tett, R. P., & Burnett, D. D. (2003). A personality trait-based interactionist model of job performance. *Journal of Applied Psychology, 88*, 500–517.

Tett, R. P., & Christiansen, N. (2007). Personality tests at the crossroads: A response to Morgeson, Campion, Dipboye, Hollenbeck, Murphy, and Schmitt (2007). *Personnel Psychology, 60*, 967–993.

Tett, R. P., & Guterman, H. A. (2000). Situation trait relevance, trait expression, and cross-situational consistency: Testing a principle of trait activation. *Journal of Research in Personality, 34*, 397–423.

Tett, R. P., Jackson, D. N., Rothstein, M., & Reddon, J. R. (1999). Meta-analysis of bidirectional relations in personality–job performance research. *Human Performance, 12*, 1–29.

Tett, R. P., & Meyer, J. P. (1993). Job satisfaction, organizational commitment, turnover intention, and turnover: Path analyses based on meta-analytic findings. *Personnel Psychology, 46*, 259–293.

Tett, R. P., & Murphy, P. J. (2002). Personality and situations in co-worker preference: Similarity and complementarity in worker compatibility. *Journal of Business and Psychology, 17*, 223–243.

Tett, R. P., & Simonet, D. V. (2011). Faking in personality assessment: A "multisaturation" perspective on faking as performance. *Human Performance, 24*, 302–321.

Uher, J. (2008). Three methodological core issues of comparative personality research. *European Journal of Personality, 22*, 475–496.

Uher, J. (2011). Individual behavioral phenotypes: An integrative meta-theoretical framework: Why "behavioral syndromes" are not analogs of "personality." *Developmental Psychobiology, 53*, 521–548.

Van Mechelen, I. (2009). A royal road to understanding the mechanisms underlying person-in-context behavior. *Journal of Research in Personality, 43*, 179–186.

Verbeke, W., Dietz, B., & Verwaal, E. (2011). Drivers of sales performance: A contemporary meta-analysis. Have salespeople become knowledge brokers? *Journal of the Academy of Marketing Science, 39*, 407–428.

Wall, T. D., Jackson, P. R., & Mullarkey, S. (1995). Further evidence on some new measures of job control, cognitive demand and production responsibility. *Journal of Organizational Behavior, 16*, 431–455.

Warr, P., Bartram, D., & Martin, T. (2005). Personality and sales performance: Situational variation and interactions between traits. *International Journal of Selection and Assessment, 13*, 87–91.

Yang, J., & Diefendorff, J. M. (2009). The relations of daily counterproductive workplace behavior with emotions, situational antecedents, and personality moderators: A diary study in Hong Kong. *Personnel Psychology, 62*, 259–295.

Yeo, G., Loft, S., Xiao, T., & Kiewitz, C. (2009). Goal orientations and performance: Differential relationships across levels of analysis and as a function of task demands. *Journal of Applied Psychology, 94*, 710–726.

Zhang, Z., & Peterson, S. J. (2011). Advice networks in teams: The role of transformational leadership and members' core self-evaluations. *Journal of Applied Psychology, 96*, 1004–1017.

Zweig, D., & Webster, J. (2004). Validation of a multidimensional measure of goal orientation. *Canadian Journal of Behavioural Science/Revue Canadienne des Sciences du Comportement, 36*, 232–248.

6

Individual Differences in Work Motivation

Current Directions and Future Needs

John J. Donovan, Tanner Bateman, and Eric D. Heggestad

The field of work motivation has long recognized the potential role of stable individual differences as determinants of motivational tendencies and behavior (e.g., Atkinson, 1957; McClelland, 1951; Murray, 1938). Although research on these individual differences slowed significantly from the late 1960s to the early 1980s (Hough & Schneider, 1996), the past two decades have witnessed a flurry of empirical and conceptual work on the identification and examination of individual differences that demonstrate meaningful relationships with motivated behavior, including goal orientation (e.g., Payne, Youngcourt, & Beaubien, 2007), regulatory focus (Higgins, 1999), the trait of conscientiousness from the Big Five representation of personality (e.g., Barrick, Mount, & Strauss, 1993), and motivational traits (Kanfer & Heggestad, 1997). Given this research interest, the goal of this chapter is to synthesize the accumulated evidence for three of the more promising individual difference frameworks (goal orientation, regulatory focus, motivational traits), while also providing an assessment of the limitations within these research literatures and offering suggestions for advancing our understanding of how individual differences influence work motivation.

Individual Differences in Work Motivation

Work motivation is most commonly defined as a set of forces (whether internal or external) that are responsible for the initiation, intensity, and duration of behavior exhibited by workers (Pinder, 2008). Since empirical and conceptual work in this domain began more than a century ago, there have been a number of diverse theoretical models proposed to explain the nature of work motivation and the processes underlying it (Campbell & Pritchard, 1976; Kanfer, 1990). However, in recent years, this literature has largely gravitated toward an emphasis on the importance of goals or standards for behavior as the key drivers of motivation (Locke, 1991; Lord, Diefendorff, Schmidt, & Hall, 2010), based in large part on the extensive research support for the relationship between goals and motivated behavior (for comprehensive reviews, see Kanfer, 1990; Locke & Latham, 2002). Although there are stylistic and conceptual differences among them, goal setting theory (Locke & Latham, 1990), social cognitive theory (Bandura, 1986), and control theory (e.g., Campion & Lord, 1982) all share the common perspective that motivated behavior is derived primarily from the establishment and pursuit of goals. More specifically, individuals are proposed to (a) establish goals and estimate the likelihood of success in achieving those goals, (b) assess progress toward goal attainment by monitoring their behavior relative to those goals, and (c) alter their cognitions and/or behavior in response to feedback they receive and the observation of discrepancies between the goals and behavior.

It is important to realize, however, that while these models suggest there are generalizable self-regulatory processes that govern work motivation *across individuals*, there is also a clear recognition that there are *individual differences within* these processes (e.g., Austin & Klein, 1996; Farr, Hofmann, & Ringenbach, 1993; Kanfer, 1990). As such, research seeking to identify and evaluate individual differences that may influence these processes is essential for developing a full understanding of the factors that drive motivation in organizations.

Early Research on Individual Differences in Motivation

Murray's (1938) *Explorations in Personality* provided much of the foundational material for subsequent research into motivation and individual differences. Within this volume, Murray (1938) described a catalog of over 20 psychogenic *needs* and the assessment tools used to measure them, including the very influential *Need for Achievement (nAch)* construct and the associated Thematic Apperception Test (TAT). A psychogenic *need*, as described by Murray, indicates an organic readiness that serves to organize perceptions and guide actions toward a desired end state, or satiation. Importantly, psychogenic *needs*, such as *nAch*, were originally conceptualized as motives or drives that were anticipated to have similar influences on behavior to the more basic viscerogenic (or physiological) needs, such as hunger and safety (Atkinson & McClelland, 1948; Murray, 1938).

Within Murray's idea of motivated behavior, psychogenic *needs* are important only in the context of a perceived situation or *press*. Specific *need–press* relationships are termed *thema* and represent an early form of interactionism in which the active agent, with some level of *need*, responds to a perceived *press* to produce behaviors aimed at satiating a currently unsatisfactory state. This dynamism between a person's *need* and an often perceived *press* produces chronic responses. For instance, a person with strong *nAch* experiences an internal force to perform well on tests due to the specific *thema*, or interplay between their motive to increase competence and their perception of the achievement situation or *press*. Unfortunately, Murray's (1938) work on psychogenic *needs* was largely devoid of broader theoretical propositions and, as such, provided very little in terms of overarching theories of personality or motivation. Nonetheless, Murray's initial conceptualization of *nAch*, *press*, and the advent of the TAT had an extensive impact on personality-based motivation research.

Shortly thereafter, McClelland and colleagues (e.g., McClelland, Clark, Roby, & Atkinson, 1949) began work to refine the TAT measurement of *nAch*. During this line of study, researchers began to utilize *nAch* as an individual difference construct capable of predicting motivated behaviors such as risk taking (Atkinson, 1957), student ability (Uhlinger & Stephens, 1960), and entrepreneurial success (Wainer & Rubin, 1969). Weak relationships between individual differences in *nAch* and goal setting also began to emerge (Atkinson & Litwin, 1960). Within this line of research, concern about the construct validity of *nAch* began to turn into the explication of what we now know as the achievement motive.

Clark, Teevan, and Ricciuti (1956) conceptualized *nAch* as a singular construct with variation occurring along one continuum from hope of success to fear of failure. Alternatively, Atkinson and Litwin (1960) argued for independent *nAch* and anxiety constructs, presenting evidence that *nAch* did not correlate with validated measures of anxiety (i.e., Test Anxiety Questionnaire; Sarason, 1978). Generally, the independent construct conceptualizations—with separate achievement and anxiety constructs—won favor, resulting in specification of the motive to approach success and the motive to avoid failure.

Research concerning individual differences in motivation slowed considerably during the 1960s through the early 1980s as researchers focused on situational determinants of motivation (Hough

& Schneider, 1996). Beginning in the mid-1980s, however, research on individual differences in motivation began to resurface, typically exploring the roles of constructs such as self-efficacy and goal-setting mechanisms (e.g., Matsui, Okada, & Kakuyama, 1982; Yukl & Latham, 1978) as mediators of the relationships between individual differences constructs (e.g., *nAch*) and behavior. Although other individual differences constructs, such as conscientiousness, goal orientation, motivational traits, and regulatory focus, have generally supplanted *nAch* as the focal representation of individual differences in motivation, the original conceptualization occasionally makes an appearance in contemporary literature (e.g., Tuerlinckx, DeBoeck, & Lens, 2002). From Murray's original conceptualization through the work of McClelland, Atkinson, and colleagues, the critical distinction between approach and avoidance tendencies remains central to contemporary perspectives on individual differences in motivation.

In personality research, conscientiousness has been lauded as the broad personality trait that is most related to work motivation (Schmidt & Hunter, 1992). Although it is a general personality trait characterized by dependability, mindfulness, and self-control, it is also composed of proactive volitional components akin to achievement orientation and hard work (Barrick et al., 1993; Costa & McCrae, 1992). It is through these approach-oriented drives that conscientiousness provides important individual difference information regarding levels of energized, directed, and maintained behaviors. The influence of Murray's early work can certainly be seen in those aspects of the conscientiousness that lie in the positive agency (i.e., approach-oriented) domain (Kanfer & Heggestad, 1997).

While aspects of motivation are certainly captured within the behavioral tendencies represented by conscientiousness, it is clear that this set of behaviors captures far more than motivationally specific individual differences. For instance, conscientiousness also captures tendencies to be neat and tidy, which are not considered specific elements of work motivation (for more coverage on the structure of common personality taxonomies and traits such as those of the Five-Factor Model [FFM], see Chapter 2, this volume). As such, scholars have focused on more narrowly defined aspects of personality to provide a more accurate conceptualization of individual differences in motivation. Three of the more promising, motivationally specific, individual difference constructs currently being explored in the work motivation literature are goal orientation (e.g., Dweck & Leggett, 1988), motivational traits (Kanfer & Heggestad, 1997), and chronic regulatory focus (Higgins, 1997). The first two of these can be tied closely to the historical concept of *nAch* and, in many ways, represent modern instantiations of the original concept. What's more, all three frameworks utilize the classic approach and avoidance distinctions as underpinnings to their theoretical propositions show promise in work motivation research and are related to other motivational constructs and outcomes such as self-efficacy, goal setting, feedback reactions, and task performance. We now turn toward a synthesis of research and exploration of future directions for these three conceptualizations of individual differences in motivation.

Goal Orientation

During the past two decades, perhaps no individual difference construct has received more research attention in the work motivation domain than goal orientation. The goal orientation construct was originally developed in the educational literature by Dweck and colleagues (e.g., Dweck, 1975) to describe different approaches to achievement settings, as well as explain how these approaches impact critical motivational outcomes, such as effort, persistence, and the degree to which individuals seek challenge. Introductory efforts in the work motivation realm by Kanfer (1990) and Farr et al. (1993) identified several potential implications of goal orientation for this area of inquiry, and since that time, research interest on the role of goal orientation in motivational processes has flourished (DeShon & Gillespie, 2005). Although a detailed review of the background of this construct is beyond the scope of this chapter (see Dweck, 1989; Farr et al., 1993; Kanfer, 1990), the following narrative will help provide context for understanding current research efforts, and will illuminate some problems in the conceptualizations of goal orientation that are currently in use.

Development of the Goal Orientation Construct

Based on their early work with children, Dweck and colleagues (e.g., Diener & Dweck, 1978; Dweck, 1975; Dweck & Reppucci, 1973) observed that children experiencing failure at a task tended to demonstrate one of two behavioral response patterns. The first behavioral pattern, termed a helpless pattern, was characterized by negative self-cognitions, such as attributing failure to personal inadequacy. These children also expressed pronounced levels of negative affect, developed an aversion to the task being performed, experienced performance-related anxiety, and demonstrated significant decrements in performance. The second behavioral pattern, termed a mastery pattern, was characterized by the belief that unsolved problems are challenges to be mastered. Children exhibiting this behavioral pattern remained optimistic that their performance-related efforts would lead to success, while also exhibiting positive affect throughout task performance. The tendency for children to engage in either of these two response patterns across various task performance situations was subsequently termed as "goal orientation" (e.g., Dweck, 1975). More specifically, an individual's goal orientation referred to the goals (i.e., mastery vs. performance) that he or she chronically pursued in achievement settings. Children exhibiting a helpless behavior pattern were characterized as holding a "performance orientation," while those exhibiting the mastery pattern were said to hold a "learning orientation." It is worth noting that, although this early work recognized that children displayed similar orientations across different settings, it also readily recognized the strong impact that situational characteristics had on the orientations displayed, suggesting that goal orientation was composed of both stable (i.e., dispositional) and situational components.

Within this early work, goal orientation was largely conceptualized as a single continuum, with the concepts of learning orientation and performance orientation anchoring the endpoints. This was due, in part, to the emphasis placed on theory of ability as a determinant of goal orientation. Individuals were proposed to hold either an *entity* view of ability (i.e., ability is fixed and cannot be altered), which leads to a performance orientation, or an *incremental* view of ability (i.e., ability is malleable and can be developed through experience and effort), which leads to a learning orientation. Later work (e.g., Dweck, 1989; Heyman & Dweck, 1992) posited that individuals could simultaneously display elements of both learning and performance orientations (e.g., be focused on outperforming others while also improving upon prior performance), suggesting that goal orientation was actually composed of two independent dimensions: learning goal orientation and performance goal orientation. Within this framework, a performance goal orientation (alternatively termed an "ego-orientation") refers to the adoption of an implicit goal of striving to demonstrate, and by doing so, gain favorable judgments of one's task competence and to avoid negative judgments of competence. Individuals displaying a strong performance goal orientation can be characterized by (a) a tendency to avoid challenges, (b) negative affect and negative ability attributions in response to failure, (c) low levels of persistence in the face of difficulty, and (d) a generalized fear of negative evaluations by others (Dweck & Leggett, 1988). In contrast, a learning goal orientation (alternatively labeled mastery orientation) refers to a striving to understand something new or to increase levels of competence in a given task or activity (Dweck, 1989; Dweck & Leggett, 1988). Correspondingly, individuals with a strong learning goal orientation are characterized by (a) challenge-seeking behaviors, (b) positive affect related to task performance, and (c) high levels of persistence in the face of difficulty.

Goal Orientation and Work Motivation

Around the time that the two-dimensional conceptualization of goal orientation was being solidified, efforts were being made to introduce them into the work motivation literature and identify the implications of goal orientation for this field (e.g., Farr et al., 1993; Kanfer, 1990). In one of the more influential efforts, Farr et al. (1993) outlined a series of propositions regarding how goal orientation dimensions might be linked to work motivation, suggesting that they likely influence self-regulatory processes such as goal setting/goal acceptance, feedback seeking, and reactions to performance feedback. However, they also recognized that the existing goal orientation literature suffered from several limitations, including inconsistent measurement strategies and inconsistent construct definitions that would need to be remedied before goal orientation could be meaningfully integrated into the work motivation domain.

In response, Button, Mathieu, and Zajac (1996) set out to provide a foundation upon which future motivation research could build by developing a two-dimensional measure of goal orientation that addressed some of the conceptual and measurement issues present in the educational literature, while also providing the beginnings of a nomological network. The resulting 16-item measure of dispositional goal orientation served as a catalyst for a significant body of research in the coming years by providing an easily utilized measure that was applicable to a wide variety of contexts. One unintended consequence, however, was that much of the ensuing research tended to assume that goal orientation was solely a dispositional variable, despite Button et al.'s (1996) clear acknowledgment that goal orientation had both stable and situational components, as well as past research demonstrating that goal orientation was susceptible to situational cues (e.g., Jagacinski & Nicholls, 1987). This assumption led researchers to insert goal orientation into research studies with relatively little forethought given to the importance of the situation in determining how goal orientation might influence behavior, while also relying on the measurement of this construct at a single point in time to predict a variety of long- and short-term outcomes.

While Button et al.'s (1996) focus was their extensive scale development efforts, the results obtained across their validation studies provided two additional noteworthy findings. First, although the theoretical foundations of this construct posited that individuals' goal orientation was largely a function of their theory of ability (incremental vs. entity), the findings of Button et al. (1996) suggested otherwise. Specifically, while an incremental theory of ability was moderately correlated with individuals' level of learning goal orientation, holding an entity theory of ability was only weakly linked to the strength of their performance goal orientation. A second noteworthy (yet often ignored) finding in Button et al. (1996) was the observation that, while there was a positive correlation between levels of dispositional goal orientation and the situational learning and performance goals exhibited by individuals, these situational goals were empirically distinct from dispositional goal orientation. Button et al. (1996) suggested that dispositional goal orientation provides a default orientation that may be influenced, altered, or overridden by situational characteristics. This once again reinforces the notion that goal orientation is not *either* a situational *or* dispositional construct, but instead likely manifests at *both* the situational and dispositional levels.

Not long after the publication of Button et al. (1996), a distinct perspective on goal orientation[1] was proposed by VandeWalle (1997). The conceptualization of goal orientation forwarded by VandeWalle (1997) diverged from that of Button et al. (1996) in two significant ways. First, VandeWalle suggested that goal orientation was more appropriately defined as a three-dimensional construct, formed by bifurcating performance goal orientation into two dimensions (performance-prove and performance-avoid). A performance-prove orientation (alternatively termed performance-approach) was characterized by a desire to demonstrate and gain favorable judgments of one's competence by others, while a performance-avoid goal orientation was primarily focused on avoiding negative evaluations of one's competence by others. The logic behind this split was that, similar to the approach/avoid distinction advocated in much of the individual differences literature, the construct definition of a performance goal orientation actually contained two distinct motives (gaining favorable judgments and avoiding negative evaluations), with unique sets of motivational outcomes and processes accompanying each. As such, this bifurcation would create a goal orientation framework with more conceptual clarity than a two-dimensional definition. Second, VandeWalle (1997) viewed goal orientation as domain specific, suggesting that individuals may chronically exhibit different goal orientations in each major life domain (e.g., work, academics, athletics). This domain specificity is in direct contrast to the general, dispositional approach to goal orientation of Button et al.'s (1996) measure, which attempted to describe a general orientation that applied across domains. Citing work by Ajzen (1987) and Dweck (1991), VandeWalle (1997) argued that broad measures assessing goal orientation across different contexts are too general to usefully predict motivated behavior in specific domains. The use of domain-specific measures, on the other hand, provides the proper level of specificity for most research questions, and therefore should enhance prediction of relevant motivational outcomes in these domains.

Consistent with these perspectives, VandeWalle (1997) developed and validated a 13-item, three-dimensional measure of work-domain goal orientation. Interestingly, the results of this construct validation effort mirrored the findings of Button et al. (1996) regarding the relatively weak influence of theory of ability (incremental vs. entity) on goal orientation, suggesting that this may not be a critical determinant of goal orientation as conceptualized in the early work on goal orientation. Instead, it may be that, as proposed by Duda and Nicholls (1992), the more critical determinant of goal orientation is beliefs regarding the causes or reasons for success (high ability vs. high effort).

Although researchers have developed alternative viewpoints and measurement strategies (e.g., Horvath, Scheu, & DeShon, 2001) in the time since these two perspectives were originally forwarded, the conceptualizations and operationalizations of the goal orientation construct formulated by Button et al. (1996) and VandeWalle (1997) remain the most influential in the motivation literature to date.

Work-Motivation Research Findings for Goal Orientation

A large portion of the research on goal orientation conducted to date has focused on its impact on self-efficacy perceptions[2] (Payne et al., 2007). This is not surprising given that many view self-efficacy as a key pathway through which distal constructs influence behavior (e.g., Barrick et al., 1993; Judge & Ilies, 2002; Matsui et al., 1982; Phillips & Gully, 1997), as well as the central role given to self-efficacy in self-regulation models of motivation (Bandura, 1989; Locke & Latham, 2002). In general, these studies have shown a moderate, positive correlation between task-specific self-efficacy and learning goal orientation (e.g., Chen, Gully, Whiteman, & Kilcullen, 2000; Phillips & Gully, 1997; VandeWalle, Brown, Cron, & Slocum, 1999). In contrast to this relatively clear link, the relationship between performance goal orientation and self-efficacy has been much more difficult to pin down. For example, while some have found that a strong performance goal orientation is associated with lower levels of self-efficacy (e.g., Ford, Smith, Weissbein, Gully, & Salas, 1998; Phillips & Gully, 1997), others have found that a strong performance goal orientation is positively related to self-efficacy (e.g., Breland & Donovan, 2005; Kozlowski et al., 2001), or observed no significant relationship between the two variables (e.g., Bell & Kozlowski, 2002; Chen et al., 2000). The split of performance goal orientation into the performance-prove and performance-avoid dimensions advocated by VandeWalle (1997) appears to have helped clarify this situation somewhat in the sense that performance-avoid orientation generally exhibits a significant (albeit weak) negative relationship with self-efficacy (e.g., Payne et al., 2007; VandeWalle, Cron, & Slocum, 2001). However, the remaining dimension (performance-prove orientation) has not displayed any consistent relationship with self-efficacy, as evidenced by the population correlation reported by Payne et al. (2007; $\rho = .03$) and by the nonsignificant findings observed in the literature (e.g., VandeWalle et al., 2001).

Moving beyond self-efficacy, goal orientation has also been linked to feedback-seeking behaviors (Ashford & Cummings, 1983), although the research literature in this area is not nearly as extensive. Research has generally shown that the degree to which individuals seek out feedback is positively correlated with the strength of one's learning goal orientation (e.g., Payne et al., 2007: $\rho = .24$; Porath & Bateman, 2006; VandeWalle & Cummings, 1997; VandeWalle, Ganesan, Challagalla, & Brown, 2000), and negatively correlated with their level of performance-avoid goal orientation (Payne et al., 2007: $\rho = -.27$; Porath & Bateman, 2006). As with self-efficacy, the influence of performance-prove goal orientation on feedback seeking tends to be somewhat inconsistent, with some studies finding positive effects (e.g., Porath & Bateman, 2006), and others reporting negative relationships (Tuckey, Brewer, & Williamson, 2002) or no significant relationship (Payne et al., 2007: $\rho = -.01$). Perhaps the most interesting findings regarding the link between goal orientation and feedback-seeking behavior are those indicating that it may be more informative (and precise) to examine how the goal orientation dimensions are related to the type of feedback that individuals seek (e.g., diagnostic vs. normative), although relatively few studies have been published on this topic to date (e.g., Janssen & Prins, 2007; Park, Schmidt, Scheu, & DeShon, 2007).

Moving past self-efficacy and feedback seeking, the literature linking goal orientation to motivational processes has been more scattered, with a smaller number of studies suggesting that goal orientation is linked to (a) the extent to which individuals revise their performance goals after receiving performance feedback (Cron, Slocum, VandeWalle, & Fu, 2005; Donovan & Hafsteinsson, 2006; Schmidt, Dolis, & Tolli, 2009), (b) the learning strategies and metacognitive processes exhibited by individuals (e.g., Lee, Sheldon, & Turban, 2003; Schmidt & Ford, 2003), (c) experienced anxiety in achievement settings (e.g., Chen et al., 2000), and (d) the performance trajectories displayed by individuals (e.g., Chen & Mathieu, 2008). Interestingly, a handful of studies have also found that the effects of goal orientation on self-regulatory and motivational processes may depend on task characteristics (e.g., Barron & Harackiewicz, 2001; Yeo, Loft, Xiao, & Kiewitz, 2009). For example, research by Steele-Johnson and colleagues (Mangos & Steele-Johnson, 2001; Steele-Johnson, Beauregard, Hoover, & Schmidt, 2000) suggests that the beneficial effects of a strong learning goal orientation may be lessened when individuals are asked to perform routine, simple, or nonchallenging tasks.

Taken as a whole, one can draw several generalized conclusions regarding the impact of goal orientation on motivational processes and outcomes based on these findings. First, learning goal orientation tends to display the most consistent and unambiguous link with critical outcome variables such as self-efficacy, while performance goal orientation (particularly the performance-prove dimension) tends to be much more inconsistent. Second, learning goal orientation is frequently observed to have a positive effect on motivational outcomes, while performance-avoid goal orientation tends to have a negative influence on self-regulatory variables. Third, much of the research efforts to date have focused on the prediction of self-efficacy, with much less research attention allocated to other outcomes and/or processes. Fourth, despite early assertions that theory of ability is a primary determinant of goal orientation (e.g., Dweck, 1986), research conducted in the work motivation domain has not supported this assertion (Button et al., 1996; Payne et al., 2007; VandeWalle, 1997).

At a more general level, the research findings clearly indicate that goal orientation has the potential to exert a significant influence on critical self-regulatory processes and/or outcomes. However, we believe that these findings need to be interpreted with some care, as there are a number of significant methodological and conceptual issues that have plagued goal orientation research. As noted by DeShon and Gillespie (2005), "Despite the widespread study of goal orientation, the literature on this construct is in disarray" (p. 1096). Given the recent reviews providing detailed discussion of the conceptual and methodological limitations in this literature (e.g., DeShon & Gillespie, 2005; Payne et al., 2007), we will not present an exhaustive review of these limitations, but instead emphasize what we feel are the most critical issues.

Critical Issues in the Goal Orientation Literature

At the most basic level, although one would assume that researchers would have settled on a particular conceptualization of goal orientation by now, there exists a fundamental disagreement about the appropriate number of goal orientation dimensions (i.e., two vs. three).[3] This lack of agreement is rather troubling, not to mention surprising, given that many researchers have embraced the notion that a three-dimensional conceptualization best represents this construct space (e.g., Elliot & Church, 1997; Elliot & Harackiewicz, 1996), and the complete lack of counter-arguments, suggesting the superiority of a two-dimensional approach. Nonetheless, research in this area continues to utilize the two-dimensional structure (e.g., Chen & Mathieu, 2008), or, with even greater limitations, to operationalize performance goal orientation as an either/or phenomenon in which individuals hold *either* a performance orientation *or* a learning orientation (e.g., Mangos & Steele-Johnson, 2001). These inconsistencies have produced a fragmented research literature that makes it difficult to draw firm conclusions about the impact of the goal orientation dimensions on motivational processes. At a more general level, these inconsistencies also indicate a lack of conceptual and theoretical clarity surrounding goal orientation. While some have attempted to deal with these inconsistencies post hoc (e.g., "translating" the results of research using a two-dimensional perspective into a three-dimensional framework; Payne et al., 2007), this simply hides the significant lack of agreement in the literature regarding how to define goal orientation.

A second issue concerns the wide array of measures that have been used to operationalize goal orientation in the research literature. As noted by DeShon and Gillespie (2005), there is no agreement or consistency in the measures utilized, with many researchers opting to use "home-grown" measures that contain significant alterations of established measures (e.g., Seijts, Latham, Tasa, & Latham, 2004), or are created solely for use in a particular study (e.g., Caldwell, Herold, & Fedor, 2004). This inconsistency is even more problematic when one considers the diversity of content represented in different measures of putatively the same construct in the sense that (a) some of these measures are specific to a particular setting or domain (e.g., VandeWalle, 1997), while others assess goal orientation across a variety of contexts (e.g., Button et al., 1996), and (b) some studies measure goal orientation as a stable, dispositional trait (e.g., Bell & Kozlowski, 2002), while others assess it as a situational variable that fluctuates according to changes in the environment (e.g., Dragoni, 2005). Unfortunately, these notable differences among measures are largely ignored when researchers draw conclusions and make generalizations about goal orientation based upon the results of their particular study.

Conclusion

While the goal orientation construct is clearly one of the more popular individual differences in the current work motivation literature, our review also makes clear that there are significant issues/limitations that need to be addressed before we can draw firm conclusions about this construct and its role in predicting motivated behavior in organizational environments. Thus, despite the significant body of research that has accumulated on goal orientation in the work-motivation domain, we believe that there is much more work to be done on this construct.

Motivational Traits and Skills

Seeking to integrate motivational approaches to personality and self-regulatory perspectives on motivation, Kanfer and Heggestad (1997) proposed a framework that included both motivational personality traits and motivational skill constructs. Motivational traits were defined "as stable, trans-situational individual differences in preferences related to approach and avoidance of goal-directed effort expenditures" (Heggestad & Kanfer, 2000, p. 753). Consistent with long-standing perspectives that motivation involves both appetitive and avoidance-oriented behaviors, Kanfer and Heggestad (1997) built the trait aspect of their framework around two broadly defined motivational trait complexes: achievement-related traits and anxiety-related traits (see Figure 6.1). While the achievement trait complex encompasses traits characterized by approach-oriented tendencies, the anxiety trait complex encompasses traits characterized by avoidance-oriented tendencies. Motivational skill constructs were aligned with each of the trait complexes. More specifically, the authors suggested that motivation control skills were associated with the achievement trait complex, and emotion control skills were associated with the anxiety trait complex. We discuss the motivational trait and skill (MTS) components of the framework in greater detail in the following sections.

Motivational Traits

Having defined the motivational trait domain in terms of the two broad trait complexes, Kanfer and Heggestad (1997; Heggestad & Kanfer, 2000) set out to identify specific motivational traits within each complex. Based on reviews of the achievement motivation literature and conceptualizations of achievement-oriented traits within more broadly defined taxonomic representations of the personality trait domain, Kanfer and Heggestad (1997) defined two motivational traits within the achievement complex. The first trait, personal mastery, represents a tendency to take on tasks and challenges with an eye toward self-development. That is, individuals with a high standing on this trait engage in and put forth effort toward tasks with the hope of learning something new or improving their levels of task competence. These individuals are competitive with themselves, and continually seek to improve

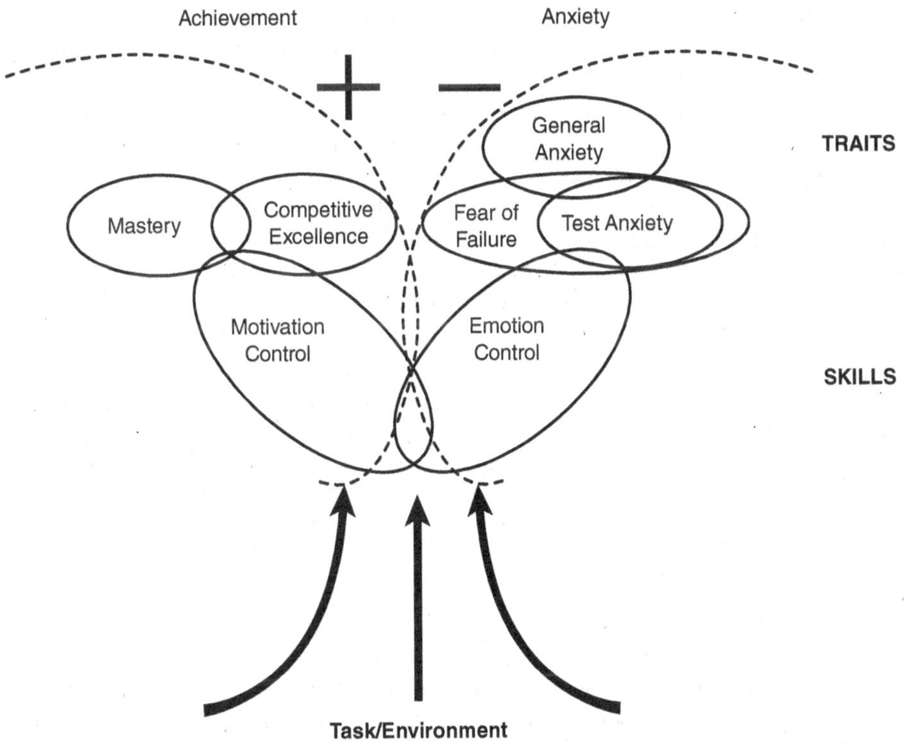

Figure 6.1 Kanfer and Heggestad's (1997) Motivational Traits and Skills (MTS) Framework.

their skills. This form of approach-oriented motivation can be traced back to the early work of Henry Murray (1938), who suggested that the *nAch* could be characterized by a striving "To excel one's self" (p. 164), and captures characteristics similar to various other constructs proposed within the achievement motivation literature—for example, Helmreich and Spence's (1978) mastery, Dweck and Leggett's (1988) learning orientation, and Hough's (1992) trait of achievement.

Kanfer and Heggestad's (1997) second trait, competitive excellence, can also be traced back to the work of Murray (1938), who noted that the need for achievement can also be characterized by a striving "to rival and surpass others" (p. 164). Competitive excellence represents a tendency to seek out and engage in competition with others, and those with a high standing on this trait evaluate their performances based on comparisons to the performance of others. These individuals have a strong desire to gain respect and approval from others, can be competitive to a fault, and may even create competition in situations where it is inappropriate.

Kanfer and Heggestad (1997) suggested that there was a lack of clarity in the literature associated with the anxiety complex, and suggested that it is best represented by the communality between general anxiety, fear of failure, and test anxiety. Based on early work related to anxiety (e.g., Atkinson, 1957; McClelland, 1951; Murray, 1938), Heggestad and Kanfer (2000) initially specified two traits within the anxiety complex. Subsequent empirical examination of the anxiety-based scales designed to represent those traits failed to find evidence that they were distinct constructs. As a revision to their perspective, the authors posited a single trait within the anxiety complex, achievement anxiety, which captures "the avoidance aspects of behavior represented in classic conceptualizations of *n*Infavoidance (Murray, 1938), fear of failure (McClelland et al., 1953), and the motive to avoid failure (Atkinson, 1957; Atkinson & Feather, 1966)," as well as "a tendency to experience anxiety responses within achievement (i.e., failure-threatening) situations" (Heggestad & Kanfer, 2000, pp. 756–757).

There is quite clearly a conceptual overlap between these motivational traits and constructs within the goal orientation framework. Personal mastery and learning goal orientation both represent self-referent, approach-oriented motivational constructs concerned with self-improvement and task mastery. Competitive excellence and performance-prove goal orientation both represent other-referent, approach-oriented motivational constructs concerned with doing better than others and proving one's worth in a normative sense. Meanwhile, achievement anxiety and performance-avoid goal orientation both represent avoidance-oriented constructs concerned with avoiding negative outcomes. It is important to consider, however, that personal mastery and competitive excellence conceptualize and account for unique portions of the achievement trait complex ignored by goal orientation. These include hard work, *nAch* (Murray, 1938), competitive acquisitiveness (Jackson, Ahmed, & Heapy, 1976), and dominance (Cassidy & Lynn, 1989). Similarly, achievement anxiety conceptually accounts for portions of the anxiety construct space that performance-avoid goal orientation fails to consider; specifically, *nInfavoidance* (Murray, 1938), debilitating anxiety (Alpert & Haber, 1960), and worry-emotionality (Morris, Davis, & Hutching, 1981). Although there is notable overlap, we believe that the construct coverage provided by the MTS framework provides more theoretical breadth and possibly a more comprehensive account of both the broadly defined achievement and anxiety trait domains.

Motivational Skills

In addition to motivational traits, the framework proposed by Kanfer and Heggestad (1997) included motivational skills, defined as "integrated, self-regulatory competencies engaged during goal striving" (p. 39). Essentially, motivational skills are strategies individuals can employ to maintain effort, persistence, and/or attention on a task when they experience difficulties in goal-directed action. Drawing on the work of Kuhl (1985; see also Kanfer & Ackerman, 1996), Kanfer and Heggestad identified two broad motivational skill constructs within their framework: motivation control and emotion control.

Motivation control skills represent strategies to maintain high levels of attention and effort toward task performance for well-learned tasks that have become rote or overlearned, and where vigilance is a key determinant of success. In these situations, motivation control skills include strategies that aid the individual in maintaining levels of effort and attention despite boredom and the inclination toward a lack of attention. Examples of motivation control skills include setting performance goals for oneself or creating imaginary rewards and punishments for different levels of performance.

While motivation control skills are used to maintain effort levels, emotion control skills are used to deal with emotional states that arise during task performance. In general, these are self-regulatory strategies that allow an individual to maintain attention despite intrusive, focus-diverting emotional states, such as worry. Kanfer, Ackerman, and Heggestad (1996) suggested that "emotion control skills involve the use of self-regulatory processes to keep performance anxiety and other negative emotional reactions (e.g., worry) at bay during task engagement" (pp. 186–187). Thus, in emotion-arousing situations, such as test-taking situations, individuals with strong emotion control skills are better able to maintain focus on the task and perform at a higher level than those with less well-developed emotion control skills. Specific emotion control strategies include relaxation techniques, deep breathing, and positive self-talk.

Traits, Skills, and Environments

Motivational skills are thought to develop from motivational trait standing as well as experiences in relevant environmental contexts. More specifically, individuals with higher levels of personal mastery and competitive excellence are naturally inclined to use motivation control skills in relevant contexts. Furthermore, the motivational control skills of these individuals should grow and develop over time as their trait standings are likely to lead them to select and enter into environments (Buss, 1987) which call for the use of those skills. Likewise, individuals with lower levels of achievement anxiety (i.e., indicating low trait-anxiety levels) are more likely to engage in effective emotion control skills (Kanfer et al., 1996) and are likely to experience situations that aid in the growth and development of those skills.

Given that there are two distinct traits, personal mastery and competitive excellence, associated with motivation control skills, it is expected that the use of specific motivation control strategies employed in a particular context will depend on the relative standing across these motivational traits. For instance, a person with a relatively high standing on personal mastery and a low standing on competitive excellence may engage different motivation control strategies than a person with the opposite standing across the two traits.

Consistent with the notion that motivational skills are influenced by environmental or contextual factors, some research has shown that providing motivational skill training can improve levels of task performance. For example, Bell and Kozlowski (2008) and Kanfer and Ackerman (1996) developed training programs for both emotion control and motivation control skills. Results from these studies indicated that those provided with emotion control training had increased levels of performance earlier in task learning than did those who did not receive the training. Likewise, they found that individuals given motivation control training performed better after the task was well learned than did those not provided training. As such, it is a person's standing on motivational traits as well as the contexts that they experience over time that lead to motivational skills development.

Research on Motivational Traits and Skills

To date, a significant portion of the research devoted to this framework has focused on the development and validation of the Motivational Trait Questionnaire (MTQ; Heggestad & Kanfer, 2000; Kanfer & Ackerman, 2000; Kanfer & Heggestad, 1999), an instrument designed to assess the motivational traits specified in this framework. The evidence obtained in this regard has provided strong support for the construct validity of the measure, demonstrating favorable psychometric properties and appropriate levels of convergent validity with related constructs, such as conscientiousness and achievement (e.g., Heggestad & Kanfer, 2000).

Beyond validation of the MTQ, several studies have examined the relationships between motivational trait constructs, key motivational processes, and organizational outcomes. Although the research has been somewhat sporadic, links between motivational traits and the key motivational processes of self-efficacy (e.g., Arshadi, 2009; Bateman & Donovan, 2010) and goal setting (e.g., Heimerdinger & Hinsz, 2008; Hinsz & Jundt, 2005) have been explored. Research linking motivational traits to organizational outcomes is also sparse but beginning to show promise. Diefendorff and Mehta (2007), for instance, found that personal mastery was negatively correlated with interpersonal and organizational deviance, while achievement anxiety was positively related to organizational deviance. Additionally, Ang, Ng, and Goh (2004) examined how motivational traits were related to self-development organizational citizenship behavior (OCB) and self-ratings of in-role performance. They found that competitive excellence was positively associated with self-development OCB and self-ratings of performance while achievement anxiety was positively associated with self-development OCB but negatively associated with self-ratings of performance.

With regard to the independent effects of motivational skills on outcomes, studies have shown that motivational skills training results in increased levels of performance in training contexts (e.g., Bell & Kozlowski, 2008; Kanfer & Ackerman, 1996). Additionally, preexisting individual differences in motivational skills have been shown to relate to outcomes such as training performance (Kanfer et al., 1996; Keith & Frese, 2005). In an interesting line of research, Wanberg, Kanfer, and Rotundo (1999) found that motivation control skills were positively associated with job search intensity within a sample of unemployed individuals actively engaged in the job search process. Furthermore, motivation control was still predictive of job search intensity when these researchers examined a subsample of people who were still unemployed 3 months after the initial data collection.

Issues With the MTS Framework

Perhaps the most critical issue with this framework is the surprising lack of research attention that has been devoted toward examining and clarifying the role of the identified motivational traits in motivational processes. The empirical research on this framework is sparse, at best, despite the clear potential that this model has for understanding motivated behavior. Although the most consistent findings regarding the framework connect motivational traits with proximal determinants of action (i.e., self-efficacy and goal setting; Bateman & Donovan, 2010; Hinsz & Jundt, 2005), to the best of our knowledge, only two studies (Creed, King, Hood, & McKenzie, 2009; Porath & Bateman, 2006) have investigated the critical mediating role of the proposed motivational skills. Unfortunately, both studies used measures of goal orientation rather than motivational trait measures to explore these relationships. Nonetheless, preliminary support for the mediated model was provided by Creed et al. (2009) who found that motivation control mediated the relationship between learning goal orientation and job-seeking intensity. Findings by Porath and Bateman (2006) were less supportive of the model, suggesting that emotion control skills were negatively related to sales performance and that emotion control skills mediated relationships between learning goal orientation and performance, neither of which is posited by the framework. Given that it is difficult to draw confident conclusions about the MTS framework based upon a handful of studies that have yet to fully test the proposed relationships, it is clear that more research is needed in this area before we can move toward integrating these constructs into more inclusive models of work motivation.

Conclusion

The MTS framework provides many of the necessary components to make it a useful tool in person-centered motivation research. It is cohesive in its treatment of motivational traits and provides proximal pathways through which they affect motivational processes and behavior. To date, the research literature is sparse but promising. Further research is needed to test the linkages between motivational traits and motivational skills, as well as further elucidate the relationships between traits, skills, and organizationally relevant outcomes, such as creativity, task performance, and teamwork.

Regulatory Focus Theory

Regulatory focus theory also conceptualizes human motivation in terms of approach and avoidance but moves beyond classic hedonic principles—approaching pleasure and avoiding pain (Higgins, 1997)—by applying approach and avoidance distinctions to phenomena both within and outside of the person (Higgins, 1999). The crux of regulatory focus theory is a distinction between two coexisting systems of self-regulation, the promotion system and the prevention system. The promotion system develops from nurturance and growth needs, which drive individuals to pursue aspirations, advancement, and *ideal* end states. The promotion system seeks to maximize positive outcomes in the form of *gains* while simultaneously ensuring against *nongains*. In contrast, the prevention system is born out of security and safety needs, which drive individuals to meet responsibilities, obligations, and *ought* end states. The prevention system seeks to maximize the absence of negative outcomes in the form of *nonlosses* while simultaneously ensuring against negative outcomes in the form of *losses*.

A person's regulatory focus is determined by the accessibility of either the promotion or the prevention system. In regulatory focus theory, the variability in access to either system can come from any source in the motivational realm. For instance, the person (e.g., individual differences and goal pursuit strategies), the desired end state (i.e., the goal), or the situation (e.g., laboratory priming or achievement setting) may each initiate the promotion or the prevention system; it is only a matter of which source is accessed that determines a person's regulatory focus for a given episode. In personality terms, a chronic regulatory focus is an individual difference characterized by strong preferences for either the promotion or the prevention of a regulatory system (Higgins & Tykocinski, 1992).

Goal pursuit strategies for those with a chronic promotion focus are driven by discrepancies between their actual state and their *ideal* end state. Promotion-focused individuals are likely to employ eager strategies that maximize *gains* and ensure against *nongains* to remedy any discrepancies. Consider the job of an air traffic controller, which requires individuals to arrange, space, and anticipate an ever-changing array of incoming and outgoing airplanes. Chronically promotion-focused individuals are likely to choose a goal based on *gains/nongains*, in this case, to move airplanes as quickly as possible. They will be driven by any discrepancies between their actual rate of landing and departing airplanes versus their *ideal* (i.e., faster) rate of moving airplanes. Eager goal pursuit strategies could include decreasing the space between airplanes, increasing air speeds, or decreasing allotted time to taxi on the runway. Obviously, these strategies are designed to increase the rate at which airplanes are landing (*gains*) while ensuring against any slowing of the rate at which airplanes land (*nongains*).

Meanwhile, chronically prevention-focused individuals are driven by discrepancies between their actual state and their *ought* end state. Because *oughts* are framed as obligations or responsibilities, prevention-focused individuals are likely to choose a goal based on *nonlosses/losses*, or to move airplanes as safely as possible. These individuals will be driven by discrepancies between their actual probability of landing airplanes safely and their *ought* probability of landing airplanes safely (i.e., landing planes with an increasing probability of safety—a *nonloss*). Prevention-focused individuals are likely to employ vigilant goal pursuit strategies such as increasing the space between airplanes, decreasing air speeds, and allotting more time to taxi on the runway. All of which are designed to maximize safety (*nonlosses*) and ensure against collisions (*losses*).

What stands in contrast to other approach- and avoidance-based theories of motivation is that the promotion and prevention systems are both capable of good performance on the same task by self-regulating in effective (albeit different) ways. Regulatory focus also allows for either system to approach desired end states (either *gains* or *nonlosses*) while avoiding undesired end states (either *nongains* or *losses*). Other individual differences theories (e.g., goal orientation, *nAch*, motivational traits) restrict their individual difference constructs to either approach or avoidance self-regulatory behaviors (i.e., approaching success or avoiding failure). Thus, Higgins and colleagues' chronic promotion and prevention foci provide a more flexible and accurate way of describing human motivation than simply approaching success (pleasure) or avoiding failure (pain).

Regulatory Fit

When congruence occurs between one's regulatory focus and their goal pursuit strategy, Higgins and colleagues (e.g., Avnet & Higgins, 2003; Freitas & Higgins, 2002) argue that people experience a phenomenon called regulatory fit. When fit occurs, the strategy employed to pursue the goal actually sustains and/or increases a person's orientation or regulatory focus for that goal. Fit, then, is a unique phenomenon that increases the motivational intensity of one's goal pursuit by creating a "feels right" sensation that sustains the self-regulation process. Alternatively, when misfit occurs (i.e., when a person's regulatory focus does not fit with their goal pursuit strategies), self-regulation is disrupted and performance suffers. Importantly, fit sustains self-regulation equally well for either promotion- or prevention-focused individuals because it is based solely on the congruence between pursuit strategy and the active regulatory focus system.

Empirical Evidence for Regulatory Focus

Much of the initial research on this perspective occurred in laboratory settings where subjects' regulatory focus was established via induction or assessed as chronic regulatory focus and then related to sensitivities to qualitatively different types of information. Higgins and Tykocinski (1992), for example, found that chronic and induced promotion focus predicted free recall of *gains/nongains* information but not *nonloss/loss* information (vice versa for chronic prevention focus). Higgins, Shah, and Friedman (1997) conducted a series of studies in which promotion-focused and prevention-focused individuals reacted with different emotions to goal attainment and goal failure. Specifically, promotion-focused individuals reacted with emotions along a continuum from cheerfulness to dejection while prevention-focused individuals reacted with emotions along a continuum from quiescence to agitation, demonstrating nicely that promotion- or prevention-focused individuals react with qualitatively different and theoretically appropriate emotional responses to goal attainment and goal failure. This particular body of research is very useful for understanding the various "sensitivities" and "reactions" that are associated with promotion and prevention regulatory focus (for a more thorough review, see Higgins, 1999).

Researchers have begun to diverge from the study of systematic sensitivities toward research focusing on regulatory focus's role in general goal processes. Shah, Higgins, and Friedman (1998), for example, found that goal attainment was higher for subjects with a chronic promotion focus when incentives to perform were also framed in a promotion focus (i.e., a monetary reward), rather than when incentives to perform were framed in a prevention focus (i.e., a monetary nonloss). The same pattern of relationships was found for subjects with a chronic prevention focus and when incentives were framed in either matching or mismatching regulatory foci. Förster, Higgins, and Idson (1998) found systematically different ways in which subjects with either a promotion or a prevention focus exhibited the "goal looms larger" effect. Those with a chronic promotion focus increased effort at a higher rate for an "aspiration" goal as the goal loomed larger than did prevention-focused subjects, while prevention-focused subjects increased effort at a higher rate for a "responsibility" goal than did promotion-focused subjects.

Regulatory focus has also begun to provide useful information regarding feedback in goal pursuit processes. Generally, researchers have found that performance feedback is differentially effective for increasing motivation and subsequent task performance based on the chronic regulatory focus of the feedback target. More specifically, success feedback (i.e., positive feedback) increases intentions to invest further effort and task performance only for those with a chronic promotion focus. Conversely, failure feedback (i.e., negative feedback) increases intentions to invest further effort and task performance for those with a chronic prevention focus (Förster, Grant, Idson, & Higgins, 2001; Idson & Higgins, 2000; Van-Dijk & Kluger, 2004). Findings to date suggest that regulatory focus plays a significant role in self-regulation models of motivation that emphasize reactions to feedback in goal pursuit processes.

Issues in Regulatory Focus Research

Much of the research conducted on regulatory focus to date has occurred in controlled laboratory settings. While this essential research has provided a basic understanding of the principles underlying the perspective and can guide future theory building and research, our understanding of how useful regulatory focus is for predicting motivated behavior in real-world settings remains limited. As such, it is important for researchers to move into more applied settings and test the tenets of regulatory focus in the field, where clear-cut distinctions between the promotion and prevention systems become more opaque. Furthermore, in field settings, the utility of using promotion or prevention regulatory focus as an individual difference depends upon the ability of a researcher/practitioner to accurately identify promotion or prevention information from all sources. A particular challenge is that regulatory focus theory posits that sources of variation occur both within the person (i.e., chronic or induced regulatory focus) and outside of the person (i.e., tasks, feedback, context, etc.), and, as such, they all must be properly accounted for to be able to accurately predict motivated behaviors. Leadership research has demonstrated promise in this regard. For instance, Kark and Van-Dijk (2007) found empirical support for a model of motivation-to-lead and motivation-to-follow using regulatory focus principles in which individuals were more likely to follow a leader with a congruent regulatory focus. Subsequently, DeCremer, Mayer, Van-Dijke, Schouten, and Bardes (2009) demonstrated that the effectiveness of specific leadership styles depends upon the regulatory focus of followers.

A second issue in the regulatory focus literature is the limited nature of associated outcomes. As noted previously, much of this research has focused on the relationship between regulatory focus and information sensitivity or information encoding. The narrowness of these outcomes, however, provides limited perspective on the impact of chronic regulatory focus on a variety of important outcomes. More specifically, without research examining relationships with proximal motivational constructs (e.g., self-efficacy, goal setting) and tangible dependent variables (e.g., task performance, citizenship behavior, teamwork, creativity, etc.), we lack a general sense of regulatory focus's utility for explaining work motivation behaviors. Two studies, presented by Keller and Bless (2006), found that chronic promotion and prevention focus, in conditions of regulatory fit, predicted math test performance and spatial ability test performance in secondary school students. At present, however, studies such as these are the exception rather than the rule in research literature.

The regulatory focus literature also suffers from a lack of a common measurement strategy for assessing chronic regulatory focus. Although not as diverse as goal orientation measures, researchers have used multiple measures to assess chronic regulatory focus with little evidence of cohesion. Haws, Dholakia, and Bearden (2010) showed that five measures of chronic regulatory focus suffer from a lack of convergence, as well as variations in predictive ability and reliability. While this may be a function of regulatory focus's relatively short history, it is a significant limitation that may hinder researchers' ability to synthesize findings now and into the future.

Conclusion

Regulatory focus theory has provided a set of motivational principles that may provide the field with some cohesion by simultaneously accounting for sources of variance within and outside of the person. By doing so, regulatory focus theory provides a potentially important individual difference construct (chronic regulatory focus) within a cohesive framework from which hypotheses of motivated work behavior can be derived. For instance, regulatory focus may moderate the relationship between constructs such as goal orientation and task performance based on the inherent promotion or prevention focus of different tasks or task context. Presently, more research is needed to demonstrate the ability of regulatory focus theory to predict behavior in field settings and to be related to more various outcomes (e.g., task performance). Now and in the future, it is essential for research to provide cohesion for the measurement of chronic regulatory focus, either in the emergence of a single "best" measure or guidance as to which measure to use for a given application.

Future Directions for Theory and Research

Throughout this chapter, we have noted shortcomings of the three motivational conceptualizations presented. While it is certainly necessary and useful to identify problematic areas, it is equally important to identify the critical next steps for theorists and researchers in this domain that help to address these issues as well as maximize the value of future information we collect in individual differences research. Toward this end, this section presents our perspective on a few critical next steps.

Consolidate and Integrate the Individual Differences Literature

Although we have chosen to focus on three of the more popular individual difference approaches to work motivation, we do not mean to imply that these are the only individual differences that exist in relevant research. In fact, even a cursory review of the work-motivation literature reveals an overabundance of individual difference constructs that have been used to explain motivated behavior. While this suggests that researchers in this domain are being thorough in attempts to identify important individual differences, it also raises the critical question of how all of these constructs relate to one another. Given that there appears to be quite a bit of conceptual overlap among the various constructs, we feel it is time for researchers in this area to do a little housecleaning. Efforts to establish interrelationships among existing individual difference constructs, carefully evaluating the unique contribution of newly proposed individual differences (over and above those that already exist), are critical if we are to continue making meaningful progress without overwhelming researchers with a plethora of redundant constructs representing the motivational domain.

These types of efforts will require that researchers not only evaluate the current set of constructs to ensure that newly introduced constructs are meaningfully distinct (i.e., not conceptually redundant), but also that they investigate historical research to ensure that similar constructs have not already been proposed, measured, and studied. To illustrate, the construct of fear of negative evaluation (Leary, 1983) is remarkably similar to notions of performance goal orientation (primarily a performance-avoid orientation), yet there is very little acknowledgment of the earlier construct or efforts to determine how performance goal orientation increments what we had previously learned from research on the fear of negative evaluation (for an exception, see VandeWalle, 1997). Undoubtedly, much of the current work on individual differences in motivation borrows heavily from the *nAch* and achievement motive literatures (e.g., Atkinson, 1957; Murray, 1938), yet there is often little recognition of the research conducted in this early literature when developing or utilizing newly formed individual difference constructs. It seems that we tend to have a very short memory in the individual differences domain in the sense that new constructs are frequently proposed without proper acknowledgment of existing constructs that may have provided redundant information about individuals. Until this issue is addressed, we fear that this research domain will suffer from continued issues of construct redundancy and "old wine in new bottles."

In sum, we believe that this field would benefit more from attempts to develop an integrative framework of extant individual differences, than from introducing new constructs. The development of this type of framework would allow us to not only identify and eliminate redundant constructs but also guide research to unexplored areas or areas in need of clarification. To this end, we believe that the MTS framework (e.g., Kanfer & Heggestad, 1997) represents an excellent first step. This model's efforts at integrating previously developed constructs and underlying themes within individual differences literature is precisely the type of work that is needed.

To illustrate the integrative nature of the MTS more precisely, the work of Kanfer and colleagues (e.g., Heggestad & Kanfer, 2000) explicitly outlines how the MTS framework not only incorporates Murray's (1938) work on needs and subsequent research on the achievement motive but also incorporates more recent constructs such as goal orientation and aspects of conscientiousness. The conceptual overlap with the goal orientation construct is particularly relevant, given the immense popularity of goal orientation in the research literature. As noted previously, personal mastery and learning goal orientation both represent self-referent, approach-oriented motivational constructs concerned with self-improvement and task mastery, while competitive excellence and performance-prove goal orientation both represent other-referent, approach-oriented motivational constructs concerned with normative comparisons and doing better than others. Similarly, achievement anxiety and performance-avoid goal orientation both represent avoidance-oriented constructs concerned with avoiding negative outcomes. Given this overlap and the fact that the MTS framework also captures unique aspects of the achievement and anxiety trait complexes that are ignored by goal orientation, the MTS framework holds great potential in helping to make sense of a scattered and disorganized individual differences literature by offering an opportunity for consolidation under the heading of three broad motivational traits. Although this framework has yet to receive extensive research attention, our hope is that future researchers devote more time not only to examining the propositions outlined by Kanfer and Heggestad but also toward assessing the utility of their framework for integrating the individual differences literature.

It is worth noting at this point that, although the MTS framework incorporates the goal orientation framework quite nicely, it is less clear as to how regulatory focus would fit into this integrative model. While regulatory focus embraces the approach/avoidance framework that is common to both MTS and goal orientation, the link between regulatory focus and these other constructs is unclear at present due to the lack of theoretical and empirical work examining this linkage. As such, the move toward an integrated model of individual differences will require additional work examining how regulatory focus is related to/distinct from the constructs in the MTS framework. During this process, it is important for researchers to consider the possibility that regulatory focus is not simply another set of individual differences that needs to be consolidated within the three motivational traits or three goal orientation dimensions. Instead, it is equally likely that regulatory focus may serve as a moderator of the effects of the MTS/goal orientation variables on important self-regulatory outcomes. As noted previously, research has demonstrated the impact of regulatory focus on sensitivities to certain types of information in the environment, suggesting that regulatory focus has the potential to influence how motivational traits may manifest themselves in a given situation. Furthermore, the effects of the MTS variables in a given situation may be dependent upon the degree of regulatory fit/misfit experienced by the individual. Although these possibilities are simply speculation at this point, we believe that future integrative efforts would benefit from their exploration, rather than simply focusing on the main effects of regulatory focus within an integrated model of individual differences.

Recognize the Multifaceted Nature of Goal Orientation

A significant debate within the individual differences literature in recent years revolves around the nature of the goal orientation construct: Is goal orientation a trait, a state, a domain-specific trait, or a quasi-trait that displays the properties of both a state and trait (Button et al., 1996; DeShon & Gillespie, 2005; Payne et al., 2007; VandeWalle, 1997)? As noted previously, there is substantial disagreement about how goal orientation should be conceptualized and measured. The result is a literature in which researchers are conceptualizing and measuring goal orientations in wildly different manners and at the same time attempting to draw conclusions about a generalizable, unified goal orientation construct. To illustrate,[4] while Phillips and Gully (1997) utilized a trait-based view of goal orientation in which goal orientation was assumed to be a stable, universal trait that applied equally to all situations, Steele-Johnson et al. (2000) conceptualized goal orientation as a situational construct that could be manipulated through the use of instructional sets, and VandeWalle et al. (2001) measured goal orientation as a domain-specific individual difference that is assumed to vary *across* life's major domains yet stay relatively stable *within* those domains. The fact that these researchers view goal orientation from such different perspectives is not problematic in and of itself. Instead, the problem arises when these researchers all attempt to make generalized conclusions about a single goal orientation construct based upon these diverse conceptualizations and operationalizations.

While one response to this situation would be to suggest that we, as a field, come to a single, agreed-upon conceptualization of goal orientation, we feel that this approach is unlikely to be successful and (more importantly) would inaccurately characterize the true nature of the goal orientation construct space. Instead, rather than trying to find a single "correct" answer to the question of whether goal orientation is a state, a trait, or a domain-specific trait, we believe that this research literature would benefit more from a recognition that goal orientation is a multifaceted individual difference construct that exists at multiple levels.

Specifically, we propose that future research would benefit from actively acknowledging that goal orientation as a construct exists at (a) the general, dispositional level, (b) the domain-specific level (e.g., goal orientation in work environments), and (c) the situational or state level (see Figure 6.2). While this notion may be viewed as somewhat of a "cop out," we feel that it is both justified and more accurate than trying to pigeon-hole a multilevel construct into a singular conceptualization, especially given the vast research literature demonstrating that goal orientation is both amenable to situational influence *and* stable over time (depending on how it is operationalized), and that individuals may adopt different goal orientations in different domains of their life (e.g., work vs. academic environments). Recognition of the multilevel nature of goal orientation would necessitate that researchers be more precise in formulating discussions of goal orientation as it relates to a particular study (and method of operationalization) instead of discussing goal orientation as a general construct. In doing so, this would likely render some of the issues identified within the goal orientation literature moot (DeShon & Gillespie, 2005), while helping to alleviate some of the inconsistent findings currently plaguing the literature.

To facilitate this move toward a multifaceted perspective on goal orientation, we suggest that researchers begin to adopt a standardized terminology when discussing goal orientation at these multiple levels. The term "chronic goal orientation" could be used to describe a general tendency

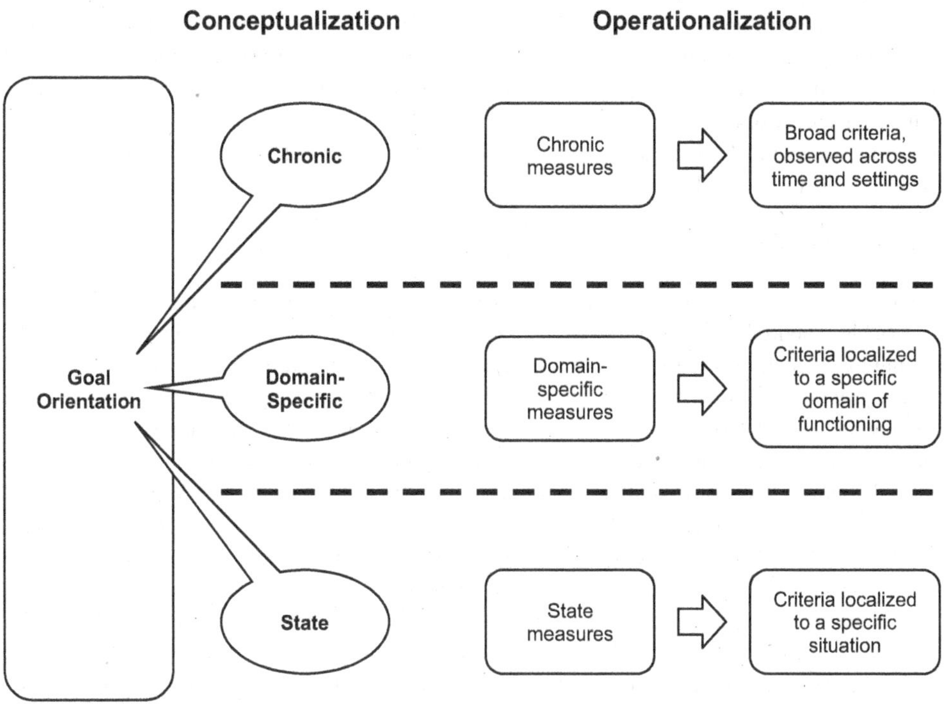

Figure 6.2 Multilevel Conceptualization and Operationalization of the Goal Orientation Construct.

held by individuals across situations in their life (e.g., Button et al., 1996). "Domain-specific goal orientation" would describe goal orientation tendencies that are specific to a particular domain, which might be based upon one's chronic goal orientation but is not assumed to be identical or even closely related to this chronic orientation (since individuals are likely to match their orientations to the situations they are placed in). "State goal orientation" would describe the goal orientations that an individual holds at a particular point in time, influenced strongly by situational characteristics (e.g., competition with others, reward structure, recent success or failure) and therefore expected to be variable over time.

The end result of this multilevel perspective on goal orientation is that researchers would begin to generate bodies of knowledge that address specific levels of goal orientation (chronic, domain-specific, state), rather than operating under the mistaken premise that goal orientation is a single, unified individual difference with either two or three dimensions. As an added bonus, this perspective may also facilitate the development and adoption of standardized measures of goal orientation, rather than the hodgepodge of measures that characterizes the current goal orientation literature (DeShon & Gillespie, 2005). This should create a much cleaner, focused research literature that facilitates drawing conclusions about the nature of goal orientation, while also allowing researchers and practitioners to "match" their operationalization of goal orientation to the outcomes they are interested in predicting. Consistent with work by Fishbein and Ajzen (1975; Ajzen, 1991), researchers would be able to match their operationalization of goal orientation to the level of specificity of the outcomes they wish to predict, which should result in stronger, more consistent observed relationships. Given that most research in the work motivation domain is interested in predicting proximal antecedents of motivated behavior (e.g., self-efficacy), this would suggest that measures of state goal orientation (rather than the more commonly used measures of chronic or domain-specific goal orientation) would hold the most value for motivation researchers. This would represent a significant departure from the current goal orientation literature, but likely would be accompanied by the emergence of clearer relationships between goal orientation and motivational constructs (a trend that can be seen in the meta-analytic work by Payne et al., 2007). Ultimately, while the transition to this multilevel perspective would require considerable work and adjustment by researchers, we feel that the benefits in the long run would be well worth it.

Examine Individual Differences From a Person-Oriented Perspective

In general, researchers examining individual differences in the work-motivation literature tend to take a "variable-oriented" approach in that they explore and report the main effects of each individual difference on the outcomes of interest separately, with little consideration of how various combinations of these constructs might interact or work together to influence these outcomes. To illustrate, researchers who study goal orientation tend to examine the independent effects of the three goal orientation dimensions on outcomes such as self-efficacy, with no consideration given to the simultaneous effects of individuals' standing on all three dimensions (i.e., in terms of a goal orientation profile) on this outcome (DeShon & Gillespie, 2005; for notable exceptions, see Porter, Webb, & Gogus, 2010; Yeo, Sorbello, Koy, & Smillie, 2008). This is particularly troubling given the repeated suggestions in the literature that the goal orientation dimensions likely work together to produce motivational outcomes (e.g., a strong performance goal orientation is not problematic when accompanied by a strong learning goal orientation; Button et al., 1996).

It is unfortunate that this failure to examine how individual differences work in concert to influence outcomes of interest is not limited to the goal orientation literature, but characterizes much of the research on individual differences in work motivation. The obvious importance of interactions among the individual differences constructs, or profiles of constructs, is in understanding their impact in real-world settings (i.e., where all individual differences are present and operating simultaneously). Our continued focus on studying the independent effects of each individual difference construct is likely providing a very limited, if not factually incorrect, understanding of how they operate in organizational environments. To illustrate, there is some initial work in the goal orientation domain suggesting that the inconsistent results observed across studies for the performance-prove goal orientation dimension may be due to a failure to consider the individual's simultaneous standing on the remaining goal orientation dimensions (e.g., Donovan, Esson, & Backert, 2007). That is, the effects of the performance-prove goal orientation dimension may depend on the level of learning and performance-avoid goal orientation held by that individual. For example, work by Donovan et al. (2007) suggested that a strong performance-prove goal orientation is associated with high levels of self-efficacy when coupled with a strong learning goal orientation, yet associated with lower levels of self-efficacy when paired with a strong performance-avoid goal orientation. As such, research examining the isolated, main effects of this dimension without considering the levels of all three dimensions together is likely to provide us with a misleading understanding of the true effects of performance-prove goal orientation.

To remedy this issue, we believe that future theory and research should move toward a "person-oriented" perspective (e.g., Magnusson, 2000), in which patterns or profiles of individual differences are examined with respect to motivational outcomes. Researchers have noted that a pattern approach to studying individual differences may account for more variance in outcome variables than individual dimensions alone (e.g., Barron & Harackiewicz, 2001; Foti & Hauenstein, 2007) and may help to clarify some of the inconsistent findings in the goal orientation literature (Harackiewicz, Barron, Pintrich, Elliot, & Thrash, 2002). As such, we believe that a person-centered approach holds considerable potential for research in work motivation and should be embraced by empirical and theoretical work in the individual differences domain.

Recognize the Impact of the Situation

We have known for a long time that both traits and situations are important drivers of behavior. As we discussed earlier, Murray discussed the influences of both needs (i.e., traits) and presses (i.e., situational characteristics) on resulting behavior as early as 1938. Yet, today's researchers still lament that the impact of situations is not sufficiently recognized in motivation research (e.g., Johns, 2006; Kanfer, 2009). We echo that sentiment. In contemporary research, interactionist theories such as trait activation (Tett & Guterman, 2000; Chapter 5, this volume) have begun to provide insight into situation characteristics that impact relationships between individual differences and behavior. More specifically, researchers have found that situations provide trait-relevant cues that prompt expression of trait-relevant behaviors and that without relevant cues, relationships between individual differences and behavior become constrained (Lievens, Chasteen, Day, & Christiansen, 2006). Unfortunately, modern theories of individual differences in motivation do not regularly account for situational effects, and the result is an incomplete body of findings.

More complete models of individual differences in motivation should consider situational influences. The three-level model of goal orientation (Figure 6.2) and MTS theory have already built in locations where systematic situational influence is likely to manifest itself. For instance, state-goal orientation is likely to be tied to the characteristics of a given task, while domain-goal orientation is likely to depend upon social cues from the specified life-domain. Importantly, both propositions can be situated nicely with Christiansen and Tett's (2008) contention that trait-relevant situational features operate in three distinct levels: task, social, and organizational. MTS theory argues motivational skills constructs—learned self-regulatory competencies that depend simultaneously on traits and situations—and is where situational influence is likely to manifest itself. In this framework, the effectiveness of self-regulatory behaviors for a given task depend on both the person's level of development of the motivational skill and the extent to which those motivational skills provide competence for the situation at hand. Fortunately, Tett and Burnett (2003) provide five features of the situation (i.e., job demands, distracters, constraints, releasers, and facilitators) that may determine the adequacy of a given self-regulation strategy for a particular situation. However, research systematically linking situational features, motivational skills, and motivational traits in models of work behavior has yet to be completed. Specifically, while the goal orientation and MTS frameworks simply acknowledge how situations might influence the motivational processes, they do not provide a nuanced account of the important characteristics of the situations and how those specific characteristics might operate to influence motivational process and outcomes.

In contrast, regulatory focus theory's promotion and prevention systems appear better able to capture and understand systematic variance in situations, self-regulation, and individuals. As such, we may be able to use these principles to help clarify relationships between traits from other theories (i.e., MTS), behavior, and situations. Consider, for example, specifying a model in which performance is determined by individual differences, self-regulation, and the characteristics of the task itself. The task can be defined in terms of characteristics that initiate either the promotion or the prevention system and a researcher can then use principles from regulatory focus to predict the self-regulatory behaviors that would be most effective for the task. From MTS theory, the most effective motivational skills would be those that are congruent with the regulatory system that has been initiated by the task. In the same way, researchers may predict which individual differences constructs (i.e., motivational traits) would be most congruent with the activated regulatory system and most likely to yield effective regulatory behaviors. Such an "overlay" of regulatory focus theory onto existing theories of individual differences in motivation such as MTS and GO (goal orientation) is not out of the realm of possibility, especially considering that the genesis of all theories discussed in this chapter are derived from the critical distinction between approach and avoidance motivation.

Conclusion

Our primary goal for this chapter was to review and evaluate three of the more promising individual difference frameworks present in the work-motivation literature. In doing so, we hope that we have not only identified strengths and limitations of each of these frameworks, but that we have provided a roadmap for future researchers to follow in the hopes of continuing to make meaningful progress in this field. As we have noted several times, although motivation scholars have been working on the study of individual differences in motivation for quite some time, there is still much work that remains to be done, particularly with respect to (a) integrating the various individual difference constructs, (b) examining individual differences from a multilevel perspective, (c) looking at the effects of individual differences from a person-oriented perspective, and (d) acknowledging and studying the impact of the situation.

Practitioner's Window

Practitioners of the organizational sciences have long been interested in employee motivation. The trait motivation perspectives discussed in this chapter have potential practical implications for selection, employee management, and development.

Selection

- As organizations desire a hard-working, goal-oriented workforce, the chronic motivational constructs described in this chapter could be usefully incorporated into hiring processes.
- It must be noted that each of these perspectives includes multiple traits, each of which may not be relevant for a particular job. Thus, as with all selection systems, the choice of predictors should be guided by an understanding of the criterion. For example, performance in jobs that require individuals to engage in continuous learning or to work autonomously in unstructured environments may be well predicted by personal mastery or learning orientation but not by competitive excellence or performance-prove orientation.

Management

- Research suggests that individuals will perform best when the work context is aligned with their chronic motivational tendencies. For example, a person with a high standing on competitive excellence may perform best in jobs that reward outperforming others.
- Thus, if a manager were aware of an employee's chronic motivational tendencies, then he or she might be able to structure jobs to maximize that employee's motivation.

Development

- Chronic motivational dispositions are difficult to change; it is their stability over time and across situations that makes them traits. However, research reviewed in this chapter suggests that motivational skills training and feedback mechanisms can be developed to "overcome" or maximize the utility of a person's dispositional tendencies.
- Leaders with motivational traits that are not optimal for his or her current or future roles may benefit from motivational skills training, counteracting any chronic detriments. For example, if

a leader has a detrimental standing on achievement anxiety, then emotion control training may help him or her perform better in the future.

In terms of feedback, providing performance information in ways that are congruent with a worker's chronic motivational tendency is much more likely to successfully change behavior and increase performance.

Notes

1 In recent years, both four-dimensional (Elliot & McGregor, 2001) and six-dimensional (Elliot & Thrash, 2001) approaches to goal orientation have appeared in the literature. However, due to the limited research conducted to date on these perspectives, as well as the fact that these approaches may have restricted applicability to a broad range of situations, we focus our attention here on the two- and three-dimensional approaches to goal orientation that dominate this literature.

2 Although a number of studies have examined goal setting (or the tandem of self-efficacy and goal setting together) as a direct outcome of goal orientation (e.g., VandeWalle, Cron, & Slocum, 2001), we focus here on the literature linking goal orientation to self-efficacy, as this is a well-established precursor to goal setting (Locke & Latham, 1990), and a number of studies have suggested that the effects of goal orientation on goal setting are mediated by self-efficacy (e.g., Diefendorff, 2004; Phillips & Gully, 1997).

3 This lack of clarity regarding a goal orientation definition is even more apparent when one considers the broader array of alternative approaches to goal orientation that have been proposed (Elliot & McGregor, 2001; Elliot & Thrash, 2001).

4 Please note that we are not suggesting that these studies are deficient or problematic in any way, but instead we are suggesting to simply use them to highlight the diversity of conceptualizations forwarded in the goal orientation literature.

References

Ajzen, I. (1987). Attitudes, traits, and actions: Dispositional prediction of behavior in personality and social psychology. In L. Berkowitz (Ed.), *Advances in experimental social psychology* (Vol. 20, pp. 1–63). New York, NY: Academic Press.

Ajzen, I. (1991). The theory of planned behavior. *Organizational Behavior and Human Decision Processes, 50*, 179–211.

Alpert, R., & Haber, R. N. (1960). Anxiety in academic situations. *Journal of Abnormal and Social Psychology, 61*, 207–215.

Ang, S., Ng, K., & Goh, K. (2004). Motivational traits and self-development OCB: A dimensional and configural analysis. In D. L. Turnipseed (Ed.), *Handbook of organizational citizenship behavior* (pp. 265–287). New York, NY: Nova Science Publishers.

Arshadi, N. (2009). Motivational traits and work motivation: Mediating role of self-efficacy. *Journal of Education and Psychology, 3*, 67–80.

Ashford, S. J., & Cummings, L. L. (1983). Feedback as an individual resource: Personal strategies of creating information. *Organizational Behavior and Human Performance, 32*, 370–398.

Atkinson, J. W. (1957). Motivational determinants of risk-taking behavior. *Psychological Review, 64*, 359–372.

Atkinson, J. W., & Feather, N. T. (1966). *A theory of achievement motivation*. New York, NY: Wiley.

Atkinson, J. W., & Litwin, G. H. (1960). Achievement motive and test anxiety conceived as motive to approach success and motive to avoid failure. *Journal of Abnormal and Social Psychology, 60*, 52–61.

Atkinson, J. W., & McClelland, D. C. (1948). The projective expression of needs. II. The effect of different intensities of the hunger drive on thematic apperception. *Journal of Experimental Psychology, 38*, 643–658.

Austin, J. T., & Klein, H. J. (1996). Work motivation and goal striving. In K. R. Murphy (Ed.), *Individual differences and behavior in organizations* (pp. 209–257). San Francisco: Jossey-Bass.

Avnet, T., & Higgins, E. T. (2003). Locomotion, assessment, and regulatory fit: Value transfer from "how" to "what." *Journal of Experimental Social Psychology, 39*, 525–530.

Bandura, A. (1986). *Social foundations of thought and action: A social cognitive theory*. Englewood Cliffs, NJ: Prentice Hall.

Bandura, A. (1989). Self-regulation of motivation and action through internal standards and goal systems. In L. A. Pervin (Ed.), *Goal concepts in personality and social psychology* (pp. 19–85). Hillsdale, NJ: Lawrence Erlbaum Associates.

Barrick, M. R., Mount, M. K., & Strauss, J. P. (1993). Conscientiousness and performance of sales representatives: Test of the mediating effects of goal setting. *Journal of Applied Psychology, 78*, 715–722.

Barron, K. E., & Harackiewicz, J. M. (2001). Achievement goals and optimal motivation: Testing multiple goal models. *Journal of Personality and Social Psychology, 80*, 706–722.

Bateman, T., & Donovan, J. J. (2010, April). *Motivational traits as predictors of task self-efficacy*. Paper presented at the 25th annual conference of the Society for Industrial and Organizational Psychology, Atlanta, GA.

Bell, B. S., & Kozlowski, S. W. J. (2002). Goal orientation and ability: Interactive effects on self-efficacy, performance, and knowledge. *Journal of Applied Psychology, 87*, 497–505.

Bell, B. S., & Kozlowski, S. W. J. (2008). Active learning: Effects of core training design elements on self-regulatory processes, learning, and adaptability. *Journal of Applied Psychology, 93*, 296–316.

Breland, B. T., & Donovan, J. J. (2005). The role of state goal orientation in the goal establishment process. *Human Performance, 18*, 23–53.

Buss, D. M. (1987). Selection, evocation, and manipulation. *Journal of Personality and Social Psychology, 53*, 1214–1221.

Button, S. B., Mathieu, J. E., & Zajac, D. M. (1996). Goal orientation in organizational research: A conceptual and empirical foundation. *Organizational Behavior and Human Decision Processes, 67*, 26–48.

Caldwell, S. D., Herold, D. M., & Fedor, D. B. (2004). Toward an understanding of the relationship between organizational change, individual differences, and changes in person–environmental fit: A cross-level study. *Journal of Applied Psychology, 89*, 868–882.

Campbell, J. P., & Pritchard, R. D. (1976). Motivation theory in industrial and organizational psychology. In M. D. Dunnette (Ed.), *Handbook of industrial and organizational psychology* (pp. 63–130). Chicago: Rand McNally.

Campion, M. A., & Lord, R. G. (1982). A control systems conceptualization of the goal setting and changing process. *Organizational Behavior and Human Performance, 30*, 265–287.

Cassidy, T., & Lynn, R. (1989). A multifactorial approach to achievement motivation: The development of a comprehensive measure. *Journal of Occupational Psychology, 62*, 301–312.

Chen, G., Gully, S. M., Whiteman, J. A., & Kilcullen, R. N. (2000). Examination of relationships among trait-like individual differences, state-like individual differences, and learning performance. *Journal of Applied Psychology, 85*, 835–847.

Chen, G., & Mathieu, J. E. (2008). Goal orientation dispositions and performance trajectories: The roles of supplementary and complementary situational inducements. *Organizational Behavior and Human Decision Processes, 106*, 21–38.

Christiansen, N. D., & Tett, R. P. (2008). Toward a better understanding of the role in situations in linking personality, work behavior, and job performance. *Industrial and Organizational Psychology: Perspectives on Science and Practice, 3*, 312–316.

Clark, R. A., Teevan, R., & Ricciuti, H. N. (1956). Hope of success and fear of failure as aspects of need for achievement. *The Journal of Abnormal and Social Psychology, 53*, 182–186.

Costa, P. T., Jr., & McCrae, R. R. (1992). *Revised NEO Personality Inventory and Five-Factor Inventory professional manual*. Odessa, FL: Psychological Assessment Resources.

Creed, P. A., King, V., Hood, M., & McKenzie, R. (2009). Goal orientation, self-regulation strategies, and job-seeking intensity in unemployed adults. *Journal of Applied Psychology, 94*, 806–813.

Cron, W. L., Slocum, J. W., VandeWalle, D., & Fu, Q. (2005). The role of goal orientation on negative emotions and goal setting when initial performance falls short of one's performance goal. *Human Performance, 18*, 55–80.

DeCremer, D., Mayer, D. M., Van-Dijke, M., Schouten, B. C., & Bardes, M. (2009). When does self-sacrificial leadership motivate prosocial behavior? It depends on followers' prevention focus. *Journal of Applied Psychology, 94*, 887–899.

DeShon, R. P., & Gillespie, J. Z. (2005). A motivated action theory account of goal orientation. *Journal of Applied Psychology, 90*, 1096–1127.

Diefendorff, J. M. (2004). Examination of the roles of action-state orientation and goal orientation in the goal-setting and performance process. *Human Performance, 17*, 375–395.

Diefendorff, J. M., & Mehta, K. (2007). The relations of motivational traits with workplace deviance. *Journal of Applied Psychology, 92*, 967–977.

Diener, C. I., & Dweck, C. S. (1978). An analysis of learned helplessness: Continuous changes in performance, strategy, and achievement cognitions following failure. *Journal of Personality and Social Psychology, 36*, 451–462.

Donovan, J. J., Esson, P. L., & Backert, R. G. (2007, April). *An examination of goal orientation patterns and task-specific self-efficacy*. Paper presented at the 22nd Annual Conference of the Society for Industrial and Organizational Psychology, New York, NY.

Donovan, J. J., & Hafsteinsson, L. G. (2006). The impact of goal-performance discrepancies, self-efficacy and goal orientation on upward goal revision. *Journal of Applied Social Psychology, 36*, 1046–1099.
Dragoni, L. (2005). Understanding the emergence of state goal orientation in organizational work groups: The role of leadership and multi-level climate perceptions. *Journal of Applied Psychology, 90*, 1084–1095.
Duda, J. L., & Nicholls, J. G. (1992). Dimensions of achievement motivation in schoolwork and sport. *Journal of Educational Psychology, 84*, 290–299.
Dweck, C. S. (1975). The role of expectations and attributions in the alleviation of learned helplessness. *Journal of Personality and Social Psychology, 31*, 674–685.
Dweck, C. S. (1986). Motivational processes affecting learning. *American Psychologist, 41*, 1040–1048.
Dweck, C. S. (1989). Motivation. In A. Lesgold & R. Glaser (Eds.), *Foundations for a psychology of education* (pp. 87–136). Hillsdale, NJ: Erlbaum.
Dweck, C. S. (1991). Self-theories and goals: Their role in motivation, personality, and development. In R. A. Dienstbier (Ed.), *Nebraska symposium on motivation: Vol. 38. Perspectives on motivation* (pp. 199–235). Lincoln: University of Nebraska Press.
Dweck, C. S., & Leggett, E. L. (1988). A social-cognitive approach to motivation and personality. *Psychological Review, 95*, 256–273.
Dweck, C. S., & Reppucci, N. D. (1973). Learned helplessness and reinforcement responsibility in children. *Journal of Personality and Social Psychology, 25*, 109–116.
Elliot, A. J., & Church, M. A. (1997). A hierarchical model of approach and avoidance achievement motivation. *Journal of Personality and Social Psychology, 72*, 218–232.
Elliot, A. J., & Harackiewicz, J. M. (1996). Approach and avoidance achievement goals and intrinsic motivation: A mediational analysis. *Journal of Personality and Social Psychology, 70*, 461–475.
Elliot, A. J., & McGregor, H. A. (2001). A 2 * 2 achievement goal framework. *Journal of Personality and Social Psychology, 80*, 501–519.
Elliot, A. J., & Thrash, T. M. (2001). Achievement goals and the hierarchical model of achievement motivation. *Educational Psychology Review, 13*, 139–156.
Farr, J. L., Hofmann, D. A., & Ringenbach, K. L. (1993). Goal orientation and action control theory: Implications for industrial and organizational psychology. In C. L. Cooper & I. T. Robertson (Eds.), *International review of industrial and organizational psychology* (Vol. 8, pp. 191–232). West Sussex, UK: John Wiley & Sons.
Fishbein, M., & Ajzen, I. (1975). *Belief, attitude, intention, and behavior: An introduction to theory and research*. Reading, MA: Addison-Wesley.
Ford, J., Smith, E. M., Weissbein, D. A., Gully, S. M., & Salas, E. (1998). Relationships of goal orientation, metacognitive activity, and practice strategies with learning outcomes and transfer. *Journal of Applied Psychology, 83*, 218–233.
Förster, J., Grant, H., Idson, L. C., & Higgins, E. T. (2001). Success/failure feedback expectancies and approach/avoidance motivation: How regulatory focus moderates classic relations. *Journal of Experimental Social Psychology, 37*, 253–260.
Förster, J., Higgins, E. T., & Idson, L. C. (1998). Approach and avoidance strength during goal attainment: Regulatory focus and the "goal looms larger" effect. *Journal of Personality and Social Psychology, 75*, 1115–1131.
Foti, R., & Hauenstein, M. A. (2007). Pattern and variable approaches in leadership emergence and effectiveness. *Journal of Applied Psychology, 92*, 347–355.
Freitas, A. L., & Higgins, E. T. (2002). Enjoying goal-directed action: The role of regulatory fit. *Psychological Science, 13*, 1–6.
Harackiewicz, J. M., Barron, K. E., Pintrich, P. R., Elliot, A. J., & Thrash, T. M. (2002). Revision of goal theory: Necessary and illuminating. *Journal of Educational Psychology, 94*, 638–645.
Haws, K. L., Dholakia, U. M., & Bearden, W. O. (2010). An assessment of chronic regulatory focus measures. *Journal of Marketing Research, 47*, 967–982.
Heggestad, E. D., & Kanfer, R. (2000). Individual differences in trait motivation: Development of the Motivational Trait Questionnaire. *International Journal of Educational Research, 33*, 751–777.
Heimerdinger, S. R., & Hinsz, V. B. (2008). Failure avoidance motivation in a goal setting situation. *Human Performance, 21*, 383–395.
Helmreich, R. L., & Spence, J. T. (1978). The work and family orientation questionnaire: An objective instrument to assess components of achievement motivation and attitudes toward family and career. *JSAS Catalog of Selected Documents in Psychology, 8*, 35.
Heyman, G. D., & Dweck, C. S. (1992). Achievement goals and intrinsic motivation: Their relation and their role in adaptive motivation. *Motivation and Emotion, 16*, 231–247.
Higgins, E. T. (1997). Beyond pleasure and pain. *American Psychologist, 52*, 1280–1300.

Higgins, E. T. (1999). Persons and situations: Unique explanatory principles or variability in general principles? In D. Cervone & Y. Shoda (Eds.), *The coherence of personality: Social cognitive bases of consistency, variability, and organization* (pp. 61–93). New York, NY: Guilford Press.

Higgins, E. T., Shah, J., & Friedman, R. (1997). Emotional responses to goal attainment: Strength of regulatory focus as moderator. *Journal of Personality and Social Psychology, 72*, 515–525.

Higgins, E. T., & Tykocinski, O. (1992). Self-discrepancies and biographical memory: Personality and cognition at the level of psychological situation. *Personality and Social Psychology Bulletin, 18*, 527–535.

Hinsz, V. B., & Jundt, D. K. (2005). Exploring individual differences in a goal setting situation using the motivational trait questionnaire. *Journal of Applied Social Psychology, 35*, 551–571.

Horvath, M., Scheu, C. R., & DeShon, R. P. (2001, April). *Goal orientation: Integrating theory and measurement.* Paper presented at the 16th annual conference of the Society for Industrial and Organizational Psychology, San Diego.

Hough, L. M. (1992). The "big five" personality variables–construct confusion: Description versus prediction. *Human Performance, 5*, 139–155.

Hough, L. M., & Schneider, R. J. (1996). Personality traits, taxonomies, and applications on organizations. In K. Murphy (Ed.), *Individual differences in organizations* (pp. 31–88). San Francisco: Jossey-Bass.

Idson, L. C., & Higgins, E. T. (2000). How current feedback and chronic effectiveness influence motivation: Everything to gain versus everything to lose. *European Journal of Social Psychology, 30*, 583–592.

Jackson, D. N., Ahmed, S. A., & Heapy, N. A. (1976). Is achievement a unitary construct? *Journal of Research in Personality, 10*, 1–21.

Jagacinski, C. M., & Nicholls, J. G. (1987). Competence and affect in task and ego involvement: The impact of social comparison information. *Journal of Educational Psychology, 79*, 107–114.

Janssen, O., & Prins, J. (2007). Goal orientations and the seeking of different types of feedback information. *Journal of Occupational and Organizational Psychology, 80*, 235–249.

Johns, G. (2006). The essential impact of context on organizational behavior. *Academy of Management Review, 31*, 386–408.

Judge, T. A., & Ilies, R. (2002). Relationship of personality and to performance motivation: A meta-analysis. *Journal of Applied Psychology, 87*, 797–807.

Kanfer, R. (1990). Motivation theory and industrial/organizational psychology. In M. D. Dunnette & L. Hough (Eds.), *Handbook of industrial and organizational psychology. Volume 1: Theory in industrial and organizational psychology* (pp. 75–170). Palo Alto, CA: Consulting Psychologists Press.

Kanfer, R. (2009). Work motivation: Identifying use-inspired research directions. *Industrial and Organizational Psychology, 2*, 77–93.

Kanfer, R., & Ackerman, P. L. (1996). A self-regulatory skills perspective to reducing cognitive interference. In I. G. Sarason, B. R. Sarason, & G. R. Pierce (Eds.), *Cognitive interference: Theories, methods, and findings* (pp. 153–171). Mahwah, NJ: Erlbaum.

Kanfer, R., & Ackerman, P. L. (2000). Individual differences in work motivation: Further explorations of a trait framework. *Applied Psychology: An International Review, 49*, 470–482.

Kanfer, R., Ackerman, P. L., & Heggestad, E. (1996). Motivational skills and self-regulation for learning: A trait perspective. *Learning and Individual Differences, 8*, 185–209.

Kanfer, R., & Heggestad, E. D. (1997). Motivational traits and skills: A person-centered approach to work motivation. In B. M. Staw & L. L. Cummings (Eds.), *Research in organizational behavior* (Vol. 19, pp. 1–56). Greenwich, CT: JAI Press.

Kanfer, R., & Heggestad, E. (1999). Individual differences in motivation: Traits and self-regulatory skills. In P. L. Ackerman, P. C. Kyllonen, & R. D. Roberts (Eds.), *Learning and individual differences: Process, trait, and content determinants* (pp. 293–309). Washington, DC: American Psychological Association.

Kark, R., & Van-Dijk, D. (2007). Motivation to lead, motivation to follow: The role of the self-regulatory focus in leadership processes. *Academy of Management Review, 32*, 500–528.

Keith, N., & Frese, M. (2005). Self-regulation in error management training: Emotion control and meta cognition as mediators of performance effects. *Journal of Applied Psychology, 90*, 677–691.

Keller, J., & Bless, H. (2006). Regulatory fit and cognitive performance: The interactive effect of chronic and situationally induced self-regulatory mechanisms on test performance. *European Journal of Social Psychology, 36*, 393–405.

Kozlowski, S. W., Gully, S. M., Brown, K. G., Salas, E., Smith, E. M., & Nason, E. R. (2001). Effects of training goals and goal orientation traits on multidimensional training outcomes and performance adaptability. *Organizational Behavior and Human Decision Processes, 85*, 1–31.

Kuhl, J. (1985). Volitional mediators of cognition-behavior consistency: Self-regulatory processes and action vs. state orientation. In J. Kuhl & J. Beckman (Eds.), *Action control: From cognition to behavior* (pp. 101–128). New York, NY: Springer-Verlag.

Leary, M. R. (1983). A brief version of the Fear of Negative Evaluation Scale. *Personality and Social Psychology Bulletin, 9*, 371–376.

Lee, F. K., Sheldon, K. M., & Turban, D. B. (2003). Personality and the goal-striving process: The influence of achievement goal patterns, goal level, and mental focus on performance and enjoyment. *Journal of Applied Psychology, 88*, 256–265.

Lievens, F., Chasteen, C. S., Day, E. A., & Christiansen, N. D. (2006). Large-scale investigation of the role of trait activation theory for understanding assessment center convergent and discriminant validity. *Journal of Applied Psychology, 91*, 247–258.

Locke, E. A. (1991). The motivation sequence, the motivation hub, and the motivation core. *Organizational Behavior and Human Decision Processes, 50*, 288–299.

Locke, E. A., & Latham, G. P. (1990). *A theory of goal setting and task performance*. Englewood Cliffs, NJ: Prentice Hall.

Locke, E. A., & Latham, G. P. (2002). Building a practically useful theory of goal setting and task motivation: A 35-year odyssey. *American Psychologist, 57*, 705–717.

Lord, R. G., Diefendorff, J. M., Schmidt, A. M., & Hall, R. J. (2010). Self-regulation at work. In S. T. Fiske (Ed.), *Annual review of psychology* (Vol. 61, pp. 543–568). Palo Alto, CA: Annual Reviews.

Magnusson, D. (2000). The individual as the organizing principle in psychological inquiry: A holistic approach. In L. R. Bergman, R. C. Cairns, L. Nilsson, & L. Nystedt (Eds.), *Developmental science and the holistic approach* (pp. 33–48). Mahwah, NJ: Elbaum.

Mangos, P. M., & Steele-Johnson, D. (2001). The role of subjective task complexity in goal orientation, self-efficacy, and performance relations. *Human Performance, 14*, 169–186.

Matsui, T., Okada, A., & Kakuyama, T. (1982). Influence of achievement need on goal setting, performance, and feedback effectiveness. *Journal of Applied Psychology, 67*, 645–648.

McClelland, D. C. (1951). *Personality*. New York, NY: Henry Holt.

McClelland, D. C., Atkinson, J. W., Clark, R. A., & Lowell, E. L. (1953). *The achievement motive*. New York, NY: Appleton-Century-Crofts.

McClelland, D. C., Clark, R. A., Roby, T. B., & Atkinson, J. W. (1949). The projective expression of needs, IV. The effect of the need for achievement on thematic apperception. *Journal of Experimental Psychology, 39*, 242–255.

Morris, L. W., Davis, M. A., & Hutchings, C. H. (1981). Cognitive and emotional components of anxiety: Literature review and a revised Worry-Emotionality Scale. *Journal of Educational Psychology, 73*, 541–555.

Murray, H. A. (1938). *Explorations in personality*. New York, NY: Oxford University Press.

Park, G., Schmidt, A. M., Scheu, C. R., & DeShon, R. P. (2007). Process model of feedback seeking. *Human Performance, 20*, 119–145.

Payne, S. C., Youngcourt, S. S., & Beaubien, J. M. (2007). A meta-analytic examination of the goal orientation nomological net. *Journal of Applied Psychology, 92*, 128–150.

Phillips, J. M., & Gully, S. M. (1997). Role of goal orientation, ability, need for achievement, and locus of control in the self-efficacy and goal setting process. *Journal of Applied Psychology, 82*, 792–802.

Pinder, C. (2008). *Work motivation in organizational behavior* (2nd ed.). New York, NY: Psychology Press.

Porath, C. L., & Bateman, T. S. (2006). Self-regulation: From goal orientation to job performance. *Journal of Applied Psychology, 91*, 157–192.

Porter, C. O. L. H., Webb, J. W., & Gogus, C. I. (2010). When goal orientations collide: Effects of learning and performance orientation on team adapatability in response to workload imbalance. *Journal of Applied Psychology, 95*, 935–943.

Sarason, I. G. (1978). The test anxiety scale: Concept and research. In C. D. Spielberger & I. G. Sarason (Eds.), *Stress and anxiety* (Vol. 5, pp. 193–216). New York, NY: Wiley.

Schmidt, A. M., Dolis, C. M., & Tolli, A. P. (2009). A matter of time: Individual differences, contextual dynamics, and goal progress effects on multiple-goal self-regulation. *Journal of Applied Psychology, 94*, 692–709.

Schmidt, A. M., & Ford, J. K. (2003). Learning within a learner control training environment: The interactive effects of goal orientation and metacognitive instruction on learning outcomes. *Personnel Psychology, 56*, 405–429.

Schmidt, F. L., & Hunter, J. E. (1992). Development of a causal model of processes determining job performance. *Current Directions in Psychological Science, 1*, 89–92.

Seijts, G. H., Latham, G. P., Tasa, K., & Latham, B. W. (2004). Goal setting and goal orientation: An integration of two different yet related literatures. *Academy of Management Journal, 47*, 227–239.

Shah, J., Higgins, E. T., & Friedman, R. S. (1998). Performance incentives and means: How regulatory focus influences goal attainment. *Journal of Personality and Social Psychology, 74*, 285–293.

Steele-Johnson, D., Beauregard, R. S., Hoover, P. B., & Schmidt, A. M. (2000). Goal orientation and task demand effects on motivation, affect, and performance. *Journal of Applied Psychology, 85*, 724–738.

Tett, R. P., & Burnett, D. D. (2003). A personality trait-based interactionist model of job performance. *Journal of Applied Psychology, 88*, 500–517.

Tett, R. P., & Guterman, H. A. (2000). Situation trait relevance, trait expression, and cross-situational consistency: Testing a principle of trait activation. *Journal of Research in Personality, 34*, 397–423.

Tuckey, M., Brewer, N., & Williamson, P. (2002). The influence of motives and goal orientation on feedback seeking. *Journal of Occupational and Organizational Psychology, 75*, 195–216.

Tuerlinckx, F., DeBoeck, P., & Lens, W. (2002). Measuring needs with the thematic apperception test: A psychometric study. *Journal of Personality and Social Psychology, 82*, 448–461.

Uhlinger, C. A., & Stephens, M. W. (1960). Relation of achievement motivation to academic achievement in students of superior ability. *Journal of Educational Psychology, 51*, 259–266.

VandeWalle, D. (1997). Development and validation of a work domain goal orientation instrument. *Educational and Psychological Measurement, 57*, 995–1015.

VandeWalle, D., Brown, S. P., Cron, W. L., & Slocum, J. W. (1999). The influence of goal orientation and self-regulation tactics on sales performance: A longitudinal field test. *Journal of Applied Psychology, 84*, 249–259.

VandeWalle, D., Cron, W. L., & Slocum, J. W. (2001). The role of goal orientation following performance feedback. *Journal of Applied Psychology, 86*, 629–640.

VandeWalle, D., & Cummings, L. L. (1997). A test of the influence of goal orientation on the feedback-seeking process. *Journal of Applied Psychology, 82*, 390–400.

VandeWalle, D., Ganesan, S., Challagalla, G. N., & Brown, S. P. (2000). An integrated model of feedback-seeking behavior: Disposition, context, and cognition. *Journal of Applied Psychology, 85*, 996–1003.

Van-Dijk, D., & Kluger, A. N. (2004). Feedback sign effect on motivation: Is it moderated by regulatory focus? *Applied Psychology: An International Review, 53*, 113–135.

Wainer, H. A., & Rubin, I. M. (1969). Motivation of research and development entrepreneurs: Determinants of company success. *Journal of Applied Psychology, 53*, 178–184.

Wanberg, C. R., Kanfer, R., & Rotundo, M. (1999). Unemployed individuals: Motives, job-search competencies, and job-search constraints as predictors of job seeking and reemployment. *Journal of Applied Psychology, 84*, 897–910.

Yeo, G., Loft, S., Xiao, T., & Kiewitz, C. (2009). Goal orientations and performance: Differential relationships across levels of analysis and as a function of task demands. *Journal of Applied Psychology, 94*, 710–726.

Yeo, G., Sorbello, T., Koy, A., & Smillie, L. (2008). Goal orientation profiles and task performance growth trajectories. *Motivation and Emotion, 32*, 296–309.

Yukl, G. A., & Latham, G. P. (1978). Interrelationships among employee participation, individual differences, goal difficulty, goal acceptance, goal instrumentality, and performance. *Personnel Psychology, 31*, 305–323.

7

Implicit Personality and Workplace Behaviors

Nicholas L. Vasilopoulos, Brian P. Siers, and Megan N. Shaw

In this chapter, we focus on the relationship between implicit personality and workplace behaviors. Implicit personality refers to the component of the self-system that operates at a subconscious level. Historically, organizational researchers have paid little attention to implicit personality, largely due to concerns about the psychometric properties of available measures such as the *Thematic Apperception Test* (TAT; Murray, 1938). Things began to change in the later part of the 20th Century with the development of psychometrically sound, objective measures that capture implicit processes, such as *conditional reasoning tests* (CRTs; James, 1998) and *implicit association tests* (IATs; Greenwald, McGhee, & Schwartz, 1998).

The organization of this chapter is as follows. First, we summarize three dual-process models that distinguish between *implicit* (or subconscious) and *explicit* (or conscious) systems that operate together to define a global personality system.[1] Next, we describe four measures of implicit personality that have received interest from organizational researchers. We then link the personality systems to important workplace behaviors. Finally, we discuss the practical implications of assessing implicit personality and offer suggestions for future research.

Dual-Process Models of Personality

Several models have been offered to describe how implicit processes guide behavior.[2] In this section, we provide an overview of three dual-process models referenced by organizational researchers investigating both implicit and explicit components of personality—the *Cognitive–Experiential Self-Theory* (CEST; Epstein, 1994), the *Reflective Impulsive Model* (RIM; Strack & Deutsch, 2004), and the *Cognitive–Affective Personality System* (CAPS; Mischel & Shoda, 1995). The decision to focus on dual-process models reflects our belief that any discussion of implicit processes that does not consider interactions with explicit processes is necessarily incomplete. We do, however, discuss models offered to describe the processes that underlie responses to specific implicit measures later in this chapter. Finally, we present examples to show how the general principles of dual-process models can be used to describe the behavior of three consultants meeting with a disgruntled client.

CEST

In CEST (Epstein, 1994, 2003), information is processed through *rational* and *experiential* self-systems. The rational system includes representations and associations between the self and environment formed through a logical evaluation of available information. Information processing in the rational system is conscious, slow, and effortful. The experiential system, on the other hand, includes representations and associations of the self and environment formed through significant and/or repetitive past experiences. Information processing in the experiential system is subconscious, fast, automatic, and effortless. At its most basic level, the experiential system includes associative links developed over time through the principles of classical conditioning. These basic associations generate emotional states in direct response to environmental cues. At more complex levels, the experiential system includes associative networks that define one's general "beliefs" about the self and the world in relation to the satisfaction of four basic needs—*maximizing pleasure and minimizing pain, maintaining coherence and stability of one's conceptual system, enhancing one's self-esteem*, and *relating with others*. These beliefs are formed through the principles of operant conditioning and observational learning and are responsible for the intuitions and heuristic processing that occurs in the absence of strong situational cues.

While the two personality systems are distinct, they interact to influence how individuals process information and make sense of the world (Epstein, 2003; Epstein & Pacini, 1999). The experiential system influences the rational system through emotions that either hinder or facilitate information processing and/or through beliefs that frame how information is perceived and evaluated. The rational system influences the experiential system through insights that help individuals resist harmful impulses and/or through self-regulatory processes that enable individuals to change associations within the experiential system.

CEST also identifies features of the situation that can influence the extent to which one system is likely to drive behavior. The rational system is the primary driver of behavior in situations that provide clear goals and allow for an extended response. Emotional states generated by the experiential system serve as the primary driver of behavior in situations that call for an immediate response. The implicit beliefs that define the complex associations of the experiential system serve as the primary drivers of behaviors in situations that are routine and well learned, as well as in situations that are ambiguous.

CEST also specifies individual differences in the preference for using the rational and experiential systems (Epstein, 2003). These differences are assessed through the *need for cognition* and *faith in intuition* scales on the *Rational Experiential Inventory* (REI; Epstein, Pacini, Denes-Raj, & Heier, 1996). Individuals with a high need for cognition prefer using the rational system, whereas individuals with high faith in intuition prefer using the experiential system.

RIM

Proposed by Strack and Deutsch (2004), RIM shares many of the features of CEST. It offers two systems of reality—a *reflective system* and an *impulsive system*—that differ in terms of their representations and information processing. The reflective system includes a network of associations between representations formed through a rational evaluation of goal-relevant information. As in CEST, information processing is deliberate, slow, and effortful. The impulsive system includes associations between schemata formed through personal experiences. Information processing is automatic, fast, and effortless.

The reflective and impulsive systems initiate behavior through the activation of the same behavioral schemata. The systems differ, however, in the processes that lead to the activation of behavioral schemata. The reflective system activates behavioral schemata through "intentions" that provide a specific course of action. The impulsive system activates behavioral schemata through associative networks that generate emotional states that initiate approach/avoidance motivational tendencies (Deutsch & Strack, 2006; Strack & Deutsch, 2004).

Like CEST, RIM views the reflective and impulsive systems as bidirectional in that each system can provide cues that influence the other system. The higher-order executive functions in the reflective system regulate, overcome, or compensate for impulsive urges. The impulsive system induces overall positive or negative states of arousal that either facilitate or hinder the operation of the reflective system (Deutsch & Strack, 2008; Russell, 2003).

Although the two systems often operate in parallel, the impulsive system is always involved in information processing, whereas the reflective system is sometimes disengaged. Because it is always active, the impulsive system plays a more central role in driving behavior. The relative influence of the two systems is largely a function of arousal. The impulsive system is more influential when arousal is either low (e.g., performing a routine, inconsequential task) or high (e.g., performing a high-stakes, consequential task). The systems are equally influential when arousal is moderate (e.g., performing a challenging task).

CAPS

Mischel and Shoda (1995, 1998) proposed CAPS to account for stable individual differences and within-person situational variability in behaviors. This system involves the interplay of situational and self-relevant information that is mediated through five types of *cognitive–affective units* (CAUs). (1) *Encoding strategies* determine how an individual categorizes information in the environment. (2) *Expectancies and beliefs* reflect the individual's prediction of the outcomes that result from behaviors. (3) *Goals and values* represent the valence associated with a given outcome and provide for behavioral consistency across situations. (4) *Competencies and self-regulatory* strategies represent an individual's level of intelligence as well as his or her self-regulatory strategies, established goals and objectives, and self-imposed consequences for effective/ineffective behaviors. (5) *Affective responses* are the emotions and feelings that occur in response to situational cues that drive physiological reactions. For any given individual, CAPS is defined in terms of the accessibility of each CAU, the relationships among the CAUs, and relationships between the CAUs and key features of the situation.

CAPS differs from more traditional perspectives of personality in that inconsistencies in behaviors across situations are viewed as systematic and predictive rather than as error (Shoda, Mischel, & Wright, 1994). A key difference between CAPS and the other models covered in this chapter is that it emphasizes the role of situational cues in defining personality. In CAPS, CAUs form complex associative networks that interact with the situation to create the "states" that guide behavior. This network is defined by intraindividual constructions of *if . . . then* situation–behavior relationships that explain both inconsistencies and consistencies in behavior. For example, an individual may act introverted when interacting with someone for the first time (if p then q_1) and extroverted when interacting with family and friends (if r then s_1). On the surface, the individual appears to behave inconsistently across the situations. However, a closer look at the situations reveals a consistent pattern behavior—the individual is introverted when interacting with unfamiliar others (if p_k then q), and extroverted when interacting with familiar others (if r_k then s). Thus, behavioral consistency is expected across similar situations, but not necessarily all situations.

Like CEST and RIM, CAPS specifies a rational (or "cool") and implicit (or "hot") information-processing system. Unlike the other models, CAPS emphasizes the role of the rational system in driving behavior. Specifically, the "cooling strategies" employed by the rational system actively control impulsive tendencies. It is through this self-regulatory process that individuals are able to effectively cope with fears and frustrations, and ensure long-term attainment of goals (Mischel & Ayduk, 2002).

Comparing the Dual-Process Models of Personality

Each model covered in this section provides a framework for understanding how explicit and implicit systems work together to define a global personality system that drives behavior. In many ways these models are very similar; however they also differ in potentially meaningful ways. These similarities and differences are summarized below.

Model Similarities

Each model acknowledges the existence of two distinct systems that influence thought and behavior—an explicit system defined by logical propositions and conscious-level information processing, and an implicit system defined by emotions, beliefs, and subconscious-level processing. The models view the systems as interacting to influence information processing and guide behavior. The implicit system generates emotions, attitudes, and motivational orientations that can influence how information is processed by the explicit system. The explicit system, on the other hand, provides the rational thought needed to counteract harmful implicit impulses.

Another common feature of dual-process models is that they recognize that environmental cues play a key part in the activation of the explicit and implicit systems. The explicit system is most influential in situations that present clear goals or require performing challenging tasks over an extended period of time. The implicit system is most influential in situations that present ambiguous goals, require performing well-learned (i.e., automatic) tasks, or call for an immediate response.

Model Differences

While each model specifies separate processing systems, there are some differences in how the systems are characterized. In CEST and RIM, the implicit system is always engaged and hence more influential than the explicit system. In CAPS, the deliberate processing of situational cues serves as the driver of behavior, with implicit processes initiating behavior only when cognitive resources are limited. The models also differ in how they define the role of emotions. In CEST and RIM, emotions initiate behaviors that are often beneficial and adaptive. In contrast, CAPS assumes that emotions distort judgment and hence must be controlled through self-regulation.

Although CEST and RIM are very similar, there are differences that are worthy of consideration. For example, the experiential system defined in CEST includes basic associations that generate emotions as well as complex associations that define beliefs about the world that allow for intuition and imagination. In contrast, the impulsive system defined in RIM is more narrowly defined in that it only includes associations among schemata that direct approach/avoidance behaviors. By addressing the role of implicit beliefs and intuition, CEST provides a richer foundation when describing the complex implicit processes that can guide behavior.

Dual-Process Models at Work: The Story of Three Consultants

Before moving on to a discussion of measures used to assess implicit personality, we offer an example to show how the general principles of dual-process models can be applied to explain the behaviors of three consultants—Alex, Pat, and Chris—during a face-to-face meeting with an upset client.

Setting the Stage

The consultants in this example have qualitatively different implicit beliefs about the world. Alex's implicit beliefs are generally negative. He views himself as incompetent, people as unkind, and the world as unpredictable. Pat's implicit beliefs are both positive and negative. She views herself as competent; however she views people as unkind and the world as unpredictable. Chris's implicit beliefs are generally positive. He views himself as competent, people as kind, and the world as predictable.

In order to demonstrate how individual differences in implicit personality can influence behavior, it is necessary to define the relevant features of the situation. In this example, each consultant meets with a client who is upset with the quality of a report. Specifically, the client is visibly angry and accuses the consultant of failing to provide remedies for the problems the consultant was hired to address. In actuality, the report addressed all of the issues specified in a contract signed by the consultant and client before the start of the project. Four characteristics of this situation can play a role in influencing how the consultants respond. First, the client's expression of anger can lead to a heightened state of arousal. Second, the nature of a face-to-face interaction is such that it requires making a relatively quick response. In dual-process models, high levels of arousal and the need to make an immediate response increase the likelihood that the implicit system is the primary driver of behavior. Third, all face-to-face interactions require attending to and evaluating information in the environment. The processing of information in the environment is handled by the explicit system. The fourth characteristic—the existence of a contract showing that the consultant addressed all agreed-upon concerns—provides objective information that can be used to control impulsive urges through explicit processes.

Consultants at Work

While each consultant is likely to become aroused by the client's expression of anger, they should respond to the situation in very different ways. Alex's negative beliefs lead him to feel extremely threatened and fearful. He perceives the client's behavior as a criticism of his abilities, and an attempt to hurt his feelings and get him fired. This leads Alex to experience an extremely high state of arousal that hampers his ability to think rationally and motivates him to engage in behaviors that protect his self-esteem and job security. At first, Alex sits silently while the client lists his concerns. When he finally responds, Alex stumbles over his words and apologizes profusely. The client ends the meeting by stating, "I will never work with you again, even if you offer to work for free!" Soon after the meeting, it dawns on Alex that he completed all of the work specified in the contract. Alex considers calling the client but decides against it, telling himself, "There is no way he'll work with me again, even if he was wrong. If only I remembered to mention the contract during the meeting."

Pat also feels threatened by the situation, although she becomes angry rather than fearful in response. While Pat does not perceive the client's behavior as a criticism of her abilities, she does see it as evidence that he enjoys berating people and would like nothing better than to get her fired. This leads Pat to experience a state of arousal that hinders her ability to control implicit urges and motivates her to engage in behaviors intended to mete out justice. At first, Pat is taken aback by the client's behavior because she did exactly what they agreed to. Shortly after the meeting starts, Pat interrupts the client, telling him to "Stop talking so I can respond" and proceeds to remind him about the terms of the contract. When the client admits that he may have been too harsh, Pat responds, "You are not only too harsh, you are dead wrong!" She goes on to tell the client everything he did to make her job more difficult than it needed to be. The meeting ends with the client stating, "I may have been wrong, but I don't need to put up with this abuse!" After the meeting, Pat begins to question her behavior in the meeting, telling herself "I was right, but I wish I hadn't lost my cool. The last thing I need is to lose my job."

Unlike the others, Chris does not perceive the client's behavior as a threat. Instead, he sees it as an indication that the client may be bothered by something that has nothing to do with the quality of his work. This leads Chris to become slightly aroused by the situation, although his ability to reason and control impulses is relatively unaffected, and motivates him to get to the bottom of whatever is troubling the client. At first, Chris lets the client talk without interruption. Once the client begins to calm down, Chris asks him to provide specific examples of how he failed to live up to the terms of the contract. After thinking it over, the client admits that Chris had performed the work they agreed to and apologizes for his behavior. Chris responds by saying, "No need to apologize, I'm just happy we had the chance to have this conversation." The meeting ends with the client stating, "You are the best consultant I have ever worked with. I hope my behavior doesn't make you think twice about working with me in the future." After the meeting, Chris is relieved that he was able to address the client's concern and starts a new task.

Admittedly, the examples included in this section are simple. In reality, there are several factors that might have influenced how each consultant responded. That being said, the examples show how differences in implicit personality can lead to different behaviors in a similar situation.

Measures of Implicit Personality

Several indirect measures have been developed to assess implicit personality (Boyle, Matthews, & Saklofske, 2008).[3] In this section, we focus on four indirect measures of personality that are often considered by organizational researchers—IATs, CRTs, *situational judgment tests* (SJTs), and *word completion tasks* (WCTs). These measures can be organized into three categories of indirect measures recently proposed by Uhlmann et al. (2012). An IAT is an example of an *association-based* measure that assesses the strength of associations between concepts in the implicit system. A CRT and an SJT are examples of *interpretation-based* measures that assess how implicit beliefs and motivations guide the interpretation of ambiguous stimuli.[4] Finally, a WCT is an example of an *accessibility-based* measure that assesses how spontaneously a concept is activated in the presence of a situational cue.

IAT

An IAT is a measure of implicit cognition that allows for a comparison of the difference in response latencies between separate target–attribute category pairings (Greenwald et al., 1998). To explain the results of the research on IATs, Greenwald et al. (2002) offered the *Unified Theory of Implicit Social Cognition* (UTISC) as a framework for integrating constructs that operate at the implicit level to define knowledge about the self and others. Self-knowledge is defined through the *self-concept* and *self-esteem*. The self-concept includes associations between the self and different roles and responsibilities (e.g., supervisor, father), and the self and different traits (e.g., intelligent and conscientious). Self-esteem reflects the valence of the associations that define the self-concept (e.g., intelligence and conscientiousness are viewed positively, leading to positive self-esteem).[5]

An IAT created to assess implicit personality includes target categories that distinguish between the self and others (e.g., me/not me), and attribute categories that represent opposite ends of a trait continuum (e.g., dependable/undependable).[6] The IAT presents category labels in the upper right- and left-hand sides of the computer screen and stimuli related to the categories in the middle of the screen (e.g., "I" and "You" for the target category; "controlled" and "reckless" for the attribute category). Examinees complete five blocks that require using a keyboard to pair the stimuli to the related category (e.g., press "a" to pair a stimulus with a category presented on the upper left-hand side of the screen, and "s" to pair a stimulus with the category on the upper right-hand side of the screen).

IAT blocks 1 and 2 are used to familiarize examinees with the target and attribute categories and are not scored. Block 3 pairs target and attribute categories from earlier blocks (referred to as the *initial combined task*). Block 4 presents the same stimuli as block 1; however the location of the target categories is reversed. Block 5 pairs the target and attribute categories from blocks 2 and 4 (referred to as the *reversed combined task*). A description of each block is presented in Table 7.1.

Table 7.1 Task Sequence for an IAT Measuring Dependability

Block	*Trials*	*Task*	*Response Key Assignment*	
			Left Key	*Right Key*
1	20	Target discrimination	Me	Not me
2	20	Attribute discrimination	Dependable	Undependable
3	40	Initial combined task	Me/dependable	Not me/undependable
4	20	Reversed target discrimination	Not me	Me
5	40	Reversed combined task	Not me/dependable	Me/undependable

The original IAT scoring algorithm compared the difference in log transformed response latencies for the last 20 trials in blocks 3 and 5 (Greenwald et al., 1998).[7] Subsequently, Greenwald, Nosek, and Banaji (2003) developed alternative scoring algorithms (labeled *D*) that improve on the initial approach by including information from practice trials (i.e., the first 20 trials in blocks 3 and 5 previously used as practice), incorporating a penalty for sorting errors, and adjusting response latencies for differences in processing speed. While the revised scoring algorithms controlled for systematic biases unrelated to the construct being assessed, some researchers have argued that the algorithms are fundamentally flawed because they are based on difference scores. For example, Blanton and colleagues (e.g., Blanton, Jaccard, Christie, & Gonzales, 2007; Blanton, Jaccard, Gonzales, & Christie, 2006; Blanton et al., 2009) argued for treating response latencies from blocks 3 and 5 separately rather than using a *D* score. Their position is based on the finding that the correlation between the latencies in blocks 3 and 5 is essentially zero after controlling for individual differences in processing speed. This finding suggests that the two latency scores represent different constructs, and as a result, computing a single score masks meaningful information in the respective latency scores.

Reliability and Construct Validity

While the debate regarding the use of *D* scores continues, research generally supports the idea that IATs provide information that is not captured through self-report measures of the same trait. For example, Grumm and von Collani (2007) examined the reliability and construct validity of IATs designed to measure the Five-Factor Model (FFM) of personality. Acceptable split-half reliabilities were obtained for four of the five IATs, with estimates ranging from .82 for the conscientiousness IAT to .64 for the agreeableness IAT. The results also provided evidence of construct validity, with small to moderate correlations observed between all five IATs and corresponding self-report measures, ranging from .41 for extroversion to .18 for conscientiousness. With one exception (i.e., correlation between an extroversion IAT and a self-report measure of neuroticism), nonsignificant correlations were observed between IATs and self-report measures of different traits.

More recently, Siers and Christiansen (2008) conducted multitrait–multimethod (MTMM) analyses to evaluate the construct validity of IATs developed to measure extroversion, conscientiousness, and emotional stability. The analyses compared correlations between the IATs, self-report measures, and peer ratings of the same traits. Correlations between the IAT and the self-report measure of the same trait were small to moderate in magnitude, ranging from −.08 for emotional stability to .25 for extroversion. The results also revealed significant amounts of method and error variance in IAT scores. Much of the method variance was explained by a tendency to associate one's self with positive attributes. This finding has important implications when designing an IAT because most pro-trait descriptors (e.g., dependable, reliable) are more positively valenced than con-trait descriptors (e.g., undependable, unreliable). To address this potential confound, researchers should use equally valenced adjectives (e.g., 10 positively valenced and 10 negatively valenced) to ensure the IAT assesses the intended personality trait rather than implicit self-esteem (the tendency to associate with positive concepts; see Haines & Sumner, 2006).

The moderate correlations between IATs and corresponding self-report measures are consistent with the .24 true score correlation reported in the meta-analytic study by Hofmann, Gawronski, Gschwendner, Le, and Schmitt (2005). In that study, correcting for statistical artifacts accounted for 44% of the variance in the distribution of correlation coefficients, suggesting the relationship between IATs and corresponding self-report measures is moderated by a third factor. Follow-up analyses indicated that the relationship between an IAT and a self-report measure is stronger to the extent the self-report measure (1) involved spontaneous rather than deliberate responses, (2) assessed affective rather than cognitive constructs, and (3) involved relative rather than absolute comparisons.

Criterion-Related Validity

To date, few studies have explored the criterion-related validity of personality IATs in an organizational setting. Asendorpf, Banse, and Mücke (2002) conducted two studies that examined the criterion-related validity of a shyness IAT and a self-report semantic differential scale that included the same set of bipolar adjectives presented in the IAT (e.g., timid–daring). The results of the first study revealed that the shyness IAT was a better predictor of spontaneous behaviors (e.g., facial expressions), whereas the semantic differential scale was a better predictor of controlled behaviors (e.g., speck duration). The second study examined the effect of faking on both the predictor (i.e., IAT and self-report shyness measures) and the criterion (i.e., simulated job interview). Participants in the experimental condition were told that appearing shy will harm their chances of getting the job. Participants in the control condition were given no information about the consequence of appearing shy. As hypothesized, scores on the shyness IAT were similar across conditions, whereas the scores on the self-report shyness scale were significantly lower in the job applicant condition. This suggests that participants were able to manipulate (or fake) their responses on the self-report measure but not the IAT. Finally, participants in the job applicant condition were able to reduce controlled shyness behaviors but not spontaneous shyness behaviors.

In another study, Back, Schmukle, and Egloff (2009) examined the relationship between IATs and self-report measures of the FFM, and a wide range of behaviors, many of which are similar to those of interest to organizational researchers (e.g., voluntary helping behavior, knowledge test). All self-report measures correlated significantly with conceptually matched behaviors. In contrast, only the neuroticism IAT and extroversion IAT significantly correlated with conceptually matched criteria. The neuroticism and extroversion IATs also added incrementally to the prediction of behaviors above that was provided by the corresponding self-report measure alone. Finally, Siers and Christiansen (2008) explored the criterion-related validity of personality IATs and found no significant correlations with job performance.

CRT

The CRT paradigm rests on the assumption that individuals develop *justification mechanisms* as a way of reconciling behaviors they consistently engage in (James, 1998; James & Lebreton, 2007). These justification mechanisms reflect implicit motives that can be captured through CRTs. The CRT methodology has primarily been used to assess achievement motivation (CRT-AM) and aggression (CRT-A). Because most of the research on CRTs conducted in an organizational setting has focused on the measurement of tendencies toward aggression, we discuss the reliability and validity evidence for the CRT-A.

The CRT-A posits six different justification mechanisms or implicit biases that are used by individuals to rationalize their desire to inflict harm on others (James, 1998). These mechanisms involve the following: (1) a *hostile attribution bias* that people in general want to harm others, (2) a *potency bias* that social interactions are competitive, (3) a *retribution bias* that retaliation is justified to "right" a perceived "wrong," (4) a *victimization by powerful others bias* that those who are dominant in a social hierarchy inflict harm on those who are less dominant, (5) a *social discounting bias* that social norms restrict individual freedom, and (6) a *derogation of target bias* that the intended target of aggression is immoral.

In completing a CRT, examinees are told that they are taking a test of logical reasoning ability. Each CRT item presents a problem along with a series of attributions or conclusions that can be drawn about the problem. Two of the options are linked to a justification mechanism related to the underlying motive. The other options serve as distracters and are not scored. For example, a CRT-A item might include a prosocial option, an aggressive option, and two neutral distracter options.

Reliability and Construct Validity

Much of the information regarding the psychometric characteristics of the CRT-A is presented in an empirical review conducted by James et al. (2005). Overall, the results suggest that the CRT-A is a reliable and valid measure of aggressive tendencies. An exploratory factor analysis revealed that the CRT-A includes five factors that map to the justification mechanisms used to develop the measure. Internal consistencies for those factors ranged from .87 for the social discounting bias factor to .74 for the potency bias factor.

Regarding construct validity, the pattern of correlations between the CRT-A and self-report measures of aggression was similar to that observed for the IAT. Of the four samples that included scores on the CRT-A and a corresponding self-report measure, moderate effects were reported in three, with correlations ranging from .14 to .26. As previously stated, the modest correlations between the CRT-A and self-report measures of aggression are consistent with the idea that the measures assess related, but distinct, constructs.

Criterion-Related Validity

Criteria in CRT-A studies are often counterproductive work behaviors (CWBs) and overall job performance. Of the 11 studies reviewed by James et al. (2005) that examined criterion-related validity, the unweighted mean validity estimate was .44. Five of the studies were conducted in an organizational setting, with an unweighted mean validity of .40. While the initial results for the CRT-A seem promising, critics argue that they overestimate the true validity of CRT-A measures. For example, Berry, Sackett, and Tobares (2010) reanalyzed the data presented by James et al. along with the results from unpublished studies not included in the earlier review. The inclusion of unpublished studies led them to arrive at different conclusions about the validity of the CRT-A in an organizational setting. Among the studies conducted in organizational contexts, the estimated validity was .20 for CWBs and .14 for ratings of job performance. More recently, Banks, Kepes, and McDaniel (2011) assessed the effect of publication bias on the meta-analytic validity estimates for CRT-A. After adjusting for publication bias, the observed validity of the CRT-A was .08.

SJT

SJTs present applicants with job-related scenarios and several behaviorally-based options for how to respond to the situation described (Motowidlo, Dunnette, & Carter, 1990). Early applications of

SJTs developed scoring keys based on expert judgments of what the correct response "should be." SJTs keyed in this way are designed to assess procedural knowledge rather than personality, and have shown to be effective predictors of job performance (McDaniel, Morgeson, Finnegan, Campion, & Braverman, 2001).

More recently, Motowidlo and colleagues proposed that SJTs can also be used to assess implicit personality (Motowidlo & Beier, 2010; Motowidlo, Hooper, & Jackson, 2006a, 2006b). They speculated that two evaluations underlie the relationship between SJT scores and job performance. The first evaluation is made to determine the appropriateness of certain behaviors in the specific work context. The second evaluation is made to assess the utility of expressing various personality traits. To describe the role of personality in determining the appropriate response to a situation, Motowidlo et al. (2006a) offered the *Implicit Trait Policy* (ITP) *Hypothesis*, which states that individuals are more likely to view behaviors consistent with their personality as being effective (e.g., an extrovert will view interacting with others as contributing to effectiveness to a greater extent than an introvert).

SJTs designed to assess an ITP require examinees to rate the effectiveness of each behavioral response option. Each response option is keyed according to its trait elevation (high or low). An ITP score is computed as the effect size of the relationship between expert judgments of behavioral effectiveness and the trait elevation of the SJT response option. This effect size can be calculated several ways including as a *D* score or correlation coefficient (see Motowidlo et al., 2006a for a description of these calculations and their appropriateness).

Reliability and Construct Validity

In general, SJTs have acceptable levels of reliability. For example, Motowidlo et al. (2006a) reported an alternate form reliability estimate of .71 for two agreeableness SJTs. These researchers also provided evidence of construct validity. Significant correlations were observed when the SJT and corresponding self-report measure assessed agreeableness (.31) and extroversion (.37), but not conscientiousness (.15, *ns*).

Criterion-Related Validity

Few studies have explored the criterion-related validity of SJTs designed to assess ITPs. The limited evidence suggests that such SJTs can serve as effective predictors of relevant criteria. Motowidlo et al. (2006a) had participants complete a role-play exercise designed to elicit trait-related behaviors. Raters scored videos of the role-play exercises to provide behavioral trait scores for participants. Behavioral ratings of agreeableness correlated significantly with the agreeableness SJT but not with the self-report measure of agreeableness. None of the correlations involving extroversion were significant (for more coverage regarding SJTs that assess personality see Chapter 19, this volume).

WCT

WCTs have been offered as a way to assess both attitudes and traits in organizational settings (e.g., Johnson & Steinman, 2009). A WCT presents examinees a list of incomplete words and instructs them to complete all of the words as fast as possible. For each incomplete word, one of the viable responses is tied to an underlying psychological construct. For example, Johnson, Tolentino, Rodopman, and Cho (2010) developed a WCT to assess affectivity, with 10 word fragments assessing positive affectivity (PA) and 10 word fragments assessing negative affectivity (NA). An example of a word fragment assessing PA is "_ O Y," with a point given when the letter "J" is inserted to spell the word "J O Y." An example of a word fragment assessing NA is "_ _ N S E," with a point given when the letters "T" and "E" are inserted to spell the word "T E N S E."

Reliability and Construct Validity

Available research suggests that WCTs have adequate reliability. Johnson et al. (2010) reported test–retest reliabilities of .72 for the WCT-PA scale and .64 for the WCT-NA scale. More recently, Johnson and Saboe (2011) reported test–retest reliabilities of .68 for a WCT measuring interdependence self-concept and .65 for a WCT measuring individualism self-concept. These researchers also reported adequate interrater agreement when scoring WCTs, with Cohen's Kappa consistently exceeding .85.

Research generally supports the construct validity of WCTs. Johnson et al. (2010) reported correlations between WCT scales that ranged from −.16 to −.26, providing some evidence that the WCT-PA and WCT-NA scales measure different constructs. They also reported significant correlations between the WCT scales and conceptually matched PANAS scales (Watson, Clark, & Tellegen, 1988), with correlations ranging from .34 to .53.

Criterion-Related Validity

Johnson et al. (2010) also provided criterion-related validity evidence for the WCT trait affectivity scale using 120 employee/supervisor pairs. Criteria included employees' self-reported CWBs as well as supervisor ratings of subordinate performance, and subordinate citizenship behaviors directed toward the organization (OCBO) and toward other individuals (OCBI). The WCT-PA scale correlated negatively with CWBs (−.30) and positively with task performance (.55), OCBOs (.54), and OCBIs (.48). The WCT-NA scale correlated positively with CWBs (.35) and negatively with task performance (−.40), OCBOs (−.39), and OCBIs (−.37). Both WCT scales added to the prediction provided by the PANAS scales, with incremental validities ranging from 7% for self-reported CWBs to 26% for supervisor ratings on OCBOs.

More recently, Johnson and Saboe (2011) collected data from 118 employee/supervisor pairs to examine the criterion-related validity of individualistic and interdependent WCTs. Criteria included subordinate-reported CWBs and supervisor ratings of OCBOs, OCBIs, quality of leader–follower exchanges, and overall job performance. As expected, the individualistic WCT correlated with CWBs, and the interdependence WCT correlated with all other criteria. With one exception, the correlations between the WCTs and the criteria were higher than those observed for the individual, relational, and collective scales on the self-report *Levels of Self-Concept Scale* (LSCS; Selenta & Lord, 2005).[8] For each criterion, the WCTs added to the prediction provided by the LSCS, accounting for between 9% and 33% of additional variance in the model.

Summarizing the Research on Indirect Measures of Personality

While positive results have been reported for indirect measures of personality, it is difficult to draw a definitive conclusion about their utility. Overall, there have been relatively few studies conducted in an organizational context. Of the indirect measures covered in this chapter, the CRT-A has been the most researched. Although James et al. (2005) reported substantial validities for the CRT-A, others have questioned its validity (Banks et al., 2011; Berry et al., 2010). It is likely that the other indirect measures covered in this section will go through similar scrutiny in the near future. Thus, as is the case in many areas of organizational research, more studies are needed to fully evaluate the utility of indirect measures of personality.

Mapping Personality Systems to Workplace Behavior

In this section, we propose a parsimonious framework in an effort to provide general guidance on how to use measures of implicit personality in organizational research.[9] We begin by considering the utility of adopting a general model of personality that differentiates between the different levels of the implicit system. This discussion covers the constructs operating at each level and offers suggestions on which measures are likely to provide the most robust assessment of the constructs. We then map the personality systems to performance domains that are often studied by organizational researchers. Our discussion seeks to balance the complexities that arise when considering interactions between personality and the situation with the desire to keep things simple. To accomplish this, we discuss how the features of broad performance domains can influence the level of arousal individuals experience, which in turn determines how the personality systems are likely to guide information processing and drive behaviors.

Defining Personality in the Workplace

Our discussion of the relationship between the different personality systems and work behavior is couched within the dual-process models described earlier. Of these models, CAPS provides the most detailed description of the representations and operations that define explicit personality (i.e., network of CAUs). In some ways, the description of the explicit system is better suited to explain the cognitive processes that underlie decision making than personality. This is not surprising given that cognitive ability plays an important part in explicit processing (Epstein, 2003). Fortunately, models of personality familiar to organizational researchers encapsulate many of the key features of the explicit system. For example, according to *socioanalytic theory* (Hogan, 1983), an individual's *identity* represents the strategies he or she uses to satisfy two basic motivations—the need to get along with others and the need to get ahead. These strategies are assessed through self-report measures that require examinees to rate the extent to which a behavior or trait is self-descriptive. For the most part, these measures organize personality according to an FFM derived through factor-analytic studies of both self-ratings and peer ratings (McCrae & Costa, 1987).

In defining the implicit system, we draw from CEST the importance of differentiating basic and complex associations between representations of the self and the environment. Basic implicit associations initiate the emotional responses that serve as the primary driver of behavior when arousal is high. These basic associations can be assessed using accessibility-based measures, such as the WCT,[10] as well as simple association-based measures, such as the Single-Category IAT (Karpinski & Steinman, 2006). Complex implicit associations, on the other hand, define basic beliefs and motivational orientations that primarily guide behavior when the level of arousal is either low or moderate. Complex implicit associations are best assessed using interpretation-based measures such as a CRT or an SJT, as well as more integrated association-based measures, such as the Self-Concept IAT (Schnabel, Banse, & Asendorpf, 2006). Table 7.2 presents the levels of personality included in the framework, the level of arousal that activates the personality system, the constructs that define each system, and examples of the measures used to assess them.

Table 7.2 Measures of Implicit and Explicit Personality

System	*Activating Arousal Level*	*Constructs*	*Example Measures*
Implicit—basic	High	Emotions	WCT, Single-Category IAT
Implicit—complex	Low, moderate	Implicit beliefs	CRT, Self-Concept IAT
Explicit	Moderate	Personality traits	Self-reports

Relating Personality Systems to Performance Domains

In this section, we consider the relationship between the systems of personality and four performance domains often used by organizational researchers. The distinction between *task* and *contextual* performance (Borman & Motowidlo, 1993, 1997) is used to show the relationship between the personality systems and formal and informal behaviors. Task performance refers to formally defined behaviors that produce or support the organization's technical core, whereas contextual performance refers to informal behaviors that are voluntary and indirectly contribute to productivity by influencing the situational and psychological factors that facilitate task performance. *Adaptive* performance (Pulakos, Arad, & Donovan, 2000) is used to show how personality systems guide behavior when there is a fundamental shift in the work environment. Finally, CWBs (Spector & Fox, 2002) are used to show how personality systems drive behaviors that negatively impact the organization. As discussed below, each of these performance domains is defined by one or more of the situational features postulated by dual-process models to influence arousal, and as a result, the extent to which a personality system is active.

Task Performance

In discussing the relationship between personality systems and task performance, we differentiate between *typical* and *maximal* performance (Sackett, 2007; Sackett, Zedeck, & Fogli, 1988). Typical performance refers to modal work behaviors that occur routinely without oversight in pursuit of well-defined work goals and objectives. Maximal performance, on the other hand, refers to work behaviors exhibited over a short duration in an evaluative setting with clear, task-specific directions.

Depending on complexity, typical performance can lead individuals to experience low to moderate levels of arousal. Low levels of arousal occur when typical task performance involves behaviors that are well learned and there is little to no need to attend to the environment. This type of typical task performance is "automatic" in that it is guided by general approach-avoidance tendencies that are best assessed through indirect measures of complex associations.[11] On the other hand, moderate levels of arousal occur when typical tasks are challenging and/or there is a clear need to attend to the environment. In these instances, both indirect measures of complex associations and direct measures should predict performance. The motivational orientations assessed through indirect measures guide the processing and evaluation of relevant information, whereas the rational propositions assessed through direct measures underlie the deliberate processes that initiates behavior.

The defining characteristics of maximal performance (i.e., consequential performance over a short duration) should lead individuals to become highly aroused (Epstein, 2003). Thus, indirect measures of basic associations are likely to serve as a useful predictor of maximal task performance. That being said, repeated exposure to the situation should, to some extent, mitigate the extent to which emotional states drive maximal performance. In this case, indirect measures that assess the beliefs and motivational orientations existing at the complex reaches of the implicit system may add to the prediction of maximal task performance. Finally, direct measures may provide useful information in cases where individuals have sufficient time to employ coping mechanisms that enable them to engage in rational processing.

Contextual Performance

Contextual performance can be categorized as behaviors representing either *job dedication* or *interpersonal facilitation* (Van Scotter & Motowidlo, 1996). Behaviors representing job dedication include volunteering to work on projects, putting in extra work hours, adhering to organizational rules and behaviors, and exercising personal disciplines. Behaviors representing interpersonal facilitation include helping others complete difficult tasks, praising others for a job well done, and treating others fairly.

Indirect measures of complex associations are likely to predict both job dedication and interpersonal facilitation. In the absence of strong situational cues, implicit beliefs and motivational orientations provide a blueprint for how to interact with the environment. For example, individuals who put in extra effort are likely to possess an implicit need for achievement. Similarly, individuals who volunteer to help others are likely to possess an implicit need for affiliation. It is also possible that direct measures will serve as useful predictors of contextual performance, although to a lesser extent than indirect measures of complex associations. This is especially true for behaviors related to interpersonal facilitation. These behaviors involve interacting with others, and as a result, involve accessing conscious-level representations of the self and the environment (for coverage of personality and citizenship performance, see Chapter 26, this volume).

Adaptive Performance

Adaptive performance is defined as an effective response to a significant change in the situation. The most well-known taxonomy of adaptive performance, offered by Pulakos et al. (2000), includes eight dimensions of adaptability: handling emergency or crisis situations; handling work stress; solving problems creatively; dealing with uncertain or unpredictable situations; learning new work tasks, technologies, and procedures; demonstrating interpersonal adaptability; demonstrating cultural adaptability; and demonstrating physically-oriented adaptability. Adaptive performance is similar to maximal performance in that they both occur under heightened levels of arousal. However, the two performance domains differ in potentially meaningful ways when the goal is to evaluate the utility of indirect measures of personality. For our purposes, maximal performance occurs as part of a defined role, such as the cashiers who checked out customers during a busy time of day in the study by Sackett et al. (1988). Adaptive performance, on the other hand, occurs when individuals are required to change their behavior in order to successfully address a change in the environment. The need to respond to a changing environment has important implications for which personality system is most likely to guide behavior.

In an effort to keep things simple, we link the implicit and explicit systems to three general categories of adaptive performance. *Adapting to stress* includes the dimensions of handling emergencies and dealing with work stress. *Adapting to uncertainty* includes solving problems creatively, dealing with uncertainty, and, to some extent, learning new tasks and skills. *Adapting to others* includes demonstrating interpersonal adaptability and demonstrating cultural adaptability.[12] These dimensions are not intended to be orthogonal, nor are they intended to be definitive. Instead, we propose these categories as a way to think about the key features of adaptive performance and their relationship to the different personality systems.

ADAPTING TO STRESS

Any situation that induces stress is highly arousing and thus is likely to be predicted by indirect measures of basic implicit associations. Indirect measures of complex implicit associations can also predict how individuals adapt in stressful situations because they frame how information is processed and evaluated. For example, individuals who hold an implicit belief that the world is generally benevolent and predictable are likely to interpret stressful events as less threatening and controllable than are individuals who hold more negative implicit beliefs about the world. Direct measures may also provide useful information, especially if implicit beliefs mitigate the level of arousal the individual experiences in response to the stressful situation. That being said, indirect measures of basic associations should provide the most utility when the goal is to predict adaptive performance in stressful situations.

ADAPTING TO UNCERTAINTY

The prevailing feature of the dimensions of adaptability included in this category is that individuals are responding to the fact that they do not possess the knowledge, skills, or abilities needed to handle the situation. In these instances, indirect measures of complex implicit associations should serve as the best predictors of performance. These complex components of personality are responsible for the creativity needed to solve novel problems (Epstein, 2003; Norris & Epstein, 2011), the implicit personality policies and heuristics that guide decisions and behaviors under uncertainty (Motowidlo et al., 2006a), and the motivational orientations that guide how individuals approach learning new tasks (Dweck, 1986). Indirect measures of basic associations and direct measures can also predict how individuals adapt to uncertainty, but to a lesser extent than indirect measures of complex associations. Indirect measures of basic associations are more likely to predict behavior when the uncertainty is perceived as very threatening. Direct measures are more likely to predict behavior when rational processes are needed to successfully perform.

ADAPTING TO OTHERS

Both direct and indirect measures can predict performance in situations that require adapting to others. Indirect measures of basic associations are likely to serve as strong predictors in situations where adapting to others is immediate and perceived as threatening (as in the examples of the consultants presented earlier). Both indirect measures of complex associations and direct measures are likely to predict behaviors in situations that involve adapting to others over time. However, indirect measures should be the stronger predictor because implicit beliefs about the world will guide how information is processed and interpreted by the explicit system.

CWBs

Several taxonomies have been offered to describe CWBs. For example, Robinson and Bennett (1995) organized CWBs into four categories—*personal aggression* (e.g., bullying and harassment), *production deviance* (e.g., unwarranted absenteeism and work slowdown), *property deviance* (e.g., damaging equipment, theft), and *political deviance* (e.g., gossiping, finger pointing). While these categories include different behaviors, the antecedents of these behaviors are either an emotional response to a situational cue (e.g., Chen & Spector, 1992; Fox, Spector, & Miles, 2001; Spector, 1978; Spector & Fox, 2002) or a cognitive response to a perceived injustice (Greenberg, 1990; Skarlicki, Folger, & Tesluk, 1999).

EMOTION-DRIVEN CWBS

Indirect measures of basic associations are likely to be the strongest predictors of CWBs that occur as the result of an emotional response to a situational cue. Indirect measures of complex implicit processes can contribute to the prediction of CWBs that unfold over time. For example, individuals who exhibit personal aggression in response to repeated exposure to situational cues may hold the belief that people are malevolent and untrustworthy or possess a retribution bias justification mechanism that predisposes them to act aggressively toward others when they feel threatened. While direct measures may predict emotionally driven CWBs, their impact is likely smaller than that found for indirect measures.

INJUSTICE-DRIVEN CWBS

In many cases, CWBs occur as the result of a perceived injustice on the part of the organization. Both indirect measures of complex associations and direct measures are likely to predict CWBs that involve production deviance. The choice of which measure provides the stronger prediction depends on the clarity of the perceived injustice. Indirect measures of complex associations should serve as the stronger predictor when the injustice is relatively unclear (i.e., individuals working in the organization do not agree that the injustice occurred). Direct measures should serve as stronger predictors in situations where the injustice is clear (i.e., individuals working in the organization overwhelmingly agree that the injustice occurred). For more coverage of personality and CWB, see Chapter 27, this volume.

Given the complexity of both personality and organizational behaviors, our framework necessarily fails to address all possible facets of personality–performance relationships. That being said, the framework provides researchers general guidance on which measures of personality are most applicable for different types of performance. A summary of linkages between personality systems and the performance domains is presented in Table 7.3.

Future Research

The major thrust of this chapter is to promote better understanding of the role of implicit personality in organizational settings. Potential lines of research include identifying factors that moderate the relationship between the personality systems and work behaviors, further establishing the construct validity of indirect measures, examining the fakeability of indirect measures, and developing additional indirect measures to capture lower-level implicit processes.

Table 7.3 Mapping Implicit and Explicit Personality to Performance

Performance Domain	*Personality System*		
	Implicit—Basic	*Implicit—Complex*	*Explicit*
Task performance			
Typical task performance	W	S	M
Maximal task performance	S	M	W
Contextual performance			
Job dedication	W	S	M
Interpersonal facilitation	W	S	S
Adaptive performance			
Adapting to stress	S	M	W
Adapting to uncertainty	M	S	M
Adapting to others	W	S	S
Counterproductive behaviors			
Emotion driven	S	M	W
Injustice driven	W	S	S

Notes: "S" indicates a strong relationship between personality system and performance domain; "M" indicates a moderate relationship between personality system and performance domain; "W" indicates a weak relationship between personality system and performance domain.

Moderators of the Personality–Performance Relationship

While there are a plethora of potential moderators of the relationship between personality systems and work behavior, we focus on four factors that we suspect can have a large effect. Three of the potential moderators—impulsivity, trait anxiety, and working memory capacity—are relatively stable individual differences. The fourth potential moderator—amount of relevant experience—can change within the individual.

Impulsivity

One factor that can influence the extent to which direct and indirect measures predict work behavior is the individual's level of impulsivity. Individuals high in impulsivity tend to "act before thinking" and "wear their personality on their sleeve." In contrast, individuals with low impulsivity tend to think through options before acting when possible. In general, indirect measures of personality should be more predictive of performance among individuals high in impulsivity compared to individuals low in impulsivity. This is especially likely for indirect measures of basic associations. This occurs because basic implicit associations are more influential in impulsive individuals (Epstein, 2003). This effect should hold across all performance domains hypothesized to be predicted by indirect measures of personality.

Trait Anxiety

The moderating effect of trait anxiety should be similar to that expected for impulsivity. Highly anxious individuals are sensitive to emotional cues in the environment and hence are more likely to become aroused across situations. According to CEST, basic associations within the implicit system are the primary driver of behaviors when arousal is high. If this is true, indirect measures of basic associations should be stronger predictors of performance for individuals with high trait anxiety than for individuals with lower levels of trait anxiety.

Working Memory Capacity

Another individual difference that can influence the ability to utilize the explicit system is working memory capacity (e.g., Barrett, Tugade, & Engle, 2004). Individuals with high working memory capacity are better able to evaluate and integrate goal-relevant information in complex situations that require making a decision about how to behave. In contrast, individuals with low working memory capacity struggle to process goal-relevant information in complex situations, and as a result, engage in behaviors that are more likely to be guided by their implicit beliefs.

Task Experience

Another factor that might moderate the relationship between implicit personality and performance is the amount of the individual's experience performing the task or working in a particular situation. We propose that indirect measures are more predictive of performance among individuals with little experience in situations of interest to the researcher. Without the benefit of experience, individuals face a relatively ambiguous situation that requires them to rely on their own implicit beliefs and motivations. Ambiguity is a salient characteristic of projective tests historically developed to assess implicit personality. If increases in experience lessen ambiguity, it should also reduce the influence of the implicit system.

Construct Validity of Indirect Measures

While there is some evidence supporting the construct validity of indirect measures, the results are far from conclusive. A recurring question in the literature is what constitutes evidence of convergent validity for indirect measures. For example, are low observed correlations among different indirect measures of similar constructs evidence of poor convergence or good discrimination? To reformulate the question, *should* implicit measures of the same construct correlate with one another? We predict that these relationships are often low because indirect measures that assess different types of associations within the implicit system are lumped together as implicit. Throughout this chapter, we have posited that the different levels of the implicit system can guide behavior in different situations. A MTMM analysis of different indirect measures using the taxonomy proposed by Uhlmann et al. (2012) would go a long way toward determining whether those different indirect measures tap different underlying processes.

Correlations between indirect and direct measures of similar constructs are also difficult to interpret as evidence of construct validity. Nosek (2005) concluded that IATs and self-reports assess conceptually distinct but empirically related constructs. While indirect/direct relationships are quite robust for some indirect measures (e.g., Johnson & Saboe, 2011), others are generally weak and highly variable (Nosek, 2005). It would seem that the theoretical foundations for indirect measurement (outlined above) would be supported by null relationships between indirect and direct measures. However, as Haines and Sumner (2006) point out, these correlations were used to select the "best" method of creating a revised scoring algorithm for the IAT (Greenwald et al., 2002). These logical inconsistencies complicate the interpretation of indirect/direct correlations as evidence for convergence/discrimination.

A final hurdle in the establishment of construct validity is that it is unlikely measures reflect processing that is *all indirect* or *all direct*. Responses to measures, regardless of type, are likely influenced by multiple implicit and explicit information-processing systems. For example, Conrey, Sherman, Gawronski, Hugenberg, and Groom (2005) used multinomial modeling to demonstrate that conceptual activation influenced IAT scores, as did a number of other factors (i.e., guessing, ability to determine correct answer) that independently influenced responding. This is also likely the case for other indirect measures, particularly those (CRT, SJT, and WCT) where there is less time pressure and more deliberation in responding. In sum, once different implicit information-processing systems are identified, we also must determine the extent to which scores on a related indirect measure reflect processing in that system.

Fakeability of Indirect Measures

One question that future research can address is whether examinees can successfully fake indirect measures of personality. Research suggests that IAT and CRT measures are less susceptible to faking than are direct measures (e.g., LeBreton, Barksdale, Robin, & James, 2007; Steffens, 2004). More research is needed to determine the extent to which coaching affects the ability to successfully distort responses on indirect measures of personality. For example, will applicants be able to fake an IAT when they are given specific strategies to override their implicit tendencies?

A recurring debate in organizational research focuses on whether or not applicant faking adversely impacts the validity of personality tests. It has been argued that faking has little impact on the validity of self-report personality measures (Ones, Viswesvaran, & Reiss, 1996). While this position is not necessarily accepted by all researchers, there is theoretical justification for it. As mentioned earlier, Hogan (1983) proposed that individuals display their identity (i.e., how we think about ourselves, and how we want others to perceive us) in an intentional manner to get along with others in order to get ahead (i.e., achieve our goals and fulfill affiliation needs). As such, faking on a self-report measure under these circumstances may be correlated with performance and hence unlikely to adversely impact prediction (it may actually improve it). Unfortunately, socioanalytic theory does not apply to the mechanisms assumed to underlie responses to indirect measures. Thus, in addition to examining whether or not examinees can fake responses to indirect measures, researchers should explore the extent to which faking on indirect measures reduces validity (for more coverage on personality tests and faking, see Chapter 12, this volume).

Developing New Indirect Measures of Personality

Researchers should investigate whether the available measures adequately capture the different levels within the implicit self-system. The importance of understanding the level of operation within the implicit system that is most relevant when using indirect measures is mentioned throughout this chapter. With the exception of the IAT, it is unlikely that the indirect measures covered in this chapter provide meaningful information about the association among schemata operating at lower levels of implicit associations. All of the indirect measures discussed rely on written stimuli (either words or written scenarios) to induce a response. These stimuli seem appropriate when the goal is to capture schemata represented at higher-level associations. However, it is unclear that these stimuli are sufficient to activate the emotion-laden schemata that define lower-level associations. We propose that researchers interested in capturing basic associations of the implicit system use performance-based measures that require individuals to respond to cues that are similar (if not identical) to those that are likely to induce the emotional response and subsequent behavior of interest.

Like any measurement approach, performance-based measures pose problems that, if not addressed, make their use problematic (e.g., subjective scoring, marginal psychometric properties). Fortunately, recent advances in technology and measurement make performance-based measurement a reasonable alternative to current implicit measures. A good example of this is a *standardized dynamic test* (SDT) proposed by Embretson (2000). SDTs can differ on three dimensions: *cue type*, *cue scheduling*, and *cue design*. Cue type refers to the effect that the cue is expected to have on test performance. *Positive* cues are used to facilitate performance (e.g., introducing new information), whereas *negative* cues are used to hinder performance (e.g., removing relevant information). Cue scheduling refers to the timing with which the intervention is presented. In *blocked* scheduling, multiple cues are presented together (e.g., a module of several problem-solving strategies), whereas in *progressive* scheduling, cues are presented separately throughout the session (e.g., providing misleading information at different points in the test session). Finally, cue design refers to the relationship between the test session and the measurement of performance. *Concurrent* designs present cues at the same time as the items used to measure performance (e.g., problem-solving strategy is given at the same time as the item assessing problem-solving ability), whereas *separate* designs present cues before the items used to measure performance (e.g., problem-solving strategy is given as part of an instructional module, which is followed by items assessing problem-solving ability).

The potential of using SDTs to assess implicit personality is suggested by Embretson (2000), who used an SDT to assess the ability to engage in abstract reasoning under stress. The negative cue used to induce stress was time allowed to complete a section of an abstract reasoning test. The results showed that the change in scores under time constraint added significantly to the prediction of performance of military personnel in high stress jobs when included in the regression analysis including ability test scores under normal time, a measure of impulsivity, and a measure of the FFM personality dimensions.[13] While these results are encouraging, more research is needed to explore the possibility of incorporating the SDT framework to develop implicit measures of personality.

Conclusion

Research conducted over the past 20-plus years suggests that researchers and practitioners might benefit from using indirect measures to assess implicit personality in an organizational context. However, given the relative dearth of research conducted to date, it is difficult to ascertain the true utility of indirect measures.

Practitioner's Window

Our discussion has offered hypotheses that researchers can follow. There are, however, several practical implications that can guide current decisions about using implicit measures to predict work behaviors. If we were forced to recommend one take away from this chapter, it would be the importance of the environment in determining the relationship between personality and performance. Throughout this chapter, we emphasize the important role that features of the situation can play in determining which component of the implicit system is most influential. The emphasis on the environment has several implications for practitioners.

- First, emphasize the need to conduct a thorough job analysis in order to gather the information needed to identify the critical aspects of the environment that can influence the activation of the different personality systems.
- Second, it is unreasonable to expect that an overall personality score will provide robust prediction of behaviors. Instead, researchers should design and implement measures of personality that predict behavior in specific, high-stakes settings.
- Another potential concern associated with using indirect measures for applied purposes is applicant reactions. In addition to examining applicant reactions to each indirect measure, it would be interesting to see if applicants react differently to the measures.
- Finally, many indirect measures (e.g., SJT and CRT) require a lot of time and resources to develop and validate. Therefore, it is important to consider both the upfront and maintenance costs associated with administering indirect measures for high-stakes purposes such as personnel selection.

Notes

1 Hereafter, we use the term "personality systems" when referring to both the implicit and explicit systems.

2 Other models offered to describe how implicit processes can drive behavior include Fazio's (1990) model of *Motivation and Opportunity as Determinants* of attitude behavior (MODE), Cloninger's (2004) *Theory of Temperament, Character, and Personality Coherence*, Kuhl's (2000) *Personality Systems Interaction Theory*, and Cervone's (2004) *Knowledge and Appraisal Personality Architecture*.

3 Hereafter, we use the term "indirect" when referring to measures designed to assess implicit personality, and the term "direct" when referring to self-report measures designed to assess explicit personality.

4 Uhlmann et al. (2012) do not include situational judgment tests (SJTs) in their taxonomy. We suggest SJTs designed to assess an individual's "Implicit Trait Policy" is an interpretation-based measure (Motowidlo, Hooper, & Jackson, 2006a).

5 The UTISC defines knowledge of others in terms of *stereotypes* and *attitudes*. Stereotypes are associations between two groups or between a group and defining attributes. Attitudes reflect the valence of the associations that define the stereotypes. We focus on self-knowledge because it defines the associations included in implicit association tests (IATs) designed to assess implicit personality.

6 This approach to constructing IAT measures of personality traits is identical to Haines and Sumner's (2006) description of IATs assessing "implicit self-concept." This is contrasted with "self-esteem" IATs that have categories labeled "positive" and "negative" rather than as traits.

7 Greenwald, McGhee, and Schwartz (1998) initially proposed two different approaches to scoring the IAT. The first involved the use of raw response latencies. Another involved the use of log transformed latencies. The logic of using log transformed latencies involved a need to "use a statistic that had satisfactory stability of variance for analyses" (p. 1467).
8 The sole exception was the correlation between the Levels of Self-Concept Scale (LSCS)-relational scale and behaviors directed toward other individuals (OCBIs).
9 Achieving parsimony necessitates skimming over (or omitting) components from earlier work offered to explain the role of personality in organizations. Interested readers should refer to other frameworks applying implicit measures in organizations (e.g., Bing, LeBreton, Davison, Migetz, & James, 2007; Uhlmann et al., 2012), as well as general models of the personality–performance relationship (e.g., Tett & Burnett, 2003).
10 Word completion tasks (WCTs) have been used to assess complex implicit representations (e.g., Johnson, Tolentino, Rodopman, & Cho, 2010).
11 Some may argue that this proposition flies in the face of the finding that personality accounts for little variance in strong situations (e.g., Meyer, Dalal, & Bonaccio, 2009). While this may be accurate when discussing direct measures, we suggest that indirect measures of complex associations provide information about general tendencies that guide behaviors across situations.
12 Demonstrating physically-oriented performance is not included as it does not fit clearly into any of the categories. It is not considered separately because it is less likely to be predicted by personality than the other dimensions of adaptability.
13 A criticism of dynamic tests is that they rely on change scores that have suspect psychometric properties. Embretson argues that problems with change scores can be overcome using item response theory (IRT).

References

Asendorpf, J. B., Banse, R., & Mücke, D. (2002). Double dissociation between implicit and explicit personality self-concept: The case of shy behavior. *Journal of Personality and Social Psychology, 83*, 380–393.

Back, M. D., Schmukle, S. C., & Egloff, B. (2009). Predicting actual behavior from the explicit and implicit self-concept of personality. *Journal of Personality and Social Psychology, 93*, 533–548.

Banks, G. C., Kepes, S., & McDaniel, M. A. (2011). *Publication bias and the validity of conditional reasoning tests.* Paper presented at the annual meeting of the Society for Industrial and Organizational Psychology, Chicago.

Barrett, L. F., Tugade, M. M., & Engle, R. W. (2004). Individual differences in working memory capacity and dual-process theories of the mind. *Psychological Bulletin, 130*, 553–573.

Berry, C. M., Sackett, P. R., & Tobares, V. (2010). A meta-analysis of conditional reasoning tests of aggression. *Personnel Psychology, 63*, 361–384.

Bing, M. N., LeBreton, J. M., Davison, H. K., Migetz, D. Z., & James, L. R. (2007). Integrating implicit and explicit social cognitions for enhanced personality assessment: A general framework for choosing measurement and statistical methods. *Organizational Research Methods, 10*, 136–179.

Blanton, H., & Jaccard, J., Gonzales, P., & Christie, C. (2006). Decoding the Implict Association Test: Implications for criterion prediction. *Journal of Experimental Social Psychology, 42*, 192–212.

Blanton, H., Jaccard, J., Christie, C., & Gonzales, P. M. (2007). Plausible assumptions, questionable assumptions and post hoc rationalizations: Will the real IAT, please stand up? *Journal of Experimental Social Psychology, 43*, 399–409.

Blanton, H., Klick, J., Mitchell, G., Jaccard, J., Mellers, B., & Tetlock, P. E. (2009). Strong claims and weak evidence: Reassessing the predictive validity of the IAT. *Journal of Applied Psychology, 94*, 567–582.

Borman, W. C., & Motowidlo, S. J. (1993). Expanding the criterion domain to include elements of contextual performance. In N. Schmitt & W. C. Borman (Eds.), *Personnel selection in organizations* (pp. 71–98). San Francisco: Jossey-Bass.

Borman, W. C., & Motowidlo, S. J. (1997). Task and contextual performance: The meaning for personnel selection research. *Human Performance, 10*, 99–109.

Boyle, G. J., Matthews, G., & Saklofske, D. H. (Eds.). (2008). *The Sage handbook of personality theory and assessment. Volume 2: Personality measurement and testing.* Los Angeles: Sage.

Cervone, D. (2004). The architecture of personality. *Psychological Review, 111*, 183–204.

Chen, P. Y., & Spector, P. E. (1992). Relationships of work stressors with aggression, withdrawal, theft, and substance abuse: An exploratory study. *Journal of Occupational and Organizational Psychology, 65*, 177–184.

Cloninger, C. R. (2004). *Feeling good: The science of well being.* New York, NY: Oxford University Press.

Conrey, F. R., Sherman, J. W., Gawronski, B., Hugenberg, K., & Groom, C. (2005). Separating multiple processes in implicit social cognition: The quad-model of implicit task performance. *Journal of Personality and Social Psychology, 89*, 469–487.

Deutsch, R., & Strack, F. (2006). Duality models in social psychology: From dual processes to interacting systems. *Psychological Inquiry, 17*, 166–172.
Deutsch, R., & Strack, F. (2008). Variants of judgment and decision making: The perspective of the reflective-impulsive model. In H. Plessner, C. Betsch, & T. Betsch (Eds.), *Intuition in judgment and decision making* (pp. 39–53). Mahwah, NJ: Erlbaum.
Dweck, C. S. (1986). Motivational processes affecting learning. *American Psychologist, 41*, 1040–1048.
Embretson, S. E. (2000). Multidimensional measurement from dynamic tests: Abstract reasoning under stress. *Multivariate Behavioral Research, 35*, 505–542.
Epstein, S. (1994). Integration of the cognitive and the psychodynamic unconscious. *American Psychologist, 49*, 709–724.
Epstein, S. (2003). Cognitive-experiential self-theory in personality. In T. Millon & M. J. Learner (Eds.), *Comprehensive handbook of psychology. Volume 5: Personality and social psychology* (pp. 159–184). Hoboken, NJ: Wiley & Sons.
Epstein, S., & Pacini, R. (1999). Some basic issues regarding dual-process theories from the perspective of cognitive-experiential self-theory. In S. Chaiken & Y. Trope (Eds.), *Dual-process theories in social psychology* (pp. 462–482). New York, NY: Guilford.
Epstein, S., Pacini, R., Denes-Raj, V., & Heier, H. (1996). Individual differences in intuitive-experiential and analytical-rational thinking styles. *Journal of Personality and Social Psychology, 71*, 390–405.
Fazio, R. H. (1990). A practical guide to the use of response latency in social psychological research. In C. Hendrick & M. S. Clark (Eds.), *Research methods in personality and social psychology* (pp. 74–97). Thousand Oaks, CA: Sage.
Fox, S., Spector, P. E., & Miles, D. (2001). Counterproductive work behavior (CWB) in response to job stressors and organizational justice: Some mediator and moderator tests for autonomy and emotions. *Journal of Vocational Behavior, 59*, 291–309.
Greenberg, J. (1990). Employee theft as a reaction to underpayment inequity: The hidden cost of pay cuts. *Journal of Applied Psychology, 75*, 561–568.
Greenwald, A. G., Banaji, M. R., Rudman, L. A., Farnham, S. D., Nosek, B. A., & Mellott, D. S. (2002). A unified theory of implicit attitudes, stereotypes, self-esteem, and self-concept. *Psychological Review, 109*, 3–25.
Greenwald, A. G., McGhee, D. E., & Schwartz, J. L. K. (1998). Measuring individual differences in implicit cognition: The implicit association test. *Journal of Personality and Social Psychology, 74*, 1464–1480.
Greenwald, A. G., Nosek, B. A., & Banaji, M. R. (2003). Understanding and using the implicit association test: I. An improved scoring algorithm. *Journal of Personality and Social Psychology, 85*, 197–216.
Grumm, M., & von Collani, G. (2007). Measuring Big-Five personality dimensions with the implicit association test—Implicit personality traits or self-esteem? *Personality and Individual Differences, 43*, 2205–2217.
Haines, E. L., & Sumner, K. E. (2006). Implicit measurement of attitudes, stereotypes and self-concepts in organizations: Teaching old dogmas new tricks. *Organizational Research Methods, 9*, 536–553.
Hofmann, W., Gawronski, B., Gschwendner, T., Le, H., & Schmitt, M. (2005). A meta-analysis on the correlation between the implicit association test and explicit self-report measures. *Personality and Social Psychology Bulletin, 10*, 1369–1385.
Hogan, R. (1983). A socioanalytic theory of personality. In M. M. Page (Ed.), *1982 Nebraska symposium on motivation* (pp. 55–89). Lincoln: University of Nebraska Press.
James, L. R. (1998). Measurement of personality via conditional reasoning. *Organizational Research Methods, 1*, 131–163.
James, L. R., & Lebreton, J. M. (2007). *Assessing the implicit personality through conditional reasoning*. Washington, DC: American Psychological Association.
James, L. R., McIntyre, M. D., Glisson, C. A., Green, P. D., Patton, T. W., LeBreton, J. M., . . . Williams, L. J. (2005). A conditional reasoning measure for aggression. *Organizational Research Methods, 8*, 69–99.
Johnson, R. E., & Saboe, K. N. (2011). Measuring implicit traits in organizational research: Development of an indirect measure of employee implicit self-concept. *Organizational Research Methods, 14*, 530–547.
Johnson, R. E., & Steinman, L. (2009). The use of implicit measures for organizational research: An empirical example. *Canadian Journal of Behavioural Science, 41*, 202–212.
Johnson, R. E., Tolentino, A. L., Rodopman, O. B., & Cho, E. (2010). We (sometimes) know not how we feel: Predicting job performance with an implicit measure of trait affectivity. *Personnel Psychology, 63*, 197–219.
Karpinski, A., & Steinman, R. B. (2006). The single category Implicit Association Test as a measure of implicit social cognition. *Journal of Personality and Social Psychology, 91*, 16–32.
Kuhl, J. (2000). A functional-design approach to motivation and volition: The dynamics of personality systems interactions. In M. Boekaerts, P. R. Pintrich, & M. Zeidner (Eds.), *Self-regulation: Directions and challenges for future research* (pp. 111–169). San Diego, CA: Academic Press.

LeBreton, J. M., Barksdale, C. D., Robin, J. D., & James, L. R. (2007). Measurement issues associated with conditional reasoning tests: Indirect measurement and test faking. *Journal of Applied Psychology, 92*, 1–16.

McCrae, R. R., & Costa, P. T. (1987). Validation of the five-factor model of personality across instruments and observers. *Journal of Personality and Social Psychology, 52*, 81–90.

McDaniel, M. A., Morgeson, F. P., Finnegan, E. B., Campion, M. A., & Braverman, E. P. (2001). Predicting job performance using situational judgment tests: A clarification of the literature. *Journal of Applied Psychology, 86*, 730–740.

Meyer, R. D., Dalal, R. S., & Bonaccio, S. (2009). A meta-analytic investigation into the moderating effects of situational strength on the conscientiousness–performance relationship. *Journal of Organizational Behavior, 30*, 1077–1102.

Mischel, W., & Ayduk, O. (2002). Self-regulation in a cognitive-affective personality system: Attentional control in the service of the self. *Self and Identity, 1*, 113–120.

Mischel, W., & Shoda, Y. (1995). A cognitive-affective system theory of personality: Reconceptualizing situations, dispositions, dynamics, and invariance in personality structure. *Psychological Review, 102*, 246–268.

Mischel, W., & Shoda, Y. (1998). Reconciling processing dynamics and personality dispositions. *Annual Review of Psychology, 49*, 229–258.

Motowidlo, S. J., & Beier, M. E. (2010). Differentiating specific job knowledge from implicit trait policies in procedural knowledge measured by a situational judgment test. *Journal of Applied Psychology, 95*, 321–333.

Motowidlo, S. J., Dunnette, M. D., & Carter, G. W. (1990). An alternative selection procedure: The low-fidelity simulation. *Journal of Applied Psychology, 75*, 640–647.

Motowidlo, S. J., Hooper, A. C., & Jackson, H. L. (2006a). A theoretical basis for situational judgment tests. In J. A. Weekley & R. E. Ployhart (Eds.), *Situational judgment tests: Theory, measurement, and application* (pp. 57–81). Mahwah, NJ: Erlbaum.

Motowidlo, S. J., Hooper, A. C., & Jackson, H. L. (2006b). Implicit policies about relations between personality traits and behavioral effectiveness in situational judgment items. *Journal of Applied Psychology, 91*, 749–761.

Murray, H. A. (1938). *Explorations in personality*. New York: Oxford University Press.

Norris, P., & Epstein, S. (2011). An experiential thinking style: Its facets and relations with objective and subjective criterion measures. *Journal of Personality, 79*, 1044–1080.

Nosek, B. A. (2005). Moderators of the relationship between implicit and explicit evaluation. *Journal of Experimental Psychology: General, 134*, 565–584.

Ones, D. S., Viswesvaran, C., & Reiss, A. D. (1996). Role of social desirability in personality testing for personnel selection: The red herring. *Journal of Applied Psychology, 81*, 660–679.

Pulakos, E. D., Arad, S., & Donovan, M. A. (2000). Adaptability in the workplace: Development of a taxonomy of adaptive performance. *Journal of Applied Psychology, 85*, 612–624.

Robinson, S. L., & Bennett, R. J. (1995). A typology of deviant workplace behaviors: A multidimensional scaling study. *Academy of Management Journal, 38*, 555–572.

Russell, J. A. (2003). Core affect and the psychological construction of emotion. *Psychological Review, 110*, 145–172.

Sackett, P. R. (2007). Revisiting the origins of the typical-maximum performance distinction. *Human Performance, 20*, 179–185.

Sackett, P. R., Zedeck, S., & Fogli, L. (1988). Relations between measures of typical and maximum job performance. *Journal of Applied Psychology, 73*, 482–486.

Schnabel, K., Banse, R., & Asendorpf, J. B. (2006). Assessment of implicit personality self-concept using the Implicit Association Test (IAT): Concurrent assessment of anxiousness and angriness. *British Journal of Social Psychology, 45*, 373–396.

Selenta, C., & Lord, R. G. (2005). *Development of the levels of Self-Concept Scale: Measuring the individual, relational, and collective levels*. Unpublished manuscript.

Shoda, Y., Mischel, W., & Wright, J. C. (1994). Intraindividual stability in the organization and patterning of behavior: Incorporating psychological situations into the idiographic analysis of personality. *Journal of Personality and Social Psychology, 67*, 674–687.

Siers, B. P., & Christiansen, N. D. (2008). On the validity of implicit association tests of personality traits. In P. Raymark (Chair), *Alternative approaches to personality assessment*. Symposium conducted at the Society for Industrial and Organizational Psychology (SIOP) Conference, San Francisco.

Skarlicki, D. P., Folger, R., & Tesluk, P. (1999). Personality as a moderator in the relationship between fairness and retaliation. *Academy of Management Journal, 42*, 100–108.

Spector, P. E. (1978). Organizational frustration: A model and review of the literature. *Personnel Psychology, 31*, 815–829.

Spector, P. E., & Fox, S. (2002). An emotion-centered model of voluntary work behavior: Some parallels between counterproductive work behavior and organizational citizenship behavior. *Human Resource Management Review, 12*, 269–292.

Steffens, M. C. (2004). Is the implicit associate test immune to faking? *Experimental Psychology, 51*, 165–179.

Strack, F., & Deutsch, R. (2004). Reflective and impulsive determinants of social behavior. *Personality and Social Psychology Review, 8*, 220–247.

Tett, R. P., & Burnett, D. D. (2003). A personality trait-based interactionist model of job performance. *Journal of Applied Psychology, 88*, 500–517.

Uhlmann, E. L., Leavitt, K., Menges, J. I., Koopman, J., Howe, M., & Johnson, R. E. (2012). Getting explicit about the implicit: A taxonomy of implicit measures and a guide for their use in organizational research. *Organizational Research Methods, 15*(4), 553–601.

Van Scotter, J. R., & Motowidlo, S. J. (1996). Interpersonal facilitation and job dedication as separate facets of contextual performance. *Journal of Applied Psychology, 81*, 525–531.

Watson, D., Clark, L., & Tellegen, A. (1988). Development and validation of brief measures of positive and negative affect: The PANAS scales. *Journal of Personality and Social Psychology, 54*, 1063–1070.

8

Multilevel Perspectives on Personality in Organizations

Anupama Narayan and Robert E. Ployhart

The study of personality in industrial–organizational (I/O) psychology has been active since the early 1990s. In the 20 years following Barrick and Mount (1991) and Tett, Jackson, and Rothstein (1991), researchers have sought to understand how and why personality is related to a variety of individual outcomes, such as job performance and contextual performance (e.g., Hurtz & Donovan, 2000), job attitudes (e.g., job satisfaction; Judge, Heller, & Mount, 2002), leadership (e.g., Bono & Judge, 2004), and subjective well-being (Hayes & Joseph, 2003). Although there remains some debate over the usefulness of personality traits in some contexts (e.g., personnel selection; Tett & Christiansen, 2007), in general the published record shows that I/O psychologists have embraced personality, especially in terms of traits, as a set of individual difference variables important for understanding workplace behavior.

The vast majority of this research has focused on relationships at the individual level, usually linking individual personality characteristics to individual behavior and outcomes (e.g., personality traits and job performance). While this research is important, we argue that it may underestimate the value and effects of personality in organizations. Specifically, personality is likely to have a strong influence on the manner in which group and team members interact, which, in turn, may influence group and team performance and behavior (e.g., Hofmann & Jones, 2005). Furthermore, recent research (e.g., Ployhart, Weekley, & Baughman, 2006) suggests that organization-level manifestations of personality, whether as an aggregate of individual personality (such as proposed within the attraction–selection–attrition model; Schneider, 1987), or as correlates of aggregate personality (e.g., organizational reputation, values, culture, or brand), may contribute to important business outcomes.

However, at this point, there is more theory than empirical research examining the nature, antecedents, and consequences of collective personality. The purpose of this chapter is to raise awareness that personality, operating in aggregate at the group and organizational levels, can have a powerful influence on individual and collective action in the workplace. We begin with a brief history of the role of personality, especially as it relates to individual behaviors in work contexts. Second, we provide an overview of multilevel theory, specifically highlighting the processes and nature of emergent phenomena, a distinction between composition and compilation models, and the broad statistical framework that models these processes. Third, we move from a discussion of multilevel issues to the area of collective personality at the unit level. This includes three perspectives that have been used to conceptualize personality at the unit level, as well as other variables that have been used to describe collective personality, especially at the organizational level (e.g., reputation). Fourth, we discuss new effects for collective personality, especially how personality relates to the emergence of human capital resources, and demonstrate how and why human capital resources are related to unit (organizational)-level phenomena. Finally, we offer directions for future research and our practitioner's window.

Personality at the Individual Level: A Brief Overview

Personality is an inherently complex psychological characteristic that is an outcome of many interacting influences ranging from genetics to culture. Since its inception, researchers in this field have focused on the scientific study of psychological individuality or differences that distinguish one person from the other. Allport (1937) defined personality as "the dynamic organization within the individual of those psychophysical systems that determine his unique adjustment to the environment" (p. 48). Recently, it has been defined as a complex organization of cognition, affect, and behavior that gives pattern and direction to an individual's life (Pervin, 1996). The term "personality" (R. T. Hogan, 1991) usually focuses on either the underlying structures, dynamics, processes, and propensities of individuals that lead to consistencies in their behavior, or the way in which these consistencies are observed and described by others. Thus, personality at its root is primarily associated with the individual (for a recent review, see Oswald & Hough, 2011).

Personality measures predict multiple work-related outcomes. Robust relationships have been found between personality traits and criteria including job satisfaction (Judge, Bono, & Locke, 2000), work attitudes (Judge, Heller, et al., 2002), trust (e.g., Mooradian, Renzl, & Matzler, 2006), leadership (Judge, Bono, Ilies, & Gerhardt, 2002), knowledge sharing (Matzler, Renzl, Müller, Herting, & Mooradian, 2008), conflict and facilitation between work and family roles (Wayne, Musisca, & Fleeson, 2004), job performance (e.g., Barrick & Mount, 1991), and organizational citizenship behavior (Organ, 1994). Such examples highlight that personality psychology has a strong presence in I/O psychology. Personality psychology, primarily, has been based on the individualist model of the person in which understanding the individual has been the primary focus. It refers simultaneously to characteristics that are (1) ascribed to individuals, (2) stable over time, and (3) psychological in nature (R. T. Hogan, 1991). Thus, personality is primarily a microlevel construct, in that it is defined as a property of an individual. Yet, there is evidence to suggest collectives of people, groups, teams, and even organizations may manifest "collective personalities." The "personality" of teams, groups, and organizations is a collective phenomenon sharing some of the elements of individuals' personalities, but combined and bundled in such a way that the aggregate construct is different conceptually and empirically. To understand why and how requires an understanding of multilevel theory and principles.

Multilevel Theory

Several authors (e.g., Bliese, 2000; Chan, 1998; Chen, Mathieu, & Bliese, 2004; Hitt, Beamish, Jackson, & Mathieu, 2007; Kozlowski & Klein, 2000; Morgeson & Hofmann, 1999; Rousseau, 1985) have thoroughly discussed the nature, structure, and validation of multilevel constructs (e.g., efficacy) across levels of analysis (e.g., individual and team). We briefly review some key concepts here as they relate to collective personality, with specific emphasis on emergent phenomena.

The primary purpose of multilevel theory is to explain how constructs operating at elemental levels (e.g., individuals) emerge in collections of those elements and how those collective structures influence the interaction between elements and their collectives (Morgeson & Hofmann, 1999). Constructs, which are synonymous with concepts, are theoretical abstractions, focused at organizing and making sense of a phenomenon (Pedhazur & Schmelkin, 1991). The level of the construct is the level at which it is expected to manifest (individual, dyad, team, and organization). These levels are referred to by organizational researchers as focal units or, more simply, as units (Rousseau, 1985).

Thus, focal units are the entities regarding which researchers would like to make generalizations (e.g., individuals, groups, and organizations; Hitt et al., 2007). For example, self-efficacy is a belief in one's ability to successfully perform a specific behavior or set of behaviors required to obtain a certain outcome (Bandura, 1977). Thus, the focal unit for self-efficacy is the individual. In contrast, collective efficacy, as defined by Bandura (1997, p. 477), is "a group's shared belief in its conjoint capabilities to organize and execute the courses of action required to produce given levels of attainment." Collective efficacy identifies the group as the focal unit (for additional coverage of how personality manifests within groups or teams, see Chapter 33, this volume).

Rousseau (1985) proposed that researchers should simultaneously consider the levels of theory, measurement, and analysis for the constructs of interest. Level of *theory* refers to the focal level at which constructs or phenomena are expected to exist. "Level of *measurement* refers to the unit to which the data are directly attached . . . [whereas] the level of *analysis* is the unit to which data are assigned for hypothesis testing and statistical analysis" (Rousseau, 1985, p. 4). In the self-efficacy example, the theory, measurement (i.e., as self-report), and analysis all operate at the individual level. For clear understanding of a multilevel phenomenon, it is important that these three facets (theory, measurement, and analysis) are aligned to minimize level-related confounds, or what are referred to as "fallacies of the wrong level." For example, self-efficacy is related to individual job performance; extrapolating this individual-level linkage to suggest that team efficacy is related to team performance would be a misspecification or fallacy of the wrong level. To avoid this fallacy, team efficacy must be conceptualized and analyzed at the collective level. The levels of theory and analysis for collective efficacy are at the unit (e.g., team and firm) level, yet the level of measurement is at the individual level because it is expected that team efficacy emerges from the shared cognitions of individuals. This difference in levels of theory versus measurement requires a consideration of multilevel processes.

Multilevel perspectives focus on processes that integrate two or more levels (Kozlowski & Klein, 2000). Microlevel phenomena are based on understanding individual-level processes, such as how individual personality is linked to individual outcomes, including job performance (e.g., Barrick & Mount, 1991) and organizational citizenship behaviors (e.g., Organ & Ryan, 1995). Macrolevel phenomena are primarily focused on understanding higher-level (e.g., firm, organization, and team) processes, such as the relationship between organizational strategy and organizational performance (Hitt et al., 2007; Molloy, Ployhart, & Wright, 2011). Cross-level models target relationships between dependent and independent variables operating at different levels (Rousseau, 1985).

Emergent Phenomena

An emergent phenomenon relates to a construct that originates in the cognitions, affects, behaviors, and characteristics of individuals, yet is manifested at the unit level through interactions and exchanges of individuals in a given context (Kozlowski & Klein, 2000; Marks, Mathieu, & Zaccaro, 2001). Emergent phenomena have two primary characteristics: (1) a set of bottom-up processes and (2) an interactive nature. Bottom-up processes have their theoretical origins at a lower level (individual, dyad, and team) but have emergent properties at a higher level (team, department, and organization). These higher-level properties of the unit have their origins in the individuals who compose the unit (e.g., team members) and are created through interactions among the members of that unit. An emergent phenomenon is thus the property of a unit and can further be either a state or a process (Marks et al., 2001). Emergent states are constructs that characterize dynamic properties of the unit level and vary as a function of inputs, processes, and outcomes (e.g., trust and cohesion). Thus, emergent states describe cognitive, motivational, and affective states of the unit level (e.g., teams). Emergent processes refer to the nature of unit member *interactions* (e.g., coordination and communication). For example, members in a team develop a process of communication leading the team to be more or less cohesive.

Composition and Compilation Models

There are two main types of emergent phenomena in multilevel analysis. The main distinguishing feature is whether emergence occurs due to processes creating homogeneity (composition) or to processes creating heterogeneity (compilation). Figure 8.1 illustrates the nature of composition and compilation models. On the left side of the figure, each of four individuals "looks" the same, and hence the unit-level construct is the average of the individual-level constructs and so "looks" like an oval. On the right side of the figure, each of four individuals "looks" different, like the pieces of a jigsaw puzzle. However, each shape (person) complements the other, and hence the manner in which the members complement each other creates a unique aggregate-level construct that is based on variability and is thus distinct from any specific individual.

Composition models are based on the premise that there is homogeneity (high similarity) among lower-level observations. This homogeneity creates a distinct aggregate-level construct that has different antecedents and consequences than its individual-level origins (Bliese, 2000; Kozlowski & Klein, 2000). Psychological and organizational climate offer an example of a composition model (James & Jones, 1974). If individuals in an organization have *similar* perceptions regarding supportive organizational climate then their scores on this facet of organizational climate can be aggregated to create an organizational climate variable that reflects homogeneity/similarity among organizational members on this construct. Thus, organizational climate is defined as the shared psychological climate in an organization (e.g., James, 1982). Organizational climate is a bottom-up process that manifests at the organizational level and is based on homogeneity (high similarity) among lower-level observations (psychological climate).

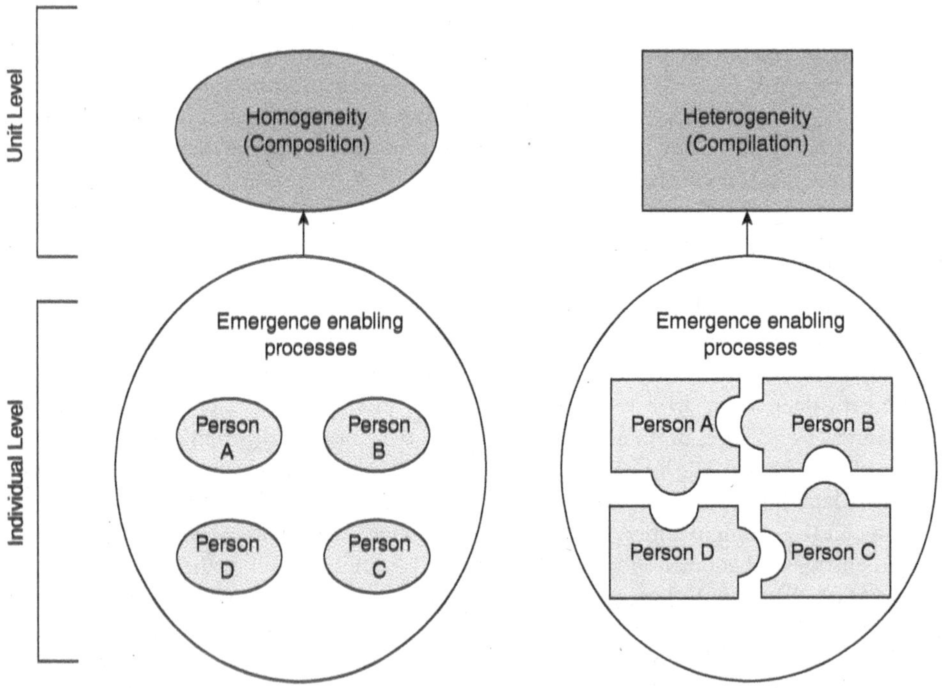

Figure 8.1 Illustrations of Homogeneity (Composition) and Heterogeneity (Compilation) Forms of Emergence.

Compilation models, in contrast, describe processes in which lower-level phenomena are combined in complex and often nonlinear ways to reflect unit-level phenomena that are not reducible to their constituent parts (Chan, 1998; Kozlowski & Klein, 2000). Constructs that emerge through compilation do not represent shared properties across levels but rather are qualitatively different (i.e., constructs are characterized by patterns). Compilation models are based on the premise that heterogeneity (discontinuity/variability) among lower-level observations creates a distinct unit-level construct (Kozlowski & Klein, 2000). Adaptive team performance is an example of a compilation process: It is an emergent phenomenon that builds recursively, whereby one or more team members use their resources to functionally change existing cognitive or behavioral goal-directed action or structures to meet demands (Burke, Stagl, Salas, Pierce, & Kendall, 2006). Team members do not perform identical activities in the same manner. For a team to have adaptive performance, individual members perform actions that are different from one another yet the configuration or pattern of these actions emerges bottom-up to characterize team performance as adaptive. In this manner, team members' different yet complementary expertise is what allows the team to adapt. As a property of the team, adaptive team performance is a continuous bottom-up process that evolves over time.

Most scholarly attention has focused on composition models. Chan (1998) and Kozlowski and Klein (2000) offered a typology of composition models that can be used to specify the nature of an emergent process. There are five basic forms: (1) additive, (2) direct consensus, (3) referent-shift consensus, (4) dispersion, and (5) process composition. Additive composition models posit that the meaning of the unit-level construct is an average of the lower-level perceptions, regardless of the variance among those perceptions. For example, an additive model of team efficacy will consist of the average level of team members' self-efficacy perceptions.

In direct consensus composition models, beyond creating the unit-level construct as an average of the lower-level perceptions, an index of consensus among those perceptions is developed. Researchers following this model will first assess consensus among members using within-group agreement of scores at the lower level (e.g., r_{wg}) to justify aggregation of lower-level scores to represent scores at the higher level (e.g., James, Demaree, & Wolf, 1984; Kozlowski & Hattrup, 1992; Ostroff, 1993; Ostroff & Rothausen, 1997). Referent-shift consensus composition models retain within-group consensus as an index of agreement of lower-level attributes. However, in a referent-shift model, the referent in the wording of the items refers to the collective (team/organization). Self-efficacy at the team level is an example of referent-shift consensus composition (e.g., Guzzo, Yost, Campbell, & Shea, 1993; Kozlowski et al., 1994). The basic content of efficacy perceptions in the original construct (self-efficacy) remains unchanged in the new form (collective efficacy), but the referent of the content is changed from the self to the team.

Dispersion models focus on the variance of scores on any lower-level units or attributes (e.g., individual self-efficacy) instead of consensus (similarity). This model captures different types of emergence that may range from low dispersion of attributes (supplementary) to high dispersion (complementary). For example, team personality dispersion models have been calculated using the lowest member score (minimum method), the highest member score (maximum method; e.g., Halfhill, Sundstrom, Lahner, Calderone, & Nielsen, 2005), and the spread of team member scores (variance method; e.g., Mohammed & Angell, 2003; Neuman, Wagner, & Christiansen, 1999). In a recent meta-analysis, Prewett, Walvoord, Stilson, Rossi, and Brannick (2009) found that minimum and variance measures of the team trait related to team performance in tasks with frequent work exchanges, but not in tasks with few work exchanges.

Finally, process composition models specify parallel nomological networks among similar constructs across levels of analysis. This form of composition model is also known as homologous models (Chen, Bliese, & Mathieu, 2005; Kozlowski & Klein, 2000). Homologous multilevel models propose parallel relationships between parallel constructs at different levels of analysis. For example, multiple reviews and meta-analyses in the goal setting literature at the individual level have indicated that there is substantial support for the basic principles of goal setting theory. It has been widely supported that specific, difficult goals, when accepted, lead to better performance than specific, easy goals, general goals such as "do your best" goals, or no goals (for reviews, see Locke & Latham, 1990; Locke, Shaw, Saari, & Latham, 1981; Tubbs, 1986). This relationship is robust and has been demonstrated in a variety of settings in the field as well as the laboratory. Similarly, at the group level, O'Leary-Kelly, Martocchio, and Frink (1994) found that groups with specific goals showed higher instances of positive results than did groups for which goals were ambiguous. Thus, the goal–performance relationship regarding goal specificity is homologous across individual and team levels.

Readers interested in exploring the role of personality at multiple levels should become familiar with the process of multilevel analysis in conjunction with multilevel theory because multilevel theory provides the underlying principles and methods needed to articulate how collective personality emerges from individual personality. A complete discussion of multilevel theory and principles is beyond the scope of this chapter, but the references provided above provide an excellent starting point. In terms of multilevel analyses, four widely used texts offering detailed introductions include Raudenbush and Bryk's (2002) *Hierarchical Linear Models*, Kreft and de Leeuw's (1998) *Introducing Multilevel Modeling*, Snijders and Bosker's (1999) *Multilevel Analysis*, and Hox's (2010) *Multilevel Analysis: Techniques and Applications*.

Summary

Originating from bottom-up processes, emergent phenomena are higher-level variables that are distinct conceptually and empirically from their lower-level origins. The higher- and lower-level phenomena will also have different antecedents and consequences, and, hence, generalizing findings from one level to the other can be inappropriate (Rousseau, 1985). Applied to personality at work, this means that generalizing individual-level findings about personality–outcome relationships to higher levels is potentially misleading and inappropriate. This is not a trivial implication, as it means that most of what we know about personality *within* teams and organizations may say little about how personality helps create differences *between* teams and between organizations—differences in terms of performance, competitive advantage, or differentiation in the eyes of applicants, consumers, or investors (see Ployhart, 2012, for a discussion of this issue). It means, for example, that hiring individuals with greater conscientiousness might not necessarily help the firm become more competitive. It also means that the traits that most generate firm-level competitive advantage may differ from those that most predict individual job performance.

Thus, for scholars wishing to fully understand unit-level personality, it becomes imperative that they appropriately conceptualize how and why individual personality traits will coalesce or configure into higher-level phenomena. Based on multilevel theory and principles, we posit that there are two broad mechanisms through which individual personality may manifest into collective personality. The first is through interaction and coordination processes that contribute to collective personality emergence. The second is through correlates of collective personality. In the following sections, we discuss in greater depth these conceptualizations of collective personality at the unit level (team/organization) and then provide some new directions for collective personality with a particular focus on human capital emergence.

Personality at the Unit Level

Collective Personality Emergence

Individual personality traits form the origins of collective personality constructs, but understanding why requires consideration of the processes underlying the emergence of personality. There are three broad ways that collective personality emergence has been considered.

Group Composition

First, theory and research on groups and teams has demonstrated that both the composition and compilation of group member personality traits contribute to what is known as group composition (Kozlowski & Ilgen, 2006). In this research, the nature of the group's tasks determines the nature and degree of the group members' coordination and communication patterns. Some group tasks require similarity in terms of personality traits (composition), while other tasks require that the group contains complementary yet distinct personality traits (compilation) (Moynihan & Peterson, 2004). For example, Barrick, Stewart, Neubert, and Mount (1998) found that different ways of configuring a group's personality created different group composition "constructs" that, in turn, had different relationships with group outcomes. They found a negative relationship between variance in conscientiousness and team performance, indicating that teams that did not have a very low conscientious member reported less conflict, more communication, and more workload sharing. This effect would not be apparent through an examination of team conscientiousness using the mean score operationalization. Driskell and Salas (Chapter 33, this volume) further examine the relationship of the Big Five personality traits to team performance and different ways in which these individual traits may be combined using various techniques to create team personality composites. Team performance frameworks likewise suggest that different group personality compositions will affect different types of team processes and mediating states (Kozlowski & Klein, 2000; Marks et al., 2001). For example, mean emotional stability is a strong predictor of team cohesion (Barrick et al., 1998), whereas mean team agreeableness positively predicts performance based on increased cohesion and helping behaviors (e.g., Kamdar & Van Dyne, 2007; O'Neill & Kline, 2008). Multiple studies and theoretical articles have advanced our understanding of the role of personality in teams and this area is constantly expanding. In general, team composition is considered to be an important input factor for emergent team processes, states, and team performance (e.g., Bell, 2007; Guzzo & Shea, 1992; LePine, Buckman, Crawford, & Methot, 2011; Mannix & Neale, 2005; Mohammed & Angell, 2003).

Homogeneity Hypothesis

Second, theory and research on the attraction–selection–attrition model (ASA; Schneider, 1987) has considered personality emergence in the form of the homogeneity hypothesis. The ASA model posits that organizations become more homogeneous (similar) in the knowledge, skills, abilities, or other characteristics (KSAOs) of their members, due to processes of attracting, selecting, and retaining members similar to others in the organization. The homogeneity hypothesis suggests that firms become homogeneous in these characteristics to the point where it is possible to differentiate firms based on aggregates of individuals' characteristics. Indeed, there is empirical research suggesting that organizations can be differentiated from each other in terms of the modal personalities of the people within those organizations (Ployhart et al., 2006; Schaubroeck, Ganster, & Jones, 1998; Schneider, Smith, Taylor, & Fleenor, 1998). These studies show that organizations can be differentiated in terms of the dominant personality characteristics of people within them—that is, the firms have become relatively homogenous with respect to their personality traits. The ASA model posits links between the individual applicant, incumbent, and the organization. Recent research has examined the ASA framework at multiple levels of analysis (Giberson, Resick, & Dickson, 2005; Ployhart et al., 2006; Satterwhite, Fleenor, Braddy, Feldman, & Hoopes, 2009). For example, Satterwhite et al. (2009) compared the homogeneity of a set of personality characteristics for 6,582 incumbents in eight occupations at eight organizations. They found that the homogeneity hypothesis was supported both within organizations and occupations, with higher homogeneity within occupations than within organizations.

Human Capital Resources

Finally, theory and research on human capital resource emergence is demonstrating how and why individual KSAOs (including personality traits) become distinct unit-level phenomena. Ployhart and Moliterno (2011) developed a theory connecting micro- and macroperspectives on (micro) individual differences and (macro) strategic resources. Resources are firm-level assets that can be accessed or controlled by an organization to develop or implement strategy (Barney, 1991). Using multilevel principles, Ployhart and Moliterno (2011) argued that firm-level human capital resources emerge from individual KSAOs due to task demands and enabling psychosocial states (e.g., cohesion and shared memory). In this manner, the theory explains how personality traits may become strategically valuable human capital resources allowing firms to differentiate themselves from competitors. Strategic human resources research finds that human capital resources, based on aggregates containing personality traits, may not only comprise unit-level resources, but also contribute to unit financial and accounting performance metrics over time (Ployhart, Van Iddekinge, & MacKenzie, 2011; Ployhart, Weekley, & Ramsey, 2009; Van Iddekinge et al., 2009).

Thus, a multilevel approach to understanding the nature of collective personality offers unique information that is not captured by a single-level focus. This can help us understand how and under what conditions individual KSAOs lead to organizational performance—and when they do not. Indeed, it is only through multilevel processes that it becomes clear how individual personality may lead to collective personality (human capital resources) and, in turn, influence organizational performance and other unit-level outcomes and processes. This is important and necessary because the current macrolevel literature uses other constructs (e.g., culture and reputation) in lieu of collective personality rather than assess attributes of individual employees directly. In the next section, we explore two widely used unit-level correlates of collective personality that have fallaciously been used as proxies for it.

Correlates of Collective Personality

"We treat organizations as if they were living, breathing entities with predictable behavioral tendencies" (Staw, 1991, p. 814). Recently, Whetten, Felin, and King (2009) suggested that organizations can be considered as social actors who have motives, drives, and intentions. Yet, it is the individuals in an organization who have motives, drives, and intentions that contribute to the development of such trait references regarding the organization. Trait/personality references about an organization are related to the organization's culture and the image/reputation of the organization as an employer. In either instance, individuals inside and outside the organization relate to organizational culture and reputation using trait terms similar to how people make trait inferences about other people (Dutton & Dukerich, 1991). For example, the perception of an organization as being affordable yet fashionable will attract individuals who value these traits and associate them with their self-concept/identity. These perceptions then get further propagated by the employees of the organization, who also identify themselves as endorsing affordable and fashionable goods. Thus, like individuals, organizations have cultures, values, identities, and reputations that may reflect collective personality and can be considered as correlates of corporate/organizational personality.

Culture

Corporate culture is a macrolevel construct focused on the ways in which shared meanings or underlying interpretive processes, values, beliefs, and assumptions characterize an organization (e.g., Moran & Volkswein, 1992; Rousseau, 1990; Schein, 1990). It has been used as a proxy for collective personality. The "trait approach" to culture (Saffold, 1988) suggests that organizations possessing strong, well-formed "personalities" with the right combinations of values, beliefs, symbols, rituals, norms, philosophies, and other cultural traits are more effective. However, it is the individuals within the organization that possess personalities, not organizations. Organizations that have strong cultures are likely to have individuals with a strong sense of common values, beliefs, and norms that facilitate the process. Furthermore, personality of the organizational members should play a role in developing a sense of common values and norms.

Just as personality helps understand the distinctiveness, coherence, and uniqueness of an individual, organizational culture is unique to a firm. Pathological–organizational types reflect similarities with the types of dysfunctions common to the neurotic styles among individuals (De Vries & Miller, 1986; Shapiro, 1965). For example, Miller and Friesen's (1978, 1984) "stagnant bureaucracies" were characterized by lack of clear goals, initiative, delayed and slow response to external changes, and managerial apathy, frustration, and inaction. The depressive personality style exhibits similar properties. However, even though depressive personality and stagnant bureaucracies get manifested in similar ways, they refer to different levels of conceptualization and are not synonymous constructs. Just as an individual with specific personality traits develops patterns of norms, beliefs, and values over time, similarly, individuals with specific personalities in an organization *interact* in identifiable patterns of behaviors that emerge at the unit level forming a collective personality that can be associated with distinct organizational culture (or norms, values, and beliefs) over time. Thus, we propose that researchers conceptualize collective personality as a construct that emerges from the unique combination of individual personalities in an organization and then explore its relationship with organizational culture to assess similarities and differences between the structure and function of these unit-level constructs instead of using culture as a proxy for collective personality.

Brand and Reputation

Personality is also understood as an individual's distinctive interpersonal characteristics, especially as described by those who have seen this individual in a variety of situations (MacKinnon, 1944). This aspect of personality is functionally equivalent to a person's reputation (R. Hogan, Hogan, & Roberts, 1996). Likewise, collective personality is associated with the notion of organizational reputation or brand, which refers to "the set of human characteristics associated with a brand" (Aaker, 1997, p. 347). Reputation or brand serves a symbolic or self-expressive function and association with the product/organization (Belk, 1988; Kleine, Schultz Kleine, & Kernan, 1993). It is argued that the symbolic use of brands is possible because consumers often instill brands with human personality traits (termed animism; e.g., Gilmore, 1919).

Brooks and Highhouse (2006) proposed that corporate reputation is a general, stable assessment of a company shared by outsiders. Corporate reputation is a global (i.e., general), temporally stable, evaluative judgment about a firm that is shared by multiple constituencies. This includes both a perception of corporate image (i.e., view of the organization held by those external to the organization; Bernstein, 1984) and corporate identity (i.e., view of the organization held by employees of the company; Albert & Whetten, 1985). Corporate philosophy and values (Stuart, 1999) are key features of corporate personality, which, in turn, is a key component of the corporate identity management process. An organization develops and maintains its reputation and image by communicating its identity, "the underlying 'core' or basic character of the firm" (Barnett, Jermier, & Lafferty, 2006, p. 33). Favorable organizational reputation (such as corporate social performance) can lead to attracting applicants (Turban & Greening, 1997) and investors (Srivastava, McInish, Wood, & Capraro, 1997), and charging premium prices for products and services (Rindova, Williamson, Petkova, & Sever, 2005).

Like organizational culture, brand and reputation are properties of the collective and are considered as a proxy for collective personality. However, it is important to differentiate between the function and structure of these variables to clarify the characteristics that these constructs may have in common with personality before they are used as proxies for collective personality. For example, in the 2011 Harris Interactive Survey, Google was reported as having the best company reputation in the country (Hernandez, 2011). The company was lauded for its workplace environment, financial performance, vision, leadership, and social responsibility by more than 30,000 individuals in the USA. This information provides us with a reflection of the complex combination of individual characteristics that emerge at the unit level, but it is not an index of collective personality or human capital resources at Google. Organizational culture and reputation relate directly and indirectly to organizational performance and success. Thus, it is important to conceptualize and understand the process by which organizational-level personality is defined and created as this has implications for various organizational-level attributes and outcomes.

Relationships Between Collective Personality and Culture

Organizational culture, reputation, and brand will directly and indirectly be affected by the way collective personality is conceptualized and assessed. Figure 8.2 provides a graphical overview of these relationships. First, collective personality should influence the emergence of organizational culture. As culture is a set of shared perceptions and assumptions, it seems likely that the personality of the people within the organization will influence the extent to which those cultural perceptions and assumptions become shared in the first place. One might expect that the more heterogeneous the organization's collective personality, the less likely there will be a dominant organizational culture and the greater the likelihood that there will be multiple subcultures (a situation not unlike what happens in mergers and acquisitions). Second, collective personality should influence the types of

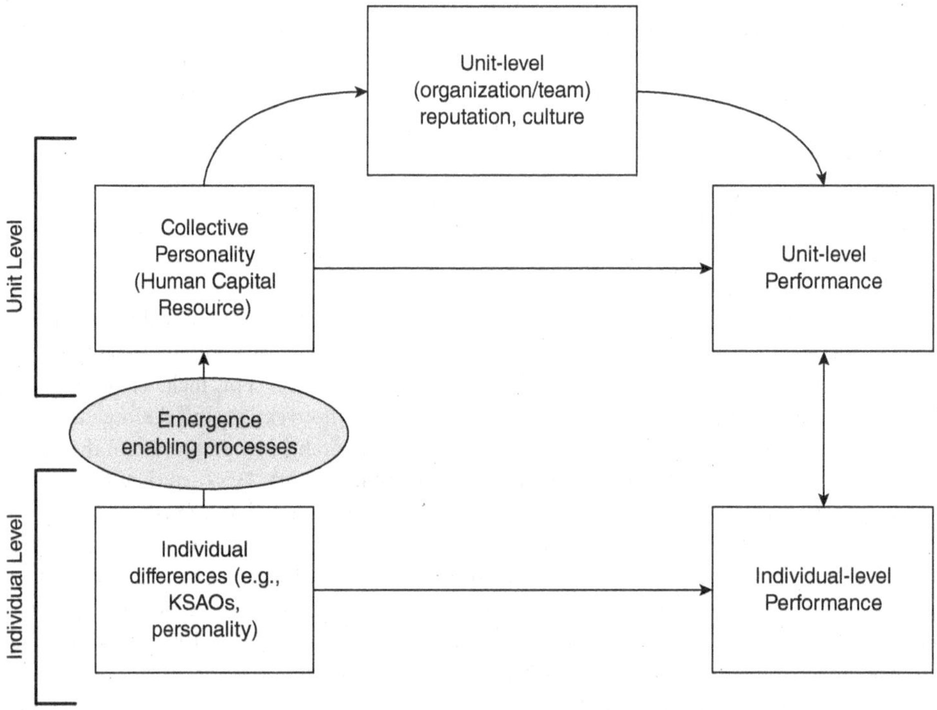

Figure 8.2 Core Relationships Associated With Collective Personality.

cultures that emerge in an organization. For example, an organization staffed with more agreeable employees may develop a culture that minimizes disagreements and critical thinking, whereas an organization staffed with highly conscientious employees may focus on bureaucracies and policies rather than innovation and risk taking.

Third, collective personality should influence the types of organizational reputation and brand that are created and maintained. Much has been written about Steve Jobs in recent years, but nearly all such writings suggest that the reputation and brand of Apple closely mirror Jobs' personality and the collective personality he created within the upper management of Apple. Their emphases on form *and* function are what differentiate Apple from many competitors who offer products of similar, if not frequently better, product features. Interestingly, the role of the organizational founder's personality on climate and culture was central in Schneider's (1987) original writing on the ASA model, but has scarcely been considered in scholarly research. Overall, researchers need to study how collective constructs, including personality, culture, and reputation, are interrelated within and across levels.

Finally, Figure 8.2 suggests that correlates of collective personality, such as culture or reputation, should not be conceptualized as surrogates for collective personality. They are related, but distinct, constructs. Inferences about collective personality may be observed from the study of culture and reputation, but scholars must realize that they do not inform questions about how collective personality emerges.

Implications and Directions for Future Research

Most applied personality research has been limited to an examination of individual-level traits and personality–criterion relationships. This research is important and we now know a great deal about how to conceptualize and measure personality, as well as how personality influences a variety of individual workplace criteria. However, we have argued that such individual-level relationships may not generalize to the organizational level, and that the traits and processes most predictive of organizational performance may differ from those most predictive of individual performance. There are theoretical reasons, and some empirical evidence, to suggest collective personality should exist, and should contribute to organizational outcomes. Thus, there is an opportunity to broaden applied personality research by studying it at higher levels. In this section we discuss some of those possibilities.

New Effects for Collective Personality

Collective personality has the potential to differentiate organizations in terms of their performance, competitive advantage, and innovation. Careful reading of Schneider's (1987) ASA model suggests that personality homogeneity should create consequences for the organization's structure, processes, and culture. This is highly consistent with research on intangible resources (particularly human capital) within the strategic human resource discipline and resource-based theory (Ployhart & Moliterno, 2011). In this literature, it is expected that firms differ in their performance due to differences in their internal resource endowments, and the manner by which the firm bundles, leverages, and deploys those resource endowments (Barney, 1991; Penrose, 1959; Sirmon, Hitt, & Ireland, 2007). Resources that are valuable and rare can generate competitive advantage, defined in terms of generating above-normal returns from a resource relative to competitors. For example, two firms may both have similar levels of human capital resources, but if Firm A can better leverage this resource, then it can generate a competitive advantage over Firm B. Resources that are also inimitable and difficult to substitute can generate sustained competitive advantage. For example, the brand reputation of Lexus allows it to charge a price premium relative to competitors, even though the car itself does not differ much from competitors. Finally, firms can generate shorter-term advantages, or at least competitive parity, through reducing costs or increasing profits. Human capital resources may improve operational performance by increasing productivity, efficiency, or innovation (Crook, Todd, Combs, Woehr, & Ketchen, 2011).

Moving personality research from the individual level to the collective level provides the opportunity for organizational-level operational performance, competitive advantage, and consumer differentiation to be examined as outcomes. That is, a unit-level study of collective personality allows direct examination of collective personality–unit criteria relationships (as shown in Figure 8.2). This research is likely to be most informative when it blends scholarship from micro (individual differences) and macro (resource-based theory) literatures (Molloy et al., 2011). For example, what is the structure and function of collective personality resources? Do collective personality resources contribute to competitive advantage or operational performance? If so, then under what circumstances is this relationship optimal? Acquiring and maintaining collective personality resources are likely to be challenging, but one should theoretically expect that firms with better collective conscientiousness human capital or with better collective agreeableness human capital should outperform their rivals. Furthermore, these unit-level trait–firm performance relationships are likely to be conditional on a variety of cultural, industry, and environmental factors (Barney, 1991; Crook et al., 2011).

One particularly interesting question is whether collective personality resources can generate competitive advantage. Collective personality resources are difficult to create because they are based on aggregations of individuals (Barney, 1991; Ployhart & Moliterno, 2011). There are also no widespread proxies of personality, as compared to those that exist for cognitive ability (e.g., Grade Point Average, level of education). As a result, collective personality resources should be extremely difficult for competitors to imitate, although correlates of collective personality (e.g., brand) should be easier to change than collective personality itself. If so, then collective personality resources may provide a powerful means of generating competitive advantage and differentiating the firm from competitors.

Finally, it is interesting to note that the prediction of higher-level performance criteria is often mediated by unit-level states (e.g., cohesion and trust) and behavioral coordinative processes (e.g., shared memory; Kozlowski & Ilgen, 2006; Marks et al., 2001). Even if collective personality is not directly predictive of unit operational performance and competitive advantage, it is nevertheless likely to be highly predictive of emergent states and mediating processes (Marks et al., 2001; Moynihan & Peterson, 2004). For example, Barrick et al. (1998) found that certain types of collective personality were related to team performance through their effects on cohesion. There is much to be learned about how different types of collective personality composition or resources may differentially relate to these mediating processes. However, conducting this research is vital for understanding *why* collective personality may contribute to operational performance and competitive advantage.

Stronger Effects for Collective Personality

Earlier, we noted how generalizing individual-level personality–criterion relationships to the unit level may be fallacious. Individual-level relationships may not generalize to higher levels simply because the criteria at each level of analysis are different. Research seems to suggest that the consequences of personality are most observable when studying interactions among people (e.g., Moynihan & Peterson, 2004). Hence, shifting the focus from relatively isolated individual performance behaviors to unit member interaction, coordination, and interdependent performance is likely to allow the effects of personality to be more observable. It is quite possible that collective personality could have even stronger relationships to collective processes (e.g., coordination and cohesion) and unit performance than what the individual-level literature might suggest.

Yet, even if the criterion-related validities are similar across levels, managers may find evidence of collective personality–unit-level performance relationships more compelling. For example, Ployhart et al. (2009) used a measure of service orientation (a composite based primarily on personality with the addition of some basic math ability) to predict change in store financial performance in a retail chain. The predictor showed good validity at the individual level (r = .23 uncorrected), but more impressive evidence was provided by an aggregate (collective) version of these scores contributing to store financial metrics such as adjusted sales, controllable profit, and sales per employee. In terms of practical significance, they found that increasing the mean service orientation scores just 1 standard deviation would produce over $4,000 in sales per employee per quarter. Similarly, a one-unit increase in store-level service orientation would result in a nearly $60,000 increase in adjusted controllable profit per quarter.

Future research needs to begin to study the relationships between collective personality and firm-level outcomes. For example, it would be interesting to examine collective (aggregate) scores on each of the Five-Factor Model (FFM) constructs, to see whether each collective FFM construct has a relationship with firm performance outcomes similar to or different from individual-level validities. If the results from collective personality research on unit performance continue to be supportive, then it is possible that organizational decision makers may have much more confidence in the value and importance of personality assessment.

The Process of Collective Personality Emergence

Research needs to build from and extend the ASA model (Schneider, 1987) and the multilevel model of human capital resource emergence (Ployhart & Moliterno, 2011) to examine more specifically how and why individual personality becomes collective personality. First, researchers need to understand the environmental and group factors that enhance or suppress personality emergence. The group and team literatures can offer guidance by identifying the critical features of tasks, environments, and psychosocial factors that affect different forms of emergence (e.g., Kozlowski & Ilgen, 2006; Marks et al., 2001). Second, research needs to consider different types of collective personality structures. Most research has focused on composition models in which collective personality is based on the mean personality scores of the employees within the unit (Ployhart et al., 2009; Schneider et al., 1998). However, other research suggests that various types of compilation may be important (e.g., Barrick et al., 1998). Research is needed to determine under which types of task and environmental complexity, and for what types of performance outcomes, will different types of collective personality operationalizations be appropriate. It is worth noting that, of the two forms of emergence, collective personality resources based on compilation are likely to be more important drivers of competitive advantage because they are harder to imitate. As an illustration, sports teams such as the Miami Heat show it is (relatively) easy to hire a star athlete, or even acquire several stars, but much more difficult to get them to work together collaboratively and effectively.

Conclusion

There is every reason to expect that collective personality exists and has organizational-level consequences, but these reasons have little to do with what is found in the published empirical literature. Currently, there is more theory than hard data to argue for the importance of collective personality. Researchers need to expand their focus from individual-level personality studies to consider the broader, multilevel context of organizations. In particular, we believe that collective personality is likely to have theoretically interesting and practically important relationships with unit operational performance and competitive advantage. Continued individual-level personality research is important, but by itself unlikely to inform questions of organizational performance and competitive advantage. Regardless of whether the findings of collective personality are similar to or different from those found at the individual level, they are likely to add much insight into our understanding of personality in the workplace.

Practitioner's Window

One of the most pressing issues facing organizational leaders is how to differentiate their firm from rivals to achieve a competitive advantage. In the last decade, it is increasingly clear that a firm's human capital is a strategically valuable resource that can generate superior performance and hence competitive advantage. A firm's human capital resource is based on its employees' collective knowledge, skills, and other characteristics. The collective personality of a firm's employees may provide a particularly valuable form of human capital resource because it contributes to many organizational processes and outcomes, yet is difficult for competitors to observe or imitate. To date, human capital resources based on collective personality have been found to contribute to greater business unit financial, accounting, productivity, and marketing metrics (e.g., growth in sales, controllable profit, and customer satisfaction). Yet, valuable human capital resources do not form by accident, and it is important for managers to actively build and maintain the desired stock and quality of collective personality. Building and maintaining a sufficient stock can be achieved by:

- Recruiting and hiring individuals with the needed types of personality traits;
- Changing the nature of the unit's coordination demands to facilitate the emergence of collective personality (e.g., use of team-based work structures);
- Managing, or changing, the company's culture to support the emergence of better collective personality;
- Measuring the extent to which the desired stock of collective personality is manifested, so that baselines can be set, goals developed, and evaluation metrics specified.

References

Aaker, J. (1997). Dimensions of brand personality. *Journal of Marketing Research, 34*, 347–356.

Albert, S., & Whetten, D. A. (1985). Organizational identity. In L. L. Cummings & B. I. M. Staw (Eds.), *Research in organizational behavior* (pp. 263–295). Greenwich, CT: JAI Press.

Allport, F. H. (1937). Introduction: The Hanover round table—Social psychology of 1936. *Social Forces, 15*, 455–462.

Bandura, A. (1977). Self-efficacy: Toward a unifying theory of behavioral change. *Psychological Review, 48*, 191–215.

Bandura, A. (1997). *Self-efficacy: The exercise of control.* New York: Freeman.

Barnett, M., Jermier, J., & Lafferty, B. (2006). Corporate reputation: The definitional landscape. *Corporate Reputation Review, 9*, 26–38.

Barney, J. B. (1991). Firm resources and sustained competitive advantage. *Journal of Management, 17*, 99–120.

Barrick, M. R., & Mount, M. K. (1991). The Big Five personality dimensions and job performance: A meta-analysis. *Personnel Psychology, 44*, 1–26.

Barrick, M. R., Stewart, G. L., Neubert, M. J., & Mount, M. K. (1998). Relating member ability and personality to work-team processes and team effectiveness. *Journal of Applied Psychology, 83*, 377–391.

Belk, R. W. (1988). Possessions and the extended self. *Journal of Consumer Research, 15*, 139–168.

Bell, S. T. (2007). Deep-level composition variables as predictors of team performance: A meta-analysis. *Journal of Applied Psychology, 92*, 595–615.

Bernstein, D. (1984). *Company image and reality: A critique of corporate communications*. Eastbourne, UK: Holt, Rinehart & Winston.
Bliese, P. D. (2000). Within-group agreement, non-independence, and reliability: Implications for data aggregation and analysis. In K. J. Klein & S. J. Kozlowski (Eds.), *Multilevel theory, research, and methods in organizations: Foundations, extensions, and new directions* (pp. 349–381). San Francisco: Jossey-Bass.
Bono, J. E., & Judge, T. A. (2004). Personality and transformational and transactional leadership: A meta-analysis. *Journal of Applied Psychology, 89*, 901–910.
Brooks, M. E., & Highhouse, S. (2006). Familiarity breeds ambivalence. *Corporate Reputation Review, 9*, 105–113.
Burke, C., Stagl, K. C., Salas, E., Pierce, L., & Kendall, D. (2006). Understanding team adaptation: A conceptual analysis and model. *Journal of Applied Psychology, 91*, 1189–1207.
Chan, D. (1998). Functional relations among constructs in the same content domain at different levels of analysis: A typology of composition models. *Journal of Applied Psychology, 83*, 234–246.
Chen, G., Bliese, P. D., & Mathieu, J. E. (2005). Conceptual framework and statistical procedures for delineating and testing multilevel theories of homology. *Organizational Research Methods, 8*, 375–409.
Chen, G., Mathieu, J. E., & Bliese, P. D. (2004). A framework for conducting multilevel construct validation. In F. J. Yammarino & F. Dansereau (Eds.), *Research in multilevel issues: Multilevel issues in organizational behavior and processes* (Vol. 3, pp. 273–303). Oxford, UK: Elsevier.
Crook, T. R., Todd, S. Y., Combs, J. G., Woehr, D. J., & Ketchen, D. J. (2011). Does human capital matter? A meta-analysis of the relationship between human capital and firm performance. *Journal of Applied Psychology, 96*, 443–456.
De Vries, M., & Miller, D. (1986). Personality, culture, and organization. *Academy of Management Review, 11*, 266–279.
Dutton, J. E., & Dukerich, J. M. (1991). Keeping an eye on the mirror: Image and identity in organizational adaptation. *Academy of Management Journal, 34*, 517–554.
Giberson, T. R., Resick, C. J., & Dickson, M. W. (2005). Embedding leader characteristics: An examination of homogeneity of personality and values in organizations. *Journal of Applied Psychology, 90*, 1002–1010.
Gilmore, G. W. (1919). *Animism or thought currents of primitive peoples*. Boston: Marshall Jones.
Guzzo, R. A., & Shea, G. P. (1992). Group performance and intergroup relations in organizations. In M. D. Dunnette & L. M. Hough (Eds.), *Handbook of industrial and organizational psychology* (2nd ed., Vol. 3, pp. 269–313). Palo Alto, CA: Consulting Psychologists Press.
Guzzo, R. A., Yost, P. R., Campbell, R. J., & Shea, G. P. (1993). Potency in groups: Articulating a construct. *British Journal of Social Psychology, 32*, 87–106.
Halfhill, T., Sundstrom, E., Lahner, J., Calderone, W., & Nielsen, T. M. (2005). Group personality composition and group effectiveness: An integrative review of empirical research. *Small Group Research, 36*, 83–105.
Hayes, N., & Joseph, S. (2003). Big 5 correlates of three measures of subjective well-being. *Personality and Individual Differences, 34*, 723–727.
Hernandez, B. E. (2011, May 5). *Google's reputation is no. 1*. Retrieved from http://www.nbcbayarea.com/blogs/press-here/Googles-Reputation-is-No-1-121118214.html
Hitt, M. A., Beamish, P. W., Jackson, S. E., & Mathieu, J. E. (2007). Building theoretical and empirical bridges across levels: Multilevel research in management. *Academy of Management Journal, 50*, 1385–1399.
Hofmann, D. A., & Jones, L. M. (2005). Leadership, collective personality, and performance. *Journal of Applied Psychology, 90*, 509–522.
Hogan, R., Hogan, J., & Roberts, B. W. (1996). Personality measurement and employment decisions: Questions and answers. *American Psychologist, 51*, 469–477.
Hogan, R. T. (1991). Personality and personality measurement. In M. D. Dunnette & L. M. Hough (Eds.), *Handbook of industrial and organizational psychology* (2nd ed., Vol. 2, pp. 873–919). Palo Alto, CA: Consulting Psychologists Press.
Hox, J. J. (2010). *Multilevel analysis: Techniques and applications* (2nd ed.). Mahwah, NJ: Erlbaum.
Hurtz, G. M., & Donovan, J. J. (2000). Personality and job performance: The Big Five revisited. *Journal of Applied Psychology, 85*, 869–879.
James, L. R. (1982). Aggregation bias in estimates of perceptual agreement. *Journal of Applied Psychology, 67*, 219–229.
James, L. R., Demaree, R. G., & Wolf, G. (1984). Estimating within-group interrater reliability with and without response bias. *Journal of Applied Psychology, 69*, 85–98.
James, L. R., & Jones, A. P. (1974). Organizational climate: A review of theory and research. *Psychological Bulletin, 81*, 1096–1113.
Judge, T. A., Bono, J. E., Ilies, R., & Gerhardt, M. W. (2002). Personality and leadership: A qualitative and quantitative review. *Journal of Applied Psychology, 87*, 765–780.

Judge, T. A., Bono, J. E., & Locke, E. A. (2000). Personality and job satisfaction: The mediating role of job characteristics. *Journal of Applied Psychology, 85*, 869–879.
Judge, T. A., Heller, D., & Mount, M. K. (2002). Five-factor model of personality and job satisfaction: A meta-analysis. *Journal of Applied Psychology, 87*, 530–541.
Kamdar, D. A., & Van Dyne, L. (2007). The joint effects of personality and workplace social exchange relationships in predicting task performance and citizenship performance. *Journal of Applied Psychology, 92*, 1286–1298.
Kleine, R. E., Schultz Kleine, S., & Kernan, J. B. (1993). Mundane consumption and the self: A social-identity perspective. *Journal of Consumer Psychology, 2*, 209–235.
Kozlowski, S. W. J., Gully, S. M., Nason, E. R., Ford, J. K., Smith, E. M., Smith, M. R., & Futch, C. J. (1994, April). *A composition theory of team development: Levels, content, process, and learning outcomes*. Paper presented at the 9th Annual Conference of the Society for Industrial and Organizational Psychology, Nashville, TN.
Kozlowski, S. W. J., & Hattrup, K. (1992). A disagreement about within-group agreement: Disentangling issues of consistency versus consensus. *Journal of Applied Psychology, 77*, 161–167.
Kozlowski, S. W. J., & Ilgen, D. R. (2006). Enhancing the effectiveness of work groups and teams. *Psychological Science in the Public Interest, 7*, 77–124.
Kozlowski, S. W. J., & Klein, K. J. (2000). A multilevel approach to theory and research in organizations: Contextual, temporal, and emergent processes. In K. J. Klein & S. W. J. Kozlowski (Eds.), *Multilevel theory, research, and methods in organizations: Foundations, extensions, and new directions* (pp. 3–90). San Francisco: Jossey-Bass.
Kreft, I., & de Leeuw, J. (1998). *Introducing multilevel modeling*. London: Sage.
LePine, J. A., Buckman, B. R., Crawford, E. R., & Methot, J. R. (2011). A review of research on personality in teams: Accounting for pathways spanning levels of theory and analysis. *Human Resource Management Review, 21*, 311–330.
Locke, E. A., & Latham, G. P. (1990). *A theory of goal setting & task performance*. Englewood Cliffs, NJ: Prentice Hall.
Locke, E. A., Shaw, K. N., Saari, L. M., & Latham, G. P. (1981). Goal setting and task performance: 1969–1980. *Psychological Bulletin, 90*, 125–152.
MacKinnon, D. W. (1944). The structure of personality. In J. McVicker Hunt (Ed.), *Personality and the behavior disorders* (Vol. 1, pp. 3–48). New York: Ronald Press.
Mannix, E., & Neale, M. A. (2005). What differences make a difference? The promise and reality of diverse teams in organizations. *Psychological Science in the Public Interest, 6*, 31–55.
Marks, M. A., Mathieu, J. E., & Zaccaro, S. J. (2001). A temporally based framework and taxonomy of team processes. *Academy of Management Review, 26*, 356–376.
Matzler, K., Renzl, B., Müller, J., Herting, S., & Mooradian, T. (2008). Personality traits and knowledge sharing. *Journal of Economic Psychology, 29*, 301–313.
Miller, D. A., & Friesen, P. H. (1978). Archetypes of strategy formulation. *Management Science, 24*, 921–933.
Miller, D. A., & Friesen, P. H. (1984). *Organizations: A quantum view*. Englewood Cliffs, NJ: Prentice Hall.
Mohammed, S., & Angell, L. C. (2003). Personality heterogeneity in teams: Which differences make a difference for team performance? *Small Group Research, 34*, 651–677.
Molloy, J. C., Ployhart, R. E., & Wright, P. M. (2011). The myth of "the" management divide: Bridging system-level and disciplinary divides. *Journal of Management, 37*, 581–609.
Mooradian, T. A., Renzl, B., & Matzler, K. (2006). Who trusts? Personality, trust, and knowledge sharing. *Management Learning, 37*, 523–540.
Moran, E., & Volkswein, J. (1992). The cultural approach to the formation of organizational climate. *Human Relations, 45*, 19–48.
Morgeson, F. P., & Hofmann, D. A. (1999). The structure and function of collective constructs: Implications for multilevel research and theory development. *Academy of Management Review, 24*, 249–265.
Moynihan, L. M., & Peterson, R. S. (2004). The role of personality in group processes. In B. Schneider & D. B. Smith (Eds.), *Personality and organizations* (pp. 317–345). Mahwah, NJ: Erlbaum.
Neuman, J. A., Wagner, S. H., & Christiansen, N. D. (1999). The relationship between work team personality composition and the job performance of teams. *Group & Organization Management, 24*, 28–45.
O'Leary-Kelly, A. M., Martocchio, J. J., & Frink, D. D. (1994). A review of the influence of group goals on group performance. *Academy of Management Journal, 37*, 1285–1301.
O'Neill, T. A., & Kline, T. J. B. (2008). Personality as a predictor of teamwork: A business simulator study. *North American Journal of Psychology, 10*, 65–78.
Organ, D. W. (1994). Personality and organizational citizenship behavior. *Journal of Management, 20*, 465–478.
Organ, D. W., & Ryan, K. (1995). A meta-analytic review of attitudinal and dispositional predictors of organizational citizenship behavior. *Personnel Psychology, 48*, 755–802.

Ostroff, C. (1993). The effects of climate and personal influences on individual behavior and attitudes in organizations. *Organizational Behavior and Human Decision Processes, 56*, 56–90.

Ostroff, C., & Rothausen, T. J. (1997). The moderating effect of tenure in person–environment fit: A field study in educational organizations. *Journal of Occupational and Organizational Psychology, 70*, 173–188.

Oswald, F. L., & Hough, L. M. (2011). Personality and its assessment in organizations: Theoretical and empirical developments. In S. Zedeck (Ed.), *APA handbook of industrial and organizational psychology: Selecting and developing members for the organization* (Vol. 2, pp. 153–184). Washington, DC: American Psychological Association.

Pedhazur, E. J., & Schmelkin, L. (1991). *Measurement, design, and analysis: An integrated approach*. Hillsdale, NJ: Lawrence Erlbaum Associates.

Penrose, E. T. (1959). *The theory of the growth of the firm*. New York: John Wiley.

Pervin, L. A. (1996). *The science of personality*. Oxford, UK: John Wiley & Sons.

Ployhart, R. E. (2012). The psychology of competitive advantage: An adjacent possibility. *Industrial and Organizational Psychology, 5*, 62–81.

Ployhart, R. E., & Moliterno, T. P. (2011). Emergence of the human capital resource: A multilevel model. *Academy of Management Review, 36*, 127–150.

Ployhart, R. E., Van Iddekinge, C., & MacKenzie, W. (2011). Acquiring and developing human capital in service contexts: The interconnectedness of human capital resources. *Academy of Management Journal, 54*, 353–368.

Ployhart, R. E., Weekley, J. A., & Baughman, K. (2006). The structure and function of human capital emergence: A multilevel examination of the attraction–selection–attrition model. *Academy of Management Journal, 49*, 661–677.

Ployhart, R. E., Weekley, J. A., & Ramsey, J. (2009). The consequences of human resource stocks and flows: A longitudinal examination of unit service orientation and unit effectiveness. *Academy of Management Journal, 52*, 996–1015.

Prewett, M. S., Walvoord, A. A. G., Stilson, F. R. B., Rossi, M. E., & Brannick, M. T. (2009). The team personality–team performance relationship revisited: The impact of criterion choice, pattern of workflow, and method of aggregation. *Human Performance, 22*, 273–296.

Raudenbush, S. W., & Bryk, A. S. (2002). *Hierarchical linear models: Applications and data analysis methods* (2nd ed.). Thousand Oaks, CA: Sage.

Rindova, V. P., Williamson, I. O., Petkova, A. P., & Sever, J. (2005). Being good or being known: An empirical examination of the dimensions, antecedents, and consequences of organizational reputation. *Academy of Management Journal, 48*, 1033–1049.

Rousseau, D. M. (1985). Issues of level on organizational research. *Research in Organizational Behavior, 7*, 1–37.

Rousseau, D. M. (1990). Assessing organizational culture: The case for multiple methods. In B. Schneider (Ed.), *Organizational climate and culture* (pp. 153–192). San Francisco: Jossey-Bass.

Saffold, G. (1988). Culture traits, strengths and organizational performance: Moving beyond strong culture. *Academy of Management Review, 13*, 546–558.

Satterwhite, R. C., Fleenor, J. W., Braddy, P. W., Feldman, J., & Hoopes, L. (2009). A case for homogeneity of personality at the occupational level. *International Journal of Selection and Assessment, 17*, 154–164.

Schaubroeck, J., Ganster, D. C., & Jones, J. R. (1998). Organization and occupation influences in the attraction–selection–attrition process. *Journal of Applied Psychology, 83*, 869–891.

Schein, E. H. (1990). Organizational culture. *American Psychologist, 45*, 109–119.

Schneider, B. (1987). The people make the place. *Personnel Psychology, 40*, 437–454.

Schneider, B., Smith, D. B., Taylor, S., & Fleenor, J. (1998). Personality and organizations: A test of the homogeneity of personality hypothesis. *Journal of Applied Psychology, 83*, 462–470.

Shapiro, D. (1965). *Neurotic styles*. New York: Basic Books.

Sirmon, D. G., Hitt, M. A., & Ireland, R. (2007). Managing firm resources in dynamic environments to create value: Looking inside the black box. *Academy of Management Review, 32*, 273–292.

Snijders, T. A. B., & Bosker, R. (1999). *Multilevel analysis: An introduction to basic and advanced multilevel modeling*. London: Sage.

Srivastava, R., McInish, T. H., Wood, R., & Capraro, A. J. (1997). The value of corporate reputation: Evidence from the equity markets. *Corporate Reputation Review, 1*, 62–68.

Staw, B. M. (1991). Dressing up like an organization: When psychological theories can explain organizational action. *Journal of Management, 17*, 805–819.

Stuart, H. (1999). Towards a definitive model of the corporate identity management process. *Corporate Communications: An International Journal, 4*, 200–207.

Tett, R. P., & Christiansen, N. D. (2007). Personality tests at crossroads: A response to Morgeson, Campion, Dipboye, Hollenbeck, Murphy, and Schmitt. *Personal Psychology, 60*, 967–993.

Tett, R. P., Jackson, D. N., & Rothstein, M. (1991). Personality measures as predictors of job performance: A meta-analytic review. *Personnel Psychology, 44*, 703–742.

Tubbs, M. E. (1986). Goal setting: A meta-analytic examination of the empirical evidence. *Journal of Applied Psychology, 71*, 474–483.

Turban, D. B., & Greening, D. W. (1997). Corporate social performance and organizational attractiveness to prospective employees. *Academy of Management Journal, 40*, 658–672.

Van Iddekinge, C., Ferris, G. R., Perrewe, P. L., Perryman, A. Z., Blass, F. R., & Heetderks, T. D. (2009). Effects of selection and training on unit-level performance over time: A latent growth modeling approach. *Journal of Applied Psychology, 94*, 829–843.

Wayne, J. H., Musisca, N., & Fleeson, W. (2004). Considering the role of personality in the work–family experience: Relationships of the big five to work–family conflict and facilitation. *Journal of Vocational Behavior, 64*(1), 108–130.

Whetten, D. A., Felin, T., & King, B. G. (2009). The practice of theory borrowing in organizational studies: Current issues and future directions. *Journal of Management, 35*, 537–563.

Section II

Assessment of Personality at Work

9

History of Personality Testing Within Organizations

Michael J. Zickar and John A. Kostek

The history of personality testing within organizations is as fascinating as it is important. Review of this history is particularly valuable given that this area is marked by cycles and phases, more so than other topics within organizational research. As will be seen, concerns at one point of time seem to fade for several years or decades, only to reappear, often with researchers at the later date only vaguely aware that their predecessors grappled with similar issues. Therefore, we think it is fruitful to review the history of personality testing for contemporary researchers to put their efforts into a broader context that they might not get if they only read current research articles. There are lots of interesting events, mistakes, and episodes in this history. We have written elsewhere in more detail about some of these episodes (see Gibby & Zickar, 2008; Zickar, 2001b; Zickar & Gibby, 2006), but in this chapter we put together a broader history of this important topic. We briefly review the origins of personality theory and then focus on the developments of personality testing within the field during the 20th Century. Finally, we summarize this history and identify some lessons learned.

An Extremely Brief Introduction to the Origin of Personality

Early Greek philosophers and scientists debated what made individuals differ from each other and what guided their behavior. Many of those thinkers focused on the soul as the source of behavior and came up with their own theories of what the soul entailed. Usually, these theories included aspects that related to sensing, perceiving, and thinking, as well as immortal strivings and spiritual matters (see Sachs, 2001, for a description of Aristotle's description of the soul). The Greek physician and thinker, Galen (*ca.* A.D. 130 to 217), proposed that a person's temperament was determined by the proportion of four different humors or liquids within the body: yellow bile, black bile, blood, and phlegm. People who had an excess of one particular humor would act in accordance to that dominant humor. Thus, if someone had an excess of yellow bile in their system, they would be bitter and nasty. If they had too much blood, they would be sanguine and, therefore, happy and volatile. If they had too much black bile, then they were prone to sadness. And if phlegm dominated their system, then they would consequently be relaxed and sluggish. Galen's theory of temperament was an influential one and, although later discarded in favor of other theories, provides one of the first theories that linked biological factors to human behavior, an insight that is often taken for granted in current personality research (see Watson, 1978). It should be noted that Galen's theory was not a strict theory of personality as we would think of it today (he was more concerned with classifying pathological individuals who needed medical attention).

The first introduction of the word *personality* into the lexicon of language to describe humans has been attributed to French philosopher Victor Cousin (1792–1867) who coined the word *personnalité*, which he used to describe an awareness of the self. He advocated introspection as a way to better understand one's personnalité (see Smith, 1997). Although Cousin did not scientifically study personality, his idea of better understanding the self is one of the impetuses for modern-day personality testing. Much of personality testing within organizations is used for selection, but the use of personality testing for self-awareness and self-development is also very popular and consistent with Cousin's original conceptualization. It is important to note that the word "personality" is a relatively modern construction.

The first scientific investigation into individual differences related to temperament was conducted by phrenologists, who believed that the shape and size of the cranium was related to both personal tendencies (similar to what we might call personality traits now) and cognitive functioning. A French anatomist, Franz Gall (1758–1828), published the first works on phrenology in the 1810s in a four-volume work entitled: *Anatomy and physiology of identifying many intellectual and moral dispositions of men and animals by the configuration of their heads*. Gall and his followers traveled the world promoting their "science" of individual differences, gaining popularity among fellow scientists as well as a general public interested in trying to better understand their own lives. Interestingly, even the famous American poet Walt Whitman was fascinated by phrenology (see Hungerford, 1931).

Although phrenology has been largely disproven (and much derided) by contemporary scientists, two important points were made by this quite popular movement. First, although the explanation of the causes of differences seems amusing by today's standards (e.g., protuberant eyes are related to strong memory), phrenology encouraged people to think systematically about how people differ from each other. Prior to the phrenologists, much of the investigation into humans was focused on determining how humans differ from animals, usually in terms of spiritual dimensions. Second, phrenology got the public to think that there may be a biological basis to personality. This was similar to Galen's early conception of personality linked to variations in bodily fluids. But in the intervening time, much of the writing on human functioning was focused on linking God's will to individuals' lives. Although the content of phrenology seems amusing by our standards, its importance as a foundation to the scientific study of personality needs to be acknowledged (see Davies, 1955, for more about phrenology).

At the beginning of modern psychology, several developments were central to later advances in personality testing and it is important to briefly review them to provide a context for the initial foray of personality testing within organizations. Although current students and many academics scoff at the ideas of Sigmund Freud (1856–1939), his late 19th Century and early 20th Century investigations into the workings of the mind had an enormous impact on the field of psychology and were very important for later events in the history of personality testing. Freud's theory of human behavior tried to link human behavior to repressed sexual urges, to childhood events, and to the hidden and dark realm of the unconscious. Freud's theory of personality included the *id* ruled by the pleasure principle, the *ego* ruled by the reality principle, and the *super-ego* ruled by the morality principle. These three forces were in constant conflict with each other and, at various stages in one's life, different forces would assume control. Freud never concerned himself with how to measure these aspects of personality, instead working on explicating his theory through a large volume of investigations and speculations as well as developing a method of "talking cures" that helped patients resolve conflicts. Freud's writings and his visit to America in 1909 had an enormous impact on the field of psychology near the time that personality testing began in earnest. The reader is referred to Peter Gay's extensive biography of Freud for a vast description of his life and work (Gay, 1988).

Around the same time as Freud's writings, important advances were being made in the measurement of mental characteristics, nearly exclusively in the areas of intelligence, psychomotor skills, and perceptual abilities. Sir Francis Galton (1822–1911) was inspired by his cousin Darwin's writings linking individual differences within a species to survival, and developed some of the first measures of what he thought was intelligence. He measured reaction times, the circumference of the cranium, and memory in an effort to categorize humans on various dimensions. Although his measures might now be judged far from being construct valid measures of intelligence, Galton should be given credit for the first standardized measures (see Forrest, 1974). Galton focused mostly on measuring intelligence and psychomotor skills, but he was convinced that measurement of character was possible. After much deliberation, he concluded, "the character which shapes our conduct is a definite and durable 'something,' and therefore that it is reasonable to attempt to measure it" (Galton, 1884, p. 181). He proposed measuring aspects of character via physiological devices such as pulse and blood flow, though he never developed these measures of character. He did ask geniuses in a study motivated by hereditary to rate themselves on Galen's typology, asking the respondents to judge whether they were "distinctly nervous, sanguine, bilious, or lymphatic?" (Galton, 1874, pp. 199–200). Galton never pursued these ideas systematically, though he might be given credit as developing the first self-report personality scale.

Meanwhile, advances in the measurement of intelligence continued. Alfred Binet was hired by the French minister of education to develop measures to identify "defective children." France had moved to compulsory education and had quickly realized that putting large groups of varying abilities of children into one class provided challenges of making sure that all students were challenged to the best of their ability. Binet's test was developed empirically by having items that differentiated between different levels of cognitive functioning. Binet's test was brought to the United States, translated into English, and modified by Stanford psychologist Lewis Terman into what was then named the Stanford–Binet Test. This test was used not only to identify students at the low end of cognitive functioning, but later to identify high-ability students as well (see Sokal, 1987, for more background information). Binet and his successors' advances in measuring mental ability, as well as an awareness of the challenges and failures in functioning highlighted by Freud and his followers, provided inspiration to psychology researchers during World War I (WWI).

Prior to WWI, there were a few direct attempts to measure aspects that we would now believe are related to personality, though these efforts were all in the area of psychopathology. Butcher (2010) identifies several efforts, including Heymans and Wiersma (1906), who developed a 90-item rating that physicians used to rate human character, and others, including Jung (1907) and Kent and Rosanoff (1910), took Freud's ideas of free association to try to measure aspects of people's characters. These research efforts can be considered precursors to the next wave of personality tests, and in many cases, developers of the next round of tests cited this work. It was not until the events of WWI, though, that personality measurement reached its first significant accomplishment.

WWI and Personality Research

The United States had a relatively small and unprepared military force at the beginning of the 20th Century. It had been a decade and a half since the last military expeditions (the Spanish-American War in 1898 and the Philippine-American War, 1898–1902) and so there were relatively few seasoned, battle-ready veterans that the United States could rely on when it geared up for the largely unexpected conflagration that had dominated the European continent beginning in 1914. When the United States entered the war in 1917, it needed a rapid mobilization of forces. In brief, it needed to rapidly create a massive organization with a vast variety of occupations without a ready pool of trained workers. Psychologists became involved early on in the efforts by developing tests of mental ability to determine whether military recruits had the skills to be put into cognitively challenging jobs such as artillery, leadership, and logistics. Also, it developed standardized trade tests to determine whether recruits had specialized knowledge in important fields, such as electricity, carpentry, and mechanics. Many important testing advances were developed in a short amount of time to deal with problems that arose. At no other point in history were the advances in development and testing more rapid than the short period of time psychologists worked in the war effort. See Kevles (1968) and Yerkes (1921) for summaries of the WWI efforts, as well as an evaluation of their impact.

During this time, Robert S. Woodworth joined the war effort. Woodworth was a former student of James McKeen Cattell and shared his mentor's interest in mental testing; in addition, he had worked in a medical college before settling back at Columbia, where he worked until his retirement. During the war, Woodworth was tasked with developing a test that would solve a particularly important problem being faced by new recruits, the *shell-shocked soldier*. Young recruits without any military experience were being trained in a short amount of time and then shipped off to Europe to fight in the trenches of France and Belgium in a last-ditch effort by the Allied Forces to end a war that had dragged on longer than most people had originally expected. A large number of these recruits, once experiencing enemy fire for the first time, would freeze and prove useless under the stress of battle. Woodworth's test was expected to identify beforehand recruits who might not fare well under battle, with the thought that these recruits could then be assigned to noncombat roles, where they could still help the war effort (see Gibby & Zickar, 2008, for more background information).

After interviewing patients who had experienced neuroses due to the war, Woodworth collected a series of symptoms that were then administered to a sample of "normals." Items that were endorsed with high frequency by normals were eliminated and the resulting inventory was called the *Psychoneurotic Tendencies* scale. This empirically developed scale was piloted on a group of soldiers and the Surgeon General subsequently recommended use of the test on a trial basis; unfortunately the test was developed too late to be used on a large operational scale.

After the war, Woodworth revised the test and renamed it as the *Woodworth Personal Data Sheet* (WPDS). The applied psychologists who worked on the war effort began to market the tools they had developed for soldier placement to industry, in an effort to help them select people for job vacancies. Woodworth's test was marketed to organizations that wanted to screen out maladjusted workers. That market for screening individuals for personality traits and personality flaws was spurred in part by one of the many hucksters who peddled nonscientific solutions to organizations and a public who were hungry for all things psychological.

Katherine Blackford and Personality Hucksterism

Katherine Blackford was an influential voice in personality assessment at the beginning of the 20th Century. She developed a classification system in which people's personality, as well as their skills and abilities, could be identified by examining their physical traits. She called her system of classifications "character analysis" and she claimed that photographs often provided sufficient information for her to make judgments about the quality and nature of a person. Although nearly all of her claims have been questioned, if not falsified, she was still an important voice at the turn of the century in attempting to measure personality in a systematic, if not scientific, manner.

Though no record exists today, Blackford claimed to have received her M.D. with honors from the College of Physicians and Surgeons in 1898. Her early study and practice of medicine led her to the conclusion that mental states and physical ailments were often connected. She began to study how physical traits relate with particular personality types. She traveled the United States and Canada extensively, as well as several other countries around the world, collecting observations in a variety of different environments. Her research and practice culminated in several publications spanning from 1910 to 1924. During this time, she lectured and consulted with companies about the value of analyzing character and developing scientific plans of employment.

Blackford's theories regarding physical traits and personality were rooted in Darwinian biology. That is, she believed that natural selection was responsible for particular physical traits as well as personality traits, and, therefore, the two covary. Blackford outlined nine fundamental physical variables that she believed could be used to distinguish a person's personality characteristics. They were (1) color, (2) form, (3) size, (4) structure, (5) texture, (6) consistency, (7) proportion, (8) expression, and (9) condition. The two most important of her physical variables were color and form. Blackford went to great lengths to discuss pigmentation and hair color. In her book *Blondes and Brunets* (Blackford & Newcomb, 1917), Blackford describes the evolution of races in different parts of the world and how she believed it influenced both physical and mental characteristics of the people of that region. She was also keenly concerned with form. Her writings describe how minute physical details, such as how convex or concave the face was, can indicate quite different personality expressions. Great attention was paid to the size, shape, and relative location of a person's eyes, nose, mouth, and general form of the face. Some of her writings even indicated that valuable personality information could be surmised from a person's hands and physical demeanor.

Blackford published several books describing her plan for scientific employment and explaining the benefits of using character analysis in making decisions regarding employment. She also published lessons on how to hone one's character analyzing skills, describing what physical traits should be looked for and the associated personality trait. Her writings were geared toward business people who needed help selecting people for jobs. Character analysis, in Blackford's words, was "an art based on common sense and experience. Anyone can learn it and use it" (Blackford, 1918, p. 9).

Scholars and researchers alike began testing the theories and claims that Blackford had laid forth. Cleeton and Knight (1924) specifically concluded that "Physical measurements which underlie character analysis agree neither with themselves nor with other measures of character" (p. 231). Their findings, along with other research testing the validity of Blackford's claims, all but put an end to the practice of character analysis in the United States. Although many if not all of the claims set forth by Blackford's theories on measuring personality have been refuted, she remains an important figure in the early study of personality, as she helped create a demand for thinking about personality in the business world, and some of the efforts to disprove her theories led to more rigorous approaches to personality measurement.

1920s and 1930s Personality Testing

Blackford's declining popularity and the introduction of the WPDS into the workplace led other psychologists to develop their own personality tests. Some of these tests have faded from the annals of history, whereas others have stuck around in one form or another. The first wave of personality tests following the WPDS included the *Colgate Tests of Emotional Outlets* (Laird, 1925), the *Mental Hygiene Inventory* (House, 1927), the *Personality Schedule* (Thurstone & Thurstone, 1929), and *X-O Tests for Investigating the Emotions* (Pressey & Pressey, 1919). These tests were largely developed for research purposes and, for the most part, focused on the adjustment dimension similar to the WPDS.

This concentration on the adjustment dimension was likely due to several factors. First, most of the early psychology work, especially from the psychoanalytic school, had focused on problems with adjustment. Organizational sociologist Elton Mayo claimed that the number 1 reason why workers performed poorly was irrational thinking and emotional control problems (see Gibby & Zickar, 2008). In addition, management at the time was obsessed with the threat of unionization. Labor organizations were gaining in political strength and were asserting their rights over the workplace through political negotiation when possible, and militant confrontation, if necessary. Management, spurred on by Mayo, believed that people joined labor unions, not to better their lives by increasing workplace safety and the size of their paycheck, but because they were emotionally maladjusted.

Hence, they turned to personality inventories as a way to screen out potential agitators and labor radicals (see Zickar, 2001b).

After President Roosevelt's National Labor Relations Act of 1935, it became illegal in the hiring process to ask applicants if they were sympathetic to organized labor, and so personality tests served as an indirect way of flouting the law. Psychologist Doncaster Humm, who had developed the *Humm–Wadsworth Temperament Test* along with industry executive Guy Wadsworth, marketed the test for such purposes. The obsession with adjustment was a problem that plagued the early days of personality testing within industry. It was only after personality testing expanded to focus on additional personality traits targeting more normal dimensions related to human behavior that results became more favorable.

Multidimensional Tests of Personality

Soon after the development of the aforementioned unidimensional personality tests, additional tests were designed that expanded the construct domain of personality tests. The *Bernreuter Personality Inventory* (BPI) was the first such test and was published by Robert Bernreuter in 1931 as part of his dissertation work at Stanford, conducted under Lewis Terman. Bernreuter took items from existing scales such as the Thurstone and Laird scales and reported scores on four dimensions: Neurotic Tendency, Self-Sufficiency, Introversion–Extraversion, and Dominance–Submission. The *Humm–Wadsworth Temperament Scale* (HWTS), previously mentioned, was also developed at this time (1934) and assessed seven dimensions (hysteroid, manic, depressive, autistic, paranoid, epileptoid, and self-mastery), with those dimensions being linked back to the clinical writings of Dr. Aaron Rosanoff. Both of these tests were true commercial products, complete with advertising as well as, at least in the case of the HWTS, full-time staff dedicated solely to sales, promotion, and research involving the instrument. The Bernreuter had unverified reports of sales of 1,000,000 administrations per year by Stanford University Press (see Gibby & Zickar, 2008).

The next important development of multidimensional personality tests was the *Minnesota Multiphasic Personality Inventory* (MMPI) developed by Hathaway and McKinley (1940) in the late 1930s. Previous scales had been developed largely by rational means with researchers writing ideas based on theory and intuition (Woodworth's scale was an exception). Hathaway and McKinley popularized and refined the empirical approach that was used by Woodworth by writing a large number of items, administering them to a group of psychiatric patients, and then comparing their scores to a normal sample. Items that discriminated between these two groups then comprised a scale, such as Schizophrenia, Hysteria, and Depression. Separate diagnoses had individual scales, though items could overlap across scales. Later researchers took the MMPI items and constructed additional scales using the empirical method (e.g., Panton, 1960). Although the MMPI was designed to provide diagnostic information for identification of psychopathology, researchers quickly sought to use it for occupational purposes.

Harmon and Wiener (1945) used the MMPI in their work with World War II (WWII) veterans who were being rehabilitated back into the civilian workforce. They believed that one of the reasons why veterans had trouble being successful at work was psychological problems due to military action, and so they used the MMPI as part of their work with the Veteran's Administration. This work seemed consistent with the original intent of the MMPI's developers because it focused on psychopathology. Subsequent research, however, used the MMPI for industrial purposes that had no direct connection to psychopathology. For example, Verniaud (1946) administered the MMPI to 97 women in three different occupations to determine the personality characteristics needed to be successful in clerical, department store, and optical workers. He realized that using an instrument designed for clinical work might be considered inappropriate for the workplace but argued: "instruments sensitive enough to be of value in identifying extreme deviates may be of value in identifying personality differences among functionally normal individuals" (Verniaud, 1946, p. 604). Companies used the MMPI for selection until the 1990s, when several organizations were sued for violations under the Americans with Disabilities Act, forbidding medical inquiries prior to a job offer being made. In addition, items on the MMPI that dealt with religious matters were deemed to violate certain state privacy laws. The MMPI is still used in some occupations related to safety (e.g., police officers), where preoffer inquiries are still permitted.

Another important test that needs to be mentioned is the *Myers–Briggs Type Indicator* (MBTI). This test is perhaps the most well-known and most administered personality test both in industry and among the general public. The Myers–Briggs was developed by Katharine Briggs, who was inspired by Jungian psychology, and her daughter, Isabel Myers, who had read an article in *Readers' Digest* about the HWTS and became inspired to develop a test that would help people be assigned to jobs most suited to their personality (see Saunders, 1991). The mother–daughter team drove around Pennsylvania promoting their test to principals, deans, and managers. After initially self-publishing the test, the authors turned to Educational Testing Services (ETS) as publisher, the MBTI being ETS' first foray into personality testing. Later, the test was published by CPP, Inc. with support given by the Center for Applications of Psychological Type (CAPT).

The MBTI uses a series of four dichotomies to classify individuals into a specific type; based on the test, individuals would be assigned Thinking versus Feeling, Sensing versus Intuition, Introverted versus Extraverted, and Judgment versus Perception. The test became popular with people using their four-letter MBTI code (e.g., INJF) as a way to communicate easily with others about their inner personality, with some people remembering their code just as they would other personally identifying information. The percentage of Americans who have taken the MBTI is probably higher than that for any other personality inventory, though the volume of sales is hard to quantify given that it is administered by a proprietary company. In 2003, CPP celebrated the 60th anniversary of the MBTI, boasting that 89 of the Fortune 100 used the test with more than 2 million administrations per year.

Despite its popularity (or perhaps in part because of it), the MBTI remains a controversial instrument among personality researchers. It has been criticized on several grounds. First, Myers and Briggs had no formal training in psychology or test construction. Their inspiration for constructing the test came from lay readings of psychology, largely those by Jung, who himself was viewed skeptically by psychologists who did not ascribe to the psychodynamic approach. Second, many psychologists were uncomfortable with simplistic type theory, where people were assigned one of two possible outcomes for a particular dimension. Most psychologists viewed personality as a continuum with people falling somewhere along a range in between two polar ends. Instead of saying you were either an introvert or an extravert, most psychologists wanted to be able to make statements such as "you are slightly introverted." These criticisms were leveled at the MBTI early on in its shelf-life and are still being made today. Despite these criticisms, the MBTI remains popular and some psychologists have worked to extract more meaningful psychometric information from the instrument, demonstrating that continuous scoring is possible and that the results correspond to other more scientifically grounded personality instruments (see Harvey & Murry, 1994). These psychologists have taken the approach that "if you can't beat them, join 'em!" (see Chapter 16 of this volume for more complete coverage of the MBTI, and type measures more broadly, in work settings).

After the development and commercial success of the Bernreuter, HWTS, MMPI, and MBTI, a large number of multifaceted personality instruments were developed in the 1950s and 1960s. These instruments were generally characterized by a wider range of personality constructs than in previous measures, with most targeting many additional traits besides adjustment. In addition, these inventories tended to be developed with sophisticated statistical methods that had not generally been available to the first wave of personality test developers. In many cases, factor analysis was used to refine scales and, in some cases, even to determine the nature of the constructs being assessed. For other scales, sophisticated empirical scoring methods, similar to that of the MMPI, were used to form scales. Inventories developed during this time include the *16PF* (Cattell & Stice, 1957), the *California Psychological Inventory* (Gough, 1956), the *Guilford and Zimmerman Temperament Survey* (Guilford & Zimmerman, 1949), and the *Personality Research Form* (Jackson, 1967). Another important feature of all of these tests was that they were designed explicitly for assessment of personality within normal populations. These tests much more closely resemble the personality tests of today compared to their predecessors; in fact, some of these tests are still being used commercially, though often with refinements.

Projectives in Industry

While objective personality tests were proliferating from the 1920s to the 1950s, a different philosophical approach to testing was also being developed. The notion of projective testing grew from Sigmund Freud's work on the unconscious. Freud believed that most of the important aspects of life were buried in the unconscious and, in order to resolve issues and conflicts, the therapist had to employ creative methods for bringing that unconscious material into conscious awareness. Freud employed dream analysis and free association as two techniques to pry into the unconscious thoughts of his patients.

In 1921, Swiss psychiatrist Hermann Rorschach developed the Rorschach Inkblot Test, which has remained the most popular projective test. In this test, respondents react to 10 ambiguous designs, each on a separate card, and are asked "What might this be?" for each card. Rorschach, who was a leader in the Swiss psychoanalytic community and who had come from an artistic background, had piloted several hundred inkblots and picked the 10 with the most diagnostic value. He published his work in a book called *Psychodiagnostik* detailing the test (Rorschach, 1921). Researchers in the United States (e.g., Beck, 1938; Exner, 1974) took this test and developed methods for interpreting and scoring it to the point that the test became one of the most frequent of all types of tests administered within psychology (see Sundberg, 1954). Because of the one-on-one nature of the administration, in which a card was presented to an individual participant and their response interpreted by a clinician, the Rorschach was of limited use in organizational settings. Validation studies have attempted to predict work behavior (see Carter, Daniels, & Zickar, in press; Dulsky & Krout, 1950) and a separate scoring system was designed to predict management talent (called the *Perceptanalytic Executive Scale*; Piotrowski & Rock, 1963). Despite these efforts, the Rorschach never became as popular in organizational use as in clinical use.

Although projective tests were difficult to apply to large-scale selection efforts (which was the bread-and-butter work of industrial–organizational [I/O] psychologists), the tests had great appeal to managers, who believed it was important to figure out what was in the unconscious minds of their workers. The nature of projective tests can also alleviate worries surrounding applicant faking. Projective tests became popular within industry as part of training and development exercises championed by the new humanism that was infusing psychology. T-groups or encounter groups (see Highhouse, 2002) often included projective tests as ways for employees to better learn about themselves. In addition, selection of executives, which was, by its nature, done on a small scale, was another avenue where projective tests were considered.

After the Rorschach, a wide range of tests was considered for organizational use. The *Cornell Word Form*, a word association test based on Jung's free association research, asked respondents to provide two responses to each stimulus word and, based on that, provided scores thought to be related to employee performance (Weider, 1951). Sentence completion tests were more popular in organizational uses. In such tasks, respondents were asked to complete sentences such as "My family doctor . . ." Several versions were created that were used widely in organizational settings, including the *Personnel Reaction Blank* (Gough & Peterson, 1952) and the *Miner Sentence Completion Scale* (Miner, 1960). Finally, picture arrangement tasks were used, in which a series of ambiguous objects had to be arranged in an order the respondent thought most meaningful. The *Tomkins–Horn Picture Arrangement Test* (Tomkins & Miner, 1957) also asked respondents to write a sentence to describe their arrangement of the objects. Although each of these methodologies had its own limited number of advocates, none had as widespread use as another projective test, the *Thematic Appreciation Test* (TAT; Morgan & Murray, 1935).

The TAT was developed by Henry Murray along with Christiana Morgan in the 1930s and included 31 ambiguous pictures in which participants were asked to write a story in response to each picture (see Murray, 1938). Murray had received a Ph.D. in biochemistry from Cambridge and was working in the natural sciences when he met Morgan, who, as an artist, was intrigued by Jungian psychology (see Anderson, 1999). Murray changed career paths and became director of the Harvard Psychological Clinic and devoted his life to the TAT, focusing on enumerating human motives that he believed were elicited during the response to the TAT. Murray was interested in using the TAT to probe the depths of the unconscious and to get people to best share secrets and fears that would not be possible through traditional personality assessment.

David McClelland was interested in motives and conducted research to see if experimental manipulation would influence TAT scores. He deprived participants of food over varying periods of time and found that results did track the amount of food deprivation, and in ways that were not always consistent with self-reports of hunger (see McClelland, 1999). McClelland used the TAT to measure three motives: achievement, affiliation, and power.

The need for achievement construct is one that has had the most impact on I/O practice, given the importance of the motivation construct. The TAT was used in several important lines of research. McClelland worked with the U.S. Navy to develop a TAT-type interview to assess competencies among race relations officers (McClelland, 1999). The TAT has been used in many studies predicting work-related behavior. For example, Collins, Hanges, and Locke (2004) recently examined the meta-analytic relation between measures of need for achievement and entrepreneurial performance and found 21 studies that had used the TAT with such criteria. They found that the TAT of need for achievement correlated with performance ($r = .16$) and career choice ($r = .20$), similar to levels for other tests. In a meta-analysis of 105 samples that included the TAT and a self-reported measure of motivation, Spangler (1992) found that, on average, the correlations were slightly higher in predicting behavioral outcomes for the TAT. Finally, research has shown that the correlations between self-report measures of motivation and the TAT assessment of need for achievement are relatively small (McClelland, 1999). This suggests that the trait, as assessed by the projective test, is assessing a different aspect of motivation than the conscious self-report measure.

Ultimately, projective tests never saw the volume that traditional personality tests did for several reasons. As previously mentioned, the practical aspects of administration and scoring were large barriers to organizations. The requirement of individual administration with a trained psychologist to score the results dissuaded many organizations. Additionally, evaluations of projective tests often resulted in poor reliabilities. Low inter-rater reliability computed by having two psychologists interpret the same answers and poor validity plagued the development and utility of projective tests (e.g., Carter et al., in press). Efforts were made to produce more consistency in scoring and, hence, increase reliability, though these efforts were mixed. For example, Exner (1974) created the Comprehensive Scoring system for the Rorschach that had test scorers evaluate responses on a series of dimensions including content of answer, form of answer, and others. Despite these efforts, the reliability of projective tests is typically much lower than for objective personality tests.

To this day, projective tests retain an allure within organizations with occasional pleas for more research and development of new projective tests. In addition, in clinical psychology, there remains an active debate on the reliability and validity of projective tests as well as their role in clinical therapy (see Lilienfield, Wood, & Garb, 2000). We suspect that this allure for projective testing will continue in the future, as organizations seek tests that are more resistant to faking and as test developers seek more interactive and engaging personality items. Similarly, individual assessment and executive coaching, which have always maintained close ties with counseling psychology, will probably continue to use projective testing. Ryan and Sackett (1987) found that 50% of people doing individual assessment for selection report using projective tests; an internet search with the terms "projective testing" and "executive coaching" shows that projective tests are still used by individual assessors and executive coaches.

The Dark Days of Personality Testing

Within organizations, personality testing experienced a dark period that has been likened to the dark days that plagued Western civilization between the flowering of Greek and Roman ideals and the Renaissance in the 15th Century that rejuvenated the Western intellectual tradition. The dark days were brought about by a series of writings and events that happened largely during the 1960s. The decline in personality testing occurred because of I/O psychologists' concern about low validities of personality tests, social psychologists' attacks on the importance of personality, and popular press attacks on the use of personality tests in the business and governmental realms.

One of the most important attacks on personality came from within I/O psychology itself. Prominent personnel psychologist Robert Guion had published several critiques on personality testing, focusing on its low validity. In an oft-cited quotation, Guion and Gottier concluded, "it is difficult in the face of this summary to advocate, with a clear conscience, the use of personality measures in most situations as a basis for making employment decisions about people" (Guion & Gottier, 1965, p. 160). This quote and related writings were cited as evidence that personality testing was not useful in industry, despite later writings by Guion to clarify that they meant to spur additional validation research, not kill a line of research (see Guion, 1967).

Another line of attack came from social psychologist Walter Mischel, who published a book called *Personality and Assessment* that questioned whether personality traits were useful in predicting behavior. Mischel (1968) argued that the correlations between personality traits and individual acts of behavior were so low as to be meaningless. He also argued that behavior was not consistent across situations and that traits exist only in the eyes of the personality theorists. He argued that, at best, it was the interaction between personality and the situation that was important to understand, but that a focus solely on personality traits was not productive. His writings provoked a large number of defenses of personality, examining various methodological and conceptual reasons for the low correlations between personality and behavior. As later theorists have written, the field in the long term benefited from this confrontation between the situation and personality (Kenrick & Funder, 1988), though, in the short term, it created another reason for people to look unfavorably upon personality tests.

Besides suffering scientific attacks, personality testing was also attacked in the public sphere. In 1964, Senator Sam Ervin attacked the use of the MMPI for the selection of Peace Corps volunteers. There were protests on governmental personality testing and the humorist Art Buchwald created his own personality test, *The Art Buchwald Personality Inventory*, to highlight what he thought was the silliness of many of the individual items within personality tests (see Armine, 1965, for a summary). This episode reminded the public of earlier criticisms of personality tests, which were viewed as tools for management to spy on workers and to enforce corporate hegemony (see Gross, 1962; Whyte, 1956).

Personality never died during the dark days, but it was used in limited ways and a decline in the number of publications was observed. However, important developments continued to be made. For example, Robert Hogan created his *Hogan Personality Inventory* (originally called Hopkins Personality Inventory; see R. Hogan, 2006) and demonstrated validity in predicting certain outcomes. As an editor of *Journal of Personality and Social Psychology*, he also fought to keep personality research alive despite a bias against such research by social psychologists (see R. Hogan, 2006). Personality research became dormant within organizational research. It would take the advent and application of a new statistical technique to reignite the interest surrounding personality.

The Resurgence or the Renaissance

The year 1991 was a pivotal year in the resurgence of personality testing in organizations. The technique of meta-analysis had been developed independently in the early 1970s by the team of Frank Schmidt and Jack Hunter as well as by a group of educational researchers. Meta-analysis revolutionized the way substantive reviews were done by providing a quantitative methodology for combining effect sizes across a variety of studies into a single effect size that best represented the relationship between two separate constructs (see Hunt, 1997). Starting in the 1980s, researchers began meta-analyzing the relationship of nearly every construct studied in I/O psychology. There was a race to determine the generalizable validity of all popular selection devices in predicting job performance. For example, there were meta-analyses of the validity of cognitive ability tests (Schmidt, Hunter, & Pearlman, 1981), employment interviews (Wiesner & Cronshaw, 1988), and assessment centers (Gaugler, Rosenthal, Thornton, & Bentson, 1987).

In 1991, two teams of researchers were working independently on meta-analyses of the relationship of personality traits to job performance. Barrick and Mount (1991) published their meta-analysis first in the March issue of *Personnel Psychology*, with Tett, Jackson, and Rothstein (1991) publishing theirs in December. Both of these articles are citation classics, with the Barrick and Mount article cited 3,873 times and Tett et al. cited 1,053 times (via Google Scholar [January 23, 2012]). The two articles have been dissected and were critiqued with many of the debates focusing on whether the analysis should have controlled for directional hypotheses (Barrick and Mount did not; Tett et al. did).

After these meta-analyses, I/O psychologists embraced personality testing with an explosion of publications and new instruments. The two meta-analyses were cited to demonstrate that personality tests, especially those targeting conscientiousness, had job-related validity. Personality tests suddenly became popular again with consultants promoting the tests as a way to increase validity of a test battery while reducing adverse impact. The constructs had small correlations with cognitive ability and relatively small amounts of adverse impact, leading people to view personality as a perfect complement in a large battery. In addition, these meta-analyses reified the Big Five taxonomy of personality.

The Big Five had first been identified by Tupes and Christal (1961). Psychologists had worked to identify the basic trait structure of personality, beginning with Gordon Allport, who had gone through the dictionary identifying adjectives that could be used to describe human personalities, finding nearly 18,000 (see Allport & Odbert, 1936). Raymond Cattell then reduced that large number of terms down to 4,500 and then identified 35 variables, which reduced to 12 factors after conducting a factor analysis (Cattell, 1947). Tupes and Christal factor analyzed eight samples of correlation matrices of the 35 Cattell variables and found a stable five-factor solution. Unfortunately, the original research was published in Air Force tech reports and did not reach wide circulation until the tech report was published in 1992 in the *Journal of Personality*, to help the original document reach a wider audience (see Christal, 1992; Tupes & Christal, 1961, 1992). By 1992, the Five-Factor Model had gained a wider audience through a group of researchers inspired by the Tupes and Christal tech reports.

It took two personality researchers in the 1980s and 1990s, Robert McCrae and Paul Costa Jr., to widely disseminate and support that work through a series of publications (e.g., McCrae & Costa, 1987). They and other researchers such as Digman (e.g., Digman & Inouye, 1986) used more modern versions of factor analysis (Tupes and Christial had relied on hand calculations) and found the Big Five personality traits, largely as identified by Tupes and Christal. The Barrick and Mount and Tett et al. meta-analyses brought that taxonomy to a larger I/O research audience and resulted in wide-scale (though not universal; see Block, 1995) acceptance of this taxonomy.

The acceptance of the Big Five taxonomy spurred development of several personality inventories that were modeled on the Big Five (e.g., Costa & McCrae, 1985) and it encouraged other personality test developers to report Big Five construct scores from their own mix of subscales. It should be noted that Hogan developed perhaps the earliest Big Five inventory after having been exposed to the Big Five taxonomy through Jerry Wiggins in the 1970s (see R. Hogan, 2006). In addition to influencing the development of subsequent personality inventories, the Big Five taxonomy drove the research agenda of personality research in organizations for many years, with research conducted to understand the importance of individual Big Five traits for predicting organizational outcomes and to refine and understand the hierarchical nature of the trait structure. Once the Big Five personality structure was accepted, research flourished and advances focused on several different areas, including both theoretical and methodological issues. See Goldberg (1993) and John and Srivastava (1999) for more details on the history of the Big Five.

Theoretical Work

Much of the work after the resurgence focused on trying to better understand the trait–criteria relationships. Driven mostly by Barrick and Mount's (1991) main findings, early researchers focused on conscientiousness as the trait that was most generalizable across a variety of jobs (e.g., J. Hogan & Ones, 1997). Other researchers examined the relations between other Big Five traits to find specific jobs and criteria that would be better predicted by traits besides conscientiousness (e.g., Stewart, 1996). Other researchers investigated the interactions of personality traits with each other or with other constructs, such as motives, attempting to increase predictability (e.g., Winter, John, Stewart, Klohnen, & Duncan, 1998). In general, this research showed promise and demonstrated that the initial validities identified by Barrick and Mount (1991) and Tett et al. (1991) could be improved upon.

Additionally, some researchers focused on developing theories on how personality manifested itself at work. Perhaps the grandest of the theories developed was the trait activation theory presented by Tett and Burnett (2003), which posited that certain situations make particular personality traits more salient and, hence, "activate" those traits. This concept had been present in the literature tracing back to Murray (1938), but the main contribution was the exhaustive nature of their classifying different types of features that might act as trait activators and trait inhibitors. Their framework was so broad that it could not be tested in any single study, though it has inspired a promising line of research (see Chapter 5, this volume). In addition, socioanalytic theory, proposed by Robert Hogan, provided a theoretical explanation of the social nature of personality traits and their perceptions (R. Hogan, 1983; see Chapter 4, this volume).

Methodological Issues

Researchers have debated the effects of faking, some citing evidence that the correlations of personality tests among applicants (where faking should be prevalent) were not much different from research on incumbent samples (where faking should be nonexistent) (see Hough, Eaton, Dunnette, Kamp, & McCloy, 1990). Others showed that faking had significant impact on the rank ordering of candidates (Rosse, Stecher, Miller, & Levin, 1998). Some focused on how to detect respondents who were faking (e.g., Zickar & Drasgow, 1996), though these techniques typically have not worked at the rate where they could be used operationally. Others focused on methods to prevent or reduce the amount of faking (Dwight & Donovan, 2003), with research being promising, though likely not to scare off sophisticated test takers who still wanted to fake. Finally, researchers began to develop theories and process models to better understand faking (e.g., McFarland & Ryan, 2000), with the idea that perhaps a better theoretical understanding would help with prevention and detection. This focus on faking is one that has been present from the beginning of personality measurement; the methodological tools used to answer the questions have become more sophisticated but the concern of researchers and managers is not new (see Zickar & Gibby, 2006, for a separate historical review on faking and social desirability; see also Chapter 12, this volume, for detailed coverage of faking personality tests in employment settings).

Other researchers focused on whether personality constructs should be measured at the broad level or more narrowly at the facet level (a level below the Big Five) (see Ones & Viswesvaran, 1996; Paunonen, Rothstein, & Jackson, 1999). Arguments were made for both sides, though this debate had been considered in other domains such as cognitive ability and work attitudes. The conclusion in personality, as well as the other domains, tended to be that narrow traits should be used to predict narrow criteria and broad traits should be used for broad criteria (Chapter 14, this volume, deals explicitly with the issue of personality trait breadth).

Other methodological advances include application of more sophisticated psychometric techniques such as item response theory (Zickar, 2001a) to improve the measurement and understanding of personality. The use of computers and the internet to measure personality has been another methodological advance with many studies being conducted to determine whether there were statistical differences between traditional paper-and-pencil measures and computerized tests (e.g., Chuah, Drasgow, & Roberts, 2006). The flexibility of administration and the ease of scoring as well as the possibility of administering items adaptively made personality assessment more accessible.

Lessons Learned

What Goes Around, Comes Around

In many ways, personality testing is one of the most faddish areas in all of I/O psychology. Personality testing has gone in and out of vogue throughout its history and many of the concerns that are currently expressed were expressed at the start of personality testing. In addition, the search for alternative personality testing methods besides self-report, objectively scored tests has been ever present. Although projective tests are currently not very popular in I/O psychology, it is possible that in the near future that may change. A review of the early history of personality testing is sobering at times.

Personality Testing Is Influenced by External Events

Although there is a tendency for people within a field to think that the actors within that field have dictated the direction of the field, throughout the history of personality testing it is evident that exterior events have shaped the field. WWI created a need for measuring personality-related constructs and jump-started the development of objective personality tests. Later events that exerted influence on personality testing included the labor–management battles of the 1930s, and the revolt against corporate culture in the 1950s and 1960s.

Battle Between Normal and Abnormal

Personality testing grew out of the need to understand the abnormal range of personality and, as was shown in this review, the first wave of personality tests was heavily focused on the trait of adjustment or, what we would call today, neuroticism or emotional stability. The validity for predicting work-related outcomes improved as personality tests focused more on the normal range of personality traits. This question of whether to focus on the normal or the abnormal is one that personality testers will continue to face. In fact, one popular personality trait focuses on the "dark side" of personality traits to predict negative work outcomes. R. Hogan and Hogan (2001) posit that psychopathology is a main reason why there is so much malfeasance and ineptitude among corporate leaders; their scale is designed to screen out the "dark side" leaders. There will always be a need, in some cases, to assess psychopathology within workplaces. The field will continue to grapple with where on the spectrum from normal to abnormal is best to focus its energy.

Development Versus Selection

Another theme that is present throughout the history of personality testing is the use of personality for self-development versus personnel selection decisions. Both of these usages are quite popular in organizations, though the demands and concerns for personality testing differ across the two usages. It is likely that most of the millions of administrations of the MBTI each year are used for employee development exercises, and not for hiring decisions. I/O psychologists are generally more concerned with the issues related to personality testing in the context of hiring, and often fail to appreciate the importance of personality testing for the use of self-insight and development. Counseling and clinical psychologists are more likely to be interested in the latter. Both usages, though, have been important through the history of personality testing within organizations and need to be considered.

Conclusions

Personality testing has come a long way in the near-centennial since Woodworth's test. The field has gone through a series of boom–bust cycles with a current growth cycle. Reviewing this history, however, should give pause to anyone who thinks that personality research will continue on a linear or exponential growth trend. As a review of history suggests, personality testing is a field that has attracted a large level of scientific interest combined with passionate interest from a lay public concerned with better understanding of themselves. We expect the future of personality testing to maintain both the interest of researchers and a public hungry for self-understanding.

Practitioner's Window

The history of personality testing within industry is helpful to review. Some key points for practitioners are as follows:

- Personality testing has always had to cope with nonscientific influences

As reviewed in this chapter, the early days of personality testing were filled with charlatans like Katherine Blackford who believed you could determine someone's personality from their hair color and body shape. The history of personality testing has been filled with these types of quacks who take advantage of the public's hunger for self-knowledge.

- Personality testing is often influenced by external events

Personality testing developed due to a need in World War I to screen recruits for proclivity for shell shock. Personality testing has been used to thwart pro-union legislation and has been subject to public and legislature backlash. All of these external events have influenced personality testing within organizations.

- Personality testing has served two functions within organizations

Organizations have used personality testing for making better hiring decisions as well as to help employees gain self-insight that will spur personal development. Each of these purposes has distinct concerns. Most psychologists specialize on one purpose or the other.

- Personality testing has benefited from advanced statistical procedures

The development of statistical techniques such as factor analysis, item response theory, and meta-analysis has helped people better understand the personality domain. Although early researchers often had good insights about the personality domain, they often lacked the statistical methods to refine those insights.

References

Allport, G. W., & Odbert, H. S. (1936). Trait names: A psycho-lexical study. *Psychological Monographs, 47*, i–171.

Anderson, J. W. (1999). Henry A. Murray and the creation of the Thematic Apperception Test. In L. Geiser & M. I. Stein (Eds.), *Evocative images: The Thematic Apperception Test and the art of projection* (pp. 23–38). Washington, DC: American Psychological Association.

Armine, M. (1965). The 1965 congressional inquiry into testing: A commentary. *American Psychologist, 20*, 859–870.

Barrick, M. R., & Mount, M. K. (1991). The Big Five personality dimensions and job performance: A meta-analysis. *Personnel Psychology, 44*, 1–26.

Beck, S. J. (1938). Personality structure in schizophrenia: A Rorschach investigation in 81 patients and 64 controls. *Nervous Mental Disorders Monograph Series, 63*, ix–88.

Blackford, K. M. H. (1918). *Reading character at sight*. New York: Independent Corporation.

Blackford, K. M. H., & Newcomb, A. (1917). *Blondes and brunets*. New York: Henry Alden.

Block, J. (1995). A contrarian view of the Big Five. *Psychological Bulletin, 117*, 187–215.

Butcher, J. N. (2010). Personality assessment from the nineteenth to the early twenty-first century: Past achievements and contemporary challenges. *Annual Review of Clinical Psychology, 6*, 1–20.

Carter, N. T., Daniels, M. A., & Zickar, M. J. (in press). Projective testing: Foundations and uses for human resources management. *Human Resources Management Review*.

Cattell, R. B. (1947). Confirmation and clarification of primary personality factors. *Psychometrika, 12*, 197–220.

Cattell, R. B., & Stice, G. E. (1957). *The Sixteen Personality Factors Questionnaire*. Champaign, IL: Institute for Personality and Ability Testing.

Christal, R. E. (1992). Author's note on "Recurrent personality factors based on trait ratings." *Journal of Personality, 60*, 221–224.

Chuah, C. C., Drasgow, F., & Roberts, B. W. (2006). Personality assessment: Does the medium matter? No. *Journal of Research in Personality, 40*, 359–376.

Cleeton, G. C., & Knight, F. B. (1924). Validity of character judgments based on external criteria. *Journal of Applied Psychology, 8*, 215–231.

Collins, C. J., Hanges, P. J., & Locke, E. A. (2004). The relationship of achievement motivation to entrepreneurial behavior: A meta-analysis. *Human Performance, 17*, 95–117.

Costa, P. T., Jr., & McCrae, R. E. (1985). *The NEO Personality Inventory manual*. Odessa, FL: Psychological Assessment Services.

Davies, J. D. (1955). *Phrenology, fad and science: A 19th century American crusade*. New Haven, CT: Yale University Press.

Digman, J. M., & Inouye, J. (1986). Further specification of the five robust factors of personality. *Journal of Personality and Social Psychology, 50*, 116–123.

Dulsky, S. G., & Krout, M. H. (1950). Predicting promotion potential on the basis of psychological tests. *Personnel Psychology, 3*, 345–351.

Dwight, S. A., & Donovan, J. J. (2003). Do warnings not to fake reduce faking? *Human Performance, 16*, 1–23.

Exner, J. E., Jr. (1974). *The Rorschach: A comprehensive system*. New York: Wiley.

Forrest, D. W. (1974). *Francis Galton: The life and work of a Victorian genius*. London: Elek.

Galton, F. (1874). *English men of science: Their nature and nurture*. New York: D. Appleton.

Galton, F. (1884). Measurement of character. *Fortnightly Review, 42*, 179–185.

Gaugler, B. B., Rosenthal, D. B., Thornton, G. C., & Bentson, C. (1987). Meta-analysis of assessment center validity. *Journal of Applied Psychology, 72*, 493–511.

Gay, P. (1988). *Freud: A life for our time*. New York: W. W. Norton.

Gibby, R. E., & Zickar, M. J. (2008). A history of the early days of personality testing in American industry: An obsession with adjustment. *History of Psychology, 11*, 164–184.

Goldberg, L. R. (1993). The structure of phenotypic personality traits. *American Psychologist, 48*, 26–34.

Gough, H. G. (1956). *California Psychological Inventory*. Palo Alto, CA: Consulting Psychologists Press.

Gough, H. G., & Peterson, D. R. (1952). The identification and measurement of predispositional factors in crime and delinquency. *Journal of Consulting Psychology, 16*, 207–212.

Gross, M. (1962). *The brain watchers*. New York: Random House.

Guilford, J. P., & Zimmerman, W. S. (1949). *The Guilford–Zimmerman Temperament Survey manual of instructions and interpretations*. Beverly Hills, CA: Sheridan Supply.

Guion, R. M. (1967). Personnel selection. *Annual Review of Psychology, 18*, 105–216.

Guion, R. M., & Gottier, R. F. (1965). Validity of personality measures in personnel selection. *Personnel Psychology, 18*, 135–164.

Harmon, L. R., & Wiener, D. N. (1945). Use of the Minnesota Multiphasic Personality Inventory in vocational advisement. *Journal of Applied Psychology, 29*, 132–141.

Harvey, R. J., & Murry, W. D. (1994). Scoring the Myers–Briggs Type Indicator: Empirical comparison of preference score versus latent-trait methods. *Journal of Personality Assessment, 62*, 116–129.

Hathaway, S. R., & McKinley, J. C. (1940). A multiphasic personality schedule (Minnesota): I. Construction of the schedule. *Journal of Personality, 10*, 249–254.

Heymans, G., & Wiersma, E. (1906). Beitrage zur spezillen psychologie auf grund einer massen-unterschung [Contributions to Differential Psychology]. *Zeitschrift für Psychologie, 43*, 81–127.

Highhouse, S. (2002). A history of the T-group and its early applications in management development. *Group Dynamics, 6*, 277–290.

Hogan, J., & Ones, D. S. (1997). Conscientiousness and integrity at work. In R. Hogan, J. A. Johnson, & S. R. Briggs (Eds.), *Handbook of personality psychology* (pp. 849–870). San Diego, CA: Academic Press.

Hogan, R. (1983). A socioanalytic theory of personality. In M. Page & R. Dienstbier (Eds.), *1982 Nebraska symposium on motivation* (pp. 55–89). Lincoln: University of Nebraska Press.

Hogan, R. (2006). Who wants to be a psychologist? *Journal of Personality Assessment, 82*, 119–130.

Hogan, R., & Hogan, J. (2001). Assessing leadership: A view from the dark side. *International Journal of Selection and Assessment, 9*, 40–51.

Hough, L. M., Eaton, N. K., Dunnette, M. D., Kamp, J. D., & McCloy, R. A. (1990). Criterion-related validities of personality constructs and the effect of response distortion on those validities. *Journal of Applied Psychology, 75*, 581–595.

House, S. D. (1927). *A mental hygiene inventory: A contribution to dynamic psychology*. New York: Columbia University.

Hungerford, E. (1931). Walt Whitman and his chart of bumps. *American Literature, 2*, 350–384.

Hunt, M. (1997). *How science takes stock: The story of meta-analysis*. New York: Russell Sage Foundation.

Jackson, D. M. (1967). *Personality Research Form manual*. Goshen, NY: Research Psychologists' Press.

John, O. P., & Srivastava, S. (1999). The Big Five trait taxonomy: History, measurement, and theoretical perspectives. In L. A. Pervin & O. P. John (Eds.), *Handbook of personality: Theory and research* (2nd ed., pp.102–138). New York: Guilford Press.

Jung, C. G. (1907). On psychological relations of the association experiment. *Journal of Abnormal Psychology, 31*, 249–257.

Kenrick, D. T., & Funder, D. C. (1988). Profiting from controversy: Lessons from the person–situation debate. *American Psychologist, 43*, 23–34.

Kent, G. H., & Rosanoff, A. (1910). A study in association in insanity. *American Journal of Insanity, 67*, 37–96.

Kevles, D. J. (1968). Testing the army's intelligence: Psychologists and the military in World War I. *Journal of American History, 55*, 565–581.

Laird, D. A. (1925). Detecting abnormal behavior. *Journal of Abnormal and Social Psychology, 20*, 128–141.

Lilienfield, S. O., Wood, J. M., & Garb, H. N. (2000). The scientific status of projective techniques. *Psychological Science in the Public Interest, 1*, 27–66.

McClelland, D. C. (1999). How the test lives on: Extensions of the Thematic Apperception Test approach. In L. Geiser & M. I. Stein (Eds.), *Evocative images: The Thematic Apperception Test and the art of projection* (pp. 163–175). Washington, DC: American Psychological Association.

McCrae, R. R., & Costa, P.T., Jr. (1987). Validation of the five-factor model of personality across instruments and observers. *Journal of Personality and Social Psychology, 52*, 81–90.
McFarland, L., & Ryan, A. M. (2000). Variance in faking across noncognitive measures. *Journal of Applied Psychology, 85*, 812–821.
Miner, J. B. (1960). The effect of a course in psychology on the attitudes of research and development supervisor. *Journal of Applied Psychology, 44*, 224–232.
Mischel, W. (1968). *Personality and assessment.* New York: Wiley.
Morgan, C. D., & Murray, H. A. (1935). A method of investigating fantasies: The Thematic Apperception Test. *Archives of Neurology & Psychiatry, 34*, 289–306.
Murray, H. A. (Ed.). (1938). *Explorations in personality: A clinical and experimental study of fifty men of college age.* New York: Oxford University Press.
Ones, D. S., & Viswesvaran, C. (1996). Bandwidth–fidelity dilemma in personality measurement for personnel selection. *Journal of Organizational Behavior, 17*, 609–626.
Panton, J. H. (1960). A new MMPI scale for the identification of homosexuality. *Journal of Clinical Psychology, 16*, 17–21.
Paunonen, S.V., Rothstein, M. G., & Jackson, D. N. (1999). Narrow reasoning about the use of broad personality measures for personnel selection. *Journal of Organizational Behavior, 20*, 389–405.
Piotrowski, Z. A., & Rock, M. R. (1963). *The Perceptanalytic Executive Scale: A tool for the selection of top managers.* New York: Grune & Stratton.
Pressey, S. L., & Pressey, L. W. (1919). "Cross-out" tests with suggestions as to a group scale of the emotions. *Journal of Applied Psychology, 3*, 138–150.
Rorschach, H. (1921). *Psychodiagnostik.* Berne, Switzerland: Bircher.
Rosse, J. L., Stecher, M. D., Miller, J. A., & Levin, R. A. (1998). The impact of response distortion on preemployment personality testing and hiring decisions. *Journal of Applied Psychology, 83*, 634–644.
Ryan, A. M., & Sackett, P. R. (1987). A survey of individual assessment practices by I/O psychologists. *Personnel Psychology, 40*, 455–488.
Sachs, J. (2001). *Aristotle's On the Soul and On Memory and Recollection.* Santa Fe, NM: Green Lion Press.
Saunders, F.W. (1991). *Katharine and Isabel: Mother's light, daughter's journey.* Palo Alto, CA: Consulting Psychologists Press.
Schmidt, F. L., Hunter, J. E., & Pearlman, K. (1981). Task differences and validity of aptitude tests in selection: A red herring. *Journal of Applied Psychology, 66*, 166–185.
Smith, R. (1997). *The Norton history of the human sciences.* New York: W. W. Norton.
Sokal, M. M. (Ed.). (1987). *Psychological testing and American society.* New Brunswick, NJ: Rutgers University Press.
Spangler, W. D. (1992). Validity of questionnaire and TAT measures of need for achievement: Two meta-analyses. *Psychological Bulletin, 112*, 140–154.
Stewart, G. L. (1996). Reward structure as a moderator of the relationship between extraversion and sales performance. *Journal of Applied Psychology, 81*, 619–627.
Sundberg, N. D. (1954). A note concerning the history of testing. *American Psychologist, 9*, 150–151.
Tett, R. P., & Burnett, D. D. (2003). A personality trait-based interactionist model of job performance. *Journal of Applied Psychology, 88*, 500–517.
Tett, R. P., Jackson, D. N., & Rothstein, M. (1991). Personality measures as predictors of job performance: A meta-analytic review. *Personnel Psychology, 44*, 703–742.
Thurstone, L. L., & Thurstone, T. G. (1929). *Personality schedule.* Chicago, IL: University of Chicago.
Tomkins, S. S., & Miner, J. B. (1957). *The Tomkins-Horn Picture Arrangement Test.* New York: Springer.
Tupes, E. C., & Christal, R. E. (1961). *Recurrent personality factors based on trait ratings* (Technical Report ASD-TR-61-97). Lackland Air Force Base, TX: Personnel Laboratory, Air Forces Systems Command.
Tupes, E. C., & Christal, R. E. (1992). Recurrent personality factors based on trait ratings. *Journal of Personality, 60*, 225–251.
Verniaud, W. M. (1946). Occupational differences in the Minnesota Multiphasic Personality Inventory. *Journal of Applied Psychology, 30*, 604–613.
Watson, R. I. (1978). *The great psychologists* (4th ed.). Philadelphia: J. B. Lippincott.
Weider, A. (1951). Some aspects of an industrial mental hygiene program. *Journal of Applied Psychology, 35*, 383–385.
Whyte, W. H. (1956). *The organization man.* New York: Simon & Schuster.
Wiesner, W. H., & Cronshaw, S. F. (1988). A meta-analytic investigation of the impact of interview format and degree of structure on the validity of the employment interview. *Journal of Occupational Psychology, 61*, 275–290.

Winter, D. G., John, O. P., Stewart, A. J., Klohnen, E. C., & Duncan, L. E. (1998). Traits and motives: Toward an integration of two traditions in personality research. *Psychological Review, 105*, 230–250.

Yerkes, R. M. (Ed.). (1921). *Psychological examining in the United States Army*. Washington, DC: U.S. Army.

Zickar, M. J. (2001a). Conquering the next frontier: Modeling personality data with item response theory. In B. Roberts & R. Hogan (Eds.), *Personality psychology in the workplace* (pp. 141–158). Washington, DC: American Psychological Association.

Zickar, M. J. (2001b). Using personality inventories to identify thugs and agitators: Applied psychology's contribution to the war against labor. *Journal of Vocational Behavior, 59*, 149–164.

Zickar, M. J., & Drasgow, F. (1996). Detecting faking using appropriateness measurement. *Applied Psychological Measurement, 20*, 71–87.

Zickar, M. J., & Gibby, R. E. (2006). A history of faking and socially desirable responding on personality tests. In R. Griffith & M. H. Peterson (Eds.), *A closer examination of applicant faking behavior* (pp. 21–42). Greenwich, CT: Information Age.

10

A Review and Comparison of 12 Personality Inventories on Key Psychometric Characteristics

Matthew S. Prewett, Robert P. Tett, and Neil D. Christiansen

Following decades of uncertainty, personality testing has become a popular, if not prominent, part of research and practice is human resource management. The utility of personality testing is still debated (e.g., Morgeson et al., 2007), but a wealth of research supports the view that personality measures can, under relevant conditions, significantly predict key job outcomes (Tett & Christiansen, 2007). There have been hundreds of local validation studies concerning personality, and enough meta-analytic evidence even to warrant a second-order meta-analysis (e.g., Barrick, Mount, & Judge, 2001). When examining the multitude of validity studies, personality inventories generally show modest overall coefficients but notable relationships for specific criteria and contexts (e.g., J. Hogan & Holland, 2003; Judge, Bono, Ilies, & Gerhardt, 2002; Prewett, Walvoord, Stilson, Rossi, & Brannick, 2009).

Given the promise of personality testing in human resource management, it is not surprising that the number of commercially available personality inventories is quite large. A wealth of research has examined the utility of personality traits in selection and development, but little information is available on the strengths and weaknesses of most instruments, and even less on comparisons among them. Although some comparisons between select inventory characteristics are currently available in the literature for a few personality inventories (e.g., Goffin, Rothstein, & Johnston, 2000), there is no comprehensive examination of relevant psychometric properties for many popular or reputable personality inventories. The lack of a formal comparative review undermines a reasoned choice among instruments. A trait with meta-analytic validation support may lack validity evidence when measured in a specific inventory. Alternatively, a meta-analytic validity coefficient may underestimate the validity of a superior performing inventory (Goffin et al., 2000). Personality tests of poor quality yield a short-term consequence of failing to assist test users in the decision regarding whom to hire or promote, but also a long-term consequence of undermining the perceived value of personality assessment as a whole in work settings. Developmental feedback to employees may also suffer should a specific test fail to accurately measure one or more job-relevant traits. The benefit of using any particular personality test clearly rests on its psychometric qualities, and choosing tests based solely on other qualities (e.g., price, name recognition, and promotional materials) would risk failure in personality testing locally and on the grander scale.

The primary purpose of this chapter is to offer a comparison of selected, popular personality inventories on key psychometric qualities, in part as a guide to users seeking to choose among those tests in light of local needs, and further as a gauge of the general state of personality assessment, as represented by some of the major players. A secondary aim is to highlight important psychometric qualities that any test user should examine when choosing from among available alternatives beyond just those measures considered here. More specifically, we evaluated 12 generally recognized and reputable personality inventories: *16 Personality Factor Questionnaire* (*16PF*), *California Psychological Inventory* (*CPI*), *Caliper Profile*, *Global Personality Inventory—Adaptive* (GPI-A), *Hogan Personality Inventory* (*HPI*), *Minnesota Multiphasic Personality Inventory II* (MMPI-2), *Myers–Briggs Type Indicator* (*MBTI*), *Neuroticism–Extraversion–Openness Personality Inventory—3* (*NEO-PI-3*), *Occupational Personality Questionnaire-32n and -32i* (*OPQ-32*), *Personality Research Form* (*PRF*), and *Wonderlic 5* (formerly the *Personal Characteristics Inventory* or *PCI*). Our methods for selecting these particular instruments are described in a later section. From this analysis, we draw conclusions for specific inventories and implications for personality assessment more generally. We begin with a description of our major evaluative criteria.

Psychometric Criteria Used for Evaluation

Because the main purpose of our review was to assist decision making in an HR context, we specifically focused on evidence that would be particularly relevant for such contexts. We identified six broad test qualities: (1) conceptual framework and development, (2) reliability and measurement approach, (3) construct validity, (4) criterion-related validity, (5) response validity, and (6) normative information. Specific criteria within these factors were evaluated according to the availability, detail, and quality of the evidence presented in the given test manual. Although manuals were penalized for excluding relevant information, we also searched the extant literature to determine if this information could be obtained elsewhere. Inventories with incomplete or poor evidence for a psychometric property received a poor evaluation on that dimension, whereas inventories with complete and strong evidence received a positive evaluation. Each of our six evaluation criteria is discussed in greater detail, as follows.

Conceptual Framework and Development

Personality inventories vary substantially in their theoretical foundations, with implications for content validation (e.g., in writing items to capture specific traits) and construct validation more generally (e.g., regarding how well empirical findings support theoretical expectations). Scales derived from independently corroborated personality taxonomies were judged more favorably than those based on less established structures. For example, the Five-Factor Model (FFM) of personality has withstood an enormous amount of empirical scrutiny in psychological and applied research (e.g., Costa & McCrae, 1985; Digman & Inouye, 1986), yielding overall support for the model. However, we did not penalize inventories for adopting a unique or non-FFM model, so long as the adoption was justified from both theoretical and empirical standpoints. The PRF, for example, was originally developed from Murray's (1938) taxonomy of psychogenic needs, but the scale and item development process led to significant revisions based on both theoretical and empirical grounds. Given its strong focus on trait constructs, the PRF was evaluated highly in this regard. Another non-FFM inventory, the MBTI, did not appear to revise deficiencies in the underlying psychoanalytic theory nor did it act upon the empirical evidence for content deficiency. We found this noteworthy because psychoanalytic theories of personality (e.g., Jung, 1971) have generally received modest empirical support and were historically developed through philosophical writings and individual case studies (Esterson, 2001).

Related to the issue of scale development, the process of item/scale writing and revision was also considered. Inventories with items written using a combination of theory and empirical testing were most favorably rated. Whereas all 12 inventories were developed using statistical analysis, those for which the methods were described in detail were favored. Measures developed using only mechanical methods were rated lower, as atheoretical approaches are more vulnerable to deficiency (i.e., omitting relevant content) and/or contamination (i.e., including irrelevant content; Cronbach

& Meehl, 1955). Contamination and deficiency may be ameliorated through repeated sampling and empirical testing with diverse criteria, but content representation is more readily ensured by reliance on an established construct domain (e.g., Mowen & Voss, 2008). Inventories developed using a balance of rational and empirical strategies were evaluated more favorably than those based primarily on either strategy alone.

Finally, evaluation of the framework and development dimension reflected the item format and scoring method. Computer adaptive tests were generally evaluated more favorably in this regard due to their more efficient testing times, while retaining measurement accuracy equal to or greater than that of traditional tests (e.g., Chernyshenko et al., 2009; Houston, Borman, Farmer, & Bearden, 2005; van der Linden & Glas, 2003). Inventories using a continuous scale or profile scores were evaluated more favorably than those simply categorizing respondents as high or low, or as one type or another. This is due to the informational advantage of interval over ordinal scales: interval scales permit comparisons along the entire score continuum, whereas ordinal scales separate only high scorers from low.

Reliability

Reliability refers to the degree that a test is free from random measurement error, and is typically assessed by the consistency with which a measure yields the same score for the same individual. This includes consistency across time (test–retest) and across item content (internal consistency). Internal consistency, the most commonly reported reliability type, is routinely indexed using Cronbach's alpha per subscale. Alpha captures both consistency among items as well as scale length[1] (Cronbach, 1951; Nunnally, 1978). Holding alpha constant, shorter scales are generally preferred to longer scales, as long as the items as a set capture the entirety of the targeted domain. Use of "duplicate items," or items that have only slight wording differences, can contribute to reliability while adding no unique information on the person's trait standing. Alpha ranges between 0 and 1, with values of .70 or higher generally considered acceptable (Nunnally, 1978). Inventories whose scales exceeded this threshold were evaluated favorably. Test–retest reliability is relevant to evaluating personality measures because personality is presumed to be an enduring and stable characteristic. Test–retest reliability coefficients vary by the time lag separating test administrations, with longer time lags yielding lower test–retest correlations. Correlations between the same measures should be high ($r > .70$) for shorter intervals (e.g., 1 month), while some decay is expected over longer intervals. Establishing a test–retest reliability benchmark for longer intervals is difficult, as the quality of the coefficient depends in part upon the length of the interval. However, correlations above .50 for intervals longer than 1 year appear to be a reasonable expectation in light of the relatively stable nature of targeted personality traits.

A couple of inventories used a measurement model based upon item response theory (IRT), which is typically more accurate at the extremes of a trait distribution than is a classical test theory (CTT) approach. For tests using IRT, reliability was assessed by examining the conditional standard error of measurement in results, which indicates the measurement accuracy at each level of the trait distribution. Ideal point models were also preferred to the classical dominance models (e.g., 3 parameter or 3PL), as these models generally reflect more realistic assumptions about the nature of personality measurement. A full review of IRT is clearly beyond the scope of this chapter. Interested readers are referred to de Ayala (2008).

Construct Validity

Construct validity is any evidence-based inference that the assessment instrument is measuring the targeted concept. This unitarian approach to validity (Guion, 1980) includes content, convergent, discriminant, structural, and criterion-related evidence as more specific indicators. We considered each source of evidence in our comparative evaluation of the 12 personality inventories. Criterion-related evidence was judged separately, given its special relevance to personality test use in personnel selection (see below).

Content validity refers to how well the test's items capture the defined content domain. A scale that excludes relevant aspects of the focal trait suffers from deficiency, and one that captures more than the focal trait suffers from contamination. This type of validity, when assessed, is usually examined by having experts judge the scale's items for relevance to the targeted trait.

The issues of bandwidth and fidelity are also relevant to construct validity. Bandwidth refers to the range of traits measured by an inventory, whereas fidelity describes the precision in assessing specific traits (Cronbach, 1960). The two features "trade off" given a constant testing time interval. Personality inventories with low bandwidth provide limited coverage over the personality construct domain. Scales with poor fidelity tend to rely only on the measurement of broad factors, with little reliability or validity evidence presented for more specific, narrow traits. Although researchers have noted the trade-offs in using broad versus narrow traits for prediction (e.g., J. Hogan & Roberts, 1996), a strong personality inventory can and should exhibit both bandwidth and fidelity to allow flexibility in user decision making. Considerable focus has been devoted to the utility of scales with high bandwidth and fidelity, yet very little attention has been given to empirical measures of a scale's bandwidth and fidelity. Given the general evidence in research that personality consists of at least five factors, we concluded that a scale exhibited poor bandwidth if it appeared to inadequately capture major elements of personality that are supported in independent research. Poor fidelity was indicated by an insufficient number of narrow traits presented in validity evidence. High correlations amongst different facets within a factor, defined as correlations that approached the reported reliability coefficients for the facet scale, were also interpreted to indicate poor fidelity because facet scores in such cases offer little unique information about the test-taker.

Convergent validity is supported when two different measures targeting the same or conceptually similar constructs correlate strongly and positively (e.g., >.50; Crocker & Algina, 2008). If the measures target conceptually opposite constructs, then convergent validity is supported by strongly negative correlations. Discriminant validity is evident when measures targeting distinct (i.e., conceptually unrelated) constructs are also empirically unrelated (Crocker & Algina, 2008). Convergent and discriminant validity coefficients are prototypically examined using a multitrait-multimethod (MTMM) matrix, which provides correlations between different traits (e.g., dominance and nurturance) measured in different ways (e.g., self-report and other-report). Convergent validity is shown in the monotrait-multimethod correlations (e.g., dominance assessed both ways), and discriminant validity in both the multitrait-monomethod (e.g., dominance and nurturance assessed by self-report) and multitrait-multimethod correlations (e.g., self-reported dominance correlated with other-reported nurturance). Outside of MTMMs, convergent evidence tends to be offered more often and in greater detail than discriminant evidence.

Structural validity, in the present context, refers to how well an inventory's subscales intercorrelate in forming clusters that match theoretical expectations (e.g., the FFM). For this evaluation criterion, we noted primarily the congruence between observed and expected structures. We also noted the method of factor extraction, selection, and the estimation of model-data fit. Confirmatory extraction methods (e.g., confirmatory factor analysis [CFA]) provide a stronger test of the inventory's proposed structure than do exploratory methods, such as principal components analysis (PCA). When a model is specified a priori, CFA can estimate model-data fit while accounting for measurement and sampling error, controls not offered in PCA (Brown, 2006). PCA may be helpful in analyzing item properties or reducing test length during development, but a CFA provides the strongest test of an established framework. Accordingly, studies using CFA received stronger evaluations, provided the structural integrity of the inventory was supported.

Factor selection is determined by model-data fit indices (e.g., root mean square error of approximation [RMSEA]) in CFA and by a variety of indices in PCA, including examination of eigenvalues, scree plots, proportion of variance explained by extracted dimensions, and factor interpretation

(Brown, 2006). Inventories reporting structural validation were judged more favorably if dimensions were identified in light of multiple-fit indices and/or extraction criteria. Finally, inventories tested against competing factor models received stronger evaluations than those tested against only the proposed model. This judgment is made because demonstrating adequate fit to one model does not preclude the possibility of achieving better fit to an alternative model.

Criterion-Related Validity

Criterion-related validity is supported to the degree that scores on the given scale correlate with a valued job-relevant outcome (e.g., job performance). Correlations between personality predictors and job performance are more generalizable to selection settings when both trait and performance scores are collected on applicants (Guion & Cranny, 1982). As relatively few applicants are hired in most predictive studies, however, the *N* available for validation in such studies is often limited. Accordingly, criterion validity estimates are more often based on samples of existing employees. Methodology of validation studies was considered to the degree that it impeded the interpretation of results, contained inadequate measures of job-relevant criteria, and/or was conducted using nonwork samples such as undergraduate college students. The size and variety of samples used to estimate criterion-related validity were also considered. Criterion-related validity evidence was evaluated more favorably if the validity evidence was provided for specific jobs or job families in addition to overall coefficients. Evaluations of the strength of specific correlations took into account the job demands and criteria involved. In some cases, the manuals provided a job analysis summary to help guide evaluations, but in other cases the evaluations of job demands depended on the validation study description. In determining the number and types of occupations that were represented in validity evidence, job families were grouped using O*NET as a resource.

Response Validity

Self-report personality inventories are known to be susceptible to intentional and unintentional response distortion. Faking is a deliberate attempt to improve one's standing on a personality scale so as to appear more favorable to the organization. Self-deception is nondeliberate (i.e., honest) over- or underestimation of one's true standing on a given trait. The effects of faking and self-deception on the validity of personality inventories are matters of ongoing debate (see Chapter 12, this volume). Although the correlation between a trait score and job criterion exhibits little change when correcting for social desirability (Ones, Viswesvaran, & Reiss, 1996), the rank order of candidates for selection is typically different when social desirability is controlled (e.g., Rosse, Stecher, Levin, & Miller, 1998). In general, personality test developers are advised to minimize susceptibility to response distortion[2] and to otherwise examine its potential impact on validity. Research is still examining the degree that forced-choice formats tend to reduce faking compared to traditional normative scales, but preliminary evidence generally supports such formats (e.g., Cheung, 2002; Christiansen, Burns, & Montgomery, 2005; Martin, Bowen, & Hunt, 2002). Thus, we considered the item format when evaluating scales on this dimension.

Response validity was also evaluated on the degree that social desirability was considered in scale development, as well as the degree that any empirical analyses were conducted to assess the effect of social desirability (e.g., correlations between trait items and social desirability). In the case of forced-choice formats, statements should be optimally matched on social desirability to help deter faking. Inventories were also rewarded for the inclusion of scales targeting detection of impression management, social desirability, and/or similar biases. The inclusion of guidelines for using these scales (e.g., statistical control and identification of extreme cases) is also an important consideration and should be included in a technical manual (Christiansen, Goffin, Johnston, & Rothstein, 1994). Estimates of the magnitude of faking were also considered in the evaluation. This is evidence that is typically gathered through experimental manipulations of test instructions (e.g., fake good vs. fake bad vs. answer honestly) or comparisons of similar samples under conditions with differing faking incentives.

In addition to social desirability, commonly identified response biases are inconsistent responding and acquiescence (Paulhus, 1991). Inconsistency suggests random or deliberately variable responding. An inventory was evaluated favorably if documentation was offered on how to identify and deal with inconsistency (e.g., inclusion of an infrequency scale with cut scores to identify cases that might be dropped from analysis). Acquiescence bias is the tendency to agree with self-descriptive statements regardless of content. Scales including an imbalance of true- and false-keyed items raise the question as to whether a high (or low) score means the respondent is high/low on the targeted trait or high/low on acquiescence. Acquiescence bias is minimized by inclusion of equal numbers of true- and false-keyed items, and so personality inventories were favored in our evaluation to the degree their scales are balanced in item keying, and guidelines are offered regarding interpretation of scale scores in light of possible acquiescence bias. A couple of scales also provided an acquiescence index that attempts to quantify the degree that participants agree with positively keyed statements across traits.

Normative Information

Norms are population-specific properties of a score distribution. The most commonly reported properties are means and standard deviations. Personality norms are useful to the degree they allow the test user to identify where an individual respondent falls on the trait continuum relative to a relevant population. Populations vary in their breadth of representation. "General norms" ideally target populations representing the entirety of possible test takers. In reality, however, norms labeled as "general" are typically based on convenience samples with limited representation of geographical location (e.g., United States vs. other countries), demographics (e.g., age and education), employment backgrounds, and so forth. More specific norms are often available (e.g., by sex, blue- vs. white-collar), but the same concerns arise over (actual) representativeness of targeted populations. As inventories are developed for application to specific types of working samples, normative information was evaluated more favorably if it reflected working versus general populations.

Normative sample size is a further concern. Tett et al. (2009) reported that norms tend to stabilize at practically reliable levels at N of around 300. Beyond $N = 100$, population specificity becomes the more important issue. Interestingly, samples drawn from different organizations within the same job (e.g., sales) varied about as much in their scale means as samples drawn from different jobs (sales vs. trucking). In light of all these issues, inventories were judged favorably to the degree they offered normative data (e.g., means and standard deviations) on diverse populations and supported the representativeness of those populations with adequate sample size ($n > 300$) and thorough description of both basic demographic properties (e.g., mean age and gender split) and sampling procedures in support of population representativeness.

Method

In testament, perhaps, to the growing popularity of personality assessment, a quick on-line search revealed over 100 such instruments (in English alone). Systematic review of even the top 50 would reasonably fill an entire volume. Here, instead, we targeted just the most commonly used instruments and/or those reputed to be exceptional. To help shorten the list, a simple survey was developed so as to place each of 100 selected personality inventories into one of five categories: (A) "This inventory is neither popular nor exceptional," (B) "This inventory is not popular, but it is an exceptional test," (C) "This inventory is popular and commonly used in industry," (D) "This inventory used to be popular, but it no longer is," and (E) "I am not at all familiar with this inventory." Categorization under "B" or "C" was counted as a point for inclusion, and, under "A" or "D," as a point for exclusion. "E" allocations were treated as missing data, though a test that was widely unknown stood little chance of inclusion. "Popular" tests were identified as those believed to have a "5% share of the market or more." The survey was completed independently by the study authors, as well as by seven other researchers and practitioners in the field of personality testing with no direct ties to any of the test publishers.

Nine of the 12 inventories included in our review had unanimous or near unanimous ratings for inclusion, based upon the percentage classifying the scales under "B" or "C." Two of the remaining scales (the Caliper and GPI-A) were unknown to a greater percentage of the sample, but those familiar with them provided unanimous ratings for inclusion. The MMPI-2 received highly variable evaluations for inclusion, reflecting substantial disagreement about its purpose and utility in work settings. We decided to include it in this review based upon its historical relevance, as well as the existing controversy over its use in human resource management. Finally, one scale (i.e., the *Dominance, Influence, Steadiness, and Conscientiousness Profile* or *DiSC*) received ratings for inclusion, but it was excluded because a manual could not be obtained for this inventory despite repeated requests to the publisher for a copy. We urge caution in the use of this inventory until the potential user is able to examine the DiSC manual. The 12 inventories are introduced briefly (in alphabetical order) before we turn to our evaluations of them.

Personality Inventories Reviewed in This Chapter

16PF

The original 16PF was created by Raymond Cattell in 1949 based on his factor analysis of a wide range of personality items (Karol & Russell, 2009). Revised in 1993, the 16PF includes 185 primary items on a three-point scale that target the original 16 facets. The 16PF also permits the organization of traits according to the FFM.

Caliper Profile

The *Caliper*, originally called the *Multiple Personality Inventory* (MPI), was published in 1961 following local validation studies for sales positions. The MPI was partially constructed from items on the *MMPI*, the *Strong Interest Inventory*, and the *Bernreuter Personality Test* (Caliper, 2009). The year of the most recent revision is not reported. The Caliper consists of 112 items with a variety of formats (Likert, semi-ipsative, and multiple choice), but the personality items are all semi-ipsative, though scored using a CTT approach. These items target 22 traits that can be organized under the FFM.

CPI

The CPI was originally published in 1956 using 194 items from the MMPI and generating new items using "folk" concepts of personality (Gough & Bradley, 1996). These folk concepts are described as aspects of social behavior that are cross-culturally significant, and that nonpsychologists intuitively understand. Revised in 1987, the CPI consists of 434 true–false items on 18 scales, which can be organized into four major profiles, or combinations of traits. A shortened version of the instrument designed for human resource management may be found in the CPI 260.

GPI-A

The GPI-A is a recently developed measure that adapted the original GPI to an adaptive test based on IRT (Previsor, 2010). As a result, the GPI varies in length, but it typically consists of 130 forced-choice items, yielding a composite score and scores for 13 dimensions of personality.

HPI

The HPI was originally developed in 1986 by Hogan and Hogan, using the FFM and a "socio-analytic" approach to item generation, similar to folk concepts from the CPI's development. Most recently revised in 2007, the HPI consists of 206 true–false items targeting seven primary scales (R. Hogan & Hogan, 2007). These factors reflect the Big Five traits, except extraversion and openness to experience are each split into two factors.

MBTI

The MBTI was originally developed in 1942 by Myers and Briggs based on Carl Jung's theory of psychological archetypes (Myers, McCauley, Quenk, & Hammer, 2009). The MBTI currently has two forms that are scored using a traditional 3PL IRT model; one form targets four binary dimensions to form 16 personality types (Form M or "Step 1"), and the other form estimates the probability of belonging to 20 subtypes organized under the four global personality types (Form Q or "Step 2"). Form M, most recently revised in 2009, consists of 51 true–false items ultimately categorizing respondents as Extraverted or Introverted, Sensing or Intuitive, Thinking or Feeling, and Judging or Perceiving. Form Q, also revised in 2009, has 144 forced-choice items for its 20 subtypes.

MMPI-2

The MMPI was originally developed in 1939 to measure psychopathology and personality structure in 10 different dimensions (Butcher, Dahlstrom, Graham, Tellegen, & Kaemmer, 1989). The MMPI-2, released in 1989, consists of 567 true–false items, with a shorter version of 338 items released in 2003 (MMPI-2-RF).

NEO-PI-3

The original NEO-PI was developed in 1985 by Costa and McRae, using Likert scale items to measure the FFM. The most recent version of the NEO (NEO-PI-3) includes a short version targeting the five factors using 60 items, and a longer version aiming to assess 30 facets (six per factor) for a total of 240 items (McRae & Costa, 2010).

OPQ-32

The OPQ was first developed in 1984 and has since evolved into three primary measures that examine 32 traits, permitting an approximate FFM organization. One of the forms uses a normative format with 230 Likert scale items (OPQ-32n), whereas the other two forms include 104 items in ipsative format, which may be scored using either a CTT (OPQ-32i) or an IRT (OPQ-32r) approach (Bartram, Brown, Fleck, Inceoglu, & Ward, 2006). As the *–r* and *–i* forms reflect the same item pool, we did not focus upon the OPQ-32r because it is a more recent measure with relatively little validation evidence available.

PRF

Created in the 1960s by Doug Jackson (e.g., Jackson, 1966), the PRF is based on the "construct approach" to scale development, blending rational and empirical methods. The most popular form, E, contains 352 true–false items targeting 20 of Murray's psychogenic needs (e.g., need for autonomy), plus desirability and infrequency scales. Although not constructed to assess a particular broad-scale taxonomy, the PRF supports both five- and six-factor structures closely aligned with the FFM.

Wonderlic 5

Formerly known as the PCI, the *Wonderlic 5* targets the broad factors of the FFM and 21 narrow traits using 150 items (Wonderlic, 2011). Although the format of these items is not described in the manual, it appears they are single stimulus, true–false, or Likert-type items.

Evaluation Procedure

Given the broad array of elements to consider when evaluating the psychometric properties of an inventory, a rating system was developed to assess agreement among multiple judges. The 12 selected instruments were assessed on each of the six noted psychometric dimensions by three raters with extensive knowledge on personality and psychometric issues. For example, construct validity was assessed in terms of the quality of evidence provided on convergent, discriminant, and structural validity. These evaluations were then interpreted collectively to yield a final dimension rating along an ordinal scale: (1) *weak*, (2) *moderately weak*, (3) *moderately strong*, and (4) *strong*. A simple ordinal scale was chosen to reflect an overall impression of the inventory. It was deemed that finer distinctions using an interval rating scale would likely hinder agreement by raters, primarily because of the wide variety of indices that raters must weigh when arriving at a judgment. The final ratings reflect judgments of absolute quality. Although this approach may lead to low variance in ratings for dimensions where most inventories perform well or poorly, it provides a uniform standard for evaluation of individual tests as well as in aggregate, reflecting performance of the testing field more broadly.

Rating values were anchored with specific criteria and examples so as to provide raters a common frame of reference. A particular challenge in evaluation was combing the statistical coefficients presented from multiple trait scales in order to arrive at a single judgment. Raters were instructed to examine the percentage of poor to excellent coefficients in arriving at a judgment and were given benchmarks for each of the anchors on the rating scale. For example, reliability was regarded very positively if less than 5% of scales displayed internal consistencies below .70. Though these benchmarks served as useful guidelines, raters were not bound to follow them if the inventory presented a complex or unusual case. Scales developed to remove social desirability, for example, will typically remove some artificially shared variance among items, thus reducing item–total correlations and internal consistency, accordingly. If raters felt confident that this objective was met, they tended to adopt more lenient reliability benchmarks. Inter-rater reliability was estimated using Kendall's tau-b (τ_b) to measure the association between each pair of ratings. Initial estimates ranged from .37 to .77, with a median τ_b of .50. Further examination of specific ratings revealed a few cases where a disagreement between two raters was greater than one rank, which likely exerted a strong influence on the reliability indices. The initial ratings were sent to the group, where raters could opt to submit revised ratings after the merits of the disagreements were debated. The reliability estimates for the final ratings ranged from .59 to .77 with the median $\tau_b = .73$. This was judged as acceptable, particularly because each evaluation had a clear majority for a specific value. The final evaluations reported here reflect the modal evaluation from the final set of ratings.

Results

Table 10.1 provides an abridged summary of the psychometric characteristics for each inventory. Other than the field "relevant studies in literature," all of the information presented in the table reflects only the information that was available in the inventory manual. More thorough coverage of each inventory is offered next.

Table 10.1 Summary of Psychometric Characteristics for 12 Personality Inventories

Characteristic	*16PF*	*Caliper*	*CPI*	*GPI-A*	*HPI*	*MBTI*	*MMPI-2*	*NEO-PI-3*	*OPQ-32n*	*OPQ-32i*	*PRF*	*Wonderlic*
Development												
Framework	Lexical factors	Predictive validity	Folk concepts	SME derived	Socio-analytic	Jung's type preferences	Clinical psychology	FFM	SME derived	SME derived	Murray's needs	FFM
Approach	Empirical	Empirical	Empirical	Rational	Construct	Construct	Empirical	Construct	Construct	Construct	Construct	Construct
Measurement												
Model	CTT	CTT	CTT	IRT (ideal point)	CTT	IRT (dominance)	CTT	CTT	CTT	CTT	CTT	CTT
Reported indices	α; test–retest	α; test–retest	α; test–retest	Conditional *SEM*	α; test–retest	α; test–retest	α; test–retest	α; test–retest	α; test–retest	α; test–retest	α; test–retest	α; test–retest
Construct validity												
No. factors/traits in validity evidence	5 factors; 16 traits	6 factors; 22 traits	3 factors; 20 traits	0 factors; 13 traits	7 factors; 0 traits	4 types; 20 subtypes	16 factors; 0 facets	5 factors; 30 traits	5 factors; 32 traits	5 factors; 32 traits	20 prime scales	5 factors; 17 facets
MTMM correlations	Variety of trait scales	Variety of other scales	Biodata; trait scales	Cognitive ability	Interest and trait scales	Interest and trait scales	None	Variety of trait scales	Variety of trait scales	1 trait and 1 ability scale	Interest and trait scales	Variety of trait scales
Structural analysis	EFA	EFA	EFA	Scale intercorrelations	EFA; CFA	EFA; CFA	Scale intercorrelations	EFA	EFA; CFA	Equivalence w/OPQ-32n	EFA	EFA
Criterion validity												
No. of job families with coefficients	6	3	0	2	6	1	0	0	6	4	0	4
Methodology	Correlations from select studies	Meta-analyses w/composites	Supportive studies mentioned	Local validation studies	Meta-analyses w/ factor scores	Correlations from select studies	Correlations with patient variables	Correlations with biodata	Correlations from select studies	Correlations from select studies	Correlations with biodata	Correlations from select studies

Characteristic	*16PF*	*Caliper*	*CPI*	*GPI-A*	*HPI*	*MBTI*	*MMPI-2*	*NEO-PI-3*	*OPQ-32n*	*OPQ-32i*	*PRF*	*Wonderlic*
Relevant studies in literature	Studies in different contexts	Very few studies	Mostly law enforcement	None	Studies in different contexts	Very few studies	Mostly law enforcement	Studies in different contexts	Studies in different contexts	Very few studies	Studies in different contexts	Studies in different contexts
Response validity												
Item format	3-point true–false	Semi-ipsative	True–false	Unidimensional pairs	True–false	Unidimensional pairs	True–false	Likert scale	Likert scale	Ipsative	True–false	Unclear
Desirability consideration	Judgment and analysis	Matched statements	No discussion	Rational judgment	Considered not an issue	Weighted scoring	Analysis with scale	Considered not an issue	Analysis with scale	Reliance on item format	Judgment and analysis	Analysis with scale
Acquiescence consideration	Assessed in scale	No discussion	No discussion	No discussion	Balanced item keys	No discussion	Analysis with scale	Balanced item keys	Not discussed	Not discussed	Balanced item keys	Not discussed
Validity scales included	IM, ACQ, INF	None	Social desirability	None	None	None	INF, ACQ, IM	None	Social desirability	INF	INF, desirability	IM, INF
Reported norms												
Sample characteristics	Based upon U.S. Census	Working population	Variety of occupations	Two job levels	Working population	Working population	Clinical populations	General population	Variety of occupations	Variety of occupations	General population	Variety of occupations
Reported indices	Means, SDs, percentiles	None	Means, SDs	Means, SDs	Means, SDs, percentiles	Means, SDs, distributions	Means, SDs, frequencies	Means, SDs, percentiles	Means, SDs	Means, SDs	Means, SDs, percentiles	Means, SDs, percentiles

Notes: 16PF: 16 Personality Factor Questionnaire; CPI: California Personality Inventory; GPI-A: Global Personality Inventory—Adaptive; HPI: Hogan Personality Inventory; MBTI: Myers–Briggs Type Indicator; MMPI-2: Minnesota Multiphasic Personality Inventory II; NEO-PI-3: Neuroticism–Extraversion–Openness Personality Inventory—Revised; OPQ-32n and -32i: Occupational Personality Questionnaire-32n and -32i; PRF: Personality Research Form; FFM: Five-Factor Model; SME: subject matter expert; CTT: classical test theory; IRT: item response theory; α: Cronbach's alpha; MTMM: multitrait-multimethod correlations; EFA: exploratory factor analysis; IM: impression management; ACQ: acquiescence; INF: infrequency; SD: standard deviation.

Analysis of Specific Inventories

16PF

The 16PF generally received positive, but not exceptional, evaluations. It was originally derived empirically through factor analytic methods, but later revisions used the FFM as the guiding theory in conjunction with Cattell's 16 facets. This framework is rated as "moderately strong" due to the comprehensive lexical approach used to develop items and use of factor analysis in support. Item writing and revision were conducted using a rational approach using the original 16 factors. However, the predominantly empirical method by which the test was developed prevented a higher rating of "strong." In particular, a re-analysis of Cattell's original work yielded a five-factor solution that reflected the FFM (Costa & McCrae, 1976). This result, as well as factor analyses reported in the 16PF manual, raises the question of whether 16 facets are appropriate, especially given the instrument's predominantly empirical foundations. A strong framework of personality facets should exhibit both theoretical and empirical depth that the 16PF currently lacks.

The reliability coefficients for the 16PF are generally acceptable, with many alpha and test–retest coefficients above .70 (Karol & Russell, 2009). A few questionable alpha and test–retest reliability coefficients (<.70) prevented a rating of "strong" for this dimension. Construct validity also received "moderately strong" ratings, supported by the MTMM pattern of correlations with the CPI, MBTI, NEO-PI-3, and PRF scales. A problem with the pattern of correlations presented in the MTMM, however, was the absence of correlations between higher order factors for the 16PF and higher order factors for other inventories. Instead, higher order factors from the 16PF are correlated with narrow facets from other inventories, creating an asymmetrical comparison. Other construct validity evidence was presented from a common (exploratory) factor analysis that organized the 16 different trait items beneath the FFM global factors. Although the manual states that the 16-factor structure has been replicated many times, many factor analyses produce the FFM instead. Additional validation data would appear suitable for testing the 16PF's definitive structure.

The "moderately strong" rating on criterion-related validity reflects the supportive validity evidence presented in the manual and described in relevant research. However, the validity evidence presented in the manual was limited. The 16PF described validation studies for several job families, but these studies were relatively few in number. Given the long history of the inventory, a more thorough summary or review of the validity evidence seemed appropriate. Furthermore, criterion-related validity was typically presented as multiple correlations from a composite of 16PF predictors. Although useful in gauging an inventory's potential, this method of analysis makes it difficult to determine the unique value of each scale in relation to job performance. An exception to both these limitations is a meta-analysis examining each of the 16 factors as they relate to customer service performance. Many of the reported correlations are quite modest, with the highest uncorrected value equal to .21 (Karol & Russell, 2009, p. 190).

External published research offers more detailed evidence of the criterion-related validity of the 16PF. For example, research on managerial effectiveness found that 16PF scales selected based on job analysis had an average validity of .23, with traits relating to extraversion having the strongest relations (Christiansen et al., 1994; see also Tett & Christiansen, 2007). Bing and Lounsbury (2000) examined the 16PF traits related to job performance of team leaders in a Japanese manufacturing plant, with composite scores of openness to experience (r = .36) and emotional stability (r = .26) emerging as the best predictors. A study on corrections officers (Schuerger, Kochevar, & Reinwald, 1982) found that 16PF traits involving conscientiousness were positively related to performance ratings (r = .29) but those related to extraversion showed a negative relationship (r = −.31). The 16PF showed modest relationships with performance for blue-collar jobs such as service and maintenance employees, where the results found better performance for those higher in conscientiousness ($r = .15$) and lower in openness to experience ($r = -.14$). To summarize, the 16PF demonstrated adequate criterion-related validity in the available research literature.

With regards to response validity, the 16PF includes scales designed to measure acquiescence, impression management, and infrequency. Also favoring the measure, items were screened for desirability and then dropped if they correlated too highly with the impression management scale. However, the three-point anchor format (true–false with a "?" as the midpoint) appears to be susceptible to response distortion, distortion that is further suggested by significant correlations between the trait and impression management scale scores. The 16PF manual recommends correcting for impression management scores, but such corrections remain controversial (Ellingson, Sackett, & Hough, 1999). Although these scales are helpful as interpretive aids and in detection of invalid cases, they do little to prevent the appearance of response biases in the first place. Finally, there is no indication if items are balanced in keying to control acquiescence bias, though such a bias may be detected by the response patterns that manifest from the included acquiescence scale. These issues prevented a "strong" rating for the 16PF's response validity in favor of a "moderately strong" one.

Finally, the normative sample for the 16PF was derived from a large sample proportional to U.S. census data. This sampling approach is fine for drawing general comparisons, but it strains occupation-specific comparisons. Means and standard deviations are provided for specific industries (e.g., health care), but position-specific information is not available within these industry statistics. Occupation-specific normative information could be obtained from the extant research that uses the 16PF, but these studies can be difficult for a practitioner to find, and they often present limited sample and statistical information on the scale norms. Accordingly, we rated the normative information for the 16PF in workplace applications as "moderately weak," despite the careful methodology employed in its procurement.

Caliper Profile

A positive feature of the *Caliper Profile* is its evidence for criterion-related validity, reported as meta-analytic estimates of the multiple correlations between a Caliper scale composite and job-relevant criteria. These multiple correlations ranged from .29 to .39 (Caliper, 2009). Details are lacking, however, regarding the scale selection for the predictor composite. Although a priori theoretical selection is implied through the presentation of job analyses for specific validation studies, the specific method and scales used in estimating the meta-analytic validity coefficients are not reported. A more informative approach, in our view, would meta-analyze the correlations between each scale or factor and each criterion separately and then in combination. This approach would have indicated the relative importance of different subscales, which is more useful in the application of a personality inventory than a multiple correlation across both contexts and traits. Finally, a review of external research yielded only a couple of available studies using the Caliper Profile. Kangis and Lago (1997) found that the Caliper predicted managerial assessments of sales performance, but not objective criteria. A more recent study compared the forced-choice items from the Caliper Profile to a normative format where each statement was rated on a Likert scale (Converse et al., 2008). Results indicated that both formats generated significant correlations with leadership and absenteeism criteria, and there was little difference in the validity between formats. Given its job-specific presentation and strong coefficients, the Caliper was evaluated as "moderately strong" in its criterion-related validity evidence.

A further strength of the Caliper Profile is the effort taken to ensure response validity. The Caliper's semi-ipsative format appears helpful in reducing response distortion, and a concerted effort was made to match paired statements on social desirability. The user is also instructed on how to check for inconsistent response patterns. A bit more detail on the development of statement pairs would be useful with regards to social desirability, but Caliper still received a "strong" rating for response validity.

In the other areas of evaluation, we found the Caliper to display both strengths and weaknesses, earning "moderately weak" ratings for framework, reliability, and construct validity. The Caliper used an empirical development approach based upon the predictive validity of specific items from other personality scales. Although this development approach has yielded adequate criterion-related validity, the lack of a theoretical framework seems to have adversely affected the measure's reliability and construct validity. Internal consistency reliability varies quite a bit across the trait scales in the Caliper. The median value is .67, with 13 of 21 subscales reporting alphas from .38 to .68 (Caliper, 2009, p. 20). We suspect these weak coefficients are partially the product of a strictly criterion-oriented approach in scale construction, and partially the drawback of using a semi-ipsative format, which tends to produce a more heterogeneous response pattern. Although the semi-ipsative format is well intentioned to reduce response distortion, such formats may be better employed using an IRT model. This is because CTT scoring methods for ipsative formats often force respondents to endorse one trait at the expense of another (e.g., Johnson, Wood, & Blinkthorn, 1988), whereas an IRT model allows for a more accurate estimation of candidate true scores (Chernyshenko et al., 2009). Test–retest reliability coefficients for the Caliper are generally strong, but they demonstrated an odd pattern: A third of the scales exhibited stronger test–retest correlations over a 1-year interval than a 2-week interval (Caliper, 2009, p. 21). These results may be attributed to the small samples used in estimating test–retest reliability (n = 40 and 21, respectively), reflecting another weakness in the reliability evidence presented.

Regarding construct validity, the Caliper provided some questionable MTMM coefficients and factor analytic methods. Several scales exhibited approximately equal correlations across multiple FFM dimensions targeted by other inventories. For example, the Caliper's "Assertiveness" scale correlated quite similarly with the NEO's Emotional Stability, Extraversion, and Openness scales, ranging from .37 to .44 between the three FFM factors (Caliper, 2009, pp. 64, 70). It also correlated strongly with multiple 16PF scales. Along similar lines, correlations between Caliper subscales and measures of similar scales in other inventories did not always display convergence. "Accommodation," defined as the desire to help others, only correlates with facets of agreeableness (e.g., altruism) ranging from .29 to .36. Finally, factor analysis showed substantial cross-loadings of several scales across the five factors. Although a PCA did support a five-factor solution, little detail was provided on the criteria used for factor selection and the comparative evaluation of alternative solutions.

Finally, the Caliper received a "weak" rating on normative information primarily for the lack of relevant statistics provided in the manual. If this normative information is only provided after purchase of the inventory, then it serves little use in the initial selection of inventories, which is a primary focus of this review. The Caliper manual did include information on the normative sample, which is representative of a working population. However, this information is not given for different occupations, and it was unclear if occupation-specific normative data are available to nonclients.

CPI

The CPI had several noteworthy strengths and weaknesses. On the plus side, it provided the most useful normative information for HR management among the inventories reviewed, providing the relevant scale statistics for a multitude of occupations and settings. The demographic representation in the norms was not as clear as it could have been, but the occupational specificity earned the CPI a "strong" rating on this dimension. The CPI received "moderately strong" ratings for reliability for having just a couple of inadequate coefficients ($\alpha < .60$) among the 20 scales (Gough & Bradley, 1996). A notable weakness is the inefficiency of scales in the full inventory version, with a relatively large number of items per scale.

Response validity was also rated as "moderately strong" because of multiple indices of response validity (social desirability, inconsistency, etc.) and the presentation of research that illustrates the effect of response distortion on CPI scale scores. We would have preferred to see more concrete analyses and guidelines regarding the use of the response validity scales, particularly because the scale yields much higher scores under "fake good" conditions, demonstrating that the test can be faked[3] (Gough & Bradley, 1996).

With regards to negative features, the CPI gains a rating of "moderately weak" for using mostly empirical methods for developing and refining its "folk concepts" framework. The applied empirical methods did not adequately test the emerging framework in our view, as they failed to validate the proposed underlying structure. Construct validity was also rated as "moderately weak." Although patterns of convergent and discriminant validity coefficients were relatively consistent with the scales from the MMPI, NEO-PI-R, Holland's typology, and other scales, several concerns emerged with regards to structural validity. First, the 20 narrow traits were not evaluated using factor analysis, nor identified for their relative utility. Second, the methodology in determining the global factor structure from the PCA appeared questionable. Factors were selected using the Kaiser rule (1970), with eigenvalues > 1 determining factor retention. Lack of reliance on factor analytic methods is not surprising given the test authors' emphasis on prediction over structural integrity (Gough & Bradley, 1996). We question this perspective, as construct validity is the crux of any test, and structural evidence contributes uniquely to judging validity. More precise factor analytic methods could offer grounds for reducing the number of items and scales on the CPI, yielding equal if not improved utility with faster testing times and streamlined interpretations.

The CPI manual presented weak criterion-related validity evidence, primarily because very few criteria presented in the manual are work-related. Criterion-related validity for specific occupations is not reported, though some correlations are provided for job satisfaction, stress, and academic criteria such as grade point average. A shorter, more specialized version of the CPI, the CPI-260, provides several composite scales geared toward specific occupational purposes, such as managerial potential, work orientation, and creative temperament. Although support was noted for each of these scales, criterion-related validity coefficients were not provided (the presented meta-analytic coefficients included scales from other inventories). When examining independent research on the CPI, the majority of available studies have been in law enforcement. Although validity evidence is lacking for other occupations, studies involving law enforcement selection are more likely to have been based on scores derived from actual applicants rather than current employees with less motivation to distort their responses. Pugh (1985) showed police candidates' CPI scores were related to extraversion (Dominance = .23, Sociability = .20, and Self-Acceptance = .22) as well as openness to experience (Achievement via Independence = .20 and Intellectual Efficiency = .30). Along the same lines, Hiatt and Hargrave (1988) found that CPI scores could differentiate between subsequent evaluations of which officers were or were not satisfactory performers, with those higher on scales related to openness to experience and conscientiousness being more likely to be satisfactory and those related to agreeableness less likely. Outside of law enforcement, Hakstian and Farrell (2001) found that CPI scales relating to openness to experience were related to performance of telemarketers ($r = .22$) and customer service employees ($r = .25$). Gluskinos and Brennan (1971) reported that performance of operating room staff in a hospital was a function of scores on the CPI scales of Responsibility ($r = .33$) and Socialization ($r = .23$), both of which are related to conscientiousness. In summary, the CPI has been used with success in certain contexts, but lacks sufficient variety and depth in its validity evidence to earn a positive evaluation.

GPI-A

The GPI-A has several advantages over other inventories, but it is largely untested when compared to older inventories. A major strength of the GPI-A is its adaptive testing format developed using an ideal point IRT model. Whereas dominance IRT models assume an ever-increasing likelihood of endorsing an item, an ideal point model is a more reasonable assumption for personality tests because respondents may disagree with a statement because it describes too high or too low a trait level (Chernyshenko, Stark, Drasgow, & Roberts, 2007). Developers also considered multiple models of personality and the purpose of the scale (i.e., to assist human resource management), ultimately producing an inventory that measures 13 traits that were designed to be more narrow than the FFM, but broader than facet-level traits seen in other inventories. However, the only apparent empirical analysis of this emerging taxonomy is the content-related validity ratings of subject matter experts (SMEs) and intercorrelations among scale scores.

Although the GPI was developed primarily by rational methods, the resulting taxonomy warrants empirical validation beyond the aforementioned indices. In terms of item analysis, descriptive statistics of the item pool were provided, but statistics for the validated items would have also been useful in evaluation. In general, we found very little information on the empirical analyses of items other than SME ratings. Finally, whereas most other inventories utilize fewer (e.g., five) major factors, we considered the possibility that 13 primary factors may be too narrow for certain purposes. Given that broad factor scores tend to relate more strongly to indices of overall job performance (Ones & Viswesvaran, 1999), the GPI-A manual should consider the construction of primary factors from the resulting 13 trait scores. The GPI-A manual argued that use of broad factors would likely violate the unidimensionality requirement of IRT. However, this would not prevent the use of broader factor scores based upon the resulting scores from the 13 primary scales. Thus, the GPI-A's framework and development received a "moderately strong" rating for a methodology that is generally sound but lacking the traditional empirical justification for the emergent trait taxonomy.

The taxonomy is also difficult to evaluate due to the limited construct validity evidence presented. Although scales that are predominantly unidimensional are desired for IRT analyses (Hulin, Drasgow, & Parsons, 1983), there are no factor analytic solutions presented to establish that (1) an alternative factor solution may provide more or less global traits than those identified by SMEs and (2) the retained traits are indeed unidimensional for use in IRT. In fairness, the GPI-A did show some evidence for the distinctions between trait scales through mostly weak interscale correlations (Previsor, 2010). The GPI-A also demonstrated discriminant validity through low correlations with cognitive ability tests, but there was no convergent validity evidence available (e.g., through classic MTMM matrices). The lack of factor analytic evidence and MTMM correlations with different personality inventories comprised the primary limitations of the GPI-A. Given the low interscale correlations, however, the fidelity of the measures to the established constructs appears to be quite strong. All told, the GPI-A received a "moderately weak" rating for construct validity evidence.

Although reliability and the conditional standard error of measurement (*SEM*) were not provided in the manual, supplemental information provided by the test authors indicated that the GPI-A uses statistical thresholds for measurement error and reliability ($SEM = .38$; $\alpha = .85$) as a stopping rule for each scale, provided that at least eight items have been administered. This procedure promotes accurate measurement of each respondent's trait level, even for those with very high or very low levels (which is not a given in traditional personality measurement). However, the GPI-A did not provide evidence for test–retest reliability, which one might argue is important for adaptive measures because a different set of items may be provided with each administration. The omission of test–retest reliability, as well as the absence of measurement characteristics in the actual test manual, limited our rating to "moderately strong" on reliability for the GPI-A.

The GPI-A received "moderately weak" evaluations on both the criterion-related validity and normative information dimensions. A major strength of the criterion-related evidence was a meta-analysis linking a variety of GPI-A scales with job criteria. The correlations reported in this meta-analysis ranged from modest to strong. On the one hand, correlations between trait scales and narrow dimensions of job performance were fairly modest with no specific scale correlating more strongly than .20 with any dimension of job performance. On the other hand, correlations built upon different composites of the GPI-A were quite strong with narrow dimensions of job performance, reaching as high as .38 for the "selling" dimension of managerial performance. Unfortunately, these correlations were only broken down into two job-level categories: management and entry-level positions. There has also been no independent research published on how the GPI-A relates to work outcomes, but this is mostly a reflection of how recently the GPI-A was developed.

Normative information for the GPI-A consists of specific scale statistics for different job levels used in the study. As with the validity information, however, statistics for different occupations would be more helpful. The normative information also did not appear to include demographic information, raising uncertainty in the representativeness of the normative samples. The detail in the statistics and the use of a working population, however, earned a "moderately strong" rating for the GPI-A's normative information.

In terms of response validity, the GPI-A's forced-choice format is designed to reduce susceptibility to response distortion. Unlike the use of ipsative formats that other forced-choice tests have used, however, the GPI-A presents statements on the same trait dimension, and it is frequently the case that one statement is naturally more desirable to endorse than another due to the desirability of having high or low levels for a specific trait. Although social desirability was mentioned in the development of trait statement pairs, there is no indication that social desirability of statements was explicitly evaluated through empirical analyses. Taken together, these elements raise questions regarding the GPI-A's ability to suppress response distortion, particularly compared to multidimensional pairings of items or ipsative measures. Use of an ipsative format would make particular sense for the GPI-A because it utilizes an IRT model for scoring, which would effectively address some of the scoring issues related to ipsative measures using traditional test theory (as discussed earlier with the Caliper Profile).

HPI

The HPI received generally favorable ratings, particularly for development and criterion-related validity. This strong rating stemmed from the comprehensive and well-designed validity studies that meta-analyzed the coefficients between specific scales and criteria for seven job families. Correlations with overall performance generally showed small to modest relationships with different occupations, with a maximum correlation of .29 between Ambition and managerial performance. Correlations with more specific performance dimensions had a much broader range and were quite strong in some specific cases (R. Hogan & Hogan, 2007). For example, Ambition correlated .51 with specific dimensions of management performance. In our view, the HPI manual provided the most comprehensive documentation of criterion-related validity in this review. Research on the HPI is largely conducted by those affiliated with the developers (Hogan Assessment Systems), so it is unclear which of the studies available in the extant literature is also included in the meta-analyses as a technical report. However, an examination of the research does provide more specific detail on the types of studies that are likely included in the meta-analysis. For example, research on sales representatives found that those higher on Ambition (r = .15) and lower on Adjustment (r = −.15) were evaluated more favorably by supervisors (J. Hogan, Hogan, & Gregory, 1992). J. Hogan, Hogan, and Murtha (1992) examined HPI correlates of managerial performance and found that Ambition (r = .21), Intellectance (r = .13), and Adjustment (r = .12) all were related to success. A study by Muchinsky (1993) on clerical employees showed that the HPI scales of Intellectance (r = .22) and Adjustment (r = .22) predicted supervisor ratings of overall performance, as did the occupational composite scales of Service Orientation (r = .19), Clerical Aptitude (r = .22), and Managerial Potential (r = .26). Finally, Tett, Steele, and Beauregard (2003) found that Prudence (r = .13), Intellectance (r = .12), and Likability (now Interpersonal Sensitivity; r = .11) explained supervisor ratings of field representatives.

The HPI also showed careful development of the personality framework and inventory, using socioanalytic theory to write items for the FFM and altering the model based on empirical testing. Specifically, the HPI used factor analytic data to split extraversion from the FFM into Sociability and Ambition and to split openness to experience into Inquisitive and Learning Orientation. However, a few of the convergent validity coefficients with other FFM inventories were lower than preferred, and model-data fit from factor analyses were good, but not exceptional. Another issue with scale content is that the HPI focuses its validation efforts on the broad factors, whereas the trait facets ("homogenous item composites" or HICs) do not appear to be validated (and also suffer from generally low reliabilities). Thus, one may argue that the HPI exhibits acceptable bandwidth in its measurement of personality, but it lacks fidelity. Taken together, these considerations reflect our rating of "strong" for framework and "moderately strong" for construct validity.

The reliability of the broad factor measures in the HPI is generally strong, with a notable exception for Interpersonal Sensitivity (α = .57; R. Hogan & Hogan, 2007). Given the poor reliability for this primary scale, we rated the HPI as "moderately strong" for reliability. Acceptable test–retest reliability coefficients and score agreement (as indicated by the intraclass correlation coefficients [ICCs]) were also presented in the manual. As the HICs were not included in validity studies, we did not evaluate them with regards to reliability, though we note that several HICs displayed poor internal consistency.

A primary weakness of the HPI is the lack of consideration given to response biases. Although it includes a scale to detect unlikely responses (whether by acquiescence or faking), little guidance is offered for making decisions on scale results (e.g., normative data, screening, and score adjustment), and the normative format is conducive to response distortion. These issues resulted in a rating of "moderately weak" for the HPI on response validity. Finally, normative information was rated as "moderately strong" to reflect the detailed statistics provided for different demographic groups. However, normative information for specific occupations is not provided, even though it is provided for criterion-related validity.

MBTI

Although the MBTI has intuitive appeal with its typology system, its psychometric characteristics generally received tepid ratings. In speaking to the MBTI's strengths, its use of IRT in the most recent revision does provide improved precision in placing the cut score and categorizing respondents, as evidenced by a high percentage of agreement between a respondent's self-label and the results of the test (Myers et al., 2009). The normative information, developed from many years of use, is comprehensive and organized by job families. This normative information would have received a stronger rating save for a limited description of the normative sample characteristics. The coefficients for both test–retest and internal consistency reliability were also quite strong. These features factored into the "moderately strong" ratings given to normative information and reliability. The primary issue with measurement was the conditional *SEM*, which was relatively large at the high and low ends of the preference distribution.

This pattern for the *SEM* likely stems from the MBTI's typology format. Unlike other inventories, the MBTI does not conceptualize personality in terms of continuous traits, but rather as dichotomous types with an underlying continuum of "preference" toward a certain type. This distinction is noteworthy, as the scores yielded by the MBTI do not reflect an estimation of one's standing on a trait distribution, but rather the expected probability that one belongs to a particular category (Quenk et al., 2001, p. 16). In keeping with the typology system, all of the MBTI items were specifically developed to focus on the center of the distribution in order to fulfill the primary objective of separating respondents into two categories.[4] Although having items focus exclusively on the center of a distribution increases the accuracy for categorizing respondents (e.g., as Extraverts vs. Introverts), it also decreases differentiation within these classifications (e.g., separating moderate Extraverts from extreme Extraverts). As a result, it would be quite difficult to rank-order candidates accurately on a particular dimension in order to facilitate decision making for selection or promotion. Even for uses outside of selection, the dichotomous scales offer employers limited feedback and development options about the differing degrees of workers' personalities and work styles.

Although the MBTI manual includes an extensive discussion of the underlying theory behind the typology system and uses empirical methods to assess item performance, the particular choice of a psychodynamic theory appears to have harmed the construct validity of the scales. Jung's theory of archetypes, with its heavy emphasis on a collective unconscious, has received little empirical support compared to other theories of personality. Indeed, Jung's work is rarely used in psychology today outside of the MBTI (e.g., Bernstein, 2011). One result of the reliance on Jung's approach is the omission of personality factors relevant to human resource management. In particular, the dimensions of the MBTI show weak correlations with neuroticism, ranging from .04 to .21 (Myers et al., 2009), suggesting that this factor is not measured. This deficiency can limit the MBTI's usefulness in work settings; for example, neuroticism has garnered significant correlations with job-relevant outcomes that would not be detected by the MBTI (Salgado, 2002). Thus, we rated the framework as "moderately weak," to reflect the adequate development methods used but a flawed underlying framework and a measurement system that focuses upon classification rather than estimation of a true score.

Beyond the issue of poor bandwidth, the MBTI presented a mixed case for construct validity. In support of the MBTI's construct validity was the inclusion of a wide variety of correlates with other measures. Correlations varied in whether they supported the pattern expected for convergent and discriminant validity evidence. For example, though many of the Extraversion–Introversion facet scales correlated strongly with Dominance and Sociability measures from the CPI, the Judging–Perceiving subtypes did not strongly correlate with the Responsibility and Self-Control CPI scales, as one would expect. Notably, a CFA was conducted, which was employed in few other inventories. The reported fit indices indicated adequate model-data fit (e.g., RMSEA = .08), but it is not apparent that any competing models were tested, or whether any additional steps might improve model-data fit. This result may indicate that the MBTI adequately captures the outlined typologies in its theory. In weighing the positives and negatives with regards to construct validity, we decided to also rate it as "moderately weak" due to poor inventory bandwidth and too many question marks regarding convergence with other scales.

In addition to framework issues, the MBTI showed relatively weak relations to job-relevant outcomes. Criterion-related validity for Form Q was first presented as a multiple correlation across 24 scale scores (i.e., the four major personality types and all 20 subscales; Quenk et al., 2001, p. 139). Even with this rather large number of predictors, multiple R ranges from .32 to .40, indicating modest predictive efficiency. Correlations between work-related attitudes and specific individual subscales also reflected surprisingly modest relationships, with only a few correlations stronger than (–).20. These correlations were also not reported for different job families, and do not contain the same depth as the meta-analyses presented for other inventories. The manual cites research that the MBTI provided some benefit in group interventions (Myers et al., 2009), but such evaluation studies in the literature are scant. It was also unclear whether the MBTI offers greater utility in such interventions than other available methods (e.g., mentoring, exercises, and alternative scales). Finally, the evidence presented in the MBTI manual rests upon attitudes and preferences for teamwork rather than empirical evaluations of team functioning and performance (Quenk et al., 2001, p. 174). A review of the existing literature also revealed a limited amount of empirical research that relates MBTI profiles to work outcomes. Although there may be a link between types and satisfaction with certain occupations, no published research has linked MBTI profiles to job performance (for a more detailed discussion of the MBTI, see Chapter 16, this volume). When examining the evidence together, we assigned a "weak" rating to the MBTI for criterion-related validity.

Finally, response validity for the MBTI was evaluated as "moderately weak." Although the inventory employs an IRT forced-choice model, model details (e.g., dominance model and ideal point) and item format (ipsative, unidimensional, etc.) are not well detailed. It is implied, however, that the inventory uses a 3PL dominance IRT model and forced-choice items with unidimensional statements that reflect opposing types (Quenk et al., 2001). The manual emphasizes that item responses should not be considered "correct" or "incorrect," and this may indeed be feasible for intervention or development purposes. However, it is often human nature to interpret any test within an organizational context as having "better" or "worse" responses and scores, such that responses may still be influenced by social desirability. In addition, testing for selection and promotion must necessarily prefer certain types of responses over others in order to find the test useful. Thus, applicants have incentive to distort their responses, yet the social desirability of items was not mentioned in development nor measured through a validity index. Much like the GPI-A, response validity was evaluated as "moderately weak" due to poor accounting of potential sources of social desirability.

MMPI-2

The MMPI-2 was generally rated unfavorably, primarily because it was developed for use in clinical rather than organizational settings. The clinical approach of the MMPI-2 is clearly reflected in the manual, which discusses the underlying framework in terms of psychopathologies and presents normative and validation data from clinical populations. As a result, the MMPI-2 received "moderately weak" ratings for development and construct validity not because there was a lack of evidence for these characteristics, but because the scale development and approach were not appropriate for human resource management. Likewise, criterion-related validity coefficients and normative information were presented with clinical populations and criteria rather than job-relevant outcomes. The use of MMPI-2 in organizational contexts is typically limited to law enforcement, likely because a clinical assessment of candidates is typically justified and permissible by law (Weiss & Weiss, 2010). Even in these contexts, however, research has generally recommended using the MMPI-2 only as an assessment for duty fitness and clinical intervention for police officers. Validity evidence of the MMPI-2, and even the propriety of its use, is questionable outside of law enforcement. These considerations led to ratings of "weak" for criterion-related validity.

The reliability and response validity dimensions also received "moderately" weak ratings. The MMPI has several response validity scales intended to explicitly detect response distortion and infrequency, but items were not developed or assessed to account for social desirability. Indeed, many items carry a strong desirability component, such that response distortion appears to be an issue. Although odd response patterns may be detected by different scales, it still results in questionable measurement of a candidate's standing. Internal consistency coefficients are also questionable for the MMPI, with 6 of the 10 clinical scales showing reliabilities less than .70. These modest reliabilities are also achieved inefficiently, with a large number of items for each scale. Another issue with the measurement properties of the MMPI is that the score distributions are slightly skewed, which is expected for clinical populations due to extreme scores. However, such skewed distributions may bias the significance tests for the statistics presented in the manual.

NEO-PI-3

The NEO-PI-3 was evaluated quite favorably with regards to its development, reliability, and construct validity, but unfavorably on other dimensions. The rational and empirical development of items toward the empirically supported framework (FFM) contributed to the NEO's strong reliability and construct validity. The NEO-PI-3 demonstrated acceptable internal consistencies (all αs > .70), as well as a variety of convergent and discriminant validity coefficients corresponding to expected patterns. The manual also facilitates interpretation of convergent validity by organizing scales from different inventories by their content similarities. The NEO-PI-3 demonstrates wide coverage of the personality domain, targeting six facets in each of the five broad factors. Fidelity is also supported by correlations among facets that are not overly high ($r < .60$). Taken together, the NEO-PI-3 offers a convincing case for a "strong" rating on framework, reliability, and construct validity.

The NEO-PI-3 is relatively new, but much of the validation presented in the manual and past editions reflects nonwork criteria. Since the emergence of the FFM, however, the scales from the NEO have appeared in more studies published in the area of personality and job performance than any other commercial inventory. For example, an early study found that scores on the Agreeableness ($r = .20$), Extraversion ($r = .17$), Openness to Experience ($r = .16$), and Conscientiousness ($r = .12$) domain scales were predictive of flight attendant training success (Cellar, Miller, Doverspike, & Klawsky, 1996). Salgado and Rumbo (1997) examined the performance of financial services managers and reported that Conscientiousness ($r = .32$) and Neuroticism ($r = -.23$) were the strongest predictors. Neuman and Wright (1999) considered performance of human resource representatives at the individual and team levels. Their results showed that Agreeableness predicted task performance at the individual ($r = .23$) and team ($r = .36$) levels, as well as interpersonal effectiveness ($r = .35$ and .36, respectively); Conscientiousness related only to task performance at the individual ($r = .23$) and team ($r = .27$) levels. A study on firefighters by Fannin and Dabbs (2003) reported that Extraversion was positively correlated with performance ($r = .27$) but the relationship was negative for Openness to Experience ($r = -.26$) and Agreeableness ($r = -.18$). Finally, Furnham and Fudge (2008) found that only sales employees higher in Openness to Experience ($r = .16$) and lower in Agreeableness ($r = -.22$) were more likely to meet their sales goals in terms of health club memberships. These studies represent but a small sample of the published studies using the NEO to explain work criteria.

Although the lack of work-related criteria in the manual creates additional work for interested users in finding relevant validity data, criterion-related validity was evaluated as "moderately strong" due to the wide array of studies involving the NEO-PI in the personnel psychology and business literatures. However, such leniency was not granted for normative information, which was also lacking in the manual. Specifically, normative information was given for the general population and no occupation-specific samples or statistics. Although some information may be obtained from external studies, this information is not reported as reliably as are correlations with criteria. Thus, the normative information from the NEO-PI-3 received a "moderately weak" rating in this review.

Response validity is also questionable in the NEO-PI-3 because of an item format that is susceptible to response distortion (i.e., single stimulus Likert scale) and the lack of consideration for social desirability in item selection. The inventory authors argued that response distortion should have equal effects upon test takers, such that the relative ranks would be preserved (McRae & Costa, 2010, p. 55), but research has generally not supported this view (e.g., Rosse et al., 1998; Tett, Freund, Christiansen, Fox, & Coaster, 2012). They further argued against the use of social desirability and response inconsistency scales, but the user, nonetheless, is referred to several in the literature if they desire to measure these constructs. Although the NEO appeared to be highly susceptible to response distortion, it did provide a balanced set of item keys to help detect acquiescence bias. Based upon each of these considerations, the NEO-PI-3 received a "moderately weak" rating for response validity. It would seem to be an appropriate measure for use with samples where there is no apparent motivation to distort (e.g., employee development). Validity for use in hiring is less certain, however, based upon the test manual.

OPQ-32n and OPQ-32i

The OPQ-32n and OPQ-32i were rated separately as they reflected different inventories with different properties, but they are summarized together here as they follow the same taxonomy and validation procedure. The OPQ-32 proposes a unique taxonomy of personality developed from SME judgments. Although this taxonomy may be collapsed into the global factors of the FFM, much of the reliability and validity evidence is presented for the 32 trait scales and specialized composite scales. Although item development occurred in a rational manner from the developed personality structure, subsequent analyses of scale and item properties prompted inventory revision. However, greater detail on the 32-scale structure is warranted, as this is the highest number of scales among the inventories reviewed here. The item stems from the normative scale were used to create the ipsative statements in the OPQ-32i. We felt this development was sufficient to warrant a "moderately strong" rating.

Both inventories received generally positive ratings across dimensions, especially for their strong assessment of reliability, detailed presentation of normative information, and thorough assessment of criterion-related validity. The OPQ-32 also shows exceptional reliability; all but one of the scales having internal consistency above .70 (Bartram et al., 2006). The normative scale also exhibits strong test–retest reliabilities, mostly above .80 (Bartram et al., 2006). However, the ipsative format does not present test–retest reliability. The normative tables in the manual provide detailed information on a diverse sample and a well-executed normative study, including an examination of adverse impact and the reporting of norms among different demographic and occupational groups. Thus, the OPQ inventories performed strongly in the presentation of normative information.

With regards to criterion-related validity, the OPQ-32n and OPQ-32i provided both individual and composite correlations for multiple criteria. Correlations were reported for the ratings of theoretically relevant competency dimensions over multiple sources (self, supervisor, or peer ratings). The OPQ was also one of the few inventories to present evidence from both predictive and concurrent validity studies, and it was one of the few to assess incremental validity over another method (cognitive ability tests in this instance). Many of the reported correlations reflected acceptable relationships for the expected criteria. As the OPQ-32i is a more recent test, however, much of the validity evidence is presented with regards to the OPQ-32n. This created a divergence in ratings for criterion-related validity, where the OPQ-32n was rated as "strong," but the OPQ-32i was rated as "moderately strong." However, one may argue that the OPQ-32i exhibits just as strong validity evidence as the OPQ-32n because the two measures are quite similar in other properties, based on the equivalence tests offered.

In addition to what is found in the manual, a considerable amount of independent research has been published with regard to the validity of different forms of the OPQ-32. For example, Robertson and Kinder (1993) examined the results of 20 previously unpublished validation studies based on samples from a range of occupations such as manufacturing and financial services. For each study, one to five OPQ scales were linked to one of a dozen criterion dimensions a priori by the consensus of 27 consultants. On average, each of the hypothesized scales correlated .15 with the targeted dimension and composites of the predicted scale scores correlated .20 across the dimensions. Another published study, which examined two samples totaling more than 700 managers, also found meaningful relationships between the hypothesized OPQ scales and performance criteria. For example, in the cross-validation sample of 270 managers, the Conceptual scale emerged as the best predictor of tasks involving analysis and planning (r = .35), the controlling scale for leadership criteria (r = .30), Affiliative for interpersonal skills criteria (r = .28), and Persuasive for entrepreneurial activities (r = .11). Barrick, Stewart, and Piotrowski (2002) organized the scales into the FFM, confirming earlier meta-analytic results (e.g., Barrick & Mount, 1991) that composites of scales related to Conscientiousness (r = .26) and Extraversion (r = .21) were the best predictors of sales performance.

Construct validity evidence was also based mostly upon the OPQ-32n, which received a "strong" rating, compared to a "moderately strong" rating for the OPQ-32i. The pattern of correlations with other inventories generally supports convergent validity. As an example, the "Outgoing" scale correlates more strongly with HPI-Sociability (r = .59) than with any other HPI scale. One limitation of construct validity is the lack of information on factor analysis. Although support was noted for the FFM using both an exploratory and confirmatory approach, the structure of the 32 facet scales was not tested using such a method. Although the specific trait structure was reviewed rationally during development, empirical analyses of the trait structure could reduce the number of scales (and thus items) needed for administration.

Not surprisingly, the primary difference in the ratings between the ipsative (OPQ-32i) and normative (OPQ-32n) scales was on the response validity dimension. Whereas the ipsative format was designed to mitigate response distortion, the normative format appears susceptible to such distortion. The OPQ-32n includes a social desirability scale to serve as an indicator of faking, but recommendations regarding the use of this scale are not provided. The normative form also includes a method of measuring response inconsistency, but the balance of differently keyed items is not presented with regards to acquiescence bias. Independent research has indicated that the ipsative format is much more resilient when comparing responses for different conditions of faking (Martin et al., 2002). Thus, we rated the OPQ-32i as "moderately strong" on response distortion but the OPQ-32n as "moderately weak." Given the relative equivalence in criterion-related validities, we recommend use of the ipsative format of the OPQ due to its greater resilience to response distortion.

PRF

The PRF was rated strongly on its development and construct validity evidence. The inventory originally targeted specific traits according to Murray's (1938) psychogenic needs, with extensive theoretical and empirical revision throughout its development. Elements such as social desirability were also considered during item development. The strong construct development method used in the PRF also resulted in highly supportive evidence for construct validity with a large number of convergent and discriminant validity coefficients that conform to expected patterns. Other scales assessed included personality measures such as the CPI, as well as values, interests, and other forms of personal information. Theoretical and factor analytic information was further used to place the PRF scales into eight factors, although independent research has found that five- and six-factor models provide good fit. A point of criticism for the PRF is that much of its validity evidence is older, derived from 30 to 40 years ago. Thus, although the presented construct validity evidence is strong, the manual needs to be updated to reflect more up-to-date normative and validity information.[5]

Several PRF scales exhibited modest internal consistencies ($\alpha < .70$), though these scales covered a fair amount of content and were relatively close to .70. With strong test–retest reliability coefficients ($r > .80$), the PRF received a "moderately strong" rating for reliability. The PRF also received a "moderately strong" rating for response validity due to the careful nature with which items were constructed to minimize social desirability. Several validity scales were utilized in analyses to assess faking and acquiescence bias, including the examination of scale correlations with these response bias scales. Although the PRF generally yields little effect of response bias on scale scores, other research has found that PRF scores can be faked reasonably well (Braun & Asta, 1969). Criterion-related validity and normative information received unfavorable ratings, primarily due to the lack of job-specific information reported in the manual. Although normative information was gathered for an employment sample, this information was not further broken down by specific occupational families.

Although the PRF manual contains only scarce results relating to validity, the *PRF Research Bibliography*, compiled by the test publisher, lists several hundred such studies, approximately 10% of which examine relationships with work outcomes. For example, Day and Silverman (1989) showed that the PRF predicted job performance beyond cognitive ability, with the average absolute correlation of those traits with a conceptual link to an accounting job of .31. Similarly, a study of managerial performance found PRF factor scores to be related to satisfaction, performance, and promotability, with traits related to self-reliance and independence emerging as the best predictors of overall effectiveness (Gellatly, Paunonen, Meyer, Jackson, & Goffin, 1991). Goffin et al. (2000) also examined managerial effectiveness, reporting that PRF traits related to extraversion and dominance predicted performance (r = .39 and .41, respectively) and that scores from the PRF predicted beyond those of the 16PF (although the reverse was not found). Although the coefficients and methodologies employed by these research studies are strong, we rated the PRF as "moderately strong" in criterion-related validity for failing to provide such information in the manual. In addition, the PRF still lacks depth in the available research on work-related outcomes.

Wonderlic 5

The Wonderlic 5 generally reported positive, though not exceptional, evidence for its psychometric quality. Scale items were rationally targeted to the FFM, though fewer narrow traits were considered than in most other FFM scales. Specifically, Agreeableness, Emotional Stability, and Openness were each represented by only two facets, while Extraversion and Conscientiousness were represented by only three. No explanation was offered for the narrower focus, and the relatively few facets per factor raises concerns regarding bandwidth. Furthermore, little detail was provided on the empirical and rational processes used to refine and develop test items. Although these flaws are noteworthy, the Wonderlic 5 appeared to adopt a sound, construct-based approach to its development, earning a rating of "moderately strong" on this dimension.

Overall, the Wonderlic 5 showed strong reliability, with internal consistency coefficients ranging from .82 to .87 for the factors and .70 to .80 for the specific subscales. The manual also reported test–retest reliabilities for three separate samples over different time intervals, all with acceptable coefficients. Although the sample sizes that provided these estimates were small relative to those reported in other inventories, they still produced strong coefficients. Overall, we rated the reliability evidence for the Wonderlic 5 as "strong."

The construct validity evidence for the Wonderlic 5 was rated as "moderately strong." The measure showed similar patterns with Norman's *Bipolar Adjective Checklist*, the HPI, and Goldberg's *Big Five-Factor Markers*. Discriminant validity was demonstrated through low correlations with general mental ability (GMA), save for a moderate and interpretable correlation with Openness to Experience. The manual also offered good evidence for structural validity based on exploratory factor analysis (EFA). Specifically, the 12 facet subscales have the strongest loadings on their respective host factors, with only one cross-loading above .35. Structural validity was also supported by facet correlations, whereby within-factor correlations were above .56, and between-factor correlations were no greater than .39. A positive feature of the Wonderlic 5 is the inclusion of validation evidence for weighted composite scales that are specific to different skill sets (e.g., a "teamwork" scale). However, the weights assigned to the global factors for these specialized occupation scales were derived from prior meta-analytic estimates across multiple inventories rather than from estimates specific to the Wonderlic inventory. As meta-analyses vary in the instruments used and the relative representation of different traits, such estimates have questionable applicability to any specific inventory. Though the Wonderlic 5 correlates with other measures of the FFM, these correlations do not imply interchangeability, particularly given the disparities in the number of facets examined from inventory to inventory. Thus, we question the wisdom of the weighting system for the specialized occupation scales.

The criterion-related validity evidence for the Wonderlic 5 is mixed. Median validity estimates across several jobs and criteria are generally low (ranging from .02 to .25), but specific scales exhibit acceptable validity coefficients when examined with the expected jobs and criteria. However, some of the validation samples were quite small (N < 100) and, although meta-analytic evidence was presented in favor of the FFM for use in predicting job performance, it was not specific to the inventory. Thus, criterion-related validity evidence was somewhat limited when examining studies specific to the Wonderlic 5. Much of the external research on the inventory was conducted by the scale developers (when it was known as the PCI). These studies showed positive validity evidence, particularly for jobs emphasizing interpersonal interactions and teamwork. Positive relationships were found between Conscientiousness, Extraversion, and Emotional Stability and performance for jobs involving interpersonal interactions (Mount, Barrick, & Stewart, 1998). In addition, different versions of aggregated scores for the global factors yield significant correlations with team performance, and quite strong correlations with various team process variables (Barrick, Stewart, Neubert, & Mount, 1998).

The global factors of the inventory have also shown adequate prediction of both individual- and organization-focused counterproductive work behaviors (Mount, Ilies, & Johnson, 2006). Conscientiousness also related positively to goal-setting and commitment, as well as supervisor ratings of performance (Barrick, Mount, & Strauss, 1993). Although the Wonderlic 5 has demonstrated positive validation evidence for contextual performance and interpersonal skills, there is little external research involving other criteria. Additional validation studies that link specific scales, jobs, and criteria would also offer more precise evaluation of criterion-related validity. The Wonderlic 5 received a "moderately strong" evaluation on criterion-related validity based on its overall supportive but incomplete body of evidence.

The Wonderlic 5 includes assessments for both intentional and unintentional response distortion and several other response validity scales (infrequency, impression management, etc.). It also provides an explicit warning against faking in selection contexts, which is a generally recommended practice (and yet is surprisingly rare amongst the inventories). These measures generated a positive impression amongst raters. However, corrections for impression management appeared to impact scale validity, as indicated by the lower validity coefficients in some scales when correcting for the response validity scales. These differences in validity coefficients ranged from .00 to .08; differences the test authors noted were not statistically significant. Although this is a fair point, the z-test for correlation differences typically has low power, and some of the differences in validity coefficients yield interpretation differences. For example, the correlation between Emotional Stability and performance moves from being statistically significant ($r = -.17$) to nonsignificant ($r = -.09$). The effect size with Conscientiousness also exhibited a potentially impactful drop ($\Delta r = -.05$) to produce a modest corrected correlation ($r = .22$). It should be noted, however, that, with the inclusion of the response validity scales, a user may choose to identify and screen invalid responses (a controversial choice), which may yield higher corrected validity coefficients. Based on the balance of evidence, the Wonderlic 5 received a "moderately strong" rating for response validity.

Normative information for the five scales is quite detailed, with both raw interval scores and descriptive statistics provided for a variety of jobs and settings. Not only do the norms allow identification of potentially invalid responses, they also provide helpful benchmarks for the types of distributions one should expect in different settings. Perhaps the only weakness in the Wonderlic 5's normative information is the lack of detail provided on the characteristics of the specific samples included. However, we believed that the variety of occupations and the statistical detail made up for this deficiency, giving the normative information a rating of "strong."

Comparisons Across Inventories

To facilitate comparisons of our evaluations across inventories, Table 10.2 presents the resulting evaluations from our review of each inventory, as well as an abbreviated explanation of the evaluation for quick reference. Considering the total number of favorable ratings (moderately strong or strong), as well as the relative importance of the dimensions that receive a favorable rating, we may draw some general conclusions when comparing our evaluations across inventories. Overall, the HPI,

Table 10.2 Evaluation Summaries for the Selected Personality Inventories

Scale	Framework and Development	Reliability and Measurement Error	Construct Validity	Criterion-Related Validity	Response Validity	Normative Information
16PF	*Moderately strong* Sound item development; 16 trait structure requires more conceptual and empirical development	*Moderately strong* Strong reliability coefficients, with some exceptions	*Moderately strong* MTMM correlations and factor analysis support validity; no facet correlations between inventories	*Moderately strong* Support noted from research and 5 job types examined; modest multiple correlations presented	*Moderately strong* Measures IM and response biases; personality scores correlate with IM	*Moderately weak* Norm sample is representative of the United States, but info is not given by occupation
Caliper	*Moderately weak* Items chosen from other scales based upon criterion-related validity	*Moderately weak* Weak internal consistency; lack of detail on the development of the semi-ipsative format	*Moderately weak* Some equally strong correlations with convergent and discriminant factors; poor factor analysis	*Moderately strong* Strong multiple correlations by job type using meta-analysis; little information on method or specific scales	*Strong* Semi-ipsative format with statements matched on desirability	*Weak* Norm sample is representative of working population, but statistics are not given
CPI	*Moderately weak* Initial development using the MMPI and "folk" concepts; followed by empirical analysis	*Moderately strong* Strong reliability coefficients, with a few exceptions; inefficient scales (many items)	*Moderately weak* Broad variety of correlates, but no supporting summary; weak factor analysis	*Moderately weak* Includes few correlations with job-relevant outcomes; mostly validated with law enforcement	*Moderately strong* Provides several response validity scales; but faking can improve scores	*Strong* Detailed normative information provided for a variety of job families
GPI-A	*Moderately strong* Computer adaptive scale using ideal point IRT model; 13 trait taxonomy warrants further investigation	*Moderately strong* *SEM* fixed to acceptable threshold before test is complete; no test–retest coefficients	*Moderately weak* No factor analysis reported to validate the unique factor structure; few MTMM correlations provided	*Moderately weak* Modest correlations between multiple scales and criteria; reported only by job level (vs. job type)	*Moderately weak* Forced-choice scale, but item statements tap the same trait with differing levels of social desirability	*Moderately strong* Provides means and SDs for different job levels, but not for different job families

Scale	Framework and Development	Reliability and Measurement Error	Construct Validity	Criterion-Related Validity	Response Validity	Normative Information
HPI	*Strong* Initial items developed from the FFM, then refined through analyses	*Moderately strong* Mostly strong reliability coefficients for the factor scales	*Moderately strong* Factor analysis and MTMM matrix support the structure; no validity with narrow traits	*Strong* Correlations with a variety of job criteria using meta-analysis, organized by job types	*Moderately weak* Validity scale identifies "unlikely" responses, but little else provided	*Moderately strong* Norms provided for different demographic groups, but not for different occupations
MBTI	*Moderately weak* Construct approach, but scale specifically developed to reflect a theory with little empirical support	*Moderately strong* Strong reliabilities, but a high *SEM* for low and high scores on a scale	*Moderately weak* Neuroticism or related construct is not measured; supportive MTMM with other scales	*Weak* Few work-relevant criteria reported; modest correlations with these criteria	*Moderately weak* Susceptible to faking; performs an adjustment based upon a prediction ratio for responses	*Moderately strong* Normative information for different occupations, but limited sample description
MMPI-2	*Moderately weak* Developed in a clinical setting and focuses upon pathologies	*Moderately weak* Several scales exhibit questionable coefficients; skewed score distributions	*Moderately weak* Scales validated with clinical behaviors, but not with personality scales for normal populations	*Weak* No work-related samples examined in validation studies; screening tool for law enforcement	*Moderately weak* Several response validity scales, but some items have strong desirability component	*Moderately weak* Normative information given for clinical populations
NEO-PI-R	*Strong* Rational item writing based upon the FFM; modified based upon empirical analyses	*Strong* Strong reliabilities on factor scales; acceptable coefficients for facets	*Strong* Correlation patterns and factor analysis support validity	*Moderately strong* Few work criteria in manual; many supportive external studies	*Moderately weak* Likert response scales are easily faked and no assessment of desirability	*Moderately weak* Diverse college and adult samples, but no job-related normative information
OPQ-32n	*Moderately strong* A tested but unique model of personality, and does not reconcile it with other models	*Strong* High reliability coefficients for almost all scales	*Strong* Correlation patterns support validity; factor analysis used to support broad factors but not the facets	*Strong* Provides supporting correlations between scales and work competencies from many studies	*Moderately weak* Provides several scales to assess response validity; format is conducive to faking	*Strong* Detailed normative information given for a variety of job families

(Continued)

Table 10.2 Continued

Scale	Framework and Development	Reliability and Measurement Error	Construct Validity	Criterion-Related Validity	Response Validity	Normative Information
OPQ-32i	*Moderately strong* A tested but unique model of personality, and does not reconcile it with other models	*Strong* High reliability coefficients, but little detail given on the IRT model	*Moderately strong* Correlation patterns support validity; factor analysis not provided	*Moderately strong* Provides supporting correlations between scales and job criteria, but few studies are presented	*Moderately strong* Ipsative format to discourage faking; examinations of response distortion not provided	*Strong* Detailed normative information given for a variety of job families
PRF	*Strong* Rational and empirical item development, with careful attention to social desirability	*Moderately strong* Several modest reliabilities, but strong effort to remove artificial variance	*Strong* Supporting patterns of MTMM correlations and factor analytic evidence	*Moderately strong* No work-related sample or criteria presented in validation	*Moderately strong* Items designed to prevent response distortion, and several validity scales to detect response biases	*Moderately weak* Detailed info provided for a diverse sample, but no job-specific info
Wonderlic 5	*Moderately strong* A tested foundation for the measure but little information on development	*Strong* High reliability coefficients, though smaller sample sizes used in estimation	*Moderately strong* Supportive MTMM coefficients and factor analysis; questionable weights for the special occupation scales	*Moderately strong* Adequate correlations with several criteria for several job types; relies too much upon the generalized validity of the FFM	*Moderately strong* Provides three validity scales with usage suggestions; validity coefficients are weak after faking correction	*Strong* Detailed normative information on several job families

Notes: 16PF: 16 Personality Factor Questionnaire; CPI: California Personality Inventory; GPI-A: Global Personality Inventory—Adaptive; HPI: Hogan Personality Inventory; MBTI: Myers–Briggs Type Indicator; MMPI-2: Minnesota Multiphasic Personality Inventory II; NEO-PI-3: Neuroticism–Extraversion–Openness Personality Inventory—Revised; OPQ-32n and -32i: Occupational Personality Questionnaire-32n and -32i; PRF: Personality Research Form; FFM: Five-Factor Model; MTMM: multitrait-multimethod correlations; IM: impression management; *SEM*: standard error of measurement; IRT: item response theory; SD: standard deviation.

OPQ-32 scales, PRF, and Wonderlic 5 performed well compared to most of the other inventories, with mostly favorable ratings across dimensions. In particular, these inventories tended to provide sound criterion-related validity evidence (e.g., for specific job families) and offered a wealth of statistical, methodological, and contextual information that is appropriate for organizational testing. They were also judged favorably for the use of appropriate methodology and measurement, and having sound psychometric properties in other areas.

Judged less favorably overall were the CPI, MBTI, and MMPI-2. The main reasons were poor reporting of relevant statistics, weak methodology, a lack of work-relevant validation evidence, and/or weak coefficients relative to professional standards. The MBTI has vulnerabilities in its measurement and construct validity due to reliance on binary typologies, and limited supporting evidence for criterion-related validity. These concerns generally echo the conclusions drawn by other researchers (e.g., Hunsley, Lee, & Wood, 2003). The CPI also failed to report much validity evidence with job-relevant criteria (beyond that of law enforcement). Furthermore, the CPI exhibited poor methodology in testing its structural validity and framework of "folk concepts." Based upon the general design and purpose of the MMPI-2, its use appears acceptable for the purposes of a psychological assessment if such an assessment is appropriate for the job. However, the MMPI was not developed and validated using a normal working population, such that we see no current argument for using it as an assessment of work-relevant personality traits outside of law enforcement and other areas where psychopathology is especially relevant.

Inventories receiving generally moderate reviews include the 16PF, Caliper, GPI-A, and NEO-PI-3. Although the GPI-A received mixed reviews on its current evidence, it is a recently developed scale with ample opportunity to build a supportive body of research. The more established scales of the Caliper, 16PF, and NEO-PI-3 have genuinely strong qualities, but also some questionable characteristics requiring some effort to remedy. We conclude that these scales may be somewhat useful in human resource management, but they lack desired qualities evident in the more favorably rated inventories (e.g., regarding normative data or validity for selected contexts).

Discussion

The main purpose of this chapter was to evaluate and summarize the psychometric strengths and weaknesses of several popular and/or reputable personality inventories used in industry. Overall, our review shows a fair degree of variability among inventories in their measurement properties and associated methods of development. Results highlight the need for a careful examination of the available options when selecting a personality inventory for practice or research. Our review also suggests that several inventories warrant stronger consideration over others for use in work settings, depending on the intended purpose. We also identified concerns in specific areas for every inventory that warrant caution. An inventory for which reliability is a noted concern, for example, could pose problems in distinguishing between two respondents with similar scores. Several manuals lacked informative statistics, which we charitably assumed reflected an error in reporting rather than an error of omission during scale development. Thus, we recommend that users of these inventories consult the extant literature for more detailed information or request this information from test publishers. Although the information presented in personality manuals is useful, more information is needed in order to make an optimally informed selection of an inventory, particularly from independent sources.

On a related point, human resource practitioners and researchers should always consider the job and criteria in light of testing purpose when choosing a personality inventory. An encouraging sign from many of the reviewed inventories is the emphasis placed on job analysis and finding an appropriate match between a personality scale and an occupation. Several manuals provided example job descriptions for the validity studies reported. We appreciated the presentation of this information, but users should examine the degree to which the jobs presented in an inventory manual are similar to the positions for which the inventory is being used in practice. In particular, validity information for a more relevant position may be found in a local validation study that is referenced in the test manual. In evaluating such studies, one should also ensure that the contextual and criterion variables reflect the variables valued by the user.

Limitations Across Personality Inventories

Beyond the issues already discussed in this chapter, a number of concerns relevant to personality measurement were not addressed by any of the reviewed inventories. These concerns reflect relevant psychometric indices that human resource management will have to address in local validation studies until such indices are incorporated into the personality inventories. We next discuss the impact that each index can have upon the utility of personality inventories.

Incremental Validity

Although personality inventories are generally accepted as useful in applied psychology, there are many researchers who argue that personality inventories are simply not useful after accounting for other selection tools (e.g., Morgeson et al., 2007; Murphy & Dziewecynski, 2005). One way to promote the merit of personality testing is to demonstrate that such inventories provide unique information beyond other methods. For example, it is unclear from the manuals if the benefit provided by the MBTI in team building outperforms other types of interventions, or whether a structured interview may provide prediction of performance as sound as do the self-report inventories reviewed here. In general, research has indicated that personality scores can demonstrate incremental validity over other methods (e.g., McManus & Kelly, 1999; Salgado & De Fruyt, 2005). Thus, it will likely benefit personality inventories to examine the incremental validity of a scale composite over other assessment methods. Incremental validity can also be assessed relative to other personality inventories, which would provide strong evidence for the use of one inventory over another. Such comparisons have been reported (e.g., Goffin et al., 2000), but much more research is needed along such lines to assess the relative merits of each inventory. Incremental validity may be examined using a variety of methods, including the use of multiple regression, dominance analysis, path analysis, or structural equation modeling. This information would be vital in showing the relative importance of a given personality inventory.

Content and Structural Validity

Although all inventory manuals indicated that items were reviewed by SMEs for content, detail on corresponding methods and analyses were rarely provided. Direct indices of content validity typically report the results of SME ratings on the degree that the dimensions and items are useful and necessary for measuring the content domain. This process may have helped prevent some of the poor consistencies observed in the empirically developed inventories, as well as the issues of content deficiency that are noted for a couple of inventories.

On a related matter, we were struck by the wide variety of taxonomies that were used for what is theoretically the same content domain. Even when using a similar framework (FFM), each inventory presented a unique number of traits organized under the global factors. Such differences appear minor in individual comparisons, but, taken as a whole, this observation has implications for the field of personality testing. These differences in inventory traits suggest that the structure of a personality inventory is, to some degree, idiosyncratic. Although there is generally broad agreement on five or six global factors, there is general disagreement on the more narrow traits that compose those factors. Deciding upon the proper number of dimensions is admittedly a difficult task, with opposing incentives of parsimony and comprehensiveness. There are a variety of statistical methods that can aid decision making in this regard, but they were not reported for the inventories. In particular, there appeared to be little effort by most test authors/publishers to test the structure of their facet scales using one or more confirmatory factor models. Based upon the uncertainty in the narrow facet structure, slight differences in the trait structures between inventories will not likely impact their utility, so long as a sufficient number of traits are assessed to retain adequate bandwidth and fidelity.

Applicant Reactions

All of the reviewed inventories failed to provide empirical information of applicant reactions to the test battery. Although secondary to predictions of job-relevant behaviors, an applicant's reaction to selection procedures can influence organizational attractiveness, intentions to accept a job offer, and related outcomes relevant to the organization (Hausknecht, Day, & Thomas, 2004). To prevent negative reactions, item content was typically developed to avoid offending applicants. However, variables other than the propriety of item content may influence applicant reactions, such as the test format, perceived relevance of the content to the job (face validity), and the included instructions to test takers during administration. Although independent research has examined applicant reactions in a few inventories (e.g., Converse et al., 2008), this research area is completely neglected in the reviewed inventory manuals.

Conclusion

The benefit of a personality inventory depends heavily on its psychometric characteristics, as well as the traits, criteria, and contexts on which these test statistics are based. As a result, human resource management specialists and researchers should gather relevant information to determine the most appropriate inventory and methods for their purpose. This review of personality inventories can serve as one such reference in this decision-making process. Our results indicate notable variability in test quality, and we urge practitioners to take care when deciding upon personality inventories for use in work settings.

Practitioner's Window

The choice of a specific personality inventory has noteworthy implications for personnel selection, promotion, and development. Although a general psychometric review of personality testing can provide a useful "state of the art" overview, the benefits a given organization can expect to gain from personality testing depend upon the specific inventory chosen.

In selecting a personality inventory, practitioners should examine (1) the method of scale development (methods using a balance of theory and empirical analysis are preferred over those using either strategy alone); (2) scale reliabilities (i.e., consistency in test scores over time and across items within the given subscale); (3) construct validity evidence (supporting the given test as a measure of the defined trait, including the strength and direction of correlations among subscales that fit what those scales are intended to assess); (4) criterion-related validity evidence (supporting the test as a predictor of relevant outcome variables, e.g., job performance); (5) response validity evidence (showing consideration of known response biases, e.g., social desirability, in scale development and/or scoring); and (6) normative information (supporting unambiguous comparisons between individuals and relevant populations).

Applying the above criteria to 12 commonly used personality inventories yielded the following overall evaluations:

Inventories with overall positive evaluations

- Hogan Personality Inventory (HPI)
- Occupational Personality Questionnaires (OPQ-32n and OPQ-32i)
- Personality Research Form (PRF)
- Wonderlic 5

Inventories with overall mixed evaluations

- 16PF
- Caliper Profile
- Global Personality Inventory—Adaptive (GPI-A)
- Neuroticism–Extraversion–Openness Personality Inventory-3 (NEO-PI-3)

Inventories with overall modest evaluations

- California Personality Inventory (CPI)
- Minnesota Multiphasic Personality Inventory-2 (MMPI-2)
- Myers–Briggs Type Inventory (MBTI)

Notably, no single measure received strongly positive evaluations on all criteria, and no single measure was uniformly low on all criteria. All measures, in fact, have key strengths in some areas for some applications. Test users are urged to seek credible, independent evidence (i.e., beyond that available from the test publisher) regarding the psychometric properties of available tests in light of the above criteria before choosing one test over others for use in selecting or developing workers. We especially urge test users to base test selection on more than simply what most other organizations are using or on the surface appeal of test brochures.

Notes

1 Aggregation over more items increases reliability by allowing the random overestimates to cancel out the random underestimates.
2 The Society for Industrial and Organizational Psychology Principles states that "efforts should be made to minimize predictor contamination" (p. 18). Response distortion is a key candidate for contamination of personality test scores.
3 Fakability is not unique to the CPI. All self-report personality inventories show susceptibility to response distortion.
4 In terms of IRT, the MBTI items contain only those *b* parameters that are close to zero in their location along the preference distribution.
5 Both the manual and the test itself are in the process of being revised at this writing.

References

Barrick, M. R., & Mount, M. K. (1991). The Big Five personality dimensions and job performance: A meta-analysis. *Personnel Psychology, 44*, 1–26.

Barrick, M. R., Mount, M. K., & Judge, T. A. (2001). The FFM personality dimensions and job performance: Meta-analysis of meta-analyses. *International Journal of Selection and Assessment, 9*, 9–30.

Barrick, M. R., Mount, M. K., & Strauss, J. P. (1993). Conscientiousness and performance of sales representatives: Test of the mediating effects of goal setting. *Journal of Applied Psychology, 78*, 715–722.

Barrick, M. R., Stewart, G. L., Neubert, M. J., & Mount, M. K. (1998). Relating member ability and personality to work-team processes and team effectiveness. *Journal of Applied Psychology, 83*, 377–391.

Barrick, M. R., Stewart, G. L., & Piotrowski, M. (2002). Personality and job performance: Test of the mediating effects of motivation among sales representatives. *Journal of Applied Psychology, 87*, 43–51.
Bartram, D., Brown, A., Fleck, S., Inceoglu, I., & Ward, K. (2006). *The OPQ32 technical manual*. London: SHL Group.
Bernstein, D. A. (2011). *Essentials of psychology* (5th ed.). Belmont, CA: Wadsworth Cengage.
Bing, M. N., & Lounsbury, J. W. (2000). Openness and job performance in US-based Japanese manufacturing companies. *Journal of Business and Psychology, 14*, 515–523.
Braun, J. R., & Asta, P. (1969). Changes in *Personality Research Form* scores (PRF, Form A) produced by faking instructions. *Journal of Clinical Psychology, 25*, 429–430.
Brown, T. A. (2006). *Confirmatory factor analysis for applied research*. New York: Guilford Press.
Butcher, J. N., Dahlstrom, W. G., Graham, J. R., Tellegen, A., & Kaemmer, B. (1989). *The Minnesota Multiphasic Personality Inventory-2 (MMPI-2): Manual for administration and scoring*. Minneapolis, MN: University of Minnesota Press.
Caliper. (2009). *Caliper technical manual* (5th ed.). Princeton, NJ: Caliper Research Department.
Cellar, D. F., Miller, M. L., Doverspike, D. D., & Klawsky, J. D. (1996). Comparison of factor structures and criterion related validity coefficients for two measures of personality based on the five factor model. *Journal of Applied Psychology, 81*, 694–704.
Chernyshenko, O. S., Stark, S., Drasgow, F., & Roberts, B. W. (2007). Constructing personality scales under the assumptions of an ideal point response process: Toward increasing the flexibility of personality measures. *Psychological Assessment, 19*, 88–106.
Chernyshenko, O. S., Stark, S., Prewett, M. S., Gray, A., Stilson, F., & Tuttle, M. (2009). Normative scoring of multidimensional pairwise Preference Personality Scales using IRT: Empirical comparisons with other formats. *Human Performance, 22*, 105–127.
Cheung, M. W. L. (2002). Reducing uniform response bias with ipsative measurement in multiple-group confirmatory factor analysis. *Structured Equation Modeling: A Multidisciplinary Journal, 9*, 55–77.
Christiansen, N. D., Burns, G. N., & Montgomery, G. E. (2005). Reconsidering forced-choice item formats for applicant personality assessment. *Human Performance, 18*, 267–307.
Christiansen, N. D., Goffin, R. D., Johnston, N. G., & Rothstein, M. G. (1994). Correcting the 16PF for faking: Effects on criterion-related validity and individual hiring decisions. *Personnel Psychology, 47*, 847–860.
Converse, P. D., Oswald, F. L., Imus, A., Hedricks, C., Roy, R., & Butera, H. (2008). Comparing personality test formats and warnings: Effects on criterion-related validity and test taker reactions. *International Journal of Selection and Assessment, 16*, 155–169.
Costa, P. T., Jr., & McCrae, R. R. (1976). Age differences in personality structure: A cluster analytic approach. *Journal of Gerontology, 31*, 564–570.
Costa, P. T., Jr., & McCrae, R. R. (1985). *The NEO Personality Inventory manual*. Odessa, FL: Psychological Assessment Resources.
Crocker, L., & Algina, J. (2008). *Introduction to classical & modern test theory*. New York: Wadsworth.
Cronbach, L. J. (1951). Coefficient alpha and the internal structure of tests. *Psychometrika, 16*, 297–334.
Cronbach, L. J. (1960). *Essentials of psychological testing* (2nd ed.). New York: Harper & Row.
Cronbach, L. J., & Meehl, P. E. (1955). Construct validity in psychological tests. *Psychological Bulletin, 52*, 281–302.
Day, D.V., & Silverman, S. B. (1989). Personality and job performance: Evidence of incremental validity. *Personnel Psychology, 42*, 25–36.
de Ayala, R. J. (2008). *The theory and practice of item response theory*. New York: Guilford Press.
Digman, J. M., & Inouye, J. (1986). Further specification of the five robust factors of personality. *Journal of Personality and Social Psychology, 50*, 116–123.
Ellingson, J. E., Sackett, P. R., & Hough, L. M. (1999). Social desirability corrections in personality measurement: Issues of applicant comparison and construct validity. *Journal of Applied Psychology, 84*, 155–166.
Esterson, A. (2001). The mythologizing of psychoanalytic history: Deception and self-deception in Freud's account of the seduction theory episode. *History of Psychiatry, 12*, 329–352.
Fannin, N., & Dabbs, J. M. (2003). Testosterone and the work of firefighters: Fighting fires and delivering medical care. *Journal of Research in Personality, 37*, 107–115.
Furnham, A., & Fudge, C. (2008). The five factor model of personality and sales performance. *Journal of Individual Differences, 29*, 11–16.
Gellatly, I. R., Paunonen, S.V., Meyer, J. P., Jackson, D. N., & Goffin, R. D. (1991). Personality, vocational interest, and cognitive predictors of managerial job performance and satisfaction. *Personality and Individual Differences, 12*, 221–231.
Gluskinos, U., & Brennan, T. F. (1971). Selection and evaluation procedure for operating room personnel. *Journal of Applied Psychology, 55*, 165–169.

Goffin, R. D., Rothstein, M. G., & Johnston, N. G. (2000). Predicting job performance using personality constructs: Are personality tests created equal? In R. D. Goffin & E. Helmes (Eds.), *Problems and solutions in human assessment: Honoring Douglas N. Jackson at seventy* (pp. 249–264). Norwell, MA: Kluwer Academic.

Gough, H. G., & Bradley, P. (1996). *The California Psychological Inventory*. Mountain View, CA: CPP.

Guion, R. M. (1980). On trinitarian doctrines of validity. *Professional Psychology, 11*, 385–398.

Guion, R. M., & Cranny, C. J. (1982). A note on concurrent and predictive validity designs: A critical reanalysis. *Journal of Applied Psychology, 67*, 239–244.

Hakstian, A. R., & Farrell, S. (2001). An Openness Scale for the California Psychological Inventory. *Journal of Personality Assessment, 76*, 107–134.

Hausknecht, J. P., Day, D. V., & Thomas, S. C. (2004). Applicant reactions to selection procedures: An updated model and meta-analysis. *Personnel Psychology, 57*, 639–683.

Hiatt, D., & Hargrave, G. E. (1988). Predicting job performance problems with psychological screening. *Journal of Police Science & Administration, 16*, 122–135.

Hogan, J., Hogan, R., & Gregory, S. (1992). Validation of a sales representative selection inventory. *Journal of Business and Psychology, 7*, 161–171.

Hogan, J., Hogan, R., & Murtha, T. (1992). Validation of a personality measure of managerial performance. *Journal of Business and Psychology, 7*, 225–237.

Hogan, J., & Holland, B. (2003). Using theory to evaluate personality and job-performance relations: A socioanalytic perspective. *Journal of Applied Psychology, 88*, 100–112.

Hogan, J., & Roberts, B. (1996). Issues and non-issues in the fidelity/bandwidth tradeoff. *Journal of Organizational Behavior, 17*, 627–637.

Hogan, R., & Hogan, J. (2007). *Hogan Personality Inventory* (3rd ed.). Tulsa, OK: Hogan Assessment Systems.

Houston, J. S., Borman, W. C., Farmer, W. L., & Bearden, R. M. (2005). *Development of the Enlisted Computer Adaptive Personality Scales (ENCAPS) for the United States Navy, phase 2* (Institute Report No. 503). Minneapolis, MN: Personnel Decisions Research Institutes.

Hulin, C. L., Drasgow, F., & Parsons, C. K. (1983). *Item response theory: Application to psychological measurement*. Ann Arbor, MI: Dow Jones-Irwin.

Hunsley, J., Lee, C. M., & Wood, J. M. (2003). Controversial and questionable assessment techniques. In S. O. Lilienfeld & S. J. Lynn (Eds.), *Science and pseudoscience in clinical psychology* (pp. 39–76). New York: Guilford Press.

Jackson, D. N. (1966). *A modern strategy for personality assessment: The Personality Research Form* (Research Bulletin No. 33c). London, Canada: University of Western Ontario.

Johnson, C. E., Wood, R., & Blinkthorn, S. F. (1988). Spuriouser and spuriouser: The use of ipsative personality tests. *Journal of Occupational Psychology, 61*, 153–162.

Judge, T. A., Bono, J. E., Ilies, R., & Gerhardt, M. W. (2002). Personality and leadership: A qualitative and quantitative review. *Journal of Applied Psychology, 87*, 765–780.

Kaiser, H. F. (1970). A second generation little jiffy. *Psychometrika, 35*, 401–415.

Kangis, P., & Lago, H. (1997). Using Caliper to predict performance of salespeople. *International Journal of Manpower, 18*, 565–575.

Karol, D., & Russell, M. (2009). *The 16PF Questionnaire manual* (5th ed.). Chicago: Institute for Personality and Ability Testing.

Martin, B. A., Bowen, C.-C., & Hunt, S. T. (2002). How effective are people at faking on personality questionnaires? *Personality and Individual Differences, 32*, 247–256.

McManus, M. A., & Kelly, M. L. (1999). Personality measures and biodata: Evidence regarding their incremental value in the life insurance industry. *Personnel Psychology, 52*, 137–148.

McRae, R. R., & Costa, P. T., Jr. (2010). *NEO Inventories for the NEO-PI-3, NEO-FFI-3, and NEO-PI-R*. Odessa, FL: Psychological Assessment Resources.

Morgeson, F. P., Campion, M. A., Dipboye, R. L., Hollenbeck, J. R., Murphy, K., & Schmitt, N. (2007). Reconsidering the use of personality tests in personnel selection contexts. *Personnel Psychology, 60*, 1029–1049.

Mount, M., Barrick, M. R., & Stewart, G. L. (1998). Five-factor model of personality and performance in jobs involving interpersonal interactions. *Human Performance, 11*, 145–164.

Mount, M., Ilies, R., & Johnson, E. (2006). Relationship of personality traits and counterproductive work behaviors: The mediating effect of job satisfaction. *Personnel Psychology, 59*, 591–622.

Mowen, J. C., & Voss, K. E. (2008). On building better construct measures: Implications of a general hierarchical model. *Psychology & Marketing, 25*, 485–505.

Muchinsky, P. M. (1993). Validation of personality constructs for the selection of insurance industry employees. *Journal of Business and Psychology, 7*, 475–482.

Murphy, K. R., & Dziewecynski, J. L. (2005). Why don't measures of broad dimensions of personality perform better as predictors of job performance? *Human Performance, 18*, 343–357.

Murray, H. A. (1938). *Explorations in personality*. Cambridge, MA: Harvard University Press.

Myers, I. B., McCauley, M. H., Quenk, N. L., & Hammer, A. L. (2009). *The Myers–Briggs Type Inventory*. Mountain View, CA: CPP.

Neuman, G. A., & Wright, J. (1999). Team effectiveness: Beyond skills and cognitive ability. *Journal of Applied Psychology, 84*, 376–389.

Nunnally, J. C. (1978). *Psychometric theory*. New York: McGraw–Hill.

Ones, D. S., & Viswesvaran, C. (1999). Bandwidth–fidelity dilemma in personality measurement for personnel selection. *Journal of Organizational Behavior, 17*, 609–626.

Ones, D. S., Viswesvaran, C., & Reiss, A. D. (1996). Role of social desirability in personality testing for personnel selection: The red herring. *Journal of Applied Psychology, 81*, 660–679.

Paulhus, D. L. (1991). Measurement and control of response bias. In J. P. Robinson, P. R. Shaver, & L. S. Wrightsman (Eds.), *Measures of personality and social psychological attitudes* (Vol. 1, pp. 17–59). San Diego, CA: Academic Press.

Previsor. (2010). *Global Personality Inventory—Adaptive, technical manual*. Roswell, GA: Previsor.

Prewett, M. S., Walvoord, A. G., Stilson, F. R. B., Rossi, M. E., & Brannick, M. D. (2009). The team personality—team performance relationship revisited: The impact of criterion choice, pattern of workflow, and method of aggregation. *Human Performance, 22*, 273–296.

Pugh, G. (1985). The California Psychological Inventory and police selection. *Journal of Police Science & Administration, 13*, 172–177.

Quenk, N. L., Hammer, A. L., & Majors, M. S. (2001). *MBTI step II manual*. Mountain View, CA: CPP.

Robertson, I. T., & Kinder, A. (1993). Personality and job competences: The criterion-related validity of some personality variables. *Journal of Occupational and Organizational Psychology, 66*, 225–244.

Rosse, J. G., Stecher, M. D., Levin, R. A., & Miller, J. L. (1998). The impact of response distortion on preemployment personality testing and hiring decisions. *Journal of Applied Psychology, 83*, 634–644.

Salgado, J. F. (2002). The Big Five personality dimensions and counterproductive work behavior. *International Journal of Selection and Assessment, 10*, 117–225.

Salgado, J. F., & De Fruyt, F. (2005). Personality in personnel selection. In A. Evers, N. Anderson, & O. Voskuijl (Eds.), *International handbook of personnel selection* (pp. 174–198). London: Blackwell.

Salgado, J. F., & Rumbo, A. (1997). Personality and job performance in financial services managers. *International Journal of Selection and Assessment, 5*, 91–100.

Schuerger, J. M., Kochevar, K. F., & Reinwald, J. E. (1982). Male and female corrections officers: Personality and rated performance. *Psychological Reports, 51*, 223–228.

Tett, R. P., & Christiansen, N. D. (2007). Personality tests at the crossroads: A response to Morgeson, Campion, Dipboye, Hollenbeck, Murphy, and Schmitt (2007). *Personnel Psychology, 60*, 967–993.

Tett, R. P., Fitzke, J. R., Wadlington, P. L., Davies, S. A., Anderson, M. G., & Foster, J. (2009). The utility of personality test norms: Effects of sample size and sample representativeness. *Journal of Occupational and Organizational Psychology, 82*, 639–659.

Tett, R. P., Freund, K. A., Christiansen, N. D., Fox, K. E., & Coaster, J. (2012). Faking on self-report emotional intelligence and personality tests: Effects of faking opportunity, cognitive ability, and job type. *Personality and Individual Differences, 52*, 195–201.

Tett, R. P., Steele, J. R., & Beauregard, R. S. (2003). Broad and narrow measures on both sides of the personality–job performance relationship. *Journal of Organizational Behavior, 24*, 335–356.

van der Linden, W. J., & Glas, C. A. W. (2003). *Computerized adaptive testing: Theory and practice*. Dordrecht, The Netherlands: Kluwer Academic.

Weiss, P. A., & Weiss, W. U. (2010). Using the MMPI-2 in police psychological assessment. In P. A. Weiss (Ed.), *Personality assessment in police psychology: A 21st century perspective* (pp. 59–71). Springfield, IL: C.C. Thomas.

Wonderlic. (2011). *Personal Characteristics Inventory (PCI), technical manual*.

11

Personality and the Need for Personality-Oriented Work Analysis

Thomas A. O'Neill, Richard D. Goffin, and Mitchell Rothstein

The Practical and Scientific Need for Personality-Oriented Work Analysis

In this chapter, we discuss personality-oriented work analysis (POWA). Instead of referring to *job analysis*, we use the term *work analysis* (WA) in light of the recent shift toward studying not just the job itself but also the context and system within which the job is embedded (Morgeson & Dierdorff, 2011). There is an immediate need for a consolidation of the POWA literature as this topic has critical practical and scientific implications. Practically, defensible methods are needed for identifying job-relevant personality traits. This could result in stronger legal defenses if personnel decisions based on personality are challenged. Criterion validation studies that may identify job-relevant traits may often not be feasible (e.g., in small N situations), whereas a solid POWA may buttress the use of personality testing in organizations.

Practically, POWA could save time and energy by reducing the number of traits that need to be assessed for a variety of organizational purposes (e.g., administrative, developmental) and for explaining why a trait is important (or not). Scientifically, there is a need for systematic approaches to identifying potentially job-relevant traits, as the literature is currently somewhat inconclusive. Important for both science and practice, when traits are identified as relevant to the criterion on conceptual grounds, criterion validities tend to be about twice as large as when purely exploratory methods are used (Tett, Jackson, & Rothstein, 1991; Tett, Jackson, Rothstein, & Reddon, 1999). Uncovering some of the most promising approaches to linking traits to job performance a priori, therefore, may be an important avenue for increasing criterion-validity coefficients, which have recently come under fire for being too low (Morgeson et al., 2007). Accordingly, a consolidation of the research could establish current best practices in POWA as well as key directions for further research.

We begin with a review of the current evidence on personality–job performance relations in order to establish personality's association with job performance. We then review traditional approaches to WA, recognizing that they have difficulty in identifying job-relevant personality traits. We also review competency modeling (CM), as some aspects of recent applications may be useful in POWA. Next, we report on the research that has explicitly set out to investigate POWA techniques. This lays the groundwork for current best practices and promising future research directions, which are the final topics covered.

Personality–Job Performance Relations: Where Does the Evidence Stand?

At the time of this writing, it has been two decades since the publication of two meta-analyses investigating relationships between personality variables and job performance criteria, in which a major breakthrough occurred in our understanding of these relationships (Barrick & Mount, 1991; Tett et al., 1991). Prior to these publications, the conventional wisdom among personnel selection researchers and industrial/organizational psychologists generally was that personality measures had no value in the prediction of job performance and was therefore not useful for personnel selection purposes (see Rothstein & Goffin, 2006). These prevailing beliefs were strongly influenced by an early narrative review of the literature by Guion and Gottier (1965), which concluded that, at that time, there was little evidence to support the validity of personality–job performance relations in personnel selection. In the decades that followed, hundreds of research studies continued to be published investigating these relationships, but the complexity of those studies (dozens of different personality traits, different types of criterion measures, and innumerable job types and levels), in addition to multiple methodological difficulties (cf. Tett et al., 1991), made conclusions very difficult to reach.

It was not until 1991 that advanced meta-analytic research methods were applied to personality–job performance relations and established that personality variables made a valid contribution to the prediction of job performance (e.g., Barrick & Mount, 1991). Tett et al.'s (1991) meta-analysis focused on the importance of the specificity of trait–criterion relations and determined that when a confirmatory research strategy was used in a source study, in which theoretical considerations or conceptual analyses helped identify personality measures hypothesized to be linked to conceptually related performance criteria, validity coefficients were more than twice the magnitude as in source studies that used an exploratory strategy to investigate personality–job performance relations.

The above meta-analytic studies, as well as many others that have subsequently been published (e.g., Borman, Penner, Allen, & Motowidlo, 2001; Hurtz & Donovan, 2000; Salgado, 1997; Vinchur, Schippmann, Switzer, & Roth, 1998), have established two notable findings. First, personality explains nontrivial variance in job performance. For example, in a second-order meta-analysis (meta-analysis of meta-analyses) conscientiousness predicted job performance at $\rho = .24$ across jobs (Barrick, Mount, & Judge, 2003). Second, personality–criterion linkages are situation specific; in other words, the predictiveness of a given trait depends on the work context (O'Neill, Goffin, & Tett, 2009; Rothstein & Jelley, 2003; Tett & Christiansen, 2008; Tett et al., 1991; Tett et al., 1999). This point was articulated in Tett and Christiansen's (2007) review of seven meta-analyses, which reported that 80% credibility intervals had an average width of .30. In other words, 80% of ρs reported in primary studies will be included in the range of .30. This means that for a personality trait with a "true" validity coefficient of .20, 80% of the validity coefficients from primary studies would fall within .05 and .35, indicating wide variation due to study context (e.g., jobs, occupations, industries).

In light of the above, personality–job performance relations are valid and useful in personnel selection, but the meta-analytic evidence clearly supports situational specificity in these relationships (Tett & Christiansen, 2008). As Rothstein and Jelley (2003) conclude,

> Unlike the case of general mental ability, it is simply not possible to use meta-analytic results from personality studies to develop validity generalization arguments to justify the selection of a particular personality measure across all or most jobs. Clearly, personality measures compared to measures of general mental ability are relatively more situationally specific . . .
>
> *p. 255*

One of the most critical implications of situational specificity when personality assessment is being considered for personnel selection purposes is that the personality traits to be assessed in job applicants must be matched to the requirements of the work. Linking any type of measure to be used as a predictor of future job performance is one of the primary functions of traditional job or WA procedures. Such procedures should establish the content validity of traits (i.e., the conceptual overlap between traits and job requirements), criterion validity (i.e., by identifying traits likely to yield empirical relations with work criteria), and a legal basis upon which the use of personality in personnel selection can be defended. Thus, we turn next to a brief description of traditional work analytic methodologies and their potential to identify work-relevant personality traits for personnel selection purposes.

Common Approaches to Identifying Worker Specifications

Traditional (Non-POWA) WA

A general definition of WA has been provided by Morgeson and Dierdorff (2011, p. 4): "the systematic investigation of (a) work role requirements and (b) the broader context within which work roles are enacted." WA methods provide the foundation for a myriad of essential purposes (Cascio & Aguinis, 2005), including personnel selection, job performance measurement/management, efficiency/safety, job classification, and many others (see Levine, Ash, Hall, & Sistrunk, 1983). The actual processes involved in acquiring the basic information used in WA can vary widely but generally include one or more of the six methods summarized in Table 11.1. Additionally, the focus of information collection in WA can be either *work oriented* or *worker oriented* (Cascio & Aguinis, 2005). A work-oriented focus places the emphasis on context-specific aspects of the tasks or activities, such as *checks the altimeter to make sure that altitude is appropriate for the respective operation*. Alternatively, a worker-oriented focus seeks to capture the generic human behaviors that are implicated in work activities, such as *pays attention to digital and analogue displays and interprets the information appropriately*.

Traditional WA and Personnel Selection: Two Key Linkages

Once the targeted work or job has been subjected to a thorough WA, additional work analytic steps must be undertaken to substantiate two linkages that are crucial to the establishment of a personnel selection tool's content validity (Goldstein, Zedeck, & Schneider, 1993; Society for Industrial and Organizational Psychology [SIOP], 2003). First, the work behaviors or tasks that have been catalogued through the WA must be linked to the requisite employee attributes. Second, the requisite attributes must be linked to the preemployment tests (or vice versa). With few exceptions (e.g., Goffin & Woycheshin, 2006), these two linkages rely directly on the guided judgments of job

Table 11.1 General Methods of Acquiring Work Analysis Information

Method	*Synopsis of Typical Practice*
Observation	Trained analyst observes incumbents at work and records key information. Could also involve electronic or computer-based monitoring of work behavior.
Use of archival data	An existing source of work information is exploited, such as O*NET or a published list of competencies.
Interview	Trained analyst asks incumbents or supervisors a series of questions about the target job(s).
Survey	Structured or semistructured questionnaires are administered to incumbents or supervisors of the target job(s).
Logbooks or work diaries	Incumbents systematically record their work activities (electronically or by writing).
SME panels	A panel of SMEs is tasked with developing lists of work activities, critical incidents, worker specifications, and/or ratings of any of the preceding items.

Note: SME: subject matter expert.

analysts, incumbents, or supervisors (see Goldstein et al., 1993, for a detailed description), often within the context of subject matter expert (SME) workshops or surveys.

Using traditional WA approaches to uncover and substantiate the employee attributes that one will test for in a personnel selection competition brings to bear a rigorous, systematic methodology (Shippmann et al., 2000). Nonetheless, with regard to its use in establishing the personality requirements of work, we see an important limitation. Mainstream WA approaches rely on taxonomies of human attributes wherein personality is, at best, poorly articulated. For example, the major WA methods in Brannick and Levine's (2002) book refer to only a small number of vague personality-like attributes that do not map readily onto established taxonomies of personality traits, most importantly the Five-Factor Model (FFM) (e.g., Costa & McCrae, 1992) or its close variants (e.g., Jackson, Paunonen, Fraboni, & Goffin, 1996). In contrast, when one considers broad as well as narrow traits, recent research has made clear that there are numerous work-relevant personality traits that should be considered in personnel selection scenarios (e.g., Paunonen, Lonnqvist, Verkasalo, Leikas, & Nissinen, 2006; Rothstein & Goffin, 2006). In fairness, traditional WA methods (e.g., Fine, 1988; Lopez, Kesselman, & Lopez, 1981; McCormick & Jeanneret, 1988; Primoff, 1975) fittingly take into account the cognitive, physical, perceptual, and other attributes that have dominated past research on the predictors of job performance. However, now that personality has been established as a legitimate predictor in its own right (see Rothstein & Goffin, 2006; Tett & Christiansen, 2007), personality-oriented WA methods are needed.

Traditional WA can be criticized for being limited to a bottom-up strategy (Morgeson & Dierdorff, 2011). In other words, it takes a micro perspective and tends to ignore macro issues, such as organizational strategy. This limitation and the subsequent development of CM as an alternative or adjunct to traditional WA are discussed in the following.

CM

The inferences advanced by WA regarding required employee attributes tend to be informed solely by consideration of work behavior. What is missing is due consideration of the overall strategy, structure, and culture of the larger organization within which work behavior must fit (Pearlman & Sanchez, 2010). The practice of CM has gained considerable ground over WA in recent years because of its explicit consideration of organizational context and use of a top-down strategy for inferring the attributes workers should possess in order to contribute to the greater good of the organization (Sanchez & Levine, 2009). Top-down approaches focus on the organization's strategic direction, expected human resource needs, and so forth in order to ensure the organization is equipped to meet its future goals. Although there is a lack of unanimity in terms of how CM should be defined, there does seem to be a common core of CM principles (Shippmann et al., 2000). In particular, competency-based approaches to personnel selection seek to identify attributes employees should possess to ensure that their work behaviors will be consistent with the culture and structure of the organization and will contribute to the organization's overall business strategy (Catano, Wiesner, Hackett, & Methot, 2010; Pearlman & Sanchez, 2010).

Generally, CMs focus on ensuring that the employee attributes that are valued in personnel selection will facilitate success at the organization level is praiseworthy and provides a needed counterbalance to the more narrow focus of WA. Unfortunately, the process of CM has been characterized as lacking sufficient methodological rigor (Shippmann et al., 2000), which causes serious concern within the litigious environment of preemployment testing (Cascio & Aguinis, 2005). Moreover, the human attributes or competencies that CM promotes have been described as "troubling concepts, because their multi-faceted nature makes them unlikely to meet well-accepted criteria for construct validity" (Sanchez & Levine, 2009, p. 58). For personnel selection purposes, the overly broad, multifaceted nature of competencies virtually precludes their unambiguous linkage to well-established personality tests that are relied upon in typical preemployment testing practices (but see Lievens & Sanchez, 2007).

In sum, the above overview of traditional WA and CM methodologies suggests that they tend to be ill-suited to linking personality traits to work performance. Whereas traditional WA can be excessively narrow and task focused, CM can be abstract, lacking in both detail and methodological rigor. What is needed is a literature review that consolidates research findings with respect to those studies that were conducted for the specific purpose of identifying the most promising personality traits to target in preemployment testing and related functions.

Current POWA Research

In light of the limitations of current work analytic methods for uncovering job-relevant personality variables, we searched and reviewed the POWA literature. Our literature review identified two general methodological approaches to conducting POWA. First, the *behavioral approach* asks SMEs to rate a set of behavioral statements on the extent to which each is manifested on the job or is viewed as important for job outcomes. Second, the *trait approach* asks SMEs to rate a set of individual traits on the extent to which the trait is helpful, or harmful, for job outcomes. We review studies falling into each of these approaches to POWA, as well as other studies advocating unique approaches. Following this, we review critical areas of research that appear to be underdeveloped in the POWA literature. We begin, however, by defining POWA and explaining our consideration of validity and reliability as it applies to POWA.

POWA Definition, Validity, and Reliability

We adopted the following definition of POWA: The systematic investigation of (a) work role requirements and (b) the broader context within which work roles are enacted *with a specific focus on the personality substrate of work* (adapted from the WA definition provided by Morgeson & Dierdorff, 2011). At its core, we suggest that an effective POWA allows one to advance strong inferences regarding the personality variables that are likely to facilitate performance in a particular job or set of work behaviors. This is consistent with Morgeson and Campion's (2000) suggestion to focus on the *validity of the inferences* made in WA, as opposed to accuracy of the data itself, which cannot be known definitively (see Sanchez & Levine, 2000, for problems with the accuracy-based model). While the focus on accuracy assumes there are "true scores" underlying the data (e.g., regarding the level of proficiency needed to complete some specific task), we posit that POWA focuses on inferences regarding the extent to which a trait is relevant to job performance in a given job. Therefore, persuasive evidence of the validity of a POWA technique accrues to the extent that the technique identifies traits that are empirically correlated with a targeted outcome such as job performance (see SIOP, 2003). Stronger validity investigations of this sort may identify work outcomes through WA and adopt rigorous measures of the outcomes (e.g., Goffin et al., 2011). Weaker designs may attempt to measure outcomes by employing "proxy" variables, such as respondents' perceptions of their potential performance in a job in which they have never worked (Fraboni, 1995) or job interview scores (e.g., Costa, McCrae, & Kay, 1995). When a weaker design has been used, we are less convinced of the technique's validity given that the criteria are not direct and rigorous measures of job outcomes. In addition to criterion-validity evidence, a valuable design component of a POWA-validity investigation includes an assessment of the extent to which the POWA technique produces different profiles of trait-relevance scores across jobs that are expected to vary on trait requirements (e.g., Raymark, Schmit, & Guion, 1997). This sheds light on the extent to which the POWA methodology produces job-relevance information that discriminates across jobs.

Of course, supporting the validity of a POWA technique requires reliability of measurement. In the case of multi-item scales that assess trait relevance, such as those used in the behavioral approach, the items must be internally consistent (e.g., Raymark et al., 1997). When multiple raters are involved, interrater reliability becomes a concern. Zero-order correlations, intraclass correlations, and the like provide information about the proportion of systematic variance attributable to raters and the across-rater consistency of the ratings (see Goffin et al., 2011). In a similar vein, one could also consider interrater agreement (i.e., consensus). For example, rater agreement would be high if every rater indicated that a trait was "highly relevant" to job outcomes (e.g., O'Neill, Lewis, & Carswell, 2011). Interrater agreement is a useful supplement to interrater correlations because correlations assess consistency of ratings, whereas interrater agreement assesses similarity, in terms of absolute levels, of ratings. Strong reliability provides the foundation for the validity of any POWA technique.

Behavioral Approach

Personality-Related Position Requirements Form

OVERVIEW OF METHOD

Raymark et al. (1997) developed the Personality-Related Position Requirements Form (PPRF), an off-the-shelf assessment tool, which asks respondents to indicate the extent to which each of a list of 107 personality-linked behavioral statements is required for job performance. Traits with high ratings are viewed as likely to be required for effective job performance. Based on responses to the behavioral statements, the PPRF provides scores on the Big Five factors as well as on 12 narrow traits subsumed within the Big Five.

RATING SCALE

The common item stem is "effective performance in this position requires the person to," and following this stem is each of the 107 statements of the PPRF. The response scale includes 0 (*not required*), 1 (*helpful*), and 2 (*essential*) (see Figure 11.1a).

RATING SOURCE

The instructions indicate that the PPRF can be completed by incumbents, supervisors, or panels. However, a test publishing agency that has marketed the companion instrument (see Guion, 2011; Guion, Highhouse, Reeve, & Zickar, 2005) posited that any individual who is highly familiar with the position can provide ratings (Sequential Employment Testing, 2011). In addition, that agency recommended that at least 10 individuals per position complete the inventory.

VALIDITY EVIDENCE

In their empirical evaluation of the PPRF, Raymark et al. (1997) had 283 respondents in 12 occupations complete the PPRF. Scale scores of the extent to which the jobs require the 12 PPRF narrow traits were generally not highly correlated, thereby supporting their distinctiveness (correlations ranged from .13 to .68; median = .35). Alpha coefficients for the scale scores were in the acceptable range, from a low of .60 to a high of .90. Interrater reliability was also high for the 12 narrow traits within occupations, ranging from .76 to .92. Average interrater reliabilities for four *individual jobs* in which there were multiple raters for each job ranged from .85 to .97.

(a) Effective performance in this position requires the person to lead group activities through exercise of power and authority.

Not Required	**Helpful**	**Essential**
☐	☐	☐

(b) Is not easily irritated by others.

Does Not Improve Performance	**Minimally** Improves Performance	**Moderately** Improves Performance	**Substantially** Improves Performance
0	1	2	3

(c) Abstract interpretations of information must be made.

1	2	3	4	5	6	7
Extremely	*Moderately*	*Slightly*	*Neutral*	*Slightly*	*Moderately*	*Extremely*

UNCHARACTERISTIC of my job (1–3)   **CHARACTERISTIC** of my job (5–7)

(d) ABASEMENT

- Individual accepts blame and criticism during this clerkship rotation, even when not deserved.

-2	-1	0	+1	+2
Disastrous effect on performance in this clerkship rotation	Negative effect on performance in this clerkship rotation	No effect on performance in this clerkship rotation	Would help person perform successfully in this clerkship rotation	Essential for successful performance in this clerkship rotation

(e) How <u>important</u> is WRITING to the performance of *your current job*?

Not Important	Somewhat Important	Important	Very Important	Extremely Important
•	•	•	•	•

Figure 11.1 Rating Scales Used in POWA. (a) Rating Scale Proposed by Raymark, Schmit, and Guion (1997), (b) Rating Scale Proposed by Hogan and Holland (2002), (c) Rating Scale Proposed by Fraboni (1995), (d) Rating Scale Proposed by Goffin et al. (2011) (Only the Partial Trait Definition Is Included—See Goffin et al. for the Full Trait Definitions, Instructions, and Rating Form), and (e) Rating Scale Proposed by Hubbard, McCloy, and Campbell (2000).

Raymark et al. found substantial differences in the PPRF profile shapes across the 12 occupations, thereby supporting the PPRF's discriminating potential. An exception was for conscientiousness-related variables, but this may be reflective of conscientiousness being required for most of the occupations studied.

In a follow-up study on the PPRF, Cucina, Vasilopoulos, and Sehgal (2005) provided mixed evidence regarding the PPRF's ability to identify personality variables that were predictive of university student grade-point average (GPA). Some of the traits within openness to experience and conscientiousness were identified by the PPRF as "helpful" for academic performance, and these personality factors were in fact predictive of GPA. However, general leadership and emotional stability were also identified as "helpful" for academic performance, but the relevant personality factors were not associated with GPA. Cucina et al. also found that 6%–18% of the variance in PPRF ratings was explained by respondent personality, which suggests that the raters' own personality characteristics tended to bias their requirement ratings of PPRF variables.

EVALUATION OF THE PPRF

The PPRF is likely one of the more credible, publicly available approaches to POWA that was developed using a strong program of research (Aguinis, Mazurkiewicz, & Heggestad, 2009), and we further discuss the PPRF under *Rater Training*. There are, however, at least five potential limitations to consider. First, Raymark et al.'s investigation did not involve a consideration of the validity of SME ratings for predicting actual trait–performance correlations. That is, we are aware of no study in which actual personality–job performance correlations were predicted by PPRF trait-requirement ratings. Cucina et al. (2005) reported some evidence of validity, but this was within a student sample that relied on an artificial scenario and criterion (GPA rather than job performance); hence, generalizability to employees is uncertain. Second, the PPRF response scale does not allow the rater to indicate whether the personality variable could be harmful for job performance (Goffin et al., 2011). For example, imagine if the cluster of "cooperative or collaborative work tendency" was rated as "not required" for job performance, but the job heavily involved negotiations that required assertive and/or aggressive behaviors. In reality, the cooperation dimension may be a valid predictor of performance but in the negative direction of association. The PPRF would overlook such bidirectional relations. Third, the PPRF attributes are not explicitly mapped onto an established personality trait measure (Goffin et al.); therefore, the job analyst is left to infer connections between PPRF dimensions and personality scales himself or herself (e.g., Millon, 1994). Fourth, although the 12 narrow traits were organized under the Big Five taxonomy, most traits were found to be keyed on more than one personality factor (see Cucina et al., 2005), and the Big Five taxonomy itself is likely a deficient framework for predicting all work behaviors (see Hough, 1992; O'Neill & Hastings, 2010). Fifth, Raymark et al. did not have extensive coverage of blue-collar jobs defined by the "things" factor of Functional Job Analysis, which means that the PPRF's usefulness for those jobs is unclear.

The Performance Improvement Characteristics Form

OVERVIEW OF METHOD

The Performance Improvement Characteristics (PIC) form was developed in order to identify which of the seven broad factors measured by the Hogan Personality Inventory (HPI; Hogan & Hogan, 1992) will be most predictive of job performance in a given job (Hogan & Holland, 2002). The PIC comprises 5–9 items per factor and has a total of 48 items. Items targeting each factor are averaged in order to obtain a trait-relevance score for each of the seven factors.

RATING SCALE

A 4-point response scale is intended to identify the extent to which each item, assigned to one of the seven HPI factors, may be helpful for job performance. The 4-point scale uses anchors ranging from 0 (*does not improve performance*) to 4 (*substantially improves performance*) (see Figure 11.1b). For example, a PIC item assessing the trait relevance of the Prudence factor is "Rarely deviates from standard procedures" (Hogan & Holland, 2002, p. 4).

RATING SOURCE

Hogan and Holland (2002) reported that all participants completing the PIC form were "subject matter experts" (p. 5). We assume this term referred to anyone familiar with the job, as the response format does not imply that participants must be job incumbents (it does not use a personal referent, such as "my job").

VALIDITY EVIDENCE

Hogan and Holland (2002) reported internal consistency reliabilities ranging from .76 for Adjustment to .87 for Likeability. Test–retest reliabilities averaged .72 after 3 months. Hogan and Holland also reported substantially different profiles across six jobs (e.g., cashier, sales, office manager), thereby supporting the PIC's ability to differentiate trait relevance across jobs. Tett, Holland, Hogan, and Burnett (2002) used meta-analytic moderator correlations in order to investigate the validity of the PIC. Correlations between PIC trait-relevance ratings and actual HPI trait validities, averaged across studies, should be high to the extent that the PIC can identify job-relevant personality variables. Meta-analysis summarizing 30 studies involving the HPI revealed that four of the seven HPI personality scales had positive meta-analytic correlations between PIC ratings and validity coefficients. This range was from .12 (Likeability) to .40 (Adjustment). Three of the HPI traits, however, had validity coefficients that were negatively related to PIC ratings: Ambition (−.09), School Success (−.16), and Intellectance (−.28), suggesting that PIC ratings were actually inversely related to criterion validities for these factors. Interestingly, PIC ratings displayed a tendency to correlate positively with mean incumbent levels of HPI traits across jobs (i.e., studies). This finding suggests that SMEs using the PIC may be swayed as much by the personality traits of current employees in the target jobs as they are by the actual demands of the job.

EVALUATION OF THE PIC

Although Tett et al.'s (2002) meta-analytic study was not strongly supportive of the PIC's ability to identify job-relevant personality factors, there were a couple of limitations to that study. First, the proportion of variance explained by artifacts tended to be quite large, leaving little residual variance across studies for most traits to exhibit differential validity. Thus, finding support for PIC predictions in the form of positive correlations with trait validities may have been statistically unlikely. Another interpretational difficulty was the small sample size of 30 studies, which introduces concerns about the stability of correlations between trait validities and PIC scores. Of course, the response format of the PIC potentially suffers from the same problem of the PPRF in that neither allows for bidirectionality of trait–criterion linkages. That is, choosing the response option *does not improve performance* could mean that the trait is unrelated to job performance or that it is negatively related to job outcomes. This could reduce the validity of PIC ratings. Overcoming one of the PPRF limitations, the PIC items were developed deductively. Thus, the linkage between items and specific personality factors was at the forefront from the beginning of test development instead of later. This has the advantages of allowing easier mapping of PIC results onto an established personality measure that can then be used for selection or other purposes.

The Work Activities and Situations Inventory

OVERVIEW OF METHOD

The Work Activities and Situations Inventory (WASI) provides scores for each of the 15 traits measured by the Jackson Personality Inventory (JPI; Jackson, 1994) and 12 values measured by the Work Value Survey (WVS; Fraboni & Jackson, 1992; as cited in Fraboni, 1995). There are eight items per scale, both positively and negatively keyed, that can be averaged in order to provide scores that are intended to reflect the potential behavioral manifestations of each trait or value within work contexts. A trait with high scores under this POWA technique should imply that individuals scoring high on the trait will perform better in the job, and be more satisfied, because the behaviors manifested on the job will be consistent with the individual's personality (Fraboni, 1995).

RATING SCALE

The WASI asks raters to indicate the extent to which the behavior in the item is characteristic of his or her job using a 7-point scale ranging from *extremely uncharacteristic of my job* to *extremely characteristic of my job* (see Figure 11.1c). For example, a positively keyed trait complexity item is "Abstract interpretations of information must be made" (Fraboni, 1995, p. 43).

RATING SOURCE

Given that the rating scale response options include references to "my job," it would appear that Fraboni (1995) intended that job incumbents complete the WASI. This is likely because the items are largely behavioral, and incumbents are typically purported to be in a good position to report on daily, on-the-job behavior by virtue of their direct experience (e.g., Goldstein et al., 1993).

VALIDITY EVIDENCE

Fraboni (1995) examined whether incumbents would generate profiles that reliably distinguished personality and value-related manifestations of traits and values across jobs. Incumbents working in 12 jobs completed the POWA forms for personality and work values and then these profiles were correlated across jobs. Low correlations would suggest that incumbents discriminated personality and value-related manifestations across jobs. Indeed, most profile correlations were sufficiently low to suggest that the WASI variables were differentially manifested across jobs (e.g., telecommunication engineer and vocational counselor correlated at .12), and jobs with similar content did in fact produce high-profile correlations (e.g., sales coordinator and senior sales coordinator correlated at .91).

Fraboni (1995) asked university students to rate their estimated levels of job performance and satisfaction after reading job descriptions derived from interviews with individuals in 5 of the 12 jobs studied earlier (i.e., in the second study). Participants also self-reported their personality and work values by completing the JPI and the WVS. Having already collected the WASI data from incumbents in the second study, profile comparisons via correlations between the POWA variable scores and the self-reported personality scale scores created a "fit" estimate. If WASI ratings are reasonably valid, highly similar profiles of WASI scale scores and self-rated personality and values scale scores should result in perceptions of greater performance and satisfaction in those five jobs. Across the five jobs, the average correlation between the fit estimate and perceptions of job performance was .13; the average correlation between fit and perceptions of job satisfaction was .44.

EVALUATION OF THE WASI

Importantly, Fraboni's (1995) WASI overcomes some limitations of the PPRF that were discussed above. First, Fraboni developed items deductively from two assessments: the JPI (Jackson, 1994) and the WVS (Fraboni & Jackson, 1992; as cited in Fraboni, 1995). Second, the nature of the response scale allows for bidirectional relations between traits and job relevance, which potentially results in more information regarding the direction of trait–criterion linkages (see also Goffin et al., 2011, below). Third, the focus is on traits with narrow definitions, which avoids problems of multidimensionality wherein components of a broad factor may be differentially relevant to the job. Fraboni reasoned that narrow traits might also have the advantage of being less prone to the "Barnum effect," which, in the present context, would result in POWA statements being so general that they are viewed as relevant (or irrelevant) to virtually any job. Not being tied to the Big Five taxonomy allows for a consideration of a broader range of traits, some of which would be underrepresented by the Big Five (e.g., Risk Taking, Energy Level; Paunonen & Jackson, 1996).

The main limitation of Fraboni's (1995) work is that the sample used to investigate validity involved correlating students' perceptions of what their job performance and satisfaction would be in jobs they had likely not experienced. Thus, their actual job performance and satisfaction in those jobs could not be ascertained. Other issues involved some low-scale reliabilities (e.g., α was .28 for Empathy), and the rating scale that elicits a rating regarding the extent to which a variable is "characteristic of the job." It is not clear whether a variable that is rated as characteristic of the job would actually be indicative of whether the variable is needed for effective job performance or, as Fraboni intended, job satisfaction.

Trait Approach

Goffin et al. (2011)

OVERVIEW OF METHOD

Goffin et al. (2011) investigated their POWA technique in a sample of medical interns who were trainees that had rotated through six "jobs." The jobs were 6-week clerkship rotations in the following areas of specialization: Family Medicine, Internal Medicine, Obstetrics, Pediatrics, Psychiatry, and Surgery. A pool of 21 potentially job-relevant personality traits was identified for use in the POWA using the input of two industrial and organizational (I/O) psychologists, an M.D. familiar with the positions, and two senior I/O graduate students. Trait definitions were adapted from their respective manuals with the POWA process in mind (i.e., that they should be descriptive of job-relevant behavior). In order to maximize the validity of the ratings, 15 raters received training involving an overview of the purpose of the POWA exercise, the trait definitions, and the rating scale, followed by an opportunity to practice the POWA rating technique on two hypothetical positions.

RATING SCALE

As shown in Figure 11.1d, the trait rating scales utilized anchors ranging from *disastrous effect on performance in this clerkship rotation* (−2) to *essential for successful performance in this clerkship rotation* (+2), and included an option for *no effect on performance in this clerkship rotation* (0).

RATING SOURCE

Fifteen medical doctor trainees who had completed the six job rotations were recruited to participate in a 30- to 60-min POWA rating session. During this rating session, the trainees completed POWA ratings for each of the six job rotations in which they had already worked. The logic of using interns as the rating source was that they had completed all six positions, allowing them to potentially (a) make relative distinctions between trait-relevance ratings across jobs and (b) have a strong understanding of the job requirements by virtue of recent experience in all the positions.

VALIDITY EVIDENCE

A total of 330 trainees who had completed the six rotations filled out established personality inventories measuring all 21 of the traits that were rated in the POWA. Additionally, job performance ratings for each intern's effectiveness in each of the six medical specialties were obtained from their supervisors. The unique feature of having personality scores on the 21 traits from 330 trainees and criterion data reflective of job performance in each of the six positions allowed Goffin et al. (2011) to report criterion validities across traits and jobs. The effectiveness of their POWA technique, therefore, could be investigated by considering whether their POWA trait-relevance ratings collected from the 15 medical trainees were associated with actual trait validities. Accordingly, criterion validities of the 21 personality traits were correlated with SME trait-relevance ratings, yielding one correlation for each of the six positions. The POWA ratings were predictive of criterion validities at r = .42, on average, with a range from .17 (psychiatry) to .62 (internal medicine). Moreover, the trait-relevance ratings were highly reliable, ranging from .81 (obstetrics) to .94 (psychiatry).

EVALUATION OF GOFFIN ET AL. (2011)

There are a few aspects of Goffin et al.'s POWA technique and research methodology that may be advantageous. First, their trait-relevance rating format makes it salient to the respondent that personality traits can be positively, negatively, or unrelated to job outcomes (see Figure 11.1d). Second, asking respondents who had recently experienced numerous positions to provide job-relevance ratings may have emphasized across-job differences in personality trait relevance. Most other studies reviewed appear to have used SMEs who had recently only participated in rating a single job. When rating a single job, the desirability of the trait, or some other bias, may be expected to drive ratings more so than when across-job differences are less salient. Third, the medical interns who provided the POWA ratings were likely quite high on cognitive ability because of the admission requirements for medical school. Fourth, it seems quite plausible that the training procedure completed by each of the 15 POWA respondents was instrumental to obtaining valid POWA ratings. We examine more closely Goffin et al.'s training protocol shortly. Regarding their study methodology, it is advantageous that the validity of Goffin et al.'s technique was rigorously evaluated by considering the capacity for trait-relevance ratings to predict actual criterion-validity coefficients in different jobs. This provides a strong test of their POWA technique.

Neuroticism–Extraversion–Openness Job Profiler

OVERVIEW OF METHOD

The Neuroticism–Extraversion–Openness (NEO) Job Profiler (Costa et al., 1995) provides trait-relevance scores for the 30 facets underlying the FFM, as measured by the NEO Personality Inventory—Revised (PI-R) (Costa & McCrae, 1992). It is a form that lists and defines each personality variable and asks SMEs to rate each on its desirability for job performance.

RATING SCALE

The 4-point rating scale ranges from −2 (*very undesirable*) to +2 (*very desirable*). SMEs are asked to only provide ratings for traits considered relevant. Traits considered irrelevant receive a score of 0.

RATING SOURCE

Costa et al. (1995) recommend that the NEO Job Profiler be completed by job analysts, supervisors, or incumbents who are successful on the job. The individual completing the NEO Job

Profiler is asked to draw on his or her knowledge of the job in order to report on the desirability of each facet for the position; thus, one would expect that only individuals familiar with the position should be included.

VALIDITY EVIDENCE

Costa et al. (1995) conducted an empirical evaluation of the NEO Job Profiler in a sample of police officers. Their prediction was that police officers who were recommended for advancement would have different NEO facet scores than would police officers recommended with reservations or not recommended, and that the NEO Job Profiler should predict these differences. The results were mixed. On the one hand, there was partial support for the validity of the NEO Job Profiler, as facets judged to be very desirable or very undesirable tended to be associated with differences in interviewer recommendations. On the other hand, however, there were notable exceptions. For example, individuals high on Tender-Mindedness, Trust, and Compliance tended to be recommended for a position, but job experts rated these traits as *undesirable* for the job. This may be partly due to the use of interview recommendations as a criterion for judging the validity of the NEO Job Profiler, however, as this is, at best, only an indirect assessment of job performance that may have been potentially confounded by levels of these trait variables.

EVALUATION OF NEO JOB PROFILER

The fact that Costa et al.'s (1995) empirical findings regarding the NEO Job Profiler were mixed suggests that more research is needed before implementing this tool. This is particularly important because the interview criterion they used would not be perfectly correlated with job performance, which would likely result in even lower associations between trait-relevance ratings and actual on-the-job performance. Furthermore, an obvious limitation is that the user would be restricted to the FFM, and, clearly, there are other traits that are of potential interest (see Paunonen & Jackson, 2000). We also see possible causes for concern regarding the trait definitions. They are provided on a bipolar basis, which may not be readily understandable by laypeople, and, considering this, the definitions are surprisingly short (cf. Fraboni, 1995; Goffin et al., 2011). Finally, although Costa et al. recommended that the instrument be used to generate weights for the 30 facets for use in computing an individual's composite score, no validity evidence was provided for this practice. Reliabilities were also recommended to be calculated on these composite scores, but, to our knowledge, none have been reported.

Other POWA Studies

In addition to the behavioral and trait approaches to POWA, we found a few empirical POWA studies not fitting well into these categories. Detrick and Chibnall (2006) illustrated an approach to POWA that involved asking 100 police trainers to think of the best entry-level law enforcement officer that they had supervised and to rate that officer's personality using the NEO observer-report form (see Costa & McCrae, 1992). The NEO observer-report form is an adapted form that is used for collecting "peer" ratings of personality. The averages of the trainers' ratings of each employee's personality traits were expected to provide a personality profile of an "ideal" police officer. The main drawback to the profile approach used by Detrick and Chibnall (2006) is that its method of application in a selection context has not been extensively researched. Another concern is that POWA ratings targeted toward a specific incumbent's personality are likely to contain some person-specific idiosyncrasies. Thus, the potential of the "ideal employee" approach, as well as profile approaches in general, remains uncertain.

In a study of military officers, Sumer, Sumer, Demirutku, and Cifci (2001) conducted semistructured interviews in order to identify the qualities and attributes of individuals that were needed for effective performance. Perhaps not surprisingly, transcripts of the interviews essentially resulted in a "laundry list" of 72 trait-like attributes. Each of these attributes was then rated on its (a) relevance to the job and (b) importance to the job. Relevance and importance ratings of each trait were then multiplied. The matrix of correlations among the relevance × importance ratings was then submitted to factor analysis with the goal of uncovering factors of personality-related variables that would be potentially related to successful performance in the military. We do not consider Sumer et al.'s factor-analytic findings in detail, however, as application of factor analysis on importance ratings has conceptual difficulties that render substantive interpretations problematic (but see also Hogan & Holland, 2002). As noted by Cranny and Doherty (1988), factor analyses of such ratings do not produce factors underlying the job—they produce factors consisting of systematic disagreement of job experts in the importance of traits across jobs. Thus, their meaning is likely to be misinterpreted and would rarely be of interest. More generally, our feeling is that asking SMEs to simply enumerate the qualities needed for the job is not likely to lead to valuable insights into the job relevance of personality traits.

Jenkins and Griffith (2004) reported that their POWA identified four traits as potentially relevant to the position of accountant. A personality scale measuring the four traits—Warmth, Emotional Stability, Openness to Change, and Understanding—was subsequently developed. A criterion-validation study found that only their measure of Emotional Stability failed to relate significantly and positively to job performance. Moreover, the scale developed for selection was viewed more positively by incumbents in that they rated its relevance for job performance higher than the relevance of traits in the 16PF, which they also completed. This supports POWA techniques that result in measurement of traits that potentially have greater face validity, thereby increasing positive applicant reactions.

Key Underdeveloped Areas in Existing Research

Trait Activation Theory

One gap in the research reviewed above is that there tends to be little theory underlying the POWA methodologies employed. Most current theorizing seems to be limited to assuming that if a trait or behavior is judged to be relevant for performance in a particular job, then employees high on that trait will be stronger performers than are employees low on that trait. In order to address this gap, Tett and Burnett (2003) offered trait activation theory (see Chapter 5, this volume). Trait activation theory goes beyond the identification of trait–performance linkages by attempting to identify the situational features that make a trait relevant to performance in a given job. It attempts to explain *why* a trait may be relevant. As summarized by Tett and Christiansen (2008), trait activation theory posits that (a) personality traits may be viewed as latent propensities to engage in certain behaviors, (b) traits become activated by situations that carry trait-relevant cues, and (c) trait-related behavior positively affects job performance when that behavior is valued by the organization. Accordingly, the role of POWA may be to uncover the traits that will be activated by situational cues in the employment environment and that also have implications for job performance.

One characteristic of trait activation theory important to POWA is that it identifies potential classes and levels of situational features that may have implications for whether a trait will be relevant for job performance. In this regard, trait activation theory provides a bridge that facilitates the importation of desirable CM features, such as a consideration of the organization's strategy and its business goals, into the POWA methodology. As we noted earlier, traditional WA has tended to overlook these organization-level issues (but see Dierdorff, Rubin, & Morgeson, 2009; Shippmann et al., 2000). Another advantage of trait activation theory is that it provides theoretical explanations and a theoretical framework that promotes an understanding of why traits are needed for effective job performance. Finally, trait activation theory directs attention to multiple levels: task, social, and organizational (we discuss these in more detail under "Future Research Needs in POWA"). Previous approaches to POWA (reviewed above) have not addressed all three, which suggests untapped potential. Accordingly, we see trait activation theory as a valuable, and currently underresearched, framework for influencing the future development of POWA methodology.

Applications of O*NET in POWA

Another area of potential relevance to POWA is the Occupational Information Network, also known as the O*NET (see Peterson et al., 2001). O*NET is an occupational database that contains WA information on over 900 occupations and 25,000 jobs involving over 100,000 incumbents (Coaster & Christiansen, 2009; Morgeson & Dierdorff, 2011). The most applicable feature of the O*NET content model for POWA is likely its work styles, which comprise 7 higher-order and 17 lower-order constructs resembling personality variables that may be relevant to job outcomes (Peterson et al., 2001). A database of importance ratings, completed with scales such as the one shown in Figure 11.1e, was completed by job incumbents in order to link work styles to jobs (Hubbard, McCloy, & Campbell, 2000). Given its tremendous potential for offering trait-relevance information that links work styles to job performance in a multitude of jobs, there is a need to review some preliminary research that has investigated the potential value of the O*NET for conducting POWA. We uncovered three such studies.

Coaster and Christiansen (2009) adopted a meta-analytic approach to investigating the validity of O*NET work style ratings. A total of 154 studies containing correlations between Big Five personality variables and job performance was collected from the research literature. Each study was assigned an occupational code using the O*NET classification system. For each occupation, the O*NET importance ratings for 16 work styles were recorded. Each work style was mapped onto the closest-resembling Big Five personality factor (e.g., Cooperation was mapped onto agreeableness; Initiative was mapped onto conscientiousness). If the O*NET work style importance ratings have any validity for use in POWA, then importance ratings for each Big Five variable should be associated with the validity coefficients obtained from the primary studies coded into occupational classifications. Correlations between importance ratings and validity coefficients across Big Five factors were as follows: extraversion (.15), openness to experience (.14), agreeableness (.01), emotional stability (–.03), and conscientiousness (–.16). Thus, O*NET importance ratings of work values had some validity for extraversion and openness to experience, but there was essentially no validity for agreeableness and emotional stability, and there was an inverse relation for conscientiousness.

Dierdorff and Morgeson (2009) employed variance component analyses of responsibility, knowledge, skill, and trait importance ratings. It was theorized that responsibilities, knowledge, and skill ratings would have more variance attributable to the construct measured than to idiosyncratic rater bias compared to work style ratings. Dierdorff and Morgeson's rationale was that personality ratings are highly abstract, unobservable, and unspecific, causing them to be more difficult to rate and, hence, open to subjectivities that translate into rater idiosyncrasies that constitute error. In support of their prediction, work style ratings had approximately twice as much rater-attributable variance than did responsibility, knowledge, and skill categories of the O*NET importance ratings. Moreover, inter-rater reliability analyses revealed an average-weighted coefficient of .45 for work styles, versus .65 for responsibilities, .70 for knowledge, and .69 for skill. Dierdorff and Morgeson interpreted these findings as suggesting that traits, being difficult to observe and highly abstract, require an inferential leap that is perhaps too great for obtaining strong measurement properties.

Tett and Anderson (2011) investigated whether O*NET job descriptions could be used to identify personality traits predictive of job performance in 16 managerial occupations. Criterion-validity evidence, in the form of multisource performance ratings collected with a proprietary measure, the

CPI 260® (Gough & Bradley, 2005), was available on the 16 managerial occupations. The 16 managerial occupations were mapped onto O*NET job titles in order to obtain O*NET job descriptions. Next, five SMEs inspected the job descriptions and rated the relevance of 25 personality variables for each job. These relevance ratings were rated on a scale including 1 (*relevance clearly stated in the O*NET information*), 2 (*relevance implied*), and 3 (*relevance not demonstrated*). The findings indicated that traits identified as relevant to job performance did not have stronger average trait validities than did the average validity coefficients computed across all jobs (i.e., the trait's baseline validity for the jobs included). The authors concluded that O*NET job descriptions contain insufficient detail to permit accurate trait-relevance ratings.

In light of the three aforementioned studies, it would appear that the O*NET work style ratings, and job descriptions, offer limited opportunity for POWA. In some respects, this is not surprising. First, ratings of work styles employ an importance rating scale that does not allow for bidirectionality (see Figure 11.1e). Second, definitions of work styles are very broad and abstract (Dierdorff & Morgeson, 2009). This leaves the respondent having to apply his or her own idiosyncratic interpretation to work style meanings. Similarly, job descriptions in the O*NET are likely to be too broad as the personality-related requirements of the job were not correctly identified by SMEs who had studied the job descriptions (Tett & Anderson, 2011). Given the difficulty of inferring linkages between work role requirements to human capabilities and attributes, broad and abstract descriptions should be avoided (Morgeson & Dierdorff, 2011). Moreover, it seems likely that job incumbents providing the importance ratings in this research had little training to assist them in making valid trait-relevance inferences. This begs the question: What type of training can be used to improve the validity of trait-relevance ratings? We address this issue next as we explore current best practices in POWA.

Current "Best Practices" in POWA

We suggest that there are currently at least three critical issues involved in maximizing the value of POWA. First, the extent to which respondents who provide POWA ratings may benefit from POWA training deserves further consideration. Second, special attention needs to be paid to the construction of the POWA rating forms. Third, selection of the individuals who provide POWA ratings is also in need of research. Our best-practice recommendations are based on current research on POWA and, in some cases, general WA research.

Rater Training

As the literature we review below suggests, it is essential to provide appropriate training to individuals who are involved in the POWA. Because all forms of POWA are at least minimally subject to human judgment, biases are always a potential threat to validity. For example, as incumbents may routinely be the source of the trait-relevance ratings, self-serving biases may occur such that the employee rates socially desirable traits as needed for effective job performance. Implicit trait biases may also occur such that the employee rates the job relevance of each trait in accordance with his or her own perceived trait scores (Aguinis et al., 2009; Morgeson & Campion, 1997). Indeed, both Cucina et al. (2005) and Aguinis et al. (2009) found evidence supporting the existence of these biases when extensive rater training was absent. These biases have the potential to lead to systematic inflation of trait-relevance ratings, and the job analyst would be wise to employ training interventions that have the potential to minimize rater bias. We are aware of three studies that have described POWA rater training procedures in detail, which we consider below.

Aguinis et al. (2009) reported on an experimental field study demonstrating the potential effectiveness of frame-of-reference (FOR) training on trait-relevance ratings using the PPRF. In the standard instructions condition, participants received the typical PPRF instructions, which ask the participant to rate the extent to which each item describes the job using the 3-point scale shown in Figure 11.1a. In the FOR training condition, the instructions were much more elaborate. Examples were provided in order to demonstrate how to use the rating form. Respondents were told to consider not how they perform the job, but how anyone should perform the job in order to be successful. This may minimize the occurrence of ratings that are reflective of idiosyncratic work behaviors. Incumbents also completed three "practice" trait-relevance ratings based on short scenario vignettes, and feedback was provided. Finally, after completing the instructions and training, job incumbents in each condition completed the PPRF for their current position. Both conditions were administered on computer.

Across the Big Five personality factors and the six jobs analyzed, Aguinis et al. (2009) reported correlations between incumbents' own personality scores and their PPRF trait-relevance scores that averaged .20 lower in the FOR training condition compared to the standard instructions condition. Moreover, *d* values measuring the standardized difference in PPRF trait-relevance ratings between FOR training and standard instructions conditions were around .50, suggesting that the FOR training condition reduced inflation of POWA ratings. Interrater reliability was also superior in the FOR training condition in four of the six positions rated.

Lievens and Sanchez (2007) used a quasi-experimental design to investigate the effect of FOR training on job-relevance ratings of competencies. Human resource practitioners were randomly assigned to either a FOR training or control condition. In the FOR training condition, raters participated in a 1-day training workshop in which they (a) were introduced to CM and were given a historical overview, (b) were provided with a list of 40 defined competencies along with behavioral examples of each, (c) conducted a retranslation activity in which trainees were asked to recategorize the behavioral examples into appropriate competencies, (d) discussed their categorizations from the retranslation phase and received feedback from the facilitator, (e) learned to use a rating scale for linking competencies to jobs (1 = *essential*, 2 = *important*, 3 = *not important*) (i.e., similar to Figure 11.1a), (f) read job descriptions for two jobs and practiced the competency-relevance rating task, and (g) obtained feedback on these practice ratings. The control group received a day-long training session on a selection-interview technique. One week after the training was administered, the experimental- and control-group participants were asked to independently provide job-relevance ratings of competencies for the job of "method engineer." A job description was provided along with background information regarding the company's history, products, and business objectives.

The results of Lievens and Sanchez's (2007) study indicated that the ratings collected from those who attended the FOR training program were associated with more favorable properties relative to the control condition. Specifically, variance attributable to competencies in the training condition tended to be nearly twice that of the control condition. This indicates that ratings were more reflective of the competencies involved than of rater idiosyncrasies in the FOR training condition relative to the control condition. Furthermore, reliability of ratings was stronger in the FOR condition. For example, in order to reach an interrater reliability coefficient of .70, nine raters were needed in the control condition, whereas only four were needed in the FOR condition. The most favorable ratings, however, were obtained from seasoned experts. These individuals were consultants who had received the FOR training and subsequently gained 1–5 years of experience in the application of CM. Variance attributable to the competencies being rated was 18% higher, and variance attributable to rater idiosyncrasies was 13% lower, than it was for the less experienced trainees. In order to reach an interrater reliability coefficient of .70, only three expert raters were needed. Finally, there was support for the accuracy of the ratings obtained from those who completed the FOR training; training groups had a greater proportion of correctly identified "essential" competencies than did the control group. This was determined by comparing job-relevance ratings from FOR and control participants against incumbent and trainer job-relevance ratings from the organization in which the method engineer job existed.

Goffin et al. (2011) conducted POWA involving a training program. A sample of 15 SMEs attended 30- to 60-min sessions in which POWA data were collected. Most of these were one-on-one sessions, thereby avoiding potential biasing factors, such as conformity pressures, associated with group contexts (see Morgeson & Campion, 1997). Participants were then given an example rating form and had the meaning of the anchors clearly described (see Figure 11.1d). Next, two positions were described and appropriate job-relevance ratings for extraversion were shown. In one position, sales associate, extraversion was expected to be rated as positively related to job performance. In another position, computer technician, extraversion was expected to be rated as negatively related to job performance. Thus, this example demonstrated the potential for bidirectionality; that is, the same trait could be helpful for performance in one position but harmful for performance in another position. Participants were provided with a description of 21 personality traits identified by the research team as potentially related to job performance in at least one of the six rotations. Trait definitions were adapted from their respective manuals (e.g., NEO, PPRF) in order to reflect the study's context by referring to clerkship-relevant behaviors and directly to the rotations where appropriate. Each trait was extensively described, as shown by two to three bullet points explaining the nature of each trait, and the facilitator pointed out how traits differed from each other. After undergoing this training, participants rated the 21 traits for their relevance to job performance, one rotation at a time. Participants were free to ask the trainer questions at any time.

As discussed earlier, Goffin et al. (2011) found that trait-relevance ratings were predictive of criterion-validity coefficients, and interrater reliability coefficients from the 15 interns who participated in the training were also strong. Likely helpful was the detailed rating form (described further under *Building the POWA Rating Forms*), the two examples demonstrating the potential for bidirectionality of trait–performance linkages, and the one-on-one setting that may have instilled a high level of accountability regarding the ratings. Also note that Goffin et al.'s approach is quite similar to the FOR studies by Aguinis et al. (2009) and Leivens and Sanchez (2007).

Goffin et al.'s training can be summarized as: participants (a) received instructions detailing the purpose of the activity, (b) were given a "Trait Description Sheet" that provided clear and detailed definitions of each trait, (c) reviewed the Trait Description Sheet with the facilitator to further describe less familiar traits and ensure the rater could distinguish each trait, (d) completed a sample rating form that familiarized them with the meaning of the scale anchors, and (e) participated in a practice rating exercise that involved rating the positions of sales associate and computer technician on the extraversion factor. This is essentially a FOR training package.

Taken together, the above findings suggest that the advantages of FOR training principles found in other research and meta-analysis (Woehr & Huffcutt, 1994) seem to generalize to POWA methodology. We therefore recommend that a solid FOR training program be carried out when collecting job-relevance ratings as part of a POWA.

Building the POWA Rating Forms

Almost all of the POWA methodologies involve the use of surveys. One critical issue, therefore, is that the surveys must be designed in a way that maximizes the reliability and validity of the data obtained. In this respect, we see at least three salient issues. Instructions must be clear, the response scale must be chosen carefully, and the breadth of measurement must be considered. We elaborate on these three issues below.

Instructions

It has become evident from reviewing the training procedures above that instructions must be extremely clear regarding the SME trait-relevance rating task. Indeed, SMEs may find that the meaning of trait-relevance ratings is not entirely obvious without detailed and understandable explication. In terms of best practices in POWA survey instruction, it seems that it is preferable to administer instructions in a face-to-face context. First, this communication medium allows for nonverbal communication that may indicate a host of issues resolvable by the job analyst. For example, if the SME appears puzzled, the job analyst can ask if any clarification is needed. Second, face-to-face interaction also allows the SME to request and receive more detail regarding a specific aspect of the rating task either during training or while completing the survey. Third, there is a possibility that SMEs will treat the task more seriously and be more motivated to provide thoughtful, considered responses for which they will feel accountable when in a face-to-face setting. Although Aguinis et al. (2009) used a web-based format, it is possible that even more reliable and valid ratings could have been obtained in face-to-face meetings, such as in Goffin et al. (2011). Until future research sheds light on this issue, we suggest collecting trait-relevance ratings "in person" unless that option is not feasible.

In addition to clear instructions, it may also be necessary to provide examples of how to use the rating scale. Developing a rating booklet that begins with hypothetical scenarios to which the respondent may provide "practice" job-relevant ratings, followed by feedback, would appear promising. Employing Goffin et al.'s (2011) methodology that involved describing how a trait could be helpful in one job but harmful in another job—that is, bidirectionality—would likely help the respondent see that traits are not always related to performance in the same magnitude or direction (O'Neill et al., 2009). Finally, in refining the instructions, it is advisable to conduct pilot studies in order to identify areas for improvement in organization and language in order to further enhance clarity.

Response Format

In light of our literature review and an inspection of the scale response formats shown in Figure 11.1, we believe that a critical, and often overlooked, issue involved in collecting trait-relevance ratings involves the choice of response scale. Our concern is largely with the use of scales that do not allow for bidirectional linkages between performance and traits. For example, the PPRF uses a potentially impoverished scale that only includes three response options: not required, helpful, and essential. Unfortunately, response scales of this nature ignore the possibility that a behavior or trait could be related to job performance *negatively*. That is, they overlook traits and behaviors that could be strong predictors of job performance because they are related negatively to job performance. Rating scales of the type used by Goffin et al. (2011), Fraboni (1995), and Hastings and O'Neill (2009) would appear to accommodate bidirectionality and are, in our view, preferred. We favor these scales because they seem to correspond more clearly to what the job analyst typically wants the SMEs to actually predict, which is the validity coefficient. Moreover, numerous studies—not necessarily POWA focused but still relevant—have used Goffin et al.'s scale, or one very similar, to identify criterion-relevant personality traits with considerable success (Hastings & O'Neill, 2009; O'Neill & Hastings, 2010; O'Neill et al., 2009; Paunonen, 1998; Paunonen & Ashton, 2001). Importance ratings and the like that attempt to tap how "essential" or "required" the trait is for job outcomes appear to have a less strong conceptual linkage to validity coefficients, which could make the rating task more difficult and ambiguous for SMEs. Thus, we see Goffin et al.'s (2011) scale as a promising response format for future POWA research and practice.

Breadth and Specificity

Personality traits are organized hierarchically. Broad personality variables, such as the Big Five, are each composed of numerous facets that represent homogeneous narrow personality traits (see, for example, Paunonen, 1998). As one moves down the hierarchy, the unit-of-analysis becomes more narrow and more information can be obtained when measurement proceeds at that level (for more coverage of the breadth of personality assessment, see Chapter 14, this volume). We believe that there are at least three reasons to include narrow traits in rating forms used for the collection of trait-relevance ratings. First, more information and understanding can be gleaned from narrow, rather than broad, personality variables. Consider the personality factor of conscientiousness. That factor contains different homogeneous traits, such as achievement and order (see Jackson et al., 1996). Clearly, there are jobs where one of these traits could be helpful for job performance and the other could be unimportant or even harmful (e.g., LePine, 2003). Considering only aggregate ratings of trait relevance, that is, the trait relevance of the conscientiousness factor, would overlook the differential prediction of the facets. This could lower the utility of the POWA. Second, it may also be difficult to write specific, precise definitions of broad factors as they are heterogeneous variables comprising numerous noninterchangeable facets (O'Neill & Hastings, 2010). To the extent that broad personality variables have imprecise definitions, our concern is that raters will have difficulty in providing meaningful trait-relevance ratings (Tett & Christiansen, 2007). On the other hand, narrow traits have clear and specific definitions that may encourage valid trait-relevance ratings. Third, when narrow traits are the focus, the job analyst always has the option of staying at the narrow level or aggregating ratings into overall factors. If all narrow traits subsumed within a factor are rated similarly, those ratings can be aggregated into an overall factor score that adequately summarizes the lower-level ratings. But if only factors are measured, there is no possibility of disaggregating those ratings in order to investigate whether SMEs would provide differential trait-relevance ratings across facets of the same factor. Accordingly, we suggest that trait-relevance ratings include the narrow-trait level. If space permits, job-relevance ratings could also be collected at the factor level (e.g., as in Goffin et al., 2011).

There is the issue of specificity on the criterion side of the equation, too. In the event that job performance is multidimensional, which it almost certainly is (Campbell, Gasser, & Oswald, 1996; Murphy & Shiarella, 1997), traits and behaviors could be linked to specific dimensions of the job. Alternatively, as suggested by Tett and Burnett's (2003) trait activation theory, traits could be relevant to different aspects of the work environment, such as the task, social, or organizational levels. One obvious drawback of linking traits or behaviors to specific facets of job performance is the increased burden placed on raters, because many more ratings will be required. Another potential drawback is that research on criterion measurement has found that multidimensional job performance ratings tend to load highly on a single factor (Viswesvaran, Schmidt, & Ones, 2005), which potentially limits the payoffs of asking raters to consider narrow elements of the criterion. Thus, at present, it seems practically and scientifically acceptable to link traits to job performance using relevance ratings for the position, but in some instances, there may be interest in making linkages to job dimensions or other features (e.g., features at the task, social, and organizational levels of Tett & Burnett's [2003] trait activation theory).

In summary, at present, it might be advisable to collect trait-relevance ratings at the narrow-trait level because trait definitions are specific and concrete, and this is expected to help raters identify linkages between traits and job performance. Conversely, the use of very specific criterion facets may offer diminishing returns given that the extant empirical evidence tends to indicate that multidimensional job performance ratings are dominated by a general factor.

Choosing the Rating Source

When conducting a POWA that involves an inferential process relating behaviors or traits to job performance, an important question concerns who should be involved in providing the ratings. Incumbents would appear to have the advantage of being highly familiar with their job and the behaviors they perform (Goldstein et al., 1993). On the other hand, collecting POWA ratings from supervisors may be advantageous because supervisors tend to be aware of the most important aspects of job performance, and they may provide trait-relevance ratings that reflect this (Morgeson & Dierdorff, 2011). Incumbents may get caught up in small details that are not as consequential as are other more central features of the job. Another attractive characteristic of supervisors is that they may have wider exposure to different jobs, thereby highlighting trait relevance through across-job comparisons. Indeed, validity of ratings is higher when individuals are asked to think in relative terms (Goffin & Olson, 2011). Although it is too early to make firm recommendations, one suggestion is to involve incumbents when using the behavior-based POWA approach (which requires specific hands-on knowledge of the job) and supervisors when using the trait-based POWA approach (which requires more of a big picture appreciation of the job).

There are alternatives to relying solely on surveys of incumbents or supervisors for job-relevance ratings. One could collect information about the job using any of the other five methods listed in Table 11.1. In particular, if the task of making inferences regarding the job relevance of traits ultimately falls to job analysts, there may be some advantages. Dierdorff and Wilson (2003) found that job analysts provide more reliable ratings than do job incumbents. Tett et al. (1999) found that if a researcher employed job analytic information to advance hypotheses regarding trait–performance linkages, validity coefficients tended to be almost double those of purely exploratory studies where no hypothesis was developed. This suggests that job analysts, in this case the researchers, are astute at inferring trait–criterion linkages. Another alternative is to make the collected job-related information available to individuals with expertise in WA, personality trait theory, measurement, or technical aspects of the job or work environment and then have them provide trait-relevance ratings (i.e., technical experts). These individuals tend to provide superior reliability of ratings (Dierdorff & Wilson, 2003). Although we did not uncover any research that has used technical experts in studies on POWA, Paunonen's work (1998) and O'Neill and Hastings's work (2010) have shown that graduate students in psychology are surprisingly accurate at identifying personality traits predictive of behavioral criteria (e.g., counterproductive workplace behavior). Thus, asking these technical experts may be a viable option for linking traits or behaviors to job performance through POWA.

A consideration of the rating source suggests that each source has its advantages and disadvantages. Facets of the situation, as described above, should facilitate the choice of rating source.

Future Research Needs in POWA

Trait-relevance judgments are often difficult to make (Goldstein et al., 1993). Knowledge, skills, abilities, and the like appear to be easier to link to job performance than personality variables, possibly because personality may be viewed more abstractly and idiosyncratically than other more concrete work antecedents (Dierdorff & Morgeson, 2009). As POWA is a relatively nascent area of WA, there are many avenues for future research. We touched on two potentially overlooked areas earlier: trait activation theory and the O*NET. We will now identify a few more areas that we see as promising.

Rater Characteristics

Dispositional Intelligence

One novel and highly pertinent construct that may be helpful for identifying raters who have the capability to provide valid trait-relevance ratings is *dispositional intelligence*. According to Christiansen, Wolcott-Burnam, Janovics, Burns, and Quirk (2005), individuals high on dispositional intelligence have a strong understanding of (a) how traits are manifested in behavioral terms, (b) how traits tend to coexist with one another, and (c) how situations are likely to call forth trait-relevant behaviors. Christiansen et al. developed a psychometrically sound 45-item measure of dispositional intelligence and found that it strongly and positively related to individuals' ability to judge others' personality in interview and acquaintanceship situations. Although understudied, the nature of dispositional intelligence makes it an attribute that has serious potential for identifying individuals capable of making valid trait-relevance ratings.

General Mental Ability and Personality

Rater characteristics such as general mental ability (GMA) and personality may have implications for trait-relevance ratings. Given the difficulty of forming inferences regarding trait relevance, individuals higher on GMA may have advantages. These individuals likely have a stronger understanding of the job and the importance of its various components (Cornelius & Lyness, 1980). Higher GMA also implies strong verbal abilities, which may facilitate comprehension of personality trait terms and definitions. In support, Christiansen et al. (2005) found that GMA was positively related to accuracy in rating others' personality. That does not, however, directly answer the question of whether GMA would facilitate valid trait-relevance ratings. Moreover, in Goffin et al.'s (2011) study, which was highly supportive of the validity of the trait-relevance ratings collected, the raters were likely high in GMA given they were M.D.s in training. On the other hand, individuals with higher cognitive ability may be assigned different levels of responsibility involving a wider variety of tasks than those lower on GMA (Morgeson & Dierdorff, 2011). This could render trait-relevance ratings less generalizable to employees at opposite ends of the GMA continuum. The direction and extent to which trait-relevance rating validities will covary with GMA requires further examination.

Personality variables related to conscientiousness may result in more motivation to report on trait relevance as accurately and dutifully as possible. For example, some support was found for the proposition that employees more motivated to take a personality test would provide more accurate self-reports (O'Neill, Goffin, & Gellatly, 2010). Perhaps those findings could be extended to POWA. Other traits related to agreeableness and to extraversion may be useful for raters as these individuals may be in tune with the interpersonal role requirements of the position. Recall, however, that there is also a tendency to project one's own traits onto trait-relevance ratings, as per implicit personality theories (Aguinis et al., 2009). Research is needed to disentangle the personality traits of individuals who provide highly effective trait-relevance ratings while simultaneously controlling for the possibility of biases attributable to the rater's own personality.

Other Promising Rater Characteristics

Familiarity with the job, length of tenure, job experience, and performance level are all likely to be related to the validity of trait-relevance ratings. These variables would likely be related to knowledge of the behavioral requirements of the job, as well as the factors that are critical for effective job performance in the position. Experienced employees with a reasonable tenure and familiarity with the job would seem to have advantages, although it is also possible that these individuals have a different perspective from their less experienced counterparts and that this could lead to valid differences in the trait requirements of the position. Familiarity with the job becomes relevant when supervisors or job analysts provide trait-relevance ratings because these individuals typically do not have access to as much direct experience on the job as do incumbents. But it is unclear whether a moderate level of familiarity is sufficient and whether knowledge of very subtle work details is needed. In fact, it is possible that a focus on extremely specific details may result in overlooking the key behaviors that are the most critical for job performance and the corresponding traits that underlie them. Finally, low performers, compared to high performers, are less likely to be aware of the critical behaviors needed in order to succeed, thereby limiting their capability to link traits to the required behaviors. The possibilities explored here are largely speculative, however, and research investigating rater characteristics is needed in order to shed light on how to identify raters for POWA.

Contextual Considerations

We believe that the ongoing movement toward integrating contextual considerations in WA, such as top-down issues involving organizational strategy, culture, and structure (e.g., Catano et al., 2010; Dierdorff, Rubin, & Morgeson, 2009; Shippmann et al., 2000), strongly applies to POWA. These approaches make the case that the situation in which the worker and the job exist has implications for what traits will be valued on the job (Dierdorff & Surface, 2007; Johns, 2006; Tett & Burnett, 2003). For example, Dierdorff et al. (2009) presented U.S.-population representative evidence that there are essentially three broad managerial work requirements (i.e., conceptual, interpersonal, and administrative) but that the importance of each work requirement varies across managerial occupations (e.g., finance, education, construction). Dierdorff and Surface also offered, and found support for, three elements of context that could influence the importance of role requirements across managerial occupations: task, social, and physical (see also Johns, 2006). Similarly, trait activation theory (Tett & Burnett, 2003), discussed earlier, suggests that beyond work tasks, there are social and organizational variables that affect the likelihood that a trait will be "activated" and will be relevant in a particular job. We see tremendous opportunity for leveraging this theory in POWA research (e.g., Tett & Guterman, 2000). Tett and Burnett provided a sample trait-relevance rating form that integrates principles from their trait activation theory (see the Appendix in their study). Finally, rigorous approaches to CM, such as the training procedure investigated by Lievens and Sanchez (2007), offer concrete methodology that appears promising for identifying trait relevance while also taking into account the situational features within which the job is embedded. In sum, there are inklings of research investigating contextual variables and these early attempts have been fruitful. More quality research integrating contextual and situational factors in POWA would likely be valuable.

Conclusion

The purpose of this chapter was to consolidate the somewhat scattered literature on POWA in order to identify the most promising techniques and identify corresponding research gaps. The two basic approaches are behavior based and trait based. At the current juncture, we see neither as clearly superseding the other. However, in the way of best practices, there were clear trends. Rigorous rater training, rating form construction, and selection of rating sources appear critical. Future research examining these issues, as well as rater characteristics and contextual variables, is needed. Practically, strong POWA methodologies are encouraged for enhancing the legal defensibility of using personality testing, as a supplement to criterion-validity studies (or as an alternative when these are not feasible), and for honing in on a smaller number of the most relevant traits in order to reduce testing time. Scientifically, POWA is needed to identify, a priori, those traits that are most likely to be job relevant in order to maximize criterion validities. POWA may also serve a theory-building function, as it is useful for understanding why traits relate to job performance. We are eager to see future applications of POWA and expect associated developments to enhance reliance on personality testing in work settings.

Practitioner's Window

Current best practices for conducting a POWA:

- Cover a full range of potentially work-relevant personality facets with clear definitions (there is no need to use only one personality model or inventory).
- Consider facets under broad factors of a taxonomy (e.g., HEXACO facets).
- Collect POWA data that have clear and direct linkages to existing, validated personality tests.
- Use specific, concrete, and easily understood work-descriptive items (filled out in a facilitated face-to-face situation if possible).
- If online administration of POWA materials is unavoidable, provide sufficient training and instructions (e.g., videos).
- Because research suggests that a given trait can be either helpful or harmful depending on the job or job context, use response formats that allow for bidirectional relationships between traits and job performance.
- Consider targeting work features at different levels (e.g., task, social, and organizational levels).
- Allow for identification of trait-level optimality, distinct from importance, where appropriate.
- Provide frame-of-reference training to participants making POWA judgments.
- Use interpretable and flexible reporting tools (e.g., tools that identify employee personality profiles to facilitate succession planning).
- Include a manual detailing the applications of POWA findings (e.g., intended uses, development methods, norms, reliability, validity).
- Aim for an O*NET-like repository for tracking POWA data across job families, industries, and organizational and national cultures. With such a repository, POWA information could be transported into local contexts in order to make a case for the personality requirements of a specific job.

References

Aguinis, H., Mazurkiewicz, M. D., & Heggestad, E. D. (2009). Using web-based frame-of-reference training to decrease biases in personality-based job analysis: An experimental field study. *Personnel Psychology, 62*, 405–438.

Barrick, M. R., & Mount, M. K. (1991). The Big Five personality dimensions and job performance: A meta-analysis. *Personnel Psychology, 44*, 1–26.

Barrick, M. R., Mount, M. K., & Judge, T. A. (2003). Personality and performance at the beginning of the new millennium: What do we know and where do we go next? *International Journal of Selection and Assessment, 9*, 9–30.

Borman, W. C., Penner, L. A., Allen, T. D., & Motowidlo, S. J. (2001). Personality predictors of citizenship performance. *International Journal of Selection and Assessment, 9*, 52–69.

Brannick, M. T., & Levine, E. L. (2002). *Job analysis: Methods, research, and applications for human resource management in the new millennium*. Thousand Oaks, CA: Sage.

Campbell, J., Gasser, M. B. P., & Oswald, F. L. (1996). The substantive nature of job performance variability. In K. R. Murphy (Ed.), *Individuals and behavior in organizations* (pp. 258–299). San Francisco: Jossey-Bass.

Cascio, W. F., & Aguinis, H. (2005). *Applied psychology in human resource management* (6th ed.). Upper Saddle River, NJ: Prentice Hall.

Catano, V. M., Wiesner, W. H., Hackett, R. D., & Methot, L. L. (2010). *Recruitment and selection in Canada* (4th ed.). Toronto, Ontario, Canada: Thomson Nelson.

Christiansen, N. D., Wolcott-Burnam, S., Janovics, J. E., Burns, G. N., & Quirk, S. W. (2005). The good judge revisited: Individual differences in the accuracy of personality judgments. *Human Performance, 18*, 123–149.

Coaster, J. A., & Christiansen, N. D. (2009, April). Effects of occupational requirements on the validity of personality tests. In D. Bartram (Chair), *Trait, criterion, and situational specificity in personality–job performance relations*. New Orleans, LA.

Cornelius, E. T., & Lyness, K. S. (1980). A comparison of holistic and decomposed judgment strategies in job analysis by incumbents. *Journal of Applied Psychology, 65*, 155–163.
Costa, P. T., & McCrae, R. R. (1992). *The Revised NEO Personality Inventory (NEO-PI-R) and NEO Five-Factor Inventory (NEO-FFI) professional manual*. Odessa, FL: Psychological Assessment Resources.
Costa, P. T., McCrae, R. R., & Kay, G. G. (1995). Persons, places, and personality: Career assessment using the revised NEO personality inventory. *Journal of Career Assessment, 3*, 123–139.
Cranny, C. J., & Doherty, M. E. (1988). Importance ratings in job analysis: Note on the misinterpretation of factor analyses. *Journal of Applied Psychology, 73*, 320–322.
Cucina, J. M., Vasilopoulos, N. L., & Sehgal, K. G. (2005). Personality-based job analysis and the self-serving bias. *Journal of Business and Psychology, 20*, 275–290.
Detrick, P., & Chibnall, J. T. (2006). NEO-PI-R personality characteristics of high-performing entry-level police officers. *Psychological Services, 3*, 274–285.
Dierdorff, E. C., & Morgeson, F. P. (2009). Effects of descriptor specificity and observability on incumbent work analysis ratings. *Personnel Psychology, 62*, 601–628.
Dierdorff, E. C., Rubin, R. S., & Morgeson, F. P. (2009). The milieu of managerial work: An integrative framework linking work context to role requirements. *Journal of Applied Psychology, 94*, 972–988.
Dierdorff, E. C., & Surface, E. A. (2007). Placing peer ratings in context: Systematic influences beyond ratee performance. *Personnel Psychology, 60*, 93–126.
Dierdorff, E. C., & Wilson, M. A. (2003). A meta-analysis of job analysis reliability. *Journal of Applied Psychology, 88*, 635–646.
Fine, S. (1988). Functional job analysis. In S. Gael (Ed.), *The job analysis handbook for business, industry, and government* (Vol. 2, pp. 1019–1035). New York: Wiley.
Fraboni, M. F. (1995). *Personality-oriented job analysis* (Unpublished doctoral dissertation). London: University of Western Ontario.
Goffin, R. D., & Olson, J. M. (2011). Is it all relative? Comparative judgments and the possible improvement of self-ratings and ratings of others. *Perspectives on Psychological Science, 6*, 48–60.
Goffin, R. D., Rothstein, M. G., Reider, M. J., Poole, A., Krajewski, H. T., Powell, D. M., Jelley, R. B., Boyd, A. C., & Mestdagh, T. (2011). Choosing job-related personality traits: Developing valid personality-oriented job analysis. *Personality and Individual Differences, 51*, 646–651.
Goffin, R. D., & Woycheshin, D. E. (2006). An empirical method of determining employee competencies/KSAOs from task-based job analysis. *Military Psychology, 18*, 121–130.
Goldstein, I. L., Zedeck, S., & Schneider, B. (1993). An exploration of the job analysis–content validity process. In N. Schmitt and W. C. Borman (Eds.), *Personnel selection in organizations* (pp. 3–34). San Francisco: Jossey Bass.
Gough, H. G., & Bradley, P. (2005). *CPI 260TM manual*. Mountain View, CA: CPP.
Guion, R. M. (2011). *Assessment, measurement, and prediction for personnel decisions* (2nd ed.). New York: Routledge.
Guion, R. M., & Gottier, R. F. (1965). Validity of personality measures in personnel selection. *Personnel Psychology, 8*, 135–164.
Guion, R. M., Highhouse, R., Reeve, C., & Zickar, M. J. (2005). *The self-descriptive index*. Bowling Green, OH: Sequential Employment Testing.
Hastings, S. E., & O'Neill, T. A. (2009). Predicting workplace deviance using broad and narrow personality traits. *Personality and Individual Differences, 47*, 289–293.
Hogan, R., & Hogan, J. (1992). *Hogan Personality Inventory manual*. Tulsa, OK: Hogan Assessment Systems.
Hogan, R., & Holland, B. (2002, April). *Evaluating personality-based job requirements*. Paper presented at the annual meeting of the Society for Industrial and Organizational Psychology, Toronto, Ontario, Canada.
Hough, L. M. (1992). The "Big Five" personality variables–construct confusion: Description versus predictions. *Human Performance, 5*, 139–155.
Hubbard, M., McCloy, R., & Campbell, J. (2000). *Revision of O*NET data collection instruments*. Raleigh, NC: National Center for O*NET Development.
Hurtz, G. M., & Donovan, J. J. (2000). Personality and job performance: The big five revisited. *Journal of Applied Psychology, 85*, 869–879.
Jackson, D. N. (1994). *Jackson Personality Inventory—Revised manual*. Port Huron, MI: Sigma Assessment Systems.
Jackson, D. N., Paunonen, S. V., Fraboni, M., & Goffin, R. D. (1996). A five-factor versus six-factor model of personality structure. *Personality and Individual Differences, 20*, 33–45.
Jenkins, M., & Griffith, R. (2004). Using personality constructs to predict performance: Narrow or broad bandwidth. *Journal of Business and Psychology, 19*, 255–269.
Johns, G. (2006). The essential impact of context on organizational behavior. *Academy of Management Review, 31*, 386–408.

LePine, J. A. (2003). Team adaptation and postchange performance: Effects of team composition in terms of members' cognitive ability and personality. *Journal of Applied Psychology, 88*, 27–39.
Levine, E. L., Ash, R. A., Hall, H., & Sistrunk, F. (1983). Evaluation of job analysis methods by experienced job analysts. *Academy of Management Journal, 26*, 339–348.
Lievens, F., & Sanchez, J. I. (2007). Can training improve the quality of inferences made by raters in competency modeling? A quasi-experiment. *Journal of Applied Psychology, 92*, 812–819.
Lopez, F. M., Kesselman, G. A., & Lopez, F. E. (1981). An empirical test of trait-oriented job analysis technique. *Personnel Psychology, 34*, 479–502.
McCormick, E. J., & Jeanneret, P. R. (1988). Position Analysis Questionnaire (PAQ). In S. Gael (Ed.), *The job analysis handbook for business, industry, and government* (Vol. 2, pp. 825–842). New York: Wiley.
Millon, T. (1994). *Millon index of personality styles: Manual*. San Antonio, TX: The Psychological Corporation.
Morgeson, F. P., & Campion, M. A. (1997). Social and cognitive sources of potential inaccuracy in job analysis. *Journal of Applied Psychology, 82*, 627–655.
Morgeson, F. P., & Campion, M. A. (2000). Accuracy in job analysis: Toward an inference-based model. *Journal of Organizational Behavior, 21*, 819–827.
Morgeson, F. P., Campion, M. A., Dipboye, R. L., Hollenbeck, J. R., Murphy, K., & Schmitt, N. (2007). Reconsidering the use of personality tests in personnel selection contexts. *Personnel Psychology, 60*, 683–729.
Morgeson, F. P., & Dierdorff, E. C. (2011). Work analysis: From technique to theory. In S. Zedeck (Ed.), *APA handbook of industrial and organizational psychology* (Vol. 2, pp. 3–41). Washington, DC: APA.
Murphy, K. R., & Shiarella, H. (1997). Implications of the multidimensional nature of job performance for the validity of selection tests: Multivariate frameworks for studying test validity. *Personnel Psychology, 50*, 823–854.
O'Neill, T. A., Goffin, R. D., & Gellatly, I. R. (2010). Test-taking motivation and personality test validity. *Journal of Personnel Psychology, 9*, 117–125.
O'Neill, T. A., Goffin, R. D., & Tett, R. P. (2009). Content validation is fundamental for optimizing the criterion validity of personality tests. *Industrial and Organizational Psychology: Perspectives on Science and Practice, 2*, 509–513.
O'Neill, T. A., & Hastings, S. E. (2010). Explaining workplace deviance behavior with more than just the "Big Five." *Personality and Individual Differences, 50*, 268–273.
O'Neill, T. A., Lewis, R. J., & Carswell, J. J. (2011). Employee personality, justice perceptions, and the prediction of workplace deviance. *Personality and Individual Differences, 51*, 595–600.
Paunonen, S. V. (1998). Hierarchical organization of personality and prediction of behavior. *Journal of Personality and Social Psychology, 74*, 538–556.
Paunonen, S. V., & Ashton, M. C. (2001). Big five factors and facets and the prediction of behaviour. *Journal of Personality and Social Psychology, 81*, 411–424.
Paunonen, S. V., & Jackson, D. N. (1996). The Jackson Personality Inventory and the five-factor model of personality. *Journal of Research in Personality, 30*, 42–59.
Paunonen, S. V., & Jackson, D. N. (2000). What is beyond the Big Five? Plenty! *Journal of Personality, 68*, 821–835.
Paunonen, S. V., Lonnqvist, J., Verkasalo, M., Leikas, S., & Nissinen, V. (2006). Narcissism and emergent leadership in military cadets. *The Leadership Quarterly, 17*, 475–486.
Pearlman, K., & Sanchez, J. I. (2010). Work analysis. In J. L. Farr & N. T. Tippins (Eds.), *Handbook of employee selection* (pp. 74–98). New York: Routledge.
Peterson, N. G., Mumford, M. D., Jeanneret, P. R., Fleishman, E. A., Morgeson, F. P., Pearlman, K., ... Dye, D. M. (2001). Understanding work using the Occupational Information Network (O*NET): Implications for research and practice. *Personnel Psychology, 54*, 451–492.
Primoff, E. S. (1975). *How to prepare and conduct job element examinations*. Washington, DC: U.S. Civil Service Commission.
Raymark, P. H., Schmit, M. J., & Guion, R. M. (1997). Identifying potentially useful personality constructs for employee selection. *Personnel Psychology, 50*, 723–736.
Rothstein, M. G., & Goffin, R. D. (2006). The use of personality measures in personnel selection: What does current research support? *Human Resource Management Review, 16*, 155–180.
Rothstein, M. G., & Jelley, R. B. (2003). The challenge of aggregating studies of personality. In K. R. Murphy (Ed.), *Validity generalization: A critical review* (pp. 223–262). Mahwah, NJ: Lawrence Erlbaum Associates.
Salgado, J. F. (1997). The five factor model of personality and job performance in the European community. *Journal of Applied Psychology, 82*, 30–43.
Sanchez, J. I., & Levine, E. L. (2000). Accuracy or consequential validity: Which is the better standard for job analysis data? *Journal of Organizational Behavior*, 809–818.
Sanchez, J. I., & Levine, E. L. (2009). What is (or should be) the difference between competency modelling and traditional job analysis? *Human Resource Management Review, 19*, 53–63.

Sequential Employment Testing (2011). Retrieved in 2011 from http://www.sequentialemptest.com/intro.html.

Shippmann, J. S., Ash, R. A., Battista, M., Carr, L., Eyde, L. D., Hesketh, B., . . . Sanchez, J. I. (2000). The practice of competency modeling. *Personnel Psychology, 53*, 703–740.

Society for Industrial and Organizational Psychology. (2003). *Principles for the validation and use of personnel selection* (4th ed.). Bowling Green, OH: Author.

Sumer, H. C., Sumer, N., Demirutku, K., & Cifci, O. S. (2001). Using a personality-oriented job analysis to identify attributes to be assessed in officer selection. *Military Psychology, 13*, 129–146.

Tett, R. P., & Anderson, M. G. (2011, April). *O*NET as a source of personality trait–job relevance.* Paper presented at the annual meeting of the Society for Industrial and Organizational Psychology, Chicago, IL.

Tett, R. P., & Burnett, D. (2003). A personality trait-based interactionist model of job performance. *Journal of Applied Psychology, 88*, 500–517.

Tett, R. P., & Christiansen, N. D. (2007). Personality tests at the crossroads: A response to Morgeson, Campion, Dipboye, Hollenbeck, Murphy, and Schmitt (2007). *Personnel Psychology, 60*, 967–993.

Tett, R. P., & Christiansen, N. D. (2008). Personality assessment in organizations. In G. Boyle, G. Matthews, & D. Saklofske (Eds.), *Handbook of personality and testing* (pp. 720–742). Los Angeles: Sage.

Tett, R. P., & Guterman, H. A. (2000). Situation trait relevance, trait expression, and cross-situational consistency: Testing a principle of trait activation. *Journal of Research in Personality, 34*, 397–423.

Tett, R. P., Holland, B., Hogan, J., & Burnett, D. D. (2002, April). *Validity of trait-based job analysis using moderator correlations.* Paper presented at the annual meeting of the Society for Industrial and Organizational Psychology, Toronto, ON, Canada.

Tett, R. P., Jackson, D. N., & Rothstein, M. (1991). Meta-analysis of personality–job performance relationships. *Personnel Psychology, 47*, 157–172.

Tett, R. P., Jackson, D. N., Rothstein, M., & Reddon, J. R. (1999). Meta-analysis of bidirectional relations in personality–job performance research. *Human Performance, 12*, 1–29.

Vinchur, A. J., Schippmann, J. S., Switzer, F. S., & Roth, P. L. (1998). A meta-analytic review of predictors of job performance for salespeople. *Journal of Applied Psychology, 83*, 586–597.

Viswesvaran, C., Schmidt, F. L., & Ones, D. S. (2005). Is there a general factor in ratings of job performance? A meta-analytic framework for disentangling substantive and error influences. *Journal of Applied Psychology, 90*, 108–131.

Woehr, D. J., & Huffcutt, A. I. (1994). Rater training for performance appraisal: A qualitative review. *Journal of Occupational and Organizational Psychology, 67*, 189–205.

12

Personality Testing and the "F-Word"

Revisiting Seven Questions About Faking

Richard L. Griffith and Chet Robie

The use of personality measures has expanded at a rapid pace since their re-emergence as accepted predictors of job performance in the 1990s, and this expansion is likely to increase with the growth of unproctored Internet assessment (Tippins, 2009). This escalation in application was accompanied by a surge of personality research, reflected in the breadth and depth of the theoretical and empirical work contained in this volume. While some researchers may argue otherwise (e.g., Murphy & Dzieweczynski, 2005), our field has gained a much better understanding of the role of personality in the workplace in the last quarter century. However, one nagging concern, faking behavior, has continued to stymie personality researchers and practitioners. Discussion of the "F-word" is often unwelcome language in industrial-organizational (I/O) circles. But we feel a little adult language is necessary to get to the bottom of one of our more challenging measurement quandaries.

Applicant faking behavior is defined as a volitional attempt at increasing one's score on a personality assessment in order to obtain a desired outcome (McFarland & Ryan, 2000). While we have gained some insight into faking behavior, these lessons have accumulated at a slow pace and have yet to yield much in the way of actionable interventions. Researchers have examined the phenomenon of faking for 80 years (Zickar & Gibby, 2006). Unfortunately, this long-standing program of research has not resulted in commensurate gains in knowledge and has been a source of frustration (Morgeson et al., 2007). The examination of faking has often been viewed as a fruitless endeavor described as a red herring (Ones, Viswesvaran, & Reiss, 1996), a chase down the rabbit hole (Hayes, 2007), a quest for the Holy Grail, and tilting at windmills (Hough & Oswald, 2008). Thus, faking research is often viewed as an old dog that still chases its tail.

Recently, the faking research environment has changed substantially. There has been a dramatic increase in published research that focuses on the actual phenomenon of faking, rather than the once ubiquitous proxy measure of social desirability that has proven to be a poor stand-in. Two edited books have been published (Griffith & Peterson, 2006; Ziegler, MacCann, & Roberts, 2012a, 2012b) and two special editions of journals have focused on the topic.[1] There has also been considerable growth in both the number and depth of the theories proposed to explain the phenomenon (e.g., Resource Allocation Theory—Komar, Komar, Robie, & Taggar, 2010; Trait Activation Theory—Tett & Simonet, 2011; Trait Contract Classification Theory—Griffith, Lee, Peterson, & Zickar, 2011; Valence–Instrumentality–Expectancy (VIE) Theory—Ellingson & McFarland, 2011). However, faking research is still lacking a dominant theoretical paradigm to organize this increased focus.

The absence of an organizing framework increases the likelihood that the lessons learned from the research will be scattered and key findings will fall through the cracks.

The goal of this chapter is to review the contemporary faking research so that it may serve as a foundation for future work conducted in this area. Rather than reinvent the wheel, we chose a framework offered by Tett et al. (2006) to organize this chapter. In their book chapter, Tett et al. reviewed all applicants faking research conducted prior to 2005 by examining a series of seven nested questions. These seven questions (presented in Figure 12.1) will guide our discussion. First, we will briefly discuss the early research evidence, touching on the key issues covered in the seven questions.

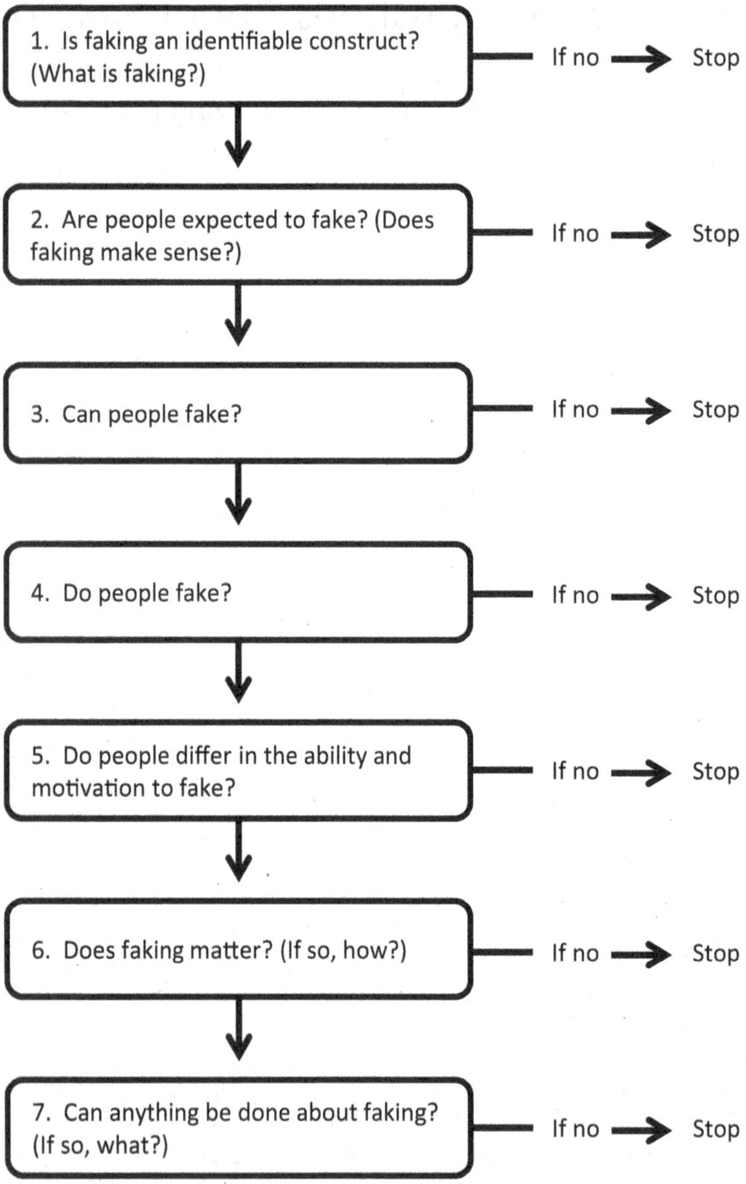

Figure 12.1 Seven Nested Questions About Faking on Personality Tests.

Then, for each question, we will first discuss the conceptual/theoretical work conducted after 2005 and then present the empirical research published during that time frame. We will then synthesize the findings and offer our opinions regarding an answer to each question. Finally, we will discuss the contemporary research as a whole and will identify necessary and untapped areas of research. The PsycINFO database was used to identify articles with the keywords "faking" and "personality" from 2006 to mid-2012. We excluded all unpublished studies. In addition, we excluded all studies that utilized measures of social desirability as a proxy measure for faking behavior.[2] In short, these measures have proven to be invalid measures of faking behavior, and thus, the results of these studies are potentially misleading. We will discuss this lack of validity, our evidence for such claims, and the implications in later sections of this chapter.

Early Research Evidence

While a full review of the history of faking research is outside the scope of this chapter, our discussion of the broad research consensus prior to 2005 will provide useful context for the contemporary research. As in many research areas, faking research has come in waves. The first wave ensued shortly after personality measures were developed (e.g., Vernon, 1934). A second wave, referred to as a pivotal battle in "the personality wars" (Hogan, 2007), focused on the measurement and meaning of social desirability (e.g., Edwards, 1957) and subsided only when the notion about personality itself was vigorously attacked (Mischel, 1968). For a detailed review of the early history of faking research, readers are encouraged to leaf through Zickar and Gibby (2006). For this review, we will concentrate on the third wave, which ensues after the "rebirth" of personality in the 1990s.

During this period, three questions were the focus of faking research: (1) Can applicants fake?; (2) Do applicants fake?; and (3) Does faking matter? A long history of instructed faking research culminating in the meta-analysis from Viswesvaran and Ones (1999) was sufficient for a "yes" answer to the first question. Thus, there was little debate about the ability of subjects to fake items when given instructions to do so.

In terms of the second question, researchers generally pointed to a difference in the scores of applicants and incumbents (e.g., Hough, 1998) as indirect evidence that faking was occurring. Little research directly tested the prevalence of faking in an applicant setting. Anderson, Warner, and Spencer (1984) used a bogus task methodology where they asked applicants to report their experience on a list of nonexistent tasks. The authors stated that 45% of job applicants reported that they engaged in one or more bogus tasks. In a similar design, Pannone (1984) found that 35% of respondents self-reported using a nonexistent piece of equipment. While research supported the occurrence of faking, the data were far from conclusive, and researchers were left with a less than satisfactory answer to question 2.

Most research during the third wave of faking research focused on the third question, "Does faking matter?" This question was generally interpreted as "Does faking affect the validity of personality measures?" In terms of construct validity, meta-analytic studies suggested that *social desirability* had little effect on the relationships between Big Five constructs (Ones et al., 1996), while studies using factor analysis (e.g., Schmit & Ryan, 1993; Zickar & Robie, 1999) and item response theory (IRT) analysis (e.g., S. Stark, Chernyshenko, Chan, Lee, & Drasgow, 2001; Zickar & Robie, 1999) found that construct validity was affected by faking resulting in changes to factor structure and theta estimates.

A number of studies examined the effect of faking on criterion-related validity. Many of these studies found validities remained intact when *social desirability* was partialed out of the personality performance relationship (Barrick & Mount, 1996; Christiansen, Goffin, Johnston, & Rothstein, 1994; Hough, Eaton, Dunnette, Kamp, & McCloy, 1990; Ones et al., 1996). However, studies examining rank order changes did find that faking affected decision quality (Christiansen et al., 1994; Zickar

& Drasgow, 1996). Due to the reliance on social desirability measure methodology, the general consensus during this period was that faking did not significantly impair our measurement efforts.

While a significant amount of knowledge was gained during the third wave of faking research, many questions remained. In fact, the number and complexity of those questions increased as reflected by the seven questions posed by Tett et al. (2006). We will now turn our attention to the contemporary review of those questions.

Question 1: Is Faking an Identifiable Construct?

If progress is to be made in any research effort, a general agreement on the definition of a phenomenon of interest is essential. Without answering the question "What is faking?" there is little hope of finding answers to the remaining research questions. Historically, the dominant view of faking largely stemmed from the view that applicant faking behavior was synonymous with the construct of social desirability, which had a great influence on the assumptions underlying research. However, contemporary theoretical literature offers more nuanced descriptions of faking behavior.

Conceptual Progress

Ten publications have focused on the delineation and theoretical refinement of applicant faking behavior (Goffin & Boyd, 2009; Griffith et al., 2011; Griffith, Malm, English, Yoshita, & Gujar, 2006; J. A. Johnson & Hogan, 2006; Kim, 2011; Marcus, 2009; Paulhus & Trapnell, 2008; Sackett, 2011; Tett & Simonet, 2011; Ziegler et al., 2012a, 2012b). The major developments in the conceptualization of applicant faking revolve around three main issues. First, the focus of recent theoretical work suggests that applicant faking is multifaceted. The second issue is the introduction of multiple perspectives on faking behavior, namely a new examination of faking through the lens of the applicant. Third, conceptual and theoretical work has begun to focus on the process of faking.

First, recent theoretical work has reinforced the idea that faking behavior has multiple influences, such as individual differences, motivation, and situational cues. One example of this multifaceted perspective is offered by Griffith et al. (2011), who suggested that by viewing faking as having distinct subcomponents, more accurate theoretical predictions may be developed. The authors propose a Trait Contract Classification Theory of faking, in which applicant individual differences in communication strategies interact with situational variables leading to four distinct forms of faking behavior: self-presentation, exaggeration, reactive responding, and deceptive responding. The authors suggested that these categories of faking may have a positive, neutral, or negative impact on the organization.

Tett and Simonet (2011) proposed a multisaturation perspective, in which faking is viewed as performance, wherein opportunity, ability, and motivation to fake interact to determine the propensity and success of faking behavior. This conceptualization of faking as performance emphasizes the behavioral view of the phenomenon and describes faking in terms of trait–situation (situation and ability) interactions. The authors then use classical test theory to demonstrate how different combinations of traits and situations may impact the psychometric properties of personality measures. The fact that faking variance results from the interaction of the situation and individual differences is echoed by Ziegler et al. (2012a, 2012b). The authors suggest that motivation to achieve a desired outcome results in situation–trait interactions that lead to spurious measurement error, which can cloud measurement efforts. Sackett (2011) decomposed the variance associated with responses to personality inventories and also suggested that faking be viewed as situation-specific intentional distortion.

Second, recent theorists have begun to frame applicant faking from the view of an important stakeholder in the process, namely the applicant (e.g., N. R. Kuncel & Borneman, 2007). Marcus (2009) extended and refined the conceptualization of faking as a natural consequence of social interaction offered by J. A. Johnson and Hogan (2006) to include the motivations and perceptions of the individual completing a personality assessment in high-stakes situations. Marcus proposed that faking researchers have focused too closely on the concept of accuracy. Marcus suggested this focus stems from taking the organizational or psychometric perspective when viewing faking behavior and proposed that faking behavior may be best understood by taking multiple perspectives (e.g., psychometric, organizational, and applicant) into account. The author suggested that it is natural for applicants to attempt to make a positive impression on employers; thus, faking would be better viewed through the lens of socioanalytic theory (J. A. Johnson & Hogan, 2006). In this view, the applicant's intent is not to deceive but to communicate their public reputation and future intentions to the employer.

N. R. Kuncel, Borneman, and Kiger (2012) provide additional insight into the goal structure of the applicant, suggesting that while responding to personality items, applicants must simultaneously balance the intrapsychic goals of being *impressive*, *credible*, and *true to the self.* Marcus (2009) views self-presentation as a natural consequence of the applicant context and can be best understood as "an adaptation to situational demands" (p. 418). Marcus suggested that the act of self-presentation be viewed independent of a particular ethical slant, in contrast to Goffin and Boyd (2009), who proposed that applicants who fake may do so because of a faulty moral code (however, no published empirical work has examined this proposition).

The third conceptual issue that has risen from the literature on the nature of faking is an increased emphasis on the process of faking behavior. While considerable attention is still placed on the impact of faking on criterion-related validity and hiring decisions, contemporary views of faking now include more discussion regarding "how applicants fake." An example of this focus on process is Goffin and Boyd (2009). The authors refine previous models of faking behavior (McFarland & Ryan, 2000; Snell, Sydell, & Lueke, 1999) by focusing at the item level and by defining key antecedents based on applicant perceptions rather than objective measurement (e.g., perceived vs. actual ability). Perhaps the most noteworthy advancement provided by Goffin and Boyd is their attempt at explicating the cognitive processes applicants engage in when faking a personality measure. The authors present a decision tree that provides a step-by-step description of the sequence leading to an applicant answering "honestly" or successfully faking. The exact mechanism proposed by Goffin and Boyd (2009) is likely to be too mechanical to reflect actual faking behavior, given that faking is likely to have both rational and irrational drivers. However, it is an important step toward gaining a clearer picture of the behavior as a process rather than a static state.

Research Progress

Although a considerable amount of theoretical development of faking has taken place in recent literature, empirical tests of these contemporary views have yet to catch up. A small number of the articles we reviewed addressed the question "What is faking?" Several of these articles provide support for trait–situation interaction views of faking (McFarland & Ryan, 2006; Mueller-Hanson, Heggestad, & Thornton, 2006), while the others discuss process issues in faking (Honkaniemi & Feldt, 2008; Robie, Brown, & Beaty, 2007).

McFarland and Ryan (2006) integrated the theory of planned behavior (TPB; Ajzen, 2001) with the McFarland and Ryan (2000) model to present a theory of why and how applicants fake. The findings of the study support TPB, as attitudes toward faking, subjective norms, and perceived behavioral control were all predictive of faking behavior. In addition, McFarland and Ryan tested a number of situational variables (e.g., warnings regarding the presence of a lie scale) as well as individual differences related to the ability to fake (e.g., knowledge of the construct being measured). The findings suggested that warnings did reduce faking behavior, but hypotheses regarding knowledge of the construct were not supported. Mueller-Hanson et al. (2006) tested a similar model of the psychological processes underlying faking, concluding that both dispositional and attitudinal antecedents contributed to faking behavior.

Honkaniemi and Feldt (2008) suggested that not all faking is created equal. They proposed that applicants are more likely to fake on items they perceive to be job-related and on agentic or egoistic traits rather than communal or moralistic traits. Given that responses to agentic trait (e.g., conscientiousness) items are more influenced by the ego, the authors hypothesized that warning applicants against misrepresentation should reduce faking on agentic traits but not on moralistic traits. However, their findings did not support this conclusion. Warnings against misrepresentation reduced scores across both categories of items. Thus, applicants either had a more general strategy of faking or saw moralistic traits as job relevant.

Summary

Is faking an identifiable construct? There does seem to be a growing consensus regarding the definition and measurement of faking. Contemporary views of faking tend to emphasize that faking is an intentional behavior and that, like all behaviors, it may have multiple motivations and antecedents. Thus, there also seems to be growing consensus that applicant faking behavior is multifaceted and may be composed of a set of correlated behaviors or strategies aimed at improving assessment outcomes for the applicant. While the behavior may be studied from multiple viewpoints, conventional wisdom at this point suggests that faking is, in fact, an identifiable construct. However, rather than viewing it as a construct in the traditional sense (i.e., latent trait), our review suggests that faking is a multifaceted goal-oriented behavior.

Question 2: Are People Expected to Fake?

Conceptual Progress

The second question asks, given the situational presses of the application context, is faking a probable (or likely) response? That is, does it make sense for an applicant to intentionally choose to alter his/her responses to manipulate the impression a future employer may have? An underlying assumption for the majority of faking research is that faking may be the normative behavior, leading some researchers to pose the question, "Why wouldn't an applicant fake?" (Griffith & McDaniel, 2006). If applicants provide fraudulent responses on other selection tools such as the resume (Bonanni, Drysdale, Hughes, & Doyle, 2006) and interviews (Levashina & Campion, 2007), why would we expect them to provide honest responses to personality measures? Ryan and Boyce (2006) suggested that concerns regarding faking are frequently voiced by clients and colleagues. Robie, Tuzinski, and Bly (2006) found that more than 70% of practitioners they surveyed thought faking was a serious problem. However, Ryan and Boyce (2006) stated that faking researchers are simply echoing the "voice of the common man" (p. 357) and attempting to verify whether this received wisdom is in fact correct. While the notion about pervasive faking is intuitive, this normative assumption has rarely been explored in depth.

A recent conceptual development draws from the general deception literature. Rather than look at faking as an isolated organizational event, this literature points to analogous opportunities for deceit in other areas of life. Griffith and McDaniel (2006) suggested that the applicant situation shares similarities with other competitive forces in nature and that an evolutionary perspective would predict that, under those conditions, faking may be an expected behavior. The authors suggest that despite societal norms that view deception as an undesirable behavior, people frequently lie, and thus question why applicants would behave differently. Dilchert, Ones, Viswesvaran, and Deller (2006) echo this perspective, suggesting that applicants were born to lie and that "all high-stakes assessments are likely to elicit deception" (p. 210). Kim (2011) offers the most elaborate examination of faking in light of the deception literature to date. Kim stated that deception is a basic human tendency and refined the conceptual understanding of faking by grounding his work in process models of human deception and situations with similar competitive pressures (e.g., academic cheating). However, the effect of the applicant context may not be uniform across all applicant circumstances. For example, Ellingson (2012) discusses how the motivation to fake may differ across job levels.

Research Progress

Robie, Emmons, Tuzinski, and Kantrowitz (2011) examined how competitive pressures may influence applicant faking behavior. Specifically, they tested whether declining economic conditions and increasing unemployment may increase the motivation to fake and whether resulting changes in motivation may lead to changes in the scores on measures of personality and intelligence. The authors examined selection and promotion data collected over 4 years in the United States during which unemployment increased 5%. The data suggested that as unemployment increased, personality scores increased significantly across the 4 years. Robie (2006) tested whether competitive forces, such as the selection ratio, might increase applicant faking. While selection ratios are not likely to be known to applicants, they may be intuited or inferred from economic conditions. Robie (2006) attempted to manipulate the perceived selection ratios of respondents by presenting them with different competitive chances at obtaining a reward (e.g., 2 of 25 vs. 18 of 25). The results suggested that altering the chances of success did not induce changes in faking behavior.

Research by Aronson and Reilly (2006) found that a cognitive bias may be responsible for the inflation of applicants' scores. The authors examined how motivated reasoning may impact schema-related processing of self-relevant information. Based on response processes proposed by Holden, Fekken, and Cotton (1991), the authors suggested that motivated self-schemas serve to filter information about the self, shaping which memories are selected when applicants are evaluating item content. This selective memory search then serves to confirm and reinforce the activated schema that is consistent with the desired self. The authors tested these propositions by introducing job descriptions designed to elicit either conscientiousness or openness. Their results suggested that under motivated conditions, respondents recalled more autobiographical events that were consistent with the activated trait, and this activation led to significantly higher mean scores on the measure of that trait. Krahé, Becker, and Zollter (2008) suggested that even without an explicit motivation to fake, situational cues may prime applicants to elevate their scores and may trigger underlying motivations to fake.

Summary

Both conceptual and empirical work suggests that the demands inherent in the applicant context are likely to elicit faking behavior. Whether through the situational appraisal of a competitive environment or through more subtle cognitive priming, applicant responding is strongly influenced by contextual cues. In addition, the literature on deception suggests that faking may be a dominant response that needs to be actively suppressed. Motivated deception is common in everyday interactions, and the strength of this dominant response would be expected to increase given the fertile application setting. First, in an increasingly disconnected corporate world, applicants are not likely to have a meaningful relationship with a future employer. Companies are more likely to be viewed as impersonal entities, and applicants may not feel the same sense of attachment (and thus felt obligation to be truthful) they would if entering a mom-and-pop shop (cf. neutralization theory in the criminology literature; Trahan, 2011). Second, applicants generally have little concern over the consequences of getting caught (Griffith & McDaniel, 2006). The absence of these two factors, which have been theoretically and empirically linked to deception (Ekman & Frank, 1993), makes it likely that a substantial number of applicants will engage in faking behavior.

Question 3: Can People Fake?

The issue of whether respondents have the ability to fake personality measures is perhaps the question that has the most consensus and may now be considered "settled law." It is generally agreed that when instructed to do so, most participants are able to elevate their scores on measures of personality.[3] This question has been supported by often-cited meta-analytic evidence (Viswesvaran & Ones, 1999) examining general personality measures mapped onto the Big Five personality dimensions. Several studies conducted since 2005 (e.g., Simón, 2007; Sisco & Reilly, 2007) add support to the notion that, when instructed, respondents can fake general measures of personality. Recent research has focused on other types of noncognitive measures, such as integrity tests and emotional intelligence measures, based on the assumption that not all noncognitive measures (Hartman & Grubb, 2011; Tett, Freund, Christiansen, Fox, & Coaster, 2011) or measurement formats (Kanning & Kuhne, 2006; McDaniel, Beier, Perkins, Goggin, & Frankel, 2009) are equally fakable.

Conceptual Progress

There were no published book chapters or theoretical articles that focused on this question.

Research Progress

Using both between- and within-subjects designs, Byle and Holtgraves (2008) examined whether participants were able to fake a covert integrity test when given the description of a desirable job and instructed to set themselves apart by looking good on the test. The results revealed that participants who were instructed to fake had significantly higher scores on the measure in both the between-subjects design (d = .46) and the within-subjects design (d = 1.08).

Using a within-subjects design, Grubb and McDaniel (2007) tested the fakability of a common measure of emotional intelligence, Bar-On's *Emotional Quotient Inventory* (EQI). The EQI is a mixed-model measure of emotional intelligence and thus has items that are similar in nature to personality items. When honest scores were compared with scores derived from directed faking, the faked condition scores were significantly higher (d = .83). Hartman and Grubb (2011) found a similar degree of faking, again using a within-subjects design. These studies as well as other recent research (Day & Carroll, 2008; Tett et al., 2011) suggest that trait-based measures of emotional intelligence are susceptible to applicant faking.

Kanning and Kuhne (2006) compared honest, applicant, and faked scores across five-item formats: problem-solving items, knowledge items, forced-choice items, Likert-type scales, and situational judgment items. Their results revealed that the Likert-type scale and situational judgment test formats were susceptible to faking instructional sets. However, the situational judgment test used in the study was scored in a nonlinear fashion and contained a top cutoff that would have eliminated many of the successful fakers in a real applicant setting. The forced-choice instrument was not successfully faked.

Ziegler, Schmidt-Atzert, Bühner, and Krumm (2007) compared faking good and bad on measures of achievement motivation across self-report, semiprojective, and objective item formats. Semiprojective measures present respondents with ambiguous stimuli, often pictures, and then ask them to rate stimulus-relevant statements. Objective tests are measures of behavior or performance and thus should be fake resistant. All three formats were susceptible to faking bad. In the fake good condition, however, only the objective measure was fake resistant. Significant differences were found for both semiprojective and self-report formats.

With a similar focus, McDaniel et al. (2009) compared the degree of faking on Likert-type versus implicit association test (IAT) items targeting conscientiousness and extraversion under both honest and maximum faking instructional sets. As expected, the results for the Likert-type measures demonstrated a significant difference (ω^2 = .95 and .91 for extraversion and conscientiousness, respectively). The IAT results were mixed. There was a significant difference between honest and faking conditions for the extraversion measure (ω^2 = .48) but not for the conscientiousness measure (for more coverage of implicit measures of personality, see Chapter 7, this volume).

Summary

Contemporary research seems to be consistent with the accepted notion that, when instructed, applicants can fake. However, differences in the degree of success in faking behavior may be moderated by response format and individual differences in faking ability. Both of these issues will be discussed in more depth in subsequent sections.

Question 4: Do People Fake?

The study of faking behavior in laboratory settings was influential in answering the question of respondents' ability to fake personality inventories. However, reliance on laboratory studies opened the door for critics who suggested that while applicants could fake, they did not actually do so in applied settings. This critique was especially puzzling given the answers to questions 2 and 3. If some applicants were expected to fake and demonstrated the ability to do so, it seemed anomalous that faking would not be present in the applicant setting. Yet these claims persisted. Thus, a considerable amount of recent faking research has more closely examined the prevalence of faking behavior under true applicant conditions.

Conceptual Progress

A recent book chapter focused directly on the question "Do applicants fake?" Griffith and Converse (2012) synthesized previous research on faking and applicant deception across a number of research designs, collecting evidence from studies examining applicant–incumbent differences in validity (Hough, 1998), bogus items (Anderson et al., 1984), within-subjects applicant designs (Arthur, Glaze, Villado, & Taylor, 2010; Ellingson, Sackett, & Connelly, 2007; Griffith, Chmielowski, & Yoshita, 2007; Peterson, Griffith, Isaacson, O'Connell, & Mangos, 2011), and self-reported faking (Donovan, Dwight, & Hurtz, 2003; Robie, Brown, & Beaty, 2007). In addition, they assessed the prevalence of other forms of applicant deception, such as resume fraud and faking an employment interview. Griffith and Converse (2012) concluded that, on average, 30% of applicants engage in faking behavior, with a confidence interval of ±10%.

Research Progress

Three studies provided evidence of applicant faking at the group level of analysis (Birkeland, Manson, Kisamore, Brannick, & Smith, 2006; J. P. Bott, O'Connell, Ramakrishnan, & Doverspike, 2007; Ellingson et al., 2007). Ellingson et al. (2007) analyzed a within-subjects archival dataset on promotion candidates who had completed the *California Psychological Inventory* (CPI) twice within a 7-year period. In some instances, participants responded in a developmental context, where the authors suggested that the employees would likely be less motivated to fake. In other instances, the assessment tools were used for the purposes of promotion. After the parameters were adjusted to account for the confounding variables of time lag and developmental feedback, the authors concluded that there were small increases in the respondents' scores in the more motivated settings.

J. P. Bott et al. (2007) analyzed between-subjects personality data collected from applicants and incumbents and found effect sizes exceeding one standard deviation (*SD*). Using meta-analysis,

Birkeland et al. (2006) found considerable differences between applicants and incumbents, with uncorrected *ds* ranging from .11 (extraversion) to .45 (conscientiousness) and corrected effect sizes exceeding one-half *SD*. Both of these studies add to the large body of evidence demonstrating higher scores in applicant settings when compared to incumbent samples.

Griffith et al. (2007) examined the prevalence of applicant faking using a within-subjects design in an actual applicant setting. When applicant and nonmotivated conditions were compared, a significant amount of faking occurred at the group level (d = .61). Griffith et al. also examined the percentage of individuals in the sample who faked their scores by creating a confidence interval based on the reliability of the measure around each respondent's honest score. If an individual's applicant score exceeded the upper bound of the interval, he/she was considered as having faked the measure. Two intervals (1.96 × *SEM* and 1.96 × *SED*) were calculated resulting in an estimated prevalence of faking between 22% and 31%. Peterson et al. (2011) also examined the prevalence of applicant faking in a within-subjects design utilizing an actual applicant sample. Using a confidence interval of 1.96 *SED*, Peterson et al. (2011) found that 24% of applicants faked a conscientiousness measure.

Arthur et al. (2010) found that a considerable number of applicants faked in the selection setting using a within-subjects design. The authors also established a confidence interval around the research scores based on the reliability of the measures. Participants who exceeded this interval when responding as applicants were subsequently categorized as fakers (35.81% on agreeableness, 34.12% on conscientiousness, 33.11% on emotional stability, 35.81% on extraversion, and 14.53% on openness). The authors found a similar pattern of results in a second study with the same design.

Two studies examined faking by analyzing data whereby candidates were retested after initially failing an assessment. Hogan, Barrett, and Hogan (2007) suggested that applicants failing the initial assessment would demonstrate an increase in motivation at subsequent retesting and therefore would be more likely to fake. Hogan et al. found negligible increases in scores during the retesting administration and suggested the study demonstrated evidence that little faking occurs in applied settings. We suggest that caution be used when interpreting Hogan et al.'s retesting study as evidence either for or against the occurrence of faking. Hogan et al.'s assumption that applicant motivation increased in the second administration was not measured during the study, and thus, the pattern of findings is open to multiple interpretations. Without a confirmed difference in motivation seen in high-stakes and low-stakes comparisons (e.g., Ellingson et al., 2007), the study is essentially a test–retest reliability study and offers little in the way of assessing the prevalence of faking. One cannot rule out that faking was consistent across both administrations. In addition, other large-scale retesting studies have found evidence of score inflation. Hausknecht (2010) also examined a dataset in which candidates who both passed and failed an initial assessment were retested. The candidates who passed the initial assessment demonstrated very little improvement in scores. However, candidates who failed the initial assessment had large score increases in the second administration with effect sizes exceeding d = .60. In a similar study, Landers, Sackett, and Tuzinski (2011) found a mean effect size of .86. A simulation conducted by Warmsley and Sackett (in press) suggests that differences in the cut score and the weight of the personality test in the battery may account for the discrepant results in retesting studies.

In a qualitative study examining the prevalence of faking, Robie et al. (2007) recruited a small sample of participants through a newspaper advertisement asking them to complete a research survey with the assurance that the top three respondents would receive US$100. Participants were instructed to complete a personality measure as if applying for a retail position. In addition, they were instructed to think aloud while completing the measure, and their verbal protocol was recorded. The authors coded the protocols and classified the participants as honest (only accessing self-relevant information), slight fakers (beginning with self-relevant information, but then shading toward the idealized response), or extreme fakers (only referencing idealized responses for the position). Twenty-five percent of the sample was comprised of fakers, with one participant classified as an extreme faker, and two as slight fakers.

Summary

While not unequivocal, the majority of research conducted since 2006 suggests that a substantial number of applicants do fake personality measures. Estimates of the prevalence of faking vary, but on average, 30% of respondents inflate their scores in selection contexts. A number of moderators (e.g., response format, professional level of the applicant, and cultural influences) may influence the dispersion around the 30% estimate. It is worth noting that the degree of faking seen in applicant settings is considerably less than those found in faking studies based on instructional sets (Griffith et al., 2007). Thus, future research interested in understanding faking should examine this "typical" applicant setting rather than the "maximal" influence of instructed faking.

Question 5: Do People Differ in the Ability and Motivation to Fake?

Conceptual Progress

We found four chapters or articles that specifically address the motivation to engage in faking behavior. Ellingson (2012) and Ellingson and McFarland (2011) each discuss how the job level of the applicant may impact choices regarding self-presentation. Ellingson (2012) suggested that faking may be more likely for entry-level positions, where the exchange between the employer and employee is driven by monetary concerns, and where opportunity to market one's self is low. However, when professionals are seeking employment, they are more marketable due to the accumulation of valuable job skills. Ellingson and McFarland (2011) extend this notion by integrating the marketability variable within the VIE theory of work motivation (Vroom, 1964). The authors suggested that applicants are more likely to engage in faking behavior when (1) they believe that faking is necessary for a job offer (instrumentality), (2) the employment opportunity is desirable (valence), and (3) candidates feel secure in their ability to fake successfully (expectancy). Offering another explanation for the differences in faking motivation between unskilled and professional applicants, Sackett (2011) suggests that the two groups may differ in temporal orientation, such that applicants with a short-term orientation may choose an immediate reward (obtaining the job) regardless of less positive, long-term consequences. Professional applicants, in contrast, may view the employment context more as a partnership and thus may adopt a more long-term perspective. Griffith et al. (2011) extend this idea, proposing that applicants who view the employment situation in terms of a relationship rather than a monetary exchange will be less likely to fake. They propose that an applicant's anticipatory psychological contract (APC; De Vos, De Stobbeleir, & Meganck, 2009) is a likely predictor of faking behavior. Applicants with a transactional APC will be more likely to fake, while those with a relational APC will be more inclined to respond honestly.

Research Progress

Several faking studies since 2006 have been addressing the question, "Do people differ in the ability and motivation to fake?" (Book, Holden, Starzyk, Wasylkiw, & Edwards, 2006; J. Bott, Snell, Dahling, & Smith, 2010; Levashina, Morgeson, & Campion, 2009; McFarland & Ryan, 2006; Mueller-Hanson et al., 2006; Raymark & Tafero, 2009). Tett et al.'s (2006) conclusion in this area was "that people indeed vary in abilities and motives directly relating to response distortion and that the expression of such individual differences depends in part on the situation" (p. 57).

Three of the studies examined individual difference variables as influences on faking (Book et al., 2006; Levashina et al., 2009; MacNeil & Holden, 2006). Individuals who scored higher on a measure of psychopathy were able to successfully "fake good" on a personality inventory, whereas individuals who scored lower on the measure of psychopathy were more apt to be caught faking using a validity index that quantifies dissimulation (Book et al., 2006). The authors suggested that individuals higher in psychopathic traits may be more skilled in using deception to exploit other individuals. Along similar lines, MacNeil and Holden (2006) asked participants high on the trait of psychopathy to make a good impression while attempting to avoid detection. The results suggested that overall psychopathy scores were unrelated to successful faking; however, three subcomponents of psychopathy (Machiavellian egocentricity, blame externalization, and stress immunity) were related to faking good. Levashina et al. (2009) found that individuals higher in mental ability were less likely to fake on a biodata inventory; when they did fake, however, they were more successful than individuals lower in mental ability. Several explanations were proffered for why individuals higher in mental ability did not fake as much, including high test self-efficacy, a greater awareness of possible sanctions for faking, and a greater likelihood of selectively faking on the inventory.

The remaining studies were partial tests of models proposed by McFarland and Ryan (2000) and Snell et al. (1999) that examined both individual difference and situational perception variables as influences on faking (J. Bott et al., 2010; McFarland & Ryan, 2006; Mueller-Hanson et al., 2006; Raymark & Tafero, 2009). J. Bott et al. (2010) reported a positive relationship between emotional stability and score elevation on a measure of conscientiousness—directly contradicting findings from McFarland and Ryan (2000). J. Bott et al. (2010) also found that instrumentality and the interaction between expectancy and instrumentality were related to score elevation. The latter result is consistent with and extends those of Schmit and Ryan (1992), who found that the criterion-related validity of a personality test was higher for a subsample with less positive test-taking motivation compared to a sample with higher test-taking motivation.

Two studies by McFarland and Ryan (2006) used the TPB (Ajzen, 2001) to examine the relationships between individual difference and situational perception variables, on the one hand, and intention to fake and actual faking behavior, on the other. In Study 1, attitudes toward faking, subjective norms, and perceived behavioral control were all positively related to intention to fake. In Study 2, the authors found that intention to fake was positively related to actual faking behavior but knowledge of the construct being measured did not moderate the relationship between intention to fake and actual behavior. In a similar vein, Mueller-Hanson et al. (2006) found that perceptions of the situation (composed of belief in importance of faking, perceived behavioral control, and subjective norms), emotional stability, and conscientiousness were related to intention to fake, but ability to fake was not related to intention to fake. The latter finding is consistent with the results from Levashina et al. (2009). Willingness to fake (composed of Machiavellianism, lack of rule-consciousness, and self-monitoring) was significantly negatively related to faking. The authors interpreted this unexpected finding as possibly because the effect of willingness to fake on intentions to fake operates through perceptions of the situation.

Raymark and Tafero (2009) examined the degree to which self-monitoring, knowledge of the constructs being measured, job familiarity, and openness to ideas accounted for variance in ability to fake on a personality measure. Some participants were asked simply to "fake good," whereas others were asked to fake toward the requirement of a specific job (e.g., "accountant"). Only knowledge of the constructs being measured was positively related to faking ability for the "fake good" condition, and only openness to ideas was positively related to ability to fake as an accountant. König, Melchers, Kleinmann, Richter, and Klehe (2006) argued that applicants who have the ability to identify what kind of behavior is evaluated positively in a personnel selection situation can use this information to adapt their behavior accordingly. They examined the relationship between the ability to identify evaluation criteria (ATIC; Kleinmann, 1993) and integrity test scores and found a significant relationship. A specific ability to determine the "correct response" in a personality assessment would be a valuable tool for an individual with the motivation to distort his/her responses.

In sum, the recent literature in this area confirms Tett et al.'s (2006) conclusion that response distortion is a function of both ability and motivation to fake. We have learned more about which individual and motivational variables affect both faking ability and intention to fake. Moreover, several of the studies have used a theory-based approach that may help future researchers to more easily build on their contributions.

Question 6: Does Faking Matter?

Conceptual Progress

Two chapters in our post-2005 survey of studies substantively address how faking may impact the validity of personality measures in the applicant setting (Holden & Book, 2012; Peterson & Griffith, 2006). Peterson and Griffith (2006) focus on the effects of faking on criterion-related validity, arguing that faking should moderately attenuate validity coefficients and that this attenuation is largely due to nonlinearity in the data. They walk through three scenarios: the faker as poor performer, the faker as a good performer, and the faker as an equivalent performer. They conclude that fakers are likely to demonstrate equivalent levels of performance as nonfakers, but that this pattern would likely lead to moderate attenuation of validity coefficients due to the faking scores serving as a statistical outlier. Holden and Book (2012) suggested that the results regarding faking and validity are mixed. In experimental studies, faking has a consistent detrimental effect on criterion-related validity. However, the pattern is less clear under more natural conditions. The authors make an important distinction regarding the overall reported validity for a given scale and the validity of the responses of an individual who has faked. They concluded that the validity of individual responses is affected by faking behavior, resulting in lower quality hiring decisions.

Research Progress

A large number of empirical faking studies since 2006 could be categorized as addressing the question "Does faking matter?" (J. P. Bott et al., 2007; Bradley & Hauenstein, 2006; Christiansen, Rozek, & Burns, 2010; Converse et al., 2008; Converse, Peterson, & Griffith, 2009; Ferrando & Anguiano-Carrasco, 2009a, 2009b; Heggestad, George, & Reeve, 2006; Holden, 2007; Holden & Passey, 2010; M. Johnson, Sivadas, & Kashyap, 2009; Komar, Brown, Komar, & Robie, 2008; Konstabel, Aavik, & Allik, 2006; Marcus, 2006; Peterson et al., 2011; Peterson, Griffith, & Converse, 2009; Schmitt & Oswald, 2006; Stewart, Darnold, Zimmerman, Parks, & Dustin, 2010; Winkelspecht, Lewis, & Thomas, 2006). Tett et al.'s (2006) conclusions in this area were:

> First, the role of social desirability in content validation of personality tests used for selection has received little empirical attention and warrants more. Second, studies of mean differences, confirmatory factor analyses, and IRT in applicant and incumbent samples suggest that response distortion adversely influences the construct validity of personality tests. Third, the criterion validity of personality seems surprisingly robust to response distortion. Fourth, however, such distortion may have a nontrivial impact on personality-based hiring decisions. Fifth, it is not obvious how faking can affect construct validity and hiring decisions without also affecting criterion-related validity. Scientists rely on theory and conceptual integration to guide their efforts and recommendations to practitioners, and the challenge of reconciliation in this case is one most worthy of pursuit in future research.
>
> *p. 62*

We will review how each of the above areas has been addressed since 2006, using Tett et al.'s (2006) subsections.

Content-Related Evidence

We could find no research from 2006 to the present that examined the content validity of personality items using expert judges or ratings of social desirability.

Construct-Related Evidence

We could find no research from 2006 to the present that examined the possible effects of response distortion on discriminant and convergent validity. However, several studies used factor analytic-type techniques to address construct validity in light of response distortion (Bradley & Hauenstein, 2006; M. Johnson et al., 2009). Bradley and Hauenstein (2006) compared incumbent versus applicant Big Five correlation matrices across a range of studies (i.e., a meta-analytic factor analysis) and found frequent but small moderating effects. The authors suggested that the differences were so small across sample type as to not affect the construct validity of personality measures from a practical point of view. In contrast, a study of salespersons on a personality-based measure of sales potential (M. Johnson et al., 2009) found an "ideal employee" factor much the same as was found by Schmit and Ryan (1993).

Two studies have used IRT-based techniques since 2006 to address the construct validity issue (Ferrando & Anguiano-Carrasco, 2009a, 2009b). Both studies, using student samples, found a high level of invariance across "honest" and "fake good" samples on personality item responses.

Finally, Heggestad, George, et al. (2006) found that faked responses contained more transient error (i.e., variance specific to the time of measurement, e.g., due to mood and mind-set) than did honest responses. The authors note that these results suggest that alpha obtained under faking conditions will overestimate the reliability of personality scores, leading to undercorrection in estimating criterion-related validity and underestimation of the standard error of measurement.

Criterion-Related Evidence

Five studies since 2006 have examined the possible effects of faking on the criterion-related validity (using performance measures) of personality measures (Converse et al., 2009; Komar et al., 2008; Marcus, 2006; Peterson et al., 2011; Schmitt & Oswald, 2006). Four of those studies used a simulation design (Converse et al., 2009; Komar et al., 2008; Marcus, 2006; Schmitt & Oswald, 2006). Schmitt and Oswald (2006) found that *corrections for faking* did not affect the criterion-related validity of personality measures. Komar et al. (2008) found that faking did affect the criterion-related validity of personality measures, with the most pronounced effects occurring when selection ratios and the proportion of fakers are low and the relationship between faking and performance is negative. Extending Komar et al.'s (2008) findings, Converse et al. (2009) reported that the negative effects of faking on criterion-related validity are substantially reduced but not eliminated by the inclusion of additional predictors (e.g., cognitive ability and the interview). Finally, Marcus (2006) found degradations in validity due to faking on a measure of integrity across a range of conditions. The reduction in criterion-related validity evidenced in these simulations was confirmed by Peterson et al. (2011) in a field study using actual applicant data. Within-subjects personality data were collected in both unmotivated and applicant settings, and scores were correlated with a measure of counterproductive work behavior. As expected, the unmotivated scores were significantly correlated. However, the correlation in the applicant setting was severely attenuated.

Several other studies since 2006 examined the possible effects of faking on the criterion-related validity (using observer reports) of personality measures (Holden, 2007; Holden & Passey, 2010; Konstabel et al., 2006). There is disagreement in this area, as social desirability moderated the relationship between self- and peer-reports of personality in two studies (Holden, 2007; Konstabel et al., 2006) but not in the other (Holden & Passey, 2010). Reasons for the discrepancies are unclear.

Selection Decisions

Several studies since 2006 have examined the possible effects of faking on selection decisions (Christiansen et al., 2010; Converse et al., 2009; Marcus, 2006; Peterson et al., 2009; Stewart et al., 2010; Winkelspecht et al., 2006). All found that faking affected selection decisions. Christiansen et al. (2010) reported that practitioners evaluating hypothetical applicants perceived candidates with elevated social desirability scores to be less hirable and less weight was given to the personality assessment. Two studies found that including multiple predictors substantially reduced but did not eliminate the negative effect of faking on selection decisions (Converse et al., 2009; Peterson et al., 2009). Marcus (2006) found that hiring decisions were more sensitive to faking than was criterion-related validity. Stewart et al. (2010) found that hiring decisions were indeed affected by faking and that common correction methods failed to accurately detect those who distort. Furthermore, the correction practice of partialing lie scale scores from personality traits would remove individuals who did not truly fake. The study by Winkelspecht et al. (2006) appeared to be a simple replication of previous studies showing that faking affects selection decisions (albeit this time in a laboratory setting).

Miscellaneous

Two studies are notable in that they examined the effects of faking on none of the other areas identified above (Berry & Sackett, 2009; J. P. Bott et al., 2007). J. P. Bott et al. (2007) examined the potential impact of response distortion when cut scores identified using incumbents are used on applicants. In support of the faking problem, applicant pass rates were much higher than those of incumbents. Interestingly, a simulation study by Berry and Sackett (2009) found that deriving cutoff scores from incumbents minimized displacement of deserving applicants but use of applicant-derived cutoff scores maximized mean performance resulting from the selection system. The use of either approach can be seen as a strategic tradeoff between performance and fairness to applicants.

Based on the studies from 2006 to present, we can address progress in the areas reviewed by Tett et al. (2006) as follows:

1. The role of faking in content validation still receives scant empirical attention.
2. Faking affected construct validity in some studies but not others. A differentiating factor may be whether social desirability measures were used to distinguish fakers from nonfakers or whether faking was operationalized as an "ideal employee" factor.
3. Newer research using simulation techniques finds that criterion-related validity is *not* robust to faking, and field data confirm this vulnerability.
4. The preponderance of evidence continues to suggest that faking affects selection decisions.
5. Newer research using simulation techniques has apparently resolved the contradiction of faking affecting selection decisions but not criterion-related validity.

Summary

Contemporary research suggests that the validity of personality measures is not immune to the effects of faking. While more research is needed before making definitive statements, decrements in criterion-related validity and hiring decisions are likely outcomes of applicant faking. The effect on construct validity is less clear. Research suggests that faking adds a systematic measurement error that results in responses (within and across constructs) being more correlated. This increased covariance is often overlooked because it goes undetected in examinations of internal consistency estimates and factor structure, which often improve under faking conditions. In most cases, fit statistics also improve when faked data are analyzed. When homogeneity statistics are used to examine the effects of faking, the results may be quite misleading. When it comes to faking, we may need to rethink our approach to evaluating construct validity.

Question 7: Can Anything Be Done About Faking?

Conceptual Progress

Eleven book chapters that discuss methods to detect or deter faking behavior have been published. These chapters discuss diverse approaches such as instructional sets/warnings (Pace & Borman, 2006); forced-choice response options (Converse et al., 2008; Vasilopoulos & Cucina, 2006); probabilistic or Bayesian truth approaches (N. R. Kuncel et al., 2012; Lukoff, 2012); overclaiming (Paulhus, 2012); IRT-based detection, deterrence, or measurement recovery (F. Stark, Chernyshenko, & Drasgow, 2012; Zickar & Sliter, 2012); or traditional social desirability measure approaches (Burns & Christiansen, 2006; Dilchert & Ones, 2012; Reader & Ryan, 2012).

A full review of these theoretical contributions exceeds the scope of this chapter. We offer, instead, an overview of the concepts presented in those works, organized by our own interpretive framework based on a medical metaphor.

When considering a medical procedure, the first concern a doctor has is for the safety of the patient. He or she must assess the risk of the illness or injury to the patient before making an assessment of possible treatments. Applying this logic to faking, a realistic appraisal of the danger of faking is in order. Faking is not terminal cancer. It is not a gunshot wound. It is more akin to an ugly inconvenience. Personality tests would work better without faking, but if constructed properly and well thought through they still work quite well (Tett & Christiansen, 2007). In medical terms, personality testing would be more productive with a corrective procedure, but no lifesaving miracle is needed to save the life of the patient. Since we seem to be a bit shaky on separating truth from fiction when faking occurs, let us call it an eyesight correction.

Once we have established that the patient (i.e., personality testing) is not in peril, the notion of side effects must be considered. Many interventions may reduce the impact of the original problem, but some cause other problems that can be quite severe. If you are not careful with your intervention, you might worsen the patient's quality of life. This is often the outcome of trial-and-error interventions, which have been the most frequent response to the challenge of faking (e.g., statistical correction for social desirability variance that removes valid variance—see Burns & Christiansen, 2006). If you kill the patient to kill the disease, it generally makes for a bad ending. Faking interventions must not impede our overall measurement goals.

The next assessment may then come from the patient who must determine whether the cost of the procedure is worth the ultimate outcome. A Lasik correction may cost US$3,000. A pair of contact lenses may cost US$100, and a pair of discount store eyeglasses US$9.99. A relatively equal effect can be achieved with lower cost, but the tradeoff is inconvenience and nonsophistication. So, in regard to faking solutions, you can get an almost-acceptable solution cheap or go for the fancy solution and spend a considerable amount. A traditional warning may be a relatively cheap intervention, while verification through a clinical interview may represent a more costly solution.

The effectiveness, side effects, and cost of proposed faking solutions vary greatly. For instance, on one end, you have the proposed solution of elaboration on item content (Schmitt et al., 2003). Sticking with the medical analogy, elaboration instructional sets are like a folk remedy (e.g., copper bracelets). They do not reduce faking or increase validity, but they are cheap and do no harm. On the other end, you have IRT approaches to faking detection/reduction/correction. To date, the U.S. military has invested the most in this approach, which has been very expensive, provided little payoff, and demonstrated unpleasant side effects (Zickar & Sliter, 2012). If we return to the medical analogy, using advanced statistical manipulations to address faking is like paying for a Beverly Hills liposuction, but gaining weight anyway and needing unsightly stitches. In Table 12.1, we organize the proposed faking interventions discussed since 2005 according to the effectiveness of faking interventions, the side effects, and the costs.

We would be remiss if we did not consider the most common form of faking detection and correction, the inclusion of social desirability measures. The research on these measures is clear. Measures of *SD* are not a valid proxy measure for faking behavior (Griffith & Peterson, 2008, 2011; Reader & Ryan, 2012). The use of these measures to detect applicant faking in operational settings should be discontinued. Ample evidence suggests they are not conceptually related to faking (Griffith & Peterson, 2008), and the mathematical reasoning behind the correction is flawed (Burns & Christiansen, 2006; Reader & Ryan, 2012). In addition, the empirical evidence demonstrates that when *SD* measures are used, they are wildly inaccurate, with a large number of false positives and false negatives (Peterson et al., 2011). Furthermore, they evidence subgroup differences protected under Title VII (Reader & Ryan, 2012). Finally, the researcher who has brought the most clarity to the concept of *SD* has stated that they should not be used for the purpose of detecting faking behavior (Paulhus, 2002; Paulhus, Harms, Nadine, & Lysy, 2003). It is time to drive the final nail in the coffin and stop using measures of *SD* in an effort to detect faking.

In that regard, it is also time to reevaluate our assumptions of faking based on studies using measures of *SD* as a proxy for faking behavior. A consistent pattern is that those studies always found support for the null hypothesis; that faking did not impact outcome variables (e.g., validity). The asserted position was that faking does not matter. After long examination, the more likely explanation for this pattern of findings is that measures of *SD* were not valid for their intended purpose.

Table 12.1 Faking Intervention Effectiveness, Side Effects, and Costs

Intervention	*Effectiveness*	*Side Effects*	*Side Effect Severity*	*Costs*	*Reference*
Warnings	Moderate	Suppression of honest scores	Moderate	Minimal	Pace & Borman, 2006
Forced choice	Minimal	G-loaded scores Ipsative measurement	Great	Moderate	Converse et al., 2008; Vasilopoulos & Cucina, 2006
Bayesian truth serum	Untested	N/A	N/A	Moderate	N. R. Kuncel, Borneman, & Kiger, 2012; Lukoff, 2012
Overclaiming	Moderate	Lack of content validity Applicant reactions Correlated with GMA	Moderate	Moderate	N. R. Kuncel et al., 2012; Paulhus, 1984
IRT approaches	Negligible	False positives Cumbersome interpretation of scores	Moderate	High	F. Stark, Chernyshenko, & Drasgow, 2012; Zickar & Sliter, 2012
Social desirability measures	Negligible	Fairness concerns Lack of validity Adverse impact Loss of credibility	Moderate	Slight	Burns & Christiansen, 2011; Dilchert & Ones, 2012; Reader & Ryan, 2012

Notes: GMA: general mental ability. IRT: item response theory. Dimensions are rated negligible, minimal, slight, moderate, or great.

It is our assertion that studies using measures of *SD* to study faking are relevant for historical purposes but should largely be ignored, as should the oft-used study citations that suggest that faking does not matter should be viewed with a large degree of skepticism. Why such citations continue to be used to justify the position that faking does not matter, when the evidence indicates otherwise, is unclear.

Research Progress

A large proportion of the faking studies since 2006 could be categorized as addressing the question "Can anything be done about faking?" (Bartram, 2007; Berry & Sackett, 2009; Bing, Kluemper, Davison, Taylor, & Novicevic, 2011; Converse et al., 2008; Converse et al., 2010; Eid & Zickar, 2007; Ellingson, Heggestad, & Makarius, 2012; Fan et al., 2012; Fleisher, Woehr, Edwards, & Cullen, 2011; Heggestad, Morrison, Reeve, & McCloy, 2006; Hirsh & Peterson, 2008; Holden & Book, 2009; Khorramdel & Kubinger, 2006; Komar et al., 2010; Kubinger, 2009; N. Kuncel & Tellegen, 2009; N. R. Kuncel & Borneman, 2007; LaHuis & Copeland, 2009; Landers, Sackett, & Tuzinski, 2011; LeBreton, Barksdale, Robin, & James, 2007; O'Connell, Kung, & Tristan, 2011; Robie, Komar, & Brown, 2010; Robie, Taggar, & Brown, 2009; Robson, Jones, & Abraham, 2008; Schnabel, Banse, & Asendorpf, 2006; Van Hooft & Born, 2012). We will use Tett et al.'s (2006) categorization for these studies as employing either preventative or remedial strategies. As noted by Tett et al. (2006, p. 62),

> Preventative methods attempt to limit respondents' opportunities, abilities, or motives to fake, and include the use of instructions and warnings, subtle items, forced choices, and item selection. Remedial strategies, on the other hand, are reactive, designed to reduce the negative effects of faking. The latter category includes option-keying, response latencies, detection scales, attitudes toward faking, and select-out selection.

Preventative Approaches

The effects of *warnings*, a variant of response instruction, on faking have been examined in several studies since 2006 (Converse et al., 2008; Fan et al., 2012; Kubinger, 2009; Landers et al., 2011; Robie et al., 2009; Robson et al., 2008). Two studies focused on the effects of warnings on mean differences on personality measures. The first study found that a warning did not significantly reduce faking (Kubinger, 2009). However, it should be noted that instead of utilizing a warning used in previous studies that the consequences of being identified for faking would result in a severely negative consequence (e.g., not being eligible for further consideration for the job or not eligible for a cash prize), the consequence in this case was to retake the test (i.e., an arguably less negative consequence). In contrast, Landers et al. (2011) found that a warning reduced faking for individuals who retested on a personality measure after initial failure. Three studies focused on relationships between personality measures and outcomes. One study found no incremental criterion-related validity for warned versus nonwarned groups (Converse et al., 2008) and that warnings may lead to negative test-taker reactions. Another study found that warnings did not increase convergent (i.e., consensual) validity for any personality constructs (Robson et al., 2008). One study found an increase in convergent validity for one personality variable (i.e., conscientiousness; Robie et al., 2009). A recent study included a faking warning early on during the testing process so that applicants could be given a chance for recourse (Fan et al., 2012). Fan et al.'s (2012) study could thus be seen as employing both preventative and remedial approaches.

No studies after 2006 could be found that used subtle items per se; however, indirect measures of personality can arguably be viewed as "subtle items." Two studies consider indirect measurement of personality and its effects on faking (LeBreton et al., 2007; Schnabel et al., 2006). Both showed resistance to faking; however, future research is needed to examine whether indirect measures maintain the same level of criterion-related validity as do traditional measures.

Several studies examined the degree to which forced-choice measures are resistant to faking (Bartram, 2007; Converse et al., 2008; Converse et al., 2010; Heggestad, Morrison, et al., 2006; Hirsh & Peterson, 2008). Studies by Bartram (2007) and Hirsh and Peterson (2008) found criterion-related validities of forced-choice measures to be superior in faking contexts than Likert-type alternatives. In contrast, Converse et al. (2008) found no differences in criterion-related validity between the two formats and further noted that the use of forced-choice instruments may lead to negative test-taker reactions. Similarly, Heggestad, Morrison, et al. (2006) found that forced-choice measures tend to not provide trait-level information as effectively as Likert-type measures. In contrast, Converse et al. (2010) found that equating response options based on social desirability ratings that are specific to the context of the job is likely to lead to less score inflation and better trait-level information in faking contexts.

One new area of study has been the examination of how speeding may prevent the effects of faking on personality measures. Speeding is the practice of putting a time limit on the completion of personality test measures. The cumulative evidence from several studies is that speeding does not prevent faking (Khorramdel & Kubinger, 2006; Komar et al., 2010; Kubinger, 2009; Robie et al., 2009; Robie et al., 2010).

One study is unique in its approach to preventing faking. Fleisher et al. (2011) found that a frequency-based measure of personality was more resistant to faking than a Likert-type measure. Frequency-based measures require individuals to report the absolute or relative frequency of occurrence for specific outcomes or behaviors over a specified time period.

Remedial Approaches

Research by Kuncel and colleagues suggests that option-keying may be an effective method of detecting idiosyncratic (or faked) responses (N. Kuncel & Tellegen, 2009; N. R. Kuncel & Borneman, 2007). Kuncel and colleagues provide evidence to suggest that individuals in faking contexts do not respond to every item in a linear fashion when trying to distort responses (i.e., respondents do not always choose the most extremely socially desirable option). Taking into account these nonlinearities in item-scoring can help identify faked responses, which, in turn, will enable practitioners to more easily identify distorted personality profiles. Measures of social desirability are designed with the assumption that respondents who are responding in a socially desirable manner always choose the most socially desirable options. These studies may help explain why typical measures of social desirability tend to be not very effective at modeling faking in real-world contexts (Burns & Christiansen, 2006).

Recent efforts at remediating faking have focused on the use of advanced statistical models (Eid & Zickar, 2007; Holden & Book, 2009; LaHuis & Copeland, 2009). Two studies have investigated the usefulness of mixed Rasch IRT models in identifying fakers (Eid & Zickar, 2007; Holden & Book, 2009). The remaining study used multilevel logistic regression to aid in identifying fakers (LaHuis & Copeland, 2009). One study included both item score and response times in examining response style (McIntyre, 2011). In all four studies, the models showed some success in identifying fakers. These models show some promise; however, the high level of technical expertise necessary to use them may hamper their operational usefulness.

One recent study found that retesting fakers who were identified as such via validity scales resulted in more accurate personality scores on the second administration (Ellingson et al., 2012).

Two studies have examined internal test indexes to examine how the effects of faking can be ameliorated. Another study examined the use of overclaiming (or declaring knowledge of a nonexistent person, event, or product) on the ability to identify fakers and increase criterion-related validity (Bing et al., 2011). The results suggested that the use of the overclaiming technique showed promise in both identifying fakers and increasing personality test score validity via suppressing unwanted error variance in personality test scores. O'Connell et al. (2011) examined three measures of response distortion (social desirability, covariance index, and implausible answers) and found mixed results in their efficacy for increasing criterion-related validity.

One study is unique in its approach and shows great promise in reducing the effects of faking. Van Hooft and Born (2012) used eye-tracking technology. Participants in the fake good condition had more fixations on the two extreme response options of the 5-point answering scale, and they fixated on these more directly after having read the question. Eye tracking was demonstrated to be potentially useful in detecting faking behavior, improving detecting rates over and beyond response extremity and latency metrics.

The research published from 2006 to the present that attempted to answer the question "Can anything be done about faking?" can be summarized as follows:

1. Warnings seem to result in decreased faking but not increased predictive validity.
2. Indirect measurement of personality constructs appears to reduce faking but may not meet adequate psychometric standards in comparison to Likert-type instruments.
3. Forced-choice measures of personality may both reduce faking and attain adequate levels of predictive validity if properly developed.
4. Speeding does not appear to reduce faking.
5. Taking into account nonlinearities in item responses can aid in identifying fakers.
6. Advanced statistical models may help in identifying fakers but may not at present be operationally viable.
7. Retesting potential fakers may be a viable method of dealing with faking.
8. The use of internal indexes has shown mixed results in terms of remediating faking.
9. Eye tracking and frequency estimation are two new methods that show great promise in remediating and preventing faking, respectively.

Discussion

The recent surge in the inclusion of personality measures in selection batteries has renewed the research interest in a long-standing vulnerability of these measures—applicant faking behavior. Since the publication of Tett et al. (2006), a large volume of theoretical and empirical research has been published. We attempted to organize this research according to the seven nested questions proposed by Tett et al. (2006) and to distill this research into a structured set of lessons learned. So what should the reader take away and what questions remain?

Considerable clarity has been reached on the first four questions, although continued research here is warranted. The growing consensus is that faking behavior is composed of volitional efforts to alter personality responses to achieve a desired goal of employment. Like all behaviors, faking may have multiple motivations and may be viewed from multiple perspectives. This multifaceted view of faking may be less parsimonious than the traditional view of faking as social desirability but is more realistic and more likely to lead to fruitful interventions than the less informed trial-and-error efforts of the past.

As Tett et al. (2006) suggested, the question of "Can applicants fake?" is largely settled with a resounding "yes." At the group level, subjects instructed to fake (good) score higher than those not so instructed. However, some respondents are not as successful as others. When analyzed at an individual level, a nontrivial number of participants engage in maladaptive responding, actually faking in the wrong direction. In addition, the construct measured and the format of the assessment influences the magnitude of faking. Continued research examining why some applicants are more successful than others and why some formats are more vulnerable may ultimately lead to methods of improving personality measurement.

The answer to the question "Do applicants fake?" has crystallized considerably since 2006. Applicant–incumbent differences have further been supported with meta-analytic evidence. In addition, a number of within-subjects studies have been conducted that allow an examination of the prevalence of faking behavior. While not unequivocal, the data suggest that roughly 30% (±10%) of applicants engage in faking behavior. Further research should be conducted to explain the variability in that estimate. Ultimately, completely eliminating faking behavior may be a fool's errand, but understanding the conditions leading to lower estimates may aid in the design of reduction interventions. It is important to note that the estimate of 30% was derived in samples from the United States. As personality assessments are used more in other countries, this question should be revisited. Early research suggests that estimates of faking behavior may be as low as 5% in Sweden and Iceland (König, Hafsteinsson, Jansen, & Stadelmann, 2011) and as high as 70% in Japan (Yoshita, 2010), with China and the United States evidencing similar levels of faking (König, Wong, & Cen, 2012). These cultural differences in faking not only have implications for applied measurement but also may inform us about the nature of faking behavior.

We have a long way to go before we finalize the answers to the last three questions posed by Tett et al. (2006). A relatively small portion of the research conducted since 2006 has examined the ability and motivation of the faker. Given that most theories of faking include ability and motivation as primary antecedents, this lack of research has left a notable hole in our knowledge. Understanding associated abilities will be helpful, but, truth be told, it does not take a rocket scientist to determine the optimal response to most Likert-type personality items. It is more likely that specific knowledge about the job being applied for or about the way personality measures are scored and interpreted will lead to successful faking than traditionally measured intelligence.

Some clarity has been achieved on the issue of the effect of faking on validity and hiring decisions. Perhaps the most definitive outcome of faking is reduced quality of hiring decisions. Faking leads to a considerable number of false positives and false negatives with fakers displacing honest applicants with desirable trait levels, and this is the primary issue that concerns employers. Employers hire individuals and not validity coefficients, and when faking is present in the selection setting, applicants with the desired trait levels are displaced by applicants low on the desired traits. The effect of faking on criterion-related validity, on the other hand, is still a little murky. Contemporary research suggests that criterion validity is attenuated but is not decimated. So, the good news is the sky is not falling (or the patient is not dying). The bad news is that criticisms regarding the low validities of personality measures are likely to persist until a significant amount of faking is reduced. The least clear outcome pertains to faking and construct validity. For the moment, research suggests that the nomological networks that inform our understanding of personality at work are intact but perhaps demonstrate more operational covariance that should be expected due to the effects of faking. At a group level, the aggregate observed measures of personality still reflect the theoretical constructs they were intended to measure. However, this should not be taken as a given and is largely dictated by the number of fakers in a given sample. If fakers constitute 20% of a sample, it may not be enough to erode the construct validity of the measures. If 40%, however, all bets are off.

The final question in Tett et al.'s (2006) framework ("Can anything be done about faking?") is where the rubber meets the road, and where efforts of personality researchers will be focused for some time. I/O psychology is an applied science, so it is only natural, given our action orientation, that we seek solutions to a perceived problem. However, to adequately address the last question, we may need to back up a bit and answer a few of the preceding questions better. As Griffith and Peterson (2011) suggested, we may have suffered from a case of "premature intervention," and a little patience may be warranted when tackling the last question. If we conduct our due diligence on the first six nested questions, the answer to the seventh question may be the sweetest and truly be the last time we have to use the "F-word."

Practitioner's Window

While the discussion of faking behavior can be a somewhat gloomy topic for personality researchers, at the end of the day there is no huge need for alarm. All assessments have strengths and weaknesses. To the best of our knowledge, there is no such thing as a perfect measurement tool. Rather than viewing faking as a fatal flaw for personality measurement, we see it as an opportunity to improve measures that have already demonstrated useful incremental validity in augmenting our ability-focused selection batteries. To make sure you are getting the most out of your personality measure we suggest the following:

1. Using personality measures as part of a whole-person assessment strategy. Hiring decisions should never be based on personality measures alone. Rather, they should be based on a combination of measures, some of which will be less fakable than others (e.g., cognitive ability). If you suspect an individual is, for example, exaggerating the degree to which they are outgoing and extraverted, you may want to use other methods of assessing these traits through an interview or reference check.
2. When choosing personality measures, emphasize the use of multiple narrow bandwidth constructs that are directly relevant to the job. This choice of measure will increase validity and may make faking effectively more difficult for applicants.
3. Using proactive (rather than reactive) approaches to reducing the occurrence and impact of faking from the outset of the selection process (e.g., warnings not to fake with opportunities to retest for those who do not heed the warnings). It is easier to keep the fox out of the hen house than to reconstruct the hens after the fact.
4. Weighing any faking detection or deterrent method against the costs and side effects that may accompany that method. Personality measures are comparatively inexpensive, so in the end, you get what you pay for. Faking may come with the territory of personality measures. If a vendor promises a fake-resistant method that sounds too good to be true, it likely is too good to be true.
5. Reducing reliance on self-report measures of personality, and increasing focus on objective or simulation-based assessments that may offer more direct measurements of personality.

Notes

1 *Psychology Science, 48*, 2006 and *Human Performance, 24*, 2011.
2 We retained studies using measures of *SD* as a proxy for faking behavior only in our brief history section, due to the fact that the history of faking research was largely influenced by *SD* methodology that shaped the general consensus of researchers and practitioners during the period. In this section, we note these studies by referring to social desirability, rather than the term applicant faking. It is the authors' opinion that, moving forward, only historical references to these studies are appropriate when discussing faking behavior.
3 The degree to which respondents can fake is affected by the construct being measured, item format, the transparency of the construct performance linkage, and so on. We are not implying faking is uniform. Generally, Likert-type scales evidence the most faking, with forced choice showing a lesser degree of faking. Performance-based or objective measures show the lowest amount of faking. Item format will be discussed with question 7.

References

Ajzen, I. (2001). Theory of planned behavior. *Organizational Behavior and Human Decision Processes, 50*, 179–211.
Anderson, C. D., Warner, J. L., & Spencer, C. C. (1984). Inflation bias in self-assessment examinations: Implications for valid employee selection. *Journal of Applied Psychology, 69*, 574–580.

Aronson, Z. H., & Reilly, R. R. (2006). Personality validity: The role of schemas and motivated reasoning. *International Journal of Selection and Assessment, 14*, 372–380.
Arthur, W., Jr., Glaze, R. M., Villado, A. J., & Taylor, J. E. (2010). The magnitude and extent of cheating and response distortion effects on unproctored internet based tests of cognitive ability and personality. *International Journal of Selection and Assessment, 18*, 1–16.
Barrick, M. R., & Mount, M. K. (1996). Effects of impression management and self deception on the predictive value of personality constructs. *Journal of Applied Psychology, 81*, 261–272.
Bartram, D. (2007). Increasing validity with forced-choice criterion measurement formats. *International Journal of Selection and Assessment, 15*, 263–272.
Berry, C., & Sackett, P. (2009). Faking in personnel selection: Tradeoffs in performance versus fairness resulting from two cut-score strategies. *Personnel Psychology, 62*, 835–863.
Bing, M. N., Kluemper, D., Davison, H. K., Taylor, S., & Novicevic, M. (2011). Overclaiming as a measure of faking. *Organizational Behavior and Human Decision Processes, 116*, 148–162.
Birkeland, S. A., Manson, T. M., Kisamore, J. L., Brannick, M. T., & Smith, M. A. (2006). A meta-analytic investigation of job applicant faking on personality measures. *International Journal of Selection and Assessment, 14*, 317–335.
Bonanni, C., Drysdale, D., Hughes, A., & Doyle, P. (2006). Employee background verification: Measuring the cross-referencing effect. *International Business & Economics Research Journal, 5*, 1–8.
Book, A. S., Holden, R. R., Starzyk, K. B., Wasylkiw, L., & Edwards, M. J. (2006). Psychopathic traits and experimentally induced deception in self-report assessment. *Personality and Individual Differences, 41*, 601–608.
Bott, J., Snell, A., Dahling, J., & Smith, B. (2010). Predicting individual score elevation in an applicant setting: The influence of individual differences and situational perceptions. *Journal of Applied Social Psychology, 40*, 2774–2790.
Bott, J. P., O'Connell, M. S., Ramakrishnan, M., & Doverspike, D. (2007). Practical limitations in making decisions regarding the distribution of applicant personality test scores based on incumbent data. *Journal of Business and Psychology, 22*, 123–134.
Bradley, K. M., & Hauenstein, N. M. A. (2006). The moderating effects of sample type as evidence of the effects of faking on personality scale correlations and factor structure. *Psychology Science, 48*, 313–335.
Burns, G. N., & Christiansen, N. D. (2006). Sensitive or senseless: On the use of social desirability measures in selection and assessment. In R. L. Griffith & M. H. Peterson (Eds.), *A closer examination of applicant faking behavior* (pp. 115–150). Greenwich, CT: Information Age Publishing.
Burns, G. N., & Christiansen, N. D. (2011). Methods of measuring faking behavior. *Human Performance, 24*, 358–372.
Byle, K. A., & Holtgraves, T. M. (2008). Integrity testing, personality, and design: Interpreting the personnel reaction blank. *Journal of Business and Psychology, 22*, 287–295.
Christiansen, N. D., Goffin, R. D., Johnston, N. G., & Rothstein, M. G. (1994). Correcting the 16PF for faking: Effects on criterion-related validity and individual hiring decisions. *Personnel Psychology, 47*, 847–860.
Christiansen, N. D., Rozek, R. F., & Burns, G. (2010). Effects of social desirability scores on hiring judgments. *Journal of Personnel Psychology, 9*, 27–39.
Converse, P. D., Oswald, F., Imus, A., Hedricks, C., Roy, R., & Butera, H. (2008). Comparing personality test formats and warnings: Effects on criterion-related validity and test-taker reactions. *International Journal of Selection and Assessment, 16*, 155–169.
Converse, P. D., Pathak, J., Quist, J., Merbedone, M., Gotlib, T., & Kostic, E. (2010). Statement desirability ratings in forced-choice personality measure development: Implications for reducing score inflation and providing trait-level information. *Human Performance, 23*, 323–342.
Converse, P. D., Peterson, M. H., & Griffith, R. L. (2009). Faking on personality measures: Implications for selection involving multiple predictors. *International Journal of Selection and Assessment, 17*, 47–60.
Day, A., & Carroll, S. (2008). Faking emotional intelligence (EI): Comparing response distortion on ability and trait-based EI measures. *Journal of Organizational Behavior, 29*, 761–784.
De Vos, A., De Stobbeleir, K., & Meganck, A. (2009). The relationship between career-related antecedents and graduates' anticipatory psychological contracts. *Journal of Business Psychology, 24*, 289–298.
Dilchert, S., & Ones, D. S. (2012). Application of preventive strategies. In M. Ziegler, C. MacCann, & R. Roberts (Eds.), *New perspectives on faking in personality assessments* (pp. 177–200). Oxford, UK: Oxford University Press.
Dilchert, S., Ones, D. S., Viswesvaran, C., & Deller, J. (2006). Response distortion in personality measurement: Born to deceive, yet capable of providing valid self-assessments? *Psychology Science, 48*, 209–225.
Donovan, J. J., Dwight, S. A., & Hurtz, G. M. (2003). An assessment of the prevalence, severity, and verifiability of entry-level applicant faking using the randomized response technique. *Human Performance, 16*, 81–106.
Edwards, A. L. (1957). *The social desirability variable in personality assessment and research.* Fort Worth, TX: Dryden.
Eid, M., & Zickar, M. J. (2007). Detecting response styles and faking in personality and organizational assessments by mixed Rasch models. In M. von Davier & C. H. Carstensen (Eds.), *Multivariate and mixture distribution Rasch models: Extensions and applications* (pp. 255–270). New York, NY: Springer Science + Business Media.

Ekman, P., & Frank, M. G. (1993). Lies that fail. In M. Lewis & C. Saarni (Eds.), *Lying and deception in everyday life* (pp. 184–200). London, England: Guilford Press.

Ellingson, J. E. (2012). People only fake when they need to fake. In M. Ziegler, C. McCann, & R. D. Roberts (Eds.), *New perspectives on faking in personality assessment* (pp. 19–33). New York, NY: Oxford University Press.

Ellingson, J. E., Heggestad, E. D., & Makarius, E. E. (2012). Personality retesting for managing intentional distortion. *Journal of Personality and Social Psychology, 102*, 1063–1076.

Ellingson, J. E., & McFarland, L. A. (2011). Understanding faking behavior through the lens of motivation: An application of VIE theory. *Human Performance, 24*, 322–337.

Ellingson, J. E., Sackett, P. R., & Connelly, B. S. (2007). Personality assessment across selection and development contexts: Insights into response distortion. *Journal of Applied Psychology, 92*, 386–395.

Fan, J., Gao, D., Carroll, S. A., Lopez, F. J., Tian, T. S., & Meng, H. (2012). Testing the efficacy of a new procedure for reducing faking on personality tests within selection contexts. *Journal of Applied Psychology, 97*, 886–888.

Ferrando, P. J., & Anguiano-Carrasco, C. (2009a). Assessing the impact of faking on binary personality measures: An IRT-based multiple-group factor analytic procedure. *Multivariate Behavioral Research, 44*, 497–524.

Ferrando, P. J., & Anguiano-Carrasco, C. (2009b). The interpretation of the EPQ lie scale scores under honest and faking instructions: A multiple-group IRT-based analysis. *Personality and Individual Differences, 46*, 552–556.

Fleisher, M. S., Woehr, D. J., Edwards, B. D., & Cullen, K. L. (2011). Assessing within-person personality variability via frequency estimation: More evidence for a new measurement approach. *Journal of Research in Personality, 45*, 535–548.

Goffin, R. D., & Boyd, A. C. (2009). Faking and personality assessment in personnel selection: Advancing models of faking. *Canadian Psychology, 50*, 151–160.

Griffith, R. L., Chmielowski, T., & Yoshita, Y. (2007). Do applicants fake? An examination of the frequency of applicant faking behavior. *Personnel Review, 36*, 341–355.

Griffith, R. L., & Converse, P. D. (2012). The rules of evidence and the prevalence of applicant faking. In M. Ziegler, C. MacCann, & R. Roberts (Eds.), *New perspectives on faking in personality assessments* (pp. 34–52). Oxford, UK: Oxford University Press.

Griffith, R. L., Lee, L. M., Peterson, M. H., & Zickar, M. J. (2011). First dates and little white lies: A trait contract classification theory of applicant faking behavior. *Human Performance, 24*, 338–357.

Griffith, R. L., Malm, T., English, A., Yoshita, Y., & Gujar, A. (2006). Applicant faking behavior: Teasing apart the influence of situational variance, cognitive biases, and individual differences. In R. Griffith & M. Peterson (Eds.), *A closer examination of applicant faking behavior* (pp. 151–178). Greenwich, CT: Information Age Publishing.

Griffith, R. L., & McDaniel, M. (2006). The nature of deception and applicant faking behavior. In R. L. Griffith & M. H. Peterson (Eds.), *A closer examination of applicant faking behavior* (pp. 1–19). Greenwich, CT: Information Age Publishing.

Griffith, R. L., & Peterson, M. H. (2006). *A closer examination of applicant faking behavior*. Greenwich, CT: Information Age Publishing.

Griffith, R. L., & Peterson, M. H. (2008). The failure of social desirability measures to capture applicant faking behavior. *Industrial and Organizational Psychology: Perspectives on Science and Practice, 1*, 308–311.

Griffith, R. L., & Peterson, M. H. (2011). One piece at a time: The puzzle of applicant faking and a call for theory. *Human Performance, 24*, 291–301.

Grubb, W. L., & McDaniel, M. A. (2007). The fakability of Bar-On's Emotional Quotient Inventory short form: Catch me if you can. *Human Performance, 20*, 43–59.

Hartman, N. S., & Grubb, W. L. (2011). Deliberate faking on personality and emotional intelligence measures. *Psychological Reports, 108*, 120–138.

Hausknecht, J. (2010). Candidate persistence and personality test practice effects: Implications for staffing system management. *Personnel Psychology, 63*, 299–324.

Hayes, T. (2007). A closer examination of applicant faking behavior. *Personnel Psychology, 60*, 511–514.

Heggestad, E. D., George, E., & Reeve, C. L. (2006). Transient error in personality scores: Considering honest and faked responses. *Personality and Individual Differences, 40*, 1201–1211.

Heggestad, E. D., Morrison, M., Reeve, C. L., & McCloy, R. A. (2006). Forced-choice assessments of personality for selection: Evaluating issues of normative assessment and faking resistance. *Journal of Applied Psychology, 91*, 9–24.

Hirsh, J. B., & Peterson, J. B. (2008). Predicting creativity and academic success with a "fake-proof" measure of the Big Five. *Journal of Research in Personality, 42*, 1323–1333.

Hogan, J., Barrett, P., & Hogan, R. (2007). Personality measurement, faking, and employment selection. *Journal of Applied Psychology, 92*, 1270–1285.

Hogan, R. (2007). *Personality and the fate of organizations*. Mahwah, NJ: Lawrence Erlbaum Associates.

Holden, R. R. (2007). Socially desirable responding does moderate personality scale validity both in experimental and in nonexperimental contexts. *Canadian Journal of Behavioural Science, 39*, 184–201.

Holden, R. R., & Book, A. (2009). Using hybrid Rasch-latent class modeling to improve the detection of fakers on a personality inventory. *Personality and Individual Differences, 47*, 185–190.
Holden, R. R., & Book, A. S. (2012). Faking does distort self-report personality assessment. In M. Ziegler, C. MacCann, & R. D. Roberts (Eds.), *New perspectives on faking in personality assessment* (pp. 71–86). New York, NY: Oxford University Press.
Holden, R. R., Fekken, G. C., & Cotton, D. H. G. (1991). Assessing psychopathology using structured test-item response latencies. *Psychological Assessment: A Journal of Consulting and Clinical Psychology, 3*, 111–118. doi:10.1037/1040-3590.3.1.111
Holden, R. R., & Passey, J. (2010). Socially desirable responding in personality assessment: Not necessarily faking and not necessarily substance. *Personality and Individual Differences, 49*, 446–450.
Honkaniemi, L., & Feldt, T. (2008). Egoistic and moralistic bias in real-life inventory responses. *Personality and Individual Differences, 45*, 307–311.
Hough, L. M. (1998). The millennium for personality psychology: New horizons or good ole daze. *Applied Psychology: An International Review, 47*, 233–261.
Hough, L. M., Eaton, N. K., Dunnette, M. D., Kamp, J. D., & McCloy, R. A. (1990). Criterion-related validities of personality constructs and the effect of response distortion on those validities. *Journal of Applied Psychology, 75*, 581–595.
Hough, L. M., & Oswald, F. L. (2008). Personality testing and industrial–organizational psychology: Reflections, progress, and prospects. *Industrial and Organizational Psychology, 1*, 272–290.
Johnson, J. A., & Hogan, R. (2006). A socioanalytic view of faking. In R. L. Griffith & M. H. Peterson (Eds.), *A closer examination of applicant faking behavior* (pp. 209–232). Greenwich, CT: Information Age Publishing.
Johnson, M., Sivadas, E., & Kashyap, V. (2009). Response bias in the measurement of salesperson orientations: The role of impression management. *Industrial Marketing Management, 38*, 1014–1024.
Kanning, U., & Kuhne, S. (2006). Social desirability in a multimodal personnel selection test battery. *European Journal of Work and Organizational Psychology, 15*, 241–261.
Khorramdel, L., & Kubinger, K. D. (2006). The effect of speediness on personality questionnaires: An experiment on applicants within a job recruiting procedure. *Psychology Science, 48*, 378–397.
Kim, B. H. (2011). Deception and applicant faking: Putting the pieces together. In G. P. Hodgkinson & J. K. Ford (Eds.), *International review of industrial and organizational psychology* (pp. 239–292). Chichester, UK: John Wiley & Sons.
Kleinmann, M. (1993). Are rating dimensions in assessment centers transparent for participants? Consequences for criterion and construct validity. *Journal of Applied Psychology, 78*, 988–993.
Komar, S., Brown, D. J., Komar, J. A., & Robie, C. (2008). Faking and the validity of conscientiousness: A Monte Carlo investigation. *Journal of Applied Psychology, 93*, 140–154.
Komar, S., Komar, J. A., Robie, C., & Taggar, S. (2010). Speeding personality measures to reduce faking: A self-regulatory model. *Journal of Personnel Psychology, 9*, 126–137.
König, C. J., Hafsteinsson, L. G., Jansen, A., & Stadelmann, E. H. (2011). Applicants' self-presentational behavior across cultures: Less self-presentation in Switzerland and Iceland than in the US. *International Journal of Selection and Assessment, 19*, 331–339.
König, C. J., Melchers, K. G., Kleinmann, M., Richter, G. M., & Klehe, U. (2006). The relationship between the ability to identify evaluation criteria and integrity test scores. *Psychology Science, 48*, 369–377.
König, C. J., Wong, J., & Cen, G. (2012). How much do Chinese applicants fake? *International Journal of Selection and Assessment, 20*, 247–250.
Konstabel, K., Aavik, T., & Allik, J. (2006). Social desirability and consensual validity of personality traits. *European Journal of Personality, 20*, 549–566.
Krahé, B., Becker, J., & Zollter, J. (2008). Contextual cues as a source of response bias in personality questionnaires: The case of the NEO-FFI. *European Journal of Personality, 22*, 655–673.
Kubinger, K. D. (2009). Three more attempts to prevent faking good in personality questionnaires. *Review of Psychology, 16*, 115–121.
Kuncel, N., & Tellegen, A. (2009). A conceptual and empirical reexamination of the measurement of the social desirability of items: Implications for detecting desirable response style and scale development. *Personnel Psychology, 62*, 201–228.
Kuncel, N. R., & Borneman, M. J. (2007). Toward a new method of detecting deliberately faked personality tests: The use of idiosyncratic item responses. *International Journal of Selection and Assessment, 15*, 220–231.
Kuncel, N. R., Borneman, M., & Kiger, T. (2012). Innovative item response process and Bayesian faking detection methods: More questions than answers. In M. Ziegler, C. MacCann, & R. Roberts (Eds.), *New perspectives on faking in personality assessments* (pp. 102–112). Oxford, UK: Oxford University Press.
LaHuis, D. M., & Copeland, D. (2009). Investigating faking using a multilevel logistic regression approach to measuring person fit. *Organizational Research Methods, 12*, 296–319.

Landers, R. N., Sackett, P. R., & Tuzinski, K. A. (2011). Retesting after initial failure, coaching rumors, and warnings against faking in online personality measures for selection. *Journal of Applied Psychology, 96*, 202–210.
LeBreton, J. M., Barksdale, C. D., Robin, J., & James, L. R. (2007). Measurement issues associated with conditional reasoning tests: Indirect measurement and test faking. *Journal of Applied Psychology, 92*, 1–16.
Levashina, J., & Campion, M. (2007). Measuring faking in the employment interview: Development and validation of an interview faking behavior scale. *Journal of Applied Psychology, 92*, 1638–1656.
Levashina, J., Morgeson, F., & Campion, M. (2009). They don't do it often, but they do it well: Exploring the relationship between applicant mental abilities and faking. *International Journal of Selection and Assessment, 17*, 271–281.
Lukoff, B. (2012). Is faking inevitable? Person-level strategies for reducing faking. In M. Ziegler, C. MacCann, & R. Roberts (Eds.), *New perspectives on faking in personality assessments* (pp. 240–252). Oxford, UK: Oxford University Press.
MacNeil, B. M., & Holden, R. R. (2006). Psychopathy and the detection of faking on self-report inventories of personality. *Personality and Individual Differences, 41*, 641–651.
Marcus, B. (2006). Relationships between faking, validity, and decision criteria in personnel selection. *Psychology Science, 48*, 226–246.
Marcus, B. (2009). "Faking" from the applicant's perspective: A theory of self-presentation in personnel selection settings. *International Journal of Selection and Assessment, 17*, 417–430.
McDaniel, M., Beier, M., Perkins, A., Goggin, S., & Frankel, B. (2009). An assessment of the fakeability of self-report and implicit personality measures. *Journal of Research in Personality, 43*, 682–685.
McFarland, L. A., & Ryan, A. M. (2000). Variance in faking across noncognitive measures. *Journal of Applied Psychology, 85*, 812–821.
McFarland, L. A., & Ryan, A. M. (2006). Toward an integrated model of applicant faking behavior. *Journal of Applied Social Psychology, 36*, 979–1016.
McIntyre, H. H. (2011). Investigating response styles in self-report personality data via joint structural equation mixture modeling of item responses and response times. *Personality and Individual Differences, 50*, 597–602.
Mischel, W. (1968). *Personality and assessment*. Hoboken, NJ: John Wiley & Sons.
Morgeson, F. P., Campion, M. A., Dipboye, R. L., Hollenbeck, J. R., Murphy, K., & Schmitt, N. (2007). Reconsidering the use of personality tests in personnel selection contexts. *Personnel Psychology, 60*, 683–729.
Mueller-Hanson, R. A., Heggestad, E. D., & Thornton, G. C. (2006). Individual differences in impression management: An exploration of the psychological processes underlying faking. *Psychology Science, 48*, 288–312.
Murphy, K. R., & Dzieweczynski, J. L. (2005). Why don't measures of broad dimensions of personality perform better as predictors of job performance? *Human Performance, 18*, 343–357.
O'Connell, M. S., Kung, M., & Tristan, E. (2011). Beyond impression management: Evaluating three measures of response distortion and their relationship to job performance. *International Journal of Selection and Assessment, 19*, 340–351.
Ones, D. S., Viswesvaran, C., & Reiss, A. D. (1996). Role of social desirability in personality testing for personnel selection: The red herring. *Journal of Applied Psychology, 81*, 660–679.
Pace, V. L., & Borman, W. C. (2006). The use of warnings to discourage faking on noncognitive inventories. In R. L. Griffith & M. H. Peterson (Eds.), *A closer examination of applicant faking behavior* (pp. 283–304). Greenwich, CT: Information Age Publishing.
Pannone, R. D. (1984). Predicting test performance: A content valid approach to screening applicants. *Personnel Psychology, 37*, 507–514.
Paulhus, D. L. (1984). Two-component models of socially desirable responding. *Journal of Personality and Social Psychology, 46*, 598–609.
Paulhus, D. L. (2002). Socially desirable responding: The evolution of a construct. In D. L. Paulhus (Ed.), *Educational Testing Service conference in honor of Sam Messick on the occasion of his retirement* (pp. 49–69). Mahwah, NJ: Lawrence Erlbaum Associates.
Paulhus, D. L. (2012). Overclaiming on personality questionnaires. In M. Ziegler, C. MacCann, & R. Roberts (Eds.), *New perspectives on faking in personality assessments* (pp. 151–164). Oxford, UK: Oxford University Press.
Paulhus, D. L., Harms, P. D., Nadine, B. M., & Lysy, D. C. (2003). The over-claiming technique: Measuring self-enhancement independent of ability. *Journal of Personality and Social Psychology, 84*, 890–904.
Paulhus, D. L., & Trapnell, P. D. (2008). Self-presentation of personality: An agency-communion framework. In O. P. John, R. W. Robins, & L. A. Pervin (Eds.), *Handbook of personality psychology: Theory and research* (3rd ed., pp. 492–517). New York, NY: Guilford Press.
Peterson, M. H., & Griffith, R. L. (2006). Faking and job performance: A multifaceted issue. In R. L. Griffith & M. H. Peterson (Eds.), *A closer examination of applicant faking behavior* (pp. 233–262). Greenwich, CT: Information Age Publishing.

Peterson, M. H., Griffith, R. L., & Converse, P. D. (2009). Examining the role of applicant faking in hiring decisions: Percentage of fakers hired and hiring discrepancies in single- and multiple-predictor selection. *Journal of Business and Psychology, 24*, 373–386.

Peterson, M. H., Griffith, R. L., Isaacson, J. A., O'Connell, M. S., & Mangos, P. M. (2011). Applicant faking, social desirability, and the prediction of counterproductive work behaviors. *Human Performance, 24*, 270–290.

Raymark, P. H., & Tafero, T. L. (2009). Individual differences in the ability to fake on personality measures. *Human Performance, 22*, 86–103.

Reader, M. C., & Ryan, A. M. (2012). Methods for correcting faking. In M. Ziegler, C. MacCann, & R. Roberts (Eds.), *New perspectives on faking in personality assessments* (pp. 131–150). Oxford, UK: Oxford University Press.

Robie, C. (2006). Effects of perceived selection ratio on personality test faking. *Social Behavior and Personality, 34*, 1233–1244.

Robie, C., Brown, D. J., & Beaty, J. C. (2007). Do people fake on personality inventories? A verbal protocol analysis. *Journal of Business and Psychology, 21*, 489–509.

Robie, C., Emmons, T., Tuzinski, K., & Kantrowitz, T. (2011). Effects of an economic recession on leader personality and general mental ability scores. *International Journal of Selection and Assessment, 19*, 183–189.

Robie, C., Komar, S., & Brown, D. J. (2010). The effects of coaching and speeding on Big Five and impression management scale scores. *Human Performance, 23*, 446–467.

Robie, C., Taggar, S., & Brown, D. J. (2009). The effects of warnings and speeding on scale scores and convergent validity of conscientiousness. *Human Performance, 22*, 340–354.

Robie, C., Tuzinski, K. A., & Bly, P. R. (2006). A survey of assessor beliefs and practices related to faking. *Journal of Managerial Psychology, 21*, 669–681.

Robson, S. M., Jones, A., & Abraham, J. (2008). Personality, faking, and convergent validity: A warning concerning warning statements. *Human Performance, 21*, 89–106.

Ryan, A. M., & Boyce, A. S. (2006). What do we know and where do we go? Practical directions for faking research. In R. L. Griffith & M. H. Peterson (Eds.), *A closer examination of applicant faking behavior* (pp. 357–371). Greenwich, CT: Information Age Publishing.

Sackett, P. R. (2011). Integrating and prioritizing theoretical perspectives on applicant faking of personality measures. *Human Performance, 24*, 379–385.

Schmit, M. J., & Ryan, A. M. (1992). Test-taking dispositions: A missing link? *Journal of Applied Psychology, 77*, 629–637.

Schmit, M. J., & Ryan, A. M. (1993). The Big Five in personnel selection: Factor structure in applicant and non-applicant populations. *Journal of Applied Psychology, 78*, 966–974.

Schmitt, N., & Oswald, F. L. (2006). The impact of corrections for faking on the validity of noncognitive measures in selection settings. *Journal of Applied Psychology, 91*, 613–621.

Schmitt, N., Oswald, F. L., Kirn, B. H., Gillespie, M. A., Ramsay, L. J., & Yoo, T.-Y. (2003). Impact of elaboration on socially desirable responding and the validity of biodata measures. *Journal of Applied Psychology, 88*, 979–988.

Schnabel, K., Banse, R., & Asendorpf, J. (2006). Employing automatic approach and avoidance tendencies for the assessment of implicit personality self-concept: The implicit association procedure (IAP). *Experimental Psychology, 53*, 69–76.

Simón, A. (2007). Sensitivity of the 16 PF motivational distortion scale to response bias. *Psychological Reports, 101*, 482–484.

Sisco, H., & Reilly, R. R. (2007). Five factor biodata inventory: Resistance to faking. *Psychological Reports, 101*, 3–17.

Snell, A. F., Sydell, E. J., & Lueke, S. B. (1999). Towards a theory of applicant faking: Integrating studies of deception. *Human Resource Management Review, 9*, 219–242.

Stark, F., Chernyshenko, O. S., & Drasgow, F. (2012). Constructing fake-resistant personality tests using item response theory: High-stakes personality testing with multidimensional pairwise preferences. In M. Ziegler, C. MacCann, & R. Roberts (Eds.), *New perspectives on faking in personality assessments* (pp. 214–239). Oxford, UK: Oxford University Press.

Stark, S., Chernyshenko, O. S., Chan, K.-Y., Lee, W. C., & Drasgow, F. (2001). Effects of the testing situation on item responding: Cause for concern. *Journal of Applied Psychology, 86*, 943–953.

Stewart, G., Darnold, T., Zimmerman, R., Parks, L., & Dustin, S. (2010). Exploring how response distortion of personality measures affects individuals. *Personality and Individual Differences, 49*, 622–628.

Tett, R. P., Anderson, M. G., Ho, C., Yang, T. S., Huang, L., & Hanvongse, A. (2006). Seven nested questions about faking on personality tests: An overview and interactionist model of item-level response distortion. In R. L. Griffith & M. H. Peterson (Eds.), *A closer examination of applicant faking behavior* (pp. 43–83). Greenwich, CT: Information Age Publishing.

Tett, R. P., & Christiansen, N. D. (2007). Personality tests at the crossroads: A response to Morgeson, Campion, Dipboye, Hollenbeck, Murphy, and Schmitt (2007). *Personnel Psychology, 60*, 967–993.

Tett, R. P., Freund, K. A., Christiansen, N. D., Fox, N. E., & Coaster, J. (2011). Faking on self-report emotional intelligence and personality tests: Effects of faking opportunity, cognitive ability, and job type. *Personality and Individual Differences, 52*, 195–201.

Tett, R. P., & Simonet, D. (2011). Faking in personality assessment: A "multi-saturation" perspective on faking as performance. *Human Performance, 24*, 302–321.

Tippins, N. T. (2009). Internet alternatives to traditional proctored testing: Where are we now? *Industrial and Organizational Psychology: Perspectives on Science and Practice, 2*, 2–10.

Trahan, A. (2011). Filling in the gaps in culture-based theories of organizational crime. *Journal of Theoretical & Philosophical Criminology, 3*, 89–109.

Van Hooft, E. A. J., & Born, M. P. (2012). Intentional response distortion on personality tests: Using eye-tracking to understand response processes when faking. *Journal of Applied Psychology, 97*, 301–316.

Vasilopoulos, N. L., & Cucina, J. M. (2006). Faking on noncognitive measures. In R. L. Griffith & M. H. Peterson (Eds.), *A closer examination of applicant faking behavior* (pp. 305–331). Greenwich, CT: Information Age Publishing.

Vernon, P. E. (1934). The attitude of the subject in personality testing. *Journal of Applied Psychology, 18*, 165–177.

Viswesvaran, C., & Ones, D. S. (1999). Meta-analyses of fakability estimates: Implications for personality measurement. *Educational and Psychological Measurement, 59*, 197–210.

Vroom, V. H. (1964). *Work and motivation*. New York, NY: Wiley.

Walmsley, P. T., & Sackett, P. R. (in press). Factors affecting potential personality retest improvement after initial failure. *Human Performance*.

Winkelspecht, C., Lewis, P., & Thomas, A. (2006). Potential effects of faking on the NEO-PI-R: Willingness and ability to fake changes who gets hired in simulated selection decisions. *Journal of Business and Psychology, 21*, 243–259.

Yoshita, Y. (2010). *Cultural membership and applicant faking behavior: A Japanese and American comparison* (Unpublished doctoral dissertation). Florida Institute of Technology, Melbourne.

Zickar, M. J., & Drasgow, F. (1996). Detecting faking using appropriateness measurement. *Applied Psychological Measurement, 20*, 71–87.

Zickar, M. J., & Gibby, R. E. (2006). A history of faking and socially desirable responding on personality tests. In R. L. Griffith & M. H. Peterson (Eds.), *A closer examination of applicant faking behavior* (pp. 21–42). Greenwich, CT: Information Age Publishing.

Zickar, M. J., & Robie, C. (1999). Modeling faking good on personality items: An item-level analysis. *Journal of Applied Psychology, 84*, 551–563.

Zickar, M. J., & Sliter, K. A. (2012). Searching for unicorns: Item response theory-based solutions to the faking problem. In M. Ziegler, C. MacCann, & R. Roberts (Eds.), *New perspectives on faking in personality assessments* (pp. 113–130). Oxford, UK: Oxford University Press.

Ziegler, M., MacCann, C., & Roberts, R. D. (2012a). Faking: Knowns, unknowns, and points of contention. In M. Ziegler, C. MacCann, & R. D. Roberts (Eds.), *New perspectives on faking in personality assessment* (pp. 3–18). New York, NY: Oxford University Press.

Ziegler, M., MacCann, C., & Roberts, R. D. (2012b). *New perspectives on faking in personality assessments*. Oxford, UK: Oxford University Press.

Ziegler, M., Schmidt-Atzert, L., Bühner, M., & Krumm, S. (2007). Fakability of different measurement methods for achievement motivation: Questionnaire, semi-projective, and objective. *Psychology Science, 49*, 291–307.

13

Applicant Reactions to Personality Tests

Why Do Applicants Hate Them?

Lynn A. McFarland

Personality tests tend to exhibit negative applicant reactions (e.g., Rosse, Miller, & Stecher, 1994; Smither, Reilly, Millsap, Pearlman, & Stoffey, 1993; Steiner & Gilliland, 1996) and these reactions have been found to generalize across countries and contexts (Anderson, Salgado, & Hulsheger, 2010). This is problematic for a host of reasons. Applicant reactions toward personality tests may relate to test performance, withdrawal from the selection process, and the validity of the test (Chan, Schmitt, DeShon, Clause, & Delbridge, 1997; Rynes, 1993). To the extent these perceptions relate to test performance, such perceptions may affect selection decisions (Ployhart & Ryan, 1997; Ryan, Sacco, McFarland, & Kriska, 2000; Smither et al., 1993).

This chapter will review the literature and discuss why applicant reactions are important to study and understand from a practical perspective. I will first review why applicants may feel negatively toward the use of personality tests in selection contexts. This discussion will outline the applicant reaction framework most frequently used to study this phenomenon. Next, I will explore the factors that may remediate or exacerbate such negative reactions. Finally, I will present ways that we, as a field, may help address such negative reactions.

Consequences of Applicant Reactions

Applicant perceptions toward selection procedures could have a number of implications for an organization. First, reactions toward personality tests have the potential to affect organizational attraction. Rynes (1991) argues that applicants use an organization's selection practices as a signal for how the organization operates. That is, they use this selection information to form impressions regarding what it may be like to work in the organization. Furthermore, research suggests that those most likely to opt out of a selection process are the most desirable applicants (Ployhart, McFarland, & Ryan, 2002). Therefore, bad experiences in the selection process may result in negative applicant reactions. If this deters applicants from continuing in the selection process, an organization may fail to hire the most qualified people. Furthermore, individuals who have negative reactions toward selection procedures are also less likely to recommend the organization to others (Ryan, Sacco, McFarland, & Kriska, 2000).

Second, applicant perceptions have been shown to affect future purchase intentions. Therefore, applicants may be less inclined to buy products or services from a company if they have had a bad experience in the selection process (Smither et al., 1993).

Third, test perceptions can result in lower test-taking motivation. To the extent these perceptions relate to test performance, such perceptions may affect selection decisions (Chan et al., 1997) and the validity of the test (Schmit & Ryan, 1992).

Finally, applicant reactions can have legal implications for an organization (Smither et al., 1993). The base rate of legal action resulting from selection procedures is very low, but we cannot rule out the possibility that if applicants perceive the selection process to be unfair, and think the process is unlikely to predict work behavior, they would be more likely to take legal action against the organization (for more coverage on personality testing and legal issues, see Chapter 23, this volume).

Clearly, it is in an organization's best interest to elicit strong positive applicant reactions. Doing so may result in a better hiring outcome, greater customer loyalty, and less spending on legal challenges to the selection process. However, why is it that personality tests seem to elicit such negative reactions and what might we do to remedy this situation? Before we can understand why reactions to personality measures tend to be poor, we must first examine the factors that affect reactions in general. Therefore, the next section will review one of the major (and most prevalent) applicant reaction frameworks.

Organizational Justice Theory

There are multiple theoretical frameworks that have been used to understand applicant reactions (Arvey & Sackett, 1993; Ployhart & Harold, 2004; Ryan & Ployhart, 2000). However, the majority of selection research has examined applicant reactions within an organizational justice framework (Gilliland, 1993, 1994, 1995). Because most research relevant to personality testing has been from this perspective, and because other applicant reaction conceptualizations fit nicely within this framework, this chapter will focus on variables within the organizational justice framework. For a thorough discussion of other applicant reaction frameworks, see Hulsheger and Anderson (2009).

Organizational justice theory is concerned with the fairness of the distribution of organizational outcomes and the fairness of procedures used to distribute these outcomes (i.e., procedural justice; Greenberg, 1990). Gilliland (1993) adapted the basic principles of organizational justice to provide a comprehensive model of how applicants perceive and react to selection procedures. This model has received considerable support. For example, Gilliland (1994) found that applicant reactions toward a selection process (e.g., perceptions of the job-relatedness of the test used) predicted intentions to recommend the organization to others, self-efficacy, and even job performance. Subsequent research using the model has been similarly supportive (Bauer, Maertz, Dolen, & Campion, 1998; Ployhart & Ryan, 1998; see Ryan & Ployhart, 2000, for a review).

Gilliland's (1993) model suggests that applicants hold standards, called procedural justice rules, for how they expect to be treated and how selection procedures should be administered (Leventhal, 1980). These procedural justice rules determine perceptions of process fairness, such that when the rules are satisfied the selection process is perceived as fair and when these rules are violated it is perceived as unfair. Note that according to Gilliland's model, justice rules would not directly relate to applicant test-taking motivation or behavior, but would do so indirectly through process fairness perceptions.

Five procedural justice rules have been given considerable attention in the applicant reactions literature and are most relevant for personality-testing contexts (Arvey & Sackett, 1993; Smither et al., 1993). *Face validity* (or job-relatedness) reflects whether the test looks like it measures constructs related to the job (e.g., Smither et al., 1993). Similarly, *perceived predictive validity* assesses whether applicants believe the test can predict job performance (Smither et al., 1993). *Opportunity to perform* refers to whether applicants believe the test method allows them to demonstrate their full abilities. *Selection information* refers to whether applicants believe they were provided with sufficient information for why the selection procedure should be used. Finally, *question propriety* refers to whether the exams used on the test are invasive or deal with issues deemed to be personal.

Reactions to Personality Testing

Although considerable research has demonstrated the usefulness of organizational justice theory for predicting outcomes resulting from reactions to selection processes in general and ability-based measures specifically (for a review see Anderson et al., 2010), less work has been done with regards to personality measures. Therefore, we have little understanding about how reactions toward personality tests relate to many of the important outcomes noted in the previous sections. What we do know is that reactions toward personality tests are consistently more negative than they are toward other testing approaches (Hausknecht, Day, & Thomas, 2004).

A meta-analysis conducted by Hausknecht et al. (2004) demonstrated that personality measures are significantly less favorable than interviews, work samples, and even cognitive ability tests. Below is a graph showing the results of their work (Figure 13.1).

What is odd about the findings of Hausknecht et al. (2004) is that interviews ranked highest in reactions among the selection procedures examined, and yet most interviews assess personality traits (Huffcutt, Conway, Roth, & Stone, 2001; Huffcutt, Weekley, Wiesner, Groot, & Jones, 2001). So, why is it that personality tests, specifically, are so frowned upon? To answer this, we might first consider the aspects of personality tests that are typically different from interviews.

First, personality measures ask people about their behavioral tendencies, relationships, attitudes, and preferences (Rosse et al., 1994; Walsh, Layton, & Klieger, 1966). Because of the personal nature of personality questions, applicants may feel there is an inherent infringement on their privacy when asked to respond to such measures. Thus, reactions toward personality measures may be negative because there are negative perceptions of question propriety resulting from the personal nature of the questions that are asked.

Interview questions also get at personality and yet do not seem to be perceived as negatively. Perhaps this is because interviews generally assess personality within the context of asking questions related to work (e.g., Huffcutt, Conway, et al., 2001). For instance, an interview might ask

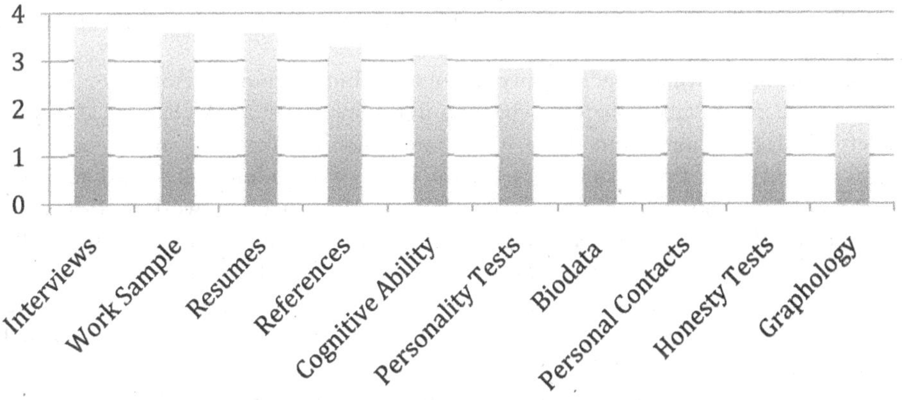

Figure 13.1 Favorability of Different Selection Measures.

how an individual deals with conflict with coworkers. Such an item would certainly capture an applicant's agreeableness, but because it is couched in a work-related context, it might not be picked up by an applicant as assessing personality or it may seem more work-related, thereby increasing perceptions of face validity and perceived predictive validity. Traditional paper and pencil personality measures are typically meant to tap characteristics that are thought to generalize across situations and therefore these items rarely reflect the job context well. For instance, a NEO-PI-R item is "I try to be courteous to everyone I meet" (Costa & McCrae, 1992). The context is unclear. Is the item referring to courteousness in the workplace, at home, among family, and so on? Such ambiguity may negatively affect applicant perceptions of face validity and the perceived predictive validity of the test or a test-taker's perception of the opportunity to perform the test. If the test is not clear, certainly an applicant might perceive it is difficult to present his or her true self.

Adding to this ambiguity, personality tests usually include all personality traits included on typical measures. So, for instance, while openness to experience may not be relevant for the job of a janitor, those items will still typically be assessed simply because a commercial test battery is used in its entirety. In many cases, only a subset of those scores will be used to make selection decisions. Therefore, the negative reactions toward personality tests may stem from the inclusion of personality traits that are clearly so irrelevant to the job in question.

Third, personality tests may result in negative perceptions of the "opportunity to perform" because of the very limited way most personality tests allow test-takers to present themselves. The majority of personality tests include a Likert scale whereby test-takers indicate the extent to which they strongly agree or strongly disagree (on a scale from 1 to 5) with the extent to which a statement represents the individual. Such a scale does not allow an applicant the chance to "tell his/her story" or explain contingencies (e.g., I'm often late to social events, but never late for work). This is another stark distinction between personality assessed via interviews and personality tests. Interviews typically allow an individual more leeway in responses. The applicant has an opportunity to qualify statements and provide the context for answers.

Fourth, interviews are one of the most common selection procedures (Posthuma, Morgeson, & Campion, 2002). Therefore, most working adults have most likely heard of or participated in an interview. Personality tests, on the other hand, are less common (Ryan, McFarland, Baron, & Page, 1999) and applicants are less likely to have familiarity with the types of items they might be asked. We already know that people tend to feel more favorable toward the familiar than the unfamiliar (Bomstein, 1989; Zajonc, 1968, 1980) and it is not unreasonable to expect this phenomenon to generalize to personality testing. This lack of familiarity with personality testing might affect the extent to which applicants think such tests are useful for selecting applicants into jobs.

Finally, although familiarity with personality tests may be limited, most personality measures are transparent in that it is fairly obvious what the items are assessing (McFarland & Ryan, 2000). Therefore, all applicants (even those who choose not to fake) will surely recognize that the items are fakable. If a test can easily be cheated, this will undoubtedly affect attitudes toward the extent to which the test is perceived to be a good predictor of work performance. If applicants perceive that some people are faking the test, and some are not, then the test really is not being consistently used across applicants (because some may choose to fake and others will not). Clearly, the faking issue poses many problems in terms of applicant reactions, and multiple justice rules may be perceived as being violated, simply because the test is perceived to be fakable.

The reasons why reactions toward personality tests may be negative lead us directly to suggestions for how to make such tests more acceptable to applicants. Strategies that may be used to elicit more positive reactions are discussed in the next section.

Strategies to Increase Positive Reactions Toward Personality Tests

The strategies that may be used to mitigate negative applicant reactions involve changing the personality test or altering the context in which the test is administered. I will begin with the ways the test itself might be altered to foster more favorable applicant reactions.

Item Transparency

Earlier, it was suggested that item transparency would have a strong influence on face validity. Johnson (1981) suggested that face validity will increase with transparency and this link has been shown. Madigan and Macan (2005) found that perceptions of transparency were positively related to overall reactions to test fairness. Going a step further, one would expect that when items are transparent that perceptions of the perceived predictive validity of the test should also increase. If applicants can identify the constructs being assessed, they should more clearly see the link between test scores and work performance.

The concern with item transparency is the potential for greater faking. If items are transparent, the constructs assessed by the items are obvious, thereby making it easier for applicants to fake the items to obtain a higher score on the test (Jackson, 1971; Lautenschlager, 1994; Mael, 1991; McFarland & Ryan, 2000; McFarland, Ryan, & Ellis, 2002; Mumford & Stokes, 1992). Therefore, there may be a tradeoff between reactions and ease of faking when it comes to the transparency of personality test items. This may make test transparency an undesirable strategy to address negative reactions toward personality tests.

Contextualize Items

Another relatively straightforward approach that may effectively increase positive reactions is to contextualize the items on the personality test. This simply involves making the items apply to work. As discussed above, most personality tests currently use very generic items that refer to generic activities (e.g., reading, going to parties) and behaviors (e.g., punctuality and ways of interacting with others; McCrae & Costa, 2008). Because it may be difficult to see the link between generic items and work performance, these tests may lack face and predictive validity. Contextualizing the items should make the link between test performance and work outcomes more obvious to the applicants, thereby increasing positive perceptions.

Contextualizing items can be done in different ways. It may involve simply adding an "at work" tag to the item. For instance, the item "I am always on time" would be changed to "I always get to work on time." Another option might be to write questions that only ask about behavior that has occurred at work such as a past behavior interview would. For example, an item like those noted above might be reworded to read "When my supervisor asks me to complete a project, I always get it done on time." On the surface, such approaches may seem easy and inexpensive. However, if all validity evidence for the test is based on the generic items, an effort will need to be made to ensure that the altered test demonstrates the same reliability and validity as the original version of the test. Research has shown that tests with context-specific tags do not necessarily have the same psychometric proprieties as the generic version of the test. Holtz, Ployhart, and Dominguez (2005) found that contextualizing items resulted in lower error variances, smaller latent variance, and higher means than a generic personality test format. Changing the context of the item can also alter the criterion-related validity of the measure (Bing, Whanger, Davison, & VanHook, 2004; Schmit, Ryan, Stierwalt, & Powell, 1995). Hunthausen, Truxillo, Bauer, and Hammer (2003) found that providing a work-specific frame-of-reference for a personality test increased the criterion-related validity of the measure. Therefore, either the equivalence of the revised test (to the old test) must be demonstrated or a new validity study must be conducted.

Whether this approach actually increases positive reactions is still not clear. Although intuitively it seems that altering personality items to be work specific should increase perceptions of face validity and perceived predictive validity, the case has yet been empirically supported. Holtz et al. (2005) did not find a difference in reactions between a context-specific and generic personality test. However, there are multiple ways to contextualize items and we have barely even scratched the surface in terms of investigating what types of changes to items have the most influence on reactions and the properties of the personality test.

Rather than contextualizing an existing personality test by adding work tags, another option is to create a test by more vividly incorporating situational information. An example of such an approach is to use situational judgment tests to assess personality constructs. This has the benefit of enhancing perceptions of face validity and perceived predictive validity (see Weekley & Ployhart, 2005, for a summary). One approach for measuring personality within situational judgment tests is to simply use situational judgment test items that correlate with personality traits, or use instructions that produce responses more affected by personality (McDaniel, Hartman, Whetzel, & Grub, 2007). A second approach is to develop the situational judgment test to specifically measure personality directly. Porr and Ployhart (2004) attempted to develop a situational judgment test (SJT) that was based on the Five-Factor Model of personality. However, such an approach is extremely time-consuming because this involves developing a test from scratch and validating the test (for more coverage regarding the assessment of personality with situational judgment measures, see Chapter 19, this volume).

Lawrence James and colleagues (James et al., 2005; LeBreton, Barksdale, Robin, & James, 2007) have developed a conditional reasoning test to assess personality (Berry, Sackett, & Tobares, 2010). This type of test is based on the notion that people use justification mechanisms to explain their behavior and that people with varying dispositions will employ different justification mechanisms. A conditional reasoning test will present what appear to be logical reasoning problems to applicants, and ask applicants to select the response that most logically follows from the initial statement. Thus, to the applicant, it would appear that logic or judgment is being assessed. The only personality trait for which a conditional reasoning test currently exists is for aggression. But, it seems that this approach has merit for increasing positive reactions, in addition to decreasing faking behavior.

Although lengthy, time-consuming, and costly, the approaches to test development employed by Ployhart and James may yield a strong payoff in validity and applicant reactions. These types of measures also tend to be less fakable because they are less transparent. Such approaches certainly warrant further examination, particularly if issues of applicant reactions and faking are of the utmost concern.

Assess Personality via Other Methods

Personality tests are typically assessed via paper and pencil. As noted previously, this might account for much of the negative reactions toward personality measures. After all, personality when assessed via the interview seems to be well received. Such differences in reactions toward the assessment of personality across these two methods suggest that it is not necessarily the case that applicants object to the use of personality measures in selection processes. Other factors may have a part to play. Perhaps paper and pencil tests are just not the best means of assessing personality if we want to ensure applicants feel they have been treated appropriately. The problem is that interviews are time-consuming and can be expensive to administer and develop. Therefore, it would not be appropriate to suggest that personality testing via paper and pencil should be abandoned, since not all organizations have the resources to start assessing personality via interviews. Interviews can be expensive to develop and administer.

Ragsdale, Christiansen, Frost, Rahael, and Burns (Chapter 22, this volume) offer an alternative that may address the negative reactions of personality tests but be less time-consuming and more cost-effective than interviews. Ragsdale et al. propose content coding of written or verbal material.

Content coding is a technique used for systematically extracting information from written or verbal material. The material coded could be responses to open-ended interview questions, text of emails, or recorded conversations with others—any information that might offer information relevant to personality. Raters, or coders, examine the content for specified characteristics such as categories, frequencies, or themes. Such a technique may directly address applicants' perceptions of the opportunity to perform by allowing them to tell their story and providing a context for their answers. In other words, this approach may have the same benefits as interviews in terms of applicant reactions. However, on the surface, a content coding approach may appear to be just as time-consuming and expensive as interviews, and it would be if done in traditional ways. However, Ragsdale et al. suggest that automated scoring systems (conducted by computers) have the potential to reduce the cost and time associated with traditional content coding (Burstein, 2003; Burstein & Marcu, 2003). It has already been shown that automated systems can be used to identify certain personality traits based on written text passages (Hirsh & Peterson, 2009; Kufner et al., 2010). This approach is described in greater detail in Chapter 22 of this book and offers a promising alternative to traditional paper and pencil testing.

Offer Applicants an Explanation for Test Use

One of the easiest and least costly ways to potentially increase positive reactions toward personality tests is to offer the applicants an explanation for their use. Explanations involve providing a reason for using the test in question. This may involve explaining to applicants that the personality test they are about to take has been shown to be a good predictor of performance on the job or that the traits being assessed by the test are ones that have been shown to be possessed by those who are most successful in the job for which they are applying. While explanations need not be lengthy, they should be accurate. For instance, if no attempt has been made to link job satisfaction with the traits being assessed, then claims that those who possess the characteristics assessed by the test are happier in the job for which they are applying should not be made.

Explanations have the potential to alter perceptions of face validity, perceived predictive validity, and selection information. Given how many justice rules this strategy may affect, it is no surprise that explanations for the use of selection tests have been found to positively affect reactions toward tests and selection processes. Holtz et al. (2005) found that job-relatedness perceptions of a personality test were significantly more positive when test-takers were told the test had been shown to be a valid measure of job performance. Truxillo, Bodner, Bertolino, Bauer, and Yonce (2009) found that reactions toward personality tests changed significantly more when explanations were provided compared to when similar explanations were provided for the use of an ability test. In other words, explanations seem to be a more effective means of manipulating applicant reactions when personality tests are used. Part of this difference in effectiveness could be that reactions toward personality tests tend to be negative to begin with (so there is more room for improvement), but the results are still very promising.

Warn Applicants Against Faking

Warning applicants against faking the personality test has been consistently shown to meaningfully reduce faking (Dwight & Donovan, 2003; McFarland, 2003). However, what implications does warning against faking have on applicant reactions? This is not as easy a question to answer as it might first appear. Warnings can take many forms. Some warnings involve telling applicants that faking can be detected, while other warnings go a step further and suggest that there are consequences for being detected as a faker (e.g., being removed from the selection process).

Other warnings try to deter faking by informing applicants that faking may be counterproductive for the applicant because, although faking might get them a higher score on the test, the applicant may end up in a job that they do not enjoy or one they cannot perform very well. Another way to subtly warn applicants against faking might be to remind them that the personality traits assessed in the personality test will be assessed in other ways later in the selection process. For example, if a personality test is the first phase of the selection process but an interview is given later, the employer might note that personality will also be assessed via the interview should the applicant go on in the process. Certainly, something like personality traits cannot technically be verified, but if the applicant is aware that personality may be evaluated in other ways later on in the process, this may reduce faking.

These different types of warnings may be used in isolation or in combination. In fact, research has found that using both warnings of faking detection and consequences for faking together are stronger deterrents against faking than just one of these warnings (McFarland, 2003). For a thorough review of the different types of warnings and their effectiveness and consequences, see Pace and Borman (2006). They identify several types of warnings.

Warnings clearly have the benefit of reducing faking, but their effect on reactions is ambiguous. Applicants may believe detection attempts are an invasion of privacy (and thus result in more negative reactions) or perhaps they would see them as leveling the playing field, making the test more fair to all applicants (increasing positive reactions). The type of warning provided will affect applicant reactions to the warnings.

Only a very small number of studies have directly examined reactions toward warnings and the results are mixed. McFarland (2003) found no negative applicant reactions toward warnings against faking when the warning involved threats of detection and/or consequences for being detected as a faker. On the other hand, Converse et al. (2008) found that warning applicants against faking that involved a consequence for being detected as a faker resulted in more negative applicant reactions.

Because the fakability of personality tests likely has a strong part to play in the negative reactions toward personality tests, it makes sense to try to do things that show applicants that faking is not necessarily occurring. However, test administrators need to be careful to balance the desire to decrease perceptions that the test is fakable with negative reactions that might result from threatening applicants with the use of such warnings. The best advice, at this point, is to positively frame warnings. Pace, Xu, Penney, Borman, and Bearden (2005) used such a warning. Prior to taking a personality test, test-takers were told to strongly consider their own best interests. They were told that faking might be harmful to them because if they faked, and were hired, they might not fit well within the organization and not enjoy the job. As these authors note, such warnings are probably most effective (in terms of reducing faking) in instances where multiple jobs are available. However, such positive framing is likely to help curb concerns about faking (thereby increasing reactions toward faking), while also potentially decreasing faking behavior itself. The same is true of the more subtle "warnings" noted earlier, which suggest that responses may be "verified" at some later point (for more information regarding personality testing and dishonest responding, see Chapter 12, this volume).

Use of Personality Tests With Other Predictors

Research suggests that some of the negative reactions toward personality tests might be mitigated if the personality test is used to make hiring decisions along with other predictors that have more positive reactions. Clearly, the use of these tests will not change reactions toward the personality test specifically. The thinking is that the negative reactions toward the personality test will be less likely to result in negative reactions toward the selection process as a whole, when used in conjunction with other measures. For example, Rosse et al. (1994) found that using a personality measure along with a cognitive ability test resulted in more positive reactions than when a personality test was used in isolation.

Very little work has currently been done to examine how different combinations of selection devices may yield varied reactions. It may be that some combinations of selection measures result in a more favorable reaction than others. Furthermore, job type may interact with their use such that a combination of tests may result in more positive reactions when used to select people into one type of job, but not another type of job. This is an area where more research is definitely needed.

Directions for Future Research

I have presented reasons why reactions toward personality tests may be so negative and suggested a variety of potential strategies that may mitigate these negative reactions. Most of the relationships discussed above are summarized in Figure 13.2 below.

As discussed, reactions are affected by both test characteristics (e.g., item transparency, test format) and the testing context (e.g., job for which applicants are applying, whether or not other measures are administered in the process, and the characteristics of those measures). These relationships are potentially moderated by individual differences (e.g., the applicant's cognitive ability, experience with personality tests, their true score on the traits being assessed). These procedural justice rules go on to affect perceptions of process fairness. Process fairness can affect all types of outcomes, including organizational attraction, future purchase intentions, the likelihood that the applicant will legally challenge the selection process, and test-taking motivation. And, as will be discussed in more detail below, test-taking motivation may affect test validity and the extent to which an applicant fakes responses. Furthermore, faking may affect test validity.

However, it is important to again point out that not all of these relationships have been empirically tested. Some are hypothesized relationships that are based on theory and research in other areas (e.g., research on cognitive ability tests). Very little work has examined reactions to personality tests in general and even less research has examined strategies for addressing negative reactions to personality tests. We cannot assume that reactions research that has been conducted with ability tests or other measures will generalize to personality-testing contexts. Cognitive ability and personality measures are inherently different. Therefore, considerable time must be spent researching reactions

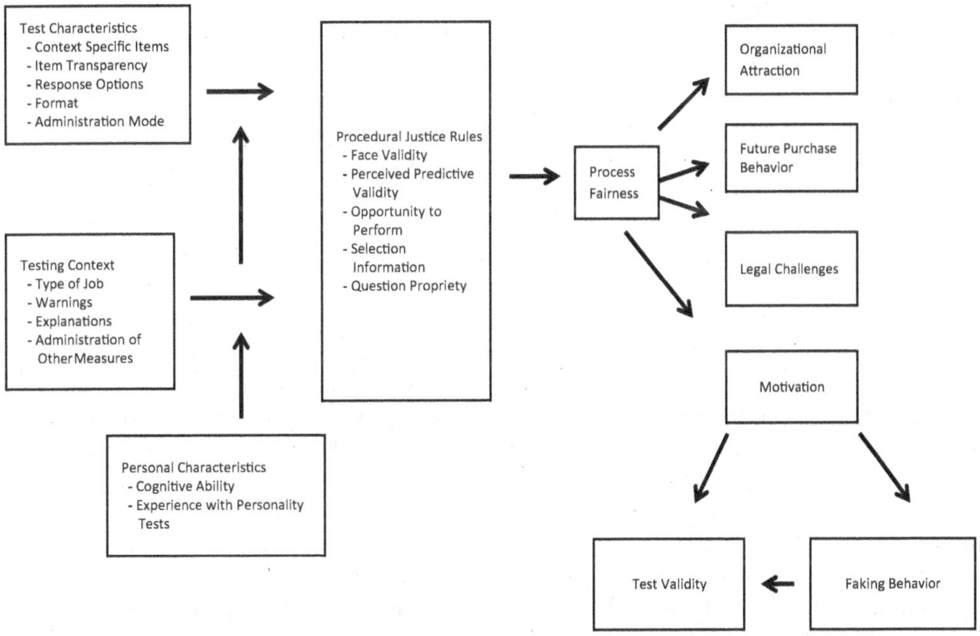

Figure 13.2 Antecedents and Consequences of Applicant Reactions to Personality Tests.

to personality tests, strategies to increase positive reactions to personality tests, and the consequences of applicant perceptions. The types of studies and research that might be conducted on this topic are nearly infinite, but below I try to isolate some of the main issues that require our attention.

Test Characteristics

I have already reviewed several characteristics of the test itself that can influence reactions, but there is still much to learn about how specific characteristics of personality measures relate to test reactions. Below I outline what I believe to be the most interesting and useful questions to answer about these relationships.

How Does Administration Mode or Test Format Affect Reactions Toward Personality Tests?

We generally think about personality tests being administered via paper and pencil methods, and the discussion here has been based on these types of measures. But, as the work of Hausknecht et al. (2004) clearly demonstrates, other methods of assessing personality may result in considerably more favorable reactions. Again, reactions toward interviews are generally much more favorable than they are toward personality tests (Kravitz, Stinson, & Chavez, 1996; Rynes & Connerley, 1993). Yet, many interviews are designed specifically to assess personality traits (Van Iddekinge, Raymark, & Roth, 2005). It may seem unusual that two methods that assess the same constructs would not elicit the same reactions, but from an applicant's perspective, the interview may have greater face and predictive validity (because the questions tend to be embedded in a job context) and greater opportunity to perform (because applicants seem to feel that they can better tell their story via an interview).

But, all of this is speculation. It is unclear why these differences actually exist. More research should be done to understand why certain methods of assessing personality are more acceptable to applicants. I have tried to determine what factors may account for the differences in reactions toward interviews and personality measures, but there are other potential formats and methods we should consider. For example, Ortner (2008) suggests that, if used within the context of computerized adaptive testing, personality measures may be even less agreeable to applicants. She notes that participants may feel they cannot properly show how they compare to others because the range of personality questions will be narrower (because adaptive tests are tailored to individuals). At this point, we do not have any data to support or refute this explanation, but such information would be very useful to both researchers and practitioners alike.

If we can determine precisely what features of measures make the assessment of personality more agreeable to applicants, we may be able to design less expensive and time-consuming methods of personality assessment that mimic those features. Such efforts may show that it is even possible to simply alter the format of paper and pencil measures to affect applicant reactions positively. For example, some have advocated the use of forced-choice tests, which require test-takers to rank multiple statements in terms of how well they describe the test-taker (or are least representative of the test-taker). This format has been shown to decrease faking behavior (Christiansen, Burns, & Montgomery, 2005; Jackson, Wroblewski, & Ashton, 2000; McCloy, Heggestad, & Reeve, 2005), but may have other unintended consequences for applicant reactions. Converse et al. (2008) found that reactions toward forced-choice scales were more negative than they were toward typical Likert scales (whereby an applicant rates how well a given description fits him or her). The authors suggest that the use of forced-choice measures may limit an applicant's perceived opportunity to perform by limiting their ability to demonstrate job-relevant personality characteristics. Furthermore, the applicant may be forced to pick a choice, when none of them are really accurate or true of them. Another possibility is that forced-choice measures are more cognitively demanding. Research has found that more cognitively demanding tests are perceived less favorably (Kluger & Rothstein, 1993). Forced-choice tests may be more difficult because more than one option may be true and it is cognitively demanding for the applicant to determine which is most true. They may also be more cognitively demanding because the "correct" answers are not as obvious as they are with personality tests that use a Likert-type scale. Of course, this is all speculation and other reasons may exist for such negative reactions toward forced-choice measures. Clearly, this is an area where additional research could aid in our understanding of the applicant reactions phenomenon and could also lead to some very useful guidance for those using personality measures in practice. Again, if we identify precisely which features of paper and pencil measures lead to negative reactions, we may be able to tweak these measures to be just as useful (in terms of validity) but yield more positive reactions.

Another issue that must be considered is the increasing prevalence of web testing. Now, more than ever, organizations are administering selection tests on the Internet and applicants take the tests without being supervised (Nye, Do, Drasgow, & Fine, 2008). It is unclear what implications this type of testing has on applicant reactions. Applicants may react more positively because they may assume that an unproctored examination is a signal that the employer is trusting. However, the alternative might be true and the applicant may think that, because the test is taken on the Internet, there may be some way the employer is able to gather other data on the applicant that may not be apparent. This is another area in desperate need of research.

How Can Personality Items Best Be Contextualized?

At this time, there is no research I am aware of that has found that contextualizing items results in more positive reactions, but very little has been done in the way of trying to understand this phenomenon. There may be particular changes to items that may result in more positive perceptions of perceived predictive validity and face validity and we need more research to try to determine precisely what types of changes lead to these more positive reactions. For instance, is it really just enough to contextualize items by including "at work" tags? Perhaps a more sophisticated approach is needed such as rewriting the item to reflect a work context entirely. Do such approaches result in the same levels of validity and positive reactions as more time-intensive approaches such as those advocated by Ployhart et al. (2004) and James et al. (2005)? At this point, these approaches have never been directly compared, so the answer is unknown.

It is also important to keep in mind that the nature of the job for which an applicant is applying will surely affect reactions toward item contextualization. For instance, if applying for a sales job, an item that asks about extraversion at work may seem appropriate to applicants. However, the same item asked within the context of a test for a firefighter position may elicit more negative reactions. Again, however, this is simply speculation and research is needed to confirm or refute this line of thinking.

Test Context

While test characteristics are certainly important and no doubt have a strong effect on applicant reactions, the testing environment is likely equally important. There are a number of unanswered questions surrounding the effects of test contexts on applicant reactions to personality measures.

How Does the Type of Job for Which One Is Applying Affect Reactions?

It seems reasonable to presume that applicant reactions toward a personality test would largely depend on the job for which applicants are applying. For instance, it seems that the role of personality for predicting performance for sales jobs should be fairly obvious and that this would have a positive effect on applicant reactions toward the use of such tests for selecting applicants into such positions. For more technical positions (e.g., engineer), the relevance of a personality test for predicting performance may be less obvious. However, there is little to no empirical support for the relationship between job type and reactions (Hausknecht et al., 2004) in general, and personality tests specifically. Research has shown that applicant perceptions of drug testing use for selection are influenced by the characteristics of the job for which one is applying (Murphy, Thornton, & Prue, 1991; Murphy, Thornton, & Reynolds, 1990). In another study, engineering applicants perceived the use of a biodata measure more favorably than plumber applicants (Forsberg & Shultz, 2009). Therefore, there is some empirical support that reactions would be influenced by job type. But, we still do not know which types of jobs personality test use would seem the most acceptable. And, more importantly, it would be useful to identify how specific job characteristics relate to perceptions of the use of personality tests in selection.

What Types of Warnings Increase Positive Reactions?

With only few exceptions (Dwight & Donovan, 2003; Pace et al., 2005), there has been very little research examining how warnings should be delivered or what content they should include for maximal effectiveness in terms of reducing faking, but also in terms of increasing positive reactions. How do applicants react to warnings that a lie scale is included on the test? Do they see this as an invasion of privacy or are reactions more positive because it is seen that the organization is attempting to make the test fair to everyone? How do these types of warnings compare with more positively framed warnings that stress issues of fit between personality traits and job satisfaction and performance? Furthermore, research suggests that combinations of warnings (e.g., using a warning about detection methods in addition to consequences for faking behavior) have been shown to have stronger effects on applicant test scores than when used in isolation (McFarland, 2003). Similar findings may hold true with regards to reactions, such that reactions are stronger when multiple warnings are used. Or perhaps different types of warnings interact, with some eliciting negative reactions and some eliciting positive reactions. We currently know very little about how these reactions interact and we could learn a lot from researching how they relate to reactions when used in isolation and when combined with other types of warnings.

What Effect Does Coaching Have on Reactions to Personality Tests?

One need only do a quick search on the Internet for personality testing to see that there are multiple websites and resources for applicants who want to learn how to "beat" personality tests. What implications does this have on personality testing? Half of what we know about reactions to personality tests is from research conducted prior to the Internet being within arm's reach of a large proportion of the population. Test-takers are much more knowledgeable now than they were just 15 years ago. It is unclear how this information might influence applicant reactions to personality tests, and the field could benefit from understanding what applicants know about personality tests before they even take the test, and if they already have strong opinions about their use in selection contexts. It may be that organizations can do very little to alter reactions if applicants already have strong opinions about personality tests even before they walk through the door.

The Role of Individual Differences in Applicant Reactions

As presented in Figure 13.2, individual differences (personal characteristics) most likely play a role in reactions toward personality tests. Considerable research has demonstrated that perceptions and behaviors are influenced by both the traits an individual possesses and the nature of the situation (Mischel, 1979; Shoda, Mischel, & Wright, 1989, 1993a, 1993b). Consistent with this view, the proposed model demonstrates that individual differences will moderate the relationships between item and context characteristics and applicant perceptions of personality tests. Demonstrating this interaction, Christiansen et al. (2005) found that individuals higher in cognitive ability had more accurate perceptions about which personality traits were related to performance in two different types of jobs. Individuals who are more capable of understanding how personality relates to job performance would likely have more favorable perceptions of personality test use (assuming the personality tests are being used appropriately) than those who are not as capable of making those connections. One can take this a step further and predict that interventions designed to remediate negative applicant reactions toward personality tests should have their strongest effects for less cognitively gifted individuals because they are the ones with less ability to see the relationships between the test and what is required on the job. Research conducted by Oostrom, Born, Serlie, and van der Molen (2010) suggests just this. They found that some individuals are predisposed to react positively to a cognitive ability and social judgment test. They further suggest that the nature of the applicant pool should be considered when designing interventions to improve applicant reactions, because modifying the test content or administration will have little effect on some individuals.

Although Hausknecht et al. (2004) did not find a relationship between demographic variables and applicant reactions toward selection procedures, they did find that some personality characteristics had a small correlation with perceptions of procedural justice. But, these results were based on a very limited number of studies and we still have a long way to go before we can rule out the role of individual differences in reactions. We are at the very beginning of our understanding of the role individual differences play in applicant perceptions and it will be interesting to see which characteristics are the strongest moderators of the relationships between test and context characteristics and test perceptions.

Consequences of Applicant Reactions

What Effect Does Motivation Have on Personality Test Validity and Faking Behavior?

This is probably the most basic question and yet the most interesting. As stated earlier, it cannot be assumed that applicant reactions research conducted within an ability-testing context will entirely generalize to personality testing because these measures are so inherently different. In fact, work that have compared the relationships between reactions and important outcomes have found differences in these relationships across contexts that use an ability test and those that use a personality test (Chan, Schmitt, Sacco, & DeShon, 1998; Truxillo et al., 2009).

There are likely several reasons that come into play that may explain these differences. Ability and personality measures have very different characteristics. With an ability test, there is a right and wrong answer, but with a personality test, the correct answer may depend on the testing context (i.e., type of job for which the applicant is applying). Furthermore, ability tests are not fakable in that, unless one is cheating, a high score is unlikely to be obtained by a person who is low in the ability being assessed. But, with personality tests, even someone low on the trait in question might be able to manipulate his or her score on the test to make it appear he or she is high on the trait, because the items are usually transparent.

This faking issue presents a unique situation when one is considering applicant reactions and their relationship with important outcomes that warrants a deeper discussion. Motivation is the main mediator within most applicant reaction frameworks between reactions and test performance. It is thought that those who have more positive reactions toward the selection devices will be more motivated to perform well on those measures, and motivation, in turn, results in a more accurate assessment of the applicants' abilities. Usually more highly motivated individuals perform better on the test, because they are trying harder. But, on ability tests, trying one's best will result in a more accurate assessment of the person's ability (if the test is valid). Such arguments have held up well when ability tests are examined and motivation has indeed been found to mediate the relationship between reactions and test performance in this way. When a personality test is used, positive applicant reactions may very well affect test performance through motivation. However, it is unlikely, based on what we know about faking behavior on such tests, that motivation will lead to more accurate responses.

Within the personality literature, most theories of faking include motivation as an antecedent to faking behavior (Ellingson & McFarland, 2011; McFarland & Ryan, 2000). In fact, many discuss test-taking motivation as synonymous with faking (Lalwani, Shrum, & Chiu, 2009) and even refer to it as "motivated responding." This suggests that test-taking motivation may lead to a less accurate assessment of one's standing on traits being assessed by a personality test. Therefore, from a faking standpoint, increasing positive applicant reactions would be predicted to increase faking through increasing test-taking motivation and this would result in a less accurate assessment of a test-taker's standing on the construct of interest.

There is existing theoretical work that suggests that positive applicant reactions will predict motivation and that motivation will go on to predict faking behavior (i.e., higher motivation will lead to greater faking; Marcus, 2009). However, this work has not directly addressed the inconsistency between such thinking and previous empirical work within the ability literature that would suggest that high test-taking motivation results in better assessment of the constructs being assessed. Schmit and Ryan (1992) found that validity was higher for more motivated applicants with cognitive tests, but lower for personality tests—supporting the idea that motivation is not necessarily a good thing where personality tests are concerned (or at least, too much of it may not be good). Or, perhaps, it is not the amount of motivation that explains these differences, but what is driving the motivation. If the individual is simply motivated to get a job, then motivation may be more likely to lead to faking. On the other hand, if motivation is driven by the desire to get a job that fits well with the individual's characteristics, then motivation may operate as it does with cognitive ability tests.

This discussion should make it obvious why we need to be very careful about generalizing results from an ability-testing to a personality-testing context. Because personality tests are unique (compared to work samples, ability tests, or judgment tests) in that they are fakable, it is unclear if our current thinking about how reactions relate to motivation and test performance will generalize. Applicant reactions are important for organizations to understand because they have such important consequences. This potential relationship requires much further examination so that we may understand the potential boundaries of applicant reactions research.

Do Reactions to Personality Tests Predict the Same Outcomes as Reactions to Other Types of Tests?

Again, because the overwhelming majority of applicant reactions research has focused on cognitive ability-testing contexts, it is unclear whether the consequences of applicant reactions are the same for personality testing. Although links between applicant reactions and important outcomes have been found in previous research within ability-testing contexts, very little research has linked applicant reactions toward personality tests to consumer behavior, acceptance of job offers, or the extent to which the applicant recommends the organization to others. These are relationships that must be explored within the context of personality testing.

Conclusion

The goal of this chapter is to shed light on the issue of applicant reactions toward personality tests—trying to understand why reactions are negative and what we might do to mitigate negative reactions. It should be clear that we know very little about these issues. I have identified areas where further research is most needed in this regard, but it is fair to say that all types of research exploring the antecedents and consequences of reactions toward personality tests, and examining the nomological network between various reactions and personality test performance and outcomes, are of the utmost importance. The increasing popularity of personality testing does not seem to be slowing and therefore these issues will have increasing importance to organizations moving forward.

Practitioner's Window

Applicant reactions toward personality tests can result in a host of negative consequences for an organization. Negative reactions may lead to an applicant's withdrawal from the selection process, negative word of mouth, and decreasing test validity, and may even increase the likelihood that applicants legally challenge the selection process.

Unfortunately, personality tests are one of the most disliked selection procedures and yet are being used with increasing frequency. It has repeatedly been shown that applicants respond more negatively toward personality tests than most other testing devices (e.g., interviews, cognitive ability tests). Some reasons for such negative reactions may be related to the format of personality tests and the fact that the response format does not allow applicants to qualify responses, applicant lack of familiarity with personality tests, and the generic nature of most personality tests.

To address the negative reactions toward personality measures, there are a number of things practitioners may do. Some of these strategies involve altering the test itself, while others involve changing the context surrounding the test.

- Alter the test
  - Increase item transparency
  - Contextualize items such that they are more clearly related to the specific work environment
  - Assess personality via other methods such as through the use of interviews or open-ended questions
- Change the testing context
  - Offer applicants an explanation for why the personality test is being used (e.g., it is job-related) and how the scores will be used to make selection decisions
  - Warn applicants against faking the test
  - Use personality tests with other predictors because applicants respond more favorably when selection decisions are made on more than just a personality test

References

Anderson, N., Salgado, J. F., & Hulsheger, U. R. (2010). Applicant reactions in selection: Comprehensive meta-analysis into reaction generalization versus situational specificity. *International Journal of Selection and Assessment, 18*, 291–304.

Arvey, R. D., & Sackett, P. R. (1993). Fairness in selection: Current developments and perspectives. In N. Schmitt & W. C. Borman (Eds.), *Personnel selection in organizations* (pp. 171–202). San Francisco: Jossey-Bass.

Bauer, T. N., Maertz, C. P., Dolen, M. R., & Campion, M. A. (1998). Longitudinal assessment of applicant reactions to employment testing and test outcome feedback. *Journal of Applied Psychology, 83*, 892–903.

Burstein, J., & Marcu, D. (2003). Automated evaluation of discourse structure in student essays. In M. Shermis & J. Burstein (Eds.), *Automated essay scoring: A cross-disciplinary perspective* (pp. 209–230). Mahwah, NJ: Lawrence Erlbaum Associates.

Berry, C. M., Sackett, P. R., & Tobares, V. (2010). A meta-analysis of conditional reasoning tests of aggression. *Personnel Psychology, 63*, 361–384.

Bing, M. N., Whanger, J. C., Davison, H. K., & VanHook, J. B. (2004). Incremental validity of the frame-of-reference effect in personality scale scores: A replication and extension. *Journal of Applied Psychology, 89*, 150–157.
Bomstein, R. F. (1989). Exposure and affect: Overview and meta-analysis of research, 1968–1987. *Psychological Bulletin, 106*, 265–289.
Burstein, J. (2003). The E-rate scoring engine: Automated essay scoring with natural language processing. In M. Shermis & J. Burstein (Eds.), *Automated essay scoring: A cross-disciplinary perspective* (pp. 113–121). Mahwah, NJ: Lawrence Erlbaum Associates.
Chan, D., Schmitt, N., DeShon, R. P., Clause, C. S., & Delbridge, K. (1997). Reactions to cognitive ability tests: The relationships between race, test performance, face validity perceptions, and test-taking motivation. *Journal of Applied Psychology, 82*, 300–310.
Chan, D., Schmitt, N., Sacco, J. M., & DeShon, R. P. (1998). Understanding pretest and posttest reactions to cognitive ability and personality tests. *Journal of Applied Psychology, 83*, 471–485.
Christiansen, N. D., Burns, G. N., & Montgomery, G. E. (2005). Reconsidering forced-choice item formats for applicant personality assessment. *Human Performance, 18*, 267–307.
Converse, P. D., Oswald, F. L., Imus, A., Hedricks, C., Roy, R., & Butera, H. (2008). Comparing personality test formats and warnings: Effects on criterion-related validity and test-taker reactions. *International Journal of Selection and Assessment, 16*, 155–169.
Costa, P. T., Jr., & McCrae, R. R. (1992). *NEO-PI-R professional manual.* Odessa, FL: Psychological Assessment Resources.
Dwight, S. A., & Donovan, J. J. (2003). Do warnings not to fake reduce faking? *Human Performance, 16*, 1–23.
Ellingson, J. E., & McFarland, L. A. (2011). Understanding faking behavior through the lens of motivation: An application of VIE theory. *Human Performance, 24*, 322–337.
Forsberg, A. M., & Shultz, K. S. (2009). Perceived fairness of a background information form and a job knowledge test. *Public Personnel Management, 38*, 33–46.
Gilliland, S. W. (1993). The perceived fairness of selection systems: An organizational justice perspective. *Academy of Management Review, 18*, 694–734.
Gilliland, S. W. (1994). Effects of procedural and distributive justice on reactions to a selection system. *Journal of Applied Psychology, 79*, 691–701.
Gilliland, S. W. (1995). Fairness from the applicant's perspective: Reactions to employee selection procedures. *International Journal of Selection and Assessment, 3*, 11–19.
Greenberg, J. (1990). Organizational justice: Yesterday, today, and tomorrow. *Journal of Management, 16*, 399–432.
Hausknecht, J. P., Day, D. V., & Thomas, S. C. (2004). Applicant reactions to selection procedures: An updated model and meta-analysis. *Personnel Psychology, 57*, 639–683.
Hirsh, J. B., & Peterson, J. B. (2009). Personality and language use in self-narratives. *Journal of Research in Personality, 43*, 524–527.
Holtz, B. C., Ployhart, R. E., & Dominguez, A. (2005). Testing the rules of justice: The effects of frame-of-reference and pre-test validity information on personality test responses and test perceptions. *International Journal of Selection and Assessment, 13*, 75–86.
Huffcutt, A. I., Conway, J. M., Roth, P. L., & Stone, N. J. (2001). Identification and meta-analytic assessment of psychological constructs measured in employment interviews. *Journal of Applied Psychology, 86*, 897–913.
Huffcutt, A. I., Weekley, J. A., Wiesner, W. H., Groot, T. G., & Jones, C. (2001). Comparison of situational and behavior description interview questions for higher-level positions. *Personnel Psychology, 54*, 619–644.
Hulsheger, U. R., & Anderson, N. (2009). Applicant perspectives in selection: Going beyond preference reactions. *International Journal of Selection and Assessment, 17*, 335–345.
Hunthausen, J. M., Truxillo, D. M., Bauer, T. B., & Hammer, B. L. (2003). A field study of frame-of-reference effects on personality test validity. *Journal of Applied Psychology, 88*, 545–551.
Jackson, D. N. (1971). The dynamics of structured personality tests. *Psychological Review, 78*, 229–248.
Jackson, D. N., Wroblewski, V. R., & Ashton, M. C. (2000). The impact of faking on employment tests: Does forced choice offer a solution? *Human Performance, 13*, 371–388.
James, L. R., McIntyre, M. D., Glisson, C. A., Green, P. D., Patton, T. W., & LeBreton, J. M. (2005). A conditional reasoning measure for aggression. *Organizational Research Methods, 8*, 69–99.
Johnson, J. A. (1981). The "self-disclosure" and "self-presentation" views of item response dynamics and personality scale validity. *Journal of Personality and Social Psychology, 40*, 761–769.
Kluger, A. N., & Rothstein, H. R. (1993). The influence of selection test type on applicant reactions to employment testing. *Journal of Business and Psychology, 8*, 3–25.
Kravitz, D. A., Stinson, V., & Chavez, T. L. (1996). Evaluations of tests used for making selection and promotion decisions. *International Journal of Selection and Assessment, 4*, 24–34.
Kufner, A. C., Back, M. D., Nestler, S., & Egloff, B. (2010). Tell me a story and I will tell you who you are! Lens model analysis of personality and creative writing. *Journal of Research in Personality, 44*, 427–435.

Lalwani, A. K., Shrum, L. J., & Chiu, C.-Y. (2009). Motivated response styles: The role of cultural values, regulatory focus, and self-consciousness in socially desirable responding. *Journal of Personality and Social Psychology, 96*, 870–882.

Lautenschlager, G. J. (1994). Accuracy and faking of background data. In G. S. Stokes, M. D. Mumford, & W. A. Owens (Eds.), *Biodata handbook* (pp. 391–419). Palo Alto, CA: Consulting Psychologists Press.

LeBreton, J. M., Barksdale, C. D., Robin, J. D., & James, L. R. (2007). Measurement issues associated with conditional reasoning tests: Indirect measurement and test faking. *Journal of Applied Psychology, 92*, 1–16.

Leventhal, G. S. (1980). What should be done with equity theory? New approaches to the study of fairness in social relationship. In K. J. Gergen, M. S. Greenberg, & R. H. Willis (Eds.), *Social exchange: Advances in theory and research* (pp. 27–55). New York: Plenum.

Madigan, J., & Macan, T. H. (2005). Improving applicant reactions by altering test administration. *Applied H.R.M. Research, 10*, 73–88.

Mael, F. A. (1991). A conceptual rationale for the domain and attributes of biodata items. *Personnel Psychology, 44*, 763–791.

Marcus, B. (2009). "Faking" from the applicant's perspective: A theory of self-presentation in personnel selection settings. *International Journal of Selection and Assessment, 17*, 417–430.

McCloy, R. A., Heggestad, E. D., & Reeve, C. L. (2005). A silk purse from the sow's ear: Retrieving normative information from multidimensional forced-choice items. *Organizational Research Methods, 8*, 222–248.

McCrae, R. R., & Costa, P. T., Jr. (2008). Empirical and theoretical status of the five-factor model of personality traits. In G. Boyle, G. Matthews, & D. Saklofske (Eds.), *Sage handbook of personality theory and assessment* (Vol. 1, pp. 273–294). Thousand Oaks, CA: Sage.

McDaniel, M. A., Hartman, N. S., Whetzel, D. L., & Grubb, W., III. (2007). Situational judgment tests, response instructions, and validity: A meta-analysis. *Personnel Psychology, 60*, 63–91.

McFarland, L. A. (2003). Warning against faking on a personality test: Effects on applicant reactions and personality test scores. *International Journal of Selection and Assessment, 11*, 265–276.

McFarland, L. A., & Ryan, A. M. (2000). Variance in faking across non-cognitive measures. *Journal of Applied Psychology, 85*, 812–821.

McFarland, L. A., Ryan, A. M., & Ellis, A. (2002). Item placement on a personality measure: Effects on faking behavior and test measurement properties. *Journal of Personality Assessment, 78*, 348–369.

Mischel, W. (1979). On the interface of cognition and personality: Beyond the person–situation debate. *American Psychologist, 34*, 740–754.

Mumford, M. D., & Stokes, G. S. (1992). Developmental determinants of individual action: Theory and practice in applying background measures. In M. D. Dunnette & L. M. Hough (Eds.), *Handbook of industrial and organizational psychology* (Vol. 3, pp. 61–138). Palo Alto, CA: Consulting Psychologists Press.

Murphy, K. R., Thornton, G. C., & Prue, K. (1991). Influence of job characteristics on the acceptability of employee drug testing. *Journal of Applied Psychology, 76*, 447–453.

Murphy, K. R., Thornton, G. C., & Reynolds, D. H. (1990). College students' attitudes toward employee drug testing programs. *Personnel Psychology, 43*, 615–631.

Nye, C. D., Do, B.-R., Drasgow, F., & Fine, S. (2008). Two-step testing in employee selection: Is score inflation a problem? *International Journal of Selection and Assessment, 16*, 112–120.

Oostrom, J. K., Born, M. P., Serlie, A. W., & van der Molen, H. T. (2010). Effects of individual differences on the perceived job relatedness of a cognitive ability test and a multimedia situational judgment test. *International Journal of Selection and Assessment, 18*, 394–406.

Ortner, T. M. (2008). Effects of changed item order: A cautionary note to practitioners on jumping to computerized adaptive testing for personality assessment. *International Journal of Selection and Assessment, 16*, 229–237.

Pace, V. L., & Borman, W. C. (2006). The use of warnings to discourage faking on noncognitive inventories. In R. L. Griffith & M. H. Peterson (Eds.), *A closer examination of applicant faking behavior* (pp. 283–304). Greenwich, CT: Information Age Publishing.

Pace, V. L., Xu, X., Penney, L. M., Borman, W. C., & Bearden, R. M. (2005, April). Using warnings to discourage personality test faking: An empirical study. Paper presented at Society for Industrial and Organizational Psychology annual conference symposium, Los Angeles, CA.

Ployhart, R. E., & Harold, C. M. (2004). The applicant attribution-reaction theory (AART): An integrative theory of applicant attributional processing. *International Journal of Selection and Assessment, 12*, 84–98.

Ployhart, R. E., McFarland, L. A., & Ryan, A. M. (2002). Examining applicants' attributions for withdrawal from a selection procedure. *Journal of Applied Social Psychology, 32*, 2228–2252.

Ployhart, R. E., & Ryan, A. M. (1997). Toward an explanation of applicant reactions: An examination of organizational justice and attribution frameworks. *Organizational Behavior and Human Decision Processes, 72*, 308–335.

Ployhart, R. E., & Ryan, A. M. (1998). Applicants' reactions to the fairness of selection procedures: The effects of positive rule violations and time of measurement. *Journal of Applied Psychology, 83*, 3–16.

Porr, W. B., & Ployhart, R. E. (2004). *Validity of empirically and constructed-oriented situational judgment tests.* Symposium presented at the annual conference of the Society for Industrial and Organizational Psychology, Chicago, IL.

Posthuma, R. A., Morgeson, F. P., & Campion, M. A. (2002). Beyond employment interview validity: A comprehensive narrative review of recent research and trends over time. *Personnel Psychology, 55*, 1–81.

Rosse, J. G., Miller, J. L., & Stecher, M. D. (1994). A field study of job applicants' reactions to personality and cognitive ability testing. *Journal of Applied Psychology, 79*, 987–992.

Ryan, A. M., McFarland, L., Baron, H., & Page, R. (1999). An international look at selection practices: Nation and culture as explanations for variability in practices. *Personnel Psychology, 52*, 359–391.

Ryan, A. M., & Ployhart, R. E. (2000). Applicants' perceptions of selection procedures and decisions: A critical review and agenda for the future. *Journal of Management, 26*, 565–606.

Ryan, A. M., Sacco, J. M., McFarland, L. A., & Kriska, S. D. (2000). Applicant self-selection: Correlates of withdrawal from a multiple hurdle process. *Journal of Applied Psychology, 85*, 163–179.

Rynes, S. L. (1991). Recruitment, job choice, and post-hire consequences: A call for new research direction. In M. D. Dunnette (Ed.), *Handbook of industrial and organizational psychology* (2nd ed. Vol. 2, pp. 399–444). Palo Alto, CA: Consulting Psychologists Press.

Rynes, S. L. (1993). Who's selecting whom? Effects of selection practices on applicant attitudes and behaviors. In N. Schmitt & W. Borman (Eds.), *Personnel selection in organizations* (pp. 240–274). San Francisco: Jossey-Bass.

Rynes, S. L., & Connerley, M. L. (1993). Applicant reactions to alternative selection procedures. *Journal of Business and Psychology, 7*, 261–277.

Schmit, M. J., & Ryan, A. M. (1992). Test-taking dispositions: A missing link? *Journal of Applied Psychology, 77*, 629–637.

Schmit, M. J., Ryan, A. M., Stierwalt, S. L., & Powell, A. B. (1995). Frame-of-reference effects on personality scale scores and criterion-related validity. *Journal of Applied Psychology, 80*, 607–620.

Shoda, Y., Mischel, W., & Wright, J. C. (1989). Intuitive interactionism in person perception: Effects of situation–behavior relations on dispositional judgments. *Journal of Personality and Social Psychology, 56*, 41–53.

Shoda, Y., Mischel, W., & Wright, J. C. (1993a). Links between personality judgments and contextualized behavior patterns: Situation–behavior profiles of personality prototypes. *Social Cognition, 11*, 399–429.

Shoda, Y., Mischel, W., & Wright, J. C. (1993b). The role of competencies in behavioral coherence: Situation similarity, cross-situational consistency and person × situation interaction. *Journal of Personality and Social Psychology, 65*, 1023–1035.

Smither, J. W., Reilly, R. R., Millsap, R. E., Pearlman, K., & Stoffey, R. W. (1993). Applicant reactions to selection procedures. *Personnel Psychology, 46*, 49–76.

Steiner, D. D., & Gilliland, S. W. (1996). Fairness reactions to personnel selection techniques in France and the United States. *Journal of Applied Psychology, 81*, 134–141.

Truxillo, D. M., Bodner, T. E., Bertolino, M., Bauer, T. N., & Yonce, C. A. (2009). Effects of explanations on applicant reactions: A meta-analytic review. *International Journal of Selection and Assessment, 17*, 346–361.

Van Iddekinge, C. H., Raymark, P. H., & Roth, P. L. (2005). Assessing personality with a structured employment interview: Construct-related validity and susceptibility to response inflation. *Journal of Applied Psychology, 90*, 536–552.

Walsh, J. A., Layton, W. L., & Klieger, D. M. (1966). Relationships between social desirability scale values, probabilities of endorsement, and invasion of privacy ratings of objective personality items. *Psychological Reports, 18*, 671–675.

Weekley, J. A., & Ployhart, R. E. (2005). Situational judgment: Antecedents and relationships with performance. *Human Performance, 18*, 81–104.

Zajonc, R. B. (1968). Attitudinal effects of mere exposure. *Journal of Personality and Social Psychology Monograph Supplement, 9*, 1–27.

Zajonc, R. B. (1980). Feeling and thinking: Preferences need no inferences. *American Psychologist, 35*, 151–175.

14

Breadth in Personality Assessment

Implications for the Understanding and Prediction of Work Behavior*

Thomas A. O'Neill and Sampo V. Paunonen

The purpose of this chapter is twofold. First, we describe how personality factors, traits, and behaviors have been conceptualized to exist in a hierarchical structure based on the breadth of the variables involved. Second, we examine how measures of these broad and narrow behavior domains can lead to different research outcomes as far as the understanding and prediction of human behavior is concerned. Based in large part on the literature of industrial and organizational (I/O) psychology, we conclude that an intermediate option is generally the best one. To paraphrase Goldilocks, personality factor measures are too broad, personality behavior measures are too narrow, but personality trait measures are just right. But first, we review some structural models that have been proposed as representing the organization of personality.

Structural Models of Personality

Establishing a unifying taxonomy of personality has been one of the major objectives of personality research. The structure of personality has been framed in two ways: hierarchical taxonomies and circumplexes. Hierarchical taxonomies aim to classify a diverse array of objects or concepts by retaining as much information about each individual object/concept as possible. Taxonomies are incredibly efficient approaches for describing multidimensional phenomena, such as personality, because they neatly arrange personality structure within a hierarchy. As an alternative to hierarchical taxonomies, the circumplex approach to identifying the structure of personality produces a two-dimensional circle of personality dimensions. Dimensions with high positive correlations are situated close to each other, and traits comprising blends of factors are allowed (not so in strict hierarchical models). We outline a few prominent models of personality structure below.

Five-Factor Model and the Big Five

The dominant model of personality is the Five-Factor Model (FFM) and its parallel counterpart the Big Five. The FFM grew out of the questionnaire-based analyses of personality structure (Costa & McCrae, 1992), whereas the Big Five emerged from lexical studies of person descriptors (for a seminal review, see Digman, 1990; see also Hough, 1997; Hough & Schneider, 1996; Saucier & Goldberg, 2003). The typical labels of the Big Five factors are extraversion, agreeableness, conscientiousness, emotional stability, and openness to experience. The structure of the factors, according to Costa and

McCrae's FFM, is thought to represent a three-level hierarchy, in which behaviors beget traits beget factors. McCrae and John (1992), and many others, have argued that the most important contribution of the Big Five is a common framework for the study of personality and behavior. This is a critical contribution because prior to the Big Five, there was no reigning taxonomy and, as a result, personality research had been criticized as scattered (e.g., Barrick & Mount, 1991).

One persistent issue with the Big Five is that the factors are not interchangeable across personality questionnaires (John & Srivastava, 1999; Saucier & Goldberg, 2003). Costa and McCrae's (1992) NEO conscientiousness factor contains six facets: competence, order, dutifulness, achievement-striving, self-discipline, and deliberation. Lee and Ashton's (2004) HEXACO conscientiousness factor contains four facets: organization, diligence, perfectionism, and prudence. The Six-Factor Personality Questionnaire (SFPQ; Jackson, Paunonen, & Tremblay, 2000) bifurcates conscientiousness into methodicalness (facets: cognitive structure, order, and low impulsivity) and achievement (facets: achievement, endurance, and low play). The Hogan Personality Inventory (HPI; R. Hogan & Hogan, 1992) birfurcates conscientiousness into ambition (facets: initiative, competitiveness, and leadership) and prudence (facets: self-discipline, responsibility, and conscientiousness). Although comparable, these factors are far from identical, which means we are still far short of the major goal of Big Five taxonomic development efforts—to provide a common framework within which research on personality can be unified. It means the same factors from different personality surveys could produce correlations with other criteria that are quite different (e.g., Steel, Schmidt, & Shultz, 2008), despite their being organized under the same label and their often interchangeable treatment.

Although the Big Five cannot be assumed to be commensurate across measures and has been critiqued for other reasons such as lacking comprehensiveness (Hough, 1997; Paunonen & Jackson, 2000), there is considerable research on the evolutionary and biological basis of the Big Five. Evolutionary perspectives position the Big Five as individual difference variables relevant to social adaptation (e.g., Nettle, 2006). Buss (1991, 1996) invoked evolutionary theory to suggest that personality variables allow an individual to identify characteristics of others in order to enhance survival. The basic premise of these and other theories is that individual differences in the Big Five evolved to support human functioning and fitness. The biological basis for the Big Five factors has been researched in twin studies. Bouchard (2004), for example, reported that the heritability of the Big Five was about 50%. According to some, that sort of evidence suggests that the Big Five may be housed in neurobiological structures and processes (Gray, 1994). For example, amygdala activation in response to seeing a happy face correlated with extraversion but not with other emotional expressions (e.g., anger and fear; Canli, Sivers, Whitfield, Gotlib, & Gabreli, 2002). Evidence of this nature has been interpreted as supporting the Big Five as basic dimensions rooted in evolutionary and biological systems (McCrae & Costa, 2008).

In summary, the Big Five is the dominant model of personality structure at the moment. It pervades the overwhelming majority of research on personality in the workplace, as we will show in subsequent sections of this chapter. As discussed briefly, however, there are potential problems with the Big Five model and, as such, it is important to consider other models that have received substantial attention.

Superordinate Factors

Some theorists have speculated that factors exist above the level of the Big Five in the personality hierarchy. The possibility of superordinate factors requires that the Big Five not be orthogonal. Despite assertions to the contrary (e.g., Costa & McCrae, 1995), some empirical findings suggest that the factor intercorrelations are large enough to support superordinate factors. Digman (1997) found replicated support for two superordinate factors, alpha (conscientiousness, agreeableness, and emotional stability) and beta (extraversion and openness to experience). Interestingly, Ones, Schmidt, and Viswesvaran (1994) found support for the factor labeled alpha by Digman, but called it integrity instead. As we will review below, that integrity factor has been referred to as a compound personality scale by Ones and colleagues, and it has exhibited strong relations with workplace behavior. Elsewhere, DeYoung and colleagues (DeYoung, 2006; DeYoung, Peterson, & Higgins, 2002) recovered the same superordinate factor structure as did Digman, naming the factors *stability* (i.e., Digman's alpha) and *plasticity* (i.e., Digman's beta). Stability was viewed as consistent patterns in maintaining motivation, social relationships, and affective experiences. Plasticity was viewed as consistent patterns of engagement in social and intellectual aspects of life. A single general factor of personality (GFP) positioned at the apex of the personality hierarchy has also been observed by some (e.g., Musek, 2007; Rushton & Irwing, 2008). In a meta-analytic investigation, stability and plasticity had factor loadings of .83 and .69, respectively, on the GFP. We return to this general factor later in the context of the prediction of job performance.

HEXACO and Supernumerary Personality Inventory

Lee and Ashton (2004) and Ashton and Lee (2001, 2007) have provided strong evidence for the existence of a sixth factor of personality, honesty-humility, residing at the level of the Big Five. They report on evidence from lexical studies involving a multitude of languages (e.g., Dutch, English, French, Hungarian, Italian, and German) that six factors form the major dimensions of personality (e.g., Ashton & Lee, 2008a; Ashton, Lee, & Goldberg, 2004). The structure of the HEXACO model comprises the factors honesty-humility, emotionality, extraversion, agreeableness, conscientiousness, and openness to experience, each with four facets. There are substantial similarities with the Big Five, although HEXACO emotionality is slightly different from Big Five emotional stability, and agreeableness in the HEXACO and Big Five have substantial points of divergence. The primary contribution of the HEXACO is the addition of honesty-humility, which contains the facets of sincerity, fairness, greed avoidance, and modesty. Lexical marker terms covered by honesty-humility include honesty, sincerity, and fair-mindedness versus greed, boastfulness, and hypocriticality. As evidence of the utility of honesty-humility, a wealth of studies has demonstrated its contribution to incremental prediction of important workplace behaviors beyond the Big Five. These behaviors include integrity (e.g., Marcus, Lee, & Ashton, 2007), workplace deviance (O'Neill, Lewis, & Carswell, 2011), unethical business decision making (Ashton & Lee, 2008a, 2008b), and sexual harassment (Lee, Gizzarone, & Ashton, 2003).

Similar to the HEXACO, Paunonen's (2002) Supernumerary Personality Inventory (SPI) identifies personality trait variables falling beyond the sphere of the Big Five. The 10 personality traits have a hierarchical organization under three factors: Machiavellianism, tradition, and masculinity–femininity. Paunonen and Jackson (2000) reported that SPI traits were not accommodated by the Big Five framework, yet SPI traits have been found to be predictive of workplace behavior (O'Neill & Hastings, 2010; Paunonen, Lonnqist, Verkasalo, Leikas, & Nissinen, 2006) and unethical behaviors (Hong, Koh, & Paunonen, 2012). We review these predictions in greater depth later. Here, we make the point that there are structures of personality beyond the Big Five that many researchers may find valuable for theory building and empirical prediction.

Circumplex Models

Circumplex models of personality are two-dimensional models in which traits are organized in a circular pattern around an origin. The arrangement captures trait correlations. Traits close to each other are positively correlated. Traits at 90-degree angles from one another are uncorrelated. Traits at opposite ends are negatively correlated. This has the advantageous feature of naturally accommodating correlations among personality dimensions, which is a feature that is less clear from personality hierarchies. Furthermore, circumplexes allow the researcher to accommodate traits that are blends of the factors that define the axes in the two-dimensional space. A given trait can be situated anywhere in the two-dimensional space, and its location is simply the weighted sum of its factor scores. Thus, the circumplex method is a powerful way to conceptualize the structure of personality.

Wiggins (1979) developed his interpersonal circumplex model from Leary's (1957) system of interpersonal traits. The two superordinate factors used to define the orthogonal axes are agency and communion. Agency involves tendencies to "get ahead" through dominance, status, and control. Communion involves tendencies to "get along" through affiliation, nurturance, and love. In light of projections of interpersonal traits on the circumplex space, Wiggins (1995) described the eight octants of the cicumplex model (in order) as warm-agreeable, gregarious-extraverted, assured-dominant, arrogant-calculating, cold-hearted, aloof-introverted, unassured-submissive, and unassuming-ingenuous.

There are a number of circumplex models of personality such as the Abridged Big Five Circumplex (e.g., Hofstee, de Raad, & Goldberg, 1992), the Interpersonal Circumplex Model (Wiggins, 1979), and others (see a volume edited by Plutchik & Conte, 1997). Despite the power and elegance of such models of personality and their use in developing personality structure, there are no current models in our literature review that provide an avenue for exploring breadth versus specificity of personality measurement. Thus, we do not address circumplex models any further in the current chapter (for additional coverage of the circumplex model, see Chapter 17, this volume).

The Hierarchical Organization of Personality

To begin our examination of the breadth and specificity of personality, we adopt the view in this chapter, already introduced, that personality variables are arranged hierarchically (see Paunonen & Hong, in press). Figure 14.1 depicts a model of this hierarchical organization first published by Eysenck (1947). Our illustration represents a partial view of the structure of a personality factor called conscientiousness (for more coverage on the structure of personality, see Chapter 2, this volume). At the base of the model, there are specific acts of a person, or behavioral responses to internal and environmental stimuli (e.g., the person made his bed this morning). Residing at the next level above are identifiable patterns of those specific behavioral responses, what might be called habits, routines, or characteristic behaviors (e.g., the person often tidies his room). In turn, several related habitual patterns of behavior are components of what are commonly referred to as personality traits (e.g., the person is orderly). Many such traits have been proposed, and factor-analytic investigations have shown that they tend to combine into a fewer number of broad personality factors, such as the conscientiousness factor exemplified in Figure 14.1.

The model illustrated in Figure 14.1 constitutes a simplification of the structure that has been advocated as characterizing human personality characteristics. First of all, the model represents only one factor of personality, conscientiousness, whereas multiple factors are presumed to exist. Second, it shows only five traits as components of conscientiousness, whereas others could be added. Third, each component at each level is connected to only one component above it, whereas more complex linkages likely apply. Fourth, one could postulate additional levels to the hierarchy beyond the four shown, such as one or more higher-order factors, or meaningful clusters of characteristic behaviors that reside between the habitual response level and the trait level. All four of these issues have been the subject of much empirical research examining the various vertical and horizontal aspects of the personality hierarchy.

A salient question raised by the model of personality structure represented in Figure 14.1 concerns the relative empirical utility of different levels of the hierarchy. Which level serves best psychology's goal of understanding and predicting human behavior? Because of the extreme specificity of behavioral acts, they are probably too narrow to provide reliable predictors as a general rule (e.g., see

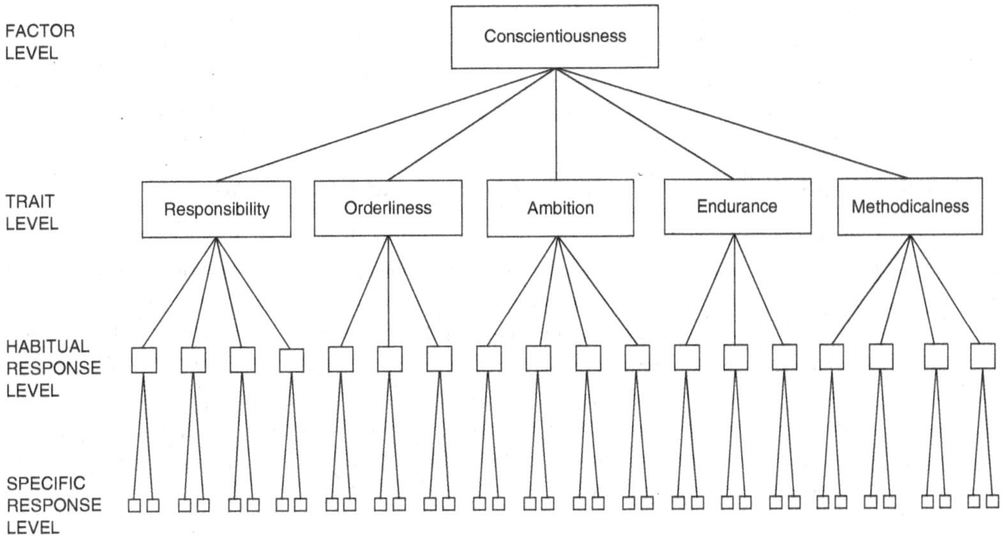

Figure 14.1 A Hierarchical Model of Personality Organization (after Eysenck, 1947).

Green, 1978; Paunonen & Jackson, 1985; Rushton, Jackson, & Paunonen, 1981). A notable exception in a work context might be behaviors identified by the Critical Incident Technique of Flanagan (1954), which, as the name implies, are specific workplace behaviors that are decisive regarding good/bad job performance. Generalized behavior tendencies, characteristic behaviors, or habits are next up the hierarchy. Such variables are actually at the core of the typical personality questionnaire or inventory that, when aggregated, yield an estimate of personality trait level. As with individual instances of behavior, however, we believe that characteristic behaviors or habits tend to be, on their own, too specific to provide optimal empirical utility (but see J. Hogan, Hogan, & Busch, 1984, regarding their so-called homogeneous item composites, such as "Generates Ideas").

The stratum of the personality hierarchy at which most modern assessment and prediction research is done is fairly high up, at the level of the personality trait or the personality factor. And, we see definite signs of movement away from the former toward the latter. This movement appears true in many areas of psychology, including I/O, and it seems to have its beginnings in the early 1980s following the more-or-less formal introduction of the so-called Big Five personality factors, or FFM, to our science (see Digman, 1996, for a detailed account).

As we alluded to above, the personality factor level is the level at which much of the contemporary research in I/O operates (e.g., Barrick & Mount, 1991, 2005; Berry, Ones, & Sackett, 2007; Judge, Heller, & Mount, 2002; Mount & Barrick, 1995, 1998; Mount, Barrick, & Stewart, 1998). Although personality traits appear at present to be understudied in our view, trait-level research may be increasing in some circles (Christiansen & Robie, 2011; Hough & Furnham, 2003; O'Neill & Hastings, 2010; Paunonen et al., 2006; Rothstein & Goffin, 2006; Tett & Christiansen, 2007). Of course, debates involving broad versus narrow measurement issues in personality have arisen, focusing mostly on the relative merits of considering personality at the level of the ubiquitous Big Five factors versus at the level of those factors' constituent traits or facets (e.g., Barrick & Mount, 2003; Ones & Viswesvaran, 1996; Paunonen, 1993, 1998; Paunonen, Rothstein, & Jackson, 1999; Rothstein & Jelley, 2003). Sometimes these exchanges have involved personality variables claimed to be even broader than the Big Five (e.g., Digman, 1997; Rushton & Irwing, 2008).

In the sections below, we review some of the established measures of personality traits and personality factors that are commonly used in I/O research and practice. We also describe so-called compound personality measures and consider their relation to the personality hierarchy. These accounts are then followed by separate sections in which we note issues that arise with each type of assessment.

The Assessment of Personality Traits, Factors, and Compounds

Components of the personality hierarchy are generally measured with self-report personality questionnaires, inventories, or rating scales. A respondent is normally asked to choose some option from a list of alternatives that best describes his or her response to a personality statement or item. As already mentioned, such items typically refer to the behavior tendencies at the habitual response level of the personality hierarchy. Several items' responses are generally aggregated to come up with a trait score. The trait scores themselves can then be combined to yield a factor score (sometimes trait or factor scores are obtained relatively directly by, for example, asking the respondent to indicate his or her position on a single personality trait/factor continuum). We describe some of the more popular trait and factor measures in the sections below, followed by description of what are called compound personality scales.

Personality Trait Measures

There are a number of omnibus personality questionnaires that directly operationalize lower-level personality traits, three examples of which are listed in Table 14.1 (for additional coverage on common personality inventories, see Chapter 10, this volume). In addition to the Personality Research Form (PRF; Jackson, 1984; see Table 14.1), classic measures include the Jackson Personality Inventory (JPI; Jackson, 1994), the Comrey Personality Scales (CPS; Comrey, 2008), the California Personality Inventory (CPI; Gough, 1987), and the 16PF (Cattell & Mead, 2008). These instruments, each of which provides scores on a relatively large number of traits, have been employed frequently in empirical prediction research. For example, the scales of the HPI (R. Hogan & Hogan, 1992) have been used extensively in I/O research to predict work outcomes (see R. Hogan & Holland, 2003; R. Hogan & Shelton, 1998).

Not all traits of personality fall within the domain of the FFM (Paunonen & Jackson, 2000; see Saucier & Goldberg, 1998), thereby suggesting that the Big Five framework might not be completely comprehensive (Hough, 1992, 1997). Of interest to those wishing to measure personality traits not captured by the FFM is the SPI (Paunonen, 2002). The SPI was designed to measure 10 lower-level traits that are essentially beyond the Big Five (see Table 14.1). Correlations with those factors have been found to be minimal (Lee, Ogunfowora, & Ashton, 2005; O'Neill & Hastings, 2010), even in cross-cultural samples (Paunonen, Haddock, Forsterling, & Keinonen, 2003). Of relevance to I/O psychology, SPI traits have been found to explain variance in workplace behaviors (Lee et al., 2003; O'Neill & Hastings, 2010; Paunonen et al., 2006) and even health-risky behaviors (Hong & Paunonen, 2009).

Perhaps the most popular measure of lower-level personality dimensions currently is the NEO Personality Inventory—Revised (NEO-PI-R; Costa & McCrae, 1992), designed to measure 30 personality traits. As described below, those traits are presumed to represent facets of the higher-level Big Five personality factors (see Table 14.1). Each trait or facet score is derived as an aggregated response computed over several self-report personality statements describing characteristic behaviors. The NEO-PI-R scales have been used in prediction studies and have been found to be related to important work-relevant criteria such as career risk taking (Nicholson, Soane, Fenton-O'Creevy, & Willman, 2005), leadership effectiveness (Judge & Bono, 2000), supervisor ratings of job performance (Piedmont & Weinstein, 1994), and performance of police recruits during basic training (Black, 2000; Detrick & Chibnall, 2006).

Table 14.1 Some Factors of the Personality Hierarchy and Their Constituent Traits, as Represented by the PRF, SPI, and NEO-PI-R Questionnaires

PRF	*SPI*	*NEO-PI-R*
Agreeableness	**Machiavellianism**	**Neuroticism**
Abasement	Seductiveness	Anxiety
Aggression (–)	Manipulativeness	Angry hostility
Defendence (–)	Egotism	Depression
	Thriftiness (–)	Self-consciousness
Extraversion		Impulsiveness
Affiliation	**Tradition**	Vulnerability
Dominance	Conventionality	
Exhibition	Religiosity	**Extraversion**
		Warmth
Independence	**Masculinity–femininity**	Gregariousness
Autonomy	Femininity	Assertiveness
Social recognition (–)	Integrity	Activity
Succorance (–)	Risk taking (–)	Excitement-seeking
	Humorousness (–)	Positive emotions
Openness to experience		
Sentience		**Openness to experience**
Change		Fantasy
Understanding		Aesthetics
		Feelings
Achievement		Actions
Achievement		Ideas
Endurance		Values
Play (–)		
		Agreeableness
Methodicalness		Trust
Cognitive structure		Straightforwardness
Order		Altruism
Impulsivity (–)		Compliance
		Modesty
		Tender-mindedness
		Conscientiousness
		Competence
		Order
		Dutifulness
		Achievement striving
		Self-discipline
		Deliberation

Notes: PRF: Personality Research Form; SPI: Supernumerary Personality Inventory; NEO-PI-R: NEO Personality Inventory—Revised. Factors, shown in bold, are from Jackson, Paunonen, Fraboni, and Goffin (1996) for the PRF; Paunonen (2002) for the SPI; Costa and McCrae (1992) for the NEO-PI-R. A minus sign in parentheses (–) indicates a trait scale that is negatively keyed on its factor.

Personality Factor Measures

Without question, the most widely accepted model of personality structure in psychology today is the Big Five (Goldberg, 1990, 1992, 1993), also known as the FFM (Costa & McCrae, 1992). Those five personality factors, suggested by some to be universal and comprehensive, are commonly labeled as extraversion, agreeableness, conscientiousness, emotional stability, and openness to experience. As already illustrated with our example of conscientiousness in Figure 14.1, each factor is thought to comprise several lower-level personality traits and, thus, to reside at the top of the personality hierarchy. The FFM emerged from factor-analytic studies of the everyday personality lexicon, supported by parallel studies of published personality questionnaires (for reviews, see Block, 1995; Digman, 1990; John, 1990; McCrae & John, 1992). Notwithstanding some serious criticisms related to the reductionistic quality of the FFM and the inevitability of finding the Big Five in typical personality measures due to variable pre-selection (e.g., Block, 1995, 2001), the Big Five factors have had a profound impact on I/O psychology (Mount & Barrick, 1998; Viswesvaran & Ones, 2000). They have been shown to predict various aspects of work behavior in numerous meta-analyses (e.g., Barrick & Mount, 1991; Barrick, Mount, & Judge, 2001; Judge, Bono, Ilies, & Gerhardt, 2002; Tett, Jackson, & Rothstein, 1991).

As already mentioned, Costa and McCrae's (1992) NEO-PI-R was designed specifically to measure 30 facets of the Big Five factors, so naturally those facet scales can be combined to yield factor scales. Specifically, as shown in Table 14.1, each of the five-factor scores is obtained through the aggregation of scores on six lower-level personality facets. The facets defining any particular factor have, of course, been shown to be empirically related to the same broad personality domain, much as we have represented for the conscientiousness factor in Figure 14.1. Furthermore, the factors themselves are theoretically orthogonal, although empirically some factor scales are moderately correlated (see Costa & McCrae, 1992, p. 100). A subset of items from the NEO-PI-R has been incorporated into a shorter questionnaire, called the NEO Five-Factor Inventory (NEO-FFI; Costa & McCrae, 1992), which provides scores on each of the Big Five personality factors but not on their constituent facets. The factors of the NEO-PI-R and NEO-FFI have been shown to have utility in the prediction of workplace criteria (e.g., Crant, 1995; Thoresen, Bradley, Bliese, & Thoresen, 2004).

There are models of personality structure other than the Big Five. Jackson, Paunonen, Fraboni, and Goffin (1996) factor-analyzed the PRF in several data sets and found support for six factors (see Table 14.1). Their alternative framework involved bifurcating conscientiousness into two distinct factors: one involving industriousness and ambition (achievement), and the other orderliness and organization (methodicalness). The separation of conscientiousness into two distinct factors facilitates considerations of how achievement and methodicalness might relate differentially to various work criteria, a view supported by Hough (1992) and by Stewart (1999), among others. The SFPQ was subsequently developed in order to measure those six broad dimensions of personality (Jackson et al., 2000).

One higher-level factor of personality that is not well represented by the NEO-PI-R or the SFPQ is a dimension related to honesty. Lee and Ashton (2004) have argued persuasively, with empirical data, that such a factor, in addition to the Big Five, can be recovered from most lexical studies of personality (also see Ashton & Lee, 2007, 2008a). This has been found to be true even in those studies originally reporting only five factors (see Ashton, Lee, Perugini, et al., 2004) and in studies reporting cross-cultural lexical data (Ashton, Lee, Perugini, et al., 2004; Boies, Yoo, Ebacher, Lee, & Ashton, 2004; Lee & Ashton, 2008). Their six-factor model has been operationalized through the HEXACO-PI inventory (Ashton & Lee, 2009; Lee & Ashton, 2004), which includes the honesty-humility factor and slight rotational variants of the traditional Big Five. Honesty-humility has been found to be negatively related to many counterproductive organizational behaviors such as sexual quid pro quos, unethical decision making, and harmful behaviors directed toward the organization and its members (Ashton & Lee, 2008b; Marcus, Lee, et al., 2007; O'Neill et al., 2011).

There are a few researchers who have argued for personality variables of even greater breadth than the Big Five. Digman (1997) reported that agreeableness, conscientiousness, and emotional stability tend to form one factor, whereas extraversion and openness to experience tend to form another factor. He called these superordinate factors alpha and beta, respectively. At an even broader level, some have argued for one unitary, general, factor of personality, much like the *g* of intelligence (Musek, 2007; Rushton, Bons, & Hur, 2008; Rushton & Irwing, 2008, 2009a, 2009b, 2009c, 2009d; van der Linden, te Nijenhuis, Cremers, & van de Ven, 2011). That factor is theorized to represent evolutionary adaptations that favor survival, growth, and reproduction (Rushton & Irwing, 2008), and is purportedly independent of a social desirability response set (Rushton & Erdle, 2010). To our knowledge, no one has yet developed a specific measure of the *g* of personality. Nor has this broad factor been used extensively in the I/O area to predict work behaviors (but see van der Linden et al., who reported modest relations between a GFP and dropout from military training in two samples).

Compound Personality Measures

A relatively recent trend in I/O psychology is to develop so-called compound personality measures as predictors of work behaviors. Such a measure comprises several personality factor scores, or personality trait scores, that are aggregated into a single composite designed to optimally predict a particular criterion (see Hough & Ones, 2001; Ones, Viswesvaran, & Dilchert, 2005; Schneider & Hough, 1995; Schneider, Hough, & Dunnette, 1996). Schneider et al. (1996) described compound personality measures as "linear combinations of narrower personality facets that do not all covary" (p. 641). Purpose-built compound measures have been developed where, instead of measuring the various personality components with separate inventories, items measuring them are blended into a single questionnaire, yielding a single score for a respondent (e.g., the Managerial Potential Scale; see J. Hogan, Hogan, & Murtha, 1992). Examples of compound scale domains, as listed by Hough and Ones (2001), include measures of integrity, customer service orientation, emotional intelligence, emotionality, and social competence. Other examples include measures related to violence and aggression, stress tolerance, and drug and alcohol use (see Ones et al., 2005).

Ones et al. (2005) and Ones and Viswesvaran (2001a) reported evidence suggesting that the strongest prediction of job outcomes offered by personality occurs when criterion-focused compound measures are employed. Furthermore, Ones et al. (2005) argued that the construct validity of the measures is supported by the fact that most of them are highly correlated with personality dimensions—in particular, citing the compound measure of integrity (targeted to predict counterproductivity) and its correlation with the Big Five factors of agreeableness, conscientiousness, and emotional stability (see also Ones et al., 1994; Ones, Viswesvaran, & Schmidt, 1993). Ones et al. (2005) interpreted those statistical relations as suggesting that so-called compound personality measures are "squarely personality measures as 70% to 100% of the variance in them are accounted for by three of the Big Five dimensions" (p. 395). Those authors further concluded that, by their nature, the composites are likely even more broad than are any of the Big Five factors and warrant a superordinate position on the personality hierarchy (see also Ones & Viswesvaran, 1996).

Issues With Broad/Narrow Personality Assessments

We stated our opinion at the beginning of our chapter that the level of the personality hierarchy represented by the common personality trait is the optimal level for most empirical research in I/O psychology. Despite this belief, in the following sections, we raise issues that can arise with measurement at all levels of the personality hierarchy; that is, with narrow trait measures, broad factor measures, and compound measures. These issues pertain equally to both the statistical prediction of behavior as well as the theoretical understanding of behavior. Because assessment at the narrowest levels, the individual behavioral act or specific habit, is not well represented in the present research domain, we ignore this stratum of the personality hierarchy in our subsequent discussion.

Trait Measures

Assuming a personality trait scale has demonstrable levels of construct validity, that measure yields scores on a single, unitary personality dimension. The individual items in the scale all measure the same trait. This means that each item yields the same true score for a respondent, but with an unknown random error component added (Lord & Novick, 1968). Because those random errors cancel out with aggregation, the more items in the measure, the more reliable and valid the resultant trait scores (which is the main reason behaviors at the bottom of the personality hierarchy, individually, generally show poor prediction of job performance). This aggregation means that longer measures of unitary traits are likely to be (a) better predictors of relevant criteria and (b) more interpretable in terms of an underlying psychological construct.

Lower-level trait measures can have disadvantages. First, a good construct-valid trait scale might be unacceptably long and time-consuming, leading to respondent antagonism. Even worse in this regard, measuring the various facets of a multifaceted criterion (more on this later) might require several such measures. Another potential problem is that a large number of trait measures used in a prediction study can capitalize on chance and produce spurious predictor–criterion relations that do not cross-validate. An omnibus trait questionnaire (e.g., the NEO-PI-R) could also have the disadvantage, particularly compared with custom-built compound measures, of containing several irrelevant measures, each having trait-specific variance that pertains to none of the aspects of the criterion of interest. These disadvantages notwithstanding, the advantages of trait measures are many, as should become apparent with our discussion below of issues surrounding other types of measures.

Factor Measures

We see more issues with factor-level measures than with trait-level measures in prediction research. It is unquestionably very seductive to a researcher to have today's option of administering a short personality questionnaire with exactly five (factor) scales to analyze, as compared with the alternative of a much longer omnibus questionnaire having 20 or more (trait) scales. Of course, constraints on time and resources sometimes dictate that the assessment needs to be brief. And, if a few factor scales can predict the criterion of interest with acceptable accuracy, then the use of such a measure might be a useful expedient. But that expedient can come at a cost.

A personality factor never accounts for 100% of its constituent traits' variance because, by definition, the factor represents the traits' common variance. Trait measures also have trait-specific variance, and it is this variance, not shared with the other traits or with the factor, that can be exploited for predictive purposes (Paunonen, 1998; Paunonen & Nicol, 2001). In other words, a factor may not be an optimal predictor of a criterion if the uniqueness of one of its facets correlates with that criterion. What appears to be an increasingly common practice in psychology—ignoring personality traits in favor of investigating only personality factors—ultimately treats trait-specific variance as irrelevant, even though that trait-specificity may offer the most powerful prediction of the criterion. How much variance in a typical personality trait measure can be attributed to an underlying Big Five factor and how much to the specific trait itself? As one example, consider that the five principal components underlying the 30 facet scales of the NEO-PI-R (Costa & McCrae, 1992) account for about 57% of the variance in the facets, leaving 43% to trait-specific (and error) factors.

We do not intend to suggest that the common variance represented by a personality factor can never be the best predictor of some criterion. That common variance could indeed be most predictive, thereby supporting a factor-level approach. Or, the trait-specific variance could add to prediction, thereby supporting a trait-level approach. Which of these alternatives exists is usually not a simple question to answer, requiring extensive theoretical and empirical work, including personality-based work analyses where applicable. Such research can lead to one of three scenarios regarding the comparison of trait versus factor predictors, each mandating their own prediction solutions. We call these three scenarios "factor dominance," "trait dominance," and "facet bidirectionality."

It is, of course, entirely possible that a broad personality factor will correlate with a criterion more strongly than will any of its facets. We refer to this occurrence as *factor dominance*, because the broad factor's common variance is more predictive than any one facet's trait-specific variances. In the case of factor dominance, the researcher will benefit most from developing theory regarding commonalities among facets instead of any one facet's uniqueness. Alternatively, there is the possibility that a broad factor correlates less strongly with the criterion than does one or more of its facets. We refer to this occurrence as *trait dominance*, because trait-specific variance predominates over common variance. The result of this is that the predictive power of a specific facet will be washed out if it is aggregated with its cohort, but less criterion-relevant, facets. Also, from an interpretive point of view, a factor-level analysis here could be costly theoretically, as inferences regarding the cause of the personality–criterion linkage will tend to be less comprehensive than they would be with a facet-level interpretation.

Even more problematic for factor-level prediction than a condition of trait dominance is what we refer to as *facet bidirectionality*. This occurs when at least one facet is positively related to the criterion and another facet is negatively related to the same criterion. If facets of a broad factor correlate with a criterion in opposite directions, these will tend to cancel out and the factor-level correlation will be near zero (Tett, Steele, & Beauregard, 2003). The researcher might then conclude that there is no relation between the domain of personality measured by the factor and the criterion when, in fact, there clearly are statistical relations at the facet level, relations that can be theoretically informative.

We suggest that empirical evidence should be used to determine statistical utilities of different personality measurement levels; that is, the extent to which it is common variance or trait-specific variance that drives the prediction. It is also necessary to examine the nature of the personality variables and the criterion in order to advance theoretical understanding of why the specific personality components are most useful (O'Neill, Goffin, & Tett, 2009; see Lievens, Buyse, & Sackett, 2005). Of course, there is nothing to stop the researcher from analyzing and reporting relations at both the factor and facet levels (Christiansen & Robie, 2011). In fact, with the omnibus personality inventories we described earlier, assessing predictor–criterion relations at the facet level does not preclude one from evaluating those relations at the factor level using the same questionnaire data (see Table 14.1). This applies to the PRF (Costa & McCrae, 1988; Jackson et al., 1996), the JPI (Paunonen & Jackson, 1996), the CPS (Comrey, 2008), the CPI (McCrae, Costa, & Piedmont, 1993), the 16PF (Cattell & Mead, 2008), and many others (see Boyle, Matthews, & Saklofske, 2008).

Compound Measures

Our issue with compound personality scales is that, unlike personality trait scales or factor scales, such composites have little or no psychological meaning. Each is the weighted (or unweighted) aggregation of many distinct and even uncorrelated personality variables that have been assembled on the basis of their incremental capacity in predicting a criterion. Note that there is no targeted, unitary construct to be measured; therefore, the test's scores can have no useful psychological interpretation beyond their predictive ability. This is in contrast to most personality trait or factor measures, for which there is generally a formal theory of a dimension's existence beyond its measuring instrument.

Most modern-day personality measures have been developed following well-established, deductively driven, construct-oriented techniques of test construction (Jackson, 1967, 1970). Items measuring a personality trait are proposed to represent an (imperfect) sample of trait-relevant behaviors selected from a homogeneous domain of parallel behaviors that reflect the underlying personality construct. Those items are largely psychometrically and conceptually interchangeable, and removal of any items will, theoretically, not affect test-score interpretations. This is consistent with the critical realist perspective (Campbell, 1960; Loevinger, 1957; Messick, 1981), in which constructs cause responses to relevant, imperfectly measured stimuli and are theorized to be real entities that exist independent of their measures (see also Borsboom, 2005; Edwards, 2011).

Compound personality measures are developed empirically using essentially a criterion-oriented approach to test construction (see Ones & Viswesvaran, 2001a). Variables or items are selected for the final test form based on the strength of their statistical relationship to some criterion of interest. The method, of course, favors variables that are each predictive but that are mutually orthogonal. The resultant scale score, which can represent the sum of the several heterogeneous components, whether differentially weighted or not, only has meaning as far as the particular prediction criterion is concerned. No psychological meaning can be applied to those scores. Furthermore, removing any one component from such a measure can drastically change the very limited meaning it does have (i.e., regarding criterion prediction). Also, two people can have the same total score on a compound measure, but have completely contrary scores at the measure's component level. As such, they would engender equal expectations about criterion performance, but perhaps for entirely different reasons. And those reasons might be important.

Edwards and Bagozzi (Bagozzi, 2007; Edwards, 2011; Edwards & Bagozzi, 2000) have used the term *formative measures* in referring to measures of the type represented by compound personality scales. The term is meant to denote the fact that the construct represented by the scores on such a scale is not known until after the instrument has been constructed—the measure itself forms or induces the underlying construct (Edwards, 2011). In contrast, typical personality trait or factor scales are reflective measures, because their scores reflect constructs known in advance, the scales having been purposely designed to assess them. Edwards and Bagozzi have shared our concerns with formative measures, noting several theoretical and psychometric problems. These include their multidimensionality, poor internal consistency, lack of model identification in structural analyses, problems with construct validation, and more (Edwards, 2011; also see Williams, Edwards, & Vandenberg, 2003).

Regarding the notion of construct validity, one might question whether it is even relevant to compound personality scales. Loevinger (1957) recognized that evidence for the construct validity of a measure is, at once, validation of the test and validation of the construct it purports to measure (see also Paunonen & Hong, in press). But what would be the psychological construct underlying scores on, say, a managerial potential scale, or a customer service orientation scale? We submit that such scores are best thought of as outcome variables, much like socioeconomic status (SES). The variable's score represents a certain type of person (this notion of typology is discussed more fully in a subsequent section) and is computed as the aggregate of multiple construct indicators that might have nothing more in common than their ability to predict a respondent's similarity to some prototypical group member. Although the notion of construct validity could be pertinent to the individual components of the compound measure, it might be difficult to relate total scores on that measure (e.g., managerial potential, or customer service orientation, or SES) to any one underlying latent psychological construct, despite their predictive ability.

Compound personality scales, being formative measures, simply yield numbers that are correlated highly with a criterion. They are "conceptual polyglots" according to Edwards (2011, p. 379; also see Borsboom, 2005). They have no connection to an underlying construct, as the construct does not exist apart from the formative variables that induce it (Judge & Kammeyer-Mueller, 2012). The resulting scores can have no theoretical meaning beyond the constructivist's language used to describe them, or beyond their prediction of the criterion (see Borsboom, Mellenbergh, & Van Heerden, 2003). Contrary to some viewpoints (Ones et al., 2005), compound personality scales have no place in the personality hierarchy as represented in Figure 14.1 (Schneider et al., 1996), except insofar as they are polyglots of traits or factors. Now, some have claimed that, because a (formative) compound scale correlates with some (reflective) personality scale(s), it means that the former measures a personality construct (e.g., Ones, 1993; Ones & Viswesvaran, 2001a, 2001b; Ones et al., 1994). But this is like claiming that SES is a personality variable because an SES index correlates with achievement motivation and self-esteem. Neither claim is valid.

The Bandwidth-Matching Hypothesis

In the preceding sections, our bias for the use of lower-level trait measures in prediction research rather than higher-level factor measures is apparent. The former measures, because they embody both common factor variance as well as a trait-specific variance, have the potential to yield the most accurate prediction and conceptualization of the criterion behavior of interest. Compound measures might provide optimal criterion prediction in highly circumscribed conditions, but any subsequent understanding of the criterion behavior can only come from a parsing of the compound measure followed by analysis of its individual components. There is another possibility, however, with the recommendation for predictor breadth not fixed to any one level of the personality hierarchy. We are referring to the so-called bandwidth-matching procedure.

Bandwidth-matching is based on the belief that the breadth of the predictor variable(s) should match the breadth of the criterion variable (R. Hogan & Roberts, 1996; Judge & Kammeyer-Mueller, 2012; Ones & Viswesvaran, 1996; Smith, 1976). Thus, if the workplace criterion is broad and multidimensional (e.g., job performance, counterproductive workplace behavior, and leadership style), the bandwidth-matching hypothesis predicts that equally broad predictors, such as those based on the factors of personality, will provide optimal prediction. For narrower, more specific criteria (e.g., maintaining a tidy workspace, engaging in friendly interpersonal interactions, and low absenteeism), the hypothesis suggests that perhaps narrow personality trait measures will be most predictive. For particularly complex and multifaceted criteria, compound personality scales that measure the disparate facets of the criterion could provide the best match in breadth.

The bandwidth-matching hypothesis sounds convincing at first blush. However, critical examination of the method and its implementation reveals a general problem. It would appear that a rule-of-thumb involving the use of predictor–criterion matching simply on the basis of bandwidth cannot be a fruitful one for optimizing personality–criterion relations, in general. The deficiency with this logic is that it ignores the fact that the match of the measures should be not only in terms of breadth but also in terms of content (Judge & Kammeyer-Mueller, 2012; Tett & Christiansen, 2007; Tett, Guterman, Bleier, & Murphy, 2000). Consider Smith's (1976) recommendation: "If possible, the relative degree of specificity in the manipulation or predictor should be matched to the specificity of the criterion measure" (p. 749). But if this advice is followed too literally, it is possible that only some of the facets of the personality measure will overlap with facets of the criterion, and criterion-irrelevant variance in the remaining facets will interfere with achieving maximum prediction, regardless of the matching bandwidths.

Whether choosing a predictor battery that resides at the level of the personality trait or the personality factor, or is level-matched with the criterion, a sensible precondition is a critical and formal evaluation of the criterion. We refer here to a personality-oriented work analysis (Tett & Christiansen, 2008). Outside of chance occurrences, where the facets of the predictor happen to be aligned perfectly with the facets of the criterion, greater utility will be observed when predictor traits are hand-picked based on their match to facets of the criterion through a proper empirical evaluation (Tett et al., 2003). A personality-oriented work analysis identifies distinct, job-relevant, personality predictors that have strong overlap with distinct dimensions of the criterion (Goffin et al., 2011; O'Neill et al., 2009; Paunonen et al., 1999; Tett & Burnett, 2003; Chapter 11, this volume). Paunonen et al. (1999) described some fundamental considerations for selecting narrow personality traits that can lead to optimal prediction even for broad criteria (see also Nunnally, 1978). The essence of those considerations was that, in ideal circumstances, traits should be selected based on their theoretical and empirical connection to facets of job performance, their capacity to contribute incremental prediction beyond other job-relevant traits, and their cross-validated weighting in an equation that produces optimal prediction. Note that a composite measure yielded by such a procedure is a formative measure, a term we defined earlier and applied to compound personality scales. But there is an important difference between our recommended statistical approach and the compound personality approach—in the former case, we exhort that no attempt be made to apply a meaningful personality interpretation to the resultant composite variable beyond its mathematical relation to the criterion. Any such interpretation might be applied to the individual components of the composite measure, of course, but not to their aggregate. Such interpretive restraint has not always been the case with proponents of compound personality scales (e.g., Ones et al., 2005).

Suffice it to say, any claim regarding the use of the bandwidth-matching hypothesis as the single basis on which to identify a potentially predictive predictor battery is insufficient (Tett & Christiansen, 2007). This maxim overlooks the more important issue of matching predictor and criteria on the basis of thematic linkages (i.e., content overlap) and other considerations (Christiansen & Robie, 2011; Goffin et al., 2011; Schneider et al., 1996; Tett & Christiansen, 2008; Tett et al., 2000). Besides, as discussed above, several narrow trait measures, carefully chosen, can predict a broad criterion as well as, or better than, a broad factor that matches that criterion in breadth (Nunnally, 1978). Notice that we said several trait measures; it would hardly be a fair test of the bandwidth-matching hypothesis to evaluate the predictive accuracy of a single narrow trait predictor against a multidimensional criterion.

Formal evaluations of the bandwidth-matching hypothesis do not exist. What would be needed now are empirical studies that explicitly manipulate predictor–criterion match in the number of underlying dimensions, and the content of those dimensions. So far, conclusions about the validity of bandwidth-matching have been based on post hoc analyses of prediction studies not designed to test that hypothesis. Because of the absence of explicit research on this topic, we discuss it no further in this chapter.

Research Findings

In the following sections, we review some of the existing literature regarding the prediction of work-related criteria with personality measures of various types. In light of the findings we report, and other issues to be discussed, we then advance some proposals regarding breadth of assessment in personality. We also offer some practical recommendations for making decisions regarding the type of personality predictors to use, broad versus narrow, in real workplace settings.

Personality Traits, Personality Factors, and the Prediction of Behavior

We review some published findings below concerning the prediction of job-relevant criteria using measures of personality characteristics. The criteria include overall job performance, counterproductive workplace behaviors, leadership and managerial performance, team performance, and other work and nonwork behaviors.

Job Performance

A meta-analysis by Dudley, Orvis, Lebiecki, and Cortina (2006) investigated the incremental prediction of conscientiousness facets beyond the conscientiousness factor. Narrow facets of conscientiousness considered were order, achievement, dependability, and cautiousness. Five job performance criteria were available: overall job performance, task performance, job dedication, interpersonal facilitation, and counterproductive behavior. Across the five job performance criteria, the average variance explained by the conscientiousness factor was .05, whereas the average percentage of incremental prediction of the four narrow traits, as a group, beyond the conscientiousness factor was .11. Thus, narrow facets of conscientiousness considerably augmented the predictive power of the conscientiousness factor.

A meta-analysis by Barrett, Miguel, Hurd, Lueke, and Tan (2003) examined the conscientiousness factor and its facets in police-selection contexts. Findings suggested that the conscientiousness factor did not predict job performance across jobs, whereas the CPI facet of responsibility did. Vinchur, Schippmann, Switzer, and Roth (1998) reported on a meta-analysis that compared conscientiousness and extraversion factors to their respective facets in the prediction of objective sales performance. Whereas the validity for conscientiousness was .31, the validities for its facets of achievement and dependability were .41 and .18, respectively. Similarly, whereas the validity for extraversion was .22, the validities for its facets of potency (defined as impact, influence, and energy) and affiliation were .26 and .15, respectively. Building on Vinchur et al.'s (1998) work, Warr, Bartram, and Martin (2005) examined three samples of sales people and confirmed that potency and achievement were stronger predictors of sales performance than were their factors of conscientiousness and extraversion, respectively.

Stewart (1999) reported that trait order was a stronger predictor of sales performance than was the conscientiousness factor during orientation and training. Once employees had learned the job and had reached a performance maintenance stage, however, achievement was a stronger predictor of sales performance than was the conscientiousness factor. Hough (1992) found that the performance of health care providers was positively related to trait dependability and negatively related to trait achievement, with both correlations at .24. Subsequent analyses performed by Christiansen and Robie (2011) revealed that aggregating Hough's facet-level correlations to the level of the conscientiousness factor would have resulted in a trivial factor-level relation with health care performance. Finally, a study investigating interaction effects of the conscientiousness factor and its facets with general mental ability found that only one of the personality variables, achievement, interacted with general mental ability in order to predict customer service representatives' task performance (Perry, Hunter, Witt, & Kenneth, 2011). The authors proposed that a contingency of the general mental ability (GMA)–performance relation may involve the employee's motivation to deploy his or her capabilities, which, according to the authors, is captured better by trait achievement than by other conscientiousness facets or by the factor.

Counterproductive Work Behavior

Counterproductive workplace behaviors are volitional, hostile behaviors directed toward the organization or its members (Bennett & Robinson, 2000). Ashton (1998) found that Responsibility and Risk Taking, narrow trait scales of the JPI (Jackson, 1994), correlated more strongly with a measure of counterproductive workplace behavior than did any Big Five factor. The most predictive Big Five factor was conscientiousness ($r = -.22$), whereas Responsibility and Risk Taking predicted counterproductivity at $r = -.40$ and .30, respectively.

O'Neill and Hastings (2010) found that narrow trait scales of Paunonen's (2002) SPI, such as Risk Taking, Integrity, Manipulativeness, Religiosity, Seductiveness, and Egotism, explained variance incremental to the Big Five, much more so than did the Big Five beyond those narrow traits. Hastings and O'Neill (2009) found that conscientiousness and agreeableness factors were more strongly correlated with counterproductive work behavior than were their constituent facets (i.e., factor dominance). For neuroticism, however, the factor was not significantly related to counterproductive workplace behavior, whereas its facet, anger, was a significant predictor, in the negative direction (i.e., trait dominance). Similarly, whereas extraversion was not related to counterproductive workplace behavior, its facets of friendliness and excitement seeking were related to counterproductivity in opposite directions (i.e., facet bidirectionality). These opposite correlations at the facet level likely served to cancel out, through aggregation, any prediction by the extraversion factor. In a study examining Lee and Ashton's (2004) honesty-humility facet of fairness, O'Neill et al. (2011) found that only conscientiousness offered superior prediction of counterproductive workplace behavior than did the fairness facet. Moreover, the fairness facet was more predictive than was its factor (for more coverage on personality and counterproductive work behavior, see Chapter 27, this volume).

Leadership and Managerial Performance

A consistent finding emerging from a series of studies investigating extraversion and its facets using Jackson's (1994) PRF and Jackson et al.'s (2000) SFPQ is that the facet Dominance tends to be a stronger predictor than do the other facets, such as Exhibition and Affiliation (Goffin, Rothstein, & Johnston, 1996, 2000; Marcus, Goffin, Johnston, & Rothstein, 2007). Similarly, Paunonen et al. (2006) reported that trait egotism, defined as having a high opinion of one's self and feeling confident in one's own capabilities, was more strongly related to peer ratings of leadership behavior than was any of the Big Five factors. Judge, Heller, et al.'s (2002) meta-analytic findings suggested that several facets can outperform their factors in the prediction of leadership performance. Those authors found that the facets of dominance and sociability were more predictive than was their underlying extraversion factor, and that the achievement and dependability facets of conscientiousness were more predictive than was their underlying conscientiousness factor (for more coverage on personality and leadership, see Chapter 34, this volume).

Tett et al. (2003) found that narrow traits of the same factor often correlated in different magnitudes with managerial criteria. These findings were observed across two samples. For example, in the first sample trait order correlated negatively with managerial criteria to which trait achievement was positively correlated (e.g., coordinating with others and problem awareness). In the second sample, the curiosity facet of openness to experience was positively related to technical performance, whereas the culture facet of the same factor was predictive in the negative direction (i.e., facet bidirectionality). Hough (1992) found that trait achievement was positively related to managerial performance, whereas trait dependability had a slight negative relation. Based on Hough's findings, Christiansen and Robie (2011) showed that a composite correlation involving a conscientiousness factor and managerial performance would be relatively trivial. Like Tett et al. (2000), that finding is an example of facet bidirectionality and a corresponding cancellation effect. Finally, in a study using multisource ratings of managerial performance, Christiansen and Robie (2011) found that none of the factor-level criterion correlations exceeded all of their respective facet-level criterion correlations. Moreover, multiple regression analyses revealed that facets explained at least twice the variance in managerial ratings than did Big Five factors.

Team Performance

O'Neill and Allen (2011) investigated factor and facet relations among conscientiousness and team performance. Engineering design teams worked on complex design projects involving the construction of prototypes and lengthy reports that detailed their design solutions. When team member self-report personality scores were averaged and correlated with team task performance, facets of conscientiousness were not more predictive than was the conscientiousness factor. But when a team's overall personality variable scores were operationalized as the maximum within-team member score, the facet of organization from the PRF (Jackson, 1994) was more strongly related to team performance than was the conscientiousness factor. Colquitt, Hollenbeck, Ilgen, LePine, and Sheppard (2002) predicted that openness to experience and some of its facets would benefit teams performing a decision-making task in a computer-mediated environment compared with a face-to-face environment. As expected, openness to experience moderated the effect of communication medium on team decision-making performance, but the facets actions and fantasy were stronger moderators than was their factor.

LePine (2003) conducted a laboratory study in which teams participated in decision-making exercises using a military command and control simulator. Teams' capacity to adapt to a change in the computer communication medium in which members interacted (i.e., adaptive performance) was positively related to team members' mean achievement scores and negatively related to mean dependability scores. LePine argued that achievement-oriented individuals' high motivation drives them to persevere in the face of change, whereas individuals high on dependability prefer stability, order, and routine. The latter set of attributes appears to be related to preferences for structure, which may explain the poor reactions to unexpected environmental changes. LePine also remarked that the nontrivial facets of conscientiousness likely would have cancelled out had they been aggregated into a conscientiousness factor (for more coverage on personality and work teams, see Chapter 33, this volume).

Other Work Criteria

LePine, Colquitt, and Erez (2000) conducted a decision-making study in which participants were tasked with determining proper threat levels to incoming aircraft in a computer simulation. The importance of various cues for accurately identifying threat levels were learned through experience, at which point an unforeseen change in the weights of various cues was introduced. Performance after the unexpected change was the criterion (i.e., adaptive performance). Supporting LePine's (2003) team research findings above, LePine et al. found that individuals' adaptation was negatively related to conscientiousness facets of order, deliberation, and dutifulness, whereas achievement-related facets were unrelated to adaptive performance. Moon (2001) investigated escalation of commitment decisions, which involved asking participants whether they would continue investing in a project that had appeared to be failing despite the possibility of huge profits if the project could get back on track. Moon found that the dutifulness facet of conscientiousness was positively related to de-escalation of commitment (i.e., cutting losses), whereas the achievement facet of conscientiousness was positively related to escalation of commitment (i.e., throwing potentially good money after bad). The conscientiousness factor was unrelated to decisions. In a follow-up study, Moon, Hollenbeck, Humphrey, and Maue (2003) found that the neuroticism factor was unrelated to levels of commitment in escalation decisions, whereas the facet of depression was positively related to de-escalation of commitment and the facet of anxiety was positively related to escalation of commitment.

Non-Work Behavior

Paunonen (1998) collected 12 behavioral variables, GPA, and sex using his Behavioral Report Form (e.g., smoking behavior, dating behavior, traffic violations, and religiosity) in order to compare the prediction offered by broad and narrow personality variables. In the first of two studies, he found that the average proportion of incremental criterion variance accounted for by Big Five factors, beyond narrow traits of the PRF (Jackson, 1984), was 2.1% across the 14 criteria. Narrow traits augmented the prediction of the Big Five factors, however, at an average of 10.2% across criteria. In the second study, Paunonen collected the same behavioral criteria and used the same Big Five measure, but this time he employed the JPI (Jackson, 1994) as the trait measure. Similar to Study 1, the Big Five factors explained an average of 2.5% of incremental variance in behavioral criteria beyond the narrow traits, whereas JPI traits explained an average of 10.7% of incremental variance beyond the Big Five factors.

In a follow-up study to Paunonen (1998), Paunonen and Ashton (2001a) used 40 criteria that included self-reported behavior (using the Behavioral Report Form), experimenter ratings (e.g., physical attractiveness), university records (i.e., GPA), and objective records (e.g., tardiness to appointments) in order to compare the predictive ability of broad and narrow personality variables. Instead of pitting all the narrow traits against the Big Five, as in Paunonen's (1998) studies, 20 graduate students were involved in providing judgmental ratings regarding the relevance of each trait to each criterion. The top five most relevant narrow traits for each behavioral criterion were then compared with the Big Five factors, thereby eliminating the possibility of capitalizing on chance due to a larger number of predictors. In a series of analyses, Paunonen and Ashton found that the relevant five preselected narrow traits were, on average, at least as predictive as were the Big Five Factors across the 40 behavioral criteria, and the narrow traits accounted for an average of 8% of incremental variance beyond the Big Five. Extending this work across cultures, Paunonen and colleagues used the Behavioral Report Form in Canada, England, Germany, and Finland (Paunonen et al., 2003). One key finding from that study was that, across cultures, important prediction of behavior was lost through aggregation of SPI trait predictors to the factor level. For example, the trait of Risk Taking in the SPI explained significant variance in traffic violations (in all countries except in England), whereas traffic violations were not explained by SPI factors or Big Five factors in any country.

In meta-analytic research examining broad versus narrow personality variables in the prediction of nine health behaviors (e.g., drug use, risky sex, and tobacco use), Bogg and Roberts (2004) reported differential prediction by six conscientiousness facets. Traditionalism tended to exhibit the strongest negative relations with health behaviors, whereas industriousness exhibited some of the lowest corresponding relations. The result of aggregating facets into a conscientiousness factor had the effect of lowering prediction relative to at least one facet for every health behavior examined (providing a demonstration of trait dominance).

Summary

Our review above suggests that narrow traits often account for nontrivial proportions of variance in a variety of criteria and that this prediction cannot be fully understood through the use of broad factors. That is, whereas there are a few instances of factor dominance, there are many instances of trait dominance, and even facet bidirectionality. As we will explain later, in the event of the latter two scenarios, a facet-level analysis is to be preferred. It is worth noting that numerous related studies are consistent with the general theme of the literature reviewed here (e.g., Ashton, Jackson, Paunonen, Helmes, & Rothstein, 1995; Mershon & Gorsuch, 1988; O'Connor & Paunonen, 2007; Paunonen, 2000; Paunonen & Ashton, 2001b; Paunonen & Nicol, 2001; Rothstein, Paunonen, Rush, & King, 1994).

Compound Personality Scales

Recall that compound personality scales are (weighted or unweighted) aggregates of personality variables that can be minimally correlated with each other and maximally correlated with a targeted criterion. As mentioned earlier, types of compound personality scales include instruments designed to predict customer service orientation, counterproductive workplace behavior (i.e., integrity), managerial potential, stress tolerance, violence, and drug use. Ones and Viswesvaran (2001a) observed meta-analytic correlations as high as .48 for violence scales predicting violent behaviors and .34 for customer service scales predicting customer service behaviors. Ones and Viswesvaran (2001b) also found meta-analytic generalizability evidence regarding the prediction of nontargeted criteria, such as drug and alcohol scales and customer service scales predicting supervisory ratings of job performance.

In evaluating compound measures of integrity, Ones and Viswesvaran (2001b) reported that they predict counterproductive workplace behavior with correlations reaching .39 (see also Ones et al., 1993). Predictions with Big Five personality variables tend to be lower; for example, Barrick and Mount (1991) found average meta-analytic operational correlation coefficients for the Big Five factors to range from .05 for openness to experience to .23 for conscientiousness. Although there is some debate about Barrick and Mount's methodology, and several reasons to believe personality factors could be stronger predictors than those results suggest (see O'Neill et al., 2009; Tett & Christiansen, 2007; Tett et al., 1991), it is not surprising to find that compound personality scales offer superior prediction over any single personality scale (trait or factor) considered in isolation.

Compound personality scales are generally designed with a criterion-oriented approach, such that only the most predictive traits, uncorrelated with each other, are included in the derivation of the overall composite personality scale score (see Hough & Ones, 2001; Hough & Schneider, 1996). In addition, each personality variable within the measure could be assigned an optimal weight for the prediction of the intended criterion. Any subset of those personality variables, therefore, will necessarily be less predictive than will be the larger number of variables built into the compound personality measure (Schneider et al., 1996). Compound personality scales yield strong prediction of work criteria because predictive accuracy is the sole (statistical) standard by which such measures are developed. In its extreme form, there is little difference between this approach to assessment and the empirical, atheoretical, construction of a regression equation arithmetically formulated to predict some criterion of interest.

Proposals Regarding Measurement Breadth

The preceding literature review of studies related to the breadth of personality assessment and prediction outcomes leads us to offer some proposals regarding the choice of broad versus narrow assessment tools in prediction research and practice. Our first proposal involves reiterating our concerns regarding the importance of the two primary goals of psychology as a science. Behavior prediction is one goal, and behavior understanding is the other. Not all measurement strategies, however, are equally effective at satisfying both goals.

Psychological Meaning Is Important

In our literature review, we focused mostly on the predictive power of personality measures varying in breadth. The predictive accuracy of work behavior is, of course, important. However, the theoretical understanding provided by different personality measurement levels is at least as important, and it should not be overlooked. Indeed, any prediction that is not accompanied by understanding is a hollow victory and of minimal use to researchers who wish to develop theories of behavior, or to practitioners who need to defend their implementation of specific assessment instruments (O'Neill et al., 2009; Tett et al., 2003).

Throughout our discussion, we have strongly hinted at the fact that psychology's goal of theoretical understanding might be best served with assessments at the trait level. But this need not always be the case. Earlier, we offered a framework outlining three potential outcomes for correlations of broad versus narrow personality variables with criteria (see Steel et al., 2008). One such outcome is factor dominance, which occurs when a personality factor is more predictive than any of the traits underlying that factor. From a theoretical perspective, this means that the common variance shared among traits is most predictive, thereby suggesting that the driver of prediction is whatever those traits have in common. To illustrate, some empirical research has suggested that the conscientiousness and agreeableness factors outperform their facets in the prediction of workplace counterproductivity (Hastings & O'Neill, 2009). Elsewhere, in the prediction of engineering design team performance, broad conscientiousness, operationalized as the mean within-team member conscientiousness score, was more predictive than any of its facets (O'Neill & Allen, 2011). Also, Black (2000) found that the conscientiousness factor was more strongly related to police recruits' written examination scores than were conscientiousness facets. From a theoretical point of view, those findings supporting factor dominance are telling. It is the variance common to the facets that is most important to the criterion, and the interpretation of personality–criterion relations should reflect this. The specific variance in trait measures that makes them distinct from one another is not important to the understanding of criterion determination in such cases.

A situation in which theoretical understanding is strongest at the narrow-trait level is, of course, with instances of trait dominance. In such situations, summarizing the trait-level relationships using an aggregated factor-level score will obscure important and informative relations that occur at the trait level. Knowing which of a factor's facets correlate with a criterion, and which do not correlate, is critical to understanding the aspects of personality that are most critical to criterion behavior. Cases of trait bidirectionality are also important in this regard. Consider a study by Paunonen et al. (2006), who found that broad personality factors were not strongly related to leadership effectiveness in military officers in training whereas some narrow traits were. Those narrow traits comprised what Paunonen et al. referred to as bright and dark sides of narcissism. The bright side was operationalized using the SPI trait of Egotism, which involves having a strong sense of self-confidence and self-importance, and a feeling of being superior to others. The dark side of narcissism was operationalized using the SPI trait of Manipulativeness, which involves exploiting others through insincere flattery and ingratiation, and the use of deception for pursuing one's own goals. The authors found a suppressor effect such that officers judged as the best leaders by their peers were those who were high on Egotism ("good" narcissism) and low on Manipulativeness ("bad" narcissism). Both of those traits, however, are constituents of the same SPI Machiavellianism factor (see Table 14.1). It is clear, therefore, that using that broad factor for the prediction of leadership would result in both (a) weaker accuracy coefficients overall, due to trait cancellation effects, and (b) lost information about the nature of the leadership criterion, being complexly affected by different, relatively narrow behavior domains.

Facet bidirectionality occurs surprisingly often. For example, dimensions of conscientiousness were found to show bidirectional relations in numerous studies reviewed by Christiansen and Robie (2011) and in some meta-analyses (e.g., Hough, 1992). Jackson et al.'s (2000) SFPQ was created, in part, because previous research supported the bifurcation of conscientiousness into achievement and methodicalness on grounds of factor analysis and differential-predictions (e.g., Jackson et al., 1996; Paunonen & Jackson, 1996). When bidirectional relations exist at the trait level, considering only factor-level relations will preclude seeing those potentially important trait–criterion linkages.

Compound Personality Scales Have Limited Meaning

Ones and Viswesvaran (2001a, 2001b) and Ones et al. (1993) reported evidence that agreeableness, conscientiousness, and emotional stability correlate strongly with most compound personality scales (see also Ones et al., 2005). They then argued that such scales are essentially measuring a super-factor of personality that comprises linear combinations of the three personality factors with which they correlate. We question this line of reasoning. Because a composite variable (e.g., a compound personality scale) correlates highly with a certain class of criteria (e.g., personality trait or factor scales), it does not mean that the former and the latter refer to the same underlying constructs (recall our earlier example of an index of SES correlating with measures of personality traits).

Our review of compound personality scales suggests that they can be, not surprisingly, very predictive of criteria. Their prediction is almost a definitional quality, given that such scales are designed purely on the basis of predictive power. Now, some have observed that a compound personality scale's predictive power often extends beyond the derivation criterion. That is, compound scales have been shown to have generalizability in predicting criteria other than those upon which they were constructed, which may be psychologically meaningful (Ones & Viswesvaran, 2001a). We have two comments to make about this aspect of compound scales. First, we suspect that any prediction that has generalized across different criteria occurs because those criteria tend to be mutually correlated (drug use, alcohol use, and job performance), and not because the compound scales measure any broad personality construct underlying the criterion behaviors (see Ones et al., 2005). Second, the generalizability property of compound scales, in and of itself, lends them no special psychologically relevant meaning—for example, just because a customer service orientation measure has some accuracy for predicting consumer complaints and, say, absenteeism does not itself indicate that the test has construct validity for measuring some unitary psychological domain. Also, recall the point we alluded to in our earlier discussion of problems with compound personality scales—a measure's predictive ability does not necessarily bear on its construct validity.

Compound personality scales are like measures of personality types rather than measures of personality traits. Personality types refer to subgroups of some population of people, where the members of each subgroup share certain personality characteristics (Allport, 1937, p. 295ff). Furthermore, the personality traits shared by members of a subgroup or type could be positively correlated, negatively correlated, or uncorrelated in the general population. Consider a typology developed by Stein (1963) to classify Peace Corps volunteers. He administered measures of some 20, theoretically independent, Murray needs (Murray, 1938; see also Jackson, 1984) to a group of such volunteers and discovered four types. What distinguished those types were their modal profiles across the Murray needs. That is, the members within a group shared their high trait scores and their low trait scores (more or less) with each other, resulting in a modal personality profile or type, but those modal profiles were different for the four subgroups.

It might be useful to illustrate our concerns about compound personality scales by considering an example from Stein's (1963) typology of Peace Corps volunteers. The top three traits for his Type 1 volunteer were Affiliation, Nurturance, and Counteraction (determination). Now, in practice, one would apply a weighting scheme to those three Murray needs (or to all 20 needs) to produce an aggregate index of Type 1 Peace Corps personality for a respondent. But those aggregate scores can have no meaning with respect to any hypothetical unitary personality construct. For instance, what psychological interpretation could one apply to a high total score on a composite measure of Affiliation plus Nurturance plus Counteraction, besides the obvious fact that the respondent resembles a prototypical Type 1 volunteer? Any meaningful interpretation would have to take place at the level of Affiliation, Nurturance, and Counteraction, individually. The parallels are obvious here between our example of assessing Peace Corps volunteer types and assessing customer service orientation, managerial potential, stress tolerance, or any number of other compound personality variables.

Both Broad and Narrow Measures Can Have Utility

Our advocacy for trait-level measures of personality in this chapter, and our various criticisms of assessment at other levels of breadth, should not be taken to imply that the latter approaches have little utility in I/O and other areas of psychology—quite the contrary. There are times when factor-level measures are desirable. There are even times when the compound personality scales are to be preferred. We list in the sections that follow some of the considerations that would lead us to choose personality measures representing various components of the personality hierarchy (see also Judge & Kammeyer-Mueller, 2012).

Narrow Personality Measures

Assessment of narrow personality variables would be advantageous in the cases of trait dominance and facet bidirectionality. In trait dominance, one facet of a factor is a stronger predictor than the factor itself. Theoretically, this means that trait-specific variance is most important for understanding why personality is predictive in that context. The facet-level approach illuminates the drivers of the factor's predictive potency; therefore, it promotes understanding of trait–criterion linkages and enables identification of which traits are, and are not, implicated in the criterion behaviors (Tett et al., 2000). Besides enhancing prediction and understanding, this approach allows the practitioner to facilitate work-analytic rationales, supporting the use of the trait(s) for making decisions about personnel (e.g., selection and development) and thereby enhancing legal defensibility (considered further below).

In the event of facet bidirectionality, the situation is even worse if a broad assessment approach is adopted over a trait approach. Facets assigned to the same factor that relate to the criterion in different directions can render factor-level assessments incredibly misleading. The likely conclusion of a factor-level analysis here would be that the personality factor (and its facets) are irrelevant, missing the important facet-level relations (Hastings & O'Neill, 2009; O'Neill & Allen, 2011; Tett et al., 2003). Because such bidirectionality within factors is not a rarity (as revealed in our literature review), it is our view that early investigations into personality–criterion relations should first consider analyses at the level of the personality trait or facet, in order to rule out any plausible bidirectional relations within a factor.

Broad Personality Measures

If the common variance among the facets underlying a factor is theoretically and empirically suspected to be more relevant than the facet-specific variance (i.e., factor dominance exists), priority should be given to the broad factor. A trait-level approach could involve wasted time and resources assessing personality dimensions for which there is little practical or theoretical payoff. As reviewed earlier, there is some empirical evidence to suggest that conscientiousness and agreeableness factors dominate their facets in the prediction of counterproductivity (e.g., Hastings & O'Neill, 2009). For these factors, it is possible that higher-order common variance (perhaps related to Digman's [1997], alpha factor), or the variance that is shared by the factors' respective facets, is more predictive of, and relevant for, counterproductive workplace behavior than is trait-specific variance (but see Ashton, 1998). Applying short, factor-based measures might result in optimal criterion prediction, possibly leaving more time for other assessments.

Note that the rationale above regarding the appropriate application of broad factor assessments presupposes direct comparison of factor-level and trait-level measures. In other words, empirical evidence must be reasonably conclusive in its demonstration that factors are more predictive than their constituent facets, and theory must explain why common variance is more important than trait-specific variance. This, then, requires that a trait-level approach be formally compared with a broader-level approach (Christiansen & Robie, 2011; O'Neill & Allen, 2011). Supporting the application of broad factors in prediction research requires a convincing demonstration that factor dominance reigns over trait dominance and facet bidirectionality for the prediction task at hand.

In summarizing the two sections above, a researcher or practitioner wishing to maximize the prediction and understanding of criterion behaviors should start with trait-level assessments. Because of the sheer number of personality traits that could be measured, a personality-based work analysis should be implemented to help guide selection of the important predictors. If cases of trait dominance and facet bidirectionality can be ruled out, while factor dominance prevails, then a broad factor-based assessment procedure would be recommended.

Compound Personality Measures

Despite specific concerns raised above, we are not opposed to using compound measures for predictive purposes. Indeed, as described earlier, a work analysis to develop a cross-validated regression equation involving multiple, independent variables would be ideal for criterion prediction. By virtue of being formative measures (Edwards, 2011), however, there may be little knowledge gained in testing an individual with such a device, beyond what it tells us about expected criterion performance. In terms of the critical realist perspective, there is no attempt with a compound personality scale to measure any known psychological attribute. Consequently, some may find it discomforting to make important decisions about personnel (e.g., selection, placement, promotion, and succession planning) based on such test scores. And, to the extent that test items do not appear relevant to the job, there may be increased risk of litigation (Rynes & Connerley, 1993). Thus, we propose that test users ensure that there are data supporting a firm understanding of the relevance of test items to the criterion (e.g., content validity evidence).

Notwithstanding the issues we raise regarding compound personality scales, they can be highly predictive of targeted criteria (and related criteria), and, accordingly, highly practical. In fact, we see little difference between the basic procedure for constructing compound personality measures and formal work analysis involving theoretical (e.g., expert opinions) and empirical (e.g., cross-validated regression weights) inputs for selecting a battery of criterion predictors. One notable variation is that the differential regression weights determined by the latter procedure are normally replaced with unit weights under the former procedure. With such a change, we would expect the resultant compound scale to be somewhat less predictive of derivation criteria than would be the corresponding regression-based composite. A unit-weighted compound measure, however, might be more generalizable across new respondent samples and different criteria (see Ones & Viswesvaran, 2001a, 2001b).

Our recommendation regarding the use of compound personality scales for research purposes is that, where possible, one should parse the total scale score into its components—and, assuming those components constitute psychometrically sound measures in themselves, report those individual scores as well as the total composite score. For example, J. Hogan et al. (1984) offered a measure of Service Orientation as a weighted composite of 14 HPI homogeneous item composites (i.e., essentially narrow trait or, even, habitual response scales). A researcher using such a measure should have the option of considering the respondents' standings on not only the composite scale but also the various component scales. The added information cannot fail but to contribute to the scientific understanding of criterion behavior.

Practical Issues Should Not Be Ignored

Most of the concerns we have expressed thus far with measurement at different levels of the personality hierarchy have pertained to issues of prediction and understanding. But there are other, perhaps more specific, concerns as well. These relate to limitations of the physical assessment context, considerations regarding exploratory research, the availability of measures, and effects on adverse impact. We discuss these issues in turn below.

Testing Time Limitations

Assessing personality at the factor level has great appeal to the practitioner (and even some researchers). The FFM, for example, represents five simplified dimensions of behavior. Those factors presumably account for most of the important, personality-based, variation in human behavior. The factor definitions are so straightforward that even a lay person can understand them. And, in practice, an assessment instrument containing five measures is, from a time and cost perspective, more desirable than one containing more measures.

Regarding assessment costs, some researchers have explicitly recommended the use of broad factors when assessment time is limited (e.g., Ones & Viswesvaran, 1996), arguing that more coverage of personality content can be achieved through broad rather than narrow measurement. This issue is at the heart of the bandwidth–fidelity tradeoff (but see Paunonen et al., 1999, pp. 396–397). An important caveat to this view, however, is that it is only logical and defensible in cases of factor dominance. In such situations, short measures of factors can indeed provide high utility, and there is little to be gained by more specific measurements (Tett et al., 2000). In the event of trait dominance or facet bidirectionality, however, there is a strong possibility that factor-level measurement will be deficient. If only a subset of traits within a factor are criterion-relevant, and these traits can be identified through work analysis and criterion validation, measurement of only those job-relevant (narrow) characteristics with targeted, highly reliable measures can actually provide superior returns, not only in terms of prediction and understanding, but also in testing time.

Exploratory Research Considerations

One might wonder about the optimal breadth of personality measurement when an organization conducts exploratory research in early attempts to identify job-relevant personality variables. Indeed, one might reason that research should begin with broad assessment in order to uncover trends that may identify promising avenues for more refined directions in the future. Logically, however, this approach is problematic. If trait dominance or facet bidirectionality underlies personality–criterion relations, a factor-level approach would quite likely result in suboptimal prediction. Observing such a low prediction, the researcher or practitioner might erroneously conclude that the personality dimension has no relevance for the criterion and may consider it no further. Our view is that exploratory research needs to begin with a facet-level approach. When testing time is limited, the most relevant traits, based on an understanding of the context and the criterion (ideally through personality-oriented work analysis), can be selected for inclusion in the survey instrument in order to maximize payoffs. And if factor dominance prevails in a particular context, it will be apparent even in facet-level data, assuming the relevant factors are adequately represented in the assessment.

Measure Availability

We recognize that, in actual practice, it is entirely likely that an organization would not find it feasible to conduct a formal criterion-oriented validation study designed to identify the facets of work that are important to job success and the personality dimensions that predict them. The cost of such an exercise might be prohibitive (note, however, that Paunonen & Ashton, 2001a, have shown that even psychology graduate students acting as expert judges can do remarkably well in identifying a priori the personality traits associated with student-related criteria such as grade point average, alcohol consumption, smoking behavior, etc.). In such cases, available off-the-shelf compound personality scales based on the prediction work of others might be appropriate for the assessment needs at hand. Some compound personality scales have, in fact, produced meta-analytic evidence (Ones & Viswesvaran, 2001b) suggesting moderate to strong predictive ability that has generalized across a variety of worker outcomes (e.g., job performance, counterproductivity, drug and alcohol use, stress tolerance, and customer service). And, many of those predictions were found to be stronger than any individual trait's prediction (Ones et al., 2005).

We observe here that if a compound personality scale is adopted based on research conducted in some other work context, the practitioner should be concerned, not only about the generality of its predictive ability, but also about the relevance of the measure's item content to the criterion of interest. Without ostensible content validity for the assessment at hand, test users might be more likely to pursue litigation because the test appears to them to have little job relevance (Rynes & Connerley, 1993). Also, any legal defenses could be compromised by the lack of such evidence. (For further details regarding content validity, see Goldstein, Zedeck, & Schneider, 1993; Society for Industrial and Organizational Psychology [SIOP], 2003. For an accessible summary of legal criteria to meet for defending test use through content validity, see Gutman & Dunleavy, 2009.) This issue is particularly salient for a compound personality scale, because its items do not typically relate to one unitary construct.

Adverse Impact

Adverse impact is most often identified when a minority group's selection ratio (e.g., number hired/ number of applicants) is less than 80% of the majority group's selection ratio (e.g., Roth, Bobko, & Switzer, 2006). All else equal, adverse impact will occur when individuals in the majority score more favorably than individuals in the minority on a test used for personnel selection decisions (Sackett & Wilk, 1994; Schmitt, Rogers, Chan, Sheppard, & Jennings, 1997). Interestingly, Powell, Goffin, and Gellatly (2011) found that adverse impact against women tended to be more pronounced at the narrow-trait level than at the broad-factor level. In that study, the authors considered factor measures of conscientiousness and extraversion, plus their facets, applied to a sample of oil refinery applicants. Because men tend to score higher on the industriousness facet of conscientiousness and the dominance facet of extraversion, selecting on the basis of those two facets will potentially lead to adverse impact against women. But the conscientiousness and extraversion factors also have facets on which women tend to score higher; that is, diligence (for conscientiousness) and affiliation (for extraversion). Accordingly, when selecting oil workers on the basis of the broad factors of conscientiousness and extraversion, Powell et al. (2011) found little adverse impact, whereas selecting for the same male-dominated job on the basis of the narrow traits of industriousness and dominance did lead to adverse impact. Incidentally, those two traits happened to be highly job-relevant traits for the managerial positions considered by those researchers.

Powell et al.'s (2011) findings suggest that selecting on narrow traits has the potential to lead to greater adverse impact than does selecting on personality factors. Adverse impact will be strongest where trait means differ substantially by subgroup (e.g., White vs. Hispanic; male vs. female) and selection ratios are low (i.e., there are few positions and many applicants). This could be an issue for managerial positions wherein certain traits, such as industriousness, dominance, and so forth, are typically strong predictors of performance but tend to have scores that favor men. Nevertheless, our belief is that these findings should not deter the human resources practitioner from evaluating the utility of narrow traits for selection. There is room in U.S. litigation to support the use of selection tests that lead to adverse impact if it can be shown that the job cannot be performed well without a certain trait level, or that there is no alternative test that provides similar levels of prediction of job performance (see Aamodt, 2010; Cascio & Aguinis, 2005). Moreover, even though some traits may favor one subgroup, trait measures (or other tests) that favor another subgroup that are also job relevant can be included in the selection battery in order to compensate (see Bobko, Roth, & Potosky, 1999; Schmitt et al., 1997). This will have the effect of lowering or eliminating adverse impact when scores from both tests are combined. For example, if women tend to score higher than men on traits such as cooperation, altruism, and affiliation, selecting on these traits may lead to little adverse impact if one also selects on traits that favor men (e.g., industriousness, adjustment; see Hough, Oswald, & Ployhart, 2001).

The use of narrow traits for personnel selection does not automatically lead to adverse impact, nor will the use of narrow traits necessarily put the organization at risk for treating minority groups unfairly. Regarding the potential for litigation, narrow traits, as opposed to broad factors, may actually reduce the likelihood that an applicant will challenge a hiring decision in court. When used in selection, narrow traits identified as important for job performance through job analysis should promote perceptions of job relevance of personality tests. This is because narrow traits, if theoretically and empirically related to job performance, are likely to represent content-homogeneous sets of items that will be viewed, by respondents and jurists alike, as appropriate in light of the job requirements. Conversely, broad factor measures containing elements that are relatively heterogeneous could be interpreted by the job applicant as having components that appear irrelevant, inappropriate, and unfair, especially if not all components are important for the job (see Jenkins & Griffith, 2004; Tett et al., 2000). Should perceptions of injustice occur, the chance of an individual pursuing legal action is greater (see Chan, Schmitt, DeShon, Clause, & Delbridge, 1997; Lind, Greenberg, Scott, & Welchans, 2000). In short, adverse impact issues related to breadth of measurement are complex and situation-specific, and we see no reason to conclude a priori that either broad or narrow traits have an advantage here.

Conclusion

One purpose in preparing this chapter was to review a general model of personality structure—a hierarchical conceptualization based on the breadth of the variables involved. Another purpose was to arrive at some recommendations regarding the level of the hierarchy at which measurement should proceed in order to maximize the prediction and understanding of work behavior. Based on several considerations, including a critical review of the literature in this area, we reached several conclusions.

1. An intermediate level of breadth will tend to be the optimal level of measurement. Specifically, this is at the level of the personality trait or facet. Factor-level measurements are too broad and behavior-level measurements are too narrow, in general.
2. Trait-level measures generally have an advantage over broader factor-level measures in promoting an understanding of human behavior. The narrower personality assessments refer to relatively unambiguous, unidimensional constructs that are likely to be critical elements in any complex network of personality–work behavior associations.
3. Trait-level measures have an advantage over broader factor-level measures in maximizing the prediction of personality-relevant work criteria. This occurs because different components of trait-specific variance, variance that is normally absent in factor-based composites, can predict the different facets of a multifaceted criterion.
4. Factor-level personality assessments have good utility for behavior prediction and understanding in some cases, specifically under conditions of factor dominance. This is present when the common variance underlying a factor's traits is the most important aspect of the work criterion.
5. Compound personality scales are formative measures. As such, they do not measure any a priori theoretically postulated personality constructs, and their scores have no meaning beyond their statistical relations to the derivation criteria.
6. The strong predictive power of compound personality scales can be advantageous when prediction is the primary goal. The same end, however, can be better served by developing cross-validated regression equations using distinct, construct-valid, lower-level trait measures as predictors. An added benefit is that knowledge of the individual traits' statistical criterion relations can advance understanding of the determinants of work behavior.

7. Practical concerns such as test-time limitations, exploratory research considerations, measure availability, and adverse impact need to be considered in choosing personality assessments. These issues, by themselves, do not unequivocally favor either a broad or narrow approach, so other features of the assessment situation will generally determine whether broad or narrow assessments are to be preferred.
8. We see room for much more research on the issue of the specificity of personality measurement and the prediction of work behavior. However, we must emphasize that any empirical comparison of measuring instruments must begin with measures that are roughly equivalent in their basic psychometric properties. Different levels of reliability or validity can contribute to different degrees of predictive accuracy with regard to independent criteria, and the cause of those differences in prediction might be mistaken as due to differences in the underlying breadth of the measures.
9. We strongly believe that decisions about which measures to use in any particular work context should ultimately be based on a careful personality-oriented work analysis, a procedure designed to determine the aspects of the work criterion that are likely to be related to specific dimensions of personality. A less desirable alternative is to use off-the-shelf measures and to rely on the research findings reported by others.

Practitioner's Window

Dealing With Specificity Issues in Practice

- The optimal level of measurement for most cases will be the personality trait level. This level has little ambiguity caused by heterogeneity, which becomes problematic at higher levels of the personality hierarchy (i.e., for factors).
- Trait-level measurement promotes understanding and, not uncommonly, prediction (even when the criterion is broad).
- Factor-level measures may be preferred *after* it has been conclusively shown that all traits within a factor correlated relatively similarly with a criterion (i.e., factor dominance). Thus, the trait level precedes the broad level.
- Compound personality scales are formative measures and, accordingly, the scores from such tests have no meaning beyond prediction. Convergent validity studies tend not to be sufficient to strongly support the construct-validity argument.
- Whereas compound personality scales may be advantageous for practitioners who cannot conduct local validation studies, it might be wise to assess their content validity prior to application. Content validity evidence could be used to support a conceptual linkage to the job in question, lending additional evidence, other than strictly prediction-related evidence, for their application.
- Alternatives to compound personality scales, such as cross-validated regression equations comprising homogeneous trait scales, will provide as much prediction as do compound personality scales. However, the latter will have the advantage of (a) being derived through local criterion-validity evidence and (b) allowing for understanding of how the traits were combined to derive the overall score.
- Practical necessity may call for the use of compound personality scales, but cross-validated regression equations comprising homogeneous trait scales are ideal when circumstances allow.
- Practical constraints of the organizational context involving test-time limitations, exploratory research considerations, measure availability, and adverse impact can have implications for selecting measurement breadth.
- Identifying the optimal breadth of personality assessment for a given situation may be further aided by a personality-oriented work analysis (see Chapter 11, this volume).

Acknowledgement

* The preparation of this chapter was supported by the Social Sciences and Humanities Research Council of Canada grant 430-2012-0059 and 410-2010-2586 to the first and second author, respectively.

References

Aamodt, M. G. (2010). *Industrial/organizational psychology: An applied approach* (6th ed.). Belmont, CA: Thomson Wadsworth.

Allport, G. W. (1937). *Personality: A psychological interpretation*. New York: Holt.

Ashton, M. C. (1998). Personality and job performance: The importance of narrow traits. *Journal of Organizational Behavior, 19*, 289–303.

Ashton, M. C., Jackson, D. N., Paunonen, S. V., Helmes, E., & Rothstein, M. G. (1995). The criterion validity of broad factor scales versus specific facet scales. *Journal of Research in Personality, 29*, 432–442.

Ashton, M. C., & Lee, K. (2001). A theoretical basis for the major dimensions of personality. *European Journal of Personality, 15*, 327–353.

Ashton, M. C., & Lee, K. (2007). Empirical, theoretical, and practical advantages of the HEXACO model of personality structure. *Personality and Social Psychology Review, 11*, 150–166.

Ashton, M. C., & Lee, K. (2008a). The HEXACO model of personality structure and the importance of the H factor. *Social and Personality Psychology Compass, 2*, 1952–1962.

Ashton, M. C., & Lee, K. (2008b). The prediction of honesty-humility-related criteria by the HEXACO and five-factor models of personality. *Journal of Research in Personality, 42*, 1216–1228.

Ashton, M. C., & Lee, K. (2009). The HEXACO-60: A short measure of the major dimensions of personality. *Journal of Personality Assessment, 91*, 340–345.

Ashton, M. C., Lee, K., & Goldberg, L. R. (2004). A hierarchical analysis of 1,710 English personality-descriptive adjectives. *Journal of Personality and Social Psychology, 87*, 707–721.

Ashton, M. C., Lee, K., Perugini, M., Szarota, P., De Vries, R. E., Di Blas, L., . . . De Raad, B. (2004). A six-factor structure of personality-descriptive adjectives: Solutions from psycholexical studies in seven languages. *Journal of Personality and Social Psychology, 86*, 356–366.

Bagozzi, R. P. (2007). On the meaning of formative measurement and how it differs from reflective measurement: Comment on Howell, Breivik, and Wilcox (2007). *Psychological Methods, 12*, 229–237.

Barrett, G. V., Miguel, R. F., Hurd, J. M., Lueke, S. B., & Tan, J. A. (2003). Practical issues in the use of personality tests in police selection. *Public Personnel Management, 32*, 497–517.

Barrick, M. R., & Mount, M. K. (1991). The Big Five personality dimensions and job performance: A meta-analysis. *Personnel Psychology, 44*, 1–26.

Barrick, M. R., & Mount, M. K. (2003). Impact of meta-analysis methods on understanding personality–performance relations. In K. R. Murphy (Ed.), *Validity generalization: A critical review* (pp. 197–222). Mahwah, NJ: Lawrence Erlbaum.

Barrick, M. R., & Mount, M. K. (2005). Yes, personality matters: Moving on to more important matters. *Human Performance, 18*, 359–372.

Barrick, M. R., Mount, M. K., & Judge, T. A. (2001). Personality and performance at the beginning of the new millennium: What do we know and where do we go next? *International Journal of Selection and Assessment, 9*, 9–30.

Bennett, R. J., & Robinson, S. L. (2000). Development of a measure of workplace deviance. *Journal of Applied Psychology, 85*, 349–360.

Berry, C. M., Ones, D. S., & Sackett, P. R. (2007). Interpersonal deviance, organizational deviance, and their common correlates: A review and meta-analysis. *Journal of Applied Psychology, 92*, 410–424.

Black, J. (2000). Personality testing and police selection: Utility of the "Big Five." *New Zealand Journal of Psychology, 29*, 2–9.

Block, J. (1995). A contrarian view of the five-factor approach to personality description. *Psychological Bulletin, 117*, 187–215.

Block, J. (2001). Millennial contrarianism: The five-factor approach to personality description 5 years later. *Journal of Research in Personality, 35*, 98–107.

Bobko, P., Roth, P. L., & Potosky, D. (1999). Derivation and implications of a meta-analysis matrix incorporating cognitive ability, alternative predictors, and job performance. *Personnel Psychology, 52*, 561–589.

Bogg, T., & Roberts, B. W. (2004). Conscientiousness and health-related behaviors: A meta-analysis of the leading behavioral contributions to mortality. *Psychological Bulletin, 130*, 887–919.

Boies, K., Yoo, T., Ebacher, A., Lee, K., & Ashton, M. C. (2004). Psychometric properties of scores on the French and Korean versions of the HEXACO Personality Inventory. *Educational and Psychological Measurement, 64*, 992–1006.

Borsboom, D. (2005). *Measuring the mind.* Cambridge, UK: Cambridge University Press.

Borsboom, D., Mellenbergh, G. J., & Van Heerden, J. (2003). The theoretical status of latent variables. *Psychological Review, 110*, 203–219.

Bouchard, T. J., Jr. (2004). Genetic influence on human psychological traits: A survey. *Current Directions in Psychological Science, 13*, 148–151.

Boyle, G. J., Matthews, D. H., & Saklofske, D. H. (2008). *The SAGE handbook of personality theory and assessment* (*Vol. 2*, pp. 113–135). Los Angeles: SAGE.

Buss, D. M. (1991). Evolutionary personality psychology. In M. R. Rosenzweig & L. W. Porter (Eds.), *Annual review of psychology* (*Vol. 42*, pp. 459–492). Palo Alto, CA: Annual Reviews Inc.

Buss, D. M. (1996). Social adaptation and five major factors of personality. In J. S. Wiggins (Ed.), *The Five-Factor Model of personality: Theoretical perspectives* (pp. 180–207). New York: Guilford Press.

Campbell, D. T. (1960). Recommendations for APA test standards regarding construct, trait, or discriminant validity. *American Psychologist, 15*, 546–553.

Canli, T., Sivers, H., Whitfield, S. L., Gotlib, I. H., & Gabreli, J. D. E. (2002). Amygdala response to happy faces as a function of extraversion. *Science, 296*, 2191.

Cascio, W. F., & Aguinis, H. (2005). *Applied psychology in human resource management* (6th ed.). Upper Saddle River, NJ: Prentice Hall.

Cattell, H. E. P., & Mead, A. D. (2008). The Sixteen Personality Factor Questionnaire (16PF). In G. J. Boyle, G. Matthews, & D. H. Saklofske (Eds.), *The SAGE handbook of personality theory and assessment* (*Vol. 2*, pp. 135–160). Los Angeles: SAGE.

Chan, D., Schmitt, N., DeShon, R. P., Clause, C. S., & Delbridge, K. (1997). Reactions to cognitive ability tests: The relationships between race, test performance, face validity perceptions, and test-taking motivation. *Journal of Applied Psychology, 82*, 300–310.

Christiansen, N. D., & Robie, C. (2011). Further consideration of the use of narrow trait scales. *Canadian Journal of Behavioral Science, 43*, 183–194.

Colquitt, J. A., Hollenbeck, J. R., Ilgen, D. R., LePine, J. A., & Sheppard, L. (2002). Computer-assisted communication and team decision-making performance: The moderating effect of openness to experience. *Journal of Applied Psychology, 87*, 402–410.

Comrey, A. L. (2008). The Comrey Personality Scales. In G. J. Boyle, G. Matthews, & D. H. Saklofske (Eds.), *The SAGE handbook of personality theory and assessment* (*Vol. 2*, pp. 113–135). Los Angeles: SAGE.

Costa, P. T., & McCrae, R. R. (1988). From catalog to classification: Murray's needs and the Five-Factor Model. *Journal of Personality and Social Psychology, 55*, 258–265.

Costa, P. T., & McCrae, R. R. (1992). *The revised NEO Personality Inventory (NEO-PI-R) and NEO Five-Factor Inventory (NEO-FFI) professional manual.* Odessa, FL: Psychological Assessment Resources.

Costa, P. T., Jr., & McCrae, R. R. (1995). Solid ground in the wetlands of personality: A reply to Block. *Psychological Bulletin, 117*, 216–220.

Crant, J. M. (1995). The proactive personality scale and objective job performance among real estate agents. *Journal of Applied Psychology, 80*, 532–537.

Detrick, P., & Chibnall, J. T. (2006). NEO-PI-R personality characteristics of high-performing entry-level police officers. *Psychological Services, 3*, 274–285.

DeYoung, C. G. (2006). Higher-order factors of the Big Five in a multi-informant sample. *Journal of Personality and Social Psychology, 91*, 1138–1151.

DeYoung, C. G., Peterson, J. B., & Higgins, D. M. (2002). Higher-order factors of the Big Five predict conformity: Are there neuroses of health? *Personality and Individual Differences, 33*, 533–552.

Digman, J. M. (1990). Personality structure: Emergence of the Five-Factor Model. *Annual Review of Psychology, 41*, 417–440.

Digman, J. M. (1996). The curious history of the Five-Factor Model. In J. S. Wiggins (Ed.), *The Five-Factor Model of personality: Theoretical perspectives* (pp. 1–20). New York: Guilford Press.

Digman, J. M. (1997). Higher-order factors of the Big Five. *Journal of Personality and Social Psychology, 73*, 1246–1256.

Dudley, N. M., Orvis, K. A., Lebiecki, J. E., & Cortina, J. M. (2006). A meta-analytic investigation of conscientiousness in the prediction of job performance: Examining the intercorrelations and the incremental validity of narrow traits. *Journal of Applied Psychology, 91*, 40–57.

Edwards, J. R. (2011). The fallacy of formative measurement. *Organizational Research Methods, 14*, 370–388.

Edwards, J. R., & Bagozzi, R. P. (2000). On the nature and direction of relationships between constructs and measures. *Psychological Methods, 5*, 155–174.

Eysenck, H. J. (1947). *Dimensions of personality*. London: Routledge & Kegan Paul.
Flanagan, J. C. (1954). The critical incident technique. *Psychological Bulletin, 51*, 327–358.
Goffin, R. D., Rothstein, M. G., & Johnston, N. G. (1996). Personality testing and the assessment center: Incremental validity for managerial selection. *Journal of Applied Psychology, 81*, 746–756.
Goffin, R. D., Rothstein, M. G., & Johnston, N. G. (2000). Predicting job performance using personality constructs: Are personality tests created equal? In R. D. Goffin & E. Helmes (Eds.), *Problems and solutions in human assessment: Honoring Douglas N. Jackson at seventy* (pp. 249–264). Boston, MA: Kluwer.
Goffin, R. D., Rothstein, M. G., Reider, M. J., Poole, A., Krajewski, H. T., Powell, D. M., . . . Mestdagh, T. (2011). Choosing job-related personality traits: Developing valid personality-oriented job analysis. *Personality and Individual Differences, 51*, 646–651.
Goldberg, L. R. (1990). An alternative "Description of personality": The Big-Five factor structure. *Journal of Personality and Social Psychology, 59*, 1216–1229.
Goldberg, L. R. (1992). The development of markers for the Big-Five factor structure. *Psychological Assessment, 4*, 26–42.
Goldberg, L. R. (1993). The structure of phenotypic personality traits. *American Psychologist, 48*, 26–34.
Goldstein, I. L., Zedeck, S., & Schneider, B. (1993). An exploration of the job analysis–content validity process. In N. Schmitt & W. C. Borman (Eds.), *Personnel selection in organizations* (pp. 3–34). San Francisco: Jossey-Bass.
Gough, H. G. (1987). *The California Psychological Inventory administrator's guide*. Palo Alto, CA: Consulting Psychologists Press.
Gray, J. A. (1994). Personality dimensions and emotion systems. In P. Ekman & R. Davidson (Eds.), *The nature of emotion: Fundamental questions* (pp. 329–331). New York: Oxford University Press.
Green, B. F. (1978). In defense of measurement. *American Psychologist, 33*, 664–679.
Gutman, A., & Dunleavy, E. (2009). On the legal front: The supreme court ruling in Ricci v. Destefano. *Industrial and Organizational Psychologist, 47*, 57–71.
Hastings, S. E., & O'Neill, T. A. (2009). Predicting workplace deviance using broad and narrow personality traits. *Personality and Individual Differences, 47*, 289–293.
Hofstee, W. K., de Raad, B., & Goldberg, L. R. (1992). Integration of the Big Five and circumplex approaches to trait structure. *Journal of Personality and Social Psychology, 63*, 146–163.
Hogan, J., Hogan, R., & Busch, C. M. (1984). How to measure service orientation. *Journal of Applied Psychology, 69*, 167–173.
Hogan, J., Hogan, R., & Murtha, T. (1992). Validation of a personality measure of managerial performance. *Journal of Business and Psychology, 7*, 225–237.
Hogan, R., & Hogan, J. (1992). *Hogan Personality Inventory manual*. Tulsa, OK: Hogan Assessment Systems.
Hogan, R., & Holland, B. (2003). Using theory to evaluate personality and job-performance relations: A socioanalytic perspective. *Journal of Applied Psychology, 88*, 100–112.
Hogan, R., & Roberts, B. W. (1996). Issues and non-issues in the fidelity–bandwidth trade-off. *Journal of Organizational Behavior, 17*, 627–637.
Hogan, R., & Shelton, D. (1998). A socioanalytic perspective on job performance. *Human Performance, 11*, 129–144.
Hong, R. Y., Koh, S., & Paunonen, S. V. (2012). Supernumerary traits beyond the Big Five: Predicting materialism and unethical behavior. *Personality and Individual Differences, 53*, 710–715.
Hong, R. Y., & Paunonen, S. V. (2009). Personality traits and health-risk behaviors in university students. *European Journal of Personality, 23*, 675–696.
Hough, L. M. (1992). The "Big Five" personality variables–construct confusion: Description versus prediction. *Human Performance, 5*, 139–155.
Hough, L. M. (1997). The millennium for personality psychology: New horizons or good old daze? *Applied Psychology: An International Review, 47*, 233–261.
Hough, L. M., & Furnham, A. (2003). Use of personality variables in work settings. In I. Weiner (Ed.), *Handbook of psychology* (pp. 131–169). Hoboken, NJ: John Wiley & Sons.
Hough, L. M., & Ones, D. S. (2001). The structure, measurement, validity, and use of personality variables in industrial, work, and organizational psychology. In N. R. Anderson, D. S. Ones, H. K. Sinangil, & C. Viswesvaran (Eds.), *Handbook of industrial, work, & organizational psychology* (*Vol. 1*, pp. 233–277). New York: SAGE.
Hough, L. M., Oswald, F. L., & Ployhart, R. E. (2001). Determinants, detection and amelioration of adverse impact in personnel selection procedures: Issues, evidence and lessons learned. *International Journal of Selection and Assessment, 9*, 152–194.
Hough, L. M., & Schneider, R. J. (1996). The frontiers of I/O personality research. In K. R. Murphy (Ed.), *Individual differences and behavior in organizations* (pp. 31–88). San Francisco: Jossey-Bass.
Jackson, D. N. (1967). *Personality Research Form manual*. Goshen, NY: Research Psychologists Press.
Jackson, D. N. (1970). A sequential system for personality scale development. In C. D. Spielberger (Ed.), *Current topics in clinical and community psychology* (pp. 61–96). New York: Academic Press.

Jackson, D. N. (1984). *Jackson Personality Research Form manual*. Port Huron, MI: Research Psychologists Press.
Jackson, D. N. (1994). *Jackson Personality Inventory—Revised manual*. Port Huron, MI: Sigma Assessment Systems.
Jackson, D. N., Paunonen, S. V., Fraboni, M., & Goffin, R. D. (1996). A five-factor versus six-factor model of personality structure. *Personality and Individual Differences, 20*, 33–45.
Jackson, D. N., Paunonen, S. V., & Tremblay, P. F. (2000). *Six Factor Personality Questionnaire: Manual*. Port Huron, MI: Sigma Assessment Systems.
Jenkins, M., & Griffith, R. (2004). Using personality constructs to predict performance: Narrow or broad bandwidth. *Journal of Business and Psychology, 19*, 255–269.
John, O. P. (1990). The "Big Five" factor taxonomy: Dimensions of personality in the natural language and in questionnaires. In P. A. Lawrence (Ed.), *Handbook of personality: Theory and research* (pp. 66–100). New York: Guilford Press.
John, O. P., & Srivastava, S. (1999). The Big-Five factor taxonomy: History, measurement, and theoretical perspectives. In L. A. Pervin & O. P. Johns (Eds.), *Handbook of personality: Theory and research* (2nd ed., pp. 102–138). New York: Guilford Press.
Judge, T. A., & Bono, J. E. (2000). Five-Factor Model of personality and transformational leadership. *Journal of Applied Psychology, 85*, 751–765.
Judge, T. A., Bono, J. E., Ilies, R., & Gerhardt, M. W. (2002). Personality and leadership: A qualitative and quantitative review. *Journal of Applied Psychology, 87*, 765–780.
Judge, T. A., Heller, D., & Mount, M. K. (2002). Five-Factor Model of personality and job satisfaction: A meta-analysis. *Journal of Applied Psychology, 87*, 530–541.
Judge, T. A., & Kammeyer-Mueller, J. D. (2012). General and specific measures in organizational behavior: Considerations, examples, and recommendations for researchers. *Journal of Organizational Behavior, 33*, 161–174.
Leary, T. (1957). *Interpersonal diagnosis of personality*. New York: Ronald Press.
Lee, K., & Ashton, M. C. (2004). Psychometric properties of the HEXACO Personality Inventory. *Multivariate Behavioral Research, 39*, 329–358.
Lee, K., & Ashton, M. C. (2008). The HEXACO personality factors in the indigenous personality lexicons of English and 11 other languages. *Journal of Personality, 76*, 1001–1053.
Lee, K., Gizzarone, M., & Ashton, M. C. (2003). Personality and the likelihood to sexually harass. *Sex Roles, 49*, 59–69.
Lee, K., Ogunfowora, B., & Ashton, M. C. (2005). Personality traits beyond the Big Five: Are they within the HEXACO space? *Journal of Personality, 73*, 1437–1463.
LePine, J. A. (2003). Team adaptation and post-change performance: Effects of team composition in terms of members' cognitive ability and personality. *Journal of Applied Psychology, 88*, 27–39.
LePine, J. A., Colquitt, J. A., & Erez, A. (2000). Adaptability to changing task contexts: Effects of general cognitive ability, conscientiousness, and openness to experience. *Personnel Psychology, 53*, 563–593.
Lievens, F., Buyse, T., & Sackett, P. R. (2005). The operational validity of a video-based situational judgment test for medical college admissions: Illustrating the importance of matching predictors and criterion construct domains. *Journal of Applied Psychology, 90*, 442–452.
Lind, A., Greenberg, J., Scott, K. S., & Welchans, T. D. (2000). The winding road from employee complainant: Situational and psychological determinants of wrongful-termination claims. *Administrative Sciences Quarterly, 45*, 557–590.
Loevinger, J. (1957). Objective tests as instruments of psychological theory. *Psychological Reports, 3*, 635–694.
Lord, F. M., & Novick, M. R. (1968). *Statistical theories of mental test scores*. Reading, MA: Addison-Wesley.
Marcus, B., Goffin, R. D., Johnston, N. G., & Rothstein, M. G. (2007). Personality and cognitive ability as predictors of typical and maximum managerial performance. *Human Performance, 20*, 275–285.
Marcus, B., Lee, K., & Ashton, M. C. (2007). Personality dimensions explaining relationships between integrity tests and counterproductive behavior: Big Five, or one in addition? *Personnel Psychology, 60*, 1–34.
McCrae, R. R., & Costa, P. T., Jr. (2008). The five-factor theory of personality. In L. A. Pervin, R. W. Robins, & O. P. John (Eds.), *Handbook of personality: Theory and research* (3rd ed., pp. 159–181). New York: Guilford Press.
McCrae, R. R., Costa, P. T., & Piedmont, R. L. (1993). Folk concepts, natural language, and psychological constructs: The California Psychological Inventory and the Five-Factor Model. *Journal of Personality, 61*, 1–26.
McCrae, R. R., & John, O. P. (1992). An introduction to the Five-Factor Model and its applications. *Journal of Personality, 60*, 175–215.
Mershon, B., & Gorsuch, R. L. (1988). Number of factors in the personality sphere: Does increase in factors increase predictability of real-life criteria? *Journal of Personality and Social Psychology, 55*, 675–680.
Messick, S. (1981). Constructs and their vicissitudes in educational and psychological measurement. *Psychological Bulletin, 89*, 575–588.
Moon, H. (2001). The two faces of conscientiousness: Duty and achievement striving in escalation of commitment dilemmas. *Journal of Applied Psychology, 86*, 533–540.

Moon, H., Hollenbeck, J. R., Humphrey, S. E., & Maue, B. (2003). The tripartite model of neuroticism and the suppression of depression and anxiety within an escalation of commitment dilemma. *Journal of Personality, 71*, 347–368.

Mount, M. K., & Barrick, M. R. (1995). The Big Five personality dimensions: Implications for research and practice in human resource management. *Research in Personnel and Human Resources Management, 13*, 153–200.

Mount, M. K., & Barrick, M. R. (1998). Five reasons why the "Big Five" article has been frequently cited. *Personnel Psychology, 51*, 849–857.

Mount, M. K., Barrick, M. R., & Stewart, G. L. (1998). Five-Factor Model of personality and performance in jobs involving interpersonal interactions. *Human Performance, 11*, 145–165.

Murray, H. A. (1938). *Explorations in personality*. New York: Oxford University Press.

Musek, J. (2007). A general factor of personality: Evidence for the Big One in the Five-Factor Model. *Journal of Research in Personality, 41*, 1213–1233.

Nettle, D. (2006). The evolution of personality variation in humans and other animals. *American Psychologist, 61*, 622–631.

Nicholson, N., Soane, E., Fenton-O'Creevy, M., & Willman, P. (2005). Personality and domain-specific risk taking. *Journal of Risk Research, 8*, 157–176.

Nunnally, J. C. (1978). *Psychometric theory* (2nd ed.). New York: McGraw-Hill.

O'Connor, M. C., & Paunonen, S.V. (2007). Big Five personality predictors of post-secondary academic performance. *Personality and Individual Differences, 43*, 971–990.

O'Neill, T. A., & Allen, N. J. (2011). Personality and the prediction of team performance. *European Journal of Personality, 25*, 31–42.

O'Neill, T. A., Goffin, R. D., & Tett, R. P. (2009). Content validation is fundamental to optimizing the criterion validity of personality tests. *Industrial and Organizational Psychology, 2*, 509–513.

O'Neill, T. A., & Hastings, S. E. (2010). Explaining workplace deviance behavior with more than just the "Big Five." *Personality and Individual Differences, 50*, 268–273.

O'Neill, T. A., Lewis, R. J., & Carswell, J. J. (2011). Employee personality, justice perceptions, and the prediction of workplace deviance. *Personality and Individual Differences, 51*, 595–600.

Ones, D. S. (1993). *The construct validity of integrity tests* (Unpublished doctoral dissertation). University of Iowa, Iowa City.

Ones, D. S., Schmidt, F. L., & Viswesvaran, C. (1994, April). *Do broader personality variables predict job performance with higher validity?* Paper presented at the annual meeting of the Society for Industrial and Organizational Psychology, Nashville, TN.

Ones, D. S., & Viswesvaran, C. (1996). Bandwidth–fidelity dilemma in personality measurement for personnel selection. *Journal of Organizational Behavior, 17*, 609–626.

Ones, D. S., & Viswesvaran, C. (2001a). Integrity tests and other criterion-focused occupational personality scales (COPS) used in personnel selection. *International Journal of Selection and Assessment, 9*, 31–39.

Ones, D. S., & Viswesvaran, C. (2001b). Personality at work: Criterion-focused occupational personality scales used in personnel selection. In B. W. Roberts & R. Hogan (Eds.), *Personality psychology in the workplace* (pp. 63–92). Washington, DC: APA.

Ones, D. S., Viswesvaran, C., & Dilchert, S. (2005). Personality at work: Raising awareness and correcting misconceptions. *Human Performance, 18*, 389–404.

Ones, D. S., Viswesvaran, C., & Schmidt, F. L. (1993). Comprehensive meta-analysis of integrity test validities: Findings and implications for personnel selection and theories of job performance. *Journal of Applied Psychology, 78*, 679–703.

Paunonen, S.V. (1993, August). *Sense, nonsense, and the Big Five factors of personality*. Paper presented at the annual meeting of the American Psychological Association, Toronto, Ontario, Canada.

Paunonen, S. V. (1998). Hierarchical organization of personality and the prediction of behavior. *Journal of Personality and Social Psychology, 74*, 538–556.

Paunonen, S.V. (2000). Big Five factors of personality and replicated predictions of behavior. *Journal of Personality and Social Psychology, 84*, 411–424.

Paunonen, S. V. (2002). *Design and construction of the Supernumerary Personality Inventory (Research Bulletin 763)*. London, Ontario, Canada: University of Western Ontario.

Paunonen, S.V., & Ashton, M. C. (2001a). Big Five factors and facets and the prediction of behaviour. *Journal of Personality and Social Psychology, 81*, 411–424.

Paunonen, S.V., & Ashton, M. C. (2001b). Big Five predictors of academic achievement. *Journal of Research in Personality, 35*, 78–90.

Paunonen, S.V., Haddock, G., Forsterling, F., & Keinonen, M. (2003). Broad versus narrow personality measures and the prediction of behavior across cultures. *European Journal of Personality, 17*, 413–433.

Paunonen, S.V., & Hong, R.Y. (in press). On the properties of personality traits. In P. R. Shaver & M. Mikulincer (Eds.), *Handbook of personality and social psychology*. New York: APA.

Paunonen, S.V., & Jackson, D. N. (1985). The validity of formal and informal personality assessments. *Journal of Research in Personality, 19*, 331–342.
Paunonen, S. V., & Jackson, D. N. (1996). The Jackson Personality Inventory and the Five-Factor Model of personality. *Journal of Research in Personality, 30*, 42–59.
Paunonen, S.V., & Jackson, D. N. (2000). What is beyond the Big Five? Plenty! *Journal of Personality, 68*, 821–835.
Paunonen, S.V., Lonnqist, J., Verkasalo, M., Leikas, S., & Nissinen, V. (2006). Narcissism and emergent leadership in military cadets. *The Leadership Quarterly, 17*, 475–486.
Paunonen, S.V., & Nicol, A. A. A. M. (2001). The personality hierarchy and the prediction of work behaviors. In B.W. Roberts & R. Hogan (Eds.), *Personality psychology in the workplace* (pp. 161–191). Washington, DC: APA.
Paunonen, S.V., Rothstein, M. G., & Jackson, D. N. (1999). Narrow reasoning about the use of broad personality measures for personnel selection. *Journal of Organizational Behavior, 20*, 389–405.
Perry, S. J., Hunter, E. M., Witt, L. A., & Kenneth, J. H. (2011). P = f (Conscientiousness × Ability): Examining the facets of conscientiousness. *Human Performance, 23*, 343–360.
Piedmont, R. L., & Weinstein, H. P. (1994). Predicting supervisor ratings of job performance using the NEO Personality Inventory. *Journal of Psychology: Interdisciplinary and Applied, 128*, 255–265.
Plutchik, R., & Conte, H. R. (Eds.). (1997). *Circumplex models of personality and emotions*. Washington, DC: APA.
Powell, D. M., Goffin, R. D., & Gellatly, I. R. (2011). Gender differences in personality scores: Implications for differential hiring rates. *Personality and Individual Differences, 50*, 106–110.
Roth, P. L., Bobko, P., & Switzer, F. S. (2006). Modeling the behavior of the 4/5ths rule for determining adverse impact: Reasons for caution. *Journal of Applied Psychology, 91*, 507–522.
Rothstein, M. G., & Goffin, R. D. (2006). The use of personality measures in personnel selection: What does current research support? *Human Resource Management Review, 16*, 155–180.
Rothstein, M. G., & Jelley, R. B. (2003). The challenge of aggregating studies of personality. In K. R. Murphy (Ed.), *Validity generalization: A critical review* (pp. 223–262). Mahwah, NJ: Lawrence Erlbaum Associates Publishers.
Rothstein, M. G., Paunonen, S.V., Rush, J. C., & King, G. A. (1994). Personality and cognitive ability predictors of performance in graduate business school. *Journal of Educational Psychology, 86*, 516–530.
Rushton, J. P., Bons, T. A., & Hur, Y.-M. (2008). The genetics and evolution of a general factor of personality. *Journal of Research in Personality, 42*, 1136–1149.
Rushton, J. P., & Erdle, S. (2010). No evidence that social desirability response set explains the general factor of personality and its affective correlates. *Twin Research and Human Genetics, 13*, 131–134.
Rushton, J. P., & Irwing, P. (2008). A general factor of personality from two meta-analyses of the Big Five: Digman (1997) and Mount, Barrick, Scullen, and Rounds (2005). *Personality and Individual Differences, 45*, 679–683.
Rushton, J. P., & Irwing, P. (2009a). A general factor of personality (GFP) from the Multidimensional Personality Questionnaire. *Personality and Individual Differences, 47*, 571–576.
Rushton, J. P., & Irwing, P. (2009b). A general factor of personality in 16 sets of the Big Five, the Guilford–Zimmerman Temperament Survey, the California Psychological Inventory, and the Temperament and Character Inventory. *Personality and Individual Differences, 47*, 558–564.
Rushton, J. P., & Irwing, P. (2009c). A general factor of personality in the Comrey Personality Scales, the Minnesota Multiphasic Personality Inventory-2, and the Multicultural Personality Questionnaire. *Personality and Individual Differences, 46*, 437–442.
Rushton, J. P., & Irwing, P. (2009d). A general factor of personality in the Millon Clinical Multiaxial Inventory-III, the dimensional assessment of personality pathology, and the personality assessment inventory. *Journal of Research in Personality, 43*, 1091–1095.
Rushton, J. P., Jackson, D. N., & Paunonen, S. V. (1981). Personality: Nomothetic or idiographic? A response to Kenrick and Stringfield. *Psychological Review, 88*, 582–589.
Rynes, S. L., & Connerley, M. L. (1993). Applicant reactions to alternative selection procedures. *Journal of Business and Psychology, 7*, 261–277.
Sackett, P. R., & Wilk, S. L. (1994). Within-group norming and other forms of score adjustment in psychological testing. *American Psychologist, 49*, 929–954.
Saucier, G., & Goldberg, L. R. (1998). What is beyond the Big Five? *Journal of Personality, 66*, 495–524.
Saucier, G., & Goldberg, L. R. (2003). The structure of personality attributes. In M. Barrick & A. M. Ryan (Eds.), *Personality and work* (pp. 1–29). San Francisco: Jossey-Bass.
Schmitt, N., Rogers, W., Chan, D., Sheppard, L., & Jennings, D. (1997). Adverse impact and predictive efficiency of various predictor combinations. *Journal of Applied Psychology, 82*, 719–730.
Schneider, R. J., & Hough, L. M. (1995). Personality and industrial/organizational psychology. In C. L. Cooper & I. T. Robertson (Eds.), *International review of industrial and organizational psychology* (*Vol. 10*, pp. 75–129). New York: Wiley & Sons.
Schneider, R. J., Hough, L. M., & Dunnette, M. D. (1996). Broadsided by broad traits: How to sink science in five dimensions or less. *Journal of Organizational Behavior, 17*, 639–655.

Smith, P. C. (1976). Behavior, results, and organizational effectiveness: The problem of criteria. In M. D. Dunnette (Ed.), *Handbook of industrial and organizational psychology* (pp. 745–775). Chicago: Rand McNally.

Society for Industrial and Organizational Psychology (SIOP). (2003). *Principles for the validation and use of personnel selection* (4th ed.). Bowling Green, OH: Author.

Steel, P., Schmidt, J., & Shultz, J. (2008). Refining the relationship between personality and subjective well-being. *Psychological Bulletin, 134*, 138–161.

Stein, M. I. (1963). Explorations in typology. In R. W. White (Ed.), *The study of lives* (pp. 280–303). New York: Oxford.

Stewart, G. L. (1999). Trait bandwidth and stages of job performance: Assessing differential effects for conscientiousness and its subtraits. *Journal of Applied Psychology, 84*, 959–968.

Tett, R. P., & Burnett, D. (2003). A personality trait-based interactionist model of job performance. *Journal of Applied Psychology, 88*, 500–517.

Tett, R. P., & Christiansen, N. D. (2007). Personality tests at the crossroads: A response to Morgeson, Campion, Dipboye, Hollenbeck, Murphy, and Schmitt (2007). *Personnel Psychology, 60*, 967–993.

Tett, R. P., & Christiansen, N. D. (2008). Personality assessment in organizations. In G. Boyle, G. Matthews, & D. Saklofske (Eds.), *Handbook of personality and testing* (pp. 720–742). Los Angeles: SAGE.

Tett, R. P., Guterman, H. A., Bleier, A., & Murphy, P. J. (2000). Development and content validation of a "Hyperdimensional" taxonomy of managerial competence. *Human Performance, 13*, 205–251.

Tett, R. P., Jackson, D. N., & Rothstein, M. (1991). Meta-analysis of personality–job performance relationships. *Personnel Psychology, 47*, 157–172.

Tett, R. P., Steele, J. R., & Beauregard, R. S. (2003). Broad and narrow measures on both sides of the personality–job performance relationship. *Journal of Organizational Behavior, 24*, 335–356.

Thoresen, C. J., Bradley, J. C., Bliese, P. D., & Thoresen, J. D. (2004). The Big Five personality traits and individual job performance growth trajectories in maintenance and transitional job stages. *Journal of Applied Psychology, 89*, 835–853.

van der Linden, D., te Nijenhuis, J., Cremers, M., & van de Ven, C. (2011). General factors of personality in six datasets and a criterion-related validity study at the Netherlands armed forces. *International Journal of Selection and Assessment, 19*, 157–169.

Vinchur, A. J., Schippmann, J. S., Switzer, F. S., & Roth, P. J. (1998). A meta-analytic review of predictors of job performance for salespeople. *Journal of Applied Psychology, 83*, 586–597.

Viswesvaran, C., & Ones, D. S. (2000). Measurement error in Big Five factors. *Educational and Psychological Measurement, 60*, 224–235.

Warr, P., Bartram, D., & Martin, T. (2005). Personality and sales performance: Situational variation and interactions between traits. *International Journal of Selection and Assessment, 13*, 87–91.

Wiggins, J. S. (1979). A psychological taxonomy of trait-descriptive terms: The interpersonal domain. *Journal of Personality and Social Psychology, 37*, 395–412.

Wiggins, J. S. (1995). *Interpersonal Adjective Scales: Professional manual.* Odessa, FL: Psychological Assessment Resources.

Williams, L. J., Edwards, J., & Vandenberg, R. J. (2003). Recent advances in causal modeling methods for organizational and management research. *Organizational Research Methods, 29*, 903–936.

15

Cross-Cultural Issues in Personality Assessment

Filip De Fruyt and Bart Wille

Importance of Personality Assessment in a Globalized Economy

Personality assessment is an established part of many selection procedures in Western countries (Furnham, 2008; Sackett & Lievens, 2008), despite its questioned predictive validity throughout the years. Opponents (e.g., Morgeson et al., 2007a, 2007b) have mainly questioned the small magnitude of the predictive correlations and further criticized the fakability of self-descriptions in at-stake contexts such as job selection procedures. Proponents (Ones, Dilchert, Viswesvaran, & Judge, 2007; Tett & Christiansen, 2007) meta-analytically reviewed validity coefficients and concluded that validities (1) are not trivial; (2) generalize across different contexts and cultures, with job characteristics acting as a moderator; (3) have demonstrated utility for selection decisions; and (4) are not necessarily worse than validities obtained with alternative methods of selection assessment (Rolland & De Fruyt, 2009). Although most authors agree that many individuals will put their best feet forward when describing their personality (in a selection context), there are varying opinions on how to handle and consider impression management. In addition to selection, personality assessment is used more and more in the context of career development and coaching, so its prominence and impact in the industrial and organizational (IO) field is steadily increasing. Given the range of criteria that are predicted by traits, it is to be expected that the frequency of personality assessments in IO professional practice will amplify in a globalized economy, where direct and indirect contacts with colleagues and customers representing diverse cultural backgrounds will be the norm rather than the exception. This multicultural context generates a series of questions and challenges that are beyond the description of personality differences for members of a single culture. With respect to *personality description*, questions at stake include the following: (1) What kind of trait model (and accompanying operationalization) should one use to describe an individual's personality within and across cultural contexts, which gets at whether one can use inventories that are developed in one culture to assess applicants with a different cultural background? (2) What norms should one use when comparing individuals from diverse cultural backgrounds applying for jobs in which they will have to collaborate intensively? (3) Do applicants from diverse cultural backgrounds perceive assessment contexts differently? In other words, are self-enhancing strategies in personality descriptions in development or selection contexts perceived alike across cultural groups? (4) What about the accuracy of personality stereotypes of cultural groups? Given their potential impact in selection processes, it is important to know whether such stereotypes reflect a kernel of truth or do not match observed differences among cultural groups. With respect to the *predictive validity* of personality, a key question is whether culture acts as a moderator of personality–criterion relationships.

The current chapter will first explore the two key constructs, that is, culture and personality, examining major models describing basic dimensions of culture and introducing a model assumed to tap the common core of personality differences observable within and across cultures, respectively. The subsequent section reviews personality findings that showed to be largely universal across cultures. The next part discusses methodological and psychometric requirements for comparing personality scores across cultures, followed by an analysis of the importance of personality dimensions and mean-level personality differences among cultures. Tett and Burnett's (2003) trait-based interactionist model of job performance is subsequently discussed, taking into account the potential impact of culture-level variables. The implications of these findings for IO professional practice are discussed in a practitioner's window. This chapter closes with a section identifying major knowledge gaps and perennial issues in the field of cross-cultural personality assessment in IO psychology.

Culture and Its Core Dimensions

The definition of culture, how to distinguish among cultural groups, and the kind of core dimensions that are necessary to describe cultures have been the subject of intensive debate and research in the past decades. Matsumoto (2000) provided an overarching description integrating different key attributes and defined culture as:

> A dynamic system of rules, explicit and implicit, established by groups in order to ensure their survival, involving attitudes, values, beliefs, norms, and behaviors, shared by a group but harbored differently by each specific unit within the group, communicated across generations, relatively stable but with the potential to change across time.
>
> *p. 24*

This definition clearly acknowledges that individuals within a particular culture differ in terms of assimilating and manifesting various cultural attributes and further underscores that cultures have the potential to change over time. Both attributes affect how traits will have to be delineated from observable behavior. There have been several attempts to investigate core dimensions of cultural differences and cultural value frameworks in particular (for an excellent review, see Nardon & Steers, 2009). Two of these models were specifically developed within an IO framework and had considerable impact on this area, that is, Geert Hofstede's (1980, 2001) four-dimensional model of cultural differences and the work of the Global Leadership and Organizational Behavior Effectiveness (GLOBE) group (R. J. House, Hanges, Javidan, Dorfman, & Gupta, 2004).

Hofstede's Model

In the 1960s and 1970s, Hofstede (1980, 2001) had access to international survey data completed by a large sample of service and marketing personnel employed in 40 countries of a firm initially referred to as "Hermes" (later on revealed to be "IBM"). The survey was intended to assess and compare morale across divisions of IBM located in multiple countries. Hofstede factor analyzed aggregated scores across employees within these 40 societies and found that four major dimensions best represented the variance. The first dimension, "Power distance," reflects how societies find solutions to deal with the basic problem of human inequality. Cultures characterized by high power distance are organized very hierarchically often with a set of formal rules on how to navigate within this hierarchy. In cultures with high power distance, people accept authority and comply with orders and directions given by those higher in the hierarchy. A second dimension, "Uncertainty avoidance," describes how cultures cope with stress in the face of an unknown future. Societies characterized by high uncertainty avoidance will invest in different programs and institutions to deal with harm and disaster; they value stability and do not tolerate deviant ideas and behavior. One of the most well-known dimensions of Hofstede's model is "Individualism–collectivism," describing how individuals are integrated into primary groups. In collectivistic cultures, a person's identity is strongly bound to family relationships and the "in-group" to which one belongs, whereas in more individualistic societies, a person's identity is more related to individualistic strivings and achievements. In collectivistic societies, the group will take care of the person, whereas in individualistic societies, people have to take care of themselves and their direct family. Finally, the fourth factor, "Masculinity–femininity," describes how societies are organized around the division of emotional roles between men and women. In more masculine societies, assertiveness, making a career, and earning money are considered important, whereas more feminine societies value cooperation and getting along. Hofstede's research and dimensions were first criticized as having a strong Western bias, because African and Asian countries were underrepresented among his initial set of 40 countries. The Chinese Culture Connection (1987) challenged this ethnocentric viewpoint with a more emic research program, proposing an additional factor: "Confucian work dynamism." Hofstede (2001) later added this dimension to his model under the label "Long-term versus short-term orientation," reflecting differences among cultures in the choice of focus for people's efforts: the future or the present.

Hofstede (2001, p. 500; Exhibit A.5.1) ranked different cultures in terms of their scores on the cultural value dimensions. For example, the United States was ranked as highly individualistic (rank 1 of 53), lower on power distance (rank 38), higher on masculinity (rank 15), and lower on uncertainty avoidance (rank 43) relative to 53 other countries, whereas Japan was ranked as less individualistic (rank 22–23 of 53), somewhat more power distant (rank 33), top in masculinity (rank 1), and higher on uncertainty avoidance (rank 7). These country rankings were used in numerous studies and correlated with other national-level data such as indicators of economic activity and wealth, health, and happiness, but also aggregate personality and national character ratings. However, as Matsumoto's definition of culture underscored, cultures are dynamic entities, and an update of this ranking of countries as well as a reexamination of the comprehensiveness and the content of Hofstede's model may be required after three decades of fast economical, societal, and political changes.

GLOBE

A second major research effort in the search for the dimensions of cultural values has been undertaken by a consortium of 160 researchers from many parts of the world under the direction of Robert J. House. The GLOBE research program (Chokhar, Brodbeck, & House, 2007; R. House, Javidan, Hanges, & Dorfman, 2002; R. J. House et al., 2004) was designed to examine implicit leadership theories and attributes of effective leadership in various cultural contexts. Data of about 17,000 managers employed in 951 organizations in 62 societies across the world were examined. In GLOBE, culture is defined as "the shared motives, values, beliefs, identities, and interpretations or meanings of significant events that result from common experiences of members of collectives that are transmitted across generations" (R. J. House & Javidan, 2004).

GLOBE defines nine major dimensions of cultural differences plus an additional six to describe leadership behavior. These nine dimensions are institutional collectivism or "the degree to which organizational and societal institutional practices encourage and reward the collective distribution of resources and collective action," in-group collectivism or "the degree to which individuals express pride, loyalty, and cohesiveness in their organizations or families," power distance or "the degree to which members of a society expect and agree that power should be stratified and concentrated at higher levels of an organization or government," performance orientation or "the degree to which an organization or society encourages and rewards members for performance improvement and excellence," gender egalitarism or "the degree to which a society minimizes gender role differences while promoting gender equality," future orientation or "the degree to which individuals in organizations or societies engage in future-oriented behaviors such as planning, investing in the future, and delaying individual or collective gratification," humane orientation or "the degree to which members of a society encourage and reward individuals for being fair, altruistic, friendly, generous, caring, and kind to others," assertiveness or "the degree to which members of a society are assertive, confrontational, or aggressive in social relationships," and finally uncertainty avoidance or "the extent to which members of a society seek certainty in their environment by relying on established social norms, rituals, and bureaucratic practices" (R. J. House, Quigley, & de Luque, 2010, p. 118, Table 1).

These dimensions were subsequently used to cluster 61 nations participating in GLOBE according to cultural values and beliefs into 10 a priori proposed clusters: South Asia, Anglo, Arab, Germanic Europe, Latin Europe, Eastern Europe, Confucian Asia, Latin America, Sub-Sahara Africa, and Nordic Europe. This clustering received considerable empirical support (Gupta, Hanges, & Dorfman, 2002). For example, the Arab cluster includes Egypt, Morocco, Turkey, Kuwait, and Qatar, and these societies are found to be highly group oriented, hierarchical, masculine, and low on future orientation (Kabasakal & Bodur, 2002). One of the major purposes of GLOBE was to examine leadership practices and how good leadership was perceived within these clusters. For example, in the Arab cluster, mid-level managers defined outstanding leadership as characterized by team-oriented and charismatic features, but also that an outstanding leadership style is not reflected by extreme positions on leadership traits (Kabasakal & Bodur, 2002). This example well illustrates how cultures may differentially value leadership behavior and hence value the personality traits that are associated with this competency (Bono & Judge, 2004). In addition, evidence is provided for the distinction between the cultural values and the cultural practices part in the assessment of the GLOBE dimensions, with only the values, but not the practices, being associated with features of outstanding leadership behavior. Javidan, House, Dorfman, Hanges, and de Luque (2006, p. 903) concluded that, "In other words, leaders' reported effectiveness is associated with the society's cultural values and aspirations, but the society's effectiveness is associated with its cultural practices."

Both Hofstede and the GLOBE consortium have been very influential in alerting IO psychologists to the notion of cultural differences and providing the field with dimensional models to denote cultural attributes. Both approaches strongly contrast with the many "easy" operationalizations of culture that simply rely on race or nationality as markers of an individual's culture and disregard the cultural heterogeneity beyond directly accessible markers. Different comparative reviews and mutual criticisms (Hofstede, 2006, 2010; Javidan et al., 2006) have further sharpened our thinking about cross-cultural differences, its applications, and its challenges. It is clear now that cultural value dimensions have main effects on a series of outcome variables, such as emotions, attitudes and perceptions, behaviors, and job performance (Taras, Kirkman, & Steel, 2010), but cultural values can also moderate relationships between other predictors (e.g., personality) and these outcomes.

One Model Fits All? The Universal Structure of Personality

Personality and culture show reciprocal relationships, with the expression of personality traits affected by culture and individuals' unique personality affecting and shaping that culture (Chao & Moon, 2005). The Five-Factor Theory distinguishes between basic tendencies and characteristic adaptations (McCrae & Costa, 1996). Basic tendencies (i.e., the traits from the Five-Factor Model, FFM) are considered as causal entities that are largely independent from cultural factors but are assumed to influence various characteristic adaptations, such as interests, motives, work competencies, and values. Individuals' value systems are also shaped by cultures' shared meaning systems. An important assumption of the Five-Factor Theory is that the structure of personality should be relatively invariant across different cultures. The question at stake becomes whether this FFM can be used for cross-cultural personality descriptions.

Cross-Cultural Replicability of the Big Five

Over the past decades, personality psychologists reached a relative consensus on the importance of five major personality dimensions, the so-called Big Five, to represent the major variance among personality descriptions. Lexical studies conducted in different languages mainly converged on the nature and number of factors suggesting that extraversion, agreeableness, neuroticism, conscientiousness, and intellect were necessary and sufficient to account for the communalities enclosed in self- and peer descriptions on large sets of personality-descriptive adjectives (Goldberg, 1982). From a different angle, Costa and McCrae (1992) introduced the FFM of personality, complementing their initial Neuroticism–Extraversion–Openness (NEO) model, already capturing the domains of neuroticism, extraversion, and openness to experience, with the domains of agreeableness and conscientiousness. Openness to experience deviates from the lexical Big Five intellect factor because it reflects a broader content including receptivity to a range of experiences and a fluid and permeable structure of consciousness that is not well represented in the natural language by trait adjectives (McCrae, 1994). They further demonstrated that this FFM was able to accommodate all main factors recurrently observable across major personality inventories. Although the terms "Big Five" and "FFM" are often used interchangeably to refer to the consensus on their importance as major constructs of personality, they have clearly different historical roots.

Cross-cultural psychologists have pointed our attention to the distinction between emic and etic approaches with respect to the use of psychological constructs in cross-cultural research (Matsumoto, 2000). Indeed, most FFM research has been *etic* in origin, examining the replicability of instruments that were to a large extent originally designed in Western cultures, in a multitude of countries across the globe. Such investigations have been done widely with the NEO Personality Inventory—Revised (NEO-PI-R; Costa & McCrae, 1992; Rolland, 2002) and its successor the NEO-PI-3 (McCrae, Costa, & Martin, 2005). There is massive evidence that the FFM structure is replicable in self- and peer ratings in cultures across all continents, at least when administered to people with sufficient reading command of the native language. Moreover, the FFM structure also showed to be valid across different age groups from adolescence (NEO-PI-3; De Fruyt, De Bolle, McCrae, Terracciano, & Costa, 2009) to adulthood (NEO-PI-R; McCrae & Terracciano, 2005b), making it the model par excellence to study gender and developmental trends from a cross-cultural perspective (see further in this chapter). De Fruyt, Aluja, Garcia, Rolland, and Jung (2006) further illustrated that the factor structure of the NEO-PI-R remained preserved across the IQ distribution in selection contexts, whereas Marshall, De Fruyt, Rolland, and Bagby (2005) demonstrated that the NEO structure was replicable across different administration contexts, including not-at-stake situations, career counseling (mild at-stake), and selection situations (high-stakes context). Together, these studies suggest that the FFM is applicable for cross-cultural assessment of personality in IO applications.

Dimensions Beyond the Big Five

There have been also *emic*, also called indigenous approaches toward personality description, where researchers started within a particular culture to comprehensively sample personality descriptors bottom–up and examine their underlying structure, rather than importing (top–down) a personality inventory designed in a different culture. For example, Meiring, Van de Vijver, Rothmann, and De Bruin (2008) examined the structure of personality descriptors in 11 languages spoken in South Africa, Church and his team (Katigbak, Church, Guanzon-Lapena, Carlota, & del Pilar, 2002) suggested additional indigenous dimensions to account for the commonality in Filipino college student personality ratings, and Benet-Martinez and John (1998) examined the personality structure in the Spanish language in Hispanic minorities. Overall, these authors demonstrated that there is evidence for a common cross-cultural personality-descriptive vocabulary as well as emic traits that may have particular relevance and importance for a specific culture. Cheung and Leung (1998), however, strongly argued in favor of Chinese indigenous personality measures.

Personality psychologists have suggested additional factors beyond the Big Five within Western cultures. For example, Paunonen and Jackson (2000), reconsidering an initial selection of personality adjectives made by Saucier and Goldberg (1998), suggested 10 possible dimensions that are difficult to position within the Big Five: (1) religious, devout, reverent; (2) sly, deceptive, manipulative; (3) honest, ethical, moral; (4) sexy, sensual, erotic; (5) thrifty, frugal, miserly; (6) conservative, traditional, down to earth; (7) masculine–feminine; (8) egoistical, conceited, snobbish; (9) humorous, witty, amusing; and (10) risk-taking and thrill-seeking. Likewise, further elaborating within the lexical research paradigm, Ashton, Lee, and Son (2000) suggested "honesty–humility" as a sixth major factor, reflecting attributes such as fairness and sincerity. Reviewing these supplements, it is unclear whether some are to be considered as facets or blends of the Big Five or are indeed replicable major dimensions above and beyond the basic five. For example, a reanalysis of the data initially used by Ashton et al. (2004) as support for the honesty–humility dimension, by the same group of authors (except Ashton and Lee), showed that no more than three factors, that is, extraversion, agreeableness, and conscientiousness, were replicable across 14 datasets from 12 different cultures, with "honesty–humility" turning up as a facet of agreeableness (De Raad et al., 2010). This reanalysis further demonstrated that also a well-known personality factor like "neuroticism/emotional stability," which is represented in almost every single theory or model on personality differences, was not replicable. Overall, this work by De Raad et al. (2010) well illustrates the limits of the lexical paradigm analyzing the passive personality-descriptive vocabulary to denote the major dimensions of personality.

Up until now, it is unclear whether these additional or emic-derived traits predict criteria of importance for IO psychology, beyond the dimensions and facets already enclosed in broad personality taxonomies for which there exists cross-cultural support. Contrary to the personality field, comprehensiveness is not necessarily the most important requirement for a personality-descriptive taxonomy to be used in IO psychology. For applied purposes, such as selection assessment, predictive validity is ultimately most important, and rather than being comprehensive, a personality measure should reflect those traits that are most useful to understand the criterion of interest such as job performance or leadership emergence, for example. This implies that a personality measure fit for IO applications should assess not only several facets of conscientiousness, such as "self-discipline," "achievement," and "planning," but also traits that form blends between conscientiousness with other broad personality domains such as "control" (forming a blend with neuroticism) and "proactivity" (blending with extraversion) (Rolland & De Fruyt, 2009) because there is evidence that conscientiousness and related traits are predictors of work performance.

General Versus Contextualized Personality Inventories in IO Psychology

Many personality inventories in the past were developed from a clinical angle, for example the Eysenck Personality Questionnaire (EPQ; Eysenck & Eysenck, 1975) or the Minnesota Multiphasic Personality Inventory (MMPI; Butcher & Williams, 2000), followed by a generation of inventories focusing at the description of trait variation observable in the general population such as the NEO-PI-R (Costa & McCrae, 1992) or the scales from Goldberg's International Personality Item Pool (IPIP; Goldberg et al., 2006). The legislation on job selection assessment in many countries, including the United States (Americans with Disabilities Act) and many European countries (e.g., France; Loi n° 92-1446 du 31 Décembre 1992), explicitly requires that assessments should have demonstrable relevance for the work context. The implication for personality assessment is that personality inventories administered in the context of job selection or career coaching should be directly relevant to judge on an individual's suitability for a particular job or contribute to an understanding of functioning at work. General personality inventories, however, often include many items that are not immediately work related, making such instruments potentially contestable when used in IO professional practice. From a different angle, in an attempt to increase validities of personality assessments for IO applications, Lievens, De Corte, and Schollaert (2008) convincingly demonstrated that the inclusion of a frame-of-reference substantially increases the validity of personality descriptions to predict performance criteria. They showed that adding a frame-of-reference to the general instructions for personality description (e.g., "Describe how you generally behave at work or at school") or adding word tags to the items (e.g., "I am curious *at work*") leads to higher validities for predicting criteria considered important in the framed contexts.

These two evolutions led to an increased use of contextualized personality inventories specifically designed to assess personality at work either through the administration of work-related personality-descriptive items or through the addition of a "work-frame" to the instructions or a combination of these. Introducing "work context" in the items, on top of the personality behavioral descriptive part, makes such inventories inevitably more culture-bound. For example, an item like "A negative evaluation at work bothers me for days" (as an indicator of frustration tolerance) (Personality for Professionals Inventory [PfPI]; Rolland & De Fruyt, 2009) introduces an organizational and cultural practice into a personality-descriptive item. Merging context and behavioral description introduces extra challenges to demonstrate equivalence of measures across cultures (see further in this chapter).

Structure of Maladaptive/Dark Side Traits

Over the past years, IO psychology witnessed a growing attention for the assessment of aberrant traits and personality dysfunction (De Fruyt & Salgado, 2003; Salgado & De Fruyt, 2005; Wu & Lebreton, 2011). This transfer followed a growing awareness in human resources to pay more attention to dark side behaviors at work, partly accelerated by the multiple examples of mismanagement and the economical crisis after the millennium. Before this shift, human resources as a discipline was heavily under the influence of positive psychology, with more attention for the bright than the dark side of functioning.

There have been few attempts to assess maladaptive aspects of personality in the work context, with Robert and Joyce Hogan among the first to call the attention of IO psychologists to the dark side of personality (R. Hogan, Hogan, & Roberts, 1996). In clinical psychology and psychiatry, aberrant personality traits are described on Axis II of the *Diagnostic and Statistical Manual of Mental Disorders* (4th ed., text rev.; *DSM-IV-TR*; American Psychiatric Association, 2000), which articulates 10 specific personality disorders, including the paranoid, schizoid, schizotypal, antisocial, borderline, histrionic, narcissistic, avoidant, dependent, and obsessive–compulsive personality disorder. Recent developments in clinical psychology, however, support the view that personality disorders do not represent qualitatively distinct categories, but should be conceived as continua of personality tendencies (Van Leeuwen, Mervielde, De Clercq, & De Fruyt, 2007) that affect broad areas in people's lives, including behavior at work (De Fruyt, De Clercq, et al., 2009). The validity of general personality-descriptive models, such as the FFM, to understand personality pathology has been extensively investigated (Costa & Widiger, 2002). This research line has demonstrated that general and maladaptive personality traits substantially overlap and that personality disorders can be described along the FFM dimensions, suggesting that differences between normality and abnormality are quantitative rather than qualitative.

Although well documented in Western countries, this assumption has not been examined widely outside North America or Western Europe, except for a study by Rossier, Rigozzi, and Personality Across Culture Research Group (2008) replicating these associations in nine French-speaking African countries. The paradigm shift, in which personality disorders are better understood dimensionally, together with the observation that general personality traits also capture core features of personality pathology, suggests that these constructs and assessment methodology might be applied successfully in IO psychology. The cross-cultural replicability of the FFM, together with the work by Rossier et al. (2008), is a first step in examining whether the evaluation of personality dysfunction may extend cross-culturally. Given the results of the GLOBE research group on the perception of leadership, it is to be expected that narcissistic leadership will be more perceived as dysfunctional in, for example, the Arab cluster relative to Germanic European countries, where outstanding leadership is defined by team-oriented and charismatic features, in the absence of extreme positions on leadership traits (Kabasakal & Bodur, 2002).

Replicable Findings Across Cultures

Due to the relative consensus on the cross-cultural replicability of more structural aspects of personality, considerable progress has been made in the past decade to examine cross-cultural patterns of gender and age differences. Data have been accumulated not only through meta-analytic summaries of convenience samples, but also via targeted sampling across various cultures using a single comprehensive personality inventory. The major advantage of this last approach is that one circumvents the necessity to classify different scales assumed to assess a similar construct when compiling the meta-analytic database. The Personality Profiles of Cultures (PPOC; McCrae & Terracciano, 2005a, 2005b) and the Adolescent Personality Profiles of Cultures Project (APPOC; De Fruyt, De Bolle, et al., 2009), a consortium of international research partners collecting data with the NEO-PI-R (Costa & McCrae, 1992) or its more reader and adolescent friendly version, the NEO-PI-3 (Costa, McCrae, & Martin, 2008; McCrae, Martin, & Costa, 2005), have considerably contributed to this field. Given their comprehensive and hierarchical character, as well as their replicability across a range of cultures, the NEO measures are well suited to examine gender and age differences across the globe.

Universal Gender Differences

In a follow-up on previous narrative (Maccoby & Jacklin, 1974) and meta-analytic reviews (Feingold, 1994) of gender differences on a more narrow set of traits, Costa, Terracciano, and McCrae (2001) investigated gender differences in NEO-PI-R self-ratings obtained in 24 samples of adults and 14 samples of young adults across the FFM domains and their 30 facets. They further examined gender differences as a function of socioeconomic status (SES) indicators of cultures, including Hofstede's (2001) dimensions, in addition to gross domestic product, female literacy, life expectancy, and fertility rate, indicated by the number of children. Although convenience samples were largely taken from Western cultures and often with undergraduates serving as young adult samples, the data lent itself to an examination of gender differences due to the replicable factor structure of the NEO-PI-R across countries. Observed gender differences were further compared with gender stereotypes assessed with the Bem Sex Role Inventory (Bem, 1974) to investigate whether stereotypes have some "kernel of truth."

Costa et al.'s (2001) findings can be easily summarized as follows: (1) At the FFM domain level, females score higher on neuroticism and agreeableness, and the orientation of these differences also generalizes to their facets. For extraversion and openness, gender differences seem to cancel out against each other at the domain level, but there are consistent gender differences at the facet level. Men score higher on E5: excitement-seeking and E3: assertiveness, whereas women have on average higher scores on E1: warmth, E2: gregariousness, and E6: positive emotions. Men further obtain higher scores on O5: openness to ideas, whereas women score higher on O2: aesthetics, O3: feelings, and O4: actions. Negligible gender differences are observed for conscientiousness. Important from the perspective of the current chapter is that these patterns generalize within (across young and older adults) and across cultures, suggesting stable cross-cultural patterns. (2) If gender differences are observed, they are usually limited to half a standard deviation, with most differences reflecting a quarter standard deviation. (3) There is a strong agreement between gender stereotypes (Bem, 1974) and observed gender differences, underscoring the "kernel of truth" hypothesis regarding gender stereotypes. (4) Both nature and size of the differences are largely consistent with previous literature on a more limited set of traits and meta-analytic evidence described by Feingold (1994). The findings further suggest that gender differences also generalize from young to late adulthood. (5) If gender differences show up to some extent in personality ratings of one trait, the size of these differences generalizes across the other traits, suggesting that gender differentiation orientation generalizes within a culture. This finding inspired Costa et al. (2001) to rank societies in terms of gender role differentiation, showing that Zimbabwe had the lowest gender role differentiation, with small to negligible gender differences among traits, whereas Belgium showed the largest differences across the FFM. (6) Costa et al. (2001) correlated this ranking of sex role differentiation with the criteria characterizing cultures and found that if gender differences are observed, they are more sizeable in countries with a larger gross domestic product, literacy and life expectancy of women, and lower fertility. These findings are intriguing and surprising because also the Scandinavian countries such as Norway, Sweden, and Denmark are at the top end of the observed gender differentiation ranking. These countries were among the first Western societies in action to reduce gender inequality and glass ceiling effects, and especially, in these countries, gender differences are more pronounced. These findings obtained from convenience samples and self-ratings were largely confirmed in research by the PPOC and APPOC research teams examining gender differences in a much broader set of cultures (50 different countries across all continents) in which individuals were requested to describe somebody they knew well (McCrae & Terracciano, 2005b, p. 553, Table 4).

Universal Age Differences

A parallel route was followed accumulating the findings on cross-cultural age trends for personality ratings, first starting with analyses of mainly convenience samples obtained from a limited set of societies, followed by a more systematic description of age effects across a broad range of cultures by the (A)PPOC research teams. McCrae et al. (1999) started to examine whether the age trends observed in the normative NEO-PI-R sample generalized across five additional cultures (Germany, Italy, Portugal, Croatia, and South Korea) in an attempt to figure out whether these age trends reflect common maturation processes (in the case of similar patterns across cultures) or whether age patterns were more culture-bound (in the case of different age trends). In line with the patterns observed in the United States, neuroticism, extraversion, and openness showed average declines with age in adulthood, whereas agreeableness and conscientiousness showed mean-level increases. The magnitude of these changes was small to moderate. These age trends were further confirmed at the FFM domain level for extraversion, openness, and conscientiousness in a broad set of 50 cultures by the PPOC research team, underscoring the notion that these age patterns reflect either common maturation patterns showing up relatively independent of cultural differences (McCrae & Costa, 1996) or are bound to common cultural processes that assert relatively common influences on traits across cultures.

One Method Fits All? Measurement Challenges When Comparing Cultures

A series of measurement issues and biases have to be taken into account before constructs and measures can be meaningfully compared across cultures. Cross-cultural researchers have distinguished among construct, method, and item bias (Van de Vijver & Leung, 1997a, 1997b), and the absence of bias is referred to as equivalence or invariance. Church (2010) provides an excellent introduction to the terminology and measurement challenges within cross-cultural measurement.

Church (2010) describes that construct or conceptual bias occurs "when the definitions of the construct only partially overlap across cultures" (p. 154). For example, the content of a construct like intelligence is in some cultures constrained to cognitive functioning, whereas it includes more social competences in other cultures. The personality trait of assertiveness has a more negative connotation in the Netherlands, Belgium, and Germany, though it is considered mainly as a desirable and extraverted attribute in the United States (De Fruyt, Mervielde, Hoekstra, & Rolland, 2000). Church (2010) distinguishes among three forms of method bias: sample, instrument, and administration bias. Cross-cultural comparisons may be distorted through sample differences on possible confounding factors and design characteristics of the instrument (e.g., the use of Likert scales or the sorting of items across a Q-sort format may be familiar in one culture, but less frequently adopted in another culture), and finally the way the data are administered may be experienced differently by cultural groups and induce response differences (Church, 2010). For example, selection assessments may be perceived as more threatening in individualistic countries with a high power distance. A third kind of bias is item bias or differential item functioning (DIF): "DIF occurs when individuals with the same level or amount of a trait, but from different cultural groups, exhibit a different probability of answering the item in the keyed direction" (Church, 2010, p. 154). In a recent study, Church et al. (2011) examined DIF in factor loadings and intercepts from a multigroup confirmatory factor analysis (CFA) of NEO-PI-R data obtained in the United States, the Philippines, and Mexico, showing that 40%–50% of the items exhibited some form of DIF. Moreover, DIF at the item level also affected the facet level, suggesting that the comparison of mean-level facet and domain scores across cultural groups should be done with caution.

In addition, Church (2010) defines different forms of equivalence, including conceptual, linguistic, and measurement equivalence. Different degrees of overlap between how constructs are defined across cultures are indicated by conceptual equivalence, whereas linguistic equivalence points to the accuracy of translations. For example, the NEO-PI-R item "I wouldn't enjoy vacationing in Las Vegas," as a reverse indicator of E5: Excitement-seeking, may have to be amended to better fit a local culture, when one would consider using the NEO-PI-R in, let us say, Iran. Finally, different levels of measurement equivalence or measurement invariance will have to be demonstrated (Vandenberg & Lance, 2000). In line with the CFA framework, weak factorial or configural invariance is demonstrated when the same number of latent constructs and the same pattern of salient and nonsalient factor loadings is presented across (cultural) groups. Metric invariance (strong factorial invariance) can be concluded when factor loadings (slopes) can be constrained to be equal across cultures without significant loss of model fit (Church, 2010). Finally, scalar invariance can be demonstrated when the item intercepts are also equal across cultural groups.

Steenkamp and Baumgartner (1998) have argued that mean scores of (cultural) groups are only meaningfully comparable when configural, metric, and scalar invariances have been established, showing that the factorial structure (configural), the scale intervals (metric), and the zero point of the scale are the same across different groups. Scalar equivalence is about the meaning of scores for different groups (Van de Vijver & Leung, 1997a); in other words: Does a particular raw score indicate the same level of a trait in different groups and have the same interpretation in all cultures? If scalar equivalence is demonstrated, then we can derive meaningful conclusions from such comparisons. The demonstration of some form of scalar equivalence is hence a prerequisite for making comparisons among any groups (McCrae & Terracciano, 2008).

The determination of scalar equivalence is hotly debated among cross-cultural personality researchers (McCrae & Terracciano, 2005a). A main group of cross-cultural psychologists uses multigroup CFAs (MCFAs) to examine scalar equivalence, although the requirements for CFA are very stringent. Alternatively, Item-Response Theory (IRT)-based methods to examine DIF can be used to establish scalar equivalence (Reise & Henson, 2003), but large sample sizes are required and analyses become more complex when items with Likert scales have to be analyzed.

Adopting these methods for comparing sets of personality-descriptive items across cultures shows that many items have DIF, but also that DIF forwards to the facet level, and does not cancel out across multiple items compiling a facet (Church et al., 2011). A second way to demonstrate scalar equivalence is through the use of bilingual retest studies, in which bilingual respondents administer a personality inventory twice. Under the condition of equivalence, means for the two language versions of the inventory should be equal (McCrae & Terracciano, 2005b). The MCFA approach is further criticized because it generally assumes that the indicators of a trait are interchangeable, and this is usually not the case.

McCrae and Terracciano (2005a, 2008) proposed a different route to demonstrate scalar equivalence and argue that scalar equivalence is not an absolute property, but a matter of degree for which a pattern of evidence should be demonstrated, preferably via several of the previously suggested methods, because all have their specific drawbacks. Instead, they suggest a top–down approach where the group means are considered as scale scores, and their construct validity is investigated. A potential difficulty here is that one needs data from a large number of cultures and appropriate criteria at the culture level. McCrae and Terracciano (2008) argue that if one is able to pinpoint a nomological network of convergent and discriminant validity for a culture-level construct, the mean scores must have some degree of scalar equivalence (see further in this chapter).

Self-Reports Versus Multi-Informant Ratings

Although observer ratings have been used frequently in personality research (Hofstee, 1994), this source of assessment input has been underresearched and underutilized in IO psychology (Connelly & Ones, 2010; see Chapter 20, this volume). There are two reasons to assume that reports by knowledgeable others (peers, supervisors, or subordinates) will be used progressively more, that is, evidence for increased validity above and beyond self-descriptions and the expanding use of 180° or 360° feedback in the course of career development and coaching trajectories.

Barrick, Mount, and Strauss (1993) were among the first to report in the international literature that observer ratings of the FFM had validities to predict work performance that were almost twice the validities of self-ratings in sales people. Similar findings were reported by Oh and Berry (2009) using 360° ratings of managerial performance. Operational validities for supervisor ratings predicting task and contextual performance were significant for four of the FFM dimensions, except for agreeableness, and generally increased when combined with peer and subordinate ratings. When further complemented with self-ratings, the operational validities ranged from .23 (agreeableness) to .45 (openness to experience) for task performance and from .37 (openness to experience) to .50 (extraversion) for contextual performance. The adjusted multiple *R*s for the FFM dimensions rated by all raters were .53 and .58 for managerial task and contextual performance, respectively. These findings suggest that the inclusion of observer ratings increases validity coefficients and that this increase is also a function of the different rater perspectives. In comparison with studies relying on self-ratings, the other FFM dimensions also show up as significant dimensions explaining facets of work performance. Oh, Wang, and Mount (2010) meta-analytically summarized validity coefficients available in 16 studies reporting on 20 independent samples, with observer personality ratings and work performance criteria rated by different sources. For all FFM dimensions, including openness to experience, validities for observer ratings were higher than for self-ratings and increased with the number of raters available. The meta-analytic work by Connelly and Ones (2010, Table 11) shows convergent results and also pleas to involve multiple raters to improve reliability and validity.

Despite evidence that observer ratings have incremental validity beyond self-descriptions and that validity of the assessments increases with the number of observers, it is not clear whether subordinate or 180° ratings are easy to obtain in all cultures. This is a highly underresearched area in IO psychology. One can assume, for example, that in cultures characterized by large power distance, inviting employees to rate the attributes of their supervisor may be perceived as odd, whereas in more collectivistic cultures, peers may have difficulty perceiving a target as an independent self, describing the target's personality more in terms of fulfilling (work) roles and relationships with significant others in the in-group (Heine, 2001). Such cultural attributes may have a profound impact on the personality descriptions and induce different forms of administration, construct, and rating bias when working with observer ratings.

Impression Management Tendencies and Culture

In general, personality psychologists agree that candidates will put their best feet forward in selection assessments affecting the means of personality scales. To demonstrate this phenomenon, De Fruyt, De Clercq, et al. (2009) argue for taking the assessment context into account and comparing an individual's score relative to others' scores obtained under similar assessment conditions. For IO applications, the implication is that test developers will have to provide different norm sets obtained in low-, mild-, or high-stakes assessment contexts (for more coverage on faking personality tests, see Chapter 12, this volume). Personnel coaching and development programs are usually considered in Western societies as mild at-stake situations, whereas selection assessment is usually conceived as a high-stakes situation, although it remains an empirical question whether these conditions are perceived likewise across the globe. Anyway, for within-culture comparisons, locally built norms are necessary, and there should be convergence between the context of application and the context in which the normative data have been collected.

There is further evidence that cultures differ in terms of motivation for self-enhancement. A recent meta-analysis across 91 cross-cultural comparisons by Heine and Hamamura (2007) showed an average effect size of .84 in self-enhancement between Western and East Asian samples. These differences can be partly explained due to the different cost–benefit ratio for self-enhancement for North Americans versus East Asians. Self-enhancement contributes to self-esteem and generates positive feelings among North Americans, but negatively impacts East Asians, threatening their within-group integration and relationships (Heine & Buchtel, 2009). There is further evidence that East Asians hold more dialectical views about themselves, including positive and negative views, whereas North Americans underscore the positive views. Whether these self-enhancing tendencies also differentially operate in selection contexts is unclear.

Mean-Level Personality Differences Across Cultures

Aggregate Personality Ratings and Geographical Patterns

There is a long tradition of speculation about a geographical distribution of personality traits; in other words: "where one lives reveals what one is like" (Allik & McCrae, 2004, p. 13), although there are hardly any empirical studies comparing personality ratings across multiple cultures. The main reason is that several requirements (see previously in this chapter) must be fulfilled before mean trait ratings can be meaningfully compared. Although personality traits have been mainly studied at the level of individuals, the past years have witnessed a growing attention for aggregate ratings of personality, that is, a mean computed for a trait across a sample of individuals living in a particular culture that is subsequently used as a variable characterizing that cultural group. The level of analysis hence shifts from the individual to the culture level. If such differences across cultures can be replicable, systematic, and valid, then such aggregate ratings may be of considerable value for IO psychological applications. Assume, for example, that there would be systematic differences across cultures in terms of aggregate ratings of conscientiousness; one could examine whether such differences are associated with culture-level variables such as gross domestic product, wealth, productivity, or absenteeism data.

Likewise, the demonstration of meaningful average personality differences among U.S. states would necessitate the compilation of specific norms per region.

Primary evidence for the existence of regional personality differences in the United States has been provided already some decades ago by Krug and Kulhavy (1973) using Cattell's Sixteen Personality Factor Questionnaire (Cattell, Eber, & Tatsuoka, 1970) and more recently by Plaut, Markus, and Lachman (2002) using a measure of the Big Five. Corroborating this research line, Rentfrow, Gosling, and Potter (2008) examined regional personality differences in scores on the Big Five Inventory (John & Srivastava, 1999) in an impressive sample of near to 620,000 Internet respondents. A comparative analysis across these three studies shows that aggregate trait levels are to a considerable extent consistent across different geographical locations for neuroticism and openness to experience and somewhat consistent for extraversion and agreeableness, despite differences in sampling, measures, and a time frame of 30 years (Rentfrow, 2010). No consistent patterns for conscientiousness were observed. Moreover, regional personality differences were associated with important culture-level variables, including social connectedness (social capital), political orientation, and health. For example, state-level agreeableness was correlated .35 ($p < .05$), conscientiousness −.44 ($p < .05$), and state-level neuroticism −.52 ($p < .05$) with social capital, and people living in left-leaning states were higher in openness and lower in conscientiousness relative to right-leaning civilians (Rentfrow, 2010; Rentfrow et al., 2008).

Taking a cross-cultural angle, Allik and McCrae (2004) analyzed NEO-PI-R self-reports from 27,965 college students and adult men and women from 36 different cultures. Allik and McCrae (2004) considered means comparable because scalar equivalence was roughly demonstrated through a set of bilingual studies showing similar personality profiles across translations, together with evidence for the construct validity of within-culture aggregate personality ratings (see further in this chapter). They found that standard deviations for the 30 NEO-PI-R facets were systematically larger among European cultures than among Asian and Black African cultures. Multidimensional scaling showed personality traits to be geographically distributed, with neighboring countries exhibiting more similar personality profiles. A multidimensional scaling plot of 36 cultures, rotated toward a horizontal dimension positively associated with extraversion and openness and negatively with agreeableness, and a vertical axis associated with neuroticism and low conscientiousness, showed a clear separation between European and American cultures on the right, and Asian and African cultures on the left. The United States and Canada were located near the bottom on the right of the plot, together with the Baltic and the Scandinavian countries. Although geographical proximity grouping was not perfect, it was certainly not random. A similar analysis on data collected with observer ratings in the course of PPOC (McCrae & Terracciano, 2005a), followed by a rotation to maximize associations with extraversion (horizontal axis) and neuroticism (vertical axis), again showed a plot of cultures that were historically and ethnically related. Summarizing the patterns across these two studies, the first relying on self-reports and the second on observer ratings, shows that Europeans and Americans are higher in extraversion and somewhat higher in openness compared to Asians and Africans.

In addition to comparing means across cultures, one can also factor analyze aggregate personality ratings from multiple cultures, also called ecological factor analysis (EFA). McCrae and Terracciano (2005a) adopted EFA on aggregated personality ratings of individuals from 51 cultures and showed that four factors of the FFM, neuroticism, openness, agreeableness, and conscientiousness, replicated the individual-level structure, with extraversion showing close approximation, loaded by five extraversion facets and some other facets that did not load the individual-level extraversion factor. They concluded that the FFM is not only applicable at the individual level, but also that there is a culture-level FFM, with a specific culture-level extraversion factor that is somewhat different from the individual-level dimension.

Finally, Stankov (2011) used hierarchical linear modeling (HLM) to examine individual, country, and societal cluster differences on Big Five personality traits, attitudes, values, and social norms in a sample of 2,029 students from across the globe. Instead of computing an average per culture, HLM enables one to decompose observed variance across different nested levels. Individuals were nested under 45 countries (level 2), and these were nested in nine societal clusters (level 3) culled from GLOBE. Both personality traits (7.41% of the variance) and values (7.48%) were only slightly affected by country and societal cluster differences, and variance was mainly explained at the level of the individual, ranging from 87.23% for openness to 95.77% for agreeableness. Social norms were assessed with the nine GLOBE dimensions. Also their variance was to a large extent explained at the level of the individual (average of 84.07%), with 5.97% and 9.95% accounted for by the country and societal cluster level, respectively. The results reported by Stankov (2011) suggest that cultural influences on Big Five personality trait scores are limited, although results should be interpreted with caution because sample size is limited, especially at levels 2 and 3 of the analysis.

Do Aggregate Ratings Predict Something Meaningful?

In the course of the PPOC-project, McCrae et al. (2005a) correlated aggregate personality observer ratings obtained with the NEO-PI-R (Costa & McCrae, 1992) with culture-level variables. Aggregate personality ratings turned out to be replicable within cultures and showed meaningful associations with Hofstede's dimensions, values (Inglehart & Norris, 2003; Schwartz, 1994), well-being, gross domestic product, and the human development index. Several of these associations were replicated in APPOC (McCrae et al., 2009). Aggregate observer means converged with aggregate self-reports for the domains of neuroticism, extraversion, and openness to experience, but not for agreeableness and conscientiousness, although significant convergent associations were found for four agreeableness and four conscientiousness facets.

The validity of aggregate traits and the nature of the previously described significant associations with culture-level criteria have been the subject of intense debate (for a discussion on culture-level criteria associations with conscientiousness, see Heine, Buchtel, & Norenzayan, 2008). As a reply, Mõttus, Allik, and Realo (2010) examined associations between self-reports on conscientiousness facets and a broad range of culture-level criteria across 42 cultures, including the 36 cultures from McCrae (2002), expanded with 3 African cultures, Lithuania, Poland, and Finland. The associations with the observer ratings reported in PPOC (McCrae & Terracciano, 2005a) were also examined. They provided clear a priori hypotheses about the expected relationships, examined associations at the facet instead of the domain level, and used a range of criteria (e.g., atheism, smoking, democracy, obesity, alcohol consumption, and gross domestic product) that were really representative of the culture and its population. Without correcting for gross domestic product, 29% of the correlations were significant at $p < .01$. Controlling for national wealth reduced the number of significant correlations by almost half. Confirmation of hypotheses was different across the six conscientiousness facets and self- versus observer ratings.

National Character Ratings

National character ratings are a different type of culture-bound personality rating, that is, descriptions of the personality of a typical individual representing a national or a cultural group. Such descriptions can be auto or hetero stereotypes with the first reflecting ratings provided by in-group members, whereas hetero stereotypes are provided by people of a different culture. These national character ratings are subsequently compared to observed descriptions of in-group members to examine whether such ratings have validity or are just stereotypes in the eye of the beholder without a kernel of truth.

Terracciano et al. (2005) examined the correspondence between national character ratings on a measure of the FFM and APPOC observer ratings on the NEO-PI-R (McCrae & Terracciano,

2005a) across 49 cultures. There was no correspondence between the two sets of ratings. For example, Indonesia, Nigeria, Turkey, Poland, and Japan obtained the highest national character scores for neuroticism, though the observed means (expressed in T-scores) on the NEO-PI-R for neuroticism for these countries ranged from 47.8 (Nigeria) to 51.4 (Turkey). The authors concluded that national character ratings appeared to reflect unfounded stereotypes.

The inaccuracy of geographical personality stereotypes has been further confirmed in studies by McCrae, Terracciano, Realo, and Allik (2007) with Northern and Southern Italians and by Realo et al. (2009) comparing Russian self-reported averages with perceptions by civilians of neighboring countries. Rogers and Wood (2010), however, did find that Americans' geographical personality stereotypes for openness to experience and neuroticism showed considerable accuracy when compared with the results reported by Rentfrow et al. (2008), with above-chance accuracy for agreeableness and extraversion. They further show what regional indicators might contribute to accuracy such as population density and political voting patterns. Rogers and Wood (2010) conclude their work by saying that geographical personality stereotypes may have some accuracy under certain conditions.

Does "Big Five" Also Reflect Universal Importance and Validity?

Although there is considerable support for the factors that are minimally necessary to structure personality traits and help define their nomological net, this evidence does not imply that personality traits as concepts are perceived equally important in all cultures (Heine & Buchtel, 2009), and all Big Five dimensions are equally important for understanding personality at work across cultures.

People from different cultures do not equally weigh personality information. There is evidence that people from more collectivistic societies rely more on situational factors and are less inclined to use personality information than people from individualistic cultures to explain differences in behavior (Heine & Buchtel, 2009; Morris & Peng, 1994). Although the factor structure of traits seems to be roughly replicable across cultures, this does not imply that all Big Five dimensions are equally important within each single culture. For example, within Western-industrialized and individualistic societies, getting-ahead traits such as extraversion and conscientiousness may be considered more important, whereas in more collectivistic cultures, more communal and getting-along traits like agreeableness may be valued more. Likewise, it can be hypothesized that more interpersonal traits such as extraversion and agreeableness will be esteemed differently as a function of the power distance level of a culture. These examples clearly show that replicability of factor structure across cultures and importance of factors within specific cultures are two different questions, and actually, there is a dearth of studies examining the importance of the Big Five dimensions across cultures. Moreover, the significance of Big Five dimensions within a particular culture may change over time. For example, Western-industrialized countries in which traits like extraversion and conscientiousness were considered important dimensions for adaptation and functioning may notice a shift toward increased importance of openness to experience-related traits such as innovation, creativity, and self-reflection. Finally, the importance of personality traits relative to other individual differences such as intelligence, attitudes, skills, and values may change across time in a rapidly transforming world economy. The current meta-analyses on predictor–criterion validities summarize validity coefficients reported in individual studies published across a broad time period, often decades ago. Given the largely changing economies of the past 20 years, it might be interesting to examine cohort differences in validity coefficients.

Validity generalization is a crucial issue for IO applications and practices that are similarly applied in different cultures. The majority of the meta-analyses on the predictive validity of trait measures relied on individual studies conducted with Westerners (Barrick & Mount, 1991; Connelly & Ones, 2010; J. Hogan & Holland, 2003; Oh et al., 2010; Salgado, 1997). As far as we know, there is no meta-analytic evidence that validities of personality measures generalize to non-Western cultures. Such confirmation is not only absent for the FFM, but is also deficient for indigenous traits. For example, it would be interesting to examine whether traits resulting from indigenous personality research in China (Cheung et al., 1996), such as "interpersonal relatedness," predict aspects of job performance, such as contextual performance, better than the FFM. At the level of the FFM, it would be interesting to investigate whether the same traits predict similar criteria across cultures, and whether the magnitude of these predictive validities is moderated by cultural characteristics. For example, Heine and Buchtel (2009) recently suggested that personality may be less predictive of behavior in collectivistic cultures, due to the presumed larger impact of norms, prescribed roles, and pressure from the social network on the person's behavior.

Tett and Burnett's (2003, p. 503, Figure 1) trait-based interactionist model of job performance can be used to better understand how culture may impact the validity of traits to predict work behavior and job performance. They distinguish work behavior from job performance, because the latter involves an evaluation within a specific context that may be valued differently across cultures. Work behavior may lead to intrinsic rewards for the individual, due to the possibility of expressing his/her personality, whereas job performance leads to extrinsic rewards such as salary, feedback, and recognition from others.

Tett and Burnett's (2003) trait-activation theory further distinguishes moderators of the trait–work behavior relationship at the task, social, and organizational levels (for more coverage of trait-activation potential, see Chapter 5, this volume). For example, orderliness as a trait may be positively related to job performance for accounting tasks (task level) in a team valuing precision and punctuality (social level) and in a detail and outcome-oriented company (organization level), but fail to predict performance in task, social, and organizational environments with a different focus. Moreover, personality expression may be further affected by job demands (tasks and duties inherent in the job), distractors (factors interfering with performance), constraints (factors restricting the manifestation of the trait), releasers (factors counteracting a constraint), and facilitators (factors making triggers more salient that are already in the situation). An accounting job includes many tasks demanding orderliness, as too much small talk with colleagues during working hours may distract from the primary tasks; the increased use of information technology may constrain the impact of personality, whereas an unforeseen bug in a program may counteract such constraint, making individual differences again more salient. Finally, dealing with a file of a highly valued customer may act as a facilitator for precision and attention to detail.

Reviewing this model, it is clear that culture may impact upon the task, social, and organizational moderators affecting the personality trait–work behavior relationship. Moreover, culture will also affect the evaluation of work behavior and the extrinsic rewards associated with good work performance. For example, in societies with many strong norms and low tolerance of deviant behavior, the so-called tight cultures, versus loose cultures with weak social norms and higher tolerance of deviant behavior (Gelfand et al., 2011), one can expect that bad performance leads to lower extrinsic rewards and negative feedback. This tendency may be strengthened in individualistic societies, holding persons more accountable for their individual contribution and strivings. In addition, it may be expected that tight (Gelfand et al., 2011) and high uncertainty avoidant and more feminine cultures (Hofstede, 2001) will put more constraints on the expression of individual differences, hence impacting the strength of the trait–work behavior relationship that can be observed.

Finally, validity generalization studies often and correctly pay a lot of attention to the predictor side of the equation. However, one should be also thoughtful about the nature and construct validity of the criteria that one wants to predict. Job performance indicators may be perceived very differently across the globe. For example, "waiter service" in a restaurant is defined and perceived very differently across cultures due to divergence in the way labor is organized and multiple cultural expectations. What is considered as good performance in most restaurants in the United States (speed of service, removing plates as soon as one person around the table has finished her/his meal, asking whether the meal is good and fits your expectations multiple times in a time frame of 20 min) leads to dismissal in Western Europe where eating is considered as a social event requiring time to enjoy the food and company, and where you make a reservation for a table for the entire evening. In the United States, people line up until a table is free and multiple shifts of service have to be completed at a single table on an evening. This cultural difference is also reflected at the financial level: In many U.S. restaurants, you are financially punished when one has to serve more than five people at a table, whereas you may have a discount in Western Europe. This example well illustrates how (job) performance criteria may be perceived very differently across cultures.

Knowledge Gaps and Perennial Issues

The previous review has made clear that considerable progress has been made in the past 20 years with respect to cross-cultural personality assessment, though it is also obvious that these developments emerge at a slow pace and most often follow rather than precede calls and questions emerging from the applied field of personality assessment. Four major challenges can be identified requiring immediate attention.

Indigenous Versus Universal Traits

It is clear that a common set of traits, integrated within the FFM, can be used to denote personality differences across the globe, but it remains to be investigated whether indigenous traits predict variance in IO criteria above and beyond the more universal traits. Despite the universality of this trait taxonomy, we know almost nothing about the importance within particular cultures of the major factors enclosed in the FFM. A similar problem arises with respect to validity generalization. Most validation studies have been conducted with Westerners, but validities remain to be demonstrated in, for example, African and South American cultures. For IO applications, comprehensiveness of trait taxonomies will be less important, though inventories will have to include those traits that are most useful for predicting IO criteria. Studies examining the moderating role of culture on personality–criterion relationships could be conducted along Tett and Burnett's (2003) trait-based interactionist model of job performance described previously, distinguishing the major variables affecting this relationship.

General Versus Work-Related Personality Inventories

Legislation within several countries and recent research recommends the use of work-related over general personality inventories for IO applications. The addition of a "work" frame-of-reference to instructions and/or items (Lievens et al., 2008) and complementing self-descriptions of personality with, preferably multiple, observer ratings (Connelly & Ones, 2010; Oh et al., 2010) enhances reliability and validity of the assessments in Western cultures. The adoption of work-related personality inventories, including items referring to observable work behavior, will facilitate the involvement of multiple raters such as subordinates, direct colleagues, or supervisors. It remains to be examined, however, under what circumstances such observer ratings add validity, and whether societal and organizational cultures moderate such relationships. In addition, scalar invariance will have to be demonstrated within cultures, before self- and observer ratings can be meaningfully compared and integrated.

Heterogeneity Within Cultures

Although migration and various forms of intercultural transmission have been universal phenomena throughout history, the way in which cultural differences are perceived and have to be handled in societies has dramatically changed in the recent past. Whereas immigrants were previously assumed to adapt and assimilate as quickly and profoundly as possible to the language, habits, and culture of the receiving society, Western societies nowadays consider diversity and a plethora of cultural backgrounds as a strength that should be taken into account, respected, and sometimes preserved. As a result, societies have definitely become more heterogeneous in terms of the cultural backgrounds of their members. In addition, individuals within a particular society may belong to different (cultural) groups at the same time or cultural boundaries may have become permeable and fuzzy. For example, children from Moroccan immigrants born in Germany may share characteristics with the host German culture, but will also resemble features and values from their Moroccan roots. Moreover, people within a culture may be members of multiple groups at the same time, that is, reflecting a different cultural heritage and background, SES (raised in a low-SES family and via upward mobility moved to a higher class, or the other way around), and gender. These different group attributes will interact, and personality inventory developers and assessment practitioners will have to face this complex reality. Practitioners and researchers will have to disentangle, for example, whether poor psychometric problems observed in a heterogeneous group within a single society are attributable to problems with understanding particular items (due to insufficient language command of the visiting culture's native language) or reflect measurement inequivalence.

Differences Between Cultures and the Feasibility of Multicultural Norms

Several studies were reviewed in this chapter suggesting that personality traits show a geographical distribution within the United States (Rentfrow, 2010) and across the globe (McCrae & Terracciano, 2005a; Stankov, 2011). There are diverging opinions, however, with respect to the comparability of such means, requiring the demonstration of some form or a degree of scalar equivalence. The heterogeneity of cultural backgrounds represented within societies and the fact that individuals often belong to multiple groups (e.g., age, gender, and an ethnic minority group) at the same time introduces very complex "equivalence" questions to be dealt with. Given the increasing cultural diversity of the workforce, the global economy, and contacts with customers from a broad range of cultures, it is to be expected that the importance of personality traits will increase and it is not an understatement to conclude that we are just at the beginning of a flourishing field of research and consulting. The challenge for academia and research will be to take the lead in this debate and provide the applied field with recommendations and workable suggestions.

Practitioner's Window

Given the increasing multiculturalism within individual societies and the steadily growing number of contacts across nations in the global economy, human resource practitioners will be faced more and more with questions on culture's consequences for the description and comparison of personality. The previous overview has made a number of points clear that may help the practitioner when facing these questions.

(a) The trait structure represented by the FFM is valid for describing general personality traits across different cultures. More indigenous dimensions may supplement this description. Major age trends for the FFM traits are largely culturally universal, and gender differences seem to be more pronounced and generalizable in Western cultures.
(b) There are a series of FFM or Big Five inventories available in different languages (academic and commercial), although these are not substitutes for each other and cannot be used interchangeably. For comparative purposes, practitioners should use the same Big Five/FFM inventory across

cultures, examining whether these translations/adaptations meet (part of) the requirements for making such comparisons.

(c) There are no compelling data on the importance of FFM traits across cultures. For example, extraversion may be considered more important in individualistic societies, whereas agreeableness may be valued more in feminine-oriented cultures.

(d) In addition to culture, one should also take into account the assessment context. There is massive evidence that the assessment context (low- versus medium- or high-stakes) impacts the personality scores within Western cultures, necessitating specific norms obtained in similar assessment contexts to make meaningful comparisons.

(e) It is inconclusive whether self-enhancement/impression management strategies are used differently across cultures and across contexts within these cultures.

(f) Cultures do not differ dramatically in terms of mean-level personality scores. Differences between varying at-stake contexts have probably a larger impact on the distribution of personality scores than differences between cultures.

(g) Individuals' personality descriptions should be preferable compared against normative distributions obtained from individuals from the same cultural background administered the inventory in the same (low-, medium-, or high-stakes) assessment context. In the absence of such norms, preference should be given to norms taking into account the assessment context, given the smaller magnitude of differences between cultures.

(h) For multicultural selection, such as in the case of ex-patriots, it is also recommended to compare individuals' scores to the normative distributions obtained in the host culture (as a supplement to point g). Likewise, for the selection of applicants from diverse cultural backgrounds who have to work together, it is recommended to assemble a cross-cultural normative set, representing the different cultural groups.

(i) There are not enough studies in non-Western cultures to conclude that the validity of personality traits to predict various forms of work behavior and performance is universal in nature and strength. Tett and Burnett's (2003) trait-based interactionist model of job performance provides a valuable framework for understanding how culture may moderate this relationship.

(j) In addition to paying attention to the predictor side of the equation, that is, personality traits, practitioners should also carefully analyze the nature of the criterion. As specified in Tett and Burnett's (2003) model, not all work behaviors are valued equally across cultures.

(k) There is an increased use of contextualized and maladaptive personality measures, in addition to general traits. Also the use of observer ratings in addition to self-ratings is highly encouraged. Whether these new assessment practices are generalizable across cultures remains an open question.

(l) Finally, aggregate personality ratings make sense and are replicable, although do not correspond to national character stereotypes. Practitioners should hence be very cautious relying on stereotypes of cultural groups.

References

Allik, J., & McCrae, R. R. (2004). Toward a geography of personality traits—Patterns of profiles across 36 cultures. *Journal of Cross-Cultural Psychology, 35*, 13–28.

American Psychiatric Association. (2000). *Diagnostic and statistical manual of mental disorders* (4th ed., text rev.). Washington, DC: Author.

Ashton, M. C., Lee, K., Perugini, M., Szarota, P., de Vries, R. E., Di Blas, L., & De Raad, B. (2004). A six-factor structure of personality-descriptive adjectives: Solutions from psycholexical studies in seven languages. *Journal of Personality and Social Psychology, 86*, 356–366.

Ashton, M. C., Lee, K., & Son, C. (2000). Honesty as the sixth factor of personality: Correlations with Machiavellianism, primary psychopathy, and social adroitness. *European Journal of Personality, 14*, 359–368.

Barrick, M. R., & Mount, M. K. (1991). The Big Five personality dimensions and job-performance—A meta-analysis. *Personnel Psychology, 44*, 1–26.

Barrick, M. R., Mount, M. K., & Strauss, J. P. (1993). Conscientiousness and performance of sales representatives—Test of the mediating effects of goal-setting. *Journal of Applied Psychology, 78*, 715–722.

Bem, S. L. (1974). The measurement of psychological androgyny. *Journal of Consulting and Clinical Psychology, 42*, 115–162.

Benet-Martinez, V., & John, O. P. (1998). Los Cinco Grandes across cultures and ethnic groups: Multitrait multi-method analyses of the Big Five in Spanish and English. *Journal of Personality and Social Psychology, 75*, 729–750.

Bono, J. E., & Judge, T. A. (2004). Personality and transformational and transactional leadership: A meta-analysis. *Journal of Applied Psychology, 89*, 901–910.

Butcher, J. N., & Williams, C. L. (2000). *Essentials of MMPI-2 and MMPI-A interpretation* (2nd ed.). Minneapolis: University of Minnesota Press.

Cattell, R. B., Eber, H. W., & Tatsuoka, M. M. (1970). *Handbook for the Sixteen Personality Factor Questionnaire (16PF)*. Champaign, IL: Institute for Personality and Ability Testing.

Chao, G. T., & Moon, H. (2005). The cultural mosaic: A metatheory for understanding the complexity of culture. *Journal of Applied Psychology, 90*, 1128–1140.

Cheung, F. M., & Leung, K. (1998). Indigenous personality measures: Chinese examples. *Journal of Cross-Cultural Psychology, 29*, 233–248.

Cheung, F. M., Leung, K., Fan, R. M., Song, W., Zhang, J.-X., & Zhang, J.-P. (1996). Development of the Chinese Personality Assessment Inventory. *Journal of Cross-Cultural Psychology, 27*, 181–199.

Chinese Culture Connection. (1987). Chinese values and the search for culture-free dimensions of culture. *Journal of Cross-Cultural Psychology, 18*, 143–174.

Chokhar, J. S., Brodbeck, F. C., & House, R. J. (2007). *Culture and leadership across the world: The GLOBE book of in-depth studies of 25 societies*. Mahwah, NJ: Lawrence Erlbaum.

Church, A. T. (2010). Measurement issues in cross-cultural research. In G. Walford, E. Tucker, & M. Viswanathan (Eds.), *The Sage handbook of measurement* (pp. 151–177). Los Angeles: Sage.

Church, A. T., Alvarez, J. M., Mai, N. T. Q., French, B. F., Katigbak, M. S., & Ortiz, F. A. (2011). Are cross-cultural comparisons of personality profiles meaningful? Differential item and facet functioning in the revised NEO Personality Inventory. *Journal of Personality and Social Psychology, 101*, 1068–1089.

Connelly, B. S., & Ones, D. S. (2010). An other perspective on personality: Meta-analytic integration of observers' accuracy and predictive validity. *Psychological Bulletin, 136*, 1092–1122.

Costa, P. T., & McCrae, R. R. (1992). *Revised NEO Personality Inventory and Five-Factor Inventory professional manual*. Odessa, FL: Psychological Assessment Resources.

Costa, P. T., McCrae, R. R., & Martin, T. A. (2008). Incipient adult personality: The NEO-PI-3 in middle-school-aged children. *British Journal of Developmental Psychology, 26*, 71–89.

Costa, P. T., Terracciano, A., & McCrae, R. R. (2001). Gender differences in personality traits across cultures: Robust and surprising findings. *Journal of Personality and Social Psychology, 81*, 322–331.

Costa, P. T., & Widiger, T. A. (2002). *Personality disorders and the five-factor model of personality* (2nd ed.). Washington, DC: American Psychological Association.

De Fruyt, F., Aluja, A., Garcia, L. F., Rolland, J. P., & Jung, S. C. (2006). Positive presentation management and intelligence and the personality differentiation by intelligence hypothesis in job applicants. *International Journal of Selection and Assessment, 14*, 101–112.

De Fruyt, F., De Bolle, M., McCrae, R. R., Terracciano, A., & Costa, P. T. (2009). Assessing the universal structure of personality in early adolescence: The NEO-PI-R and NEO-PI-3 in 24 cultures. *Assessment, 16*, 301–311.

De Fruyt, F., De Clercq, B. J., Miller, J., Rolland, J. P., Jung, S. C., Taris, R., & Van Hiel, A. (2009). Assessing personality at risk in personnel selection and development. *European Journal of Personality, 23*, 51–69.

De Fruyt, F., Mervielde, I., Hoekstra, H. A., & Rolland, J. P. (2000). Assessing adolescents' personality with the NEO-PI-R. *Assessment, 7*, 329–345.

De Fruyt, F., & Salgado, J. F. (2003). Editorial: Personality and IWO applications: Introducing personality at work. *European Journal of Personality, 17*, S1–S3.

De Raad, B., Barelds, D. P. H., Levert, E., Ostendorf, F., Mlacic, B., Di Blas, L., . . . Katigbak, M. S. (2010). Only three factors of personality description are fully replicable across languages: A comparison of 14 trait taxonomies. *Journal of Personality and Social Psychology, 98*, 160–173.

Eysenck, H. J., & Eysenck, S. B. G. (1975). *The Eysenck Personality Questionnaire*. Sevenoaks, UK: Hodder & Stoughton.

Feingold, A. (1994). Gender differences in personality—A meta-analysis. *Psychological Bulletin, 116*, 429–456.
Furnham, A. (2008). HR professionals' beliefs about, and knowledge of, assessment techniques and psychometric tests. *International Journal of Selection and Assessment, 16*, 300–305.
Gelfand, M. J., Raver, J. L., Nishii, L., Leslie, L. M., Lun, J., Lim, B. C., & Yamaguchi, S. (2011). Differences between tight and loose cultures: A 33-nation study. *Science, 332*, 1100–1104.
Goldberg, L. R. (1982). From Ace to Zombie: Some explorations in the language of personality. In C. D. Spielberger & J. D. Butcher (Eds.), *Advances in personality assessment* (*Vol. 1*, pp. 203–234). Hillsdale, NJ: Erlbaum.
Goldberg, L. R., Johnson, J. A., Eber, H. W., Hogan, R., Ashton, M. C., Cloninger, C. R., & Gough, H. G. (2006). The international personality item pool and the future of public-domain personality measures. *Journal of Research in Personality, 40*, 84–96.
Gupta, V., Hanges, P. J., & Dorfman, P. (2002). Cultural clusters: Methodology and findings. *Journal of World Business, 37*, 11–15.
Heine, S. J. (2001). Self as a cultural product: An examination of East Asian and North American selves. *Journal of Personality, 69*, 881–906.
Heine, S. J., & Buchtel, E. E. (2009). Personality: The universal and the culturally specific. *Annual Review of Psychology, 60*, 369–394.
Heine, S. J., Buchtel, E. E., & Norenzayan, A. (2008). What do cross-national comparisons of personality traits tell us? The case of conscientiousness. *Psychological Science, 19*, 309–313.
Heine, S. J., & Hamamura, T. (2007). In search of East Asian self-enhancement. *Personality and Social Psychology Review, 11*, 4–27.
Hofstede, G. (1980). *Culture's consequences: International differences in work-related values*. Beverly Hills, CA: Sage.
Hofstede, G. (2001). *Culture's consequences: Comparing values, behaviors, institutions, and organizations across nations* (2nd ed.). Thousand Oaks, CA: Sage.
Hofstede, G. (2006). What did GLOBE really measure? Researchers' minds versus respondents' minds. *Journal of International Business Studies, 37*, 882–896.
Hofstede, G. (2010). The GLOBE debate: Back to relevance. *Journal of International Business Studies, 41*, 1339–1346.
Hofstee, W. K. B. (1994). Who should own the definition of personality? *European Journal of Personality, 8*, 149–162.
Hogan, J., & Holland, B. (2003). Using theory to evaluate personality and job-performance relations: A socio-analytic perspective. *Journal of Applied Psychology, 88*, 100–112.
Hogan, R., Hogan, J., & Roberts, B. W. (1996). Personality measurement and employment decisions—Questions and answers. *American Psychologist, 51*, 469–477.
House, R., Javidan, M., Hanges, P., & Dorfman, P. (2002). Understanding cultures and implicit leadership theories across the globe: An introduction to Project GLOBE. *Journal of World Business, 37*, 3–10.
House, R. J., Hanges, P. J., Javidan, M., Dorfman, P. W., & Gupta, V. (2004). *Culture, leadership, and organization: The GLOBE study of 62 societies*. Thousand Oaks, CA: Sage.
House, R. J., & Javidan, M. (2004). Overview of GLOBE. In R. J. House, P. J. Hanges, M. Javidan, P. W. Dorfman, & V. Gupta (Eds.), *Culture, leadership, and organizations: The GLOBE study of 62 societies* (pp. 9–26). Thousand Oaks, CA: Sage.
House, R. J., Quigley, N. R., & de Luque, M. S. (2010). Insights from Project GLOBE: Extending global advertising research through a contemporary framework. *International Journal of Advertising, 29*, 111–139.
Inglehart, R., & Norris, P. (2003). *Rising tide: Gender equality and cultural change around the world*. New York: Cambridge University Press.
Javidan, M., House, R. J., Dorfman, P. W., Hanges, P. J., & de Luque, M. S. (2006). Conceptualizing and measuring cultures and their consequences: A comparative review of GLOBE's and Hofstede's approaches. *Journal of International Business Studies, 37*, 897–914.
John, O. P., & Srivastava, S. (1999). The Big Five trait taxonomy: History, measurement, and theoretical perspectives. In L. A. Pervin & O. P. John (Eds.), *Handbook of personality: Theory and research* (2nd ed., pp. 102–139). New York: Guilford Press.
Kabasakal, H., & Bodur, M. (2002). Arabic cluster: A bridge between East and West. *Journal of World Business, 37*, 40–54.
Katigbak, M. S., Church, A. T., Guanzon-Lapena, M. A., Carlota, A. J., & del Pilar, G. H. (2002). Are indigenous personality dimensions culture specific? Philippine inventories and the five-factor model. *Journal of Personality and Social Psychology, 82*, 89–101.
Krug, S. E., & Kulhavy, R. W. (1973). Personality differences across regions of the United States. *Journal of Social Psychology, 91*, 73–79.
Lievens, F., De Corte, W., & Schollaert, E. (2008). A closer look at the frame-of-reference effect in personality scale scores and validity. *Journal of Applied Psychology, 93*, 268–279.

Maccoby, E. E., & Jacklin, C. N. (1974). *The psychology of sex differences*. Stanford, CA: Stanford University Press.
Marshall, M. B., De Fruyt, F., Rolland, J. P., & Bagby, R. M. (2005). Socially desirable responding and the factorial stability of the NEO-PI-R. *Psychological Assessment, 17*, 379–384.
Matsumoto, D. (2000). *Culture and psychology: People around the world*. Belmont, CA: Wadsworth/Thomson Learning.
McCrae, R. R. (1994). Openness to experience—Expanding the boundaries of Factor V. *European Journal of Personality, 8*, 251–272.
McCrae, R. R. (2002). NEO-PI-R: Data from 36 cultures: Further intercultural comparisons. In R. R. McCrae & J. Allik (Eds.), *The five-factor model of personality across cultures* (pp. 105–125). New York: Kluwer Academic/Plenum.
McCrae, R. R., & Costa, P. T. (1996). Toward a new generation of personality inventories: Theoretical contexts for the five-factor model. In J. S. Wiggins (Ed.), *The five-factor model of personality: Theoretical perspectives* (pp. 51–87). New York: Guilford Press.
McCrae, R. R., Costa, P. T., de Lima, M. P., Simoes, A., Ostendorf, F., Angleitner, A., & Piedmont, R. L. (1999). Age differences in personality across the adult life span: Parallels in five cultures. *Developmental Psychology, 35*, 466–477.
McCrae, R. R., Costa, P. T., & Martin, T. A. (2005). The NEO-PI-3: A more readable revised NEO Personality Inventory. *Journal of Personality Assessment, 84*, 261–270.
McCrae, R. R., Martin, T. A., & Costa, P. T. (2005). Age trends and age norms for the NEO Personality Inventory-3 in adolescents and adults. *Assessment, 12*, 363–373.
McCrae, R. R., & Terracciano, A. (2005a). Personality profiles of cultures: Aggregate personality traits. *Journal of Personality and Social Psychology, 89*, 407–425.
McCrae, R. R., & Terracciano, A. (2005b). Universal features of personality traits from the observer's perspective: Data from 50 cultures. *Journal of Personality and Social Psychology, 88*, 547–561.
McCrae, R. R., & Terracciano, A. (2008). The five-factor model and its correlates in individuals and cultures. In F. J. R. Van de Vijver, D. A. Van Hemert, & Y. Poortinga (Eds.), *Multilevel analysis of individuals and cultures* (pp. 249–283). Mahwah, NJ: Erlbaum.
McCrae, R. R., Terracciano, A., De Fruyt, F., De Bolle, M., Gelfand, M. J., & Costa, P. T. (2009). The validity and structure of culture-level personality scores: Data from ratings of young adolescents. *Journal of Personality, 78*, 815–838.
McCrae, R. R., Terracciano, A., Realo, A., & Allik, H. (2007). Climatic warmth and national wealth: Some culture-level determinants of national character stereotypes. *European Journal of Personality, 21*, 953–976.
Meiring, D., Van de Vijver, F., Rothmann, I., & De Bruin, D. (2008). Uncovering the personality structure of the 11 language groups in South Africa: SAPI project. *International Journal of Psychology, 43*, 364.
Morgeson, F. P., Campion, M. A., Dipboye, R. L., Hollenbeck, J. R., Murphy, K., & Schmitt, N. (2007a). Are we getting fooled again? Coming to terms with limitations in the use of personality tests for personnel selection. *Personnel Psychology, 60*, 1029–1049.
Morgeson, F. P., Campion, M. A., Dipboye, R. L., Hollenbeck, J. R., Murphy, K., & Schmitt, N. (2007b). Reconsidering the use of personality tests in personnel selection contexts. *Personnel Psychology, 60*, 683–729.
Morris, M. W., & Peng, K. (1994). Culture and cause: American and Chinese attributions for social and physical events. *Journal of Personality and Social Psychology, 67*, 949–971.
Mõttus, R., Allik, J., & Realo, A. (2010). An attempt to validate national mean scores of conscientiousness: No necessarily paradoxical findings. *Journal of Research in Personality, 44*, 630–640.
Nardon, L., & Steers, R. M. (2009). The culture theory jungle: Divergence and convergence in models of national culture. In R. S. Bhagat & R. M. Steers (Eds.), *Cambridge handbook of culture, organizations, and work* (pp. 3–22). Cambridge, UK: Cambridge University Press.
Oh, I. S., & Berry, C. M. (2009). The five-factor model of personality and managerial performance: Validity gains through the use of 360 degree performance ratings. *Journal of Applied Psychology, 94*, 1498–1513.
Oh, I. S., Wang, G., & Mount, M. K. (2010). Validity of observer ratings of the five-factor model of personality traits: A meta-analysis. *Journal of Applied Psychology, 96*, 762–773.
Ones, D. S., Dilchert, S., Viswesvaran, C., & Judge, T. A. (2007). In support of personality assessment in organizational settings. *Personnel Psychology, 60*, 995–1027.
Paunonen, S. V., & Jackson, D. N. (2000). What is beyond the Big Five? Plenty! *Journal of Personality, 68*, 821–835.
Plaut, V. C., Markus, H. R., & Lachman, M. E. (2002). Place matters: Consensual features and regional variation in American well-being and self. *Journal of Personality and Social Psychology, 83*, 160–184.
Realo, A., Allik, J., Lonnqvist, J. E., Verkasalo, M., Kwiatkowska, A., Koots, L., . . . Renge, V. (2009). Mechanisms of the national character stereotype: How people in six neighbouring countries of Russia describe themselves and the typical Russian. *European Journal of Personality, 23*, 229–249.

Reise, S. P., & Henson, J. M. (2003). A discussion of modern versus traditional psychometrics as applied to personality assessment scales. *Journal of Personality Assessment, 81*, 93–103.

Rentfrow, P. J. (2010). Statewide differences in personality toward a psychological geography of the United States. *American Psychologist, 65*, 548–558.

Rentfrow, P. J., Gosling, S. D., & Potter, J. (2008). A theory of the emergence, persistence, and expression of geographic variation in psychological characteristics. *Perspectives on Psychological Science, 3*, 339–369.

Rogers, K. H., & Wood, D. (2010). Accuracy of United States regional personality stereotypes. *Journal of Research in Personality, 44*, 704–713.

Rolland, J. P. (2002). The cross-cultural generalizability of the five-factor model. In R. R. McCrae & J. Allik (Eds.), *The five factor model of personality across cultures* (pp. 7–28). New York: Kluwer Academic/Plenum.

Rolland, J. P., & De Fruyt, F. (2009). *PfPI: Inventaire de Personnalité au Travail*. Paris: ECPA.

Rossier, J., Rigozzi, C., & Personality Across Culture Research Group. (2008). Personality disorders and the five-factor model among French speakers in Africa and Europe. *La Revue Canadienne de Psychiatrie, 53*, 534–544.

Sackett, P. R., & Lievens, F. (2008). Personnel selection. *Annual Review of Psychology, 59*, 419–450.

Salgado, J. F. (1997). The five factor model of personality and job performance in the European Community. *Journal of Applied Psychology, 82*, 30–43.

Salgado, J. F., & De Fruyt, F. (2005). Personality in personnel selection. In A. Evers, N. Anderson, & O. Voskuijl (Eds.), *The Blackwell handbook of personnel selection* (pp. 174–198). Oxford, UK: Blackwell.

Saucier, G., & Goldberg, L. R. (1998). What is beyond the big five? *Journal of Personality, 66*, 495–524.

Schwartz, S. H. (1994). Beyond individualism/collectivism: New cultural dimensions of values. In U. Kim, H. C. Triandis, C. Kagitcibasi, S.-C. Choi, & G. Yoon (Eds.), *Individualism and collectivism: Theory, method, and applications* (*Vol. 18*, pp. 85–119). Thousand Oaks, CA: Sage.

Stankov, L. (2011). Individual, country and societal cluster differences on measures of personality, attitudes, values, and social norms. *Learning and Individual Differences, 21*, 55–66.

Steenkamp, J.-B. E. M., & Baumgartner, H. (1998). Assessing measurement invariance in cross-national consumer research. *Journal of Consumer Research, 25*, 78–90.

Taras, V., Kirkman, B. L., & Steel, P. (2010). Examining the impact of culture's consequences: A three-decade, multilevel, meta-analytic review of Hofstede's cultural value dimensions. *Journal of Applied Psychology, 95*, 405–439.

Terracciano, A., Abdel-Khalek, A. M., Adam, N., Adamovova, L., Ahn, C., Ahn, H. N., . . . McCrae, R. R. (2005). National character does not reflect mean personality trait levels in 49 cultures. *Science, 310*, 96–100.

Tett, R. P., & Burnett, D. D. (2003). A personality trait-based interactionist model of job performance. *Journal of Applied Psychology, 88*, 500–517.

Tett, R. P., & Christiansen, N. D. (2007). Personality tests at the crossroads: A response to Morgeson, Campion, Dipboye, Hollenbeck, Murphy, and Schmitt (2007). *Personnel Psychology, 60*, 967–993.

Vandenberg, R. J., & Lance, C. E. (2000). A review and synthesis of the measurement invariance literature: Suggestions, practices, and recommendations for organizational research. *Organizational Research Methods, 3*, 4–70.

Van de Vijver, F. J. R., & Leung, K. (1997a). *Methods and data analysis for cross-cultural research*. Thousand Oaks, CA: Sage.

Van de Vijver, F. J. R., & Leung, K. (1997b). Methods and data analysis of comparative research. In J. W. Berry, Y. H. Poortinga, & J. Pandey (Eds.), *Handbook of cross-cultural psychology: Theory and method* (*Vol. 1*, pp. 257–300). Boston: Allyn & Bacon.

Van Leeuwen, K. G., Mervielde, I., De Clercq, B. J., & De Fruyt, F. (2007). Extending the spectrum idea: Child personality, parenting and psychopathology. *European Journal of Personality, 21*, 63–89.

Wu, J., & Lebreton, J. M. (2011). Reconsidering the dispositional basis of counterproductive work behavior: The role of aberrant personality. *Personnel Psychology, 64*, 593–626.

16

Type Theory Revisited

Implications of Complementary Opposites for the Five-Factor Model of Personality and Organizational Interventions

James H. Reynierse

> Even if the typological framework has no reality—and the present results point in that direction—the attitudes and functions still may exist as continuous traits, and have considerable meaning, while lacking the structural properties attributed to them. It would be wise to bear this possibility in mind in studies of the attitudes and functions, and their utility as measures in the personality domain.
>
> *Stricker & Ross, 1964a, p. 70*

P. B. Myers (2008), son of Isabel Briggs Myers and her coauthor of the type classic *Gifts Differing* (I. B. Myers & Myers, 1980), had this to say about the Myers–Briggs Type Indicator (MBTI) and the broader psychological community:

> My own view is that the MBTI has been widely enough used and copied that it is high time responsible, professional researchers in the academic psychological community recognize there must be something to the theory and the instrument, and it is not going to go away. They ought to take it seriously and get over their biases against an instrument that was developed by nonpsychologists, is based on Jung, and is easily understood and applied by people who are not trained psychologists. I assume that these biases factor into the general academic disdain for the indicator.
>
> *p. 11*

Certainly, this is a provocative statement particularly for any differences that alienate academics and practitioners. But there is no disputing that the MBTI is a highly popular personality measurement instrument that is used extensively in the world of work and many organizational environments. Bayne (2005, p. xi) identified the MBTI as the "most widely used personality measure for nonclinical populations . . . that dominates applied personality theory in the way that Big Five theory dominates personality research." In general, about 2 million individuals take the MBTI annually, although some estimates are higher, including a high estimate of 3 million (Spoto, 1995), with American rates relatively stable and international sales growing. Reviewers have described the MBTI as user-friendly (Mastrangelo, 2001), positive, and nonthreatening (Sundberg, 1965), all factors that contribute to its popularity. Formal and informal comments from practitioners and workshop participants indicate high customer satisfaction with both the instrument and programs that include the MBTI (Druckman & Bjork, 1991; Kerr, 2007).

Overall, the MBTI is well liked by those who use it—for reasons related to its structure as complementary opposite, preference pairs, and the positive language that is part of its interpretative framework—factors that distinguish it from traditional trait measures of personality. Complementary opposites are fundamentally Jungian and set the stage for many positive features of the MBTI. For example, type dimensions are described by opposite bipolar descriptors, for example extraversion and introversion, and both are viewed as normal and positive. By contrast, for the trait equivalent, only relatively high scores, that is, high extraversion, are viewed positively, and low scores toward the introversion pole of the scale are viewed in negative terms and defined as less of or a deficiency in extraversion (Newman, 1995a; Quenk, 1993b).

The MBTI is an American success story for entrepreneurial and enterprise ventures. But the MBTI also exists in a professional context where there are implications for psychological theory, practice, and measurement standards.

There is an underlying premise that will inform much of what I introduce here, that is, many of the perceived problems with the MBTI are problems of theory rather than problems of measurement. This is not new but is implicit in much of the criticism of the MBTI (e.g., Fleenor, 2001; Mastrangelo, 2001; McCrae & Costa, 1989; Mendelsohn, 1965; Pittenger, 1993b, 2005; Stricker & Ross, 1964a, 1964b; Wiggins, 1989). What is new is my belief that the theory can be fixed. Fix the theory and the MBTI has value for interpreting and applying type principles—although not all "commonly held" type principles will survive revision. As part of this, I will argue that the MBTI is an underutilized instrument that, in fact, measures much more and provides more information about individuals than is commonly presented or recognized. In general, I will examine the empirical and conceptual issues along with their implications for practice and theory in four sections. First, I will present the classical framework of the MBTI and Jungian type theory; second, I will address the primary objections and criticisms (including my own) to both the MBTI and the type theory; third, I will present an MBTI-derived revised type theory that expands the explanatory scope of the MBTI and reinterprets several type constructs within the structure of the Five-Factor Model (FFM) of personality (Reynierse, 2012); and fourth, I will discuss acceptability and quality issues for practitioner activities in organizations. In the course of this discussion, I will introduce concepts and research evidence that have significance for work and understanding organizations from a type perspective. But the primary emphasis will be on revisions to type theory that provide a framework for interpreting individual MBTI scores, that is anchored in demonstrated empirical relationships, that has broad applicability, and where practice routinely follows the spirit of an evidentiary-based science that informs both theory and practice (e.g., Baker, McFall, & Shoham, 2008).

Classical Type Theory

Classical MBTI Type Theory

The conceptual framework of the MBTI follows, with some modifications, the typology of Jung (1923/1971), including the extraversion and introversion attitudes, Jung's four functions—the perceiving functions of sensing and intuition and the judging functions of thinking and feeling—the organization of these dimensions as complementary opposites, and the idea of type dominance. In general, it is a positive and optimistic account of human nature that was intended to promote "understanding of both similarities and differences among human beings" (I. B. Myers & Myers,

1980, p. ix). Positive language is generally used to describe each person's individual preferences and type but with the implicit understanding that one's comfort level and use will be less for the non-preferred, opposite preferences. From this perspective, everyone has gifts that can be used effectively, and each type is characterized by strengths and limitations.

The underlying theory (I. B. Myers, 1962, 1980; I. B. Myers & Myers, 1980) posits that personality is structured around four preference pairs that represent different uses of people's perception and judgment and has been summarized by many (e.g., Bayne, 2005; Brownsword, 1987; Lawrence, 1979; Lawrence & Martin, 2001; I. B. Myers & McCaulley, 1985; I. B. Myers, McCaulley, Quenk, & Hammer, 1998; Quenk, 1993a, 1993b). According to the theory, there are two fundamental ways of perceiving the world or collecting information, either by sensing, that is, through the use of our five senses, or by intuition, that is, by relationships and possibilities that occur outside of the senses and which Jung called "hunches" (Beebe, 2004). Similarly, there are two different ways of making judgments or deciding things, either by thinking, that is, through impersonal, objective logic, or by feeling, that is, through personal, subjective values. The theory includes four preference pairs, E–I, S–N, T–F, and J–P, that are measured by four corresponding, bipolar MBTI scales, that is, individual preferences for Extraversion (E) or Introversion (I), Sensation (S) or Intuition (N), Thinking (T) or Feeling (F), and Judgment (J) or Perception (P). The preference pairs are viewed as complementary opposites and each of these pairs is presumed to provide important information regarding the use of perception (either S or N) and judgment (either T or F), that is, *they have particular significance for interpreting the four Jungian functions.* According to the classic model (I. B. Myers & Myers, 1980, p. 9), the role of the preference pairs can be summarized as follows:

- The preference for E or I represents whether one prefers the outer world of people and things or the private world of self and ideas. Furthermore, it identifies where the dominant (favorite or superior) function is expressed, that is, whether it is extraverted or introverted;
- The preference for S or N represents which perceiving function is preferred and used;
- The preference for T or F represents which judging function is preferred and used;
- The preference for J or P represents whether the preferred perceiving function (either S or N) or the preferred judging function (either T or F) is extraverted, that is, expressed in the outer world.

Note that the J–P preference pair is categorically different from the other three MBTI preference pairs, where E–I, S–N, and T–F are direct, straightforward measures of these preferences. By contrast, J–P is primarily a "pointer variable" within the assignment rules of type dynamics, where it determines how someone prefers to deal with the outer world, that is, which functions are extraverted. E–I, although measured directly at one level of analysis, is also part of the assignment rules of type dynamics determining whether the dominant function is extraverted or introverted.

The arrangement of these four preference pairs provides for unique combinations and the resulting psychological types. These combinations, presented in the first column of Table 16.1, produce the conventional arrangement of the MBTI preferences into 16 four-letter types, for example, ISTJ for someone with MBTI scores that show preferences for I + S + T + J or ENFP for someone with MBTI scores that show preferences for E + N + F + P. The scores are simply *added together* in a straightforward manner to identify each four-letter type with each individual preference contributing independently. But the theory is explicit that additional information about personality is both measured and summarized in these four-letter types that extend well beyond the strictly additive, surface qualities of the individual preferences. Table 16.1 includes the additional type dynamics information for each type.

Table 16.1 The 16 Types and Their Straightforward MBTI and Dynamical Interpretative Meanings

MBTI Type	*Straightforward Interpretation*	*Dynamical Interpretation*	
ESTJ	E + S + T + J	Dominant Thinking extraverted	Auxiliary Sensing introverted
ESTP	E + S + T + P	Dominant Sensing extraverted	Auxiliary Thinking introverted
ESFJ	E + S + F + J	Dominant Feeling extraverted	Auxiliary Sensing introverted
ESFP	E + S + F + P	Dominant Sensing extraverted	Auxiliary Feeling introverted
ISTJ	I + S + T + J	Dominant Sensing introverted	Auxiliary Thinking extraverted
ISTP	I + S + T + P	Dominant Thinking introverted	Auxiliary Sensing extraverted
ISFJ	I + S + F + J	Dominant Sensing introverted	Auxiliary Feeling extraverted
ISFP	I + S + F + P	Dominant Feeling introverted	Auxiliary Sensing extraverted
ENTJ	E + N + T + J	Dominant Thinking extraverted	Auxiliary Intuition introverted
ENTP	E + N + T + P	Dominant Intuition extraverted	Auxiliary Thinking introverted
ENFJ	E + N + F + J	Dominant Feeling extraverted	Auxiliary Intuition introverted
ENFP	E + N + F + P	Dominant Intuition extraverted	Auxiliary Feeling introverted
INTJ	I + N + T + J	Dominant Intuition introverted	Auxiliary Thinking extraverted
INTP	I + N + T + P	Dominant Thinking introverted	Auxiliary Intuition extraverted
INFJ	I + N + F + J	Dominant Intuition introverted	Auxiliary Feeling extraverted
INFP	I + N + F + P	Dominant Feeling introverted	Auxiliary Intuition extraverted

The Whole Type, Interaction, Type Dynamics Model

Although the MBTI consists of four scales that measure four preference pairs, there was always greater meaning attributed to the 16 types, for example, ISTJ, ENFP, and so on. The third edition of the *MBTI Manual* (I. B. Myers et al., 1998) was explicit that

> From a typological perspective, the fundamental unit of analysis is the whole type . . . And that researchers should consider using whole types as the independent variables in their analyses . . . as such analyses would provide better tests of theory, regardless of the fact that types are identified by the results of four separate dichotomies.
>
> *p. 201*

Commitment to whole types embraced an interaction-type dynamics model, where each of the 16 types was no longer additive but reflected unique, dynamic interactions, for example, an ISTJ becomes I × S × T × J, and an ENFP becomes E × N × F × P. Accordingly, type interactions, the nature of the whole types, and type dynamics relationships are the three central theoretical constructs that *must* be demonstrated to confirm type theory.

Type dynamics refers to the hierarchical ordering of Jung's functions (Sensing, Intuition, Thinking, and Feeling); the identification of this order as the Dominant, Auxiliary, Tertiary, and Inferior functions; and the expression of these functions in the Extraverted and Introverted attitudes. According to theory, the Jungian functions represent opposite perceiving (Sensing or Intuition) and judging (Thinking or Feeling) processes that must be differentiated in order to provide focus and direction for any individual. From this perspective, there are opposite attitudes (Extraversion and Introversion) for expressing the functions, with each type expressing the dominant function in its preferred attitude. Similarly, there are opposite attitudes (Judgment and Perception) for dealing with the outer world, that is, that determine which functions are extraverted. Explicit within type dynamics is the idea that, for any individual, the four functions are ordered in terms of individual preference and effectiveness—that is, they form a hierarchy where dominant > auxiliary > tertiary > inferior. Or to put it another way, the dominance hierarchy describes a gradient of use, where the dominant function is most highly developed and most likely to be used, whereas the inferior function is least developed and least likely to be used.

The justification for type dynamics is not based on empirical evidence but relies on exegesis of Jung's (1923/1971) identification of a principal or dominant process and a secondary or auxiliary function "whose nature is not opposed to the dominant function . . . Experience shows that the secondary function is always one whose nature is different from, though not antagonistic to, the primary function" and the corresponding observation that "besides the conscious primary function there is a relatively unconscious, auxiliary function *which is in every respect different from the nature of the primary function*" (pp. 405–406, italics added). Accepting Jung's comments at face value provides a "rule of thumb" for determining whether the auxiliary function occurs in the extraverted or introverted attitude, that is, since the auxiliary "is in every respect different," logically it must be opposite from the dominant or primary function.

Brownsword (1987) provided a general framework for conceptualizing type dynamics within the framework of the MBTI measure and identified three rules for forming type dynamics groups that preserved Jung's observation that the *auxiliary function is in every respect different from the nature of the primary or dominant function*. First, Js extravert their judging function, T or F, but introvert their perceiving function, S or N. By contrast, Ps extravert their perceiving function, S or N, but introvert their judging function, T or F. Thus, type dynamics uses J–P as a "pointer variable" in which the J–P preference pair identifies how someone deals with the outer world, that is, which functions are extraverted. Second, for Es, the extraverted function is dominant and the introverted function is auxiliary. By contrast, for Is, the introverted function is dominant and the extraverted function is auxiliary. Third, the opposite of the dominant is the inferior, which is introverted if the dominant is extraverted, but extraverted if the dominant is introverted. Similarly, the opposite of the auxiliary is the tertiary, which is introverted if the auxiliary is extraverted, but extraverted if the auxiliary is introverted. From this perspective and following the attitude balance rule of type dynamics (Wilde, 2011), both the dominant and the tertiary functions occur in the preferred attitude and the auxiliary and inferior functions in the less preferred attitude in an alternating fashion (E–I–E–I and I–E–I–E). The *MBTI Manual* (I. B. Myers & McCaulley, 1985; I. B. Myers et al., 1998) outlined a similar set of rules except that only the dominant function operates in the preferred attitude, whereas the auxiliary, tertiary, and inferior functions occur in the less preferred, opposite attitude (E–I–I–I and I–E–E–E).

The additive and dynamic models summarized in Table 16.1 are two reoccurring views of psychological type. Both are recognized and used as explanatory concepts and few (if any) would deny that the MBTI preferences have straightforward meaning. There are two fundamental problems, however, when type theorists "toggle" at will between the alternative uses. First, nowhere in the theory is there a conceptual "toggle switch" to provide direction for when to shift from one use to the other; and second, whereas there is substantial empirical support for the additive model based on the MBTI preferences, there is scant support for the dynamic model.

Empirical Problems for MBTI Type Theory

In this section, I examine the logical structure and evidence against the "whole type, interaction, type dynamics model" of psychological type, emphasizing the conceptual language of type theory. Although these concepts are combined within type interactions, whole types, and type dynamics, relationships are distinct conceptual issues. Elements of this model were embedded in the theory from the start but had a higher profile with the publication of the third edition of the *MBTI Manual* (I. B. Myers et al., 1998). Yet the evidence presented there (Myers et al.) in support of these concepts was sparse and often contradictory (Reynierse, 2009). Only a brief summary of the arguments against the model can be presented here and the interested reader should consult the original papers for key issues related to type interactions (Hicks, 1984, 1985; Reynierse & Harker, 2001a), whole types (Reynierse & Harker, 2000), and type dynamics (Reynierse, 2009; Reynierse & Harker, 2008a, 2008b).

Type Interactions

Interactions are central to psychological type and the preference combinations recognized by classical MBTI type theory (Hicks, 1984, 1985). The critical issues were framed by Hicks and others (e.g., Block & Ozer, 1982; Mendelsohn, Weiss, & Feimer, 1982; Weiss, Mendelsohn, & Feimer, 1982). Theoretically, each individual combination and type represents a unique configuration where the whole is greater than the sum of the individual parts, that is, the effects for any combination and type reflect additional meaning beyond any additive relationship of the individual preferences. Thus, traditional type theory emphasizes the synergistic nature of type interactions in which the interaction produces new, emergent forms. In this sense, type *theory* is couched exclusively in terms of positive, primary augmenting effects that magnify or enhance the effect, whereas many *empirical type interaction effects* are in fact secondary and mitigating, that is, decrease or lessen it (Reynierse & Harker, 2001a, 2005a). In fact, type interactions are very complicated, often distorted by statistical artifacts, and disappear or become trivial when effects are examined further (Reynierse & Harker, 2001a, 2005a). In general, several large-scale studies of type interactions report identical trends for self-ratings of personal preferences (I. B. Myers et al., 1998), independent observer ratings for lexical descriptors (Reynierse & Harker, 2000, 2001a), self-report, questionnaire scale scores (Reynierse & Harker, 2005a), business values (Reynierse, Harker, Fink, & Ackerman, 2001), and personal values important for teamwork (Sundstrom, Koenigs, & Huet-Cox, 1996). In each study, there were many significant effects for the individual preferences and two-way interactions, few effects for the three-way interactions, and the four-way interactions occurred only rarely, effects and relationships that are difficult to interpret and reconcile with the prevailing whole type, interaction, type dynamics model.

Limited support for type interactions was found repeatedly in type-related sources. Hicks (1984) did not find a predicted E–S × S–N interaction for bookishness (books read per year) but found an unanticipated modest S–N × T–F interaction. Some investigators have examined the interactions but found none (e.g., Faucett, Morgan, Poling, & Johnson, 1995; Otis & Loucks, 1997) and lower-order interactions were reported somewhat more frequently (e.g., Hammer, 1985; Hester, 1996; Oxford & Ehrman, 1988), results that are consistent with other research where type interactions were limited (e.g., McCrae & Costa, 1989; Stricker & Ross, 1964a).

Whole Types

Direct analyses of the whole types, for example one-way analyses of variance (ANOVAs) of the 16 MBTI types (Table 16.1), was the research model endorsed by the *MBTI Manual* (I. B. Myers et al., 1998) and the approach of Pearman and Fleenor (1996, 1997). The entire idea of whole types ignores the loss of information that occurs with type dichotomies (e.g., Cohen, 1983; McCrae & Costa, 1989) and begs the question as to why MBTI type interaction effects occur only rarely at the locus of the four-way interaction and, when obtained, are quite weak. In a study based on ratings of 276 lexical descriptor-dependent variables, Reynierse and Harker (2000) examined all the interaction terms but found only three significant four-way interactions. Results for a similar study, based on ratings of 73 personal preference-dependent variables reported in the *MBTI Manual* (p. 202, Table 9.19), also found only three significant four-way interactions (Myers et al.). All of these interactions were relatively trivial with variance accounted for ranging from 1.44% to 6.01% (Reynierse & Harker, 2001a, 2005a) and 0.7% to 2.2% (Myers et al.). Regardless, analyses of whole types are not sufficient to demonstrate that effects occur at the locus of the types, that is, the assumed four-way interaction, when in fact it is more likely that the effects can be entirely explained by lower-order preferences or interactions. Unless studies employ procedures that *examine and exclude* the contributions of all main effects for the individual preferences and their lower-order interactions, whole type studies are meaningless and uninterpretable because they cannot isolate the locus of any significant type effects—they could occur anywhere (Reynierse & Harker, 2001a, 2005a).

Whole type research can use taxometric techniques (Meehl, 1992; Ruscio & Ruscio, 2008; Waller & Meehl, 1998) to distinguish categorical (type) from dimensional (continuous) effects. Arnau, Green, Rosen, Gleaves, and Melancon (2003) empirically addressed this issue using taxometric methods with three Jungian personality measurement instruments—the MBTI, the *Singer–Loomis Type Deployment Inventory* (SL-TDI), and the *Personal Preferences Self-Description Questionnaire* (PPSDQ). Results showed that there was not a nonarbitrary taxon or clear categorical type for any of the Jungian type measures—all were uniformly continuous rather than categorical dimensions.

Type Dynamics

Whole type research based on the MBTI assignment rules of type dynamics produced many contradictory results and errors of diagnosis (Reynierse, 2009; Reynierse & Harker, 2008a, 2008b), including 54 (20%) contradictory effects (e.g., Auxiliary was superior to Dominant) for the Grant–Brownsword type dynamics model and 50 (18.5%) contradictory effects for the *Manual* model. Furthermore, their results for E and I were based strictly on the E–I preference pair, where they uniformly tracked the E–I preferences, rather than the expression of effects in the E and I attitudes. What mattered was being an Extravert or Introvert, and the dominant and auxiliary status of any function was irrelevant (Reynierse & Harker, 2001a, 2005a).

The entire idea that the MBTI measures four-letter whole types as part of an interaction, type dynamics model at the point of the dichotomy can be questioned, if not rejected a priori, based on the convoluted language of type dynamics and that the structural properties of the MBTI include four bipolar, preference scales rather than whole type scales. The prevailing whole type, interaction, type dynamics model identified with the MBTI is fraught with empirical and logical problems. This model abandons the individual preference pairs, confounds the four-way interaction with all other type variables, gives special status to the four-way interaction—the weakest empirical type effect—and discards all others. Abandoning the preferences comes at a very high empirical cost, particularly since the MBTI preferences have been demonstrated frequently, have a strong empirical foundation, and the MBTI instrument was constructed and validated for these individual preferences—not whole types.

Carl Alfred Meier's View of Jungian Psychological Type

According to Meier (1975/1989, 1977/1995), Jung distinguished four basic elements of consciousness which he identified as the four functions—sensation (S), thinking (T), feeling (F), and intuition (N)—and introduced core principles that are relevant for this discussion of the MBTI. Meier's interpretation identified the Jungian meaning of the four functions (first principle),[1] the concept of complementary opposites (second principle), that the opposites are mutually exclusive (third principle), and type dominance (fourth principle). Meier (1975/1989) also identified the relationship of the dominant (the differentiated function) to the inferior function (fifth principle). Meier (1977/1995) makes two additional points. First, "the starting point for Jung's typology was the fact that people usually have a preference for one specific 'intellectual talent' and exploit it to the full." And second, the main or primary function, that is, "the intellectual talent that is exploited to the full," is expressed mainly in two different ways, either "internally, to the ego, or externally, to the outside world" (p. 13). These two possibilities are, of course, introversion and extraversion. Meier then defines introversion in terms of reference to the "subject," that is, self or ego, and its connection to one's inner world and unconscious side. By contrast, extraversion is defined in terms of an "object" (material things) referent, and the relation of the "subject" or self to the outside world. For Meier, these are the two attitude types that are distinguished by their external, that is, visible, characteristics.

Meier's (1977/1995) primary objective was to examine Jung's concept of individuation and to describe the individuation path or process in the development of human personality. Individuation is Jung's term for type development over the life span of every individual where "there must be an attempt to make all four functions conscious in the course of time—in other words, to differentiate them as much as possible" (Meier, p. 56). Recall that, earlier, Meier noted that individuals often have "one specific intellectual talent and exploit it to the full," an indication that there is overreliance on one psychological function and type development is incomplete. From this perspective, a mature, better developed personality permits conscious use of the four functions (i.e., each function in both its extraverted and introverted forms) when the situational context is appropriate.

Implications for Jung's Typology and the MBTI

Meier's (1975/1989, 1977/1995) interpretation of Jung identified the four functions (first principle), complementary opposites (second principle), that the components of each pair are mutually exclusive (third principle), type dominance (fourth principle), the relationship of the dominant (the differentiated function) to the inferior function (fifth principle), the expression of type dominance by introverts and extraverts (the two attitudes), and the path to a mature personality through type development or individuation. The four functions and the two attitudes can be equated with three of the four MBTI preference pairs, each of which is constructed as complementary opposites and are presumably mutually exclusive. The Jungian types reflect the *dominant status* of each of the four functions and where each functional type is identified with "the fact that people usually have a preference for one 'intellectual talent' and exploit it to the full" (Meier, 1977/1995, p. 13). The implication for the MBTI is that the dominant MBTI preference, that is, the preference used most often and relied upon by an individual, is the type. Furthermore, the extent to which any individual can effectively use additional (multiple) functions is determined by one's type development through the process of individuation.

The expression of the functions depends on whether someone is an extravert or introvert without any consideration of the attitude balance rule (Wilde, 2011). Although Jung's concept of extraversion and introversion is couched in terms of expression in the external world of objects and things versus the internal world of self and ideas, it also includes the same or similar social extraversion, for example being friendly and a good mixer (Meier, 1977/1995), as that described by the FFM of personality (e.g., McCrae & Costa, 1989) and many other personality measures (e.g., Stricker & Ross, 1964b). It is accurate that Jung and Meier discuss type dominance in terms of the dominant function being in one attitude and the inferior function in its opposite (fifth principle). But this is a reliably obtained empirical effect that reflects the complementarity of type opposites and straightforward preference pair differences when evaluated on external variables (Reynierse, 2009; Reynierse & Harker, 2008b).

Meier's (1977/1995) discussion of the four functions shows that Jung's typology is about four orienting functions of consciousness. In other words, Jungian psychology is about *types of consciousness* and not *types of people*, a distinction made explicit by Beebe (2004) and Geldart (2010).

It is also clear that there is nothing in Meier's (1977/1995) interpretation of Jung's typology that in any way promotes or otherwise identifies psychological type with preference interactions, whole types, or any dynamic relationships implied by the elementary structure of the MBTI type system. Rather, it is a straightforward structural system based on preferences (the functions and attitudes), complementary opposites, and a dominant or primary functional preference that is favored, relied on, "exploited to the full," and probably often to the exclusion of other, potentially useful preferences until type development (individuation) is complete and in a mature, adult form. That Jungian type is couched in terms of "frequency of use" suggests that the phenomena of psychological type may not be fairly or properly evaluated by nomothetic procedures that establish general laws of human behavior based on group data and that idiographic analyses of individual cases based on systematic observation of individuals over time would be better and more appropriate (e.g., Denzin, 1994). But that is a question for another time and is beyond the scope of this chapter.

It is also clear that McCrae and Costa's (1989) conclusion that Jungian theory was "either incorrect or inadequately operationalized by the MBTI" must be taken seriously (p. 17). There is considerable similarity between the descriptive theoretical framework of psychological type as presented by Meier (1977/1995) and its basis for a *straightforward* Jungian interpretation of the MBTI and the FFM of personality. I. B. Myers (1962, 1980; I. B. Myers & Myers, 1980) may have intended to operationalize Jung differently but ultimately created an MBTI instrument that successfully measures Jungian concepts and that fits the FFM factor structure. The type community, however, has been reluctant to accept the conceptual relationships of the FFM for either practice or theory (e.g., Quenk, 1992, 1993a; Rytting & Ware, 1993), although there is some indication that acceptance has occurred at an empirical level (Schaubhut, Herk, & Thompson, 2009). Regardless, in much of the remainder of this chapter, I will argue that the MBTI preferences and their arrangement as complementary opposites are an alternative and defensible interpretation of the meaningfulness of FFM dimensions.

The Objections and Criticisms to the MBTI and Type Theory

Some of these criticisms were presented earlier and emphasized the conceptual language of type theory. Here, criticism will be presented more broadly.

In the Foreword to the Argentine Edition of *Psychological Types*, Jung (1923/1971) identified some of his objectives in writing his book. Two of his points are particularly relevant.

First, he noted:

> If one is plunged, as I am for professional reasons, into the chaos of psychological opinions, prejudices, and susceptibilities, one gets a profound and indelible impression of the diversity of individual psychic dispositions, tendencies, and convictions, while on the other hand one increasingly feels the need for some order among the chaotic multiplicity of points of view. This need calls for a critical orientation and for general principles and criteria, not too specific in their formulation, which may serve as *points de repère* in sorting out the empirical material.
>
> *p. xiv*

Second, and commenting on his perception that "far too many readers have succumbed to the error of thinking that Chapter X (General Description of the Types) represents the essential content and purpose of the book, in the sense that it provides a system of classification," Jung adds:

> This regrettable misunderstanding completely ignores the fact that this kind of classification is nothing but a childish parlour game . . . My typology is far rather a critical apparatus to sort out and organize the welter of empirical material, but not in any sense to stick labels on people at first sight. It is not a physiognomy and not an anthropological system, but a critical psychology dealing with the organization and delimitation of psychic processes that can be shown to be typical.
>
> *pp. xiv–xv*

The implication is that, for Jung, psychological types are primarily convenient shorthand for finding order out of a chaos of individual variability and *not* a system for labeling people. Jung accepts the infinite variability of individual people but not an infinite set of psychological concepts or explanations for this variability. The "types" are Jung's attempt to identify significant differences among people and "shorten the list" of explanatory concepts that are necessary to understand them. Bayne (1995) presented a similar interpretation of psychological type.

What then is Jung's primary objective? Review of the first nine chapters of *Psychological Type*—where Jung examined the role of "type" in philosophy, literature, and Western thought—suggests that Jung was primarily interested in demonstrating the role of complementary opposites in the history of Western thought and he is only marginally interested in categorization or classification. For example, Jung identified the type problem in classical and medieval thought and emphasized that it is the "effects of the psychological pairs of opposites we are discussing" (p. 11). In this sense, the opposites were the starting point and basis for Jung's concept of mind or psyche.[2]

General Reviews

There are several comprehensive commentaries that have critically analyzed the theoretical and psychometric basis of the MBTI, including Barbuto (1997), Carlson (1985), Carlyn (1977), Druckman and Bjork (1991), and Pittenger (1993a, 1993b, 2005). In some cases (particularly Druckman & Bjork, and Pittenger), analysis included implications for practice, notably the issue of type stability. Coe (1992), in a generally favorable review, addressed appropriate uses and potential misuses of the MBTI for human resource practices and personnel administration, and warned about using the MBTI for selecting employees and the temptation to stereotype or "typecast" others. At the same time, Coe found the MBTI useful for teambuilding, improving communications and decision making, diagnosing organizational dysfunctions, facilitating organizational change and conflict resolution, and generally strengthening employee and supervisory relations. In addition, research papers have often included critical analysis and identified core issues (e.g., Furnham, 1996; McCrae & Costa, 1989; Reynierse & Harker, 2000, 2008a, 2008b; Stricker & Ross, 1964a, 1964b). Similarly, Spoto (1995) examined the MBTI from an explicitly Jungian perspective and Bayne (2005) examined the evidence for the MBTI for both theory and practice.

The Whole Type, Interaction, Type Dynamics Model

Earlier, I discussed the problems of the whole type, interaction, type dynamics theoretical basis of Jungian type theory as identified by the MBTI. There is a long history of criticism of this model that comes from a traditional trait view of personality, often using the language of psychometrics rather than the language of type theory, but which is consistent with my earlier comments. In the course of this discussion, I will present further evidence that is critical of this model but will also make comments intended to show that the criticism applies *only* to the classical MBTI model of type but *not* to a revised theory of MBTI type that is firmly anchored in the FFM of personality and Carl Alfred Meier's (1977/1995) interpretation of Jung's typology.

Qualitative Differences of the Types

A premise of type theory is that there are qualitative, categorical differences between types that distinguish them from the quantitative, dimensional differences of traits. This implies that the MBTI measure (and other type instruments) can identify mutually exclusive groups of people based on a nonarbitrary cutting point or true zero point for separating the independent types. One prediction from the type view is that the distribution of dichotomous preference scores should be bimodal with independent means and standard deviations. But evidence for bimodality of the MBTI preferences is often weak or absent. Rather, MBTI scores usually have a bell-shaped distribution that clusters around the median and is similar to trait distributions (Harvey & Murry, 1994; Hicks, 1984; McCrae & Costa, 1989; Stricker & Ross, 1964a).

However, bimodality for the MBTI preferences has been reported, sometimes with striking results. For example, when scoring was based on item response theory, bimodality was observed (Harvey & Murry, 1994). Furthermore, Rytting, Ware, and Prince (1994) examined the distribution of continuous MBTI preference scores for a sample of 348 CEOs of moderate-size companies. This group of CEOs had uniformly clear strength-of-preference scores, including higher frequencies in the middle and lower frequencies in the tails of the frequency distribution—that is, clear bimodality for each MBTI preference scale (e.g., E or I)—and with few scores (less than 2%) near the midpoint of the continuous scale (e.g., E–I), a convincing U-shaped distribution. Rytting, Ware, Prince, File, and Yokomoto (1994) then analyzed another sample of successful individuals from a study of philanthropy. This sample of major donors also produced a bimodal distribution of MBTI preference scores, which was similar to that for the CEOs. In both samples, participants were successful, self-confident high performers with high to moderate individual preference scores on the MBTI scales, suggesting a mature level of type development and individuation. By contrast, there is little reason to expect bimodality when the subject pool consists of young adults (12th graders or college undergraduates) whose adult personalities are just beginning to develop and type development is incomplete.

Reliability of the Four-Letter Type Classification System

In general, estimates of MBTI reliability are high—.73–.93 for E–I, .69–.93 for S–N, .56–.91 for T–F, and .60–.89 for J–P—for 26 separate test–retest measures ranging from 1 week to 2.5 years. A retest interval of 4 years had lower correlations of .51 (E–I), .58 (S–N), .45 (T–F), and .45 (J–P) (Harvey, 1996; Myers & McCaulley, 1985). Reviewers agree that the MBTI-reported reliabilities are adequate, generally high, and comparable to those of other measurement instruments (e.g., Carlson, 1985; Carlyn, 1977; Devito, 1985; Druckman & Bjork, 1991; McCarley & Carskadon, 1983; McCrae & Costa, 1989; Pittenger, 1993b, 2005). However, about 50% of subjects are reclassified for their type category on retesting despite high test reliabilities for the individual preferences (Howes & Carskadon, 1979; McCarley & Carskadon, 1983).

Druckman and Bjork (1991) argued that traditional measures of reliability do not address the key theoretical issue of MBTI type stability. Similarly, Pittenger (1993b) noted that standard test–retest measures of reliability based on continuous preference scales is a trait measurement procedure that is inappropriate for the explicit type classification system of the MBTI, particularly the formation of the 16 four-letter types. Their point is that reliability for a type measure requires stable classification for the four-letter type over the test–retest interval. In other words, if the MBTI system is framed in terms of 16 four-letter *whole* types, the *whole* type must be stable and should not change with repeated testing.

Harvey (1996) evaluated type stability rates for the I. B. Myers and McCaulley (1985) reliability studies that included strength of preference data. The studies included two test–retest intervals, a short inter-test interval (ITI) of 5 weeks and a long ITI of 4–5 years, and three levels of preference clarity (slight, moderate, and clear) for each of the four MBTI scales. Results indicated that both the short ITI and higher preference clarity conditions uniformly showed strong type agreement between test and retest with at least 95% type agreement on all scales. Type agreement rates were lower for the slight preference group near the cutoff score with rates in the 60%–70% range for the short ITI and 50%–60% for the long ITI conditions. Similar results for MBTI Form M were reported by Schaubhut et al. (2009).

Collectively, these results indicate that the majority of test–retest type assignment differences occur where the preference clarity score is numerically low, that is, is close to the cutoff point used to dichotomize the preferences, and that measurement error near this point accounts for most of the reported type instability under test–retest conditions. In other words, where preference clarity is uncertain and an individual preference is undifferentiated from its opposite, test–retest variability is high and the undifferentiated preference is likely to change when retested, a result that is not particularly surprising from either a type or statistical perspective. At the same time, whether or not the test–retest reliability data have a satisfactory type explanation does not mean this justifies the continued use of 16 four-letter whole types. All of the improvement lies with the four MBTI scales—not four-letter *whole* types—and it is disingenuous to use continuous scale scores for measurement purposes and then present this in an interpretative framework based on dichotomies.

Factor Analytic Studies

Initially, the MBTI was criticized by many for its factor structure, including whether or not it measured four independent, robust factors that correspond to the four MBTI measurement scales (e.g., McCrae & Costa, 1989; Pittenger, 1993b; Stricker & Ross, 1964b). In the interim, considerable research was directed toward the basic structure of personality and there is now substantial agreement that five basic elements can describe personality. This FFM is closely associated with the NEO-PI, a personality test developed by McCrae and Costa. The NEO-PI identifies five unipolar factors—Neuroticism (Emotional Stability), Extraversion, Openness to Experience, Agreeableness, and Conscientiousness—that correspond to the Comfort–Discomfort (C–D), Extraversion–Introversion (E–I), Sensing–Intuition (S–N), Thinking–Feeling (T–F), and Judging–Perceiving (J–P) scales of MBTI Form J. The MBTI is more widely recognized, however, for its four-factor structure, which was confirmed often (Furnham, 1996; Jackson, Parker, & Dipboye, 1996; Johnson, 1995; Johnson & Saunders, 1990; McCrae & Costa, 1989; Schaubhut et al., 2009; Thompson & Borrello, 1986a, 1986b; Tischler, 1994).

There is significant convergence between the NEO-PI scales and the MBTI scales, as each NEO-PI scale correlates highly with the corresponding MBTI scales (Furnham, 1996; Johnson, 1995; McCrae & Costa, 1989), evidence that supports the validity of both the NEO-PI and the MBTI (Bayne, 2005; Rytting & Ware, 1993), and is summarized in Table 16.2. There are two ways of evaluating this congruence between the MBTI and the FFM of personality. One interpretation (Pittenger, 1993b) is that the MBTI is a special case of the more general FFM and can be understood within this system. Alternatively, the MBTI has a four-factor solution that provides empirical justification for its scales and reassurance that it is measuring what it is supposed to measure.

Concluding Comment on Type Stability and Consistency

The criticisms of MBTI stability by Pittenger and others is a legitimate concern for an MBTI scoring and assignment procedure that equates type with 16 four-letter whole types based exclusively on dichotomization at the preference, cutting points. At the very least, this is a rigid, limited assignment procedure that lumps a large range of individual scores into a small set of identical four-letter whole types and with considerable lost information. But where continuous scoring is used that considers strength of preference, where distinctions are made based on preference clarity, and where it is recognized that the four-letter types represent only a convenient additive relationship of four separate preferences, the whole type problem is resolved. The empirical evidence indicates that the MBTI does not form or establish four-letter whole type effects but does produce and establish scores for four separate, independent bipolar scales.

Notably, the errors of the MBTI identified and discussed in this section are not errors of measurement but errors of interpretation. The fault is not with the MBTI per se but with users who accept a

Table 16.2 Correlations of MBTI Scale Scores With NEO-PI Scales (Corresponding Scale Correlations in Bold)

MBTI Scales	*NEO-PI Factors (Scales)*				
	N	*E*	*O*	*A*	*C*
McCrae and Costa (1989) MBTI-Form G					
Men (*N* = 267)					
E–I (Introversion)	.16**	**−.74*** **	.03	−.03	.08
S–N (Intuition)	−.06	.10	**.72*** **	.04	−.15*
T–F (Feeling)	.06	.19**	.02	**.44*** **	−.15*
J–P (Perception)	.11	.15*	.30***	−.06	**−.49*** **
Women (*N* = 201)					
E–I (Introversion)	.17*	**−.69*** **	−.03	−.08	.08
S–N (Intuition)	.01	.22**	**.69*** **	.03	−.10
T–F (Feeling)	.28***	.10	−.02	**.46*** **	−.22**
J–P (Perception)	.04	.20**	.26***	.05	**−.46*** **
Johnson (1995) MBTI-TDI (N = 335)					
C–D (Discomfort)[a]	**.65*** **	.31**	−.13	.18*	.12
E–I (Introversion)	−.39***	**−.67*** **	.16*	.14	.14
S–N (Intuition)	−.16*	−.22*	**.61*** **	.18*	.24**
T–F (Feeling)	−.14	−.25**	.23*	**.40*** **	.01
J–P (Perception)	−.42***	−.06	−.17*	−.21*	**−.56*** **
Furnham (1996) MBTI-Form G (N = 160)					
E–I (Introversion)	.25**	**−.70*** **	−.22**	.00	.04
S–N (Intuition)	.05	.11	**.48*** **	−.04	−.16
T–F (Feeling)	.19	.04	−.24***	**.47*** **	−.23**
J–P (Perception)	.00	.02	.17**	−.06	**−.52*** **[b]

Source: Reynierse (2012).

[a] MBTI-TDI Comfort–Discomfort scale.

[b] The correct value is −.52 as shown here, not .52 as shown in Furnham (1996); personal communication, Adrian Furnham.

* $p < .05$; ** $p < .01$; *** $p < .001$.

flawed theory of psychological type and ignore long-standing criticism (e.g., Stricker & Ross, 1962). In short, they primarily indicate *human error* and not test error or measurement error.

Additional Issues

Other issues have been identified, often repeatedly, and cover a variety of methodological, theoretical, and empirical issues. Due to space constraints, I will address only three. Interested readers should examine the papers of critics identified earlier, particularly Pittenger (1993a, 1993b, 2005) and Stricker and Ross (1962, 1964a, 1964b) for comprehensive discussion of the issues, and Barbuto (1997) for a Jungian perspective.

Is the MBTI Ipsative?

The MBTI has often been criticized for being a forced-choice, ipsative measurement instrument (e.g., Arnau, Thompson, & Rosen, 1999; Boyle, 1995; Furnham, 1996; Girelli & Stake, 1993; Jackson et al.,

1996; McCrae & Costa, 1989; Mitchell, 2001; Pittenger, 2005). This criticism tends to be general and with only limited discussion. By contrast, Anastasi (1976), Devito (1985), and Hicks (1970) recognized the forced-choice nature of the MBTI but indicate that it is not ipsative. Hicks presented a detailed discussion of ipsative and forced-choice measures, including particular attention to the MBTI.

Hicks (1970) distinguished absolute measures, where individual scale scores are independent and are free to vary on each scale, from ipsative measures, where individual scores are relative to the score levels on other scales. Hicks then offers a "stringent definition of ipsative" where

> any score matrix is said to be ipsative when the sum of the scores obtained over the attributes measured for each respondent is a constant. That is, an ipsative measure yields a mean over all assessed attributes, this mean being the same for each person.
>
> *p. 169*

Constraints are imposed on scale scores for ipsative measures because items from *different* scales are paired with each other and individuals make a forced choice among them. Since the total score is fixed and invariant for ipsative scoring, each forced choice affects the scale score for both scale variables. This is not the case for the MBTI and its bipolar scale structure. Hicks noted that "the critical item-format characteristic of the MBTI is the fact that items representing a given bipolar scale are never paired with items representing another bipolar scale" (p. 171). In other words, MBTI forced-choice items are only compared with items from the opposite pole of the same scale so that the sums of the scale scores are always independent and are absolute measures for each scale. From a methodological perspective, the forced-choice format of the MBTI is a legitimate measurement practice comparable to the paired comparison technique in psychophysics. More formally, MBTI forced-choice data fall comfortably into Quadrant I (preferential choice data) of Coombs' (1964) data classification system.

The Problem of the Jungian Types

Although the MBTI is based on Jung, the MBTI types are not Jung's types. In fact, neither the straightforward four-letter MBTI types nor the four-letter dynamical types (Table 16.1) are Jung's types. In both cases, 16 different types are identified. However, the dynamical interpretation is based on only eight preference combinations (pairs) as *measured by the four MBTI scales*—ES, EN, ET, EF, IS, IN, IT, and IF—because the expression of type dynamics includes *only* the combination of Extraversion or Introversion with the individual functions (Sensing, Intuition, Thinking, or Feeling) *and does not measure the Jungian function types, that is, Se, Ne, Te, Fe, Si, Ni, Ti, and Fi, directly*. In this sense, the intended meaning of Extraversion and Introversion is identified only where the dominant function is expressed, for example, Se means dominant Sensing extraverted. I. B. Myers (1962, 1980) may have intended that her 16 four-letter dynamical types (Table 16.1) were separate forms of the eight Jungian types and in fact were part of the original MBTI type descriptions. For example, there are two forms of the Extraverted Thinking Types where T is dominant, one with sensing as auxiliary (ESTJ) and another with intuition as auxiliary (ENTJ).

Accepting this interpretation, however, is inconsistent with the structural properties of the MBTI, particularly an E–I scale that measures similar social extraversion as other personality measures (e.g., McCrae & Costa, 1989; Schaubhut et al., 2009; Stricker & Ross, 1964b) more clearly than an intended "orientation" role (Reynierse, 2009; Reynierse & Harker, 2008a, 2008b; Stricker & Ross, 1962, 1964a). Even worse, it reduces a restrictive set of 16 four-letter MBTI types to 8 two-letter Jungian types.

Although the eight-function model is an accurate interpretation of Jung and is widely accepted, it occurs in an empirical vacuum where there is scant supporting data. Equating psychological type with the eight Jungian function types is, at best, a very limited and incomplete version of type; at worst, it is subject to many of the criticisms of the classical type theory and psychometric concerns discussed earlier in this chapter and elsewhere. For example, although the Jungian function types are identified conceptually as "whole types," where the function and attitude are inseparable, taxometric analyses showed that, where tested, the Jungian function types were uniformly continuous rather than categorical dimensions (Arnau et al., 2003). Furthermore, it is doubtful that the eight Jungian SL-TDI scales are independent, as there were unusually high correlations between the scales ranging from .31 to .71 for the eight Jungian scales and from .50 to .75 for the six Preference scales under test–retest reliability conditions (Arnau, Rosen, & Thompson, 2000). And when correlations were measured within the same time period they were even higher, ranging from .53 to .76 for the eight Jungian scales and from .69 to .90 for the Preference scales, suggesting that all of these very high correlations were due to the commingling of the functions and attitudes.[3]

Interpretation of the MBTI preference relationships can vary based on personal allegiance to particular interpretations of Jung and subjective interpretations regarding how successfully the MBTI operationalizes Jung's theory of types. What we know with certainty is that the MBTI consists of four relatively straightforward measurement scales and interpretation should be cautious and restricted to what is objectively measured by these scales. Anything beyond the straightforward measure is conjecture and outside the MBTI as an objective measurement instrument. Adoption or substitution of the Jungian function types for interpreting the MBTI may reflect Jungian purity of thought or belief, but in the absence of evidence is merely conjecture or prejudice.

MBTI Type Theory Is Nonsituational

Pittenger (2005) discussed the idea that type theory, couched in fixed descriptions of the 16 four-letter types, has little to say about an individual's response to situational or contextual events. He noted:

> Reading McCaulley's (2000) description of the type preferences suggests that situational factors have little or no influence on individuals' behaviors or cognitions. Indeed, little in the MBTI theory appears to acknowledge the Person X Situation interaction that is a common component of contemporary social-cognitive theory (Mischel & Shoda, 1995; Shoda & Mischel, 2000).
>
> *p. 217*

This criticism applies to a type system based on a limited set of 16 four-letter whole types that are fixed at the dichotomy but not necessarily to a preference-based type system.

Tett and Burnett (2003) presented a Person × Situation interaction model and taxonomy for work-related and job performance factors that was integrated with FFM trait dimensions (for more information regarding this theory, see Chapter 5, this volume). One unique feature of their model is that it addressed bidirectional, situational effects of personality on job performance as the model incorporated both positive and negative factors, for example, job demands where there is the opportunity to act in a positive way to meet work requirements, versus distracters that are inherently negative and interfere with performance. Application of the Tett and Burnett model to the MBTI preferences is particularly appropriate since the complementary opposite structure of the MBTI preference pairs are naturally bipolar and bidirectional.

Salter (1995) developed a taxonomy of environmental types that was MBTI related and later introduced the *Salter Environmental Type Assessment* (SETA) to examine the fit between environmental demands and the MBTI preferences (Salter, 2003). The SETA has a four-factor structure that parallels the MBTI preferences, and the Person × Situation interaction research with it has occurred primarily in educational settings. Belling (2009) used the SETA to examine transfer of learning from executive development programs back to the workplace and found that Fs identified the greatest number of barriers for transfer whereas Ns and Ts identified the most facilitators for transfer to the executive workplace. At another level of analysis, the complexity of situational effects of personality on performance is apparent when the MBTI preference multidimensionality content of situations is considered (Reynierse, 2009; Reynierse & Harker, 2008b). This concept is discussed further in the next section on a revised type theory.

Principles of a Revised Type Theory

The revised type theory summarized below is abstracted from Reynierse (2012). The revised theory represents a synthesis of Jungian type theory, particularly the ideas of Meier (1977/1995) discussed earlier, with the FFM of personality, particularly the many contributions of McCrae and Costa (1989, 2003, 2008). Within this revised type theory, the MBTI has an expanded role for understanding and interpreting human personality.

An overarching objective of the revised type theory is the construction of a system that can account for a wide range of human personality characteristics and behavior. In this sense, the theory recognizes both human individuality (variation) and behavioral complexity. The theory is explicitly dynamic but views this dynamic character as occurring in the Person × Situation interaction, that is, where an individual is active in a potentially infinite set of ever-changing "real-world" events and experiences. How then can a model of personality account for a large array of personality characteristics and potentialities based on a limited set of theoretical principles and measured personality concepts? The model presented here is my solution to this problem. In my revised type theory, complexity occurs primarily as an emergent effect of preference complementarity and is expressed as type preference combinations plus their ordinal relationships.

The major principles of this revised type theory are as follows:

Principle 1: All individual human beings differ with their own personal identity and individuality formed by their own unique genetic, ontogenetic, epigenetic, and experiential background.

The starting point of this revised type theory is explicitly biological and consistent with Darwinian evolution and modern biological thought that rejected typological thinking and replaced it with population thinking (Mayr, 1982, 1988, 1991). Everyone is different and unique. The significant psychological question is not whether or not individuals differ—that is a given—but rather to what extent are individuals similar? In other words, what psychological dimensions are shared and include substantial commonality among many individuals?

My view of "psychological types" is that they are inexact, unfixed, and probabilistic. It follows Meier (1977/1995), who noted that "people usually have a preference for one specific 'intellectual talent' and *exploit it to the full*" (p. 13, italics added). The type then is the "intellectual talent" that any individual relies on, that is, is most comfortable with, when interacting with everyday events or situations in the world. In this system, the types are identified with each of the eight MBTI preferences. The dominant or primary MBTI preference for any individual is generally the "individual talent" that is "exploited to the full" and is used extensively.

The "types" themselves are conveniences that sort an otherwise chaotic arrangement of infinite variability into psychologically meaningful categories that are representative of human activity. In short, the "types" are intended to identify psychologically meaningful order out of the chaos of individual variation and uniqueness.

Principle 2: The individual MBTI preferences are the fundamental unit of analysis for type theory.

The straightforward individual preferences are the starting point for type theory and identify significant differences that distinguish one person from another. This position is consistent with Jung's

(1923/1971) four functions but extends Jung to include each of the MBTI preferences. Within this framework, each of the individual preferences—Extraversion (E), Introversion (I), Sensing (S), Intuition (N), Thinking (T), Feeling (F), Judging (J), and Perceiving (P)—has independent meaningfulness and equivalent status relative to each other.[4] Each preference is functional, that is, has utility when used appropriately, but can also be dysfunctional when used inappropriately or excessively.

The empirical evidence for the independence and primacy of the MBTI preferences is overwhelming. All three editions of the *MBTI Manual* (I. B. Myers, 1962; I. B. Myers & McCaulley, 1985; I. B. Myers et al., 1998), the *MBTI Form M Manual Supplement* (Schaubhut et al., 2009), Harvey's (1996) review of MBTI validity, and many *Journal of Psychological Type* articles, for example Harker, Reynierse, and Komisin's (1998) research with lexical descriptors, provide substantial validation for the individual preferences.

Ultimately, each preference is part of a fundamental brain structure and organization that lurks in the background at all times and is available for use to meet environmental demands when needed. In this sense, the individual preferences are postulated as generic, neurological processes that can act alone or in combination with other preferences.

Principle 3: The individual preferences are arranged as sets of complementary opposites.

The arrangement of the MBTI preferences as complementary opposite pairs can expand type categories—both for individual type profiles and the situational demands that routinely occur as part of life and human existence. Specifically, preference complementarity produces unique patterns of conscious experience and expressed behavior that are part of the information identified by the MBTI measure, for example, the empirical fact that a large percentage of managers at all levels are T and J. For example, lower management in business organizations is primarily S, T, and J, but become increasingly N at higher management levels (Reynierse, 1993; Roach, 1986; Walck, 1992) where the demands differ. Similarly, start-up entrepreneurs are generally N, T, and P (Carland & Carland, 1992; Reynierse, 1997), whereas growth executives are N, T, and J (Fasiska, 1992)—results that are consistent with the fact that creative individuals in general have high levels of P (Thorne & Gough, 1991) and that entrepreneurs have high scores on a scale of change (Sexton & Ginn, 1990). Opposition occurs naturally due to the bipolar structure of the preference pairs and follows Meier's (1977/1995) third fundamental principle that, within the individual pair, the two functions are in opposition to each other and are mutually exclusive. They are complementary since, for any preference pair, one preference fulfills (or compensates for) what the other lacks. This arrangement of opposites is the source for any individual's personal strengths and limitations when dealing with real-world situations. Colloquially, we understand this by the expression "we cannot be all things to all people."

There is some risk that any Jungian function or MBTI preference can be so highly differentiated that it is used indiscriminately and to the exclusion of the nonpreferred preference. Although the preferred preference is a source of psychological strength, it can be used inappropriately. Similarly, the opposite preference can be the source of significant personal weakness within any individual and the source of considerable annoyance, conflict, and misunderstanding between a person with one preference and another person with the opposite preference (Meier). Although opposite preferences provide complementary strategies for interacting in the world, they also have the potential for exaggerating differences between individuals.

This theoretical system accepts both the Jungian concept of complementary opposites and the MBTI nomenclature for the E–I, S–N, T–F, and J–P preference pairs. From this perspective, the MBTI preference pairs can be briefly described as follows:

- E–I represents two kinds of social orientation—outgoing and personable (Extraverted) or private and reserved (Introverted). This is essentially the same social extraversion of the FFM and other structural models of personality. In this restricted sense, E–I includes the Jungian preferences for the external and internal worlds where Es are expressive and responsive to the external world of people and things, whereas Is are outwardly less expressive but attend to and monitor their internal world of feelings and ideas. Within this framework, the workings of the conscious human mind are private and internalized (Introverted), whereas the expression of the conscious mind is public and externalized (Extraverted).

- S–N represents two kinds of intellect—practical, applied, and literal (Sensing) or abstract, symbolic, and conceptual (Intuition)—and should not be conflated with "measured intelligence." This approximates the Jungian concept of two ways of perceiving or finding things out where Ss gather factual information about situations from their sensory experiences, whereas Ns see connections and relationships.
- T–F represents two kinds of orientation to others (interpersonal relations or outlook)—demanding and tough-minded, that is, task before people (Thinking), or responsive and tender-minded, that is, people before task (Feeling). Again, this approximates the Jungian concept of two ways of making judgments or coming to conclusions where Ts are demanding, logical, objective, and impersonal, whereas Fs are responsive, sensitive, subjective, and caring.
- J–P represents two kinds of life-style orientation—structured, organized living (Judging), or spontaneous, flexible living (Perceiving). This approximates the FFM dimension of conscientiousness but also includes two ways of dealing with authority. Js tend to accept authority, standardized work procedures, and the need to conform and work comfortably within organizations, whereas Ps question authority, dislike standardized routines, and are more rebellious and entrepreneurial.

Principle 4: The individual preferences are free to combine with each other and in any order.

The compound arrangements of the preferences provide for behavioral complexity, human diversity, and an expanded array of type categories. In this sense, there are many type effects that are fundamentally multidimensional. Such preference multidimensionality was identified by Harker et al. (1998) as their research with lexical descriptors showed that many items were significant for more than one MBTI preference. But, historically, many preference multidimensionality effects were presented—but not interpreted—in every edition of the *MBTI Manual*. For example, the reported correlations of the MBTI preference scores with the *16 Personality Factors Questionnaire*, the *Millon Index of Personality Styles*, and the *California Psychological Inventory* show that many of their scales were also significant for multiple MBTI preferences. Similar preference multidimensionality effects were reported for many interest inventories including the *OAIS: Opinion, Attitude, and Interest Scales*, *Kuder Occupational Interest Survey*, and the *Strong–Campbell Interest Inventory* (e.g., I. B. Myers & McCaulley, 1985; I. B. Myers et al., 1998). Cumulative research with the MBTI clearly shows that multidimensional combinations of the preferences are the norm and occur often.

The rich array of potential combinations of the preferences has been described in greater detail elsewhere, for example Reynierse (2000) and Reynierse and Harker (2001a), where these combinations applied to individual type profiles. Later, Reynierse and Harker (2008b) showed that the preferences can combine in any order, for example "conservative" is an SJ item, whereas "structure oriented" is a JS item, and "enterprising" is a TE item, whereas "seeks action" is an ET item. In each case, both specific MBTI content and the ordinal relationship of this content have meaningfulness for psychological effects. For example, Sensing (S) is primary for the SJ item "conservative" and Judging (J) has a secondary contributory role. Additional complexity is sometimes observed, for example, the item "structure oriented" also combines with the "T" preference (JST). Examples of such preference multidimensional order effects are presented in Table 16.3. Ultimately, how any individual responds in a particular situation depends on the MBTI preference multidimensionality composition

Table 16.3 Preference Multidimensionality Effects for Lexical Descriptors With Their Correlations and Difference Scores ($p < .0001$) From Reynierse and Harker (Unpublished Data; $N = 770$)

Primary MBTI Preference	*MBTI Preference Pairs, r-scores and Difference Scores (ds)*			
	EI r-scores (ds)	*SN r-scores (ds)*	*TF r-scores (ds)*	*JP r-scores (ds)*
Extraversion (E) primary				
Fun loving (EFP)	33 (.51)		–.18 (.27)	–.18 (.22)
Verbal (EN)	.33 (.56)	–.16 (.30)		
Expresses feelings easily (EF)	.31 (.64)		–.17 (.30)	
Stimulating (EN)	.28 (.41)	–.21 (.35)		
Seeks action (ET)	.28 (.50)		.18 (.32)	
Introversion (I) primary				
Reserved (IJS)	–.44 (.91)	.17 (.36)		.18 (.33)
Avoids drawing attention to self (IS)	–.31 (.62)	.19 (.41)		
Timid (IF)	–.29 (.53)		–.22 (.44)	
Meek (ISF)	–.21 (.36)	.20 (.42)	–.18 (.40)	
Serious (IJ)	–.19 (.28)			.17 (.21)*
Sensing (S) primary				
Conservative (SJ)		.28 (.49)		.17 (.31)
Likes tested routines (SJI)	–.15 (.29)	.28 (.54)		.28 (.45)
Likes tried methods (SJ)		.27 (.41)		.22 (.29)
Concrete (SJT)		.25 (.39)	.14 (.25)*	.16 (.29)
Factual (SJT)		.25 (.35)	.14 (.31)	.23 (.36)
Cautious (SJI)	–.12* (.22)*	.22 (.35)		.17 (.21)*
Traditional (SJ)		.21 (.31)		.19 (.32)
Intuition (N) primary				
Unconventional (NP)		–.29 (.46)		–.25 (.38)
Idea oriented (NT)		–.27 (.47)	.16 (.27)	
Conceptual thinker (NT)		–.24 (.42)	.16 (.22)*	
Inventive (NT)		–.20 (.29)	.17 (.28)	
Thinking (T) primary				
Competitive (TE)	.16 (.38)		.29 (.67)	
Assertive (TE)	.21 (.43)		.23 (.42)	
Enterprising (TE)	.15 (.26)		.23 (.37)	
Decisive (TJ)			.22 (.35)	.21 (.41)
Aggressive (TE)	.20 (.47)		.20 (.41)	
Industrious (TJ)			.19 (.29)	.16 (.25)
Feeling (F) primary				
Emotional (FE)	.13 (.28)*		–.32 (.66)	
Dreamy (FP)			–.24 (.52)	–.20 (.36)
Lenient (FP)			–.25 (.35)	–.13 (.25)
Hesitant (FIS)	.18 (.34)	.11** (.25)	–.22 (.35)	

Table 16.3 (Continued)

Primary MBTI Preference	*MBTI Preference Pairs, r-scores and Difference Scores (ds)*			
	EI r-scores (ds)	*SN r-scores (ds)*	*TF r-scores (ds)*	*JP r-scores (ds)*
Judging (J) primary				
Scheduled (JS)		.16 (.19)*		.44 (.77)
Structure oriented (JST)		.23 (.34)	.16 (.33)	.39 (.70)
Organized (JS)		.16 (.27)*		.34 (.63)
Orderly (JS)		.17 (.25)*		.33 (.61)
Likes things settled (JS)		.24 (.34)		.27 (.45)
Thorough (JT)			.16 (.25)	.26 (.39)
Exact (JTS)		.17 (.26)*	.18 (.32)	.24 (.47)
Practical (JS)		.18 (.23)		.19 (.25)
Perceiving (P) primary				
Spontaneous (PEN)	.24 (.45)	−.13 (.25)		−.27 (.35)
Uncomfortable with routines (PN)		−.23 (.35)		−.26 (.44)
Impulsive (PE)	.19 (.39)			−.26 (.40)

Notes: Negative correlations are associated with E, S, T, and J; positive correlations are associated with I, N, F, and P.

* $p < .001$; ** $p < .01$.

or content of that activity, for example a uniquely TE "enterprising" situational demand, and the unique location of "T" and "E" on that individual's personal type dominance hierarchy. If both T and E are well developed and high on the dominance hierarchy, that person will likely perform often and comfortably on enterprising tasks. That the "preferences can combine in any order" provides a mechanism for type effects to occur in different situations.

Principle 5: The combination of individual preferences is additive rather than interactive.

Although conventional type theory assumes that the preferences interact to form unique types, the extent that type interactions occur are *at best* modest, are subordinate to the preferences, and occur most often at the most basic level, that is, at the level of the two-way interactions (Reynierse, 2009; Reynierse & Harker, 2000, 2001a). Examination of the effects suggests that obtained type interactions were very complicated, uncertain, the result of statistical artifacts, and vanishingly small (Reynierse & Harker, 2001a, 2005a).

When the combination of two or more preferences is additive, the unique contribution is straightforward, often substantial, and occurs at the locus of each component MBTI preference rather than with the whole pair (or whole type). From this perspective, the "whole types" are constructed through the addition of the parts, that is, the individual preferences that describe them. For example, an ISTJ reflects its independent I + S + T + J composition.

Individual personalities, as illustrated by someone's MBTI scores, usually reflect a range of individual scores. The whole type then, for example ISTJ, only incompletely describes that person since any dimensional differences among the scale scores are ignored when the four-letter whole type is emphasized. Sometimes, however, an individual has multiple (usually two) high MBTI scores that stand out and are comparable, for example, high N + T (NT), high T + N (TN), high E + F (EF), or high F + E (FE). High pairs are important for accurately describing these individuals, and the pairs, again constructed through the addition of the high-scale score parts, are significant type forms for such individuals (Reynierse, 2000, 2009). Regardless, the additive nature of each type combination applies to both individual MBTI type profiles and the preference multidimensionality content or composition of type-related situations.

Principle 6: The expression of psychological type is fundamentally contextual and situational.

Table 16.3 presents statistically significant MBTI preference relationships for several lexical descriptors. At one level, this is conventional validation evidence for the MBTI preferences. At another level, they identify the MBTI composition or content for each descriptor. One interpretation of this material is that these descriptors are lower-order psychological traits that are subordinate to the superordinate MBTI preferences. Such traits can also be viewed as characteristics of individual people (the type profiles) or as behavioral activities necessary to respond to environmental demands. Whether viewed as a constellation of related traits or situational demands, preference multidimensionality (i.e., the activation or presence of two or more MBTI preferences) is often necessary to describe them. Each descriptor has meaning for human activity when there is a corresponding, specific environmental demand. The MBTI content relationships (Table 16.3) provide an estimate of the contextual or situational requirements to act or respond appropriately in specific situations.

There is a fundamental distinction between the type effects that characterize individual people (the type profiles) and the type conditions that are descriptive of individual psychological events. Preference multidimensionality identifies the specific MBTI composition or content that is relevant for such situational or contextual events (Reynierse, 2009; Reynierse & Harker, 2008b). Each of these psychological events is situational and limited in scope and represents just a fragment of the broader capacity of human nature. The lexical descriptors identified in Table 16.3 are examples of such situational or contextual conditions and reflect the fact that only some type constructs are necessary to describe them. The remaining, unused preferences are idle for that particular situation (Reynierse & Harker, 2001a, 2005a).

Principle 7: MBTI preference scores matter and indicate strength of preference.

The MBTI measure and type theory are usually expressed in categorical terms where individuals are sorted into the preference pairs or *dichotomies*, ignoring individual preference scale scores. But dichotomization of any measurement variable comes with considerable cost in lost statistical power and information contained in the full range of scale scores (Cohen, 1983). However, MBTI preference scores matter a great deal and recognition of the scale scores expands both the conceptual and statistical power of the MBTI instrument (e.g., Reynierse & Harker, 2005b).

Based on the strength (difference score from the 100 base) of participants' individual continuous scores, Reynierse and Harker (2005b) ranked each participant on each of the eight MBTI preferences. The attraction of continuous scores is that they are relative measures that reflect the difference between a preference and its opposite, where relatively large-scale scores toward each end of the continuum indicate relatively large differences between a preference and its opposite, whereas scale scores close to the midpoint indicate relatively small differences. Thus, ranks 1–4 correspond to each person's four-letter type, ranging from strongest to weakest for the four preferred preferences. Ranks for the four opposite preferences can be estimated by taking the inverse of each continuous score and applying this to the nonpreferred preferences, a procedure that considers the forced-choice nature of the MBTI preference scales and the application of an unfolding technique for determining the order of "mirror image" ranks (Coombs, 1964). The outcome is that the eight preferences are then ranked 1–8 for each individual. Accordingly, Reynierse and Harker were able to examine eight separate levels of each MBTI preference, that is, when a particular preference was ranked 1, 2, 3, . . . 8, and then analyze performance on different dependent variables across these ranks, for example, an F item such as "Sympathetic" for individuals where the F preference was ranked 1, 2, 3, . . . or 8.

Statistical analyses based on these rankings were unusually systematic and orderly as the ranking of the preferences consistently produced a general gradient of effects in which the higher-ranking preferences showed the significantly stronger effects, intermediate ranks were progressively weaker, and the lower-ranking preferences showed the weakest effects.[5]

Principle 8: Type dominance is a function of strength of preference and the dominant preference is simply the independently high-value preference.

The falsification of type dynamics (Reynierse, 2009; Reynierse & Harker, 2008a, 2008b) came at considerable cost since it identified significant problems with the long-standing, objective MBTI procedure for identifying type dominance within individuals. This "principle," then, is intended to preserve the importance of type dominance conceptually within type theory and show that the MBTI provides a reliable *estimate* of type dominance information that has utility for understanding individual personality.

Identification of type dominance is an extension of Principle 7, the Reynierse and Harker (2005b) research presented there, and our considerable research on preference multidimensionality (Reynierse, 2009, 2012; Reynierse & Harker, 2008b). Preference multidimensionality is complex and generally beyond the scope of this chapter. For our immediate objectives, preference multidimensionality includes two fundamental ideas: first, two or more MBTI preferences are often necessary to describe significant type effects; and second, preference effects are proportional to their independent contributions where the independently larger preference has a greater effect than the independently smaller preference. Structurally, the dominant preference is simply the *independently high-value preference*, particularly when that preference stands out and is markedly higher than any other preference in someone's four-letter type. In other words, each individual's MBTI preference scores are a reliable estimate of the strength or rank order of each of the preferences. Furthermore, this dominance is dependent on the individual situation or context and varies from one psychological state to another *depending on the relevant MBTI content for a particular situation.*

Table 16.4 summarizes dominance relationships for the IS item "Avoids drawing attention to self" for several alternative type dominance models. In each case, the analysis was for mean observer ratings (where lower rating scores indicate a greater effect)[6] from related studies with the same database (Reynierse & Harker, 2008a, 2008b). Note that the S type dynamics condition includes the following MBTI types (Table 16.1); that is, for Dominant Sensing (ESTP, ESFP, ISTJ, and ISFJ), Auxiliary Sensing (ESTJ, ESFJ, ISTP, and ISFP), Tertiary Sensing (ENFJ, ENTJ, INFP, and INTP), and Inferior Sensing (ENFP, ENTP, INFJ, and INTJ).[7] Note too that only the Dominant and Auxiliary conditions include the Sensing (S) types, whereas the Tertiary and Inferior conditions always include the Intuition (N) types, the opposite of Sensing. The E–I controls compare the rating scores for the straightforward effects for E and I across the type dynamics, dominance conditions. Now, it is also the case that the IS item "Avoids drawing attention to self" has specific MBTI content that is summarized in Table 16.3 and where the I content ($r = .31$; $ds = .62$) is greater than the S content ($r = .19$; $ds = .41$). This represents the aggregated preference multidimensionality content for this item based on the effects. Thus, preference multidimensionality specifically predicts order effects that are very different from the predicted order effects of type dynamics. Four MBTI content conditions can be formed based on this content, that is, where the I content is primary because it is greater, and the S content is secondary because it is less. These include conditions in which both relevant preferences are shared (both I and S), only the primary preference is shared (I only), only the secondary preference is shared (S only), and neither relevant preference was shared (both E

Table 16.4 Mean-Independent Observer Ratings for Type Dynamics, E–I Controls, and Preference Multidimensionality Equivalent Dominance Hierarchy Conditions for the IS Item "Avoids Drawing Attention to Self"[a]

Alternative Model	*Condition*	*Dominant*	*Auxiliary*	*Tertiary*	*Inferior*
Grant–Brownsword	S	2.35	2.43	2.73	2.85
	Se	2.72	1.94	3.01	2.54
	Si	2.22	2.77	2.46	3.07
Manual Model	S	2.35	2.43	2.73	2.85
	Se	2.72	1.94	2.46	2.54
	Si	2.22[b]	2.77	3.01	3.07
E–I controls	E	2.72	2.77	3.01	3.07
	I	2.22	1.94	2.46	2.54
		MBTI Content Conditions			
		Both I and S	*I Only*	*S Only*	*Neither*
Preference multidimensionality	IS	2.13	2.50	2.75	3.05

[a] Lower rating scores indicate a greater effect.

[b] The only statistically significant effects were that dominant (Si) > auxiliary, tertiary, and inferior. Auxiliary (Si) was not significantly better than tertiary ($p = .105$) and was marginally better than inferior ($p = .054$).

and N are shared but not I and S). Note that these four conditions include the following MBTI types (Table 16.1): Both I and S (ISTJ, ISTP, ISFJ, and ISFP), I Only Primary (INTJ, INTP, INFJ, and INFP), S Only Secondary (ESTJ, ESTP, ESFJ, and ESFP), and Neither I nor S (ENTJ, ENTP, ENFJ, and ENFP).

The E–I controls show a substantial, straightforward effect for E and I and a modest preference pairs difference for the type dynamics conditions—results that track the E and I preferences directly rather than the type dynamics predictions for expressing the Jungian functions in the E and I attitudes. The combined S condition is the same for both the Grant–Brownsword and the *Manual* models of type dynamics (2.35, 2.43, 2.73, and 2.85) and where dominant = auxiliary > tertiary = inferior, an effect that identifies only a preference difference but does not contradict type dynamics. The Grant–Brownsword Se condition (2.72, 1.94, 3.01, and 2.54) and where auxiliary > dominant, tertiary, and inferior and inferior > tertiary includes two effects (auxiliary > dominant and inferior > tertiary) that contradict type dynamics. The Grant–Brownsword Si condition (2.22, 2.77, 2.46, and 3.07) and where dominant > auxiliary, tertiary, and inferior supports type dynamics but the finding tertiary > auxiliary contradicts it. The *Manual* Se condition (2.72, 1.94, 2.46, and 2.54) and where auxiliary > dominant, tertiary, and inferior includes auxiliary > dominant that contradicts type dynamics. The *Manual* Si condition (2.22, 2.77, 3.01, and 3.07) and where dominant > auxiliary > tertiary and inferior provides support for type dynamics. At the same time, the combined S solution, the Grant–Brownsword Se and Si solutions, the *Manual* Se solution, and the *Manual* Si solution—the best solution among them—are each *inferior* to the preference multidimensionality solution where there is a perfect hierarchy and Both (2.13) > I Primary (2.50) > S Secondary (2.75) > Neither (3.05). Empirically, type dynamics predictions produced many contradictions to theory (Reynierse & Harker, 2008a). By contrast, for the approximately 500 tests of preference multidimensionality ordinal relationships, in every case, without exception, the effects were consistent with the predictions of preference multidimensionality and were completely free from contradiction (Reynierse, 2009; Reynierse & Harker, 2008b).

Within this revised type theory, the key points are that type dominance includes eight positions (not four as occur for the original Jungian type hierarchy)—one for each of the eight MBTI preferences; that each position in the hierarchy can be estimated by the strength of preference rank based on MBTI preference scores; and that the same rules apply for assigning preference ranks under aggregated research conditions as apply when forming MBTI profiles for individuals. The aggregated data provide information about the general effect and lawfulness of type dominance conceptually; the individual type profiles provide an estimate of the eight-position type dominance hierarchy for that individual.

The conventional four-letter MBTI types (Table 16.1) include many unidentified type variants and hide considerable type information about everyone, in particular preference strength and preference order, information that is important for type dominance relationships. The objective of formatting types as eight-letter types is intended to make this hidden information visible (and useful). For example, consider a traditional INFP with MBTI continuous scores of I = 125, N = 145, F = 119, and P = 145 with ranks of N (first), P (first), I (third), and F (fourth); the inverse of these scores is T (fifth), E (sixth), J (eighth), and S (eighth).[8] Note that both N and P are essentially equivalent and primary preferences for this individual, and which preference is in fact dominant will be determined by the situation and context. The dominance hierarchy for this individual can be summarized as NPIFtejs for "N situations," but PNIFtesj is an equally accurate description for "P situations," information that is not apparent from the traditional "INFP" classification system but which distinguishes this individual from other conventionally scored "INFPs" with different dominance hierarchies. Depending upon context and the strength of the individual preferences, this is the source of significant differences within each person's behavioral repertoire.

A Concluding Note on Type Acceptability and Quality

The FFM of personality provides a structure that is conceptually attractive and organizes the empirical facts effectively. It presents an elegant empirical structure that satisfies the objectives of researchers and theorists engaged in the tasks of psychological science, an audience it serves well. At the same time, the trait structure of the FFM is less effective for the "art" of the practitioner who often operates in a "fuzzy" environment where the objectives are murky, trade-offs are real, and compromise and consensus are essential to move forward and take concrete action steps. By contrast, the MBTI is explicitly functional and can more easily address these organizational realities.

Applications of the MBTI and type theory for work and organizational interventions occur in many forms and have been summarized for an MBTI emphasis (e.g., Bridges, 1992; Demarest, 1997; Hirsh & Kummerow, 1987; McCaulley, 2000) and from a Jungian perspective (Stein & Hollwitz, 1992). In general, these applications are descriptive rather than empirical and ultimately their utility rests with the perceived "practical differences" that occur in organizational interventions where the successful application is itself supporting evidence for a pragmatism-based theory of truth (James, 1907/1943). Wherever people are involved and have differences, there is a potential market for a consultant or trainer who has the MBTI in their toolkit. Users of the MBTI and type theory are keenly aware of potential misuses of type (e.g., Coe, 1992; McCaulley, 2000) and are reluctant to use the MBTI for selection applications. The argument is that the "MBTI indicates preferences, not skills . . . and all types can be found in all careers" (McCaulley, 2000, p. 131), and making hiring, promotion, or assignment decisions based on MBTI type scale scores *alone* is discouraged. The user-friendly, nonthreatening, positive character of the MBTI is an attractive feature for the consultant working within organizations because it is congruent with goals for developing organizational growth, promotes advocacy and a collegial climate for conducting the intervention, and reduces the risk that the process is perceived as adversarial.

The MBTI as a diagnostic measure and consulting tool has several advantages over most psychological measures (McCaulley, 2000, p. 131):

- The questions are less threatening and invasive;
- The basic constructs are recognized in everyday life as people are already familiar with differences between outgoing and quiet people, between practical and innovative people, between tough-minded and warm-hearted people, and between organized and spontaneous people;
- The MBTI provides a clear, simple, logical model for understanding the people side within TJ organizations.

In my introductory comments, I indicated that the complementary structure of the MBTI preferences promotes a positive framework for interpreting type constructs. One way this occurs is that type dimensions are described by opposite bipolar descriptors where *both poles are viewed as normal and positive*. By contrast, for the FFM trait equivalents only relatively high scores, for example high extraversion, high agreeableness, and so on, are viewed positively, and low scores are viewed in negative terms and defined as less of or a deficiency for that dimension, for example low extraversion, low agreeableness, and so on (Bayne, 1994; K. D. Myers, Quenk, & Kirby, 1995; Newman, 1995a; Quenk, 1993b). From the type perspective, each pole of the preference pairs is functional, has utility, and can be advantageous or disadvantageous, depending on situational circumstances.

Pittenger (1993a) made several critical comments about MBTI type descriptions including that they are generally flattering and therefore are believed to be accurate regardless of their truth or validity, but misses the point on their flattering and positive tone. Type descriptors are explicitly positive and favorable *only* for the relevant MBTI type or preference that is described primarily in terms of distinctive strengths (e.g., Bayne, 1994). There is always the implicit understanding that the complementary opposite, nonpreferred type or complementary opposite, nonpreferred preference is a limitation or weakness, despite that it too is presented in positive terms. And in the privacy of an individual counseling session, both strengths and weakness are routinely discussed.

Both complimentary and unflattering descriptors were identified for the MBTI preferences when independent observers rated individuals that they knew well (Harker et al., 1998; Reynierse & Harker, 2001b). That both complimentary and unflattering descriptors are reliably associated with the MBTI preferences is not a surprise but rather represent appropriate qualities that are descriptive of *equally valid opposite categories*—the complementary opposites—and that correspond to their potential strengths and weaknesses. It was also apparent that the meaningfulness of natural language descriptors included an element of social acceptability and that independent observers were reluctant to make unflattering ratings for those they know well (Reynierse & Harker, 2001a, 2005a). Everyone is more comfortable with positive language to describe people whether in their private lives or at work.

The problem is compounded for the descriptive language trait theory uses to describe people and again contrasts with the descriptive language used in type theory. Consider the extraversion and introversion descriptors used by type and trait theories. Type descriptors, for example gregarious, enthusiastic, initiator, expressive, and auditory for extraversion and intimate, quiet, receptor, contained, and visual for introversion, are uniformly positive or neutral. By contrast, trait descriptors, for example sociable, fun-loving, affectionate, bold, friendly, and spontaneous, are uniformly positive only for relatively high extraversion scores, and the trait descriptors for low scores, the introversion pole of the scale, often include less flattering terms, for example retiring, reclusive, sober, reserved, timid, aloof, and inhibited, that have frequent negative connotation (Newman, 1995a). The general principle applies to other FFM trait dimensions compared to their MBTI bipolar equivalents

Table 16.5 Representative FFM-Positive and -Negative Trait Descriptors

Source	*Dimension*	*Positive Pole Descriptors*	*Negative Pole Descriptors*
Norman (1963)	Extraversion or surgency	Talkative	Silent
		Frank, open	Secretive
		Adventurous	Cautious
		Sociable	Reclusive
	Agreeableness	Good-natured	Irritable
		Not jealous	Jealous
		Mild, gentle	Headstrong
		Cooperative	Negativistic
	Conscientiousness	Fussy, tidy	Careless
		Responsible	Undependable
		Scrupulous	Unscrupulous
		Persevering	Quitting, fickle
	Culture	Artistically sensitive	Artistically insensitive
		Intellectual	Unreflective, narrow
		Polished, refined	Crude, boorish
		Imaginative	Simple, direct
Wiggins (1979)	Gregarious/extraverted	Gregarious	Aloof
		Friendly	Antisocial
		Genial	Impersonal
		Neighborly	Unneighborly
		Good-natured	Distant
		Extraverted	Introverted
		Outgoing	Shy
		Vivacious	Bashful
		Enthusiastic	Unsparkling
		Cheerful	Undemonstrative
	Warm/agreeable	Warm	Cold
		Tender-hearted	Cold-hearted
		Kind	Cruel
		Sympathetic	Unsympathetic
		Appreciative	Ruthless
		Agreeable	Quarrelsome
		Courteous	Discourteous
		Respectful	Disrespectful
		Cooperative	Uncooperative
		Well-mannered	Uncivil
Goldberg (1990)	Surgency (extraversion)	Jolly	Lethargic
		Talkative	Aloof
		Outgoing	Quiet
		Boisterous	Modest
		Venturous	Joyless
		Energetic	Apathetic

(Continued)

Table 16.5 (Continued)

Source	*Dimension*	*Positive Pole Descriptors*	*Negative Pole Descriptors*
	Agreeableness	Trustful Friendly Generous Cooperative Tolerant Tactful	Vengeful Testy Critical Sarcastic Argumentative Abrasive
	Conscientiousness	Ambitious Organized Orderly Serious Predictable Dignified	Lazy Messy Erratic Rude Inconsistent Awkward
	Intellect	Intelligent Creative Logical Informed Thoughtful	Simple Ignorant Illogical Narrow Dull

(Newman). For example, Table 16.5 identifies several descriptive labels for the positive and negative poles of FFM traits (Goldberg, 1990; Norman, 1963) and interpersonal domain trait descriptors (Wiggins, 1979). Although there are exceptions, for the most part the descriptors identified in Table 16.5 and in the original papers include many descriptors that follow the identical pattern—primarily positive descriptors for the positive pole of the trait dimension but negative and often harsh descriptive language for the negative, that is, opposite, pole. Bayne (2005) agreed with this assessment of trait descriptors but viewed McCrae and Costa's NEO-PI descriptors as more balanced than most and concluded that "The tone is still less even-handed than in the MBTI descriptions, but moving in that direction, if a little grudgingly" (p. 23).

Newman (1995b) recognized the negative aspects of human personality but, as a practitioner, considered it wise to use positive or value-neutral language for dealing with people and criticized trait theorists for "describing much of society in quite unflattering terms" (p. 69). Both the complementary opposite structure and the nonjudgmental descriptive language of the MBTI (e.g., Devito, 1985) contribute to its popularity and acceptability.

Maier (1963, 1973) addressed the general problem for promoting effective decision making in organizations and distinguished the objective, impersonal *quality* (Q) of the decision from the more subjective *acceptability* (A), that is, how those who must execute the decision feel about it. The data for Q depend on the objective facts of the external situation, whereas data for A depend on the subjective feelings of people. Maier's formula for an effective decision (ED) is as follows:

$$ED = Q \times A$$

Both are important.

Consultants adopt the MBTI for use in organizations because they view it as a useful tool for their practice. But they also recognize that the MBTI is a valid measure (Q) and that its user friendliness (A) will establish a positive tone for participants and promote open discussion of the issues for group problem solving and decision making. *Acceptability* is an important consideration for the practice of psychology. The MBTI as a measurement instrument promotes acceptability due to its complementary structure and positive descriptive language. But it also promotes both quality and acceptability through the problem solving and decision-making *process* as this same complementary structure fosters recognition of differences for the organizational issues.

The MBTI problem-solving process (Lawrence, 1979), known colloquially as the "Zig-Zag" model, identifies the sequence that the Jungian functions—S, N, T, or F—are used in problem solving (e.g., Demarest, 1997; Hirsh & Kummerow, 1987; McCaulley, 2000). The sequential process has the following steps:

- Sensing (S)—The first step is a fact-finding stage to identify the relevant facts for each issue;
- Intuition (N)—The second step is a brainstorming stage to identify implications, possibilities, and alternatives;
- Thinking (T)—The third step is an analytical stage that examines the effects or consequences (e.g., pros and cons and costs) of adopting the different options;
- Feeling (F)—The final step is an evaluative stage that examines the impact of the decision and action plans for stakeholders (people issues).

The MBTI problem-solving model resembles principles discussed by Maier (1963) that increase the productivity of group problem solving while increasing both quality and acceptability throughout the process. For example, both models start with the available facts, separate the idea-getting process from the idea-evaluation process, delay the decision making or choice situation, and explicitly incorporate concerns for acceptability and people issues.

Quality is too easily equated with validity, although here the MBTI does quite well (Harvey, 1996; Schaubhut et al., 2009; Thorne & Gough, 1991), particularly for convergent and discriminant validity studies with other measures and analyses of the MBTI factor structure. There is little doubt that these studies provide support for the MBTI scales, that is, the individual preference pairs, and that they measure what they are intended to measure (Schaubhut et al., 2009). There is considerable information on interests and career choice (Hammer, 1996; I. B. Myers & McCaulley, 1985; I. B. Myers et al., 1998) and limited material on job satisfaction where global measures are equivocal, but clearer relationships occur when facets of the job are examined separately, for example, the T–F scale is related to satisfaction with coworkers (Kummerow, 1998). There is little, if any, evidence for the effectiveness of the MBTI when used in organizational interventions, particularly for process consulting (Gauld & Sink, 1985).

No one should be surprised that it is difficult to measure the effectiveness of the MBTI—or any individual measure of personality—on what is achieved for complex group activities. The process consultant working within an organization has "specialist" experience for that particular organizational problem and the MBTI is only one exercise of many that is part of the structured, often proprietary, format for finding solutions to the problem. The role of the MBTI is to make everyone aware of differences among the individuals, provide a model for understanding these differences, and as a reminder when these differences are blocking effective participation for the broader, organizational task. My own view is that success is determined by the client. If the organization's objectives are met, that is what counts. Any successful organizational intervention is, from a Pragmatism tradition, sufficient evidence for the truth (or validity) of the "theory" and methods behind the application (James, 1907/1943).

Case studies provide qualitative validation for the successful intervention but are admittedly rarely generalizable to similar cases. One of my successes was with a large bank following a turbulent merger that affected employee morale, customer dissatisfaction, and many business issues, including profitability (Reynierse & Leyden, 1991). The process involved many steps including an organization culture survey (Reynierse & Harker, 1986), a values clarification exercise (Reynierse, Harker, & Fink, 2000), and an organizational change model (Reynierse, 1994). Although not discussed in the case study (Reynierse & Leyden, 1991), the MBTI was a significant part of the process, particularly the team-building, action planning, and task force activities with 60 key employees. The intervention reversed the low employee morale and employees "bought-in" to the new strategic focus. Effectiveness was evident in the workplace and in the marketplace and was documented in the case study (Reynierse & Leyden, 1991). The success of the program validated all the key elements—the cultural survey, values clarification exercise, organizational change model, and the MBTI. It is difficult to identify any tangible effects that the MBTI contributed to the process other than that it was nonthreatening, the participants enjoyed it, and they recognized the implications for the problem-solving model. Maybe the primary benefit was for my role as process consultant and organizational change agent as it gave me insights about each participant that I used repeatedly to facilitate the process. The differences that previously included hostility, negativity, and rivalry were neutralized in the context of the MBTI, and the participants—from both merged banks—worked productively with each other.

I have emphasized throughout this chapter that the MBTI as a measure, based on the straightforward preferences alone, is useful for identifying significant differences between individuals and can promote a positive experience when used with either individuals or groups. Perhaps that is all that one can ask for. Thorne (2007), responding to criticism of several personality tests including the MBTI and Big Five measures, gave this sage advice:

> Once upon a time, a professor told me not to fault a Volkswagen for not being a Cadillac. His point was that users of personality tests sometimes fault the test for not doing things that the test doesn't claim to do.
>
> *p. 327*

Practitioner's Window

- This chapter discusses historic criticism of the MBTI, its Jungian basis, and presents a revised theory of type that addresses this criticism.
- Many of the perceived problems with the MBTI are problems of theory rather than problems of measurement.
- The MBTI is an underutilized instrument that, in fact, measures much more and provides more information about individuals than is commonly presented or recognized.
- Type interactions, whole types, and type dynamics relationships are the core principles of classical MBTI type theory. The whole type, interaction, type dynamics model identified with the MBTI has not been demonstrated and has many empirical and logical problems.
- Carl Alfred Meier was a long-time associate of C. G. Jung and prolific contributor to the development of Analytical Psychology. The theoretical basis of psychological type presented by Meier (1977/1995) provides context for a *straightforward* Jungian interpretation of the MBTI and the FFM of personality.
- A revised theory of type is presented where the eight MBTI preferences are the principal types rather than the four-letter types of classical type theory.
- Within this revised type theory, the dominant type is simply the highest ranking preference.
- The MBTI includes the five-factor structure of the FFM of personality but ordinarily relies on the more common four factors that conform to the four scales, E–I, S–N, T–F, and J–P.
- The MBTI preferences and their arrangement as complementary opposites are an alternative and defensible interpretation of the meaningfulness of FFM dimensions. This is enhanced by a functional orientation related to use in real-world situations, including work, and a positive framework that promotes acceptability by users.

Recommendations for Research

This recommended research is for the straightforward MBTI preferences as measured by the MBTI scales.

- Type theory predicts changes in the use of Jung's functions through type development or individuation. Longitudinal studies are necessary to examine individual growth or change over time for Jung's functions over the full range of adult development. Given the prominent role of type development or individuation in type theory, this should be a high priority area for future research.
- More broadly, type theory asserts that, for any individual, the dominant preference will appear earlier in development than less dominant preferences (functions). Longitudinal studies that begin with infancy could examine whether evidence for the MBTI preferences appear sequentially rather than in fixed stages and that this is related to type dominance in adulthood. Evidence for epigenetic, molecular switches related to the MBTI preferences should also be examined as part of developmental research.
- Type theory emphasizes that the types are characterized by their frequency of use, yet type research does not measure or report either individual or aggregated data for actual use of the MBTI preferences. Type research should make an effort to measure and report frequency of use data for the MBTI preferences and for many independent variables.
- Idiographic analyses of individual cases based on systematic observation of individuals over time may be more appropriate than the aggregated group data usually presented. These studies should ideally incorporate time-sampling procedures and objective observational techniques for each observed participant.
- Type research for the Person × Situation interaction should be expanded to many different situations for both aggregated research with groups and idiographic analyses with individuals over time.
- Jung's model is broadly cognitive yet there is little research on the relationship of the MBTI preferences to broadly cognitive issues. Since the MBTI and type theory are couched in terms of two contrasting perceiving and judging functions, research on perceptual organization, judgment, and choice are good places to start.
- Practical intelligence is a neglected area in psychology but is part of the S–N preference pair in type theory. It is an important problem, particularly for the world of work, and future research should address this issue.
- There is considerable similarity between Maier's group problem-solving model and that of the MBTI model. Research based on the MBTI and the two models in various settings would have particular value for process consulting and problem solving in organizations.

Acknowledgments

I thank Bob McPeek, Director of Research, and Jamie Johnson, Coordinator of Research Services (now retired), at the Center for Applications of Psychological Type (CAPT). Both gave me continuous support for the duration of this project and provided access to many relevant documents and publications from the extensive CAPT library. I also thank Walter J. Geldart and Bob McPeek for our many conversations on various aspects of type theory and my developing radical revisions of type theory. This chapter has benefited from their insights and constructive comments.

Notes

1 In the first principle, Meier (1975/1989) described the Feeling function in terms of what "its *value is*." Beebe (2004, p. 89), quoting Jung (1957/1977, p. 306), indicated that another term used to describe Feeling is "whether it is agreeable or not," usage that coincides with the FFM term and dimension of Agreeableness.

2 John Beebe (personal communication) indicates that 10 different pairs of opposites emerge as a basis of psyche (or mind) in *Psychological Types*. These include introversion/extraversion, rational/irrational, superior/inferior, superior/auxiliary, conscious/unconscious, sensation/intuition, thinking/feeling, anima/animus, anim(a or us)/persona, and ego/self. An additional pair of complementary opposites not covered in *Psychological Types* is between ego and shadow. According to Beebe, the Jungian interpretation is that the "tensions between these opposites are what create the dynamics that can be analyzed typologically."

3 The original Arnau et al. (2000) paper was concerned with test–retest reliability and the published correlations were for Time 1 and Time 2 of the test–retest period. Randy Arnau ran the correlations for Time 1 of their test–retest conditions following correspondence with me. As expected, under these conditions within a given time point, the correlations were even higher and ranged from .527 to .760 for the eight Jungian scales and from .687 to .895 for the six Preference scales, suggesting that the eight Jungian SL-TDI scales lack independence (Randolph Arnau, personal communication).

4 The J and P preferences as used here are conceptually different than their historical use in MBTI type theory. However, I use the symbols "J" and "P" because they are universally part of MBTI nomenclature and are widely known and accepted.

5 There were 28 comparisons for each of the 174 items in this research for a total of 4,872 individual comparisons. Of the many significant differences—often with extremely low probabilities, for example, at $p < .0000$ or lower—the only significant reversals were an E item where rank 3 < rank 2, an I item where rank 4 < rank 3, an F item where ranks 3 and 4 < rank 2, and a P item where rank 5 < rank 4, a trivial frequency of reversals confined largely to adjacent ranks.

6 The 5-point rating scale in these studies was 1 = *strongly applies*, 2 = *most of the time*, 3 = *some of the time*, 4 = *seldom applies*, and 5 = *definitely not*. A sixth box was available for raters who were unable to make a judgment or did not understand the meaning of a particular word or phrase. Reverse scoring was not used for statistical analyses.

7 The S condition is the general case that includes both the Se and Si Jungian types. The Se condition for the Grant–Brownsword model includes the following MBTI types for Dominant Sensing (ESTP and ESFP), Auxiliary Sensing (ISTP and ISFP), Tertiary Sensing (ENFJ and ENTJ), and Inferior Sensing (INFJ and INTJ); the Si condition includes the following MBTI types for Dominant Sensing (ISTJ and ISFJ), Auxiliary Sensing (ESTJ and ESFJ), Tertiary Sensing (INFP and INTP), and Inferior Sensing (ENFP and ENTP). The *Manual* model differs only for Tertiary Sensing where Se includes INFP and INTP and Si includes ENFJ and ENTJ.

8 There are frequently issues of questionnaire uncertainty when individual test profiles are constructed, a measurement problem related to the type stability problem for type dichotomies at the cutting point. The eight-position type dominance hierarchy does not solve this problem. Although beyond the scope of this chapter, two points can be made here. First, the aggregated research data based on continuous scoring are immune from this problem; and second, interpretation of individual profiles is intended to identify broad, qualitative effects where interpretation is informed by the aggregated, empirical research. Where questionnaire results are clear and relatively certain, interpretation can occur with greater confidence; where uncertain, interpretation should be more cautious. It is my understanding that increasingly FFM dimensions are interpreted as being bidirectional with a bipolar structure. To the extent that this is accurate, then FFM dimensions too are affected by the problem of questionnaire uncertainty, at least for determining which pole to use for interpretation.

References

Anastasi, A. (1976). *Psychological testing* (4th ed.). New York: Macmillan Publishing Co.

Arnau, R. C., Green, B. A., Rosen, D. H., Gleaves, D. H., & Melancon, J. G. (2003). Are Jungian preferences really categorical? An empirical investigation using taxometric analysis. *Personality and Individual Differences, 34*, 233–251.

Arnau, R. C., Rosen, D. H., & Thompson, B. (2000). Reliability and validity of scores from the Singer–Loomis Type Deployment Inventory. *Journal of Analytical Psychology, 45*, 409–426.

Arnau, R. C., Thompson, B., & Rosen, D. H. (1999). Alternative measures of Jungian personality constructs. *Measurement and Evaluation in Counseling and Development, 32*, 90–104.

Baker, T. B., McFall, R. M., & Shoham, V. (2008). Current status and future prospects of clinical psychology: Toward a scientifically principled approach to mental and behavioral health care. *Psychological Science in the Public Interest, 9*, 67–103.

Barbuto, J. E. (1997). A critique of the Myers–Briggs type indicator and its operationalization of Carl Jung's psychological types. *Psychological Reports, 80*, 611–625.

Bayne, R. (1994). The "Big Five" versus the Myers-Briggs. *The Psychologist, 7*, 14–16.
Bayne, R. (1995). "I don't like being put in a box": A review of some major criticisms of the Myers–Briggs. *Selection & Development Review, 11*, 4–5.
Bayne, R. (2005). *Ideas and evidence: Critical reflections on MBTI® theory and practice*. Gainesville, FL: CAPT.
Beebe, J. (2004). Understanding consciousness through the theory of psychological types. In J. Cambray & L. Carter (Eds.), *Analytical psychology: Contemporary perspectives in Jungian analysis* (pp. 83–115). Hove, UK and New York: Brunner Routledge.
Belling, R. (2009). The influence of psychological type on transfer of managers' learning. *Journal of Psychological Type, 69*, 101–110.
Block, J., & Ozer, D. J. (1982). Two types of psychologists: Remarks on the Mendelsohn, Weiss, and Feimer contribution. *Journal of Personality and Social Psychology, 42*, 1171–1181.
Boyle, G. J. (1995). Myers–Briggs Type Indicator (MBTI): Some psychometric limitations. *Australian Psychologist, 30*, 71–74.
Bridges, W. (1992). *The character of organizations: Using Jungian type in organizational development*. Palo Alto, CA: Consulting Psychologists Press.
Brownsword, A. W. (1987). *It takes all types!* San Anselmo, CA: Baytree Publication Company.
Carland, J. C., & Carland, J. W. (1992). Managers, small business owners and entrepreneurs: The cognitive dimension. *Journal of Business & Entrepreneurship, 4*, 55–66.
Carlson, J. G. (1985). Recent assessments of the Myers–Briggs Type Indicator. *Journal of Personality Assessment, 49*, 356–365.
Carlyn, M. (1977). An assessment of the Myers–Briggs Type Indicator. *Journal of Personality Assessment, 41*, 461–473.
Coe, C. K. (1992). The MBTI: Potential uses and misuses in personnel administration. *Public Personnel Management, 21*, 511–522.
Cohen, J. (1983). The cost of dichotomization. *Applied Psychological Measurement, 7*, 249–253.
Coombs, C. H. (1964). *A theory of data*. New York: John Wiley & Sons.
Demarest, L. (1997). *Looking at type in the workplace*. Gainesville, FL: CAPT.
Denzin, N. K. (1994). Idiographic–nomothetic psychology. In R. J. Corsini (Ed.), *Encyclopedia of psychology* (2nd ed., pp. 204–205). New York: John Wiley & Sons.
Devito, A. J. (1985). Review of Myers–Briggs Type Indicator (MBTI). In J. V. Mitchell (Ed.), *The ninth mental measurements yearbook* (pp. 1030–1032). Lincoln, NE: University of Nebraska-Lincoln.
Druckman, D., & Bjork, R. A. (Eds.). (1991). *In the mind's eye: Enhancing human performance*. Washington, DC: National Academy Press.
Fasiska, E. J. (1992). Managerial type determination and its role in the development of an Entrepreneurial Quotient (EQ) instrument. *International Journal of Value-Based Management, 5*, 17–37.
Faucett, J. M., Morgan, E. R., Poling, T. H., & Johnson, J. (1995). MBTI type and Kohlberg's postconventional stages of moral reasoning. *Journal of Psychological Type, 34*, 17–23.
Fleenor, J. W. (2001). Review of the Myers–Briggs Type Indicator, Form M. In B. S. Plake & J. C. Impara (Eds.), *The fourteenth mental measurements yearbook*. Lincoln, NE: Buros Institute of Mental Measurements. See Test Number 251. Retrieved from http://www.unl.edu/buros/
Furnham, A. (1996). The big five versus the big four: The relationship between the Myers–Briggs Type Indicator (MBTI) and NEO-PI five factor model of personality. *Personality and Individual Differences, 21*, 303–307.
Gauld, V., & Sink, D. (1985). The MBTI as a diagnostic tool in organizational development interventions. *Journal of Psychological Type, 9*, 24–29.
Geldart, W. J. (2010). *The EPIC roles of consciousness: Emergent patterns of individual consciousness*. Denver, CO: Outskirts Press, Inc.
Girelli, S. A., & Stake, J. E. (1993). Bipolarity in Jungian type theory and the Myers–Briggs Type Indicator. *Journal of Personality Assessment, 60*, 290–301.
Goldberg, L. R. (1990). An alternative "Description of personality": The Big-Five factor structure. *Journal of Personality and Social Psychology, 59*, 1216–1229.
Hammer, A. L. (1985). Psychological type and media preferences in an adult sample. *Journal of Psychological Type, 10*, 20–26.
Hammer, A. L. (1996). Career management and counseling. In A. L. Hammer (Ed.), *MBTI applications: A decade of research on the Myers–Briggs Type Indicator* (pp. 31–54). Palo Alto, CA: Consulting Psychologists Press.
Harker, J. B., Reynierse, J. H., & Komisin, L. (1998). Independent observer ratings and the correlates of MBTI preferences with their behavioral descriptors. *Journal of Psychological Type, 45*, 5–20.
Harvey, R. J. (1996). Reliability and validity. In A. L. Hammer (Ed.), *MBTI applications: A decade of research on the Myers–Briggs Type Indicator* (pp. 5–29). Palo Alto, CA: Consulting Psychologists Press.

Harvey, R. J., & Murry, W. D. (1994). Scoring the Myers–Briggs Type Indicator: Empirical comparison of preference score versus latent-trait methods. *Journal of Personality Assessment, 62*, 116–129.
Hester, C. (1996). The relationship of personality, gender, and age to adjective check list profiles of the ideal romantic partner. *Journal of Psychological Type, 36*, 28–35.
Hicks, L. E. (1970). Some properties of ipsative, normative, and forced-choice normative measures. *Psychological Bulletin, 74*, 167–184.
Hicks, L. E. (1984). Conceptual and empirical analysis of some assumptions of an explicitly typological theory. *Journal of Personality and Social Psychology, 46*, 1118–1131.
Hicks, L. E. (1985). Dichotomies and typologies: Summary and implications. *Journal of Psychological Type, 10*, 11–13.
Hirsh, S. K., & Kummerow, J. M. (1987). *Introduction to type in organizational settings*. Palo Alto, CA: Consulting Psychologists Press.
Howes, R. J., & Carskadon, T. G. (1979). Test–retest reliabilities of the Myers–Briggs Type Indicator as a function of mood changes. *Research in Psychological Type, 2*, 29–31.
Jackson, S. L., Parker, C. P., & Dipboye, R. L. (1996). A comparison of competing models underlying responses to the Myers–Briggs Type Indicator. *Journal of Career Assessment, 4*, 99–115.
James, W. (1943). *Pragmatism*. New York: Meridian Books. (Original work published 1907.)
Johnson, D. A. (1995). The Myers–Briggs Type Differentiation Indicator (TDI) measures the Big Five. In J. Newman (Ed.), *Measures of the five factor model and psychological type: A major convergence of research and theory* (pp. 81–100). Gainesville, FL: CAPT.
Johnson, D. A., & Saunders, D. R. (1990). Confirmatory factor analysis of the Myers-Briggs Type Indicator—Expanded analysis report. *Educational and Psychological Measurement, 50*, 561–571.
Jung, C. G. (1971). *Psychological types*. Princeton, NJ: Princeton University Press. (Original work published 1923.)
Jung, C. G. (1957/1977). *The Houston films*. In W. M. McGuire & R. F. C. Hull (Eds.), *C.G. Jung speaking* (pp. 276–352). Princeton, NJ: Princeton University Press.
Kerr, P. L. (2007). The edge of reality. *Australian Psychological Type Review, 9*, 33–36.
Kummerow, J. M. (1998). Uses of type in career counseling. In I. B. Myers, M. H. McCaulley, N. L. Quenk, & A. L. Hammer (Eds.), *MBTI manual: A guide to the development and use of the Myers–Briggs Type Indicator* (3rd ed., pp. 285–324). Palo Alto, CA: Consulting Psychologists Press.
Lawrence, G. (1979). *People types & tiger stripes: A practical guide to learning styles*. Gainesville, FL: CAPT.
Lawrence, G. D., & Martin, C. R. (2001). *Building people, building programs*. Gainesville, FL: CAPT.
Maier, N. R. F. (1963). *Problem-solving discussions and conferences: Leadership methods and skills*. New York: McGraw-Hill Book Company.
Maier, N. R. F. (1973). *Psychology in industrial organizations* (4th ed.). Boston: Houghton Mifflin Company.
Mastrangelo, P. M. (2001). Review of the Myers-Briggs Type Indicator, Form M. In B. S. Plake & J. C. Impara (Eds.), *The fourteenth mental measurements yearbook*. Lincoln, NE: Buros Institute of Mental Measurements. See Test Number 251. Retrieved from http://www.unl.edu/buros/
Mayr, E. (1982). *The growth of biological thought*. Cambridge, MA: Harvard University Press.
Mayr, E. (1988). *Toward a new philosophy of biology*. Cambridge, MA: Harvard University Press.
Mayr, E. (1991). *One long argument*. Cambridge, MA: Harvard University Press.
McCarley, N. G., & Carskadon, T. G. (1983). Test–retest reliabilities of scales and subscales of the Myers-Briggs Type Indicator and of criteria for clinical interpretive hypotheses involving them. *Research in Psychological Type, 6*, 14–20.
McCaulley, M. H. (2000). Myers–Briggs Type Indicator: A bridge between counseling and consulting. *Consulting Psychology Journal: Practice and Research, 52*, 117–132.
McCrae, R. R., & Costa, P. T., Jr. (1989). Reinterpreting the Myers–Briggs Type Indicator from the perspective of the five-factor model of personality. *Journal of Personality, 57*, 17–40.
McCrae, R. R., & Costa, P. T., Jr. (2003). *Personality in adulthood: A five-factor perspective* (2nd ed.). New York: Guilford Press.
McCrae, R. R., & Costa, P. T., Jr. (2008). The five-factor theory of personality. In O. P. John, R. W. Robins, & L. A. Pervin (Eds.), *Handbook of personality: Theory and research* (pp. 159–181). New York: Guilford Press.
Meehl, P. E. (1992). Factors and taxa, traits and types, differences of degree and differences in kind. *Journal of Personality, 60*, 117–174.
Meier, C. A. (1989). *Consciousness*. Boston: Sigo Press. (Original work published 1975.)
Meier, C. A. (1995). *Personality: The individuation process in light of C.G. Jung's typology*. Einsiedeln, Switzerland: Daimon. (Original work published 1977.)
Mendelsohn, G. A. (1965). Review of Myers–Briggs Type Indicator (MBTI). In O. K. Buros (Ed.), *The sixth mental measurements yearbook* (pp. 321–322). Highland Park, NJ: The Gryphon Press.

Mendelsohn, G. A., Weiss, D. S., & Feimer, N. R. (1982). Conceptual and empirical analysis of the typological implications of patterns of socialization and femininity. *Journal of Personality and Social Psychology, 42*, 1157–1170.

Mischel, W., & Shoda, Y. (1995). A cognitive–affective theory of personality: Reconceptualizing situations, dispositions, dynamics, and invariance in personality structure. *Psychological Review, 102*, 246–268.

Mitchell, W. D. (2001). A full dynamic model of type. *Journal of Psychological Type, 59*, 12–28.

Myers, I. B. (1962). *Manual: The Myers–Briggs Type Indicator.* Palo Alto, CA: Consulting Psychologists Press.

Myers, I. B. (1980). *Introduction to type* (3rd ed.). Palo Alto, CA: Consulting Psychologists Press.

Myers, I. B., & McCaulley, M. H. (1985). *Manual: A guide to the development and use of the Myers–Briggs Type Indicator* (2nd ed.). Palo Alto, CA: Consulting Psychologists Press.

Myers, I. B., McCaulley, M. H., Quenk, N. L., & Hammer, A. L. (1998). *MBTI manual: A guide to the development and use of the Myers–Briggs Type Indicator* (3rd ed.). Palo Alto, CA: Consulting Psychologists Press.

Myers, I. B., & Myers, P. B. (1980). *Gifts differing.* Palo Alto, CA: Consulting Psychologists Press.

Myers, K. D., Quenk, N. L., & Kirby, L. K. (1995). The MBTI comfort–discomfort dimension is not a measure of NEO-PI neuroticism: A position paper. *Journal of Psychological Type, 35*, 3–9.

Myers, P. B. (2008). Reflections on the MBTI® now and into the future. *Bulletin of Psychological Type, 31*, 10–11.

Newman, J. (1995a). A brief history of the science of personality. In J. Newman (Ed.), *Measures of the five factor model and psychological type: A major convergence of research and theory* (pp. 1–18). Gainesville, FL: CAPT.

Newman, J. (1995b). Trait theory, type theory and the biological basis of personality. In J. Newman (Ed.), *Measures of the five factor model and psychological type: A major convergence of research and theory* (pp. 63–79). Gainesville, FL: CAPT.

Norman, W. T. (1963). Toward an adequate taxonomy of personality attributes: Replicated factor structure in peer nomination personality ratings. *Journal of Abnormal and Social Psychology, 66*, 574–583.

Otis, G. D., & Loucks, J. L. (1997). Rebelliousness and psychological distress in a sample of introverted veterans. *Journal of Psychological Type, 40*, 20–30.

Oxford, R., & Ehrman, M. (1988). Psychological type and adult learning strategies: A pilot study. *Journal of Psychological Type, 16*, 22–32.

Pearman, R. R., & Fleenor, J. (1996). Differences in observed and self-reported qualities of psychological types. *Journal of Psychological Type, 39*, 3–17.

Pearman, R. R., & Fleenor, J. (1997). 16 patterns of leadership effectiveness: A multivariate analysis of observational variables and the MBTI. In L. Demarest & T. Golatz (Eds.), *Proceedings: The Myers–Briggs Type Indicator and leadership* (pp. 183–212). Gainesville, FL: Center for Applications of Psychological Type.

Pittenger, D. J. (1993a). Measuring the MBTI . . . and coming up short. *Journal of Career Planning and Employment, 54*, 48–53.

Pittenger, D. J. (1993b). The utility of the Myers–Briggs Type Indicator. *Review of Educational Research, 63*, 467–488.

Pittenger, D. J. (2005). Cautionary comments regarding the Myers–Briggs Type Indicator. *Consulting Psychology Journal: Practice and Research, 57*, 210–221.

Quenk, N. L. (1992). The whole is greater than the sum of its parts: Observations on the dynamics of type. *Bulletin of Psychological Type, 15*, 5–10.

Quenk, N. L. (1993a). *Beside ourselves: Our hidden personality in everyday life.* Palo Alto, CA: Consulting Psychologists Press.

Quenk, N. L. (1993b). Personality types or personality traits: What difference does it make? *Bulletin of Psychological Type, 16*, 9–13.

Reynierse, J. H. (1993). The distribution and flow of managerial types through organizational levels in business and industry. *Journal of Psychological Type, 25*, 11–23.

Reynierse, J. H. (1994). Ten commandments for CEOs seeking organizational change. *Business Horizons, 37*, 40–45.

Reynierse, J. H. (1997). An MBTI model of entrepreneurship and bureaucracy: The psychological types of business entrepreneurs compared to business managers and executives. *Journal of Psychological Type, 40*, 3–19.

Reynierse, J. H. (2000). The combination of preferences and the formation of MBTI types. *Journal of Psychological Type, 52*, 18–31.

Reynierse, J. H. (2009). The case against type dynamics. *Journal of Psychological Type, 69*, 1–21.

Reynierse, J. H. (2012). Toward an empirically sound and radically revised type theory. *Journal of Psychological Type, 72*, 1–25.

Reynierse, J. H., & Harker, J. B. (1986). Measuring and managing organizational culture. *Human Resource Planning, 9*, 1–8.

Reynierse, J. H., & Harker, J. B. (2000). Waiting for Godot, the search for the Holy Grail, and the futility of obtaining meaningful whole-type effects. *Journal of Psychological Type, 53*, 11–18.

Reynierse, J. H., & Harker, J. B. (2001a). The interactive and additive nature of psychological type. *Journal of Psychological Type, 58*, 6–32.

Reynierse, J. H., & Harker, J. B. (2001b). Social acceptability of natural language descriptors associated with the MBTI preferences. *Journal of Psychological Type, 59*, 29–35.

Reynierse, J. H., & Harker, J. B. (2005a). Type interactions: MBTI relationships and self-report questionnaire scale scores. *Journal of Psychological Type, 64*, 57–75.

Reynierse, J. H., & Harker, J. B. (2005b). Type versus trait: Taxons, real classes, and carving nature at its joints. *Journal of Psychological Type, 64*, 77–87.

Reynierse, J. H., & Harker, J. B. (2008a). Preference multidimensionality and the fallacy of type dynamics: Part I (Studies 1–3). *Journal of Psychological Type, 68*, 90–112.

Reynierse, J. H., & Harker, J. B. (2008b). Preference multidimensionality and the fallacy of type dynamics: Part II (Studies 4–6). *Journal of Psychological Type, 68*, 113–138.

Reynierse, J. H., Harker, J. B., & Fink, A. A. (2000). A credible and strategy-relevant set of business values. *International Journal of Value-Based Management, 13*, 259–271.

Reynierse, J. H., Harker, J. B., Fink, A. A., & Ackerman, D. (2001). Personality and perceived business values: Synergistic effects for the Myers–Briggs Type Indicator and management ratings. *International Journal of Value-Based Management, 14*, 259–271.

Reynierse, J. H., & Leyden, P. J. (1991). Implementing organizational change: An ordinary effort for an extra-ordinary situation. In R. J. Niehaus & K. F. Price (Eds.), *Bottom line results from strategic human resource planning* (pp. 133–148). New York: Plenum Press.

Roach, B. (1986). Organizational decision-makers: Different types for different levels. *Journal of Psychological Type, 12*, 16–24.

Ruscio, J., & Ruscio, A. M. (2008). Categories and dimensions: Advancing psychological science through the study of latent structure. *Current Directions in Psychological Science, 17*, 203–207.

Rytting, M., & Ware, R. (1993). Reinterpreting the NEO-PI from the perspective of psychological type. In *Conscious choices, unconscious forces: Proceedings of the X Biennial, International Conference of the Association for Psychological Type* (pp. 213–218). Kansas City, MO: Association for Psychological Type.

Rytting, M., Ware, R., & Prince, R. A. (1994). Bimodal distributions in a sample of CEOs: Validating evidence for the MBTI. *Journal of Psychological Type, 31*, 16–23.

Rytting, M., Ware, R., Prince, R. A., File, K. M., & Yokomoto, C. (1994). Psychological types and philanthropic styles. *Journal of Psychological Type, 30*, 3–9.

Salter, D. W. (1995). Design and testing of the Environmental Personality Type Assessment. *Journal of Psychological Type, 34*, 29–35.

Salter, D. W. (2003). Revisiting the taxonomy of environmental types and introducing the Salter Environmental Type Assessment. *Journal of Psychological Type, 62*, 55–66.

Schaubhut, N. A., Herk, N. A., & Thompson, R. C. (2009). *MBTI®: Form M Manual Supplement*. Mountain View, CA: CPP, Inc. Retrieved from https://www.cpp.com/products/mbti/index.aspx

Sexton, D. L., & Ginn, C. W. (1990). The psychological aspects of rapid growth: Trait intensities of the 1988 *Inc.* 500 founders and cofounders. In J. A. Hornaday, F. Tarpley, J. A. Timmons, & K. Vesper (Eds.), *Frontiers of entrepreneurship research* (pp. 17–18). Wellesley, MA: Babson College.

Shoda, Y., & Mischel, W. (2000). Reconciling contextualism with the core assumptions of personality psychology. *European Journal of Psychology, 14*, 407–428.

Spoto, A. (1995). *Jung's typology in perspective* (Rev. ed.). Wilmette, IL: Chiron Publications.

Stein, M., & Hollwitz, J. (Eds.). (1992). *PSYCHE at work*. Wilmette, IL: Chiron Publications.

Stricker, L. J., & Ross, J. (1962). *A description and evaluation of the Myers–Briggs Type Indicator (Research Bulletin #RB-62-6)*. Princeton, NJ: Educational Testing Service.

Stricker, L. J., & Ross, J. (1964a). An assessment of some structural properties of the Jungian typology. *Journal of Abnormal and Social Psychology, 68*, 62–71.

Stricker, L. J., & Ross, J. (1964b). Some correlates of a Jungian personality inventory. *Psychological Reports, 14*, 623–643.

Sundberg, N. D. (1965). Review of Myers–Briggs Type Indicator (MBTI). In O. K. Buros (Ed.), *The sixth mental measurements yearbook* (pp. 322–325). Highland Park, NJ: The Gryphon Press.

Sundstrom, E., Koenigs, R. J., & Huet-Cox, G. D. (1996). Personality and perceived values: Myers–Briggs Type Indicator and coworker ratings on SYMLOG. In S. E. Hare & A. P. Hare (Eds.), *SYMLOG field theory: Organizational consultation, value differences, personality and social perception* (pp. 155–173). Westport, CT: Praeger.

Tett, R. P., & Burnett, D. D. (2003). A personality trait-based interactionist model of job performance. *Journal of Applied Psychology, 88*, 500–516.
Thompson, B., & Borrello, G. M. (1986a). Construct validity of the Myers–Briggs Type Indicator. *Educational and Psychological Measurement, 46*, 745–752.
Thompson, B., & Borrello, G. M. (1986b). Second-order factor structure of the MBTI: A construct validity assessment. *Measurement and Evaluation in Counseling and Development, 18*, 148–153.
Thorne, A. (2007). A kick in the pants for personality psychology—The cult of personality testing [review of the book]. *American Journal of Psychology, 120*, 327–330.
Thorne, A., & Gough, H. (1991). *Portraits of type: An MBTI research compendium*. Palo Alto, CA: CPP Books.
Tischler, L. (1994). The MBTI factor structure. *Journal of Psychological Type, 31*, 24–31.
Walck, C. L. (1992). Psychological type and management research: A review. *Journal of Psychological Type, 24*, 13–23.
Waller, N. G., & Meehl, P. E. (1998). *Multivariate taxometric procedures: Distinguishing types from continua*. Newberry Park, CA: Sage.
Weiss, D. S., Mendelsohn, G. A., & Feimer, N. R. (1982). Reply to comments of Block and Ozer. *Journal of Personality and Social Psychology, 42*, 1182–1189.
Wiggins, J. S. (1979). A psychological taxonomy of trait-descriptive terms: The interpersonal domain. *Journal of Personality and Social Psychology, 37*, 395–412.
Wiggins, J. S. (1989). Review of Myers–Briggs Type Indicator. In J. C. Conoley & J. J. Kramer (Eds.), *The tenth mental measurements yearbook* (pp. 537–538). Lincoln, NE: University of Nebraska-Lincoln.
Wilde, D. J. (2011). *Jungian personality theory quantified*. London: Springer-Verlag.

17

Trait Interactions and Other Configural Approaches to Personality

Mindy K. Shoss and L. A. Witt

Need-An-Expert company needed an expert and hired Ann for her advanced technical skills. Shortly after Ann was hired, her coworkers began to complain that she treats them as if they were her subordinates. She makes many, often unreasonable, demands and is easily angered if they can't meet them. She is highly critical and frequently antagonistic. To make matters worse, she refuses to share resources or information with others, but expects others to share with her. Ann is low in: (a) conscientiousness, (b) extraversion, (c) openness to experience, (d) emotional stability, (e) agreeableness.

Managers, who, by the nature of their position, observe and try to shape others' behavior, note the considerable variability in how individuals respond to events in the workplace (Dunn, Mount, Barrick, & Ones, 1995). Despite the intuitive relationship between personality and behavior, meta-analytic research suggests that these relationships may be quite weak (e.g., Hurtz & Donovan, 2000). Why is it that personality appears to explain much less variance in behavior than we would expect? One line of thought suggests that our expectations are misguided, that is, we attribute variation in behavior to personality when they are really driven by situations (i.e., fundamental attribution error; Ross, 1977). Another suggests that situations evoke or trigger the expression of specific personality traits such that traits may only be relevant predictors of behavior in a given context (Tett & Burnett, 2003). Another alternative is that validities found in research studies are lower than true validities because of measurement limitations, such as faking (Mueller-Hanson, Heggestad, & Thornton, 2003).

In addition to these possibilities, we suggest that personality appears to have limited utility for explaining important behaviors, attitudes, and cognitions because of the way we have typically examined personality variables in research. By this, we are referring to the common practice in the organizational sciences to consider traits as competing predictors in a regression model. By focusing on the unique relationships of traits with outcomes, this approach fails to consider that it may be the specific *configuration* of traits that is most relevant for understanding and predicting workplace variables. At least intuitively, we know that one word or one trait provides a limited representation of a person—one that likely omits important and relevant information. Even the simplest of icebreakers generally allows one to describe oneself on more than one dimension.

Accordingly, we suggest that: (a) personality traits in combination influence behavior, and, therefore, (b) considering an individual's standing on multiple personality traits can provide a more powerful way of understanding and capturing personality's influence on behavior. For example, we began the chapter asking about Ann. From the description, you may have selected that she is low on agreeableness. However, her behavior is better understood by also considering her standing on other traits, such as emotional stability. Indeed, such characteristics as demanding, selfish, ill-tempered, and antagonistic are indicative of a blend of low agreeableness and low emotional stability (Hofstee, De Raad, & Goldberg, 1992). In contrast, those low in agreeableness but high in emotional stability might be better described as insensitive. Therefore, a more accurate answer is that Ann is low in both agreeableness and emotional stability. As another example, consider two individuals, Bill and Joe, who are both high in extraversion. According to personality theory, they are both likely to be attracted to working with others (Costa & McCrae, 1992). However, whereas Bill tends to be personable, Joe tends to be domineering. These differences are certainly important for those with whom they work. We can understand these differences by considering Bill and Joe's respective standings on agreeableness in conjunction with their levels of extraversion: Bill is friendly and compassionate, whereas Joe is not (Hofstee et al., 1992).

This chapter is devoted to the theoretical rationale behind and practical approaches to considering multiple traits simultaneously in the explanation and prediction of behavior in the workplace. Our ultimate goal is to improve our understanding of personality's influence on workplace behavior, and, as a result, to develop ways of more completely capturing personality that may be useful for both research and practice. In the following sections, we first describe the circumplex model of personality and theory behind trait-by-trait interactions. Then, we expand the trait-by-trait interaction concept to consider the interactions of more than two traits. We then discuss alternative approaches for conceptualizing profiles of traits. Finally, we discuss issues related to the use of these approaches in personnel selection.

Circumplex Model

Although the Five-Factor Model (FFM) of personality has dominated personality research in organizations, we emphasize five criticisms that have been leveled against it. First, different personality assessments do not always classify certain traits as falling under the same factors, and there is some disagreement as to what each factor actually represents. Perhaps the greatest disagreement has been over the meaning of the fifth factor, which has been labeled openness to experience by some (McCrae & Costa, 1985) and intellect by others (Goldberg, 1992; Hogan, 1986). These labels reflect differences in the adjectives assigned to each factor; those who view this factor as openness to experience tend to assign such terms as intellect and analytical to the conscientiousness factor instead (J. A. Johnson & Ostendorf, 1993). Debates exist over other factors as well. For example, researchers have discussed characteristics involving conformity with reference to agreeableness, conscientiousness, and openness to experience (Costa, McCrae, & Dye, 1991; J. A. Johnson, 1983; McCrae & Costa, 1985). A second and related issue is that the FFM's theoretically orthogonal factors are often correlated in research (J. A. Johnson & Ostendorf, 1993). This is problematic, as it suggests that the five factors might not be "pure," that is, there is likely some overlap. Hence, the FFM may not accurately describe personality. These overlaps are also problematic as they make the factor locations unstable and contribute to the confusion over the meaning of each factor (Hofstee et al., 1992). Along these lines and third, although there is some consensus about the five-factor structure (e.g., Fiske, 1949; Goldberg, 1992; John & Srivastava, 1999; McCrae & Costa, 1999; Norman, 1963), some scholars have advocated fewer as well as more factors (e.g., Benet & Waller, 1995; Block, 1995). Fourth, some have criticized the FFM for being overly broad and, for this reason, failing to capture nuances in personality that might meaningfully predict outcomes (Ten Berge & De Raad, 1999). Fifth, some have noted that many characteristics tend to "fall in the fuzzy regions between the factors" (John & Srivastava, 1999, p. 106; see also Arthur, Woehr, & Graziano, 2001). Goldberg (1993) suggested that most personality variables "must be viewed as blends of two or more factors" (p. 186). These last two issues are largely interrelated. By covering a relatively broad conceptual space, the factors in the FFM inherently include characteristics that may be more accurately described as a combination of two factors.

The circumplex model (i.e., Abridged Big Five Dimensional Circumplex, AB5C; Hofstee et al., 1992; J. A. Johnson & Ostendorf, 1993) addresses a number of these issues by integrating the FFM and illustrating the adjectives that fall within blends of traits. The circumplex model, like the FFM, is based on the fact that five factors can be extracted from an analysis of personality attributes (i.e., the lexical approach). Unlike the FFM, the circumplex model takes into account the secondary loadings of trait attributes (by using an oblique instead of orthogonal model), suggesting that the particular *blend* of personality characteristics is most relevant. The AB5C model considers blends of two traits at a time. The blends take a circular form. One bipolar trait represents the vertical diameter of the circle. The other trait represents the horizontal diameter. Attributes are mapped on to this two-dimensional space and are distributed at 30° angles around the circle according to their loadings on the two factors (Hofstee et al., 1992; J. A. Johnson & Ostendorf, 1993). As a result, the circumplex model yields 45 combinatorial measures.[1]

The circumplex model uses Roman numerals to designate factors, instead of descriptive labels. Factor I corresponds to extraversion in the FFM, Factor II to agreeableness, Factor III to conscientiousness, Factor IV to emotional stability, and Factor V to openness to experience or intellectance. The model uses a plus sign (+) to indicate one end of the bipolar trait (e.g., careful) and a minus sign (–) to indicate the other (e.g., careless). The circumplex model suggests that each factor has pure traits as well as traits representing blends with other factors. Pure traits are those that do not have a secondary loading on another factor or have secondary loadings that are substantially smaller than the primary loadings; thus, they constitute the core definitions of their respective factors. At its core, Factor I (i.e., extraversion) is captured by such traits as sociable (I+) and secretive (I–), Factor II (i.e., agreeableness) by gentle (II+) and headstrong (II–), Factor III (i.e., conscientiousness) by careful (III+) and careless (III–), Factor IV (i.e., emotional stability) by calm (IV+) and anxious (IV–), and Factor V (i.e., openness) by creative (V+) and unimaginative (V–; J. A. Johnson & Ostendorf, 1993).

The majority of personality characteristics fall in between these factors. For example, traits that represent tendencies to experience positive emotions reflect blends between Factors I (primary) and II (secondary; i.e., extraversion and agreeableness; J. A. Johnson & Ostendorf, 1993). Conformity-related traits reflect combinations of Factors III (primary) and V (secondary; e.g., rule abiding, conscientiousness, and openness) as well as combinations of I (primary) and V (secondary; e.g., submissive, extraversion, and openness). We note additional examples throughout the chapter.

The nuances provided by considering blends of traits illustrate the greatest advantages of using a circumplex approach over the traditional method of considering each trait independently. For example, purposefulness is characterized by III+IV+ (high conscientiousness and high emotional stability), whereas perfectionism is characterized by III+IV– (high conscientiousness and low emotional stability; J. A. Johnson & Ostendorf, 1993). Whereas purposefulness might be a desirable trait among employees, perfectionism might not be (Hewitt & Flett, 1991). By considering both the primary and secondary loadings of traits, the circumplex model elucidates the space between the traits. As a result, it covers more "conceptual territory than the Big Five factors in isolation" while providing a more nuanced view of personality (Judge & Erez, 2007, p. 575; see also Hofstee, 2003). Particularly notable, the circumplex model includes personality characteristics that the FFM has been criticized for overlooking. That is, whereas the FFM is criticized for inadequately representing such nuanced characteristics as aggressive, hostile, impulsive, sensual, and humorous (Hough & Ones, 2001), the circumplex model captures them (harsh: II–I+, combative: II–II–, impulsive: III–IV–, sensual: V+IV–, and humorous: II+I+; Hofstee et al., 1992).

The circumplex model has also helped resolve prior inconsistencies among different measures of the Big Five. For example, J. A. Johnson and Ostendorf (1993) offered this summary:

> McCrae and Costa's (1985b) view that positive emotions and warmth belong to Factor I caused their Factor I and II scales to take on a I+II+ and II+I+ character, respectively; this differs from the other researchers whose Factor I scales were I+I+ and Factor II scales were II+IV+. McCrae and Costa's Factor III scale received a III+V+ designation, reflecting their view that intellect belongs to this factor rather than to the fifth factor. This view is consistent with the interpretation of Factor III as organized purposefulness or intellectual achievement. In contrast, Hogan and Johnson's (1981) scale was III+II+, reflecting a view of Factor III as interpersonal maturity and impulse control. Finally, McCrae and Costa's (1985b) Factor V scale, which they said measures openness to experience, received a V+I+ designation. The other researchers, who favored an intellect interpretation of Factor V, used V+III+ scales.
>
> *p. 570*

The circumplex model also helps explain why researchers have often found correlations between measures of each of the FFM factors. If, for example, a measure of conscientiousness asks about a respondent's standing on characteristics that load on both conscientiousness and openness to experience, this measure is likely to correlate with measures of openness to experience. This also explains why including personality traits independently in a multiple regression model might be problematic. It might be that the characteristics included in the overlapping portions of two traits are meaningfully related to behavior but instead become partialled out when both of the traits are used to predict outcomes. Although this may not influence overall model fit (i.e., the proportion of variance in the outcome explained, R^2), it certainly may influence the size and significance of the regression coefficients and, therefore, the interpretation of the results.

As alluded to previously, the nuanced view of personality provided by the circumplex model may help achieve greater insight into the role of personality in shaping work behaviors, attitudes, and cognitions than that provided by the FFM alone. For example, although one might expect openness to experience to be particularly important in today's competitive and dynamic knowledge-based workplace, meta-analytic research has not revealed a strong correlation between openness to experience and job performance (Barrick & Mount, 1991).[2] B. Griffin and Hesketh (2004) noted that prior research findings that openness to experience has null or small relationships with job performance may be due to the fact that openness tends to involve openness to both inward (e.g., fantasy) and outward (e.g., accepting of others' ideas) experiences, which have conflicting implications for performance. However, the circumplex model can allow us to pinpoint the aspects of openness that might be particularly relevant for explaining employees' performance. In an AB5C analysis of the Revised NEO Personality Inventory (NEO-PI-R), J. A. Johnson (1994) found that the fantasy subscale of the NEO-PI-R openness scale reflected a nonconscientious version of openness to experience (V+III–), whereas the actions subscale, which most clearly reflects openness to outward experiences, reflects an extraverted version (V+I+). Thus, as alluded to previously, the circumplex model lends itself to a more comparable level of specificity between personality and job demands than is provided by the FFM.

As an additional example, consider the blends of Factors V (i.e., openness to experience) and III (i.e., conscientiousness). Such traits as analytical, curious, and intellectual reflect a V+III+ combination—what Peabody and Goldberg (1989) labeled as controlled intellect. However, the combination of changeable and unorthodox reflects a V+III– blend—what Peabody and Goldberg called expressive intellect. Both of these combinations may predict performance in jobs that require adapting one's knowledge, skills, abilities, and other characteristics to change. However, the V+III+ combination may be most predictive in situations or jobs where doing so requires learning or incremental strategizing (e.g., an engineer). In contrast, the V+III– combination may be most predictive in situations or jobs that require one to readily change mental sets, such as an entrepreneur (LePine, Colquitt, & Erez, 2000). Similarly, V+ (i.e., artistic, creative) may predict performance in jobs that require creativity (e.g., interior decorator) better than performance in jobs where adaptation requires more intellectual analyses (e.g., CEO). In line with these ideas, J. A. Johnson (1994) suggested that the openness to ideas and aesthetics facets of openness to experience (alternatively, intellectance and origence; Welsh, 1975) may map on to Holland's (1985) vocational types in a circumplex manner such that, for example, the investigative-artistic (e.g., psychologist) type reflects high ideas and high aesthetics, whereas the realistic-investigative type (e.g., engineer) reflects high ideas and low aesthetics. Thus, we suggest that considering trait blends may result in a greater correspondence between personality and performance in specific jobs.

Research on the circumplex model is still in its infancy. Although it provides a useful framework for understanding the different ways that personality might manifest, a number of questions remain to be answered. For example, how viable is this approach for use in applied research and practice given that it involves 45 facets? In the aim for precision, do we lose some of the manageability afforded by the FFM? If so, is this cost offset by the gains? Additionally, the circumplex model only takes into account two factors at a time, although blends of more than two factors may be important for explaining outcomes—a point to which we return later. In the following section, we discuss an alternative to the circumplex model that shares a focus on binary trait combinations—trait-by-trait interactions.

Trait-by-Trait Interactions

Despite the benefits of the circumplex model in identifying nuances in personality, only a handful of studies have employed this framework in nonmeasurement-oriented studies (e.g., Burke & Witt, 2004; Judge & Erez, 2007; Witt, 2002). Judge and Erez (2007) suggested that researchers may be hesitant to use the AB5C model because of uncertainty regarding how to include such information in analyses. Following work by Witt and colleagues (e.g., Burke & Witt, 2004; Witt, Burke, Barrick, & Mount, 2002), they suggested that trait interactions provide an indirect assessment of trait blends, such that similar information could be gleaned by considering the interactions between two traits as predictors of workplace outcomes. Although circumplexes have been described as "having a structure definable in terms of a uniform system of additive components" in a two-dimensional space (Gurtman & Pincus, 2003, p. 407), trait interactions (as opposed to trait additions) indirectly assess these blends because they similarly involve a two-dimensional space and consider one trait as shaping the expression of another. In other words, both trait interactions and the circumplex model suggest that different combinations of high and low levels of two traits have different substantive interpretations, whereas additive models of traits suggest that the combination of levels of traits reflects different degrees of a single substantive interpretation. As Judge and Erez (2007) noted, trait interactions are advantageous to circumplex measures because they allow researchers to use statistical methods and measures with which they are already familiar (as well as data already collected with FFM measures) to analyze hypotheses generated from this approach. This may be particularly useful for selection research and practice. If combinations of traits add incremental variance in predicting performance, organizations that already use personality in selection could achieve additional validity in their selection systems without additional data collection cost.

Indeed, studies have found that trait-by-trait interactions have predictive validity over and above the individual traits themselves. For example, the interaction between conscientiousness and agreeableness predicts high-maintenance employee behavior, helping behaviors, and performance ratings (Burke & Witt, 2004; King, George, & Hebl, 2005; Witt, Burke, et al., 2002). The nature of this interaction indicates that although those high in conscientiousness are dependable and efficacious, they may come across as demanding and insensitive if they are also low in agreeableness. Judge and Erez (2007) found that the combination of extraversion and emotional stability (reflecting happiness) was more predictive of performance among customer service employees than either alone. Additionally, research by Ode and colleagues (Ode & Robinson, 2009; Ode, Robinson, & Wilkowski, 2008) found that agreeableness moderated the relationship between neuroticism and depressive symptomology, such that agreeableness helped those high in neuroticism better regulate their emotions. In a more comprehensive approach to trait-by-trait interactions, recent work by Penney, David, and Witt (2011) set forth a number of hypotheses regarding the predictive value of the binary trait interactions of conscientiousness and emotional stability with each other as well as with agreeableness and extraversion for various dimensions of workplace performance.

Do trait-by-trait interactions and the circumplex model yield identical information? From a measurement standpoint, trait-by-trait interactions are assessed by multiplying scale scores on paired FFM measures. The circumplex model can be assessed using Goldberg's (1999) International Personality Item Pool (IPIP) AB5C (http://ipip.ori.org/; Hofstee et al., 1992) scales; others have created scales from adjectives identified as particular trait blends in prior research (J. A. Johnson, 1994). However, Bäckström, Larsson, and Maddux (2009) noted that some of the IPIP's AB5C scales differ somewhat from the blends presented in Hofstee et al.'s (1992) original model. In particular, they note that the pure factor for Factor V (Openness) provides the weakest correspondence. Whereas creativity constitutes the pure trait in Hofstee et al. (1992) and J. A. Johnson and Ostendorf's (1993) AB5C analyses, the IPIP measure treats intellect as the pure version of this factor. An alternative approach to using the AB5C-IPIP scale might be to take advantage of the fact that different measures of the FFM factors appear to capture different blends and administer the scale that best captures the blend being investigated. For example, J. A. Johnson and Ostendorf (1993) found that Goldberg's (1992) agreeableness scale reflects a II+IV+ blend, whereas McCrae and Costa's (1985) agreeableness scale reflects a II+I+ blend. Researchers could therefore base their selection of scales on whether such traits as cooperative and flexible (II+IV+) or generous and warm (II+I+) are most relevant to the phenomenon under investigation. However, given that there are not as many personality measures as there are blends in the AB5C model, this approach may have limited utility.

Conceptually, the circumplex model and trait-by-trait interactions have different foci. The circumplex model aims to pinpoint a specific intersection or blend of traits, with the goal of more comprehensively representing the structure of personality. In contrast, trait-by-trait interactions model the conditional effect of one trait on another when predicting a given outcome in order to examine how one trait (e.g., extraversion) shapes the expression of another (e.g., openness) across the full theoretical range of both variables. Thus, differences exist with regard to the specificity of these two approaches. As Judge and Erez (2007) summarized,

> An intersection between two traits located along a circumplex is a more specific concept in that it stipulates a "unique geometric configuration" (Ansell & Pincus, 2004, p. 169). A circumplex measure has precise reference points that are fixed and, in the Big Five circumplex, each point represents a particular configuration of two traits, with "conceptual-empirical anchors" (Carson, 1996, p. 242). Each configuration is specific, different from other configurations, and can describe individuals. As Ansell and Pincus (2004, p. 170) noted, in a circumplex measure, a "fixed radius is seen when traits are successfully projected to locations at equal distances from the center of the circumplex, and continuous form implies directionality of traits," which differs from a statistical interaction.
>
> *p. 578*

Consider our example regarding openness to experience in the previous section. Using the circumplex model, we could focus on those characteristics that have primary loadings on openness but secondary loadings on one of the other four factors (or vice versa). Specifically, if we were interested in the blend of openness to experience (as the primary factor) and extraversion (as the secondary factor) in the circumplex model, we would focus on characteristics related to experimenting (V+I+) and conventional (V–I–; J. A. Johnson & Ostendorf, 1993). If we were considering traits closer to extraversion (i.e., extraversion as primary factor), we would focus on such characteristics as daring

(I+V+) and follower (I–V–). In contrast, trait-by-trait interactions consider the two traits together without giving one primary importance. That is, theoretically, trait-by-trait interactions capture all characteristics that are blends of the two traits without considering on which factor they primarily load, in essence including all traits that fall within the 45% angle between two bipolar traits in the circumplex circle (see Figure 17.1). Personality combinations using trait interactions, therefore, are described in much broader terms than are trait blends in the circumplex model. For example, those low in openness but high in extraversion might be described as vocally disliking change, whereas those low in openness and low in extraversion might be described as being quietly disinterested in new things. As trait interactions capture multiple blends within each circumplex, the circumplex model is likely to be useful for developing theory regarding how trait combinations manifest in workplace outcomes.

Judge and Erez (2007) compared the predictive validities of the intersection and interaction of extraversion and emotional stability. They used the IV+/I+ versus IV–/I– AB5C-IPIP measure to assess the intersection and calculated the interaction between measures of extraversion and emotional stability from the Big Five Inventory (BFI; John, Donahue, & Kentle, 1991). Judge and Erez found that both the circumplex measure and the interaction significantly predicted performance among

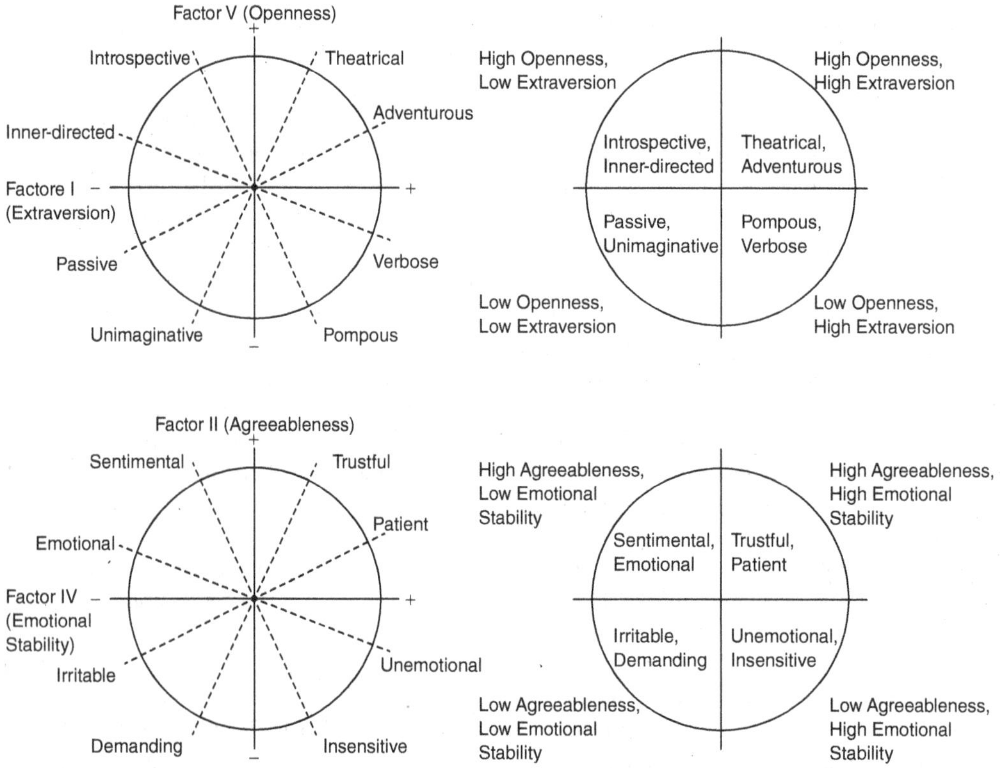

Figure 17.1 Examples of Intersections (Left) and Interactions (Right) of Openness and Extraversion (Top) and Agreeableness and Emotional Stability (Bottom).

Adjectives taken from Hofstee, De Raad, and Goldberg (1992).

employees of a health and fitness center, even when the other was included in the model. They suggested that although the results indicate that these two approaches provide unique information, they have similar interpretations—that workers with "happy" personalities are better performers. What unique information does each approach capture? Comparing the items from the AB5C-IPIP and the BFI yields some insight. The AB5C-IPIP measure includes items along the lines of self-esteem or confidence (e.g., "feel comfortable with myself," "am sure of my ground"), which are not reflected in either the emotional stability or extraversion scales in the BFI. Similarly, the BFI scales include items regarding energy (e.g., "is full of energy," "generates a lot of enthusiasm") and expressiveness (e.g., "has an assertive personality," "tends to be quiet") that do not map on well to the AB5C-IPIP measure. However, these items correspond somewhat to those in the AB5C-IPIP I+/IV+ versus I–/IV– measure (e.g., "have a lot of fun," "find it difficult to approach others"), suggesting that Judge and Erez's findings may have differed if they had assessed traits with primary loadings on extraversion (e.g., I+IV+) in addition to or instead of assessing traits with primary loadings on emotional stability (e.g., IV+I+).

An important question is whether these differences reflect real substantive differences between the two approaches or are artifacts of measurement. More research is needed to answer this question, but we suspect that it is a little of both. From a theoretical standpoint, trait interactions capture the blended characteristics described in the circumplex model; however, as previously noted, the two approaches differ with regard to their specificity (see Figure 17.2). As Saucier and Goldberg (2003) and others (e.g., Goldberg, 1993; Hough, 1992; John, Hampson, & Goldberg, 1991) noted, narrow constructs may be more predictive of specific instances of behavior than the broad constructs of which they are a part. From a methodological standpoint, traits with high secondary loadings tend to get omitted from inventories assessing the FFM (Bäckström et al., 2009); therefore, measures corresponding to the circumplex model might be assessing traits that are not covered in FFM *measures*. This could explain the lack of overlap between the circumplex and BFI measures discussed in the paragraph above. However, the utility of this explanation is somewhat difficult to assess at present given that Judge and Erez (2007) represented the circumplex approach with only a narrow range of trait characteristics—those with primary loadings on emotional stability and secondary loadings on openness that fall on one bisection of the circumplex (IV+I+ vs. IV–I–). Thus, future research is needed to compare the predictive validities of trait-by-trait interactions with multiple dimensions of trait blends in the circumplex model.

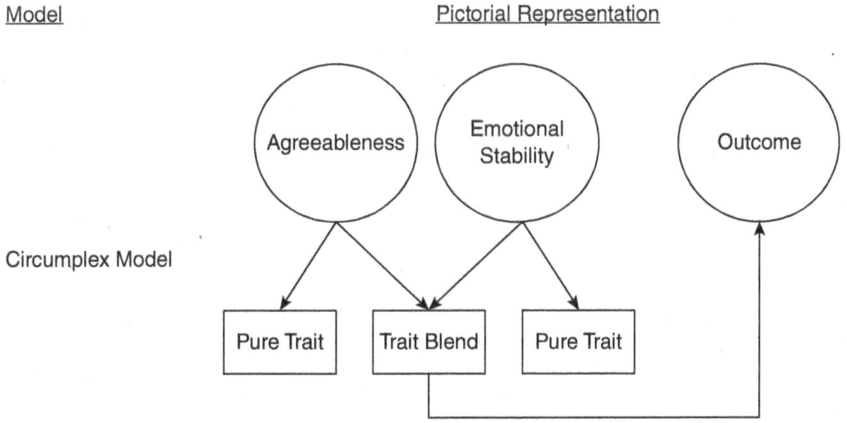

Figure 17.2 Graphical Representation of Five Configural Approaches to Personality.

(Continued)

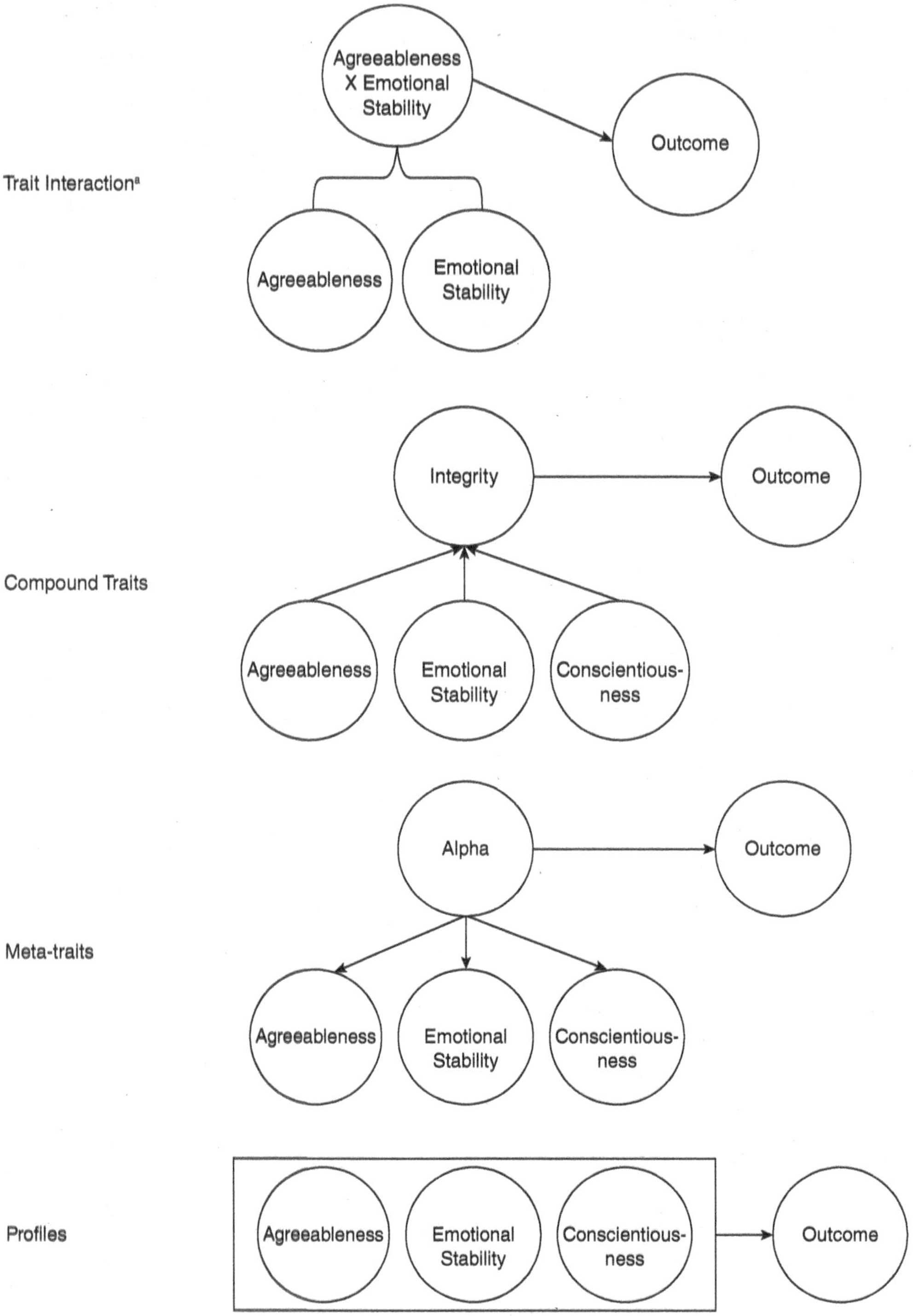

Figure 17.2 (Continued)

[a] Interactions between three or more traits are omitted for simplicity.

Trait-by-Trait Interactions: 3-, 4-, and 5-Way Interactions

The circumplex model is limited in its focus on only two factors at a time, meaning that it does not consider if characteristics have loadings on more than two factors (Witt, 2002). Similarly, trait-by-trait interactions have primarily only focused on the interaction of two traits. However, given the usefulness of trait interactions and trait blends, might it not be more useful to consider 3, 4, or all 5 personality factors in combination?

This idea is intriguing, as it would allow for a more holistic view of personality. Certainly, it may be achieved using 3-, 4-, and 5-way interactions, which can be easily computed in many of the statistical software packages commonly used today. However, there are a number of challenges inherent in this approach that we believe have dissuaded researchers from exploring it. The first set of challenges is practical. It is difficult to detect two-way interactions, let alone interactions of many variables. Power size considerations are compounded by the need to sample individuals falling into each 3-, 4-, or 5-dimensional quadrant.

The second set of challenges is theoretical. Personality theory has just begun to identify the trait combinations that may be most useful for predicting certain outcomes. However, an explanation as to whether traits have additive or interactive effects on outcomes has not yet been developed. It may be that additive models of traits are relevant to some outcomes, whereas multiplicative models are more relevant to others. Alternatively, some traits may primarily operate in a multiplicative sense (i.e., by shaping the expression of others), whereas others have only main effects.

Campbell, Gasser, and Oswald (1996) called for examination of specific facets of performance rather than overall job performance. Indeed, consideration of specific facets permits us to look at how various combinations of the Big Five traits are likely to influence work behavior in different ways. To illustrate the considerations needed to develop theory on trait configurations, we examine the combinations of the FFM traits predicting five different performance-related work behaviors—task performance, adaptive performance, organizational citizenship behavior (OCB), person-focused counterproductive work behavior (CWB), and organization-focused CWB. We emphasize that, because our interest is linking personality traits with performance-related work behaviors, we are focusing on performance constructs that reflect employee behaviors (i.e., "goal-relevant actions that are under the control of the individual"; Campbell, McCloy, Oppler, & Sager, 1993, p. 40) as opposed to the outcomes of those actions (i.e., effectiveness). Measures of effectiveness (e.g., sales volume) are important but are reflective not only of personality and other individual differences but also of factors beyond the control of employees, such as store location (Binning & Barrett, 1989; Campbell et al., 1993; Rotundo & Sackett, 2002). In contrast, employee behaviors (e.g., creating positive relationships with customers and making sales calls on time) are more directly reflective of personality (as well as other individual differences).

Borman and Motowidlo (1993, 1997a, 1997b) distinguished between task performance and contextual performance as distinct facets of job performance. Task performance reflects behaviors involving a job's primary substantive tasks/duties. Consequently, task performance behaviors are unique to a job. In contrast, contextual performance behaviors are neither formally prescribed nor unique to a specific job. In general, OCB refers to cooperative behavior targeted at helping coworkers and/or the organization, such as cooperating, following rules, helping, and volunteering (Organ, 1988, 1997). Characteristic of all jobs, they affect both social capital and operational effectiveness (for more coverage of the underlying processes between personality and performance, see Chapter 3, this volume; for more coverage of personality and predicting citizenship performance, see Chapter 26, this volume).

Adaptive performance refers to two related sets of behaviors: (a) enhancing one's skill set in response to or in anticipation of a changing environment and (b) cooperating with workplace changes, such as the introduction of new procedures (e.g., B. Griffin & Hesketh, 2003; M. A. Griffin,

Neal, & Parker, 2007; J. W. Johnson, 2001). Shoss, Witt, and Vera (2012) emphasized that adaptive performance reflects behavior rather than ability or intent. In addition, they noted that firms need employees who can successfully handle the ambiguity and anxiety that accompany change and who are also willing and capable of developing and applying new skills. Thus, personality may be particularly relevant for understanding and predicting adaptive performance. Furthermore, given the changing nature of work, adaptive performance is a performance outcome that organizations may do well to consider when developing selection systems.

CWB is a performance-related outcome that refers to behavior that is inconsistent with the interests of an organization or its members (Sackett & DeVore, 2001). Organization-focused CWB is targeted toward organizations; examples include theft, wasting time, and performing work slowly or incorrectly. In contrast, person-focused CWB is targeted toward individuals; examples include ignoring, insulting, and making fun of others. We make predictions for two types of person-focused CWB—(a) person-focused CWB motivated by desires for retaliation and (b) person-focused CWB motivation by achievement of a task-relevant tactical end (cf. Penney, Hunter, & Perry, 2011)—based on our expectation that personality traits differentially relate to these two types (for more coverage of personality and CWB, see Chapter 27, this volume).

We offer in Table 17.1 the 32 possible combinations of the Big Five traits at low and high levels and how the levels of the traits might be associated in most jobs with low, moderate, and high levels of task performance, adaptive performance, OCB, retaliation-driven person-focused CWB, instrumentally driven person-focused CWB, and organization-focused CWB. We present the combinations of the Big Five traits labeled as groups (i.e., Groups 1–32). For simplicity, the table summarizes our *general* expectations regarding multitrait interactions in relations with distinct criteria, irrespective of possible situational moderators. In particular, these general expectations primarily assume jobs that require very little creativity or interpersonal interaction. However, in the text that follows, we supplement our description of these expectations by indicating how they may differ in the case of jobs that do require creativity or high levels of interpersonal interaction.[3] We emphasize that these predictions are speculative.

As shown in Table 17.1, we suggest that conscientiousness and emotional stability are the primary drivers of *task performance*. Individuals low in conscientiousness are not motivated to exert effort to succeed on tasks. Because they tend to experience angst easily, individuals low in emotional stability often divert their effort toward managing their angst and away from their task performance. Hence, we anticipate that workers with low levels of both conscientiousness and emotional stability are unlikely to manifest effective levels of task performance behaviors (Groups 1–8). In contrast, task performance is likely to be high in Groups 25–32 because both conscientiousness and emotional stability are at high levels. We anticipate that Groups 17–24 (high emotional stability, low conscientiousness) likely manifest moderate levels of effective task performance behavior; although they may experience a low need for achievement (i.e., low conscientiousness), they are calm and able to focus on completing tasks (i.e., high emotional stability). In other words, high levels of emotional stability compensate somewhat for low levels of conscientiousness. However, we doubt that it works the other way around, thus suggesting that the effects of conscientiousness and emotional stability on task performance are interactive rather than (or as well as) additive. Even though they are motivated to achieve, the highly conscientious workers low in emotional stability are unlikely to be able to focus effectively on job tasks and therefore perform at low levels (Groups 9–16).

We emphasize that we anticipate this to be the case in most but not all jobs. For example, in jobs requiring creativity and out-of-the-box thinking, task performance might be moderate or high (instead of low) in Groups 10, 12, 14, and 16; that is, we expect openness to experience to play a role in the extent to which low emotional stability detracts from task performance in these job families. The combination of creativity (i.e., high in openness to experience), diligence, and desire

Table 17.1 General Predictions Regarding Multitrait Interactions and Performance Criteria

Group	*Emotional Stability*	*Conscientiousness*	*Agreeableness*	*Extraversion*	*Openness*	*Task Performance*	*Adaptive Performance*	*OCB*	*Person-Focused CWB I*	*Person-Focused CWB II*	*Organization-Focused CWB*
1	Low	Low	Low	Low	Low	Low	Low	Low	Low	Low	High
2	Low	Low	Low	Low	High	Low	Low	Low	Low	Low	High
3	Low	Low	Low	High	Low	Low	Low	Low	High	Low	High
4	Low	Low	Low	High	High	Low	Low	Low	High	Low	High
5	Low	Low	High	Low	Low	Low	Low	Low	Low	Low	Low
6	Low	Low	High	Low	High	Low	Low	Low	Low	Low	Low
7	Low	Low	High	High	Low	Low	Low	Low	Low	Low	Low
8	Low	Low	High	High	High	Low	Low	Low	Low	Low	Low
9	Low	High	Low	Low	Low	Low	Low	Low	Low	Moderate	Moderate
10	Low	High	Low	Low	High	Low	Moderate	Low	Low	Moderate	Moderate
11	Low	High	Low	High	Low	Low	Low	Low	Moderate	Moderate	Moderate
12	Low	High	Low	High	High	Low	Moderate	Low	Moderate	High	Moderate
13	Low	High	High	Low	Low	Low	Low	Moderate	Low	Low	Low
14	Low	High	High	Low	High	Low	Moderate	Moderate	Low	Moderate	Low
15	Low	High	High	High	Low	Low	Low	Moderate	Low	Moderate	Low
16	Low	High	High	High	High	Low	Moderate	Moderate	Low	Moderate	Low
17	High	Low	Low	Low	Low	Moderate	Low	Low	Low	Low	Low
18	High	Low	Low	Low	High	Moderate	Low	Low	Low	Low	Low

(Continued)

Table 17.1 (Continued)

Group	*Emotional Stability*	*Conscientiousness*	*Agreeableness*	*Extraversion*	*Openness*	*Task Performance*	*Adaptive Performance*	*OCB*	*Person-Focused CWB I*	*Person-Focused CWB II*	*Organization-Focused CWB*
19	High	Low	Low	High	Low	Moderate	Low	Low	Low	Low	Low
20	High	Low	Low	High	High	Moderate	Low	Low	Low	Low	Low
21	High	Low	High	Low	Low	Moderate	Low	Low	Low	Low	Low
22	High	Low	High	Low	High	Moderate	Low	Low	Low	Low	Low
23	High	Low	High	High	Low	Moderate	Low	Low	Low	Low	Low
24	High	Low	High	High	High	Moderate	Low	Low	Low	Low	Low
25	High	High	Low	Low	Low	High	Low	Moderate	Low	Moderate	Low
26	High	High	Low	Low	High	High	High	Moderate	Low	High	Low
27	High	High	Low	High	Low	High	Low	Moderate	Low	High	Low
28	High	High	Low	High	High	High	High	Moderate	Low	Highest	Low
29	High	High	High	Low	Low	High	Low	High	Low	Low	Low
30	High	High	High	Low	High	High	High	High	Low	Moderate	Low
31	High	High	High	High	Low	High	Low	High	Low	Moderate	Low
32	High	High	High	High	High	High	High	High	Low	High	Low

Notes: OCB: organizational citizenship behavior; CWB: counterproductive work behavior. Person-focused CWB I is motivated by retaliation goals. Person-focused CWB II is motivated by achievement of a task-relevant tactical end.

for achievement (i.e., high conscientiousness) may allow individuals to cope with their angst (i.e., low emotional stability) in ways that are productive for their jobs; for example, they may be likely to express it through the creative arts or leverage it to make emotionally compelling products or pitches. In contrast, task performance in jobs requiring creativity might be lowest in Groups 9, 11, 13, and 15 (i.e., low in openness to experience, high conscientiousness, and low emotional stability). These individuals are likely to be inflexibly obsessed with the minute details of each task and to be reluctant to develop and/or try alternative strategies for achieving tasks. Stated another way, openness is likely to be influential for task performance in creative jobs only when conscientiousness is high and emotional stability is low.

Furthermore, agreeableness might influence the expression of conscientiousness and emotional stability relevant for task performance in jobs that require interacting with others. Those who are highly conscientious but low in both agreeableness and emotional stability (Groups 9–12) are unlikely to be high performers in team settings, as this combination of characteristics makes them appear demanding and ill tempered to others; they are also likely to be easily angered if others do not share their same level of detail-orientation and achievement striving (perhaps especially so if they are extraverted; Groups 11 and 12). Those with high levels of both conscientiousness and emotional stability, paired with a low level of agreeableness (Groups 25–28), might, in contrast, achieve moderate levels of performance, as high levels of emotional stability might reduce the opportunities for low agreeableness to be manifested but may not completely compensate for low agreeableness. High levels of agreeableness might compensate somewhat for low levels of emotional stability among those who are highly conscientious working in team settings, allowing these individuals (Groups 13–16) to reach moderate levels of performance (as opposed to the low levels of performance in jobs that require little interpersonal interaction that is depicted in the table). Among workers low in conscientiousness, we expect that high levels of both agreeableness and emotional stability allow them to achieve a moderate level of performance; they may not want to let others down, and therefore may feign higher levels of conscientiousness than they really have. As suggested by Judge and Erez (2007), extraversion may also influence an individual's success in jobs that require interacting with others, as high levels of extraversion in conjunction with emotional stability relate to the emotions and arousal (i.e., activation) individuals espouse.

We suggest that conscientiousness and openness to experience are the primary drivers of *adaptive performance*, such that high levels of both traits are needed. Motivated to exert effort in general (i.e., conscientiousness) and consider change (i.e., openness to experience), such individuals are generally likely to adapt well. We expect that high levels of both are needed for adaptive performance. Conscientiousness may be detrimental for adaptive performance if openness is low, as these individuals are more conventional and may rigidly adhere to the traditional ways of doing things (Hofstee et al., 1992; J. A. Johnson & Ostendorf, 1993). High openness is unlikely to translate into adaptive performance if conscientiousness is low. Accordingly, we expect those high in conscientiousness and low in openness (Groups 9, 11, 13, 15, 25, 27, 29, and 31), those low in conscientiousness and high in openness (Groups 2, 4, 6, 8, 18, 20, 22, and 24), and those low in both traits (Groups 1, 3, 5, 7, 17, 19, 21, and 23) to engage in low levels of adaptive performance. Emotional stability is likely a secondary driver. Individuals high in both conscientiousness and openness to experience but low in emotional stability are predisposed to adapt but are likely handicapped somewhat by a tendency to focus or ruminate on their angst; hence, they may be likely to have suboptimal levels of energy with which to engage in adaptive performance behavior. Accordingly, we anticipate that Groups 10, 12, 14, and 16 are likely to manifest moderate levels of adaptive performance behaviors. In contrast, because workers high in conscientiousness, openness to experience, and emotional stability are motivated to adapt and have the emotional energy to do so, we anticipate that Groups 26, 28, 30, and 32 are likely to manifest high levels of adaptive performance behaviors. Agreeableness may also play a tertiary role in adaptive performance, especially with regard to being cooperative with workplace changes or adapting to new members in one's workgroup. Thus, high levels of agreeableness may compensate at least to some extent for lower levels of openness or emotional stability in these situations.

We suggest that conscientiousness, agreeableness, and emotional stability are the primary drivers of *OCB*, and that high levels of all three are associated with high levels of OCB. Persons who experience little angst, and therefore spend little energy on coping with it (i.e., high emotional stability), are motivated to exert effort (i.e., high conscientiousness), are cooperative (i.e., high agreeableness), and are likely to seek out opportunities to contribute beyond core task performance behaviors. Hence, we anticipate that Groups 29–32 are likely to manifest high levels of OCB. We anticipate that, regardless of the levels of agreeableness and emotional stability, individuals low in conscientiousness will not put forth much effort to do more than is required and to do it well. That being said, individuals low in conscientiousness and emotional stability but high in agreeableness may attempt some OCB behaviors, such as volunteering for extra tasks, due to their agreeableness, but they are unlikely to engage in these behaviors effectively. Thus, we expect Groups 1–8 and 17–24 to engage in low levels of OCB. However, among workers high in conscientiousness, high levels of either agreeableness or emotional stability are likely to compensate for low levels in the other and yield moderate levels of OCB. For example, highly conscientious workers high in agreeableness but low in emotional stability may engage in OCB as an emotion-focused coping mechanism; whereas their low emotional stability may prevent them from manifesting high levels of OCB, their general motivation (i.e., high conscientiousness) and cooperative nature (i.e., high agreeableness) may predispose them to do nice things to feel better. Highly conscientious workers high in emotional stability but low in agreeableness are unlikely to seek opportunities to be nice, per se, but they are predisposed to exert effort and observe opportunities to be successful. Hence, we anticipate that Groups 13, 14, 15, 16, 25, 26, 27, and 28 engage in moderate levels of OCB. Finally, we expect that those high in conscientiousness but low in both emotional stability and agreeableness (Groups 9–12) will engage in low levels of OCB. Workers who are easily upset and are not interested in or considerate of others are likely to pursue other ways to achieve their goals.

As noted above, we suggest that personality trait predictors of engagement in person-focused CWB vary based on the motivation to manifest the CWB—retaliation or a tactic to achieve a task-relevant end. For the sake of simplicity, we ignore for the moment the tactical motivations underlying person-focused CWB and limit our example to linking the FFM traits with *retaliatory person-focused CWB*. We argue that agreeableness, extraversion, and emotional stability are the primary drivers of retaliatory person-focused CWB. Because they are motivated to be liked, individuals high in agreeableness are likely to view person-focused CWB as an inappropriate way in which to treat others and therefore refrain from doing so. Those high in emotional stability have fewer opportunities to engage in person-focused CWB, as they less frequently experience anger and hurt. Those low in extraversion may find themselves in fewer situations that might motivate person-focused CWB because introverts prefer to avoid interaction with others. Thus, we anticipate that all but Groups 3, 4, 11, and 12 manifest low levels of retaliatory person-focused CWB.

We suggest that high conscientiousness serves as a governor limiting CWB among those predisposed to manifest it. Hence, we view conscientiousness as a secondary rather than a primary driver of retaliatory person-focused CWB. We expect this to primarily be a function of the impulse-control aspect of conscientiousness. Thus, we anticipate that extraverts low in agreeableness and emotional stability are likely to manifest high levels of retaliatory person-focused CWB if they are also low in conscientiousness. We expect high levels of conscientiousness to constrain person-focused CWB among those high in extraversion and low in agreeableness and emotional stability, but not completely. Accordingly, we expect that: (a) Groups 3 and 4 engage in high levels and (b) Groups 11 and 12 engage in moderate levels of retaliatory person-focused CWB.

Our expectations differ markedly for jobs that require teamwork or high levels of interpersonal interaction. In this case, we expect agreeableness and emotional stability to be the primary drivers of person-focused CWB. Those low in agreeableness who are easily upset by others (i.e., low emotional stability) are likely to manifest high levels of person-focused CWB (Groups 1–4 and 9–12) in interpersonally demanding settings. Conscientiousness is likely to do little to restrain this behavior because repeated interactions with others provide many opportunities for emotional reactions; these serve to drain one's impulse-control resources available at a given moment. In fact, conscientiousness may contribute to retaliatory person-focused CWB, especially in situations where team members provoke emotional responses by failing to meet performance goals or doing work incorrectly. Likewise, introversion is unlikely to restrict this behavior because introverts are unable to avoid others in team settings. As a result, introversion might even be associated with increased retaliatory person-focused CWB because having to interact with others is emotionally draining for these individuals.

We discuss *organization-focused CWB* before discussing tactically driven person-focused CWB. We suspect that the motivation to manifest organization-focused CWB is largely retaliation and not a tactic to achieve a task-related end. Extraversion and openness to experience are probably not salient to organization-focused CWB. Instead, we view agreeableness and emotional stability as the primary drivers. High-agreeableness workers are cooperative. Emotionally stable workers are unlikely to get angry and feel the need to retaliate against the organization. We argue that the presence of one compensates for the lack of the other, that is, persons high in either agreeableness or emotional stability engage in low levels of organization-focused CWB. We view conscientiousness as a secondary driver of organization-focused CWB; as stated above, we view conscientiousness as a governor limiting CWB among workers predisposed to manifest it. Thus, we anticipate that persons low in agreeableness and emotional stability are likely to manifest high (moderate) levels of organization-focused CWB if they are also low (high) in conscientiousness. Accordingly, we expect that Groups 1–4 engage in high levels and Groups 9–12 engage in moderate levels of organization-focused CWB. We expect all other groups (Groups 5–8 and 13–32) to engage in low levels of organization-focused CWB.

Up to this point, our description of the influences of the various combinations of the FFM traits on performance-related behaviors has featured primary and secondary drivers of the behaviors. In other words, we have suggested that not all of the traits jointly influence task performance, adaptive performance, OCB, retaliatory person-focused CWB, and organization-focused CWB. To provide an illustration of how the five traits might jointly influence a performance-related behavior, we return to person-focused CWB manifested as a tactic intended to achieve a task-relevant end, such as the acquisition of resources. For the purposes of this example, we assume that instrumental (i.e., tactically oriented) person-focused CWB is considered inconsistent with cultural norms.

We suggest that conscientiousness is the primary driver of instrumental person-focused CWB. Highly motivated to achieve, high-conscientiousness workers are likely to exert effort to manifest instrumental person-focused CWB for the purpose of acquiring work-related resources in order to get the job done; in contrast, low-conscientious workers have no such need to achieve. Without the motivation to get things done (i.e., high conscientiousness), the question of whether to engage in instrumental person-focused CWB for tactical purposes is unlikely to arise. Accordingly, we anticipate that workers low in conscientiousness (i.e., Groups 1–8 and 17–24) manifest low levels of instrumental person-focused CWB, regardless of their standing on the other four traits. However, we consider each of the other four traits to be secondary drivers of instrumental person-focused CWB. Thus, the extent to which highly conscientious workers engage in instrumental person-focused CWB depends on their standing on the other four traits.

We consider emotional stability to be the primary second driver. However, because we suggest that emotional stability shapes the expression of the other secondary drivers, we discuss it last. We suggest that, in general, persons high in agreeableness avoid instrumental person-focused CWB because they are cooperative and want to be liked; in contrast, low-agreeableness workers have no such need to avoid unpleasantness. Highly conscientious workers who are low (high) in agreeableness probably have few (many) concerns about manifesting instrumental person-focused CWB. Introverts prefer to avoid unnecessary interaction with others and thus generally refrain from person-focused CWB; in contrast, extraverts have no such preference to avoid others. Highly conscientious extraverts who are low (high) in agreeableness probably manifest high (moderate) levels of instrumental person-focused CWB, whereas highly conscientious introverts who are low (high) in agreeableness probably manifest moderate (low) levels of instrumental person-focused CWB.

We suggest that highly conscientious persons who are also high in openness to experience are more likely to manifest instrumental person-focused CWB—an unconventional approach to acquiring resources—than those low in openness to experience.[4] Taken together, we would expect those who are high in conscientiousness, extraversion, and openness to experience but low in agreeableness to engage in high levels of instrumental person-focused CWB to acquire resources—for the moment not considering emotional stability. However, high conscientiousness accompanied by unfavorable levels (i.e., unfavorable to the expression of instrumental person-focused CWB, meaning high agreeableness, low extraversion, or low openness to experience) in one or two of the other three traits is likely to somewhat restrict instrumental person-focused CWB.

Where does emotional stability fit? As previously noted, we suggest that emotional stability is the main secondary driver. Emotionally unstable individuals are easily upset and tend to be focused on coping with their angst. Depending on the other traits, these individuals may be emotionally unavailable to exert high levels of effort toward instrumental person-focused CWB. However, among the highly conscientious, we believe that favorable levels of one or two of the other traits can somewhat compensate for low emotional stability (in the sense that those low in emotional stability are less likely to engage in person-focused CWB for instrumental purposes) and yield moderate levels of instrumental person-focused CWB (Groups 9–11 and 14–16). We further expect that favorable levels of the other three traits can fully compensate for low emotional stability; thus, we expect Group 12 to engage in high levels of person-focused CWB.

We expect that high levels of emotional stability can compensate fully (partially) for levels of one (two) of the other three traits—agreeableness, extraversion, and openness to experience—that are unfavorable to the expression of instrumentally driven person-focused CWB and therefore yield high levels of these behaviors among those in Groups 26, 27, and 32, and moderate levels among those in Groups 25, 30, and 31. Emotional stability is unlikely to compensate for unfavorable levels of all of the other three traits; hence, we expect Group 29 to engage in low levels of instrumental person-focused CWB. Thus, considering all five traits, workers high in all traits but agreeableness (Group 28) are likely to manifest the highest levels of instrumental person-focused CWB. In contrast, high levels of conscientiousness accompanied by high levels of agreeableness and low levels of extraversion, emotional stability, and openness to experience (Group 13) are likely to manifest low levels of instrumental person-focused CWB.

We have suggested that the criterion variable determines whether specific traits have additive or interactive effects on outcomes. We emphasize that our discussion of the nature of the joint relationships of the Big Five traits with these performance-related work outcomes is speculative. Hence, we call for empirical work to test our suppositions and theoretical work to fine tune the nature of these relationships. Efforts to do so that include specification of the characteristics of the jobs and organizational context would likely be of considerable utility. We argue that such efforts will yield a more holistic view of personality and how personality influences performance-related work outcomes.

Alternative Approaches

There are a number of alternative configural approaches to personality that have, to varying extents, been discussed by organizational researchers. We focus here on compound traits, metatraits, and profiles.

Compound Traits

Schneider, Hough, and Dunnette (1996) defined a compound trait as "linear combinations of narrower personality facets that do not all covary" (p. 641). Two of the most commonly discussed compound traits are integrity and customer service orientation (Ones & Viswesvaran, 2001a). As Ones and Viswesvaran (2001b) described, these compound traits were developed for use in selection systems to maximize prediction of their respective criterion (e.g., by asking about tendencies toward being personable and courteous to others). To understand how these measures relate to other variables typically used in selection as well as to "help explain why these scales are valid predictors of behavior on the job" (p. 72), researchers have examined them in conjunction with the FFM traits (see Ones & Viswesvaran, 2001a, 2001b, for a review). Ones and Viswesvaran (2001a) concluded that: (a) integrity reflects the combination of conscientiousness, agreeableness, and emotional stability, and (b) customer service orientation reflects the combination of agreeableness, emotional stability, and conscientiousness; the traits are weighted in these orders. This linear, additive, model suggests that each of these component personality traits are viewed as positively contributing, to a greater or lesser extent, to these broader individual difference characteristics (e.g., integrity). This implies a compensatory process wherein a high level of one of the traits that make up the compound trait could compensate for a low level of another, particularly so if the trait with the higher score is weighted more heavily. It is worth noting that Ones and Viswesvaran (2001a, 2001b) appeared to reach the conclusion that integrity and customer service, for example, constitute compound traits after viewing evidence that the FFM traits predict them, rather than by first considering whether the aggregate of FFM traits constitutes a meaningful multidimensional construct and then seeking to define that construct (cf. Law, Wong, & Mobley, 1998).

Despite being considered to be "broad" traits (Ones & Viswesvaran, 1996), Schneider et al. (1996) examined common measures of integrity and customer service and suggested that these compound traits were actually "constellations of narrow personality traits" (p. 644), such as responsible, hostile, and sociable. As noted before, many of these characteristics are captured by factor blends in the circumplex model (responsible: III+II+, critical/disagreeable/irritable: II−IV−, and sociable: I+I+; J. A. Johnson & Ostendorf, 1993). Therefore, although compound traits appear to have higher validity than their constituent traits (Ones & Viswesvaran, 1996), it is not clear whether compound traits actually reflect distinct constructs wherein the whole is greater than the sum of its parts, or if these findings reflect issues in measurement similar to those discussed above with regard to trait interactions versus circumplex trait blends (e.g., measures of the compound trait are narrower than measures of the traits that comprise it). Furthermore, we are unaware of research that has compared the relationships between compound traits and trait interactions. It is possible that trait interactions more strongly relate to compound traits (e.g., integrity and customer service orientation) than do the individual traits that make up the interaction. The implications of such a finding would be twofold: (a) that compound traits (or specific compound traits) may be best conceptualized as a blend of traits or as reflecting a specific combinatory profile, and (b) that compound traits may contribute little to no incremental validity when compared with trait interactions (for more coverage of compound traits and breadth in personality assessment see Chapter 14, this volume).

Metatraits

In contrast to compound traits, which involve the additive combinations of potentially nonoverlapping traits, higher-order latent traits are a type of configural approach that attempts to explain covariance among what Eysenck (1991) labeled "mid-level" traits. For example, a growing amount of research has focused on core self-evaluations (Judge, Erez, & Bono, 1998), which Judge et al. defined as "fundamental premises that individuals hold about themselves and their functioning in the world"

(p. 161). Judge et al. argued that core self-evaluations explain the shared variance among emotional stability, locus of control, self-esteem, and generalized self-efficacy. Researchers have found that core self-evaluations predict outcomes, such as job performance and well-being, better than the individual core traits (Judge, Erez, Bono, & Thoresen, 2003).

Similarly, some research has examined higher-order factors of the FFM traits. This research has suggested the existence of two higher-order factors—Alpha and Beta (DeYoung, 2006; Digman, 1997). Alpha is the commonality between emotional stability, conscientiousness, and agreeableness and is often labeled *stability or socialization* as it "appears to reflect stable functioning in emotional, motivational, and social domains" (DeYoung, Peterson, Séguin, Pihl, & Tremblay, 2008, p. 947; also DeYoung, 2006; Digman, 1997). Beta is the commonality between extraversion and openness and is often labeled *plasticity or personal growth.* It reflects a general willingness to explore new ideas and activities. These traits have also been, respectively, labeled communion and agency (Abele & Wojciszke, 2007; Wiggins, 1991), emphasizing how they shape one's interpersonal goals in interactions (e.g., getting along vs. getting ahead; Digman, 1997). In one of the few studies in the organizational sciences to investigate the predictive validity of these factors, Kim and Glomb (2010) found that agency was positively associated with victimization, and that both communion and agency interacted with cognitive ability to predict victimization. Other researchers suggest that there might be a "General Factor of Personality" that underlies these two higher-order factors (Erdle, Irwing, Rushton, & Park, 2010) and is independent of method variance (Rushton et al., 2009). The theoretical rationale for a general factor stems from differential k-theory (Rushton, 1985) and suggests that this general factor reflects general evolutionarily based strategies toward species' reproduction and survival. Consistent with this argument, Musek (2007) found evidence supporting the existence of a higher-order factor underlying the Alpha and Beta factors described above. A concern with these metatraits is the same leveled against the Big Five model—they are so broad that they obscure meaningful variations in personality. For example, although Rushton and Irwing (2008) found that a general factor explained approximately 44% of the variance in Alpha and Beta, this translated into only 20% of variance in the FFM factors (e.g., agreeableness, conscientiousness). Research is needed on the comparative utility of these various higher-level factors for explaining workplace outcomes.

Profiles

Personality profiles are commonly used in other areas of psychology, such as pathology (Carlson & Furr, 2007) and husband–wife similarity (Gaunt, 2006). In those domains, the profile includes a person's scores on a series of traits. Cronbach and Gleser (1953) identified three distinct elements of profiles—elevation, scatter, and shape. Elevation refers to the average score (i.e., the overall height of the profile), whereas scatter refers to the variability among scores (i.e., the extremity of peaks and valleys). Shape reflects an individual's overall pattern of scores (i.e., which particular trait scores are high and low) and is most relevant for our purposes.

Furr (2009) pointed out that the shapes of profiles, and the shape-similarity between profiles, can be characterized in terms of normativeness and distinctiveness (also Furr, 2010). He suggested that normativeness can distort indications of similarity because

> any two profiles are likely to be similar, even without an intrinsic connection between the two profiles. For example, one target's self-rated personality profile is likely to be somewhat, if not very, similar to an informant-rated profile of another target. This is likely because (a) each target's self-rated profile is likely to be similar to the normative self-rated profile, (b) each informant-rated profile is likely to be similar to the normative informant-rated profile, and (c) the normative self-rated profile is likely to be similar to the normative informant-rated profile.
>
> *p. 1272*

As a result, Furr recommended considering each profile's normativeness separately from its distinctiveness. He also suggested comparing profiles' scatter and elevation (he provides SAS code for calculating these on his website) and, perhaps, looking at the interaction between these elements.

Within organizational science, the most common use of profiles is in the person–organizational fit literature (Edwards, 2007). Here, a profile of an employee's personality, interests, or values is compared to a profile designed to reflect that of the organization. Many different approaches have been used to compare profiles, including D^2, Euclidean distance, absolute value of D, and Q. However, these approaches have been criticized for combining conceptually different elements into a single score and for treating positive and negative misfit as equivalent (Edwards, 1993). Furthermore, these approaches are inherently compensatory in the sense that poorer fit on one point can be compensated by better fit on another. Recent approaches using polynomial regression and response surface mapping (Edwards, 2007) have helped to resolve these issues. Unfortunately, these latter approaches consider differences in only one variable (e.g., personality trait) at a time. Future research is needed to integrate Edwards' and Furr's approaches to profile comparison, as both have unique advantages. Whereas Furr's approach to profiles considers differences in more than one trait at a time, it appears that Edwards' provides a more comprehensive consideration of similarity (e.g., distinguishing positive and negative differences).

An issue that remains crucial for the use of profiles is the difficulty in determining a comparison profile. An employee's personality profile could be compared to scores on the same set of variables: (a) obtained at another point in time, (b) reported by an informant (e.g., coworker, spouse), or (c) reflective of another person. These comparisons are relevant when similarity (e.g., over time, between people) is theoretically related to outcome of interest.

However, what about the use of profiles to explain outcomes where the theoretical process is unrelated to similarity? Cluster analysis and related approaches (e.g., latent profile analysis) might be useful in this regard. For example, Cortina and Magley (2009) used cluster analysis to identify profiles of coping with incivility and then used discriminant function analysis to determine those factors that maximally discriminated between the clusters. Meyer, Stanley, and Parfyonova (2012) used latent profile analysis to determine commitment profiles (e.g., continuance dominant, fully committed) and compared how these profiles predicted a variety of well-being and performance outcomes. Although these studies did not examine personality, personality could certainly be used in these contexts. Latent profile and cluster analyses may also be useful in examining whether there are common personality profiles (i.e., combinations reflected in our groups in Table 17.1) and whether these profiles meaningfully explain/predict behavior.

Summary and Recommendations for Research and Practice

Figure 17.2 illustrates the five main configural approaches discussed throughout the chapter as well as how each could be used for predicting outcomes. Our aim in Figure 17.2 is not to provide a complete structural model for each (e.g., outcomes would be regressed on traits as well as their interaction in trait-by-trait interactions) but rather to illustrate the key similarities and differences between the approaches.

Note that the depictions of compound and metatraits are virtually identical, except for the direction of the arrows connecting the compound and metatrait with agreeableness, conscientiousness, and emotional stability. This distinction reflects that between formative and latent constructs. The former, which are also called aggregate constructs, reflect those constructs that are formed by the combination of their indicators (i.e., indicators "cause" the construct; Bollen & Lennox, 1991; Diamantopoulos & Siguaw, 2006; Edwards & Bagozzi, 2000). A common example of a formative construct is CWB, where the individual behaviors are not necessarily interchangeable, but together comprise the construct (Spector et al., 2006). In contrast, the latter, which are also called superordinate constructs, consider the indicators as reflecting an underlying construct (i.e., the construct "causes" the indicators). The implication is that formative constructs do not consider indicators to be interchangeable, and therefore, indicators may have different sets of antecedents and unique effects on outcomes (R. E. Johnson, Rosen, & Levy, 2008). In contrast, latent constructs suggest a certain degree of interchangeability because indicators are driven by a single construct; therefore, indicators would be expected to result from similar antecedents and to have similar effects on outcomes. Research is needed to examine compound and metatraits with regard to these assumptions. This is particularly important given that the same indicators appear in some compound and metatraits (e.g., integrity and alpha both have agreeableness, emotional stability, and conscientiousness as indicators). Thus, an integrative view of these approaches may be necessary to avoid return to the "good old daze" (Hough, 1997, p. 233) of disjointed personality constructs.

Research is needed to examine the relative validities of all of the configural approaches presented here. That being said, we have noted the growing amount of evidence that suggests that configural approaches, whether trait interactions, trait blends, compound traits, or higher-order traits, appear to provide incremental validity over nonconfigural approaches in predicting a wide range of outcomes. Assuming that the compatibility principle of attitude–behavior relationships (Ajzen, 1988; Harrison, Newman, & Roth, 2006) might also be applied to personality–behavior relationships, we expect the trait blends in the circumplex model (and other narrow approaches) to best predict precise and narrow dependent variables, whereas trait interactions (and other broader approaches) likely best predict broader dependent variables such as the dimensions of performance discussed in this chapter (Saucier & Goldberg, 2003).

As previously noted, our primary aim in this chapter was to describe how configural approaches, in particular trait interactions, may yield a more comprehensive understanding of personality in the workplace. A related, secondary aim is to suggest that these ways of more comprehensively capturing personality have practical utility for improving the validity of personnel selection systems. All of the aforementioned approaches—circumplex, trait interactions, compound scales, metatraits, and profiles—can be implemented in personnel selection. However, three considerations are relevant to choosing among them: (a) ease of measurement/implementation, (b) ease of interpretation, and (c) validity. Trait-by-trait interactions are likely one of the easiest approaches to implement. As previously noted, organizations that already use personality in selection could potentially see additional validity in their selection systems without any additional cost for data collection. Trait interactions are also relatively easy to interpret, as they allow one to understand the implications of changing one trait while keeping the other(s) constant. Following Witt and colleagues (e.g., Witt, 2002; Witt, Burke, et al., 2002), the circumplex model could be used to develop theory regarding how trait interactions relate to behavior. Thus, an advantage of trait interactions is that they capture the nuances provided by the circumplex model while maintaining the simplicity of the FFM traits as an organizing framework. However, the interpretation of trait interactions becomes more difficult as the number of traits in the interaction increases. Turning to the other approaches, compound and higher-order traits are easy to use and relatively easy to interpret. In contrast, we see profiles as more difficult to implement and interpret. As noted above, research is needed to examine the comparative validities of these approaches for predicting important workplace outcomes.

In addition to theoretical issues, there are a number of practical issues that need to be considered when using configural approaches in applied settings. Many of those issues (e.g., faking and situational specificity) apply generally to the use of personality in selection. Others (e.g., setting cutoffs) present unique challenges associated with configural approaches. We highlight situational specificity and setting cutoffs as two key considerations and briefly discuss each in turn.

As alluded to throughout the chapter and supported by a considerable body of research, context plays an important role in shaping the personality–performance relationship (Hochwarter, Witt, & Kacmar, 2000; Tett & Christiansen, 2007; Witt, Kacmar, Carlson, & Zivnuska, 2002). Thus, situational specificity is an important consideration when using personality in a selection setting (as well as when developing theory linking personality to performance; see Chapter 5, this volume). A major emphasis of our chapter is the need to consider personality holistically. In doing so, we recognize the very complex relationship between traits and outcomes. Likewise, we encourage researchers to consider the context in which various aspects of personality may emerge. For example, Judge and Erez (2007) examined the interaction between emotional stability and extraversion as a predictor of performance in customer service employees. To this aim, some have suggested adapting personality scales so that they are more relevant for the work context (i.e., specifying in the instructions for respondents to indicate the extent to which each item reflects how they are "at work"), consistent with the idea of commensurate measurement (Heggestad & Gordon, 2008). Although doing so may increase personality–performance relationships, we caution that benefits from contextualizing personality assessments might be at the cost of being able to draw from and contribute to personality theory more generally. Furthermore, we suggest that research is needed to understand what assessments of personality situated at work are actually measuring; for example, respondents may simply be indicating organizational or workgroup norms regarding behaviors. Therefore, we again suggest that efforts to develop theory as to how personality traits in combination influence behavior need to also include a consideration of context.

Setting critical scores with multiple predictors to establish protocol for hiring decisions can sometimes be complicated, even when considering only the additive effects of the predictors. Setting critical scores presents unique challenges for using trait interactions and profile approaches. Clearly, the standards for replication need to be higher for the use of selection systems that include predictors with joint effects that are interactive than those that are only additive. Rigorous evidence of replication would be needed particularly when different combinations of the traits are being used to predict different criterion variables in the same selection system. Moreover, setting cutoff scores, which may change periodically because they may reflect such additional considerations as the number of applicants, the number of openings, and the immediacy of the need for the opening(s) to be filled (see Maurer, 2005, for an excellent discussion of the issues surrounding critical and cutoff scores), present considerable challenges when employing predictors whose joint effects are not additive. Consequently, we emphasize the need for research to investigate specifically the effects of setting critical and cutoff scores on the validity of selection systems using trait profiles.

Conclusion

As noted by Hough and Oswald (2005),

> Organizational researchers study real-world phenomena, where human behavior and performance are complex, and therefore when a correlation between a single variable for personality and a single variable for performance is relatively low, we should not be too surprised or be too quick to dismiss its usefulness.
>
> *p. 381*

The configural approaches described here constitute ways for organizational researchers to consider the complexities of personality by considering personality more holistically. In doing so, such approaches have exciting potential to provide a greater understanding of how personality influences important outcomes in the workplace. We encourage research to systematically investigate the issues and questions described here in order to realize this potential.

Practitioner's Window

Two of the most powerful uses of personality data are selection and employee development. For years, many, if not most, practitioners have primarily considered conscientiousness and emotional stability in developing selection systems. Moreover, many have primarily, if not only, considered the *main effects* of conscientiousness and emotional stability. Additionally, it is likely that the development of many selection systems reflects inadequate consideration of multiple performance-related work outcomes as criterion variables. At the same time, employee and leader development practices have typically discussed with their clients the effects of traits only in terms of main effects. Whereas much work remains to be done, we argue that simultaneous consideration of the effects of all five traits on specific performance-related work outcomes is likely to provide not only more accurate and rigorous selection outcomes but also higher-utility employee and leader development practices. In particular, key points noted in the chapter include the following:

- One personality trait may shape the expression of another. Therefore, there is a need to consider specific configurations of traits when using personality to explain or predict behavior in the workplace.
- The extant evidence suggests that configural approaches (e.g., trait interactions, trait blends, and compound traits) appear to provide incremental validity over nonconfigural approaches in predicting a wide range of outcomes.
- Trait interactions are likely to be the easiest approach to implement in practice because they allow for the use of familiar methods and measures. Therefore, trait interactions may allow organizations to achieve additional validity in selection systems without additional data collection cost.
- Careful attention needs to be paid to both performance criteria and context when developing personality-based systems for selection or employee development.

Notes

1 The circumplex model uses both ends of the Five-Factor Model (FFM) dimensions (e.g., IV+ is calm; IV− is anxious; J. A. Johnson & Ostendorf, 1993). There are 90 unipolar facets, which are discussed in terms of 45 bipolar facets (e.g., sociable vs. unsociable: I+II+ vs. I–II–; Hofstee, De Raad, & Goldberg, 1992). Forty of these are blends of two factors. Five capture "pure" traits, where the loading on the primary factor is at least 3.73 as large as the loading on a secondary factor (Hofstee et al., 1992).

2 Of course, there may be reasons other than a lack of consideration of trait blends for the low meta-analytic correlation between openness to experience and performance. In particular, this low correlation may be evidence of situational specificity, such that openness to experience may contribute positively to performance in some situations and negatively in others. Although Barrick and Mount (1991) found a relatively weak interval, Hurtz and Donovan (2000) reported a considerably wider interval for the openness–task performance relationship.

3 These are just two of the many possible job demands that may influence how multitrait interactions influence performance criteria.

4 It is conceivable that those low in openness to experience may be more likely to engage in instrumental person-focused CWB for other tactical reasons—for example, to enforce the standard ways of doing things.

References

Abele, A., & Wojciszke, B. (2007). Agency and communion from the perspective of self versus others. *Journal of Personality and Social Psychology, 93*, 751–763.

Ajzen, I. (1988). *Attitudes, personality, and behavior.* Milton Keynes, UK: Open University Press.

Ansell, E. B., & Pincus, A. L. (2004). Interpersonal perceptions of the five-factor model of personality: An examination using the structural summary method for circumplex data. *Multivariate Behavioral Research, 39*, 167–201.
Arthur, W., Jr., Woehr, D. J., & Graziano, W. G. (2001). Personality testing in employment settings: Problems and issues in the application of typical selection practices. *Personnel Review, 30*, 657–676.
Bäckström, M., Larsson, M. R., & Maddux, R. E. (2009). A structural validation of an inventory based on the abridged five factor circumplex model (AB5C). *Journal of Personality Assessment, 91*, 462–472.
Barrick, M. R., & Mount, M. K. (1991). The Big Five personality dimensions and job performance: A meta-analysis. *Personnel Psychology, 44*, 1–26.
Benet, V., & Waller, N. G. (1995). The Big Seven factor model of personality description: Evidence for its cross-cultural generality in a Spanish sample. *Journal of Personality and Social Psychology, 69*, 701–718.
Binning, J. F., & Barrett, G.V. (1989). Validity of personnel decisions: A conceptual analysis of the inferential and evidential bases. *Journal of Applied Psychology, 74*, 478–494.
Block, J. (1995). A contrarian view of the five-factor approach to personality description. *Psychological Bulletin, 117*, 187–215.
Bollen, K., & Lennox, R. (1991). Conventional wisdom on measurement: A structural equation perspective. *Psychological Bulletin, 110*, 305–314.
Borman, W. C., & Motowidlo, S. J. (1993). Expanding the criterion domain to include elements of contextual performance. In N. Schmitt & W. C. Borman (Eds.), *Personnel selection* (pp. 71–98). San Francisco: Jossey-Bass.
Borman, W. C., & Motowidlo, S. J. (1997a). Introduction: Organizational citizenship behavior and contextual performance. *Human Performance, 10*, 67–69.
Borman, W. C., & Motowidlo, S. J. (1997b). Task performance and contextual performance: The meaning for personnel selection research. *Human Performance, 10*, 99–109.
Burke, L., & Witt, L. (2004). Personality and high-maintenance employee behavior. *Journal of Business and Psychology, 18*, 349–363.
Campbell, J. P., Gasser, M. B., & Oswald, F. L. (1996). The substantive nature of performance variability. In K. R. Murphy (Ed.), *Individual differences and behavior in organizations* (pp. 258–299). San Francisco: Jossey-Bass.
Campbell, J. P., McCloy, R. A., Oppler, S. H., & Sager, C. E. (1993). A theory of performance. In N. Schmitt & W. C. Borman (Eds.), *Personnel selection in organizations* (pp. 35–70). San Francisco: Jossey-Bass.
Carlson, E., & Furr, R. M. (2007). *Evaluating a trait profile approach to personality pathology.* Poster presented at the Association for Research in Personality Pre-Conference of the 8th Annual Meeting of the Society for Personality and Social Psychology, Memphis, TN.
Cortina, L. M., & Magley, V. J. (2009). Patterns and profiles of response to incivility in organizations. *Journal of Occupational Health Psychology, 14*, 272–288.
Costa, P. T., & McCrae, R. R. (1992). Normal personality assessment in clinical practice: The NEO Personality Inventory. *Psychological Assessment, 4*, 5–13.
Costa, P. T., Jr., McCrae, R. R., & Dye, D. A. (1991). Facet scales for agreeableness and conscientiousness: A revision of the NEO Personality Inventory. *Personality and Individual Differences, 12*, 887–898.
Cronbach, L. J., & Gleser, G. (1953). Assessing similarity between profiles. *Psychological Bulletin, 6*, 456–473.
DeYoung, C. G. (2006). Higher-order factors of the Big Five in a multi-informant sample. *Journal of Personality and Social Psychology, 91*, 1138–1151.
DeYoung, C. G., Peterson, J. B., Séguin, J. R., Pihl, R. O., & Tremblay, R. E. (2008). Externalizing behavior and the higher-order factors of the Big Five. *Journal of Abnormal Psychology, 117*, 947–953.
Diamantopoulos, A., & Siguaw, J. (2006). Formative versus reflective indicators in organizational measure development: A comparison and empirical illustration. *British Journal of Management, 17*, 263–282. doi:10.1111/j.1467-8551.2006.00500.x
Digman, J. M. (1997). Higher-order factors of the Big Five. *Journal of Personality and Social Psychology, 73*, 1246–1256.
Dunn, W., Mount, M., Barrick, M., & Ones, D. (1995). Relative importance of personality and general mental ability in managers' judgments of applicant qualifications. *Journal of Applied Psychology, 80*, 500–509.
Edwards, J. R. (1993). Problems with the use of profile similarity indices in the study of congruence in organizational research. *Personnel Psychology, 46*, 641–665.
Edwards, J. R. (2007). Polynomial regression and response surface methodology. In C. Ostroff & T. A. Judge (Eds.), *Perspectives on organizational fit* (pp. 361–372). San Francisco: Jossey-Bass.
Edwards, J. R., & Bagozzi, R. P. (2000). On the nature and direction of the relationship between constructs and measures. *Psychological Methods, 5*, 155–174.
Erdle, S., Irwing, P., Rushton, J. P., & Park, J. (2010). The general factor of personality and its relation to self-esteem in 628,640 Internet respondents. *Personality and Individual Differences, 48*, 343–346.

Eysenck, H. J. (1991). Dimensions of personality: 16, 5, or 3? Criteria for a taxonomic paradigm. *Personality and Individual Differences, 12*, 773–790.

Fiske, D. W. (1949). Consistency of the factorial structures of personality ratings from different sources. *Journal of Abnormal Social Psychology, 44*, 329–344.

Furr, R. M. (2009). Profile analysis in person–situation integration. *Journal of Research in Personality, 43*, 196–207.

Furr, R. M. (2010). The double-entry intraclass correlation as an index of profile similarity: Meaning, problems, and alternatives. *Journal of Personality Assessment, 92*, 1–15.

Gaunt, R. (2006). Couple similarity and marital satisfaction: Are similar spouses happier? *Journal of Personality, 74*, 1401–1420.

Goldberg, L. R. (1992). The development of markers for the Big Five factor structure. *Psychological Assessment, 4*, 26–42.

Goldberg, L. R. (1993). The structure of phenotypic personality traits. *American Psychologist, 48*, 26–34.

Goldberg, L. R. (1999). A broad-bandwidth, public-domain, personality inventory measuring the lower-level facets of several five-factor models. In I. Mervielde, I. J. Deary, F. De Fruyt, & F. Ostendorf (Eds.), *Personality psychology in Europe* (Vol. 7, pp. 7–28). Tilburg, The Netherlands: Tilburg University Press.

Griffin, B., & Hesketh, B. (2003). Adaptable behaviours for successful work and career adjustment. *Australian Journal of Psychology, 55*, 65–73.

Griffin, B., & Hesketh, B. (2004). Why openness to experience is not a good predictor of job performance. *International Journal of Selection and Assessment, 12*, 243–251.

Griffin, M. A., Neal, A., & Parker, S. K. (2007). A new model of work role performance and positive behavior in uncertain and interdependent contexts. *Academy of Management Journal, 50*, 327–347.

Gurtman, M. B., & Pincus, A. L. (2003). The circumplex model: Methods and research applications. In J. A. Schink & W. F. Velicer (Eds.), *Handbook of psychology: Research methods in psychology* (Vol. 2, pp. 407–428). New York: Wiley.

Harrison, D. A., Newman, D. A., & Roth, P. L. (2006). How important are job attitudes? Meta-analytic comparisons for integrative behavioral outcomes and time sequences. *Academy of Management Journal, 49*, 305–326.

Heggestad, E. D., & Gordon, H. L. (2008). An argument for context-specific personality assessments. *Industrial and Organizational Psychology, 1*, 320–322.

Hewitt, P. L., & Flett, G. L. (1991). Perfectionism in the self and social contexts: Conceptualization, assessment, and association with psychopathology. *Journal of Personality and Social Psychology, 60*, 456–470.

Hochwarter, W. A., Witt, L. A., & Kacmar, M. K. (2000). Perceptions of organizational politics as a moderator of the relationship between conscientiousness and job performance. *Journal of Applied Psychology, 85*, 472–478.

Hofstee, W. K. (2003). Structures of personality traits. In T. Millon & M. J. Lerner (Eds.), *Handbook of psychology: Personality and social psychology* (Vol. 5, pp. 231–254). Hoboken, NJ: Wiley.

Hofstee, W. K., De Raad, B., & Goldberg, L. (1992). Integration of the Big Five and circumplex approaches to trait structure. *Journal of Personality and Social Psychology, 63*, 146–163.

Hogan, R. (1986). *Hogan Personality Inventory manual.* Minneapolis, MN: National Computer Systems.

Holland, J. L. (1985). *Vocational Preference Inventory (VPI) manual.* Odessa, FL: Psychological Assessment Resources.

Hough, L. M. (1992). The "Big Five" personality variables–construct confusion: Description versus prediction. *Human Performance, 5*, 139–155.

Hough, L. M. (1997). The millennium for personality psychology: New horizons or good old daze. *Applied Psychology: An International Review, 47*, 233–261.

Hough, L. M., & Ones, D. S. (2001). The structure, measurement, validity, and use of personality variables in industrial, work, and organizational psychology. In N. Anderson, D. S. Ones, H. Sinangil, & C. Viswesvaran (Eds.), *Handbook of industrial, work, and organizational psychology* (pp. 233–277). London, England: Sage.

Hough, L. M., & Oswald, F. L. (2005). They're right . . . well, mostly right: Research evidence and an agenda to rescue personality testing from 1960's insights. *Human Performance, 18*, 373–387.

Hurtz, G., & Donovan, J. (2000). Personality and job performance: The Big Five revisited. *Journal of Applied Psychology, 85*, 869–879.

John, O. P., Donahue, E. M., & Kentle, R. L. (1991). *The Big Five Inventory—Versions 4a and 54.* Berkeley: University of California, Berkeley, Institute of Personality and Social Research.

John, O. P., Hampson, S. E., & Goldberg, L. R. (1991). The basic level in personality-trait hierarchies: Studies of trait use and accessibility in different contexts. *Journal of Personality and Social Psychology, 60*, 348–361.

John, O. P., & Srivastava, S. (1999). The Big Five trait taxonomy: History, measurement, and theoretical perspectives. In L. A. Pervin & O. P. John (Eds.), *Handbook of personality: Theory and research* (2nd ed., pp. 102–138). New York: Guilford Press.

Johnson, J. A. (1983). Criminality, creativity, and craziness: Structural similarities in three types of nonconformity. In W. S. Laufer & J. M. Day (Eds.), *Personality theory, moral development, and criminal behavior* (pp. 81–105). Lexington, MA: Lexington Books.

Johnson, J. A. (1994). Clarification of factor five with the help of the AB5C model. *European Journal of Personality, 8*, 331–334.

Johnson, J. A., & Ostendorf, F. (1993). Clarification of the five-factor model with the Abridged Big Five Dimensional Circumplex. *Journal of Personality and Social Psychology, 65*, 563–576.

Johnson, J. W. (2001). The relative importance of task and contextual performance dimensions to supervisor judgments of overall performance. *Journal of Applied Psychology, 86*, 984–996.

Johnson, R. E., Rosen, C. C., & Levy, P. E. (2008). Getting to the core of core self-evaluation: A review and recommendations. *Journal of Organizational Behavior, 29*, 391–413.

Judge, T., & Erez, A. (2007). Interaction and intersection: The constellation of emotional stability and extraversion in predicting performance. *Personnel Psychology, 60*, 573–596.

Judge, T., Erez, A., & Bono, J. (1998). The power of being positive: The relation between positive self-concept and job performance. *Human Performance, 11*, 167–187.

Judge, T., Erez, A., Bono, J., & Thoresen, C. (2003). The Core Self-Evaluations Scale: Development of a measure. *Personnel Psychology, 56*, 303–331.

Kim, E., & Glomb, T. M. (2010). Get smarty pants: Cognitive ability, personality, and victimization. *Journal of Applied Psychology, 95*, 889–901.

King, E. B., George, J. M., & Hebl, M. R. (2005). Linking personality to helping behaviors at work: An interactional perspective. *Journal of Personality, 73*, 585–608.

Law, K. S., Wong, C. S., & Mobley, W. H. (1998). Toward a taxonomy of multidimensional constructs. *Academy of Management Review, 23*, 741–755.

LePine, J. A., Colquitt, J. A., & Erez, A. (2000). Adaptability to changing task contexts: Effects of general cognitive ability, conscientiousness, and openness to experience. *Personnel Psychology, 53*, 563–593.

Maurer, T. J. (2005). Distinguishing cutoff from critical scores in personnel testing. *Consulting Psychology Journal: Practice and Research, 57*, 153–162.

McCrae, R. R., & Costa, P. T., Jr. (1985). Updating Norman's "adequate taxonomy": Intelligence and personality dimensions in natural language and in questionnaires. *Journal of Personality and Social Psychology, 49*, 710–721.

McCrae, R. R., & Costa, P. T., Jr. (1999). A five-factor theory of personality. In L. Pervin & O. P. John (Eds.), *Handbook of personality* (2nd ed., pp. 139–153). New York: Guilford Press.

Meyer, J. P., Stanley, L. J., & Parfyonova, N. M. (2012). Employee commitment in context: The nature and implication of commitment profiles. *Journal of Vocational Behavior, 80*, 1–16.

Mueller-Hanson, R., Heggestad, E. D., & Thornton, G. C. (2003). Faking and selection: Considering the use of personality from select-in and select-out perspectives. *Journal of Applied Psychology, 88*, 348–355.

Musek, J. (2007). A general factor of personality: Evidence for the Big One in the five-factor model. *Journal of Research in Personality, 41*, 1213–1233.

Norman, W. T. (1963). Toward an adequate taxonomy of personality attributes: Replicated factor structure in peer nomination personality ratings. *Journal of Abnormal and Social Psychology, 66*, 574–583.

Ode, S., & Robinson, M. (2009). Can agreeableness turn gray skies blue? A role for agreeableness in moderating neuroticism-linked dysphoria. *Journal of Social & Clinical Psychology, 28*, 436–462.

Ode, S., Robinson, M., & Wilkowski, B. (2008). Can one's temper be cooled? A role for agreeableness in moderating neuroticism's influence on anger and aggression. *Journal of Research in Personality, 42*, 295–311.

Ones, D. S., & Viswesvaran, C. (1996). Bandwidth–fidelity dilemma in personality measurement for personnel selection. *Journal of Organizational Behavior, 17*, 209–226.

Ones, D. S., & Viswesvaran, C. (2001a). Integrity tests and other criterion-focused occupational personality scales (COPS) used in personnel selection. *International Journal of Selection and Assessment, 9*, 31–39.

Ones, D. S., & Viswesvaran, C. (2001b). Personality at work: Criterion-focused occupational personality scales (COPS) used in personnel selection. In B. Roberts & R. T. Hogan (Eds.), *Personality psychology in the workplace* (pp. 63–92). Washington, DC: American Psychological Association.

Organ, D. W. (1988). *Organizational citizenship behaviors: The good soldier syndrome*. Lexington, MA: Lexington Books.

Organ, D. W. (1997). Organizational citizenship behavior: It's construct clean-up time. *Human Performance, 10*, 85–97.

Peabody, D., & Goldberg, L. R. (1989). Some determinants of factor structures from personality-trait descriptors. *Journal of Personality and Social Psychology, 46*, 384–403.

Penney, L. M., David, E. M., & Witt, L. A. (2011). A review of personality and performance: Identifying boundaries, contingencies, and future research directions. *Human Resources Management Review, 21*, 297–310.

Penney, L. M., Hunter, E. M., & Perry, S. J. (2011). Personality and counterproductive work behaviour: Using conservation of resources theory to narrow the profile of deviant employees. *Journal of Occupational and Organizational Psychology, 84*, 58–77.

Ross, L. (1977). The intuitive psychologist and his shortcomings: Distortions in the attribution process. In L. Berkowitz (Ed.), *Advances in experimental social psychology* (Vol. 10, pp. 173–220). New York: Academic Press.

Rotundo, M., & Sackett, P. R. (2002). The relative importance of task, citizenship, and counterproductive performance to global ratings of job performance: A policy-capturing approach. *Journal of Applied Psychology, 87*, 66–80.
Rushton, J. P. (1985). Differential K theory: The sociobiology of individual and group differences. *Personality and Individual Differences, 6*, 441–452.
Rushton, J. P., Bons, T. A., Ando, J., Hur, Y. M., Irwing, P., Vernon, P. A., . . . Barbaranelli, C. (2009). A general factor of personality from multitrait-multimethod data and cross-national twins. *Twin Research and Human Genetics, 12*, 356–365.
Rushton, J. P., & Irwing, P. (2008). A general factor of personality (GFP) from two meta-analyses of the Big Five: Digman (1997) and Mount, Barrick, Scullen, and Rounds (2005). *Personality and Individual Differences, 45*, 679–683.
Sackett, P. R., & DeVore, C. J. (2001). Counterproductive behaviors at work. In N. Anderson, D. S. Ones, H. K. Sinangil, & C. Viswesvaran (Eds.), *Handbook of industrial, work and organizational psychology* (Vol. 1, pp. 145–164). Thousand Oaks, CA: Sage.
Saucier, G., & Goldberg, L. R. (2003). The structure of personality attributes. In M. R. Barrick & A. M. Ryan (Eds.), *Personality and work: Reconsidering the role of personality in organizations* (pp. 1–29). San Francisco: Jossey-Bass.
Schneider, R. J., Hough, L. M., & Dunnette, M. D. (1996). Broadsided by broad traits: How to sink science in five dimensions or less. *Journal of Organizational Behavior, 17*, 639–655.
Shoss, M. K., Witt, L. A., & Vera, D. (2012). When does adaptive performance lead to higher task performance? *Journal of Organizational Behavior, 33*, 910–924.
Spector, P. E., Fox, S., Penney, L. M., Bruursema, K., Goh, A., & Kessler, S. (2006). The dimensionality of counterproductivity: Are all counterproductive behaviors created equal? *Journal of Vocational Behavior, 68*, 446–460.
Ten Berge, M., & De Raad, B. (1999). Taxonomies of situations from a trait psychological perspective: A review. *European Journal of Personality, 13*, 337–360.
Tett, R. P., & Burnett, D. (2003). A personality trait-based interactionist model of job performance. *Journal of Applied Psychology, 88*, 500–517.
Tett, R. P., & Christiansen, N. D. (2007). Personality tests at the crossroads: A response to Morgeson, Campion, Dipboye, Hollenbeck, Murphy, and Schmitt (2007). *Personnel Psychology, 60*, 967–993.
Welsh, G. S. (1975). *Creativity and intelligence: A personality approach.* Chapel Hill, NC: Institute for Research in Social Science.
Wiggins, J. S. (1991). Agency and communion as conceptual coordinates for the understanding and measurement of interpersonal behavior. In W. M. Grove & D. Ciccetti (Eds.), *Thinking clearly about psychology: Personality and psychopathology* (Vol. 2, pp. 89–113). Minneapolis: University of Minnesota Press.
Witt, L. A. (2002). The interactive effects of extraversion and conscientiousness on performance. *Journal of Management, 28*, 835–851.
Witt, L. A., Burke, L., Barrick, M., & Mount, M. (2002). The interactive effects of conscientiousness and agreeableness on job performance. *Journal of Applied Psychology, 87*, 164–169.
Witt, L. A., Kacmar, K. M., Carlson, D. S., & Zivnuska, S. (2002). Interactive effects of personality and organizational politics on contextual performance. *Journal of Organizational Behavior, 23*, 911–926.

18

Assessing Personality in Selection Interviews

Patrick H. Raymark and Chad H. Van Iddekinge

Over the past few decades, there has been a substantial amount of research on the use of personality assessments for personnel selection. The results of this research suggest that certain personality variables (e.g., conscientiousness, emotional stability) can predict job performance across a variety of jobs (e.g., Barrick & Mount, 1991; Hurtz & Donovan, 2000), and that the criterion-related validities of personality variables may be enhanced when confirmatory rather than exploratory research strategies are used (Tett, Jackson, & Rothstein, 1991; Tett, Jackson, Rothstein, & Reddon, 1999). In addition, when considered within a multivariate framework, evidence suggests that small sets of carefully selected personality variables may predict job performance at a level similar to that produced by cognitive ability (Tett & Christiansen, 2007). Despite this favorable evidence for the criterion-related validity of personality measures, several authors have called for additional research on the use of alternative methods of assessing job applicant personality (Morgeson et al., 2007; Ployhart, 2006a).

Another line of research suggests that the selection interview remains one of the most popular, if not *the* most popular, approaches to evaluating job applicants (Wilk & Cappelli, 2003). These positive reactions to the selection interview are not only found for organizational decision makers (e.g., Lievens, Highhouse, & De Corte, 2005) but also for job applicants (e.g., Hausknecht, Day, & Thomas, 2004). In addition, several meta-analyses have concluded that structured interviews can obtain respectable levels of criterion-related validity (e.g., Huffcutt & Arthur, 1994; McDaniel, Whetzel, Schmidt, & Maurer, 1994; Wiesner & Cronshaw, 1988; Wright, Lichtenfels, & Pursell, 1989), while providing a relatively low level of adverse impact (e.g., Huffcutt & Roth, 1998). Although there is evidence that many selection interviews are designed to assess personality (e.g., Huffcutt, Conway, Roth, & Stone, 2001), surprisingly few studies have attempted to examine the extent to which selection interviews are an effective means for this purpose. In this chapter, we will further explore the potential for the selection interview to enhance personality assessment in organizational settings and will describe some of the challenges associated with this approach. To provide a foundation for the remainder of this chapter, we begin with a brief description of the current state of research on the selection interview.

The Selection Interview

Evidence suggests that the interview remains one of the most prevalent selection techniques used by organizations (Konig, Klehe, Berchtold, & Kleinmann, 2010). Furthermore, meta-analytic results indicate that selection interviews can produce useful levels of both reliability and criterion-related validity, especially if the interviews contain a certain amount of structure (e.g., use of a consistent set of job-related questions for all applicants; McDaniel et al., 1994). Beyond their zero-order relations with job performance, there is also evidence that ratings on structured selection interviews can explain additional variance in job performance beyond that of cognitive ability tests (e.g., Berry, Sackett, & Landers, 2007). A recent summary of the interviewing literature has concluded that the selection interview can produce criterion-related validity estimates that are "highly comparable with mental ability tests, job knowledge tests, work samples/simulations, and other top predictors" (Huffcutt & Culbertson, 2011, p. 190).

Nonetheless, there are a couple of reasons why we need to be careful before drawing any broad conclusions about the validity of selection interviews. First, several authors (e.g., Arthur & Villado, 2008) have cautioned about the failure to distinguish selection methods from selection constructs. The interview is a selection method, and as such, it has the potential to assess a wide range of psychological constructs (Harris, 1998; Macan, 2009). For example, an interview loaded with problem-solving questions may result in interview ratings that are highly correlated with cognitive ability measures, whereas an interview loaded with motivation-related questions is more likely to produce interview ratings that are strongly related to personality measures. Not only do selection interviews have the potential to assess a variety of different constructs, but each of these constructs may have different relations with job performance. Consistent with this point, there is a considerable amount of unexplained variance in validity estimates for selection interviews across studies, even when the validities are examined within more homogenous subcategories like different levels of structure (Huffcutt & Arthur, 1994). Thus, at this point, it is not clear whether the generally favorable validity coefficients for the selection interview are primarily a function of the interviewing methodology or the dimensions/constructs selection interviews are designed to assess.

Second, and relatedly, attempts to assess the construct validity of selection interviews have often failed to distinguish between interview research that is descriptive (e.g., how do ratings on selection interviews relate to other variables?) from that which is prescriptive (e.g., can selection interviews be designed to assess certain constructs?). We do see value in the attempts to further understand what constructs might be assessed by interviews that are currently being used in organizations. At the same time, however, the reactive nature of such research (e.g., trying to infer or deduce constructs after the interview has already been developed or conducted) may provide little insight into the potential of the selection interview to assess personality.

We will interweave both of these broad points throughout the remainder of this chapter. Specifically, we will focus on the usefulness of the selection interview as a method to assess personality, and as such, we will explore how certain characteristics of the interviewing methodology may enhance or detract from the assessment of personality. In addition, we will attempt to separate the question of how well selection interview ratings correlate with other measures of personality (e.g., descriptive research) from the question of whether selection interviews can be designed to accurately assess targeted personality traits (prescriptive research). We begin by examining the issue of interview development and then discuss how this development process may impact the ability of selection interviews to accurately assess applicant personality.

Interview Development

In the case of unstructured interviews, very little advanced thought may be given to the questions that the interviewer will ask or to how answers to those questions will be evaluated. In such interviews, the interviewer may identify a few things to ask applicants after a brief scan of their application materials (Ryan & Sackett, 1987), or the interviewer may rely upon generic interview questions like "Please describe your strengths and weaknesses." Structured interviews, on the other hand, often rely on job analysis data to identify specific, job-related examples that can then be turned into interview questions (the job analysis data may also provide behavioral anchors for the response rating scales). As such, structured interview questions are based on job-related scenarios in which the behaviors of good performers are clearly different from that of poor performers (Campion, Palmer, & Campion, 1997). Job applicants are asked how they have responded to similar scenarios in the past (in the case of a behavior description interview) or how they would respond to the scenario if it occurred in the future (in the case of a situational interview).

As noted earlier, structured interviews have consistently demonstrated higher levels of reliability and validity when compared to unstructured interviews (e.g., McDaniel et al., 1994). However, the reason for this enhanced validity is not clear. One explanation is related to the enhanced consistency that is associated with structured interviews (e.g., use of the same questions, same response scales, and questions asked in the same order). In fact, some research suggests that differences in criterion-related validity between structured and unstructured interviews may be due to the greater reliability of structured interviews (Schmidt & Zimmerman, 2004).

A second explanation is that structured interviews do a better job of assessing constructs that are important for job performance (perhaps because the questions are tied directly to job analysis results; Huffcutt, Conway, et al., 2001). Consistent with the idea of content-oriented test construction (Tenopyr, 1977), the development of structured interview questions attempts to maximize the content overlap between the predictor (the interview questions) and the criterion (job performance; Campion et al., 1997). This content-oriented approach to predictor development (also used in the development of other predictors such as situational judgment tests [SJTs]) is thought to enhance predictive validity by focusing on samples rather than on signs of job behavior (Wernimont & Campbell, 1968). In this approach, the predictor content is drawn directly from the performance domain (in the form of critical incidents), often without any attempt to identify the constructs necessary to perform these job behaviors. Thus, although the content-oriented approach to predictor development has the potential to result in favorable criterion-related validities (cf., Murphy, 2009), it often does so without a thorough understanding of which constructs may be measured (Ployhart, 2006b).

In an attempt to further our understanding of the constructs interviews are designed to measure, Huffcutt, Conway, et al. (2001) surveyed the selection interview literature and identified a list of 338 interview dimensions (which were subsequently classified into one of seven sets of interview constructs). The results suggested that (a) personality traits and social skills were the sets of constructs that were most frequently measured in selection interviews, and (b) the constructs assessed by high-structure interviews tended to be different from those assessed by low-structure interviews. Specifically, applied social skills (e.g., communication, interpersonal, and leadership) were more likely to be assessed by high-structure than low-structure interviews, whereas mental capability (e.g., general intelligence) and a few personality characteristics (e.g., agreeableness and emotional stability) were more likely to be assessed by low-structure than high-structure interviews. These results also dovetail with meta-analytic results. For example, Huffcutt, Roth, and McDaniel (1996) found that low-structure interviews tend to produce higher correlations with cognitive ability measures than do high-structure interviews, and Salgado and Moscoso (2002) reported that the correlation between interview ratings and personality test scores are higher for conventional (i.e., unstructured) interviews than for behavior interviews. Specifically, these latter authors reported the following corrected correlations between unstructured (and structured) interview ratings and the Five-Factor Model dimensions: emotional stability = .38 (.08), extraversion = .34 (.21), openness to experience = .30 (.09), agreeableness = .26 (.12), and conscientiousness = .28 (.17).

We would like to note a few points about the above literature. First, we suggest caution when using author-reported interview dimension labels as a basis to determine the constructs that may be measured in structured selection interviews. As a result of the content-sampling approach to question development, a common focus of structured interview questions is on work-related behavioral composites (e.g., customer service orientation, teamwork, commitment; Bobko, Roth,

& Potosky, 1999; Campion et al., 1997). These work-focused performance constructs differ from person-focused predictor constructs (e.g., Big Five personality factors) in several ways (Binning & Barrett, 1989). One difference is that performance constructs tend to focus on organizational goals (e.g., "he/she follows all rules and regulations relating to safety procedures") rather than underlying dispositions (e.g., "he/she is conscientious"). Another difference is that performance constructs are often created and defined by organizational decision makers rather than researchers (who are more likely to clearly define their constructs and ground them in theory). A third difference is that performance constructs are used to further understand and predict behavior in job settings, whereas person-focused predictor constructs tend to reference behavioral tendencies as they occur across a variety of settings. This difference in focus between performance constructs and person constructs is also reflected in the emerging line of research demonstrating that work-specific personality measures often do a better job of predicting job performance and other organizational outcomes (e.g., job satisfaction, turnover intentions) than do general measures of the same personality constructs (e.g., Bowling & Burns, 2010; Hunthausen, Truxillo, Bauer, & Hammer, 2003; Pace & Brannick, 2010).

Taken as a whole, performance constructs are not as well defined nor as deeply embedded in the given nomological network as are predictor constructs (Binning & Barrett, 1989). Perhaps as a result of the lack of definitional precision, it can be difficult to identify clean connections between performance constructs and their underlying predictor constructs (e.g., Raymark, Schmit, & Guion, 1997). For example, attempts to decompose a performance construct (e.g., customer service orientation) into underlying predictor constructs (e.g., conscientiousness, agreeableness, and extraversion) may result in a set of variables both contaminated and deficient with regard to the parent performance construct. Thus, an examination of the correlations between structured interview ratings (which often assess performance constructs) and measures of person-focused predictor constructs (including personality variables) may not tell us much about the construct validity of interview ratings. A cleaner approach to assessing the construct validity of structured interview ratings would be to examine relations between structured interview ratings and alternative measures of the performance constructs. However, such an approach to construct validation would require interview researchers to (a) do a better job of defining the performance constructs that selection interviews are intended to assess and (b) develop high-quality alternative measures of those constructs.

Second, we note that an examination of correlations between interview ratings and test scores may obscure important relations due to the focus on the overall interview evaluation (which may be based on numerous interview questions that do not share a lot of construct overlap). Such correlations fail to consider the possibility that different parts of a selection interview could be focused on very different personality constructs. In recent years, a few studies have taken a more micro approach to interview construct validity by examining how ratings on individual interview questions (or subsets of interview questions) relate to alternate measures of the underlying constructs. The results of two of these studies (e.g., Roth, Van Iddekinge, Huffcutt, Eidson, & Schmit, 2005; Van Iddekinge, Raymark, Eidson, & Attenweiler, 2004) suggest that an overall impression factor may permeate interview ratings, thereby preventing individual interview items from being differentially related to various constructs. These findings are consistent with the literature suggesting that a single-factor solution explains much of the variance in interview ratings (e.g., Huffcutt, Weekley, Wiesner, DeGroot, & Jones, 2001; Pulakos & Schmitt, 1995; Roth & Campion, 1992). In contrast, the results of two other studies (Allen, Facteau, & Facteau, 2004; Van Iddekinge, Raymark, & Roth, 2005) suggest that individual interview ratings can produce favorable levels of convergent and discriminant validity (we will discuss some possible reasons for these divergent findings later in this chapter). Overall, these results indicate that interview researchers could be missing out on valuable construct-related evidence by focusing on overall interview ratings. At the least, we suggest that more of this fine-grained research is needed to further our understanding of how various characteristics of the selection interview may impact the reliability and validity of interview-based personality judgments.

Third, the literature focused on identifying interview constructs serves to illuminate the distinction between descriptive ("what *do* selection interviews measure?") and prescriptive ("what *can* selection interviews measure?") research. For example, meta-analyses of the relations between interview ratings and personality constructs rarely consider whether the source interviews were intended or designed to assess those constructs (e.g., Salgado & Moscoso, 2002). In fact, in order to reduce common rater variance, Huffcutt (2011) excluded studies from his review in which the focal personality constructs were formally assessed as part of the interview. As a result, these summaries may provide little insight as to how well selection interviews can measure personality variables when it is specifically designed to do so (Ployhart, 2006a; Posthuma, Morgeson, & Campion, 2002).

Can Interviewers Accurately Assess Personality?

We have identified two streams of research that may inform whether interviewers are capable of providing accurate ratings of applicants' personality. The first line of research we consider is the person perception literature. This literature has explored the broader question of whether, and under what conditions, a variety of observers can accurately assess the personality of a target individual. The organizing framework for this discussion is provided by the Realistic Accuracy Model (RAM) of person perception (Funder, 1999). Following a review of this literature, we highlight research that has taken a more systematic approach to assessing the potential of selection interviews to produce construct valid ratings of job applicant personality.

Person Perception Literature

Funder's (1999) RAM of person perception provides an integrative framework for understanding the factors that may influence the accuracy of personality judgment. In short, this model posits two factors that influence trait expression and two factors that influence trait perception. Concerning trait expression, accurate personality perception is considered a function of whether the environment allows the trait to be expressed (relevance) and whether it allows the observer to perceive the trait expression (availability). Concerning trait perception, the model specifies that accurate personality perception is a function of whether observers notice trait-relevant cues (detection) and whether they appropriately combine these cues to form an impression of the target (utilization).

Attempts to examine factors that impact trait expression and perception have largely focused on situations in which the observer tries to infer traits based on the behavior of the target. However, interviewers may infer personality characteristics based on the behavior of the applicant within the interview, as well as on the content of the applicant's responses to the interview questions (i.e., applicant self-reports of prior or intended behavior). Regardless of the source of the behavioral information, the RAM suggests four factors that may moderate the accuracy of personality judgments: (a) the ability of the observer to accurately evaluate targets (i.e., the "good judge"), (b) the ease with which a particular target can be judged (i.e., the "good target"), (c) the ease with which differences on a trait can be easily assessed (i.e., the "good trait"), and (d) the quality of the available information relative to the trait judgment (i.e., "good information").

The Good Judge

Research has supported the notion that there may be important differences between individuals in their ability to judge the personality characteristics of another person. For example, Letzring (2008) asked unacquainted triads to engage in unstructured interactions prior to making personality judgments. The results revealed that social skill, agreeableness, and emotional stability were predictive of the accuracy of personality judgments. Other research (e.g., Vogt & Colvin, 2003) has identified a variety of additional characteristics (e.g., sympathy, empathy, interpersonal orientation) that predict how accurately judges can assess the personality of others.

Within the domain of the selection interview, there is evidence of individual differences in interviewer validity (e.g., Posthuma et al., 2002; Van Iddekinge, Sager, Burnfield, & Heffner, 2006). In addition, research suggests that different interviewers may focus on different sets of personality traits (van Dam, 2003), and that the choice of focal personality traits may be a function of the interviewer's own personality characteristics (Hilliard & Macan, 2009; Sears & Rowe, 2003). Finally, interviewer dispositional intelligence (i.e., the knowledge of how personality is related to behavior) has been found to predict the accuracy of personality judgments made in simulated interviews (Christiansen, Wolcott-Burnam, Janovics, Burns, & Quirk, 2005). Thus, there is an emerging line of research indicating that there are individual differences across interviewers in what personality constructs are assessed, as well as in their proficiency in making personality judgments of job applicants.

The Good Target

The idea of a "good target" is that there are individual differences across targets in the extent to which the observers can accurately judge their personality (Funder, 1999). For example, some individuals may be more expressive and thus provide more easily discernible clues to their personality. Alternatively, individuals may differ in their tendency to engage in behaviors that make it more difficult to accurately judge their personality. For example, the idea of a "good target" within the context of a selection interview may be a function of job applicant impression management (IM) behaviors. A considerable amount of research has demonstrated that job applicants frequently use a variety of IM tactics during the course of an interview, and that the use of these tactics is positively related to interviewer evaluations (e.g., Barrick, Shaffer, & DeGrassi, 2009; Ellis, West, Ryan, & DeShon, 2002; Higgins & Judge, 2004; McFarland, Ryan, & Krista, 2003). The finding that IM tactics are highly used within selection interviews should not be surprising, as many interview questions explicitly ask the applicant to engage in behaviors that essentially invite IM (e.g., self-promotion, descriptions of overcoming obstacles). The central importance of IM tactics within selection interviews is reflected in the recent theoretical model developed by Huffcutt, Van Iddekinge, and Roth (2011), who proposed that various forms of interviewee social effectiveness (including IM) are a primary determinant of interviewee performance. However, what remains unclear is how the use of these IM tactics may influence interviewers' ability to assess the personality characteristics of the job applicant.

Relations between applicant personality and the use of IM tactics within selection interviews have been explored in a pair of recent studies (e.g., Peeters & Lievens, 2006; Van Iddekinge, McFarland, & Raymark, 2007). In both studies, applicants' motivation to manage impressions was proposed to moderate the relations between personality variables and IM. Although the results provided mixed support for this particular hypothesis, Van Iddekinge et al. did find that the use of IM tactics partially mediated the relations between applicant personality and interview ratings. However, this literature tells us little about how the use of IM may, in turn, impact on how interviewers judge the personality characteristics of an applicant. However, data reported by Kristof-Brown, Barrick, and Franke (2002) suggest that IM may provide one mechanism for how applicant personality influences relatively broad interview ratings (e.g., perceived overall person–job fit).

The Good Trait

The idea of a "good trait" concerns the ease with which a particular personality trait can be assessed by an observer. According to Funder (1999), the level of visibility and evaluativeness of a trait are the primary determinants of whether it can be accurately assessed by observers. For example, traits more likely to result in observable behaviors (e.g., expressive social behaviors often linked to extraversion) should be easier for observers to judge than traits more strongly tied to the internal thoughts and feelings of the individual (i.e., thought processes linked to openness or the affective component of emotional stability). The evaluativeness of a trait refers to whether social norms and values may impact the desired level of the trait. According to Funder, traits high in evaluativeness (e.g., facets of emotional stability) should be harder to assess by others because the target will be motivated to conceal the undesirable behaviors. In contrast, traits low in evaluativeness (e.g., facets of extraversion) should be easier to assess since the level of such traits is typically not accompanied by social evaluations.

There is considerable empirical support for the "good trait" propositions of the RAM. For example, observer ratings of extraversion (a trait considered to be high in visibility and low in evaluativeness) have been found to be more accurate than observer ratings of other personality characteristics (e.g., Borkenau & Liebler, 1992; John & Robbins, 1993). More recently, two meta-analyses have found that the self-other correspondence for ratings of extraversion (a "good" trait) are consistently higher than the self-other correspondence for ratings of agreeableness (e.g., Connelly & Ones, 2010; Connolly, Kavanaugh, & Viswesvaran, 2007). The RAM also suggests that what is considered a "good trait" could vary across settings. For example, the literature on situation–trait relevance proposes that the likelihood of a trait being expressed is tied to the presence of trait-relevant situational cues (Tett & Burnett, 2003; Tett & Guterman, 2000). Thus, the trait demands of a particular job may influence the relative desirability of different traits, which in turn may influence whether applicants exhibit those traits within the selection interview. Consistent with this trait activation perspective, recent research suggests that individuals will emphasize different sets of personality traits for different focal jobs (e.g., Raymark & Tafero, 2009; Tett, Freund, Christiansen, Fox, & Coaster, 2012). In summary, the identification of what constitutes a "good trait" in a particular interview setting (specifically, its level of evaluativeness) may be partially dependent on the trait demands of the focal job.

Good Information

"Good information" refers to the quality of the personality-related information available to the observer. One of the ways that "good information" has been investigated is to compare the accuracy of personality ratings made by individuals that differ in their familiarity with the target (due to enhanced quality or frequency of interaction with the target). Overall, this literature suggests that observer familiarity with a target is related to enhanced accuracy of personality judgments, but that the increase in accuracy is due to the quality of the relationship (interpersonal intimacy) rather than to mere frequency of interaction (Connelly & Ones, 2010). Certainly, one of the potential limitations of the selection interview as a means to assess applicant personality concerns the challenge of acquiring "good information" within the bounds of the interview context.

On a related note, a few authors have proposed that the quality of personality-related information obtained in a selection interview may be inversely related to the level of interview structure (e.g., Binning, LeBreton, & Adorno, 1999; Blackman & Funder, 2002). In support of this view, a study by Blackman (2002a) found that personality ratings resulting from an unstructured interview produced higher levels of self-interviewer and peer-interviewer rating agreement than did personality ratings resulting from a structured interview. In addition, an examination of the interview transcripts revealed that the interviewers in the unstructured interview condition asked significantly fewer personality-oriented questions than did the interviewers in the structured interview condition. Thus, Blackman concluded that the higher level of rating convergence for the unstructured interviews can be attributed to the relaxed and open atmosphere associated with an unstructured interview and not because the unstructured interview is more likely to include personality-related questions. Overall, Blackman and Funder (2002) have argued that the reason why unstructured interviews may do a better job of assessing personality is that the unconstrained nature of such interviews allows interviewers to obtain a richer set of behavioral cues relevant to personality judgment.

In summary, Funder's RAM suggests that the accuracy of observer ratings of target personality is a function of the (a) judge, (b) target, (c) trait, and (d) information. With this model as a backdrop, we will now review the empirical literature on the criterion-related validity of observer ratings of personality.

Validity of Observer Ratings of Personality

One way to assess the validity of observer ratings of personality is to assess their relationship with corresponding self-reports. A meta-analysis of correlations between self-reports and observer ratings of the Big Five personality factors resulted in true score correlations ranging from .46 for agreeableness to .62 for extraversion (Connolly et al., 2007). While these results indicate an appreciable level of consistency across self-report and observer ratings of personality, it is also clear that these two methods of personality assessment are not redundant. However, from our perspective, the more important question is whether observer ratings provide some degree of unique, trait-relevant information not captured by self-report measures (for more coverage on personality from the perspective of an observer, see Chapter 20, this volume).

The idea that observer ratings of personality might provide a valuable supplement to self-ratings is supported by socioanalytic theory (R. Hogan & Shelton, 1998; R. T. Hogan, 1991). This theory suggests that self-reports of personality assess the identity of the individual, whereas observer ratings assess the reputation of the individual. Furthermore, because observer ratings of personality are typically based on the individual's past behavior, and past behavior is a good predictor of future behavior, this theory suggests that observer ratings of personality could produce stronger criterion-related validities than do self-report measures (for more coverage of the socioanalytic theory of personality, see Chapter 4, this volume).

Two recent meta-analyses provide some insight into the relative value of observer ratings of personality in the prediction of job performance (Connelly & Ones, 2010; Oh, Wang, & Mount, 2011). Both studies concluded that observer ratings of the Big Five are significant predictors of job performance, with estimated mean operational validities across the Big Five ranging from .11 to .29 (Connelly & Ones) and from .21 to .37 (Oh et al.). Furthermore, both studies noted that observer ratings of personality produce a significant increment in validity beyond that of their corresponding self-report ratings (average validity increase of .09 and .13 in the studies by Connelly & Ones and Oh et al., respectively). However, we caution that these comparisons of observer and self-report measures of personality may be confounded by the fact that research investigating observer reports is more likely to be confirmatory in nature (which results in larger validities; Tett et al., 1999).

Most of the primary studies included in the above meta-analyses used coworkers to provide the observer ratings of personality; thus, it is not clear whether the apparent validity advantages associated with peer ratings may generalize to interviewer ratings of personality. As suggested by the RAM, if peers have greater access to "good information" than do interviewers (due to higher quality interactions), then the results suggesting incremental validity of observer ratings may not generalize to interviewers. However, one possible advantage for interviewers is that they can base their personality judgments on the behavior of the target individual, as well as on the applicant's self-report of behavior in other settings (i.e., in response to interview questions). With this as a foundation, we now turn to research examining the validity of interviewer ratings of personality.

Interviewer Ratings of Personality

One study that provides insight into the ability of interviewers to provide accurate personality ratings was conducted by Barrick, Patton, and Haugland (2000). These authors compared how three sets of "other" ratings of personality (e.g., close friends, interviewers, and strangers) correlated with self-ratings of personality. The results revealed that stranger ratings of personality produced the lowest level of convergence with self-ratings ($\bar{r}$ = .09), interviewer ratings provided a much higher level of convergence ($\bar{r}$ = .27), and ratings provided by close friends produced the highest level of convergence ($\bar{r}$ = .39). Thus, this research suggests that interviewers can assess applicant personality with some degree of accuracy, but perhaps not as accurately as that achieved by others who have a higher level of personal familiarity with the target. However, Barrick et al. noted that these results may underestimate the potential of the selection interview as a means to assess personality, as these interviews were not specifically designed to assess personality (nor were the interviewers explicitly instructed that they were to assess applicant personality).

Surprisingly, very little research has examined the construct and criterion-related validity of interviews that are specifically designed to assess applicant personality. Within the domain of clinical psychology, Trull et al. (1998) found encouraging psychometric support for the Structured Interview for the Five-Factor Model of Personality (SIFFM). However, the generalizability of this work to selection interviews is unclear as the SIFFM is structured more like an oral version of a typical self-report personality measure (e.g., dozens of items, Likert-type rating scale) than a selection interview.

One study that does provide insight as to whether a structured selection interview can be designed to assess personality was conducted by Van Iddekinge et al. (2005). In this study, several job-related interview questions were identified as being possibly useful for assessing one of the three relatively narrow personality characteristics (e.g., altruism, self-discipline, and vulnerability). After repeated modifications to the initial sets of questions, subject matter expert (SME) ratings were used to identify three questions that clearly assessed the intended personality construct but not the other two constructs to be included in the interview (i.e., three uniquely relevant questions per trait). Pairs of experienced interviewers conducted mock interviews using these questions, and they were required to evaluate each interview response on a behaviorally anchored rating scale before moving on to the next interview question. In addition, interviewees completed a self-report measure of the same three personality traits. The results of multitrait–multimethod (MTMM) and confirmatory factor analyses (CFAs) provided support for the construct validity of the personality ratings. For example, the mean correlation within a personality dimension and across the two interviewers was .66, whereas the mean correlation across personality dimensions and within interviewers was .38. In addition, a similar pattern of results was found when comparing interviewer ratings of personality with the self-report measures of personality.

Two unique characteristics of this study deserve additional consideration. First, the construct-oriented approach to interview development differs markedly from the traditional content-oriented approach. That is, the job-related interview questions and response scales were repeatedly modified so as to more clearly measure person-focused predictor constructs (e.g., altruism) rather than job-focused performance constructs (e.g., customer service orientation). We suspect that this construct-oriented approach to question development is partially responsible for the clarity of measurement that was obtained. Second, this interview was specifically designed to assess a relatively small number of narrow and conceptually independent constructs. The limited number of focal constructs meant that three interview questions could be asked for each construct (which may have enhanced reliability). In summary, the practicality of this construct-oriented approach to interview development may be limited to situations in which the organizational goal is to assess a small number of relatively distinct personality constructs. This concern aside, the results of Van Iddekinge et al. (2005) demonstrated that it is possible to develop a personality-focused structured selection interview that has evidence of construct validity. In the next section, we explore reasons why the selection interview may provide a valuable alternative methodology for assessing applicant personality.

Potential Advantages of Using the Selection Interview to Assess Personality

Several authors have commented that the primary weakness of personality assessment for personnel selection is the reliance on the self-report methodology (e.g., Morgeson et al., 2007). In this section, we explore some of the reasons why selection interviews may provide a valuable alternative to standard self-report measures for the assessment of personality in selection settings.

Information Richness and Detail

A primary reason why the selection interview has potential for enhancing personality assessment in selection settings concerns the richness of the data that results from the response generation process. Specifically, self-report measures of personality require job applicants to indicate only how likely they are to engage in a variety of behaviors. In contrast, structured interviews require the applicant to generate detailed responses to job-related scenarios based on how they have responded in the past or how they would anticipate responding in the future. This response generation process can provide the interviewer with considerable detail concerning how an applicant may approach a variety of settings, as well as to their motivations for choosing certain behaviors. This additional detail is simply not possible with typical self-report methodologies of personality assessment and such detail may be uniquely informative of job-relevant personality traits.

Presence of Behavioral Cues Relevant to Personality Assessment

Another reason why the selection interview holds promise as a means to personality assessment is that the interviewer has access to two sources of information: the content of the applicant's responses and the behaviors exhibited by the applicant during the interview. For example, if an interviewer is interested in assessing some facet of conscientiousness, he or she may acquire useful information from applicants' responses to conscientiousness-related questions, as well as from applicant behaviors within the interview that suggest conscientiousness (does the applicant seem prepared for the interview?). The potential validity of this behavioral information is reflected in research demonstrating that extraverts provide more elaborate interview responses than do introverts (Caldwell & Burger, 1998), and that individuals high in emotional stability demonstrate behaviors suggesting higher composure during an interview (Cook, Vance, & Spector, 2000). Similarly, research on interpersonal communication has found that certain vocal cues (e.g., pitch variability, speech rate) are associated with perceptions of extraversion (DeGroot & Motowidlo, 1999). Other research has found that auditory cues are related to the accuracy of state anxiety ratings (meta-analytic $\bar{r}$ = .49), and that visual cues were predictive of the accuracy of both state anxiety and trait anxiety ratings ($\bar{r}$s of .24 and .31; Harrigan, Wilson, & Rosenthal, 2004).

The above literature suggests that interviewers may gain insight into an applicant's personality by closely observing various behaviors during the interview. Beyond this passive observation of interviewee behavior, it may also be possible to actively construct situations within the interview that are designed to prompt behaviors relevant for a focal personality construct. For example, behaviors relevant to emotional stability may be elicited by an interview that is infused with artificial time constraints and an interviewer who repeatedly interrupts responses. Alternatively, behaviors relevant to impatience may be elicited by an interview in which the questions are asked very slowly, with numerous drawn-out pauses. There are likely a variety of other ways in which the interview design could be altered so as to intentionally elicit behavioral manifestations of personality characteristics. However, we are unaware of any research that has examined whether such manipulations of interview structure are an effective means of enhancing personality assessment, as well as what effect such manipulations may have on applicant reactions to the interview.

Overall, a considerable amount of research has supported the idea that observations of "thin slices" of behavior can result in surprisingly high levels of judgment accuracy (e.g., Ambady & Rosenthal, 1992). Specifically, this research suggests that observers can make reasonably accurate predictions of various objective behavioral outcomes (e.g., existence of deception, supervisor ratings of effectiveness) based on viewing only 30 seconds of nonverbal behaviors. A related line of research on spontaneous trait inferences has demonstrated that observers quickly and automatically infer traits based on the behavior of another person (e.g., Uleman, Newman, & Moskowitz, 1996). Furthermore, these automatic personality judgments tend to produce strong relations with self-ratings of personality, even in instances in which the observer and the target do not have an opportunity to interact (Albright, Kenny, & Malloy, 1988). Thus, this literature suggests that interviewers may be able to make reasonably accurate personality judgments based on a relatively small sample of behavior.

One factor that may influence whether these interviewee behaviors are noticed, encoded, and used in interviewer personality judgments is the cognitive demands placed on the interviewer. Specifically, social perception research suggests that, when perceivers are cognitively busy, behavioral (nonlinguistic) information may be especially influential since this information is more likely to be processed automatically than is verbal (linguistic) information (Gilbert & Krull, 1988). Focusing more specifically on the selection interview, Huffcutt (2011) proposed three main sources of construct-related variance in interview ratings: job-related interview content, interviewee performance factors, and personal/demographic characteristics. Next, he reported mean correlations between interview ratings and the specific factors contained within each of these three sources of construct-related variance. The results suggested that factors related to interviewee performance (e.g., IM and social skills) are more highly related to interview ratings than are content factors (e.g., personality, job experience). Although other studies have found that the content of what an applicant says is more important than how they say it (e.g., Riggio & Throckmorton, 1988), the results of Huffcutt (2011) suggest that job applicant behaviors within the selection interview can have a substantial impact on interview ratings.

Opportunity to Follow Up and Clarify Responses

Another potential advantage to using a selection interview to assess personality variables concerns the ability to probe responses that may lack clarity. Although numerous reviews have emphasized the importance of asking the same questions to each applicant (e.g., Campion et al., 1997), some authors have suggested that a loosening of some of the tenets of structured interviewing may result in a broader sample of interpersonal behaviors, which in turn may result in an enhanced ability to assess personality (e.g., Binning et al., 1999; Lanyon & Goodstein, 1997). On a related note, Huffcutt and Arthur (1994) found that the criterion-related validities for completely structured interviews (Level 4 interviews, $\bar{r}$ = .57) were comparable to the criterion-related validities of interviews that were not completely structured (Level 3 interviews, $\bar{r}$ = .56). Thus, at this point, it is not clear whether a completely structured interview may enhance or harm the construct validity of interview-based personality judgments. However, we encourage future researchers to explore this question, as well as the broader question of how the various components of interview structure may influence the construct validity of interview ratings.

Minimization of Self-Presentation Effects

A considerable amount of research has been directed toward the question of whether job applicants fake their responses on self-report personality measures (e.g., McFarland & Ryan, 2000; Rosse, Stecher, Miller, & Levin, 1998), as well as to the impact of faking on the criterion-related validity of these assessments (e.g., Hough, Eaton, Dunnette, Kamp, & McCloy, 1990; see Chapter 12, this volume). Concerns over faking behavior have led to the development of a scale specifically designed to assess faking behavior in the selection interview (Levashina & Campion, 2007). Preliminary evidence suggests that people admit to engaging in deceptive behavior within the selection interview. However, there are a variety of reasons why faking may be less of a concern when personality is assessed via a selection interview than when it is assessed via a traditional self-report method. For example, when attempting to fake on a self-report measure of personality, applicants need only to identify the desirable end of the scale for each item and respond appropriately. In contrast, when attempting to fake on an interview, applicants need to generate and describe job-related examples that are plausible, detailed, and relevant to the questions being asked. Furthermore, applicants who attempt to fake during an interview may instead produce a negative impression if they are perceived as lying or overly exaggerating their positive qualities (e.g., Fletcher, 1990; Jones & Pittman, 1982). Finally, the interviewee must also monitor a variety of nonverbal behaviors while they are concurrently trying to generate plausible and detailed interview responses. Overall, research suggests that it may be very difficult to effectively convey an image that is inconsistent with one's personality (Pontari & Schlenker, 2000).

In addition, there is empirical evidence that selection interviews may be resistant to applicant attempts to fake responses. Specifically, Van Iddekinge et al. (2005) compared the impact of instructions to fake on both a self-report measure of personality and an interview designed to assess the same personality constructs. The results revealed that faking instructions produced much higher score increases in the self-report personality measures than in the interview ratings of personality. Thus, not only do selection interviews enable the collection of a very rich set of behavioral data that can be used to assess applicant personality, they also may lessen concerns about applicant faking.

Challenges in Using the Selection Interview to Assess Personality

Many of the advantages associated with using the selection interview to assess personality center around the fact that interviews provide a richer source of personality-related information than does a typical self-report personality measure. However, many of the interview characteristics that promote information richness also may increase the difficulty in accurately assessing personality with the selection interview. A couple of these issues are discussed below.

Multidimensional Nature of Interview Questions

As noted earlier, interview questions derived from critical incidents have the advantage of being clearly tied to effective performance on the job in question. However, one of the challenges to evaluating responses to such questions is that their content is often multidimensional in nature (Roth et al., 2005). For example, consider the following interview question:

> You are about to take your lunch break, but before leaving, you decide to make sure that a coworker in an adjacent department is going to cover for you while you are gone. Instead, the

coworker informs you that he is also just about to leave for lunch. You know that this coworker is not scheduled for lunch until later. What would you do and why?

In some respects, this is not a particularly complex question, and yet it could potentially assess several different personality characteristics, including components of emotional stability (e.g., self-control), extraversion (e.g., assertiveness), agreeableness (e.g., altruism), and conscientiousness (e.g., dutifulness). Furthermore, it is possible that other interviewer questions may tap the same (or partially overlapping) sets of personality characteristics. As noted earlier, when interviews are developed from the results of a critical incident analysis, the resulting questions tend to focus on performance constructs, and thus the conceptual connections to person-focused predictor constructs may be tenuous. Obviously, this lack of construct clarity may limit the ability of structured interviews to accurately assess person-oriented constructs.

Open-Ended Response Format

A related concern is that the open-ended nature of the selection interview may result in interviewees taking their response in a direction not anticipated by the interview developer. Consider again the interview question in which the applicant is asked how they would respond if a coworker places them in an awkward situation by deciding to take lunch at an unscheduled time. Here are a few ways in which the applicant could respond:

1. Delay one's own lunch and take it when the opportunity arises;
2. Report the situation to the supervisor and let him/her handle it;
3. Confront the coworker and forcefully state that they need to follow the schedule;
4. Try to find another coworker to cover the lunch period in your department;
5. Take the regularly scheduled lunch break and let the coworker explain their absence if a problem arises.

Once again, the multidimensionality of the interview question is revealed by the fact that each of these responses may provide insight into different personality characteristics. Furthermore, a job applicant may expand on their answer by discussing a variety of additional topics, from how they would treat this coworker in the future ("I would certainly never help out this person in the future if they asked me for something") to how they think the organization should handle such instances ("I would try to find a way to ensure that the organization reprimands workers for unauthorized lunches"). Such unanticipated responses (resulting from the open-ended nature of the selection interview) may provide insight into various motivations and personality characteristics, despite the fact that they were not intended to be assessed. In fact, these unanticipated responses may be particularly salient to interviewers (owing to their uniqueness) and thus may be unduly weighted in interview ratings. At this point, however, it is unclear how interviewers integrate such interview responses that do not specifically address the focal point of the interview question.

Other Issues Impacting the Usefulness of Interview-Based Personality Ratings

Mode of Administration

A few additional issues are relevant to the discussion of whether the selection interview can be used to accurately assess job applicant personality. First, there are various presentation formats in which a selection interview can be administered. Some examples involve the use of a telephone (Bauer, Truxillo, Paronto, Weekley, & Campion, 2004; Silvester & Anderson, 2003), video-recording technology (Van Iddekinge, Raymark, Roth, & Payne, 2006), videoconferencing (Chapman, Uggerslev, & Webster, 2003; Straus, Miles, & Levesque, 2001), and written interviews (e.g., Whetzel, Baranowski, Petro, Curtin, & Fisher, 2003). One of the general trends in this literature is that face-to-face interviews tend to produce more favorable interview ratings than do interviews conducted using one of the alternative modes of administration (e.g. Silvester, Anderson, Haddleton, Cunningham, & Gibb, 2000; Van Iddekinge, Raymark, et al., 2006). In addition, Blackman (2002b) found that the correlations with self-report measures of personality were lower when an interview was conducted via telephone than when it was conducted face to face. Overall, these findings suggest that the mode of interview administration can substantially influence the level of interview ratings and perhaps the validity of these ratings. Given that the use of technology for assessment purposes is likely to increase (e.g., Skype interviews?), future research needs to further explore the specific mechanisms by which these different technologies may influence the interviewer judgment process.

Interview Transparency

An interview design characteristic that may impact the construct validity of interview-based personality ratings is whether the focal constructs are transparent to the interviewees prior to the interview. Klehe, Konig, Richter, Kleinmann, and Melcher (2008) found that applicants who were informed about the dimensions on which they would be assessed achieved higher interview ratings than applicants who were not informed about the interview dimensions. Perhaps of more interest, these authors reported higher levels of construct validity for the transparent interviews than for the nontransparent interviews. Although the underlying mechanism for this effect remains unclear, it seems reasonable to assume that transparent interviews may enable interviewees to better recognize how their various job-relevant experiences map onto individual interview questions.

Summary and Future Directions

The selection interview has long been used to assess job applicant personality, but surprisingly little is known about the validity of personality ratings derived from selection interviews. In this chapter, we noted that the lack of understanding may be rooted in the failure to adequately distinguish selection methods from selection constructs, as well as in the tendency to examine issues related to interview construct validity in a post hoc and reactive manner. Nonetheless, research indicates that there is a strong level of convergence among observer ratings of personality, as well as between observer and self-ratings. We also reviewed research suggesting that observers can make reasonably accurate ratings of personality based on thin slices of behavior, and that selection interviews may be somewhat resistant to faking attempts on the part of the applicant. Taken as a whole, our review of the interviewing and associated literatures is suggestive of the potential for the selection interview to provide accurate ratings of job applicant personality. Nonetheless, below we have identified several additional issues relating to the validity of interviewer-based personality judgments that we believe are in need of additional research attention.

Perhaps the most pressing issue concerns the construct validity of interview ratings. As noted, researchers need to be aware of the fact that there may not be a direct correspondence between the performance constructs measured in typical structured interview questions and the psychological constructs represented by the vast majority of individual difference measures. One approach to dealing with this disconnect is to alter the content of structured interview questions so that they more cleanly tap the person constructs that are thought to be important for performing the focal job (e.g., Van Iddekinge et al., 2005). A second approach is to further develop and define the performance constructs that are assessed in selection interviews and then develop alternative measures of these constructs so as to be able to better assess the construct validity of structured interview ratings.

Yet another possible approach to examining the construct validity of interview ratings can be found in the literature on SJTs. Specifically, Ployhart (2006b) proposed the Predictor Response Process (PRPR) model as a means to "unite contemporary conceptualizations of validity with research on psychological response processes and methodological models for testing such questions" (p. 84). This model starts with the assumption that different sets of knowledge, skills, abilities, and other attributes (KSAOs) are important for different parts of the PRPR (i.e., item comprehension, information retrieval, judgment, and response). Once these relations are identified and specified, it is then possible to further explore the meaning of scores drawn from multidimensional predictors (like SJTs or selection interviews) by isolating and modeling the sources of variance that influence the different stages of the predictor response process. The PRPR model has been successfully applied to SJTs (e.g., Friede Westring et al., 2009; MacKenzie, Ployhart, Weekley, & Ehlers, 2010); we encourage interview researchers to apply this model to the domain of selection interviews.

The next broad issue concerns the relations between various components of interview structure and assessments of applicant personality. Concerning the issue of question consistency, it is unclear whether a strict reliance on a predetermined set of interview questions may enhance or detract from the ability of the interviewer to assess personality. Although the research by Blackman (2002a) suggested that a lower level of interview structure may enhance the ability to make personality judgments, it is unclear which components of interview structure (e.g., question consistency, evaluation standardization) may be responsible for these effects. A related issue concerns an elaboration of the factors that may determine whether specific interviewers can accurately assess job applicant personality (especially within the context of an unstructured or semistructured interview). A specification of interviewer individual differences is only part of this equation; an alternative approach would involve training interviewers in techniques that would enhance their judgments of applicant personality (e.g., Powell & Goffin, 2009).

A third issue concerns the several promising lines of research relating to how IM tactics may relate to interviewer ratings of applicant personality. A meta-analysis (Barrick et al., 2009) found that the use of IM tactics is highly related to interview ratings but not to subsequent job performance. Furthermore, the use of IM tactics had a larger impact on unstructured than structured interview ratings. However, future research is needed to address whether the use of IM tactics enhances or degrades the construct validity of interview ratings of personality. In addition, future research could further examine how interviewer behaviors may impact the use of IM tactics. For example, research suggests that the influence of IM behaviors may be a function of interviewer individual differences (e.g., Lievens & Peeters, 2008; Silvester, Anderson-Gough, Anderson, & Mohamed, 2002). In fact, one study found that IM tactics may have less of an influence on interviewers who have received interview training (Howard & Ferris, 1996). Finally, future research might explore whether IM tactics are differentially linked to specific personality judgments within the selection interview. For example, a high level of self-promotion may have a larger impact on ratings of extraversion than on ratings of conscientiousness, whereas the reverse pattern may be true for the IM tactics of overcoming obstacles.

These are but a few ideas for future research examining the potential of the selection interview as a useful method for the assessment of personality; there are certainly many others. The vast amount of research conducted on this topic over the past decade suggests that there is a considerable amount of optimism and interest in identifying ways to enhance interviewer judgments of personality. We look forward to continued advances within this line of research.

Practitioner's Window

Below are some suggestions for practitioners who are interested in assessing personality within a selection interview.

1. Use personality-oriented job analysis techniques (e.g., Raymark et al., 1997) to help identify personality variables relevant for the focal job.
2. Clearly define the constructs of interest. Consider whether it is possible for multidimensional constructs to be broken down into narrower, facet-level constructs. For example, if conscientiousness is determined to be job relevant, is it the attention to detail facet, the dependability facet, and/or another facet of conscientiousness that is most relevant?
3. Consider which personality variables may be most economically assessed via self-report measures. Try to limit the number of interview-assessed constructs to five or less, so that each can be assessed with multiple questions. Give preference to constructs for which behavioral manifestations are most likely (i.e., Funder's "good traits").
4. Identify critical job incidents in which employees would need to demonstrate the target personality traits. Use SMEs to judge whether the critical incidents and behavioral response anchors map onto the intended constructs. Modify and simplify items to minimize multidimensionality.
5. Use panel interviews when possible, and have each interviewer evaluate each response prior to moving on to the next question.
6. Consider if there are structural characteristics of the interview (e.g., how the questions are asked) that may elicit behaviors relevant for the focal constructs.

References

Albright, L., Kenny, D. A., & Malloy, T. E. (1988). Consensus in personality judgments at zero acquaintance. *Journal of Personality and Social Psychology, 55*, 387–395.

Allen, T. D., Facteau, J. D., & Facteau, C. L. (2004). Structured interviewing for OCB: Construct validity, faking, and the effects of question type. *Human Performance, 17*, 1–24.

Ambady, N., & Rosenthal, R. (1992). Thin slices of expressive behavior as predictors of interpersonal consequences: A meta-analysis. *Psychological Bulletin, 111*, 256–274.

Arthur, W., Jr., & Villado, A. J. (2008). The importance of distinguishing between constructs and methods when comparing predictors in personnel selection research and practice. *Journal of Applied Psychology, 93*, 435–442.

Barrick, M. R., & Mount, M. K. (1991). The Big Five personality dimensions and job performance. *Personnel Psychology, 44*, 1–26.

Barrick, M. R., Patton, G. K., & Haugland, S. N. (2000). Accuracy of interviewer judgments of job applicant personality traits. *Personnel Psychology, 53*, 925–951.

Barrick, M. R., Shaffer, J. A., & DeGrassi, S. W. (2009). What you see may not be what you get: Relationships among self-presentation tactics and ratings of interview and job performance. *Journal of Applied Psychology, 94*, 1394–1411.

Bauer, T. N., Truxillo, D. M., Paronto, M. E., Weekley, J. A., & Campion, M. A. (2004). Applicant reactions to different selection technology: Face-to-face, interactive voice response, and computer-assisted telephone screening interviews. *International Journal of Selection and Assessment, 12*, 135–148.

Berry, C. M., Sackett, P. R., & Landers, R. N. (2007). Revisiting interview–cognitive ability relationships: Attending to specific range restriction mechanisms in meta-analysis. *Personnel Psychology, 60*, 837–874.

Binning, J. F., & Barrett, G. V. (1989). Validity of personnel decisions: A conceptual analysis of the inferential and evidential bases. *Journal of Applied Psychology, 74*, 478–494.

Binning, J. F., LeBreton, J. M., & Adorno, A. J. (1999). Assessing personality. In R. W. Eder & M. M. Harris (Eds.), *The employment interview handbook* (pp. 105–123). Thousand Oaks, CA: Sage.

Blackman, M. C. (2002a). Personality judgment and the utility of the unstructured employment interview. *Basic and Applied Social Psychology, 24*, 241–250.
Blackman, M. C. (2002b). The employment interview via the telephone: Are we sacrificing accurate personality judgments for cost efficiency? *Journal of Research in Personality, 36*, 208–223.
Blackman, M. C., & Funder, D. C. (2002). Effective interview practices for accurately assessing counterproductive traits. *International Journal of Selection and Assessment, 10*, 109–116.
Bobko, P., Roth, P. L., & Potosky, D. (1999). Derivation and implications of a meta-analytic matrix incorporating cognitive ability, alternative predictors, and job performance. *Personnel Psychology, 52*, 561–589.
Borkenau, P., & Liebler, A. (1992). Trait inferences: Sources of validity at zero acquaintance. *Journal of Personality and Social Psychology, 62*, 645–657.
Bowling, N. A., & Burns, G. N. (2010). A comparison of work-specific and general personality measures as predictors of work and non-work criteria. *Personality and Individual Differences, 49*, 95–101.
Caldwell, D. F., & Burger, J. M. (1998). Personality characteristics of job applicants and success in screening interviews. *Personnel Psychology, 51*, 119–136.
Campion, M. A., Palmer, D. K., & Campion, J. E. (1997). A review of structure in the selection interview. *Personnel Psychology, 50*, 655–702.
Chapman, D. S., Uggerslev, K. L., & Webster, J. (2003). Applicant reaction to face-to-face and technology-mediated interviews: A field investigation. *Journal of Applied Psychology, 88*, 944–953.
Christiansen, N. D., Wolcott-Burnam, S., Janovics, J. E., Burns, G. N., & Quirk, S. W. (2005). The good judge revisited: Individual differences in the accuracy of personality judgments. *Human Performance, 18*, 123–149.
Connelly, B. S., & Ones, D. S. (2010). An other perspective on personality: Meta-analytic integration of observers' accuracy and predictive validity. *Psychological Bulletin, 136*, 1092–1122.
Connolly, J. J., Kavanaugh, E. J., & Viswesvaran, C. (2007). The convergent validity between self and observer ratings of personality: A meta-analytic review. *International Journal of Selection and Assessment, 15*, 110–117.
Cook, K. W., Vance, C. A., & Spector, P. E. (2000). The relation of candidate personality with selection-interview outcomes. *Journal of Applied Social Psychology, 30*, 867–885.
DeGroot, T., & Motowidlo, S. J. (1999). Why visual and vocal interview cues can affect interviewers' judgments and predict job performance. *Journal of Applied Psychology, 84*, 986–993.
Ellis, A. P. J., West, B. J., Ryan, A. M., & DeShon, R. P. (2002). The use of impression management tactics in structured interviews: A function of question type? *Journal of Applied Psychology, 87*, 1200–1208.
Fletcher, C. (1990). The relationships between candidate personality, self-presentation strategies, and interviewer assessments in selection interviews: An empirical study. *Human Relations, 43*, 739–749.
Friede Westring, A. J., Oswald, F. L., Schmitt, N., Drzakowski, S., Imus, A., Kim, B., & Shivpuri, S. (2009). Estimating trait and situational variance in a situational judgment test. *Human Performance, 22*, 44–63.
Funder, D. C. (1999). *Personality judgment: A realistic approach to person perception*. San Diego, CA: Academic Press.
Gilbert, D. T., & Krull, D. S. (1988). Seeing less and knowing more: The benefits of perceptual ignorance. *Journal of Personality and Social Psychology, 54*, 193–202.
Harrigan, J. A., Wilson, K., & Rosenthal, R. (2004). Detecting state and trait anxiety from auditory and visual cues: A meta-analysis. *Personality and Social Psychology Bulletin, 30*, 56–66.
Harris, M. M. (1998). The structured interview: What constructs are being measured? In R. Eder & M. Harris (Eds.), *The employment interview: Theory, research and practice* (2nd ed., pp. 143–157). Thousand Oaks, CA: Sage.
Hausknecht, J. P., Day, D. V., & Thomas, S. C. (2004). Applicant reactions to selection procedures: An updated model and meta-analysis. *Personnel Psychology, 57*, 639–683.
Higgins, C. A., & Judge, T. A. (2004). The effect of applicant influence tactics on recruiter perceptions of fit and hiring recommendations: A field study. *Journal of Applied Psychology, 89*, 622–632.
Hilliard, T., & Macan, T. (2009). Can mock interviewers' personalities influence their personality ratings of applicants? *The Journal of Psychology: Interdisciplinary and Applied, 143*, 161–174.
Hogan, R., & Shelton, D. (1998). A socioanalytic perspective on job performance. *Human Performance, 11*, 129–144.
Hogan, R. T. (1991). Personality and personality measurement. In M. D. Dunnette & L. M. Hough (Eds.), *Handbook of industrial and organizational psychology* (2nd ed., Vol. 2, pp. 873–919). Palo Alto, CA: Consulting Psychologists Press.
Hough, L. M., Eaton, N. K., Dunnette, M. D., Kamp, J. D., & McCloy, R. A. (1990). Criterion-related validities of personality constructs and the effect of response distortion on those validities. *Journal of Applied Psychology, 75*, 581–595.
Howard, J. L., & Ferris, G. R. (1996). The employment interview context: Social and situational influences on interviewer decisions. *Journal of Applied Social Psychology, 26*, 112–136.
Huffcutt, A. I. (2011). An empirical review of the employment interview construct literature. *International Journal of Selection and Assessment, 19*, 62–81.

Huffcutt, A. I., & Arthur, W., Jr. (1994). Hunter and Hunter (1984) revisited: Interview validity for entry-level jobs. *Journal of Applied Psychology, 79*, 184–190.

Huffcutt, A. I., Conway, J. M., Roth, P. L., & Stone, N. J. (2001). Identification and meta-analytic assessment of psychological constructs measured in employment interviews. *Journal of Applied Psychology, 86*, 897–913.

Huffcutt, A. I., & Culbertson, S. S. (2011). Interviews. In S. Zedeck (Ed.), *APA handbook of industrial and organizational psychology. Vol. 2: Selecting and developing members for the organization* (pp. 185–203). Washington, DC: American Psychological Association.

Huffcutt, A. I., & Roth, P. L. (1998). Racial group differences in employment interview evaluations. *Journal of Applied Psychology, 83*, 179–189.

Huffcutt, A. I., Roth, P. L., & McDaniel, M. A. (1996). A meta-analytic investigation of cognitive ability in employment interview evaluations: Moderating characteristics and implications for incremental validity. *Journal of Applied Psychology, 81*, 459–473.

Huffcutt, A. I., Van Iddekinge, C. H., & Roth, P. L. (2011). Understanding applicant behavior in employment interviews: A theoretical model of interviewee performance. *Human Resource Management Review, 21*, 353–367.

Huffcutt, A. I., Weekley, J. A., Wiesner, W. H., DeGroot, T. G., & Jones, C. (2001). Comparison of situational and behavior description interview questions for higher-level positions. *Personnel Psychology, 54*, 619–644.

Hunthausen, J. M., Truxillo, D. M., Bauer, T. N., & Hammer, L. B. (2003). A field study of frame-of-reference effects on personality test validity. *Journal of Applied Psychology, 88*, 545–551.

Hurtz, G. M., & Donovan, J. J. (2000). Personality and job performance: The Big Five revisited. *Journal of Applied Psychology, 85*, 869–879.

John, O. P., & Robbins, R. W. (1993). Determinants of interjudge agreement on personality traits: The Big Five domains, observability, evaluativeness, and the unique perspective of the self. *Journal of Personality, 61*, 521–551.

Jones, E. E., & Pittman, T. S. (1982). Toward a general theory of strategic self-presentation. In J. Suls (Ed.), *Psychological perspectives on the self* (pp. 231–262). Hillsdale, NJ: Erlbaum.

Klehe, U., Konig, C. J., Richter, G. M., Kleinmann, M., & Melcher, K. G. (2008). Transparency in structured interviews: Consequences for construct and criterion-related validity. *Human Performance, 21*, 107–137.

Konig, C. J., Klehe, U.-C., Berchtold, M., & Kleinmann, M. (2010). Reasons for being selective when choosing personnel selection procedures. *International Journal of Selection and Assessment, 18*, 17–27.

Kristof-Brown, A., Barrick, M. R., & Franke, M. (2002). Applicant impression management: Dispositional influences and consequences for recruiter perceptions of fit and similarity. *Journal of Management, 28*, 27–46.

Lanyon, R. I., & Goodstein, L. D. (1997). *Personality assessment* (3rd ed.). New York: John Wiley & Sons.

Letzring, T. D. (2008). The good judge of personality: Characteristics, behaviors, and observer accuracy. *Journal of Research in Personality, 42*, 914–932.

Levashina, J., & Campion, M. A. (2007). Measuring faking in the employment interview: Development and validation of an interview faking behavior scale. *Journal of Applied Psychology, 92*, 1638–1656.

Lievens, F., Highhouse, S., & De Corte, W. (2005). The importance of traits and abilities in supervisors' hirability decisions as a function of method of assessment. *Journal of Occupational and Organizational Psychology, 78*, 453–470.

Lievens, F., & Peeters, H. (2008). Interviewers' sensitivity to impression management tactics in structured interviews. *European Journal of Psychological Assessment, 24*, 174–180.

Macan, T. (2009). The employment interview: A review of current studies and directions for future research. *Human Resource Management Review, 19*, 203–218.

MacKenzie, W. I., Jr., Ployhart, R. E., Weekley, J. A., & Ehlers, C. (2010). Contextual effects on SJT responses: An examination of construct validity and mean differences across applicant and incumbent contexts. *Human Performance, 23*, 1–21.

McDaniel, M. A., Whetzel, D. L., Schmidt, F. L., & Maurer, S. (1994). The validity of employment interviews: A comprehensive review and meta-analysis. *Journal of Applied Psychology, 79*, 599–616.

McFarland, L. A., & Ryan, A. M. (2000). Variance in faking across noncognitive measures. *Journal of Applied Psychology, 85*, 869–879.

McFarland, L. A., Ryan, A. M., & Krista, S. D. (2003). Impression management use and effectiveness across assessment methods. *Journal of Management, 29*, 641–661.

Morgeson, F. P., Campion, M. A., Dipboye, R. L., Hollenbeck, J. R., Murphy, K. R., & Schmitt, N. (2007). Reconsidering the use of personality tests in personnel selection contexts. *Personnel Psychology, 60*, 683–729.

Murphy, K. R. (2009). Content validation is useful for many things, but validity isn't one of them. *Industrial and Organizational Psychology, 2*, 453–464.

Oh, I.-S., Wang, G., & Mount, M. K. (2011). Validity of observer ratings of the five factor model of personality traits: A meta-analysis. *Journal of Applied Psychology, 96*, 762–773.

Pace, V. L., & Brannick, M. T. (2010). Improving prediction of work performance through frame-of-reference consistency: Empirical evidence using openness to experience. *International Journal of Selection and Assessment, 18*, 230–235.
Peeters, H., & Lievens, F. (2006). Verbal and nonverbal impression management tactics in behavior description and situational interviews. *International Journal of Selection and Assessment, 14*, 206–222.
Ployhart, R. E. (2006a). Staffing in the 21st century: New challenges and strategic opportunities. *Journal of Management, 32*, 868–897.
Ployhart, R. E. (2006b). The predictor response model. In J. A. Weekley & R. E. Ployhart (Eds.), *Situational judgment tests: Theory, measurement, and application* (pp. 135–155). Mahwah, NJ: Lawrence Erlbaum.
Pontari, B. A., & Schlenker, B. R. (2000). The influence of cognitive load on self-presentation: Can cognitive busyness help as well as harm social performance? *Journal of Personality and Social Psychology, 78*, 1092–1108.
Posthuma, R. A., Morgeson, F. P., & Campion, M. A. (2002). Beyond employment interview validity: A comprehensive narrative review of recent research and trends over time. *Personnel Psychology, 55*, 1–81.
Powell, D. M., & Goffin, R. D. (2009). Assessing personality in the employment interview: The impact of training on rater accuracy. *Human Performance, 22*, 450–465.
Pulakos, E. D., & Schmitt, N. (1995). Experience based and situational interview questions: Studies of validity. *Personnel Psychology, 48*, 289–308.
Raymark, P. H., Schmit, M. J., & Guion, R. M. (1997). Identifying potentially useful personality constructs for employee selection. *Personnel Psychology, 50*, 723–736.
Raymark, P. H., & Tafero, T. L. (2009). Individual differences in the ability to fake on personality measures. *Human Performance, 22*, 86–103.
Riggio, R. E., & Throckmorton, B. (1988). The relative effects of verbal and nonverbal behavior, appearance, and social skills in evaluations made in hiring interviews. *Journal of Applied Social Psychology, 18*, 331–348.
Rosse, J. G., Stecher, M. D., Miller, J. L., & Levin, R. A. (1998). The impact of response distortion on preemployment personality testing and hiring decisions. *Journal of Applied Psychology, 83*, 634–644.
Roth, P. L., & Campion, J. E. (1992). An analysis of the predictive power of the panel interview and preemployment tests. *Journal of Occupational and Organizational Psychology, 65*, 51–60.
Roth, P. L., Van Iddekinge, C. H., Huffcutt, A. I., Eidson, C. E., Jr., & Schmit, M. J. (2005). Personality saturation in structured interviews. *International Journal of Selection and Assessment, 13*, 261–273.
Ryan, A. M., & Sackett, P. R. (1987). A survey of individual assessment practices by I/O psychologists. *Personnel Psychology, 40*, 455–488.
Salgado, J. F., & Moscoso, S. (2002). Comprehensive meta-analysis of the construct validity of the employment interview. *European Journal of Work and Organizational Psychology, 11*, 299–324.
Schmidt, F. L., & Zimmerman, R. D. (2004). A counterintuitive hypothesis about employment interview validity and some supportive evidence. *Journal of Applied Psychology, 89*, 553–561.
Sears, G. J., & Rowe, P. M. (2003). A personality-based similar-to-me effect in the employment interview: Conscientiousness, affect-versus competence-mediated interpretations, and the role of job relevance. *Canadian Journal of Behavioral Science, 35*, 13–24.
Silvester, J., & Anderson, N. (2003). Technology and discourse: A comparison of face-to-face and telephone employment interviews. *International Journal of Selection and Assessment, 11*, 206–214.
Silvester, J., Anderson, N., Haddleton, E., Cunningham, S., & Gibb, A. (2000). A cross-modal comparison of telephone and face-to-face selection interviews in graduate recruitment. *International Journal of Selection and Assessment, 8*, 16–21.
Silvester, J., Anderson-Gough, F. M., Anderson, N. R., & Mohamed, A. R. (2002). Locus of control, attributions and impression management in the selection interview. *Journal of Occupational and Organizational Psychology, 75*, 59–76.
Straus, S. G., Miles, J. A., & Levesque, L. L. (2001). The effects of videoconference, telephone, and face-to-face media on interviewer and applicant judgments in employment interviews. *Journal of Management, 27*, 363–381.
Tenopyr, M. L. (1977). Content–construct confusion. *Personnel Psychology, 30*, 47–54.
Tett, R. P., & Burnett, D. D. (2003). A personality trait-based interactionist model of job performance. *Journal of Applied Psychology, 88*, 500–517.
Tett, R. P., & Christiansen, N. D. (2007). Personality tests at the crossroads: A response to Morgeson, Campion, Dipboye, Hollenbeck, Murphy, and Schmitt (2007). *Personnel Psychology, 60*, 967–993.
Tett, R. P., Freund, K. A., Christiansen, N. D., Fox, K. E., & Coaster, J. (2012). Faking on self-report emotional intelligence and personality tests: Effects of faking opportunity, cognitive ability, and job type. *Personality and Individual Differences, 52*, 195–201.
Tett, R. P., & Guterman, H. A. (2000). Situation trait relevance, trait expression, and cross-situational consistency: Testing a principle of trait activation. *Journal of Research in Personality, 34*, 397–423.

Tett, R. P., Jackson, D. N., & Rothstein, M. (1991). Personality measures as predictors of job performance: A meta-analytic review. *Personnel Psychology, 44*, 703–742.

Tett, R. P., Jackson, D. N., Rothstein, M., & Reddon, J. R. (1999). Meta-analysis of bi-directional relations in personality–job performance research. *Human Performance, 12*, 1–29.

Trull, T. J., Widiger, T. A., Useda, J. D., Holcomb, J., Doan, B.-T., Axelrod, S. R., . . . Gershuny, B. S. (1998). A structured interview for the assessment of the Five-Factor model of personality. *Psychological Assessment, 10*, 229–240.

Uleman, J. S., Newman, L. S., & Moskowitz, G. B. (1996). People as flexible interpreters: Evidence and issues from spontaneous train inference. *Advances in Experimental Social Psychology, 28*, 211–279.

van Dam, K. (2003). Trait perception in the employment interview: A five factor model perspective. *International Journal of Selection and Assessment, 11*, 43–55.

Van Iddekinge, C. H., McFarland, L. A., & Raymark, P. H. (2007). Antecedents of impression management use and effectiveness in a structured interview. *Journal of Management, 33*, 752–773.

Van Iddekinge, C. H., Raymark, P. H., Eidson, C. E., Jr., & Attenweiler, W. J. (2004). What do structured interviews really measure? The construct validity of behavior description interviews. *Human Performance, 17*, 71–93.

Van Iddekinge, C. H., Raymark, P. H., & Roth, P. L. (2005). Assessing personality with a structured employment interview: Construct related validity and susceptibility to response inflation. *Journal of Applied Psychology, 90*, 536–552.

Van Iddekinge, C. H., Raymark, P. H., Roth, P. L., & Payne, H. A. (2006). Comparing the psychometric characteristics of ratings of face-to-face and videotaped selection interviews. *International Journal of Selection and Assessment, 14*, 347–359.

Van Iddekinge, C. H., Sager, C. E., Burnfield, J. L., & Heffner, T. S. (2006). The variability of criterion-related validity estimates among interviewers and interview panels. *International Journal of Selection and Assessment, 14*, 193–205.

Vogt, D. S., & Colvin, C. R. (2003). Interpersonal orientation and the accuracy of personality judgments. *Journal of Personality, 35*, 238–246.

Wernimont, P. F., & Campbell, J. P. (1968). Signs, samples, and criteria. *Journal of Applied Psychology, 52*, 372–376.

Whetzel, D. L., Baranowski, L. E., Petro, J. M., Curtin, P. J., & Fisher, J. F. (2003). A written structured interview by any other name is still a selection instrument. *Applied H.R.M. Research, 8*, 1–16.

Wiesner, W., & Cronshaw, S. (1988). A meta-analytic investigation of the impact of interview format and degree of structure on the validity of the employment interview. *Journal of Occupational Psychology, 61*, 275–290.

Wilk, S. L., & Cappelli, P. (2003). Understanding the determinants of employer use of selection methods. *Personnel Psychology, 56*, 103–124.

Wright, P. M., Lichtenfels, P. A., & Pursell, E. D. (1989). The structured interview: Additional studies and a meta-analysis. *Journal of Occupational Psychology, 62*, 191–199.

19

Assessing Personality With Situational Judgment Measures

Interactionist Psychology Operationalized

Michael C. Campion and Robert E. Ployhart

Interactionist psychology refers generically to a research paradigm that seeks to simultaneously model the behavioral consequences of individual characteristics (e.g., traits) and situational characteristics. Lewin's (1936) proposition, Behavior = *f*(Person, Environment), is classic shorthand for this type of research. Many applied psychologists today assume behavior is a function of individuals (P) and their environments (E), or more specifically, their immediate situation (S). For example, research on the attraction–selection–attrition model, person–environment fit, leader–member relationships, organizational identification, and climate strength are all based on a premise that behavior is affected by the joint relationship between the person and the situation.

Despite such beliefs, most applied personality psychologists tend to focus purely on the "person" side of the function, utilizing relatively context-free assessments of personality and rarely providing a serious consideration of situations or contexts (cf. Cappelli & Sherer, 1991; Johns, 2006). That is, most applied psychologists (particularly those in the individual differences and personnel selection fields) adopt a model where Behavior = *f*(Person). If situations are "considered," it is usually limited to meta-analyses where situations are treated as sampling error or variance to be accounted for by moderators. However, a moderating effect for situations is not what Lewin proposed. Lewin did *not* mean Behavior = *f*(Person × Situation). The moderating effect of situations is a mutation of Lewin, and a consequence of framing theory and research in terms of statistics (e.g., moderated regression). Lewin instead proposed a simultaneous and dynamic relationship between the person and the situation—he did not propose interactionism occurred *after* main effects.

Modern personality and social psychologists have returned to Lewin's original thinking and adopted dynamic models of traits and situations (e.g., Mischel & Shoda, 1995; Rusbult & Van Lange, 2008). Some in applied psychology have likewise adopted such approaches by proposing that the person is an active perceiver of the situation, and hence, it is critical to understand the person in context (Tett & Burnett, 2003; see Chapter 5, this volume). Yet personality assessment remains focused on context-free measures of traits (based usually on the Five-Factor Model [FFM]). When context is considered, it is often by simply adding "at work" tags to the generic personality items (e.g., M. J. Schmitt, Ryan, Stierwalt, & Powell, 1995). Adding "at work" tags enhances the criterion-related validity of the personality scores (Lievens, De Corte, & Schollaert, 2008) but still lacks a rich consideration of work situations and contexts.

The first purpose of this chapter is to argue that scholars wishing to understand personality need to devote attention to interactionist psychology, that is, Behavior = *f*(Person, Situation). They need to make a more serious effort to understand the psychological processes linking people to situations. In turn, this requires scholars to move beyond models treating situations only as moderators (B = P *f* S), to consider the fact that people perceive, interpret, and react to situations. Stated differently, we may be able to better understand the role of personality in work behavior by taking a more serious consideration of the "S" side of the function, and the joint relationship between persons and situations. To consider personality devoid of situations is unnatural.

The second purpose of this chapter is to propose a way to measure interactionist approaches to personality in a reasonably efficient manner. We suggest methodologies are already available to model and assess interactionist psychology. In particular, situational judgment tests (SJTs) can provide a relatively simple assessment methodology for capturing person–situation relationships in applied settings. SJTs are measurement methods that present respondents with work situations and then examine how they would or should behave in those situations (N. Schmitt & Chan, 2006). SJT responses are inherently a function of the person's characteristics and the content of the situations. However, SJTs rarely produce homogeneous factors, suggesting a lack of construct validity. The reason is because the situations in SJTs are often derived without any consideration of an underlying structure. Rather, the situations in SJTs are determined purely by a descriptive examination of the content of the job and are not based on any taxonomy or underlying framework of the situations. The consequence is that SJTs have many specific subfactors clustering more around elements of situations and not around the knowledge, skill, ability, or other characteristic (KSAO) constructs they are designed to assess (a consequence similar to "exercise effects" found with assessment centers).

Thus, integrating the applied personality research on traits (where Behavior = *f*(Person)) with the research on SJTs (where Behavior = *f*(Situation)) can allow applied psychologists to operationalize interactionist psychology. Furthermore, it would allow a greater understanding of the determinants of work behavior and job performance. Such an integration could also help increase the criterion-related validity of personality assessments and increase the construct validity of SJTs. But integrating personality theory with the SJT measurement methodology requires a careful understanding of interactionist psychology. Therefore, the following section of this chapter will briefly review the historical basis of interactionist psychology and will emphasize some of the key "lessons learned" from the debate on persons and situations. We will then turn to more modern "process theories" of interactionist psychology. These lessons will then be contrasted to the existing work on SJTs. We conclude with an integration of personality and SJTs to fulfill the promise of Lewin.

Interactionist Psychology

Historical Origins

During the first half of the 20th Century, the field of personality psychology was dominated by two distinct theoretical perspectives—that of the trait theorist and that of the situationist (Endler & Magnusson, 1976; Murtha, Kanfer, & Ackerman, 1996). Trait theorists contended that traits (or personal dispositions) exist within an individual, are enduring and stable, and influence how that individual tends to behave across *all* situations. In the past, they used methodological approaches that measure cross-situational consistency in responses and cited these correlations as evidence that traits exist (Krahe, 1992). Situationists, on the other hand, argued that what govern people's behaviors are the characteristics of the situation (Endler & Magnusson, 1976). They cite trait theorists' low cross-situational behavioral consistency coefficients (usually less than .30) as evidence of the nonexistence of traits and as evidence of the importance of the situation as a determinant of behavior (Epstein, 1979; Mischel, 1968). The war between trait theorists and situationists had been taking place for decades and was widely known within the personality psychology field as the "consistency controversy."

Dating back to the late 1930s with Allport's (1937) criticism of the Hartshorne and May (1928) studies, the consistency controversy ruled the personality literature until the late 1960s when Mischel (1968) boldly stated that with a correlation coefficient "ceiling" of .30, only 10% of the variance in behavior is explained by traits. He further asserted that "with the possible exception of intelligence, highly generalized behavioral consistencies have not been demonstrated, and the concept of personality traits as broad predispositions is thus untenable." This incited the emergence of modern interactionism (see Endler & Hunt, 1966, 1968, 1969; Magnusson, Gerzen, & Nyman, 1968), an approach that recognized both traits and the situation as determinants of behavior (for a more detailed account of the history of personality testing, see Chapter 9, this volume).

Despite its widespread visibility in more recent times in adjacent research domains, interactionism has a long history in personality psychology. The notion of an interaction between a stimulus condition (situation) and a psychological organism (person) leading to a response behavior can be traced back as far as the 1920s and 1930s (see Kantor, 1924, 1926; Koffka, 1935; Lewin, 1936; Murray, 1938). It was during this time period that behavior was operationalized for the first time as a function of the continuous interaction between the psychological characteristics of the person and the psychological meaning of the situation, or Lewin's classic $B = f(P, S)$. One of the reasons that interactionism seemed so attractive following Mischel's (1968) statement was that the interaction between individuals and situations accounted for more variance than either source could alone. In an early review of the literature, Bowers (1973) found that, on average, person and situation accounted for 12.71% and 10.17% of the variance, respectively, while the interaction, on average, accounted for 20.77%.

As with trait theory and situationism, interactionist theory is not a single, well-defined theory but rather a research perspective (Krahe, 1992). Advocates differ in the degree to which they weigh the importance of the situation and the dispositional components (Buss, 1977). However, a widely accepted definition of personality from an interactionist's perspective is as follows: ". . . personality can be defined as a person's coherent manner of interacting with himself or herself and with his or her environment" (Endler, 1983, p. 179). This definition can be summed up in four fundamental postulates:

> 1) actual behavior is a function of a continuous process of multidirectional interaction or feedback between the individual and the situations he or she encounters, 2) the individual is an intentional, active agent in this interaction process, 3) on the person side of the interaction, cognitive and motivational factors are essential determinants of behavior, 4) on the situation side, the psychological meaning of situations for the individual is the important determining factor.
>
> *Magnusson & Endler, 1977, p. 4*

In conducting research following an interactionist paradigm, two tasks must be performed. First, one must examine how the relationship between person and situation evokes behavior. Second, one must evaluate and classify stimuli in a systematic fashion (Endler, 1983). The second task is fundamental to providing information about how situational cues are processed within an individual; this is meaningful because it develops a picture of how the individual perceives the social world around him or her.

Interactionist approaches are more than an additive combination of trait theory and situationism. Interactionists seek to discover a lawfulness in individual behavior or *coherence* (Krahe, 1992; Magnusson & Endler, 1977). This requires a different level of analysis. Trait theorists and situationists primarily utilize theory and methodologies that allow the researcher to distinguish *between* individuals in their explanation of behavior, that is, they seek to explain behavior from an *inter*individual perspective. Interactionists, on the other hand, seek to explain behavior from an *intra*individual perspective. That is, interactionists' primary goal in personality research is to identify ideographically predictable patterns of behavior across situations and through time (Krahe, 1992; Magnusson, 1976). They believe that by focusing on the dispositional characteristics *within* an individual, and the interactions between those characteristics and the psychological meaning of the situation, behavior can be more accurately explained or predicted.

In accordance with an intraindividual level of analysis and the goal of discovering a consistency in patterns of individual behavior, interactionists define personality as one's interaction with oneself within a given environment. That is, they postulate that it is the variables interacting *within* an individual as well as the situational stimuli that explain patterns in their behavior. These variables are known as reaction variables and mediating variables (Magnusson & Endler, 1977). Reaction variables are defined as the different types of responses that the individual shows due to the interaction between the situation and their own internal processing, and they are observable. Mediating variables are not directly observable. Mediating variables integrate to form processes that determine how one perceives situational cues, interprets them, and ultimately responds. There are three types of mediating variables involved in these processes: (1) the content of the mediating process or the psychological meaning attached to the situational information based on information intrinsic to the situation or already stored social knowledge; (2) the cognitive structure into which the content is integrated, or in other words, the cognitive schema formed by the individual linking the new content with preexisting content in some meaningful way; and (3) motivational variables, which serve to explain why specific situational cues are often selected and interpreted in a certain way (Krahe, 1992). Thus, these mediating processes are where the "action" occurs.

Situations From an Interactionist Perspective

The psychological meaning of situations for the individual is more important than the more objective nature of the situation (Magnusson & Endler, 1977). This postulate points to the importance of determining what the salient characteristics of the situation are to the individual. In other words, how do people subjectively interpret their situations? It is this interpretation of the situation that will ultimately lead to interindividual differences as well as intraindividual consistency in behavior across situations. There are two strategies typically utilized by interactionists in assigning psychological meaning to situations: the stimulus–analytical approach and the response–analytical approach. These approaches are often used in conjunction with one another to develop a more detailed understanding of situations because they refer to the perception of the situation as well as the behavior elicited by the situation.

The stimulus–analytical approach is a process whereby researchers attempt to classify situations according to their perceived meaning to the individual. The response–analytical approach refers to the process whereby researchers attempt to classify situations according to the responses elicited by the individual. The response–analytical approach can be further broken down into two different foci. The first is the reaction approach, wherein one focuses on the spontaneous affective or physical responses. The second is the action approach; this is where more complex, global actions are addressed (Krahe, 1992). Several studies have been performed showing a relationship between perceived characteristics of a situation and response patterns, which support the notion that the subjective meaning of a situation is an important source of information in understanding the consequent behavior of individuals (see Ekehammar, Schalling, & Magnusson, 1975; Krahe, 1986).

Difficulties Associated With Interactionism

As Cronbach said,

> Once we attend to interactions, we enter a hall of mirrors that extends to infinity. However far we carry our analysis—to third order or fifth order or any other—untested interactions of a still higher order can be envisioned.
>
> *Cronbach, 1957, p. 119*

This quote captures the difficulties associated not with interactionism but with conceptualizing interactionism as a statistical interaction in a regression model. Indeed, the most popular way to define interactionist psychology is to equate it with a moderated General Linear Model (GLM). This has been called the mechanistic, or statistical, interaction (see Buss, 1977, and Howard, 1979, for more comprehensive reviews). This definition of interaction posits that there is a unidirectional effect of the person × situation interaction on behavior; in this way, "true" independent and dependent variables are established (Krahe, 1992). The methodological approach typically associated with this view of interaction is the GLM, which allows the researcher to quantify the amount of variance accounted for by the independent variables individually as well as the interaction. However, one of the problems associated with this model is that the apportioning of variance allows for only a *quantitative* assessment. By not obtaining information in the form of a *qualitative* explanation, we are unable to understand the how and the why and, in most cases, to predict the when (Golding, 1975). A second problem is that the GLM cannot be used to separate the effects of the variables in a dynamic relationship. A third problem is that the GLM controls for the main effects before modeling the interaction. While this is important from a statistical perspective (one should always remove the variance for main effects before estimating the interaction), it is inconsistent with the underlying interactionist framework. For example, Lewin never said B = P + S + PS. Thus, equating interactionism with statistical interactions is a simplistic, even erroneous representation of interactionist psychology.

However, these difficulties can be obviated, and behavior can be more fully explained, through considering the psychological processes linking persons to situations. First, the situation must be defined; this includes the temporal aspects (when does it begin and end?) and the identification of the criteria upon which the person relies for interpretation. Usually, this involves the development of a precise taxonomy of situations according to their salient psychological features. Second, the units of analysis for the individual must be defined. In the past, interactionists have conceptualized the person as containing an organized set of "cognitive scripts" (see Abelson, 1981) or "cognitive categories" (see Cantor, 1981; Cantor, Mischel, & Schwartz, 1982) from which they pull to appropriate rules for action upon recognition of specific features of the situation. More modern process models of personality incorporate these elements.

From Statistical Interaction to Process Models

The development of process models linking persons to situations stemmed from the inadequacies of the previous modern interactionist frameworks. To this point, most empirical research had taken place within the mechanistic interaction framework discussed above. Following various critiques of this approach (e.g., Argyle, 1977; Furnam & Jaspars, 1983) and the increased interest in understanding the individual and the psychological meaning of situations in a more systematic way (e.g., Mischel, 1973; Shoda, Mischel, & Wright, 1994), process models were born.

As mentioned earlier, interactionist theory attempts to explain behavior through the use of an intraindividual level of analysis. Thus, several interactionism theorists have developed mediating process models in order to simultaneously explain an individual's variability in behavior across situations as well as the stability in the qualities of an individual's personality. Mediating process models are complex and draw from literature in many domains including personality, social, cognitive, and neuropsychology. Here, we describe some of the most dominant theoretical approaches.

Cognitive–Affective Personality System

One of the most noteworthy process models stemmed from an extensive set of observational studies performed by Walter Mischel, Yuichi Shoda, and Jack Wright at a summer camp for children in the late 1980s and early 1990s (see Shoda, 1990; Shoda, Mischel, & Wright, 1989, 1993a, 1993b, 1994; Wright & Mischel, 1987, 1988). In this series of experiments, children aged 7–13 years were observed interacting in five types of situations. The situations were defined according to valence (positive vs. negative) as well as object of situation (counselor vs. child peer). Over the 6-week summer, the children were recorded on several previously selected dimensions (e.g., withdrawal, prosocial behavior, and aggression). Afterward, observations were standardized and mapped onto a situation–behavior profile. This enabled each child to be compared to his or her peers via a Z-score for each situation and provided a profile stability correlation coefficient for each child across similar situations. Shoda et al. (1994) found that mean stability coefficients ranged from .19 ($p < .05$) to .47 ($p < .01$) and thus were significantly stable over the course of the experiment. It was also found that, for situations of negative valence, the mean profile stability coefficients ranged from .32 ($p < .05$) for physical aggression to .48 ($p < .05$) for verbal aggression. If it was true that intraindividual variation in behavior across situations was just measurement error (as assumed by trait theorists), these mean stability coefficients would be equal to zero; however, the overall findings indicate otherwise and show that there is a statistically significant, stable facet of intraindividual behavior across situations (Mischel & Shoda, 1995). These results led to the birth of the cognitive–affective personality system (CAPS).

Drawing from the social and cognitive learning literature (e.g., Bandura, 1982; Cantor, 1990), and the social and emotional processing literature (e.g., Markus, 1977), Mischel and Shoda (1995) developed a mediating process model called CAPS, which operates under the assumption that there are stable individual differences in aspects of situations selected, cognitive–affective units (CAUs) that become activated, and behaviors that follow. According to CAPS, every individual has his or her own unique processing system. This system is composed of feature detection units, CAUs, and behavior output units, which ultimately determine how and why individuals behave the way they do. There are five types of CAUs. The first type of CAU is encodings; these are categories or cognitions that activate and interact with other cognitions to form a network within the system forming a construal of self and others. The organization of this network represents the individual's overall life experience as well as their biological makeup. With each new experience, an addition is made to the network. The second type of CAU is expectancies or beliefs. These are expectations about the consequences of specific behaviors, beliefs about the social world, and self-efficacy. Affect is the third type of CAU and represents feelings, emotions, affective responses, and physiological responses. The fourth type of CAU is goals and values. Finally, competencies and self-regulatory plans are the fifth type of CAU. These refer to the behavioral scripts, plans, and strategies that one might choose and are meant to organize action and affect outcomes. When confronted with a situation, all of these CAUs act in concert, activating and deactivating, to produce a behavioral response. To explicate further, when situational cues are perceived by an individual, a distinct set of feature detection units are activated in response. These units then trigger the activation and constraining of cognitive and affective processing units in accordance with the individual's own distinct configuration (or characteristic attractor states of the CAUs) in their CAPS network. This sequence ends with the activation of specific behavior output units. This process ultimately activates plans, strategies, emotions, behaviors, and potentially observable behaviors (Mischel & Shoda, 1995; Shoda & LeeTiernan, 2002).

Note that specific cognitive scripts or dispositional tendencies constructed through repeated activation of specific CAU pathways over time are posited to be more automatic in situations where an individual has the ability to cope with the effects of highly demanding situations. The *cognitive demand hypothesis* suggests that as the situation increases in cognitive and psychological complexity, identifiable interindividual differences in behavior can be more easily detected because there is greater variability (Wright & Mischel, 1987). Competency demands also mean that not all personality traits are relevant to every situation, and hence only those situations that place "demands" on specific "competencies" (i.e., traits) will see variability in those competencies.

CAPS offers several implications. First, situation–behavior profiles or "personality signatures" can be mapped for individuals and lead to the development of *If . . . then . . .* statements. For example, *If* John is teased, *then* he will become aggressive. Such a mapping of behavioral profiles helps to gain a deeper understanding of an individual's processing system and leads to better prediction of the person's behavior in future psychologically similar situations (Mischel & Shoda, 1995). Second, CAPS assumes that individuals vary in their ability to discriminate between situational cues; to the degree that an individual lacks the necessary competency to construct and access their CAU networks, their behavior may be greatly affected (or unaffected) when presented with a variety of situations. This suggests that those high in cognitive and social competence may exhibit a more well-defined situation–behavior profile. Third, commonalities between individuals in their arrangement or relationships between CAUs can be seen in the congruence of their situation–behavior profiles as well as their *If . . . then . . .* behavioral patterns. It follows that those who indicate common organization of cognitions and affects may be referred to as having common processing dispositions (Mischel & Shoda, 1995). Finally, implicit in this theory is the notion that individuals can govern their own behaviors by selecting situations to avoid. As mentioned above, this network of CAUs is formed through experience, as one selects in and out of certain situations that can directly influence their future behavior.

The CAPS model was an important step forward in interactionist theory for several reasons. First, it provides a model that explains why individuals seem to be predisposed to certain behavioral patterns (Mischel & Shoda, 1995). Second, whereas previous models in interactionism only allowed for the study of main effects, CAPS provides a parsimonious, theoretically based, framework that provides the opportunity to study higher-order interactions (Mischel, 2004). Third, because CAPS draws from research in areas such as cognitive psychology, neuroscience, and social psychology, it allows for a more complete understanding of the entire process (Mischel, 2004). In recent years, CAPS has grown in theoretical detail and there has been interest in combining it with the FFM in order to aid in the explanation and prediction of when and why an individual will behave in characteristic ways (Mischel & Shoda, 1998). Its use has also been extended to research of dyadic relationships where it has been computer-coded to model *interpersonal* systems whereby each individual acts as a stimulus for the other (Shoda & LeeTiernan, 2002).

Trait Activation Theory

Barrick and Mount (1991) performed a meta-analysis to investigate the validity using the FFM personality traits in predicting job performance. It was found that several traits were linked to performance and thus an explosion in research on this topic ensued. However, in this meta-analysis, validities were aggregated across studies in a manner that does not take into account "bidirectionality" (Tett & Burnett, 2003; Tett, Jackson, Rothstein, & Reddon, 1999). Bidirectionality refers, here, to the positive or negative relationship (correlation) between the pole of a personality trait (e.g., neurotic vs. emotional stability) and its correlate (in this case, job performance). Because similar jobs have been found to have both positive and negative correlations with the same personality trait, it has been suggested that there are deeper variables that need to be investigated. This and the lack of research on situational trait relevance led to the conception of what is known as trait activation theory (TAT; Tett & Burnett, 2003; Tett & Guterman, 2000; Chapter 5, this volume).

The model proposed utilizes interactionist theory to present a framework that attempts to explain cross-situational consistency in behavior through the acknowledgment of two key situational components: *trait relevance*, defined as the quantity of cues a situation offers toward the arousal of a particular trait, and *activation potential* (or situational strength) (Tett & Guterman, 2000). The theory posits that the higher the trait activation potential (TAP) of a situation (defined as high relevance and low situational strength), the more variability will be shown in behavior. A major contribution of this theory is how the trait *relevance* of a situation imposes power over behavior, as this is an aspect that has garnered little research attention in the past (Tett & Guterman, 2000). Thus, when observations of situations similar in trait relevance are aggregated, they will indicate a higher level of cross-situational consistency in individual behavior.

There has been strong empirical support for the theory of trait activation. Tett and Guterman (2000) found that given more "concrete" situational cues and a higher level of trait relevancy, stronger correlations were found with the intentions to express the given trait in that situation. Also, Haaland and Christiansen (2002) found that assessment center exercises judged to be high in TAP for a given trait correlated twice as strongly with the same trait score on a personality inventory when compared with their low TAP counterparts. In addition to the above empirical studies, TAT has also been used as a theoretical framework for explaining the underlying processes in the measurement of job performance (e.g., Maxham, Netemeyer, & Lichtenstein, 2008).

The model proposed by Tett and Burnett (2003) treats job situations as moderators of the relationship between personality trait expression and evaluation of job performance. It hypothesizes that (1) traits are expressed in work behavior as responses to trait-relevant situational cues; (2) there are three sources, or levels, of trait-relevant cues: task, social, and environmental; and (3) work behavior and job performance are not one and the same. In this model, it is posited that a personality trait is activated according to organizational, social, and task-level cues. In this way, traits will manifest and lead to work behavior and ultimately job performance. This link between work behavior and job performance reflects the importance of the context. If the trait is valued by the organization and leads to high job performance, there will be a positive correlation between this personality trait and job performance. However, if this trait is not valued it will correlate negatively with job performance; thus, this is where bidirectionality is understood. Another aspect of the model is motivation. This is represented as intrinsic and extrinsic rewards received via the activation of a particular trait. Finally, the model accounts for the dynamic aspect of interactionist theory by linking work behavior back to the moderating situations (Tett & Burnett, 2003; see Kacmar, Collins, Harris, & Judge, 2009, for an example in application).

Summary and Implications

Interactionist psychology states that the behavior is a *function* of the person (P) *and* the situation (S): $B = f(P, S)$, rather than $B = f(P \times S)$. Modern interactionism is remembering this fact by seeking to understand the psychological processes through which people and situations are related. Process models of personality ascribe supreme importance to the psychological meaning of the situation to the person; hence, objective situational features are something that are perceived differently as a function of the person's traits. At the same time, situations do not challenge all traits in the same manner, and some traits are more relevant for solving the challenges presented in certain situations.

To model the relationships between persons and situations, process models emphasize the study of behavior from an *intra*individual perspective. There are ideographically predictable patterns in an individual's behavior across situations and through time. This requires an understanding of interindividual differences in intraindividual behavior across similar situations (Mischel, 2004). This is a very important point because it means that applied personality researchers must do more than search for situational interactions with traits, and they must do more than add "at work" tags to generic items. A serious consideration of interactionist psychology requires scholars to use process models to, first, study individual behavior over time within psychologically similar situations to identify intraindividual profiles, and second, study individuals across psychologically different situations to provide estimates of interindividual differences.

The need to study individual behavior *over time* in both psychologically similar and dissimilar situations represents a considerable break from most applied research on personality. Again, consider that most personality measurement is based on broad items that are essentially context free. Such measures provide a broad average across all situations and time. But work behavior and performance behavior occur within specific situations and within specific periods of time. Greater correspondence between situations and time on the assessment and behavior intended to be predicted will enhance understanding and criterion-related validity (Fishbein & Ajzen, 1975). Therefore, researchers need to adapt personality measurement to present participants with both psychologically similar and dissimilar situations repeatedly. SJTs may be an effective and efficient way to do so, but it would also require a major change from the way SJTs are typically studied and developed.

SJTs

The use of SJTs has a long history in selection (see McDaniel, Morgeson, Finnegan, Campion, & Braverman, 2001, for a review). One of the earlier examples came in the 1940s with How Supervise? (File, 1945), which was devised as a selection tool to measure supervisor potential. SJTs have been shown to manifest criterion-related validities considerably better than personality. For example, McDaniel, Hartman, Whetzel, and Grubb (2007) performed a meta-analysis investigating relationships between different composites of SJTs, cognitive ability, the FFM, and performance. They found that SJTs provided incremental criterion-related validity over both *g* (.03 and .05, for knowledge and behavior stems, respectively) and the FFM (.06 and .07, for behavior and knowledge stems, respectively). They also found that an SJT provides incremental criterion-related validity above a composite of *g* and the FFM (ranging from .01 to .02). Christian, Edwards, and Bradley (2010) reviewed 136 SJT studies and found that approximately 3% claimed to measure knowledge and skills, 13% measured interpersonal skills, 4% measured teamwork, 38% measured leadership, and 10% measured personality composites (the remainder were too heterogeneous to be classified according to constructs). However, even those SJTs classified as measuring a particular knowledge, skill, attribute, or other characteristic (KSAO) likely lacked construct validity evidence, as the determination of the constructs was based on judgment rather than empirical evidence.

The lack of construct validity for SJTs can quite possibly be attributed to their development process. Developing an SJT typically involves a three-step process (Motowidlo, Hanson, & Crafts, 1997). The first step in this process is collecting critical incident reports to aid in the generation of situations. The generation of these situations is usually a descriptive sampling of the situations encountered in a particular job or occupation, without any consideration of a latent underlying structure (i.e., the psychology of the situation or even its objective elements). The second step is the generation of a pool of situations and their respective responses by subject matter experts (SMEs) and/or test makers. The responses are likewise rarely sampled from a construct domain but rather sampled from the job domain. The third step is the development of scoring keys and the finalization of the test

(Motowidlo et al., 1997). Supervisors are usually the ones who will determine the final scoring keys, but sometimes an empirically based approach is used.

Thus, the typical SJT development method is lacking a theoretically based approach for structuring situational content, and this has made the assessment of the construct validity inaccessible. There is no underlying structure to the situations, so each situation is heterogeneous in terms of content and constructs. This heterogeneity carries over to the options, as each behavioral response is not focused on constructs but rather the behaviors typically found in a given situation. It is no mystery why SJTs lack construct validity, even though they are often *intended* to measure a particular construct (as shown clearly in Christian et al., 2010).

However, we argue that SJT researchers can learn from modern interactionist psychology, applying their theory and methods, to provide a theory-driven approach for developing SJTs (Ployhart, 1999). We argue that SJTs already measure (to some degree) personality by presenting the applicant with a situation; researchers must further structure the situations and behavioral responses so that the specific personality constructs can be measured.

One attempt in the SJT literature to expand the manner in which individuals interact with their situations has been proposed by Motowidlo, Hooper, and Jackson (2006). Derived from literature published in the 1950s on judgment in cognitive and social psychology (e.g., Tajfel, 1957), Motowidlo et al. (2006) developed the concept of implicit trait policies (ITPs) in order to explain why individuals judge specific behaviors to be more useful in particular situations. He utilized SJTs to test his hypotheses that (1) personality traits affect ITPs such that the higher one's standing on a particular trait, the more effective they believe behaviors displaying that quality will be, and (2) ITPs predict behavior associated with personality traits.

According to Motowidlo et al. (2006), ITPs are "implicit beliefs about causal relations between personality traits and behavioral effectiveness." This suggests that ITPs are processing systems whereby one subconsciously links one's own standing on personality traits to judgments of the effectiveness of behavioral action. This also suggests that although personality has a direct effect on ITPs, the two are not one and the same. To this end, dispositional fit may be used to explain the connection between personality and ITPs. The theory of dispositional fit states that when judgments are made regarding the effectiveness of behavior, individuals tend to judge behaviors reflecting their own traits as being more effective (Motowidlo, 2003; Motowidlo & Beier, 2010). Dispositional fit is different from ITPs in that ITPs are beliefs about the effectiveness of behaviors similar to one's own personality traits, whereas dispositional fit is an individual's tendency to actually act on that belief.

Since the theory of ITPs was conceived, there have been several additions to the model. Cognitive ability has been hypothesized to have an effect such that the more intelligent an individual is shown to be, the more quickly and thoroughly they can learn which trait expressions are more effective in certain situations (Motowidlo & Beier, 2010). Also, experience has been partitioned into two categories: (1) general and (2) specific knowledge about effectiveness of behavior. Specific knowledge, in this case, refers to specific job knowledge. Also, the notion of "differential attractiveness" has been introduced. Differential attractiveness is defined as the degree to which a behavior reflecting some trait appears to be more effective to someone who is high on that same trait (Motowidlo & Beier, 2010).

A second approach for integrating SJTs with personality attempts to more specifically link situations (or responses to situations) to personality constructs. Ployhart (1999) applied a methodology where raters evaluated the trait relevance of each situation. He then wrote response options that reflected a range of behavior in that situation that would be manifested by the relevant personality trait. The results found good criterion-related validity and some support for construct validity. A program of research by Labrador and colleagues (Labrador & Christiansen, 2008; Labrador, Christiansen, & Burns, 2006) also sought to connect personality constructs with SJTs. In one study, they found that open-ended SJT responses were more highly related to personality scores than closed-form responses (Labrador & Christiansen, 2008). Apparently, the manifestation of personality was more possible when respondents were able to express their responses using their own words. Labrador et al. (2006) sought to evaluate situations in terms of their trait relevance. Using TAT (described above), raters evaluated the TAP of each situation. They found some evidence to suggest that it is possible to write situations to focus on specific personality constructs. Thus, cumulatively, this research suggests that it is possible to develop situations that more directly tap specific personality traits.

SJTs to Assess Interactionist Psychology

As noted, most applied personality research treats behavior primarily as a function of the person ($B = f(P)$). Situational variance is treated as error variance and therefore much of the potential understanding of behavior goes unexplained, contributing in part to disappointing criterion-related validities (Morgeson et al., 2007). SJT research, on the other hand, treats behavior primarily as a function of the situation ($B = f(S)$). SJT research finds stronger criterion-related validities than personality researchers, but at the expense of construct validity (N. Schmitt & Chan, 2006). Little effort has been spent studying the integration of these two assumptions in an "interactionist approach" such that behavior is assumed to be explained by the process between person *and* situation ($B = f(P, S)$). Therefore, we propose a synergy between personality and SJTs, complementing each other's strengths while offsetting their limitations, using theory derived from interactionist psychology. In the following subsections, we identify the primary approaches we believe should produce greater construct and criterion-related validity for measuring personality within an SJT methodology. Table 19.1 provides an overview of these implications.

Table 19.1 Key Implications for Measuring Trait and Situation Elements in SJTs

1. Whenever possible, interactionist psychology should be studied longitudinally. Time is an important element in discovering coherence in personality; therefore, methodologies must adopt longitudinal designs.
2. Theory must account for bidirectional influences that exist between the person, their environment (or the situation), and their behavior. Methodologies must also address this issue. That is, methods must be able to empirically account for all of these influences, and analyses must be employed that are capable of modeling them.
3. Psychologically similar situations can be derived from a theoretical framework (such as a situational taxonomy) created a priori. Each subfactor within the framework must contain equivalent features (e.g., valence, domain, and object).
4. All subfactors within the predeveloped framework must differ from at least one other subfactor by only one feature. In this way, behavioral/personality differences can be linked to identifiable sources aiding in causal inference and interpretation.
5. Individual behavior can be modeled "over time" by contrasting sets of psychologically similar situations with psychologically dissimilar situations to identify contingencies. These contingencies result in distinct intraindividual profiles or unique behavioral signatures.
6. Responses must be derived from a trait content taxonomy developed a priori. In this way, theory will act as a guide to aid in interpretation when looking for coherence in personality.
7. Likert-type items should be used for the response format.

Isolating Personality Within Situations

The overarching goal in personality research is to identify coherence in intraindividual behavior (Mischel, 2004; Mischel & Shoda, 1995; Shoda & LeeTiernan, 2002). By doing so through the repeated measurement of behavior in situations characterized by equivalent psychological meaning, a clearer picture of one's behavioral tendencies can be obtained. This will lead to better predictive accuracy of behavior in future psychologically similar situations (Shoda & LeeTiernan, 2002). Therefore, in order to obtain a more accurate measure of personality using an SJT, we suggest that situations need to be constructed according to their salient psychological features. This has two implications for the development of SJTs.

First, test respondents need to be repeatedly presented with psychologically similar situations. Second, a cogent framework must be developed a priori because it provides the necessary theoretical groundwork for characterizing situations according to their distinct psychological characteristics. As an example, Murtha et al. (1996) have created a situational–dispositional taxonomy wherein a trait content taxonomy and a situational taxonomy are fully crossed to form the overall "situational–behavioral taxonomy." In their trait content taxonomy, a superordinate trait is broken down into subfactors that categorize personality trait dispositions (e.g., traditional). In their situational taxonomy, a superordinate trait is broken down into subfactors that characterize situations according to psychological meaning (e.g., intimate). When the two interact, they manifest a behavioral output (behavior), which is a function of both the personality input variable and the situational input variable (e.g., traditional in an intimate situation).

By characterizing situations according to their subfactors (e.g., intimate, pleasant, and stressful) and presenting multiple psychologically similar situations to an individual (as can be done on an SJT), one can determine when and perhaps why certain behaviors are enlisted. In other words, the unique psychological determinants of the individual will manifest themselves through the evaluation of the responses within each subfactor. In this way, a distinctive behavioral signature can then be established for each individual, which will make accurate predictability of behavior possible in future psychologically similar situations. Other approaches for isolating personality within situational content are provided by Labrador and Christiansen (2008), Labrador et al. (2006), and Ployhart (1999).

Structuring Situational Content

In order to construct an SJT for the purpose of measuring personality, the beginning stages of situational development must be drastically altered. Typically, critical incident reports are obtained from SMEs and job analyses are reviewed, and these are used as a framework for the construction of the situations (McDaniel et al., 2001; Motowidlo et al., 1997). Therefore, dimensions vary according to the job and are often not capable of exhibiting systematic behavioral tendencies. In contrast, the dimensions being assessed using an interactionist approach are meant to act as consistent, psychologically meaningful situational characteristics upon which individual behavior (responses) will be evaluated.

The first stage is to develop a taxonomy similar to the situational taxonomy described above in Murtha et al. (1996). In so doing, each situational subfactor will provide a dimension that will enable the development of situations according to *psychological meaning*. The psychological meaning of situations is integral to their development if they are to provide an overall measure of coherence in personality. Thus, careful attention must be devoted to at least three critical features of situations: (1) valence, which refers to whether the situation induces an overall positive or negative affective state; (2) domain or context in which the situation takes place (e.g., task, social, and environmental); and (3) object, which refers to a respondent's intended focus of attention within the given situation (e.g., peer, subordinate, and boss). After the creation of multiple subfactors that vary systematically by only *one* feature (i.e., valence, domain, and object), one can move to the next stage.

Stage 2 involves the creation of situations that adhere to two criteria. First, each situation must reflect *only one* psychological meaning or subfactor (Labrador & Christiansen, 2008; Labrador et al., 2006; Ployhart, 1999). In this way, psychological meaning will be fundamentally similar within each dimension for each respondent. Second, situations should be in line with the intended use of the SJT upon completion. In general, SJTs are developed for the purposes of selection and hiring; thus, situations could be created to reflect actual job situations. For example, consider the two following psychologically similar situations. These two situations are roughly equivalent in valence (negative), domain (social), and object (customer).

> Situation 1: You are a manager at the local grocery store and a customer walks into your store and becomes deeply distressed when she realizes her favorite type of tea is no longer on sale. She is growing increasingly unpleasant. What would you do?
>
> Situation 2: You are a customer service agent and you have just received a call from a customer who seems to be blaming you personally for her problem. What would you do?

Although an SJT does not assess respondents *over* time, it does offer the unique opportunity to measure a respondent many times in psychologically similar situations. Therefore, the final SJT should contain many distinct sets of psychologically similar questions developed from their respective subfactors. In this way, sets of situations can be created, which vary uniquely by the above features (i.e., valence, domain, and object), that will, in turn, provide an *overall*, systematic measure of the coherence in one's behavior. That is, by comparing responses on sets of situations *across* and *within* subfactors, the test maker should be able to make more informed causal inferences regarding whether and why an individual's behavior changes or remains stable in response to alterations or similarities in valence, domain, and object.

Stems, Responses, and Scoring

Most prior SJT literature has formatted responses in one of two ways. Depending on the wording, the item stem often elicits either a behavioral response (e.g., "would do") or a knowledge-based response (e.g., "should do") and correlations between the two types of stems have been shown to be quite low (Ployhart & Ehrhart, 2003). Furthermore, it has been found that these item stems affect convergent and discriminant validity. That is, "would do" stems correlate more strongly with personality, while "should do" stems correlate more strongly with cognitive ability (McDaniel et al., 2007). Thus, it seems logical that in developing an SJT to assess behavior, "would do" stems may be deemed more appropriate.

Recall that the content and situational taxonomies are developed prior to test construction; this is the point in our example that the content taxonomy should be employed to function as a set of dimensions that categorize, and aid in the construction of, the responses included in the SJT. In this way, responses can be built to exemplify specific trait-based behaviors of interest. To illustrate, a particular psychological meaning (e.g., situational cue) will be derived from the situation by the individual, which will lead to the activation of a trait-based response tendency (Tett & Guterman, 2000) that, in turn, can be matched to the response option considered to be most representative of that person's response (see Labrador & Christiansen, 2008). For example, in a selection-related personality SJT, one might be interested in how often an individual endorses a response indicating conflict avoidance behavior; thus, a response option exhibiting this content subfactor would be included in the response options. Repeated endorsement of response options constructed to exhibit this subfactor in psychologically similar situations would indicate a coherency in personality.

Response formats typically associated with SJTs tend to vary too. A brief review of the literature suggests that the most often utilized formats include the following: Likert-type scaling for each response, dual-answer multiple-choice (e.g., "most/least likely do"), and single-answer multiple-choice (e.g., "best answer"). In the case of an SJT built to measure behavioral tendencies, it would be advisable to use a Likert-type scale by response item in order to capture as much intraindividual "uniqueness" in behavior as possible. To illustrate, consider the comparison between two 10-item SJTs; the first with a single-answer multiple-choice response format and the second with a Likert-type scale for each response. The first and most obvious difference is that the second SJT, in effect, contains more information. The second and more nuanced difference is that in utilizing a scaled index of an individual's agreement with a particular response option (as opposed to an all or nothing approach), each item contains a unique intraindividual signature of the degree to which the respondent would endorse and, thus, behave in a manner consistent with that option.

Psychologically Similar Situations

As mentioned earlier, one advantage of the utilization of an SJT to measure personality is that it has the ability to measure an individual's behavioral tendencies repeatedly in situations that convey the same psychological meaning. This is important because prior personality research has found it difficult to investigate personality coherence accurately without the inclusion of multiple testing periods (e.g., Mischel & Shoda, 1995). Shoda and LeeTiernan (2002), for example, suggest that the administration of the exact same situations on multiple occasions can be correlated to find a degree of coherence for an individual. However, in practice, it is rarely the case that the exact same test is ever employed in succession. Their methodology is unique in that it does explain more variance in behavior, but there are several problems associated (e.g., respondent memory). Also, as of yet, an optimum amount of time between administrations has not been determined; too much time between sessions may eliminate memory effects but other forms of error may emerge such as maturation. In our case, because situations included in the SJT will be derived from a predetermined subfactor, they should all be functionally equivalent within the dimension. Stated differently, SJTs within a category should be roughly equivalent, where equivalence is defined in terms of competency demands.

To score this particular SJT, an individual's responses can either be plotted by situation within subfactor, or an overall "behavioral signature" can be obtained for all subfactors through the correlation of responses (possibly even factor structures). These signatures will be useful in the determination of an individual's personality for at least two reasons. First, the signatures themselves provide a comprehensive picture of how an individual tends to act when confronted with a situation of a specific psychological meaning. An "*If* . . . *then* . . . statement" can be obtained to allow better prediction of behavior in similar situations. Second, because the responses will be constructed from different subfactors and will remain the same throughout the SJT, information regarding how an individual interprets a situational subfactor can be obtained. Furthermore, given the fact that the SJT contains *multiple* situations per subfactor in addition to a response format that allows for measurement of the *degree* to which the individual would exhibit the behavioral tendency, it may be possible to ascertain what nuanced situational cues seem to elicit specific behaviors.

Conclusion

It has taken nearly 60 years for psychologists to take Lewin's (1936) statement of Behavior = *f*(Person, Environment) seriously. Yet applied personality research, and in particular the research on personality in selection contexts, has focused on behavior as a function of the person, to the neglect of the environment. We argue that research on SJTs, in contrast, has focused too much attention on the environment and not enough on the person. Using theory from interactionist psychology to integrate the applied research on personality and SJTs offers the potential to more holistically conceptualize, measure, and predict behavior in organizations. Therefore, we concluded the chapter with broad recommendations for operationalizing the promise of interactionist psychology using situational judgment measures. It is our hope that scholars will begin to more seriously study personality within context, because research that continues to neglect situations is unlikely to advance the field much further than where it is today.

Practitioner's Window

One of the often-heard complaints about personality tests is that the questions are too generic because they lack a situational context. After all, it is well known that behavior is the result of a person's characteristics and the situation as he or she perceives it. SJTs may offer an effective alternative to traditional methods of personality assessment because they are contextualized yet can still be administered to large samples. Therefore, SJTs may be developed to assess personality in work situations.

1. *Understand the Situation.* When attempting to understand behavior (i.e., personality traits), one must first understand the psychological meaning of the situation (objective features of situations are far less relevant). This can be done by identifying the situational factors most salient to people. These factors may include the situation's valence (negative or positive), domain (e.g., social), and object (e.g., customer). Managers often find themselves wondering why their subordinates behave in ways that are inconsistent with expectations; it is these very factors of situations that often contribute to those differences.
2. *Look for Coherence in Behavior.* The ultimate goal of personality assessment is to identify coherence in behavior. To do this, "behavioral signatures" must be identified. SJTs can be utilized to capture behavioral signatures because they have the unique ability to present respondents with repeated psychologically similar situations, while simultaneously allowing for the use of a response scale. Therefore, consistency within specific types of situations can be examined. The use of SJTs to identify coherent patterns in personality dispositions should result in higher levels of criterion-related validity than what is often found in generic personality tests.

References

Abelson, R. P. (1981). The psychological status of the script concept. *American Psychologist, 36*, 715–729.

Allport, G. W. (1937). *Personality: A psychological interpretation*. New York: Holt, Rinehart & Winston.

Argyle, M. (1977). Predictive and generative models of person × situation interaction. In D. Magnusson & N. S. Endler (Eds.), *Personality at the crossroads* (pp. 353–370). Hillsdale, NJ: Erlbaum.

Bandura, A. (1982). Self-efficacy mechanisms in human agency. *American Psychologist, 37*, 122–147.

Barrick, M. R., & Mount, M. K. (1991). The Big Five personality dimensions and job performance: A meta-analysis. *Personnel Psychology, 44*, 1–26.

Bowers, K. S. (1973). Situation in psychology: An analysis and critique. *Psychological Review, 80*, 307–336.

Buss, A. R. (1977). The trait–situation controversy and the concept of interaction. *Personality and Social Psychology Bulletin, 3*, 196–201.

Cantor, N. (1981). Perceptions of situations: Situation prototypes and personality prototypes. In D. Magnusson (Ed.), *Toward a psychology of situations* (pp. 229–244). Hillsdale, NJ: Erlbaum.

Cantor, N. (1990). From thought to behavior: "Having" and "doing" in the study of personality and cognition. *American Psychologist, 45*, 735–750.

Cantor, N., Mischel, W., & Schwartz, J. (1982). A prototype analysis of psychological situations. *Cognitive Psychology, 14*, 45–77.

Cappelli, P., & Sherer, P. D. (1991). The missing role of context in OB: The need for a meso-level approach. *Research in Organizational Behavior, 13*, 55–110.

Christian, M. S., Edwards, B. D., & Bradley, J. C. (2010). Situational Judgment Tests: Constructs assessed and a meta-analysis of their criterion-related validities. *Personnel Psychology, 63*, 83–117.

Cronbach, L. J. (1957). The two disciplines of scientific psychology. *American Psychologist, 12*, 671–684.

Ekehammar, B., Schalling, D., & Magnusson, D. (1975). Dimensions of stressful situations: A comparison between a response analytical and stimulus analytical approach. *Multivariate Behavioral Research, 10*, 155–164.

Endler, N. S. (1983). Interactionism: A personality model, but not yet a theory. In M. M. Page (Ed.), *Nebraska symposium on motivation* (pp. 155–200). Lincoln: University of Nebraska Press.

Endler, N. S., & Hunt, J. McV. (1966). Sources of behavioral variance as measured by the S-R Inventory of anxiousness. *Psychological Bulletin, 65*, 336–346.

Endler, N. S., & Hunt, J. McV. (1968). S-R Inventories of hostility and comparisons of the proportions of variance from persons, responses, and situations for hostility and anxiousness. *Journal of Personality and Social Psychology, 9*, 309–315.

Endler, N. S., & Hunt, J. McV. (1969). Generalizability of contributions from sources of variance in the S-R Inventories of anxiousness. *Journal of Personality, 37*, 1–24.

Endler, N. S., & Magnusson, D. (1976). Toward an interactional psychology of personality. *Psychological Bulletin, 83*, 956–974.

Epstein, S. (1979). The stability of behavior: On predicting most of the people much of the time. *Journal of Personality and Social Psychology, 37*, 1097–1126.

File, Q. W. (1945). The measurement of supervisory quality in industry. *Journal of Applied Psychology, 29*, 381–387.

Fishbein, M., & Ajzen, I. (1975). *Belief, attitude, intention, and behavior: An introduction to theory and research.* Reading, MA: Addison-Wesley.

Furnam, A., & Jaspars, J. (1983). The evidence for interactionism in psychology: A critical analysis of situation–response inventories. *Personality and Individual Differences, 6*, 627–644.

Golding, S. L. (1975). Flies in the ointment: Methodological problems in the analysis of the percentage of variance due to persons and situations. *Psychological Bulletin, 82*, 278–288.

Haaland, S., & Christiansen, N. D. (2002). Implications of trait-activation theory for evaluating construct validity of assessment center ratings. *Personnel Psychology, 55*, 137–163.

Hartshorne, H., & May, A. (1928). *Studies in the nature of character: Studies in deceit (Vol. 1)*. New York: Macmillan.

Howard, J. A. (1979). Person–situation interaction models. *Personality and Social Psychology Bulletin, 5*, 191–195.

Johns, G. (2006). The essential impact of context on organizational behavior. *Academy of Management Review, 31*, 386–408.

Kacmar, K. M., Collins, B. J., Harris, K. J., & Judge, T. A. (2009). Core self-evaluations and job performance: The role of perceived work environment. *Journal of Applied Psychology, 94*, 1570–1580.

Kantor, J. R. (1924). *Principles of psychology (Vol. 1)*. Bloomington, IN: Principia Press.

Kantor, J. R. (1926). *Principles of psychology (Vol. 2)*. Bloomington, IN: Principia Press.

Koffka, K. (1935). *Principles of Gestalt psychology*. New York: Harcourt, Brace.

Krahe, B. (1986). Similar perceptions, similar reactions: An idiographic approach to cross-situational coherence. *Journal of Research in Personality, 20*, 349–361.

Krahe, B. (1992). *Personality and social psychology: Towards a synthesis.* London: Sage.

Labrador, J. R., & Christiansen, N. D. (2008, April). *"What would you do?" Assessing personality with unstructured situational judgments.* Symposium presented at the 23rd Annual Conference of the Society for Industrial and Organizational Psychology, San Francisco.

Labrador, J. R., Christiansen, N. D., & Burns, G. N. (2006, April). *Measuring personality using Situational Judgment Tests.* Symposium presented at the 21st Annual Conference of the Society for Industrial and Organizational Psychology, Dallas, TX.

Lewin, K. (1936). *Principles of topological psychology*. New York: McGraw-Hill.

Lievens, F., De Corte, W., & Schollaert, E. (2008). A closer look at the frame-of-reference effect in personality scale scores and validity. *Journal of Applied Psychology, 93*, 268–279.

Magnusson, D. (1976). The person and the situation in an interactional model of behavior. *Scandinavian Journal of Psychology, 17*, 253–271.

Magnusson, D., & Endler, N. S. (Eds.). (1977). *Personality at the crossroads: Current issues in interactional psychology.* Hillsdale, NJ: Erlbaum.

Magnusson, D., Gerzen, M., & Nyman, B. (1968). The generality of behavioral data I: Generalization from observations on one occasion. *Multivariate Behavioral Research, 3,* 295–320.

Markus, H. (1977). Self-schemata and processing information about the self. *Journal of Personality and Social Psychology, 35,* 63–78.

Maxham, J. G., Netemeyer, R. G., & Lichtenstein, D. (2008). The retail value chain: Linking employee perceptions to employee performance, customer evaluations, and store performance. *Marketing Science, 27,* 147–167.

McDaniel, M. A., Hartman, N. S., Whetzel, D. L., & Grubb, W. L. (2007). Situational Judgment Tests, response instructions, and validity: A meta-analysis. *Personnel Psychology, 60,* 63–91.

McDaniel, M. A., Morgeson, F. P., Finnegan, E. B., Campion, M. A., & Braverman, E. P. (2001). Predicting job performance using Situational Judgment Tests: A clarification of the literature. *Journal of Applied Psychology, 86,* 730–740.

Mischel, W. (1968). *Personality and assessment.* New York: Wiley.

Mischel, W. (1973). Toward a cognitive social learning reconceptualization of personality. *Psychological Review, 80,* 252–283.

Mischel, W. (2004). Toward an integrative science of the person. *Annual Review of Psychology, 55,* 1–22.

Mischel, W., & Shoda, Y. (1995). A cognitive affective system theory of personality: Reconceptualizing situations, dispositions, dynamics, and invariance in personality structure. *Psychological Review, 102,* 246–268.

Mischel, W., & Shoda, Y. (1998). Reconciling processing dynamics and personality dispositions. *Annual Review of Psychology, 49,* 229–258.

Morgeson, F. P., Campion, M. A., Dipboye, R. L., Hollenbeck, J. R., Murphy, K., & Schmitt, N. (2007). Reconsidering the use of personality tests in personnel selection contexts. *Personnel Psychology, 60,* 683–729.

Motowidlo, S. J. (2003). Job performance. In W. C. Borman, D. R. Ilgen, & R. J. Klimoski (Eds.), *Comprehensive handbook of psychology: Industrial and organizational psychology* (*Vol. 12*, pp. 39–53). New York: Wiley.

Motowidlo, S. J., & Beier, M. E. (2010). Differentiating specific job knowledge from implicit trait policies in procedural knowledge measured by a Situational Judgment Test. *Journal of Applied Psychology, 95,* 321–333.

Motowidlo, S. J., Hanson, M. A., & Crafts, J. L. (1997). Low-fidelity simulations. In D. L. Whetzel & G. R. Wheaton (Eds.), *Applied measurement methods in industrial psychology* (pp. 241–260). Palo Alto, CA: Consulting Psychologists Press.

Motowidlo, S. J., Hooper, A. C., & Jackson, H. L. (2006). Implicit policies about relations between personality traits and behavioral effectiveness in situational judgment items. *Journal of Applied Psychology, 91,* 749–761.

Murray, H. A. (1938). *Explorations in personality.* New York: Oxford University Press.

Murtha, T., Kanfer, R., & Ackerman, P. L. (1996). Toward an interactionist taxonomy of personality and situations: An integrative situational-dispositional representation of personality traits. *Journal of Personality and Social Psychology, 71,* 193–207.

Ployhart, R. E. (1999). *Integrating personality with situational judgment for the prediction of customer service performance* (Unpublished doctoral dissertation). Michigan State University, East Lansing.

Ployhart, R. E., & Ehrhart, M. G. (2003). Be careful what you ask for: Effects of response instructions on the construct validity and reliability of Situational Judgment Tests. *International Journal of Selection and Assessment, 11,* 1–16.

Rusbult, C. E., & Van Lange, P. A. M. (2008). Why we need interdependence theory. *Social & Personality Psychology Compass, 2,* 2049–2070.

Schmitt, M. J., Ryan, A. M., Stierwalt, S. L., & Powell, A. B. (1995). Frame-of-reference effects on personality scale scores and criterion-related validity. *Journal of Applied Psychology, 80,* 607–620.

Schmitt, N., & Chan, D. (2006). Situational Judgment Tests: Method or construct? In J. A. Weekley & R. E. Ployhart (Eds.), *Situational Judgment Tests: Theory, measurement and application* (pp. 135–155). Mahwah, NJ: Erlbaum.

Shoda, Y. (1990). *Conditional analyses of personality coherence and dispositions* (Unpublished doctoral dissertation). Columbia University, New York.

Shoda, Y., & LeeTiernan, S. J. (2002). What remains invariant? Finding order within a person's thoughts, feelings, and behaviors across situations. In D. Cervone & W. Mischel (Eds.), *Advances in personality science* (pp. 241–270). New York: Guilford Press.

Shoda, Y., Mischel, W., & Wright, J. C. (1989). Intuitive interactionism in person perception: Effects of situation–behavior relations on dispositional judgments. *Journal of Personality and Social Psychology, 56,* 41–53.

Shoda, Y., Mischel, W., & Wright, J. C. (1993a). Links between personality judgments and contextualized behavior patterns: Situation–behavior profiles of personality prototypes. *Social Cognition, 4,* 399–429.

Shoda, Y., Mischel, W., & Wright, J. C. (1993b). The role of situational demands and cognitive competencies in behavior organization and personality coherence. *Journal of Personality and Social Psychology, 65*, 1023–1035.
Shoda, Y., Mischel, W., & Wright, J. C. (1994). Intra-individual stability in the organization and patterning of behavior: Incorporating psychological situations into the idiographic analysis of personality. *Journal of Personality and Social Psychology, 67*, 674–687.
Tajfel, H. (1957). Value and the perceptual judgment of magnitude. *Psychological Review, 64*, 192–204.
Tett, R. P., & Burnett, D. D. (2003). A personality trait-based interactionist model of job performance. *Journal of Applied Psychology, 88*, 500–517.
Tett, R. P., & Guterman, H. A. (2000). Situation trait relevance, trait expression, and cross situational consistency: Testing a principle of trait activation. *Journal of Research in Personality, 34*, 397–423.
Tett, R. P., Jackson, D. N., Rothstein, M., & Reddon, J. R. (1999). Meta-analysis of bidirectional relations in personality–job performance research. *Human Performance, 12*, 1–29.
Wright, J. C., & Mischel, W. (1987). A conditional approach to dispositional constructs: The local predictability of social behavior. *Journal of Personality and Social Psychology, 53*, 1159–1177.
Wright, J. C., & Mischel, W. (1988). Conditional hedges and the intuitive psychology of traits. *Journal of Personality and Social Psychology, 55*, 454–469.

20

Personality From the Perspective of the Observer

Implications for Personality Research and Practice at Work

Brian S. Connelly

People devote much of their lives to forming and revising impressions of others' stable characteristics. A manager will watch a new employee for signs of how reliable and cooperative he will be, and that new employee will watch his manager for indications of how authoritative and supportive she is or will be. Coworkers and friends monitor one another's trustworthiness, and spouses spend a lifetime learning one another's personality from the broadest tendencies to the narrowest habits. Making judgments about others' personalities is simply a fundamental component of our cognition as social animals, and these judgments—which tend to be relatively accurate—serve us well to navigate and negotiate how we interact with the world around us (Gibson, 1979; McArthur & Baron, 1983).

For almost a century, personality psychologists have used these judgments as a measurement tool for validating much of what we know about personality by simply shifting personality self-report items from the first person to the third person. From assessing personality inventories' validity (e.g., Cleeton & Knight, 1924; McCrae, 1982) to examining the consistency of behaviors across situations (e.g., Bem & Allen, 1974; Chaplin & Goldberg, 1984) to affirming that personality's genetic roots and stability over the lifespan reflect more than response tendencies (e.g., Costa & McCrae, 1988; Riemann, Angleitner, & Strelau, 1997), observers' reports have been a frequently used instrument in the tool-shed of personality research. When industrial and organizational (I/O) psychologists have drawn on personality research to understand and solve workplace problems, however, the tool of observer-reports has often been lost in the shuffle. Indeed, across decades of I/O personality research on a multitude of personality predictors, criteria, and occupations, only a handful of studies in I/O have used observer-reports of personality.

The overriding purpose of this chapter is to assimilate what is known about observer-reports of personality as a guide for how observer-reports can be used to explore what is unknown about personality at work. I have several more specific aims. First, I will review fundamental aspects of observers' judgments of personality: what makes observers' judgments accurate, what biases affect these judgments, how the context of acquaintanceship affects observers' judgments, and how accurate observer-reports are compared to self-reports. Second, I will discuss how the process of forming accurate judgments of others is a fundamental (but under-studied) component of effective socialization and teamwork in organizations. Finally, I will discuss practical ways that observer-reports of personality can be incorporated in organizational personality measurement in both selection and development contexts. To conclude, I will discuss the implications that broadening our approach to measuring personality to include observer-reports will have for our understanding of personality.

Searching for Accuracy and Avoiding Bias in Observer-Reports

Forming Accurate Judgments of Others' Personality

A first consideration in discussing accuracy and bias in observer-reports is what criteria are used to judge whether observers are accurate. Funder and West (1993) describe three classic criteria for judging whether observer-reports are accurate. Specifically, observers should agree with one another in describing targets' personalities (strong rater consensus/interrater reliability), agree with self-reports (strong self-observer correlations), and predict relevant behaviors (strong criterion-related validity). Although any of these accuracy criteria could be inflated (e.g., observers with the opportunity to communicate with one another about a target's personality may artifactually reach stronger consensus than they would from independent observation of the target's behavior), convergent findings across multiple criteria can ameliorate the effects on any one accuracy criterion. Researchers have operationalized these accuracy criteria both nomothetically (correlating ratings of one trait across a sample of individuals) and idiographically (correlating across a set of trait ratings for a particular individual, as in profile similarity correlations) (see Figure 20.1; Kenny & Winquist, 2001). Nomothetic accuracy aligns with common data-analysis practices within I/O psychologists, where (for example) participants' scores on one variable may be correlated with another variable. Idiographic accuracy, on the other hand, is more common among person-perception researchers where Q-correlations are common and has often been the accuracy index of choice for indexing accuracy on the California Q-Sort (Block, 1961). These two approaches to indexing accuracy are entirely independent data analytic procedures. Nomothetic accuracy has the advantage of linking specific traits to behaviors and resulting perceptions, whereas idiographic accuracy is useful as an indicator of how accurate an individual judge may be or how accurately an individual target may be judged.[1]

Ratings of Extraversion

Participant #	**Self-rating**	**Peer-rating**
1	5	4
2	2	1
3	3	4
4	3	2
.	.	.
.	.	.
.	.	.
n_i	4	5

$r_n = .30$

Ratings of Target Participant #3

Trait	**Self-rating**	**Peer-rating**
Callous	2	3
Expressive	4	4
Diligent	1	3
Nuanced	4	5
.	.	.
.	.	.
.	.	.
$trait_j$	3	1

$r_j = .30$

Figure 20.1 Nomothetic vs. Idiographic Accuracy.

In using these accuracy criteria, theoretical perspectives have richly described how accurate judgment of others' personality traits occurs. Drawing on Brunswik's (1956) classic lens model, Funder's (1995) Realistic Accuracy Model provides a useful four-stage framework for conceptualizing how observers form accurate judgments of targets. Observers must perceive targets in a situation that is conducive for trait expression (*relevance*), and then that expression must be perceivable to the outside world (*availability*). An individual observer then must perceive the trait expression (*detection*) and appropriately assemble the trait cues to form an accurate perception (*utilization*). For example, a person perceiving others' sense of humor at a funeral would likely be prone to inaccuracies because (a) funerals tend not to prime targets' funny bone (i.e., low relevance), (b) humor tends to not be expressed to others at funerals (i.e., low availability), (c) any expression of humor is likely to be soft and subtle (i.e., low detection), and (d) humor could be misinterpreted as disrespect (i.e., low utilization). Thus, accurate perception can only be achieved if each stage of the process is satisfied, with deficiencies at each point deteriorating the link between the observer's perception and the underlying target's trait.

Of course, this process of perceiving others' traits does not unfold perfectly every time. Person-perception researchers have studied hundreds of moderators of the accuracy process, which Funder (1995) groups into four categories: A *good judge* must rate a *good target* on a *good trait* by using *good information*. Good judges tend to be more accurate raters of others' personality by using their strong reasoning skills (e.g., intelligence and social skills), interpersonal sensitivity (e.g., warmth and empathy), and psychological adjustment (Colvin & Bundick, 2001; Davis & Kraus, 1997; Taft, 1955). Interestingly, good judges appear to be more accurate not only because they are better at interpreting trait cues (detection and utilization) but also because they solicit more trait expression (e.g., making targets feel at ease to increase relevance and availability; Letzring, 2008). Good targets are easy to judge by others because their behaviors are more consistent (Bem & Allen, 1974; Funder & Colvin, 1991), because they are more comfortable expressing their traits (Colvin, 1993; Human & Biesanz, 2011), and even because they are more attractive (Lorenzo, Biesanz, & Human, 2010). Good traits tend to be more visibly expressed (e.g., extraversion) rather than internally held (e.g., neuroticism) and to be neutral in desirability (e.g., openness) rather than extreme in desirability (e.g., agreeableness; John & Robins, 1993). Finally, researchers have examined the effects of good information by varying the time that an observer has known the target and the cues used to draw trait inferences (e.g., viewing videos of targets with vs. without audio). Although most researchers presume that more information is likely to be better, the effects of simply increasing observation of targets level off in mere minutes (Kenny, Albright, Malloy, & Kashy, 1994). In addition, limiting visual or auditory information appears to have minimal impact on accuracy for some traits (Borkenau & Liebler, 1992).

Connelly and Ones (2010) meta-analyzed the accuracy of observer-reports to systematically examine good trait and good information hypotheses from Funder's Realistic Accuracy Model. Figure 20.2 summarizes the (test–retest reliability corrected) self-observer correlations and the inter-rater consensus correlations from their meta-analysis, separated by the trait being rated and the type of relationship observers had with targets. These figures display some important trends. First, note that some traits are generally more accurately observed than others. For example, Extraversion tends to be an especially "good trait" because it is very visible. In contrast, Emotional Stability and Openness to Experience are very internal traits describing inner thoughts and feelings; accordingly, these traits generally are low in desirability. Thus, trait visibility appears to generally make an impact across all observer types.

Second, different types of relationships that observers have with targets represent different sources and amounts of information from which observers can draw trait inferences. Not surprisingly, family members, friends, and roommates[2] tended to be the most accurate observers, and strangers were the least accurate observers. However, note that work colleagues are only marginally more accurate than

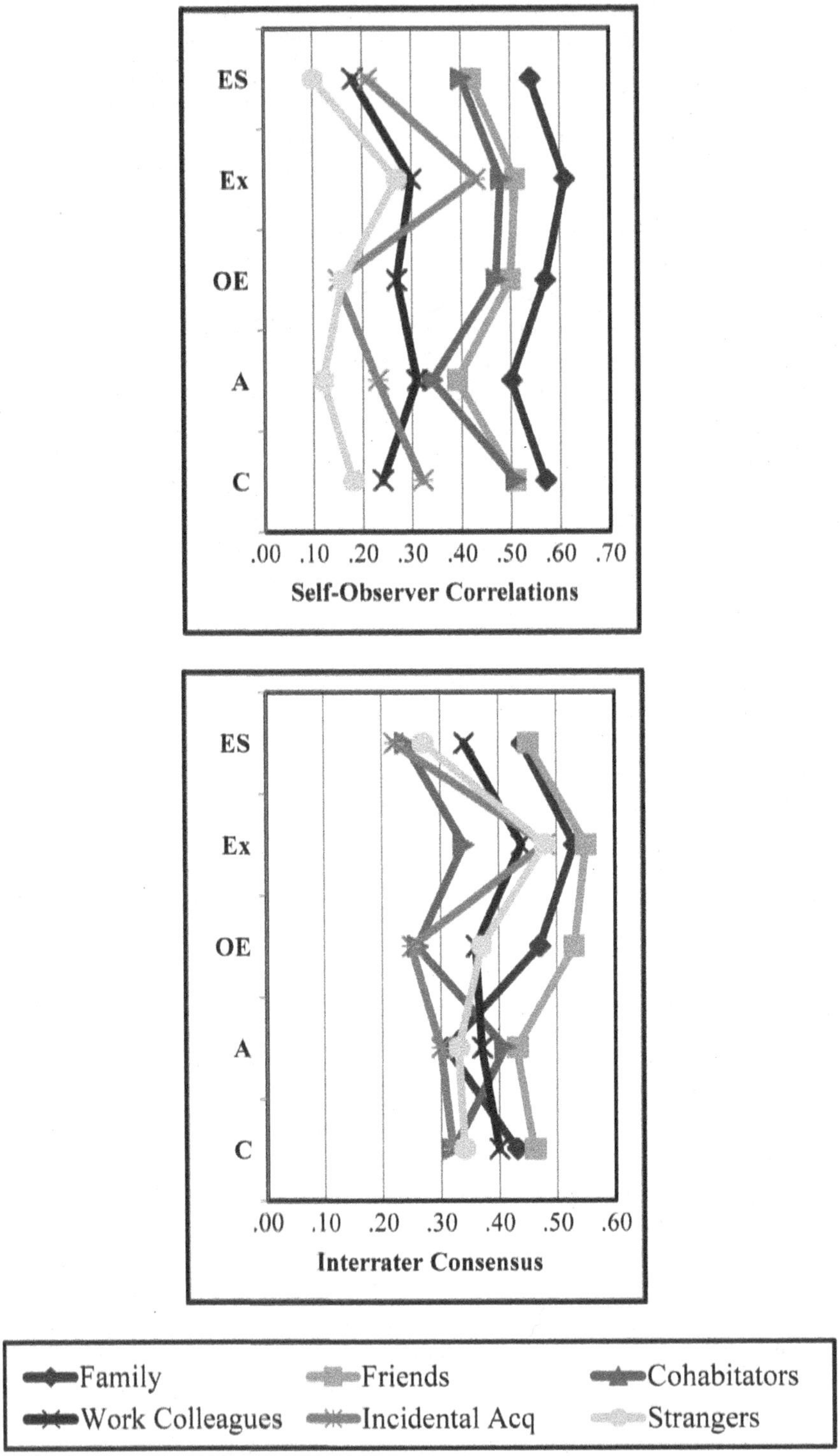

Figure 20.2 Accuracy Correlations From Connelly and Ones (2010).

Note: Correlations are test–retest corrected correlations from Tables 5 and 3 for self-observer and interrater consensus correlations, respectively.

total strangers and achieve approximately the same accuracy as incidental acquaintances (who are observers who become only briefly acquainted with targets through a shared activity). Even though we may spend 40 hr/week (or more) around our coworkers, their perceptions of our personality are only marginally more accurate than those we have just met. This suggests that sheer quantity of information is not a sufficient condition for accuracy; rather, high-quality information that comes from having an intimate friendship or family relationship with the target is required to boost accuracy beyond what is generally perceivable.

Third, note that the "good information" effects for different types of observers are more pronounced for some traits than others. For example, the benefits of observers with intimate relationships with targets (family members, friends, and roommates) are more pronounced for the two least visible traits, Emotional Stability and Openness to Experience. Thus, intimacy provides observers with unique access to internally held information, for which accuracy might not otherwise be possible. However, the benefits of intimacy acquaintanceship are not pronounced for all traits: Agreeableness (and, to a lesser extent, Conscientiousness) do not show the same accuracy increases for observers who are family, friends, or roommates. This is probably because observers' judgments of how "likable" (i.e., Agreeable) a target is are strongly influenced by how much they like the person and choose to maintain a relationship with the targets. Thus, for traits high in desirability like Agreeableness and Conscientiousness, intimacy may not have as noticeable benefits.

Of course, observers' judgments about targets are affected not only by targets' true traits but also by perception biases (West & Kenny, 2011). For several decades, social cognitive research on such perception biases was so prevalent that observers' attributions of behavior to a stable personality trait were labeled as a fundamental error (Ross, 1977). However, more contemporary perspectives on person perception simultaneously examine the effects of targets' underlying traits and sources of bias. For example, this research has focused on observers' leniency/harshness (referred to as perceiver effects in the Social Relations Model; Kenny, 1984), reliance on stereotypes (Kenny, 1991, 2004), their projection of their own personality onto targets (Cronbach, 1955), and their unique relationship with targets (Kenny, 1984) as sources of bias. Importantly, some of these sources of bias can artifactually inflate accuracy criteria like rater consensus (e.g., commonly held stereotypes or communication between observers). On the whole, theory and data show that, though the process of reaching accurate judgments is a complicated one susceptible to perception errors, trait perceptions by observers can achieve at least moderate levels of accuracy.

The Importance of Acquaintanceship Context for Observers' Reports

One critical theoretical and pragmatic consideration in measuring personality via observer-reports is whether observers from different contexts are interchangeable judges of personality. For example, will family members paint the same picture of a target's personality as coworkers? Questions about whether targets shift the way they express their personalities as they change contexts stem directly from the legendary person–situation debate (Kenrick & Funder, 1988; Mischel, 1968). Mischel (1968) is often credited (or blamed, depending on one's perspective) for introducing the view that became pervasive among many North American psychologists in the 1970s and 1980s that an individual's behavior is so strongly influenced by situational forces that conceptualized cross-situationally stable traits are nonsensical. In addition, many psychologists studying social cognition argued that the apparent stability in behavior that observers attribute to stable traits really reflects biases in perception. These "biases" were so central to social cognition as to be regarded as the fundamental attribution error (Funder, 2001; Ross, 1977; Sabini, Siepmann, & Stein, 2001). This premise has major implications for how observers from different contexts should be expected to agree in perceiving targets' traits. That is, to the extent that personality is not stable across situations but specific to a particular context, observers from different contexts should have inconsistent views of the same targets.

Moreover, research on targets' "personality" would be fragmented and compartmentalized within specific situations. However, a substantial body of research has slain Mischel's (1968) situational-specificity dragon, with observer-report methodologies playing a major role (Edwards & Klockars, 1981; McCrae, 1982).

Even though most personality and social psychologists now recognize that individuals' behavior is at least somewhat stable across situations, contemporary perspectives in personality have also emphasized that an individual's trait expression can meaningfully vary across situations (Fleeson, 2001). Thus, multiple theoretical perspectives have emerged emphasizing the way that situations and traits may interact to guide behavior. Mischel and Shoda (1995) conceptualize personality as a Cognitive–Affective Personality System of if–then contingencies that guide the way a particular person will respond to a particular situation. For example, although it may be possible to characterize some individuals as being more aggressive than others, Mischel and Shoda argue that the most important and meaningful personality descriptions must account for individual differences in the situations that provoke aggression. Similarly, the Trait Activation Theory (Tett & Burnett, 2003; Tett & Guterman, 2000) also emphasizes the effects that situations have by differentially eliciting trait expression. Thus, although aggression may be a stable individual difference, aggressive behavior may be inconsistently expressed because some situations simply may not be relevant for its expression. From trait–interactionist perspectives, it is paramount to consider the context of interest and the situational demands it presents when measuring personality.

Observer-reports offer a naturally occurring way to measure personality within a particular context that can specifically examine cross-situational consistency and specificity of behavior. For example, in a now-classic study, Funder, Kolar, and Blackman (1995) examined how observer-reports of college student targets converged across raters from three relatively independent contexts: parents, hometown friends, and college friends. Funder et al. found that observers from different contexts converged, indicating some stability in the way that traits are expressed across these contexts. However, they also noted that observer-reports converged much more strongly within contexts than across contexts (e.g., mothers agreed more with fathers than with hometown or college friends), suggesting that there is both stability and contextual specificity in the way traits are expressed. Connelly, Geeza, and Chang (2013) meta-analyzed these cross-context observer correlations to estimate the situational specificity of trait expression. For the most intimate-acquainted observers (family, friends, and roommates), situational specificity was minimal, but for coworkers, between 20% and 50% of the reliable variance in the way traits were expressed was unique to coworkers. For complete strangers (typically viewing only one behavioral episode of targets), specificity was even higher. Thus, personality expression can meaningfully vary across contexts, particularly at work.

Finding that personality trait expression is partly stable across situations and partly specific to particular contexts raises questions about how important context-specific trait expressions are for predicting behavior. Such ideas are reflected in frame-of-reference measures of personality, where respondents are directed to self-report about how their personality is expressed in particular situations by adding situational tags to the end of personality items (e.g., "I complete tasks in a timely manner *at work*"; Bing, Whanger, Davison, & VanHook, 2004; Lievens, De Corte, & Schollaert, 2008; Schmit, Ryan, Stierwalt, & Powell, 1995). Contextualizing self-reports has provided some increases in validity coefficients for predicting job performance. However, self-raters may not be the best at disentangling their personality in general from contextually specific ways it may manifest: Frame-of-reference measures tend to correlate with general trait ratings near the limits of their reliability, and work-contextualized measures are not better predictors of coworker-ratings than are general self-report measures (Small & Diefendorff, 2006). Thus, contextually limited observer-reports may provide a better method for isolating contextually specific personality manifestations.

Some research using observer-reports has shown that access to context-specific information can compensate for poor accuracy when predicting behaviors. Specifically, Colvin and Funder (1991) found that, although strangers are less accurate in judging targets' traits, they could predict targets' behaviors as well as close acquaintances if they viewed the target in a similar situation. Thus, even though coworkers may be less accurate in judging targets' general personality, their opportunity to view targets at work may give them advantages in predicting workplace behavior. When predicting job performance, however, the unique insights that coworkers possess enhanced prediction for only one trait, Openness to Experience (Connelly & Hülsheger, in press). For Emotional Stability, Agreeableness, and Conscientiousness, the unique ways these traits were expressed at work did not predict performance beyond the stable, cross-contextual expression of the traits (Extraversion did not predict performance in this cross-occupational study). However, these findings merit replication across a larger sample of contexts (both more specific within-work contexts and beyond-work domains) and criteria (beyond overall job performance). Thus, it remains somewhat unclear when trait expressions unique to a particular context are more meaningful predictors of behavior than underlying tendencies that are stable across situations. However, it seems clear that context does affect observers' perceptions, and prediction of at least some workplace behaviors may benefit from considering these work-specific trait expressions.

The Relative Accuracy of Self- Versus Observer-Reports

Although substantial evidence suggests that self- and observer-reports overlap and converge, self- and observer-reports remain distinct in the way they represent targets (Connelly & Ones, 2010). This raises an age-old question: Do others know our personality as well as—or better than—we do ourselves (Shen, 1925; Vazire & Carlson, 2010)?

Numerous theoretical perspectives have weighed in on this question in one form or another. A longstanding tradition of concerns about self-presentation effects in self-report measures would argue that other-ratings predict target behavior better than self-reports. Whether arising from intentional misrepresentation to present a desirable impression or from unintentional self-serving biases that skew our self-perceptions (Paulhus, 1984; Paulhus & Reid, 1991), researchers have long been concerned about how—and have documented ways that—our self-representations become biased. Similarly, social psychology researchers have long documented the tension between maintaining self-perceptions that are accurate versus those that are positive and consistent (Kunda, 1990). Although individuals' self-perceptions are not entirely devoid of truth, they are typically full of overly positive distortions that are less prevalent among observer-reports (Dunning, Heath, & Suls, 2004; Vazire & Carlson, 2010).

From an alternate perspective, self-reports may be more accurate than observer-reports. Simply put, no observer has the same degree of opportunity to observe a target's behavior as does the self, or the direct access to targets' thoughts, feelings, and values. This may particularly be the case when observers are not close acquaintances of the target. From such a perspective, access to internally held thoughts and feelings may be far more important than avoiding distorted responding. In a particularly interesting study, McCrae, Stone, Fagan, and Costa (1998) interviewed couples who had completed self-report and spouse-report measures, inquiring specifically about items where self-ratings and spouse-ratings diverged. The most common reason for disagreements between self-ratings and spouse-ratings was simply that the spouses formed different interpretations of the items or considered different specific instances when reading the item. These reasons are consistent with traditional conceptualizations of measurement error and can be reduced simply by administering more like-targeted items. Disagreements from considering the target in different contexts, roles, or time periods were considerably less frequent, and intentional self-report faking, perceived contrast, and assumed similarity (observers projecting their own personality onto targets) were almost never listed as reasons for disagreements. If most of the discrepancies between self-reports and observer-reports stem from self-raters' greater opportunity to observe themselves, self-ratings may be more accurate.

Finally, several theoretical perspectives suggest that self-reports and observer-reports may each be more accurate in particular domains. Hogan and colleagues (Hogan, 1996; Hogan & Blickle, Chapter 4, this volume; Hogan & Shelton, 1998; Hogan & Warrenfeltz, 2003) have distinguished between two domains of personality: the "inner" domain reflecting how individuals appraise themselves and craft an identity, and an "outer" personality reflecting the way individuals build reputations among others. In this framing, the unique ways that self-reports reflect personality represent not just bias but also an entire domain of personality not directly accessible to observers. In the same vein, however, observer-reports are direct indicators of the outer personality an individual creates in building a reputation. Thus, whether the self or observers are more accurate depends on whether the accuracy criterion is more closely aligned with the inner or outer domain. Recently, Vazire (2010) has also argued that self-reports and observer-reports have relative advantages in making judgments of targets. In her Self–Other Knowledge Asymmetry Model, Vazire suggests that self-reports will be more accurate in judging traits that are difficult to observe, whereas observers will be more accurate in judging traits that are highly evaluative. Thus, who has a more accurate perspective of a particular trait will depend on how the trait aligns with observability and evaluativeness dimensions.

The best empirical insight on the relative accuracy of self-reports and observer-reports comes from studies that have compared their validity for predicting cognitive, affective, and behavioral criteria. Although rare, these studies suggest that observer-reports are markedly better predictors of behaviors that are critical for a person's success and well-being in life. In what has now become a landmark study, Mount, Barrick, and Strauss (1994) showed that not only can observer-reports of personality validly predict performance criteria, but they also predict them more strongly than do self-reports and incrementally to self-reports. These findings offered I/O psychology some of the first indications that reliance on self-report measures of personality may underestimate the impact that personality traits have on work behaviors. Subsequent replications showing observers' advantages over self-reports can be found in Nilsen (1995), Small and Diefendorff (2006), and Connelly and Hülsheger (in press).

Subsequently, two small-scale meta-analyses have found that ratings from a single observer are better predictors of job performance than are self-reports (Connelly & Ones, 2010; Oh, Wang, & Mount, 2011). These findings replicate even when observers are personal acquaintances who know targets only outside the workplace, suggesting that observers benefit from a clearer lens in viewing targets more than from contextually limited knowledge (Connelly & Hülsheger, in press). The predictive validity advantages extend outside of the workplace, to include prediction of grades (Connelly & Ones, 2010), military dropout (Oltmanns, Fiedler, & Turkheimer, 2004), and even the development of coronary heart disease (Smith et al., 2008). However, self-reports and observer-reports show a less consistent pattern of advantages when predicting more specific behaviors, like how strangers will perceive targets after viewing thin slices of behavior or how often a target talks to others (Connelly & Ones, 2010; Vazire & Mehl, 2008). Two studies have shown that self-reports are stronger predictors of daily logs of emotions (Abe, 2004; Spain, Eaton, & Funder, 2000), though the criteria in these studies share common method variance with self-ratings. In clinical psychology, researchers have also emphasized that observer-reports may afford more accurate insights about the existence of personality disorders than do self-reports, particularly when predicting interpersonal problems and social functioning (Clifton, Turkheimer, & Oltmanns, 2005; Oltmanns, Gleason, Klonsky, & Turkheimer, 2005; Oltmanns & Turkheimer, 2006). Thus, although further research is needed for examining boundary conditions, (a) observer-reports predict many behavioral criteria better than do self-reports, and (b) self-reports may be more accurate predictors of emotional criteria.

Workplace Implications of Accuracy in Person Perception

Predominantly, when researchers have studied accuracy in judging others' personalities, the focus has been on identifying factors that promote accurate judgment—that is, accuracy has predominantly been studied as a desirable outcome or criterion. However, whether coworkers perceive each other's personalities correctly may also have important consequences for how they work together. Thus, trait perception accuracy may be an important but neglected independent variable in research on leadership, teams, and socialization.

On the one hand, accurate trait perceptions may improve group performance by promoting more effective communication and resource allocation. Information about coworkers' personality traits is one important set of knowledge that allows us to interpret their actions and correctly predict their behaviors. Considerable research in the past decade has highlighted that workgroups and teams that have similar knowledge and schemas (shared mental models) function more fluidly and perform better as a result (Klimoski & Mohammed, 1994; Mathieu, Heffner, Goodwin, Salas, & Cannon-Bowers, 2000; Mohammed & Dumville, 2001). Although research on team mental models has focused primarily on knowledge about the structure of tasks, consistency in interpersonal knowledge may be even more important over time for the smooth functioning of workgroups. For example,

- A workgroup or team that readily identifies its most conscientious members will be better off when it comes to picking someone to create a filing system.
- Leaders who know their most neurotic subordinates can be better prepared to provide support in times of stress.
- Peers who know that a target is disagreeable may be less likely to take his or her hurtful comments personally.

Conversely, inaccurate perceptions in any of these examples would likely result in substantial miscommunications between individuals that squander organizational resources.

The self-verification theory (Swann, 1981, 1983, 1990) offers another perspective on why accuracy in perceiving coworkers' traits may be important for performance and satisfaction among workgroups. According to the self-verification theory, individuals are motivated to ensure that their peers' perceptions of them are in line with their self-perceptions. When the perceptions of one's peers are discordant with self-perceptions, individuals feel that their well-being and sense of identity are threatened. Thus, the self-verification theory would suggest that inaccuracy in coworkers' perceptions of traits should result in less satisfaction at work and increased conflict. Consistent with this hypothesis, Gill and Swann (2004) found that stronger trait perception accuracy was associated with greater dyadic relationship quality for romantic partners and for fraternity brothers.

To my knowledge, only two studies have examined how accuracy in perceiving group members' personality traits impacts group functionality. Consistent with predictions from the self-verification theory, Polzer, Milton, and Swann (2002) found that student project teams whose peer-perceptions were more closely in line with team members' self-perceptions were more socially integrated, had greater member group identification, and had less relationship conflict. However, the group's performance was not related to congruence between self-perceptions and peer-perceptions. Purvanova (2008) found that student project teams who eventually reached greater consensus performed better and were more trusting. However, this effect emerged only for student teams who had face-to-face interactions; for virtual teams (which were less accurate in observing one another's traits), accuracy did not influence performance or trust. In addition, individuals who felt that their teammates knew them better were more satisfied and felt that they learned more. Thus, despite the limited number of studies of how accuracy in groups impacts how groups function, preliminary results indicate that research on the consequences of accuracy may be as important as research on predictors of accuracy. This has many practical implications in underscoring the importance of structuring early group interactions so that they promote accurate personality judgment.

Practical Applications of Measuring Personality via Observer-Reports

Selection and Admissions Decisions

Despite a preponderance of evidence indicating that personality traits predict a wide array of valued work behaviors and attitudes (Hough & Ones, 2001; Hough & Oswald, 2008), personality measures have incurred recurrent criticisms that the predictive validity of personality measures is not strong enough to justify their use in personnel selection (Guion & Gottier, 1965; Morgeson et al., 2007). Even among many proponents of using personality measures in selection, there are pervasive concerns that meta-analytic validity coefficients for personality (Barrick & Mount, 1991; Barrick, Mount, & Judge, 2001; Hurtz & Donovan, 2000) do not reflect the extent that personality traits intuitively influence job performance. Personality researchers have offered many reasons for why these validity coefficients may underestimate the traits' predictive power: from deteriorating effects of faking (Rees & Metcalfe, 2003) to meta-analyses' focus on broad instead of narrow traits (Schneider, Hough, & Dunnette, 1996) to variability across occupations in the directionality of trait–performance relationships (Tett & Christiansen, 2007) to consideration of irrelevant contexts of trait expression (Lievens et al., 2008; Schmit et al., 1995) to the importance of using multiple traits in combination (Ones, Dilchert, Viswesvaran, & Judge, 2007) or multiple measures of the same trait (Connelly & Ones, 2007). Thus, the latent view among many I/O personality psychologists seems to be that meta-analytic validities do not fully capture the impact of personality on performance in the same way that meta-analyses of general mental ability's validity do. However, finding that a single peer's rating of traits predicts job performance more strongly than and incrementally to self-report measures suggests that observer-reports may capture traits more fully than self-reports (Connelly & Ones, 2010; Oh et al., 2011). Thus, personnel selection systems potentially stand to gain by using observer-reports instead of or in addition to self-reports.

In addition, using observer-reports means that personnel selection systems are not limited to collecting personality ratings from a single observer (Hofstee, 1994). Because correlations between raters (interrater reliabilities) tend to be somewhat modest (generally, $r_{xx} < .45$; Connelly & Ones, 2010), combining trait ratings from multiple raters stands to produce substantial gains in validity in the same way that combining modestly correlated predictors improves validity.[3] For example, a single observer-report of Conscientiousness produces an operational validity of $\rho_{ov} = .29$ (vs. $r_{ov} = .20$ for self-reports; Barrick et al., 2001), but adding a second observer would increase the validity to $\rho_{ov} = .36$ (Connelly & Hülsheger, in press). With a third rater, validities climb to $\rho_{ov} = .39$, and, with a fourth, to $\rho_{ov} = .42$. Gains in validity eventually asymptote, such that a large number of observers would produce validities of $\rho = .55$ for Conscientiousness. Single-trait validities in the .50s represent markedly stronger prediction than ever observed for self-report personality traits' prediction of performance and even surpass those of general mental ability (Schmidt & Hunter, 1998). Personality traits are strongly predictive of job performance, but researchers and practitioners' use of single raters—especially self-raters—do not capture the full extent of traits' predictive power.

A third advantage of incorporating observer-reports in personnel selection is that they can identify individuals whose self-reports overestimate their standing on traits. Research has shown that, above and beyond main effects, overestimators of personality (specifically, Agreeableness and Conscientiousness; Connelly & Hülsheger, in press), performance (Atwater, Ostroff, Yammarino, &

Fleenor, 1998), and motivation (Hirschfeld, Thomas, & McNatt, 2008) tend to perform worse. For example, even among those low in Conscientiousness (as rated by peers), individuals who (falsely) believe themselves to be higher in Conscientiousness tend to perform more poorly than those with more conservative Conscientiousness self-estimates. Such inflated self-views are a hallmark of narcissism (John & Robins, 1994), a personality disorder recently receiving considerable research attention for its negative effects in the workplace (Judge, LePine, & Rich, 2006; Judge, Piccolo, & Kosalka, 2009). Personality researchers have long been concerned that such self-deceptive enhancement could influence personality ratings and allow those who are most self-delusional to rise to the top of applicant pools (Barrick & Mount, 1996; Paulhus & Reid, 1991). Although attempts to measure self-deceptive enhancement's influence on personality traits have generally not been fruitful (Chang & Connelly, 2011; Li & Bagger, 2006; Ones, Viswesvaran, & Reiss, 1996), comparing observer-reports and self-reports offers a valuable method for identifying applicants with inflated self-views.

The idea of using observer-reports of personality for personnel selection is hardly a new one. In a series of unpublished technical reports, Tupes and colleagues (Tupes, 1957, 1959; Tupes & Christal, 1958; Tupes & Kaplan, 1961) describe a major research program developing and validating selection procedures for selecting Air Force officers from peer-ratings of cadets. In what remains the largest study to examine the validity of observer-reports for predicting performance, Tupes and colleagues found that personality ratings from cadets' peers (approximately 30 peer-ratings per target) were strongly predictive of their later performance as officers—even more predictive than well-recognized predictors like military and academic grades. This research program is also credited among the landmark studies discovering the Five-Factor model that has become the dominant personality taxonomy for theoretically aligning traits (Digman, 1990). However, this program stalled during the 1960s, and its research findings were never published. I am not aware of any formal observer-report measures of personality being used for workplace selection since the Air Force's personnel laboratory's research program led by Tupes.

Part of the absence of observer-reports in personnel selection is likely because it is more difficult to gain access to observers than to self-reports. However, organizations regularly collect information about applicants from nonself sources such as references or recommendation letter writers. Although reference checks and letters of recommendations typically are not strong predictors of performance (Reilly & Chao, 1982; Vannelli, Kuncel, & Ones, 2007), standardized procedures designed to elicit trait information from these sources have yielded stronger validities (McCarthy & Goffin, 2001; Peres & Garcia, 1962; Taylor, Pajo, Cheung, & Stringfield, 2004). Thus, soliciting trait information from observers well acquainted with targets may offer a more valid and standardized method for collecting information about targets. Zimmerman, Triana, and Barrick (2010) offer preliminary support that such procedures may be effective. Zimmerman et al. solicited ratings of Conscientiousness, Emotional Stability, leadership, and interpersonal skills from the references of applicants to an MBA program. These references' ratings were effective predictors of students' performance in school (first semester grades), team performance, and (concurrent) work performance. In the domain of educational admissions, the Educational Testing Service has launched the Personal Potential Index, a "noncognitive" measure in which references rate graduate school applicants on six attributes partially overlapping with personality traits: knowledge and creativity, resilience, communication skills, planning and organization, teamwork, and ethics and integrity (Kyllonen, 2008). Preliminary research on the instrument has supported its ability to distinguish between dimensions and to predict student performance. Thus, educational admissions may soon be more systematically capitalizing on the knowledge that references can provide about applicants' personality traits. Many similar mechanisms are likely already in place for organizations to collect observer-report information, with this research from admissions offering strong preliminary support.

The prospect of using observer-reports of personality for personnel selection raises a number of pragmatic questions meriting further research scrutiny. Among the most immediate among these is, "Who should serve as observers?" When observer-reports are collected only for research purposes, targets tend to self-nominate observers with whom they are most intimately acquainted (e.g., spouses, family, friends, and roommates). Although these individuals tend to be more accurate judges, observers who like targets also are more likely to provide inflated, range-restricted descriptions of the targets (Leising, Erbs, & Fritz, 2010). Such friendship biases are likely more pronounced in high-stakes selection settings. Thus, further research should disentangle whether the greater accuracy of intimately acquainted observers would outweigh the potential-rating inflation in selection settings.

Using observer-reports in selection also raises concerns levied against nearly all personality measures: How susceptible are observer-reports to faking and forms of response distortion? If observers are inclined to fake as much as or more than self-reports, the validity advantages for observer-reports could deteriorate. Preliminary results indicate that in a lab-simulated applicant setting, observer-reports elevate ratings of targets as much as self-reports (Connelly & Wollscheid, 2012). Even among faked scores, observers appear to exaggerate positive characteristics more than outright falsifying responses, which is not the case with self-reports. However, Zimmerman et al. (2010) showed that observer-reports could produce strong validity for predicting performance even in high-stakes contexts (though concerns that faking may not impact criterion-related validities are well warranted; Mueller-Hanson, Heggestad, & Thornton, 2006; Rosse, Stecher, Miller, & Levin, 1998). In addition, aggregating across raters may offer a method for ameliorating the effects of faking by any single observer. Further research on response distortion in observer-reports is certainly warranted, particularly in an actual applicant context.

Finally, prior to using observer-reports of personality in selection settings, research should examine whether observer-reports of personality are likely to produce adverse impact. One appealing aspect of (self-report) personality measures has been that they tend to produce minimal adverse impact, particularly against protected racial groups (Foldes, Duehr, & Ones, 2008; Hough, Oswald, & Ployhart, 2001). However, it is not necessarily the case that observer-reports would show this same pattern. Rather, research on observer-reports' accuracy has long emphasized the impact that stereotypes have on observers' judgments, particularly when observers are not closely acquainted with targets (Kenny, 2004; Kunda & Thagard, 1996). Stereotypes related to personality traits are widespread and, by and large, generally negative about protected classes of gender, race, and age. To the extent that such stereotypes affect observer-reports, selection systems may produce adverse impact and punish those already harmed by negative stereotypes. To my knowledge, no research has compared group differences for self-reports versus observer-reports of personality, though such research is clearly merited if observer-reports are to be used in selection settings.

Interviews have also been discussed as alternate methods for assessing "observer" ratings of personality (see Chapter 18, this volume, on the assessment of personality in employment interviews). Personality information is certainly conveyed readily in job interviews (Salgado & Moscoso, 2002), even from small gestures like handshakes (Stewart, Dustin, Barrick, & Darnold, 2008). Moreover, interviewers appear to be more accurate judges of personality than are general strangers (Barrick, Patton, & Haugland, 2000), though they appear less accurate than close friends and family members (cf. Connelly & Ones, 2010). Collecting personality information from interviewers as observers can remedy concerns about observers faking on behalf of applicants or applicants selecting more lenient raters (but see also Barrick, Shaffer, & DeGrassi, 2009, for an examination of impression management in interviews). In addition, training could be provided to reduce interviewer stereotypes that could obscure observers' judgments. However, the information available in an interview represents only a very "thin slice" of applicants' personality (Ambady & Rosenthal, 1992), which, though somewhat accurate, likely lacks the insight available from closer acquaintances. In addition, more structured interviews (as typically recommended) may create a "strong situation" that constrains the expression of trait-relevant information (Salgado & Moscoso, 2002; Tett & Burnett, 2003). Thus, although interviewers may to some extent be effective observers in rating personality, it is not clear that they are necessarily preferable to or a substitute for the greater depths of trait information provided by more intimately acquainted observers.

Applications for Developmental Feedback

Although the majority of personality research in I/O psychology has focused on applying personality measures for personnel selection, organizations frequently use personality measures to provide job incumbents with developmental feedback. Whether used as a stand-alone source of feedback, within the context of a personality workshop training program, as a starting point with an executive coach, or as part of team development, employees often receive personality feedback as a mechanism for increasing self-awareness about strengths and weaknesses and setting goals to improve. As is the case with selection, nearly all personality feedback is based on self-report measures (the Campbell Leadership Index and the Leader Multirater Assessment of Personality represent two exceptions as multirater personality inventories designed for providing employees with 360-degree personality feedback). However, finding that (a) single raters tend to be somewhat idiosyncratic in their perceptions of targets' traits and (b) observer-reports predict performance more strongly than self-reports suggests that developmental personality feedback may be more accurate and useful if based on (multiple) observer-reports. Intuitively, if the goal of providing personality feedback is to increase incumbents' self-awareness, these goals are more likely to be achieved when using sources other than incumbents themselves.

In addition, contrasting observers' perceptions with self-perceptions offers a mechanism for directly confronting individuals' blindspots about strengths and weaknesses. Although individuals' tendencies to overestimate their standing on positive traits is stable over time, genetically influenced, and debilitative for performance (Connelly & Hülsheger, in press; Kandler et al., 2010), information about observers' perceptions is likely a useful mechanism for correcting false trait perceptions. Similar multirater feedback on performance has been shown to be effective in bringing self-perceptions more closely in line with coworkers' perceptions and consequently in improving targets' performance (Johnson & Ferstl, 1999). In contrast, providing personality feedback based on only self-perceptions may serve to reinforce incumbents' incorrect self-perceptions. Although providing self-discordant trait information may not be well received by some targets (particularly in the short-term), this feedback about personality traits is much more likely to be useful than feedback that more likely confirms their existing self-views.

Although multirater personality feedback is uncommon in organizations, multiple raters are frequently used in giving performance feedback via 360-degree feedback. To some extent, mechanisms for providing feedback from observer-reports of personality may already be in place in many organizations. Existing 360-feedback on performance may benefit by also incorporating personality information. In fact, many 360 performance feedback instruments have marked similarities in some of their items to observer-reports of personality, frequently using items like "meets deadlines and timelines," "is assertive," and "treats others with respect," showing clear conceptual alignment with Conscientiousness, Extraversion, and Agreeableness, respectively. Despite these similarities, there are two important distinctions between how multirater personality and performance tools are constructed and implemented. First, although some item content might be overlapping, personality inventories should appropriately select items representing raters' perspectives of behavioral, affective, and cognitive tendencies that define the core of a trait domain. In contrast, the domain of performance items typically focuses exclusively on behaviors that are valued by the organization and relevant to the given job. Thus, whereas performance feedback is most useful in identifying downstream performance consequences, personality feedback may be more beneficial for diagnosing upstream causes of performance deficiencies.

Second, multirater performance and personality differ in the context under which they are provided by raters and in which they are interpreted by targets. Personality feedback is inherently more personal: It pertains not to how effectively individuals perform but by how they are perceived generally by their coworkers. Soliciting personality feedback in addition to performance feedback may solicit a broader set of developmental challenges and may be more jarring for targets to receive. How personality and performance feedback should be coupled together thus merits closer empirical scrutiny.

Conclusion

Although personality measures have substantially improved organizations' effectiveness via self-reports, observer-reports of personality have much to offer I/O research and practice. A long tradition of research among personality psychologists has supported the accuracy of observer-reports. Research within I/O psychology can strongly benefit by using observer-reports not only as an alternative to self-reports but also to test some of the most fundamental theories in our field about how traits shape employees' behaviors and attitudes. Specifically, observer-reports are relevant for testing hypotheses from the Trait Activation Theory, socioanalytic theory, frame of reference measures of personality, and self-deceptive enhancement. In addition, using observer-reports—particularly from multiple observers—can enhance and improve the ways organizations use personality measures for selection and development.

Practitioner's Window

Collecting personality reports from observers (as opposed to self-reports) has been a mainstay of core personality research, but the practice has rarely made its way into organizational research and practice. This chapter highlights four key practical points:

- Observers' ratings can be quite accurate when they come from close acquaintances and somewhat accurate when they come from work colleagues and interviewers.
- Our peers' insights into our personality are more predictive of job performance than our own self-insights. Selection systems may be improved by incorporating observer-reports of personality from multiple observers. However, further research is needed to determine (a) who should be allowed to provide ratings, (b) how observer-reports may be susceptible to intentional response distortion, and (c) whether observer-reports could introduce adverse impact as a result of observer stereotypes.
- Individuals who overestimate their standing on positive personality traits perform worse as a result. Multirater personality feedback may be an effective method for correcting this overestimation, but developmental personality feedback from self-ratings could reinforce these overestimation tendencies.
- Forming accurate judgments of our coworkers is an ongoing component of workgroup functioning and socialization. Inaccuracies and inconsistencies in how a target's personality is viewed may impair team functioning and diminish a target's satisfaction in the workplace.

Notes

1 Nomothetic accuracy and idiographic accuracy have typically been distinct frameworks for analyzing observer-reports. However, Biesanz's (2010) Social Accuracy Model uses multilevel modeling to simultaneously analyze nomothetic and idiographic accuracies. Although elaboration of the Social Accuracy Model extends beyond the purview of this chapter, the interested reader is referred to Biesanz (2010).

2 Cohabitators included two subcategories: roommates and dorm/hallmates. Roommates tended to have markedly higher accuracy than dorm/hallmates. In the studies providing interrater reliabilities, most observers classified as cohabitators are dorm/hallmates (because people tend to only have a single roommate, making calculating interrater reliabilities impossible in most samples). In contrast, studies providing cohabitators' self-observer correlations tended to use roommates.

3 The prospect of collecting personality ratings from multiple observers warrants a brief discussion of how the reliability of multiple observers should be assessed. In choosing the appropriate reliability statistic, researchers and practitioners should make two considerations: (a) the type of measurement design used and (b) whether reliability is assessed at the level of the individual rater or at the level of the aggregate. Multirater designs generally fall within three categories: *block/classic designs*, in which a given set of raters rate every target (e.g., six undergraduates watch videos of 30 targets and rate each target); *nested designs*, in which targets have unique sets of judges (e.g., each target nominates three friends as raters, but no two targets nominate the same friends as raters); and *round-robin/reciprocal designs*, in which each participant rates and is rated by every other participant (e.g., five roommates rate one another's traits such that each participant is both an observer and a target; Kenny & Albright, 1987). Type 1 intraclass correlations (ICCs) are appropriate for indexing reliability in nested designs, Type 2 ICCs are appropriate for indexing reliability in block designs (Shrout & Fleiss, 1979), and the social relations model (and associated SOREMO software) provides estimates of variability attributable to targets that indexes reliability in round-robin designs. Raw intraclass correlations and target-variance estimates generally estimate the reliability of a single rater. However, when researchers are interested in the reliability of an aggregate of raters (e.g., the reliability of an average of three friends' ratings of a target), these single-level reliability estimates can be stepped up to estimate the reliability of *k*-raters by using the Spearman–Brown formula (when there are no mean differences across raters, Cronbach's alpha is functionally equivalent to the stepped-up ICC Type 2). Appropriate reporting of intraclass correlations should note both the associated type and number of raters—for example, ICC(1, 1) denotes a Type 1 intraclass correlation at the level of a single rater, whereas ICC (2, 5) denotes a Type 2 intraclass correlation for an aggregate of five raters—though readers should be cautioned that there are substantial divergences in reporting format in the literature. Outside the observer-report/person-perception literatures, r_{wg}s are often reported as an index of interrater agreement (James, Demaree, & Wolf, 1984). Such indices are calculated for individual groups (in this case, for individual targets) and are typically used in multilevel modeling to justify aggregation to the group level (as opposed to analyzing data at lower levels). Because the decision to aggregate observer-report data is typically made a priori (as the decision to aggregate items into a total scale score), r_{wg}s tend to be less appropriate in the context of observer ratings of traits.

References

Abe, J. A. (2004). Shame, guilt, and personality judgment. *Journal of Research in Personality, 38*, 85–104.

Ambady, N., & Rosenthal, R. (1992). Thin slices of expressive behavior as predictors of interpersonal consequences: A meta-analysis. *Psychological Bulletin, 111*, 256–274.

Atwater, L. E., Ostroff, C., Yammarino, F. J., & Fleenor, J. W. (1998). Self-other agreement: Does it really matter? *Personnel Psychology, 51*, 577–598.

Barrick, M. R., & Mount, M. K. (1991). The Big Five personality dimensions and job performance: A meta-analysis. *Personnel Psychology, 44*, 1–26.

Barrick, M. R., & Mount, M. K. (1996). Effects of impression management and self-deception on the predictive validity of personality constructs. *Journal of Applied Psychology, 81*, 261–272.

Barrick, M. R., Mount, M. K., & Judge, T. A. (2001). Personality and performance at the beginning of the new millennium: What do we know and where do we go next? *International Journal of Selection and Assessment, 9*, 9–30.

Barrick, M. R., Patton, G. K., & Haugland, S. N. (2000). Accuracy of interviewer judgments of job applicant personality traits. *Personnel Psychology, 53*, 925–951.

Barrick, M. R., Shaffer, J. A., & DeGrassi, S. W. (2009). What you see may not be what you get: Relationships among self-presentation tactics and ratings of interview and job performance. *Journal of Applied Psychology, 94*, 1394–1411.

Bem, D. J., & Allen, A. (1974). On predicting some of the people some of the time: The search for cross-situational consistencies in behavior. *Psychological Review, 81*, 506–520.

Biesanz, J. C. (2010). The social accuracy model of interpersonal perception: Assessing individual differences in perceptive and expressive accuracy. *Multivariate Behavioral Research, 45*, 853–885.

Bing, M. N., Whanger, J. C., Davison, H. K., & VanHook, J. B. (2004). Incremental validity of the frame-of-reference effect in Personality Scale scores: A replication and extension. *Journal of Applied Psychology, 89*, 150–157.

Block, J. (1961). *The Q-sort method in personality assessment and psychiatric research*. Palo Alto, CA: Consulting Psychologists Press.

Borkenau, P., & Liebler, A. (1992). Trait inferences: Sources of validity at zero acquaintance. *Journal of Personality and Social Psychology, 62*, 645–657.

Brunswik, E. (1956). *Perception and the representative design of experiments*. Berkeley: University of California Press.

Chang, L., & Connelly, B. S. (2011, April). *A meta-analytic multitrait–multirater separation of substance and style in social desirability*. Paper presented at the Annual Meeting for the Society for Industrial and Organizational Psychologists, Chicago, IL.

Chaplin, W. F., & Goldberg, L. R. (1984). A failure to replicate the Bem and Allen study of individual differences in cross-situational consistency. *Journal of Personality and Social Psychology, 47*, 1074–1090.

Cleeton, G., & Knight, F. (1924). Validity of character judgments based on external criteria. *Journal of Applied Psychology, 8*, 215–231.

Clifton, A., Turkheimer, E., & Oltmanns, T. F. (2005). Self- and peer perspectives on pathological personality traits and interpersonal problems. *Psychological Assessment, 17*, 123–131.

Colvin, C. R. (1993). "Judgable" people: Personality, behavior, and competing explanations. *Journal of Personality and Social Psychology, 64*, 861–873.

Colvin, C. R., & Bundick, M. J. (2001). In search of the good judge of personality: Some methodological and theoretical concerns. In J. A. Hall & F. J. Bernieri (Eds.), *Interpersonal sensitivity: Theory and measurement* (pp. 45–65). Mahwah, NJ: Lawrence Erlbaum.

Colvin, C. R., & Funder, D. C. (1991). Predicting personality and behavior: A boundary on the acquaintanceship effect. *Journal of Personality and Social Psychology, 60*, 884–894.

Connelly, B. S., Geeza, A. A., & Chang, L. (2013). *A meta-analytic examination of cross-contextual consistency in observers' perspectives across contexts*. Unpublished manuscript.

Connelly, B. S., & Hülsheger, U. R. (in press). A narrower scope or a clearer lens? Examining the validity of personality ratings from observers outside the workplace. *Journal of Personality, 80*, 603–631. doi: 10.1111/j.1467-6494.2011.00744.x

Connelly, B. S., & Ones, D. S. (2007, April). *Multiple measures of a single conscientiousness trait: Validities beyond .35!* Paper presented at the Annual Meeting for the Society for Industrial and Organizational Psychologists, New York.

Connelly, B. S., & Ones, D. S. (2010). An other perspective on personality: Meta-analytic integration of observers' accuracy and predictive validity. *Psychological Bulletin, 136*, 1092–1122.

Connelly, B. S., & Wollscheid, P. A. (2012, July). *Lying, boasting, self-exalting: Using observer reports of personality to identify and remedy applicant faking*. Paper presented at the European Conference on Personality, Trieste, Italy.

Costa, P. T., & McCrae, R. R. (1988). Personality in adulthood: A six-year longitudinal study of self-reports and spouse ratings on the NEO Personality Inventory. *Journal of Personality and Social Psychology, 54*, 853–863.

Cronbach, L. J. (1955). Processes affecting scores on "understanding of others" and "assumed similarity." *Psychological Bulletin, 52*, 177–193.

Davis, M. H., & Kraus, L. A. (1997). Personality and empathic accuracy. In W. Ickes (Ed.), *Empathic accuracy* (pp. 144–168). New York: Guilford Press.

Digman, J. M. (1990). Personality structure: Emergence of the Five-Factor model. *Annual Review of Psychology, 41*, 417–440.

Dunning, D., Heath, C., & Suls, J. M. (2004). Flawed self-assessment: Implications for health, education, and the workplace. *Psychological Science in the Public Interest, 5*, 69–106.

Edwards, A. L., & Klockars, A. J. (1981). Significant others and self-evaluation: Relationships between perceived and actual evaluations. *Personality and Social Psychology Bulletin, 7*, 244–251.

Fleeson, W. (2001). Toward a structure- and process-integrated view of personality: Traits as density distributions of states. *Journal of Personality and Social Psychology, 80*, 1011–1027.

Foldes, H. J., Duehr, E. E., & Ones, D. S. (2008). Group difference in personality: Meta-analyses comparing five U.S. racial groups. *Personnel Psychology, 61*, 579–616.

Funder, D. C. (1995). On the accuracy of personality judgment: A realistic approach. *Psychological Review, 102*, 652–670.

Funder, D. C. (2001). The really, really fundamental attribution error. *Psychological Inquiry, 12*, 21–23.

Funder, D. C., & Colvin, C. R. (1991). Explorations in behavioral consistency: Properties of persons, situations, and behaviors. *Journal of Personality and Social Psychology, 60*, 773–794.

Funder, D. C., Kolar, D. C., & Blackman, M. C. (1995). Agreement among judges of personality: Interpersonal relations, similarity, and acquaintanceship. *Journal of Personality and Social Psychology, 69*, 656–672.

Funder, D. C., & West, S. G. (1993). Consensus, self-other agreement, and accuracy in personality judgment: An introduction. *Journal of Personality, 61*, 457–476.

Gibson, J. J. (1979). *The ecological approach to visual perception*. New York: Harper & Row.

Gill, M. J., & Swann, W. B. (2004). On what it means to know someone: A matter of pragmatics. *Journal of Personality and Social Psychology, 86*, 405–418.

Guion, R. M., & Gottier, R. F. (1965). Validity of personality measures in personnel selection. *Personnel Psychology, 18*, 135–164.

Hirschfeld, R. R., Thomas, C. H., & McNatt, D. B. (2008). Implications of self-deception for self-reported intrinsic and extrinsic motivational dispositions and actual learning performance. *Educational and Psychological Measurement, 68*, 154–173.

Hofstee, W. K. B. (1994). Who should own the definition of personality? *European Journal of Personality, 8*, 149–162.

Hogan, R. (1996). A socioanalytic interpretation of the Five-Factor model. In J. S. Wiggins (Ed.), *The Five-Factor model of personality* (pp. 163–179). New York: Guilford Press.

Hogan, R., & Shelton, D. (1998). A socioanalytic perspective on job performance. *Human Performance, 11*, 129–144.

Hogan, R., & Warrenfeltz, R. (2003). Educating the modern manager. *Academy of Management Learning & Education, 2*, 74–84.

Hough, L. M., & Ones, D. S. (2001). The structure, measurement, validity, and use of personality variables in industrial, work, and organizational psychology. In N. Anderson, D. S. Ones, H. K. Sinangil, & C. Viswesvaran (Eds.), *Handbook of industrial, work, and organizational psychology: Personnel psychology* (*Vol. 1*, pp. 233–277). Thousand Oaks, CA: Sage.

Hough, L. M., & Oswald, F. L. (2008). Personality testing and industrial-organizational psychology: Reflections, progress, and prospects. *Industrial and Organizational Psychology: Perspectives on Science and Practice, 1*, 272–290.

Hough, L. M., Oswald, F. L., & Ployhart, R. E. (2001). Determinants, detection and amelioration of adverse impact in personnel selection procedures: Issues, evidence and lessons learned. *International Journal of Selection and Assessment, 9*, 152–194.

Human, L. J., & Biesanz, J. C. (2011). Target adjustment and self-other agreement: Utilizing trait observability to disentangle judgeability and self-knowledge. *Journal of Personality and Social Psychology, 101*, 202–216.

Hurtz, G. M., & Donovan, J. J. (2000). Personality and job performance: The Big Five revisited. *Journal of Applied Psychology, 85*, 869–879.

James, L. R., Demaree, R. G., & Wolf, G. (1984). Estimating within-group interrater reliability with and without response bias. *Journal of Applied Psychology, 69*, 85–98.

John, O. P., & Robins, R. W. (1993). Determinants of interjudge agreement on personality-traits: The Big Five domains, observability, evaluativeness, and the unique perspective of the self. *Journal of Personality, 61*, 521–551.

John, O. P., & Robins, R. W. (1994). Accuracy and bias in self-perception: Individual differences in self-enhancement and the role of narcissism. *Journal of Personality and Social Psychology, 66*, 206–219.

Johnson, J. W., & Ferstl, K. L. (1999). The effects of interrater and self-other agreement on performance improvement following upward feedback. *Personnel Psychology, 52*, 271–303.

Judge, T. A., LePine, J. A., & Rich, B. L. (2006). Loving yourself abundantly: Relationship of the narcissistic personality to self- and other perceptions of workplace deviance, leadership, and task and contextual performance. *Journal of Applied Psychology, 91*, 762–776.

Judge, T. A., Piccolo, R. F., & Kosalka, T. (2009). The bright and dark sides of leader traits: A review and theoretical extension of the leader trait paradigm. *Leadership Quarterly, 20*, 855–875.

Kandler, C., Bleidorn, W., Riemann, R., Spinath, F. M., Thiel, W., & Angleitner, A. (2010). Sources of cumulative continuity in personality: A longitudinal multiple-rater twin study. *Journal of Personality and Social Psychology, 98*, 995–1008.

Kenny, D. A. (1984). *Interpersonal perception: A social relations analysis*. New York: Guilford Press.

Kenny, D. A. (1991). A general model of consensus and accuracy in interpersonal perception. *Psychological Review, 98*, 155–163.

Kenny, D. A. (2004). PERSON: A general model of interpersonal perception. *Personality and Social Psychology Review, 8*, 265–280.

Kenny, D. A., & Albright, L. (1987). Accuracy in interpersonal perception: A social relations analysis. *Psychological Bulletin, 102*, 390–402.

Kenny, D. A., Albright, L., Malloy, T. E., & Kashy, D. A. (1994). Consensus in interpersonal perception: Acquaintance and the Big-Five. *Psychological Bulletin, 116*, 245–258.
Kenny, D. A., & Winquist, L. (2001). The measurement of interpersonal sensitivity: Consideration of design, components, and unit of analysis. In J. A. Hall & F. J. Bernieri (Eds.), *Interpersonal sensitivity: Theory and measurement* (pp. 265–302). Mahwah, NJ: Lawrence Erlbaum.
Kenrick, D. T., & Funder, D. C. (1988). Profiting from controversy: Lessons from the person–situation debate. *American Psychologist, 43*, 23–34.
Klimoski, R., & Mohammed, S. (1994). Team mental model: Construct or metaphor? *Journal of Management, 20*, 403–437.
Kunda, Z. (1990). The case for motivated reasoning. *Psychological Bulletin, 108*, 480–498.
Kunda, Z., & Thagard, P. (1996). Forming impressions from stereotypes, traits, and behaviors: A parallel-constraint-satisfaction theory. *Psychological Review, 103*, 284–308.
Kyllonen, P. C. (2008). *The research behind the ETS Personal Potential Index (PPI)*. Princeton, NJ: Educational Testing Service.
Leising, D., Erbs, J., & Fritz, U. (2010). The letter of recommendation effect in informant ratings of personality. *Journal of Personality and Social Psychology, 98*, 668–682.
Letzring, T. D. (2008). The good judge of personality: Characteristics, behaviors, and observer accuracy. *Journal of Research in Personality, 42*, 914–932.
Li, A., & Bagger, J. (2006). Using the BIDR to distinguish the effects of impression management and self deception on the criterion validity of personality measures: A meta-analysis. *International Journal of Selection and Assessment, 14*, 131–141.
Lievens, F., De Corte, W., & Schollaert, E. (2008). A closer look at the frame-of-reference effect in Personality Scale scores and validity. *Journal of Applied Psychology, 93*, 268–279.
Lorenzo, G. L., Biesanz, J. C., & Human, L. J. (2010). What is beautiful is good and more accurately understood: Physical attractiveness and accuracy in first impressions of personality. *Psychological Science, 21*, 1777–1782.
Mathieu, J. E., Heffner, T. S., Goodwin, G. F., Salas, E., & Cannon-Bowers, J. A. (2000). The influence of shared mental models on team process and performance. *Journal of Applied Psychology, 85*, 273–283.
McArthur, L. Z., & Baron, R. M. (1983). Toward an ecological theory of social perception. *Psychological Review, 90*, 215–238.
McCarthy, J. M., & Goffin, R. D. (2001). Improving the validity of letters of recommendation: An investigation of three standardized reference forms. *Military Psychology, 13*, 199–222.
McCrae, R. R. (1982). Consensual validation of personality traits: Evidence from self-reports and ratings. *Journal of Personality and Social Psychology, 43*, 293–303.
McCrae, R. R., Stone, S.V., Fagan, P. J., & Costa, P. T. (1998). Identifying causes of disagreement between self-reports and spouse ratings of personality. *Journal of Personality, 66*, 285–313.
Mischel, W. (1968). *Personality and assessment*. New York: Wiley.
Mischel, W., & Shoda, Y. (1995). A cognitive–affective system theory of personality: Reconceptualizing situations, dispositions, dynamics, and invariance in personality structure. *Psychological Review, 102*, 246–268.
Mohammed, S., & Dumville, B. C. (2001). Team mental models in a team knowledge framework: Expanding theory and measurement across disciplinary boundaries. *Journal of Organizational Behavior, 22*, 89–106.
Morgeson, F. P., Campion, M. A., Dipboye, R. L., Hollenbeck, J. R., Murphy, K., & Schmitt, N. (2007). Reconsidering the use of personality tests in personnel selection contexts. *Personnel Psychology, 60*, 683–729.
Mount, M. K., Barrick, M. R., & Strauss, J. (1994). Validity of observer ratings of the Big Five personality factors. *Journal of Applied Psychology, 79*, 272–280.
Mueller-Hanson, R. A., Heggestad, E. D., & Thornton, G. C. (2006). Individual differences in impression management: An exploration of the psychological processes underlying faking. *Psychology Science, 48*, 288–312.
Nilsen, D. (1995). *An investigation of the relationship between personality and leadership performance* (Unpublished doctoral dissertation). University of Minnesota, Minneapolis.
Oh, I. S., Wang, G., & Mount, M. K. (2011). Validity of observer ratings of the Five-Factor model of personality traits: A meta-analysis. *Journal of Applied Psychology, 96*, 762–773.
Oltmanns, T. F., Fiedler, E. R., & Turkheimer, E. (2004). Traits associated with personality disorders and adjustment to military life: Predictive validity of self and peer reports. *Military Medicine, 169*, 207–211.
Oltmanns, T. F., Gleason, M. E., Klonsky, E., & Turkheimer, E. (2005). Meta-perception for pathological personality traits: Do we know when others think that we are difficult? *Consciousness and Cognition: An International Journal, 14*, 739–751.
Oltmanns, T. F., & Turkheimer, E. (2006). Perceptions of self and others regarding pathological personality traits. In R. F. Krueger & J. L. Tackett (Eds.), *Personality and psychopathology* (pp. 71–111). New York: Guilford Press.

Ones, D. S., Dilchert, S., Viswesvaran, C., & Judge, T. A. (2007). In support of personality assessment in organizational settings. *Personnel Psychology, 60*, 995–1020.
Ones, D. S., Viswesvaran, C., & Reiss, A. D. (1996). Role of social desirability in personality testing for personnel selection: The red herring. *Journal of Applied Psychology, 81*, 660–679.
Paulhus, D. L. (1984). Two-component models of socially desirable responding. *Journal of Personality and Social Psychology, 46*, 598–609.
Paulhus, D. L., & Reid, D. B. (1991). Enhancement and denial in socially desirable responding. *Journal of Personality and Social Psychology, 60*, 307–317.
Peres, S. H., & Garcia, J. R. (1962). Validity and dimensions of descriptive adjectives used in reference letters for engineering applicants. *Personnel Psychology, 15*, 279–286.
Polzer, J. T., Milton, L. P., & Swann, W. B. (2002). Capitalizing on diversity: Interpersonal congruence in small work groups. *Administrative Science Quarterly, 47*, 296–324.
Purvanova, R. K. (2008). *Linking personality judgment accuracy and the sense of feeling known to team effectiveness in face-to-face and virtual project teams: A longitudinal investigation* (Unpublished doctoral dissertation). University of Minnesota, Minneapolis.
Rees, C. J., & Metcalfe, B. (2003). The faking of personality questionnaire results: Who's kidding whom? *Journal of Managerial Psychology, 18*, 156–165.
Reilly, R. R., & Chao, G. R. (1982). Validity and fairness of some alternative employee selection procedures. *Personnel Psychology, 35*, 1–62. doi:10.1111/j.1744-6570.1982.tb02184.x
Riemann, R., Angleitner, A., & Strelau, J. (1997). Genetic and environmental influences on personality: A study of twins reared together using the self- and peer-report NEO-FFI scales. *Journal of Personality, 65*, 449–475.
Ross, L. (1977). The intuitive psychologist and his shortcomings: Distortions in the attribution process. In L. Berkowitz (Ed.), *Advances in experimental social psychology* (*Vol. 10*, pp. 173–220). New York: Academic Press.
Rosse, J. G., Stecher, M. D., Miller, J. L., & Levin, R. A. (1998). The impact of response distortion on preemployment personality testing and hiring decisions. *Journal of Applied Psychology, 83*, 634–644.
Sabini, J., Siepmann, M., & Stein, J. (2001). Target article: "The Really Fundamental Attribution Error in Social Psychological Research." *Psychological Inquiry, 12*, 1–15.
Salgado, J. F., & Moscoso, S. (2002). Comprehensive meta-analysis of the construct validity of the employment interview. *European Journal of Work and Organizational Psychology, 11*, 299–324.
Schmidt, F. L., & Hunter, J. E. (1998). The validity and utility of selection methods in personnel psychology: Practical and theoretical implications of 85 years of research findings. *Psychological Bulletin, 124*, 262–274.
Schmit, M. J., Ryan, A. M., Stierwalt, S. L., & Powell, A. B. (1995). Frame of reference effects on Personality Scale scores and criterion-related validity. *Journal of Applied Psychology, 80*, 607–620.
Schneider, R. J., Hough, L. M., & Dunnette, M. D. (1996). Broadsided by broad traits: How to sink science in five dimensions or less. *Journal of Organizational Behavior, 17*, 639–655.
Shen, E. (1925). The validity of self-estimate. *Journal of Educational Psychology, 16*, 104–107.
Shrout, P. E., & Fleiss, J. L. (1979). Intraclass correlations: Uses in assessing rater reliability. *Psychological Bulletin, 86*, 420–428.
Small, E. E., & Diefendorff, J. M. (2006). The impact of contextual self-ratings and observer ratings of personality on the personality–performance relationship. *Journal of Applied Social Psychology, 36*, 297–320.
Smith, T. W., Uchino, B. N., Berg, C. A., Florsheim, P., Pearce, G., Hawkins, M., … Hopkins, P. N. (2008). Associations of self-reports versus spouse ratings of negative affectivity, dominance, and affiliation with coronary artery disease: Where should we look and who should we ask when studying personality and health? *Health Psychology, 27*, 676–684.
Spain, J. S., Eaton, L. G., & Funder, D. C. (2000). Perspectives on personality: The relative accuracy of self versus others for the prediction of emotion and behavior. *Journal of Personality, 68*, 837–867.
Stewart, G. L., Dustin, S. L., Barrick, M. R., & Darnold, T. C. (2008). Exploring the handshake in employment interviews. *Journal of Applied Psychology, 93*, 1139–1146.
Swann, W. B. (1981). Self-verification processes: How we sustain our self-conceptions. *Journal of Experimental Social Psychology, 17*, 351–372.
Swann, W. B. (1983). Self-verification: Bringing social reality into harmony with the self. In J. Suls & A. G. Greenwald (Eds.), *Psychological perspectives on the self* (*Vol. 2*, pp. 33–66). Hillsdale, NJ: Erlbaum.
Swann, W. B. (1990). To be known or to be adored: The interplay of self-enhancement and self-verification. In E. T. Higgins & R. M. Sorrentino (Eds.), *Handbook of motivation and cognition* (*Vol. 2*, pp. 408–448). New York: Guilford Press.
Taft, R. (1955). The ability to judge people. *Psychological Bulletin, 52*, 1–23.
Taylor, P. J., Pajo, K., Cheung, G. W., & Stringfield, P. (2004). Dimensionality and validity of a structured telephone reference check procedure. *Personnel Psychology, 57*, 745–772.

Tett, R. P., & Burnett, D. D. (2003). A personality trait-based interactionist model of job performance. *Journal of Applied Psychology, 88*, 500–517.
Tett, R. P., & Christiansen, N. D. (2007). Personality tests at the crossroads: A response to Morgeson, Campion, Dipboye, Hollenbeck, Murphy, and Schmitt (2007). *Personnel Psychology, 60*, 967–993.
Tett, R. P., & Guterman, H. A. (2000). Situation trait relevance, trait expression, and cross-situational consistency: Testing a principle of trait activation. *Journal of Research in Personality, 34*, 397–423.
Tupes, E. C. (1957). *Relationships between behavior trait ratings by peers and later office performance of USAF Officer Candidate School graduates*. Lackland Air Force Base, TX: Air Force Personnel and Training Research Center.
Tupes, E. C. (1959). *Personality traits related to effectiveness of junior and senior Air Force officers* (USAF Wright Air Development Center Technical Note No. 59-198, 1959, 9).
Tupes, E. C., & Christal, R. C. (1958). *Stability of personality trait rating factors obtained under diverse conditions* (USAF Wright Air Development Center Technical Note No. 16).
Tupes, E. C., & Kaplan, M. N. (1961). *Similarity of factors underlying peer ratings of socially acceptable, socially unacceptable, and bipolar personality traits* (USAF Aeronautical Systems Division Technical Note No. 29).
Vannelli, J. R., Kuncel, N. R., & Ones, D. S. (2007, April). *Letters of recommendation: Not much to write home about*. Paper presented at the Annual Meeting of the Society for Industrial and Organizational Psychology, New York.
Vazire, S. (2010). Who knows what about a person? The self-other knowledge asymmetry (SOKA) model. *Journal of Personality and Social Psychology, 98*, 281–300.
Vazire, S., & Carlson, E. N. (2010). Self knowledge of personality: Do people know themselves? *Social and Personality Psychology Compass, 4*, 605–620.
Vazire, S., & Mehl, M. R. (2008). Knowing me, knowing you: The accuracy and unique predictive validity of self-ratings and other-ratings of daily behavior. *Journal of Personality and Social Psychology, 95*, 1202–1216.
West, T. V., & Kenny, D. A. (2011). The truth and bias model of judgment. *Psychological Review, 118*, 357–378.
Zimmerman, R. D., Triana, M. C., & Barrick, M. R. (2010). Predictive criterion-related validity of observer ratings of personality and job-related competencies using multiple raters and multiple performance criteria. *Human Performance, 23*, 361–378.

21

Assessment Centers and the Measurement of Personality

Neil D. Christiansen, Brian J. Hoffman, Filip Lievens, and Andrew B. Speer

Although personality constructs are now widely accepted as being important for understanding work behavior, self-report personality tests as a method of assessment are not without their critics (e.g., Morgeson et al., 2007). Whether misguided or not, concerns persist regarding the validity of these measures and the issue of applicant faking has yet to be fully resolved (Tett & Christiansen, 2007). Moreover, applicant reactions tend to be less favorable for personality inventories than many other assessments commonly used in employment settings (Hausknecht, Day, & Thomas, 2004). To some, self-report inventories may be a poor way to assess personality traits, and yet such inventories are the method most often used to assess these constructs. This trend goes well beyond the area of Industrial and Organizational Psychology. Consistently across the field of psychological measurement, personality is rarely formally assessed by directly *observing* a person's behavior (Baumeister, Vohs, & Funder, 2007; for more coverage of personality assessment at work based on observer reports, see Chapter 20, this volume).

An exception to the practice of relying exclusively on the results of paper-and-pencil or computerized personality tests is the processes involved in assessment centers (ACs). ACs are composed of multiple moderate to high fidelity simulations of critical job tasks and situations (exercises) where trained raters observe candidates' behavior, and the resulting ratings are used for development or selection purposes. Most often associated with the assessment of managers, the dimensions used to organize the behavioral observations are often aligned to the results of a job analysis or a competency model rather than to any established taxonomy of individual differences. Despite the difference in methods typically used to derive personality traits and AC dimensions, there is obvious overlap in the behavioral domains of each type of construct (e.g., Lievens, De Fruyt, & Van Dam, 2001).

Although personality is not usually explicitly measured in ACs, the relationship between personality and candidate behavior in ACs is intuitive. AC exercises present the opportunity to express a variety of behaviors that are likely a reflection of candidates' personality tendencies (along with abilities and skills). Those individual traits that describe behavior across many other situations should also manifest in an AC. Furthermore, AC assessors are often quick to describe AC candidates in trait terms that any personality psychologist would recognize (Gaugler & Thornton, 1989; Lievens et al., 2001). However, despite the similarities between AC behavior and personality dispositions, social and personality psychologists long ago learned that inferential errors can lead individuals to make dispositional attributions where trait inferences are at times without foundation (Funder, 1999). Rather than relying on anecdotal observations, theory and research are needed to understand how personality relates to AC processes and outcomes.

Although early views of ACs lacked much theoretical basis, recent developments have linked theories of personality at work to ACs (cf. Haaland & Christiansen, 2002; Lievens, Chasteen, Day, & Christiansen, 2006). These advances promote understanding of the construct relationships of traditional AC ratings and, in particular, how these might be related to aspects of personality. However, just because personality traits may be related to AC behaviors and their resulting dimension ratings does not mean that there is a one-to-one correspondence. The purpose of this chapter is to review both the conceptual underpinnings that relate how personality constructs are assessed in ACs as well as the empirical research that has been done in the area.

AC Method

Borrowing from methods of behavioral simulation developed before and during World War II, Douglas Bray and his team at AT&T developed the first managerial AC. The cornerstone of this approach, like early performance tests, is the focus on behavioral assessment. Physical and psychological fidelity to the criterion domain is viewed as a unique advantage of performance tests relative to other predictors and arguably accounts for the strong psychometric properties of those tests (Wernimont & Campbell, 1968) and favorable user reactions toward them (Hausknecht et al., 2004).

AC exercises have emerged as a distinct subset of performance tests. Although ACs vary widely across administrations and uses (Woehr & Arthur, 2003), they are generally distinguished by some common features. First, ACs are designed to measure behaviors important for effective performance in management and leadership roles. Next, behavioral ratings are provided by trained assessors (Spychalski, Quiñones, Gaugler, & Pohley, 1997). Finally, ACs incorporate multiple simulation exercises designed to elicit behavior relevant to multiple behavioral dimensions. As described below, these core design features have implications for the way that personality relates to the behaviors displayed in ACs and offer unique potential for the measurement of personality using the AC method.

The behaviors targeted in ACs are most commonly organized into dimensions collapsed across exercises. These dimensions typically reflect skills and competencies that are important for effective performance in leadership roles and the dimension ratings often become the focal scores when interpreting AC performance. Although there is substantial variation in the labels applied to dimensions, there is strong conceptual overlap in the underlying constructs measured in ACs (Arthur, Day, McNelly, & Edens, 2003). Accordingly, researchers and practitioners routinely collapse dimensions into broader, more generalizable "mega-dimensions" when interpreting AC performance (Arthur et al., 2003; Hoffman, Melchers, Blair, Kleinmann, & Ladd, 2011; Shore, Thornton, & Shore, 1990). As we discuss below, these broader dimension factors can be theoretically mapped onto antecedent personality constructs.

AC exercises also differ substantially across administrations. Ideally, AC exercises are designed to reflect a situation common to the focal work role and to elicit behaviors relevant to success or failure. Although exercises were historically viewed as passive vessels by which to measure dimensions, more recent work has aggregated behaviors in ACs based on exercises rather than dimensions, making exercise performance the focal AC constructs (Atkins & Wood, 2002; Collins et al., 2003; Lance, 2008). Similar to dimensions, there is considerable variability in exercises across ACs, but common forms of AC exercises include: leaderless group discussions (LGDs), in-baskets, role-plays, case analyses, and oral presentations. Clearly, these exercises demand different types of behavior for a candidate to be successful in each, making ACs an ideal avenue to measure behavior across unique work situations.

Despite clear agreement on the value of behavioral measurement, the appropriate conceptualization of the behaviors has been controversial in the AC literature. Some argue that the behaviors should be interpreted on the basis of dimensions (Arthur et al., 2003; Arthur, Day, & Woehr, 2008; Rupp, Thornton, & Gibbons, 2008), others point to evidence that the behaviors should be aggregated and interpreted corresponding to different exercises (Atkins & Wood, 2002; Jackson, Stillman, & Englert, 2010; Lance, 2008; Neidig & Neidig, 1984), and still others take a more multifaceted view of AC performance (e.g., Brannick, 2008; Hoffman et al., 2011; Lievens et al., 2006). Finally, AC performance is often conceptualized using the overall assessment rating (OAR; Gaugler, Rosenthal, Thornton, & Bentson, 1987), which is akin to general performance in the broader performance rating literature. Below we discuss the influence of personality in AC dimensions, exercises, and OARs.

Trait Activation Theory and ACs

In commercial brochures, it is commonly stated that different AC exercises measure various intrapersonal and interpersonal competencies of candidates. Typical examples are leadership or interpersonal skills. These skill-based constructs are often conceptualized as a reflection of individuals' personality and abilities. In other words, it is assumed that AC exercises allow for the assessment of behavioral expressions caused at least in part by candidates' personality. From a conceptual point of view, one might expect that candidates' behavior shown in AC exercises is related to their standing on personality traits. Trait activation theory (Tett & Burnett, 2003; Tett & Guterman, 2000; Chapter 5, this volume) provides a useful framework to shed light on this personality–AC relationship. In this section, we discuss the basic axioms of trait activation theory. Then, we demonstrate how trait activation theory is relevant to ACs.

As a recent interactionist theory, trait activation theory has foundations in the historical debate in personality and social psychology over the relative importance of traits and situations as sources of behavioral variability. The theory starts with the notion that a person's trait level is expressed as trait-relevant behavior at work. An important underlying principle of the theory is that traits will manifest as expressed work behaviors only when trait-relevant cues are present (Tett & Burnett, 2003). According to trait activation theory, these trait-relevant cues can be categorized into three broad interrelated groups: task, social, and organizational. That is, specific task features (e.g., a messy desk), social features (e.g., problem colleagues), and organizational features (e.g., team-based organizational culture) are posited to influence when and how traits manifest as behavior.

For example, a trait such as autonomy has little opportunity to be expressed in routine monotonous jobs (task level), in the presence of a controlling supervisor (social level), or in a rigid autocratic culture (organizational level), whereas it is more likely to be activated in the opposite conditions. According to trait activation theory, situations are then described on the basis of their situation trait relevance, a qualitative feature of situations that is essentially trait-specific. In essence, it provides information as to which cues are present to elicit behavior for a given latent trait. For example, when an employee is faced with organizing a scattered stack of papers and files on a desk, this situation is relevant for the trait of order (a facet of conscientiousness). Similarly, when someone is confronted with an angry customer, this situation provides cues for traits such as calmness (emotional stability).

A second principle underlying trait activation theory is that trait expression also depends on the strength of the situation (Tett & Burnett, 2003). The notion of situation strength builds on the research about strong and weak situations (Meyer, Dalal, & Bonaccio, 2009; Mischel, 1973). In contrast to situation trait relevance, situation strength is a continuum that refers to how much clarity there is with regard to how the situation is perceived. Strong situations contain unambiguous behavioral demands, where the outcomes of behavior are clearly understood and widely shared. Strong situations and their relatively uniform expectations are therefore likely to result in few differences in how individuals respond to the situation, obscuring individual differences in underlying personality traits even where relevant. Conversely, weak situations are characterized by more ambiguous expectations, enabling much more variability in behavioral responses to be observed. Staying with the same example as above, when a supervisor instructs the employee to clean the messy desk by the end of the shift (with an explicit or implied threat), it will be much more difficult to observe individual differences related to the trait of order, whereas the opposite might be true in the same situation but without clear-cut supervisory instructions.

Thus, according to trait activation theory, the greatest variability in trait-expressive behavior might be observed when individuals act in situations that (a) offer trait-relevant cues (the notion of "situation trait relevance") and (b) are ambiguous (the notion of "situation strength"). Both of these distinct situational characteristics determine a situation's trait activation potential (TAP; Haaland & Christiansen, 2002; Lievens, Tett, & Schleicher, 2009; Tett & Burnett, 2003). So, a situation's TAP is defined as the opportunity to observe differences in trait-related behaviors within a certain situation. The more probable it is to observe these differences, the higher that situation's TAP (see Tett & Burnett, 2003, for a primer on trait activation theory, and Chapter 5, this volume, for an update on the theory).

In ACs, a candidate's rating on a dimension reflects bundles of behavior observed across exercises that may be related to deeper underlying trait or traits. For example, in a role-play with a confrontational supervisor, the candidates may stammer in their verbal responses, resulting in a lower rating on the stress resilience dimension by the assessor. The same behaviors that are targeted by the AC dimension may be expressions of emotional stability. AC exercises, therefore, represent situations that differ in terms of their TAP. The more likely that behavior can be observed within an exercise that is relevant to a particular trait, the higher the exercise's activation potential would be for that trait. The TAP of AC exercises is determined by the availability of trait-relevant cues and the strength of the situation as described above. Apart from the obvious task-demands in the exercise description, advantages of AC exercises over other methods of assessment are the presence of social cues (e.g., clients, colleagues, and supervisors played by role-players or other candidates) and the situation may contain information relevant to a specific organizational culture.

In AC exercises, the strength aspect is represented by the purpose of the AC (a high-stakes selection or promotion opportunity versus a low-stakes developmental purpose) and the specific exercise instructions that provide information and expectations to candidates about what to do to be successful. For example, exercise instructions might mention that the general aim of the exercise is "to reach consensus," "to motivate the problem subordinate," "to make a good impression," or "to give an oral presentation on strategic issues." Of course, instructions and cues regarding effective behavior may come from other sources besides exercise instructions, as candidates could infer what is effective from prior experience with similar situations or from the actions of other candidates.

Taken together, the application of trait activation theory to ACs suggests that the strongest links between candidates' personality trait scores and AC exercises will be found when exercises provide ample cues for behavior related to the trait-related dimensions to be expressed, and when the situations are not too strong to reduce variability in responding to them. To this point, several studies have employed the logic of trait activation theory in ACs by using TAP ratings to determine the cross-exercise convergence of AC dimensions (Haaland & Christiansen, 2002; Lievens et al., 2006). A TAP rating represents the relevance and strength of trait expression in a given situation (Tett & Guterman, 2000). For example, a situation where behaviors related to agreeableness are expected with some frequency would have a high TAP rating for that trait. Also consistent with trait activation theory, Haaland and Christiansen (2002) found that the relationships between trait scores from a personality test and trait-relevant dimensions were stronger in exercises high in TAP than those evaluated as being low in TAP.

Lievens et al. (2006) recently utilized FFM-based TAP ratings within AC exercises. Experts of both the AC and personality domains linked the FFM traits and a list of common AC exercises. The strongest of these linkages can be seen here in Table 21.1 and represent which trait-relevant behaviors are expected to be easily observed in each AC exercise type. For instance, within the competitive LGD all the FFM traits have high TAP levels and thus behaviors related to these traits may be expected to be easily observed. On the other hand, the role-play has high TAP ratings for only

Table 21.1 Linkage Between Five-Factor Model Traits and Typical Assessment Center Exercises

	E	*A*	*C*	*ES*	*O*
Case analysis			X		
Competitive LGD	X	X	X	X	X
Cooperative LGD	X	X	X		X
In-basket			X		
Oral presentation			X	X	
Role-play	X	X			

Source: Lievens, Chasteen, Day, and Christiansen (2006).

Notes: E: extraversion; A: agreeableness; C: conscientiousness; ES: emotional stability; O: openness to experience; LGD: leaderless group discussion. A cutoff was used to establish trait–exercise linkages.

extraversion and agreeableness. So, while observations based on these traits might be relatively accurate, inferences regarding conscientiousness, emotional stability, and openness to experience would likely not be so much, as there is less potential to observe trait-related behaviors.

Thus, by using trait activation theory and TAP ratings, researchers and practitioners can determine which personality traits will be relevant for each AC exercise. Likewise, trait activation theory provides a framework for understanding how situational demands affect behavioral expression that may impact ratings on dimensions that have very strong overlap with personality traits. It also informs expectations about the construct-related validity of dimension ratings, as only when two exercises have similar TAP ratings would a high degree of behavioral convergence be expected. This notion has been evidenced by both Haaland and Christiansen (2002) and Lievens et al. (2006), each showing that AC dimension convergence is highest across exercises mutually high in a specific TAP trait and when the dimensions in question are linked to that trait.

Conceptual Overlap Between AC Dimension Ratings and Personality

In ACs, information about behavioral tendencies is evaluated as a method of predicting candidates' behavior in actual work settings, with the behavioral information organized into AC dimensions. At face value, many AC dimensions appear directly related to personality traits. For example, AC dimensions such as sensitivity, drive, and influence would seem relevant to agreeableness, achievement orientation, and extraversion. Despite these similarities, there are also fundamental differences between assessments of AC dimensions and personality traits.

With regard to the overlap between dimensions and traits, evidence shows that, in the process of rating AC dimensions, assessors often describe individuals in terms of personality traits. For example, when taking notes on candidate behaviors, assessors frequently jot down trait inferences and overall impressions rather than actual behaviors (often despite being told explicitly to avoid such attributions). Gaugler and Thornton (1989) demonstrated that 20% to 25% of notes taken by AC assessors contained trait/personality descriptors. A more systematic examination of AC note taking found that, when assessors took notes containing personality-related adjectives, 68% of them could be traced back to the FFM (Lievens et al., 2001). Of these, descriptors related to emotional stability and conscientiousness were mentioned most often. This suggests that assessors organize the behaviors they observe into trait-based schemas when dimension ratings are made.

Lievens et al.'s (2006) study provides a frame of reference for how AC dimensions map onto personality traits. As part of a study examining the convergence and discrimination of AC dimensions, Lievens et al. (2006) had experts in both the AC and personality domains link Arthur et al.'s (2003) popular taxonomy of seven AC dimensions to the FFM. Table 21.2 displays the strongest linkages between the FFM traits and AC dimensions. As shown, each FFM trait maps onto at least one of Arthur et al.'s (2003) dimensions, and each of the AC dimensions maps onto at least one of the FFM factors. For instance, there is an intuitive connection between consideration/awareness dimensions and agreeableness, as facets of agreeableness such as tender-mindedness, trust, and altruism (McCrae & John, 1992) overlap with the definition of consideration/awareness (how well one cares for and attends to the feelings and needs of others). Tolerance for stress and uncertainty, defined as "maintains effectiveness in diverse situations under varying degrees of pressure, opposition, and disappointment" (Arthur et al., 2003, p. 136), has obvious links to emotional stability. Problem solving is linked to openness. Extraversion is linked to both communication and influencing others. Conscientiousness is linked to both drive and organization and planning. Thus, despite differences in the constructs typically assessed in ACs and those typically measured with personality measures, there seems to be at least some overlap between the behavioral domains of AC dimensions and personality traits.

Although AC dimensions and personality traits focus on similar sets of behaviors, there are also noticeable differences between the two sets of constructs. First, AC dimensions and personality traits differ in terms of the variety of contexts they are intended to generalize to. Second, the two types of constructs likely differ in how unidimensional (versus multidimensional) each may be. Third, there are differences in the evaluative nature of the constructs in that AC dimensions are value laden whereas the value of trait-related behaviors depends upon situational constraints.

Personality traits are essentially constructs that explain why certain behaviors covary within and across situations. All personality theorists today acknowledge that behavior is a function of both the person and situation and, as such, that behavior will be most consistent within a given situation or across situations with similar demands (Tett & Burnett, 2003). From the perspective of conditional dispositions, trait constructs are better construed as "if-then" propositions that define patterns of behavior in terms that encapsulate both characteristics of people and situations (Mischel & Shoda, 1995). This suggests that trait measures assessed in particular contexts will contain both specific variance and more general variance ultimately attributable to the broad, cross-situational trait constructs.

Consistent with this, research confirms that how extraverted one is at work is related to how extraverted one is in other contexts (Bowling & Burns, 2010; Heller, Ferris, Brown, & Watson, 2009). However, evidence also suggests that prediction of work outcomes is enhanced when personality inventories provide a work frame-of-reference (i.e., with the addition of "at work" tags) and that such measures predict beyond broad assessments (Bing, Whanger, Davison, & VanHook, 2004; Lievens, De Corte, & Schollaert, 2008; Schmit & Ryan, 1993). Thus, there is unique variance involved in contextualized assessment.

Table 21.2 Linkage Between Five-Factor Model Traits and Arthur et al.'s (2003) Assessment Center Dimensions

	E	*A*	*C*	*ES*	*O*
Communication	X				
Consideration and awareness of others		X			
Drive			X		
Influencing others	X				
Organizing and planning			X		
Problem solving					X
Tolerance for stress and uncertainty				X	

Source: Lievens, Chasteen, Day, and Christiansen (2006).

Notes: E: extraversion; A: agreeableness; C: conscientiousness; ES: emotional stability; O: openness to experience. A cutoff was used to establish trait–dimension linkages.

Viewed this way, AC dimensions may be seen as contextualized traits assessed within common work situations, with the ratings of behavioral tendencies not being intended to generalize to other domains of life. In other words, AC designers and raters are not concerned with whether ratings of problem solving predict behavior at a family barbeque, just future behavior on the job as simulated by the given AC exercise (Callinan & Robertson, 2000). In contrast, most personality traits assessed using other methods are broader in terms of context. Thus, while the behaviors that fall under an AC dimension may overlap with aspects of a personality trait, AC dimensions are more narrowly contextualized constructs. This issue of contextualization parallels that of typical and maximal performance (e.g., Sackett, Zedeck, & Fogli, 1988), with ACs constituting maximum performance situations. Due to their short duration and high-stakes nature, ACs are likely to generate behaviors that reflect optimum levels of candidate performance, whereas personality measures typically gauge dispositions that explain candidate tendencies across a range of more common situations. These issues likely have implications for expectations of convergence between AC dimension ratings and noncontextualized personality measures, which generalize to a broader range of situations. As AC dimension scores reflect performance-related behavior, their convergence with personality should occur only to the extent that the traits are also related to performance within the given exercise (i.e., exercise has high TAP).

AC dimensions also differ in that they may not be a function of single individual difference constructs in the way that the behavioral domains of personality traits are generally understood. Similar to many performance dimensions used to evaluate work behavior on the job, individual AC dimensions may represent a hodgepodge of personality traits, abilities, knowledge, and skills. Performance dimensions are typically clusters of activities deemed important by stakeholders, tend to occur in the same venue, or even involve a common piece of equipment; they are not necessarily intended to be activities thought to have one common cause. For example, a dimension involving the retail sales portion of a job may include both dealing with customers and working a cash register, as "warehouse management" for the same position may involve keeping track of inventory levels as well as operating a forklift. From that perspective, AC dimensions may be more similar to performance dimensions that index effectiveness as an expression of what the organization values.

Consider an AC dimension such as organizing and planning. Although this dimension could certainly relate to portions of conscientiousness (such as being methodical and industrious), it is also related conceptually and empirically to general mental ability (Meriac, Hoffman, Woehr, & Fleisher, 2008) and might also be linked to facets of openness to experience. To the extent that AC dimensions are more like performance dimensions, ratings will become more akin to composites or indices rather than the scales typically used to measure other predictor constructs. Behavioral convergence would then require the many influences of dimension-related behavior (e.g., knowledge, ability, and personality) to be activated in a similar manner across AC exercises, whereas with a more unidimensional trait (e.g., industriousness), convergence might be easier to obtain.

Personality traits, in contrast, tend to be more unidimensional (at least at the conceptual level), with well-understood behavioral domains. The clarity involved in how a construct is defined and understood by raters can affect both the reliability and validity of ratings. The haphazard way that AC dimensions are often developed and used has been noted in the literature when discussing issues related to construct validity (Arthur et al., 2008; Woehr & Arthur, 2003). For example, dimensions such as inner work standards, personal breadth, inspiring trust, and social flexibility may be commonly used in ACs but are ambiguous in terms of construct domain. As such, the espoused constructs may not be the actual constructs that are being assessed. This may affect how much convergence might be expected between ratings of an AC dimension and any single unidimensional measure.

Finally, there are differences in the evaluative nature of each type of construct. AC ratings are value laden, meaning high scores on a dimension-effective performance (at least most of the time), whereas trait-relevant behaviors can be viewed either positively or negatively depending on the situation.

Because of this, a trait could be positively related to performance on one exercise but negatively related to performance on another. For instance, assertive behavior might be required in a role-play with an outspoken subordinate, but evaluated negatively in a role-play with an emotionally downtrodden coworker. When an AC dimension would not indicate effective performance in an exercise, it is generally not assessed.

This has implications for expectations regarding the cross-situational convergence of AC ratings. If trait-related behavior is valued in one exercise and not in another, and if an AC dimension and personality trait are related and a candidate expresses trait-related behavior similarly across situations, dimension scores may lack convergence (see Haaland & Christiansen, 2002). This becomes more complicated when one considers that (a) multiple personality traits may be related to any single AC dimension; (b) a behavior may be an expression of more than one trait with a given situation; and (c) even if an expression of just one trait, which trait is involved may depend on the context (interrupting may indicate impulsivity or rudeness depending on other behavioral and situational cues). To the extent that assessors are able to take these complexities into account, personality ratings may demonstrate better convergence across exercises that have trait-relevant cues and demands (as trait-related behavior still has implications for trait elevation regardless of whether behavior is regarded as effective or ineffective in that situation). If assessors are not able to take these factors into account due to lack of training or ability, convergence may be worse.

In sum, AC dimensions and personality traits overlap conceptually, but there are notable differences. AC dimensions are work-contextualized characteristics that have a high degree of behavioral overlap with many common personality traits. Although personality traits can also be viewed contextually and assessed in work-specific terms, they are generally conceptualized as having greater situational breadth than traditional AC dimensions. AC dimensions overlap with other skill and ability-based constructs more so than personality traits. They also serve as indices of performance and are designed to overlap more directly with job performance, whereas personality traits can apply to many situations and across many domains. Because AC dimensions act as indices of performance and are thus value-laden, expectations of their cross-situational consistency differ from expectations of trait-related expectations of consistency.

Empirical Relationships Between AC Ratings and Personality

There exists a rich history of studying the relationship between AC ratings and personality. Corresponding with more general trends in the AC literature, this research has operationalized AC performance in a few ways, including: the OAR, dimensional performance, and overall exercise performance. Below, we review evidence pertaining to the relationship between personality and each of the three noted approaches to operationalizing AC performance. Table 21.3 summarizes the results of meta-analytic reviews pertaining to the relationships between the FFM and OARs (Collins et al., 2003; Hoeft & Schuler, 2001), dimensions (Meriac et al., 2008), and exercises (Monahan, Hoffman, Williams, & Lance, 2012).

A first strand of studies focuses on the link between personality and OARs, reflecting the overall clinically or mechanically derived judgment made about candidates at the end of the AC. Similar to measures of job performance criteria (Viswesvaran, Schmidt, & Ones, 2005), AC ratings are characterized by a positive manifold of correlations (Arthur et al., 2003; Hoffman et al., 2011), suggesting a meaningful general factor of performance. Accordingly, the correlations among personality and the OAR give an idea of the personality characteristics that relate to general performance across the tasks and competencies needed for effective performance in the AC.

Three meta-analyses summarize this literature. Collins et al. (2003) meta-analytically investigated the relationship between the OAR and the FFM dimensions. They reported artifact-corrected correlations between $\rho = .17$ and $\rho = .50$ for the personality dimensions of agreeableness, openness,

Table 21.3 Quantitative Summaries of the Relationships Between AC Ratings and Five-Factor Model Personality Domains

	E			*A*			*C*			*ES*			*O*		
	k	*r*	ρ	*k*	*r*	ρ	*k*	*r*	ρ	*k*	*r*	ρ	*k*	*r*	ρ
Overall assessment rating															
Collins et al. (2003)	13	.36	.50	7	.12	.17				6	.26	.35	5	.18	.25
Hoeft and Schuler (2001)	10	.10	.14	7	−.05	−.07	4	−.05	−.06	8	.12	.15	5	.07	.09
Dimensions (Meriac, Hoffman, Woehr, & Fleisher, 2008)															
Consideration/awareness of others	9	.07	.10	8	.05	.07	7	.09	.14	4	.07	.10	7	.06	.09
Communication	9	.11	.16	8	.09	.13	6	.09	.12	5	.08	.11	9	.12	.17
Drive	9	.21	.29	6	.09	.12	7	.10	.14	3	.04	.06	7	.06	.08
Influencing others	11	.15	.21	11	.08	.11	6	.09	.13	6	−.01	−.02	10	.08	.11
Organizing and planning	10	.09	.13	9	.02	.03	7	.05	.07	6	.07	.09	10	.09	.12
Problem solving	10	.08	.11	10	.06	.09	6	.13	.17	5	.07	.09	10	.11	.14
Stress tolerance	9	.12	.17	7	.06	.09	3	.12	.17	7	.07	.10	7	.11	.15
Exercises (Monahan, Hoffman, Williams, & Lance, 2012)															
In-basket	7	.06	.07	3	−.02	−.03	4	.13	.16	4	.04	.05	6	.04	.06
LGD	13	.13	.15	10	.00	.00	10	.04	.05	11	.08	.09	10	.07	.08
Role-play	5	.10	.12	4	.01	.01	5	.02	.02	5	.03	.04	4	.11	.14
Case analysis	3	−.01	−.01	3	−.04	−.05	3	.02	.03	3	.05	.06	2	.12	.15
Oral presentation	3	.13	.17	2	−.10	−.13	3	.09	.11	3	.06	.08	2	.09	.14

Notes: E: extraversion; A: agreeableness; C: conscientiousness; ES: emotional stability; O: openness to experience; k: the number of independent samples; r: sample-size weighted mean observed correlation; ρ: corrected validity estimate, corrected for attenuation due to predictor and criterion unreliability; LGD: leaderless group discussion.

emotional stability, and extraversion and AC performance, with extraversion as the strongest FFM predictor of OAR. Scholz and Schuler (1993) also conducted a meta-analysis of studies in which AC scores were correlated with an array of external measures such as personality inventories. This meta-analysis revealed that the overall AC rating tended to correlate .23 (corrected for unreliability) with dominance, .30 with achievement motivation, .31 with social competence, and .26 with self-confidence. In another meta-analysis that also examined personality correlates of the OAR (Hoeft & Schuler, 2001), much lower correlations were reported with the personality traits of agreeableness ($\rho = -.07$), conscientiousness ($\rho = -.06$), openness ($\rho = .07$), extraversion ($\rho = .14$), and emotional stability ($\rho = .15$).

Taken together, these studies produced equivocal results. There are four potential explanations for the mixed findings. Most obviously, more narrow personality constructs were used across one of the supportive reviews; perhaps constructs more clearly targeted to the domain will have stronger relationships than broad bandwidth constructs, as in Scholz and Schuler's (1993) review. Second, each review targeted a somewhat different literature base. Third, some meta-analyses may have included studies wherein the OAR was based on information that came not only from AC exercises but also from personality inventories, artificially inflating observed relationships (Collins et al., 2003). Finally, the use of the OAR has been criticized because it can potentially obscure effects by combining unique aspects of performance across dimensions and exercises (Arthur et al., 2003; Arthur et al.,

2008). Instead, some have argued that theoretically mapping personality onto unique aspects of AC performance can provide a more meaningful analysis of the construct validity of AC ratings. In the next two sections, we discuss the findings of research linking personality to ratings of performance in AC dimensions and exercises.

Personality and AC Dimension Ratings

The correlation between personality and AC dimensions has important implications for understanding the nomological network of AC dimensions (Cronbach & Meehl, 1955; Shore et al., 1990) and the potential for incremental validity of AC dimensions beyond other measures (Meriac et al., 2008). It is important to investigate the construct-related validity of dimensions, given that AC dimensions are often the focus when interpreting AC performance, especially in developmental contexts. Research attempting to support the nomological network of dimensions by using external measures of personality has yielded mixed results.

Although some studies found support for a relationship between AC dimension ratings and conceptually related personality trait ratings (e.g., Dilchert & Ones, 2009; Shore et al., 1990; Thornton, Tziner, Dahan, Clevenger, & Meir, 1997), such hypothesized convergence has not always been confirmed (e.g., Chan, 1996; Fleenor, 1996; Goffin, Rothstein, & Johnston, 1996). In these latter studies, the final dimension ratings failed to demonstrate expected relationships with conceptually similar personality dimensions. Furthermore, the average correlations between final dimension ratings and conceptually dissimilar personality dimensions were equal to or even higher than those with conceptually related personality dimensions.

Meriac et al. (2008) presented a meta-analysis of the relationship between individual differences and final dimension ratings using Arthur et al.'s (2003) seven-dimensional taxonomy as an organizing framework. Their results indicated generally weak and inconsistent relationships between AC dimensions and personality (ρs ranging from −.11 to .29). There was some evidence for the nomological network of dimensions, with general mental ability correlating more strongly with problem-solving dimensions than with interpersonally oriented dimensions, and with extraversion significantly correlating with influencing others. However, the hypothesized correlations between organizing and planning and conscientiousness were weak in this review. As might be expected based on the inconsistent support in the literature, only modest support was provided for the nomological network of dimensions based on Meriac et al.'s (2008) meta-analysis.

In sum, studies of the overlap between personality constructs and AC dimension ratings show an equivocal picture. The primary studies have come to differing conclusions, and the largest existing meta-analysis provided only modest support. A possible explanation for these findings is that the labels applied to certain AC dimensions do not match the actual construct that is measured (Arthur & Villado, 2008). However, although incorporating theoretical taxonomies of AC dimensions has improved findings in some studies (Dilchert & Ones, 2009; Shore et al., 1990), it has not in other studies (Meriac et al., 2008). It is possible that closer attention needs to be paid to the dimensions underlying broad factors in existing conceptual taxonomies. For instance, Arthur et al.'s (2003) popular seven-dimensional taxonomy is rarely supported empirically; instead, 2–4 dimensions more regularly describe the structure of final dimension ratings (Hoffman & Woehr, 2009; Kolk, Born, & Van der Flier, 2004; Schmitt, 1977; Shore et al., 1990). Thus, perhaps this taxonomy specifies too many dimensions to reasonably expect differential relationship with personality variables. Similarly, there are questionable linkages between the subordinate dimensions assigned to Arthur et al.'s taxonomy. For instance, communication includes written communication, which is strongly correlated with General Mental Ability (GMA), possibly resulting in the larger-than-expected relationship between communication and intelligence and the weaker relationships between communication and personality. Similarly, organizing and planning includes subordinate dimensions of developing others and control, more routinely included under leadership behaviors (cf. Borman & Brush, 1993). This possibly explains why extraversion was the strongest personality predictor of organizing and planning in Meriac et al.'s (2008) review.

Personality and AC Exercises

Given the well-known measurement problems with AC dimensions (Lance, 2008), a third group of studies examined the relationship between personality and AC exercises by focusing on AC exercise scores instead of AC dimension scores (Craik et al., 2002; Lievens et al., 2001; Spector, Schneider, Vance, & Hezlett, 2000). Although somewhat novel to the AC literature, research stemming from other areas has frequently investigated personality predictors of overall performance in behavioral simulations (Brunell et al., 2008; Foti & Hauenstein, 2007). The central prediction is that the behaviors manifest in a given situation (exercise) will be a reflection of an individual's underlying personality in response to the demands of the situation. Because exercises differ in their general potential to activate behavior related to specific traits, it is expected that the relationship between personality scores and AC exercises will differ, depending on the type of exercise.

Although only a handful of studies have directly examined the overlap between personality and AC exercises (Craik et al., 2002; Spector et al., 2000), a recent meta-analysis presented correlations between individual differences and exercise performance (Monahan et al., 2012). A common finding in existing research is that extraversion is consistently shown to be among the best personality predictors of performance in LGDs (Craik et al., 2002; Monahan et al., 2012). This is consistent with leadership literature supporting extraversion as a key antecedent to leader emergence (Judge, Bono, Ilies, & Gerhardt, 2002) and with Lievens et al.'s (2001) findings that notes on assessors' LGD rating forms were characterized mainly by extraversion descriptors. In addition, intelligence and conscientiousness, two constructs having particularly close ties to the completion of task responsibilities, are more strongly related to in-basket performance than to performance in other exercises (Craik et al., 2002; Monahan et al., 2012). Given the task, rather than interpersonally oriented nature of the in-basket responses, this finding supports the nomological network of in-basket scores. This pattern of results is also consistent with Lievens et al.'s (2001) finding that assessors' rating sheets most frequently include conscientiousness descriptors in the in-basket exercise. Thus, some of the observed results support the predictability of exercise performance based on individual differences.

On the other hand, FFM traits were weakly and somewhat sporadically related to role-play, case analysis, and oral presentation exercises. Openness was the strongest personality correlate of role-play performance in the Monahan et al. (2012) review, and this correlation was quite weak ($\rho = .14$). This overlap with openness might reflect the ability to use one's imagination in order to "get into role" in the sometimes awkward role-play simulation. This suggestion is consistent with Meriac et al.'s (2008) results that openness is among the strongest trait predictors of stress tolerance. Finally, limited research has examined individual difference correlates of case analysis exercises and oral presentations; however, there is some evidence that extraversion predicts oral presentation performance (Monahan et al., 2012).

Basically, these studies provide some general support for trait activation theory as they show that personality is differentially related to performance on different AC exercises. However, the support is most pronounced in correlations of in-basket and LGD performance, as the correlations between other exercises and personality seem to be less predictable. These studies, however, do not test whether specific exercise stimuli elicit specific trait-related behavior. They also do not reveal whether interventions to increase the situational trait relevance and strength of AC exercises affect the link between personality and AC ratings.

Moderators of Personality–AC Rating Relationships

A common thread running through all aforementioned strands of research is that they focused on the main effect of personality on AC ratings (either conceptualized at the OAR, dimension, or exercise level). A final stream of studies has searched for moderators of the personality–AC relationship, aiming to explain under what conditions personality might relate to AC ratings (Jansen, Lievens, & Kleinmann, 2011; Kolk et al., 2004; Krajewski, Goffin, Rothstein, & Johnston, 2007).

Some of these studies have built on trait activation principles, aiming to uncover conditions that might trigger or constrain personality trait expression in ACs. In this respect, Jansen et al. (2011) discovered that relevant traits were triggered only when candidates perceived the situational demands correctly. The general hypothesis was that individual differences in people's perception of situational demands will moderate the relationship between personality traits and conceptually related AC dimension ratings because only among candidates who perceived that a given exercise required behavior related to given personality traits would those traits be expressed behaviorally. This logic was confirmed for two of the three traits: agreeableness and conscientiousness. In particular, Jansen and colleagues showed that self-report agreeableness was related to ratings on cooperation in AC exercises only among people who perceived that the situation demanded agreeable behavior. Similar results were obtained for the relationship between participants' standing on conscientiousness and their AC rating on planning and organizing.

Krajewski et al. (2007) argued that age might moderate the relationship between personality and managerial effectiveness as measured by the AC. In particular, they posited that older managers with high scores on certain job-related personality traits may express them in a more effective fashion than similar younger managers, thus causing age to moderate the relationship between personality and AC performance. Consistent with hypotheses, age moderated the relations of dominance and exhibition with AC performance, such that dominance and exhibition were more strongly related to AC performance for older as opposed to younger managers.

Finally, Kolk et al. (2004) did not focus on trait-expression moderators but examined three method-related factors that might moderate the personality–AC relationship, namely differences in rating source (other vs. self), rating domain (general vs. specific), and rating format (multiple items vs. single item). For instance, the hypothesis about rating source was that the correlation between personality and AC ratings would be higher when the rating source was held constant across the personality inventory and the AC. There was partial support for the influence of each of the three method factors, although the differences were not large.

A few noteworthy trends emerged across investigations of the influence of personality on AC ratings. First, the three most recent meta-analyses revealed relatively weak relationships between personality and AC scores, regardless of whether AC performance is operationalized using OAR, dimensional performance, or exercise performance. This weak correlation should not be surprising, given that ACs are rarely used to measure personality; instead, the competencies measured in ACs are thought to be a consequence of individual personality, ability, experience, and skills. Indeed, if ACs overlapped substantially with self-reports of personality, there would be little need to go through the time and expense of administering an AC. It is also noteworthy that the magnitude of correlations between AC ratings and the FFM are relatively consistent with those investigating the FFM and job performance ratings (e.g., Barrick & Mount, 1991).

Although the modest magnitude of the correlations is not problematic for AC ratings, the moderate support for the nomological network of individual differences and AC ratings is more troubling. Specifically, for the most part, the three most recent reviews did not provide particularly strong evidence for differential relations among AC ratings and theoretically related (and unrelated) personality constructs. However, across all three reviews, AC ratings were more strongly related to GMA than to self-reports of personality (Collins et al., 2003; Meriac et al., 2008; Monahan et al., 2012). In addition, cognitively oriented dimensions and exercises generally correlate more strongly with GMA than do interpersonally oriented dimensions and exercises. The more influential impact of GMA on performance in ACs should not be surprising, given that GMA is found to be among the strongest predictors of performance across settings and performance domains (Schmidt & Hunter, 1998).

Next, extraversion and conscientiousness emerged as the two strongest personality predictors of AC performance across all three AC scoring approaches, and emotional stability and agreeableness were less strongly related to AC performance, though these differences were not large. Still, given the theoretical links between extraversion and leadership performance (Judge et al., 2002) and conscientiousness and performance across settings (Barrick & Mount, 1991), this pattern of results provides modest evidence for the construct-related validity of AC ratings.

Using Behavioral Observations to Directly Measure Personality in Work Simulations

Despite the widespread use of personality assessment today, little work has been done to measure traits directly in work situations such as ACs. This would ease the inferential leap involved in mapping traits onto AC dimension ratings if the results of the two types of assessments are to be combined mechanically. There may also be advantages in that, as constructs, personality traits such as the FFM are well understood in terms of their behavioral domains and place in the nomological network. This may facilitate the development of predictive hypotheses based on past research or even prove beneficial in terms of the psychometric properties of the ratings. Unfortunately, there is currently very little in the way of existing formal, behavioral assessments of personality that are suitable for work situations.

However, recent research has developed a tool (the Work Simulation Personality Rating Scales [WSPRS]) to assess personality-related behavior in work simulations and provides evidence of reliability and validity in an AC context (Christiansen, Honts, & Speer, 2011). The WSPRS is a 40-item measure designed to assess behaviors relevant to the FFM and common to work situations, with eight items per FFM trait. The WSPRS items were developed based on existing AC instruments, behavioral coding schemes (Funder, Furr, & Colvin, 2000), and traditional self-report personality inventories of the FFM (Goldberg et al., 2006). The items were formed at a moderate level of abstraction and specifically for application in a work simulation context. Furthermore, the WSPRS was grounded in trait activation theory (Tett & Burnett, 2003), meaning potential utility of the instrument was assumed to be dependent upon the situation in which behavior was assessed. Only in situations in which trait behavior is relevant and where behavioral variation is expected should the instrument be expected to assess a given FFM trait accurately.

A study was conducted to evaluate the WSPRS by applying it to 123 candidates of a developmental AC consisting of five behavioral exercises (three role-plays, an LGD, and a case analysis presentation). Raters were trained using frame-of-reference procedures on sample videotapes before viewing actual videotapes of candidates within the AC. Three assessors rated each candidate using the WSPRS. Traditional AC ratings were also collected by a separate set of trained assessors, and ratings of TAP were completed as a check on the assumption that behavioral observations would be more accurate in situations deemed trait-relevant. The observer ratings of personality were then correlated with scores on a self-report personality test completed by the candidates prior to the AC.

Results revealed that behavioral observations of the WSPRS reached moderate convergence with self-rated personality scores (see Table 21.4). Uncorrected correlations between self-report and WSPRS dimension scores ranged from a low of .11 for emotional stability to a high of .31 for extraversion. The magnitude of these correlations is similar to those presented by Connelly and Ones (2010) for the correlations between self-ratings and stranger ratings (see Figure 21.1). Interestingly,

Table 21.4 Correlations Between Behavioral Observation Ratings and Self-Reported Personality

	TAP	*IRR*	*r*	ρ
Extraversion	3.88	.87	.31	.36
Agreeableness	3.41	.71	.24	.31
Openness	3.02	.83	.22	.30
Conscientiousness	2.94	.78	.18	.22
Emotional stability	2.80	.82	.11	.13

Notes: TAP: trait activation potential (these ratings are on a 1–5 scale); IRR: interrater reliability for a composite of three independent raters; r: uncorrected correlation between WSPRS composites and self-report scores; ρ: corrected correlation between WSPRS composites and self-report scores, corrected for self-report unreliability; WSPRS: Work Simulation Personality Rating Scales.

Source: Christiansen, Honts, and Speer (2011).

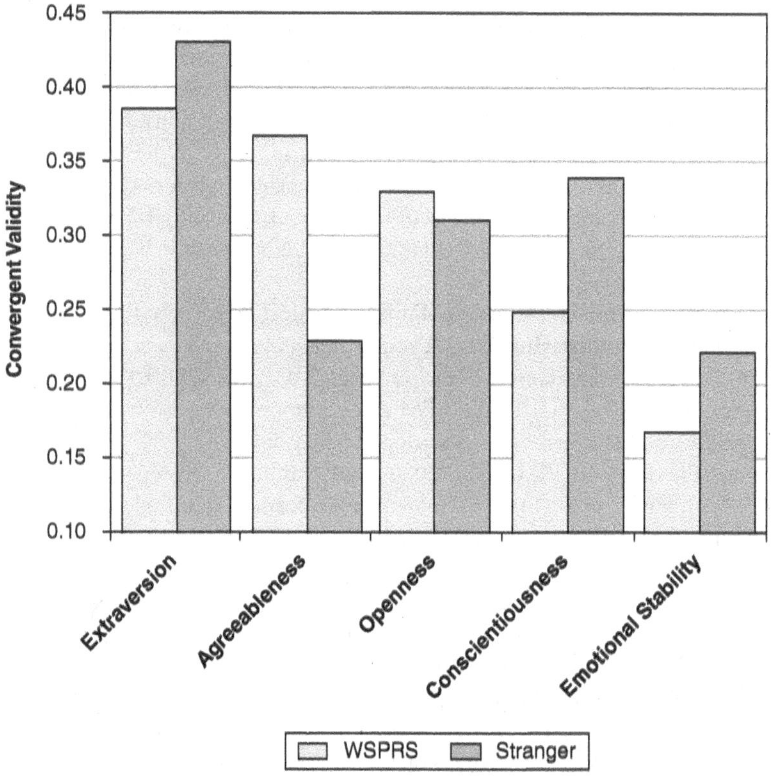

Figure 21.1 Convergent Validity Estimates From Correlating Self-Report Personality Measures With Observer Ratings of Strangers.

Notes: WSPRS: Work Simulation Personality Rating Scales. Estimates for stranger ratings taken from Connelly and Ones (2010). Correlations are corrected for both unreliability in self-report measures and interrater unreliability in the observer

the degree of self-WSPRS convergence almost directly coincided with the rank ordering of TAP for the FFM traits, in that WSPRS dimension scores correlated more strongly with corresponding self-ratings when there was ample opportunity to observe trait-related behaviors. For example, emotional stability was rated lowest in TAP and likewise had the lowest convergence with self-reports of that trait. Extraversion was highest in TAP and had the highest correlation between the WSPRS and self-report scores. The same general trend occurred in terms of interrater reliability, where the average interrater reliability of a composite of three raters ranged from .62 to .87 for the FFM dimensions (see Table 21.4). As expected, observations using the WSPRS were more reliable and more accurate for those traits that were relevant to the situation.

Table 21.5 displays a list of WSPRS items and item characteristics. Items such as "exhibits high enthusiasm and energy," "appears passive," "acts in a polite manner toward others," "contributes new and creative ideas," and "attempts to keep group organized" all had appropriate variability and moderate to high relationships with other items in their respective scales. On the other hand, some items had low variation and did not correlate well with other items. For instance, the items "behaves in a non-normative manner" and "behaves in a rude or abrupt manner" did not discriminate well amongst AC candidates. The items "argues their opinion or point" and "openly emotional and/or volatile" did not correlate with other items in their respective scales. It is unclear whether these items were poor representatives of their targeted traits or whether the situations did not allow enough opportunity for the expression of these behaviors (i.e., low baseline).

Table 21.5 Work Simulation Personality Rating Scale Item Statistics and Convergence With Self-Report Personality

	Descriptive Statistics		*Reliability*		*Self-Report Convergence*	
	M	*SD*	*IRR*	*CITC*	*r*	ρ
Extraversion						
Behaves in an influential and persuasive manner	1.92	.59	.70	.80	.32	.37
Exhibits high enthusiasm and energy	1.79	.63	.83	.83	.31	.36
Talkative	2.06	.62	.81	.82	.28	.33
Interacts confidently with others	2.23	.59	.77	.75	.28	.32
Expressive with voice, face, and/or gestures	1.97	.63	.75	.79	.26	.30
Seems detached from the situation (r)	2.49	.54	.77	.74	.25	.29
Appears passive (r)	2.34	.63	.80	.80	.24	.27
Behaves timidly (r)	2.44	.56	.75	.78	.21	.24
Agreeableness						
Makes supportive comments	2.07	.58	.54	.70	.27	.35
Expresses agreement or support	2.12	.46	.57	.70	.27	.35
Acts in a polite manner toward others	1.98	.61	.63	.69	.24	.31
Displays concern for others	2.01	.52	.62	.67	.19	.25
Supports others' decisions	2.21	.46	.56	.67	.16	.20
Behaves dismissively toward others (r)	2.56	.46	.57	.66	.12	.15
Behaves in a rude or abrupt manner (r)	2.65	.44	.56	.65	.11	.14
Argues their opinion or point (r)	1.93	.57	.65	.16	.01	.01
Openness to experience						
Says interesting things	1.89	.57	.67	.81	.25	.37
Discusses multiple aspects of ideas and topics	2.01	.52	.55	.80	.25	.36
Considers both pros and cons	1.99	.57	.66	.82	.22	.32
Exhibits a high degree of intelligence	2.02	.58	.72	.88	.18	.26
Integrates others' ideas and suggestions	2.11	.52	.55	.74	.17	.25

(Continued)

Table 21.5 (Continued)

	Descriptive Statistics		*Reliability*		*Self-Report Convergence*	
	M	*SD*	*IRR*	*CITC*	*r*	ρ
Contributes new and creative ideas	1.97	.58	.73	.72	.14	.21
Makes nonintellectual statements (r)	2.46	.48	.50	.65	.14	.20
Unconcerned with different thoughts and ideas (r)	2.46	.48	.57	.60	.09	.13
Conscientiousness						
Emphasizes goals and accomplishments	2.07	.58	.72	.74	.22	.27
Attempts to keep group organized	1.88	.61	.70	.77	.17	.21
Encourages group to stay on task	1.87	.57	.67	.80	.16	.20
Does not behave professionally (r)	2.48	.52	.70	.67	.16	.19
Prioritizes or plans activities	2.07	.58	.72	.80	.15	.18
Dresses appropriately	2.46	.56	.76	.43	.13	.15
Easily distracted and does not follow through (r)	2.56	.48	.70	.72	.07	.09
Considers all options and is thorough	2.00	.57	.66	.67	.03	.04
Emotional stability						
Appears calm and relaxed (r)	1.60	.46	.40	.44	.12	.14
Interacts poorly or awkwardly	1.57	.52	.59	.73	.08	.10
Interested in others and tasks (r)	1.77	.52	.68	.48	.08	.10
Behaves in a non-normative manner	1.36	.41	.48	.61	.08	.09
Acts irritated or annoyed	1.37	.42	.55	.25	.08	.09
Openly emotional and/or volatile	1.27	.37	.57	.19	.07	.08
Seeks reassurance from others	1.49	.48	.56	.45	.02	.02
Displays low opinion of self	1.36	.43	.58	.46	.01	.02

Source: Christiansen, Honts, and Speer (2011).

Notes: M: mean, with items on a 1–3 scale; SD, standard deviation; IRR: interrater reliability for a composite of three independent raters; CITC: corrected item total correlation; r: uncorrected correlation between WSPRS items and self-report composite scores; ρ: corrected correlation between WSPRS items and self-report composite scores, corrected for self-report unreliability; (r): an item that was reverse-coded; WSPRS: Work Simulation Personality Rating Scales.

The WSPRS scores were also correlated with the OAR to determine the degree of overlap. Essentially, the OAR represents assessment performance and is often used to make personnel decisions in operational ACs. As both the OAR and WSPRS ratings were based on the same videotaped sets of performance, it was expected that they would be highly correlated, which they were (R = .73). Extraversion emerged as the best predictor of the OAR (β = .34), followed by openness to experience (β = .24), conscientiousness (β = .16), agreeableness (β = .08), and emotional stability (β = .05).

To date, this research represents the most direct evidence that behavior relevant to personality can be readily observed in AC exercises. It also underscores how important a thorough understanding of exercise demands is in terms of how well traits can be assessed. In this AC, emotional stability in particular was hypothesized to be the most difficult to observe relevant behavior, and evidence confirmed this. If the AC were being used for a position where this trait is critical, existing exercises would need to be redesigned or additional exercises added to provide more trait-relevant cues. On the other hand, with the current exercises (three role-plays, group discussion, and a presentation), many cues were present for extraversion.

Effects of Impression Management and Response Distortion

Another potential advantage of assessing personality in the context of ACs is that it is likely to be more difficult to raise scores by engaging in impression management. Research has shown that response distortion is relatively common when personality tests are used in applicant settings and degrades their validity (see Tett & Christiansen, 2007). In most self-report inventories, it is fairly easy to identify the response that is favorable for a job (Christiansen, Burns, & Montgomery, 2005). On the other hand, research has shown that faking is more difficult when using interviews to assess personality, where applicants need to generate and describe job-related examples that are plausible, detailed, and relevant to the questions asked (Van Iddekinge, Raymark, & Roth, 2005). In addition, overtly obvious attempts at impression management may result in negative evaluations (see Chapter 18, this volume).

Although no research has directly examined the effects of impression management in AC in terms of mean shifts or validity, it would seem more challenging to raise scores in this context than when an interview or a personality inventory is used to measure personality. To achieve high scores in an AC exercise, candidates must first determine what responses will be most effective both in terms of task success and the perceptions of evaluators. This can be challenging because the situations in ACs are typically much more complicated than a question on a personality test or interview. Beyond just determining a desirable response, in ACs candidates have to actually engage in behavior that results in assessors evaluating them more favorably, rather than just saying they would do it or had done it in the past. This places greater cognitive demands on AC participants, forcing them to focus more on the task at hand and in turn limiting their ability to engage in impression management (McFarland, Ryan, & Kriska, 2003). Similar to interviews, overt attempts at impression management may be expected to result in negative evaluations in ACs, whereas they are seldom taken into account by assessors when reviewing the results of self-report personality inventories (Christiansen, Burns, & Rozek, 2010).

This is not to say that impression management does not happen in ACs. The prevalence and effects are likely to depend on the demands of the exercise where trait-relevant behavior is to be observed. For example, impression management is less common in exercises demanding technical competency than in those requiring interpersonal effectiveness in order to be successful (McFarland, Yun, Harold, Viera, & Moore, 2005). Even so, the effects of impression management on criterion-related validity may be at least partly mitigated, as those who are correctly able to identify what they are being evaluated on are also likely to perform better on the job (Kleinmann et al., 2011).

Conclusions and Future Directions for Research

Modern research on ACs and personality measurement has largely progressed independently, with limited attempts at empirical integration. In this chapter, we have attempted to highlight the similarities and differences between the constructs assessed in ACs and traditional self-report measures of personality, the theoretical and empirical overlap between ACs and personality, and ways in which AC research and practice might inform the assessment of personality. This review shows that, although performance behaviors in ACs are likely a function of personality, the constructs measured in ACs tend to be modestly related to self-reports of personality, regardless of whether AC performance is assessed in terms of dimensions, exercises, or the OAR. Nevertheless, the pattern of observed relationships does provide some support for the construct-related validity of both ACs and self-reports of personality.

Together, although ACs do tap some relevant aspects of personality, the modest correlations between the two suggest that the constructs measured in typical ACs are not interchangeable with those measured with personality scales. That said, it is difficult to know whether correlations are weak because AC dimensions and personality constructs are actually that different or because ACs and self-reports of personality reflect fundamentally unique methods of measurement (see Arthur & Villado, 2008). Future research directly comparing the psychometric soundness of behavioral and self-report based measures of personality could help to clarify this issue. The WSPRS research presented here seems a promising starting point. Similarly, it might be interesting to compare self-reports of traditional AC competencies to assessor ratings. By comparing different methods of measuring the same constructs, it might be possible to enhance the accuracy of prediction associated with these tools.

Practitioner's Window

1. Given the modest relationships that have been observed between measures of personality and AC ratings, practitioners should consider using both trait and AC dimensions as complementary sources of information.
2. Assessment of personality traits in ACs could take on a number of forms, such as:
   - The traditional approach of administering a personality inventory alongside simulation exercises. This may have merit, but trait scores and AC dimension ratings should be mechanically combined into more broad composites reflecting "mega-dimensions." We suspect many ACs have utilized personality test results subjectively when making final dimension ratings, often as part of the consensus process. In either event, traits and dimensions should be conceptually linked by experts familiar with both types of constructs.
   - An alternative approach that focuses on behavior within the AC (rather than self-report) would be to require assessors to write down adjectives descriptive of personality when observing candidates in simulation exercises. Assessors could then make judgments of relevant traits on rating scales that could be combined with dimension ratings (or not), as above.
   - Practitioners could formalize this by using specific behavioral scales, such as the WSPRS, that have recently been developed to assess personality-related traits directly in simulation exercises. Initial investigation into the reliability and validity of these scales has been promising.
3. Exercises should be evaluated in terms of trait activation potential and traits to be considered in each winnowed to those where there is ample opportunity to observe trait-relevant behavior. For that matter, practitioners should consider carefully which traditional AC dimensions can reasonably be assessed in each exercise in order to further reduce the cognitive load on the assessors. To the extent that a dimension has strong links to personality traits, it may be difficult to rate candidates accurately if behavior related to those traits is judged by experts to have little opportunity to be observed.

References

Arthur, W., Jr., Day, E. A., McNelly, T. L., & Edens, P. S. (2003). A meta-analysis of the criterion-related validity of assessment center dimensions. *Personnel Psychology, 56*, 125–154.

Arthur, W., Jr., Day, E. A., & Woehr, D. J. (2008). Mend it, don't end it: An alternate view of assessment center construct-related validity evidence. *Industrial and Organizational Psychology: Perspectives on Science and Practice, 1*, 105–111.

Arthur, W., Jr., & Villado, A. J. (2008). The importance of distinguishing between constructs and methods when comparing predictors in personnel selection research and practice. *Journal of Applied Psychology, 93*, 435–442.

Atkins, P.W., & Wood, R. E. (2002). Self- versus others' ratings as predictors of assessment center ratings: Validation evidence for 360-degree feedback programs. *Personnel Psychology, 55*, 871–904.

Barrick, M. R., & Mount, M. K. (1991). The Big Five personality dimensions and job performance: A meta-analysis. *Personnel Psychology, 44*, 1–26.

Baumeister, R. F., Vohs, K. D., & Funder, D. C. (2007). Psychology as the science of self-reports and finger movements: Whatever happened to actual behavior? *Perspectives on Psychological Science, 2*, 396–403.

Bing, M. N., Whanger, J. C., Davison, H. K., & VanHook, J. B. (2004). Incremental validity of the frame-of-reference effect in personality scale scores: A replication and extension. *Journal of Applied Psychology, 89*, 150–157.

Borman, W. C., & Brush, D. H. (1993). More progress toward a taxonomy of managerial performance requirements. *Human Performance, 6*, 1–21.

Bowling, N. A., & Burns, G. N. (2010). A comparison of work-specific and general personality measures as predictors of work and non-work criteria. *Personality and Individual Differences, 49*, 95–101.

Brannick, M. T. (2008). Back to basics of test construction and scoring. *Industrial and Organizational Psychology: Perspectives on Science and Practice, 1*, 131–133.

Brunell, A. B., Gentry, W. A., Campbell, W. K., Hoffman, B. J., Kuhnert, K. W., & DeMarree, K. G. (2008). Leader emergence: The case of the narcissistic leader. *Personality and Social Psychology Bulletin, 34*, 1663–1676.

Callinan, M., & Robertson, I. T. (2000). Work sample testing. *International Journal of Selection and Assessment, 8*, 248–260.

Chan, D. (1996). Criterion and construct validation of an assessment centre. *Journal of Occupational and Organizational Psychology, 69*, 167–181.

Christiansen, N. D., Burns, G., & Montgomery, G. E. (2005). Reconsidering the use of forced-choice formats for applicant personality assessment. *Human Performance, 18*, 267–307.

Christiansen, N. D., Burns, G., & Rozek, R. F. (2010). Effects of socially desirable responding on hiring judgments. *Journal of Personnel Psychology, 9*, 27–39.

Christiansen, N. D., Honts, C. R., & Speer, A. B. (2011, May). *Assessment of personality through behavioral observations in work simulations.* Paper presented at the 15th Conference of the European Association of Work and Organizational Psychology, Maastricht, The Netherlands.

Collins, J. M., Schmidt, F. L., Sanchez-Ku, M., Thomas, L., McDaniel, M. A., & Le, H. (2003). Can basic individual differences shed light on the construct meaning of assessment center evaluations? *International Journal of Selection and Assessment, 11*, 17–29.

Connelly, B. S., & Ones, D. S. (2010). An other perspective on personality: Meta-analytic integration of observers' accuracy and predictive validity. *Psychological Bulletin, 136*, 1092–1122.

Craik, K. H., Ware, A. P., Kamp, J., O'Reilly, C., Staw, B., & Zedeck, S. (2002). Explorations of construct validity in a combined managerial and personality assessment programme. *Journal of Occupational and Organizational Psychology, 75*, 171–193.

Cronbach, L. J., & Meehl, P. E. (1955). Construct validity in psychological tests. *Psychological Bulletin, 52*, 281–302.

Dilchert, S., & Ones, D. S. (2009). Assessment center dimensions: Individual differences correlates and meta-analytic incremental validity. *International Journal of Selection and Assessment, 17*, 254–270.

Fleenor, J. W. (1996). Constructs and developmental assessment centers: Further troubling empirical findings. *Journal of Business and Psychology, 10*, 319–335.

Foti, R. J., & Hauenstein, N. M. (2007). Pattern and variable approaches in leadership emergence and effectiveness. *Journal of Applied Psychology, 92*, 347–355.

Funder, D. C. (1999). *Personality judgment: A realistic approach to person perception.* San Diego, CA: Academic Press.

Funder, D. C., Furr, R. M., & Colvin, C. R. (2000). The Riverside Behavioral Q-sort: A tool for the description of social behavior. *Journal of Personality, 68*, 450–489.

Gaugler, B. B., Rosenthal, D. B., Thornton, G. C., & Bentson, C. (1987). Meta-analysis of assessment center validity. *Journal of Applied Psychology, 72*, 493–511.

Gaugler, B. B., & Thornton, G. C. (1989). Number of assessment center dimensions as a determinant of assessor accuracy. *Journal of Applied Psychology, 74*, 611–618.

Goffin, R. D., Rothstein, M. G., & Johnston, N. G. (1996). Personality testing and the assessment center: Incremental validity for managerial selection. *Journal of Applied Psychology, 81*, 746–756.

Goldberg, L. R., Johnson, J. A., Eber, H. W., Hogan, R., Ashton, M. C., Cloninger, C. R., & Gough, H. C. (2006). The International Personality Item Pool and the future of public-domain personality measures. *Journal of Research in Personality, 40*, 84–96.

Haaland, S., & Christiansen, N. D. (2002). Implications of trait-activation theory for evaluating the construct validity of assessment center ratings. *Personnel Psychology, 55*, 137–163.

Hausknecht, J. P., Day, D. V., & Thomas, S. C. (2004). Applicant reactions to selection procedures: An updated model and meta-analysis. *Personnel Psychology, 57*, 639–683.

Heller, D., Ferris, D. L., Brown, D., & Watson, D. (2009). The influence of work personality on job satisfaction: Incremental validity and mediation effects. *Journal of Personality, 77*, 1051–1084.
Hoeft, S., & Schuler, H. (2001). The conceptual basis of assessment centre ratings. *International Journal of Selection and Assessment, 9*, 114–123.
Hoffman, B. J., Melchers, K. G., Blair, C. A., Kleinmann, M., & Ladd, R. T. (2011). Exercises and dimensions are the currency of assessment centers. *Personnel Psychology, 64*, 351–395.
Hoffman, B. J., & Woehr, D. J. (2009). Disentangling the meaning of multisource performance rating source and dimension factors. *Personnel Psychology, 62*, 735–765.
Jackson, D. J., Stillman, J. A., & Englert, P. (2010). Task-based assessment centers: Empirical support for a systems model. *International Journal of Selection and Assessment, 18*, 141–154.
Jansen, A., Lievens, F., & Kleinmann, M. (2011). Do individual differences in perceiving situational demands moderate the relationship between personality and assessment center dimension ratings? *Human Performance, 24*, 231–250.
Judge, T. A., Bono, J. E., Ilies, R., & Gerhardt, M. W. (2002). Personality and leadership: A qualitative and quantitative review. *Journal of Applied Psychology, 87*, 765–780.
Kleinmann, M., Ingold, P. V., Lievens, F., Jansen, A., Melchers, K. G., & König, C. J. (2011). A different look at why selection procedures work: The role of candidates' ability to identify criteria. *Organizational Psychology Review, 1*, 128–146.
Kolk, N. J., Born, M. P., & Van der Flier, H. (2004). Three method factors explaining the low correlations between assessment center dimension ratings and scores on personality inventories. *European Journal of Personality, 18*, 127–141.
Krajewski, H. T., Goffin, R. D., Rothstein, M. G., & Johnston, N. G. (2007). Is personality related to assessment center performance? That depends on how old you are. *Journal of Business and Psychology, 22*, 21–33.
Lance, C. E. (2008). Where have we been, how did we get there, and where shall we go? *Industrial and Organizational Psychology: Perspectives on Science and Practice, 1*, 140–146.
Lievens, F., Chasteen, C. S., Day, E. D., & Christiansen, N. D. (2006). Large-scale investigation of the role of trait activation theory for understanding assessment center convergent and discriminant validity. *Journal of Applied Psychology, 91*, 247–258.
Lievens, F., De Corte, W., & Schollaert, E. (2008). A closer look at the frame-of-reference effect in personality scale scores and validity. *Journal of Applied Psychology, 93*, 268–279.
Lievens, F., De Fruyt, F., & Van Dam, K. (2001). Assessors' use of personality traits in descriptions of assessment centre candidates: A five-factor model perspective. *Journal of Occupational and Organizational Psychology, 74*, 623–636.
Lievens, F., Tett, R. P., & Schleicher, D. J. (2009). Assessment centers at the crossroads: Toward a reconceptualization of assessment center exercises. *Research in Personnel and Human Resources Management, 28*, 99–152.
McCrae, R. R., & John, O. P. (1992). An introduction to the five-factor model and its applications [Special issue]. *Journal of Personality, 60*, 175–215.
McFarland, L. A., Ryan, A. M., & Kriska, S. D. (2003). Impression management use and effectiveness across assessment methods. *Journal of Management, 29*, 641–661.
McFarland, L. A., Yun, G., Harold, C. M., Viera, L., & Moore, L. G. (2005). An examination of impression management use and effectiveness across assessment center exercises: The role of competency demands. *Personnel Psychology, 58*, 949–980.
Meriac, J. P., Hoffman, B. J., Woehr, D. J., & Fleisher, M. S. (2008). Further evidence for the validity of assessment center dimensions: A meta-analysis of the incremental criterion-related validity of dimension ratings. *Journal of Applied Psychology, 93*, 1042–1052.
Meyer, R. D., Dalal, R. S., & Bonaccio, S. (2009). A meta-analytic investigation into the moderating effects of situational strength on the conscientiousness–performance relationship. *Journal of Organizational Behavior, 30*, 1077–1102.
Mischel, W. (1973). Toward a cognitive social learning reconceptualization of personality. *Psychological Review, 80*, 252–283.
Mischel, W., & Shoda, Y. (1995). A cognitive-affective system theory of personality: Reconceptualizing situations, dispositions, dynamics, and invariance in personality structure. *Psychological Review, 102*, 246–268.
Monahan, E., Hoffman, B. J., Williams, A., & Lance, C. (2012). *A meta-analysis of the validity of assessment center exercises*. Paper presented at the 27th annual SIOP conference, April San Diego, CA.
Morgeson, F. P., Campion, M. A., Dipboye, R. L., Hollenbeck, J. R., Murphy, K., & Schmitt, N. (2007). Reconsidering the use of personality tests in personnel selection contexts. *Personnel Psychology, 60*, 683–729.
Neidig, R. D., & Neidig, P. J. (1984). Multiple assessment center exercises and job relatedness. *Journal of Applied Psychology, 69*, 182–186.

Rupp, D. E., Thornton, G. C., & Gibbons, A. M. (2008). The construct validity of the assessment center method and usefulness of dimensions as focal constructs. *Industrial and Organizational Psychology: Perspectives on Science and Practice, 1*, 116–120.

Sackett, P. R., Zedeck, S., & Fogli, L. (1988). Relations between measures of typical and maximum job performance. *Journal of Applied Psychology, 73*, 482–486.

Schmidt, F. L., & Hunter, J. E. (1998). The validity and utility of selection methods in personnel psychology: Practical and theoretical implications of 85 years of research findings. *Psychological Bulletin, 124*, 262–274.

Schmit, M. J., & Ryan, A. M. (1993). The Big Five in personnel selection: Factor structure in applicant and non-applicant populations. *Journal of Applied Psychology, 78*, 966–974.

Schmitt, N. (1977). Interrater agreement in dimensionality and combination of assessment center judgments. *Journal of Applied Psychology, 62*, 171–176.

Scholz, G., & Schuler, H. (1993). Das nomologische netzwerk des assessment centers: Eine metaanalyse [The nomological network of assessment centers]. *Zeitschrift für Arbeits und Organisationspsychologie, 37*, 73–85.

Shore, T. H., Thornton, G. C., & Shore, L. M. (1990). Construct validity of two categories of assessment center dimension ratings. *Personnel Psychology, 43*, 101–116.

Spector, P. E., Schneider, J. R., Vance, C. A., & Hezlett, S. A. (2000). The relation of cognitive ability and personality traits to assessment center performance. *Journal of Applied Social Psychology, 30*, 1474–1491.

Spychalski, A. C., Quiñones, M. A., Gaugler, B. B., & Pohley, K. (1997). A survey of assessment center practices in organizations in the United States. *Personnel Psychology, 50*, 71–90.

Tett, R. P., & Burnett, D. D. (2003). A personality trait-based interactionist model of job performance. *Journal of Applied Psychology, 88*, 500–517.

Tett, R. P., & Christiansen, N. D. (2007). Personality tests at the crossroads: A response to Morgeson, Campion, Dipboye, Hollenbeck, Murphy, and Schmitt. *Personnel Psychology, 60*, 967–993.

Tett, R. P., & Guterman, H. A. (2000). Situation trait relevance, trait expression, and cross-situational consistency: Testing a principle of trait activation. *Journal of Research in Personality, 34*, 397–423.

Thornton, G. C., Tziner, A., Dahan, M., Clevenger, J. P., & Meir, E. (1997). Construct validity of assessment center judgments: Analyses of the behavioral reporting method. *Journal of Social Behavior and Personality, 12*, 109–128.

Van Iddekinge, C. H., Raymark, P. H., & Roth, P. L. (2005). Assessing personality with a structured employment interview: Construct related validity and susceptibility to response inflation. *Journal of Applied Psychology, 90*, 536–552.

Viswesvaran, C., Schmidt, F. L., & Ones, D. S. (2005). Is there a general factor in ratings of job performance? A meta-analytic framework for disentangling substantive and error influences. *Journal of Applied Psychology, 90*, 108–131.

Wernimont, P. F., & Campbell, J. P. (1968). Signs, samples, and criteria. *Journal of Applied Psychology, 52*, 372–376.

Woehr, D. J., & Arthur, W., Jr. (2003). The construct-related validity of assessment center ratings: A review and meta-analysis of the role of methodological factors. *Journal of Management, 29*, 231–258.

22

Content Analysis of Personality at Work

Jennifer M. Ragsdale, Neil D. Christiansen, Christopher T. Frost, John A. Rahael, and Gary N. Burns

When assertiveness is required for successful job performance, how can we tell which of the two job candidates is likely to be more assertive? If we were to survey the current literature in industrial-organizational (I-O) psychology, we would conclude that we should find a personality inventory that measures assertiveness and administer it to each of them. In research published in psychology as a whole, the preponderance of empirical studies that examine personality constructs at work use self-report questionnaires where individuals choose answers from a fixed set of response options. As McAdams (1995) and others have noted, this process is very different from how we generally get to know people in our everyday lives, typically based on conversations and observations where responses are much less constrained. Although self-report inventories have many advantages, their practicality may come at a cost in terms of the research questions that get asked and the type of personality constructs that are studied (Dunning, Heath, & Suls, 2004). This is no less true in work settings.

The purpose of this chapter is to examine the use of content coding of written and verbal material to draw inferences about personality for research and practice in the psychology of work. Most often, the material coded will be responses to open-ended questions, but other content, such as the text of emails to coworkers or recorded conversations with customers, may also contain useful information relevant to personality. We start by providing an overview of content analysis and its history. Next, we examine the variety of materials to which content analysis can be applied and the type of personality information that content analysis typically yields. A step-by-step guide for use of content analysis techniques is then presented along with illustrative case examples. Finally, we discuss the use of automated essay scoring (AES) to reduce the time and cost of content analysis while still providing reliable and valid scores.

Background on Content Analysis

Content analysis is a technique used for systematically extracting information from written or verbal material. Thus, a large body of qualitative information can be reduced into a more manageable quantitative form (Smith, 2000). Content analysis may be used for exploratory research, theory development, hypothesis testing, or as an assessment tool used to make applied decisions about individuals. It can be applied to such qualitative material as archival records or open-ended responses that range from sentence completion to an extensive narrative (Woike, 2007). This process of scoring the material is often referred to as coding. Raters, or coders, examine the content for specified characteristics such as categories, frequencies, or themes. The consistent application of the coding process across all material is intended to yield scores that can be subjected to the same psychometric scrutiny as those derived from other assessment methods.

Use of Content Analysis in Personality Assessment

Some of the earliest research using content analysis to assess personality focused on the use of projective tests, historical documents, and verbal transcripts to make inferences about individuals' motive dispositions (Winter, 1992). Perhaps the most well-known method for assessing personality using content analysis evolved for responses to projective tests such as the Thematic Apperception Test (TAT; Murray, 1943). With this method, people are asked to tell stories about what is taking place in contextually vague pictures. These stories are coded for thematic content related to the motives of interest, such as Need for Achievement, Need for Power, and Need for Affiliation. Applications of these coding systems were soon expanded to include historical documents and other sources of text. For example, McClelland (1961) used content analysis of historical documents to show that power imagery present in historical literature declined following wars, whereas affiliation imagery increased. More recent applications include examining the content of press transcripts from world leaders for imagery related to affiliation and power (Hermann, 1979). These examples illustrate how content analysis of text has been used successfully to assess personality factors from individuals who may be unavailable to direct methods of surveying.

Although still used in some areas of psychology, content analysis is rarely applied in research or practice within I-O psychology. It is reasonable to conclude that this is due to beliefs that the limitations outweigh the potential benefits. Probably, the most salient concern is the time and effort required to collect and code the verbal responses. From the perspective of the individual being assessed, constructing an open-ended response may require more effort than selecting a number on a response scale, and not all respondents are motivated to expend the effort required to give a meaningful response. The individual's effort may be minimized by using existing sources of verbal material, recording an interview, administering an online assessment, or setting word limits. For the researcher or practitioner, it takes more than just time to read through and score the responses after they have been collected. These types of assessments require extensive training on coding systems to achieve adequate reliability. This is especially apparent when compared to self-report survey assessments, where no such training is necessary and scoring requires much less time. However, if good coders can commit to long-term involvement in projects requiring content analysis, they can engage in ongoing coding efforts as well as training of future coders. Therefore, the initial effort may result in a continuous cycle of coding and training. If such people-resources are unavailable, an alternative is to use AES software. The use of such software will be discussed later in the chapter.

Another concern is the reliability of scores derived from content analysis. Content analysis is often associated with projective measures of personality, such as the TAT, that have been frequently criticized for having poor reliability despite the best efforts of researchers to train coders (Smith, 1992). For example, the TAT may display poor internal consistency when each story is considered as an item, as it may take several stories before a theme or pattern emerges. A reasonable alternative is to utilize a test–retest design based on overall scores, but this approach has also led to generally disappointing stability estimates (Smith, 1992). On the whole, the most appropriate reliability measures may be interrater reliability estimates, as rater errors tend to be the single largest source of error in the scoring of projective tests (Kazdin, 2003).

Despite these limitations, there are benefits to employing content analytic methods (Kazdin, 2003; Woike, 2007). First, a constructed-response format allows implicit traits to manifest in the written or verbal material. Such aspects of personality are distinct from traits assessed using explicit measures as they are not readily accessible to the individual (see Chapter 7, this volume). Furthermore, using content analysis to assess motive dispositions is useful because of the potential for themes to emerge across responses (Kazdin, 2003). Second, open-ended questions need not target a specific personality construct to provide relevant information on a range of traits. Because of this, responses can even be reanalyzed for information on different variables that become of interest long after the data have been collected. Third, characteristics of the response structure can be analyzed to provide insight into personality, including elements such as the overall affective tone or conceptual and integrative complexity of the response. Fourth, open-ended questions can capture unique responses from individuals who have a low base rate of occurring and would typically not be afforded a response option on a fixed scale. Finally, as mentioned above, content analysis may be applied to available written or verbal content generated by individuals for whom there would not normally be an opportunity to observe or survey them (e.g., dead politicians). Content analysis provides a systematic way to examine the extent to which personality affects verbal content in different ways. Personality may influence the behavior expressed in the original situation being discussed, as well as the traits that played a role in creating the situation (Funder & Ozer, 1983). Beyond the situation itself, personality affects the specific story out of many that an individual chooses to tell. Finally, personality will affect the content of the story itself and how individuals represent themselves.

Content in the Workplace

Whether it is during an interview for hiring purposes or just talking to coworkers in order to determine an appropriate influencing tactic, people routinely interpret others' verbal and written communication in order to make inferences about personality and inform decision making. However, doing this in an unsystematic manner can result in key pieces of information being overlooked or the misattribution of characteristics of the message content (Smith, 2000). Content analytic methods were derived to improve the accuracy of such inferences with the hope of improving decisions made based on them.

Within the context of applying for a job, a variety of content is generated by applicants that may be subjected to content analytic procedures. The most obvious are responses to open-ended questions during the employment interview. The resume and cover letter also provide content that could be coded (e.g., Cole, Field, Giles, & Harris, 2009). For workers already on the job, they could be asked to keep work diaries of notable events. Emails, memoranda, and incident reports may be written by the individuals for whom we wish to learn more about. What is said during role-plays or group discussions from training and development activities may be recorded for transcription. With the rate at which social networking (e.g., Twitter, Facebook, LinkedIn) is being used within organizations, even more content is available for analysis. In theory, anything that is spoken or written at work could be saved for later analysis. Depending on the organization's policies about the use of technology such as email, ethical issues may arise if this were done without the consent of the individual who was being recorded or whose written work was being analyzed. This ethical gray area may be dealt with by developing clear rules about the types of email communications analyzed. For example, one might include only emails sent to other company email addresses and exclude any personal email addresses. Another alternative to managing confidentiality could involve hiring a consultant to do the analysis so that no one else within the organization would see the emails and the consultant would not divulge any identifying information. Automated scoring procedures may also be used, especially when the personal or sensitive content may be involved.

Although verbal material from job interviews, role-plays, or conversations can be coded, most often it will be advantageous to convert verbal statements to written passages by transcription. Coding is simpler when material is broken into discrete units, allowing coders to move forward and backward as needed among written passages. Of course, information about nonverbal aspects (such as pitch or tone) is lost in the transcription, but these features are not typically coded in content analysis. For written assessments, it may be useful to include some elements of tone by encouraging individuals to use emoticons. In some assessments where tone might be particularly important, adding a behavioral observation component can help address additional information that is not captured in verbal responses.

We can learn a lot about a person from the stories he or she tells (e.g., McAdams, 1985); the same is true in the context of work. For example, during an interview, hiring managers can make inferences about an applicant's personality (among other things) from the stories he or she recounts about previous work experiences with other employers. The success of McAdams' life story methods suggests that the methodology could be adapted to provide a contextualized assessment of personality at work that has the potential to access information beyond what is provided by explicit measures. In our research that will serve as an illustrative example in this chapter, individuals were asked to describe specific experiences that occurred *at work*. Some questions were directly based on the life narrative questions but were adapted to ask about a specific work experience. The content analysis cases presented later in the chapter are based on data collected using such work narratives.

Coding for Personality Constructs

One of the benefits of utilizing qualitative work-related materials is the opportunity it affords to code for numerous personality constructs; therefore, it is important to distinguish between constructs. In order to organize the ways in which personality psychologists examine the multifaceted nature of individuality, McAdams (1995) proposed a model of personality that involves three distinct levels. The first level consists of *dispositional traits* that account for consistencies in behavior across situations (e.g., McCrae & Costa, 1987). These tend to be the focus of most self-report personality inventories. The second level consists of *characteristic adaptations*, which represents the motivational, social-cognitive, and developmental aspects of personality. These include goals, motives, concerns, and strivings contextualized in time, place, or one's social role. Although less likely to be assessed by personality tests, those tests that focus on a work frame-of-reference may incorporate some information from this level. Finally, the third level consists of *integrative life stories*, which are evolving narratives of the self that speak to how individuals view themselves and their positions in the world. By applying content analysis to work-related verbal materials, attention can be focused on more than just trait descriptions of personality.

Traditionally, self-report questionnaires are used in the work setting to study personality. These are labeled *explicit* measures, due to the direct nature of their prompts and the extent to which individuals directly attribute traits to themselves. However, sometimes people act less deliberately and more impulsively and cannot access information about themselves to explain this behavior. Assessments used to capture such unconscious processes are generally called *indirect* or *implicit* measures. Across implicit methods for assessing personality, assumptions differ about how underlying traits affect responses. However, what all implicit methods hold in common is that the process whereby personality impacts responses is not obvious to the respondent.

Past research using content analysis to examine motives such as need for achievement or need for affiliation argues that this level of assessment is implicit. McClelland, Koestner, and Weinberger (1989) state:

> From the beginning of the work on the achievement motive, it has been apparent that motive dispositions coded in imaginative thought from the stories written to pictures differ from motive dispositions with the same name as measured in self-reported desires or interests.
>
> *p. 690*

Additional research demonstrates that implicit measures do not correlate strongly with explicit measures that reflect processing in the deliberative system. For example, an individual might self-report that their academic motivation is driven by a high need for achievement, while an implicit measure suggests that a power motive drives their academic behavior more than they might care to admit. From this perspective, it may come as little surprise that correlations between self-reported motives and implicit motives are not strong (e.g., McClelland et al., 1989).

Self-reported motives and implicit motives may also predict different types of behaviors and outcomes. McClelland and his colleagues argue that implicit motives should predict "spontaneous behavioral trends over time" (p. 691), while self-reported motives should better predict actions in specific situations (McClelland et al., 1989; see also McClelland, 1980). Given that some incidents in the workplace that have important consequences may involve spur-of-the-moment reactions to unexpected events, there may be value in developing practical ways to assess implicit traits and motives.

Content Analysis and Traits

Content analysis is an effective strategy in trait-based approaches to personality assessment. There is a rich history of trait assessment through sentence completion and word fragments (for a review, see Holaday, Smith, & Sherry, 2000). In addition, recent research has linked personality and content analysis of word use in several different contexts, including directed writing assignments (Hirsh & Peterson, 2009), recordings of day-to-day speech (Mehl, Gosling, & Pennebaker, 2006), and blog postings (Yarkoni, 2010). Within the workplace, these techniques have been used as projective assessment procedures with job applicants or as techniques to examine selection interviews or even resumes.

Word Frequency

People express their personality not just in what they think, feel, or do, but in the words they use to express what they think, feel, or do. In examining word use, strong findings have been found for the traits of extraversion and neuroticism in relation to words used that are associated with positive or negative emotions (Hirsh & Peterson, 2009; Pennebaker & King, 1999). For example, Yarkoni (2010) found that blog writers with higher levels of neuroticism tended to use words associated with anxiety, fear, sadness, and anger more than bloggers who were more emotionally stable. Similarly, more extraverted bloggers tended to use words referencing positive emotions, friends, social events, and sexuality than more introverted bloggers. These patterns of personality and language also hold in spoken conversation, with word use correlating with both self-report and observer ratings of personality (Fast & Funder, 2008).

Sentence Completion

The use of sentence completion tests have been a popular option for practitioners assessing personality for the last several decades (Holaday et al., 2000). With its rise in the 1930s, early sentence completion tests focused on psychodynamic theory to gain insight into patients' problems (Tendler, 1930). Since that time, sentence completion tests have primarily been used to assess motive dispositions (i.e., *The Sentence Completion Method*; Rohde, 1946) or ego development (i.e., *Sentence Completion Test of Ego Development*; Loevinger, 1987). However, these tests have also been used to assess traits. The *Personnel Reaction Blank* (Gough, 1971) was developed to measure integrity in job applicants. Although examples of these trait-based sentence completion tests are less common, development-based tests such as the *Washington University Sentence Completion Test* can be rescored to capture information on traits related to the Five-Factor Model (FFM; Hogansen & Lanning, 2001).

Word Fragments

Word fragment tests involve presenting respondents with incomplete word stems and asking them to complete each word. Stimuli in these approaches are developed in such a way that there are multiple correct answers, with the belief that implicit personality traits or attitudes will influence which word is provided. Research has linked extraversion and neuroticism to completion of positive and negative word fragments (Rusting & Larsen, 1998), with more recent research focusing on linking word completion with aggression (Anderson, Carnagey, & Eubanks, 2003). Although more aggressive word fragment responses were generated when participants were primed by exposure to violent media (Anderson et al., 2003), they typically do not correlate well with trait-based measures of aggression (Barlett & Rodeheffer, 2009). Affective traits assessed through word fragment tasks were predictive of supervisor ratings of job performance (Johnson, Tolentino, Rodopman, & Cho, 2010). For example, trait positive affectivity predicted task performance (β = .38), organization citizenship behaviors directed at the individual (OCBI; β = .37), and organization citizenship behaviors directed at the organization (OCBO; β = .40). Trait negative affectivity predicted task performance (β = −.22) and OCBO (β = −.17). Taken together, trait affectivity assessed with word fragments predicted incremental variance in task performance (ΔR^2 = .24), OCBI (ΔR^2 = .22), and OCBO (ΔR^2 = .26), beyond self-reported trait affectivity.

Personal Narratives, Stories, and Diaries

When individuals tell stories about their life or work experiences, narrative themes such as agency and communion, redemption and contamination, cognitive complexity, and affective tone may provide information about personality. For example, narrative themes have been linked to self-reports of dispositional traits (e.g., McAdams et al., 2004). As might be expected, neuroticism was related to an emotionally negative life story tone. Agreeableness was related to the communion theme, and openness to experience to the complexity of the narratives. Although research has linked narrative indices to such dispositional traits, each approach appears to provide unique information about personality (McAdams et al., 2004).

Resume Content

Similar to the other techniques described above, job applicants' resumes can be content analyzed to reveal meaningful personality information. The content within resumes has been shown to correlate with the FFM traits (Cole et al., 2009). For example, conscientiousness was linked to both grade point average (GPA) as well as membership in professional societies, whereas extraversion was linked to leadership positions and volunteer activities. In our own research, we have found that it is not only resume content that is related to personality but also stylistic features of resumes (Christiansen & Burns, 2008). In terms of content, personality traits such as extraversion manifested in how many leadership positions were listed on the resume, and those higher in agreeableness were more likely to include memberships in social organizations. With regard to stylistic characteristics, job applicants high in conscientiousness tended to use more consistent formatting and provide clear focus within sections of the resume, whereas those high in extraversion tended to produce more attractive resumes by using less traditional fonts and formatting.

Content Analysis and Motives

Motives assessed with implicit methods have been related to both the process and outcomes of work, particularly need for achievement and need for affiliation. *Need for achievement* refers to the drive to accomplish a goal related to performing at some standard of excellence or outperforming others. Alternatively, *need for affiliation* refers to the drive to establish and maintain personal relationships. For example, the achievement motive has a strong relationship with task choice and task success across a wide range of domains (Atkinson & Feather, 1996). Individuals with a high achievement motive tend to be more involved and interested in their work and are more likely to seek out feedback about their ongoing performance (Klich & Feldman, 1992; Veroff, 1982). Similarly, motive dispositions are also related to occupational choice (McClelland, 1965, 1987; McClelland & Winter, 1971), upward mobility (Andrews, 1967; Crockett, 1962), and job success (McClelland & Burnham, 1976). For example, achievement motivation has been shown to be related to being promoted (r = .43) and receiving more raises (r = .36), especially when the organization values achievement (Andrews, 1967). Conversely, individuals with a high affiliation motive tend to react more negatively and perform worse in competitive work contexts (Karabenick, 1977). This can extend to choice of coworkers, such that individuals with high affiliation motives have a tendency to choose friends to work with, whereas individuals with high achievement motives prefer experts or those most competent as their partners (French, 1956).

Another motive important for predicting how individuals respond to different situations is uncertainty orientation, which has received even less attention in the work context. The notion of uncertainty orientation grew out of Kagan's (1972) assertion that uncertainty resolution is a primary determinant of behavior. People will sometimes approach or avoid ambiguous situations depending on the availability of coping mechanisms and the extent to which the nature of involvement in the situation is voluntary. In such situations, the primary motive is to resolve the uncertainty, and other motives are considered to be secondary (Sorrentino & Short, 1986). In general, individuals identified as more uncertainty oriented are assumed to be motivated primarily by the need to approach and understand uncertainty. Those lower on uncertainty orientation, on the other hand, are motivated to maintain clarity through relying on what is already known (Raynor & McFarlin, 1986; Sorrentino & Short, 1986).

Steps in Content Coding

There are several steps to consider when developing a content coding system (Smith, 2000; Woike, 2007). We present guidelines below and use our own research on work narratives as an illustrative example of key decisions made during the process. Some of the steps include identifying what is to be measured, creating appropriate cues or questions to get the best information, determining the unit of analysis to be coded, determining how the content will be coded, and then pilot testing and revising the system. The critical steps are listed in Table 22.1.

Table 22.1 Steps in Implementing Content Analysis for Personality Assessment

Step 1: Determine your goal and what you want to assess
Step 2: Decide whether content analysis is the best approach
Step 3: Determine the material to be coded and how to obtain it
Step 4: Select or develop a content coding system
Step 5: Train coders and ensure convergence
Step 6: Pilot and revise coding system
Step 7: Collect data, code, analyze, and interpret

Step 1: Determine Your Goal and What You Want to Assess

The first step is to clarify what inferences about personality you wish to draw from the content that can be collected. This follows directly from the research question at hand. Woike (2007) identifies three types of hypotheses at this step that are not mutually exclusive. First, content analysis can focus on gleaning information about stable personality characteristics, such as traits, that can be used to order individuals for the purposes of prediction. This would be most likely in applied scenarios where one is interested in predicting who is most likely to be successful on the job or fit with a given organizational culture. Second, open-ended questions can be used to assess individuals' understanding of certain events, such as job redesign process or downsizing. In this case, the resulting information would likely be used as an intervening variable to understand why traits assessed with a traditional method result in certain work behavior or outcomes. Finally, the content coding may serve as the outcome variable that is being explained in the research by other predictors. For example, if managers kept performance diaries of subordinates, these could be assessed for explanatory style to determine if certain types of leaders (measured independently) explain performance issues in terms of controllable or uncontrollable events.

In our work narrative research, the goal was to assess the personality characteristics that would predict the work environments in which individuals are likely to excel. The resulting information could be used to place individuals in preferred environments or those that will result in success, or perhaps to manipulate aspects of the environment to motivate or support employees. After reviewing previous research, we hypothesized that those with a high need for achievement would prefer a more competitive and results-driven organization, while those with a high need for affiliation would prefer a more team-based and collaborative organizational culture. Similarly, we were interested in how individuals' orientation to uncertainty would explain their preferences in terms of work environment and how this was related to the stress process.

Step 2: Decide Whether Content Analysis Is the Best Approach

As mentioned previously, surveying employees using self-report personality inventories is typically the preferred method for assessing personality. However, there may be some situations where using surveys will not be the best approach and the time and effort necessary for content analysis is justified. Content analysis is preferred when individuals are not available for observation or surveying; the "artifacts" they have left behind in terms of recorded verbal or written material may be all that is available. If the researcher wished to include managers in their sample who were no longer with the organization along with those who are still there, such content might be the only way to draw inferences about personality. Another situation where content analysis might be preferred is when the assessment already involves content that is usually analyzed with less systematic methods such as subjective ratings, interviews, or work simulations.

The additional effort may also be justified when the constructs of interest may not be assessed very well by personality inventories or where such instruments do not yet exist. In the former case, it has been argued that implicit traits and motive dispositions assessed in less structured assessments where responses are constructed are different constructs than those measured by self-report inventories (McClelland, 1980). Researchers interested in aspects of personality that are less available to conscious introspection may consider the time and effort of content analytic methods justified. Those researchers interested in constructs where more convenient measures do not yet exist may also find the trade-off between developing and coding content versus multiple pilot studies to obtain a psychometrically sound questionnaire to their liking.

Finally, in research design, it is not always desirable to use the same method of assessment for all predictors and criteria as there are concerns about effects of common method variance. By choosing content analysis using trained coders who are blind to scores on traditional surveys used in other aspects of the design, such concerns are minimized. Of course, multiple methods of assessment are desirable when the research design and resources allow.

When we considered whether content analysis was the best approach to measure need for achievement and uncertainty orientation, we explored the possibility of using self-report ratings of motives. Research has shown that motives assessed through rating scales are more strongly related to performance when there are external rewards (McClelland et al., 1989); on the other hand, motives assessed through content analytic assessments are more strongly related to behaviors in which the task or environment is inherently characterized by rewards of interest. With regard to uncertainty orientation, we had concerns that individuals may not always be aware when they are approaching or avoiding aspects of the work environment. Since we were interested in the organization or environment in which individuals are most likely to prefer, we thought that a content analytic approach would provide the most rich, and ultimately useful, data.

Step 3: Determine the Material to Be Coded and How to Obtain It

By this stage of the process, the researchers should have a firm notion of what the material to be used will be, as it must be assumed to contain information relevant to the personality constructs of interest. However, many decisions still need to be made with regard to the exact content and data collection methods. Which exact questions will be asked of respondents? Will there be any limits to response length in terms of the minimum or maximum number of words? Will responses be anonymous or just confidential? If there are questions asked, how specific should they be? If they are broad and open (e.g., "Tell me about your last job?"), will there be too much variability in the aspects included in responses to compare across individuals? On the other hand, if the questions restrict responses to basic agreement with a statement, a close-ended survey may have sufficed. In general, questions should have enough structure so that meaningful comparisons can be made across individuals. For example, we asked respondents who were telling us about their first day of work on their current or last job to focus all answers on learning the new job and adjusting to the new environment. This process is parallel to that of developing a standardized personality test. For example, a clear item (e.g., "I like to be the center of attention") would be preferred over a bad item with multiple meanings (e.g., "I am a regular person").

At this point, researchers should also decide what the unit of analysis will be in coding. Will each page of a memorandum be coded separately or the entire document? Will the entire interview be considered a discrete unit for coding purposes, or responses to each question? One implication of this is how much time coders will spend assigning scores. The more fine-grained the unit, the more time and coders will be required to generate scores useable in quantitative analysis. Aggregating across multiple units will provide more stable scores. However, even when resources allow for it, making the units so small that the base rate of the phenomenon occurring is quite low will result in little payoff relative to using larger units that do not need to be aggregated. In the end, researchers must keep in mind at what level of analysis the tests of the hypotheses will occur and whether the benefits of aggregation outweigh the costs.

In our research, we adapted McAdams' (1985) life story interview by asking individuals to describe specific experiences that occurred *at work*. In all, six questions were included in the work narrative interview. These were designed to be broad enough so that the constructs being assessed would not be transparent, but specific enough that they would solicit responses that would contain themes that are important to the participant. Some questions were directly based on the life narrative questions but were adapted to ask about a specific work experience. See Table 22.2 for examples of the questions used.

Table 22.2 Example Work Narrative Questions

1. Discuss what happened the first day of your most recent job and how it went
2. Describe a work experience (specific situation) that was a significant turning point in your work life
3. Describe an experience at work (specific situation) when you were uncertain of what was expected of you and were unsure of how to proceed
4. Describe when a major and unexpected change occurred at work
5. Describe an ideal future workplace experience (specific situation) that you want to occur
6. Describe an experience (specific situation) when you were faced with a new challenge at work

Resource constraints dictated many of the decisions of how the narrative responses would be collected in our research. Ideally, we would have had trained interviewers asking the questions, with individuals compensated for participating in face-to-face interviews, with recorded audio responses, and had them transcribed to written text. Unfortunately, available funds were modest, and we estimated that at least US$50 would be needed to adequately compensate working individuals to show up and participate in 1-hour interviews. Transcription services can easily cost half that amount per interview. We therefore decided to use an online text-based "interview" in order to collect data from employed individuals from across the United States and reduce costs to closer to US$20 per participant. We initially prescreened potential participants with a brief survey that included an open-ended question and only followed up with those that provided a detailed response to that question. We decided against maximum time limits or the collection of identifiable information. Therefore, individuals were able to complete the online text-based interview at their own pace with complete anonymity. It was required that individuals provide detailed responses with at least 10 sentences or 200 words to each question in order to get paid and be included in the study. Each answer would be discretely coded and scores from each story would then be summed together for a final score on each dimension of interest.

Step 4: Select or Develop a Content Coding System

The next step in the process is to identify or create the systematic procedures for assigning scores to the content that will reflect elevation on the personality constructs. An important consideration is whether the coding scheme will be developed a priori, where the criteria are specified in advance, or will emerge based on reviewing the material that will be analyzed. Here, we assume that the content coding system will be determined in advance, but it should be noted that there are many applications of content analysis where the materials are inspected in order to develop a coding scheme. For example, if one were analyzing customer comments about wait staff in a restaurant, the researcher might read through all of the responses and determine that there are basically three types of comments (timeliness, demeanor, and attention to detail) and that they vary on how favorable each is. Independent coders could then categorize each comment and rate it on how favorable it is on a 5-point scale.

Whether specified in advance or not, researchers should be familiar with past efforts to code similar content. A number of coding systems have been developed in past research; therefore, a thorough review of the literature is important. Even if a coding scheme cannot be located for the exact constructs of interest, adapting a system may be easier than reinventing the wheel. Whether interested in existing coding systems or developing their own, researchers are advised to locate the edited volume *Motivation and Personality: Handbook of Thematic Content Analysis* by Smith, Atkinson, McClelland, and Veroff (1992) that has numerous examples of established systems.

Perhaps the most critical aspect of the content coding system is what types of scores are most desirable for understanding the data. Essentially, there are three types of scores that can be generated for a dimension of interest: categories, ratings, and frequencies. A categorization scheme is used to cast responses into nominal groups reflecting a broad orientation in terms of personality process or structure. For example, written emails and memoranda from an in-basket exercise could be sorted based on whether they predominantly reflect task, social, or transformational leadership. Ratings are similar but take each category as a separate dimension that is assigned a value by the coders indicating the extent along a continuum (e.g., low–high). Each discrete unit is then assigned one or more ratings; with multiple raters, the decision must be made as to whether the same raters will be used to evaluate all of the dimensions or whether some separation is desired. Frequency coding involves assigning values based on how many times something occurs rather than the extent that a response possesses some quality. Frequency counts may be used to assess the degree of a given trait. For example, one could count how many self-references were used in managers' monthly sales reports to gather information on narcissism. It is important to control for the length of the material because the frequency of trait-related terms occurring will increase with the length of the material. In some cases, this can become quite labor intensive such as if one were to instead count how many adjectives were used. At this point, researchers should also consider the possibility of using computerized scoring, which can be cost efficient for scoring frequencies but may also be trained to reproduce human ratings. We discuss this possibility in more detail below. Regardless of whether categories, ratings, or frequencies are utilized, the greater the number of discrete judgments that coders must make to assign scores, the more time will be required of them.

For the work narrative research, we needed to determine a coding system for assessing themes related to the motives of need for achievement, need for affiliation, and uncertainty orientation. The motive constructs of interest have been previously well defined and analyzed in the past (see Smith, 1992), providing us with enough information to code content with a priori rules and dimensions to guide us. However, existing scoring systems such as that developed for the TAT are labor intensive and provide more detail than would be needed in our research. We therefore chose to modify the existing scoring systems in order to simplify the process. Traditionally, the TAT coding system utilizes 12 dimensions that we integrated into four broader dimensions: (1) the extent to which there is *Need Imagery* present, (2) the extent to which there is *Instrumental Activity* performed by the person in the story, (3) the extent to which there is something *blocking or aiding* the individual in pursuit of the need, and (4) the extent to which there are *emotions* or *anticipation/frustration* related to need fulfillment/unfulfillment. Each dimension is rated on a 3-point scale: *not at all present* (0), *somewhat present* (1), and *explicit statements being made in the text* (2). Following the original TAT scoring, the last three dimensions are rated only if the first is nonzero; if Need Imagery is absent, the overall score is taken as zero. The result is a potential score of 0–8 for the response to each question. Scores are then summed across all six stories for a final score on the construct of interest. Table 22.3 provides definitions and examples of the dimensions rated in the modified coding system and example responses for each.

The coding scheme for uncertainty orientation developed by Sorrentino, Roney, and Hanna (1992) was also revised and is similar to that of the need for achievement and need for affiliation protocols. The original 10 dimensions were collapsed into four broad dimensions: (1) the extent to which a *need to master* or deal with the uncertainty is clearly stated, (2) *instrumental actions* or behaviors directed at dealing with the uncertainty, (3) *blocks* from the environment or person that interfere with dealing with the uncertainty, and (4) *affective states* associated with the success or failure in dealing with uncertainty. Corresponding to the achievement and affiliation protocols, each dimension is rated on a 3-point scale with anchors based on the dimension being *not at all present* (0), *somewhat*

Table 22.3 Achievement, Affiliation, and Uncertainty Dimensions

	nAchievement	*nAffiliation*	*Uncertainty*
Imagery			
	Competition: Engaged in activity where doing as well as or better than others is primary concern	*Feelings or desire for friendship*: Some statement of liking or desire to be liked. And/or the existence of social activities that are not instrumental for some other goal	*Uncertainty*: Statement of uncertainty, doubt of reaching outcome, and willing to approach experience
	Standard of excellence: Self-imposed requirements of performance indicated by explicit statement or concern over activities	*Reaction to separation or disruption*: Feeling bad following a separation or disruption of relationship. Concern with maintaining or restoring the relationship	*Curiosity*: Seeking to understand an unknown by expressing curiosity and actively seeks to learn more
	Long-term aspirations: Involved in a long-term achievement goal related to a standard of excellence	*Concern for others (not culturally prescribed)*: Existence of friendly, nurturing actions that are not culturally prescribed (e.g., father/son) or motivated by a sense of obligation	*Conflict*: Seeks to resolve a discrepancy between one's ideas and behaviors
Indicators			
Need directly stated	Extent to which at least one of the above achievement imagery dimensions is stated in the story indicating an achievement goal	Extent to which at least one of the above affiliation imagery dimensions is stated in the story indicating an affiliation goal	Extent to which at least one of the above uncertainty imagery dimensions is stated in the story indicating a goal of resolving uncertainty
Instrumental activities	Activities that are directly related to goal attainment, or when not completed would lead to failure	Activities that are directly related to goal attainment, or when not completed would lead to failure	Overt/covert activities directed at approaching or resolving the uncertainty
Blocks	Some characteristic of the person or environment is an obstacle to goal attainment	Some characteristic of the person or environment is an obstacle to goal attainment	Goal-directed activities are hindered in some way. Must not be the source of the uncertainty
Affective states	Affective responses to anticipated outcomes or instrumental tasks related to goal attainment	Affective responses to anticipated outcomes or instrumental tasks related to goal attainment	Feelings associated with attainment or failure to resolve or approach uncertainty

present (1), and *explicit statements being made in the text* (2). The result is a score of 0–8 for the response to each question, and scores are combined across stories.

Step 5: Train Coders and Ensure Convergence

Three things are required to train coders in scoring the content (Smith, 2000). First, there must be a clear coding manual that details rules for scoring and provides examples. This must be read carefully by all coders before training sessions, and the first step in the initial training session should be to review the manual and scoring system. Second, adequate practice materials must be available so that coders can make judgments on a realistic sample of content and then receive feedback on coding performance. Finally, there must be opportunity to discuss coding decisions in order to establish a common frame of reference. Ideally, such discussions will include an expert rater to help resolve disagreement. Often, training sessions result in refinements made to the coding protocol (i.e., adding examples, clarifying instructions).

After each session, interrater agreement (for categories) or interrater reliability (for ratings and frequencies) can be computed to determine whether adequate convergence has been achieved. For agreement, Cohen's *kappa* is often used as it takes into account the number of categories and chance agreement. With regard to interrater reliability, if all coders will evaluate all materials, then a traditional correlational model of interrater reliability is desirable; most researchers are familiar with estimates such as the average correlation between raters. If only a subset of coders will evaluate the materials from each participant, intraclass correlations may be preferred. Information about each rater can be used to identify those in need of remediation, such as the correlation between a rater and the composite of the others (e.g., the corrected item-total correlation from SPSS reliability output). Alternatively, a discrepancy score can be easily computed.

Content analysis places large demands on coders; therefore, it is important to select coders that provide accurate ratings and are reliable and committed to the project. It is recommended to train more coders than is actually needed. Only those coders who demonstrate the necessary aptitude should be selected to code for the pilot and full study. A coder can be excluded when he or she cannot achieve adequate convergence with the expert and other coders. Beyond ability, good coders are conscientious. They show up for training sessions and complete their coding on time, in the correct format. Given the time necessary to code the available content, a desirable coder will also commit to participate for the duration of the project.

The coders of the work narrative samples in our study were graduate students with no knowledge of the hypotheses in order to minimize rater effects (e.g., expectancies). Training consisted of reviewing the coding manuals and proceeding through three phases. In the first phase, coders were introduced to the construct definitions, the detailed definitions for each of the coding dimensions, and the rating protocols. Two examples were then discussed as a group, one that illustrated high need for achievement and another, high need for affiliation. An expert then demonstrated how the coding guide would be used and how each dimension would have been rated and why. The example passages are presented in Tables 22.4 and 22.5 along with coding notation, indicating how each dimension should be rated and the text within the passage that relates to it. Finally, the third phase allowed participants to practice coding, ask questions to clarify what should be coded, compare the ratings they made to those of others and the expert, and receive feedback from the expert to help improve their rating accuracy. Because our goal was to utilize only two coders per response, the benchmark was set for each coder's ratings to correlate with a composite of the others at .50. During this process, we identified two coders to be excluded from any future coding because they were unable to maintain adequate convergence with the expert and others. Training for coding uncertainty orientation followed the same procedures; the training example for this dimension is provided in Table 22.6.

Table 22.4 Narrative Response and Coding Example for High Need for Achievement

Response

My first day at my most recent job I was only given one formal day of training, which I did not think was enough time to fully understand what was needed for the job. I asked the trainer several questions, knowing that this would be the only chance I had.[3] Most of my questions were not answered, or would only be answered if that particular scenario had arrived. I was nervous[4] because I was afraid of doing a bad job.[5] I wanted to make sure and do the job well,[1,2] as many others in the past had not. I think my nervousness was justifiable, since most individuals in this position receive much more training than I received.[4] It is possible they believed that I was more competent than most, and less training would be required. I think I did the job pretty well today,[5] but certainly at first there were some difficulties. I think this shows that as long as I have some sort of direction, no matter how limited, I can accomplish anything.

Statement	*Dimension*	*Rating*	*Explanation*
1	Imagery	Present	Scored as present for concern with performing at *a standard of excellence*
2	Need stated	2	The statement relating to a *standard of excellence* was explicit
3	Instrumental activity	1	The actions described were not explicitly linked to achieving the goal of performance, but can be inferred to be linked to the goal. Should be scored either 1 or 2
4	Block/aid	1	The statement of nervousness is not a direct block to instrumental activity, but raters saw it as a statement referring to a personal block to goal attainment. There was also a statement referring to not getting enough training, indicating that this may also be a potential block
5	Anticipation of result/affect	2	This reveals that there was some anticipation of a result of failure and a description of the actual result of successful achievement of doing a good job

Note: The superscripts next to statements within the paragraph indicate the dimension relevance.

Table 22.5 Narrative Response and Coding Example for High Need for Affiliation

Response

The first day of my most recent job, I was at Teller Training. After getting to know the other tellers, I was excited to come to training the next day.[5] Because all of the training was done online or out of a manual, it seemed like the days kept dragging on. The only thing that made each day interesting was the other people I was in training with. Unfortunately none of those people were going to work at my branch, which made me really disappointed[1,2] because they were such great people. When I got to my branch after training, it just wasn't the same. Immediately I was labeled the "black sheep"[4] because I was not from the small town like every other employee there. Since then, getting up every morning to go to work has been an extreme challenge.[4] I dislike working[5] there because of how the people are and the only thing that keeps me going are the customers I have met.

Statement	*Dimension*	*Rating*	*Explanation*
1	Imagery	Present	Scored as present for a reaction to separation or disruption and/or feelings or desire for friendship
2	Need stated	2	The statement relating to a reaction to a separation or disruption was explicit
3	Instrumental activity	0	There did not appear to be any statement regarding a behavior or action to rectify the issue
4	Block	2	The statements regarding the label given to the person and the difficulty waking up in the morning seems to be an indication of a block to building friendships
5	Anticipation of result/affect	2	These statements indicate strong emotional feelings regarding the friendships or lack thereof

Note: The superscripts next to statements within the paragraph indicate the dimension relevance.

Table 22.6 Narrative Response and Coding Example for High Uncertainty Orientation

Response

After layoffs happened in my organization, I was forced to take on many new responsibilities. As I mentioned, having not been one of the employees that survived a layoff at any institution, this was very difficult for me to deal with because I was lacking critical knowledge and experience about how to perform the new duties[1] and all my other coworkers were too busy themselves to assist or train me.[4] I am familiar with the phrase trial by fire, but when you are in the midst of such a seemingly impossible workload, it is extremely daunting.[5] It is true that breaking large challenges down into smaller pieces helps, but what I have learned[2] is also very helpful is expressing your doubts and concerns to those expecting you to accomplish more than you think you can.[3] I personally don't like to admit that there is something I cannot do well and it's very difficult for me to go to my boss and explain my fears.[4] I am getting better at it, but for now, it's a balance for me to do my duties and all the additional work that has recently been placed upon me. I find that I can get things done, but sometimes not as well as I would like to do them.

Statement	*Dimension*	*Rating*	*Explanation*
1	Imagery	Present	Definite statements of uncertainty and willingness to approach or resolve it
2	Need stated	1	Not an explicit statement that author wanted/needed to learn the task, but could be inferred.
3	Instrumental activity	2	Statement of different activities used to approach/resolve uncertainty
4	Blocks	2	Explicit statement of external factors and personal obstacles that interfere with approaching/resolving uncertainty
5	Affective states	2	Explicitly stated emotion related to attempt to resolve uncertainty

Note: The superscripts next to statements within the paragraph indicate the dimension relevance.

Step 6: Pilot and Revise the Coding System

Before investing the resources in final data collection, it is useful to pilot the coding system on a small sample from the same or a similar population as what will be used in the main study. One important consideration in the pilot data is whether responses relevant to the different categories or dimensions occur often enough to warrant retaining them. It is therefore critical to inspect the variance of the scores assigned by coders. Another issue is whether the responses obtained contain enough information based on the sampling technique or whether some chance must be made in terms of length or incentives. Convergence among coders can be assessed to determine whether more training is needed or if the definitions in the coding system are specific enough for judges to reliably apply them to samples of actual content. Finally, if questions were used to elicit the text, responses can be collapsed across raters and analyzed based on corrected item-total correlations to determine whether they are all providing content relevant to the intended dimensions.

In order to pilot test the work narrative coding system with regard to motive dispositions, we recruited 41 MBA students to complete the work narrative questionnaire online. Two coders rated each response, and we analyzed the variability of the ratings, the interrater reliability of coders, corrected item-total correlations from responses to each question collapsed across raters, and preliminary evidence of validity by correlating scores with the self-report ratings of the FFM. Previous research found relationships between conscientiousness and need for achievement, and both agreeableness and extraversion were related to need for affiliation (Daugherty, Kurtz, & Phebus, 2009). It was expected that finding such relationships with work narrative scores would indicate convergent validity.

Responses to all of the questions demonstrated adequate variability for need for achievement, but scores on need for affiliation tended to be low with restricted range. The interrater reliability for the composite of the two raters was .82 for need for achievement and .79 for need for affiliation, demonstrating acceptable convergence despite the suppressed scores for need for affiliation. These estimates supported the adequacy of the manual, scoring system, and training. Finally, in order to explore convergent validity, we first controlled for narrative length. The word count for each response was correlated with need for achievement and need for affiliation, and the residuals for each were computed after removing the variance for length.

These scores were then correlated with the FFM scores from the mini-IPIP questionnaire (Donnellan, Oswald, Baird, & Lucas, 2006), with the results shown in Table 22.7. As expected, need for achievement correlated more strongly with conscientiousness ($r = .34$) than did the other explicit trait measures. Similarly, need for affiliation correlated more strongly with agreeableness ($r = .40$) than did the other traits. Need for affiliation also correlated with openness to experience ($r = .40$), suggesting those higher in openness are more concerned with affiliative behavior in the workplace. Perhaps individuals higher in openness are more curious about and open to engaging with people. Overall, the evidence of construct validity was encouraging at the pilot stage, as the aggregated motive disposition ratings correlated more with the hypothesized personality traits than with those less conceptually related.

Step 7: Collect Data, Code, Analyze, and Interpret

The last step is to collect the data that will be used for the research study. Those collecting the data should be unaware of the hypotheses. Ideally, those collecting the data will be different from those who will code the materials to reduce any biases that might enter the process. All identifiers should be removed from the materials when they are coded. It is also desirable that discrete units from the same participants not be clustered together when coded so that coders are blind to those that go together. If possible and desirable, different coders can be used for different units of content. Cross-validation using a second sample, or splitting a larger sample, can also be undertaken if careful piloting was not possible.

As with most data collection efforts, the initial steps are to clean the data of any anomalies (e.g., outliers, gross data entry errors) and examine descriptive statistics. Of course, it is important to consider the type of data coded (categories, frequencies, and ratings) prior to analyzing the data. For categorical data, the chi-square statistic may be the most appropriate test. For continuous ratings, descriptive statistics should be examined for skewed distributions or range restriction. With frequency data, it is important to consider the length of the response, or word count. As the responses get longer, it becomes more likely that the unit being coded will occur more often. It is

Table 22.7 Correlations Between Motive Dispositions and Five-Factor Model Traits From Pilot of Work Narrative Coding

Five-Factor Model Trait	*Motive Disposition*	
	Need for Achievement	*Need for Affiliation*
Conscientiousness	.34*	.11
Agreeableness	.06	.40*
Extraversion	.06	.04
Emotional stability	−.03	−.15
Openness to experience	−.02	.40*

Note: $N = 41$.

* $p < .05$.

recommended that word count be controlled especially when frequency data is collected (Woike, 2007). Hypotheses are then tested by examining category means on other study variables or by correlating the coded ratings (or frequencies) with variables of interest derived from the content materials or from other sources of data.

For the work narrative project, recall that we hypothesized that individuals with a high need for achievement will prefer organizational cultures characterized as more risk taking, challenging, and results oriented, whereas individuals with a high need for affiliation will prefer organizational cultures characterized as more friendly and familial. Thirty full-time employees were recruited to complete the survey, including the work narrative questionnaire and a cultural preference survey targeting four types of cultures (Cameron & Quinn, 1999): (a) a clan culture characterized as a friendly place to work where employees are like an extended family, (b) an adhocracy with dynamic and entrepreneurial people who are willing to take risks, (c) a market culture that is results oriented, where the major concern is getting the job done, and (d) a hierarchy described as a very formalized place to work where procedures govern what people do.

To test the hypotheses, we again controlled for word count and correlated motive scores with each of the organizational culture preferences (see Table 22.8). Need for achievement was positively related to a market culture (r = .33) and negatively related to clan culture preferences. Need for affiliation was positively related to a clan culture (r = .35) but negatively related to market culture preferences. However, contrary to the prediction, need for achievement was unrelated to an adhocracy culture preference (r = −.06). These findings indicate that assessing motives by content-analyzing stories about past work experiences that do not directly ask about culture can predict the types of workplace environments that individuals prefer.

In a separate data collection effort, 91 employees completed the work narrative survey, a self-report personality test, and measures of work-related ambiguity, psychological detachment, and coping. The results of this study are summarized in Table 22.9. The interrater reliability for the composite of the two raters coding for uncertainty orientation was .91. It was expected that uncertainty orientation has an influence at different stages of the stress process. The correlation between the implicit uncertainty orientation scores from the work narratives and the explicit neuroticism scores was .17. This result suggests that individuals higher in neuroticism are more likely to attempt to deal with and resolve ambiguous situations in the workplace. This is in line with previous findings that people higher in neuroticism are more likely to select planful problem-solving coping strategies more than their low-neuroticism counterparts (Bolger & Zuckerman, 1995). This is in contrast to our findings that neuroticism was related to less problem-focused coping (r = −.36) in favor of more emotion-focused coping (r = .45). The difference in these findings may be due to the *context-specific* nature of the work narratives, as opposed to the self-report surveys used to assess one's *general* coping strategies. Uncertainty orientation scores derived from the work narrative survey were also related to increased

Table 22.8 Correlations Between Motive Dispositions and Organizational Culture Preferences

Organizational Culture	*Motive Disposition*	
	Achievement	*Affiliation*
Clan culture	−.23	.35*
Market culture	.33*	−.50*
Adhocracy culture	−.06	−.25
Hierarchy culture	.08	.11

Note: N = 30.

* $p < .05$.

Table 22.9 Correlations Between Uncertainty Orientation and Stress-Related Variables

Measure	*1*	*2*	*3*	*4*	*5*	*6*
1. Uncertainty orientation	*.91*					
2. Neuroticism	.17*	*.88*				
3. Psychological detachment	−.23*	−.10	*.85*			
4. Work-related ambiguity	.23*	.33*	−.05	*.65*		
5. Problem-focused coping	−.04	−.36*	.02	.00	*.78*	
6. Emotion-focused coping	−.00	.45*	−.02	.00	−.27*	*.75*

Notes: $N = 91$. Reliabilities are on the diagonal.

* $p < .05$.

perceptions of workplace ambiguity ($r = .23$) and decreased psychological detachment ($r = -.23$), but was relatively unrelated to coping strategies. These findings suggest that uncertainty-oriented individuals are concerned with sources of ambiguity in the workplace, both during *and* after work hours, but the manner in which they deal with this ambiguity is situation specific, and does not seem to correspond to how they cope in general. Overall, these findings suggest that this contextualized narrative approach provides unique findings about personality and occupational stress.

Computer-Based Assessment Systems and Automated Essay Scoring

One of the most obvious challenges to coding verbal or written content is that it can be a very time-intensive process. One way to significantly reduce the time required for this process is through the use of AES software. AES uses computer technology to evaluate and score written prose (Shermis & Burstein, 2003). AES has been used to reduce time-related issues (e.g., response times, training coders, time spent coding), reduce cost, and improve reliability (Burstein, 2003; Burstein & Marcu, 2003).

Whereas the primary purpose behind the development of AES systems was to evaluate the quality of essays in terms of the assessment of writing ability, recent research has shown that AES can be used to identify certain personality traits based on written text passages (Hirsh & Peterson, 2009; Kufner, Back, Nestler, & Egloff, 2010; Lee & Cohn, 2009; Pyszcynski & Greenberg, 1987; Rude, Gortner, & Pennebaker, 2004; Stirman & Pennebaker, 2001). Typically, these studies have required participants to describe a past life experience and their reactions to it, much like the process discussed in this chapter.

For example, Hirsh and Peterson (2009) examined self-narratives generated by instructing undergraduate students to recall and write about past events and future plans. The text was scored by the Linguistic Inquiry and Word Count (LIWC) software (Pennebaker, Francis, & Booth, 2001). Results showed that scores from many of the dimensions generated by the LIWC software correlated with those from the conceptually related FFM dimensions. For example, self-report ratings of conscientiousness correlated with AES-generated scores on the *achievement* ($r = .22$) and *work* ($r = .21$) dimensions based on word counts from the default dictionaries of the software. Furthermore, scores from dimensions such as *sad* and *negative emotion* were correlated with neuroticism in the expected direction ($r = .29$ and .26, respectively).

In a study that went beyond the FFM traits, coping strategies were assessed by AES software (Lee & Cohn, 2009). Participants were required to write about a stressful college experience and then completed a coping inventory targeting three different coping styles. Again, it was found that the personality dimensions developed by the software correlated with conceptually meaningful coping strategies. For example, the dimension of *insight* generated by LIWC was negatively related to self-report scores on an emotion-focused coping measure ($r = -.19$) and scores from the *negative emotion* dimension were related negatively to problem-focused coping ($r = -.16$).

Types of Automatic Essay Scoring Systems

A variety of AES systems is available, designed to be used with written passages. Most of these programs are intended to score essays in educational contexts. Other programs have been developed that are more directly applicable to the assessment of constructs related to personality, cognitive style, and coping strategies. Typically, these programs contain dictionaries for each dimension that they aim to assess that contain words that have been conceptually linked to that particular dimension. The more often words that are linked to a particular dimension are used in a text passage, the higher the score that is assigned to that passage.

Linguistic Inquiry and Word Count

The most frequently used AES software in psychological research is undoubtedly the LIWC program (Pennebaker et al., 2001). This software contains multiple default dictionaries that are used to score each text passage and also has the possibility of creating custom dictionaries. Some of the default dictionaries include pronouns, verbs, and numbers. LIWC can also count frequencies of grammatical characteristics, such as how often past, present, and future tenses are utilized. In addition, the LIWC software includes dictionaries that represent individual difference variables relevant to personality psychology. For example, one of the dimensions included is "tentativeness," which is defined by words such as *doubt*, *guess*, and *hope* in the dictionary. Word exemplars were developed and linked to each dictionary by expert judgment.

The default dictionaries of LIWC contain a number of word categories of potential interest for deriving personality information from text. For example, social references to family, friends, or people in general can be scored. Affective processes such as general positive and negative emotions can be scored separately, along with the anxiety, sadness, and anger facets of negative affectivity. Finally, there are dimensions that resemble personality traits, such as tentative, certainty, and inhibition, as well as personal concerns, including work, achievement, leisure, money, religion, and death.

Bayesian Essay Test Scoring System

A second type of software that can be used to predict personality based on text passages is the Bayesian Essay Test Scoring System (BETSY; Rudner & Liang, 2002). This software requires a training process in which text passages are arranged into groups based on a particular variable, such as personality traits. For example, a researcher may obtain scores of participants' extraversion from self-report or behavioral observation. Based on where participants fall within the distribution of extraversion scores (low, moderate, high), the researcher could then place participants in up to five groups. The software examines the passages of each group and then identifies words used in isolation or in tandem that differentiate the groups that differ in trait elevation. For example, groups of participants in the top third and bottom third of the extraversion distribution could be contrasted based on words such as *talk*, *spoke*, *friends*, or *party* because they occurred more often in the group higher in extraversion. During this process, BETSY is trained to look for words that appear more frequently in one group than others. New text passages can then be uploaded, and BETSY will use the words identified in the training process to predict individuals' category assignments. In theory, BETSY could be trained to reproduce any human rating or test score.

Table 22.10 Words Differentiating Between Those High or Low on FFM Dimensions

Extraversion	*Agreeableness*	*Neuroticism*	*Conscientiousness*	*Openness*
Team	Patient	Mean	Information	Concerned
Successful	Explained	Terrible	Learning	Talked
Telling	Teach	Worried	Knowledge	Speak
Train	Willing	Worry	Decisions	Uncertain[a]
Speak	Relationship	Problem	Successful	Customer

Notes: FFM: Five-Factor Model. $N = 91$.

[a] Word used more by those low on the personality dimension than those high.

To illustrate, we trained BETSY to differentiate work narrative passages from groups constructed to differ on self-report FFM ratings. Although some of the words generated made little conceptual sense (such as "of" or "the"), many appear to be trait relevant. Displayed in Table 22.10 are the words used much more by the 91 employees from the uncertainty orientation sample who were high in a personality dimension compared to those low on that dimension. All words included in Table 22.10 were used at least three times more frequently by those high in a particular personality trait than those low in that trait. These could be used to score future passages using BETSY or to create custom dictionaries in the LIWC software, if desired.

Limitations and Future Directions in Computerized Content Analysis

Although promising in making content analysis easier to implement in personality assessment, there are a number of disadvantages as well. First, it is difficult for software that examines word frequencies, or the occurrence of even pairs of words, to account for negations in word strings and sentences. For example, if one person generated a response that they "would experience anxiety" if put in a situation and another that they "would be unlikely to worry," both appear similar in use of the word related to being anxious. This may make it difficult to differentiate between someone high versus low in emotional stability. Even if latent semantic meaning is taken into account, it is difficult for software to appreciate the context in the same way a human judge can. However, frequency of negation terms are routinely tracked by software such as LIWC, and it may be that a product term could be computed to account for the interaction with frequency of trait-relevant terms. Otherwise, researchers must manually examine occurrences of verb negations to take this into account (see Lee & Cohn, 2009).

Second, the default dimensions of LIWC do not contain many of the common personality traits that are typically used in organizational research. As such, the default dictionaries are ill-suited for directly assessing personality constructs and probably would serve better to measure intervening processes or as criteria that are predicted by a more traditional personality assessment. Second, in terms of the BETSY software, in order to be reliably trained to differentiate among groups, the software requires a large number of cases (upward of 500–1,000 are recommended). It is unclear whether having more text for each case can compensate for having a smaller number of cases.

One of the most promising future directions in this area is to develop user-generated dictionaries for LIWC. To take advantage of this function, researchers may wish to conduct a pilot study to identify words that tend to be used more often by those low or high in a targeted personality construct. The BETSY software may prove to be effective in this process by developing lists that can serve as a custom dictionary for LIWC. If successfully applied in this way, it may be that open-ended personality assessment would become more popular in research and practice. Separate dictionaries would likely be necessary for words where usage indicated high versus low trait elevation and the resulting scores aggregated after reversing those from the indicators of low trait elevation.

One potential application may be studying emails or memoranda in order to provide developmental feedback. For example, if a manager were facing resistance from various subordinates, computer-based analysis of emails and memos could highlight the source of an issue. If the analysis suggests the work communications are *tentative* based on frequent uses of words such as *hope*, *guess*, and *maybe*, recommendations could be provided about stronger or more persuasive ways of communicating with employees. In addition to the advantages discussed earlier, computer-scored open-ended assessment may reduce some forms of response or rater bias. Computer-based assessment will examine the data consistently across participant response and does not fatigue, whereas raters may start out following the protocol strictly only at the beginning.

Conclusions and Future Directions

Different methods of assessing personality have their advantages and disadvantages, whether it is self-report personality inventories, behavior observations, or judgments derived from employment interviews. Because of this, psychologists interested in understanding work behavior are best served by having as many tools as possible in their repertoire. Although content analysis is only rarely used for personality assessment in psychology as a whole, use in I-O research and practice has been almost nonexistent. We can certainly imagine the reaction of researchers and practitioners alike to the amount of labor involved in deriving scores from the text, no matter how it was collected. Although resource intensive to be sure, we believe that it is a mistake to ignore valid cues about the personality of people at work if verbal or written content is readily available.

Our own research on work narratives underscores how information about how people make sense of their work history can be instructive of personality. Personality impacts the narrative accounts at several points in the process. First, personality may causally influence what happened in the original situations discussed, both in terms of behavior expressing traits of the individual and the traits playing a role in creating their situations (Funder & Ozer, 1983). Personality also influences the choice of which of many stories individuals might tell in response to an open-ended question. Finally, personality will affect how respondents represent their behavior and goals in the situation described. Although our research into the rich information provided in these accounts is admittedly in the early stages, it shows at the very least that reliable coding is possible and that the scores derived will relate to work attitudes and behavior. The differential patterns of prediction displayed when compared to explicit measures also suggest that the additional time and effort may yield something not contained in self-report measures.

One area for future research involves how much open-ended responses can be faked and the extent that this will compromise the validity of the content analysis of those responses. Research has shown that applicants can readily fake self-report tests and that this distortion results in substantial decay in validity (see Tett & Christiansen, 2007, for a review). Many of the work narrative questions we have used could be asked either in an interview format or as part of an essay-type test taken by applicants. To the extent that constructed responses are more difficult to fake, validity of these assessments may be more robust to the effects of applicant distortion.

Although in its early stages, the use of computers to generate scores from text holds promise for reducing the amount of labor involved and the time before scores are available. Although primarily used with open-ended responses to specific questions, there is no reason that such software could not be trained to score other types of written documents. For example, a hiring committee could make judgments on the credentials of a set of resumes and the software could be trained to reproduce those ratings. With advances in voice recognition software, it may also be possible to extend automatic essay scoring to verbal responses by having audio files automatically "transcribed." Used in tandem, online interviews could be automated to yield real-time scores to decision makers using a phone or the microphone included on most laptop computers. Future research is needed for each step in this process.

More research is also needed to develop a better understanding of which attitudes, behaviors, and outcomes will be better predicted by which type of content. For that matter, it is not currently clear which personality constructs are assessable from which types of content. We know from TAT research that motive dispositions assessed through content analysis of stories appears to assess aspects of personality distinct from that assessed by traditional questionnaires. It is less clear which assessments predict some criteria better than others. If content analysis of verbal and written material from work is to advance, careful mapping of the nomological network of the constructs assessed is essential.

Finally, this review should serve as an invitation to expand how researchers and practitioners conceptualize personality constructs and approach the assessment of personality. Self-report personality measures have become ubiquitous due to the ease of administration and scoring. Although useful in many regards, what is captured by responses to these inventories represents only a portion of what personality psychology informs us is comprised by "personality." We believe that it is time we went back to listening more to what people say about themselves in order to understand more of their personality. At the very least, we can read what they have written rather than focusing just on which bubble they have filled in on an answer form.

Practitioner's Window

The verbal or written content that people generate provide important information about their personality that can be systematically analyzed. Although theory can be used to guide the development of the coding process, it can also be empirically driven when cues are determined based on correlates of other personality assessments. Most importantly, research has shown that content analysis can recover aspects of personality that go beyond the results of traditional self-report tests.

- The most important choice involved is the decision on what content to analyze. Workers' emails, applicants' resumes, interview transcripts, or even responses to sentence completion inventories can all serve as appropriate material for analysis.
- The personality-related constructs that have been most often assessed using content analysis have been motive dispositions such as need for achievement, need for affiliation, need for power, and uncertainty orientation. More traditional traits such as those represented by the Five-Factor Model have also been assessed. Research has shown that scores generated on these constructs predict work attitudes and behavior.
- In order to obtain reliable results, clear coding procedures and careful training of raters are necessary. Piloting and revising the procedures will also be beneficial before beginning any large-scale assessment using content analysis.
- Automated essay scoring software can reduce the amount of time and effort required to both develop and apply the scoring system. However, a large number of sample cases are required with this approach to train the software, and the research on validating the results of computerized scoring is in the early stages.

References

Anderson, C. A., Carnagey, N. L., & Eubanks, J. (2003). Exposure to violent media: The effects of songs with violent lyrics on aggressive thoughts and feelings. *Journal of Personality and Social Psychology, 84*, 960–971.

Andrews, J. D. W. (1967). The achievement motive in two types of organizations. *Journal of Personality and Social Psychology, 6*, 163–168.

Atkinson, J., & Feather, N. (Eds.). (1996). *A theory of achievement motivation*. New York, NY: Wiley.

Barlett, C. P., & Rodeheffer, C. (2009). Effects of realism on extended violent and nonviolent video game play on aggressive thoughts, feelings, and physiological arousal. *Aggressive Behavior, 35*, 213–224.

Bolger, N., & Zuckerman, A. (1995). A framework for studying personality in the stress process. *Personality Processes and Individual Differences, 69*, 890–902.

Burstein, J. (2003). The E-rate scoring engine: Automated essay scoring with natural language processing. In M. Shermis & J. Burstein (Eds.), *Automated essay scoring: A cross-disciplinary perspective* (pp. 113–121). Mahwah, NJ: Lawrence Erlbaum Associates.

Burstein, J., & Marcu, D. (2003). Automated evaluation of discourse in student essays. In M. Shermis & J. Burstein (Eds.), *Automated essay scoring: A cross-disciplinary perspective* (pp. 209–230). Mahwah, NJ: Lawrence Erlbaum Associates.

Cameron, K., & Quinn, R. (1999). *Diagnosing and changing organizational culture*. New York, NY: Addison-Wesley.

Christiansen, N. D., & Burns, G. (2006, April). *Personality judgments from resumé content and style*. Paper presented at the annual meeting of the Society for Industrial and Organizational Psychology, Dallas.

Cole, M. S., Field, H. S., Giles, W. F., & Harris, S. G. (2009). Recruiters' inferences of applicant personality based screening: Do paper people have a personality? *Journal of Business and Psychology, 24*, 5–18.

Crockett, H. (1962). The achievement motive and differential occupational mobility in the United States. *American Sociological Review, 27*, 191–204.

Daugherty, J., Kurtz, J., & Phebus, J. (2009). Are implicit motives "visible" to well-acquainted others? *Journal of Personality Assessment, 91*, 373–380.

Donnellan, B. M., Oswald, F. L., Baird, B. M., & Lucas, R. E. (2006). The mini-IPIP scales: Tiny-yet-effective measures of the Big Five factors of personality. *Psychological Assessment, 18*, 192–203.

Dunning, D., Heath, C., & Suls, J. M. (2004). Flawed self-assessment: Implications for health, education, and the workplace. *Psychological Science in the Public Interest, 5*, 69–106.

Fast, L. A., & Funder, D. C. (2008). Personality as manifest in word use: Correlations with self-report, acquaintance report, and behavior. *Journal of Personality and Social Psychology, 94*, 334–346.

French, E. (1956). Motivation as a variable in work-partner selection. *Journal of Abnormal and Social Psychology, 53*, 96–99.

Funder, D. C., & Ozer, D. J. (1983). Behavior as a function of the situation. *Journal of Personality and Social Psychology, 44*, 107–112.

Gough, H. G. (1971). The assessment of wayward impulse by means of Personnel Reaction Blank. *Personnel Psychology, 24*, 669–677.

Hermann, M. G. (1979). Who becomes a political leader? Some societal and regime influences on selection of a head of state. In L. S. Falkowski (Ed.), *Psychological models in international politics* (pp. 112–118). Springfield, IL: C.C. Thomas.

Hirsh, J. B., & Peterson, J. B. (2009). Personality and language use in self-narratives. *Journal of Research in Personality, 43*, 524–527.

Hogansen, J., & Lanning, K. (2001). Five factors in sentence completion test categories: Toward rapprochement between trait and maturational approaches to personality. *Journal of Research in Personality, 35*, 449–462.

Holaday, M., Smith, D. A., & Sherry, A. (2000). Sentence completion tests: A review of the literature and results of a survey of members of the society for personality assessment. *Journal of Personality Assessment, 74*, 371–383.

Johnson, R. E., Tolentino, A. L., Rodopman, O. B., & Cho, E. (2010). We (sometimes) know not how we feel: Predicting job performance with an implicit measure of trait affectivity. *Personnel Psychology, 63*, 197–219.

Kagan, J. (1972). Motives and development. *Journal of Personality and Social Psychology, 22*, 51–66.

Karabenick, S. (1977). Fear of success, achievement and affiliative dispositions, and the performance of men and women under individual and competitive situations. *Journal of Personality, 45*, 117–149.

Kazdin, A. (2003). *Research design in clinical psychology* (4th ed.). Boston: Allyn & Bacon.

Klich, N. R., & Feldman, D. C. (1992). The role of approval and achievement needs in feedback seeking behavior. *Journal of Managerial Issues, 4*, 554–570.

Kufner, A. C., Back, M. D., Nestler, S., & Egloff, B. (2010). Tell me a story and I will tell you who you are! Lens model analysis of personality and creative writing. *Journal of Research in Personality, 44*, 427–435.

Lee, H. S., & Cohn, L. D. (2009). Assessing coping strategies by analyzing expressive writing samples. *Stress & Health, 26*, 250–260.
Loevinger, J. (1987). The concept of self or ego. In P. Young-Eisendrath & H. James (Eds.), *The book of the self: Person, pretext, and processes* (pp. 88–94). New York, NY: New York University Press.
McAdams, D. P. (1985). *Power, intimacy, and the life story: Personological inquiries into identity*. New York, NY: Guilford Press.
McAdams, D. P. (1995). What do we know when we know a person? *Journal of Personality, 63*, 365–396.
McAdams, D. P., Anyiodoho, N. A., Brown, C., Huang, Y. T., Kaplan, B., & Macado, M. A. (2004). Traits and stories: Links between dispositional and narrative features of personality. *Journal of Personality, 72*, 761–784.
McClelland, D. C. (1961). *The achieving society*. Princeton, NJ: Van Nostrand.
McClelland, D. C. (1965). N achievement and entrepreneurship: A longitudinal study. *Journal of Personality and Social Psychology, 1*, 389–392.
McClelland, D. C. (1980). Motive dispositions: The merits of operant and respondent measures. In L. Wheeler (Ed.), *Review of personality and social psychology* (Vol. 1, pp. 10–41). Los Angeles: Sage.
McClelland, D. C. (1987). Characteristics of successful entrepreneurs. *Journal of Creative Behavior, 3*, 219–233.
McClelland, D. C., & Burnham, D. (1976). Power is the great motivator. *Harvard Business Review, 54*, 100–110.
McClelland, D. C., Koestner, R., & Weinberger, J. (1989). How do self-attributed and implicit motives differ? *Psychological Review, 96*, 690–702.
McClelland, D. C., & Winter, D. (1971). *Motivating economic achievement*. New York, NY: Free Press.
McCrae, R. R., & Costa, P. C. (1987). Validation of the five-factor model across instruments and observers. *Journal of Personality and Social Psychology, 52*, 81–90.
Mehl, M. R., Gosling, S. D., & Pennebaker, J. W. (2006). Personality in its natural habitat: Manifestations and implicit folk theories of personality in daily life. *Journal of Personality and Social Psychology, 90*, 862–877.
Murray, H. A. (1943). *Thematic apperception test manual*. Cambridge, MA: Harvard University Press.
Pennebaker, J. W., Francis, M. E., & Booth, R. J. (2001). *Linguistic inquiry and word count (LIWC)*. Mahwah, NJ: Erlbaum.
Pennebaker, J. W., & King, L. A. (1999). Linguistic styles: Language use as an individual difference. *Journal of Personality and Social Psychology,* 77, 1296–1312.
Pyszczynski, T., & Greenberg, J. (1987). Self-regulatory perseveration and the depressive self-focusing style: A self-awareness theory of depression. *Psychological Bulletin, 102*, 122–138.
Raynor, J. O., & McFarlin, D. B. (1986). Motivation and the self-system. In R. M. Sorrentino & E. T. Higgins (Eds.), *The handbook of motivation and cognition: Foundations of social behavior* (pp. 315–349). New York, NY: Guilford Press.
Rohde, A. R. (1946). Explorations in personality by the sentence completion method. *Journal of Applied Psychology, 30*, 169–181.
Rude, S., Gortner, E. M., & Pennebaker, J. (2004). Language use of depressed and depression-vulnerable college students. *Cognition & Emotion, 18*, 1121–1133.
Rudner, L.M., & Liang, T. (2002). Automated essay scoring using Bayes' theorem. *The Journal of Technology, Learning and Assessment,* 1, 3–21.
Rusting, C. L., & Larsen, R. J. (1998). Personality and cognitive processing of affective information. *Personality and Social Psychology Bulletin, 24*, 200–213.
Shermis, M., & Burstein, J. (2003). *Automated essay scoring: A cross-disciplinary perspective*. Mahwah, NJ: Lawrence Erlbaum Associates.
Smith, C. (1992). Reliability issues. In C. Smith, J. Atkinson, D. McClelland, & J. Veroff (Eds.), *Motivation and personality: Handbook of thematic content analysis* (pp. 153–178). New York, NY: Cambridge University Press.
Smith, C. (2000). Content analysis and narrative analysis. In H. Reis & C. M. Judd (Eds.), *Handbook of research methods in social and personality psychology* (pp. 313–335). New York, NY: Cambridge University Press.
Smith, C., Atkinson, J. W., McClelland, D. C., & Veroff, J. (1992). *Motivation and personality: Handbook of thematic content analysis*. New York, NY: Cambridge University Press.
Sorrentino, R. M., Roney, C. J. R., & Hanna, S. E. (1992). Uncertainty orientation. In C. P. Smith (Ed.), *Motivation and personality: Handbook of thematic content analysis* (pp. 419–427). New York, NY: Cambridge University Press.
Sorrentino, R. M., & Short, J. C. (1986). Uncertainty orientation, motivation and cognition. In R. M. Sorrentino & E. T. Higgins (Eds.), *The handbook of motivation and cognition: Foundations of social behavior* (pp. 379–403). New York, NY: Guilford Press.
Stirman, S. W., & Pennebaker, J. W. (2001). Word use in poetry of suicidal and non-suicidal poets. *Psychosomatic Medicine, 63*, 517–522.

Tendler, A. D. (1930). A preliminary report on a test for emotional insight. *Journal of Applied Psychology, 14*, 122–136.

Tett, R. P., & Christiansen, N. D. (2007). Personality tests at the crossroads: A response to Morgeson, Campion, Dipboye, Hollenbeck, Murphy, and Schmitt (2007). *Personnel Psychology, 60*, 967–993.

Veroff, J. (1982). Assertive motivations: Achievement versus power. In A. J. Stewart (Ed.), *Motivation and society* (pp. 99–132). San Francisco: Jossey-Bass.

Winter, D. (1992). Content analysis of archival materials, personal documents, and everyday verbal productions. In C. Smith, J. Atkinson, D. McClelland, & J. Veroff (Eds.), *Motivation and personality: Handbook of thematic content analysis* (pp. 110–125). New York, NY: Cambridge University Press.

Woike, B. (2007). Content coding of open-ended responses. In R. Robins, C. Fraley, & R. Krueger (Eds.), *Handbook of research methods in personality psychology* (pp. 292–307). New York, NY: Guilford Press.

Yarkoni, T. (2010). Personality in 100,000 words: A large scale analysis of personality and word use among bloggers. *Journal of Research in Personality, 44*, 363–373.

Section III

Applications of Personality to the Psychology of Work

23

Legal Issues in Personality Testing

Mark J. Schmit and Ann Marie Ryan

Over the past 50 years, the use of personality testing in employee selection has not come under the same type of legal scrutiny as other more cognitive-based tests. However, there have been a number of U.S. court cases concerning personality testing. In addition, and probably just as important, the popular press has propagated the opinion that negative applicant perceptions and complaints regarding personality testing are fairly common, whether this is true or not. In this chapter, we will first provide evidence of employer usage of personality tests in employee selection, employer experience with legal claims and applicant complaints, and practitioner views on the use and legality of personality tests. Then, we will discuss relevant U.S. employment law and past cases regarding personality testing, summarizing potential legal issues surrounding personality tests and the validation of these tests. This is followed by discussions of applicant reactions to personality testing for hiring purposes and other issues that may be related to complaints about such testing. We conclude that, although the use of personality testing in employee selection has not faced intense legal inquiry, there are certainly issues that the practitioner should consider before using these tools, in addition to research that should be conducted to advance the legal and effective use of these tools in practice.

Legal Compliance

There are three primary documents that human resource (HR) professionals should consult to understand whether their personality testing is in compliance with legal and professional standards. The legal standards can be found in the *Uniform Guidelines on Employee Selection Procedures* ("Uniform Guidelines"; Equal Employment Opportunity Commission [EEOC], 1978). Professional standards include the *Standards for Educational and Psychological Tests* (American Educational Research Association [AERA], 1999) and the *Principles for the Validation and Use of Employee Selection Procedures* (Society for Industrial and Organizational Psychology [SIOP], 2003). HR professionals can also find more practitioner-oriented direction from comprehensive textbooks on the topic of employee selection (e.g., Gatewood, Field, & Barrick, 2011). These sources provide detailed and technical specifications for HR professionals; however, some HR professionals may need to seek additional help from other professionals such as industrial and organizational psychologists or employment lawyers who are intimately familiar with these sources.

Definition of Personality Testing

A discussion of legal issues related to the use of personality testing in employee selection must begin by defining and setting the scope of the term *personality testing*. The personality characteristics and related behavioral tendencies of individuals can be measured through multiple methods. In the realm of employee selection, these methods include interviews, biodata tests, situational judgment tests, and simulations (both live and electronic) among others. In this chapter, we will limit our discussion to the traditional personality test that measures personality traits or tendencies through self-report inventories, where respondents use scales or item comparisons to describe how well individual items describe their own behavioral or attitudinal tendencies. Such inventories are typically administered via paper-and-pencil surveys or in a similar electronic version. This definition and scope narrows the realm of personality testing to only those measures that attempt to directly measure personality or behavioral constructs. Still, throughout this chapter and where appropriate, we will mention other trends in personality assessment and the legal implications of these trends away from the traditional methods.

Survey of Usage and Challenges

Many recent popular press and professional journal articles declare that there have been substantial increases in personality testing used for employee selection and promotion. There are additional claims of widespread use among organizations. However, very little data exist to support these claims. The best data come from the American Management Association (AMA, 2001), but they are data that have not been updated in 10 years. Still, the AMA data neither suggest an increase in usage nor widespread usage. The number of organizations using personality tests for employee selection or promotion was 17.60% in 1999, 16.30% in 2000, and 13.10% in 2001. If anything, these data suggest a decline in usage over this particular 3-year timeframe. Clearly, the existing research on usage is sparse and does not explore specific job-level usage, legal or complaint issues, or practitioner experiences or reasons for using or not using personality tests in employee-selection programs. Accordingly, we conducted a more comprehensive usage survey with HR professionals from the membership of the Society for Human Resource Management (SHRM).

A sample of HR professionals was randomly selected from SHRM's membership database, which included approximately 255,000 individual members at the time the survey was conducted. In May 2011, an e-mail that included a hyperlink to the SHRM survey was sent to 3,000 randomly selected SHRM members from the sampling frame. Of these, 2,803 were successfully delivered to respondents, and 495 HR professionals responded, yielding a response rate of approximately 18%. The final sample was generally representative of the SHRM membership population. The SHRM population of members is highly representative of the organizations in the United States that employ at least one HR professional. For interpretation of the results, the margin of error, using a 95% confidence interval, is ±5% points.

The first question in the survey asked about the use of personality tests in the selection of employees. As shown in Table 23.1, approximately 18% of organizations currently use personality tests for employee selection. Table 23.2 presents the results of a second question that asked those who conduct personality testing what job levels they use the tests for in practice. The findings suggest that more organizations use personality tests for exempt (i.e., salaried) jobs, particularly at the mid-manager level.

These findings, together with the AMA (2001) trend data, do not suggest a strong increase in the use of personality testing for personnel selection and promotion. In fact, after accounting for measurement error in both data sources, there appears to have been no change in usage over the past 12 or so years.

The third question in the survey asked HR professionals how personality test results are used in their organization to make hiring and/or promotion decisions. This was posed as an open-ended question. The responses were content analyzed, and we identified five categories of responses. The first category of responses was labeled as *computational methods*. Respondents in this category indicated that they used the tests in a variety of ways that involve the computation of a score and the

Table 23.1 Use of Personality Testing

Does your organization currently use a personality test in the hiring and/or promotion of employees? (This would include personality tests used as part of an assessment center or individual assessment process.)

	n	%
Yes	89	18
No	396	80
Unsure	10	2
Total	495	100

Table 23.2 Use of Personality Testing by Job Level

For which of the following job groups is personality testing used in your organization as part of the hiring and/or promotion process?

	All	*Most*	*Some*	*Few/select jobs*	*Do not use for this category of employee*
Nonexempt jobs (hourly)	30% (*n* = 27)	5% (*n* = 4)	8% (*n* = 7)	22% (*n* = 20)	35% (*n* = 31)
Entry-level exempt jobs (professional, supervisor, individual contributors, etc.)	43% (*n* = 38)	4% (*n* = 4)	15% (*n* = 13)	13% (*n* = 12)	25% (*n* = 22)
Mid-level managers (managers, director, etc.)	56% (*n* = 50)	7% (*n* = 6)	9% (*n* = 8)	4% (*n* = 4)	24% (*n* = 21)
Executives (vice presidents, senior vice presidents, executive vice presidents, chiefs)	45% (*n* = 40)	7% (*n* = 6)	1% (*n* = 1)	7% (*n* = 6)	40% (*n* = 36)

Note: *N* = 89.

use of that score in a multiple hurdle or composite score fashion (generally with scores from other decision-making tools, such as an interview score) to reach a decision about a job applicant. A second category of responses we identified was labeled as *clinical methods*. Responses in this category included a variety of ways that organizations use personality test information in combinations with other information to arrive at a selection decision for an individual candidate. In this category of responses, it appeared that the method of integrating scores from multiple data-gathering tools was not done in a computational manner and generally left to the discretion of the hiring manager, HR professional, or third-party consultant/psychologist. Responses in this category often used the term *fit* to describe the method. That is, they used the test results to determine cultural fit, job fit, team fit, and so forth. The third category of responses was closely related to the second category but still unique; we labeled this category of responses as *interpersonal fit* methods. Responses in this category indicated that organizations use personality tests to identify placement of a candidate with a compatible manager or coworker. A fourth category of responses was labeled *interview* methods. Responses in this category indicated that personality tests were used to guide the development of candidate-specific interview questions. Finally, a fifth set of responses were grouped into a category we labeled *development methods*. Responses in this category suggested that, although personality test scores were collected during the preemployment testing phases, the results were used for development purposes rather than for making selection decisions.

From a legal perspective, computational methods are preferable to clinical methods. Computational methods ensure consistency in decisions; clinical methods, though useful for highly trained professionals such as psychologists, can lead to inconsistent or even outright illegal decision making. For example, if a hiring manager frequently or always uses the personality test to justify the hiring of men over women, this would be an overt case of disparate treatment against women. Even simple inconsistency in the application of test results in a series of hiring decisions can have negative consequences for the validity of a test and thereby undermine the usefulness of the test in selecting the best possible applicants for a job. The interpersonal fit method is an even more extreme use of a clinical method and could result in both disparate treatment and disparate impact on minority groups. Approximately 25% of the respondents whose organizations used personality tests for selection decisions fell into these two categories that represent legally vulnerable methods.

Table 23.3 presents the results of the fourth question asked in the survey—a question asking about the most common method of personality test administration. Clearly, the trend is away from monitored tests, and even more pronounced is the trend toward unproctored Internet testing from any location of the applicant's choosing. Among the responses in the *Other* category were the following: the test is taken online at a company facility but not monitored; the test is sent to the candidate and then sent by the candidate to a test-processing vendor; the test is administered by an outside agency with a monitor; partial testing is available online from anywhere and then followed up with more extensive testing in a monitor company facility; two tests are used—one is administered online and the second is given in person once the candidate has progressed to a face-to-face interview.

The last two administration methods in the list follow the same pattern of unproctored Internet testing followed by proctored follow-up testing. This administration sequence has been viewed by some testing experts as best practice in light of the test security and unknown nature of the test taker and test conditions existing in an online testing condition (Tippins, 2009; Tippins et al., 2006), though this approach is also more costly than simple unproctored Internet administration and can suffer other psychometric challenges, such as the disqualification of some proportion of qualified candidates based on a short and less reliable measure used as a prescreen (Pearlman, 2009).

Although there is some initial research to suggest that proctored and unproctored tests have similar validities (Beaty et al., 2011), fairness issues may still surface if applicants (and/or their attorneys)

Table 23.3 Common Methods of Administration

What is the most common method your organization uses to administer the personality test(s) in the hiring and/or promotion process?

	n	%
The test is administered in person and the administrator oversees the candidate testing process, including checking identification of the test taker, administering the test either by paper-and-pencil or by computer, and monitoring the test taker and test-taking environment during the entire process	15	20
The test is administered in person but the administrator does not monitor the test taker or test environment throughout the entire process	12	16
The test is administered online and the test taker can take it from anywhere he or she has Internet access	42	56
Other	6	8
Total	75	100

feel an unfair advantage is being given to majority group members in this scenario and/or data show adverse impact. Initial research demonstrates that groups may perform differentially based on the conditions under which the test is administered (Weiner & Morrison, 2009). Without control over conditions, as is the case with Internet testing conducted in sites of the applicant's choice, it is a gamble to assume that all groups of individuals will perform similarly under standardized versus unstandardized conditions. The result could be unexpected adverse impact findings after large numbers of applicants have been both hired and rejected, potentially leaving an organization with a large-scale liability.

The next question in the survey asked the respondents who use personality testing whether they have experienced any formal legal filings as a result of their use (see Table 23.4). Only one HR professional (<2%) responded affirmatively. The claim was that some items and/or the test as a whole were biased against a specific gender group. The low frequency of such reports was not unexpected, because we were unable to locate many employment-related legal cases associated with personality testing, as discussed in a later section of this chapter.

However, an examination of the results of the next survey question suggests that although personality tests used for employee selection may not often come under formal legal scrutiny, it does not mean that most applicants hold them in high regard from a fairness perspective. The results presented in Table 23.5 for this question indicate that 12% of those respondents using personality tests for employee selection received written or verbal complaints about the tests. This is substantially higher than the number of formal legal filings identified in Table 23.4. To further investigate the nature of complaints regarding these tests, we asked respondents to identify the general categories in which these complaints could be classified.

Table 23.6 provides results regarding the nature of complaints regarding personality tests used in employee selection. The majority of complaints were in the category of questionable job-relatedness of the test. Two of the open-ended responses in the *Other* category also fell loosely into this category

Table 23.4 Legal Challenges to Personality Testing Used in Employee Selection

Have you had any legal challenges (not simply by verbal complaints, but a formal legal filing or notice from a lawyer) to your organization's use of personality testing in the hiring and/or promotion process?

	n	%
Yes	1	<2
No	69	88
Unsure	8	10
Total	78	100

Table 23.5 Applicant Complaints Regarding Personality Testing Used in Employee Selection

Have applicants made any verbal or written complaints (not including formal legal complaints) about your use of a personality test in the hiring and/or promotion process?

	n	%
Yes	9	12
No	63	83
Unsure	4	5
Total	76	100

Table 23.6 Applicant Complaints Regarding Personality Testing Used in Employee Selection

What has been the nature of the verbal or written complaints? (select all that apply)

	n	%
Some items on the test were viewed as personally invasive	2	25
Some items on the test were viewed as potentially revealing of a disability covered under the American's with Disabilities Act (ADA)	0	0
Some items or the test as a whole was viewed as biased against a specific racial or ethnic group	0	0
Some items or the test as a whole was viewed as biased against a specific gender group	1	13
Some items or the test as a whole was viewed as biased against a specific age group	0	0
Some items or the test as a whole was viewed as biased against another protected group	0	0
The test was not job-related	4	50
The test or items in the test violated a specific state law	0	0
The test was not consistently administered	0	0
Other (please specify)	3	38
Total	8	

as the complaints stated that the applicants did not believe the test provided a complete measure of all the personal characteristics required by the job. The other open-ended complaint questioned the scoring of the test.

Job-relatedness of personality tests used in employee selection is often questioned by those who are unfamiliar with the concept of personality traits and the measurement of these traits. General personality test items, by their very nature, can seem personal, invasive, or, at best, not directly job-related to the average applicant. However, research has now shown that even rather minor changes to standard personality tests, such as adding "at work" tags to item stems, can lead to incremental gains in validity in predicting job performance (Bing, Whanger, Davison, & VanHook, 2004; Holtz, Ployhart, & Dominguez, 2005; Hunthausen, Truxillo, Bauer, & Hammer, 2003; Lievens, De Corte, & Schollaert, 2008; Schmit, Ryan, Stierwalt, & Powell, 1995). Accordingly, it is likely that the majority of complaints can be staved off by using a test that more directly links to the job, or at least has an appearance of being work-related in general.

The next question asked of the HR professionals in this study was on their views on the usefulness of personality tests in employee selection. Table 23.7 presents the response patterns of the participants.

Table 23.7 Human Resource Professionals' Views on Personality Testing

Which of the following best indicates your professional view of personality tests? (select one)

	n	%
Personality tests are useful in predicting job-related behavior and/or organizational fit	43	9
When properly vetted and validated, personality tests can be useful in predicting job-related behavior and/or organizational fit	291	62
Personality tests are generally not useful in predicting job-related behavior and/or organizational fit	63	14
The use of personality testing may leave applicants with negative views of the organization and therefore should not be used or at least used very sparingly	36	8
Other (please specify)	33	7
Total	466	100

The majority of HR professionals believed that personality tests can be useful predictors of job performance, particularly when properly vetted and validated. Only 14% did not believe personality tests are useful in employee selection, and 7% believed the negative impressions created by these types of tests may not be balanced by their potential usefulness.

The open-ended responses of the 7% in the *Other* category were content analyzed. The responses were grouped into four categories: (a) lack of knowledge of, or experience with, personality tests; (b) personality tests are better suited for use in employee development programs, rather than selection or promotion; (c) personality tests are not a strong predictor of job performance; and (d) personality test information can easily be misused by hiring managers, which can create potential legal or business risks.

Recent research by SHRM (2011) suggests that about 18% of organizations are now using social networking or professional websites in the screening of employees—coincidentally equal to the number of organizations that use personality tests. Many of the HR professionals who use these sites indicated that reputational or personality-related information is used from the sites in making screening decisions. Accordingly, we asked HR professionals two questions in the current study to compare their views of the usefulness and legal risks of reputational information gleaned from social networking sites versus personality tests when used for employee selection. We only asked these two questions of HR professionals who indicated that their organization used personality tests for employee selection. Tables 23.8 and 23.9 present the results of these two survey questions.

Table 23.8 Usefulness of Reputational Information Versus Personality Tests

Do you agree or disagree with the statement "The reputational or personality-related information that is available about job candidates through Internet search engines (e.g., Google) or on social networking or professional websites is more useful in making hiring decisions than personality tests"?

	n	%
Strongly agree	1	1
Agree	36	43
Disagree	41	49
Strongly disagree	5	6
Total	83	100

Table 23.9 Legal Risk of Reputational Information Versus Personality Tests

Do you agree or disagree with the statement "The use of reputational or personality-related information that is available about job candidates through Internet search engines (e.g., Google) or on social networking or professional websites is legally less risky than the use of personality tests in making hiring and/or promotion decisions"?

	n	%
Strongly agree	2	2
Agree	29	34
Disagree	49	58
Strongly disagree	5	6
Total	85	100

The data suggest that 44% of HR professionals in organizations who use personality tests for employee selection believe that reputational information on social or professional networking sites can be more useful than personality tests, but 64% believe that this approach is more legally risky than the use of personality tests. Given the fact that social websites provide (a) inconsistent or nonexistent information about applicants, (b) both potential job-related and non-job-related information, and (c) information that may be illegal to use in making employee-selection decisions (e.g., gender, race, and religion), the use of reputational information from social or professional networking websites is far more open to future legal challenge than validated personality tests consistently administered to job applicants as part of a screening process.

The findings from the SHRM survey suggest that although personality testing is not widely used for selection and promotion decisions, there are enough organizations using the tests—and in some cases, large companies are using these tests with thousands of job applicants—to justify legal scrutiny of the practice. In addition, several of the survey questions raised potential legal vulnerabilities based on the existing practices of the organizations employing personality tests for selection or promotion of employees. In the next section of this chapter, we consider the legal issues and challenges that personality tests used for these purposes have faced in the past.

Legal Challenges

A number of U.S. state and federal court cases relate to personality testing, although none of them are Supreme Court cases (Black, 1994). Cases have dealt with issues of (a) employment discrimination, in terms of adverse impact against protected groups; (b) violations of the Americans with Disabilities Act (ADA); and (c) invasion of privacy claims. While our focus is on U.S. laws, we highlight relevant law elsewhere when appropriate.

Discrimination Claims

Stabile (2002) notes that plaintiffs have generally not been successful in challenging the use of personality tests under Title VII claims of employment discrimination. For example, in *Reynolds v. State of Arizona* (1993), a female applicant for a patrol officer job with the Arizona Department of Public Safety alleged that the use of personality tests, including the Minnesota Multiphasic Personality Inventory (MMPI) and California Psychological Inventory (CPI), adversely affected female applicants, but the evidence did not support a claim of adverse impact. In *Colbert v. H-K Corporation* (1971) the court upheld the personality testing procedures as job-related as they were professionally developed, and evidence of their relationship to job performance had been established. In *Re Vey* (1991, 1993, 1994), a plaintiff was deemed ineligible for full-time police work based on personality testing. In this case, the city presented a list of traits and examples of how they related to job functions; while the court majority upheld the employer's view, the dissenting opinion noted that this was not an established validation method (Mook, 1996).

Although legal claims regarding personality testing and discrimination have typically been unsupported in the United States, this does not preclude the possibility of a successful claim if an employer does not take care to establish validity evidence in support of the use of the test. While many see personality tests as advantageous because of a lack of adverse impact, Arthur, Woehr, and Graziano (2001) note that this may be true only in the case of race and not gender, as there are personality scales where sex differences exist. Indeed, Hough, Oswald, and Ployhart (2001) provided a meta-analysis of subgroup differences in personality measures and indicated minimal ethnic group differences, but some sizable gender differences (women score higher on agreeableness, dependability, and affiliation, and lower on surgency or dominance and masculinity). Mook (1996) notes that even though a test may not have produced adverse impact in the past in studies by the publisher, an employer should examine adverse impact in its administration. Menjoge (2003) suggests that because gender and cultural groups may differ on average on certain traits, personality tests might be used to exclude certain groups. However, for both Mook's and Menjoge's points, presentation of high-quality validity evidence by an employer would be a sufficient defense.

To what extent is adverse impact likely with personality measures? As noted, both Hough et al. (2001) as well as Foldes, Duehr, and Ones (2008) found little evidence of ethnic group differences in personality measures. Indeed, Foldes et al. noted that over 70% of the effects they reported in their meta-analysis were small or negligible. However, it is important to note that adverse impact is influenced not only by group differences but also by selection ratios. Thus, given a small group difference (e.g., Foldes et al. mention Emotional Stability and Extraversion), there may be conditions when adverse impact could occur, although we did not find any evidence of this in our review of cases. To reiterate, it is always good practice to have validation evidence to support selection method use, regardless of whether the potential for adverse impact is low.

On an international basis, one can draw similar conclusions regarding the use of personality tests. In their review of the legal environment for selection in 22 countries, Myors et al. (2008) noted that protection from discrimination often covers many of the same groups in the United States, although additional groups (e.g., sexual orientation and marital status) are sometimes a focus as well. Readers should consult the specifics of a given jurisdiction to determine whether protections might relate to groups where there are established differences in personality scores.

The composition and method of using norm groups may be another consideration that could be involved in legal claims of discrimination, although this has not been tested. Arthur et al. (2001) noted that, in personality research, the use of separate normative data for interpreting the scores of males and females is common, but the use of within-group norms in employment would be in violation of the Civil Rights Act of 1991. Sackett and Wilk (1994) note that the aim of this provision was to prevent after-the-fact score adjustments done simply to eliminate adverse impact, and that accurate score interpretation via separate norms was likely not a consideration in its formulation. Arthur et al. (2001) note that the use of separate gender norms has not yet been put to a legal test, and this is still true today. In terms of global test use, Bartram (2012) notes that a practice of aggregating data within but not between countries is not always justifiable psychometrically, and one can develop muticultural, multinational, and multilingual norms where construct comparability can be established. Thus, we would once again conclude that if one is following recommended good practice regarding norm development and use (e.g., Bartram, 2008), there is no reason to expect a successful legal challenge to using global rather than single group normative data.

We also should add that personality test data may be used in multiple ways: as a scored instrument evaluated via norms and cut-scores, in matching to a profile of successful candidates, or as input to a narrative report. Indeed, the survey data presented earlier illustrate variability in use. The SIOP Principles clearly emphasize the importance of validation evidence to support *how* an assessment is used, so variations in use may lead to both differences in magnitude of group differences as well as requiring different types of evidence to support the validity of the use. While validation evidence for more clinical combinations of personality data with other test and interview data does exist (see Silzer & Jeanneret, 2011, for a recent review), Morris, Kwaske, and Daisley (2011) noted that there is considerable variability in validity depending on who is the assessor. In other words, when one moves from using personality scores in traditional ways to greater reliance on subjective expert judgment in interpreting and using personality tests, data in support of use are less consistent and compelling (Kuncel & Highhouse, 2011).

Furthermore, Menjoge (2003) noted that norm groups for many personality tests are not culturally diverse and therefore one can question whether using such normative data in score interpretation can lead to bias against minority groups. Stabile (2002) also suggests that work could be done to demonstrate that norms themselves discriminate because norm groups are often noninclusive or nonrepresentative. Cut-scores and norms groups that are derived using incumbent samples run this risk if the organization does not include a diverse population of incumbents in the jobs that are targeted (Hausdorf & Risavy, 2010). Once again, while there does not seem to be any case law on this issue, it seems that it is always good practice to understand how norms and associated cut-scores were developed for a given test (Tett et al., 2009).

Invasion of Privacy

Invasion of privacy cases are often brought under specific state privacy laws (Black, 1994). In *Soroka v. Dayton Hudson Corp* (1991), a class action suit was brought against Target, which used the MMPI and CPI in preemployment screening for security positions. The claim was that items about religious beliefs, sex life, and sexual orientation violated California state law regarding invasion of privacy (O'Meara, 1994). While the suit was settled without admission of wrongdoing or liability, the case is often mentioned in the literature because it brought a focus on examining individual test items, not just overall personality scales.

The definition of "invasive" may be in the eyes of the beholder. That is, there are some individuals who feel employers have no right to ask about things that others feel are job-related (e.g., prior conflict situations and criminal record). However, employers can conduct reviews of personality test items to determine whether there should be a concern that test takers will view items as offensive and non-job-related. They can also follow test development practices mentioned earlier to create items related to work contexts.

Invasion of privacy cases can also be brought under the Fourth, Fifth, or Fourteenth Amendments to the U.S. Constitution for claims of a search and seizure, violation of guarantee against self-incrimination, or violation of a liberty interest in depriving employment, respectively (Vetter, 1999). For example, in *McKenna v. Fargo* (1978, 1979), the court found the use of various psychological tests (including the MMPI, the Edwards Personal Preference Schedule, and several projective tests) in screening firefighters was supported by validity evidence presented by the city. They concluded that any intrusion on constitutionally based privacy was justified by a compelling state interest in public safety (Mook, 1996).

Another case, *Dziewoir v. City of Marengo* (1989), involved personality screening for a police officer job and the due process clause of the Fourteenth Amendment. Black (1994) notes that the case illustrates that while a test such as the MMPI might lead to high scores on scales related to schizophrenia or other disorders, if the employer does not put labels on the individual because of the test that results in the individual's reputation being injured to the extent he or she is not employable, their use could be upheld.

In general, the conclusion from privacy cases is that individual personality inventory questions should be reviewed to make sure they do not intrude on privacy rights, or, if they do, that the employer can demonstrate a compelling interest that would justify requiring answers to those questions, such as public safety (Mook, 1996).

Some vendors of personality tests do not provide organizations with item-level data. Although this may help to diminish concerns regarding invasion of privacy if the fact is clearly communicated to the job applicant, there may still be concerns about the truth of the statement and whether it is necessary to ask for the information in the first place, particularly if it is information that does not appear to have a direct link to job requirements.

Outside of the United States, the key principles in privacy laws (e.g., European Union's Data Protection Directive, Organisation for Economic Co-operation and Development Guidelines on the Protection of Privacy and Transborder Flows of Personal Data) deal largely with limits on data collection without the knowledge of the individual, limits on use of data without consent, and protection of data collected. Thus, even though there are stronger privacy laws outside the United States, these do not focus on assessment content as problematic. Still, a savvy selection system designer would certainly want to be aware of how assessment content is viewed in local cultural groups when using a tool globally.

Disability Discrimination

Under the ADA, inquiries such as medical screens cannot be made pre-offer, although one can use a medical screen after a contingent offer is made to a candidate. Smith (2006) and Mulvihill (2006) provide thorough reviews of ADA cases related to personality testing. While the courts have sometimes viewed exams such as the MMPI as medical screens (e.g., *Barnes v. Cochran*, 1996, 1997) and sometimes not (*Miller v. City of Springfield*, 1998; *Thompson v. Borg Warner Protective Services*, 1996), exams used in medical or clinical diagnostic settings are likely to be problematic. In *Karraker v. Rent-A-Center* (2005), workers seeking promotions had to take a test battery that included the MMPI. In an appellate court decision, the ruling was that because the test could reveal mental disabilities, it would be considered a preemployment medical exam and a violation of the ADA. Of interest, the test developer noted the limitations of the test and clearly conveyed its inappropriateness for use in preemployment screening, yet employers seemed unaware of that (Whitehouse, 2005). In a different case involving the MMPI (*Adkerson v. MK-Ferguson Co.*, 1991, 1992), the issue of how a test may reveal a tendency toward alcoholism was considered, which could also be a violation of the ADA.

As Camara and Merenda (2000) stated with regard to whether a test would be considered a medical screen,

> Among the questions asked are the following: (a) Is the test *designed* to reveal impairment or physical or mental health (such diagnosis is the primary intended use for personality tests developed with clinical normative populations)? (b) Is the test normally given in a medical setting (for example, a health care professional's office)? (c) Is the test administered or interpreted by a health care professional or someone trained by a health care professional? and (d) Is medical equipment used? In nearly all instances in which clinical personality tests are used for preemployment screening, the answers to the former two questions are likely to be "yes," but answers to the latter two questions would be "no."
>
> *p. 1169*

Personality tests designed specifically for preemployment screening purposes would likely yield a "no" answer to all of those questions. By steering clear of tests used in clinical diagnosis settings or with scale labels clearly connected to diagnostic categories (e.g., depression and paranoia), employers should be able to comply with ADA requirements regarding the use of personality measures.

Applicant Reactions and Nonlegal Challenges

As we mentioned at the start of this chapter, the popular press often mentions negative reactions of individuals to taking personality tests in employment contexts. In the organizational psychology literature, one also often sees references to negative views of personality tests. However, a closer look at actual studies of perceptions supports a much more nuanced conclusion.

Consider some of the studies often referenced as showing that applicants have negative reactions to personality tests. Rosse, Miller, and Stecher (1994) found that reactions to personality tests were more positive when administered with both an interview and cognitive ability test than with just an interview, but in all cases, reactions were in the favorable range (i.e., above the midpoint of the scale) on average. Yet, this article is often cited as supporting negative reactions to personality tests. Another example would be LaHuis, Perreault, and Ferguson (2003), who found that the average ratings for perceptions of personality test content validity, face validity, fairness, and opportunity to perform reactions were all above the midpoint of the scale, yet in the discussion the authors suggest that perceptions of personality assessments are too negative to overcome. Thus, there needs to be much greater care in noting whether studies find actual "negative reactions" to personality tests. In the survey we described previously in this chapter, the very small number of applicant complaints is further evidence of a lack of negative perceptions regarding personality tests by the majority of applicants.

A second important consideration is what test is used, and how the testing is administered and framed in these research studies. For example, Ambrose and Rosse (2003) demonstrated that test takers reacted more negatively when the administrator expressed concern about asking personal questions, representing a highly unlikely scenario in a typical selection context where a test would not be used if the organization had strong concerns and administrators adhered closely to a script. While Harland, Rauzi, and Biasatto (1995) did show that personality tests (16PF and CPI) given in conjunction with interviews were viewed more negatively than interviews alone, and mean ratings of the personality–interview condition were below the scale midpoint, the difference in reactions may have reflected the additional 2 hr required to take the personality test. Current trends in employment testing suggest that such lengthy testing would not be typical for screening for entry-level positions (although more in-depth testing might occur for higher level/managerial or special duty of care positions, such as police positions). In addition, studies vary in the use of tests designed for research purposes versus those designed specifically for use in employment contexts. The latter are not used as frequently in studies of perceptions, making it difficult to interpret whether reactions are to personality testing in general or to the specific, non-face-valid test employed.

A third consideration is where the study is conducted. Reactions to personality tests may have some cross-cultural variance; for example, Anderson and Witvliet (2008) found that Dutch participants reacted more favorably to personality measures than did those in the United States, and suggested this may be a function of familiarity, as personality tests may have wider usage in Europe. In the most recent and comprehensive look at the issue, Anderson, Salgado, and Hulsheger (2010), in a meta-analysis of studies of reactions to various types of selection tools across 17 countries, concluded that personality inventories are generally positively evaluated. Interestingly, Anderson et al. also demonstrated that the average evaluation of personality test respect for privacy, right of employers to use, scientific evidence supporting, face validity, and opportunity to perform were all above the scale midpoint.

In sum, applicant dislike of personality testing is too often assumed, and the empirical basis for the claim suggests a much more nuanced conclusion is warranted—not all personality testing is reacted to negatively. Research should proceed to examine reactions to tests developed for use in employment contexts that are presented to actual applicants with the types of framing and explanations that are prototypical of those contexts (e.g., explanation for why the test is used and what it assesses in general), rather than using tests that are atypical in length and not content for employment contexts.

Unexplored Issues

One issue related to personality test use in selection contexts that may have legal implications surrounds how faking is treated, specifically in relation to (a) the use of corrections and (b) the use of verification, retesting, or follow-up testing.

Corrections for Faking

Reeder and Ryan (2011), in a recent review of methods for correcting personality test scores for faking, noted that the legal defensibility of using such corrections (i.e., lowering scores of individuals or rejecting too high-scoring applicants because of a belief that such scores were faked) seems tenuous (e.g., Arthur et al., 2001; Christiansen, Goffin, Johnston, & Rothstein, 1994; Luther & Thornton, 1999).They also note that because there is evidence of subgroup differences on the social desirability scales that are used in many forms of corrections (see Hough et al., 2001, for a meta-analysis), corrections may create or increase adverse impact (Dudley, McFarland, Goodman, Hunt, & Sydell, 2005). Reeder and Ryan concluded that the practice of correction of personality test scores would be difficult to justify in a legal challenge without clear evidence that it "(a) does not increase adverse impact, (b) does not differentially affect validity across subgroups, and (c) does increase validity for the sample as a whole" (p. 145).

Use of Verification, Retesting, or Other Forms of Follow-Up

One common practice is for those who are identified as "potential fakers" to be given a retesting on a similar or alternative test, sometimes accompanied by a statement that initial scores were invalid due to high social desirability. The legal issues here would surround relative rates of being placed in the category requiring verification testing across different ethnic and gender groups. As just noted in our discussion of corrections, Hough et al. (2001) found that one of the areas of greatest minority group difference was social desirability scores. Thus, relative rates of being in this category are likely to be higher for minority groups. Organizations should take care to ensure consistency in their verification testing or retesting procedures, as well as monitoring pass rates of those tests.

Validation Issues

The validation of a test is important from both business impact and legal perspectives. A validated test confirms that the inference made from the test scores is substantiated. That is, the inference can be made that those who score higher on the test will be more likely to perform better on the job than those with lower scores. From a business perspective, the investment in a validated testing program should show a significant return on investment. From a legal perspective, if a personality test is involved in a case where adverse impact has been demonstrated, then the employer's defense is a validation study that shows the job-relatedness of the test. And, of course, the plaintiff's lawyers will challenge this validity evidence.

The trend found in the SHRM survey, presented in Table 23.3, toward using unproctored Internet testing to deliver personality tests can influence the potential legal scenario just described. Adverse impact can be shown in a couple of ways, though most courts now give deference to statistical methods (Siskin & Trippi, 2005). The finding of statistical significance is influenced by the sample size used in the statistical test. The use of the Internet to deliver tests directly to applicants' computers without any constraints on location ensures that very large numbers of applicants can easily take the test. In other words, the sample size for statistical tests is maximized under these conditions. Large organizations that use unproctored Internet testing run the risk that even relatively small differences in minority versus majority group scores will show statistical significance. Although the general finding is that group differences on personality tests are relatively small, there is evidence of some differences that could result in adverse impact under these highly sensitive statistical conditions (Foldes et al., 2008; Hough et al., 2001). Testing programs that screen large numbers of candidates through unproctored testing conditions, such as large retailers, need to consider the potential consequences of this scenario.

As noted earlier, once a demonstration of adverse impact is made, the employer will be required to show validity evidence for the test. Here again, unproctored Internet testing can present some challenges. Pearlman (2009) provides a detailed treatise of these challenges. Primary among the problems faced by an unproctored Internet test validation is showing that the conditions under which the test is validated are similar enough to generalize to the conditions of the operationalized testing program. This is a standard of professional validation principles (AERA, 1999; SIOP, 2003). Unfortunately, a testing program where a test that can be taken anywhere, at any time, by unknown persons, represents a scenario that is impossible to standardize or replicate, rendering criterion-related validity study findings that are tenuous at best. Although lawyers have not yet challenged this type of personality testing in a case to date, there is sufficient reason to believe they will eventually, and employers must be prepared for this challenge, particularly if their testing program impacts large numbers of applicants.

Another challenge for unproctored Internet testing stems from the conditions under which the test is administered. By its very nature of unstandardized conditions, the potential for disadvantaged groups to be adversely impacted is magnified. For example, under standardized, proctored testing conditions, persons with disabilities can request and often be accommodated consistent with legal guidelines. However, under unproctored Internet testing conditions, this is close to impossible, particularly on a case-by-case basis. Other issues to consider include the following: (a) unequal access to reliable computer equipment with unequal capabilities to deliver the test in the identical manner, (b) unequal familiarity with the equipment required to take the test, and (c) unequal conditions under which the test is administered. Any of these conditions may be possible to demonstrate for particular minority groups, disabled individuals, or older applicants. As noted earlier, there is initial research that demonstrates that groups may perform differentially based on the conditions under which the test is administered (Weiner & Morrison, 2009). Again, large-scale unproctored Internet personality testing programs are most vulnerable to these challenges, given the greater possibility of finding adverse impact using a statistical standard.

If criterion-related validity evidence is tenuous as a result of the testing conditions or if the employer does not have a large enough population of incumbents or applicants to conduct a criterion-related validity study, is there an alternative? The *Uniform Guidelines on Employee Selection Procedures* (EEOC, 1978), representing the guidepost for court decisions on preemployment testing, suggest that content validity methods may not be appropriate as the sole evidentiary basis for a showing of job-relatedness of personality tests. However, professional standards and principles that are given deference by the *Uniform Guidelines* (i.e., AERA, 1999; SIOP, 2003) have moved away from this separated view of matching specific methods to specific test type, and case law has followed, toward a more unified view of validation methods, generally suggesting that all forms of validation evidence are acceptable and more evidence of multiple forms is better than less. Accordingly, content validity may be an option in cases where criterion-related validity data are difficult to defend or conduct.

Content validity approaches require a direct linkage between the content of the job and the content of the test. Where traditional trait measures of personality are used, this may be a difficult task for hiring managers or HR professionals (i.e., the traditional subject matter experts [SMEs] in a content validity study) without psychological training. However, personality tests that are specifically developed for employee selection may avoid this potential problem (Davison & Bing, 2009). For example, if both test items and constructs are tied directly to the work context, then organizational SMEs would likely be able to make judgments of job-relatedness. In addition, the content domains of work-related behaviors that are markers of personality constructs are infinitely more definable than the general content domain of a construct. In other words, the representativeness of the content of a work-specific measure of a personality trait can be judged against the possible domain of content the test is meant to represent, thereby making a content validation approach acceptable under professional standards and principles (AERA, 1999; SIOP, 2003). Thus, content validation methods for personality tests should be further researched, and specific guidelines for implementation should be developed by researchers for practitioners to offer alternative approaches for those organizations most vulnerable to legal challenges (for information on personality-oriented work analysis, see Chapter 11, this volume).

Indirect Measures of Personality

Personality tests, as we defined them at the outset of this chapter, are direct measures of constructs. However, there are several methods for measuring personality that are not captured under this definition. For example, biodata, situational judgment tests, simulations, games, and interviews, among other measures, all can contain indirect measurement of personality. Frequently, these measures focus more directly on work behaviors and are thereby more job-related on the face of them than more traditional measures of personality. However, the constructs underlying these measures also frequently contain a mixture of personality and cognitive ability with undetermined and unknowable weights. Consequently, the potential for adverse impact associated with these measures is increased, and the attention given to validation efforts must be similarly amplified. This will be particularly true if these methods are used as screening devices in the unproctored Internet methodologies that are becoming the prevalent mode of personality testing.

Conclusion

Advice to employers regarding the use of personality tests abounds, and most of it is simply sound testing practice (e.g., maintain confidentiality of results, use only for purposes stated, provide accommodations for those requesting them, use the most recent versions of tests, and use tests developed by professionals). Interestingly, a number of reviews of the legality of personality testing provided the same advice—use personality tests with other assessment methods to increase the likelihood of an accurate evaluation of whether the applicant can do the job (e.g., Black, 1994; Mook, 1996; Woods & Savino, 2007). On the one hand, most organizational psychologists would agree that there are multiple aspects to job performance, with personality being only one potential set of predictors (e.g., skills, abilities, interests, and others). We would caution, though, against a fallacy that combining a personality measure with another predictor will necessarily increase validity or would absolve someone from any legal challenges to the personality test itself (Sackett & Ellingson, 1997). While some legal reviews suggest using other methods of screening (biodata and assessment centers) is less risky than using personality testing and one should avoid personality testing (Mulvihill, 2006), others note the value of objective, validated personality tests over more subjective methods of evaluation such as unstructured interviews (Nevins, 2005).

A second theme in some of the literature on personality testing and legal issues is a call for greater legal regulation of personality testing. For example, Stabile (2002) suggests that because there are so many new companies offering fast, low-cost assessments, there is a need for regulation and quality control of testing such that such companies are licensed. Stabile (2002) also suggests that employers use personality tests because they cannot obtain quality information from reference checking, as defamation suits have led to prior employers providing little or no information. From our viewpoint, many personality tests are currently administered by individuals with little or no specific training regarding psychometrics, and unfortunately, some personality tests on the market have been developed by those with little training also. The answer may not be greater regulation of the testing industry but greater employer education regarding the appropriate use of tests. It was our objective in writing this chapter to provide initial steps in this direction.

Practitioner's Window

Legal Issues in Personality Testing

If you are thinking of using personality tests for personnel selection or promotion, or are already using such tests for such purposes, here are eight key points you need to consider from a legal perspective:

1. Ensure that your test and administration process meet legal and professional standards.
2. Although personality tests have generally not been found to cause adverse impact, the collection of validation evidence is still recommended.
3. Ongoing personality testing programs should be monitored for possible adverse impact.
4. Validation evidence should be collected to support exactly how the test will be used in practice.
5. Individual personality test questions should be reviewed to make sure they do not intrude on privacy rights.
6. Personality tests designed for preemployment screening purposes should be used rather than tests designed for clinical diagnostics or other nonemployment purposes.
7. In general, applicants view personality tests positively; however, care should be taken to explain to applicants why a test is being used and, in general, what it assesses.
8. Before using unproctored Internet testing, practitioners should consider the potential legal risks and probability of future court cases around this type of usage.

References

Adkerson v. MK-Ferguson Co., 191 Mich. App. 129, 477 N.W. 2d 465 (1991), appeal denied, 441 Mich. 877, 494 N.W. 2d 475 (1992).

Ambrose, M. L., & Rosse, J. G. (2003). Procedural justice and personality testing: An examination of concern and typicality. *Group & Organizational Management, 28*, 502–526.

American Educational Research Association, American Psychological Association, National Council on Measurement in Education. (1999). *The standards for educational and psychological testing.* Washington, DC: Author.

American Management Association. (2001). *2001 AMA survey on workplace testing: Basic skills, job skills, psychological measurement: Summary of key findings.* New York: Author.

Anderson, N., Salgado, J. F., & Hulsheger, U. R. (2010). Applicant reactions in selection: Comprehensive meta-analysis into reaction generalization versus situational specificity. *International Journal of Selection and Assessment, 18*, 291–304.

Anderson, N., & Witvliet, C. (2008). Fairness reactions to personnel selection methods: An international comparison between the Netherlands, the United States, France, Spain, Portugal, and Singapore. *International Journal of Selection and Assessment, 16*, 1–13.

Arthur, W., Woehr, D. J., & Graziano, W. G. (2001). Personality testing in employment settings: Problems and issues in the application of typical selection practices. *Personnel Review, 30*, 657–676.

Barnes v. Cochran, 944 F. Supp. 897 (S.D. Fla. 1996), affirmed, 130 F.3d 443 (11th Cir. 1997).

Bartram, D. (2008). Global norms: Towards some guidelines for aggregating personality norms across countries. *International Journal of Testing, 8*, 315–333.

Bartram, D. (2012). Stability of OPQ32 personality constructs across languages, cultures and countries. In A. M. Ryan, F. T. L. Leong, & F. Oswald (Eds.), *Conducting multinational research projects in organizational psychology: Challenges and opportunities* (pp. 59–89). Washington, DC: APA Books.

Beaty, J. C., Nye, C. D., Borneman, M. J., Kantrowitz, T. M., Drasgow & Grauer, E. (2011). Proctored versus unproctored noncognitive tests as predictive of job performance. *International Journal of Selection and Assessment, 19*, 1–10.

Bing, M. N., Whanger, J. C., Davison, H. K., & VanHook, J. B. (2004). Incremental validity of the frame-of-reference effect in personality scale scores: A replication and extension. *Journal of Applied Psychology, 89*, 150–157.

Black, K. R. (1994). Personality screening in employment. *American Business Law Journal, 32*, 69–124.
Camara, W. J., & Merenda, P. F. (2000). Using personality tests in preemployment screening: Issues raised in *Soroka v. Dayton Hudson Corporation. Psychology, Public Policy, and Law, 6*, 1164–1186.
Christiansen, N. D., Goffin, R. D., Johnston, N. G., & Rothstein, M. G. (1994). Correcting the 16PF for faking: Effects on criterion-related validity and individual hiring decisions. *Personnel Psychology, 47*, 847–860.
Colbert v. H-K Corporation, 1971 WL 215 (N.D. Ga. 1971).
Davison, H. K., & Bing, M. N. (2009). Content validity does matter for the criterion-related validity of personality tests. *Industrial and Organizational Psychology: Perspectives on Science and Practice, 2*, 501–503.
Dudley, N. M., McFarland, L. A., Goodman, S. A., Hunt, S. T., & Sydell, E. J. (2005). Racial differences in socially desirable responding in selection contexts: Magnitude and consequences. *Journal of Personality Assessment, 85*, 50–64.
Dziewoir v. City of Marengo, 715 F. Supp. 1416 (N.D. Ill. 1989).
Equal Employment Opportunity Commission, Civil Service Commission, Department of Labor, & Department of Justice. (1978). Uniform guidelines on employee selection procedures. *Federal Register, 43*, 38296–38309.
Foldes, H. J., Duehr, E. E., & Ones, D. S. (2008). Group differences in personality: Meta-analyses comparing five racial groups. *Personnel Psychology, 61*, 579–616.
Gatewood, R. D., Feild, H. S., & Barrick, M. (2011). *Human resource selection* (7th ed.). Mason, OH: South-Western Publishing.
Harland, L. K., Rauzi, T., & Biasatto, M. M. (1995). Perceived fairness of personality tests and the impact of explanations for their use. *Employee Responsibilities and Rights Journal, 8*, 183–192.
Hausdorf, P. A., & Risavy, S. D. (2010). Decision making using personality assessment: Implications for adverse impact and hiring rates. *Applied HRM Research, 12*, 100–120.
Holtz, B. C., Ployhart, R. E., & Dominguez, A. (2005). Testing the rules of justice: The effects of frame-of-reference and pretest validity information on personality test responses and test perceptions. *International Journal of Selection and Assessment, 13*, 75–86.
Hough, L. M., Oswald, F. L., & Ployhart, R. E. (2001). Determinants, detection and amelioration of adverse impact in personnel selection procedures: Issues, evidence and lessons learned. *International Journal of Selection and Assessment, 9*, 152–194.
Hunthausen, J. M., Truxillo, D. M., Bauer, T. B., & Hammer, B. L. (2003). A field study of frame-of-reference effects on personality test validity. *Journal of Applied Psychology, 88*, 545–551.
Karraker v. Rent-A-Center, 411 F.3d 831, 833 (7th Cir. 2005).
Kuncel, N. R., & Highhouse, S. (2011). Complex predictions and assessor mystique. *Industrial and Organizational Psychology: Perspectives on Science and Practice, 4*, 302–306.
LaHuis, D. M., Perreault, N. E., & Ferguson, M. W. (2003). The effect of legitimizing explanations on applicants' perceptions of selection assessment fairness. *Journal of Applied Social Psychology, 33*, 2198–2215.
Lievens, F., DeCorte, W., & Schollaert, E. (2008). A closer look at the frame-of-reference effect in personality scale scores and validity. *Journal of Applied Psychology, 93*, 268–279.
Luther, N. J., & Thornton, G. C. (1999). Does faking on employment test matter? *Employment Testing Law and Policy Reporter, 8*, 129–136.
McKenna v. Fargo, 451 F. Supp. 1355 (D.N.J. 1978), affirmed, 601 F.2d 575 (3rd Cir. 1979).
Menjoge, S. S. (2003). Testing the limits of anti-discrimination law: How employers use of pre-employment psychological and personality tests can circumvent Title VII and the ADA. *North Carolina Law Review, 82*, 326–365.
Miller v. City of Springfield, 146 F.3d 612 (8th Cir. 1998).
Mook, J. R. (1996). Personality testing in today's workplace: Avoiding the legal pitfalls. *Employee Relations Law Journal, 22*, 65–88.
Morris, S. B., Kwaske, I. H., & Daisley, R. R. (2011). The validity of individual psychological assessment. *Industrial and Organizational Psychology: Perspectives on Science and Practice, 4*, 322–326.
Mulvihill, M. E. (2006). *Karraker v. Rent-A-Center*: Testing the limits of the ADA, personality testing, and employer pre-employment screening. *Loyola University Chicago Law Journal, 37*, 865–910.
Myors, B., Mariani, M., Lievens, F., Schollaert, E., Van Hoye, G., Fraccaroli, F., & Bayazit, M. (2008). Broadening international perspectives on the legal environment for personnel selection. *Industrial and Organizational Psychology: Perspectives on Science and Practice, 1*, 266–270.
Nevins, J. L. (2005). Measuring the mind: A comparison of personality testing to polygraph testing in the hiring process. *Penn State Law Review, 109*, 857–883.
O'Meara, D. P. (1994, January). Personality tests raise questions of legality and effectiveness. *HR Magazine, 39*, 97–103.
Pearlman, K. (2009). Unproctored Internet testing: Practical, legal, and ethical concerns. *Industrial and Organizational Psychology: Perspectives on Science and Practice, 2*, 14–19.

Re Vey, 124 N.J. 534, 591 A.2d 1333 (1991), appeal after remand, 272 N.J. Super. 199, 639 A.2d 724 (1993), affirmed, 135 N.J. 306, 639 A.2d 718 (1994).

Reeder, M. C., & Ryan, A. M. (2011). Methods for correcting for faking. In M. Ziegle, C. MacCann, & R. D. Roberts (Eds.), *New perspectives on faking in personality assessments* (pp. 131–150). New York: Oxford University Press.

Reynolds v. State of Arizona, 992 F.2d 1220, 1993 WL 133831 (9th Cir. 1993).

Rosse, J., Miller, J. L., & Stecher, M. D. (1994). A field study of job applicants' reactions to personality and cognitive ability testing. *Journal of Applied Psychology, 79*, 987–992.

Sackett, P. R., & Ellingson, J. E. (1997). The effects of forming multi-predictor composites on group differences and adverse impact. *Personnel Psychology, 50*, 707–721.

Sackett, P. R., & Wilk, S. L. (1994). Within-group norming and other forms of score adjustment in psychological testing. *American Psychologist, 49*, 929–954.

Schmit, M. J., Ryan, A. M., Stierwalt, S. L., & Powell, S. L. (1995). Frame-of-reference effects on personality scores and criterion-related validity. *Journal of Applied Psychology, 80*, 607–620.

Silzer, R., & Jeanneret, R. (2011). Individual psychological assessment: A practice and science in search of common ground. *Industrial and Organizational Psychology: Perspectives on Science and Practice, 4*, 270–296.

Siskin, B. R., & Trippi, J. (2005). Statistical issues in litigation. In F. J. Landy (Ed.), *Employment discrimination litigation: Behavioral, quantitative, and legal perspectives* (pp. 132–166). San Francisco: Jossey-Bass.

Smith, D. M. (2006). The paradox of personality: Mental illness, employment discrimination, and the Americans with Disabilities Act. *George Mason University Civil Rights Law Journal, 17*, 1–59.

Society for Human Resource Management. (2011). *SHRM poll: Social networking websites and online search engines for screening job candidates [online]*. Retrieved from http://www.shrm.org/Research/SurveyFindings/Articles/Pages/TheUseofSocialNetworkingWebsitesandOnlineSearchEnginesinScreeningJobCandidates.aspx

Society for Industrial and Organizational Psychology. (2003). *Principles for the validation and use of personnel selection procedures* (4th ed.). Author. Retrieved from http://www.siop.org/_Principles/principles.pdf

Soroka v. Dayton Hudson Corp., 6 Ind. Empl. Rights Case (BNA) 1491 (Cal. Ct. App. 1991).

Stabile, S. J. (2002). The use of personality tests as a hiring tool: Is the benefit worth the cost? *University of Pennsylvania Journal of Labor and Employment Law, 4*, 279–313.

Tett, R. P., Fitzke, J. R., Wadlington, P. L., Davies, S. A., Anderson, M. G., & Foster, J. (2009). The use of personality test norms in work settings: Effects of sample size and relevance. *Journal of Occupational and Organizational Psychology, 82*, 639–659.

Thompson v. Borg Warner Protective Services, 1996, U.S. Dist., Lexis 4781.

Tippins, N. T. (2009). Internet alternatives to traditional proctored testing: Where are we now? *Industrial and Organizational Psychology: Perspectives on Science and Practice, 2*, 2–10.

Tippins, N. T., Beatty, J., Drasgow, F., Gibson, W. M., Pearlman, K., Segall, D. O., & Shepherd, W. (2006). Unproctored Internet testing in employment settings. *Personnel Psychology, 59*, 189–225.

Vetter, G. R. (1999). Is a personality test a pre-job-offer medical examination under the ADA? *Northwestern Law Review, 93*, 597–639.

Weiner, J. A., & Morrison, J. D., Jr. (2009). Unproctored online testing: Environmental conditions and validity. *Industrial and Organizational Psychology: Perspectives on Science and Practice, 2*, 14–19.

Whitehouse, K. (2005, July 13). Employers face risks with use of a popular personality test. *The Wall Street Journal*, pp. B1–B2.

Woods, D. R., & Savino, D. M. (2007). Do you blush often? Questions on integrity and personality tests that legally embarrass employers. *Employee Relations Law Journal, 33*, 3–31.

24

Personality and the Analysis, Design, and Delivery of Training

Christina L. Wilson, Jason L. Huang, and Kurt Kraiger

The benefits of effective training have been well established through empirical research (for reviews, see Aguinis & Kraiger, 2009; Arthur, Bennett, Edens, & Bell, 2003; Salas et al., 2008; Salas, Tannenbaum, Kraiger, & Smith-Jentsch, 2012). Moreover, considerable progress has been made in building a science of training (Salas & Cannon-Bowers, 2001; Salas et al., 2012), particularly with respect to linking individual states and organization-level variables to training outcomes before, during, and after training (see Cannon-Bowers, Tannenbaum, Salas, & Converse, 1991; Kozlowski & Salas, 1997). Still, relevant personality variables have received less empirical attention than are perhaps deserved. In general, training is widely considered to be a cognitive, skill-based intervention, whereas personality traditionally captures enduring personal characteristics (and thus less amenable to change). To provide a framework for future research and practice, we will review the relevant literature on personality in the development, delivery, and evaluation of training, while highlighting variables and topics in need of further examination.

Goldstein and Ford (2002) defined training as "the systematic acquisition of skills, rules, concepts or attitudes that result in improved performance in another environment" (p. 1). Noe (2002) distinguished between training and development: training refers to activities designed to enhance knowledge, skill, ability, and other characteristics for which there is an immediate application, whereas development refers to activities that facilitate personal growth or enhance knowledge, skills, abilities, or other characteristics for which there is no direct or immediate application but instead prepare an individual for future aspirations (for coverage more focused on personality development, see Chapter 35, this volume). Although this distinction is very important, the activities themselves are not always distinguishable depending on whether the intention is training or development. Therefore, personality is likely relevant for activities targeted at either purpose. This being the case, we will focus our discussion on the activities themselves and will use the term "training" to refer to those activities regardless of whether their purpose is development or training.

Traditionally, the emphasis of training research is the design and delivery of the training (the training environment) around critical job tasks or knowledge and skills underlying those tasks. Although individual differences of trainees are generally agreed to be important determinants of training outcomes, less emphasis has been placed on some individual differences than on others. Noe (1986) pointed out that most training models have focused on ability, leaving other characteristics all but ignored. Indeed, cognitive ability is a strong predictor of training success (Ree, Carretta, & Teachout, 1995; Ree & Earles, 1991). However, over the past two decades, more emphasis has been placed on personality differences (e.g., Colquitt, LePine, & Noe, 2000; Martocchio & Webster,

1992; Mathieu, Tannenbaum, & Salas, 1992; Quiñones, 1995) and performance in training (e.g., S. M. Gully, Payne, Knoles, & Whiteman, 2002; Lievens, Harris, VanKeer, & Bisqueret, 2003; Washburn, Smith, Baker, & Raby, 2001). Accordingly, a review of the recent literature examining the role of personality in the design, delivery, and evaluation of training is timely. Our purpose throughout this chapter is to identify and summarize previous findings regarding the role of personality in training as well as to offer suggestions and propositions to guide future research in an attempt to fill the gaps in understanding.

As we will highlight throughout this chapter, we see two ways in which a stronger consideration of personality variables can have a positive effect on training outcomes in organizations. First, training can compensate for behaviors for which the individual lacks the propensity (or trait) to engage in naturally. Customer service skills, for example, might be trained in those lacking traits like empathy and tolerance (which make those who possess such traits more "naturally skilled" at customer service). Second, training can provide a basis for trait activation (Tett & Burnett, 2003): Features of training systems and training support environments can trigger key learning-related traits (e.g., openness to experience and learning goal orientation [LGO]), thereby facilitating training effectiveness. These considerations, as well as direct and moderating effects of personality on training decisions and training outcomes, are discussed throughout this chapter.

How Are We Using the Term Personality? Two Foci

For the purposes of this chapter, we will use two foci in our examination of personality. First, we focus on core personality traits, the Big Five. The Big Five personality characteristics (conscientiousness, agreeableness, openness to experience, neuroticism, and extraversion) have proven to be a useful categorization of personality traits across various domains (Barrick & Mount, 2005). Substantial research has been dedicated to the Big Five, and scores on these five factors have been shown to be relatively stable over time and across situations. The Big Five personality characteristics have also been shown to predict outcomes of interest, such as job performance and training outcomes (Baldwin & Ford, 1988; Barrick & Mount, 1991; Barrick, Mount, & Judge, 2001; Salas & Cannon-Bowers, 2001; Salgado 1997). However, there has been little research on the Big Five factors of personality on decision making with respect to training in general and on the process of training in particular. That is, most of the research in this domain has focused on outcomes such as learning or in-training performance (e.g., Lievens et al., 2003).

Our second focus is on a broad definition of personality characteristics beyond the Big Five, including persistent self-concept traits such as trait goal orientation, adaptability, self-efficacy, and locus of control (e.g., Colquitt et al., 2000; S. Gully & Chen, 2010; Salas & Cannon-Bowers, 2001). This focus is consistent with Tett and Guterman (2000), who defined personality as "intraindividual consistencies and interindividual uniquenesses in propensities to behave in identifiable ways in light of situational demands" (p. 398). This definition of personality is more useful for the purposes of understanding the process of training than the more narrowly defined five-factor model of personality. In fact, research in the training domain related to personality tends to include characteristics that meet this broader definition of personality, and there is substantially more research on these types of characteristics than on the Big Five.

These broad personality characteristics are generally considered dispositional. However, there is also evidence that each may be situationally activated as well. For example, Button, Mathieu, and Zajac (1996) found evidence that goal orientation has distinguishable situational and dispositional aspects. While we recognize situational influences on these and other personality characteristics, given the nascent state of personality research in training, we will tend to treat the personality variables we review as relatively stable attributes of individuals.

Framework for the Rest of This Chapter

Goldstein and Ford (2002) summarized the classic instructional system design model that identifies four key stages to training design and delivery: needs assessment, training design and delivery, transfer of training, and training evaluation. In this chapter, we organize our discussion of personality and training by roughly following these four stages. First, we will discuss how personality is relevant during the needs assessment stage of the training process, regarding what to train, who to train, and how to train. Relevant to this discussion is two ways in which training design may be affected by personality information. First, there are certain personality traits that lend themselves well to success in training (e.g., conscientiousness and openness to experience). Second, training may be useful as an intervention to redress a lack of a trait that is predictive of successful completion of job tasks. Both of these roles will be addressed where relevant within the following sections. Next, we will focus on various aspects of the delivery of training for which personality is relevant, including the characteristics of learners, characteristics of trainers, and interactions between these individual characteristics and characteristics of the environment and design of training. As stated above, personality can be considered both in terms of the design of compensatory training (for individuals lacking on key traits) and in terms of the design of training environments that activate key learning traits. Then, we will focus on the role of personality in learning and the transfer of training, the trainees' application of the knowledge and skills gained during training to their jobs (Broad & Newstrom, 1992). Finally, we will next discuss the relevance of personality in the evaluation of training, including how individual trainees' personalities may affect self-report reactions to training, as well as how personalities may interact with training design in measures of training effectiveness. Finally, we will discuss future directions for research in personality and training.

Needs Assessment

The first step in the training process is training needs assessment (Goldstein & Ford, 2002). The needs assessment phase is the information gathering and planning phase of training. What needs to be trained? Who needs to be trained? What is the context of the organization where training will take place? This phase can be considered the development of the training road map and is rife with relevance to personality. Consideration of personality variables can affect what to train, who to train, and how training should be designed to ensure that individual differences related to learning are activated. Colquitt et al. (2000) underscored the need to include personality during the needs assessment phase of training design. The authors found that scores on personality measures showed promising relationships with declarative knowledge, motivation to learn (MTL), and transfer of training. This suggests that what an individual brings into training is important to training outcomes and should be considered from the beginning of the training process.

Organization Analysis

In its classic form, needs assessment consists of three steps: organization analysis, task analysis, and person analysis (Goldstein & Ford, 2002). The purpose of the organization analysis is to determine whether or not the organization is ready to provide the required support for training. The role of personality at this phase is tangential, yet important. Training analysts do not assess individuals at this stage, but an important question is how organization-level variables (e.g., climate and learning environment) either attract certain types of learners or activate characteristics that, in turn, may have an impact later in the process. If the organization analysis reveals that there is not sufficient support for the enactment of learning behaviors associated with certain traits (e.g., goal orientation), then it becomes more critical to design effective learning environments in training.

Following from trait activation theory (Tett & Burnett, 2003; Tett & Guterman, 2000; Chapter 5, this volume), aspects of the environment may be strong enough to inhibit activation of certain traits, while masking individual differences in other traits. For example, one would not expect to witness a fistfight in a library because the situational cues at the library strongly discourage activation of aggressive traits. However, in the heat of battle, one may have difficulty in discerning differences among soldiers' aggressive tendencies because the situational cues strongly endorse behaviors that would be considered aggressive (Tett & Guterman, 2000). In contrast, there are situations in which the situational cues are weaker and individual differences are more likely to predict behavior. Applying these principles to organizational analysis, very strong organizational climates (i.e., those in which situational cues are very strong) are likely to engender specific behaviors despite individual differences in organization members. An example of this type of organization would be the military, where standard operating procedures are in place for most activities, and there is a strong culture that drives behavior in most situations, from interactions with superiors to how clothing is worn. In such organizations, personality may be less important because individual differences in the performance of a job are discouraged. Skills are more important in a situation such as the military because there are only a few correct ways to behave; thus, training is more important to ensure that all employees know exactly how to behave and how to correctly complete each task. Conversely, when an organizational climate is weak (i.e., when situational cues brought on by climate in the organization are weak), then individual differences will play a larger role in predicting behavior. For example, in an organization where innovation and creativity are key traits, and there are numerous means to succeed, the situational cues are likely to be less restrictive of individual differences in behavior and specific task completion. In this case, personality will take on a more important role in predicting success of employees, and training may be less important or may need to be more flexible so that training content may be tailored to individual styles.

Trait activation theory is further relevant to training needs assessment in terms of whether or not organizational climate activates traits that are beneficial for the success of the training process, such as MTL. MTL refers to the desire and willingness to engage in learning and development activities and to persist with learning of training content (Noe, 1986). A further discussion of MTL can be found in the "Person Analysis" section. If trait antecedents to MTL (e.g., conscientiousness and locus of control) are not activated by the organizational climate, then the training itself may need to be designed to activate these traits. Organizations with a strong culture for continuous learning, for example, are likely to activate traits relevant to MTL. In organizations lacking a pro-learning culture, training interventions may be designed explicitly to provide the situational cues that will activate learning traits. Traits that are strongly activated by organizational culture may also need to be considered as impactful during the training process. That is, training delivery decisions may be more effective if due consideration is given to traits that are identified as relevant in particular work settings. For example, an organization with a strong culture for collaboration should require individual employees to demonstrate agreeableness, and training would likely be more effective if design decisions were made in consideration of this expectation.

Note that trait activation theory has not been studied in regard to its impact on training within organizations. The arguments provided here serve as a proposal for future directions in training research.

Task Analysis

Task analysis, on the surface, does not seem to be relevant to a discussion about personality. However, there are aspects of task analysis that may require considerations of personality. The product of a task analysis is a list of key tasks that need to be trained. Traditionally, task analysis includes a detailing of the tasks and required knowledge, skills, abilities, and other attributes (KSAOs) involved in a job. "Other" attributes often refer to personality characteristics that are required to perform a function well. For example, a sales employee who exhibits extraversion is more likely to be successful than a sales employee who exhibits introversion (e.g., Barrick, Stewart, & Piotrowski, 2002). Where there is a gap between the desired attributes and attributes present in the workforce, there is a need to train. That is, when there are identified work behaviors that are related to effective performance, but individuals lack traits or characteristics likely to display those behaviors, then it is more important to design training to compensate for trait levels among employees. To be clear, an example of a task is making a presentation to a potential client; the level of extraversion may affect how that presentation is delivered. Employees naturally high in extraversion may benefit little from training on this skill, whereas employees naturally low in extraversion may benefit significantly more from training in planning and skills required to make a successful presentation. Thus, understanding the effects of personality attributes may lead to more refined decisions of what tasks to train and how they should be trained.

On the other hand, the attribute itself may be targeted for training. Some research has shown that, at least in the short term, certain personality characteristics do respond to training interventions. For example, characteristics such as self-regulation and goal orientation have been shown to change as a result of training interventions (e.g., Baumeister, Gailliot, DeWall, & Oaten, 2006; Blackwell, 2002; Leonardelli, Herman, Lynch, & Arkin, 2003; McEnrue, Groves, & Shen, 2009). If personality is considered as an "other characteristic" in the task analysis phase of the training needs assessment, then personality traits relevant for successful task performance should be considered in making decisions regarding both training objectives (to instill behaviors that compensate for a lack of natural traits) and training targets (selecting for training those individuals who are likely to benefit most from the training).

Although the task analysis stage generally focuses on identifying critical job tasks, from the perspective of personality theory, it is also important to consider the activation of traits as a function of the tasks (and how that determines training content). Certain personality characteristics may influence an employee's decision to attend or to avoid a particular training program depending on the tasks involved in the training. As an example, consider a training intervention on team problem-solving that includes role playing within the team. Such a task may be threatening to individuals low on extraversion and/or self-esteem, leading those individuals to avoid the training altogether. Decisions must be made about training content, training delivery, and training environment that will encourage participation, particularly in those individuals who stand to benefit most from the training. One solution may be to develop an error management culture within the training environment in which individuals are encouraged to share the errors that they make and to feel safe to make errors during training because errors are seen as learning opportunities rather than disastrous events to be avoided at all cost (vanDyck, Frese, Baer, & Sonnentag, 2005). Alternatively, creating a safe training environment that is free from judgment may be all that is required to encourage participation.

Person Analysis

The third step in the needs assessment phase is person analysis. Person analysis has several goals, including development of performance indicators, determination of KSAO gaps in the target population, and determination of the best approach to resolve the gaps through examination of the learning environment (Goldstein & Ford, 2002). Personality is relevant to each of these goals. Note too that person analysis as described here overlaps significantly with personality-oriented job analysis (for a detailed description of personality-oriented job analysis, see Chapter 11, this volume).

Developing performance indicators entails making decisions about what behaviors and outcomes will be used to evaluate performance as desirable or undesirable. For some training interventions, the intended outcome may be a change in the behavioral expression of a personality characteristic, such as self-efficacy (Bandura, 1997), extraversion, goal orientation, emotional intelligence (McEnrue et al., 2009), and self-regulation (Baumeister et al., 2006). In short, when training outcomes are considered, personality characteristics should not be ignored as there is compelling evidence that training interventions targeting the behavioral expression of characteristics can be effective.

During task analysis, a determination is made about required KSAOs. During person analysis, KSAO gaps in the target population are identified. This informs decisions about who should receive training and what training is required. When there is a gap between the characteristics desired and the characteristics observed, there is need for a training intervention. When those desired characteristics are personality traits, then training interventions should be focused on development of behaviors associated with those traits, as discussed above.

Another aspect of person analysis, as it relates to gap analysis, is determining the readiness of the individual to succeed in training. Holton, Bates, and Ruona (2000) defined readiness to learn as "the extent to which individuals are prepared to enter and participate in training" (p. 344). Knowles, Holton, and Swanson (2005) characterized readiness to learn as inclusive of cognitive and physical ability as well as MTL. Many personality characteristics have been found to be related to MTL as follows. Conceptually, personality may be considered one predictor or determinant of MTL.

Major, Turner, and Fletcher (2006) used a web-based survey of employees of a financial services company to determine that extraversion, openness to experience, and conscientiousness are all moderately positively related to MTL. Colquitt and Simmering (1998) also found conscientiousness to be positively related to MTL. Similarly, in a meta-analysis by Colquitt et al. (2000), achievement motivation and conscientiousness were positively related to MTL. Colquitt et al. also found that locus of control was strongly related to MTL; those with a more internal locus of control exhibited greater MTL as compared to those with a more external locus of control. Anxiety was strongly negatively related to MTL and to posttraining self-efficacy.

Goal orientation has also been shown to be related to MTL. Goal orientation consists of two separate factors: an LGO, in which the individual is driven by the desire to master a skill or learn content, and a performance goal orientation (PGO), in which the individual is driven by the desire to demonstrate his or her proficiency and skill to others (Dweck, 1986). Colquitt and Simmering (1998), in a longitudinal study, found that an LGO was positively related to MTL, while a PGO was negatively related to MTL.

One important predictor of MTL is self-efficacy or "beliefs in one's capabilities to organize and execute the courses of action required to produce given attainments" (Bandura, 1997, p. 3). Self-efficacy may be task specific or generalized. Generalized self-efficacy (GSE) is defined as "one's belief in one's overall competence to effect requisite performance across a wide variety of achievement situations" (Eden, 2001, p. 75). Individuals high in self-efficacy are more likely to participate in learning activities, work harder and persist longer in learning activities, and have fewer negative emotional reactions in response to challenge and difficulty (Bandura, 1977, 1997; Phan, 2011). Chen, Gully, Whiteman, and Kilcullen (2000) found that after controlling for ability and goal orientation, GSE was related to learning performance, primarily through an effect on task-specific efficacy. There is little doubt that self-efficacy is an important variable throughout the training process.

Goal orientation plays a direct and complex role in readiness to learn. Hofmann (1993) found that a PGO's negative effect on task performance was mediated by distracting cognitions and that the relationship between PGO and task performance was moderated by cognitive ability for final performance but not for initial performance. This suggests that those higher in cognitive ability may have more resources to overcome the distracting cognitions brought about by a PGO.

Here we see an important conceptual and practical connection between personality and training. If the person analysis reveals the overall presence (across employees) of personality variables that predict pretraining MTL, the focus of training should be on what and how to train (with the assumption that most trainees are ready to learn). However, if the analysis reveals that many or most employees lack attributes predictive of MTL, then interventions should be designed within training to enhance trainees' MTL at the outset.

Personality characteristics also have indirect effects on training outcomes through their effects on learner behaviors. As an example, setting challenging goals in training facilitates learning and performance. Several personality characteristics (LGO, self-efficacy, locus of control, and conscientiousness) predict the content of, commitment to, and level of self-set goals (Barrick, Mount, & Strauss, 1993; Brett & VandeWalle, 1999; Chen, Gully, & Eden, 2004; Chen et al., 2000; Hollenbeck & Klein, 1987; Kozlowski et al., 2001; Phillips & Gully, 1997). Phillips and Gully offer a comprehensive model of personality and goal setting that includes ability, goal orientation, and locus of control as predictors of self-efficacy, which, in turn, predicts self-set goals along with the need for achievement. Future research should focus on including core personality characteristics into the model. For example, conscientiousness is not included in the Phillips and Gully model but likely plays a role in setting goals.

Training Delivery

The delivery phase of training refers to the actual training activities themselves. This may include technology-mediated or face-to-face training, as well as training that occurs in groups or one-on-one, such as on-the-job training. As training design has been discussed previously, we will focus our attention here on the people involved directly with the training itself and interactions among those people. Specifically, we consider characteristics of the trainer and characteristics of the trainee. Later, an interaction between the training environment and the characteristics of the trainee will be discussed in detail.

Trainer Characteristics

Trainer characteristics have received little attention in the training literature despite calls for research into this aspect of training (Steiner, Dobbins, & Trahan, 1991; Wexley, 1984; Wexley & Latham, 1981). Earlier research examined trainer characteristics such as position power and perceived competence (e.g., Justis, Kedia, & Stephens, 1978). More recently, there has been a resurgence of interest in this area with research on the effects of trainer characteristics, such as practical experience (Gan, Lee, & Soutar, 2009), reputation (A. Towler & Dipboye, 2006), attractiveness (Rechlin, 2009), expressiveness and organization (A. J. Towler, 2009; A. J. Towler & Dipboye, 2001), and demographic characteristics such as race and sex (Holladay & Quiñones, 2008). However, trainer personality characteristics have been generally ignored to date, even though some trainer personality characteristics may be very important for training outcomes (Surface & Ellington, 2008). For example, in one large study of over 700 military trainees and 50-plus civilian trainers, Ellington and Surface (2009) found that trainer conscientiousness predicted trainees' intent to transfer and trainers' performance orientation and that agreeableness predicted trainees' learning self-efficacy.

The self-efficacy of the trainer is also important, as self-efficacy has been strongly linked with performance in many situations (Bandura, 1997). Self-efficacy regarding the ability to carry out the tasks required to conduct training and self-efficacy regarding bringing about the required outcomes are likely related to effective training performance on the part of the trainer. Clearly, individuals selected by the organization to conduct training should have high self-efficacy for training behaviors, but there may be considerable variability in on-the-job trainers in this characteristic because on-the-job trainers are often chosen based on their ability to perform the required tasks of the job rather than their ability or desire to deliver training. Instructor conscientiousness and agreeableness would also seem to be related to trainee learning. Future research should focus on personality characteristics of trainers and their effects on training outcomes. Attention needs to be given to the characteristics of trainers and how those characteristics interact with the training environment and trainee characteristics to predict training outcomes.

Trainee Characteristics

Big Five

In stark contrast to trainer characteristics, trainee characteristics have received a great deal of research attention. Personality characteristics, including the core traits of the Big Five as well as other traits, have been examined in relation to training outcomes. For example, Barrick and Mount (1991) meta-analyzed personality research and reported that the corrected validity coefficient for openness to experience (of trainees) on their training proficiency was significant ($\rho = .25$). The corrected validity coefficient for extraversion as a predictor of training proficiency was similar in strength ($\rho = .26$). Although none of the other Big Five factors predicted training performance, this does not rule out the relevance of conscientiousness, emotional stability, and agreeableness to training performance. It is worth bearing in mind that trait activation theory offers an overarching explanation: the presence or absence of various organization and task cues may differentially activate each trait, making it possible for a trait to be positively related to training performance in one study, while being negatively related in another. These contradictory relationships can cancel each other out, resulting in a weak meta-analytic validity coefficient.

Campbell, Castaneda, and Pulos (2010) recently conducted a meta-analytic review of personality characteristics predicting training outcomes for military aviation training. They reported small but significant corrected correlations between training success and neuroticism ($r = -.25$), extraversion ($r = .17$), and anxiety ($r = -.14$). Lievens et al. (2003) studied the factors that predict performance in cross-cultural training for expatriate managers. They found the strongest corrected relationship between openness to experience and training performance ($r = .33$). Conscientiousness also predicted training performance ($r = .20$) as did agreeableness ($r = -.26$, corrected). Emotional stability and extraversion were not found to be significant predictors of training performance in this study. Big Five factors also have been examined as predictors of MTL in two independent studies (Major et al., 2006; Rowold, 2007). Major et al. reported a significant, negative relationship between introversion and MTL ($r = -.39$) and a significant, positive relationship between MTL and openness to experience ($r = .23$). Rowold reported the relationship between MTL and extraversion as significant and positive ($r = .20$), although not as strong as the relationship reported by Major et al. The relationship between MTL and openness to experience reported by Rowold was very similar to that reported by Major et al. ($r = .20$). However, there were some differences in the findings. Major et al. found that conscientiousness predicted MTL ($r = .16$), while Rowold did not ($r = .06$). Rowold reported that agreeableness predicted MTL ($r = .34$), while Major et al. did not ($r = -.06$). Both studies used field samples of current employees; however, the study by Major et al. relied on archival personality and training data compared to surveys measuring MTL. In contrast, Rowold administered surveys at three time points to employees currently involved in a training program within their organization. The differences in the findings between these studies could be explained as sampling error or may be indicative of moderating variables in the relationship between personality characteristics and MTL. For example, the differences in data collection techniques used may account for the differences in the findings. Alternatively, different training and organizational environments may account for the different findings.

Self-Efficacy

Moving away from a focus on the Big Five factors of personality traits, there are many other characteristics that have received a great deal of research attention in the area of trainee characteristics. Among the most prolific topics is self-efficacy. Whether dispositional or situational, or generalized or task specific, self-efficacy has been shown to be a strong predictor of performance across a wide variety of situations, including training (Cole & Latham, 1997; Combs & Luthans, 2007; Eden & Aviram, 1993; Ford, Smith, Weissbein, Gully, & Salas, 1998; Martocchio, 1994; Martocchio & Webster, 1992; Mathieu, Martineau, & Tannenbaum, 1993; Mathieu et al., 1992; Mitchell, Hopper, Daniels, George-Falvy, & James, 1994; Phillips & Gully, 1997; Quiñones, 1995; Stajkovic & Luthans, 1998; Stevens & Gist, 1997). Colquitt et al. (2000) found through meta-analysis that self-efficacy, along with locus of control, conscientiousness, and anxiety, was a strong predictor of training motivation and outcomes. But self-efficacy is not only a direct predictor of performance; it has also been found to be a moderator in predicting performance. For example, Dierdorff, Surface, and Brown (2010) reported an interaction between self-efficacy and goal orientation in predicting performance during frame of reference training as well as near transfer of the trained skills. Specifically, higher levels of self-efficacy reduced the negative effects of a performance-avoid goal orientation. Note that performance-avoid goal orientation is a subdimension of a PGO wherein the goal is to avoid demonstrating lack of competence by avoiding performing on a task where there is risk of error or failure (Elliot, 1999; VandeWalle, 1996, as cited in Payne, Youngcourt, & Beaubien, 2007). Similarly, Sitzmann, Bell, Kraiger, and Kanar (2009) found that self-efficacy moderated the relationship between self-regulation and strategic performance in technology-delivered instruction, such that subjects with higher task-specific self-efficacy demonstrated stronger increases in strategic performance (i.e., learning of deeper complexities of a task) when prompted to self-regulate than subjects with lower task-specific self-efficacy in the same conditions. Given research to date on the potency of self-efficacy in affecting individual behavior, perhaps all training interventions may benefit from considering self-efficacy at the trait and state levels.

As noted above, one value for considerable personality variables is to design training differently when trainees are lacking on attributes considered important for job performance or learning. Researchers have successfully used training interventions designed to redress a lack of trait self-efficacy in trainees with promising results. For example, Eden and Zuk (1995) conducted an intervention with naval cadets attempting to increase the cadets' self-efficacy for working through seasickness. After the training intervention, cadets who underwent the training reported less seasickness and were rated as better performers than cadets in a control condition. Including self-efficacy interventions along with the delivery of any training material may be considered a best practice.

Goal Orientation

Another motivational personality trait that has been the focus of a great deal of research on trainee characteristics is goal orientation. As discussed above, goal orientation is generally composed of two dimensions: PGO and mastery goal orientation. Theoretical and empirical development in the area of goal orientation (Dweck, 1986; Dweck & Leggett, 1988; Heyman & Dweck, 1992; Licht & Dweck, 1984) has enabled training researchers to study how individuals' propensity to adopt different types of goals may influence their learning and performance. Most studies have focused on trait mastery versus PGO (see Button et al., 1996), whereas a number of studies adopted the three-dimensional approach (mastery, performance-prove, and performance-avoid; see VandeWalle, 1997). PGO can be further broken down into approach and avoid orientations. Performance-approach goal orientation is the propensity to strive to demonstrate competence through performance and a desire for positive judgments of performance. Performance-avoid goal orientation is the propensity to avoid situations that may end in negative judgments of performance (Elliot, 1999).

Brett and VandeWalle (1999) studied the effects of trait goal orientation by surveying MBA students trained for presentation skills. The authors found that mastery, performance-prove, and performance-avoid goal orientations influenced the content of goals trainees adopted during training. Both mastery and performance-prove orientations were positively related to content goals that were relevant to skill development. These developmental goals subsequently led to greater training performance.

Goal orientation can predict training outcomes. As an example, Ford et al. (1998) found that LGO predicted metacognitive activity (i.e., monitoring one's own progress and adjusting learning strategies to achieve learning goals) during training, which, in turn, predicted knowledge acquisition, skill performance, and task-specific self-efficacy. Kozlowski et al. (2001) included both dispositional goal orientation and situation-specific goal orientation into a model predicting adaptive performance after training. They found that trait learning (or mastery) goal orientation did predict task-specific self-efficacy, which, in turn, predicted adaptive performance. Additionally, situation-specific goal orientation predicted knowledge structure coherence as well as self-efficacy, both of which contributed independently to the prediction of adaptive performance after training. Adaptive performance refers to generalization of knowledge and skills from the practice task to a novel task (Pulakos, Arad, Donovan, & Plamondon, 2000).

Much of the prior discussion looks at the effects of performance orientation on learning in training. Empirical research also generally supports the positive effect of mastery orientation on training performance (e.g., Orvis, Fisher, & Wasserman, 2009; A. J. Towler & Dipboye, 2001), as mastery-oriented individuals tend to exert more effort in learning (Fisher & Ford, 1998), adopt more metacognitive learning strategies (Ford et al., 1998), and stay on task after receiving feedback (VandeWalle, Cron, & Slocum, 2001). As with self-efficacy, it is important that goal orientation be considered in the delivery of training interventions to enhance learning. The finding that situation-specific goal orientation is independently related to training outcomes is promising in that training interventions can be designed to facilitate a learning goal in trainees despite a preexisting, dispositional PGO.

Researchers have also started to investigate the interactive effects of goal orientation scales on training outcomes. Ely, Sitzmann, and Falkiewicz (2009) found that trainees' mastery and performance-avoid goal orientations interacted in affecting the time spent on an online occupational training program. Individuals who scored low on both scales were more likely to spend less time on the training than individuals who scored high on one or both of the scales. Similarly, Yeo and Neal (2004) found that mastery orientation moderated the negative effect of performance orientation, such that highly performance-oriented individuals suffered most in performance when they were also low on mastery orientation.

Locus of control was developed in social learning theory to account for the observed variation across people in their expectancies of the contingency between their behavior and observed outcomes (Rotter, 1966; Rotter, Chance, & Phares, 1972). An internal generalized expectancy is associated with seeing reinforcements, rewards, or outcomes in life as being controlled by one's actions as opposed to other forces (Spector, 1988). Noe (1986) argued that locus of control plays an important role in the training process as it may affect antecedents to trainees' MTL. For example, Phillips and Gully (1997) demonstrated a positive association between internal locus of control and self-efficacy.

However, Colquitt et al.'s (2000) meta-analytic findings suggested a complex role of locus of control in the training process: while external locus of control was negatively associated with MTL, it had a positive relationship with declarative knowledge acquisition while having no influence on either skill acquisition or posttraining self-efficacy. Taken together, it is not surprising that Blume, Ford, Baldwin, and Huang (2010) found no effect of locus of control on transfer.

Need for cognition denotes individuals' tendency to engage in and enjoy effortful cognitive activities (Cacioppo, Petty, Feinstein, & Jarvis, 1996). It is conceptualized as a trait-like motivational construct that can impact motivational states (Nair & Ramnarayan, 2000; Verplanken, 1993). The effects of need for cognition have only been examined in the training setting in a limited number of studies. Sadowski and Gulgoz (1996) found a positive influence of need for cognition on course performance in two social psychology courses. In a complex computer simulation training program, need for cognition influenced skill acquisition through state mastery goals and self-efficacy (Day, Espejo, Kowollik, Boatman, & McEntire, 2007).

Learning styles refer to individuals' preferred ways of information acquisition and processing. The fundamental thesis in the application of learning style is a person by situation interaction: learning can be maximized when an individual receives his/her preferred style of instruction. Although different conceptualizations and operationalizations of learning styles exist in the literature, the two underlying dimensions of cognitive growth identified by Kolb (1976, 1984)—active versus reflective and abstract versus concrete—provided a theoretical framework for studying learning styles. While several studies reported significant trait influences on learning styles (e.g., Furnham, 1992; Furnham, Jackson, Forde, & Cotter, 2001), few studies investigated the role of learning styles in adult training contexts. Two exceptions are noted here.

L.-Y. Lee and Li (2008) examined the extent to which expatriates' perceived need for expatriate training would interact with the match/mismatch between their learning styles and the instructors' teaching styles to influence training effectiveness. Their survey from 197 expatriates in China demonstrated that perceived need for expatriate training was more strongly associated with self-reported training effectiveness when expatriates' learning styles matched with the instruction styles. In contrast, Kappe, Boekholt, den Rooyen, and Van der Flier (2009) showed no support for the notion that learning styles would predict corresponding learning criteria in college, casting doubt on the potential use of learning styles.

Learning and Transfer

From the organization's perspective, the ultimate goal of training activities is that trainees learn the targeted knowledge and skills and then transfer the knowledge and skills acquired in the learning environment to the work context, resulting in enhanced job performance (Baldwin & Ford, 1988; Goldstein & Ford, 2002). The effects of personality variables, however, did not receive much research attention in early transfer research. In their review of the literature on transfer of training, Baldwin and Ford (1988) noted a lack of understanding of the key personality predictors of transfer and called for more research on this topic.

Big Five Traits

More recently, some research has examined the relationship of Big Five traits to transfer of training. Conscientiousness is conceptually the most relevant to training transfer, as it entails aspects of achievement striving, attention to detail, and dependability. Although qualitative reviews have reported inconsistent relationships between conscientiousness and training transfer (Burke & Hutchins, 2007; Cheng & Hampson, 2008), a recent meta-analytic study revealed that differences across studies could be largely attributed to sampling error and measurement error, with an overall positive effect of conscientiousness on transfer (ρ = .28; Blume et al., 2010). It is likely that conscientious individuals tend to be more attentive to the opportunities for transfer, devise action plans for implementation, persist in transferring despite initial setbacks, and maintain a high motivation to transfer irrespective of disturbances from the environment.

Blume et al. (2010) also discovered weaker relationships between other Big Five factors and training transfer. Neuroticism was negatively related to transfer (ρ = −.19). Perhaps individuals who score high on neuroticism are more highly affected by the differences between the training environment and transfer environment and feel less at ease to apply the knowledge and skills in the new environment. In contrast, agreeableness, extraversion, and openness did not exhibit significant association with transfer. Despite shedding light on the importance of personality factors in the transfer process, the meta-analytic findings on the Big Five reported by Blume et al. (2010) are based on a small number of studies (*K*s range = 3–6) and thus would benefit from including more investigations.

In addition to having direct effects on transfer, Big Five factors can also interact with early learning to affect later transfer. Herold, Davis, Fedor, and Parsons (2002) examined the roles of conscientiousness and emotional stability in a multistage aviation training program, in which they assessed learning at the end of a computer-based simulation and measured transfer at the time to obtain pilot certification. The authors found that conscientiousness had a positive effect on transfer only for trainees with lower initial learning scores. Faced with difficulty in learning, highly conscientious trainees managed to make up the initial deficiency over time. In contrast, emotional stability had a positive effect on transfer only for trainees who performed well on the initial learning test. Given the necessary learning, individuals high on emotional stability might have dealt better with transitioning from the safe learning environment to the anxiety-inducing transfer environment (Herold et al., 2002).

Herold et al.'s (2002) findings suggest that personality variables, as antecedents to motivating factors, may interact with individual and situational characteristics to influence transfer in a complex pattern. This provides yet another example of compensatory decision making regarding training following the measurement of personality. If a significant number of trainees are low in conscientiousness or high in neuroticism, then more care should be paid to providing support for learning in the posttraining environment.

Goal Orientation

The dispositional tendency to prove one's competence, as assessed in performance-prove orientation (VandeWalle, 1997), appears to have inconsistent effects on transfer. While some studies reported a negative effect on transfer (e.g., Ford et al., 1998; Holladay & Quiñones, 2003), other studies indicated no effect or even a positive effect (e.g., Fisher & Ford, 1998; Kozlowski et al., 2001). Blume et al. (2010) found that performance-prove orientation did not have a significant effect on transfer. In contrast, performance-avoid orientation showed a negative, albeit weak, effect on transfer (Blume et al., 2010). Thus, the general desire to avoid showing one's lack of competence (VandeWalle, 1997) tends to result in poor transfer performance.

Mastery goal orientation has also been shown to have a positive effect on both perceived self-efficacy to learn and transfer (Ford et al., 1998; Holladay & Quiñones, 2003; Kozlowski et al., 2001). The positive effect of mastery orientation on transfer is further supported in Blume et al.'s (2010) meta-analysis ($\rho = .14$).

Emerging Trends

Intervention on Psychological States

We have previously discussed the theme that consideration of personality plays a role in identifying contexts in which training should be designed to activate traits that result in behaviors promoting effective learning. This reasoning can be applied to transfer as well. Research on motivational traits has established the linkage between dispositional influences and psychological states within specific situations (e.g., Button et al., 1996; Chen et al., 2000; Kanfer, Ackerman, & Heggestad, 1996). The understanding of psychological states instrumental in the learning and transfer process offers training researchers a means to create and affect key learning states (Ford & Oswald, 2003). Bell and Kozlowski (2008) examined how error framing intervention interacted with trait goal orientation to affect state goal orientation. Error framing interacted with trait mastery goal orientation to influence state mastery orientation, such that encouraging trainees to make errors as opposed to avoid errors resulted in greater state mastery goal orientation only in trainees low on trait mastery goal orientation but not in trainees high on trait mastery goal orientation. Weissbein, Huang, Ford, and Schmidt (2011) found that a pretraining intervention on state analogs of locus of control increased trainee motivation and enhanced transfer of training. A potential venue of future research lies in the investigation of personality states. As momentary analogs of stable personality traits, personality states can be viewed as activation of their corresponding traits in situ (see Fleeson, 2001). Recent research has indicated that the activation of certain personality states in response to situational cues may be due either to a trait-like individual difference (Minbashian, Wood, & Beckmann, 2010) or a stable job characteristic (Huang & Ryan, 2011). Future training research may examine interventions that enhance transfer through heightening personality states in the training and/or transfer contexts.

Effects of Personality on Transfer Over Time

The study by Herold et al. (2002) reviewed above highlighted the importance of examining the effects of personality variables on transfer over time. Mitchell and James (2001) noted that time warrants careful consideration as it allows events to unfold. In particular, time can serve as a situational constraint that limits the effects of personality (see Mischel, 1977). Further complicating the matter is the effect of time on the transfer phenomenon: as time elapses, the transfer context evolves from near transfer to far transfer (Barnett & Ceci, 2002). More research is needed to further understand how personality affects transfer over time.

Evaluation

Building on a review of educational and cognitive science literature, Kraiger, Ford, and Salas (1993) argued that training outcomes are multidimensional and proposed three broad categories of training outcomes, including cognitive, skill-based, and affective outcomes. Each category consists of specific constructs. Cognitive outcomes include declarative knowledge, knowledge organization, and cognitive strategies; skill-based outcomes include skill compilation and automaticity; affective outcomes include attitudinal and motivational factors. The delineation of the three broad training outcomes has facilitated investigations of a nomological network around the training outcomes in subsequent training research (Ford, Kraiger, & Merritt, 2010). In this section, we discuss the effects of personality variables as they relate to these three categories of training outcomes.

Personality variables have been proposed and examined as distal antecedents to cognitive and skill-based learning outcomes (e.g., Colquitt et al., 2000; S. Gully & Chen, 2010; S. Lee & Klein, 2002; Lievens et al., 2003). Although, as discussed, personality variables such as conscientiousness, neuroticism, and mastery goal orientation may influence important mediating mechanisms during training such as MTL and self-efficacy, it should be noted that the effects of personality likely depend on the strength of the training intervention. Indeed, training interventions can differ on the level of situational strength, which denotes the presence of various situational characteristics that restrict the expression of non-cognitive individual differences (Mischel, 1977; Mullins & Cummings, 1999; Snyder & Ickes, 1985; Weiss & Adler, 1984). With the presence of a strong intervention, the effects of personality variables weaken or even dissipate. In contrast, when a training intervention resembles a weak situation, the effects of personality may emerge. For example, for a training program that is well designed (e.g., based on specific instructional principles and ample opportunities for practice, feedback, and review), personality variables may have less impact, relative to a training program that is voluntary, self-paced, and does not carry material consequences. Therefore, instead of focusing on personality's main effects, we review and discuss how personality's influence depends on treatments and characteristics in the training environment within the framework of aptitude-by-treatment interaction (ATI).

ATI

ATI refers to the interaction between an intervention and preexisting individual characteristics in determining an outcome (Cronbach, 1957, 1975; Cronbach & Snow, 1977). Cronbach (1957) argued that offering the same intervention to all individuals ignores individuals' responsiveness to the treatment. The understanding of ATI may enable assigning individuals to treatment conditions most suited to their aptitudes and thus maximize the outcome (Cronbach, 1957). Thus, students should learn better when the instructor's presentation is adapted to their ability and personality (Cronbach & Snow, 1977). As Snow (1992) noted, aptitude does not equate with intelligence but rather indicates the predisposition for certain responses across different situations. Our review will focus on ATI as it relates to personality characteristics.

Training research has revealed ATIs both on learning outcomes and on key learning processes. S. M. Gully et al. (2002) examined the interplay between error framing interventions and the personality traits of openness and conscientiousness. They implemented three error framing conditions: error encouragement—encouraging trainees to make errors; error avoidance—instructing trainees to avoid making errors; and a control condition—informing trainees to do their best without any instructions on errors. They found that openness moderated the effect of error encouragement intervention on knowledge and skill acquisition, such that individuals high, as opposed to low, in openness benefited more from error encouragement. In addition, trainee conscientiousness interacted with error framing, such that conscientiousness had a negative influence on self-efficacy for trainees in the error encouragement condition only.

A. J. Towler and Dipboye (2001) investigated how lecture organization and trainer expressiveness may influence recall and problem-solving skills at the end of a training program on employment discrimination. While an expressive trainer delivering an organized lecture resulted in the highest recall, the influence on problem-solving skills was more complex. Specifically, trainees' mastery goal orientation interacted with the two design characteristics, such that trainees with high mastery goal orientation suffered most in problem-solving performance when exposed to an organized lecture from an inexpressive trainer, whereas trainees with low mastery goal orientation were not influenced by either factor.

Schmidt and Ford (2003) studied the effects of a metacognitive intervention, which provided trainees with strategies to monitor how they were learning. The level of metacognitive activity positively predicted declarative knowledge, skill-based performance, and posttraining self-efficacy. Furthermore, performance-avoid goal orientation moderated the effect of metacognitive intervention on metacognitive activity, such that the intervention increased metacognitive activity in trainees with low performance-avoid orientation but decreased metacognitive activity in those with high performance-avoid orientation.

A careful look at the ATI findings reveals two distinct patterns of ATIs, depending on whether the treatment is specifically designed to address the aptitude domain. These two patterns map onto the two essential roles of personality in the training context discussed above. First, an intervention may be designed to affect the learning state or behavioral manifestation of a personality trait variable. That is, the intervention can compensate for behaviors the trainee lacks the propensity (i.e., trait) to activate naturally. For instance, error encouragement framing can enhance state mastery goal orientation for trainees low on trait mastery goal orientation (Bell & Kozlowski, 2008). As another example, self-leadership training can increase self-directed (i.e., conscientious) behavior for trainees with low conscientiousness (Stewart, Carson, & Cardy, 1996). Note that these are additional examples of a compensatory learning principle, such that decisions of what to train can be based in part on knowing what skills may be lacking in trainees given personal dispositions.

Such interventions seek to elevate a personality state conducive to learning and transfer, compensating low trait level on the same personality dimension. Given the conceptual overlap between the target of the intervention and the trait of interest, it is reasonable to expect a weaker intervention effect on individuals who are already high on this particular aptitude and thus having limited opportunity to benefit from the intervention (see Tett & Simonet, 2011, for a discussion of the trait level as the opportunity to fake on self-report of personality). As researchers continue to explore interventions on learning state variables to enhance learning, similar ATIs can be expected. For instance, an intervention that elevates trainees' curiosity in the training topic may boost learning to the greatest extent for trainees with low openness to experience, and such a supplement on how trainees desire cognition in the training setting may be most beneficial to trainees with low need for cognition.

Second, it is possible that the effect of an intervention depends on a trainee personality factor but does not directly influence the personality domain. This type of ATI follows trait activation theory: cues from the training context trigger learning-related traits to affect learning and transfer. For example, providing positive rather than negative performance feedback in a software training context can lead to higher learning performance in trainees with low rather than high cognitive playfulness, a construct likely related to openness to experience (Martocchio & Webster, 1992). Similarly, feedback specificity moderated the effects of trainees' trait mastery and PGO on task performance, such that mastery goal orientation led to positive early performance when low rather than high specificity feedback was provided, whereas the effect of PGO on later task performance became more positive as more specific feedback was given (Davis, Carson, Ammeter, & Treadway, 2005). Further extending this type of interaction, a personality characteristic may moderate the effect of a contextual influence, which need not be a deliberate intervention. For example, locus of control interacted with team transfer climate perception to influence trained behavior, such that a stronger association obtained between transfer climate perception and trainee behavior for more external trainees (Smith-Jentsch, Salas, & Brannick, 2001).

The continued search for better understanding of ATIs may shed light on the effectiveness of training design and interventions. For example, the overall lack of supportive evidence for transfer of training interventions (Blume et al., 2010) may be due in part to the interaction between personality characteristics and transfer interventions, such that the effects of interventions are concealed in the entire population. Investigation of ATIs might also facilitate training design considerations in relation to trainee characteristics. Specifically, incorporation of a training design element needs to be informed by the type of trainees in the training program. For example, given the interactive effect of performance-avoid goal orientation and metacognitive intervention from Schmidt and Ford (2003), a metacognitive intervention may not be desirable for a group of trainees with high performance-avoid orientation. Furthermore, through pretests on relevant personality measures, training researchers may begin to explore methods to assign trainees to training conditions optimal for their learning and transfer (see Cronbach, 1957).

Personality's Influence on Affective Outcomes

Although trainee reactions after training have been linked to personality characteristics such as mastery goal orientation and agreeableness (Sitzmann, Brown, Casper, Ely, & Zimmerman, 2008), reaction measures do not directly assess whether learning has occurred (Kraiger et al., 1993). Kraiger (2002) discussed how affective outcomes, including attitudinal and motivational outcomes, can serve as direct or indirect indicators of learning. He noted that affective outcomes directly reflect the extent of learning when the training objective is to enhance, for example, the appreciation of values or the strength of attitudes. He also suggested that affective outcomes can indirectly indicate how much learning has occurred as they often covary with practice and exposure to training material. Furthermore, with the potential influences of affective outcome variables on transfer (Blume et al., 2010; Kraiger et al., 1993), recent research has examined the effects of motivational traits on affective outcomes, primarily posttraining self-efficacy. Kozlowski et al. (2001) showed that trait mastery goal orientation significantly predicted posttraining self-efficacy. Bell and Kozlowski (2008) identified three significant state predictors of posttraining self-efficacy: state performance-prove goal orientation, state performance-avoid goal orientation, and state anxiety. The univariate associations indicated that posttraining self-efficacy was negatively related to trait performance-avoid orientation and trait anxiety. In addition, Ford et al. (1998) showed that both mastery and PGO predicted posttraining self-efficacy.

We also tentatively gleaned from the literature some relationships on other personality variables. Tews and Tracey (2008) included the Big Five as control variables in studying the effects of on-the-job supplements. Several weeks after a managerial training, managers reported the degree to which they felt efficacious to manage employee performance. This posttraining self-efficacy was negatively associated with neuroticism, after controlling for pretraining self-efficacy, prior experience, general mental ability, and the other four Big Five factors. Finally, Tziner, Haccoun, and Kadish (1991) found a weak and nonsignificant association between locus of control and motivation to transfer skills learned from an instructional design training program.

Future Research on ATIs and Affective Outcomes

Much has yet to be explored on the influence of personality on affective training outcomes. Specifically, we propose two areas for future research. First, researchers can start to delineate the extent to which affective outcomes mediate personality's influence on transfer of training. With the positive effects of posttraining self-efficacy (e.g., Gist, Stevens, & Bavetta, 1991; Kozlowski et al., 2001) and motivation to transfer (e.g., Axtell, Maitlis, & Yearta, 1997) on transfer of training, the extent to which personality variables exert their influence on transfer through the affective outcomes remains to be addressed. Second, for motivational constructs such as self-efficacy, state mastery goal orientation, and training-specific attributions, researchers may begin to determine the degree to which personality influences change in the construct domain. For example, Huang and Ford (2012) assessed drivers' driving locus of control perceptions before and after a defensive driving program. Trainees' MTL and pretraining self-efficacy predicted change of driving locus of control, which further predicted change in driving behavior. It remains to be seen what personality traits may predispose a trainee towards being influenced through training experience, and what characteristics can sustain such systematic change.

Summary and Conclusions

The role of personality in the training literature is not as extensive as in some other domains, for example personnel selection and leadership. A likely reason for this is that training is widely conceived to be a primarily cognitive, skill-based intervention, whereas personality traditionally captures enduring personal characteristics. However, research to date shows promising influences of personality on phenomena before, during, and after training. Effects have been found not only for certain core personality traits (the Big Five) but also for broader personality characteristics such as goal orientation and self-efficacy. The latter set of traits has been studied much more extensively by training researchers.

Research shows that personality variables can influence trainee states and characteristics (e.g., MTL), learning during training, as well as the transfer of training back to work. The effects of personality can be not only direct but also in combination with situational characteristics. Given evidence of the effects of personality found in research to date, we encourage future training researchers to integrate meaningful personality variables more fully into conceptual models of training impact that encompass all of the parties involved in the training process.

Practitioner's Window

Training is a planned effort to improve individuals' skills, knowledge, or attitudes in order to improve their performance in another environment. The benefits of effective training have been well established through empirical research. Since training is widely considered to be a cognitive, skill-based intervention, personality variables have received less attention in practice and research. However, there is evidence that some personality and individual difference factors predict learning and transfer of training, and other research shows that personality/individual difference factors predict trainees' MTL and self-efficacy, which, in turn, affects learning and transfer.

There are two conceptual and practical ways in which consideration of personality factors should affect decision making about training.

- *Training as compensation.* To the extent that certain personality variables (e.g., outgoingness) are either important to job performance or learning during training *and* potential trainees score low on those variables, training should be designed to cover behavior characteristics of those high on the trait.
- *Training as activation.* As discussed elsewhere in this volume, environments differ in the extent to which they activate or elicit traits that may lead to desired behaviors. To the extent that the pretraining or posttraining environments are deficient in their capacity to activate positive traits, training programs should be designed to activate those traits during training. For example, trainee resiliency can be activated through training activities in anticipation of a nonsupportive posttraining environment.

Personality variables may factor into decision making during training needs assessment, training design, training evaluation, or supporting transfer of training. Personality variables include not only the Big Five (particularly conscientiousness and agreeableness) but other individual difference variables, particularly self-efficacy and goal orientation. Goal orientation refers to whether the individual in a situation primarily attends to performing well and making a positive impression or attends to learning or mastering a new skill.

The relationships between these personality variables and training outcomes are often complex and are thus difficult to summarize. However, it is clear that assessing and understanding trainees' traits and individual differences can lead to more informed decisions about who, what, and how to train.

References

Aguinis, H., & Kraiger, K. (2009). Benefits of training and development for individuals, teams, organizations, and society. *Annual Review of Psychology, 60*, 451–474.

Arthur, W., Jr., Bennett, W., Jr., Edens, P. S., & Bell, S. T. (2003). Effectiveness of training in organizations: A meta-analysis of design and evaluation features. *Journal of Applied Psychology, 88*, 234–245.

Axtell, C. M., Maitlis, S., & Yearta, S. K. (1997). Predicting immediate and longer-term transfer of training. *Personnel Review, 26*, 201–213.

Baldwin, T. T., & Ford, J. K. (1988). Transfer of training: A review and directions for future research. *Personnel Psychology, 41*, 63–105.

Bandura, A. (1977). Self-efficacy: Toward a unifying theory of behavior change. *Psychological Review, 84*, 191–215.

Bandura, A. (1997). *Self-efficacy: The exercise of control.* New York: Freeman.

Barnett, S. M., & Ceci, S. J. (2002). When and where do we apply what we learn? A taxonomy for far transfer. *Psychological Bulletin, 128*, 612–637.

Barrick, M. R., & Mount, M. K. (1991). The Big Five personality dimensions and job performance: A meta-analysis. *Personnel Psychology, 44*, 1–26.

Barrick, M. R., & Mount, M. K. (2005). Yes, personality matters: Moving on to more important matters. *Human Performance, 18*, 359–372.

Barrick, M. R., Mount, M. K., & Judge, T. A. (2001). Personality and performance at the beginning of the new millennium: What do we know and where do we go next? *International Journal of Selection and Assessment, 9*, 9–30.

Barrick, M. R., Mount, M. K., & Strauss, J. P. (1993). Conscientiousness and performance of sales representatives: Test of the mediating effects of goal setting. *Journal of Applied Psychology, 78*, 715–722.

Barrick, M. R., Stewart, G. L., & Piotrowski, M. (2002). Personality and job performance: Test of the mediating effects of motivation among sales representatives. *Journal of Applied Psychology, 87*, 43–51.

Baumeister, R. F., Gailliot, M., DeWall, C. N., & Oaten, M. (2006). Self-regulation and personality: How interventions increase regulatory success, and how depletion moderates the effects of traits on behavior. *Journal of Personality, 74*, 1773–1801.

Bell, B. S., & Kozlowski, S. W. J. (2008). Active learning: Effects of core training design elements on self-regulatory processes, learning, and adaptability. *Journal of Applied Psychology, 93*, 296–316.

Blackwell, L. S. (2002). *Psychological mediators of student achievement during the transition to junior high school: The role of implicit theories* (Unpublished doctoral dissertation). Columbia University, New York.

Blume, B. D., Ford, J. K., Baldwin, T. T., & Huang, J. L. (2010). Transfer of training: A meta-analytic review. *Journal of Management, 36*, 1065–1105.

Brett, J. F., & VandeWalle, D. (1999). Goal orientation and goal content as predictors of performance in a training program. *Journal of Applied Psychology, 84*, 863–873.

Broad, M. L., & Newstrom, J. W. (1992). *Transfer of training: Action-packed strategies to ensure high payoff from training investments*. Reading, MA: Addison-Wesley.

Burke, L. A., & Hutchins, H. M. (2007). Training transfer: An integrative literature review. *Human Resource Development Review, 6*, 263–296.

Button, S. B., Mathieu, J. E., & Zajac, D. M. (1996). Goal orientation in organizational research: A conceptual and empirical foundation. *Organizational Behavior and Human Decision Processes, 67*, 26–48.

Cacioppo, J. T., Petty, R. E., Feinstein, J. A., & Jarvis, W. B. G. (1996). Dispositional differences in cognitive motivation: The life and times of individuals varying in need for cognition. *Psychological Bulletin, 119*, 197–253.

Campbell, J. S., Castaneda, M., & Pulos, S. (2010). Meta-analysis of personality assessments as predictors of military aviation training success. *The International Journal of Aviation Psychology, 20*, 92–109.

Cannon-Bowers, J. A., Tannenbaum, S. I., Salas, E., & Converse, S. A. (1991). Toward an integration of training theory and technique. *Human Factors, 33*, 281–292.

Chen, G., Gully, S. M., & Eden, D. (2004). General self-efficacy and self-esteem: Toward theoretical and empirical distinction between correlated self-evaluations. *Journal of Organizational Behavior, 25*, 375–395.

Chen, G., Gully, S. M., Whiteman, J. A., & Kilcullen, B. N. (2000). Examination of relationships among trait-like individual differences, state-like individual differences, and learning performance. *Journal of Applied Psychology, 85*, 835–847.

Cheng, E. W. L., & Hampson, I. (2008). Transfer of training: A review and new insights. *International Journal of Management Reviews, 10*, 327–341.

Cole, N. D., & Latham, G. P. (1997). Effects of training in procedural justice on perceptions of disciplinary fairness by unionized employees and disciplinary subject matter experts. *Journal of Applied Psychology, 82*, 699–705.

Colquitt, J. A., LePine, J. A., & Noe, R. A. (2000). Toward an integrative theory of training motivation: A meta-analytic path analysis of 20 years of research. *Journal of Applied Psychology, 85*, 678–707.

Colquitt, J. A., & Simmering, M. J. (1998). Conscientiousness, goal orientation, and motivation to learn during the learning process: A longitudinal study. *Journal of Applied Psychology, 83*, 654–665.

Combs, G. M., & Luthans, F. (2007). Diversity training: Analysis of the impact of self-efficacy. *Human Resource Development Quarterly, 18*, 91–120.

Cronbach, L. J. (1957). The two disciplines of scientific psychology. *American Psychologist, 12*, 671–684.

Cronbach, L. J. (1975). Beyond the two disciplines of scientific psychology. *American Psychologist, 30*, 116–127.

Cronbach, L. J., & Snow, R. E. (1977). *Aptitudes and instructional methods: A handbook for research on interactions*. Oxford, UK: Irvington.

Davis, W. D., Carson, C. M., Ammeter, A. P., & Treadway, D. C. (2005). The interactive effects of goal orientation and feedback specificity on task performance. *Human Performance, 18*, 409–426.

Day, E. A., Espejo, J., Kowollik, V., Boatman, P. R., & McEntire, L. E. (2007). Modeling the links between need for cognition and the acquisition of a complex skill. *Personality and Individual Differences, 42*, 201–212.

Dierdorff, E. C., Surface, E. A., & Brown, K. G. (2010). Frame-of-reference training effectiveness: Effects of goal orientation and self-efficacy on affective, cognitive, skill-based, and transfer outcomes. *Journal of Applied Psychology, 96*, 1181–1191.

Dweck, C. S. (1986). Motivational processes affecting learning. *American Psychologist, 41*, 1040–1048.

Dweck, C. S., & Leggett, E. L. (1988). A social-cognitive approach to motivation and personality. *Psychological Review, 95*, 256–273.

Eden, D. (2001). Means efficacy: External sources of general and specific subjective efficacy. In M. Erez, U. Kleinbeck, & H. Thierry (Eds.), *Work motivation in the context of a globalizing economy* (pp. 73–86). Mahwah, NJ: Lawrence Erlbaum Associates, Inc.

Eden, D., & Aviram, A. (1993). Self-efficacy training to speed reemployment: Helping people to help themselves. *Journal of Applied Psychology, 78*, 352–360.

Eden, D., & Zuk, Y. (1995). Seasickness as a self-fulfilling prophecy: Raising self-efficacy to boost performance at sea. *Journal of Applied Psychology, 80*, 628–635.

Ellington, J. K., & Surface, E. A. (2009, April). The trainer's impact in the learning environment: A multilevel examination. In S.T. Bell & A. Towler (Chairs), *The people factor: Considering trainee and trainer effects on learning*. Symposium conducted at the 24th Annual Conference of the Society for Industrial and Organizational Psychology, New Orleans, LA.

Elliot, A. J. (1999). Approach and avoidance motivation and achievement goals. *Educational Psychologist, 34*, 169–189.

Ely, K., Sitzmann, T., & Falkiewicz, C. (2009). The influence of goal orientation dimensions on time to train in a self-paced training environment. *Learning and Individual Differences, 19*, 146–150.

Fisher, S. L., & Ford, J. K. (1998). Differential effects of learner effort and goal orientation on two learning outcomes. *Personnel Psychology, 51*, 397–420.

Fleeson, W. (2001). Toward a structure- and process-integrated view of personality: Traits as density distributions of states. *Journal of Personality and Social Psychology, 80*, 1011–1027.

Ford, J. K., Kraiger, K., & Merritt, S. M. (2010). An updated review of the multidimensionality of training outcomes: New directions for training evaluation research. In S. W. J. Kozlowski & E. Salas (Eds.), *Learning, training, and development in organizations* (pp. 135–165). New York: Routledge.

Ford, J. K., & Oswald, F. L. (2003). Understanding the dynamic learner: Linking personality traits, learning situations, and individual behavior. In M. Barrick & A. M. Ryan (Eds.), *Personality and work* (pp. 229–261). San Francisco: Jossey-Bass.

Ford, J. K., Smith, E. M., Weissbein, D. A., Gully, S. M., & Salas, E. (1998). Relationships of goal orientation, metacognitive activity, and practice strategies with learning outcomes and transfer. *Journal of Applied Psychology, 83*, 218–233.

Furnham, A. (1992). Personality and learning style: A study of three instruments. *Personality and Individual Differences, 13*, 429–438.

Furnham, A., Jackson, C. J., Forde, L., & Cotter, T. (2001). Correlates of the Eysenck Personality Profiler. *Personality and Individual Differences, 30*, 587–594.

Gan, C. G., Lee, J. A., & Soutar, G. N. (2009). Preferences for training options: A conjoint analysis. *Human Resource Development Quarterly, 20*, 307–330.

Gist, M. E., Stevens, C. K., & Bavetta, A. G. (1991). Effects of self-efficacy and post-training intervention on the acquisition and maintenance of complex interpersonal skills. *Personnel Psychology, 44*, 837–861.

Goldstein, I. L., & Ford, J. K. (2002). *Training in organizations* (4th ed.). Belmont, CA: Wadsworth.

Gully, S., & Chen, G. (2010). Individual differences, attribute–treatment interactions, and training outcomes. In S. W. J. Kozlowski & E. Salas (Eds.), *Learning, training, and development in organizations* (pp. 3–64). New York: Routledge.

Gully, S. M., Payne, S. C., Knoles, K. L. K., & Whiteman, J. K. (2002). The impact of error training and individual differences on training outcomes: An attribute–treatment interaction perspective. *Journal of Applied Psychology, 87*, 143–155.

Herold, D. M., Davis, W., Fedor, D. B., & Parsons, C. K. (2002). Dispositional influences on transfer of learning in multistage training programs. *Personnel Psychology, 55*, 851–869.

Heyman, G. D., & Dweck, C. S. (1992). Achievement goals and intrinsic motivation: Their relation and their role in adaptive motivation. *Motivation and Emotion, 16*, 231–247.

Hofmann, D. A. (1993). The influence of goal orientation on task performance: A substantively meaningful suppressor variable. *Journal of Applied Psychology, 23*, 1827–1846.

Holladay, C. L., & Quiñones, M. A. (2003). Practice variability and transfer of training: The role of self-efficacy generality. *Journal of Applied Psychology, 88*, 1094–1103.

Holladay, C. L., & Quiñones, M. A. (2008). The influence of training focus and trainer characteristics on diversity training and effectiveness. *Academy of Management Learning & Education, 7*, 343–354.

Hollenbeck, J. R., & Klein, H. J. (1987). Goal commitment and the goal setting process: Problems, prospects and proposals for future research. *Journal of Applied Psychology, 74*, 18–23.

Holton, E. F., Bates, R. A., & Ruona, W. E. (2000). Development of a generalized learning transfer system inventory. *Human Resource Development Quarterly, 11*, 333–360.

Huang, J. L., & Ford, J. K. (2012). Driving locus of control and driving behavior: Inducing change through driver training. *Transportation Research Part F: Traffic Psychology and Behaviour, 15*, 358–368.

Huang, J. L., & Ryan, A. M. (2011). Beyond personality traits: A study of personality states and situational contingencies in customer service jobs. *Personnel Psychology, 64*, 451–488.

Justis, R. T., Kedia, B. L., & Stephens, D. B. (1978). The effect of position power and perceived task competence on trainer effectiveness: A partial utilization of Fiedler's contingency model of leadership. *Personnel Psychology, 31*, 83–93.

Kanfer, R., Ackerman, P. L., & Heggestad, E. D. (1996). Motivational skills & self-regulation for learning: A trait perspective. *Learning and Individual Differences, 8*, 185–209.

Kappe, F. R., Boekholt, L., den Rooyen, C., & Van der Flier, H. (2009). A predictive validity study of the Learning Style Questionnaire (LSQ) using multiple, specific learning criteria. *Learning and Individual Differences, 19*, 464–467.

Knowles, M., Holton, E. F., III, & Swanson, R. A. (2005). *The adult learner: The definitive classic in adult education and human resource management*. Burlington, MA: Elsevier.

Kolb, D. (1976). *Learning Style Inventory: Technical manual*. Boston: McBer.

Kolb, D. (1984). *Experimental learning*. Englewood Cliffs, NJ: Prentice Hall.

Kozlowski, S. W. J., Gully, S. M., Brown, K. G., Salas, E., Smith, E. M., & Nason, E. R. (2001). Effects of training goals and goal orientation traits on multidimensional training outcomes and performance adaptability. *Organizational Behavior and Human Decision Processes, 85*, 1–31.

Kozlowski, S. W. J., & Salas, E. (1997). A multilevel organizational systems approach for the implementation and transfer of training. In J. K. Ford, S. W. J. Kozlowski, K. Kraiger, E. Salas, & M. S. Teachout (Eds.), *Improving training effectiveness in work organizations* (pp. 247–287). Mahwah, NJ: Erlbaum.

Kraiger, K. (2002). Decision-based evaluation. In K. Kraiger (Ed.), *Creating, implementing, and maintaining effective training and development: State-of-the-art lessons for practice* (pp. 331–375). San Francisco: Jossey-Bass.

Kraiger, K., Ford, J. K., & Salas, E. (1993). Application of cognitive, skill-based, and affective theories of learning outcomes to new methods of training evaluation. *Journal of Applied Psychology, 78*, 311–328.

Lee, L.-Y., & Li, C.-Y. (2008). The moderating effects of teaching method, learning style and cross-cultural differences on the relationship between expatriate training and training effectiveness. *International Journal of Human Resource Management, 19*, 600–619.

Lee, S., & Klein, H. J. (2002). Relationships between conscientiousness, self-efficacy, self-deception, and learning over time. *Journal of Applied Psychology, 87*, 1175–1182.

Leonardelli, G. J., Herman, A. D., Lynch, M. E., & Arkin, R. M. (2003). The shape of self-evaluation: Implicit theories of intelligence and judgments of intellectual ability. *Journal of Research in Personality, 37*, 141–168.

Licht, B. G., & Dweck, C. S. (1984). Determinants of academic achievement: The interaction of children's achievement orientations with skill area. *Developmental Psychology, 20*, 628–636.

Lievens, F., Harris, M. M., VanKeer, E., & Bisqueret, C. (2003). Predicting cross cultural training performance: The validity of personality, cognitive ability, and dimensions measured by an assessment center and a behavior description interview. *Journal of Applied Psychology, 88*, 476–489.

Major, D. A., Turner, J. E., & Fletcher, T. D. (2006). Linking proactive personality and the Big Five to motivation to learn and development activity. *Journal of Applied Psychology, 91*, 927–935.

Martocchio, J. J. (1994). Affects of conceptions of ability on anxiety, self-efficacy and learning in training. *Journal of Applied Psychology, 79*, 819–825.

Martocchio, J. J., & Webster, J. (1992). Effects of feedback and cognitive playfulness on performance in microcomputer software training. *Personnel Psychology, 45*, 553–578.

Mathieu, J. E., Martineau, J. W., & Tannenbaum, S. I. (1993). Individual and situational influences on the development of self-efficacy: Implication for training effectiveness. *Personnel Psychology, 46*, 125–147.

Mathieu, J. E., Tannenbaum, S. I., & Salas, E. (1992). Influences of individual and situational characteristics on measures of training effectiveness. *Academy of Management Journal, 35*, 828–847.

McEnrue, M. P., Groves, K. S., & Shen, W. (2009). Emotional intelligence development: Leveraging individual characteristics. *Journal of Management Development, 28*, 150–174.

Minbashian, A., Wood, R. E., & Beckmann, N. (2010). Task-contingent conscientiousness as a unit of personality at work. *Journal of Applied Psychology, 95*, 793–806.

Mischel, W. (1977). The interaction of person and situation. In D. Magnusson & N. S. Endler (Eds.), *Personality at the crossroads: Current issues in interactional psychology* (pp. 333–352). Hillsdale, NJ: Lawrence Erlbaum.

Mitchell, T. R., Hopper, H., Daniels, D., George-Falvy, J., & James, L. R. (1994). Predicting self-efficacy and performance during skill acquisition. *Journal of Applied Psychology, 79*, 506–517.

Mitchell, T. R., & James, L. R. (2001). Building better theory: Time and the specification of when things happen. *Academy of Management Review, 26*, 530–547.

Mullins, J. W., & Cummings, L. L. (1999). Situational strength: A framework for understanding the role of individuals in initiating proactive strategic change. *Journal of Organizational Change Management, 12*, 462–479.

Nair, K. U., & Ramnarayan, S. (2000). Individual differences in need for cognition and complex problem solving. *Journal of Research in Personality, 34*, 305–328.

Noe, R. A. (1986). Trainees' attributes and attitudes: Neglected influences on training effectiveness. *Academy of Management Review, 11*, 736–749.

Noe, R. A. (2002). *Employee training and development* (2nd ed.). Boston: McGraw-Hill.

Orvis, K. A., Fisher, S. L., & Wasserman, M. E. (2009). Power to the people: Using learner control to improve trainee reactions and learning in web-based instructional environments. *Journal of Applied Psychology, 94*, 960–971.

Payne, S. C., Youngcourt, S. S., & Beaubein, J. M. (2007). A meta-analytic examination of the goal orientation nomological net. *Journal of Applied Psychology, 92*, 128–150.

Phan, H. P. (2011). Interrelations between self-efficacy and learning approaches: A developmental approach. *Educational Psychology, 31*, 225–246.

Phillips, J. M., & Gully, S. M. (1997). Role of goal orientation, ability, need for achievement, and locus of control in the self-efficacy and goal setting process. *Journal of Applied Psychology, 82*, 792–802.

Pulakos, E. D., Arad, S., Donovan, M. A., & Plamondon, K. E. (2000). Adaptability in the workplace: Development of a taxonomy of adaptive performance. *Journal of Applied Psychology, 85*, 612–624.

Quiñones, M. A. (1995). Pretraining context effects: Training assignment as feedback. *Journal of Applied Psychology, 80*, 226–238.

Rechlin, A. M. (2009). *The effect of trainer attractiveness on trainee learning* (Unpublished master's thesis). Colorado State University, Fort Collins, CO.

Ree, M. J., Carretta, T. R., & Teachout, M. S. (1995). Role of ability and prior job knowledge in complex training performance. *Journal of Applied Psychology, 80*, 721–730.

Ree, M. J., & Earles, J. A. (1991). Predicting training success: Not much more than g. *Personnel Psychology, 44*, 321–332.

Rotter, J. B. (1966). Generalized expectancies for internal versus external control of reinforcement. *Psychological Monographs: General and Applied, 80*, 1–28.

Rotter, J. B., Chance, J. E., & Phares, E. J. (1972). *Applications of a social learning theory of personality*. Oxford, UK: Holt, Rinehart & Winston.

Rowold, J. (2007). The impact of personality on training-related aspects of motivation: Test of a longitudinal model. *Human Resource Development Quarterly, 18*, 9–31.

Sadowski, C. J., & Gulgoz, S. (1996). Elaborative processing mediates the relationship between need for cognition and academic performance. *The Journal of Psychology, 130*, 303–307.

Salas, E., & Cannon-Bowers, J. A. (2001). The science of training: A decade of progress. *Annual Review of Psychology, 52*, 471–499.

Salas, E., DiazGranados, D., Klein, C., Burke, C. S., Stagl, K. C., Goodwin, G. F., & Halpin, S. M. (2008). Does team training improve team performance? A meta-analysis. *Human Factors, 50*, 903–933.

Salas, E., Tannenbaum, S. I., Kraiger, K., & Smith-Jentsch, K. A. (2012). The science of training and development in organizations: What matters in practice. *Psychological Science in the Public Interest, 13*, 74–101.

Salgado, J. F. (1997). The five factor model of personality and job performance in the European Community. *Journal of Applied Psychology, 82*, 30–43.

Schmidt, A. M., & Ford, J. K. (2003). Learning within a learner control training environment: The interactive effects of goal orientation and metacognitive instruction on learning outcomes. *Personnel Psychology, 56*, 405–429.

Sitzmann, T., Bell, B. S., Kraiger, K., & Kanar, A. (2009). A multilevel analysis of the effect of prompting self-regulation in technology-delivered instruction. *Personnel Psychology, 62*, 697–734.

Sitzmann, T., Brown, K. G., Casper, W. J., Ely, K., & Zimmerman, R. D. (2008). A review and meta-analysis of the nomological network of trainee reactions. *Journal of Applied Psychology, 93*, 280–295.

Smith-Jentsch, K. A., Salas, E., & Brannick, M. T. (2001). To transfer or not to transfer? Investigating the combined effects of trainee characteristics, team leader support, and team climate. *Journal of Applied Psychology, 86*, 279–292.

Snow, R. E. (1992). Aptitude theory: Yesterday, today, and tomorrow. *Educational Psychologist, 27*, 5–32.

Snyder, M., & Ickes, W. (1985). Personality and social behavior. In G. Lindzey & E. Aronson (Eds.), *Handbook of social psychology* (3rd ed., pp. 883–948). New York: Random House.

Spector, P. E. (1988). Development of the Work Locus of Control Scale. *Journal of Occupational Psychology, 61*, 335–340.

Stajkovic, A. D., & Luthans, F. (1998). Self-efficacy and work-related performance: A meta-analysis. *Psychological Bulletin, 124*, 240–261.

Steiner, D. D., Dobbins, G. H., & Trahan, W. A. (1991). The trainer–trainee interaction: An attributional model of training. *Journal of Organizational Behavior, 12*, 271–286.

Stevens, C. K., & Gist, M. E. (1997). Effects of self-efficacy and goal orientation training on negotiation skill maintenance: What are the mechanisms? *Personnel Psychology, 50*, 955–978.

Stewart, G. L., Carson, K. P., & Cardy, R. L. (1996). The joint effects of conscientiousness and self-leadership training on employee self-directed behavior in a service setting. *Personnel Psychology, 49*, 143–164.

Surface, E. A., & Ellington, J. K. (2008, April). Rethinking context in training effectiveness research: Instructor as learning context. In E. C. Dierdorff (Chair), *Illuminating the "Murky Ground": Linking context theory to empirical research*. Symposium conducted at the 23rd Annual Meeting of the Society for Industrial and Organizational Psychology, San Francisco.

Tett, R. P., & Burnett, D. D. (2003). A personality trait-based interactionist model of job performance. *Journal of Applied Psychology, 88*, 500–517.

Tett, R. P., & Guterman, H. A. (2000). Situation trait relevance, trait expression, and cross-situational consistency: Testing a principle of trait activation. *Journal of Research in Personality, 34*, 397–423.

Tett, R. P., & Simonet, D.V. (2011). Faking in personality assessment: A "multisaturation" perspective on faking as performance. *Human Performance, 24*, 302–321.

Tews, M. J., & Tracey, J. B. (2008). An empirical examination of posttraining on-the-job supplements for enhancing the effectiveness of interpersonal skills training. *Personnel Psychology, 61*, 375–401.

Towler, A., & Dipboye, R. L. (2006). Effects of trainer reputation and trainees' need for cognition on training outcomes. *The Journal of Psychology, 140*, 549–564.

Towler, A. J. (2009). Effects of trainer expressiveness, seductive details, and trainee goal orientation on training outcomes. *Human Resource Development Quarterly, 20*, 65–84.

Towler, A. J., & Dipboye, R. L. (2001). Effects of trainer expressiveness, organization, and trainee goal orientation on training outcomes. *Journal of Applied Psychology, 86*, 664–673.

Tziner, A., Haccoun, R. R., & Kadish, A. (1991). Personal and situational characteristics influencing the effectiveness of transfer of training improvement strategies. *Journal of Occupational Psychology, 64*, 167–177.

VandeWalle, D. (1997). Development and validation of a work domain goal orientation instrument. *Educational and Psychological Measurement, 57*, 995–1015.

VandeWalle, D., Cron, W. L., & Slocum, J. W., Jr. (2001). The role of goal orientation following performance feedback. *Journal of Applied Psychology, 86*, 629–640.

vanDyck, C., Frese, M., Baer, M., & Sonnentag, S. (2005). Organizational error management culture and its impact on performance: A two-study replication. *Journal of Applied Psychology, 90*, 1228–1240.

Verplanken, B. (1993). Need for cognition and external information search: Responses to time pressure during decision-making. *Journal of Research in Personality, 27*, 238–252.

Washburn, D. A., Smith, J. D., Baker, L. A., & Raby, P. R. (2001) Responding to uncertainty: Individual differences and training effects. *Proceedings of the 2001 Meeting of the Human Factors and Ergonomics Society*, 911–915.

Weiss, H. M., & Adler, S. (1984). Personality and organizational behavior. *Research in Organizational Behavior, 6*, 1–50.

Weissbein, D. A., Huang, J. L., Ford, J. K., & Schmidt, A. M. (2011). Influencing learning states to enhance trainee motivation and improve training transfer. *Journal of Business and Psychology, 26*, 423–435.

Wexley, K. N. (1984). Personnel training. *Annual Review of Psychology, 35*, 519–551.

Wexley, K. N., & Latham, G. P. (1981). *Developing and training human resources in organizations*. Glenview, IL: Foresman.

Yeo, G. B., & Neal, A. (2004). A multilevel analysis of effort, practice, and performance: Effects of ability, conscientiousness, and goal orientation. *Journal of Applied Psychology, 89*, 231–247.

25

Incorporating Personality Assessments Into Talent Management Processes

David Bartram and Fred Guest

Introduction

In this chapter, we examine the role of talent management in business and commerce and its importance for helping organizations to realize the value locked up in their human capital resources and for helping individuals to realize their potential through their careers. The assessment of personality, whether through the formal use of measurement instruments or informally through the implicit models held by line managers and others, plays a crucial role in many talent management decisions. The choices people make about what they want to do at work and what they do not want to do, their capabilities for working with others, their task-based competencies, and the way they shape their roles are all influenced by personalities, preferences, and preferred styles of behavior.

We will argue that personality plays a crucial role in determining the potential people have for developing those competencies the organization needs in order to attain its goals. Understanding what competencies are and how they can be developed lies at the heart of talent management. Data on personality provide important indicators of people's potential for the development of job-related competencies. As such, using personality measures in volume recruitment offers a highly efficient way of assessing the potential of a talent pool for future competency development and utilization.

In this chapter, we first define what we mean by talent management and then go on to consider how organizations can better match people to the roles they will occupy. We emphasize the need for organizations to have integrated talent management approaches so that talent management is driven by the need to achieve certain business outcomes.

A central part of this chapter is a consideration of "competencies": what they are, how personality measurement figures in their assessment, and the role they play in integrated talent management. We argue that accurate, objective measurement is critical to realizing value, and as a result, it is important that organizations eschew the use of implicit models of personality and subjective assessment for the more objective methods now available. Both ability and personality measures can be used as predictors of competencies and, through them, of job performance outcomes.

Finally, we address some specific topics, including the use of personality-based measures of competency potential in development and coaching, person–job matching, the development of competency maps, and succession planning.

Competencies as an Integrating Language

Integrated talent management requires an operating language that is sufficiently comprehensive to allow for it to act as the core performance language of the business—a single comprehensive and unifying competency framework.

Competencies have become a useful tool to integrate various human resource (HR) processes across the organization. This is mainly due to the fact that competencies are a behaviorally described language that is easily understandable by line managers and employees alike. Competency management is the process by which the strategic talent requirements of the organization are defined in behavioral terms and then integrated into the full employee life cycle to create talent architecture.

We define competencies as "sets of behaviors that are instrumental in the delivery of desired results" (Bartram, 2002). In the business environment, they are behaviors that support the attainment of organizational objectives. It is important to note that the focus here is on behaviors and not on the results or consequences of those behaviors or on personal attributes that have no behavioral expression within the work environment. Many early approaches to competencies produced "eclectic" models where competencies were defined in such a way as to include anything from personality traits to performance outcomes. We believe it is important to clearly differentiate between characteristics that provide the potential for future development and that may underlie current capability (such characteristics may be accessed through personality measurement, ability testing, measurement of motivation, etc.), performance itself as it happens in the workplace (which is primarily assessed through the judgment of others, especially line managers), and the consequences of managed performance for achieving business outcomes.

With this in mind, competencies need to be understood within the context of three other terms that are equally relevant:

Competency potential refers to what people could do, given the necessary training, development, and opportunity. It is determined largely by aspects of personality, ability, and motivation. It is by helping to define potential that personality assessment plays a key role. Measures of potential define the scope for development and change and as such are forward-looking or "lead" measures that can be used to develop talent within the organization.

Competency requirements are the demands made upon people to display certain behaviors and not others. These requirements can be both facilitators of, and barriers to, effective performance in the workplace. They can also be explicitly encouraged through line manager instruction, or implicitly through organizational norms and values. Competency requirements are what we endeavor to define as one part of the job-match process, where we compare an individual's competency potential, or current competencies, against the requirements of one or more roles or positions. As we shall see later, getting a good definition of competency requirements is as important for job matching as getting a good measure of people's competencies or competency potential.

Results are the outcomes of behavior, typically as assessed through performance reviews and appraisals. Results are generally described in terms of and measured through business outcomes. Results are typically "lag" measures as they look back on what has been achieved.

We will describe the role of personality in the prediction of competency potential in more detail later in this chapter; however, it is important to note that the nature and characteristics of the competencies in the integrated framework will have a significant influence on the value that is gained from the measurement of talent. We will argue that key to effective talent management is accurate measurement of both competency potential and competencies within the context of a known set of desired business outcomes.

Competency frameworks provide a potentially powerful mechanism for mapping measurement based on personality assessment onto a construct system explicitly designed to deal with the world of work, performance at work, and business outcomes.

The Talent Management Landscape

Talent management has become one of the most pressing topics within HR organizations today. This is to be expected, given an environment that is characterized by continuous economic instability, corporate restructuring, and belt-tightening. HR professionals are under increasing pressure to cut costs, and companies are trying to maximize employee productivity. At the same time, a lack of skills and an aging workforce have opened up significant gaps in organizations' leadership pipelines, putting corporate performance at risk. These pressures have brought talent management to the forefront of corporate HR agendas (Bersin & Associates, 2007).

Bersin and Associates (2007) believe that the new focus on talent management is forcing HR to become increasingly business focused. The "change manager" and "strategic partner" roles of Ulrich's (1997) model focus specifically on the development of organizational capabilities. In what follows, we consider the implications of this for a more strategic approach by HR to talent management and the need for organizations to integrate talent management across the employee life cycle. There is a tendency for functions to operate in vertical silos—selection, post-hire induction, succession planning, coaching and development—without these becoming "joined-up" in a way that enables information from one process to feed into and support another.

Talent Management as a Strategic Concept

One of the largest investments most organizations make is in human capital. How do you ensure that the investments you have made in human capital, your "people equity," move performance to significantly higher levels? Put differently, how do you measure, and maximize, your return on human capital investment? Schiemann (2010) introduces the concept of people equity as an integrative way to measure and manage human capital. People equity consists of three core elements: *alignment*, the extent to which the workforce is connected with the business strategy; *capabilities*, the talent, information, and resources required to execute that strategy; and *engagement*, the degree to which workers are committed to the organization. In this model, *capabilities* capture the extent to which the organization effectively matches talent, information, and resources with business strategy and customer requirements.

Talent is, by definition, a strategic concept: Talent is only "talent" if it allows the organization to meet strategic objectives more successfully. In general, the term "talent" refers to those individuals that possess the capabilities, knowledge, skills, and experience that are needed by the organization to meet strategic objectives. In current HR terminology, "talent" is used to refer to the person as a whole rather than the attributes or "talents" a person might possess. Changes in organizational strategy to ensure greater competitiveness and increase profitability have a direct effect on the definition and demand for talent. The talent management challenge is to ensure that the supply of talent can keep up with the demand for talent. This has become increasingly difficult, given the accelerated pace of change in corporate strategy needed to deal with volatile economic conditions.

Guthridge, Komm, and Lawson (2008) comment that talent management cannot be isolated from business strategy and that those that rely solely on the HR department to drive their strategy for talent are missing an opportunity to align the behavior and capabilities of the workforce with the priority of the business.

How do you cope with these moving goalposts that continuously define and redefine the demand for and supply of quality talent? It is this dilemma that lies at the core of the proverbial "war for talent."

Organizations able to clearly define the talent capabilities their strategy demands, and then measure and engage these effectively, will unlock more value from their people and realize a larger return on their investment. Talent management has become the primary HR process to drive this value.

Talent Management Defined

Generally, we can define talent management as the process of ensuring that an organization's supply of talent meets and keeps up with its demand for talent. Within the scope of this definition, the term "talent management," however, still has vastly different uses for various stakeholders in organizations. In practice, it is applied to all of the following:

Single "High-Potential" schemes.

Executive talent and succession schemes or leadership pipelines.

Large-scale enterprise resource planning (ERP) system-based approaches.

Graduate and experienced hire programs.

Risk management approaches (aimed at technical or functional specialists).

Clearly, the issues involved in identifying, developing, and tracking a small number of top executives are very different from those of an international skills audit implemented using a sophisticated, electronic talent management system. The former may involve in-depth assessment of a small number of people with intensive follow-up, coaching, and mentoring procedures, while the latter may involve online survey methods to collect large volumes of data for subsequent demographic-based analyses.

Bersin and Associates (2007) suggest that talent management requires a broader focus, moving beyond the realm of helping individual business units and functions to become more effective. The focus should be on building "organizational capabilities," not just "individual capabilities." Talent management forces the HR organization to view problems and value creation opportunities as business leaders do. HR professionals are asked to solve significant business challenges through the implementation of integrated processes, governed in partnership with the business.

Bersin and Associates (2007) define talent management as a set of business-focused organizational processes designed to attract, manage, develop, motivate, and retain key people. The goal of a talent management program is to create a highly responsive, high-performance, sustainable organization that meets its business targets. The top areas considered part of talent management today are leadership development, sourcing and recruiting, training and development, performance management, and succession planning. These five areas form the basis of talent-related processes, collectively entailing the acquisition, management, assessment, development, and succession planning of people (Bersin, 2008).

For the purposes of this chapter, it is important to note that all of these processes require some form of talent matching where individuals are measured against criteria to determine who best fits talent requirements. Just as talent is only talent if it is useful in the execution of the organization's strategy, so talent management processes are only as useful as their capability to identify "who" is talent. The matching of talent to business requirements involves a very familiar three-stage process. This is the same process that underpins all assessment for talent acquisition (e.g., selection and recruitment) and talent mobility (e.g., development, succession planning):

1. Define talent requirements;
2. Measure individuals to determine their "fit" to these requirements;
3. Realize the benefits of this process by using this "fit" information to make important talent decisions.

Defining Talent Requirements

The organization's ability to accurately define the people-capabilities that are required to meet strategy demands will have a significant effect on the success of talent management initiatives. The "define" stage of talent management typically asks the following questions:

What people-capabilities does the organization need to be successful?

Which roles are critical in the execution of the strategy?

Are certain capabilities more important than others?

What processes are in place that will provide an indication that demands for certain capabilities are changing?

These questions are typically dealt with as part of the organization's competency management, job analysis, manpower planning, and organizational design processes.

Measuring Talent Requirements

The accurate and efficient measurement of talent criteria allows the organization to determine the quantity and quality of talent. The "measure" stage of talent management typically asks the following questions:

How can talent be identified?

Which individuals have the capabilities that are required for success?

How can the organization develop the capabilities it requires?

How does the organization keep talent engaged?

Answers to these questions are sought through measurement in all stages of the employee life cycle—in attraction, selection, development, performance management, and succession planning.

Realizing the Benefits: Talent Matching

The nature of the "matching" process depends on the talent process. Typically, however, an indication of an individual's fit to requirements is used to make one of two types of decision: (1) those involving the early identification of potential (i.e., in graduate selection, high-potential leadership development, succession planning, or career guidance) or (2) placement decisions (i.e., in selection, placement, and promotion).

From a human capital perspective, a return on investment is possible only when there is a close match between clearly defined talent requirements and accurately measured people-capabilities. The extent to which the organization is able to implement talent management processes that provide decision makers with timely and accurate talent information will have a significant effect on the return on investment of their talent management processes and interventions.

Bersin and Associates (2007) aptly describe how HR value drivers affect key business value (see Figure 25.1), pointing out that the key business drivers can be delivered only if the fundamental HR

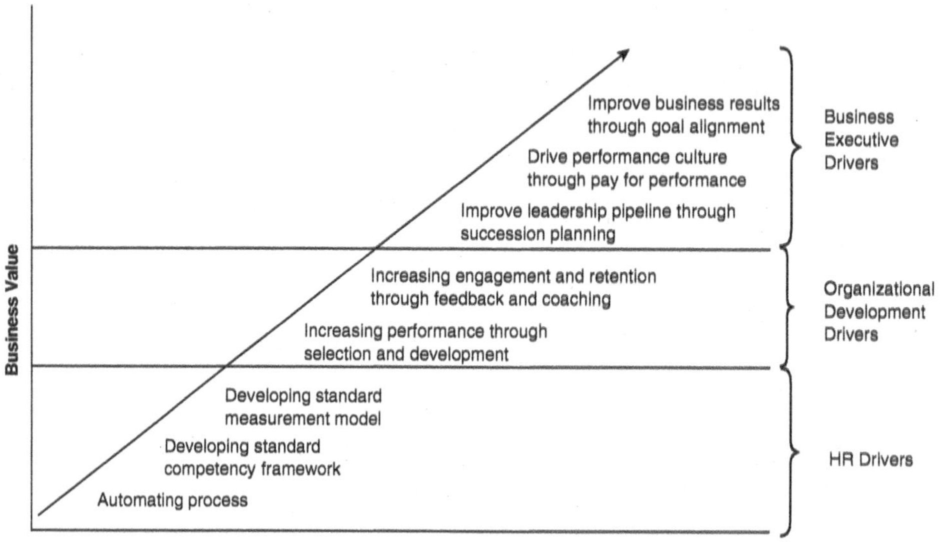

Figure 25.1 HR Drivers Affecting Business Drivers for Talent Management.

Source: Adapted from Bersin and Associates (2007).

Note: HR: human resource.

value drivers are in place. These HR drivers are (1) automated processes, (2) the development of a standard competency framework, and (3) the development of a standard measurement model.

Integrated Talent Management

In a traditional HR organization, processes such as selection and succession planning tend to be developed and managed individually. In an integrated talent management strategy, the organization seeks to integrate these processes in such a way that they achieve business-driven talent objectives. The integration points will vary, depending on the critical business problems to be addressed (Bersin & Associates, 2007).

To truly get value from talent management, talent requirements and measurement should be integrated in all processes across the employee life cycle. To become more business focused and solve larger business challenges, HR is forced to integrate traditional "practice silos." The lack of sufficient leadership talent at senior management and executive levels is directly or indirectly related to poor attraction, selection, and succession planning or compensation practices. The extent to which the organization is able to define and integrate measurement criteria across these processes becomes important to ensure consistency of implementation and value creation from the attraction to retention of appropriate executive-level talent. For example, organizations may define competency requirements for selection procedures but not carry these through to use with post-hire functions such as leadership development or succession planning. Using different competency models for the selection, development, and succession of executives limits integration and reduces the effectiveness with which the organization grows its leadership pipeline.

The importance of integration was well argued by Schippmann (1999) who proposed competency models as providing the core for what he described as "strategic job modeling." In many organizations, however, the need for integration is not driven by HR, but through the implementation of larger ERP (like SAP and Oracle) or integrated talent management systems (like PeopleSoft, StepStone, SuccessFactors, etc.). Nearly all these systems have a key objective to match business requirements with resource availability. As part of the implementation process, the system forces various HR processes to integrate measurement criteria into a single "qualifications dictionary" or database. These systems are often implemented organization-wide and across all business processes. The effect is a standardization of criteria for all HR processes and across business units. Many of these ERP or talent management systems will, for example, integrate the recruitment and selection of new employees (through applicant tracking or online assessment modules) with development or succession planning processes (through multirater questionnaire or talent profile modules). In order to compare and present individual information across modules, these systems require a standardized set of criteria.

This type of integration can have significant benefits including the following:

The opportunity to work with evidence-based people management processes.

Achieving greater integration of information across talent processes.

Saving time and effort by removing duplication of process.

Building a strong culture and platform for sharing knowledge and talent information.

Developing a shared language of performance.

Responding more quickly to changing business needs.

The way that this integration is implemented can vary dramatically. Key stages, however, include (SHL, 2007) the following:

Business strategy: Which roles are required to deliver the strategy?

Organizing framework: Who to target and how?

Capability framework: The skills, tools, and techniques to define talent requirements.

Leadership involvement: Creating a "Talent Mind-Set" in senior managers.

Rigorous assessment of potential across the organization.

Development of high-performance talent: Filling gaps through targeted development interventions and recruitment initiatives.

Building fluid talent pools—keeping it tied into the strategy.

Figure 25.2 provides an outline of what an integrated framework might look like. Clearly, if the business strategy changes, then the talent management strategy needs to be reevaluated to ensure it stays relevant. This single integrated approach is achieved by using a coherent, meaningful operating language that ensures the consistent and relevant measurement of talent requirements.

Competencies and the Importance of Accurate Measurement

As discussed earlier, developing an integrated language of performance that allows for the effective sharing of talent information is a critical part of developing an integrated talent management strategy. The competency framework is critical as it sits at the heart of all assessments. This importance is not unusual—competency models have sat at the heart of HR applications for a number of years. However, competency management in talent management is more complex as it aims not only to act as criteria for a specific talent decision (e.g., training, promotion) but also to facilitate integration between various talent processes and multiple talent decisions from the same source information.

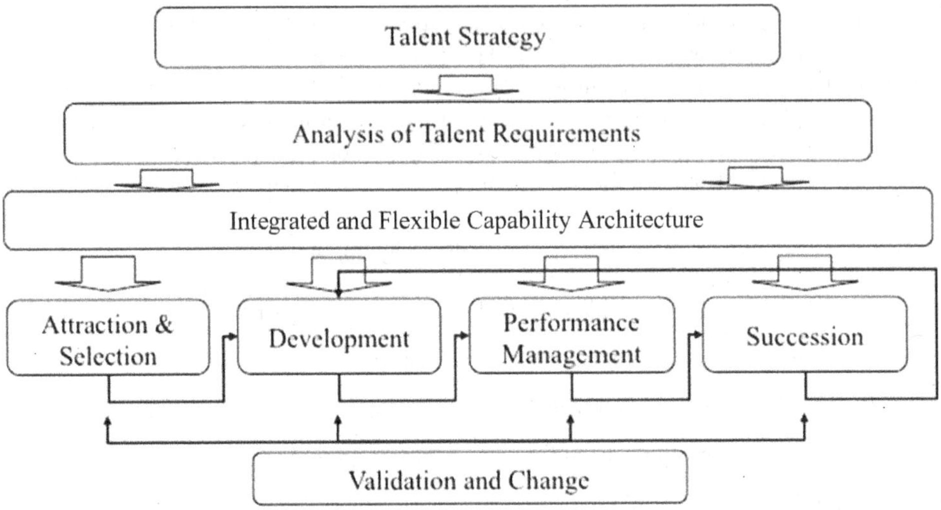

Figure 25.2 Integrated Talent Management (See Text for Explanation).

The fact that the competency framework links talent strategy to HR applications and facilitates accurate, relevant, and meaningful measurement of talent requirements necessitates that organizations pay particular attention to how competencies are defined and ultimately measured. The definition of talent requirements without the capability to measure them effectively has very little value. Talent requirements that are vaguely defined or too value based, for example "integrity" or "courage," are often particularly difficult to measure effectively, and their inclusion in competency models might have little value.

The implementation of a single unifying competency framework across the organization is fraught with difficulty, and very few organizations have been able to do so effectively. This is often the case because various stakeholders in the organization, particularly in HR, are not able to gain agreement on how this language should integrate across "silos." There are also concerns that a single unifying framework might be too inflexible to change when business or HR strategy change.

The real reason for failure might be subtler and relates to the nature of competencies as a language. As in any language, it is very easy to "misunderstand" if the user does not fully comprehend the concepts that are communicated. Competencies are often poorly described or given labels that sound similar even though the expected behavior is not similar. At best, this leads to duplication and redundancy in the model, while, at worst, it leads to unreliable and invalid measurement. To undertake accurate and useful measurement, it is of critical importance to understand the constructs that are assessed. It would also be important to understand the relationships between these constructs and how they relate to performance.

To illustrate, take for example any competency model in which competencies are described using different levels of complexity. A typical competency is "teamwork"—possibly best predicted by "agreeableness." In describing this competency at higher levels of complexity, one might start to describe behavior that relates more to "leadership of teams" than "teamwork," thus changing the most likely predictor of success at more senior levels in the organization from agreeableness to either "extraversion" or "emotional stability." In many competency models, such construct change is often not realized, and the competencies are treated as being the "same" but at different levels. This sort of "construct change" can have the unintended, negative consequence that the future leaders of the organization are recruited as "agreeable" team workers, rather than more "charismatic" leaders.

A competency-like "strategic planning" can be equally confusing. If the focus of the behavioral descriptions in this competency is on "strategic," then the most likely predictor of success would be "openness to experience"; yet, if the focus is on "planning," then the most likely predictor of success might be "conscientiousness." In recruitment, this could lead to the selection of the more rule-following, methodical planner, rather than the innovative, more flexible strategic thinker. The problem is avoided by clearly defining the competency to mean either "the capability to develop a long-term vision" or "the capability to develop short-term plans and schedules."

Organizations often develop competency frameworks that describe how a common set of competencies apply to varying levels within the organization to ensure alignment of criteria required for lower-level jobs (e.g., individual contributors) and jobs higher up in the job family or leadership pipeline (e.g., team leader, managers, or executives). A competency-like strategic planning may then be described to mean "short-term planning" at the lower levels and "strategic thinking" at the higher levels. It is important to note, however, that, due to the independent nature of the underlying personality constructs, one can hardly argue that the competency of "short-term planning" is the lower or less complex-level descriptor of the higher or more complex-level competency of "long-term thinking." They are in fact two distinct competencies predicted by two different personality constructs. Including the competency of "strategic planning" in a framework as if it were a single competency with multiple levels of complexity will lead to misalignment as individuals who "fit" job requirements at lower levels move to positions higher in the leadership pipeline.

When selecting a competency language framework for use as part of an integrated talent management strategy, the following characteristics should be taken into consideration:

The competency language should allow the organization to link competency potential (as measured by personality and other relevant traits) to behavior, and to link behavior to results directly with clearly defined relationships. This allows for the measurement of any of these components of the language while still maintaining an understanding of the bigger picture. For example, the relationship between agreeableness as a trait, teamwork as a competency, and team performance.

The intention is that the competency framework will act as a unifying performance language across talent processes and even across business units or organizations. This language should therefore describe requirements as clearly defined behavioral constructs that relate to performance. The language exists because work and people exist. It is an evidence-based reflection of the interaction between people and their work.

Competency frameworks exist independently of any specific organization, job, or HR application. The validity of a framework is therefore not dependent on the organization or the application, but on the generalizable relationships between individual potential, behavior, and performance. This "independence" provides a language framework that can be used in multiple organizations and applications without losing construct validity.

A well-developed, evidence-based competency language framework is an articulated set of relationships that defines the components of a model, how these relate to each other, and how they relate to other external construct systems (such as personality traits), and is not just an arbitrary combination of behavioral descriptors (Bartram, 2002).

The language should have sufficient depth of description to allow for the development of competency descriptions that convey performance requirements across multiple applications and levels in the organization without losing construct validity. As mentioned previously, the accurate description of behavioral requirements is critical for accurate measurement. In performance management, for example, one would like to contextualize what is meant by a competency-like "leadership" in such a way that the job incumbent can relate relevant behaviors concerning team motivation, supervising others, providing direction, and so on, to his or her specific job or context. Competency models that only describe broad constructs often do not provide enough granular descriptors that allow for depth of description without duplication or diluting constructs (as described earlier in the case of teamwork or strategic planning).

The language should have sufficient breadth and describe a broad range of competency requirements. This allows the organization to reconfigure competency models and applications as talent strategy changes. When strategy changes, the organization should not have to change the performance language, just the emphasis on what is important. Competency models that have been developed with only one strategy in mind often exclude certain behaviors from measurement deliberately. Including these behaviors at a later stage requires a significant redesign of a number of HR applications and tools (e.g., the rewrite of interview guides). Using a competency framework and related personality measures that are able to provide information on a broad range of behaviors, even if these behaviors are not considered important in the current strategic context, allows for the reprioritization of this information when required without incurring additional costs.

The language should be acceptable and applicable across the organization and in various HR processes to provide a "single source of truth" that builds a strong culture and platform for business leaders to share talent information.

Validation and Talent Management

The effective use of personality assessment in talent management depends on our ability to use information about personality (and other human attributes) in a diagnostic fashion to differentiate people's areas of potential strength and areas of developmental need. If we can do this, then we can use personality measures as the basis for assessing competency potential and feed this information into the organization's procedures for dealing with both the acquisition and internal mobility of talent (i.e., talent audits, succession planning, and individual development).

To be practical and effective, it is necessary to map the domain of personality attributes onto some practical business language that can be used by everyone in talent management procedures. This language is the language of competencies. Like all languages, it needs a vocabulary and a structure, and we need to know how to translate from this language to other languages (such as the language of the psychological domain of constructs).

Developing a Universal Competency Framework (UCF)

The SHL UCF development (see Bartram, 2005, 2006; Bartram, Robertson, & Callinan, 2002; Kurz & Bartram, 2002) was based on an analysis of a wide range of published and practitioner models. The process adopted in developing this model was similar to that described in Tett, Guterman, Bleier, and Murphy (2000), who identified 53 competencies from an analysis of published and practitioner models and arranged these into nine general categories. They also list in their paper example models from Personnel Decisions Inc., Jeanneret & Associates, and Lominger Limited. However, their nine general categories (e.g., Task Orientation, Person Orientation, Communication, Occupational Acumen and Expertise) were not intended to be structurally related to patterns of correlation between the 53 competencies.

At the time the UCF was being developed (work started on this in 1998), there was considerable confusion over the nature of the construct "competency." Boyatzis (1982) had defined competency as any underlying characteristic that is causally related to effective or superior performance (a definition that corresponds more to the present authors' notion of competency potential). Fleishman, Wetrogan,

Uhlman, and Marshall-Mies (1995) noted that the term "competency" was often used to refer to a mixture of knowledge, skills, abilities, beliefs, values, motivation, and interests. Spencer, McLelland, and Spencer (1994), following on from Boyatzis, stated that competencies can be any individual characteristic that can be shown to differentiate superior from average performance. However, Schippmann (1999) was more specific and defined competencies as "measurable, occupationally relevant, and behaviorally based characteristics or capabilities of people" (p. 20) and distinguished between "can do" and "will do" competencies. Earlier, work by Schippmann and colleagues had produced a 21-dimension task and 22-dimension job skill classification for managerial jobs based on an analysis of a number of job analysis surveys (Schippmann, Prien, & Hughes, 1991).

To develop a framework that has practical value in talent management, it is important to be very clear. To this end, we defined competencies as "sets of behaviors that are instrumental in the delivery of desired results or outcomes" (Bartram et al., 2002, p. 7). This definition focuses on two key points: first, competencies are assessable by others through their expression in behavior, and second, the only behaviors we are interested in are those that are instrumental in leading to the outcomes the organization has defined as being important. Tett et al. (2000) similarly define a competency as "an identifiable aspect of prospective work behavior attributable to the individual that is expected to contribute positively and/or negatively to organizational effectiveness" (Tett et al., 2000, p. 215). The main difference to the Bartram et al. definition lies in the explicit inclusion of negative attributes.

Work on the UCF resulted in a framework that distinguishes 112 "competency components" at the finest level of detail. These components are relatively homogeneous clusters of similar workplace behaviors that, in practice, are not found to be further differentiated in competency models (see Bartram, 2005, Appendix A, for a full list). These components can be thought of as building blocks that are aggregated to produce competencies. Sets of competencies, in turn, form competency models.

Within the UCF, one general-purpose model is defined, with 20 competencies. These are referred to as competency dimensions and provide a generic model for use by organizations that have not developed their own model. In practice, large organizations will want to develop their own models based on their analyses of talent requirements. This is where the component level of the UCF provides real value, as these building blocks can be used to generate customized models that target the key areas of behavior necessary for the talent strategy to succeed.

An important outcome of the UCF development research is the more general model, which aggregates the 112 components under eight general factors (Kurz, Bartram, & Baron, 2004). These factors have been labeled as the Great Eight as they appear to occupy a similar position within the work performance domain (see Table 25.1) to the Big Five in the personality predictor domain.

What was unique about the UCF when it was developed was that it was designed to provide the mechanism for mapping measures from one construct space (that of psychological constructs such as abilities and personality traits) to that of a different construct space (that of behavioral competencies). Most other developments in the competency area were focused instead on the description and measurement of competencies themselves. While there is clearly some overlap between the UCF model and those described by Campbell, McCloy, Oppler, and Sager (1993) and Tett et al. (2000), the UCF has the advantage of being elaborated in terms of the 112 component competencies, which, in turn, are linked both to competency assessment "criterion" measures and to personality, motivation, and ability scales in the "predictor" measurement domain. As such, the model provides a single framework for making predictions from measures of competency potential (ability, personality, and motivation) to measures of competencies (actual work performance) as elaborated on in Bartram (2005).

The Great Eight structure articulates the work performance domain consistently with a wide range of models used by practitioners in competency practice and supported empirically by the way

Table 25.1 Titles and High-Level Definitions of the Great Eight Competencies

Factor	*Competency Domain Title*	*Competency Domain Definition*	*Hypothesized Big Five, Motivation, and Ability Relationships*
1	Leading and Deciding	Takes control and exercises leadership. Initiates action, gives direction, and takes responsibility.	Need for power and control Extraversion
2	Supporting and Cooperating	Supports others and shows respect and positive regard for them in social situations. Puts people first, working effectively with individuals and teams, clients, and staff. Behaves consistently with clear personal values that complement those of the organization.	Agreeableness
3	Interacting and Presenting	Communicates and networks effectively. Successfully persuades and influences others. Relates to others in a confident and relaxed manner.	Extraversion General mental ability
4	Analyzing and Interpreting	Shows evidence of clear analytical thinking. Gets to the heart of complex problems and issues. Applies own expertise effectively. Quickly takes on new technology. Communicates well in writing.	General mental ability Openness to experience
5	Creating and Conceptualizing	Works well in situations requiring openness to new ideas and experiences. Seeks out learning opportunities. Handles situations and problems with innovation and creativity. Thinks broadly and strategically. Supports and drives organizational change.	Openness to experience General mental ability
6	Organizing and Executing	Plans ahead and works in a systematic and organized way. Follows directions and procedures. Focuses on customer satisfaction and delivers a quality service or product to the agreed standards.	Conscientiousness General mental ability
7	Adapting and Coping	Adapts and responds well to change. Manages pressure effectively and copes well with setbacks.	Emotional stability
8	Enterprising and Performing	Focuses on results and achieving personal work objectives. Works best when work is related closely to results and the impact of personal efforts is obvious. Shows an understanding of business, commerce, and finance. Seeks opportunities for self-development and career advancement.	Need for achievement Negative agreeableness

Notes: The final column shows the hypothesized relationships between the Big Five, General Mental Ability, and Motivation for the Great Eight. Where more than one predictor is shown, the second is expected to be of lesser importance than the first. The titles and definitions in Table 25.1 are taken from the SHL Universal Competency Framework™ Profiler Cards (copyright © 2004 by SHL Group plc, reproduced with permission of the copyright holder). These titles and definitions may be freely used for research purposes subject to due acknowledgment of the copyright holder.

in which competency ratings cluster when subjected to factor analysis (e.g., Gotoh, 1999; Kurz, 1999; Kurz et al., 2004). For example, Kurz et al. (2004) report an analysis of data from 365 managers drawn from four U.K. organizations in different industry sectors and from a wide range of functional areas. Two aptitude tests from the SHL Management and Graduate Item Bank were utilized: Verbal Critical Reasoning (VMG2) and Numerical Critical Reasoning (NMG2). In addition, two questionnaires were administered: the Occupational Personality Questionnaire (Concept Model; OPQ CM4.2; SHL, 1993b), which measures 30 scales using a forced-choice item format, and the Inventory of Management Competencies (IMC; SHL, 1993a), which measures 16 generic competency dimensions using a combined Likert and forced-choice format. A composite "180° performance" score for each IMC competency was calculated by averaging self- and boss ratings. These 16 performance scores were entered together with selected marker scales from the OPQ and the ability scales into a principal components factor analysis to ascertain the underlying factor structure of the competency performance and competency potential variables. Eight factors yielded eigenvalues > 1, accounting for 68% of the variance. The factor structure was largely in line with that predicted by the Great Eight model. Factor scores, generated from these data, were relatively independent, with the strongest correlations being just over 0.3. Other analyses on different data sets have produced similar degrees of fit to the model (e.g., Gotoh, 1999; Kurz, 1999). Multidimensional scaling (MDS) analyses of criterion IMC competency ratings produce a circumplex pattern with pairs of scales clustering together according to their proximity as defined by their expected Great Eight content loadings.

Factor analyses of Great Eight predictor or criterion measures tend to produce higher-level solutions. In the predictor domain, these reflect a broad motivational factor, general ability, and two broad personality factors (Digman, 1997). For the criterion domain, two factors tend to emerge, corresponding generally to Hogan's Getting Along and Getting Ahead distinction (Hogan & Holland, 2003) or Borman's Contextual and Task Performance distinction (Borman & Motowidlo, 1993).

Personality assessment instruments are only valuable for talent management if they can provide valid measures of competency potential. Bartram (2005) reports a meta-analysis of 29 validity studies covering different countries, industries, and jobs. The research looked at the relationship between measures of competency potential (based on personality and ability tests) and competencies (as assessed through supervisor ratings of performance on various aspects of a competency model) with both sets of measures being mapped onto the generic Great Eight level of description. Predictors of the Great Eight competencies based only on personality scales showed moderate to good correlations with line-manager ratings for all eight of the competencies. On their own, ability tests correlated with only four of the eight competencies. Together, ability and personality data yield operational validities ranging from 0.20 to 0.44 for the eight competencies. Operational validities for aggregated predictors with aggregated criteria were estimated to be 0.53. Furthermore, there was evidence to support the discriminant validity of the eight factors in that matched pairs of predictors and criteria (e.g., the prediction of Leading & Deciding competency correlated with the criterion measure of Leading & Deciding competency) showed consistently higher correlations than unmatched pairs (e.g., the prediction of Leading & Deciding competency correlated with the other seven criterion competencies).

Ability and Personality as Predictors of Competencies and Job Performance

Ability measures have been acknowledged as good predictors of job performance and even better predictors of training performance. The early meta-analyses (e.g., Hunter & Hunter, 1984) showed the generalizability of this finding. More recently, the academic literature has begun to support the view that personality measures also predict performance at work. Studies concentrating on the Big Five have shown that conscientiousness and emotional stability have broadly generalizable relationships with overall job performance (Barrick & Mount, 1991; Hough, 1992; Salgado, 1997, 1998).

Barrick and Mount (1991) report corrected mean validities of $r = .22$ for conscientiousness and $r = .13$ for extraversion. Focusing exclusively on confirmatory estimates (for which researchers offered conceptual rationales linking traits to criteria), Tett, Jackson, and Rothstein (1991) reported corrected mean validities ranging from $r = .16$ for extraversion to $r = .33$ for agreeableness. Salgado (1997, 1998) replicated Barrick and Mount's results with European data sets, and also found evidence for the validity of emotional stability (corrected $r = .19$). Hurtz and Donovan (2000) reported corrected correlations of $r = .22$ for conscientiousness, $r = .14$ for emotional stability, and $r = .09$ for extraversion. Thus, the evidence is generally supportive of some of the Big Five in providing moderately generalizable predictions of relatively gross job performance measures.

Many of the more recent criticisms of the evidence provided to support the validity of personality measures (Morgeson et al., 2007a, 2007b) have focused on the use of gross Big Five measures as predictors of even more general criterion measures of overall job performance. Such studies are problematic in two ways. First, they tend to focus on looking for generalizable validity across differing patterns of competency requirements, and second, they do so using aggregated measures (Bartram, Warr, & Brown, 2010). For talent management, one needs to be far more diagnostic in the use of predictor instruments. You need measures that have good divergent as well as convergent validity when considering people's potential for one or another competency.

The predictions tested in Bartram (2005) differentiated between what ability measures might predict and what personality might predict. General mental ability was expected to relate most strongly to Analyzing & Interpreting competencies, as the content of these are heavily "g" loaded. On the basis of the content of the competencies, we would also expect general mental ability measures to show some relationships with the factors of Interacting & Presenting and Creating & Conceptualizing. It is these three areas of competency, especially Analyzing & Interpreting, that contain competency components that are underpinned by job knowledge and skills, and hence most likely to be predicted by measures of general mental ability. Organizing & Executing is also likely to be correlated with general ability, but more weakly than the other three competency factors.

With respect to personality, the relationship between the Great Eight and the Big Five is not exact. A clearer pattern of results can be obtained if some aspects of the Big Five are differentiated. Notably, Big Five conscientiousness combines both dependability and achievement, and extraversion combines aspects of interacting with others on the one hand and dominance or potency on the other (Hough, 1992; Hough, Ones, & Viswesvaran, 1998; Robertson, Baron, Gibbons, Maciver, & Nyfield, 2000; Warr, Bartram, & Martin, 2005). In the Great Eight competency model, we expected the trait of dependability to relate to Organizing & Executing, while the trait of achievement should relate to Enterprising & Performing; the trait of sociability should relate to Interacting & Presenting, while dominance and potency aspects of extraversion should relate to Leading & Deciding and Interacting & Presenting competencies.

The findings strongly supported the predictions. When predictors of competency potential and criterion competency measures were matched together on a like-for-like basis, personality-based predictors had good validity across all of the Great Eight competency factors (operational validities ranged from .16 to .33). When mismatched predictor criterion pairs were considered (e.g., using Leading & Deciding competency potential to predict Adapting & Coping competencies), the average correlation was only .02. This supported the view that one needs to be specific in matching measures of competency potential to measures of actual competencies.

As expected, ability tests predicted only four of the Great Eight competencies (Interacting & Presenting, $r = .22$; Analyzing & Interpreting, $r = .40$; Creating & Conceptualizing, $r = .24$; and Organizing & Executing, $r = .16$). What is crucial for the use of personality assessment in talent management is that, while personality-based predictors showed good divergent validity for all eight of the areas of competency, *only* personality predicted Leading & Deciding, Supporting & Cooperating, Adapting & Coping, and Enterprising & Performing competencies. It is also important to note that the personality instruments used in the 29 studies were all from the SHL OPQ family of questionnaires. While these can be used to create Big Five measures, the scales cover a broader domain, including areas of motivation. Instruments constructed as Big Five measures would probably not have the scope to provide the same degree of coverage of the Great Eight competencies and would likely need to be supplemented by other measures.

Increasing the Diagnostic Power of Personality Measures as Predictors of Competencies

Good measurement is a key factor in making practical use of personality assessment in talent management. One of the main problems faced in assessing competencies in the workplace is the tendency for observers to show "halo effects." That is, they tend to rate a person as either high on everything or low on everything and find it difficult to discriminate within people. Many raters also find it difficult to discriminate between people, producing ratings that are all around the "OK" range, with no highs or lows. Typically, our predictor instruments are better constructed than our criterion ones.

One way of getting people to discriminate better is to use forced-choice rating formats. Here, they have to choose whether someone is stronger on one competency than another, and cannot say they are the same on everything. Forced-choice multiple scale instruments do have some technical psychometric issues (relating to the properties of what are known as ipsative scales). However, modern measurement models, using Item Response Theory, can now be used to produce normative scale measures from forced-choice format items (Brown & Maydeu-Olivares, 2011).

Bartram (2007) reported a meta-analysis that compared the use of rating scales as criterion measures with forced-choice item formats as criterion measures. This study managed to control all other factors: the same people were rated on both formats, the same line-manager raters were used, everyone had the same predictor instrument, and the same statements were used for both the forced-choice and the rating format criterion competency assessment. The findings were very clear. Higher operational validity coefficients (prediction of line-manager ratings of competencies) are associated with the use of forced-choice ($r = .38$) rather than rating scale ($r = .25$) item formats for the criterion measurement instrument when performance is rated by the same line managers on both formats and where the predictor is held constant. Thus, the criterion-related validity of a predictor can be increased by 50% simply by changing the format of the criterion measurement instrument.

The implication of this for talent management is that we need to focus more attention on developing good tools for the measurement of competencies. In the past, we have tended to focus on improving the measurement of competency potential while ignoring the "criterion problem."

Using Personality-Based Measures of Competency Potential in Development and Coaching

Helping individuals and their managers understand the influence of their preferences and typical modes of behavior on performance at work is one of the most valuable uses of personality questionnaires. Developmental talent interventions typically do not require any "high stakes" decisions about the suitability of talent for a particular role. Most organizations see the use of personality questionnaires in these contexts as a low-risk but high-utility option.

Individuals' personality scores are most often expressed as areas of strengths and areas for development. These results, provided as composite competency potential or "fit" scores, enable the individual, trainers, and coaches to identify typical behavior that would influence effective performance at work. Figure 25.3 provides a graphical explanation of how a set of personality scale scores can be combined using regression-based weights to create a single measure of "competency potential": in this case, a measure that would be used to predict competency in the area of planning and organizing.

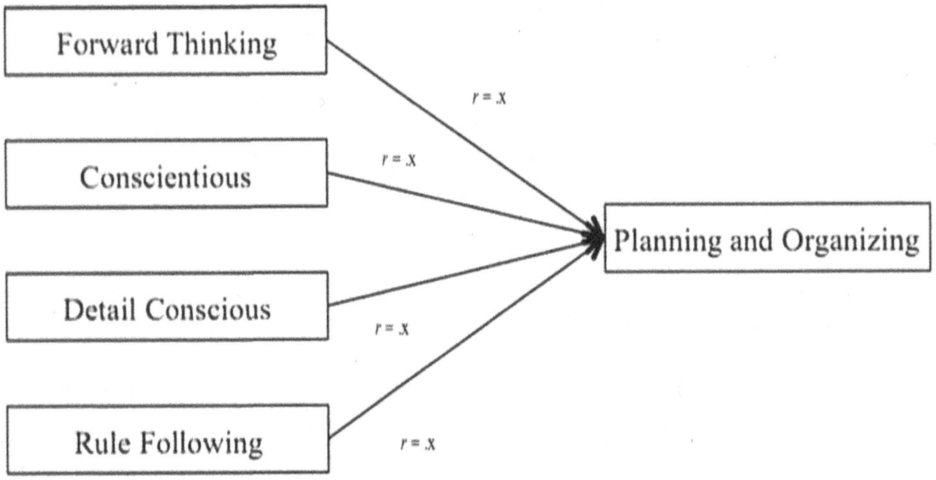

Figure 25.3 The Calculation of Composite Competency Potential Scores From a Set of Personality Trait Scales (See Text for Explanation).

Figure 25.4 provides an example of a report output from the OPQ32r (SHL, 2006, 2009). In this example of the competency "Planning and Organizing," each personality scale from the OPQ that has relevance to this particular competency (in this case "forward thinking," "conscientious," "detail

2. Supporting and Co-operating	**1 2 3 4 5**
2.1 Working with People	
✓✓ Nearly always seeks contributions from others in order to make a decision.	
✓✓ Is likely to nearly always provide support and sympathy to colleagues.	
● Occasionally seeks to understand the reasons for others' behavior.	
● Is as comfortable as most others to spend time with others.	
× Drive to be moderately competitive may affect co-operation with colleagues.	

Key to symbols:

Symbol	Short Description	Definition
✓✓	Key Strength	Strongly likely to have a positive impact
✓	Likely Strength	Likely to have a positive impact
●	Moderate	Likely to have neither a positive nor a negative impact
×	Likely Limitation	Likely to have a negative impact
××	Key Limitation	Strongly likely to have a negative impact

The overall likelihood of an individual displaying strength in each competency is shown in the bar graphs on the right hand side of the report.

1	2	3	4	5
Unlikely to be a strength	**Less likely** to be a strength	**Moderately likely** to be a strength	**Quite likely** to be a strength	**Very likely** to be a strength

Figure 25.4 Extract From an OPQ32 Universal Competency Report Output (See Text for Explanation).

Source: Reproduced with permission from SHL Group Ltd.

conscious," and "rule following"—see Figure 25.3) is represented by a behavioral statement with an indication of the strength of the individual's preference for that behavior indicated by the marks on the left. The competency potential fit score is a normed composite score and is represented by the length of the bar next to the competency name.

In addition, one is able to provide detailed development tips for specific competencies that are likely development areas. This type of information can be useful as part of talent interventions that require individual feedback, development planning, or coaching (e.g., leadership and graduate development programs). It is also particularly useful as part of career discussions.

Person–Job Matching

Talent decisions that relate to specific roles or talent criteria require that one has a better indication of the "fit" of the individual, not against specific competencies only, but against a complete job role profile or leadership model. The UCF provides a framework for the relationship between personality scales, on the one hand, and workplace behaviors, on the other. These relationships are used to provide composite scores that indicate the likelihood of an individual showing the required behaviors (or competencies) in the workplace (see Bartram, 2005, for details).

Job-specific profiles include a list of competencies essential for effective performance in that role. These profiles are determined from the results of an analysis of the most critical success factors of the role as judged by subject matter experts through competency modeling or other job analysis techniques (Bartram, 2008).

When making selection or placement decisions, the aim is to understand the extent to which an individual is suitable for a particular role or job. It is useful in these cases to have a "person–job match" score that could be used as input to decision processes. These scores are often expressed as weighted composite scores that represent the individual's "fit" against a complete role profile. Figure 25.5 provides a graphical representation. Figure 25.6 shows the outcome of a person–job match report using the UCF and competency potential scores from the OPQ32.

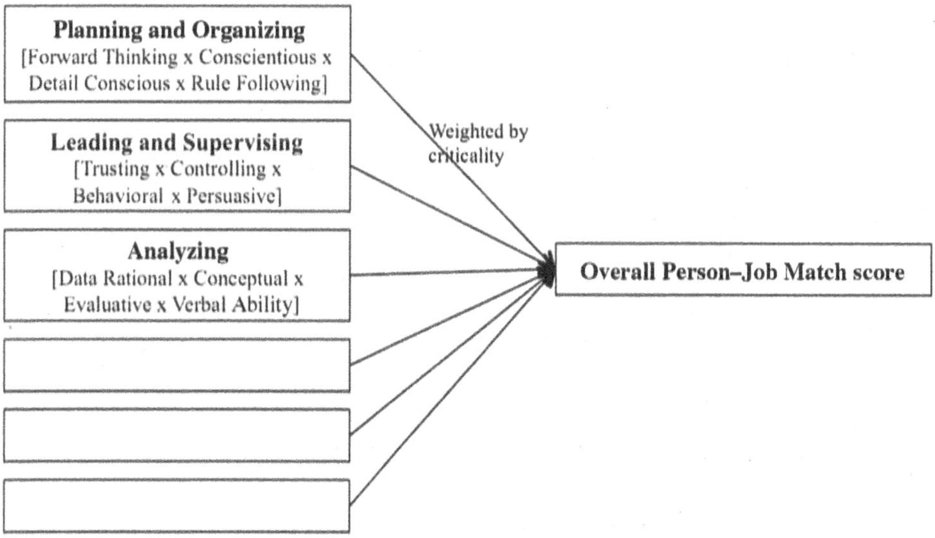

Figure 25.5 The Calculation of Weighted Composite Scores That Represent Fit Against a Job Role to Create a Person–Job Match Score.

Note: Each component of this match score is itself a competency potential measure created by the weighted addition of a small number of personality trait measures (often in combination with measures of ability or motivation where relevant).

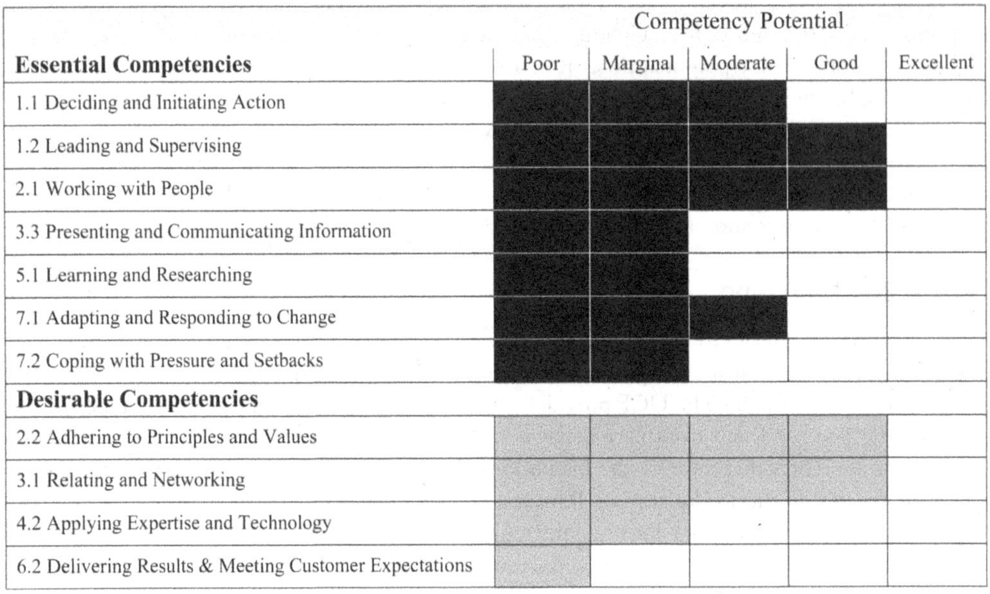

Competency Potential		Job Importance: Lower Job Importance	Job Importance: Higher Job Importance
		Unused Potential	**Areas of Strength**
	Excellent or Good Potential		7.1 Adapting and Responding to Change 3.1 Relating and Networking 2.2 Adhering to Principles and Values 2.1 Working with People 1.2 Leading and Supervising
		Undeveloped Areas	**Areas for Development**
	Moderate Potential	8.2 Entrepreneurial and Commercial Thinking 3.2 Persuading and Influencing	1.1 Deciding and Initiating Action
		Undeveloped Areas	**Areas of Concern**
	Marginal or Poor Potential	8.1 Achieving Personal Work Goals and Objectives 6.3 Following Instructions and Procedures 6.1 Planning and Organizing 5.3 Formulating Strategies and Concepts 5.2 Creating and Innovating 4.3 Analyzing 4.1 Writing and Reporting	7.2 Coping with Pressure and Setbacks 6.2 Delivering Results and Meeting Customer Expectations 5.1 Learning and Researching 4.2 Applying Expertise and Technology 3.3 Presenting and Communicating Information

Figure 25.6 Outputs From the OPQ32 UCF Person–Job Match Report.

Source: Reproduced with permission from SHL Group Ltd.

Notes: UCF: Universal Competency Framework. The upper table is the "Summary Profile of Essential and Desirable Competencies." This summary profile displays competency potential scores for competencies that were rated as either essential or desirable for the target job. Beneath that is the "Summary Match Table." This illustrates for a particular individual the relationship between their competency potential scores and the relative importance of the competency for a particular job role for each of the 20 UCF competencies (see Bartram, 2005, for further details of the UCF competencies).

Competency Maps and the Importance of Criticality Values

It is not within the scope of this chapter to discuss the practices involved in job analysis (for coverage on personality-oriented work analysis see Chapter 11, this volume). It is important to note, however, that, unless the job analysis method used provides a clear indication of the criticality or weighted importance of competency requirements, it is not possible to provide a person–job match score.

The competency criticality value is an indication of the extent to which a competency contributes to successful performance against job objectives. If one argues that job objectives are the "operationalization" of the business strategy in each role, then it stands to reason that an increased job fit would represent "more" talent, while a poor fit would represent "less" talent.

Figure 25.7 represents a map of the relative importance (E = Essential, H = Highly Important, and M = Moderately Important for job success) of each of the UCF 20 competencies for various roles: individual contributors, team leaders, manager of managers, and senior managers. The map becomes a visual representation of the talent requirements across the organization. Maps such as these are useful to determine the requirements per role for selection, determine the differences between roles for person–job matching in career or succession planning, and determine talent requirements in critical roles as part of manpower planning.

The flexibility to change critical talent requirements quickly when strategy changes is one of the key advantages of the use of a comprehensive framework like the UCF in maps similar to the one displayed in Figure 25.7.

We explained earlier in this chapter how personality could be used to predict competency potential against the components of the UCF. Person–job matching allows the organization to match personality to critical competency requirements. By changing the criticality values for competencies in the map to reflect new strategy requirements, new person–job match scores can be calculated without having to change the core competency language or the need to reassess individuals. This

UCF Dimension	Individual Contributors	Team Leaders	Manager of Managers	Senior Managers
1.1 Deciding and Initiating Action		H	H	
1.2 Leading and Supervising		E	E	M
2.1 Working with People	E	E	M	M
2.2 Adhering to Principles and Values	H	H		M
3.1 Relating and Networking	H	M		E
3.2 Persuading and Influencing			M	E
3.3 Presenting and Communicating Information	H	M	M	M
4.1 Writing and Reporting	M			
4.2 Applying Expertise and Technology	H	H	M	E
4.3 Analyzing			H	E
5.1 Learning and Researching	H	M	H	H
5.2 Creating and Innovating		H	M	
5.3 Formulating Strategies and Concepts			E	E
6.1 Planning and Organizing	H	E	E	M
6.2 Delivering Results and Meeting Customer Expectations	E	E	E	M
6.3 Following Instructions and Procedures				
7.1 Adapting and Responding to Change	H			
7.2 Coping with Pressures and Setbacks	H	M	M	
8.1 Achieving Personal Work Goals and Objectives	E		M	
8.2 Entrepreneurial and Commercial Thinking			E	E

Figure 25.7 An Example of a "Competency Map" (See Text for Explanation).

approach makes the use of personality in talent management much more flexible. It allows the organization to change the weights of more and less important competencies and not the measures of these competencies. Thus, the fit of a person, with a given set of personality scores, may change as the importance of different competency requirements are changed. This results in a different interpretation of personality preferences against talent requirements and could result in someone who was a good fit to a role needing development to continue to fit the requirements when those requirements are changed. Such evaluations can be carried out without any further assessment of people, but through a reweighting of existing data.

Much has been written about the importance of proper job analysis and the dangers of the "inferential leap" (Lievens, 2004). The usefulness of person–job match scores is highly dependent on the accuracy and specificity of competency criticality values. Person–job match scores become more useful when criticality values are highly differentiated, that is, where there is a clear distinction between which subset of competencies are essential to success in the role and which are not relevant. Job match algorithms work by weighting the fit between potential and requirements more highly for essential competencies than for desirable or less-relevant ones. As a consequence a clear articulation of the requirements underlies effective use of such algorithms. Typically, a competency model of 20 competencies might, for a given role, have five or six at most defined as "essential." Competency potential for these "essentials" may be measured by a mix of relevant abilities and narrow band personality scales (such as the scales of the OPQ32), with constraints on the number of scales per competency and on overlap in mappings of scales to competencies (to ensure good discrimination between composite predictors and differentiation between essential and other competencies). Contrary to this, the use of a person–job match approach when implementing broadly defined competency models representing company values or general leadership requirements are less successful as they tend to provide very little between-person differentiation.

If the organization is planning to use personality-based competency potential scores throughout the employee life cycle, it is essential that practitioners clearly determine which competencies contribute most to success, given a specific role or within a particular talent intervention. The unwillingness of many organizations to spend sufficient time and resources on proper job analysis often leads to poor differentiation between the requisite criteria from one role to the next or for different talent decisions. This reduces the usefulness of personality measures as part of integrated talent management interventions. All the standard industrial–organizational (I/O) psychology text books provide guidance on the fundamental of job analysis (e.g., Bartram, 2008; Landy & Conte, 2004, Module 5.4).

The Use of Person–Job Match Scores in Various Talent Management Processes

Processes Involving One Individual and a Single Competency Model

Person–job match scores, where individual preferences are matched to a single set of competency requirements, can be used for talent decisions involving the placement of individuals, for example as part of selection decisions, or for role-specific development interventions. In both cases, the aim is to understand the potential "gap" between the individual's likely behavior and the requirements of the role.

As part of an integrated talent management strategy, this information becomes the basis of selection, provides information on the success of attraction models, informs future development programs, and assists in on-boarding and performance management.

Processes Involving More Than One Individual, But a Single Competency Model

Processes involving the selection of talent often require that individuals are compared to both the criteria for success and other individuals in the talent pool. In these cases, it is possible to use competency potential person–job match scores to rank-order individuals. It is important to note, however, that this is possible only if all individuals in the pool have been compared to the same role profile, have been assessed using exactly the same measures, and if the same scoring key and norm group have been applied. Figure 25.8 shows an example of such a rank-order list (merit list).

A merit list, like the one shown in Figure 25.8, is extremely useful when large groups of individuals need to be compared, for example in graduate or volume recruitment.

Using Person–Job Matching in Succession Planning

Talent decisions made as part of succession planning processes often involve, not just competency potential information, but also information based on the measurement of current performance. In this context, "key talent" is typically those individuals who are exceptional performers and show significant potential for leadership or specialist roles. The relationship between potential and performance is typically depicted in a "9-box" grid similar to the one shown in Figure 25.9.

Here, measures aimed at assessing potential (personality and reasoning ability) are used in comparison to multiple-rater questionnaires, simulations, or other measures of actual behavior, with a common "language" (i.e., that of competencies) being used for both. This makes it easier to compare individual potential and performance and understand where it will be most effective to target development resources.

			Extremely Important					Highly Important				
Match Score		Candidate	1.1 Deciding and Initiating Action	1.2 Leading and Supervising	2.1 Working with People	2.2 Adhering to Principles and Values	3.1 Relating and Networking	5.3 Formulating Strategies and Concepts	3.2 Persuading and Influencing	4.3 Analyzing	5.2 Creating and Innovating	7.1 Adapting and Responding to Change
√√	83	Candidate 1	5	9	9	7	8	8	8	5	6	8
√√	78	Candidate 2	8	8	7	7	6	7	7	5	6	6
√√	73	Candidate 3	7	7	7	6	8	6	7	5	6	8
√	69	Candidate 4	5	7	6	7	4	9	4	9	8	6
√	68	Candidate 5	5	5	7	6	9	7	7	5	5	8
x	34	Candidate 6	5	6	6	6	6	4	6	4	3	3
xx	28	Candidate 7	4	5	2	3	4	7	4	6	5	3

Figure 25.8 Example of a Person–Job Match Merit List Report.

Note: Here the candidates are rank ordered by the size of the match score, indicating that those at the top of the list will generally better "fit" the role requirements (at least in terms of competency potential) than those lower down. Scores (Stens) are shown for each of the important competencies so the hiring manager can consider the profile of scores as well as the summary match score.

Competency Potential	**Significant Potential**	Understand circumstances, use improvenment plan or ensure fit	Maintain in role, develop for next role	Key Talent Increase challenge or promote
	Growth Potential	Understand circumstances, manage performance	Maintain in role and provide new assignments	Maintain in role, develop for lateral role
	Plateaued or Stretched	Redeploy	Support in role	Support in role with special recognition
		Below Target	**On Target**	**Over Target**
		Performance		

Figure 25.9 Example of a Typical 9-Box Grid Used to Represent the Relationship Between Potential and Performance.

Note: These are used either for identifying where an individual employee is positioned or more generally as part of broader talent mobility procedures to map groups of people.

Person–job match scores, where individual preferences are matched to a possible next job or new leadership role, provide a useful indication of potential and development need. These scores determine the individual's position on the vertical axis of the 9-box grid. As part of integrated talent management, this also provides information relating to other areas of the employee life cycle, for example urgency of development in learning and development, development plans for high potentials in performance management, the number of critical roles filled by successors in sourcing, the capacity to fill key positions in talent strategy and planning, and the forecast of compensation needs in compensation.

Application Across Roles and Groups

Person–job match scores should be calculated based on a match with clearly defined competencies that have been shown to significantly relate to successful job performance. In organizations where strategic objectives have been sufficiently aligned and cascaded throughout the various levels and roles of the organization, the assumption would be that job objectives, and, therefore, competency requirements, are strategically aligned. Matching each individual against the competencies more relevant for his or her role would provide an indication of person–job fit. Aggregating these "fit" scores provides an indication of the extent to which talent across the organization "fit" against strategic talent requirements. Figure 25.10 provides an example of the overall person–job match scores per grade. In this organization, it seems clear that the state of talent in grade D1 (junior management) is potentially problematic. This information has particular relevance for succession planning, leadership development, and sourcing.

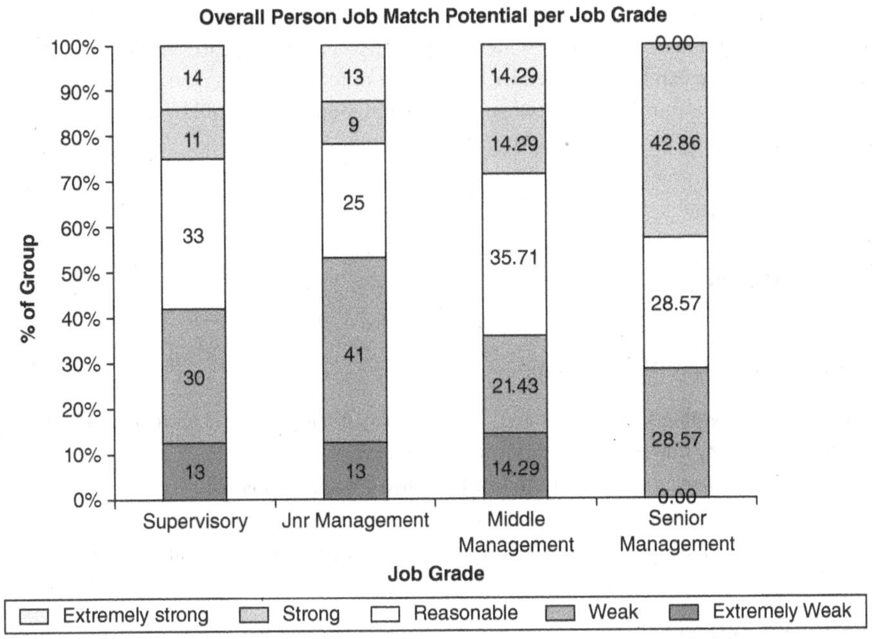

Figure 25.10 Overall Person–Job Match Potential Aggregate Reporting (See Text for Explanation).

Conclusions

The use of personality questionnaires as part of integrated talent management requires that the organization carefully consider which measures of personality to select as part of their assessment strategy. Factors to consider include the following:

The capability of the questionnaire to provide sufficiently detailed information that will result in a comprehensive measure of competency potential. Big Five measures, for example, tend to be too broad. The differences between competencies are better captured at the facet level.

The applicability of the questionnaire and benchmark groups for all job roles in the organization as opposed to only specific groups.

The efficiency of the measure—the range of report options to address various applications across the employee life cycle.

In multinational organizations, the availability of the measure in multiple languages.

Technology integration options with integrated talent management systems.

Given that assessment data will be used across multiple applications over a period of time, it would also be important to consider any changes that might be made to the assessment policy to include guidelines as regards reassessment. In cases where the organization obtains informed consent to use assessment data, it must be made clear that the data will be used across multiple talent processes for multiple talent decisions. The organization also needs to consider any assessment policy issues relating to data protection law and best practice.

In conclusion, while organizations often assert that people are their greatest asset, few really "live" this. Integrated talent management is a process that provides the opportunity to make the most of the assets on which organizations rely for their competitive advantage and indeed for their very existence. People are not all the same: They differ in how they interact with others (work colleagues, customers, suppliers), how they interact with their work tasks, and in a host of other ways. This variance provides the potential source from which competitive advantage can be gained—or lost. Much of this people-variance can be explained by underlying differences in personality. The accurate measurement of personality and its use in assessing competency potential should be a key tool in any organization's integrated talent management program.

Practitioner's Window

Establish Integrated Talent Strategy

- Obtain buy-in for integrated, evidence-based talent management practices before implementation of the competency framework and assessment of potential.
- Find a sponsor at the executive level (the Talent Executive if one is appointed).
- Get involved in the implementation of integrated talent management systems early in order to influence the specification of competency framework and measurement procedures within the system.

Define Talent Requirements

Step 1: Select a suitable criterion language (i.e., competency framework). This needs to be focused on behavior and to have sufficient depth and breadth to represent the behaviors required for success in the workplace.

Step 2: Do a detailed job analysis and profile jobs in terms of the competencies most critical for job outcomes. It is extremely important that competency profiles include an indication of importance or criticality. Indicators of proficiency are not sufficient. Ensure that the most critical competencies are defined in order to maintain sufficient differentiation in match scores between jobs.

Measure Talent Potential

Step 1: Use a personality questionnaire with a broad range of traits. For the purposes of person–job matching, broad trait-based instruments, like the Big Five, and type-based questionnaires will not be useful.

Step 2: Link traits to competencies using validity data. This can involve content-, construct-, and criterion-related evidence.

Step 3: Assess individuals using the chosen personality questionnaire. For some competencies it is useful also to include measures of cognitive ability. Multirater measures (like 360-degree questionnaires) may provide additional criterion data for future validity studies.

Step 4: Compute person–job match scores and rank individuals according to talent requirements. Using various banding or scoring formats will be useful to ensure fairness and deal with measurement error. Realize value by integrating person–job match data into broader talent management processes and systems.

Step 5: Use "competency fit" information as a *part* of the integrated talent processes, together with other assessment information, to define potential for selection, development planning, succession decisions, and leadership development.

References

Barrick, M. R., & Mount, M. K. (1991). The Big Five personality dimensions and job performance: A meta-analysis. *Personnel Psychology, 44*, 1–26.

Bartram, D. (2005). The Great Eight competencies: A criterion-centric approach to validation. *Journal of Applied Psychology, 90*, 1185–1203.

Bartram, D. (2006). *The SHL Universal Competency Framework* (SHL White Paper Series). Thames Ditton, UK: SHL Group.

Bartram, D. (2007). Increasing validity with forced choice criterion measurement formats. *International Journal of Selection and Assessment, 15*, 263–272.

Bartram, D. (2008). Work profiling and job analysis. In N. Chmiel (Ed.), *An introduction to work and organizational psychology: A European perspective* (2nd ed., pp. 3–28). Malden, MA: Blackwell.

Bartram, D., Robertson, I. T., & Callinan, M. (2002). Introduction: A framework for examining organisational effectiveness. In I. T. Robertson, M. Callinan, & D. Bartram (Eds.), *Organisational effectiveness: The role of psychology* (pp. 1–12). London: Wiley.

Bartram, D., Warr, P., & Brown, A. (2010). Let's focus on two-stage alignment not just on overall performance. *Industrial and Organizational Psychology, 3*, 335–339.

Bersin & Associates. (2007). *High-impact talent management*. Oakland, CA: Author.

Bersin, J. (2008). *Talent management: State of the industry*. Available from http://www.hreonline.com

Borman, W. C., & Motowidlo, D. J. (1993). Expanding the criterion domain to include elements of contextual performance. In N. Schmitt, W. C. Borman, & Associates (Eds.), *Personnel selection in organizations* (pp. 71–98). San Francisco: Jossey-Bass.

Boyatzis, R. E. (1982). *The competent manager: A model for effective performance*. New York, NY: Wiley-Interscience.

Brown, A., & Maydeu-Olivares, A. (2011). Item response modelling of forced-choice questionnaires. *Educational and Psychological Measurement, 71*, 460–502.

Campbell, J. P., McCloy, R. A., Oppler, S. H., & Sager, C. E. (1993). A theory of performance. In N. Schmitt, W. C. Borman, & Associates (Eds.), *Personnel selection in organizations* (pp. 35–70). San Francisco: Jossey-Bass.

Digman, J. M. (1997). Higher order factors of the Big Five. *Journal of Personality and Social Psychology, 73*, 1246–1256.

Fleishman, E. A., Wetrogan, L. I., Uhlman, C. E., & Marshall-Mies, J. C. (1995). Abilities. In N. G. Peterson, M. D. Mumford, W. C. Borman, P. R. Jeanneret, & E. A. Fleishman (Eds.), *Development of prototype occupational information network content model* (Vol. 1, pp. 1–10.39). Salt Lake City: Utah Department of Employment Security.

Gotoh, A. (1999). *The evaluation of competencies predictors across nine studies in five countries* (Unpublished MSc dissertation). Goldsmith College, London.

Guthridge, M., Komm, A. B., & Lawson, E. (2008). Making talent a strategic priority. *The McKinsey Quarterly, 1*, 49–59.

Hogan, J., & Holland, B. (2003). Using theory to evaluate personality and job-performance relations: A socio-analytic perspective. *Journal of Applied Psychology, 88*, 100–112.

Hough, L. M. (1992). The Big Five personality variables–construct confusion: Description versus prediction. *Human Performance, 5*, 139–155.

Hough, L. M., Ones, D. S., & Viswesvaran, C. (1998). *Personality correlates of managerial performance constructs*. Paper presented at the SIOP conference, Dallas.

Hunter, J. E., & Hunter, R. F. (1984). Validity and utility of alternative predictors of job performance. *Psychological Bulletin, 96*, 72–98.

Hurtz, G. M., & Donovan, J. J. (2000). Personality and job performance: The Big Five revisited. *Journal of Applied Psychology, 85*, 869–879.

Kurz, R. (1999). Automated prediction of managerial competencies from personality and ability variables. In *Proceedings of the BPS Test User Conference* (pp. 96–101). Leicester, England: British Psychological Society.

Kurz, R., & Bartram, D. (2002). Competency and individual performance: Modelling the works of work. In I. T. Robertson, M. Callinan, & D. Bartram (Eds.), *Organisational effectiveness: The role of psychology* (pp. 227–258). London: Wiley.

Kurz, R., Bartram, D., & Baron, H. (2004, January). Assessing potential and performance at work: The Great Eight competencies. In *Proceedings of the British Psychological Society Occupational Conference* (pp. 91–95). Leicester, England: British Psychological Society.

Landy, F. J., & Conte, J. M. (2004). *Work in the 21st century: An introduction to industrial and organizational psychology* (Module 5.4). New York, NY: McGraw-Hill.

Lievens, F. S. (2004). Easing the inferential leap in competency modeling: The effects of task-related information and subject matter expertise. *Personnel Psychology, 57*, 881–904.

Morgeson, F. P., Campion, M. A., Dipboye, R. L., Hollenbeck, J. R., Murphy, K., & Schmitt, N. (2007a). Are we getting fooled again? Coming to terms with limitations in the use of personality tests for personnel selection. *Personnel Psychology, 60*, 1029–1049.

Morgeson, F. P., Campion, M. A., Dipboye, R. L., Hollenbeck, J. R., Murphy, K., & Schmitt, N. (2007b). Reconsidering the use of personality tests in personnel selection contexts. *Personnel Psychology, 60*, 683–729.

Robertson, I. T., Baron, H., Gibbons, P., Maciver, R., & Nyfield, G. (2000). Conscientiousness and managerial performance. *Journal of Occupational and Organizational Psychology, 73*, 171–180.

Salgado, J. F. (1997). The five factor model of personality and job performance in the European Community. *Journal of Applied Psychology, 82*, 30–43.

Salgado, J. F. (1998). Big Five personality dimensions and job performance in army and civil occupations: A European perspective. *Human Performance, 11*, 271–288.

Schiemann, W. A. (2010). People equity: A new paradigm for measuring and managing human capital. *Human Resource Planning, 29*, 34–44.

Schippmann, J. S. (1999). *Strategic job modelling: Working at the core of integrated human resources*. Mahwah, NJ: Lawrence Erlbaum.

Schippmann, J. S., Prien, E. P., & Hughes, G. L. (1991). The content of management work: Formation of task and job skill composite classifications. *Journal of Business and Psychology, 5*, 325–354.

SHL. (1993a). *Inventory of management competencies: Manual and user's guide*. Thames Ditton, UK: Author.

SHL. (1993b). *OPQ concept model: Manual and user's guide*. Thames Ditton, UK: Author.

SHL. (2006). *OPQ32 technical manual*. Thames Ditton, UK: Author.

SHL. (2007). *Talent management issues and observations* (SHL White Paper Series). Thames Ditton, UK: Author.

SHL. (2009). *OPQ32 development and psychometric properties of OPQ32r* (Supplement to the OPQ32 Technical Manual). Thames Ditton, UK: Author.

Spencer, L. M., McLelland, D. C., & Spencer, S. (1994). *Competency assessment methods: History and state of the art*. Boston: Hay McBer Research Press.

Tett, R. P., Guterman, H. A., Bleier, A., & Murphy, P. J. (2000). Development and content validation of a "hyper-dimensional" taxonomy of managerial competence. *Human Performance, 13*, 205–251.

Tett, R. P., Jackson, D. N., & Rothstein, M. (1991). Personality measures as predictors of job performance: A meta-analytic review. *Personnel Psychology, 44*, 704–742.

Ulrich, D. (1997). *Human resource champions*. Boston: Harvard Business School Press.

Warr, P., Bartram, D., & Martin, T. (2005). Personality and sales performance: Situational variation and interactions between traits. *International Journal of Selection and Assessment, 13*, 87–91.

26

Validity of Personality for Predicting Citizenship Performance

Walter C. Borman and Jeffrey S. Conway

Introduction

This chapter briefly reviews the topic of contextual or citizenship performance, and then argues for a substantial link between certain personality constructs and citizenship performance. In particular, we (1) describe a model of citizenship performance; (2) discuss the conceptual origins of the construct (i.e., precursors to the citizenship performance concept), and how this performance domain is different from task performance; (3) present a model intended to explain the relationship between ability, personality, task, and citizenship performance; (4) discuss the several reviews and meta-analyses summarizing links between personality and citizenship performance; (5) explore reasons why these relations are not higher; and (6) offer a research agenda that may lead to a better understanding of personality–citizenship performance relationships.

The usual view of job performance typically revolves around task performance. Indeed, the most common job analysis method, task analysis, typically results in task dimensions or task categories. However, Borman and Motowidlo (1993, 1997) have focused on a separate job performance construct, citizenship performance. Citizenship performance contributes to organizational effectiveness but is important primarily because it "shapes the organizational, social, and psychological context that serves as the critical catalyst for task activities and processes" (Borman & Motowidlo, 1993). Citizenship performance includes such activities as helping others with their jobs, supporting the organization, and volunteering for additional work or responsibility. In particular, Borman and Motowidlo (1993) proposed a five-dimensional model: (1) persisting with enthusiasm and extra effort as necessary to complete own task activities successfully, (2) volunteering to carry out task activities that are not formally part of own job, (3) helping and cooperating with others, (4) following organizational rules and procedures, and (5) endorsing, supporting, and defending organizational objectives.

Origins of the Citizenship Performance Concept

Borman, Motowidlo, and colleagues were certainly not the first to recognize the importance of this criterion construct. Indeed, their work is substantially related to several earlier efforts. As far back as 1938, Barnard discussed the "informal organization" and the need for organization members to be willing to cooperate for the good of the organization. Katz (1964) emphasized that cooperative and helpful behaviors beyond formal role prescriptions are important for organizational functioning. More recently, Organ (e.g., Smith, Organ, & Near, 1983) introduced the notion of organizational citizenship behavior (OCB). OCB was defined as extra-role, discretionary behavior that helps other organization members perform their jobs or shows support for and conscientiousness toward the organization. OCB has been studied primarily in relation to its links with job satisfaction and organizational justice (Organ, 1997). Clearly OCB contains substantial elements in common with the definition of citizenship performance developed by Borman and Motowidlo (1993).

Another closely related concept is prosocial organizational behavior (POB). Brief and Motowidlo (1986) defined POB as behavior that is directed toward an individual, group, or organization, with the intention of promoting their welfare. They identified nine functional dimensions that, again, cover constructs similar to those in the five-dimensional taxonomy presented above.

A third major source of support for the citizenship performance taxonomy comes from a model of soldier effectiveness developed for the U.S. Army by Borman, Motowidlo, and Hanser (1983). The model assumed that soldier effectiveness is more than just successfully performing assigned tasks. In fact, the model comprised *only* those elements that are beyond task performance or the technical proficiency-related part of the job. Borman et al. argued that the concepts of organizational socialization, organizational commitment, and morale could be combined and integrated into a three-dimensional performance model. Morale and commitment merge to form a performance dimension labeled "determination." The combination of morale and socialization yields "teamwork," and socialization and commitment merge to form "allegiance." Each of these three dimensions was, in turn, decomposed into five subdimensions (e.g., determination into perseverance, reaction to adversity, etc.).

The three domains briefly discussed above (i.e., OCB, POB, and the model of soldier effectiveness) were grouped and integrated to form Borman and Motowidlo's (1993) five-dimensional taxonomy. They believed that this taxonomy reflected all the concepts from those domains, while providing a parsimonious representation of citizenship performance.

More recent research has explored other possible ways to configure the citizenship performance domain. Coleman and Borman (2000) prepared a list of dimensions representing all the concepts contained in the various dimension sets (i.e., OCB: Morrison, 1994; Organ, 1988; Smith et al., 1983; Van Dyne, Graham, & Dienesch, 1994; Williams & Anderson, 1991; POB: Brief & Motowidlo, 1986; model of soldier effectiveness: Borman et al., 1983). The 27 dimensions and their definitions were then sorted into categories according to their perceived content. Forty-four industrial–organizational psychologists completed the sorting task. From the sorting solutions, a pooled similarity matrix was developed and then an indirect similarity correlation matrix was derived (see Borman & Brush, 1993, for a description of this method).

Coleman and Borman (2000) conducted factor analyses, multidimensional scaling, and cluster analyses on this matrix and a consensus three-category solution emerged. This three-category system then formed the basis of a three-dimensional model of citizenship performance. The personal support dimension is virtually the same as the previous helping-others dimension; organizational support combines the conscientiousness and supporting-the-organization dimensions; and conscientious initiative combines the extra effort and volunteering dimensions (Borman, Hanson, Kubisiak, & Buck, 2000).

Citizenship Performance Distinguished From Task Performance

An important distinction between task and citizenship performance is that task activities vary across jobs, whereas citizenship activities are quite similar across jobs. In fact, task-based job analysis typically has as a purpose discovering the tasks and task dimensions that differentiate one job from other jobs. On the other hand, such activities as volunteering and cooperating with others are largely the same for different jobs.

A study that supports a distinction between task and citizenship was conducted by Conway (1996). He had a panel of industrial–organizational psychologists review the performance dimensions and their definitions in 14 published studies and sort each dimension into one of two categories, task or citizenship performance. Results showed that 55% of the dimensions were very reliably sorted into the task category and 30% of the dimensions were sorted very reliably into the citizenship category. There was some disagreement about the remaining 15%. These findings suggest that, for most performance dimensions, the distinction is clear regarding classifying them into task or citizenship performance.

A Model of Ability, Personality, Task, and Citizenship Performance

Motowidlo, Borman, and Schmit (1997) proposed a theory of individual differences in task and citizenship performance (Figure 26.1). One of the most important elements in this theory is the notion that the antecedents of task and citizenship performance will be different. Task performance should be largely a function of cognitive ability, mediated primarily by task knowledge (knowledge of principles related to technical aspects of job performance), task skill (applying technical knowledge to perform tasks effectively), and task habits (characteristic responses to task situations that either facilitate or hinder the performance of tasks). However, personality should be the central antecedent of citizenship performance, mediated primarily by citizenship knowledge (knowing how to take effective action in situations calling for helping, following rules, volunteering, etc.), citizenship skill (applying knowledge about helping and coordinating, following organizational rules and procedures, etc.), and citizenship habits (personal stylistic tendencies that facilitate or inhibit performing citizenship activities). The mediating variables, citizenship knowledge and task habits, have as antecedents *both* ability and personality. Again, the central feature of this model is that cognitive ability is the main antecedent of task performance; personality is the main antecedent of citizenship performance.

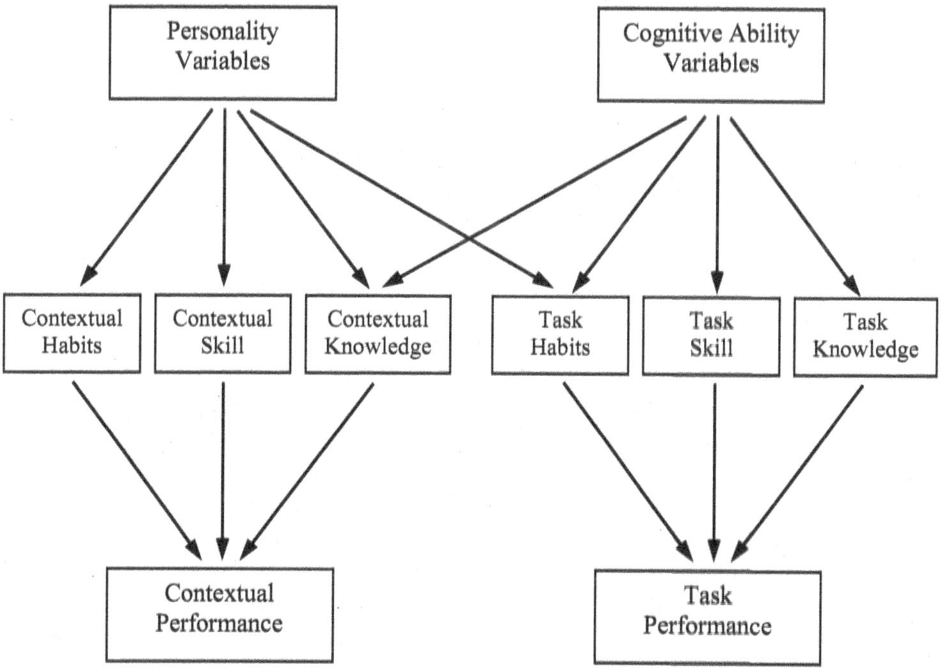

Figure 26.1 A Theory of Individual Differences in Task and Citizenship Performance.

However, there is evidence for some of the mediational paths in the Motowidlo et al. (1997) model. Bergman, Donovan, Drasgow, Overton, and Henning (2008) in combination with Brantley, Borman, and Hanson (2013) provide evidence for, respectively, citizenship knowledge as a mediating variable between personality and citizenship performance, and task knowledge and skill mediating the cognitive ability–task performance relationship. Briefly, Bergman et al. found in a study of support staff working with salespeople that customer relations knowledge mediated the relation between personality and customer service performance, a facet of citizenship performance. And Brantley et al. found that a computerized situational judgment test, a measure of task knowledge and task skill, mediated the relationship between cognitive ability and task performance.

In sum, these studies support the importance of delineating task and citizenship performance dimensions and mapping predictors onto the individual performance constructs, with a focus on emphasizing cognitive predictors for task performance, and personality predictors for citizenship performance, with some evidence for mediation as hypothesized by Motowidlo et al. (1997).

Relationships Between Personality Predictors and Citizenship Performance

The most comprehensive review of relationships between personality and citizenship performance is Organ and Ryan's (1995) meta-analysis of the organizational and dispositional correlates of OCB. Among the organizational variables they considered were job satisfaction, leadership style, organizational justice, and organizational commitment. The four personality traits included in the study were conscientiousness, agreeableness, positive affectivity, and negative affectivity.

Organ and Ryan (1995) separately considered the altruism dimension of OCB, behaviors intended to benefit individuals within an organization, and the conscientiousness, or generalized compliance dimension, of OCB, behaviors intended to benefit the organization. They also divided the findings into those that were based on self-reports and other-reports of OCB and those that were based on only other-reports.

Organ and Ryan (1995) found that, among the personality variables, only conscientiousness correlated significantly with OCB. Specifically, conscientiousness correlated .22 with the altruism component and .30 with the generalized compliance component (these r_s are corrected for criterion unreliability and restriction-in-range; total $N = 2{,}172$ and 1,818, respectively). Correlations were lower when studies employing self-ratings of OCB were excluded (corrected $r_s = .04$ and .23, respectively). However, substantially larger and more consistent relationships were found for the organizational variables. These findings led Organ and Ryan to conclude that if personality variables were related to OCB, the relationship was weak and probably mediated by the impact of personality on job satisfaction. Specifically, personality characteristics may affect satisfaction, which in turn influences OCB.

Organ and Ryan (1995) provided a comprehensive review of the literature concerning relationships between personality and OCB. However, a considerable number of additional studies bearing on the personality–citizenship performance linkage have been conducted since the Organ and Ryan meta-analysis. In this section of the chapter, we review recent studies that have examined Five-Factor Model (FFM)–citizenship performance relations.

Hurtz and Donovan (2000) conducted a meta-analysis of FFM personality dimensions and job performance correlations. In one of their analyses, they were able to separate three different criterion dimensions, task performance and two citizenship performance dimensions, job dedication, and interpersonal facilitation (Van Scotter & Motowidlo, 1996). The true (operational) validities, that is, corrected for restriction-in-range and criterion unreliability, but not predictor unreliability, for the Big Five against these three criteria are shown in Table 26.1.

Table 26.1 True (Operational) Validities for Big Five Dimensions and Three Criteria

	Task Performance	*Job Dedication*	*Interpersonal Facilitation*
Conscientiousness	.15	.18	.16
Emotional stability	.13	.13	.16
Agreeableness	.07	.08	.17
Extraversion	.06	.05	.10
Openness to experience	−.01	.01	.05

For our purposes here, it is important to note that, with a few exceptions, the validities are not appreciably higher for the citizenship performance dimensions compared to task performance. The exceptions are the conscientiousness–job dedication and the emotional stability, agreeableness, and extraversion–interpersonal facilitation relations. But, even in those cases, the differences in the validities favor the citizenship criteria only a small amount.

Borman, Penner, Allen, and Motowidlo (2001) reviewed a total of 20 studies linking personality constructs and citizenship performance, conducted between the Organ and Ryan (1995) meta-analysis and 2000. They summarized validities for several personality constructs and citizenship performance. These include conscientiousness, agreeableness, extraversion, positive and negative affectivity, locus of control, other-oriented empathy, and helpfulness. They involved from 3 to 12 studies, with total numbers from 434 to 1,963. Table 26.2 presents the results.

Table 26.2 Mean Validities for Eight Personality Constructs Against Citizenship Performance Criteria

Personality Construct	*Number of Studies*	*Weighted Mean Uncorrected Validity*	*Estimate of Corrected Validity*
Conscientiousness	12	.24	.32
Agreeableness	7	.13	
Extraversion	8	.08	
Positive affectivity	5	.16	.22
Negative affectivity	6	−.14	
Locus of control	3	.16	
Other-oriented empathy	7	.28	.33
Helpfulness	7	.22	.27

Observed weighted mean validities are low to moderate, similar to what has been found in other reviews and meta-analyses of personality–job performance relations. The highest validities are for conscientiousness, positive affectivity, other-oriented empathy, and helpfulness. The latter two variables emerged from Penner and colleagues' work on the prosocial personality, traits believed to be associated with prosocial thoughts, feelings, and actions. Their Prosocial Personality Battery (Penner, Fritzsche, Craiger, & Freifeld, 1995) was subjected to a series of factor analyses at the item level, with two factors evident: (1) other-oriented empathy, with aspects of affective and cognitive empathy and moral reasoning; and (2) helpfulness, consisting of elements associated with being effective at helping others.

We did not conduct a formal meta-analysis, but using the magnitude of the corrections found in the Barrick and Mount (1991), Tett, Jackson, and Rothstein (1991), and Organ and Ryan (1995) meta-analyses as guidance, the estimated corrected validities for these four constructs are, respectively, .32, .22, .33, and .27. These results are somewhat more optimistic for the size of the relationships between at least some personality traits and citizenship performance compared to the usual personality-task or personality-overall performance estimates.

But perhaps the best summary comparison, and certainly the most up-to-date, is by Chiaburu, Oh, Berry, Li, and Gardner (2011). These researchers meta-analyzed the relationship between the FFM personality traits and several conceptualizations of citizenship performance. Chiaburu et al. used the components citizenship toward individuals and toward the organization (OCB-I and OCB-O), as well as a construct they refer to as proactive OCB related to change (OCB-CH). The OCB-CH construct is heavily influenced by Van Dyne's (e.g., Van Dyne & LePine, 1998) work on the voice subdimension of OCB. Finally, they meta-analyzed studies where OCB was measured as a unidimensional construct.

Overall, results of the study paralleled past work, finding small positive relationships between the FFM and citizenship (full results can be seen in Table 26.3). Thus, against aggregate citizenship performance, estimated true score correlations ranged from .09 to .18, with conscientiousness having

Table 26.3 Chiaburu et al.'s Meta-Analysis Results for Five-Factor Model and Facets of Citizenship

FFM Trait	*k*	*N*	*r*	*ρ*	CV_{LL}	CV_{UL}	CI_{LL}	CI_{UL}
Aggregate OCB								
Conscientiousness	71	14,355	0.14	0.18	0.02	0.34	0.15	0.21
Agreeableness	47	10,308	0.11	0.14	0.01	0.28	0.11	0.18
Emotional stability	36	8,629	0.10	0.12	−0.03	0.27	0.08	0.17
Extraversion	34	6,700	0.07	0.09	−0.07	0.25	0.04	0.14
Openness/intellect	38	7,405	0.11	0.14	0.04	0.25	0.11	0.18
Test Test								
FFM Trait	*k*	*N*	*r*	*ρ*	CV_{LL}	CV_{UL}	CI_{LL}	CI_{UL}
OCB-O								
Conscientiousness	20	4,025	0.13	0.17	0.06	0.28	0.12	0.22
Agreeableness	15	4,598	0.12	0.17	0.00	0.34	0.10	0.24
Emotional stability	10	2,139	0.08	0.12	−0.03	0.27	0.04	0.20
Extraversion	9	2,017	0.01	0.02	−0.12	0.16	−0.07	0.11
Openness/intellect	7	1,311	0.13	0.19	0.10	0.28	0.12	0.27
OCB-I								
Conscientiousness	28	6,347	0.16	0.21	−0.01	0.43	0.14	0.28
Agreeableness	19	5,608	0.13	0.18	0.10	0.26	0.15	0.22
Emotional stability	13	3,073	0.11	0.14	0.04	0.23	0.09	0.19
Extraversion	13	3,129	0.07	0.10	−0.09	0.30	0.01	0.19
Openness/intellect	10	2,049	0.13	0.18	0.05	0.31	0.11	0.26
OCB-CH								
Conscientiousness	17	2,629	0.08	0.10	−0.03	0.24	0.04	0.17
Agreeableness	8	1,396	−0.02	−0.03	−0.17	0.11	−0.12	0.06
Emotional stability	7	1,732	0.06	0.08	−0.05	0.22	−0.01	0.17
Extraversion	6	1,144	0.10	0.13	0.13	0.13	0.07	0.19
Openness/intellect	19	3,761	0.11	0.14	0.04	0.24	0.09	0.19

Notes: r: uncorrected correlation; ρ: correlation corrected for unreliability in predictor and criterion; CV_{LL} and CV_{UL}: lower and upper bounds, respectively, of the 80% credibility interval; CI_{LL} and CI_{UL}: lower and upper bounds, respectively, of the 95% confidence interval around the corrected mean correlation (i.e., ρ).

the usual highest relation. One unexpected finding was that openness displayed larger relationships with citizenship than in previous work. Chiaburu et al. (2011) speculated that this could be due to the level of criterion specificity used in their meta-analysis. Actually, compared to validities for FFM traits against aggregate citizenship (= .134), the mean for OCB-O (= .134) was the same, for OCB-I (= .162) somewhat higher, and for OCB-CH (= .096 for absolute values) lower. In the "Future Research Directions" section of the chapter, we will make the argument that the personality–citizenship facet's relations might be higher if a lower-level taxonomy of personality is employed and the predictions for these links are based on theory (J. Hogan & Holland, 2003; Tett & Christiansen, 2007).

Another useful comparison provided by Chiaburu et al. (2011) is the mean FFM validities against citizenship performance corrected so as to be comparable to Hurtz and Donovan (2000) and FFM validities against task performance from that study. These appear in Table 26.4.

Table 26.4 True Score Correlations of Five-Factor Model Traits With Citizenship Performance and Task Performance

	Citizenship Performance	*Task Performance*
Conscientiousness	.22	.16
Agreeableness	.17	.08
Emotional stability	.15	.14
Extraversion	.11	.07
Openness/intellect	.17	−.01
Multiple *R*	.28	.19

With all five of the FFM traits, correlations with citizenship performance are higher than with task performance. In a couple of cases, these differences are significantly different (i.e., agreeableness and openness). But overall, the evidence for the core feature of the Motowidlo et al. (1997) model remains somewhat tenuous. Personality does seem to have a slightly stronger link to citizenship performance than to task performance, but the differences are not very large. Evidence is stronger for the ability–task performance relationship, with Project A data showing the cognitive ability–task proficiency relation significantly higher than ability with citizenship performance criteria (e.g., Borman, White, & Dorsey, 1995; Oppler, McCloy, Peterson, Russell, & Campbell, 2001). Finally, more evidence is needed beyond Bergman et al. (2008) and Brantley et al. (2013) for the mediation part of the model.

Why Is the Relation Not Higher Between Personality and Citizenship Performance? Future Research Directions

We are persuaded by the argument and some empirical results that personality–criterion correlations will tend to be higher when comparatively narrow traits and specific performance constructs are evident (for more information regarding the breadth of personality assessment, see Chapter 14, this volume). Of course, this will only be true when they are aligned conceptually based on theory or other conceptual matching. The Hurtz and Donovan (2000) and Chiaburu et al. (2011) meta-analyses used facets of citizenship on the criterion side, but for the predictor side, the FFM offered a fairly broad representation of personality dimensions. The Borman et al. analysis had a mix of FFM dimensions of personality and somewhat narrower traits, and for the criterion, overall citizenship performance, a mid-range level of specificity.

A better example of a narrow personality predictor-specific criterion study with theoretical links between pairs of the traits and criteria appeared in an article by Pulakos, Borman, and Hough (1988). The study had relatively narrow traits from the Personality Research Form (Jackson, 1974), the California Psychological Inventory (Gough, 1987), and the Multidimensional Personality Questionnaire (Tellegen, 1982). For criteria, Pulakos et al. identified three factors from a factor analysis of peer and supervisor ratings of Navy recruiters (N = 267) on several performance dimensions.

Subject matter expert psychologists (N = 14) estimated the relationships between each of the 11 personality dimensions and each of the three performance factors. The personality predictors were administered to the recruiters, peer and supervisor performance ratings were generated for each recruiter, and the pattern of empirical validities was compared to the pattern estimated by the SMEs. Scoring the pattern agreement as hits or misses in relation to the order of each of the predictors and the three criteria (e.g., predictor A highest for criterion 1, next highest for 2, and lowest for 3), 26 of 33 (79%) were as hypothesized. Eliminating the predicted "close-calls" (e.g., within .10 correlation points difference), 24 of 27 (89%) were as hypothesized.

Example empirical results were the personality dimension impulsiveness correlated .22 with selling skills and −.38 with organizing skills. Similarly, exhibition correlated .10 and −.17 with these performance dimensions. Order correlated near zero with selling skills and human relations skills but .40 with organizing skills. Finally, social closeness correlated .17 with human relations skills and near zero with the other two criteria. Thus, with relatively specific personality traits and performance criteria, along with reasonably strong a priori predictions of alignment, we might expect good differentiation in validities and, in some cases, higher observed personality–performance correlations.

Of course, one strategy for conducting studies that use narrow personality-specific performance measures is to generate target performance and personality constructs from scratch in each setting, for example, based on a job analysis done within each study. However, another way to approach this problem is, first, on the personality side, to develop a taxonomy similar to the FFM but at a higher level of specificity compared to the FFM. We and others have called for such a taxonomy that might be widely embraced similar to what has occurred with the FFM (e.g., Borman, Hanson, & Hedge, 1997; Hough & Furnham, 2003). There has been some progress in that direction if we consider development of facet-level representations of the FFM. For example, Costa and McCrae's (1992) NEO-PI has 30 facets, 6 for each of the FFM dimensions, and the Hogan Personality Inventory (R. Hogan & Hogan, 1992) has 43 homogeneous item composites. In either of these cases, the facets might offer a more specific taxonomy of personality for the purpose of linking personality and specific performance constructs.

Another strategy to derive a more specific taxonomy tied to the FFM might be to follow the lead of Roberts, Chernyshenko, Stark, and Goldberg (2005) who factor analyzed data from seven personality questionnaires with 36 scales measuring constructs closely related to conscientiousness. Their analyses resulted in six factors that can be interpreted as a good representation of the underlying facets of conscientiousness. This same methodology could be followed to derive facets for each of the other four FFM dimensions.

Actually, a strategy similar to Roberts et al. (2005) has been employed for facets of all five of the FFM constructs. Specifically, DeYoung, Quilty, and Peterson (2007) factor analyzed facet-level scores from two FFM personality inventories, the Revised NEO Personality Inventory (NEO-PI-R; Costa & McCrae, 1992) and the Abridged Big Five Circumplex scales from the International Personality Pool (AB5C-IPIP; Goldberg, 1999). The NEO-PI-R measures 6 facets for each FFM dimension; the AB5C-IPIP 9 per FFM dimension, for a total of 75 facets, 15 for each FFM dimension. Exploratory factor analyses of the facets within each of the FFM domains resulted in two correlated factors represented in each domain, 10 factors in all. These factors were carefully interpreted, a shorter instrument was developed with empirically derived IPIP marker items (Goldberg, 1999), and the 10 factors were cross-validated on a separate sample. Results were supportive of the 10-dimensional solution. Thus, the DeYoung et al. (2007) 10-dimensional system represents another possible, lower-level personality taxonomy.

Finally, the Occupational Information Network (O*NET) offers a hierarchical model of personality (i.e., workstyles) that builds on the FFM but includes a lower-order 17-dimensional system. In particular, a 7-dimensional higher-order taxonomy consists of achievement orientation that is typically part of conscientiousness in the FFM, but often seen as quite different from the dependability facet of that FFM dimension; social influence, similar to Hogan's Ambition and Hough's Potency dimension; interpersonal orientation, similar to the FFM's agreeableness; adjustment, very similar to emotional stability from the FFM; conscientiousness, essentially the FFM dimension of the same name without the achievement component, thus closer to dependability; independence, close to Gough's (1987) construct of masculinity and Fleishman and Gilbert's (1994) self-sufficiency; and practical intelligence, aligned most closely to the FFM construct of openness to experience, with an emphasis on the intellectance interpretation of the construct. These seven dimensions are, in turn, decomposed into the lower-order 17-dimensional system summarized in Table 26.5.

Table 26.5 Descriptions and Definitions of Lower-Order Workstyle Descriptors

		Level Scale	
Construct Label	*Operational Definition*	*Level*	*Anchor*
I. Achievement orientation			
A. Achievement/ effort	Job requires establishing and maintaining personally challenging achievement goals and exerting effort toward task mastery	High	Requires continual extensive effort toward achievement of work goals
		Medium	Requires sustained effort toward achievement of work goals
		Low	Requires only moderate levels of effort toward achievement of work goals
B. Persistence	Job requires persistence in the face of obstacles on the job	High	Requires high levels of persistence when work becomes difficult
		Medium	Requires moderate levels of persistence on the job
		Low	Requires little persistence on the job; few obstacles are encountered
C. Initiative	Job requires being willing to take on job responsibilities and challenges	High	Requires volunteering to take on new or additional work responsibilities and challenges
		Medium	Requires some willingness to take on new work responsibilities and challenges
		Low	Requires little interest in new work responsibilities or challenges; responsibilities are structured and stable

(Continued)

Table 26.5 (Continued)

		Level Scale	
Construct Label	*Operational Definition*	*Level*	*Anchor*
II. Social influence			
A. Energy	Job requires the energy and stamina to accomplish work tasks	High	Requires very high levels of energy to get tasks done
		Medium	Requires moderate levels of energy to get tasks done
		Low	Requires little energy to get tasks done; job is not very physically or mentally demanding
B. Leadership orientation	Job requires a willingness to lead, take charge, and offer opinions and direction	High	Requires a strong preference for making decisions and leading or directing other organization members
		Medium	Requires some preference for making decisions and leading or directing other organization members
		Low	Requires little or no leader decision making
III. Interpersonal orientation			
A. Cooperation	Job requires being pleasant with others on the job and displaying a good-natured, cooperative attitude encouraging people to work together	High	Requires working very smoothly and cooperatively with others on the job
		Medium	Requires generally working smoothly and cooperatively with others on the job
		Low	Requires little interaction with others
B. Concern for others	Job requires being sensitive to others' needs and feelings and being understanding and helpful on the job	High	Requires very high levels of sensitivity to others' needs and feelings and consistent caring and support for others on the job
		Medium	Requires high levels of sensitivity, caring, and support toward others on the job
		Low	Requires sensitivity, caring, and support toward others on the job, but this is not a highly important trait for this job
C. Social orientation	Job requires preferring to work with others rather than alone and being personally connected with others on the job	High	Requires a high degree of participation and working closely with other organization members
		Medium	Requires a moderate degree of participation and, at times, working closely with other organization members
		Low	Requires little participation with other organization members; usually works alone

Table 26.5 (Continued)

		Level Scale	
Construct Label	*Operational Definition*	*Level*	*Anchor*
IV. Adjustment			
A. Self-control	Job requires maintaining composure, keeping emotions in check even in very difficult situations, controlling anger, and avoiding aggressive behavior	High	Requires a very high degree of self-control and behaving in a nonthreatening manner
		Medium	Requires a high degree of self-control
		Low	Does not usually involve situations that challenge self-control
B. Stress tolerance	Job requires accepting criticism, and dealing calmly and effectively with high stress situations	High	Requires being extremely calm and tolerant of stress imposed by other people or by circumstances
		Medium	Requires being moderately calm and tolerant of stress imposed by other people or by circumstances
		Low	Does not involve much stress
C. Adaptability/ flexibility	Job requires being open to change (positive or negative) and to considerable variety in the workplace	High	Requires being highly flexible and adaptable, even to rapidly changing work situations
		Medium	Requires being moderately flexible and adaptable to changing work situations
		Low	Rarely requires being flexible to changing work situations; this job and work setting are usually stable
V. Conscientiousness			
A. Dependability	Job requires being reliable, responsible, and dependable, and fulfilling obligations	High	Requires the highest levels of responsibility and dependability in fulfilling job and work obligations
		Medium	Requires considerable responsibility and dependability in fulfilling job and work obligations
		Low	Requires responsibility and dependability, but if work is not done, it can be transferred to others
B. Attention to detail	Job requires being careful about detail and thorough in completing work tasks	High	Requires a very high degree of care and thoroughness in handling details on the job
		Medium	Requires a high degree of care and attention to detail in handling job duties
		Low	Requires attention to detail in handling job duties, but this is not a highly important trait for this job

(Continued)

Table 26.5 (Continued)

Construct Label	Operational Definition	Level Scale Level	Anchor
C. Integrity	Job requires being honest and avoiding unethical behavior	High	Requires the highest levels of integrity and a willingness to abide by a strict code of ethics or behavior
		Medium	Requires a great deal of integrity and abiding by a standard code of ethics and behavior
		Low	Does not generally require ethical choices or abiding by a code of ethics
VI. Independence			
Independence	Job requires developing own ways of doing things, guiding oneself with little or no supervision, and depending mainly on oneself to get things done	High	Requires a very high level of autonomy, with little or no dependence on others, to get the job done
		Medium	Requires a moderate level of autonomy, with some dependence on others, to get the job done
		Low	Does not work alone; requires working with others to get the job done
VII. Practical intelligence			
A. Innovation	Job requires creativity and alternative thinking to come up with new ideas for and answers to work-related problems	High	Requires a lot of creative thinking and coming up with new ideas related to work, addressing job and work issues and problems, etc.
		Medium	Requires moderate levels of creative thinking and coming up with ideas related to work, addressing job and work issues and problems, etc.
		Low	Requires little or no creative thinking
B. Analytical thinking	Job requires analyzing information and using logic to address work or job issues and problems	High	Requires being very good at analyzing complex issues, data, or problems related to work and consistently coming up with high quality, useful information
		Medium	Requires being generally good at analyzing complex issues, data, or problems related to work and coming up with high quality, useful information
		Low	Does not require analyzing complex information

Level and importance ratings were generated for each of the 17 dimensions by an average of about 10 job incumbents in each of 35 occupations. These ratings can be interpreted as the personality requirements for each of these jobs. The interrater reliabilities for the ratings were reasonably high;

k-rater reliabilities were .66 and .64, respectively, for the level and importance ratings. If the target of 30 raters per occupation would have been reached, reliabilities would almost all be above .75, with many above .85. It appears that personality requirements for occupations can be reliably rated.

Thus, we are enthusiastic about the 17-dimensional O★NET taxonomy that could provide a more specific dimension system that might better align personality dimensions with multidimensional performance criteria, potentially leading to higher validities for personality–performance relations. This is certainly not the only lower-level taxonomy that might be considered. We have discussed two other approaches to identify or develop lower-level personality taxonomies. However, an advantage of the O★NET is that it was developed specifically in a selection context to help identify the personality dimensions that represent the personality requirements of jobs in the economy.

Accordingly, we recommend considering the O★NET lower-level taxonomy as a dimension system to link to relatively specific citizenship performance dimensions, for example, our individual support, organizational support, and conscientious initiative system (Borman et al., 2001). If the narrow personality dimension-specific citizenship performance relations prove to yield higher correlations when aligned according to theoretical and conceptual considerations, higher personality–citizenship performance relationships may yet be realized.

Practitioner's Window

Below are two practice-oriented take-aways from research discussed in the chapter.

1. Organizational citizenship behavior or citizenship performance has been characterized as extra-role and not really a formal part of an employee's job. And yet, citizenship performance is often not extra-role or "discretionary" in the following sense. This is because research shows supervisory overall performance ratings are a function of roughly half task performance and half citizenship performance. So behaviors such as helping others at work, supporting and defending the organization to those inside and outside the organization, and taking initiative to complete tasks that need to get done even if not assigned to them are taken into account by supervisors when they form judgments about employees' overall performance. Accordingly, although these kinds of behaviors may not be on a formal job description, they are likely to be considered as part of performance evaluations of employees and therefore it seems important and indeed fair to make them aware that citizenship is an important evaluation criterion.
2. Job performance is sometimes characterized as a function of Ability × Motivation. Both are required for effective performance. Within this perspective, cognitive ability or g can clearly represent the ability side and personality is often argued to be the best measurable indicator of motivation. This makes sense to most laypersons' view of personnel selection. What is needed for success in most jobs is cognitive ability and the right kind of personality. And, empirical evidence suggests this is largely true. Cognitive ability is one of our best predictors of job performance, and although not as impressive, certain personality traits also seem to be useful predictors of performance. What this chapter offers is a modest modification of this view. It hypothesizes that cognitive ability is especially good at predicting performance in that part of jobs associated with technical proficiency, whereas personality is particularly useful for predicting what we call citizenship performance, effectiveness in such activities as cooperating and helping others with their jobs, supporting the organization and its objectives, and persisting with enthusiasm and extra effort as necessary to complete own task activities successfully. Our and others' research shows some support for this modification, although support for the personality–citizenship performance link is somewhat weaker.

References

Barnard, C. I. (1938). *The functions of the executive.* Cambridge, MA: Harvard University Press.

Barrick, M. R., & Mount, M. K. (1991). The Big Five personality dimensions and job performance: A meta-analysis. *Personnel Psychology, 44,* 1–26.

Bergman, M. E., Donovan, M. A., Drasgow, F., Overton, R. C., & Henning, J. B. (2008). Test of Motowidlo et al.'s (1997) theory of individual differences in task and contextual performance. *Human Performance, 21,* 227–253.

Borman, W. C., & Brush, D. H. (1993). More progress toward a taxonomy of managerial performance requirements. *Human Performance, 6,* 1–21.

Borman, W. C., Hanson, M. A., & Hedge, J. W. (1997). Personnel selection. *Annual Review of Psychology, 48,* 299–337.

Borman, W. C., Hanson, M. A., Kubisiak, U. C., & Buck, D. (2000). *Computerized Adaptive Rating Scales (CARS): Development and evaluation of the concept* (Institute Report No. 350). Tampa, FL: Personnel Decisions Research Institutes.

Borman, W. C., & Motowidlo, S. J. (1993). Expanding the criterion domain to include elements of contextual performance. In N. Schmitt & W. C. Borman (Eds.), *Personnel selection in organizations* (pp. 71–98). San Francisco: Jossey-Bass.

Borman, W. C., & Motowidlo, S. J. (1997). Task performance and contextual performance: The meaning for personnel selection research. *Human Performance, 10,* 99–109.

Borman, W. C., Motowidlo, S. J., & Hanser, L. M. (1983, August). A model of individual performance effectiveness: Thoughts about expanding the criterion space. In *Integrated criterion measurement for large scale computerized selection and classification.* Symposium conducted at the 91st Annual American Psychological Association Convention, Washington, DC.

Borman, W. C., Penner, L. A., Allen, T. D., & Motowidlo, S. J. (2001). Personality predictors of citizenship performance. *International Journal of Selection and Assessment, 9,* 52–69.

Borman, W. C., White, L. A., & Dorsey, D. W. (1995). Effects of ratee task performance and interpersonal factors on supervisor and peer performance ratings. *Journal of Applied Psychology, 80,* 168–177.

Brantley, L. B., Borman, W. C., & Hanson, M. A. (2013). *Progress toward understanding the structure and determinants of job performance: A partial test of the Motowidlo et al. theory.* Unpublished manuscript.

Brief, A. P., & Motowidlo, S. J. (1986). Prosocial organizational behaviors. *Academy of Management Review, 11,* 710–725.

Chiaburu, D. S., Oh, I., Berry, C. M., Li, N., & Gardner, R. G. (2011). The five-factor model of personality traits and organizational citizenship behaviors: A meta-analysis. *Journal of Applied Psychology, 96,* 1140–1166.

Coleman, V. I., & Borman, W. C. (2000). Investigating the underlying structure of the citizenship performance domain. *Human Resource Management Review, 10,* 25–44.

Conway, J. M. (1996). Additional construct validity evidence for the task–contextual performance distinction. *Human Performance, 9,* 309–329.

Costa, P. T., Jr., & McCrae, R. R. (1992). *Revised NEO Personality Inventory (NEO-PI-R) and NEO Five-Factor Inventory (NEO-FFI) professional manual.* Odessa, FL: Psychological Assessment Resources.

DeYoung, C. G., Quilty, L. C., & Peterson, J. B. (2007). Between facets and domains: 10 aspects of the Big Five. *Journal of Personality and Social Psychology, 5,* 880–896.

Fleishman, E. A., & Gilbert, J. A. (1994). *A taxonomy of social/interpersonal characteristics for describing worker requirements for the new occupational classification system.* Unpublished working paper, Management Research Institute, Bethesda, MD.

Goldberg, L. R. (1999). A broad-bandwidth, public domain, personality inventory measuring the lower-level facets of several five-factor models. In I. Mervielde, I. Deary, F. De Fruyt, & F. Ostendorf (Eds.), *Personality psychology in Europe* (Vol. 7, pp. 7–28). Tilburg, Netherlands: Tilburg University Press.

Gough, H. G. (1987). *Manual: The California Psychological Inventory.* Palo Alto, CA: Consulting Psychologists Press.

Hogan, J., & Holland, B. (2003). Using theory to evaluate personality and job-performance relations: A socioanalytic perspective. *Journal of Applied Psychology, 88,* 100–112.

Hogan, R., & Hogan, J. (1992). *Manual for the Hogan Personality Inventory.* Tulsa, OK: Hogan Assessment Systems.

Hough, L. M., & Furnham, A. (2003). Use of personality variables in work settings. In W. C. Borman, D. R. Ilgen, & R. J. Klimoski (Eds.) and I. B. Weiner (Editor-in-Chief), *Handbook of psychology. Volume 12: Industrial and organizational psychology* (pp. 131–169). New York: Wiley.

Hurtz, G. M., & Donovan, J. J. (2000). Personality and job performance: The Big Five revisited. *Journal of Applied Psychology, 85,* 869–879.

Jackson, D. N. (1974). *Personality research form manual.* Goshen, NY: Research Psychologists Press.

Katz, D. (1964). The motivational basis of organizational behavior. *Behavioral Science, 9,* 131–146.

Morrison, E.W. (1994). Role definitions and organizational citizenship behavior: The importance of the employee's perspective. *Academy of Management, 37*, 1543–1567.

Motowidlo, S.J., Borman, W. C., & Schmit, M.J. (1997). A theory of individual differences in task and contextual performance. *Human Performance, 10*, 71–83.

Oppler, S. H., McCloy, R. A., Peterson, N. G., Russell, T. L., & Campbell, J. P. (2001). The prediction of multiple components of entry-level performance. In J. P. Campbell & D. K. Knapp (Eds.), *Exploring the limits of personnel selection and classification* (pp. 349–388). Mahwah, NJ: Lawrence Erlbaum.

Organ, D. W. (1988). *Organizational citizenship behavior: The good soldier syndrome*. Lexington, MA: Lexington Books.

Organ, D. W. (1997). Organizational citizenship behavior: It's construct clean-up time. *Human Performance, 10*, 85–97.

Organ, D.W., & Ryan, K. (1995). A meta-analytic review of attitudinal and dispositional predictors of organizational citizenship behavior. *Personnel Psychology, 48*, 775–802.

Penner, L. A., Fritzsche, B. A., Craiger, J. P., & Freifeld, T. (1995). Measuring the prosocial personality. In J. N. Butcher & C. D. Spielberger (Eds.), *Advances in personality assessment* (Vol. 10, pp. 147–163). Hillsdale, NJ: Lawrence Erlbaum.

Pulakos, E. D., Borman, W. C., & Hough, L. M. (1988). Test validation for scientific understanding: Two demonstrations of an approach to studying predictor–criterion linkages. *Personnel Psychology, 41*, 703–716.

Roberts, B.W., Chernyshenko, O. S., Stark, S., & Goldberg, L. R. (2005). The structure of conscientiousness: An empirical investigation based on seven major personality questionnaires. *Personnel Psychology, 58*, 103–139.

Smith, C. A., Organ, D.W., & Near, J. P. (1983). Organizational citizenship behavior: Its nature and antecedents. *Journal of Applied Psychology, 68*, 653–663.

Tellegen, A. (1982). *Brief manual for the Multi-Dimensional Personality Questionnaire*. Minneapolis: University of Minnesota.

Tett, R. P., & Christiansen, N. D. (2007). Personality tests at the crossroads: A response to Morgeson, Campion, Dipboye, Hollenbeck, Murphy, and Schmitt (2007). *Personnel Psychology, 60*, 967–993.

Tett, R. P., Jackson, D. N., & Rothstein, M. (1991). Personality measures as predictors of job performance: A meta-analytic review. *Personnel Psychology, 44*, 703–742.

Van Dyne, L., Graham, J. M., & Dienesch, R. M. (1994). Organizational citizenship behavior: Construct redefinition, measurement, and validation. *Academy of Management Journal, 37*, 765–802.

Van Dyne, L., & LePine, J. A. (1998). Helping and voice extra-role behaviors: Evidence of construct and predictive validity. *Academy of Management Journal, 41*, 108–119.

Van Scotter, J. R., & Motowidlo, S. J. (1996). Interpersonal facilitation and job dedication as separate facets of contextual performance. *Journal of Applied Psychology, 81*, 525–531.

Williams, L. J., & Anderson, S. E. (1991). Job satisfaction and organizational commitment as predictors of organizational citizenship and in-role behaviors. *Journal of Management, 17*, 601–617.

27

Personality and Counterproductive Work Behavior

Jesús F. Salgado, Silvia Moscoso, and Neil Anderson

Interest concerning counterproductive and deviant behaviors at work has grown sharply in the last 20 years, and now measures of counterproductive work behaviors (CWBs) are included as criteria in many published studies. An important characteristic of these behaviors is that they are voluntary (i.e., intentional), which distinguishes them from behaviors that are mere hazards. For example, an action that provokes a physical injury or an accident will be considered a counterproductive behavior if the injury or the accident is a consequence of avoiding the use of preventive measures or norms, for instance. Also, a great deal of interest that has been given to identifying the situational and personal antecedents of CWBs. This is relevant in order to adequately manage CWB and its effects on the organizational outcomes.

The major theme in this chapter is the relationships between CWB and personality, as well as to provide an overview of the main theoretical models and conceptualizations in the domain. The organization of the chapter is as follows. There are four sections. The first section reviews the literature on CWBs, with separated subsections devoted to the diverse definitions of CWBs, the cross-cultural conceptualization of CWBs, the classificatory systems, and the prevalence of the CWBs. In the second section, we review the empirical findings on the relationship between CWB and personality variables, including subsections devoted to the Big Five, personality composites, non-Five-Factor Model (FFM)-based personality measures (e.g., locus of control, positive and negative affectivity), and the relationship between personality and CWBs in higher education. In the third section, we review some theoretical and conceptual models of CWB. Finally, in the fourth section, we suggest some personality-based strategies to manage CWBs.

Defining CWB

Sackett and DeVore (2001) have defined counterproductive behaviors as "any intentional behavior on the part of an organization member viewed by the organization as contrary to its legitimate interest" (p. 145). This definition focuses on the intentional behavior itself rather than on the consequences of the behavior, and it is one of the most widely used definitions of CWB.

However, one of the problems of this research domain has been the use of different but related labels to describe CWBs (Duffy, Ganster, & Pagon, 2002; Robinson & O'Leary-Kelly, 1998; Tepper, 2000). For example, together with CWBs and organizational deviant behaviors, other frequently used labels are as follows: antisocial behavior, social undermining, abusive supervisory behaviors, aggressive behavior at work, and, in Europe, bullying and mobbing. In the following, we provide some definitions, although variability in the terms used to describe CWB limits the integration of relevant research findings.

Organizational antisocial behavior is defined by Giacalone and Greenberg (1997) as

> any behavior that brings harm, or is intended to bring harm, to an organization, its employees, or stakeholder. It is the opposite of prosocial behavior, which is designed to help, to bring good. Antisocial behavior falls into the same category as deviant or dysfunctional behavior, terms that also have been used in the literature, although we believe the term antisocial behavior is more encompassing.
>
> *p. vii*

Giacalone and Greenberg consider that antisocial behavior includes examples such as arson, blackmail, bribery, discrimination, espionage, extortion, fraud, interpersonal violence, kickbacks, lawsuits, lying, sabotage, sexual harassment, theft, violations of confidentiality, and whistle-blowing.

Abusive supervision is defined by Tepper (2000) as "subordinate perceptions of the extent to which supervisors engage in *the sustained display of hostile, verbal and nonverbal behaviors, excluding physical contact*" (p. 178; italics in the original). This definition characterizes abusive supervision as a subjective assessment. The same individual could view a supervisor's behavior as abusive in one context and as nonabusive in another context, and two subordinates could differ in their evaluations of the same supervisor's behavior. The abusive supervisions are characterized by manifestations of public criticism, loud and angry tantrums, rudeness, inconsiderate actions, and coercion (Bies, 2000; Bies & Tripp, 1998). The abusive supervisory behaviors affect the subordinates' perceptions of organizational justice, the intention to quit, job satisfaction, life satisfaction, and organizational commitment, and create conflict between work and family life. Furthermore, abusive supervisors damage the subordinates' self-esteem, use noncontingent punishment, and fail to provide helpful feedback. Abusive supervision may also interfere with the subordinates' contextual and task performance.

Social undermining is defined by Duffy et al. (2002) as "behavior intended to hinder, over time, the ability to establish and maintain positive interpersonal relationships, work-related success, and favorable reputation" (p. 332). Examples of these behaviors are not doing promised work, withholding necessary information for doing the job, slowing work progress with the intention of harming someone, making tactless comments on a stressful event or that induce stress, ruining an individual's good reputation or irrevocably damaging that person's ability to attain success at work, intentionally saying derogatory things about a person, rejecting someone outright, belittling someone's ideas, withholding necessary information, failing to defend someone, and the "silent treatment." Duffy et al. (2002) found a considerable relationship between social undermining and CWBs. Furthermore, in support of the importance of this set of behaviors, they found that supervisor and coworker undermining have a stronger effect on job performance than do supervisor and coworker support.

There are important differences between social undermining and organizational deviance. For example, social undermining is never directed at the organization as a whole but rather is intended to harm a particular individual. Another difference is that some behaviors, such as rejection or ignoring the individual, insensitivity (e.g., laughing at someone or hurting his or her feelings), and hindrance behaviors, cannot be considered organizational deviance if they do not violate organizational norms.

Employee deviance behavior violates institutionalized expectations or norms and, in doing so, threatens the well-being of an organization and/or its members (Robinson & Bennett, 1995). Greenberg and Scott (1996) mentioned two forms of employee deviance: production deviance is the violation of norms regarding the minimal quality and quantity of work (e.g., habitual lateness), and property deviance includes behaviors intended to damage or acquire property and coworker assets (e.g., theft). Robinson and Bennett (1995) also discuss interpersonal forms of deviance, such as political game playing.

Another type of behavior considered part of CWB is aggression. Aggressive behavior at work can go from physical forms of extreme violence (e.g., homicide, physical assault, credible threats of assault) to milder forms, such as talking behind people's backs, interrupting others when they are speaking, and taking overly long breaks as a form of retaliation. European research has made a relevant contribution to the topic of "mobbing" or "bullying," first described in 1984 by Heinz Leymann in a report published by the National Board of Occupational Safety and Health in Stockholm, Sweden (Leymann, 1996). In Europe, the domain is called indistinctly "mobbing" or "bullying." The label "mobbing" is mainly used in the Nordic countries (Norway, Sweden, Denmark, and Finland) and in Germany, The Netherlands, France, Italy, and Spain, whereas "bullying" is used in the English-speaking countries.

Leymann (1996) defined mobbing as

> hostile and unethical communication, which is directed in a systematic way by one or a few individuals mainly towards one individual who, due to mobbing, is pushed into a helpless and defenceless position, being held there by means of continuing mobbing activities.
>
> *p. 168*

Zapf, Knorz, and Kulla (1996) suggested that mobbing should be understood as a subset of social stress at work, which has the basic characteristic of being related to the social relations of employees within the organization.

To summarize these definitional issues, it is clear that CWB is related to concepts such as antisocial behavior, aggressive behavior, and mobbing and bullying in the workplace. Burch and Anderson (2008) identified three important points from the literature on counterproductive behaviors at work: (1) counterproductivity is viewed as the outcome of counterproductive behaviors, (2) there is a distinction between interpersonal deviance (behaviors directed toward other people in the organization) and organizational deviance (behaviors directed at the organization), and (3) counterproductive behaviors and citizenship performance are distinct constructs. Recent research has begun to clarify the differences (and similarities) in definitions for each of these concepts.

Cross-Cultural Conceptualizations of CWB

Cross-cultural differences in the conceptualization of CWBs have received attention since the 1990s. Murphy (1994) suggested different attitudes toward stealing software in the United States and Asian countries. Munene (1995) described some organizational realities in certain African countries. For example, the "Not-in-the-seat" phenomenon in Nigeria denotes

> the widespread practice of official reporting early in the morning, hanging their jackets on their seats, and then leaving premises, not to return until several hours later. A "stranger" will attempt to wait, whereas an acclimatised or an acculturated individual will promptly proceed to whatever other business of the day is to be done.
>
> *p. 112*

Munene describes similar misbehavior in Uganda, Kenya, and other West and East African countries. For example,

> Many people believe that it is only stealing company stock or funds that is wrong. They forget their contract with their employer to work at least eight hours per day and more for officers . . . many leave their coats or hand bag in their offices and are absent most of the day. Many go to their village (rural) homes on Thursday afternoon and return on Tuesday.
>
> *p. 112*

Other deviant practices mentioned by Munene include ghost contracts, salaries unpaid as pay checks are diverted to individual use, and illegal salaries. Blunt (1980) mentioned the case of a

Kenyan security organization owner who deliberately manipulated ethnic identification in order to enhance organizational commitment, and achieve improved performance in terms of reduced turnover of staff, damage to property, and increase in written recommendations. These findings suggest that cross-cultural differences may be relevant to the prediction and management of CWBs.

A Classification of CWBs

Since the early 1980s, several authors have developed different taxonomies of CWBs for use in research and practice in organizations. For example, Hollinger and Clark (1982, 1983) offered a long list of CWBs and proposed that these could be classified into two broad categories. The first one was *property deviance*, including behaviors such as theft, property damage, and misuse of discount privileges. The second category was *production deviance*, including not being on the job in working hours (absence, tardiness, or long breaks) and behaviors that detract from production (drug and alcohol use, intentional slow or sloppy work).

Robinson and Bennett (1995) set out to extend previous typologies to include behaviors directed at individuals. They identified the underlying dimensions of these categories and then assessed their validity by developing an empirically derived typology of CWBs using multidimensional scaling. They found that CWBs varied along two dimensions. The first dimension refers to the extent to which behaviors are interpersonal and harmful to individuals versus noninterpersonal and harmful to organizations. The second dimension reflects the extent to which behaviors are minor versus serious. Combining these two dimensions yields four types of behaviors: (1) property deviance, including sabotaging equipment, stealing from the company, and accepting kickbacks; (2) production deviance, including leaving early, wasting resources, and intentionally working slowly; (3) personal aggression, including sexual harassment, verbal abuse, and stealing from coworkers; and (4) political deviance, which refers to gossip, blaming coworkers, and showing favoritism. From the point of view of the measure of CWB, Bennett and Robinson (2000) developed one 12-item scale of organizational deviance and a 7-item scale of interpersonal deviance. This classification of deviance in two dimensions has become very popular, and other authors have developed measures that include both organizational and interpersonal CWB scales (Laczo, 2002; Marcus, Schuler, Quell, & Hümpfner, 2002).

Gruys (2000) describes a unique approach to classifying CWBs at work. This author identified 87 different CWBs and, using factor analysis methods, reduced them to 11 different categories: (1) theft and related behavior (e.g., stealing cash or property, misusing an employee discount); (2) destruction of property (e.g., sabotaging production); (3) misuse of information (e.g., revealing confidential information, falsifying records); (4) unauthorized use of time and resources (e.g., wasting time, conducting personal business during work hours); (5) unsafe behavior (e.g., failing to follow safety procedures); (6) poor attendance (e.g., unexcused absence or tardiness, misusing sick leave); (7) poor-quality work (e.g., intentionally slow or sloppy work); (8) alcohol use on the job; (9) drug use (e.g., smoking marijuana at work, selling drugs at work); (10) inappropriate verbal actions (e.g., arguing with customers, verbally harassing coworkers); and (11) inappropriate physical actions (e.g., physically attacking coworkers, making unwanted sexual advances toward coworkers).

In a similar vein, Sackett and DeVore (2001) proposed a hierarchical model based on previous classifications and on the interrelationships among CWBs. This model has three levels: (1) CWB in general, (2) group factors (e.g., organizational deviance and interpersonal deviance), and (3) specific behavior domains (e.g., absence, theft, alcohol use, slow work). Thus, researchers and practitioners may focus on different levels of the model, depending on their specific objectives. For example, if they are interested in reducing individual absenteeism, they will focus primarily on the more basic level (i.e., specific behavior domains). If they are globally interested in CWB, their focus will mainly be on the upper level.

More recently, Spector et al. (2006) proposed a CWB classification based on potential antecedents (underlying motives as hostility or instrumentality). Accordingly, the CWB types are as follows: (1) abuse against others (e.g., making threats, nasty comments, ignoring the person), (2) production deviance (failure to do a task or to do it correctly), (3) sabotage (intentionally destroying something), (4) theft, and (5) withdrawal (absence, arriving late, leaving early, or taking longer breaks than authorized).

Table 27.1 provides a comprehensive summary of the CWB classification systems described above. The table covers the classifications by Hollinger and Clark (1982, 1983), Robinson and Bennett (1995), Bennett and Robinson (2000), Gruys (2000), Sackett and DeVore (2001), and Spector et al.

Table 27.1 Classifications of CWBs Proposed Since the 1980s

Author	*Categories*	*Examples of CWB*
Hollinger and Clark (1982, 1983)	1. Property deviance	Theft, property damage, or misuse of discount privileges
	2. Production deviance	Absence, tardiness, long breaks, drug and alcohol use, or intentional slow or sloppy work
Robinson and Bennett (1995)	1. Property deviance	Equipment sabotaging, stealing from company, or accepting kickbacks
	2. Production deviance	Leaving early, wasting resources, or intentionally workings low
	3. Personal aggression	Sexual harassment, verbal abuse, or stealing from coworkers
	4. Political deviance	Gossip, blaming coworkers, or showing favoritism
Bennett and Robinson (2000)	1. Interpersonal deviance	Sexual harassment, verbal abuse, stealing from coworkers, gossip, blaming coworkers, or showing favoritism
	2. Organizational deviance	Equipment sabotaging, stealing from company, accepting kickbacks, leaving early, wasting resources, or intentionally workings low
Gruys (2000)	1. Theft and related behavior	Theft of cash or property, or misuse of employee discount
	2. Destruction of property	Damage or destroy property, or sabotage production
	3. Misuse of information	Reveal confidential information or falsify records
	4. Misuse time and resources	Waste time, alter time card, or conduct personal business at work
	5. Unsafe behavior	Failure to follow or learn safety procedures
	6. Poor attendance	Unexcused absence or tardiness, or misuse sick leave
	7. Poor-quality work	Intentionally slow or sloppy work
	8. Alcohol use	Alcohol use on job, or coming to work drunk
	9. Drug use	Drug use on job, or coming to work under the influence of drugs
	10. Inappropriate verbal actions	Arguing with customers or verbally harassing coworkers
	11. Inappropriate physical actions	Physically attacking or sexual advances toward coworker

Author	*Categories*	*Examples of CWB*
Sackett and DeVore (2001)	1. Counterproductive factor	Overall counterproductivity
	2. Group factors	Interpersonal or organizational behavior
	3. Specific behavior domains	Absence, theft, alcohol use, or slow work
Spector et al. (2006)	1. Abuse against others	Making threats, nasty comments, or ignoring the person
	2. Production deviance	Failure to do a task or do it correctly
	3. Sabotage	Intentionally destroying something
	4. Theft	Theft of cash or property, giving away goods or services, misuse of employee discounts
	5. Withdrawal	Absence, arriving late, leaving early, or taking longer breaks

Note: CWB: counterproductive work behavior.

(2006), and shows the categories (main dimensions) that are included in these classification systems together with behavioral examples of each of them.

In our view, these are important contributions toward clarifying the dimensional structure underlying CWB as a broad and disparate concept involving various types of behavior and outcomes. This collection of typologies advances our understanding of CWBs and identifies it as an advanced and specified subfield of interest for exploring the connections of personality with occupational behaviors. These typologies share a number of common themes and areas, as can be seen in Table 27.1, and we would therefore argue that the subfield of CWB has "come of age" in terms of the generally agreed-upon components of behavior evident across the taxonomies.

Prevalence of CWBs

Determining the base rate of CWBs is important for many reasons, such as to clarify the magnitude of the problem and to find out how to manage it (e.g., prevention, solution). As a research question, it has also attracted the attention of several authors active in this area of personality research. However, determination of base rates of different types of CWB phenomena is difficult because many factors can affect the measurement of the frequency of deviant behaviors. For example, assessing the prevalence of CWBs can be affected by administrative errors in inventories and mismanagement, and by the undetected CWBs. This makes it harder to assess CWBs than more positive work behaviors.

Depending on the specific behavior of interest, the prevalence of CWB varies widely. Regarding theft, for example, some surveys have shown that 75% of employees admitted to having stolen from their employer at least once (McGurn, 1988). Other research has shown base rates of employee theft ranging from 12% to 50% (Slora, 1991). Hollinger and Clark (1983) found that the theft rates varied across industries with an average of 28% for manufacturing, 33% for health organizations, and 35% for retail. For the same industries, they found deviation of the production (less being produced than was possible) of 65%, 69%, and 82%, respectively. Hollinger, Slora, and Terris (1992; see also Slora, 1991) found, using an anonymous survey, that 59.5% of fast-food industry employees reported involvement in one or more of the following behaviors: taking merchandise or equipment without permission, taking company supplies, eating food at work without paying for it, stealing money from the employer, and changing company records to get paid for work not actually done. On the good side, 49.5% of employees reported never being involved in those practices. Hollinger et al.

(1992) also found that 36.1% of employees reported involvement in a variety of counterproductive actions (e.g., using employee discount privileges for friends, arriving late to work, engaging in slow or sloppy work). Slora (1991) reported that 43% of supermarket employees admitted cash and property theft, 77% admitted time theft, and 75% admitted other CWBs, such as damaging property and arguing with customers.

In the case of mobbing and bullying, European surveys provide relevant findings. For example, Leymann (1996) found that 3.5% of the Swedish employees suffered mobbing, with no differences across age groups or between the sexes. Einarsen and Skogstad (1996), based on several Norwegian surveys, found that, on average, 8.6% of respondents were bullied in the previous 6 months, with mean duration of around 18 months. They further found that 4% were bullied once or twice, 3.4% several times, and 1.2% weekly. With regard to the perpetrator, Einarsen and Skogstad found that 20% of victims were bullied both by colleagues and supervisors, and 68% by colleagues or supervisors/managers. Vartia (1996) reported that 10.1% of Finnish municipal employees claimed to have been bullied at the workplace, for reasons including envy (68%), weak superior (42%), competition for tasks or advancement (38%), and competition for the superior's favor and approval (34%). In the United Kingdom, Hoel, Cooper, and Faragher (2001) found that 10.6% of respondents from 70 organizations reported having been bullied during the last 6 months. Mikkelsen and Einarsen (2001) reported prevalence of bullying in several Danish samples between 8% and 25%. Salin (2001), in a survey of Finnish business professionals, found that between 8.8% and 24.1% of respondents reported having been bullied in the last 12 months. A recent report published by the Dortmund Institute for Social Research found that 2.7% of the German employees suffered "mobbing" in the last year. Zapf and Gross (2001), reviewing research on bullying, concluded that the prevalence of this phenomenon is between 1% and 4% in most organizations. These last estimates are considerably lower than those summarized above, and they can be due, in part, to a selection bias (i.e., those bullied may be more likely to report it than those who are not bullied).

Summarizing all of these findings, some of these prevalence percentages seem quite high, they cover studies involving several countries and levels of job function, and they are thus quite striking in their effect. The various types of CWB may be far more prevalent than the layperson or management sciences scholar outside of the personality at work field might have supposed. The noted prevalence of CWBs invites greater research attention to this behavioral domain. Given the intentional and discretionary nature of CWB, personality offers a particularly promising approach to such research. We now turn to this topic more specifically.

Personality and CWB

Relationships between personality and assorted CWBs have been examined empirically in a large number of primary studies, and in meta-analyses as well. The studies used a variety of personality measures that, for this chapter, are grouped into three broad categories: (1) the Big Five personality dimensions and their facets, (2) occupational personality composites, and (3) personality variables developed in other models (not based on the FFM). In the following sections, we examine the empirical evidence involving each group of personality constructs.

The Big Five and CWBs

Several primary studies and a number of meta-analyses have been carried out in the last decade linking the Big Five to CWBs. Salgado (2002) conducted a meta-analysis using, as criteria, absenteeism, accident rate, turnover, and deviant behavior (including actual theft, disciplinary problems, substance abuse, property damage, organizational rule breaking, and other irresponsible behaviors). All validity coefficients were corrected for criterion reliability and predictor range restriction. The results for absenteeism and accidents were very similar. In both cases, none of the Big Five dimensions were predictors of these criterion types because the coefficients were very small, ranging from .06 to .08 for absenteeism and ranging from −.09 to .08 for accidents. Turnover was predicted by all the Big Five personality dimensions. The best predictor of turnover was emotional stability with an operational validity of −.35, followed by conscientiousness with an operational validity of −.31, and agreeableness with −.22. With regard to deviant behavior, the findings showed that conscientiousness and agreeableness were valid predictors of the deviant behavior criterion (−.26 and −.20, respectively). More recently, Zimmerman (2008) conducted a meta-analysis on the relationship between turnover and the Big Five. He found that conscientiousness, emotional stability, and agreeableness predicted turnover and showed validity generalization. Extraversion and openness did not predict turnover. Zimmerman's results were similar to the previous findings by Salgado (2002).

Dalal (2005) conducted a meta-analysis on the relationship between CWB and conscientiousness, and the results showed an operational validity of −.38. In a large-sample study ($N = 900$), Sackett, Berry, Wiemann, and Laczo (2006), using the Bennett and Robinson scale (2000), found that CWB was strongly and negatively related with conscientiousness, emotional stability, and agreeableness and that CWB had modest relationship with extraversion and openness. The operational correlations were −.46, −.36, −.34, −.12, and −.07 for conscientiousness, emotional stability, agreeableness, extraversion, and openness, respectively. Sackett et al. (2006) also examined separately the correlation of the Big Five with interpersonal and organizational CWB. Conscientiousness (−.26 and −.49), emotional stability (−.34 and −.30), and agreeableness (−.39 and −.24) showed a strong and negative relationship with the two facets of CWB.

More recently, the meta-analysis by Berry, Ones, and Sackett (2007), using the distinction between interpersonal CWB and organizational CWB, found similar correlations for emotional stability (−.24 and −.18 for interpersonal and organizational CWB, respectively) and with openness to experience (−.09 and −.03). However, the results showed relevant differences with the other three personality factors. Conscientiousness correlated (−.23) with interpersonal CWB and (−.33) with organizational CWB; agreeableness correlated (−.46 and −.24) with interpersonal and organizational CWB, respectively; and the coefficients for extraversion were .02 for interpersonal CWB and −.07 for organizational CWB. The authors compared their results with Salgado's (2002) findings and considered that the differences might be due to the levels at which each meta-analysis measured deviance. That is, Berry et al. used aggregate measures of Interpersonal Deviance (ID) and Organizational Deviance (OD), while Salgado used narrower behavioral measures (e.g. absenteeism, accident rate, turnover, and deviant behavior).

Chang and Smithikrai (2010), in a large-sample study ($N = 1662$) in Thailand, assessed CWBs using a scale that was compiled from the standardized scales of Robinson and Bennett (1995) and Gruys and Sackett (2003). Results showed that the five personality factors can predict CWB with operational validities ranging between −.22 for emotional stability and −.49 for conscientiousness.

Several recent studies examined the relation between the Big Five and specific CWBs, such as theft, accidents, and incivility. With regard to theft, Levine and Jackson (2002) found that all the Big Five predicted stock loss (i.e., theft, measured in amount of money) at the aggregate departmental level in a U.K. sample ($N = 153$). Conscientiousness and agreeableness correlated negatively with theft. However, extraversion and neuroticism also showed a negative correlation when it was expected to positively correlate. In an experimental study of theft in organizations, Greenberg (2002) found that the magnitude of theft was greater (1) among employees with lower moral development, (2) when the organization stood to be victimized (as opposite to coworkers), and (3) when the organization had no ethics program. He also found that there is an interactive effect among the variables. Clarke and Robertson (2005) conducted a meta-analysis on the relationship between Big Five personality factors and accident involvement. Their results showed that low conscientiousness and agreeableness were valid and generalizable predictors of accident involvement (0.27 and 0.26); openness showed a relevant correlation (0.31), but it was not generalizable, in the sense that the 90%

credibility value included 0 (therefore, the search of moderators would be appropriate). These results contrast with Salgado's findings, but the meta-analysis by Clarke and Robertson contains between two and three times more studies, and the cumulated sample is also two or three times larger (K = 6, N = 2094 vs. K = 18, N = 4550 for conscientiousness; K = 4, N = 1540 vs. K = 14, $N \geq 3528$ for agreeableness; and K = 5, N = 1660 vs. K = 10, N = 1147 for openness). Therefore, from this point of view, Clarke and Robertson's results are more robust.

In summary, research has showed unambiguously that some of the Big Five personality dimensions have substantial relationships with CWBs. The strongest relations are for conscientiousness. Agreeableness and emotional stability are also related with CWB. In Table 27.2, we present a comprehensive summary of the findings of the main studies.

Table 27.2 Summary of the Main Findings of Meta-Analytic and Large-Sample Studies on the Relationship Among the Big Five Personality Dimensions and CWBs

Dimension	*Author*	*K*	*N*	ρ
Overall CWB				
Conscientiousness	Salgado (2002)[a]	13	6276	–.26
	Dalal (2005)[a]	10	3280	–.38
	Sackett, Berry, Wiemann, and Laczo (2006)[b]	1	900	–.46
	Chang and Smithikrai (2010)[b]	1	1662	–.49
Emotional stability	Salgado (2002)[a]	15	3107	–.06
	Sackett et al. (2006)[b]	1	900	–.36
	Chang and Smithikrai (2010)[b]	1	1662	–.22
Agreeableness	Salgado (2002)[a]	9	1299	–.20
	Sackett et al. (2006)[b]	1	900	–.34
	Chang and Smithikrai (2010)[b]	1	1662	–.43
Extraversion	Salgado (2002)[a]	12	2383	.01
	Sackett et al. (2006)[b]	1	900	–.12
	Chang and Smithikrai (2010)[b]	1	1662	–.38
Openness	Salgado (2002)[a]	8	1421	.14
	Sackett et al. (2006)[b]	1	900	–.07
	Chang and Smithikrai (2010)[b]	1	1662	–.30
Interpersonal CWB				
Conscientiousness	Berry, Ones, and Sackett (2007)[a]	11	3458	–.23
Emotional stability	Berry et al. (2007)[a]	10	2842	–.24
Agreeableness	Berry et al. (2007)[a]	10	3336	–.46
Extraversion	Berry et al. (2007)[a]	8	2360	.02
Openness	Berry et al. (2007)[a]	8	2360	–.09
Organizational CWB				
Conscientiousness	Berry et al. (2007)[a]	8	2934	–.33
Emotional stability	Berry et al. (2007)[a]	7	2300	–.18
Agreeableness	Berry et al. (2007)[a]	8	2934	–.24
Extraversion	Berry et al. (2007)[a]	5	1836	–.07
Openness	Berry et al. (2007)[a]	5	1772	–.03

Dimension	*Author*	*K*	*N*	ρ
Turnover				
Conscientiousness	Salgado (2002)[a]	5	748	−.31
	Zimmerman (2008)[a]	17	1631	−.22
Emotional stability	Salgado (2002)[a]	4	554	−.35
	Zimmerman (2008)[a]	19	1824	−.20
Agreeableness	Salgado (2002)[a]	4	554	−.22
	Zimmerman (2008)[a]	15	1532	−.27
Extraversion	Salgado (2002)[a]	4	554	−.20
	Zimmerman (2008)[a]	19	1608	−.04
Openness	Salgado (2002)[a]	4	554	−.14
	Zimmerman (2008)[a]	16	1563	.10
Absenteeism				
Conscientiousness	Salgado (2002)[a]	10	2155	−.06
Emotional stability	Salgado (2002)[a]	12	2491	.04
Agreeableness	Salgado (2002)[a]	8	1339	.04
Extraversion	Salgado (2002)[a]	10	1799	.08
Openness	Salgado (2002)[a]	8	1339	.00
Accident involvement				
Conscientiousness	Salgado (2002)[a]	6	2094	−.06
	Clarke and Robertson (2005)[a]	18	4550	−.24
Emotional stability	Salgado (2002)[a]	5	2121	−.08
	Clarke and Robertson (2005)[a]	23	3518	−.19
Agreeableness	Salgado (2002)[a]	4	1540	−.01
	Clarke and Robertson (2005)[a]	14	3528	−.23
Extraversion	Salgado (2002)[a]	7	2341	−.04
	Clarke and Robertson (2005)[a]	30	6048	.14
Openness	Salgado (2002)[a]	5	1660	.09
	Clarke and Robertson (2005)[a]	10	1147	.27

Notes: *K*: number of samples; *N*: total sample size; ρ: operational validity; CWB: counterproductive work behavior. The operational validity reported in this table was estimated as the observed validity corrected by criterion reliability and direct range restriction.

[a] Meta-analysis.

[b] Large-sample study.

Several studies examined the relationship between the facets of the Big Five and CWB. Borman, White, Pulakos, and Oppler (1991), using nine large army samples (total $N = 4362$), found that achievement orientation and dependability showed average operational correlations of −.08 and −.21, respectively. A meta-analysis by Dudley, Orvis, Lebiecki, and Cortina (2006), targeting relations between facets of conscientiousness and several CWBs (e.g., theft, disciplinary problems, and not adhering to policies and procedures), yielded corrected mean correlations of .00, −.30, −.06, and −.10 for achievement, dependability, order, and cautiousness, respectively. We present a detailed summary of these results in Table 27.3.

Table 27.3 Summary of the Main Findings of Meta-Analytic Studies on the Relationship Among the Facets of Big Five Personality Dimensions and CWBs (Operational Validity)

Dimension	*Author*	*K*	*N*	ρ
Overall CWB				
Achievement	Borman, White, Pulakos, and Oppler (1991)	9	4362	–.08
	Dudley, Orvis, Lebiecki, and Cortina (2006)	13	1026	.00
Dependability	Borman et al. (1991)	9	4362	–.21
	Dudley et al. (2006)	16	2195	–.30
Order	Dudley et al. (2006)	13	1311	–.06
Cautiousness	Dudley et al. (2006)	14	2251	–.10

Notes: K: number of samples; *N*: total sample size; ρ: operational validity; CWB: counterproductive work behavior. The operational validity reported in this table was estimated as the observed validity corrected by criterion reliability and direct range restriction.

More recently, Hastings and O'Neill (2009) found in a primary study ($N = 198$) that both personality factors and facets predicted workplace deviance, but the level of prediction depended on the personality variable. Specifically, agreeableness and conscientiousness showed slightly stronger prediction than did most of their facets, all of which were significantly related to workplace deviance. For extraversion, on the other hand, excitement seeking correlated positively with deviance ($r = .17, p < .05$), whereas friendliness correlated negatively ($r = -.15, p < .05$). A similar result was found for neuroticism (reversed emotional stability), for which facets of anger ($r = .28, p < .01$) and immoderation ($r = .17, p < .05$) yielded significant relations. Concerning openness to experience, several facets were predictive of deviance, and the factor also showed a significant correlation ($r = .20, p < .01$).

Bolton, Becker, and Barber (2010) compared the validity of the Big Five traits for predicting CWB measured globally, as well as in two dimensions (interpersonally and organizational CWB) and in five dimensions (abuse, production deviance, sabotage, theft, and withdrawal). Results ($N = 233$) showed that conscientiousness correlated with all measures (range from –.14 to –.31), but more strongly with overall CWB, organizational CWB in the two-dimensional case, and the withdrawal and sabotage dimensions in the five-dimensional case. Agreeableness also related with all measures (range from –.11 to –.33), but better predicted overall CWB, interpersonal CWB, and the abuse dimension. For emotional stability, correlations ranged from –.13 to –.27, with the strongest results obtaining for overall CWB and abuse. Extraversion predicted theft, while openness to experience predicted sabotage.

Building on the results presented in Table 27.3, we summarize the results for the Big Five and their facets with the various measures of CWB in Table 27.4. We calculate the sample-weighted average operational correlation using the results of the meta-analyses and the large-*N* studies. The results suggest that conscientiousness, emotional stability, and agreeableness are each moderately related, on average, with overall CWB, interpersonal CWB, organizational CWB, turnover, and accident involvement. Extraversion correlates with turnover, and openness shows a small correlation with turnover and accident involvement. Furthermore, conscientiousness shows a larger correlation with organizational CWB than with interpersonal CWB, and agreeableness shows a larger correlation with interpersonal CWB than with organizational CWB. With regard to facets, dependability is the only one showing relevant correlations. Nevertheless, the number of studies on the relationship between facets and CWB is small, and clearly, more research is needed to allow for more robust conclusions.

Table 27.4 Summary of the Findings of the Operational Validity of the Big Five and C Facets for Predicting Various CWB Dimensions

Criterion	*C*	*ES*	*A*	*Ex*	*O*	*D*	*Ach*	*Or*	*Ca*
Overall CWB	−.34	−.15	−.33	−.14	.02	−.24	−.05	−.06	−.10
I-CWB	−.23	−.24	−.46	.02	−.09				
O-CWB	−.33	−.18	−.24	−.07	−.03				
Turnover	−.31	−.35	−.22	−.20	−.14				
Absenteeism	−.06	.04	.04	.08	.00				
Accident	−.18	−.15	−.16	.09	.16				

Notes: C: conscientiousness; ES: emotional stability; A: agreeableness; Ex: extraversion; O: openness to experience; D: dependability; Ach: achievement; Or: order; Ca: cautiousness; CWB: counterproductive work behavior; I-CWB: interpersonal CWB; O-CWB: organizational CWB. The coefficients reported are the weighted-sample average correlations using the operational validities reported in Tables 27.2 and 27.3.

Personality Composites and CWBs

Ones and Viswesvaran (2001a) classified personality composite measures (i.e., compound scales) into one of two broad groups: Criterion-Focused Occupational Personality Scales (COPS) and Job-Focused Occupational Personality Scales (JOPS). COPS are occupational personality scales created for the purpose of predicting specific organizational criteria, such as honesty, stress tolerance, CWBs, customer service orientation, security orientation, and others. The JOPS are occupational personality scales explicitly developed for the purpose of predicting performance in specific occupational groups, such as managerial positions, sales jobs, clerical occupations, and others.

Ones and her colleagues have also extensively researched the validity of COPS for predicting CWBs, such as overall counterproductivity and specific disruptive behaviors such as theft and absenteeism. In a comprehensive meta-analysis, Ones, Viswesvaran, and Schmidt (1993) found that personality-based integrity tests predicted CWBs very efficiently given that the operational validity was .32 when the criterion included both narrow and broad disruptive behaviors, such as actual theft, admitted theft, illegal activities, absenteeism, tardiness, dismissals for actual theft, and violence. Ones et al. also reported an operational validity of .36 for personality-based integrity tests in predicting voluntary absenteeism. This contrasts with the modest validities found by Salgado (2002) for the Big Five in predicting absenteeism and suggests that personality-based integrity tests are a good option for predicting employee absenteeism.

In addition to the validity of integrity tests, Ones and Viswesvaran (2001a, 2001b) have also meta-analyzed the validity of other types of COPS for predicting CWBs. For example, they reported mean validity estimates of .29 for drug and alcohol scales, .42 for stress tolerance and customer service scales, and .46 for violence scales. All these coefficients are substantial, suggesting that COPS are robust predictors of CWB. Table 27.5 summarizes the meta-analytic results on the relation between COPS and CWBs.

Non-FFM-Based Personality Measures and CWB

In the last decade, researchers have also examined the relationship of CWB and specific deviant behaviors with a number of personality variables traditionally considered to fall outside the FFM. Among others, negative affectivity, positive affectivity, self-efficacy, self-esteem, locus of control, trait anger, and narcissism were correlated with overall CWB, interpersonal CWB,

Table 27.5 Summary of Meta-Analytic Results on the Relationship Between COPS and CWB

COPS Type	*K*	*N*	ρ
CWBs			
Integrity (personality-based tests)[a]	138	158065	.32
Stress Tolerance Scales[b]	5	594	.42
Customer Service Scales[b]	5	740	.42
Violence Scales[c]	4	533	.46
Absenteeism			
Integrity (personality-based tests)[d]	16	5435	.36

Notes: *K*: number of studies; *N*: total sample size; CWB: ρ: weighted-sample average correlation corrected for criterion unreliability and range restriction; counterproductive work behavior; COPS: Criterion-Focused Occupational Personality Scales.

[a] Ones, Viswesvaran, and Schmidt (1993).

[b] Ones and Viswesvaran (2001a).

[c] Ones and Viswesvaran (2001b).

[d] Ones, Viswesvaran, and Schmidt (2003).

organizational CWB, withdrawal, absenteeism, interpersonal aggressive behavior, organizational aggressive behavior, and occupational injuries. Although, globally, the amount of research is scarce, several meta-analyses and large-sample studies have been reported. Table 27.6 lists the most relevant studies and reports the correlations found between these personality variables and targeted CWB measures.

Three meta-analyses by Dalal (2005), Hershcovis et al. (2007), and Kaplan, Bradley, Luchman, and Haynes (2010) examined relationships between positive affectivity and overall CWB, withdrawal, interpersonal aggressive behavior, and organizational aggressive behavior. With regard to overall CWB, Dalal's (2005) results showed operational correlations of −.34 and .41, respectively, for positive affectivity ($K = 23$; $N = 4425$) and negative affectivity ($K = 23$; $N = 4101$), and Kaplan et al.'s (2010) research found that negative affectivity correlated (.30) with CWB ($K = 8$; $N = 1461$). Dalal's findings are more robust, given their larger sample. With respect to overall CWB, Crede, Chernyshenko, Stara, Dalal, and Bashshur (2007) reported correlations of −.25 and .42 ($N = 959$) for positive affectivity and negative affectivity, respectively. This study was not included in previous meta-analyses, offering independent support for Dalal's findings.

In connection with withdrawal, Kaplan et al. (2010) found very small correlations between this criterion and positive and negative affectivity (.05 and .16, respectively). They also found that negative affectivity correlated .20 with occupational injuries. Finally, the relationship of negative affectivity with interpersonal and organizational aggressive behavior was researched by Hershcovis et al. (2007). They found a similar correlation for the two types of aggressive behavior (.29 and .28, for interpersonal and organizational, respectively).

Research has also begun to examine the relationship of trait anger and interpersonal and organizational aggressive behavior, and interpersonal and organizational CWB. The meta-analysis by Hershcovis et al. (2007) found a larger correlation between trait anger and aggressive behavior. With regard to interpersonal aggressive behavior, the correlation was .43, and for organizational aggressive behavior, the correlation was .33. For their part, Fox and Spector (1999) found correlations of .64, .61, and .54 among overall CWB, organizational CWB, and interpersonal CWB with trait anger ($N = 185$; correlations corrected for criterion unreliability), respectively. In a subsequent study, Fox, Spector, and Miles (2001) found a corrected correlation of .38 for organizational CWB and the same correlation for interpersonal CWB. O'Brien and Allen (2008), in another primary

Table 27.6 Summary of the Main Findings of Meta-Analytic and Primary Studies on the Relationship Among Personality Variables and CWBs at Work

Dimension	*Author*	*K*	*N*	ρ
CWB				
Locus of control	Storms and Spector (1987)	1	160	−.17
	Fox and Spector (1999)	1	185	−.32
	Leroy (2005)	1	633	−.07
Negative affect	Dalal (2005)[a]	23	4101	.41
	Crede, Chernyshenko, Stara, Dalal, and Bashshur (2007)	1	959	.45
	Kaplan, Bradley, Luchman, and Haynes (2010)[a]	8	1461	.30
Positive affect	Dalal (2005)[a]	23	4425	−.34
	Crede et al. (2007)	1	959	−.27
Self-esteem	Chang and Smithikrai (2010)	1	1662	−.41
Trait anger	Fox and Spector (1999)	1	185	.64
Machiavellianism	O'Boyle, Forsyth, Banks, and McDaniel (2012)[a]	13	2546	.25
Narcissim	O'Boyle et al. (2012)[a]	9	2708	.43
Psychopathy	O'Boyle et al. (2012)[a]	27	6058	.07
Organizational CWB				
Locus of control	Storms and Spector (1987)	1	160	−.15
	Fox and Spector (1999)	1	185	−.35
	O'Brien and Allen (2008)	1	333	−.26
Trait anger	Fox and Spector (1999)	1	185	.61
	Fox, Spector, and Miles (2001)	1	292	.38
	O'Brien and Allen (2008)	1	333	.34
Interpersonal CWB				
Locus of control	Storms and Spector (1987)	1	160	−.14
	Fox and Spector (1999)	1	185	−.20
	O'Brien and Allen (2008)	1	333	−.13
Trait anger	Fox and Spector (1999)	1	185	.54
	Fox et al. (2001)	1	292	.38
	O'Brien and Allen (2008)	1	333	.43
Withdrawal				
Positive affect	Kaplan et al. (2010)[a]	7	2165	.05
Negative affect	Kaplan et al. (2010)[a]	9	2650	.16
Locus of control	Storms and Spector (1987)	1	160	−.14
Absenteeism				
Self-efficacy	Salgado and Moscoso (2000)[a]	4	718	−.21
Locus of control	Ng, Sorensen, and Eby (2006)[a]	6	2927	−.13
Interpersonal aggressive behavior				
Negative affect	Hershcovis et al. (2007)[a]	5	1532	.29

(Continued)

Table 27.6 (Continued)

Dimension	*Author*	*K*	*N*	ρ
Organizational aggressive behavior				
Negative affect	Hershcovis et al. (2007)[a]	4	1168	.28
Trait anger	Hershcovis et al. (2007)[a]	7	2032	.33
Occupational injuries				
Negative affect	Kaplan et al. (2010)[a]	8	1461	.20
Locus of control	Leroy (2005)	1	615	–.04

Note: CWB: counterproductive work behavior. *K*: number of studies; *N*: sample size; ρ: weighted-sample average correlation corrected for criterion unreliability and range restriction.

[a] Meta-analysis.

study, examined the relation between trait anger and interpersonal and organizational CWB. They found a corrected correlation of .43 and .34 (*N* = 333) for interpersonal and organizational CWB, respectively.

Internal–external locus of control is a personality variable that was linked with CWB in several primary studies and a meta-analysis. The first study was done by Storms and Spector (1987), who related locus of control with overall CWB, organizational CWB, interpersonal CWB, and withdrawal, and they found corrected correlations of –.16, –.17, –12, and –.21, respectively (*N* = 160). Fox and Spector (1999) examined the same relationships, and they found corrected correlations of –.32, –.32, and –.20, for overall CWB, organizational CWB, and interpersonal CWB, respectively (*N* = 185). A third study was done by Leroy (2005), who found a correlation of –.06 (*N* = 633) between locus of control and overall CWB. Finally, O'Brien and Allen (2008) reported a corrected correlation of –.34 and –.13 for organizational and interpersonal CWB, respectively (*N* = 333). Ng, Sorensen, and Eby (2006) conducted a meta-analysis in which locus of control was related with absenteeism, and they found a corrected correlation of –.13 between both variables (*K* = 6, *N* = 2927).

Two additional personality variables that were related to organizational deviant behaviors were self-esteem and self-efficacy. Chang and Smithikrai (2010) in a large-sample study (*N* = 1662) found that self-esteem correlated –.41 with overall CWB. Previously, a meta-analysis by Salgado and Moscoso (2000) found that self-efficacy correlated –.21 (*K* = 4, *N* = 718) with absenteeism.

Recently, a meta-analysis by O'Boyle, Forsyth, Banks, and McDaniel (2012) examined the relationships between the "dark triad" personality traits (Machiavellianism, narcissism, and psychopathy) and CWB. They found that two traits, Machiavellianism and narcissism, were correlated with CWB (.25 and .43, respectively).

Table 27.7 shows an integrative summary of the results of the studies commented on and reviewed above in this section. As can be seen, all the variables mentioned showed relevant correlations with the measures of CWB, and practically all of them were in the expected direction. The exception was the correlation between positive affectivity and withdrawal, which was positive when it was expected to be a negative correlation.

Personality and CWB in Higher Education

So far, all of the studies conducted on CWBs in academic settings have concentrated upon student CWB rather than staff CWB. A characteristic of the measures used in the research on academic

Table 27.7 Summary of the Findings of the Operational Validity of the Non-FFM Personality Variables for Predicting Various CWB Dimensions

Criterion	*LC*	*NA*	*PA*	*SES*	*TA*	*SEF*	*MAC*	*NAR*	*PSY*
Overall CWB	−.16	.42	−.33	−.41	.64	—	.25	.43	.07
I-CWB	−.26	—	—	—	.52	—	—	—	—
O-CWB	−.15	—	—	—	.44	—	—	—	—
Withdrawal	−.14	.16	.05	—	—	—	—	—	—
Absenteeism	−.13	—	—	—	—	−.21	—	—	—
I-Aggressive B	—	.29	—	—	.43	—	—	—	—
O-Aggressive B	—	.28	—	—	.33	—	—	—	—
Occ. injuries	−.04	.20	—	—	—	—	—	—	—

Notes: FFM: Five-Factor Model; LC: locus of control; NA: negative affectivity; PA: positive affectivity; SES: self-esteem; TA: trait anger; SEF: self-efficacy; MAC: Machiavellianism; NAR: narcissism; PSY: psychopathy; CWB: counterproductive work behavior; I-CWB: interpersonal CWB; O-CWB: organizational CWB; I-Aggressive B: interpersonal aggressive behavior; O-Aggressive B: organizational aggressive behavior; Occ.: Occupational. The coefficients reported are the sample-weighted average correlations using the operational validity estimates reported in Table 27.6.

performance is that the majority of them are referred to as "positive student performance" and "positive outcomes." In other words, researchers center on behaviors and outcomes that result or contribute to a positive outcome, be this, for example, a good grade point average (GPA) or obtaining a degree, and several meta-analyses have shown that academic outcomes are positively related to job performance (e.g., Roth, BeVier, Switzer, & Schippmann, 1996). However, in the academic settings similar to the organizational settings, there also are a number of deviant behaviors that do not contribute to good results and positive outcomes. The academic deviant behaviors can be grouped into a large category of "negative academic performance," with absenteeism and cheating probably being the most common and representative of this negative side of academic performance. For example, Romer (1993) found that the overall absenteeism in three American universities (public and private, and large, medium, and small size) was 34%, 40%, and 25%, or in other words, one-third of students were absent during any class. In another university, he also found an absenteeism rate of 45% across courses. Marburger (2001) found that (1) the daily absenteeism for a class on Principles of Microeconomics was 18.5% on average, (2) absenteeism ranged from 8.5% to 44.1% on any given day, and (3) absenteeism was significantly higher on Fridays and gradually increased as the semester progressed. In another study, Marburger (2006) compared the absenteeism of two groups of students, one with mandatory attendance and another with no mandatory attendance. He found that, on average, the first group showed 11.6% absenteeism, and the second group showed 20.7%. Similar rates of absenteeism are common across the world (Lin & Chen, 2006; Ryan, Delaney, & Harmon, 2010; Stanca, 2006; Van Walbeek, 2004). With regard to other academic deviant behaviors such as cheating, plagiarism, and falsifications, several studies have shown that they are chronic problem for the universities, and that typically between 60% and 80% of the university students reported having cheated during their university lifetime (Marsden, Carroll, & Neill, 2005; McCabe & Trevino, 1997; Robinson, Amburgey, Swank, & Faulker, 2004; Stern & Havlicek, 1986; Williams, Nathanson, & Paulus, 2010).

Using Robinson and Bennett's (1995) categories of counterproductive behaviors, namely (1) negative behaviors against production, (2) negative behavior against property, (3) serious negative behaviors toward others, and (4) minor negative behaviors toward others, and trying to apply this classification to academic proficiency, reveals several negative categories as well. An analysis of the various negative academic behaviors results in most of them falling into one of five broad categories: (1) cheating (cheating, plagiarism, and falsification), (2) not attending class (absenteeism), (3) stealing/damage to property of others and of the university, (4) breaking the rules and regulations, and (5) making a low voluntary effort and having low productivity.

The current research of personality and negative academic performance is still scarce, in part due to the fact that it is a new area of research and that academic performance is not of great interest for the industrial–organizational (I/O) psychologist. In the future, we would also expect this area to extend to the consideration of CWB in staff in academia, a topic that has received notably little research attention from scholars to date. However, in the last few years, several studies have examined the relationship between some academic negative deviant behaviors and personality variables in student samples. A summary of the research conducted on the relationship among the personality variables and the academic counterproductive behaviors appears in Table 27.8.

Oswald, Schmitt, Kim, Ramsay, and Gillespie (2004) found that conscientiousness showed an observed correlation of −.27 (N = 636) with absenteeism and −.34 with self-reported academic CWB (ACWB). Marsden et al. (2005) examined the correlation of academic self-efficacy with three measures of academic deviant behaviors (cheating, plagiarism, and falsifications) in a large sample of Australian university students. They found a correlation corrected for by criterion unreliability of −.12, −.20, and −.19 for cheating, plagiarism, and falsifications, respectively. Paulhus and his associates have carried out a series of studies on university cheating and its relations with the dark personality triad and the Big Five personality dimensions. The dark personality triad consisted of narcissism, Machiavellianism, and subclinical psychopathy. In a first study, Nathanson, Paulhus, and Williams (2006) examined the correlation of the personality measures with a behavioral measure of scholastic cheating, and they found that subclinical psychopathy and narcissism correlated (.14 and .12; disattenuated for criterion reliability) but that the Big Five did not show significant correlations. In a second study, Nathanson et al. (2006) found that the dark triad correlated .31, .13, and .12 (for subclinical psychopathy, Machiavellianism, and narcissism, respectively) and that conscientiousness, extraversion, agreeableness, emotional stability, and openness correlated (−.12, .13, −.10, −.04, and −.18, respectively; all correlations were disattenuated for criterion unreliability). More recently, Williams et al. (2010), using a self-report measure of cheating, found that the "dark triad" correlated (.66, .46, and .24; N = 228, and −.39, .19, and .16; N = 107) in two independent samples. Conscientiousness showed corrected correlations of −.33 and −.08, agreeableness of −.27 and −.26, and extraversion of −.11 and −.11 in the two samples.

Marcus, Lee, and Ashton (2007) found that conscientiousness showed an observed correlation of −.49 (N = 171) and −.48 (N = 259) with ACWB in one German sample and another Canadian sample. They also found that honesty, as defined in the Honesty-Humility, Emotionality, Extraversion, Agreeableness, Conscientiousness, and Openness to Experience (HEXACO) model of personality (Ashton & Lee, 2007), was negatively correlated with counterproductive academic behavior (−.29 and −.45). Marcus et al. (2007) also examined the relation of personality-based integrity and overt integrity tests with negative academic behaviors. They found correlations ranging from −.40 to −.67, with the personality-based integrity tests showing larger correlations. The most recent published study was done by Brunell, Staats, Barden, and Hupp (2011), who examined the relationship between narcissism and self-esteem with a measure of academic dishonesty. They found a corrected correlation for criterion unreliability of .26 and −.10 for narcissism and self-esteem, respectively.

Table 27.8 Summary of the Main Findings of Primary Studies on the Relationship Among the Big Five Personality Dimensions and Other Personality Variables With Measures of Academic CWBs

Dimension	*Author*	*K*	*N*	ρ
Self-reported ACWB				
Conscientiousness	Oswald, Schmitt, Kim, Ramsay, and Gillespie (2004)	1	636	−.34
	Marcus, Lee, and Ashton (2007; German)	1	259	−.57
	Marcus et al. (2007; Canadian)	1	171	−.53
	Williams, Nathanson, and Paulus (2010)	1	228	−.33
Emotional stability	Oswald et al. (2004)	1	636	−.13
	Marcus et al. (2007; German)	1	259	−.02
	Marcus et al. (2007; Canadian)	1	171	−.32
	Williams et al. (2010)	1	228	.10
Extraversion	Oswald et al. (2004)	1	636	.13
	Marcus et al. (2007; German)	1	259	.15
	Marcus et al. (2007; Canadian)	1	171	.08
	Williams et al. (2010)	1	228	.11
Openness to experience	Oswald et al. (2004)	1	636	−.12
	Marcus et al. (2007; German)	1	259	−.07
	Marcus et al. (2007; Canadian)	1	171	−.06
	Williams et al. (2010)	1	228	.08
Agreeableness	Oswald et al. (2004)	1	636	−.28
	Marcus et al. (2007; German)	1	259	−.02
	Marcus et al. (2007; Canadian)	1	171	−.01
	Williams et al. (2010)	1	228	−.27
Self-esteem	Brunell, Staats, Barden, and Hupp (2011)	1	99	.11
Self-efficacy	Marsden et al. (2005)	1	954	−.17
Narcissism	Williams et al. (2010)	1	228	.24
	Brunell et al. (2011)	1	99	.29
Machiavellianism	Williams et al. (2010)	1	228	.46
Psychopathy	Williams et al. (2010)	1	228	.16
Behavioral ACWB				
Conscientiousness	Nathanson, Paulhus, and Williams (2006; Study 1)	1	291	−.06
	Nathanson et al. (2006; Study 2)	1	150	−.12
	Williams et al. (2010)	1	107	−.08
Emotional stability	Nathanson et al. (2006; Study 1)	1	291	.08
	Nathanson et al. (2006; Study 2)	1	150	.04
	Williams et al. (2010)	1	107	−.04
Extraversion	Nathanson et al. (2006; Study 1)	1	291	−.03
	Nathanson et al. (2006; Study 2)	1	150	.13
	Williams et al. (2010)	1	107	.11

(Continued)

Table 27.8 (Continued)

Dimension	*Author*	*K*	*N*	ρ
Openness to experience	Nathanson et al. (2006; Study 1)	1	291	−.05
	Nathanson et al. (2006; Study 2)	1	150	−.18
	Williams et al. (2010)	1	107	−.09
Agreeableness	Nathanson et al. (2006; Study 1)	1	291	−.05
	Nathanson et al. (2006; Study 2)	1	150	−.18
	Williams et al. (2010)	1	107	−.09
Narcissism	Nathanson et al. (2006; Study 1)	1	291	.12
	Nathanson et al. (2006; Study 2)	1	150	.12
	Williams et al. (2010; Study 1)	1	107	.30
Machiavellianism	Nathanson et al. (2006; Study 1)	1	291	.09
	Nathanson et al. (2006; Study 2)	1	150	.13
	Williams et al. (2010)	1	107	.19
Psychopathy	Nathanson et al. (2006; Study 1)	1	291	.14
	Nathanson et al. (2006; Study 2)	1	150	.31
	Williams et al. (2010)	1	107	.66

Notes: CWB: counterproductive work behavior; ACWB: academic CWB. *K*: number of studies; *N*: sample size; ρ: weighted-sample average correlation corrected for criterion unreliability and range restriction.

Table 27.9 Summary of the Findings of the Operational Validity of the Personality Variables for Predicting Various Measures of Academic CWBs

Variable	*Self-reported*			*Behavioral*		
	ACWB			*ACWB*		
	K	*N*	ρ	*K*	*N*	ρ
Conscientiousness	4	1294	−.37	3	548	−.08
Agreeableness	4	1294	−.19	3	548	−.06
Emotional stability	4	1294	−.09	3	548	.05
Extraversion	4	1294	.12	3	548	.04
Openness to experience	4	1294	−.07	3	548	−.09
Narcissism	2	327	.26	3	548	.16
Machiavellianism	1	228	.46	3	548	.12
Psychopathy	1	228	.16	3	548	.29

Notes: CWB: counterproductive work behavior; ACWB: academic CWB. The coefficients for the Big Five are the weighted-sample average correlations using the operational validities reported in Table 27.8. *K*: number of studies; *N*: sample size; ρ: weighted-sample average correlation corrected for criterion unreliability and range restriction.

A quantitative synthesis of the above research appears in Table 27.9. Two main conclusions may be posited. First, conscientiousness is the best predictor of self-rated ACWB, and subclinical psychopathy is the best predictor of behavioral measures of ACWB. Second, agreeableness is a relevant predictor for self-rated ACWB, and narcissism may be a predictor of the behavioral measures of ACWB. Nevertheless, more research clearly is necessary to confirm these former conclusions as both the number of studies and the total sample size are small.

Theoretical and Conceptual Explanations of CWB

Together with the great deal of research carried out in the last few years on CWB, some contributions were directed to developing models and frameworks for explaining deviant behaviors at work. A first proposal was postulated by Martinko, Gundlach, and Douglas (2002), who presented an explanatory model based on causal attribution theory. They suggested that the causal explanations used by individuals about work events are the primary cause of the emotions and behaviors leading to CWB. In their model, causal attributions would be the proximal antecedents of CWB and situational variables, and individual differences would be the determinants of the causal attributions and the perceptions of disequilibria (e.g., perceptions of justice). Among the personality variables that are antecedents of the causal attributions, Martinko et al. (2002) included integrity, negative affectivity, emotional stability, core self-evaluations, locus of control, self-esteem, and self-efficacy. The situational variables mentioned by Martinko et al. (2002) included economic conditions, competitive environment, norms, leadership style, rewards, working conditions, task difficulty, organizational culture, and organizational policies. Although Martinko et al. (2002) did not explicitly mention it, it might be expected that the situational variables interact with particular personality traits to produce CWB (e.g., task difficulty may be a more important determinant of CWB for individuals scoring low in emotional stability than for individuals scoring high).

A second model of CWB and aggressive behavior at work was developed by Spector and Fox (2005). This stressor–emotion model of CWB gives a key role to emotions as a response to workplace stressors. According to Spector and Fox, employees perceive and appraise the conditions and events at work, and those that are perceived to be stressors induce negative emotions (e.g., including anger, anxiety, and depression) and, subsequently, CWB. In connection with personality, this model suggests two relevant impacts. First, perceived locus of control affects the appraisal of situations and the decision about engaging in CWB or any alternative constructive act. Individuals showing an internal locus of control will be less likely to perceive a stressor, experience negative emotion, and to engage in CWB. Second, low emotional stability leads individuals to experience negative emotions, and therefore they will be more sensitive to stressors and will be more likely to show CWB. A limitation of this model is that it considers CWB as a reaction to stressful work conditions, but CWB is not always a reaction and the employee can initiate it.

This last limitation was considered by Cullen and Sackett (2006), who stated that there are two types of counterproductive behaviors. One type is reactive and the second is an initiated one. In order to explain both types of CWB, Cullen and Sackett (2006) suggested an interactionist model of CWB, which includes variables of individual differences, situational variables, and the theory of planned action. According to this model, personality variables have three types of effects: direct, indirect, and moderator. For example, low levels in conscientiousness, emotional stability, agreeableness, and integrity might be initiators of CWB both directly and indirectly. Agreeableness would determine attitudes toward CWB, for example fostering unfavorable attitudes to aggressive acts. Emotional stability and extraversion would determine perception and moods associated with CWB such as perceptions of injustice and negative emotional reactions. Furthermore, some personality variables would moderate the relationships between organizational events and CWB.

For example, low emotional stability would moderate the relationship between the perceptions of environmental events and CWB, and low emotional stability, low conscientiousness, and high impulsivity would moderate the cognitive and emotional reactions to perceived environmental events.

The most recent model of CWB, developed by Spector (2011), recognizes the limitation of earlier work (Spector & Fox, 2005). The new model incorporates the possibility that CWB can be initiated by employees. In this new model, personality variables can affect employees' perceptions and appraisal of the work environment, the causal attributions, and the possibility to initiate and/or react to CWB. Spector's (2011) model includes six personality variables: hostile attribution bias, narcissism, negative affectivity, trait anger, effortful control, and locus of control. According to Spector, hostile attribution bias and narcissism mainly affect the perceptions and appraisals of events. Negative affectivity and trait anger mainly affect emotional reactions to perceived situations once they have been appraised. Locus of control and effortful control mainly affect the perceptions of control and the control of aggressive and CWB impulses. A limitation of this model is that it neglects the role of basic personality dimensions (e.g., Big Five) and personality composites (e.g., integrity) demonstrated to be important predictors in previous CWB research (see Martinko et al., 2002).

A general limitation of the four models considered here is that they see deviant behaviors only as negative ones. However, there are examples of positive deviant behaviors. For example, violating organizational norms can serve, in some cases, as a source of innovation and creativity, thus providing competitive advantages (Tziner, Fein, Sharoni, Ber-Hen, & Nord, 2010). In connection with this last point, the four models can be considered interactionist models and can be successfully merged with the personality trait-based interactionist model of job performance developed by Tett and Burnett (2003). Given that job performance is a multidimensional space in which CWBs, task performance, and contextual (i.e., citizenship) performance are major components, an explanatory model of CWB may be identified as part of a wider model of job performance. In this sense, Tett and Burnett's (2003) trait activation model admits both positive and negative deviant behaviors (for more coverage of trait activation theory see Chapter 5, this volume). A further limitation of the models reviewed above relates to where, for instance, some types of behaviors may be unwanted and even counterproductive in most circumstances, but in specific others, these may be required job components. One example is for aggression at work in professional occupations in the armed forces or in professional sports. Such aggression needs to be controlled, channeled, and target-focused, needless to say, but it is a necessary component of successful task performance in these very specific contexts. Tett and Burnett's (2003) trait activation theory explains this controlled aggression. Again, inappropriate aggression, excessive aggression, or aggression toward one's peers or superior officers would naturally be classified as CWB, and indeed may be punishable by severe sanctions and repercussions for the perpetrator.

For the specific case of mobbing and bullying, several theoretical contributions and advances have been made over the last 20 years. According to Leymann (1996), Resch and Schubinski (1996), and Vartia (1996), four factors seem to be involved in mobbing: (1) deficiencies in the work design, (2) deficiencies in leadership, (3) a socially exposed position of the victim, and (4) low morale. There is some consensus that there are three phases in the mobbing process (Leymann, 1996; Resch & Schubinski, 1996). The early phase is when the underlying conflict is still recognizable, and all parties can perceive the disputes and quarrels between the individuals involved. The middle stage is characterized by participants no longer perceiving the conflict between people, but rather between "us and the person." In this stage, the rejection of the bullied person is not only with respect to some specific behavior but also to the person as a whole and a polarization has taken place. The final stage is when the departmental limits are crossed and official measures are implemented (e.g., legal measures such as warnings or transfers). Vartia (1996) found that neuroticism and self-esteem are related to mobbing, and Björkqvist, Österman, and Hjelt-Bäck (1994) found that envy and competition were perceived as the most common causes for mobbing in a study among university employees. Niedl (1996) found that bullied people scored significantly higher than nonbullied individuals on irritation, depression, psychosomatic complaints, and anxiety. The bullied individuals further showed two types of destructive reactions: low commitment or leaving the firm.

Some Strategies to Manage CWB and Deviant Behavior at Work

In the previous sections of this chapter, we reviewed a number of advances in the research base in this area, all of which suggest that CWB and its management are important concerns for practicing managers and human resource management (HRM) professionals. Three particular conclusions may be drawn. First, CWB appears from the research evidence to date to be more prevalent than perhaps laypersons or indeed practicing line managers or HRM specialists might have supposed. As a consequence, CWBs warrant greater attention and concern from practitioners in organizations. Second, CWBs produce direct economic losses for the organization, but they also have an indirect impact on the bottom line through their effects on the organizational image, culture, climate, and attraction and retention of human capital. The third issue is that personality variables explain a relevant amount of variance in various types of CWB. In light of all these observations, strategies for managing CWB and negative deviant behaviors at work are of interest for HR researchers, practitioners, managers, and organizations.

In connection with personality variables, the robust finding that employee personality is related to CWB suggests two strategies. An initial strategy consists in preventing CWB, and, consequently, the practices of recruitment and personnel selection should include measures of the personality variables that have demonstrated a strong relation with CWB. The most important of such traits appear to be conscientiousness, agreeableness, and emotional stability. The second strategy is reduction. In order to reduce CWB at work, situational and organizational variables have to be considered, for instance perceptions of justice, leadership practices, organizational norms, rewards, organizational culture, and task difficulty. As the examination of these variables is beyond the scope of this chapter, we will concentrate on the first approach to managing CWB, prevention to enable better personnel selection practices, although we also will give some ideas for reduction of CWB. See the "Practitioner's Window" below for suggestions on how to utilize personality measures for selection with CWB in mind.

Overall, when the CWB is present or it is an actual possibility, and in connection with employee personality, supervisors and HRM specialists should take into account that some personality variables can provoke or activate CWBs, both as an employee reaction or as initiative. For example, individuals low in conscientiousness, agreeableness, and emotional stability are more prone to show negative deviant behavior. The same is true for individuals high in negative affectivity or trait anger. Therefore, managers should align leadership practices with workers' personality characteristics. For example, managers should avoid placing such individuals in stressful situations. Of course, this strategy would require a better knowledge of human personality characteristics by team leaders and supervisors, and, consequently, training them in this domain might be also a good investment for the organization.

Practitioner's Window

In order to prevent CWB, we suggest, in the first place, identifying the particular type of CWB in question that is of concern to the organization. The second step would be to identify specific, relevant personality variables and to include some measures of them during the screening process, and thereby to select-out individuals self-reporting as high on these variables. Using an evidence-based framework, and based on the findings reported in this review, our suggestions would be the following:

1. If the interest is on overall CWB, we recommend one of the following measures: (1) a composite of conscientiousness, agreeableness, and emotional stability; (2) an integrity test or similar COPS; (3) a composite of negative plus positive affectivity; and (4) a composite of narcissism plus Machiavellianism.
2. If the interest is on organizational CWB, we recommend one of the following: (1) a composite of conscientiousness, agreeableness, and emotional stability and (2) a measure of trait anger supplemented with a measure of locus of control.
3. If the interest is on interpersonal CWB, we recommend one of the following measures: (1) a composite of agreeableness, conscientiousness, and emotional stability and (2) a measure of trait anger.
4. If the interest is on absenteeism, we recommend using an integrity test supplemented with a measure of self-efficacy.
5. If the interest is on aggressive behaviors (interpersonal and/or organizational), we recommend using a measure of trait anger supplemented with a measure of negative affectivity.
6. If the interest is on accident involvement, we recommend using a composite of conscientiousness, agreeableness, emotional stability, and openness.
7. If the interest is on occupational injuries, we recommend using a measure of negative affectivity.
8. If the interest is on voluntary turnover, we recommend using a composite of conscientiousness, agreeableness, and emotional stability.

Acknowledgments

We thank Robert Tett and Neal Christiansen for the comments and suggestions on a previous version of this chapter. The contribution by Jesús F. Salgado and Neil Anderson was partially supported by the grant EDU2008-03592 and PSI2011–27943 from the Spanish Ministry of Science, and the contribution by Silvia Moscoso was partially supported by the grant PSI2008-03617 from the Spanish Ministry of Science and Innovation.

References

Ashton, M. C., & Lee, K. (2007). Empirical, theoretical, and practical advantages of the HEXACO model of personality structure. *Personality and Social Psychology Review, 11*, 150–166.

Bennett, R. J., & Robinson, S. L. (2000). Development of a measure of workplace deviance. *Journal of Applied Psychology, 85*, 349–360.

Berry, C. M., Ones, D. S., & Sackett, P. R. (2007). Interpersonal deviance, organizational deviance, and their common correlates: A review and meta-analysis. *Journal of Applied Psychology, 92*, 410–424.

Bies, R. J. (2000). Interactional (in)justice: The sacred and the profane. In J. Greenberg & R. Cropanzano (Eds.), *Advances in organizational behavior* (pp. 89–118). Stanford, CA: Stanford University Press.
Bies, R. J., & Tripp, T. M. (1998). Two faces of the powerless: Coping with tyranny. In R. M. Kramer & M. A. Neale (Eds.), *Power and influence in organizations* (pp. 203–219). Thousand Oaks, CA: Sage.
Björkqvist, K., Österman, K., & Hjelt-Bäck, M. (1994). Aggression among university employees. *Aggressive Behavior, 20*, 173–184.
Blunt, P. (1980). Bureaucracy and ethnicity in Kenya: Some conjectures for the Eighties. *The Journal of Applied Behavioral Science, 6*, 336–351.
Bolton, L. R., Becker, L. K., & Barber, L. K. (2010). Big Five trait predictors of differential counterproductive work behavior dimensions. *Personality and Individual Differences, 49*, 537–541.
Borman, W. C., White, L. A., Pulakos, E. D., & Oppler, S. H. (1991). Models of supervisory job performance ratings. *Journal of Applied Psychology, 76*, 863–872.
Brunell, A. B., Staats, S., Barden, J., & Hupp, J. M. (2011). Narcissism and academic dishonesty: The exhibitionism dimension and the lack of guilt. *Personality and Individual Differences, 50*, 323–328.
Burch, G. S. J., & Anderson, N. (2008). Personality as a predictor of work-related behavior and performance: Recent advances and directions for future research. In G. P. Hodgkinson & J. Kevin Ford (Eds.), *International review of industrial and organizational psychology* (Vol. 23, pp. 261–305). London: Wiley.
Chang, K., & Smithikrai, C. (2010). Counterproductive behavior at work: An investigation into reduction strategies. *International Journal of Human Resource Management, 21*, 1272–1288.
Clarke, S., & Robertson, I. T. (2005). A meta-analytic review of the Big Five personality factors and accident involvement in occupational and non-occupational settings. *Journal of Occupational and Organizational Psychology, 78*, 355–376.
Crede, M., Chernyshenko, O. S., Stara, S., Dalal, R. S., & Bashshur, M. (2007). Job satisfaction as a mediator: An assessment of job satisfaction's position within the nomological network. *Journal of Occupational and Organizational Psychology, 80*, 515–537.
Cullen, M. J., & Sackett, P. R. (2006). Personality and counterproductive behavior. In M. R. Barrick & A. M. Ryan (Eds.), *Personality at work: Reconsidering the role of personality in organizations* (pp. 150–183). San Francisco: Jossey-Bass.
Dalal, R. S. (2005). A meta-analysis of the relationship between organizational citizenship behavior and counterproductive work behavior. *Journal of Applied Psychology, 90*, 1241–1255.
Dudley, N. M., Orvis, K. A., Lebiecki, J. E., & Cortina, J. M. (2006). A meta-analytic investigation of conscientiousness in the prediction of job performance: Examining the intercorrelations and the incremental validity of narrow traits. *Journal of Applied Psychology, 91*, 40–57.
Duffy, M. K., Ganster, D. C., & Pagon, M. (2002). Social undermining in the workplace. *Academy of Management Journal, 45*, 331–351.
Einarsen, S., & Skogstad, A. (1996). Bullying at work: Epidemiological findings in public and private organizations. *European Journal of Work and Organizational Psychology, 5*, 185–203.
Fox, S., & Spector, P. E. (1999). A model of work frustration–aggression. *Journal of Organizational Behavior, 24*, 915–931.
Fox, S., Spector, P. E., & Miles, D. (2001). Counterproductive work behavior (CWB) in response to job stressors and organizational justice: Some mediator and moderator tests for autonomy and emotions. *Journal of Vocational Behavior, 59*, 291–309.
Giacalone, R. A., & Greenberg, J. (Eds.). (1997). *Employee crimes; Violence in the workplace; Problem employees.* Thousand Oaks, CA: Sage.
Greenberg, J. (2002). Who stole the money, and when? Individual and situational determinants of employee theft. *Organizational Behavior and Human Decision Processes, 89*, 985–1003.
Greenberg, J., & Scott, K. S. (1996). Why do workers bite the hands that feed them? Employee theft as a social exchange process. In B. M. Staw & L. L. Cummings (Eds.), *Research in organizational behavior* (pp. 111–156). Greenwich, CT: JAI Press.
Gruys, M. L. (2000). *The dimensionality of deviant employee behavior in the workplace* (Doctoral dissertation). University of Minnesota. Retrieved from Dissertations & Theses A&I database (Publication No. AAT 9972966).
Gruys, M. L., & Sackett, P. R. (2003). Investigating the dimensionality of counterproductive work behavior. *International Journal of Selection and Assessment, 11*, 30–42.
Hastings, S. E., & O'Neill, T. (2009). Predicting workplace deviance using broad versus narrow personality variables. *Personality and Individual Differences, 47*, 289–293.
Hershcovis, M. S., Turner, N., Barling, J., Arnold, K. A., Dupré, K. E., Inness, M., . . . Sivanathan, N. (2007). Predicting workplace aggression: A meta-analysis. *Journal of Applied Psychology, 92*, 228–238.

Hoel, H., Cooper, C. L., & Faragher, B. (2001). The experience of bullying in Great Britain: The impact of organizational status. *European Journal of Work and Organizational Psychology, 10*, 443–465.
Hollinger, R. C., & Clark, J. (1982). Employee deviance: A response to the perceived quality of the work experience. *Work and Occupations, 9*, 97–114.
Hollinger, R. C., & Clark, J. P. (1983). *Theft by employees*. Lexington, MA: Lexington Books.
Hollinger, R. C., Slora, K. B., & Terris, W. (1992). Deviance in the fast-food restaurant: Correlates of employee theft, altruism, and counter productivity. *Deviant Behavior: An Interdisciplinary Journal, 13*, 155–184.
Kaplan, S., Bradley, J. C., Luchman, J. N., & Haynes, D. (2010). On the role of positive and negative affectivity in job performance: A meta-analytic investigation. *Journal of Applied Psychology, 94*, 162–176.
Laczo, R. M. (2002). *An examination of the dimensionality of non-task performance* (Unpublished doctoral dissertation). University of Minnesota, Minneapolis.
Leroy, Z. P. (2005). *Personality trait and cognitive ability correlates of unsafe behaviors* (Unpublished doctoral dissertation). University of British Columbia, Canada.
Levine, S. Z., & Jackson, C. J. (2002). Aggregated personality, climate and demographic factors as predictors of departmental shrinkage. *Journal of Business and Psychology, 17*, 287–297.
Leymann, H. (1996). The content and development of mobbing at work. *European Journal of Work and Organizational Psychology, 5*, 165–184.
Lin, T.-F., & Chen, J. (2006). Cumulative class attendance and exam performance. *Applied Economics Letters, 13*, 937–942.
Marburger, D. R. (2001). Absenteeism and undergraduate exam performance. *Journal of Economic Education, 32*, 99–109.
Marburger, D. R. (2006). Does mandatory attendance improve student performance? *Journal of Economic Education, 37*, 148–155.
Marcus, B., Lee, K., & Ashton, M. C. (2007). Personality dimensions explaining relationships between integrity tests and counterproductive behavior: Big Five or one in addition? *Personnel Psychology, 60*, 1–34.
Marcus, B., Schuler, H., Quell, P., & Hümpfner, G. (2002). Measuring counterproductivity: Development and initial validation of a German self-report questionnaire. *International Journal of Selection and Assessment, 10*, 18–35.
Marsden, H., Carroll, M., & Neill, J. T. (2005). Who cheats at university? A self-report study of dishonest academic behaviors in a sample of Australian university students. *Australian Journal of Psychology, 57*, 1–10.
Martinko, M. J., Gundlach, M. J., & Douglas, S. C. (2002). Toward an integrative theory of counterproductive workplace behavior: A causal reasoning perspective. *International Journal of Selection and Assessment, 10*, 36–50.
McCabe, D. L., & Trevino, L. K. (1997). Individual and contextual influences on academic dishonesty: A multi-campus investigation. *Research in Higher Education, 38*, 379–396.
McGurn, M. (1988, March 8). Spotting thieves who work among us. *The Wall Street Journal*, p. A16.
Mikkelsen, E. G., & Einarsen, S. (2001). Bullying in Danish work-life: Prevalence and health correlates. *European Journal of Work and Organizational Psychology, 10*, 393–413.
Munene, J. C. (1995). "Not-on-seat": An investigation of some correlates of organisational citizenship behaviour in Nigeria. *Applied Psychology: International Review, 44*, 111–122.
Murphy, K. R. (1994). *Honesty in the workplace*. Pacific Groves, CA: Brooks/Cole.
Nathanson, C., Paulhus, D. L., & Williams, K. M. (2006). Predictors of a behavioral measure of scholastic cheating: Personality and competence but not demographics. *Contemporary Educational Psychology, 31*, 97–122.
Ng, T. W. H., Sorensen, K. L., & Eby, L. T. (2006). Locus of control at work: A meta-analysis. *Journal of Organizational Behavior, 27*, 1057–1087.
Niedl, K. (1996). Mobbing and well-being. *European Journal of Work and Organizational Psychology, 5*, 239–249.
O'Boyle, E. H., Jr., Forsyth, D. R., Banks, G. C., & McDaniel, M. A. (2012). A meta-analysis of the dark triad and work behavior: A social exchange perspective. *Journal of Applied Psychology, 97*, 557–579.
O'Brien, K. E., & Allen, T. D. (2008). The relative importance of correlates of organizational citizenship behavior and counterproductive work behavior using multiple sources of data. *Human Performance, 21*, 62–88.
Ones, D. S., & Viswesvaran, C. (2001a). Integrity tests and other criterion-focused occupational personality scales (COPS) used in personnel selection. *International Journal of Selection and Assessment, 9*, 31–39.
Ones, D. S., & Viswesvaran, C. (2001b). Personality at work: Criterion-focused occupational personality scales (COPS) used in personnel selection. In B. Roberts & R. T. Hogan (Eds.), *Applied personality psychology* (pp. 63–92). Washington, DC: American Psychological Association.
Ones, D. S., Viswesvaran, C., & Schmidt, F. L. (1993). Comprehensive meta-analysis of integrity test validities: Findings and implications for personnel selection and theories of job performance [Monograph]. *Journal of Applied Psychology, 78*, 679–703.

Ones, D. S., Viswesvaran, C., & Schmidt, F. L. (2003). Personality and absenteeism: A meta-analysis of integrity tests. *European Journal of Personality, 17*, 19–38.

Oswald, F. L., Schmitt, N., Kim, B. H., Ramsay, L. J., & Gillespie, M. A. (2004). Developing a Biodata Measure and Situational Judgment Inventory as predictors of college student performance. *Journal of Applied Psychology, 89*, 187–207.

Resch, M., & Schubinski, M. (1996). Mobbing—prevention and management in organizations. *European Journal of Work and Organizational Psychology, 5*, 295.

Robinson, E., Amburgey, R., Swank, E., & Faulker, C. (2004). Test cheating in a rural college: Studying the importance of individual and situational factors. *College Student Journal, 38*, 380–395.

Robinson, S. L., & Bennett, R. J. (1995). A typology of deviant workplace behaviors: A multidimensional scaling study. *Academy of Management Journal, 38*, 555–572.

Robinson, S. L., & O'Leary-Kelly, A. (1998). Monkey see, monkey do: The influence of work groups on the antisocial behavior of employees. *Academy of Management Journal, 41*, 658–672.

Romer, D. (1993). Do students go to class? Should they? *Journal of Economic Perspectives, 7*, 167–174.

Roth, P. L., BeVier, C. A., Switzer, F., III, & Schippmann, J. S. (1996). Meta-analyzing the relationship between grades and job performance. *Journal of Applied Psychology, 81*, 548–557.

Ryan, M., Delaney, L., & Harmon, M. (2010). *Micro-level determinants of lecture attendance and additional study-hours* (IZA Discussion Paper n° 5144). Retrieved from http://hdl.handle.net/10197/2658

Sackett, P. R., Berry, C. M., Wiemann, S. A., & Laczo, R. M. (2006). Citizenship and counterproductive work behavior: Clarifying relationships between the two domains. *Human Performance, 19*, 441–464.

Sackett, P. R., & DeVore, C. J. (2001). Counterproductive behaviors at work. In N. Anderson, D. S. Ones, H. Sinangil, & C. Viswesvaran (Eds.), *Handbook of industrial, work, and organizational psychology: Vol. 1* (pp. 144–164). London: Sage.

Salgado, J. F. (2002). The Big Five personality dimensions and counterproductive behaviors. *International Journal of Selection and Assessment, 10*, 117–125.

Salgado, J. F., & Moscoso, S. (2000). Autoeficacia y criterios organizacionales de desempeno [Self-efficacy and organizational performance criteria]. *Apuntes de Psicología, 18*, 179–191.

Salin, D. (2001). Prevalence and forms of bullying among business professionals: A comparison of two different strategies for measuring bullying. *European Journal of Work and Organizational Psychology, 10*, 425–441.

Slora, K. (1991). An empirical approach to determining employee deviance base rates. In J. W. Jones (Ed.), *Preemployment honesty testing: Current research and future directions* (pp. 21–38). New York: Quorum Books.

Spector, P. E. (2011). The relationship of personality to counterproductive work behavior (CWB): An integration of perspectives. *Human Resource Management Review, 21*, 342–352.

Spector, P. E., & Fox, S. (2005). The stressor-emotion model of counterproductive work behavior. In P. E. Spector & S. Fox (Eds.), *Counterproductive work behavior: Investigations of actors and targets* (pp. 151–174). Washington, DC: American Psychological Association.

Spector, P. E., Fox, S., Penney, L. M., Bruursema, K., Goh, A. & Kessler, S. A. (2006). The dimensionality of counterproductivity: Are all counterproductive behaviors created equal? *Journal of Vocational Behavior, 68*, 446–460.

Stanca, L. (2006). The effects of class attendance on academic performance: Panel data evidence for introductory microeconomics. *Journal of Economic Education, 37*, 251–266.

Stern, E. B., & Havlicek, L. (1986). Academic misconduct: Results of faculty and undergraduate student surveys. *Journal of Allied Health, 15*, 129–142.

Storms, P., & Spector, P. (1987). Relationships of organizational frustration with reported behavioral reactions: The moderating effect of locus of control. *Journal of Occupational Psychology, 60*, 227–234.

Tepper, B. J. (2000). Consequences of abusive supervision. *Academy of Management Journal, 43*, 178–190.

Tett, R. P., & Burnett, D. D. (2003). A personality trait-based interactionist model of job performance. *Journal of Applied Psychology, 88*, 500–517.

Tziner, A., Fein, E. C., Sharoni, G., Ber-Hen, P., & Nord, T. (2010). Constructive deviance, leader–member exchange, and confidence in appraisal: How do they interrelate, if at all? *Journal of Work and Organizational Psychology, 26*, 95–100.

Van Walbeek, C. (2004). Does lecture attendance matter? Some observations from a first-year economics course at the University of Cape Town. *South African Journal of Economics, 72*, 861–883.

Vartia, M. (1996). The sources of bullying—psychological work environment and organizational climate. *European Journal of Work and Organizational Psychology, 5*, 203–214.

Williams, K. M., Nathanson, C., & Paulhus, D. L. (2010). Identifying and profiling scholastic cheaters: Their personality, cognitive ability, and motivation. *Journal of Experimental Psychology: Applied, 16*, 293–307.

Zapf, D., & Gross, C. (2001). Conflict escalation and coping with workplace bullying: A replication and extension. *European Journal of Work and Organizational Psychology, 10*, 497–522.
Zapf, D., Knorz, C., & Kulla, M. (1996). On the relationship between mobbing factors and job content, social work environment and health outcomes. *European Journal of Work and Organizational Psychology, 5*, 215–239.
Zimmerman, R. (2008). Understanding the impact of personality traits on individuals' turnover decisions: A meta-analytic path model. *Personnel Psychology, 61*, 309–348.

28

What Personality Does and Does Not Predict and Why

Lessons Learned and Future Directions

Kevin R. Murphy, Paige J. Deckert, and Samuel T. Hunter

The use of personality measures in personnel selection has a long and controversial history (Guion & Gottier, 1965; Morgeson et al., 2007b). To understand current thinking about the strengths and weaknesses of personality measures as predictors of broad criteria such as job performance or organizational success or narrower criteria such as effectiveness as a leader in specific jobs that draw heavily on specific personality traits (e.g., sales extraversion), it is important to lay out the relevant historical context. Professional consensus about the role of personality measures as predictors of both broad and narrow criteria in organizations has undergone a remarkable set of changes, in some ways paralleling the substantial changes in thinking about the validity of cognitive tests as predictors of similar criteria. The common thread running through both the ability and personality testing literatures is the marked influence of meta-analysis and studies of validity generalization (e.g., Schmidt & Hunter, 1998) on our understanding of the circumstances under which measures of cognitive abilities or of broad personality dimensions will or will not predict both broad and narrow performance criteria. Table 28.1 illustrates the evolution of the literatures dealing with the validity of cognitive ability and personality measures over the last 50 years.

Table 28.1 Professional Consensus Regarding Validity as a Predictor of Job Performance

Time Period	*Cognitive Ability*	*Broad Personality Dimensions*
1960–1970	Strict situational specificity	Strict situational specificity
1970–1980	Some acceptance of generalizability	Strict situational specificity
1980–1990	Broad acceptance of generalizability	Strict situational specificity
1990–2000	Broad acceptance of generalizability	Acceptance of generalizability for some traits
2000–2010	Broad acceptance of generalizability	Increasing awareness of situational specificity

In the 1960s, it was widely believed that the validity of tests of virtually every sort varied considerably from one situation to another. The doctrine of situational specificity reflects the assumption that there were features of individual jobs, organizations, tests, and settings that caused validity estimates from different studies to vary, making it difficult to draw clear or general conclusions about the validity of different classes of predictors.

Guion and Gottier's (1965) review fit this zeitgeist perfectly. Their review cast considerable doubt on the value of personality measures, especially as predictors of job performance. They concluded that "there is no generalizable evidence that personality measures can be recommended as good or practical tools for employee selection" (p. 159), and that "it is difficult to advocate, with a clear conscience, the use of personality measures in most situations as a basis for making employment decisions about people" (p. 160). This review led to a long period of skepticism about the relevance of personality in understanding performance and effectiveness in the workplace. It was not until the 1990s that personality indices reemerged as a viable tool for understanding and predicting performance and effectiveness (Barrick & Mount, 1991).

In the 1970s and 1980s, studies of the generalizability of the validity of cognitive ability tests changed the landscape substantially (Schmidt, Gast-Rosenberg, & Hunter, 1980; Schmidt & Hunter, 1998; Schmidt, Hunter, & Caplan, 1981; Schmidt, Hunter, Pearlman, & Shane, 1979). By the mid-1980s, it was widely accepted that cognitive ability tests showed positive validity for predicting performance in virtually every job (Hartigan & Wigdor, 1989). Furthermore, with the exception of job complexity (Gutenberg, Arvey, Osburn, & Jeanneret, 1983), there appeared to be few important moderators of the validity of cognitive tests. One implication of this literature was that detailed analyses of jobs, situations, and so on were not always necessary to identify valid predictors of performance; in virtually any job, a good measure of general cognitive ability could be expected to show at least moderate (and often reasonably high) levels of validity. In stark contrast, there was still little consensus that personality measures had any real value as predictors of future performance. Guion and Gottier's (1965) conclusion that the validity of personality measures was not generalizable across indices, organizations, or situations was still widely accepted by researchers and practitioners through the 1980s.

In the context of 30 years of professional consensus that personality measures were of limited value as predictors of job performance, the meta-analyses of Barrick and Mount (1991) and Tett, Jackson, and Rothstein (1991) came as a virtual thunderbolt; in particular, Barrick and Mount's (1991) conclusion that measures of at least some of the Big Five personality dimensions (particularly conscientiousness) showed validity that generalized across situations. The Big Five taxonomy spans the domain of normal personality (Digman, 1990; Goldberg, 1993; John & Srivastava, 1999), so a showing that measures of these broad dimensions demonstrated positive correlations with job performance suggested that the long-standing skepticism about the value of personality as a predictor of performance was mistaken.

The effect of meta-analyses for the validity of personality measures was arguably even stronger than the effect of earlier meta-analyses for cognitive tests. Even in the heyday of situational specificity, most researchers and practitioners assumed that cognitive ability tests were useful in at least some situations; job analyses and local validity studies were used to try and nail those situations down. Personality inventories went from being seen as essentially useless in applications such as personnel selection to being seen as valid predictors of performance across a wide range of jobs, organizations, and situations.

The newfound consensus that personality measures showed generalizable validity led to an explosion of interest in the applications of these measures in organizations (Morgeson et al., 2007b). By the mid-1990s, concerns about the validity and usefulness of personality measures in selection contexts seemed passé. For example, a once widely cited review concluded, "From a practical standpoint, recent findings . . . suggest that the controversy over whether personality tests can be useful for prediction of employee performance is no longer pertinent" (Kanfer, Ackerman, Murtha, & Goff, 1995, p. 597). In the last decade, there has been increasing focus on the ways the interaction between the demands of jobs and particular personality traits is likely to influence the validity of personality measures as predictors of performance (e.g., Christiansen & Tett, 2008).

What Changed?

There are good reasons to believe that it is the context and not the data that led to such a sea change in beliefs about the validity of personality measures in selection contexts. First, the *levels* of validity in predicting performance and success reported in the meta-analyses of the 1990s was not all that different from that reported by Guion and Gottier (1965) or in subsequent analyses (e.g., Schmitt, Gooding, Noe, & Kirsch, 1984). That is, it is not that the basic findings of studies that relate scores on personality inventories to measures of job performance and effectiveness have changed. Rather, our standards have changed.

The methods of meta-analysis widely used in personnel psychology have appropriately directed our attention to two key questions: (1) On average, how high are the correlations between important variables (e.g., ability and performance)? and (2) Is there evidence that these correlations are consistently positive? Meta-analyses ask important questions about the variability of correlations from study to study, but the main focus has generally been on whether this variability is larger than what might be expected on the basis of sampling error, and perhaps a few other artifacts. The relative inattention to the variability in outcomes is particularly unfortunate when meta-analytic methods are applied to personality studies, because there is abundant evidence that the level of validity of various tests can vary substantially and meaningfully across jobs and situations. For example, confirmatory meta-analyses, which focus on studies where there is a theoretical match between specific personality measures and attributes of the job, tend to show higher average validities than comprehensive meta-analyses that include all studies, regardless of the match between tests and jobs (Tett & Burnett, 2003; Tett et al., 1991). Because both positive and negative correlations with particular personality dimensions might be expected in different jobs or situations (Tett et al., 1991), it is important in evaluating the validity of personality measures to pay careful attention to the variability of validity coefficients, once the effects of correctable artifacts are removed. Unfortunately, researchers have tended to follow the lead of meta-analyses in the cognitive realm, by paying attention to the mean of the corrected validity distribution and to the proportion of that distribution that is above zero.

The excitement over early meta-analytic findings (e.g., Barrick & Mount, 1991; Tett et al., 1991) was arguably due to the conclusion that the validity of these measures generalized—that is, that the lower bound of the validity distribution was likely to be above zero. Barrick and Mount (1991) found evidence of generalizable validity where others had not, not because the validities in their analysis were markedly higher than the validities in previous analyses, but rather because of the meta-analytic corrections they applied. This is not a phenomenon unique to Barrick and Mount's analysis or to meta-analyses of personality; corrections are an essential part of meta-analysis. There is a robust debate over the appropriateness of some of these corrections (Murphy & DeShon, 2000a, 2000b; Schmidt, Viswesvaran, & Ones, 2000), but regardless of the corrections used, the results are clear. Measures of broad personality dimensions (e.g., Big Five factors) show levels of validity in predicting performance across a wide range of jobs that are greater than zero in the great majority of studies (i.e., generalizable). What tends to get lost in the shuffle is that the average validities are rarely all that far from zero (Morgeson et al., 2007a, 2007b; Murphy & Dzieweczynski, 2005; Ones, Dilchert, Viswesvaran, & Judge, 2007). Because there is often meaningful variability in the validity of personality measures across jobs, finding that the mean of a validity distribution is relatively close to zero does not mean that the entire validity distribution will be close to zero. Nevertheless, the combination of relatively low average validity and relatively large variance in validity (adjusting for the effects of statistical artifacts) does tend to undercut the argument that, like cognitive ability measures, personality measures show broad applicability in predicting job performance.

A recent meta-analysis suggests that the low validity of personality measures is, in part, an artifact of the use of self-reports, and that others' reports of personality are better predictors of a range of outcomes (Oh, Wang, & Mount, 2011), but it is still not clear whether self-reports and others' reports measure the same constructs (for more coverage of personality from the perspective of observers, see Chapter 20, this volume). For example, are the lower validities of self-reports a sign that individuals do not know their own personalities (in which case, much of the existing research literature on personality is on extremely shaky ground) or is it because of biases in self-judgments vs. others' judgments? If it is biases, who is more biased? For example, others' ratings of personality might share the same biases (e.g., attractiveness) that are present in others' evaluations of performance, which would inflate validity coefficients.

The most compelling argument for the limited validity of personality measures as predictors of job performance and effectiveness comes from a paper (Ones et al., 2007) written to *refute* the claim by Morgeson and colleagues (2007b) that personality measures showed limited validity. Ones and colleagues (2007) summarize almost two decades of primary and meta-analytic work, and they do indeed show impressive validities for some personality measures as predictors of some criteria, but with regards to overall performance, their results closely mirror those cited by Morgeson and colleagues (2007a, 2007b) and Murphy and Dzieweczynski (2005). Ones and colleagues show that the uncorrected validity of a unit-weighted composite of the whole Big Five (a taxonomy that is thought to span the domain of normal personality) for predicting overall performance is .12. In other words, a composite of the Big Five accounts for 1.4% of the variance in overall performance. With generous corrections, the entire Big Five might account for as much as 4.6% of the variance in overall performance (i.e., r = .21). Ones and colleagues (2007) also examined the validity of conscientiousness alone as a predictor of performance, and they conclude that, even with the most generous corrections, this dimension of personality would explain about 4% of the variance in overall job performance (i.e., r = .20). As Sturman and Murphy (2010) have shown, the corrections used in the meta-analyses cited by Ones and colleagues (2007) substantially overestimate the attenuating effects of measurement error. Personality indices are likely to be useful for a variety of purposes, but the claim that they are *broadly* useful for predicting performance across a range of jobs, as is the case for cognitive ability measures, is not consistent with the data. Confirmatory meta-analyses suggest that personality measures can be quite useful in a number of specific circumstances, but the data do not suggest that they will typically show levels of validity that are consistently shown by other selection measures, particularly cognitive tests.

It is clear that some personality indices can show substantial validity for predicting performance in some situations (Ones et al., 2007; Ones, Viswesvaran, & Dilchert, 2005; Tett & Christiansen, 2007). Some personality-like measures (e.g., integrity tests) show levels of validity in selection contexts that are both consistent *and* substantial (Ones et al., 2007; Ones, Viswesvaran, & Schmidt, 1993). However, the proposition that these measures have broad utility for personnel selection is not supported by the data. There are some jobs, organizations, situations, and so on in which measures of specific personality characteristics might prove to be quite useful, but the hoopla surrounding the reemergence of personality measures as broadly valid selection devices seems to be (and certainly should be) dying down (Morgeson et al., 2007a, 2007b). Criticism of the observation that personality measures have limited validity have sometimes been presented with what appears to be significant force (e.g., Ones et al., 2007; Ones et al., 2005; Tett & Christensen, 2007), but a close examination of the data *as they relate to predicting overall performance or effectiveness* clearly shows the limitations of personality indices as potential selection tools.

What Went Wrong?

The question of why such high levels of enthusiasm for the use of personality measures in predicting performance across a range of jobs built up, especially in the face of such a long and consistent record of relatively low validities, is one that might have a very simple answer. For a long time, researchers and practitioners have treated validity as a binary state—that is, tests are either valid or not valid (Murphy,

2009). This tendency was greatly reinforced by the emergence of validity generalization. If you ask the question of what, exactly, generalizes in a validity generalization study, the answer is "the conclusion that a test is valid generalizes." The long-standing norm in validity generalization studies is to look at the lower bound of some sort of credibility interval (often, the 90% credibility value) and to compare the meta-analytic estimates of validity to some minimal standard. Most often, if a meta-analysis supports the claim that at least 90% of the validity distribution is above zero (or some other low value), the authors will conclude that validity generalizes; bidirectional meta-analyses make similar claims if the preponderant majority of the absolute values of validity coefficients are sufficiently above zero. This is perfectly true at a formal level, but, by sorting tests into two classes, valid and not valid, this interpretative standard has the potential to mischaracterize the research literature. For example, a test that yields validities for predicting a well-measured criterion that hover in the teens and below might end up being classified in the same way as a test that consistently yields validities in the .40 to .50 range. Both, by the binary standard, are "valid."

The personality meta-analyses of the 1990s led to a 180-degree shift in perspective on the utility of personality as a predictor in hiring. Personality measures went from being pariahs in personnel selection to rising stars. Well-done meta-analyses consistently showed that these measures were "valid" predictors of overall performance, and, in the excitement over credibility values that were consistently higher than zero, personality researchers and practitioners seem to have lost track of just what it means for a test to be, in the binary sense, "valid."

Murphy (2010) suggests that instead of asking "Is this test valid?" we should be asking questions like "valid for what?" and "how valid?" That is, the statement that a test is valid, without qualifications (how valid, valid for what, and under what circumstances?), is almost pointless. Almost any test is useful for some purposes, but some are more useful for a wider range of purposes than others. The conclusion that the validity of personality measures as predictors of performance is not zero eliminates one possibility out of an infinite set of possibilities, but it should not be thought of as an end of the process of investigating the use of these measures in selection.

Turning the Question Around

The process of overturning 30 years of negative conclusions about the value of personality measures as predictors of performance was a heady one, but unfortunately too many researchers and practitioners stopped asking critical questions once the question "Are these tests valid?" was answered. In our view, the more interesting question is not whether personality tests show *some* validity (of course they do, at least in some situations), but rather why they do not do better. Consider the results of Ones and colleagues (2007): If the full range of meta-analytic corrections is applied *and* the statistically optimal composite of the Big Five is used to predict performance, the conclusion is drawn that personality predicts about 7% of the variance in job performance. If we turn this assertion around, they are also asserting that about 93% of the variance in job performance is completely independent of the Big Five. This is an intriguing statement.

Think about two job candidates, Pat and Mike. Pat is moderately conscientious, extraverted, emotionally stable, agreeable, and open to experience. Mike is moderately undependable, withdrawn, neurotic, disagreeable, and closed-minded. If you ask the question of how much difference it would make (in terms of their overall level of performance) whether you hired Pat or Mike, common sense would suggest that it should make a lot of difference. However, the results presented by Ones and colleagues (2007) might lead you to conclude that there is not much difference in the likelihood that they will perform well in many jobs. The consistent finding, across a wide range of meta-analyses, that 90–95% of the variance in overall job performance is unrelated to broad dimensions of personality is both disappointing and surprising. To be sure, there are likely to be specific jobs, situations, and so on where the difference between Pat and Mike has profound implications for their success or failure.

Why Does Not Personality Perform Better As a General Predictor of Overall Job Performance?

One way to develop hypotheses about the general failure of personality measures as good general predictors of overall job performance is to contrast them with what is generally regarded as the best single predictor of performance: general cognitive ability (Jensen, 1980, 1998; Kuncel, Hezlett, & Ones, 2004; Ree & Earles, 1991a, 1991b; Ree, Earles, & Teachout, 1994; Sackett, Schmitt, Ellington, & Kabin, 2001; Schmidt & Hunter, 1998). Cognitive abilities predict performance reasonably well (corrected correlations of .30 or above for individual tests of general cognitive ability are common) across a wide range of situations for two reasons. First, nearly every job in just about every organization requires incumbents to engage in active information processing, which is at the heart of cognitive ability. In contrast, most jobs will require or involve some aspects of personality and draw very little on others. Some jobs are likely to require extraversion (e.g., sales), whereas others might involve conscientiousness (e.g., accounting) or agreeableness (e.g., customer service). In other words, cognitive abilities show up in virtually every job, whereas the influence of personality variables is likely to reflect the specific demands of the job or situation (Tett & Christiansen, 2007).

Second, there are structural explanations for the broad success of cognitive tests in comparison to personality measures. Murphy (1996, 2010) has argued that the best explanation for the success of general cognitive abilities across a range of situations, as well as the accompanying failure of personality variables to work well in predicting performance across a comparable range, is that cognitive abilities show stronger evidence of positive manifold (i.e., a consistent pattern of positive intercorrelations and positive correlations with criteria). As a result of positive manifold, the relations among various cognitive measures are best characterized by a hierarchically structured model, in which just about any type of information processing can be eventually related back to most general cognitive factor "g" (Ackerman & Humphreys, 1990; Allinger, 1988; Carroll, 1993; Eysenck, 1979; Guttman & Levy, 1991; Jensen, 1980; Johnson & Bouchard, 2005; Ree & Earles, 1991b; Vernon, 1964). In contrast, the major dimensions of personality, although not orthogonal (Ones et al., 2005), do not show this same pattern of positive manifold, and the notion of a single general factor that pervades all aspects of personality does not seem feasible (see, however, Gustafsson, 2001; Rushton & Irwing, 2008).

Positive manifold has striking implications for the validity of different types of tests. When positive manifold is strong, just about any battery of tests will end up measuring the same general factor as other test batteries (Murphy, 2009; Murphy, Dzieweczynski, & Yang, 2009). One implication is that the choice of specific abilities to measure particular jobs does not turn out to have much of an effect on criterion-related validity. In particular, the match or mismatch between the content of the job and the content of the tests does not have meaningful implications for the criterion-related validity of batteries of tests that show positive manifold (Murphy et al., 2009). In contrast, the match between test content and job content appears likely to be highly relevant to the criterion-related validity of personality inventories (Cucina, Vasilopoulos, & Sehgal, 2005; Hogan & Holland, 2003; Jenkins & Griffith, 2004; Raymark, Schmit, & Guion, 1997; Riggio & Taylor, 2000; Sumer, Sumer, Demirutku, & Cifci, 2001). As Tett et al. (1991) showed, the correlation between personality measures and measures of job performance is considerably larger if personality attributes were chosen on the basis of their theoretical or logical relevance to the jobs in question and weaker if there was no a priori link between personality attributes and jobs (see also Hogan & Holland, 2003; Jenkins & Griffith, 2004).

Dudley, Orvis, Lebiecki, and Cortina (2006) showed that the criterion-related validity of measures of the broad trait conscientiousness and the incremental validity of measures of specific facets of that trait (e.g., achievement, dependability, and order) varied across occupations. Measures of order and cautiousness were positively correlated with performance in skilled and unskilled jobs (corrected correlations of .34 and .20), but negatively correlated with performance in managerial jobs (corrected correlations of −.13 and −.10). This reversal of signs when the same measures are used to predict performance in two different occupations virtually never occurs in domains where tests show positive manifold, and is potentially powerful evidence that matches between job content and test content can be important, at least for this particular set of facet measures.

If the validity of a set of measures for predicting performance differs strongly across jobs, the average validity across jobs cannot be very high; if there is a reasonable balance of positive and negative validities, the average cannot be very far from zero. The explanation is simple. The validity of any single test (cognitive or personality) for predicting performance rarely exceeds .30 (with corrections, this figure is closer to .60). If we accept a figure of approximately .30 as an uncorrected validity ceiling for most individual tests, the presence of variability in validities means that there will be a substantial number of coefficients that are lower than .30, perhaps a lot lower. Average validities can approach this ceiling only when there is little variability. Thus, the presence of variability in criterion-related validity from job to job creates validity distributions in which the uncorrected means will rarely get out of the teens, and often will be even lower. A close examination of Barrick and Mount's (1991) meta-analysis, which arguably triggered the renaissance in research on the use of personality in selection, shows exactly this pattern. The dimension with the highest validity across a wide range of jobs (conscientiousness) shows an uncorrected average validity of .12.

This variability in validities across jobs, organizations, situations, and so on resembles in some ways the old assumption of situational specificity, with one critical difference. The traditional situational specificity hypothesis implies that there is some unidentified aspect of the job, the organization, or the situation that causes validities to vary. Guion and Gottier (1965) added the substantial diversity in what different personality inventories actually measure to this list of potential causes of variability in validities. Following the lead of Tett and colleagues (1991), current professional consensus suggests that the factors that influence the validity of various personality inventories in specific jobs are identifiable. In particular, the match between the behaviors required by a job and the behaviors that characterize a personality dimension has a strong impact on the criterion-related validity of measures of various personality attributes—a finding that stands, notably, in contrast to the cognitive ability literature (Tett & Burnett, 2003; Tett et al., 1991).

In an effort to identify factors that might moderate the criterion-related validity of broad personality measures, Tett and his colleagues developed a trait activation model that attempts to specify the job-level, group-level, and organization-level variables that are likely to influence the linkage between personality and performance or effectiveness (Tett & Burnett, 2003; Tett, Jackson, Rothstein, & Reddon, 1999; Chapter 5, this volume). This model suggests that a wide range of situational factors activate personality traits, and that they affect behavior only in situations in which they have in fact been activated. That is, Tett and Burnett's (2003) model suggests that, in the workplace, personality traits are expressed as responses to trait-relevant situational cues. They suggest that the tasks themselves, the work group, or the organization can all give off cues that activate specific personality traits, and that the presence or absence of these cues will moderate the relationship between personality and performance or effectiveness. These cues can enhance or reduce the relationships between personality traits and work performance.

What Does Personality Predict?

Although current data are clear in showing that personality often does a poor job predicting overall job performance, the question still lingers: What does personality predict well, if anything? The answers, it would seem, are quite a few things. For example, in a meta-analysis of subjective well-being (i.e., happiness), DeNeve and Cooper (1998) observed an uncorrected and unweighted mean correlation between neuroticism and happiness of −.30, with measures of locus of control (used as related indicators of conscientiousness) producing uncorrected coefficients of roughly the same value (r = .25–.35). Along similar lines, traits have been associated with a number of important nonworkplace outcomes, such as mortality, divorce, and alcoholism (Cooper-Hakim & Viswesvaran, 2002; Roberts, Kuncel, Shiner, Caspi, & Goldberg, 2007). Finally, a meta-analysis examining the relationship between conscientiousness-related traits and health-related behaviors revealed a number of sizable uncorrected correlations, including those for alcohol use (r = –.25), drug use (r = –.28), risky driving (r = –.25), and violence (r = –.25). The general trend emerging from these results is that nontrivial relationships exist between self-report personality tests and major life outcomes—a conclusion drawn by other personality scholars (e.g., Hough & Oswald, 2008). Such a trend, in many ways, is expected, given the macro nature of factor-level personality measures used in these types of studies and the more macro outcomes examined. Along these lines, Heggestad and Gordon (2008) noted that "many personality assessments used in personnel decision making have not been created specifically for use in selection settings, but rather as general assessments of the respondent's personality" (p. 320). Thus, when taking the approach of a general assessment of personality, it seems reasonable that measures would be predictive of major life outcomes.

As researchers of organizational behavior, however, we are typically less interested in predicting major life outcomes. Our primary interest, rather, lies in predicting behavior within the context of work. The implication here is that, by and large, there is a mismatch between the assessments being used and their desired outcomes of interest (Tett & Christiansen, 2007). Taken a step further, although the Five-Factor Model (FFM) has been essential in structuring how researchers think about personality, it is likely that greater utility lies in the facet levels of these constructs (Rothstein & Goffin, 2006). Accordingly, it would appear useful to briefly consider and contrast the predictive power of both the factor and its facets.

In consistent fashion, the personality trait showing the strongest and most generalizable criterion-related validity in the workplace has been conscientiousness. Conscientious individuals are characterized as being achievement-oriented, dependable, disciplined, organized, planful, and hard working (Barrick & Mount, 1991; Costa, McCrae, & Dye, 1991). As noted earlier in our discussion, the general trait of conscientiousness has been found to be the strongest, yet still relatively modest, predictor of overall job performance (uncorrected mean r = .12; Barrick & Mount, 1991). The trait, however, has demonstrated stronger relationships with workplace outcomes such as getting along, expatriate performance, individual teamwork, citizenship, compliance, overall counterproductivity, interpersonal deviance, procrastination, and organizational deviance. Uncorrected correlations among these outcomes range from r = .14 for getting along (Hogan & Holland, 2003) to r = –.61 for procrastination (Steel, 2007). Conscientiousness has also been studied in the leadership domain by researchers such as Judge, Bono, Ilies, and Gerhardt (2002), who found measures to be predictors of leader effectiveness (uncorrected r = .26) and leader emergence (uncorrected r = .23). Finally, conscientiousness has also been found to be predictive of team performance (uncorrected r = .29; Peeters, van Tuiji, Rutte, & Reymen, 2006), suggesting that multilevel investigation may help to elucidate relationships in future research.

Although other examples exist and are well summarized by Ones and colleagues (2007), several key observations emerge from the above meta-analytic trends. First, although conscientiousness is only minimally predictive of job performance, the trait does appear to be substantively predictive of a rather broad *range* of other workplace criteria; outcomes that run the gamut from interpersonal facilitation to career satisfaction (Hough & Oswald, 2008; Judge, Heller, & Mount, 2002). Along those lines, the second general observation emerging is that conscientiousness appears to predict secondary outcomes such as procrastination and organizational deviance better than broader primary outcomes such as overall job performance. The general/specific argument for predictors and outcomes is well documented by a number of authors (e.g., Tett & Christiansen, 2007; Van Iddekinge, Taylor, & Eidson, 2005). However, it is worth noting again that the complexity of succeeding in one's job is unlikely to be driven by a single activity, behavior, or action and, as such, is unlikely to be primarily driven by a single personality trait. Accordingly, it would appear useful to briefly consider the *specific* components comprising conscientiousness and their respective relationships to workplace outcomes (for more coverage of breadth of personality measurement, see Chapter 14, this volume).

At the more specific facet level, conscientiousness is often broken down into the dimensions of achievement, dependability, order, and cautiousness, although it is important to acknowledge that there is some debate on the precise facet factor structure (e.g., Costa et al., 1991; Roberts, Chernyshenko, Stark, & Goldberg, 2005). We consider the four-factor framework here for two reasons: first, this framework is most commonly used by researchers of organizational behavior (e.g., Ones et al., 2007), and second, it allows us to consider the notable meta-analysis by Dudley and colleagues (2006), who also employed the four-facet framework. In their meta-analysis, the researchers examined a range of workplace outcomes, including overall job performance, task performance, job dedication, interpersonal facilitation, and counterproductive work behaviors. With regard to job performance, Dudley and colleagues reported the following facet-level uncorrected correlations for achievement ($r = .10$), dependability ($r = .13$), order ($r = .05$), and cautiousness ($r = -.01$). Faring somewhat better are the uncorrected values for job dedication. Dudley and colleagues found that achievement ($r = .20$, $r = .39$) and dependability ($r = .23$, $r = .46$) facets produced the strongest correlations with job dedication, whereas order ($r = .05$, $r = .10$) and cautiousness ($r = .04$, $r = .08$) produced rather weak values, although it should be acknowledged that there is some evidence for bidirectionality (i.e., high variability around the means) in 4 of the 21 reported rho values that may have artificially reduced the observed effect sizes. The other three outcomes examined by the researchers produced mean correlations roughly between the two illustrations above.

Perhaps even more interestingly, Dudley and colleagues (2006) were able to examine whether including facet-level measures improved predictive ability over and above general measures of conscientiousness. Across all five criteria examined, the inclusion of facet-level measures substantively improved the variance explained, with ΔR^2s ranging from .037 (i.e., 3.7%) for job performance to .259 (i.e., 25.9%) for job dedication. Notably, including facet scores for counterproductive work behaviors resulted in a 13.6% increase in variance accounted for over and above global measures, driven primarily by the achievement and dependability facets.

We suggest the reader examine the meta-analysis by Dudley and colleagues (2006) for an in-depth review of their results and interpretation, but, here, we comment on the trends observed at the facet level of conscientiousness that are relevant to the present discussion. First, as to be expected, coefficients are more variable at the specific facet level than at the broader factor level. Across the five criteria examined, for example, general measures of conscientiousness yielded validity estimates ranging from .10 (task performance) to −.16 (counterproductive work behaviors). In contrast, facet values for dependability yielded estimates ranging from .23 (job dedication) to −.21 (counterproductive work behaviors). For the same outcomes, the facet of achievement produced uncorrected correlations of .20 and .00, respectively. This variability is not unexpected—with greater specificity provided by facet-level predictors, there can be greater alignment between predictor and criterion, yielding stronger coefficients. The resulting implication here is that although predictive power may be improved, greater care is needed in choosing predictors and specifying a priori why that predictor should be utilized for a given criterion (e.g., Tett & Christiansen, 2007).

The second trend emerging from the meta-analytic work of Dudley and colleagues (2006) is that specific facets closely matched or outperformed general measures of conscientiousness with regard to predictive validity. A possible implication is that, if thought is placed in choosing the appropriate predictor, facet measures may surpass general measures with regard to predictive capacity. This is the same conclusion tentatively drawn by Rothstein and Goffin (2006) in their review of selection and personality. This trend underscores recommendations by Tett and colleagues (Christiansen & Tett, 2008; Tett & Christiansen, 2007; Tett et al., 1991) to spend time and resources on careful job analyses and predictor selection.

The third trend is that, by utilizing separate facets in blocked regression analyses, predictive ability of the facet predictor set exceeded the single, broader measure. Admittedly, such a trend is at least, in part, a statistical artifact. That is, including additional predictors will nearly always improve variance accounted for, even if the predictors lack substantive rationale for inclusion. Inspection of the results, however, reveals the effects to be nontrivial—the average increase in variance accounted for (i.e., ΔR^2) when including facet-level scores was 11%, ranging from 3.7% for overall job performance to 25.9% for job dedication. Simply put, they do not appear to be simply the result of including "extra" predictors and would appear to suggest a more substantive trend driven by heterogeneous, unique contributions among predictors.

Souring the discussion somewhat is our final observation. Namely, despite the positive tone of the trends discussed above, most effects still remain in the low to modest range. Combined predictor sets (i.e., including general and specific facets), using multiple regression, accounted for 9.5% of the variance in overall job performance, 7.2% for task performance, 8.9% for interpersonal facilitation, and 20.4% for counterproductive work behaviors. The strongest effect—one that is admittedly sizable—revealed that 29.9% of variance could be accounted for in job dedication. Even this strong effect, however, still suggests that roughly 70% of the variance is attributable to other factors. On the whole, the results above indicate that facet-level results show promise in improving the predictive power of personality, but they do not appear to be a panacea for the often small to modest effects observed across studies. When issues such as bidirectionality and job relevance are taken into account, coefficients are indeed larger (see Tett & Christiansen, 2007); this general conclusion is frequently applicable for our often primary outcome of interest, overall job performance.

Do Relationships Differ by Jobs or People?

A reasonable question that emerges in a discussion on the predictive capacity of personality is whether relationships differ across jobs or among varying subgroups. It is beyond the scope of our discussion to consider each and every moderator here, but it would appear useful to consider a few key factors that might impact observed relationships. We begin by asking whether relationships hold consistently across various job domains—the answer to which is summarized well by Ones and colleagues (2007). In their review, the authors report that conscientiousness produced fairly similar uncorrected mean correlations across sales (r = .11), skilled (r = .12), customer service (r = .17), professional (r = .11), police (r = .11), and managerial (r = .12) samples. It should be noted, however, that, at the facet level, there is greater variability across jobs (Dudley et al., 2006; Ones et al., 2007). Moreover, inspection of traits other than conscientiousness reveals that it may be the exception in consistency. When examining mean correlation coefficients presented by Ones and colleagues (2007), traits such as extraversion and agreeableness vary more than conscientiousness in their prediction of workplace outcomes.

Perhaps most telling is a study by Tett and colleagues (1999) who found that, when the nature of the job was taken into account when choosing predictors, observed uncorrected meta-analytic means were r = .26, compared to r = .20 for those studies that did not. Furthermore, we see even greater differences when considering comparisons between exploratory (mean uncorrected r = .10) and confirmatory job analysis (mean uncorrected r = .26), values that corrected for upward bias. Thus, although there is some consistency across jobs for a subset of personality traits (i.e., conscientiousness), values are nontrivially improved when the nature of the job is carefully considered and predictors appropriately chosen. Generally speaking, job type and local trait job relevance matter.

Turning to the issue of differences across subgroups, use of personality was initially heralded as a method to reduce adverse impact and, notably, there were some early indications of support for this (see Campbell, 1996; Chapter 23, this volume). Although a nice idea, it has not panned out as expected. Hough, Oswald, and Ployhart (2001), for example, found that, even when broad-level constructs (e.g., conscientiousness) showed no difference between Black and White candidates, there were noticeable differences at the facet level, with effect sizes (d statistics) as large as 0.2 and 0.3, with larger effects generally favoring White candidates. It should be noted, however, that across minority groups, there was inconsistency on which group was higher, with results often being facet- and criterion-dependent. Hispanic candidates, for instance, scored higher on integrity scales than White candidates (d = 0.14), as did Asian candidates on achievement scales (d = 0.13) and Black candidates on the extraversion facet scores of potency (d = 0.12). These trends reinforce the notion that job analytic information needs to be used when creating selection batteries to assess specific characteristics, with the awareness that subgroup differences may vary based on the construct used, as well as the specificity of measurement.

What If We Combine Measures?

Several scholars have suggested that predictive capacity is increased by matching predictors and outcomes. At the heart of the argument is that job performance is a complex phenomenon and, as such, will be maximally predicted by a similarly complex construct on the predictor side (e.g., Hogan & Roberts, 1996; Ones & Viswesvaran, 1996). Indeed, Ones and colleagues (2005) report improved uncorrected correlation coefficients when larger, more macro, scales are utilized. Broader measures of integrity, for example, produced uncorrected coefficients with mean r = .41 (Ones et al., 1993), while measures of customer service orientation produced similar mean r = .39 (Ones & Viswesvaran, 2001).

In contrast, other researchers have suggested that such aggregation obscures the possible facet-level relationships and lessens overall interpretability (e.g., Hough & Oswald, 2000; Tett, Steele, & Beauregard, 2003). Although beyond the scope of this discussion to solve the bandwidth–fidelity debate, a study of the macroconstruct of integrity highlights the potentially problematic issues of utilizing broader measures in selection contexts. Van Iddekinge et al. (2005) examined 152 customer service managers by utilizing a broader measure of integrity and overall job performance. Results revealed that the broader integrity scale was actually comprised of eight subfactors and, more importantly, the subfactors differentially predicted job performance. More specifically, half of the factors *positively* predicted performance, whereas the other half *negatively* predicted performance, with correlations ranging from −.16 to .18. Therein lies the potential pitfall of macro measures: Although predictive capacity is improved overall, the cost of understanding how the predictor relates to an outcome may simply prove too high.

One rather simple way around such pitfalls is to use facet-level values in blocked multiple regression (or similar) analysis. These approaches permit researchers and practitioners to gain the unique predictive power of appropriately chosen facets while simultaneously harnessing the collective predictive capacity of the measures. Tett and Christiansen (2007) take this argument one step further and suggest that when measures of the FFM are included in a multiple regression analysis and job relevance is carefully considered, they may rival even cognitive ability in predictive capacity. Moreover, in the meta-analysis by Dudley and colleagues (2006), including facet-level components of conscientiousness improved variance accounted for across all five variables and, for two of the five, this improvement was substantial (14%–26% more variance explained). Acknowledging that personality predicts incrementally over cognitive ability, a reasonable argument exists for applying a multivariate approach to utilizing personality—at least with regard to overall variance accounted for in job performance. Along these lines, one point to bear in mind when utilizing a multivariate approach is that we must be able to demonstrate the unique validity of each facet chosen in the predictor set. Note that conscientiousness is, on average, the best predictor of job performance in the FFM (Barrick & Mount, 1991); yet even measures of this specific facet demonstrate sizable variability in validity across facets and job types (Tett & Christiansen, 2007). As such, making the case for including *other* measures, particularly at the facet level, may prove challenging. Barring such limitations and focusing carefully on job-relevant predictor and criterion choices, however, combined approaches stand as viable next steps in understanding the role of personality in selection contexts.

To summarize, in the second half of this chapter we asked, "What does personality predict well, if anything?" En route to answering this question, we observed that broader personality traits are predictive of major life outcomes such as happiness (DeNeve & Cooper, 1998) and mortality (Roberts et al., 2007). We also noted that within the context of work, personality has been related to a rather broad range of outcomes, and when we step outside the primary outcome of job performance, coefficients tend to be stronger. Moreover, if we consider data at the facet level—primarily for conscientiousness—coefficients also tend to improve. Taken a step further, including multiple facets of personality results in nontrivial predictive increases, as well. Finally, by carefully considering the job and person, choices of predictor sets are improved and overall validity coefficients increased. On the whole, then, these findings suggest that improvements can be made in the utility of personality in selection contexts. Limitations and concerns remain, however, largely centered on the notion that, even with improvements, coefficients with overall job performance remain modest, at least in comparison with other widely used predictors (Schmidt & Hunter, 1998). In addition, we must also ask ourselves if heading down a path of greater detail, specificity, and refinement will help or harm the use of personality in selection—an issue we consider in the parting comments of the chapter.

Summary and Conclusions

Debates about the use of personality measures in organizations have an unfortunate all-or-none quality, especially when these measures are used to help make high-stakes decisions. Critics of the use of personality testing in these settings (e.g., Morgeson et al., 2007a, 2007b; Murphy & Dzieweczynski, 2005) are sometimes cast as nihilists, who are unaware or unappreciative of the broad validity of personality tests as predictors of organizationally relevant criteria (e.g., Ones et al., 2007; Ones et al., 2005). This all-or-none nonsense should stop. To our knowledge, there are no responsible researchers who believe that personality is irrelevant to the workplace or who believe that personality measures should be universally used in organizations.

The question of why broad personality measures do not perform better as predictors of overall performance across a range of jobs is a broad and fascinating one. The evidence that personality measures do have real predictive value in relation to some criteria, jobs, and settings and not others clearly shows that any understanding of the role of personality in organizations is likely to require nuanced thinking.

Better Measures and Assessment Approaches

Oftentimes, the measures used to assess personality within the organization are not measures designed to assess the Big Five (Ryan & Sackett, 1987, 1992, 1998). Murphy and Dzieweczynski (2005) noted that the measures most commonly used include the *Myers–Briggs Type Inventory* (MBTI), the *California Personality Inventory* (CPI), the *Minnesota Multiphasic Personality Inventory* (MMPI), the *Sixteen Personality Factor Questionnaire* (16PF), and the *Guilford–Zimmerman Temperament Survey* (GZTS). All of these can be problematic. The MMPI is most appropriate for measuring psychopathology, rather than normal spectrum personality levels. It may have some utility in high-risk occupations, but has low predictive validity overall. The MBTI, though extremely popular, has yielded disappointingly low levels of construct and criterion-related validity (Gardner & Martinko, 1996; McCrae & Costa, 1989; Saggino, Cooper, & Kline, 2001). Without knowledge of what this test is really measuring, and very little evidence of any predictive power, it is not useful in organizational settings (see also Chapter 16, this volume, on the use of personality-type measures in the workplace). The 16PF and CPI are psychometrically sound scales, but it is not always easy to interpret the scores in terms of the FFM; furthermore, the personality dimensions that these scales are designed to measure are not consistently related to job performance. Along the same lines, the GZTS seems to lack relevance to organizational criteria, despite being used by personality researchers for years.

Second, there is compelling evidence that the method of measurement makes a real difference. Oh et al.'s (2011) recent meta-analysis shows that, at least for some FFM traits, the use of others' ratings (particularly the pooled ratings of several evaluators) rather than self-ratings can make a substantial difference in validity estimates. Precisely why this occurs (e.g., higher reliability for pooled others' ratings, biases in self-ratings and/or others' ratings) is still unclear, but it is obvious that we could do a better job measuring personality, and that this would almost certainly influence conclusions about validity.

Careful Job Analyses and Predictor Choices

Tett and colleagues (e.g., Tett & Burnett, 2003; Tett et al., 1991; Tett, Jackson, Rothstein, & Reddon, 1994) have consistently made the case that we should think of personality like a scalpel, not like a broadsword. That is, personality measures have consistently shown stronger predictive power in some settings and jobs than in others, and a careful analysis of where to use personality measures, which constructs to apply, and what criteria to choose makes all the difference. Unlike cognitive tests, it is not sensible to apply personality tests to all jobs and situations. Rather, it is necessary to know a good deal about the job and the situation in which tests will be applied before a firm prediction about the relevance and usefulness of particular personality inventories can be made.

Unfortunately, the argument for specificity cuts both ways. If the validity of measures of broad personality constructs in predicting criteria such as overall performance and effectiveness is at least sometimes low, this not only drags down the mean, but it also confirms the need for nuanced rather than scattershot thinking about the use of personality measures in organizations. Specifically, although some scholars have found mixed support for personality-oriented job analysis (e.g., Cucina et al., 2005), Tett et al. (1999) make a compelling case that job analysis with special care given to the role of personality in these jobs results in larger validity coefficients (for more complete coverage of personality-oriented work analysis, see Chapter 11, this volume).

Multilevel Consideration

Much of what happens in organizations happens in groups and teams, and personality is likely to have multilevel effects (for more complete coverage of multilevel perspectives of personality in organizations and personality in work teams, see Chapters 8 and 33, this volume). For example, Taggar (2001) examined team composition, group processes, and creativity. When teams lacked adequate interpersonal team processes, teams performed best with only one or two creative individuals. Interestingly, Taggar (2001) also found that both increases and decreases in creative performance operated in multiplicative, rather than linear, fashion when team processes were taken into account. The implications for selection are interesting and, for estimating the predictive value of creativity measures, distinctly challenging.

Multivariate Analyses

An argument can be made for focusing on more specific measures (e.g., facets) rather than relying on measures of broad traits. Using a battery of more specific facet measures rather than simply grouping them into traits would almost certainly raise validity estimates. Caution will be needed here; the biggest concern raised in Guion and Gottier's (1965) review—which arguably started the 40-year roller coaster of assessments of the validity of personality measures in organizations—was not the low validity of measures, but rather the lack of a common core. The more we move in the direction of each researcher favoring a different "basket" of facet measures, the more we will approach the kind of chaos that Guion and Gottier (1965) lamented.

In the early 1960s, the FFM was not yet firmly established, and it can be argued that the lack of a common framework for discussing personality (like the FFM) was at least in part the reason for the lack of a common core bemoaned by Guion and Gottier (1965). Current proposals for focusing on either facets or composite traits can free researchers from some of the limitations of the FFM, but great care must be taken to ensure that we do not end up back in a state where no two personality researchers use the same language or the same inventories to measure normal personality.

If We Do All of These Things, Where Will We Be?

Before turning to our final thoughts, we consider a brief illustration that parallels many of the current issues faced by personality and selection researchers—an illustration that centers on the near downfall of the leadership field (Hunt, 1999). Leadership research began, not uncoincidentally, with researchers asking which traits separated leaders from nonleaders (Bass & Bass, 2008). Known as the great-man approach, work here was fruitful and abundant for several years. As the studies began to pile up, however, scholars noticed a lack of consensus among findings (Stogdill, 1948). With the exception of qualities such as intelligence, there were few individual differences consistently associated with successful leaders. The conclusion drawn by early leadership researchers was that the context should be taken into account for richer understanding of leadership as a phenomenon to be gained. Thus began the situational-contingency approach to leadership, whereby multiple scholars attempted to identify key contextual factors that might have been obscuring important and yet-unknown relationships (e.g., Fiedler, 1964; Hersey & Blanchard, 1969). It was at this point, during the 1970s and early 1980s, that the field settled into the "gloom and doom" phase (Hunt, 1999). Scholars and practitioners saw the field as dull, boring, and nearly pointless (Mintzberg, 1982). The lack of integration, limited over-arching frameworks, and inconsistent findings led to the field standing on the precipice of extinction.

What saved the field was emergent work on charismatic and transformational leadership (Hunt, 1999). These theories were interesting, novel, and exciting. More centrally, they were fairly generalizable—findings held up across organizations, industries, and jobs (Bass & Bass, 2008). Gone were the days of gnashing and fighting about specific situations and specific subgroups. Instead, a new collection of theories invigorated an area and led to the explosion of the leadership field. In a post-transformational leadership era, the field is currently asking itself where to head next and if we have over-relied on these theories, but it would seem that enough momentum has built up from the initial burst that growth will be made on multiple fronts (Hunter, Bedell-Avers, & Mumford, 2007). It seems that leadership research is here to stay.

What might we learn from this illustration? At first glance, perhaps nothing; perhaps the parallels are weak, connections minor, and lessons unrelated. On the other hand, if we look carefully, this illustration may show us the dangers of becoming too specific, too narrow, and too disconnected. We must certainly grow with regard to refinement (e.g., using personality-oriented job analysis and acknowledging bidirectionality), but the lessons from leadership can drive home the importance of broader, guiding theory. It can also illustrate the importance of exciting young scholars about the potential in an area of research. Finally, the illustration reminds us that we must remain cognizant of the organizations, managers, and employees we study and, hopefully, aim to help. That is, although we as academics may grasp the complexities and nuances required to interpret a refined approach to utilizing personality in a selection setting, we might ask whether this specificity limits the practical utility sought by those in organizational applied settings.

Practitioner's Window

Measures of personality are useful predictors of a number of organizationally relevant criteria, but their relationships with job performance and effectiveness are more complex than is the case for measures of general cognitive ability, which predict performance well in virtually all jobs. In particular, the use of personality measures to make selection decisions requires detailed knowledge of the job, along with a clear rationale for the relevance of particular personality traits to the performance of that job.

1. The relationship between personality traits and job performance shows substantial variability across jobs. Some personality traits can be positively related to performance in some jobs and negatively related to performance in others.
2. A good job analysis is critical when applying personality measures in selection. Credible evidence that the tasks and responsibilities of particular jobs require particular personality traits is particularly important.
3. It is not only jobs but also work situations that can influence the validity and value of personality measures as predictors of performance. In particular, jobs that demand working in teams or groups or interacting with external customers may pose demands that require personality characteristics such as agreeableness or extraversion.
4. In using the results of meta-analyses to help guide decisions about the use of personality measures, it is important to pay attention to both the mean of the validity distribution and the variability in validities across jobs. Personality traits that on average do not show much predictive power may nevertheless be good predictors in some jobs.

References

Ackerman, P. L., & Humphreys, L. G. (1990). Individual differences theory in industrial and organizational psychology. In M. Dunnette & L. Hough (Eds.), *Handbook of industrial and organizational psychology* (2nd ed., *Vol. 1*, pp. 223–282). Palo Alto, CA: Consulting Psychologists Press.

Allinger, G. M. (1988). Do zero correlations really exist among measures of different cognitive abilities? *Educational and Psychological Measurement, 48*, 275–280.

Barrick, M. R., & Mount, M. K. (1991). The big five personality dimensions and job performance: A meta-analysis. *Personnel Psychology, 44*, 1–26.

Bass, B. M., & Bass, R. (2008). *Handbook of leadership: Theory, research, & managerial applications*. New York: Free Press.

Campbell, J. P. (1996). Group differences and personnel decisions: Validity, fairness, and affirmative action. *Journal of Vocational Behavior, 49*, 122–158.

Carroll, J. B. (1993). *Human cognitive abilities: A survey of factor-analytic studies*. Cambridge, UK: Cambridge University Press.

Christiansen, N. D., & Tett, R. P. (2008). Toward a better understanding of the role situations in linking personality, work behavior, and job performance. *Industrial and Organizational Psychology: Perspectives on Science and Practice, 1*, 312–316.

Cooper-Hakim, A., & Viswesvaran, C. (2002). A meta-analytic review of the MacAndrew Alcoholism Scale. *Educational and Psychological Measurement, 62*, 818–829.

Costa, P. T., McCrae, R. R., & Dye, D. A. (1991). Facet scales for agreeableness and conscientiousness: A revision of the NEO Personality Inventory. *Personality and Individual Differences, 12*, 887–898.

Cucina, J. M., Vasilopoulos, N. L., & Sehgal, K. G. (2005). Personality-based job analysis and the self-serving bias. *Journal of Business and Psychology, 20*, 275–290.

DeNeve, K., & Cooper, H. (1998). The happy personality: A meta-analysis of 137 personality traits and subjective well being. *Psychological Bulletin, 124*, 197–229.

Digman, J. M. (1990). Personality structure: Emergence of the five-factor model. *Annual Review of Psychology, 41*, 417–440.

Dudley, N. M., Orvis, K. A., Lebiecki, J. E., & Cortina, J. M. (2006). A meta-analytic investigation of conscientiousness in the prediction of job performance: Examining the intercorrelations and the incremental validity of narrow traits. *Journal of Applied Psychology, 91*, 40–57.

Eysenck, H. J. (1979). *The structure and measurement of intelligence*. New York: Springer-Verlag.

Fiedler, F. E. (1964). A contingency model of leadership effectiveness. In L. Berkowitz (Ed.), *Advances in experimental social psychology* (*Vol. 1*, pp. 149–190). New York: Academic Press.

Gardner, W. L., & Martinko, M. J. (1996). Using the Myers–Briggs type indicator to study managers: A literature review and research agenda. *Journal of Management, 22*, 45–83.

Goldberg, L. R. (1993). The structure of phenotypic personality traits. *American Psychologist, 48*, 26–34.

Guion, R. M., & Gottier, R. F. (1965). Validity of personality measures in personnel selection. *Personnel Psychology, 18*, 135–164.

Gustafsson, J. (2001). On the hierarchical structure of ability and personality. In J. Collis & S. Messick (Eds.), *Intelligence and personality: Bridging the gap in theory and measurement* (pp. 25–42). Mahwah, NJ: Erlbaum.

Gutenberg, R. L., Arvey, R. D., Osburn, H. G., & Jeanneret, P. R. (1983). Moderating effects of decision-making/information processing job dimensions on test validities. *Journal of Applied Psychology, 68*, 602–608.

Guttman, L., & Levy, S. (1991). Two structural laws for intelligence tests. *Intelligence, 15*, 79–103.

Hartigan, J. A., & Wigdor, A. K. (1989). *Fairness in employment testing: Validity generalization, minority issues, and the General Aptitude Test Battery*. Washington, DC: National Academy Press.

Heggestad, E. D., & Gordon, H. L. (2008). An argument for context-specific personality assessments. *Industrial and Organizational Psychology: Perspectives on Science and Practice, 1*, 320–322.

Hersey, P., & Blanchard, K. H. (1969). Life cycle theory of leadership. *Training and Development Journal, 23*, 26–34.

Hogan, J., & Holland, B. (2003). Using theory to evaluate personality and job-performance relations. *Journal of Applied Psychology, 88*, 100–112.

Hogan, J., & Roberts, B. W. (1996). Issues and non-issues in the fidelity–bandwidth trade-off. *Journal of Organizational Behavior, 17*, 627–637.

Hough, L. M., & Oswald, F. L. (2000). Personnel selection: Looking toward the future—Remembering the past. *Annual Review of Psychology, 51*, 631–664.

Hough, L. M., & Oswald, F. L. (2008). Personality testing in industrial-organizational psychology: Reflections, progress, and prospects. *Industrial and Organizational Psychology: Perspectives on Science and Practice, 1*, 272–290.

Hough, L. M., Oswald, F. L., & Ployhart, R. E. (2001). Determinants, detection and amelioration of adverse impact in personnel selection procedures: Issues, evidence, and lessons learned. *International Journal of Selection and Assessment, 9*, 152–194.

Hunt, J. G. (1999). Transformational/charismatic leadership's transformation of the field: An historical essay. *The Leadership Quarterly, 10*, 129–144.

Hunter, S. T., Bedell-Avers, K. E., & Mumford, M. D. (2007). The typical leadership study: Assumptions, implications, and potential remedies. *The Leadership Quarterly, 18*, 435–446.

Jenkins, M., & Griffith, R. (2004). Using personality constructs to predict performance: Narrow or broad bandwidth. *Journal of Business and Psychology, 19*, 255–269.

Jensen, A. R. (1980). *Bias in mental testing*. New York: Free Press.

Jensen, A. R. (1998). *The g factor*. Westport, CN: Praeger.

John, O. P., & Srivastava, S. (1999). The big five trait technology: History, measurement, and theoretical perspectives. In L. Pervin & O. John (Eds.), *Handbook of personality: Theory and research* (2nd ed., pp. 102–138). New York: Guilford.

Johnson, W., & Bouchard, T. J. (2005). The structure of human intelligence: It is verbal, perceptual and image rotation (VPR), not fluid and crystallized. *Intelligence, 33*, 393–416.

Judge, T. A., Bono, J. E., Ilies, R., & Gerhardt, M. W. (2002). Personality and leadership: A qualitative and quantitative review. *Journal of Applied Psychology, 87*, 765–780.

Judge, T. A., Heller, D., & Mount, M. K. (2002). Five-factor model of personality and job satisfaction: A meta-analysis. *Journal of Applied Psychology, 87*, 530–541.

Kanfer, R., Ackerman, P. L., Murtha, T., & Goff, M. (1995). Personality and intelligence in industrial and organizational psychology. In D. H. Saklofske & M. Zeidner (Eds.), *International handbook of personality and intelligence* (pp. 577–602). New York: Plenum.

Kuncel, N. R., Hezlett, S. A., & Ones, D. S. (2004). Academic performance, career potential, creativity, and job performance: Can one construct predict them all? *Journal of Personality and Social Psychology, 86*, 148–161.

McCrae, R. R., & Costa, P. T., Jr. (1989). Reinterpreting the Myers–Briggs type indicator from the perspective of the five-factor model of personality. *Journal of Personality, 57*, 17–40.

Mintzberg, H. (1982). If you're not serving Bill and Barbara, then you're not serving leadership. In J. G. Hunt, U. Sakaran, & C. N. Schriesheim (Eds.), *Leadership: Beyond establishment views* (pp. 239–259). Carbondale: Southern Illinois University Press.

Morgeson, F. P., Campion, M. A., Dipboye, R. L., Hollenbeck, J. R., Murphy, K. R., & Schmitt, N. (2007a). Are we getting fooled again? Coming to terms with limitations in the use of personality tests for personnel selection. *Personnel Psychology, 60*, 1029–1049.

Morgeson, F. P., Campion, M. A., Dipboye, R. L., Hollenbeck, J. R., Murphy, K. R., & Schmitt, N. (2007b). Reconsidering the use of personality tests in personnel selection contexts. *Personnel Psychology, 60*, 683–729.

Murphy, K. R. (1996). Individual differences and behavior in organizations: Much more than g. In K. Murphy (Ed.), *Individual differences and behavior in organizations* (pp. 3–30). San Francisco: Jossey-Bass.

Murphy, K. R. (2009). Content validation is useful for many things, but validity isn't one of them. *Industrial and Organizational Psychology: Perspectives on Science and Practice, 2*, 453–464.

Murphy, K. R. (2010). Individual differences that influence performance and effectiveness: What should we assess? In J. Scott & D. Reynolds (Eds.), *Handbook of workplace assessment: Selecting and developing organizational talent* (pp. 3–26). New York: Wiley.

Murphy, K. R., & DeShon, R. (2000a). Inter-rater correlations do not estimate the reliability of job performance ratings. *Personnel Psychology, 53*, 873–900.

Murphy, K. R., & DeShon, R. (2000b). Progress in psychometrics: Can industrial and organizational psychology catch up? *Personnel Psychology, 53*, 913–924.

Murphy, K. R., & Dzieweczynski, J. L. (2005). Why don't measures of broad dimensions of personality perform better as predictors of job performance? *Human Performance, 18*, 343–357.

Murphy, K. R., Dzieweczynski, J. L., & Yang, Z. (2009). Positive manifold limits the relevance of content-matching strategies for validating selection test batteries. *Journal of Applied Psychology, 94*, 1018–1031.

Oh, I., Wang, G., & Mount, M. K. (2011). Validity of observer ratings of the five-factor model of personality traits: A meta-analysis. *Journal of Applied Psychology, 96*, 762–773.

Ones, D. S., Dilchert, C., Viswesvaran, C., & Judge, T. (2007). In support of personality assessment in organizational settings. *Personnel Psychology, 60*, 995–1027.

Ones, D. S., & Viswesvaran, C. (1996). Role of social-desirability in personality testing for personnel selection: The red herring. *Journal of Applied Psychology, 81*, 660–679.

Ones, D. S., & Viswesvaran, C. (2001). Integrity tests and other criterion-focused occupational scales (COPS) used in personnel selection. *International Journal of Selection and Assessment, 9*, 31–39.

Ones, D. S., Viswesvaran, C., & Dilchert, C. (2005). Personality at work: Raising awareness and correcting misconceptions. *Human Performance, 18*, 389–404.

Ones, D. S., Viswesvaran, C., & Schmidt, F. L. (1993). Comprehensive meta-analysis of integrity test validities: Findings and implications for personnel selection and theories of job performance. *Journal of Applied Psychology, 78*, 679–703.

Peeters, M. A., van Tuiji, H. F. J. M., Rutte, C. G., & Reymen, I. M. M. J. (2006). Personality and team performance: A meta-analysis. *European Journal of Personality, 20*, 377–396.

Raymark, P. H., Schmit, M. J., & Guion, R. M. (1997). Identifying potentially useful personality constructs for employee selection. *Personnel Psychology, 50*, 723–736.

Ree, M. J., & Earles, J. A. (1991a). Predicting training success: Not much more than g. *Personnel Psychology, 44*, 321–332.

Ree, M. J., & Earles, J. A. (1991b). The stability of g across different methods of estimation. *Intelligence, 15*, 271–278.

Ree, M. J., Earles, J. A., & Teachout, M. S. (1994). Predicting job performance: Not much more than g. *Journal of Applied Psychology, 79*, 518–524.

Riggio, R. E., & Taylor, S. J. (2000). Personality and communication skills as predictors of hospice nurse performance. *Journal of Business and Psychology, 15*, 351–359.

Roberts, B. W., Chernyshenko, O. S., Stark, S., & Goldberg, L. R. (2005). The structure of conscientiousness: An empirical investigation based on seven major personality questionnaires. *Personality Psychology, 58*, 103–139.

Roberts, B. W., Kuncel, N. R., Shiner, R., Caspi, A., & Goldberg, L. R. (2007). The power of personality: The comparative validity of personality traits, socioeconomic status, and cognitive ability for predicting important life outcomes. *Perspectives on Psychological Science, 2*, 313–345.

Rothstein, R. G., & Goffin, R. D. (2006). The use of personality measures in personnel selection: What does current research support? *Human Resource Management Review, 16*, 155–180.

Rushton, J. P., & Irwing, P. (2008). A general factor of personality (GFP) from two meta-analyses of the Big Five: Digman (1997) and Mount, Barrick, Scullen, and Rounds (2005). *Personality and Individual Differences, 45*, 679–683.

Ryan, A. M., & Sackett, P. R. (1987). A survey of individual assessment practices by I/O psychologists. *Personnel Psychology, 40*, 455–488.

Ryan, A. M., & Sackett, P. R. (1992). Relationships between graduate training, professional affiliation, and individual psychological assessment practices for personnel decisions. *Personnel Psychology, 45*, 363–385.

Ryan, A. M., & Sackett, P. R. (1998). Individual assessment: The research base. In R. Jeanneret & R. Silzer (Eds.), *Individual psychological assessment: Predicting behavior in organizational settings* (pp. 54–87). San Francisco: Jossey-Bass.
Sackett, P. R., Schmitt, N., Ellington, J. E., & Kabin, M. B. (2001). High-stakes testing in employment, credentialing, and higher education. *American Psychologist, 56*, 302–318.
Saggino, A., Cooper, C., & Kline, P. (2001). A confirmatory factor analysis of the Myers–Briggs type indicator. *Personality and Individual Differences, 30*, 3–9.
Schmidt, F. L., Gast-Rosenberg, I., & Hunter, J. E. (1980). Validity generalization results for computer programmers. *Journal of Applied Psychology, 65*, 643–661.
Schmidt, F. L., & Hunter, J. E. (1998). The validity and utility of selection methods in personnel psychology: Practical and theoretical implications of 85 years of research findings. *Psychological Bulletin, 124*, 262–274.
Schmidt, F. L., Hunter, J. E., & Caplan, J. R. (1981). Validity generalization results for job groups in the petroleum industry. *Journal of Applied Psychology, 66*, 261–273.
Schmidt, F. L., Hunter, J. E., Pearlman, K., & Shane, G. S. (1979). Further tests of the Schmidt–Hunter Bayesian validity generalization procedure. *Personnel Psychology, 32*, 257–281.
Schmidt, F. L., Viswesvaran, C., & Ones, D. S. (2000). Reliability is not validity and validity is not reliability. *Personnel Psychology, 53*, 901–912.
Schmitt, N., Gooding, R., Noe, R., & Kirsch, M. (1984). Meta-analyses of validity studies published between 1964 and 1982 and the investigation of study characteristics. *Personnel Psychology, 37*, 407–422.
Steel, P. (2007). The nature of procrastination: A meta-analytic and theoretical review of quintessential self-regulatory failure. *Psychological Bulletin, 133*, 65–94.
Stogdill, R. M. (1948). Personal factors associated with leadership: A survey of the literature. *Journal of Psychology, 25*, 3–71.
Sturman, M., & Murphy, K. (2010, August). *Sources of error variance and their effects on supervisor's job performance ratings*. Annual Conference of the Academy of Management, Montreal, QC, Canada.
Sumer, H. C., Sumer, N., Demirutku, K., & Cifci, O. S. (2001). Using a personality-oriented job analysis to identify attributes to be assessed in officer selection. *Military Psychology, 13*, 129–146.
Taggar, S. (2001). Group composition, creative synergy, and group performance. *The Journal of Creative Behavior, 35*, 261–286.
Tett, R. P., & Burnett, D. D. (2003). A personality trait-based interactionist model of job performance. *Journal of Applied Psychology, 88*, 500–517.
Tett, R. P., & Christiansen, N. D. (2007). Personality tests at the crossroads: A response to Morgeson, Campion, Dipboye, Hollenbeck, Murphy, and Schmitt. *Personnel Psychology, 60*, 967–993.
Tett, R. P., Jackson, D. N., & Rothstein, M. (1991). Personality measures as predictors of job performance: A meta-analytic review. *Personnel Psychology, 44*, 703–742.
Tett, R. P., Jackson, D. N., Rothstein, M., & Reddon, J. R. (1994). Meta-analysis of personality–job performance relations: A reply to Ones, Mount, Barrick, and Hunter (1994). *Personnel Psychology, 47*, 157–172.
Tett, R. P., Jackson, D. N., Rothstein, M., & Reddon, J. R. (1999). Meta-analysis of bidirectional relations in personality–job performance research. *Human Performance, 12*, 1–29.
Tett, R. P., Steele, J. R., & Beauregard, R. S. (2003). Broad and narrow measures on both sides of the personality–job performance relationship. *Journal of Organizational Behavior, 24*, 335–356.
Van Iddekinge, C. H., Taylor, M., & Eidson, C. E. (2005). Broad versus narrow facets of integrity: Predictive validity and subgroup differences. *Human Performance, 18*, 151–177.
Vernon, P. E. (1964). *The structure of human abilities*. London, England: Methuen.

29

Personality and Vocational Behavior

Jo-Ida C. Hansen

Vocational psychology is the basic science that supports career counseling—the applied practice of assisting individuals to choose and adjust to occupations and jobs. Historically, vocational psychology has focused on the adjustment of the individual to work, whereas industrial–organizational (I/O) psychology has focused on solving workplace problems to achieve efficient operations and profitability. However, I/O and vocational psychology and career counseling have overlapping interests in work satisfaction and success or performance. In the extant literature, satisfaction is assessed broadly (e.g., career satisfaction) or with specificity (e.g., satisfaction with pay). Research examining satisfaction also often includes related constructs such as well-being or even physical and psychological health. Performance or success is also a multifaceted outcome variable and is assessed in the literature both subjectively (e.g., supervisor ratings) and objectively (e.g., billable hours) and includes a range of behaviors from employee turnover intentions to salary increases. Satisfaction often lines up as the individual outcome variable and performance as the organizational outcome variable, as is the case in the Theory of Work Adjustment's (TWA; Dawis & Lofquist, 1984) outcome variables of satisfaction (the individual) and satisfactoriness (the job or organization). Thus, articulating individual goals and organizational goals, and then translating those into congruent outcome behaviors, is essential for studying both satisfaction and performance. Three approaches—person–environment (P-E) fit, developmental, and social learning—have dominated the theoretical literature of vocational psychology. The P-E fit approach is the one that most clearly incorporates personality.

Of course, the relation of personality to variables other than satisfaction and performance also has been studied, and this *Handbook* provides overviews of other major constructs that relate to personality (e.g., affective cognitive and behavioral job attitudes [Chapter 32, this volume]; counterproductive work behavior [Chapter 27, this volume]; occupational stress [Chapter 31, this volume]; talent management [Chapter 25, this volume]; workplace citizenship [Chapter 26, this volume]; leadership [Chapter 34, this volume]; and teams [Chapter 33, this volume]). Therefore, this chapter will focus primarily on personality and, its relations to other vocational behavior predictors (e.g., interests, abilities, and values) and to vocational outcome behaviors representing satisfaction and performance criteria broadly defined. The following content will focus on a brief history of vocational psychology, an overview of four P-E fit models, the intersection of personality with interests, abilities, and values, and the efficacy of these traits to predict satisfaction and performance. This chapter also will introduce a neuroscientific model of interests and personality and will conclude with suggestions for practice.

History of Vocational Psychology

The historical roots of the field of vocational psychology often are traced back to the work and writing of a Boston attorney, Frank Parsons, in the early 1900s. As the United States transformed from an agrarian society to one focused on manufacturing, and as poor immigrant workers strove to improve their quality of life, the vocational guidance movement emerged to help place young workers (mostly men) into jobs and careers. Parsons' (1909) model for career counseling, which emphasized the promotion of self-understanding (i.e., true reasoning), analysis of the requirements of jobs, and the match of worker strengths with the demands of the work environment, evolved out of his work with an immigrant community center called the Civic Service House. Parsons' approach to vocational guidance in turn evolved into the trait–factor approach to career counseling and vocational psychology (now commonly called the person–environment or P-E fit model) popularized by D. G. Paterson and E. G. Williamson at the University of Minnesota (Ewing, 1990).

The goal of early P-E fit models was to promote employee job and financial security with the expectation that this stability in workers' lives would lead to political and social empowerment. The emphasis of the early P-E fit movement was on the quality of life of the individual; somewhat later, industry embraced P-E fit as a tool for increasing worker productivity. The faculty at Harvard University was especially interested in Parsons' vocational guidance work. John Brewer, in education, argued that vocational guidance should be part of the educational experience. Hugo Münsterberg, in the psychology department, focused on the assessment of individual differences as an important component in guidance; this branch of vocational guidance became known as vocational psychology (Baker & Subich, 2008; Brewer, 1932).

Parsons' influence cannot be denied, but another stream of historical events was equally influential and necessary in the evolution of vocational psychology. This second stream was the testing and assessment movement that began during World War I (WWI). This war, as well as World War II (WWII), brought together U.S. psychologists and gave them the motivation and opportunity to develop assessments that are at the core of vocational psychology and essential for studying and understanding vocational behavior.

WWI stimulated the need for efficient methods for testing aptitudes, evaluating the performance of officers, and developing skill requirements for hundreds of military jobs. Robert M. Yerkes, president of the American Psychological Association, organized a number of committees to assist the war effort. The Committee on the Classification of Personnel led the effort to develop the first paper-and-pencil tests of intelligence—the Army Alpha (a verbal test) and the Army Beta (a nonverbal test for those with limited English language skills)—that could be administered on a large-scale basis. The approach used to develop the Army Alpha and Army Beta subsequently was employed to develop group-administered tests for civilians.

Another area of psychological testing that evolved during WWI was personality assessment. The *Personal Data Sheet*, developed by Woodworth (DuBois, 1970) and intended to identify seriously disturbed men not suited for military service, was not completed in time for actual use before the war ended. However, civilian forms also were developed and became the model for inventories designed to assess emotional adjustment. Several hundred personality tests now are available for use for a range of purposes including mental health evaluations, vocational decision making, and personnel selection.

After WWI, several members of the classification committee went to the Carnegie Institute of Technology in Pittsburgh, which became a hub of activity related to applied psychology. A legacy of this period at Carnegie was the development of the Carnegie Interest Inventory, which is considered to be the first standardized interest inventory. Several inventories were later derived from the original Carnegie Inventory item pool, including the Vocational Interest Blank developed by Strong (1927). Among these early interest inventories, Strong is the only one still published (*Strong Interest Inventory*, SII; Donnay et al., 2005), and Strong's method of empirical contrast groups, which discriminates the interests of specific occupations from people-in-general, still is used for SII Occupational Scale construction. (The empirical method of contrast groups later was used for construction of the Minnesota Multiphasic Personality Inventory [MMPI; Hathaway & McKinley, 1934] and the California Psychological Inventory [CPI; Gough, 1956].)

The first Great Depression, in the 1930s, stimulated the use of psychological tests and occupational information developed in the previous decade. Donald G. Paterson, in the psychology department of the University of Minnesota, directed the Minnesota Employment Stabilization Research Institute (MESRI) which, with the support of federal funding for large-scale studies of selection in education and industry to promote job placement, became a model for integrating P-E fit theories with ability and interest assessment to help workers reenter the labor force after returning from military duty. The United States Employment Service (USES), along with public and private counseling centers, implemented the methods developed in the MESRI project. Paterson's work was broadly in the areas of employee selection and vocational counseling, which allowed him to approach issues of job fit from the perspective of the employee or job applicant as well as the organization. More recently, the field of Occupational Health Psychology (OHP) also has focused on the interplay between workers and organizations to the benefit of both management and employees (Erdheim, Zickar, & Yankelevich, 2007; Hansen, in press).

WWII demanded, as did WWI, that "almost every [military] person with any training as a psychologist become involved in some way with assessment activities, either for selection and training of military personnel or for psychological diagnosis of military casualties" (Gelso & Fretz, 2001, p. 33). Military psychologists advanced psychological testing by using factor analysis to construct multiple aptitude test batteries. This work in turn led to the development of aptitude tests for civilian use.

Following WWII, veterans who had been dislocated for several years were returning to their communities and looking for opportunities to improve their lives. For many, the GI Bill gave them the resources necessary to pursue higher education—both at the undergraduate and graduate levels—and universities realized the need to provide counseling and career development services for these returning veterans. These services emphasized the assessment of interests and abilities to aid in the career decision-making process. Paterson's work at this time, which emphasized P-E fit, led the movement that became known as the Minnesota Point of View. The model was the trait- and factor-approach that involved individual assessment of students to help them find the best match between their abilities and interests and university courses. The Minnesota Point of View, often referred to as "three interviews and a cloud of dust" or "test 'em and tell 'em" because of its heavy emphasis on assessment in the context of brief therapy, influenced vocational counseling in colleges and universities across the United States (Williamson, 1947).

Thus, the first half of the 20th Century focused on the development and use of assessment techniques. Applied psychology, including vocational, I/O, and clinical psychology, embraced testing. Vocational psychology employed assessment to measure interests, abilities, and personality; industrial psychology assessed aptitudes and abilities for selection; and clinical psychology used tests of personality and intelligence.

Personality in Vocational Psychology

Broadly construed, within vocational psychology, personality has included a range of affective or nonintellectual aspects of behavior—emotional states, interpersonal relations, motivation, interests, and attitudes. Guilford (Guilford, 1959; Guilford, Christensen, Bond, & Sutton, 1954), for example, proposed that an individual's personality included aptitudes, attitudes, interests, needs, physiological characteristics, and temperament. The organization of these traits and the patterns of the organization revealed through factor analysis provided, according to Guilford, a parsimonious, comprehensive description of personality. Most trait and factor theorists would define personality more narrowly than did Guilford and focus more on needs and temperament, and possibly attitudes, but not on aptitudes or interests. However, some definitions of vocational interests have focused on personality, as well as motivation or drive, and self-concept, and John Holland's Theory of Vocational Personality Types links interests and personality. One of the most comprehensive definitions of interests, which stresses personality and motivation variables, states:

> The interests of an individual can be defined as his [or her] like for, dislike for, or indifference to something such as an object, occupation, a person, a task, an idea, or an activity. Interests are one aspect of what is broadly considered as the motivation of an individual. Thus, interests are a part of a person's personality structure or organization. When an individual's interest is described in relation to occupations or the world of work, we speak of his [or her] vocational interests.
>
> *Layton, 1958, pp. 3–4*

While the function of interests has been widely researched and interests have been assessed extensively, the fundamental question of what interests are has not yet been answered. Most often interests simply are described as what the interest test measures.

If one were to develop a pyramid of constructs most frequently researched and most frequently assessed in career counseling settings, vocational interests would be the base, then abilities, then personality, and finally values. Within I/O selection settings, knowledge, skills, and abilities would be the base and then personality, with interests and work values less frequently assessed. Vocational psychology theorists have focused on each of these constructs—abilities, interests, personality, and values—to varying degrees. Holland's Theory of Vocational Personality Types, for example, is a matching (P-E fit) theory that focuses on interests. The TWA (Dawis & Lofquist, 1984), another P-E fit theory, features values and abilities. The Attraction–Selection–Attrition (ASA) model (B. Schneider, Goldstein, & Smith, 1995) highlights the P-E fit of the personality of workers in an organization with that organization's culture; the Multidimensional Theory of P-E Fit (Jansen & Kristof-Brown, 2006) focuses on the multiple environments a worker experiences.

Holland's Theory

Holland's Theory of Vocational Personality Types, first proposed in his 1959 paper and last updated in 1997, proposes six vocational personality types that can be used to capture vocational interests. The six types are realistic (manual and mechanical interests), investigative (scientific and academic interests), artistic (creative, aesthetic, and musical interests), social (work with others, helping), enterprising (leadership and entrepreneurial interests), and conventional (attention to detail). Holland uses these six types, or some combination of the six types, to describe both vocational interests and work environment requirements. Holland's definitions for the six types also draw on the relations of each interest type to personality, abilities, and values. For example, he describes enterprising types as aggressive and sociable, with high self-esteem and speaking abilities (and lacking scientific ability), and valuing economic and political achievement and autonomy (Holland, 1997).

Holland drew on the empirical work of Guilford et al. (1954), John Darley (1938), Strong (1943), Leona Tyler (1951), and Anne Roe (1956) to hypothesize the relations among the six Holland types. He used the hexagon to provide a visual image of the six types arranged in R-I-A-S-E-C order with the types most similar to one another adjacent on the hexagon (e.g., social is adjacent to enterprising) and the types with the least in common diametrically opposed to one another (e.g., artistic is opposite conventional).

The parsimony of Holland's Theory, as well as that of the Five-Factor Model (FFM) of Personality (Costa & McCrae, 1992a; Tupes & Christal, 1961), has contributed enormously to the investigation of the relations between interests and personality. In 1971, Holland published the Self-Directed Search (SDS), an inexpensive interest inventory designed to measure his six types. In addition, the widely used SII (Hansen & Campbell, 1985) incorporated six General Occupational Themes measuring Holland's types (Campbell & Holland, 1972; Hansen & Johansson, 1972) along with 23 Basic Interest Scales. These scales, along with those of the NEO Personal Inventory (NEO-PI; Costa & McCrae, 1992b) and the development of the International Personality Item Pool (IPIP; Goldberg, 1992), enhanced the exploration of the relations between personality and interests.

Holland's Theory posits four constructs that provide a framework for exploring worker–environment relations. Holland's *consistency* is the extent to which a person or an environment's interest code is composed of RIASEC types that are adjacent to one another on Holland's hexagon (e.g., the Holland code RI is more consistent than the Holland code RS). Holland's *differentiation* describes the degree to which one or two interests emerge that are clearly stronger than the other types. Holland's *identity* construct introduces a career maturity component to his theory. The fourth construct, *congruence*, is the most frequently researched among his constructs and lends itself to the exploration of P-E fit between workers' interests and requirements of the work environment. Several indices have been developed (e.g., Hexagon Congruence Index, Swaney & Prediger, 1985; C-Index, S. D. Brown & Gore, 1994; Sb Index, Gati, 1985) to operationalize Holland's version of P-E fit, and a plethora of research studies and meta-analyses have been conducted that examine the relation of P-E fit to job outcomes (e.g., satisfaction and performance; Hansen, in press).

ASA Model

The ASA model (B. Schneider et al., 1995) focuses on personality, attitudes, and values in the context of goals of an organization as articulated by the founder or the top management of the organization. The "personality" of the founder is reflected in ASA by the "organizational goals, and the processes, structures, and culture that emerge to facilitate achievement of these [the founder's] goals" (p. 749). Thus, ASA focuses on the personality of members of the organization; personality is broadly defined to include values, personality, attitudes, and beliefs, which according to B. Schneider et al. (1995) are the predictors of the criterion, which is organizational behavior. B. Schneider et al. (1995) point primarily to case studies to support their contention that the founders of an organization have considerable influence on the organization's culture. The result (their contention) is that organizations tend to seek and prefer homogeneity as an outcome of their selection decisions and that people, in turn, are attracted to organizations because of a fit between person and organization characteristics. B. Schneider et al. (1995) note that two of the limitations of the ASA model are the vague specification or definition of personal and organizational characteristics and the lack of elaboration on how to assess homogeneity. They conclude that this leads to "ambiguity in how fit should be operationalized" (p. 758).

Within the ASA model, attraction is viewed as a process whereby people judge organizations as attractive based on the extent to which the person perceives congruence between her or his own personal characteristics and the attributes of an organization. The second process in the ASA model is selection, which is the procedure used to recruit and hire people who have the personal characteristics the organization desires. The third process is attrition or the departure of people who do not fit the organization.

What places ASA in contrast to other theories about fit, in the organizational behavior literature, is that ASA stipulates the prediction of organizational behavior as the criterion. Other person–organization fit models, whether the situational perspective or the interactional perspective, typically predict behaviors of individuals rather than organizational behavior.

In sum, ASA hypothesizes that (a) the personality differences between organizations are larger than are the personality differences between people in the same organization, and (b) the predictors of interest are organizational behaviors such as structure, process, culture, and effectiveness. ASA also postulates that, over time, organizations may become homogeneous and this homogeneity eventually may have negative consequences (e.g., inability to adapt or change, restriction in range of new ideas, and intolerance to differing points of view).

TWA

P-E fit research has increasingly found its place in the I/O literature to complement the role it has played for decades in vocational psychology. TWA (Dawis & Lofquist, 1984), often one of the models chosen to drive this P-E research, is a theory that postulates both *P-E fit* and *P-E interaction* (Dawis, 2005) and is both a *predictive* and *process* model. *Fit* in TWA is the popular fit model that reflects the extent to which a person's characteristics (P) correspond to the expectations of the environment (E). *Interaction* provides a template for the give and take that inevitably occurs between the person and the environment. The extent to which the environment reinforces and the person's needs are congruent (this state is called "correspondence" in TWA) *predicts* the person's satisfaction. Performance (or satisfactoriness) is the correspondence of the person's abilities to the job's requirements. TWA hypothesizes that satisfaction (predicted by P-E need–reinforcer fit) predicts a person's desire to remain in a job and that job requirement–ability fit predicts the organization's willingness to retain an employee. Tenure results from the decisions to remain and to retain (Hansen, in press). The TWA *predictive* model helps people identify careers and work environments that will bring them satisfaction. But what about those instances in which a person may be dissatisfied? The TWA *process* model conceptualizes the cycle that occurs when people are dissatisfied and work to change either themselves or their environment to reduce their dissatisfaction. TWA calls effort to change the self *reactive*, and efforts to change the environment's skill requirements or reinforcers is labeled *active*. Individual differences in the length of time that people can tolerate discorrespondence have been established, and TWA refers to this construct as *flexibility*. The length of time a person is willing to attempt to reduce dissatisfaction or discorrespondence is labeled *perseverance*. The role of personality and interests is not central to the TWA model. Nonetheless, Dawis (2005) has indicated that both interests and personality, which have modest correlations with TWA constructs, values, needs, skills, and abilities, are known correlates of work outcomes and should be included in vocational research.

Multidimensional Theory of P-E Fit

Some promising efforts have been made to integrate various P-E fit theories to better capture the plethora of variables that contribute to P-E fit and the relation of fit to outcome criteria. One particularly attractive combination is blending Holland's Theory with TWA to capture interests, values, and abilities—constructs that share a small amount of variance but are not redundant—in one model (e.g., Bizot & Goldman, 1993; Lubinski & Benbow, 2000; Ton & Hansen, 2001; Tziner & Meir, 1997). Figure 29.1 provides a simple model for conceptualizing the integration of P and E traits to maximize outcomes. Person (P) traits of abilities, personality, interests, and values are matched with environmental requirements. The environment (E) might be a broad occupation (e.g., psychologist), a specific job (e.g., consulting psychologist with a personnel selection firm), or the organization itself (e.g., a consulting firm).

Jansen and Kristof-Brown (2006) recommend an integrative model that combines multiple environments that a worker experiences—vocation (V), organization (O), group (G), job (J), and person (P). Their hypotheses incorporate the individual's personality style (expressed in FFM terms) and the hierarchical structure or culture of an organization. In a nutshell, they propose that agreeable and social personality types will find P-P and P-G congruence or fit more important (or salient) than P-J

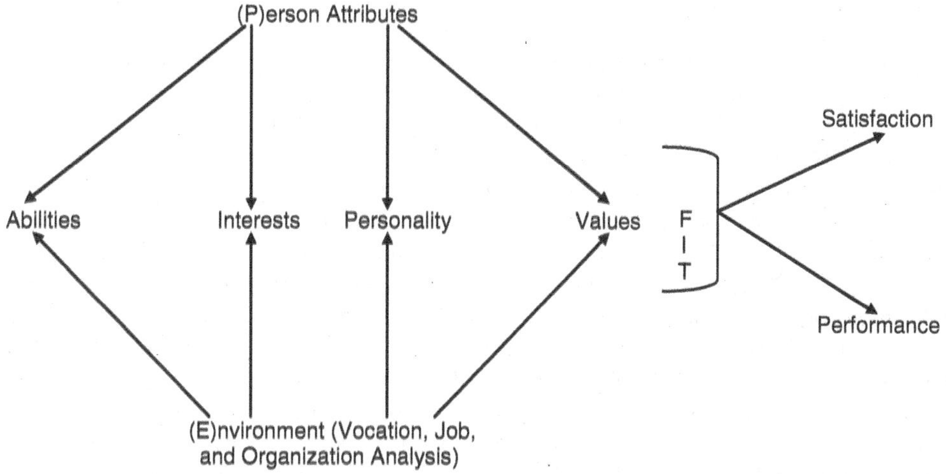

Figure 29.1 Integrative Model of P-E Fit for Abilities, Interests, Personality, and Values.
Note: P-E: person–environment.

and P-V fit. Conscientious and high achievement individuals will find P-J and P-V more salient than P-P or P-G. The salience of the organizational culture in their model is as follows: (a) large organizations with formal hierarchies lead to job (J) or group (G) salience rather than organizational (O) salience; (b) organizations with strong cultures reflect organizational (O) salience; (c) in cases where vocational identity is strong, then one expects high vocational (V) salience; (d) if the organizational culture is weak, then group (G) salience will dominate; and (e) a lack of group norms may lead to high person (P) salience.

Future P-E Fit Research: Cultural Fit

The integrative and multidimensional theories of P-E fit are stimulating research that promises to lead to a better understanding of person predictor constructs (e.g., creativity, cognitive styles, and job complexity), outcome criteria (e.g., burnout, subjective well-being, and job involvement), and moderators of the congruence (i.e., P-E fit)–outcome relation (i.e., personality, perceived fit, adjustment styles, and demographic variables). International and cross-cultural research is exploring the way in which extant P-E fit theories, most of which are based on U.S. and Western cultures, apply to diverse groups. Another direction in this area considers the match between organizational cultures and practices and the values and assumptions of national cultural or ethno-cultural orientations (e.g., Aycan, Kanungo, & Sinha, 1999; Iplic, Kilic, & Yalcin, 2011; Lyons & O'Brien, 2006; Newman & Nollen, 1996).

Personality and Vocational Predictors and Criteria

Abilities, interests, and personality, important constructs in assessment, are popular vocational psychology constructs and have been studied extensively in relation to vocational satisfaction and performance. These traits are sometimes labeled the Big Three of differential psychology, which studies the domain of individual differences. Values and needs, especially those values and needs related to work, are other constructs of interest to vocational psychology. This section provides an overview of these three constructs and their relations to personality as well as satisfaction and performance.

Interests

Evidence of the impact of interests on vocational behavior is robust for career choice outcomes. Hansen and Dik (2005), for example, found that 76% of their adult participants scored high on SII Occupational Scales that matched their current occupation. Similar results are found for the match between occupational interest scores and college major choice (Hansen & Tan, 1992). Another approach for examining the efficacy of P-E fit for various outcomes looks at the correlation of a P-E fit index with an outcome criterion such as satisfaction. The relation between P-E congruence and satisfaction is studied frequently with mixed results. For example, Tsabari, Tziner, and Meir (2005) used meta-analysis to explore this question and found a vocational interest-job congruence relation with job satisfaction of .17, which included 0 in the 95% confidence interval. However, Tsabari and colleagues also found that larger relations were reported for those studies that used Holland's SDS than for those that used the SII General Occupational Themes to measure interests ($\rho = .20$ and .09, respectively). Earlier meta-analyses found small but statistically significant correlations ($r = .13$–.20) between job satisfaction and congruence (Assouline & Meir, 1987; Tranberg, Slane, & Ekeberg, 1993). These mixed results and relatively small effect sizes have led to attempts to unearth moderator variables that may affect the correlations. For example, Dik and Hansen (2011) found that lower job involvement, intrinsic motivation, and psychological participation moderate the relation between interest-job congruence and intrinsic and/or overall job satisfaction. Specifically, and counterintuitively, they found that interest-job congruence seems to be more closely associated with satisfaction for individuals who are *less* invested in their careers. These results suggest that career development opportunities may be most critical for individuals who are least invested in their careers and work. For individuals who are highly committed to work, poor P-E congruence may be mitigated by their intrinsic motivation and they may report job satisfaction regardless of their P-E match.

The dispositional approach to job satisfaction suggests another explanation, in addition to moderation, for low P-E congruence and satisfaction correlations. Several studies have concluded that some individuals have dispositions that lead them to positive feelings about their lives including positive reactions to their work (i.e., job satisfaction). Connolly and Viswesvaran (2000), for example, found moderate relations of job satisfaction with negative affectivity ($\rho = -.33$), positive affectivity ($\rho = .49$), and affective disposition ($\rho = .36$). Ilies and Judge (2002) found that mood, measured with the positive and negative affect scales (Watson, Clark, & Tellegen, 1988), explained 29% of the within-individual variance in job satisfaction. Job satisfaction also has been shown to be related to high internal locus of control ($r = .20$) in addition to positive affect (Fritsche & Parrish, 2005). Research on twins reared together and those reared apart, which shows that 30% of the variance in job satisfaction is inherited, further supports the dispositional approach to understanding job satisfaction (Arvey, Bouchard, Segal, & Abraham, 1989).

Early research on interests and job performance often concluded that interests have little relation to performance. However, Nye, Su, Rounds, and Drasgow (2012) conducted a meta-analysis of the relations between vocational interests and performance, using a broad definition of performance (e.g., completing work, assisting coworkers, completing a degree, and course grades) that explored the relations in both educational and work settings for a variety of performance criteria, with samples that had been taken from several different inventories (e.g., SII, SDS, Kuder Preference Inventory, and Vocational Preference Inventory). They found a baseline meta-analytic correlation of .20. They also examined the relations between interest-job congruence and performance and found a baseline estimate of .36. The meta-analytic baseline estimate for the relation between interests and academic performance was .23; between congruence and academic performance, the baseline estimate was .32. Studies that add interests to ability to predict success also have shown increased predictive power over abilities alone (Hansen, 1994). Generally speaking, persons with interests in an occupation and the necessary ability do well, but persons with ability but no interest may or may not be successful.

Interests and Personality

In 1984, without the benefit of meta-analyses, Hansen concluded that the most robust correlations between interests and personality occurred between factors that measure social orientation (e.g., enterprising interests and extraversion) and those that measure independent thought (e.g., artistic interests and openness to experience). Subsequent meta-analytic research has supported Hansen's contention that related variables, such as social adjustment, emotional sensitivity, introversion–extraversion, flexibility, independent thought, creativity, dogmatism, authoritarianism, and dominance, share the most variance with interests (Larson, Rottinghaus, & Borgen, 2002; Sullivan & Hansen, 2004; Wilkinson & Hansen, 2006). In fact, scales have been developed using interest inventory items to measure personality traits such as introversion, extraversion, willingness to take risks, dogmatism, and liberalism–conservatism (Campbell, 1971; Campbell & Rossman, 1972; Hansen & Johansson, 1974). Meta-analyses conducted to examine the relations between the FFM of personality and Holland's RIASEC types (Barrick, Mount, & Gupta, 2003; Larson et al., 2002) show that the strongest relations typically are between the enterprising theme and extraversion (r = .35–.41), social theme and extraversion (r = .25–.31), and artistic theme and openness (r = .34–.48). Smaller, but significant, relations have been found between enterprising interests and conscientiousness (r = .07–.22), conventional interests and conscientiousness (r = .17–.25), and investigative interests and openness (r = .21–.28). Realistic is the one interest type that appears unrelated to personality.

Oreg, Neva, Metzer, Leder, and Castro (2009) conducted a series of studies to examine the role of an individual's dispositional resistance to change (RTC) to occupational choice. They found that people in realistic and conventional occupations scored higher on RTC (i.e., were more resistant to change) than did people in enterprising and investigative jobs. They also found two dimensions of RTC—emotional reaction to change and routine seeking—that related differentially to interests. Higher levels of emotional reaction were positively associated with artistic choices (r = .21) and negatively associated with conventional interests (r = –.25), and conversely, greater routine seeking was positively associated with conventional choices (r = .29) and negatively associated with emotional reaction (r = –.21). Understanding the relations between dispositional RTC and vocational behaviors is relevant to the demands of dynamic occupational environments that often require workers to accept change.

Another direction that change research has pursued is the role of personality and interests in predicting job instability. In a longitudinal study over a 15-year period, Wille, de Fruyt, and Feys (2010) found significant positive associations between openness and enterprising interests and job instability (r = .15 in both cases). Conventional and agreeable types were less likely to exhibit external moving behaviors (i.e., changing jobs beyond the boundaries of a current employer; r = –.12 and –.16, respectively). Leadership types (high in extraversion), on the other hand, exhibited internal job mobility (i.e., job changes within the same employer; r = .17). Negative relations were found between agreeableness and overall job instability (r = –.13).

Proactive personality is another trait that has been studied in relation to willingness to change. Bateman and Crant (1993) describe the proactive person as "one who is relatively unconstrained by situational forces, and who affects environmental change" (p. 105). In other words, proactive people seek opportunities, exhibit perseverance to bring about change, and show initiative. Fuller and Marler (2009) conducted a meta-analysis of 313 correlations from 107 studies to test the relation of proactive personality to a plethora of vocational behaviors (e.g., subjective and objective career success, taking charge, career initiative, networking, creativity, leader–member exchange [LMX], job performance, psychological empowerment, role breadth self-efficacy, flexible role orientation, job search self-efficacy, career self-efficacy, organizational and political knowledge, learning orientation, and entrepreneurial cognitions). Generally, their results showed proactive personality to be a slightly better predictor of vocational behaviors than was any one Big Five variable alone. The results indicated that people with proactive personalities tend to experience career satisfaction (ρ = .31) and job satisfaction (ρ = .30) and overall job performance (ρ = .38). Proactive personality also was related to behaviors such as entrepreneurial cognitions (ρ = .42), networking (ρ = .31), career initiative (ρ = .35), and organizational knowledge (ρ = .31), all of which contribute to career success. Finally, proactive personality also was related to psychological empowerment (ρ = .48) as well as role breadth self-efficacy (ρ = .45), flexible role orientation (ρ = .40), and felt responsibility for constructive change (ρ = .48), and to behaviors that indicate leadership potential—taking charge (ρ = .34) and high quality exchange relationships with supervisors (ρ =.30). The authors conclude that people with proactive personalities are suited to contemporary career paths (e.g., protean and boundaryless career perspectives) and careers that require continuous learning and new skill development. They also conclude that the proactive personality is a compound personality trait that is not fully captured by the Big Five personality traits.

A longitudinal study of college graduates' job search behavior (D. J. Brown, Cober, Kane, Levy, & Shalhoop, 2006) shows that proactive personality is correlated with job search self-efficacy (r = .44) and has statistically significant correlations in the small effect size range with job search behavior (r = .19), job search effort (r = .16), number of second interviews (r = .21), and number of job offers (r = .22). Conscientiousness was significantly related to search behavior (r = .18) and search effort (r = .16) but not to number of second-round interviews or job offers. Not surprisingly, perhaps, two personality variables—extraversion (ρ = .46) and conscientiousness (ρ = .38)—have been identified as predictors of job search behaviors such as search intensity and effort. Openness to experience (ρ = .27) also was related to job search behaviors, and extraversion (r = .41), openness (r = .28), and agreeableness (r = .29) were related to number of job offers (Kanfer, Wanberg, & Kantrowitz, 2001). Positive affectivity and extraversion have been found to relate to search strategies that are socially oriented (r = .40 and .35, respectively) and interviewing success (r = .35 and .30, respectively; Burger & Caldwell, 2000).

Personality and vocational interests also have been studied in relation to turnover intentions (i.e., desire or willingness to leave an organization). For example, negative affectivity is related to intentions to quit (ρ = .28) but positive affectivity is not (Thoresen, Kaplan, Barsky, Warren, & Chermont, 2003). Zimmerman (2008) conducted a meta-analysis that found similar results. Neuroticism (ρ = .29) and negative affect (ρ = .31) best predicted employees' intentions to quit, and agreeableness (ρ = .27) and conscientiousness (ρ = .20) best predicted staying in the job. A study that looked at predictors of police officers who voluntarily terminated and those who remained on the police force found three personality facets, measured with the 16PF, that predicted turnover. Those who resigned, compared to those who stayed, were more venturesome (extraversion), more affected by their feelings (neuroticism), and more tender-minded (openness to experience; Drew, Carless, & Thompson, 2008). The study by Drew et al. also did not find a difference in predictive relations between personality and resignation for women and men.

Motivation to lead (MTL) is a relatively new vocational behavior construct (relative to the long history of vocational psychology) hypothesized to be orthogonal to Holland's six vocational personality types. MTL is construed as three dimensions: affective identity (extraversion, value competition, confidence in leadership ability), social normative (sense of social duty and obligation, confidence in leadership ability), and noncalculative MTL (agreeableness, emotional stability, group or other orientation). Chan, Rounds, and Drasgow (2000) used a series of confirmatory factor analyses (CFAs) to ascertain the extent to which measures of interests, personality, MTL, and individualism–collectivism assessed different constructs and used multidimensional scaling to evaluate the relation of MTL to Holland's hexagon and MTL subscale scores on each Holland type. MTL, which correlates with social and enterprising interests, nonetheless appears to be a relatively independent (or orthogonal) construct. Interestingly, the high-point code analysis for the three subtypes of MTL were equally spread across the six vocational types. This work suggests that leadership is a general *work role* construct independent of the *work domain* captured by Holland's six types. The intersection of work roles with personality is a promising direction for vocational research. As the authors note, their work suggests the importance of evaluating constructs important to various career developmental stages. They suggest, for example, that job content (i.e., interests) may be important prior to and at the time of entry into the world of work but that work role (e.g., leadership position), driven by personality or values, may be more important as careers progress.

As Barrick et al. (2003) note, although interests and personality share variance, nonshared variance still provides the opportunity for both variables to contribute to predictions in vocational psychology. Generally speaking, interests appear to be what motivates people to engage in or avoid certain activities while personality helps to explain how a person interacts with an environment (Hansen, 1994).

Neuroscientific Model of Interests and Personality

Building on the known relations between personality and interests, basic research on the neurological underpinnings of personality has the potential to inform knowledge about the underlying processes of interests. Personality research has linked the behavioral approach system (i.e., the tendency to exhibit positive emotions) to various behaviors such as motivation, affiliation–communion, and positive emotionality. This research conceptualizes approach motivation as having two components: *affiliative/communal tendencies* (e.g., warmth and social bonding) and *agency* (e.g., gregariousness and potency). Communion and agency have been shown to have distinct neurobiological processes, and these distinct processes are theorized to shape personality. The robust relations between social interests and communal facets of personality and between enterprising interests and agentic facets of personality suggest that communion and agency may also shape the development of some interests.

One recent study (Hansen, Sullivan, & Luciana, 2011) supports the hypothesis that vocational interests are shaped by individual differences regulated by the approach system. This study also supports the often-stated hypothesis that personality and some interests develop, to an extent, in tandem and suggests that the approach system is a driving force in this process. Various definitions of interests can be reconciled if interests are in fact regulated by the approach system. For example, some interests (e.g., social and enterprising) would be expected, as early theorists proposed, to be related to positive emotions or to be related to approach behaviors such as occupational entry (this relation with interests is already well established empirically). The social neuroscientific model also offers an explanation for the repeated finding that social and enterprising interests have small relations with abilities. People with low approach motivation, on the other hand, are likely to have interests associated with specific abilities (e.g., perceptual speed with conventional interests, visual perception and reasoning with realistic and investigative interests, and ideational fluency with artistic interests).

Abilities

Abilities are an important predictor of achievement and performance. Cognitive abilities of children, adolescents, and college students, along with past performance (e.g., grade-point average [GPA]), have been shown to contribute relatively unique variance to the prediction of educational achievement ($r \approx .40$ between ability and overall GPA; Kuncel, Credé, & Thomas, 2007). Cognitive ability also has been shown to be predictive of future job performance ($\rho = .51$; Judge, Jackson, Shaw, Scott, & Rich, 2007). Meta-analytic studies also have shown that the predictive power of abilities for vocational outcomes generalizes across cultures (e.g., meta-analyses of European job performance found $\rho = .53$ and training success $\rho = .47$; Hülsheger, Maier, & Stumpp, 2007; Salgado et al., 2003). Ability assessment can play an important role in career counseling by identifying untapped potential and identifying career choices that match a person's strengths (Krane & Tirre, 2005).

Abilities and Personality

An encompassing meta-analysis of the relations between personality and ability scores was conducted by Ackerman and Heggestad (1997). They included 10 ability variables and 19 personality variables, some of which were broad constructs (e.g., well-being) and others that were quite specific (e.g., test anxiety). Not every cell in their matrix had data, but for the 161 nonempty cells, 53% were significantly different from 0 with about half being negative correlations and half being positive correlations. They concluded that personality traits positively associated with ability fell into two categories—those associated with extraversion (e.g., social potency, social closeness, and extraversion) and those associated with intellectually oriented personality traits (e.g., typical intellectual engagement [TIE], openness to experience, achievement, and intellectance). Personality traits negatively associated with ability included stress reaction, alienation, neuroticism, and psychoticism. For the most part, the statistically significant ($p < .05$) correlations are in the small effect size range (e.g., .06–.19). Interesting exceptions include the relation between (a) harm avoidance and speed and visual perception (−.21 and −.43, respectively); (b) intellectance and general intelligence (G) and visual perception (.20 and .31, respectively); (c) openness and G (.33) and crystallized intelligence (Gc), knowledge and achievement, and visual perception (.30, .28, and .24, respectively); (d) TIE and G, Gc, ideational fluency, and knowledge and achievement (.22, .35, .47, and .23, respectively); and (e) test anxiety and G, Gc, learning and memory, visual perception, fluid intelligence (Gf), and math numerical (−.33, −.24, −.22, −.23, −.25, and −.27, respectively).

In spite of relatively small effect sizes for the relation between conscientiousness and abilities (e.g., the only significant correlations found by Ackerman and Heggestad (1997) were negative correlations of −.19 with knowledge and achievement and −.15 with math numerical), many extant research studies identify conscientiousness as a personality predictor of academic and job performance (Barrick & Mount, 1991; Trapman, Hell, Hirn, & Schuler, 2007). Other personality traits also have been shown to have relations with various other specific performance outcomes such as feelings of accomplishment, training proficiency, and job performance ratings for some occupations. For example, extraversion is a predictor of performance variables for managers and sales people, and neuroticism typically is negatively related to career success (Judge & Ilies, 2002; Ng, Eby, Sorenson, & Feldman, 2005). Research that has parsed contextual performance from task performance enhances the predictive power of personality for contextual work behaviors such as law-abiding behavior (r = .58 with dependability), commendable behavior (r = .33 with achievement), irresponsible behavior (r = .24 with dependability), leadership (r = .22 with energy and .23 with work orientation), teamwork (r = .17 with agreeableness), personal discipline (r = .29 with nondelinquency and .25 with traditional values), and effort (r = .21 with achievement; R. J. Schneider & Hough, 1995).

Tett and colleagues (Tett & Burnett, 2003; Tett & Christiansen, 2007) have offered an even more nuanced approach to evaluating the evidence of validity for personality tests as predictors of job performance. Tett and Christiansen (2007) observe, based on seven well-known meta-analyses of job proficiency (Barrick & Mount, 1991), management performance (Hough, Ones, & Viswesvaran, 1998), task performance (Hurtz & Donovan, 2000), leadership (Judge, Bono, Ilies, & Gerhardt, 2002), performance ratings (Salgado, 1997), and ratings of subjective sales performance and objective sales performance (Vinchur, Schippman, Switzer, & Roth, 1998), that evidence of validity exists for all five FFM traits as predictors of performance in some situations. As an example, they note that conscientiousness "yields ρ > = .33 in 10% of studies in each of the seven meta-analyses" (p. 972). They also point to the average upper boundary of the 80% credibility interval across traits of .27 and the large breadth of the credibility intervals (i.e., ranging from .00 to .54, averaging .30) as additional evidence that "situational specificity is a dominant feature of personality-performance linkages" (p. 972). They suggest that evidence of validity for personality prediction of performance will be stronger in those instances when careful job analysis has identified the relevant personality traits to be used as predictors. They also propose, and cite evidence to support their conclusion, that narrow measures of personality (e.g., personality facets) have a predictive advantage over broad personality scales (e.g., the Big Five). Finally, they suggest that the use of personality to predict performance should reflect the multidimensional nature of personality and should treat the scales as a predictor set by using multiple regression/correlation analysis (MRC). They conclude that their approach results in predictive power for personality that equals that of cognitive ability tests (e.g., predictive validity coefficients approximately equal to .33; for a thorough discussion of a personality trait-based interaction model of job performance see Chapter 5, this volume).

Occasionally, personality is proposed as a moderator of the relation between vocational predictors and various criteria (e.g., interest-job congruence and performance). However, Blickle, Wendel, and Ferris (2010) have proposed that political skill moderates the relations between each of extraversion and openness to experience and sales performance. They investigated this hypothesis with a sample of 112 car salespersons, most of whom were men ($N = 103$). Their results indicated that salespersons high on both extraversion and political skill demonstrated more sales proficiency than did those who scored low on both. An even lower level of sales performance was reported for those participants who scored high on extraversion but low on political skill. However, the relation between openness to experience and political skill was not statistically significant. Other research along this line has shown that social effectiveness (i.e., political skill) moderates the conscientiousness–job performance relationship (i.e., conscientiousness is related to performance for socially skilled workers but unrelated or negatively related for workers low in social skill; Witt & Ferris, 2003) and the agreeableness and job performance relation (i.e., agreeableness is related to performance for politically skilled individuals but not for those low on political skill; Blickle et al., 2008).

Cognitive ability and personality have been studied in tandem to predict job search activity. Boudreau, Boswell, Judge, and Bretz (2001) found, for employed managers, that cognitive ability ($r = .11$), agreeableness ($r = .06$), neuroticism ($r = .13$), and openness to experience ($r = .07$) had statistically significant correlations with engagement in a job search. The effect sizes however were small (Boudreau et al., 2001).

Integrative Models of Personality, Interests, and Abilities

Several models have been proposed that integrate interests, personality, and cognitive abilities to form *trait complexes*. These models have honed in on four trait complexes, three of which include personality. The science/math trait complex includes visual perception and math reasoning abilities along with realistic and investigative interests (but no personality types or traits). The intellectual/cultural trait complex includes general mental ability and ideational fluency, investigative and artistic interests, and openness to experience. The social trait complex includes extraversion, social potency, and well-being personality characteristics and social and enterprising interests (but no cognitive abilities). The fourth trait complex, clerical/conventional, includes perceptual speed, conventional interests, and conscientiousness, control, and traditionalism personality characteristics (Ackerman & Heggestad, 1997).

Values and Personality

McCrae and Costa (1996) conceptualize FFM traits as basic tendencies of the person and values as more malleable and subject to development through interaction with the environment. The assessment of work values, however, has received less attention in vocational psychology than has the assessment of interests, abilities, and personality. Yet, TWA posits values and needs (in TWA, needs are the facets that aggregate to represent values) as essential components that reflect work reinforcers that are important predictors of an individual's satisfaction. However, the TWA model does not feature personality directly, and relatively little research has been done to examine the relations between work values and personality. The few studies reported in the literature indicate modest positive correlations between extraversion and agreeableness and the value, work relationships (r = .30 and .34, respectively), and between extraversion and the work values, achievement, comfortable work environment, and relationships (r = .26, .23, and .20, respectively), and a negative correlation between agreeableness and status (r = −.25; Leuty & Hansen, in press). Berings, de Fruyt, and Bouwen (2004) found, for engineering and social science undergraduate majors, relations between conscientiousness and valuing structure (r = .52), rationality (r = .31), and influence (r = .31); openness and teamwork (r = .36) and negative relations with competition (r = −.36), extraversion and influence (r = .32) and creativity (r = .29), and neuroticism and community (r = .32) and stress avoidance (r = .28). Another study (Furnham, Petrides, Tsaousis, Pappas, & Garrod, 2005) found significant positive relations between extraversion and influence/advancement (r = .28) and negative relations between agreeableness and influence/advancement (r = −.34). A study that focused on the values of physicians (Duffy, Borges, & Hartung, 2009) found negative relations between agreeableness and prestige (r = −.23). Adolescents' levels of agreeableness, conscientiousness, and openness also have been shown to become more closely related to values, as well as interests, between the 8th and 11th grades (Hirschi, 2008).

In sum, work values and personality share an average of about 20% variance (Berings et al., 2004). Thus, they are related but also have substantial unique variance. The work done by Dawis and Lofquist (1984), focused on understanding the way in which the P-E fit of worker values and needs, combined with job reinforcers, leads to satisfaction, and how the P-E fit of worker abilities with job requirements leads to satisfactoriness, provides a model for pursing the role of personality in combination with values and needs for career decision making by both employees and employers.

Conclusions

As this chapter has demonstrated, modest relations occur between personality and other predictors of vocational behaviors such as interests, abilities, and values. Thus, each construct has an opportunity to contribute unique variance to explanations and predictions of vocational behavior but at the same time can be conceptualized within one nomological net (i.e., trait complexes). Empirical evidence shows that personality is related to various vocational behaviors and vocational outcomes. Judge, Heller, and Mount (2002), for example, used meta-analysis to examine the relations between Big Five personality and job satisfaction and found small effect sizes with conscientiousness (ρ = .26), extraversion (ρ = .25), and neuroticism (ρ = −.29). Tokar, Fischer, and Subich (1998) also found that extraversion and low neuroticism were related to job satisfaction. As already noted, personality adds unique variance to that explained by cognitive ability for the prediction of performance. Personality characteristics such as locus of control, optimism, anxiety, shyness, and risk-taking (Swanson & D'Achiardi, 2005) all modestly predict job outcomes. Across individuals who have similar ability and interests, personality does add to understanding individual differences in career choices that are not apparent by studying only abilities and interests (Lubinski, 2000). Also, personality and interests in combination have been found to account for significant variance in several values. For example, the value of prestige was predicted by a combination of a lack of agreeableness and social interests, and extraversion and investigative interests for a sample of physicians. Extraversion and a lack of agreeableness also predicted a management work value for the physicians, and scholarly pursuits were predicted by investigative interests and low scores on measures of conventional interests (Duffy et al., 2009).

Today's work environments are characterized by rapid changes that can benefit from a better understanding of the role that personality and work values play in promoting adjustment to work after initial vocational decisions, often based on abilities and interests, are made. Work roles, which often are tied to personality and values, promise to augment our understanding of career paths and career choices along the developmental pathway. The explication of integrative models will most likely have the greatest impact on understanding vocational behavior as well as on translating research into practice.

Meta-analytic research is allowing the science to move to increasingly complete (i.e., inclusion of all relevant variables) models of work satisfaction and performance. Nonetheless, translating these complex models into practice will be challenging and will require detailed job analysis, goal setting exercises, and development of person and job taxonomies. As Guion and Gottier (1965) noted, "in *some* situations, for *some* purposes, *some* personality measures can offer helpful predictions. But there is nothing . . . to indicate in advance which measure should be used in which situation or for which purpose" (pp. 159–160). Thorough job analyses will promote a better match of personality traits and facets with organizational goals and job requirements for specific positions. The utility cost of these detailed analyses needs to be weighed against the benefits, and the translation of the empirical evidence to practice will require organizational commitment and creativity. P-E fit models offer templates for pursuing such translational research. What is known now about the relations between personality, interests, abilities, and values, on the one hand, and work satisfaction and performance, on the other, provides a starting point, but implementation to the fullest extent possible will require enormous efforts at job analysis as well as a willingness to implement large-scale assessment.

One question raised about P-E fit models is the extent to which self-selection of applicants or selection of employees by decision makers, who thought the applicants' personality traits or interests matched the job or organization, results in range restriction. Iddekinge, Roth, Putka, and Lanivich (2011) partially address this question in their study on vocational interests and employee performance and turnover. They conducted range restriction analyses that showed little variance difference between normative and study samples. They propose that employees may self-select and organizations may terminate incongruent employees less often than theories (e.g., Holland's Theory or ASA) predict and that chance plays a role in job selection for some people.

Research on the role of personality in the transition from work to retirement and in retirement adjustment is an area ripe for study as the baby boomer bulge approaches retirement. Currently most retirement counseling focuses on questions concerning finances, health insurance, or social security benefits with little emphasis on lifestyle exploration or the way in which personality may relate to retirement satisfaction. However, research has shown that extraversion (r = .28) and low neuroticism (r = .41) predict life satisfaction of preretirement individuals. Low neuroticism (r = .38), agreeableness (r = .23), and conscientiousness (r = .21) are related to retirement life satisfaction. Neuroticism is the largest correlate of both preretirement and retirement, satisfaction (–.41 and –.38, respectively) suggesting that emotional stability is important in later-life transitions (Robinson, Demetre, & Covney, 2010). Another study (Löckenhoff, Terracciano, & Costa, 2009), using a longitudinal design, found that personality traits did not predict future retirement, but once retirement decisions occurred those who retired exhibited increases in agreeableness and decreases in extraversion compared to those who did not retire. They also found that neuroticism related negatively to retirement satisfaction.

Personality research may be one area that begins to bridge the gap between vocational psychology and I/O psychology. The work being done in OHP, which examines the impact of worker–employer interactions on employee and organization well-being, also has the potential to bridge the gap between vocational psychology, with its emphasis on the well-being of the worker, and I/O psychology, with its emphasis on the success of the employer.

Practitioner's Window

Evidence suggests that personality assessment can be a useful component in career counseling to promote client self-understanding and to identify a match between the client's/employee's strengths and job requirements. Organizations can also use personality assessment as a component in screening applicants or employees for job placement.

1. An individual's personality relates to some, but not all, vocational interests, abilities, values, and needs.
2. Matching people's personality traits, interests, abilities, and values to the requirements of careers, jobs, and organizations tends to increase job satisfaction and job performance.
3. For professions who are involved in selection, placement, evaluation, and development of employees, a P-E fit matching model can guide organizational program development (e.g., a mentor program that matches mentor and mentee on personality traits).
4. The assessment of multiple personal traits such as personality, interests, abilities, and values helps employees and career counseling clients develop a holistic understanding of their strengths and weaknesses, which, in turn, may help them to make more efficacious career decisions.
5. Contemporary career concepts (e.g., frequent job changes, boundaryless careers, and second careers after retirement) that are person, rather than organization, focused also argue for comprehensive and integrated assessment of individual differences variables to help practitioners as they in turn work with employees and clients to help them understand their career development trajectories and to help them make career decisions.
6. While the parsimony of the FFM and RIASEC models is enticing, the use of lower-level traits (e.g., facets of the Big Five or basic interests rather than Holland's six interest types) often results in richer interpretive information for career development work with individual employees as well as incremental validity for predicting outcome criteria than does the use of higher-order measures.
7. Knowing personality, interests, abilities, and values may contribute to understanding why employees who are mismatched with their jobs have more difficulty with particular skill areas than do others. In some instances, training or compensatory strategies can be developed to help them develop the appropriate skills.
8. Congruence between individual difference variables and job requirements may be more important for students and employees who are less invested in their education and jobs than are individuals who are highly invested. Career counseling and assessment may be especially effective in helping them to make career decisions that increase their P-E congruence and hence their satisfaction and performance.
9. Monitoring person–job fit over time is important because an individual's needs and motives can change over time, may be developmentally differentiated, and may depend on contextual factors. A career development approach after selection, with periodic reassessments, is recommended.

References

Ackerman, P. L., & Heggestad, E. D. (1997). Intelligence, personality, and interests: Evidence for overlapping traits. *Psychological Bulletin, 121*, 219–245.

Arvey, R. D., Bouchard, T. J., Jr., Segal, N. L., & Abraham, I. M. (1989). Job satisfaction: Environmental and genetic components. *Journal of Applied Psychology, 74*, 187–192.

Assouline, M., & Meir, E. I. (1987). Meta-analysis of the relationship between congruence and well-being measures. *Journal of Vocational Behavior, 31*, 319–332.

Aycan, Z., Kanungo, R. N., & Sinha, J. B. P. (1999). Organizational cultures and human resource management practices. *Journal of Cross-Cultural Psychology, 30*, 501–526.

Baker, D. B., & Subich, L. M. (2008). Counseling psychology historical perspectives. In W. B. Walsh (Ed.), *Biennial review of counseling psychology* (pp. 1–260). New York, NY: Psychology Press, Taylor & Francis Group.

Barrick, M. R., & Mount, M. K. (1991). The Big Five personality dimensions and job performance: A meta-analysis. *Personnel Psychology, 44*, 1–26.

Barrick, M. R., Mount, M. K., & Gupta, R. (2003). Meta-analysis of the relationship between the five-factor model of personality and Holland's occupational types. *Personnel Psychology, 56*, 45–74.

Bateman, T. S., & Crant, J. M. (1993). The proactive component of organizational behavior: A measure and correlates. *Journal of Organizational Behavior, 14*, 103–118.

Berings, D., de Fruyt, F., & Bouwen, R. (2004). Work values and personality traits as predictors of enterprising and social vocational interests. *Personality and Individual Differences, 36*, 349–364.

Bizot, E. B., & Goldman, S. H. (1993). Prediction of satisfactoriness and satisfaction: An 8-year follow-up. *Journal of Vocational Behavior, 43*, 19–29.

Blickle, G., Meurs, J. A., Zettler, I., Solga, J., Noethen, D., & Kramer, J. (2008). Personality, political skill, and job performance. *Journal of Vocational Behavior, 72*, 377–387.

Blickle, G., Wendel, S., & Ferris, G. R. (2010). Political skill as moderator of personality–job performance relationships in socioanalytic theory: Test of the getting ahead motive in automobile sales. *Journal of Vocational Behavior, 76*, 326–335.

Boudreau, J. W., Boswell, W. R., Judge, T. A., & Bretz, R. D., Jr. (2001). Personality and cognitive ability as predictors of job search among employed managers. *Personnel Psychology, 54*, 25–50.

Brewer, J. M. (1932). *Education in guidance: An examination of the possibilities of a curriculum in terms of life activities, in elementary and secondary school and college*. New York, NY: Macmillan.

Brown, D. J., Cober, R. T., Kane, K., Levy, P. E., & Shalhoop, J. (2006). Proactive personality and successful job search: A field investigation with college graduates. *Journal of Applied Psychology, 91*, 717–726.

Brown, S. D., & Gore, P. A., Jr. (1994). An evaluation of interest congruence indices: Distribution characteristics and measurement properties. *Journal of Vocational Behavior, 45*, 310–327.

Burger, J. M., & Caldwell, D. F. (2000). Personality, social activities, job-search behavior and interview success: Distinguishing between PANAS trait positive affect and NEO extraversion. *Motivation and Emotion, 24*, 51–62.

Campbell, D. P. (1971). *Handbook for the Strong Vocational Interest Blank*. Stanford, CA: Stanford University Press.

Campbell, D. P., & Holland, J. L. (1972). A merger in vocational interest research: Applying Holland's theory to Strong's data. *Journal of Vocational Behavior, 2*, 353–376.

Campbell, D. P., & Rossman, J. E. (1972, September). *Liberalism-conservatism, men, women, and occupations*. Paper presented at the meetings of the American Psychological Association, Honolulu, HI.

Chan, K.-Y., Rounds, J., & Drasgow, F. (2000). The relation between vocational interests and the motivation to lead. *Journal of Vocational Behavior, 57*, 226–245.

Connolly, J. J., & Viswesvaran, C. (2000). The role of affectivity in job satisfaction: A meta-analysis. *Personality and Individual Differences, 29*, 265–281.

Costa, P. T., Jr., & McCrae, R. R. (1992a). Four ways five factors are basic. *Personality and Individual Differences, 13*, 653–665.

Costa, P. T., Jr., & McCrae, R. R. (1992b). *NEO-PR-I professional manual*. Odessa, FL: Psychological Assessment Resources.

Darley, J. G. (1938). A preliminary study of relations between attitude, adjustment and vocational interest tests. *Journal of Educational Psychology, 29*, 467–473.

Dawis, R. V. (2005). The Minnesota theory of work adjustment. In S. D. Brown & R. W. Lent (Eds.), *Career development and counseling: Putting theory and research to work* (pp. 3–24). Hoboken, NJ: Wiley.

Dawis, R. V., & Lofquist, L. H. (1984). *A psychological theory of work adjustment*. Minneapolis: University of Minnesota Press.

Dik, B. J., & Hansen, J. C. (2011). Moderation of P-E fit–job satisfaction relations. *Journal of Career Assessment, 19*, 35–50.

Donnay, D. A., Morris, M., Schaubut, N., Thompson, R., Harmon, L. W., Hansen, J. C., . . . Hammer, A. L. (2005). *Strong Interest Inventory manual: Research, development, and strategies for interpretation*. Palo Alto, CA: Consulting Psychologists Press.

Drew, J., Carless, S. A., & Thompson, B. M. (2008). Predicting turnover of police officers issued the Sixteen Personality Questionnaire. *Journal of Criminal Justice, 36*, 326–331.

DuBois, P. H. (1970). *A history of psychology testing*. Boston: Allyn & Bacon.

Duffy, R. D., Borges, N. J., & Hartung, P. J. (2009). Personality, vocational interests, and work values of medical students. *Journal of Career Assessment, 17*, 189–200.

Erdheim, J., Zickar, M. J., & Yankelevich, M. (2007). Remembering Donald G. Paterson: Before the separation between industrial-organizational and vocational psychology. *Journal of Vocational Behavior, 70*, 205–221.

Ewing, D. B. (1990). Direct from Minnesota—E. G. Williamson. In P. P. Heppner (Ed.), *Pioneers in counseling and development: Personal and professional perspectives* (pp. 104–111). Alexandria, VA: American Association for Counseling and Development.

Fritsche, B. A., & Parrish, T. J. (2005). Theories and research in job satisfaction. In S. D. Brown & R. W. Lent (Eds.), *Career development and counseling: Putting theory and research to work* (pp. 180–202). Hoboken, NJ: John Wiley & Sons.

Fuller, B., Jr., & Marler, L. E. (2009). Change driven by nature: A meta-analytic review of the proactive personality literature. *Journal of Vocational Behavior, 75*, 329–345.

Furnham, A., Petrides, K. V., Tsaousis, I., Pappas, K., & Garrod, D. (2005). A cross-cultural investigation into the relationships between personality traits and work values. *The Journal of Psychology, 139*, 5–32.

Gati, I. (1985). Description of alternative measures of the concepts of vocational interests: Crystallization, congruence, and coherence. *Journal of Vocational Behavior, 27*, 37–55.

Gelso, C., & Fretz, B. (2001). *Counseling psychology* (2nd ed.). Belmont, CA: Wadsworth Group/Thomson Learning.

Goldberg, L. R. (1992). The development of markers for the Big-Five factor structure. *Journal of Personality and Social Psychology, 59*, 1216–1229.

Gough, H. G. (1956). *California Psychological Inventory (CPI)*. Palo Alto, CA: Consulting Psychologists Press.

Guilford, J. P. (1959). *Personality*. New York, NY: McGraw-Hill.

Guilford, J. P., Christensen, P. R., Bond, N. A., Jr., & Sutton, M. A. (1954). A factor analysis study of human interests. *Psychological Monographs, 68*(4, Whole No. 375).

Guion, R. M., & Gottier, R. F. (1965). Validity of personality measures in personnel selection. *Personnel Psychology, 18*, 135–164.

Hansen, J. C. (1984). The measurement of vocational interests. In S. D. Brown & R. W. Lent (Eds.), *Handbook of counseling psychology* (pp. 99–136). New York, NY: John Wiley & Sons.

Hansen, J. C. (1994). The measurement of vocational interests. In M. G. Rumsey, C. B. Wallar, & J. H. Harris (Eds.), *Personnel selection and classification* (pp. 293–316). Hillsdale, NJ: Lawrence Erlbaum.

Hansen, J. C. (2013). Nature, importance, and assessment of interests. In S. D. Brown & R. W. Lent (Eds.), *Career development and counseling: Putting theory and research to work* (2nd ed.). New York, NY: Wiley.

Hansen, J. C. (in press). Person–environment fit approach to cultivating meaning. In B. J. Dik, Z. S. Byrne, & M. F. Steger (Eds.), *Purpose and meaning in the workplace*. Washington, DC: American Psychological Association.

Hansen, J. C., & Campbell, D. P. (1985). *Manual for the SVIB-SCII*. Stanford, CA: Stanford University Press.

Hansen, J. C., & Dik, B. J. (2005). Evidence of 12-year predictive validity for SII Occupational Scale scores. *Journal of Vocational Behavior, 67*, 365–378.

Hansen, J. C., & Johansson, C. B. (1972). The application of Holland's vocational theory to the Strong Vocational Blank for Women. *Journal of Vocational Behavior, 2*, 479–493.

Hansen, J. C., & Johansson, C. B. (1974). Strong Vocational Interest Blank and dogmatism. *Journal of Counseling Psychology, 21*, 196–201.

Hansen, J. C., Sullivan, B. A., & Luciana, M. (2011). A social neuroscientific model of vocational behavior. *Journal of Career Assessment, 19*, 216–227.

Hansen, J. C., & Tan, R. N. (1992). Concurrent validity of the 1985 Strong Interest Inventory for college major selection. *Measurement and Evaluation in Counseling and Development, 25*, 53–57.

Hathaway, S. R., & McKinley, J. C. (1934). *The Minnesota Multiphasic Personality Inventory* (Rev. ed.). Minneapolis: University of Minnesota Press.

Hirschi, A. (2008). Personality complexes in adolescence: Traits, interests, work evaluations, and self-evaluations. *Personality and Individual Differences, 45*, 716–721.

Holland, J. L. (1971). *The counselor's guide to the Self-Directed Search*. Odessa, FL: Psychological Assessment Resources.

Holland, J. L. (1997). *Making vocational choices: A theory of vocational personalities and work environments* (3rd ed.). Odessa, FL: Psychological Assessment Resources.

Hough, L. M., Ones, D. S., & Viswesvaran, C. (1998, April). *Personality correlates of managerial performance constructs*. Paper presented at the 13th annual conference of the Society for Industrial Organizational Psychology, Dallas, TX.

Hülsheger, U. R., Maier, G. W., & Stumpp, T. (2007). Validity of general mental ability for the prediction of job performance and training success in Germany: A meta-analysis. *International Journal of Selection and Assessment, 15*, 3–18.

Hurtz, G. M., & Donovan, J. J. (2000). Personality and job performance: The Big Five revisited. *Journal of Applied Psychology, 85*, 869–879.

Iddekinge, C. H.V., Roth, P. L., Putka, D. J., & Lanivich, S. E. (2011). Are you interested? A meta-analysis of relations between vocational interests and employee performance and turnover. *Journal of Applied Psychology, 96*, 1167–1194.

Ilies, R., & Judge, T. A. (2002). Understanding the dynamic relationships among personality, mood, and job satisfaction: A field experience sampling study. *Organizational Behavior and Human Decision Processes, 89*, 1119–1139.

Iplic, F. N., Kilic, K. C., & Yalcin, A. (2011). The simultaneous effect of person–organization and person–job fit on Turkish hotel managers. *International Journal of Contemporary Hospitality Management, 23*, 644–661.

Jansen, K. J., & Kristof-Brown, A. (2006). Toward a multidimensional theory of person–environment fit. *Journal of Managerial Issues, 18*, 193–212.

Judge, T. A., Bono, J. E., Ilies, R., & Gerhardt, M. W. (2002). Personality and leadership: A qualitative and quantitative review. *Journal of Applied Psychology, 87*, 765–780.

Judge, T. A., Heller, D., & Mount, M. K. (2002). Five-Factor model of personality and job satisfaction: A meta-analysis. *Journal of Applied Psychology, 87*, 530–541.

Judge, T. A., & Ilies, R. (2002). Relationship of personality to performance motivation: A meta-analytic review. *Journal of Applied Psychology, 87*, 797–807.

Judge, T. A., Jackson, C. L., Shaw, J. C., Scott, B. A., & Rich, B. L. (2007). Self-efficacy and work-related performance: The integral role of individual differences. *Journal of Applied Psychology, 92*, 107–127.

Kanfer, R., Wanberg, C. R., & Kantrowitz, T. M. (2001). Job search and employment: A personality-motivational analysis and meta-analytic review. *Journal of Applied Psychology, 86*, 837–855.

Krane, N. E. R., & Tirre, W. C. (2005). Ability assessment in career counseling. In S. D. Brown & R. W. Lent (Eds.), *Career development and counseling: Putting theory and research to work* (pp. 330–352). Hoboken, NJ: John Wiley & Sons.

Kuncel, N. R., Credé, M., & Thomas, L. L. (2007). A meta-analysis of the predictive validity of the Graduate Management Admission Test (GMT) and the undergraduate grade point average (UGPA) for graduate student academic performance. *Academy of Management Learning & Education, 6*, 51–58.

Larson, L. M., Rottinghaus, P. J., & Borgen, F. H. (2002). Meta-analyses of Big Six interests and Big Five personality variables. *Journal of Vocational Behavior, 61*, 217–239.

Layton, W. L. (1958). *Counseling use of the Strong Vocational Interest Blank* (Minnesota Studies in Personnel Work No. 8). Minneapolis: University of Minnesota Press.

Leuty, M., & Hansen, J. C. (in press). Building evidence of validity: Relation between work values, interests, personality, and personal values. *Journal of Career Assessment.*

Löckenhoff, C. E., Terracciano, A., & Costa, P. T., Jr. (2009). Five-factor model personality traits and the retirement transition: Longitudinal and cross-sectional associations. *Psychology and Aging, 24*, 722–728.

Lubinski, D. (2000). Scientific and social significance of assessing individual differences: "Sinking shafts at a few critical points." *Annual Review of Psychology, 51*, 405–444.

Lubinski, D., & Benbow, C. P. (2000). States of excellence. *American Psychologist, 55*, 137–150.

Lyons, H. Z., & O'Brien, K. M. (2006). The role of person–environment fit in the job satisfaction and tenure intentions of African American employees. *Journal of Counseling Psychology, 53*, 387–396.

McCrae, R. R., & Costa, P. T., Jr. (1996). Toward a new generation of personality theories: Theoretical contexts for the Five-Factor Model. In J. S. Wiggins (Ed.), *The five-factor model of personality: Theoretical perspectives* (pp. 51–87). New York, NY: Guilford Press.

Newman, K. L., & Nollen, S. D. (1996). Culture and congruence: The fit between management practices and national culture. *Journal of International Business Studies, 27*, 753–779.

Ng, T. W. H., Eby, L. T., Sorenson, K. L., & Feldman, D. C. (2005). Predictors of objective and subjective career success: A meta-analysis. *Personnel Psychology, 58*, 367–408.

Nye, C. D., Su, R., Rounds, J., & Drasgow, F. (2012). Vocational interests and performance: A quantitative summary of over 60 years of research. *Perspectives on Psychological Science, 7*, 384–403.

Oreg, S., Neva, O., Metzer, H., Leder, N., & Castro, D. (2009). Dispositional resistance to change and occupational interests and choice. *Journal of Career Assessment, 17*, 312–323.

Parsons, F. (1909). *Choosing a vocation*. Boston: Houghton Mifflin.

Robinson, O. C., Demetre, J. D., & Covney, R. (2010). Personality and retirement: Exploring the links between the Big Five personality traits, reasons for retirement and the experience of being retired. *Personality and Individual Difference, 48*, 792–797.

Roe, A. (1956). *The psychology of occupations*. New York, NY: John Wiley & Sons.

Salgado, J. F. (1997). The five factor model of personality and job performance in the European Community. *Journal of Applied Psychology, 82*, 30–43.

Salgado, J. F., Anderson, N., Moscoso, S., Bertua, C., de Fruyt, E., & Rolland, J. P. (2003). A meta-analytic study of general mental ability validity for different occupations in the European community. *Journal of Applied Psychology, 88*, 1068–1081.

Schneider, B., Goldstein, H. W., & Smith, D. B. (1995). The ASA framework: An update. *Personnel Psychology, 48*, 747–773.

Schneider, R. J., & Hough, L. M. (1995). Personality and industrial/organizational psychology. In C. L. Cooper & I. T. Robertson (Eds.), *The international review of industrial and organizational psychology* (pp. 7–129). New York, NY: John Wiley & Sons.

Strong, E. K., Jr. (1927). *Vocational Interest Blank*. Palo Alto, CA: Stanford University Press.

Strong, E. K., Jr. (1943). *Vocational interests of men and women*. Stanford, CA: Stanford University Press.

Sullivan, B. A., & Hansen, J. C. (2004). Mapping associations between interests and personality: Toward a conceptual understanding of individual differences in vocational behavior. *Journal of Counseling Psychology, 51*, 287–298.

Swaney, K., & Prediger, D. (1985). The relationship between interest-occupational congruence and job satisfaction. *Journal of Vocational Behavior, 26*, 13–24.

Swanson, J. L., & D'Achiardi, C. (2005). Beyond interests, needs/values, and abilities: Assessing other important career constructs over the life span. In S. D. Brown & R. W. Lent (Eds.), *Career development and counseling: Putting theory and research to work* (pp. 353–381). Hoboken, NJ: John Wiley & Sons.

Tett, R. P., & Burnett, D. D. (2003). A personality trait-based interaction model of job performance. *Journal of Applied Personality, 88*, 500–517.

Tett, R. P., & Christiansen, N. D. (2007). Personality tests at the crossroads: A response to Morgeson, Campion, Dipboye, Hollenbeck, Murphy and Schmitt. *Personnel Psychology, 60*, 960–993.

Thoresen, C. J., Kaplan, S. A., Barsky, A. P., Warren, C. R., & Chermont, K. (2003). The affective underpinnings of job perceptions and attitudes: A meta-analytic review and integration. *Psychological Bulletin, 129*, 914–945.

Tokar, D. M., Fischer, A. R., & Subich, L. M. (1998). Personality and vocational behavior: A selective review of the literature, 1993–1997. *Journal of Vocational Behavior, 53*, 115–153.

Ton, M., & Hansen, J. C. (2001). Using a person–environment fit framework to predict satisfaction and motivation in work and marital roles. *Journal of Career Assessment, 9*, 315–331.

Tranberg, M., Slane, S., & Ekeberg, S. E. (1993). The relation between interest congruence and satisfaction: A meta-analysis. *Journal of Vocational Behavior, 42*, 253–264.

Trapman, S., Hell, B., Hirn, J. O. W., & Schuler, H. (2007). Meta-analysis of the relationship between the Big Five and academic success at university. *Zeitschrift für Psychologie, 215*, 132–151.

Tsabari, O., Tziner, A., & Meir, E. I. (2005). Updated meta-analysis on the relationship between congruence and satisfaction. *Journal of Career Assessment, 13*, 216–232.

Tupes, E. C., & Christal, R. E. (1961). *Recurrent personality factors based on trait ratings* (U.S. Air Force ASD Technical Report No. 61–97). Lackland Air Force Base, TX: U.S. Air Force.

Tyler, L. E. (1951). The relationships of interests to abilities and reputation among first grade children. *Educational and Psychological Measurement, 11*, 255–264.

Tziner, A., & Meir, E. I. (1997). Work adjustment: Extension of a theoretical framework. In C. L. Cooper & I. T. Robertson (Eds.), *International review of industrial and organizational psychology* (Vol. 12, pp. 96–114). Hoboken, NJ: Wiley.

Vinchur, A. J., Schippman, J. S., Switzer, F. S., & Roth, P. L. (1998). A meta-analytic review of job performance for salespeople. *Journal of Applied Psychology, 83*, 586–597.

Watson, D., Clark, K. A., & Tellegen, A. (1988). Development and validation of brief measures of positive and negative affect: The PANAS scales. *Journal of Personality and Social Psychology, 5*, 1063–1070.

Wilkinson, T., & Hansen, J. C. (2006). The relationship among leisure interests, personality traits, affect, and mood. *Measurement and Evaluation in Counseling and Development, 39*, 31–41.

Wille, B., de Fruyt, F., & Feys, M. (2010). Vocational interests and Big Five traits as predictors of job instability. *Journal of Vocational Behavior, 76*, 547–558.

Williamson, E. G. (1947). Counseling and the Minnesota point of view. *Educational and Psychological Measurement*, 7, 141–155.

Witt, L. A., & Ferris, G. R. (2003). Social skill as moderator of the conscientiousness–performance relationship: Convergent results across four studies. *Journal of Applied Psychology, 88*, 809–820.

Zimmerman, R. D. (2008). Understanding the impact of personality traits on individual turnover decisions: A meta-analytic path model. *Personnel Psychology, 61*, 309–348.

30

Mood, Emotion, and Personality

Jennifer M. George

Moods and emotions are central components of how workers experience their jobs and organizations (George & Jones, 1996, 1997) and can have profound effects on thought processes, decision making, and behavior in organizations (Barsade & Gibson, 2007; Brief & Weiss, 2002; Elfenbein, 2008; George, 1996, 2011). Thus, it is not surprising that both moods and emotions have received extensive attention from researchers as has the link between personality and affect. In this chapter, I discuss the distinction between moods and emotions and highlight research on these important constructs. I then turn to a discussion of the relation between personality and affect. More specifically, I discuss three complementary perspectives on the links between personality and affect: the temperament perspective, the instrumental perspective, and the emotion regulation perspective. Finally, I discuss the construct of emotional intelligence.

Affect in the Workplace: The Distinction Between Moods and Emotions

Affect is a general term that refers to psychological states entailing feelings that are evaluative in nature in that they can be thought of as pleasant/positive/good or unpleasant/negative/bad (E. K. Gray & Watson, 2001; Parkinson, Totterdell, Briner, & Reynolds, 1996). Thus, as a relatively broad and generic construct, affect refers to both intense feelings commonly referred to as emotions and less intense feelings called moods (George, 1996). Unfortunately, in the organizational behavior literature, the distinction between moods and emotions is often vague (George, 2011; Gooty, Gavin, & Ashkanasy, 2009). That is, researchers often use the two terms interchangeably or indicate that they are studying emotions when, in fact, they are studying moods. While both moods and emotions are functional and adaptive in the workplace, they are distinct kinds of states, and appreciating the differences between moods and emotions is important for advancing research in this area.

While some treatments and definitions of emotions focus on their experiential qualities, it is important to keep in mind that emotions are automatic responses to stimuli that have implications for a person's survival or well-being (Damasio, 1999). Thus, a considerable portion of emotional processes take place at a nonconscious level, and nonconscious emotions give rise to consciously experienced emotions some, but not necessarily all, of the time (e.g., Bargh & Ferguson, 2000; Berridge & Winkielman, 2003; Damasio, 1994, 1999, 2003; George, 2009, 2011; Scherer, 2005; Winkielman, Berridge, & Wilbarger, 2005). When emotions are consciously experienced, in addition to being high intensity, they tend to be of very short duration, are triggered by and linked to a salient antecedent cause, command attention, and serve to interrupt cognitive processes and ongoing behavior (Forgas, 1992; George, 2000, 2011; E. K. Gray & Watson, 2001; Morris, 1989; Simon, 1982). Consciously felt emotions provide people with important signals about things that require their attention or cease to require it and result in action readiness to deal with events and stimuli that are important for well-being (Frijda, 1988, 2007; Parrott, 2002).

Moods are low-intensity, generalized, and pervasive affective states that are not directly tied to an antecedent cause (Brady, 1970; George, 2000; George & Brief, 1992; Morris, 1989; Nowlis, 1970; Ryle, 1950). Moods do not command attention and do not interrupt cognitive processes and behaviors (M. S. Clark & Isen, 1982; Forgas, 1992). Moods essentially provide the affective background for ongoing activities, and, in the workplace, as in everyday life, individuals are usually experiencing some kind of mood state (Watson, 2000; Watson & Clark, 1994). Thus, moods are experienced much more frequently in the workplace than are emotions (E. K. Gray & Watson, 2001). Moods have significant effects on cognitive processes and behaviors that have been well documented in the literature (e.g., Bower, 1981; Fiedler, 1991; Forgas, 1995; Forgas & George, 2001; George, 1989; George & Brief, 1992; Isen & Shalker, 1982; Isen, Shalker, Clark, & Karp, 1978). Moods can arise in the aftermath of emotions, such that once the intensity of an emotion subsides because its triggering factor has been dealt with, a mood state of a similar valence to the original emotion is experienced (George, 2000). For example, a worker may experience excitement and joy upon learning that he or she will receive a promotion in the coming months during an early morning meeting with a supervisor. Hours later in the afternoon, the worker is in a positive mood while interacting with clients.

As in everyday life, both positive *and* negative moods and emotions are functional and adaptive in the workplace (George, 2011). While the organizational literature has tended to emphasize the benefits of positive emotions and moods (Elfenbein, 2008), increasing attention has been paid to the often nuanced, important, and adaptive role that negative moods and emotions also play (e.g., Forgas, 2007; George & Zhou, 2002, 2007; Tamir, 2009; Tamir, Chiu, & Gross, 2007; Tamir & Ford, 2009). For example, while anger has been traditionally associated with what are usually considered to be undesirable outcomes in the workplace (e.g., Aquino, Douglas, & Martinko, 2004; Aquino, Tripp, & Bies, 2001; Bies & Tripp, 1998), Gibson and Callister (2010) highlight research in their recent review pointing to the beneficial functions of anger (e.g., Bies, 1987; Frijda, 1986; Tafrate, Kassinove, & Dundin, 2002). For instance, experienced and expressed anger can be beneficial in terms of providing organizational members with information about sources of injustice and unfairness that can be useful in efforts to reduce inequities (Bies, 1987; Gibson & Callister, 2010).

Moreover, the dual-tuning model (George, 2011; George & Zhou, 2007) suggests that, in order to understand the role that affect plays in the workplace, the combined effects of positive and negative affect should be considered. More specifically, the dual-tuning model suggests that positive moods and/or emotions experienced over a time period have different effects on behavior in the workplace to the extent that negative moods and/or emotions are also experienced over that time period and vice versa (George, 2011). Thus, for example, George and Zhou (2007) hypothesized and found, in a sample of workers in an oil field services company, that creativity was highest when both positive and negative moods were high (at different times) and supervisors provided a supportive context for creativity.

Both emotion and mood refer to feeling *states* that fluctuate and change over time, albeit at different rates. As such, a wide diversity of approaches has been used to measure and/or manipulate moods and emotions in organizational and social psychology research ranging from self-report survey methods, diary keeping, and experience sampling methodology to laboratory inductions and behavior and video coding (Barsade & Gibson, 2007). For example, in a diary study, Weiss, Nicholas, and Daus (1999) had managerial workers record their mood states four times a day for 16 days; average mood levels over the 16 days were significantly associated with job satisfaction. Relatedly, it may be the case that one mechanism by which personality affects job attitudes like job satisfaction and affective commitment is via state affect (Elfenbein, 2008). Given the focus of this handbook and chapter, it is now time to turn to the relation between personality and affect more directly and, hence, shift gears to a *trait* approach.

Personality and Affect: The Temperament Perspective

The two major personality dimensions or traits that underlie the experience of positive and negative affect are extraversion or positive affectivity/emotionality and neuroticism or negative affectivity/emotionality. Converging evidence suggests that these two personality traits are dimensions of temperament (L. A. Clark & Watson, 2008; Eysenck, 1992, 1997; Tellegen, 1985; Watson, 2000; Watson & Clark, 1993). While the definition of temperament is not without controversy, temperament essentially refers to innate biological factors that underlie the experience and regulation of emotion and mood (Allport, 1937; L. A. Clark & Watson, 2008; Watson, 2000).

While trait approaches have traditionally strived to identify broad dimensions of personality irrespective of their origins, research on the genetic underpinnings of personality traits (e.g., Bouchard & Loehlin, 2001; Loehlin, McCrae, Costa, & John, 1998; Tellegen et al., 1988) suggests that dimensions of personality, like extraversion and neuroticism, have a considerable genetic component (L. A. Clark & Watson, 2008). Genetic underpinnings of extraversion and neuroticism, in combination with research documenting that these traits are related to individual differences in the experience of positive and negative affect, respectively (e.g., Meyer & Shack, 1989; Tellegen, 1985; Watson & Clark, 1984, 1992, 1997), support the temperament approach to understanding the relation between personality and affect (L. A. Clark & Watson, 2008).

Essentially, the temperament perspective suggests that extraversion and neuroticism have direct effects on the experience of affect, such that individuals high on extraversion are prone to experience positive affect and individuals high on neuroticism are prone to experience negative affect (McCrae & Costa, 1991; Zelenski & Larsen, 1999). According to this perspective, extraversion and neuroticism cause individuals to be more susceptible to experiencing positive and negative affective states, respectively (Larsen & Katelaar, 1989, 1991; Zelenski & Larsen, 1999).

Given the prominence of the Five-Factor Model as well as other hierarchical models of the structure of personality, such as the Big Two and the Big Three (e.g., Digman, 1990, 1997; McCrae & Costa, 1987, 1997; Tellegen, 1985; Watson & Clark, 1993; see below), it is important to understand how these models relate to the temperament perspective. L. A. Clark and Watson (2008) suggest that the Big Three provides a useful structure for understanding temperament that has the added value of being linked to biological underpinnings (e.g., Eysenck, 1992, 1997; Tellegen, 1985). The Big Three has its origins in the theorizing and research of Eysenck (1967, 1992, 1997) and, as described by L. A. Clark and Watson (2008), comprises the traits of neuroticism/negative emotionality (N/NE), extraversion/positive emotionality (E/PE), and disinhibition versus constraint (DvC). L. A. Clark and Watson describe these Big Three dimensions as follows.

Individuals high on N/NE tend to view the world around them in a negative light—as stressful, troublesome, and menacing. They are more likely to experience negative emotions and moods and view their circumstances as problematic. In contrast, individuals low on N/NE tend to be relatively calm, content with their circumstances, and stable. Thus, individuals high on N/NE self-report experiencing higher levels of negative affect in a variety of situations (Watson, 2000; Watson & Clark, 1984). For example, L. A. Clark and Watson (2008) report results from four longitudinal college student samples in which the Big Three, mood, and other variables were measured. In Study 1, respondents indicated how they felt that day (i.e., "today") on the Positive and Negative Affect Schedule (PANAS; Watson, Clark, & Tellegen, 1988) for an average of 44 consecutive days; in Study 2, respondents indicated how they felt that day for an average of 48 consecutive days; in Study 3, respondents indicated how they felt "over the past few days" for an average of 42 two-day time segments; and in Study 4, respondents indicated how they felt "over the past week" for an average of 13 week-long time periods. Correlations between N/NE and average mood ratings over the whole time period for each study ranged between .41 (Studies 1 and 2) and .60 (Study 3).

N/NE has also been found to be significantly related to physical symptom reporting (e.g., Brown & Moskowitz, 1997; Larsen, 1992; Watson, 1988, 2000; Watson & Pennebaker, 1989), and it has been suggested that N/NE might also be associated with poorer coping and inferior responses to actual sickness, partly due to the fact that individuals high on N/NE might engage in more rumination (David & Suls, 1999; John, Naumann, & Soto, 2008; Scheier & Carver, 1993). Consistent with this reasoning, research suggests that rumination and worry might partially or fully mediate relations between neuroticism and anxiety and depression (Muris, Roelofs, Rassin, Franken, & Mayer, 2005; Nolen-Hoeksema, Wisco, & Lyubomirsky, 2008).

E/PE reflects individual differences in positive engagement with the environment (L. A. Clark & Watson, 2008). Individuals high on E/PE have an active and energetic orientation toward life; approach life with a sense of zest, good cheer, and self-assurance; are more likely to experience positive emotions and moods; and enjoy social interactions. Individuals low on E/PE are more quiet and reserved, are less likely to experience positive emotions and moods, and approach life with less energy and self-assurance (L. A. Clark & Watson, 2008). Thus, individuals high on E/PE self-report experiencing higher levels of positive affect in a variety of situations (L. A. Clark & Watson, 2008; Watson & Clark, 1992, 1997). For example, in the four studies described above, correlations between E/PE and average positive mood ratings over the whole time period of the studies ranged from .35 (Study 1) to .49 (Study 3). Research has also documented that individuals high on E/PE engage in more social activities and behavior than individuals low on E/PE (L. A. Clark & Watson, 2008; Watson & Clark, 1997).

It is important to note that N/NE and E/PE in the Big Three are analogous to neuroticism and extraversion in the Big Five (L. A. Clark & Watson, 2008; Watson & Clark, 1992, 1993; Watson, Kotov, & Gamez, 2006). Nonetheless, Wilt and Revelle (2009, p. 36) suggest that it may be premature to treat extraversion and positive emotionality as "redundant constructs." And indirect evidence suggests that neuroticism might be more nuanced than negative emotionality (Hong, 2010). Also, despite their seemingly oppositional orientation (i.e., positive/negative), N/NE and E/PE are independent personality factors (Meyer & Shack, 1989; Tellegen, 1982, 1985; Tellegen et al., 1988; Watson & Clark, 1984; Watson & Pennebaker, 1989); thus, people can be high on both, low on both, or high on one and low on the other (George, 1996).

Consistent with the temperament perspective, research supports the genetic and biological bases of N/NE and E/PE (L. A. Clark & Watson, 2008; George, 1996). For instance, Tellegen et al. (1988) found that about 40% of the variance in E/PE and 55% of the variance in N/NE was attributable to genetic factors in a study of fraternal and identical twins brought up apart and together. As another example, a longitudinal twin study in which N/NE and E/PE were measured at two points in time 6 years apart and at ages ranging from 18 to 59 years strongly supported a genetic underpinning of N/NE and E/PE at all ages (Viken, Rose, Kaprio, & Koskenvuo, 1994). Viken et al. (1994) found heritabilities similar to those of Tellegen et al. (1988), although they tended to decrease by small degrees based on respondents' ages. Research has also focused on the biological underpinnings of N/NE and E/PE (L. A. Clark & Watson, 2008; Depue & Collins, 1999; Eysenck, 1997; Tellegen, 1985). For instance, research suggests that E/PE may be linked to dopamine activity in the brain (Depue, Luciana, Arbisi, Collins, & Leon, 1994).

While N/NE and E/PE are clearly the factors linked to positive and negative affect in the Big Three model (and for that matter in the Big Five model as well), for the sake of completeness, it is useful to also consider DvC, describing tendencies to act in an undercontrolled or overcontrolled fashion. Individuals who are on the disinhibition (undercontrolled) end of the continuum are characterized by impulsivity, a certain degree of recklessness, and a relative lack of concern for the consequences of their actions; experiences and feelings in the present moment are key drivers of their actions (L. A. Clark & Watson, 2008). Individuals on the constrained (overcontrolled) end of the continuum are careful planners who are concerned with the long-term consequences of their actions and steer clear of risk and/or danger (L. A. Clark & Watson, 2008; Watson & Clark, 1993). While DvC does not tend to be strongly associated with positive affect or negative affect, it nonetheless might have implications for the experience of affect (L. A. Clark & Watson, 2008). In particular, L. A. Clark and Watson (2008) suggest that

> . . . the DvC dimension is related more to the style of affective regulation than to the overall affective level . . . Disinhibited individuals experience greater reinforcement from positive stimuli and simultaneously are capable of diverting attention away from negative stimuli. This combination leads them to focus more strongly on the rewards than the risks of behavior and thus to engage in a wide range of pleasurable behaviors. Nonetheless, they are not immune to the negative consequences of these behaviors, and so also report a greater number of behavior-related problems. The end result is a zero balance in terms of overall affective level . . . but a broader range of affective experience.
>
> *p. 275*

The temperament perspective suggests that genetically determined innate and biological factors (i.e., N/NE and E/PE) influence the extent to which people experience negative and positive affect in their everyday lives, including in the workplace. Thus, it should come as no surprise that measures of N/NE and E/PE are significantly associated with negative and positive affect at work. For instance, among a sample of employees in an oil field services company, George and Zhou (2007) found that positive mood at work was significantly and positively related to a measure of E/PE, and negative mood at work was significantly and positively related to a measure of N/NE. Other studies document these relations. For example, among a sample of managers, George (1995) found that positive mood at work was positively and significantly related to a measure of E/PE; in a sample of salespeople, George (1989) found that positive mood at work was significantly and positively related to a measure of E/PE, and negative mood at work was significantly and positively related to a measure of N/NE; and among a sample of professionals and managers in an insurance company, Brief, Burke, George, Robinson, and Webster (1988) found that a measure of N/NE was significantly and positively related to negative mood at work.

Consistent with the overall conclusions regarding DvC and affect discussed above, in the workplace one would expect that DvC would be largely unrelated to the experience of positive and negative affect. However, it might be the case that disinhibited individuals experience a wider range of affective states in the workplace than do individuals who are more constrained (L. A. Clark & Watson, 2008). This is an interesting topic for future research to explore.

Additional support for the temperament perspective comes from psychobiological approaches to personality (Heller, Watson, & Ilies, 2004). Based on the pioneering work of J. A. Gray (1981, 1994), it has been suggested that E/PE and N/NE are aspects of two evolved and adaptive biobehavioral systems (Heller et al., 2004). The behavioral activation system (BAS) is responsible for responses to indicators of conditioned reward and nonpunishment and orients people to engage in activities that will be rewarding or pleasurable (Heller et al., 2004). The behavioral inhibition system (BIS) is responsible for responses to indicators of conditioned punishment and nonreward and orients people to avoid or withdraw from activities that will be punishing or painful (Heller et al., 2004; Watson, Wiese, Vaidya, & Tellegen, 1999). Individuals high on E/PE are thought to have a strong BAS and to be highly sensitive to signals of reward (Depue & Collins, 1999; Heller et al., 2004; Lucas, Diener, Grob, Suh, & Shao, 2000). Individuals high on N/NE have a strong BIS (Depue & Collins, 1999; Heller et al., 2004). Studies that find that individuals high on extraversion are more sensitive to positive mood inductions and individuals high on neuroticism are more sensitive to negative mood inductions are consistent with this reasoning (Gross, Sutton, & Katelaar, 1998; Heller et al., 2004; Rusting & Larsen, 1997).

Importantly, in addition to the broad dimensions of positive and negative affect, moods and emotions have also been studied at more specific/discrete levels. For example, Diener, Smith, and Fujita (1995) focus on understanding the nature of the intercorrelations between the discrete positive emotions of love and joy and the intercorrelations between the discrete negative emotions of shame, anger, fear, and sadness. The PANAS-X scale has measures of four negative affective states (fear, sadness, guilt, and hostility), three positive affective states (joviality, self-assurance, and attentiveness), and four "other" affective states (shyness, fatigue, serenity, and surprise) (Watson, 2000, p. 11).

Relations between these more specific and discrete affective states and personality may be more complex and nuanced than the preceding discussion implies. For example, while Watson and Clark found strong associations between specific positive affects and E/PE and between specific negative affects and N/NE, they also found that attentiveness was more highly associated with conscientiousness than with E/PE, and hostility was related to both N/NE and low agreeableness. Shiota, Keltner, and John (2006) suggest that it is useful to distinguish between specific positive emotion dispositions and their nuanced relations with the Five-Factor traits. Associations between complex discrete emotions such as empathy (Johnson-Laird & Oatley, 2008) and both global and specific dimensions of personality are also likely to be nuanced (Eisenberg, 2000). Additionally, some researchers suggest that personality traits and affective states can be represented by circumplex structures (e.g., Fisher, 1997; Myllyniemi, 1997).

Personality and Affect: The Instrumental Perspective

The instrumental perspective suggests that, in understanding relations between personality and affect, it is important to consider how traits such as E/PE and N/NE result in behaviors, actions, and situations that generate affective experience. It is widely recognized that a variety of situational and contextual factors influence people's affective states, even though people may not be very good at determining what influences those states (Watson, 2000).

With regard to the workplace, Brief and Weiss (2002) review a variety of situational influences on affect. They categorize these situational influences as follows: stress-inducing events and conditions, leaders, work groups, the physical environment, and organizational rewards and punishments (Brief & Weiss, 2002). As Watson and others suggest, environmental factors that influence positive affect are unlikely to influence negative affect and vice versa. For example, stress-inducing events and conditions influence negative affect but not positive affect (Watson, 1988, 2000; Watson & Pennebaker, 1989). On the other hand, social activities, interactions, and physical activity tend to be associated with positive affect but not negative affect (Watson, 2000).

In fact, a wide variety of factors in organizational settings, ranging from the monumental (e.g., layoffs) to the more mundane everyday hassles (e.g., computer problems), have the potential to influence negative affect; likewise, a wide variety of factors in organizational settings ranging again from the more monumental (e.g., receiving a substantial raise or a sought-after promotion) to the more mundane (e.g., a pleasant conversation with coworkers over lunch) have the potential to influence positive affect (Brief & Weiss, 2002; George, 1996; George & Brief, 1992; Weiss & Cropanzano, 1996). For example, experience-sampling studies document the link between workplace events and moods (e.g., Fuller et al., 2003; Miner, Glomb, & Hulin, 2005).

Interestingly enough, after reviewing the research on environmental and situational determinants of affect, Watson (2000) speculates that

> . . . positive mood is related more to action than to thought, and that it is easier to induce a state of elevated Positive Affect through *doing* rather than through *thinking*. Conversely, hard and

intensive *thinking* is more likely to lead to Negative Affect than to Positive Affect, especially if the thinking is directed inward. toward oneself.

p. 102

The instrumental perspective suggests that E/PE and N/NE result in actions, behaviors, and circumstances that generate positive affect and negative affect, respectively (Watson, 2000). For example, this perspective would suggest that individuals high on E/PE experience more pleasant activities and engage in more social interaction (Watson, 1988; Watson, Clark, McIntyre, & Hamaker, 1992) than individuals low on E/PE, and these activities and interactions cause them to experience more positive affect (Watson, 2000). Thus, the instrumental perspective proposes indirect effects of E/PE and N/NE on affect; essentially, E/PE and N/NE are instrumental in fostering circumstances that result in the experience of positive and negative affect, respectively (Zelenski & Larsen, 1999). For example, coworkers of a worker high in E/PE might be more likely to engage in favorable social interactions with the worker and express positive affect when interacting with the worker; these favorable social interactions and expressions of positive affect, in turn, result in the worker being more likely to experience positive affect.

Watson (2000) and Heller et al. (2004) review research bearing on the instrumental perspective. For example, individuals high on E/PE report engaging in more frequent and involved social activities and socializing than individuals low on E/PE (Watson, 1988; Watson et al., 1992). Watson et al. (1992) report the results of two studies that directly address this issue. In the first study, students self-reported the number of times they participated in 15 distinct social activities at the end of each week for a total of 13 weeks; overall engagement in social activities was significantly and positively associated with extraversion. In the second study, students self-reported the amount of time they spent involved in 21 distinct social activities each day over the course of several weeks; overall time spent in social activities was significantly and positively related to extraversion.

Headey and Wearing (1989) studied the link between E/PE and N/NE, on the one hand (measured at Time 1), and the occurrence of favorable or desirable events (e.g., marriage) and adverse or undesirable events (e.g., unemployment) over the following 2, 4, and 6 years, on the other hand. For each of the three 2-year time periods, E/PE was significantly and positively associated with the occurrence of favorable events and unrelated to the occurrence of adverse events. Likewise, for each time period, N/NE was significantly and positively associated with the occurrence of adverse events and unrelated to the occurrence of favorable events. Specifically pertaining to the workplace, E/PE was significantly and positively related (and N/NE unrelated) to favorable job events in each 2-year time period, and N/NE was significantly and positively related (and E/PE unrelated) to adverse job and financial events in each time period. Sample favorable job events included "promoted at work," "your boss praised you for your work," and "your ability to do your job well increased"; sample adverse financial and job events included "you had a financial crisis," "continuous financial worry," "unemployed or seeking work," "sacked or laid off," "you found out you were not going to be promoted," and "trouble or arguments with people at work" (Headey & Wearing, 1989, p. 736). Favorable events experienced during one of the time periods were significantly and positively associated with positive affect at the end of the time period; unfavorable events occurring in one of the time periods were significantly and positively associated with negative affect and also negatively associated with positive affect at the end of the time period (Headey & Wearing, 1989).

Despite such supportive findings, the instrumental perspective, alone, is not able to account for all of the relations between personality and affect (Heller et al., 2004; Watson, 2000). That is, personality continues to be significantly related to affect even when controlling for events, activities, and life circumstances (Heller et al., 2004; Watson, 2000). For example, research has found that E/PE continues to be positively and significantly associated with positive affect controlling for social activity (e.g., Watson et al., 1992) and N/NE continues to be positively and significantly associated with negative affect controlling for difficult life circumstances (Ormel & Wohlfarth, 1991). Moreover, the instrumental perspective does not explain why individuals high on E/PE or N/NE might perform actions and create circumstances for themselves that generate positive and negative affect, per se (Watson, 2000).

On the whole, support for both the temperament and instrumental perspectives and the fact that each on its own might be incomplete suggests that they be viewed as complementary accounts of personality–affect linkages. Hence, in understanding the link between personality and affect in the workplace, it is important to keep in mind that personality has the potential to influence: (a) the level of positive and negative affect experienced, (b) differential reactivity to affect-inducing events and conditions, and (c) the conditions, circumstances, and events that give rise to affective experience.

Personality and Affect: The Emotion Regulation Perspective

At the outset, this section should really be referring to the "Affect Regulation Perspective" rather than the "Emotion Regulation Perspective," given that theorizing and research on emotion regulation concerns both emotions and moods; however, work in this area uses the term "emotion regulation" (e.g., Gross, 2007, 2008a; John & Gross, 2007), and I follow suit here so as to be consistent with the literature I draw from.

Emotion regulation is concerned with the ways in which individuals influence the affective states they experience (Gross, 1998) and can be nonconscious or conscious and automatic or controlled (Gross, 2008a, 2008b; Mauss, Evers, Wilhelm, & Gross, 2006). While emotion regulation is often used to mitigate negative emotions and moods (Gross, 2008a, 2008b; Gross, Richards, & John, 2006), positive affective states are also regulated depending upon the context (Erber, Wegner, & Therriault, 1996; Gross, 2008a, 2008b) and individuals may regulate to increase negative emotions when doing so has instrumental value (Tamir, 2005; Tamir, Mitchell, & Gross, 2008). Thus, for example, an individual may try to downregulate a positive mood when entering into a serious discussion about a problematic organizational issue or commiserating with a coworker who has been unfairly treated. As another example, in anticipation of a workplace confrontation, workers may seek to experience anger (Tamir et al., 2008). Thus, while people typically prefer to experience positive affective states and avoid negative ones, people are also willing to forego positive affective states and experience negative states when doing so is beneficial for goal attainment or has other instrumental purposes (Parrott, 1993; Tamir, 2005; Tamir et al., 2007; Tamir et al., 2008). For example, trait-consistent mood states can be beneficial under certain circumstances (Tamir & Robinson, 2004; Tamir, Robinson, & Clore, 2002).

There are multiple ways in which people seek to regulate their affective states and, relevant to the purposes of this chapter, how people regulate their affect may be influenced by personality. In particular, Gross (2008a) suggests that the five categories of emotion regulation processes identified by Gross and Thompson (2007, p. 10)—situation selection, situation modification, attentional deployment, cognitive change, and response modulation—all have the potential to be impacted by individual differences or personality. Before continuing, it is important to recognize that, while on the surface the experience and regulation of emotion might appear to be distinct processes, in reality they may be highly interconnected. As Gross and Thompson (2007) indicate,

> The notion of emotion regulation presupposes that it is possible (and sensible) to separate emotion generation from emotion regulation. However, emotion regulation is so tightly intertwined with emotion generation that some theorists view emotion regulation as part and parcel of emotion (Campos, Frankel, & Camras, 2004; Frijda, 1986).
>
> *p. 18*

Situation selection concerns the steps people take to help to ensure that they will be in situations that will lead to desired affective states and emotions (or will help them to avoid undesired affective states and emotions) (Gross, 2008a; Gross & Thompson, 2007). For example, a faculty member might purposely choose to avoid scheduling meetings that will include a particularly disagreeable colleague to avoid the negative affective states that typically result from interacting with this person. Situation modification refers to the steps people take to modify or alter the actual nature of a situation so as to influence its emotion/affect-generating qualities (Gross, 2008a; Gross & Thompson, 2007). Extending the prior example, when attending a meeting with the disagreeable colleague, the faculty member might deliberately choose a seat far from where the disagreeable colleague is sitting to limit the chance of eye contact and any kind of direct conversation.

Attentional deployment concerns how and where people focus their attention in a situation to influence the emotions that the situation gives rise to and can include distraction, concentration, and rumination (Gross, 2008a; Gross & Thompson, 2007). With distraction, a person might focus attention away from the situation or away from emotion-eliciting aspects of the situation. Concentration can amplify the experiential qualities of a situation as in the case of a state of flow (Csikszentmihalyi, 1975). Rumination involves directing attention to one's negative feelings, the situation in which they have arisen, and their consequences, and tends to heighten and/or prolong negative affective experience. This type of attentional deployment is discussed in more depth later in this chapter (Bushman, 2002; Gross, 2008a; Nolen-Hoeksema, McBride, & Larson, 1997; Ray, Wilhelm, & Gross, 2008).

Cognitive change refers to altering how one thinks about an emotion-inducing situation or altering beliefs about one's ability to deal appropriately with the situation (Gross, 2008a, 2008b; Gross & Thompson, 2007). Response modulation entails regulating one's emotion-related physiological responses, experiential responses, or behaviors (Gross, 2008a, 2008b; Gross & Thompson, 2007). Thus, response modulation can range from engaging in exercise or using drugs and alcohol to trying to control one's expression of emotion (Gross, 2007).

One form of response modulation that may have important consequences for behavior in the workplace and well-being is suppression. Suppression occurs when individuals try to inhibit the expression of experienced emotions (Gross, 1998; Gross & John, 2003). For example, a team member might try to hide his or her anger when another team member makes a costly mistake, a medical resident might try to hide the fear experienced during the first episode of performing a difficult and complex procedure, and a supervisor might try to avoid laughing when an inexperienced subordinate has an amusing misunderstanding of a work situation. Suppression can be cognitively effortful and has the potential to lead to negative outcomes (Gross, 2008b). For example, individual differences in the propensity to rely on suppression to regulate emotions has been linked to feelings of inauthenticity, lower positive affect, higher negative affect, lower life satisfaction, and less favorable relations with others (Gross & John, 2003).

While certain specific individual differences have been identified that may influence one's propensity to engage in one or more of these emotion regulation processes and/or their effectiveness, for the purposes of this chapter it is perhaps more useful to consider the role of more global dimensions of personality. In particular, John and Gross (2007) discuss some of the ways in which the Big Five personality traits might influence these five self-regulation processes.

Conscientiousness describes individual differences in determination, organization, impulse control, and conformity (Costa & McCrae, 1992; George & Zhou, 2001; J. Hogan & Ones, 1997). People high on conscientiousness tend to be dependable, reliable, and self-controlled; are determined with a robust sense of will and purpose and a desire to achieve; are goal-oriented and work hard to achieve goals; follow rules and conform to norms; and generally are responsible and careful (Costa & McCrae, 1992; George & Zhou, 2001; Goldberg, 1992; R. Hogan & Blake, 1996).

John and Gross (2007) suggest that at least three of the five emotion regulation processes described above may be facilitated by a high level of conscientiousness. Given that individuals high on conscientiousness control their impulses, are organized, and plan for the future, they may be especially proficient at situation selection and, thus, able to steer clear of situations that might result in undesired affective states (John & Gross, 2007). For example, a worker high on conscientiousness likely would plan to ensure that important deadlines are met and thus avoid stressful situations arising out of a lack of time and failure to fulfill commitments. Those high on conscientiousness might also be especially proficient at situation modification due to their high levels of organization and determination (John & Gross, 2007). For example, a highly conscientious worker who is feeling frustrated during a team meeting over a lack of progress toward goal attainment might use his or her determination, organization, and goal orientation to help the team get back on track and make more progress. Attention deployment should also be facilitated by conscientiousness, as being determined, willing to work hard, and striving to achieve goals should help the highly conscious focus their attention in adaptive ways (John & Gross, 2007).

With regard to E/PE, John and Gross (2007) suggest that individuals low on E/PE may be prone to engage in situation selection, while those high on E/PE would not be so inclined given their overall energetic and welcoming approach to life. On the other hand, E/PE is predicted to be positively associated with situation modification, given that individuals high on E/PE might use their high energy, social orientation, and approach motivation to try to change things for the better (John & Gross, 2007). Finally, individuals low on E/PE might be more inclined to engage in the suppression form of response modulation (John & Gross, 2007).

Individuals high on N/NE are expected to engage in less of, and be less effective in, most of the emotion regulation strategies (John & Gross, 2007), in part due to their tendencies to think that people cannot alter their emotions and also to think that their own emotions are intense and hard to manage (Gross & John, 1998).

Openness to experience captures individual differences in curiosity, independence, imagination, sensitivity to aesthetics, and approach to novel ideas, experiences, and unconventionality; the high end of this dimension characterizes those who embrace novelty, variety, and deep experience, whereas the low end characterizes those more inclined toward routine, familiar, traditional, and customary kinds of experiences (Costa & McCrae, 1992; McCrae, 1996; McCrae & Costa, 1997). Individuals high on openness to experience have high levels of access to different feelings, thoughts, approaches, ideas, and perspectives, encounter a wider range of experiences, may be more adaptive to change, and may be more willing and able to come up with new approaches that are inconsistent with the status quo (George & Zhou, 2001; McCrae & Costa, 1997).

Given their openness to their own feelings and also their cognitive complexity and creativity, individuals high on openness might be prone to engage in situation modification, attention deployment, and cognitive change (John & Gross, 2007). Since they are open to their own feelings, they might not be likely to engage in response modulation; and situation selection might depend upon the nature of the situation under consideration (John & Gross, 2007).

An interpersonally oriented dimension, "Agreeableness contrasts a *prosocial and communal orientation* toward others with antagonism, and includes traits such as altruism, tender-mindedness, trust, and modesty" (John, Naumann, & Soto, 2008, p. 138). John and Gross (2007) make few predictions regarding the effects of agreeableness on emotion regulation processes because these effects might depend upon the interpersonal dynamics of the situation. They suggest that individuals high on agreeableness might be less inclined to engage in situation modification, given their greater orientation toward others than to their own self-interest (John & Gross, 2007).

Nonetheless, it is important to recognize that agreeableness might influence others to behave toward a focal individual in ways that have the potential to influence the focal individual's affective experience. As Widiger and Smith (2008) suggest,

> an antagonistic individual is more likely to evoke unfriendly responses from others than is an agreeable person. In a very real sense, those two individuals end up living in different psychological worlds: In one world, others tend to be hostile and mean; in the other world, others tend to be warm and friendly.
>
> *p. 756*

Clearly, multiple aspects of personality are likely relevant to emotion regulation processes. However, much more research is needed to determine the extent and nature of these linkages. Additionally, this research might build from work that focuses on much more specific individual differences underlying emotion regulation (Gross & John, 2003; John & Gross, 2007).

Emotional Intelligence

While the construct of emotional intelligence is not without controversy (Cherniss, 2010), in this chapter I adopt the four-branch model of emotional intelligence put forth by Salovey, Mayer, and colleagues (Mayer, Roberts, & Barsade, 2008; Mayer & Salovey, 1997; Salovey & Mayer, 1990) and, more generally, view emotional intelligence as an ability (Côté, 2010; Mayer et al., 2008) rather than as a mixture of personality, ability, and other constructs. As such, one might wonder why I am covering emotional intelligence in a chapter on personality and affect. I am doing so for at least four reasons. First, as an ability, emotional intelligence is an individual difference variable (as are personality traits). Second, emotional intelligence may influence some of the constructs and processes discussed in this chapter. Third, emotional intelligence has the potential to have both direct and indirect effects on the experience of affect in organizations. And fourth, emotional intelligence (construed as an ability) has been linked to traits in the Five-Factor Model. For example, Brackett and Mayer (2003) found that emotional intelligence as measured by the Mayer–Salovey–Caruso Emotional Intelligence Test (MSCEIT; Mayer, Salovey, & Caruso, 2002) was correlated .25 with openness to experience and .28 with agreeableness.

The four-branch model of emotional intelligence suggests that overall emotional intelligence is composed of four types of ability: (a) perception, appraisal, and expression of emotion; (b) knowledge about emotions; (c) use of emotion to enhance cognitive processes and decision making; and (d) management of emotions (George, 2000; Mayer et al., 2008; Mayer & Salovey, 1997; Salovey & Mayer, 1990). Integrating these areas, Mayer and Salovey (1997) define emotional intelligence as "The ability to perceive emotions, to access and generate emotions so as to assist thought, to understand emotions and emotional knowledge, and to reflectively regulate emotions so as to promote emotional and intellectual growth" (p. 5). Before proceeding, it is important to note that the term "emotional" in emotional intelligence has a broad reference point in that it refers to both moods and emotions (George, 2000).

While there are complexities and nuances involved in the emotional intelligence construct, below I provide a brief overview of the four areas in the four-branch model. This overview is based on the work of Mayer, Salovey, and colleagues (e.g., Mayer, DiPaolo, & Salovey, 1990; Mayer & Salovey, 1993, 1995, 1997; Salovey, Hsee, & Mayer, 1993; Salovey & Mayer, 1990, 1994; Salovey, Mayer, Goldman, Turvey, & Palfai, 1995).

The perception, appraisal, and expression of emotion branch is concerned with both the self and other people. With regard to the self, individuals differ in their own awareness of their experienced emotions and the extent to which they can accurately express these emotions through verbal and nonverbal pathways (George, 2000). Accurate appraisal of one's own emotions can be beneficial with regard to being able to use emotional input in making choices, decisions, and judgments. Accurate expression of emotion to others facilitates effective communication, which can help people accomplish their goals and meet their needs (George, 2000).

Some people are ambivalent about expressing their own emotions, and ambivalence over expressing emotions is associated with depression, anxiety, decrements in well-being, certain psychiatric problems, and lower levels of social support (Emmons & Colby, 1995; Katz & Campbell, 1994; King & Emmons, 1990, 1991). Two forms of ambivalence over expressing emotions have been documented (King & Emmons, 1991). In one form, people actually do wish to express their emotions, worry about doing so, and so do not express them (Emmons & Colby, 1995). In the other form, the expression of emotions is followed by regret over having expressed them. Both forms are associated with the maladaptive outcomes described above and more generally can interfere with developing and maintaining supportive interpersonal relationships (George, 2000).

The accurate expression of emotions also varies across people. At one extreme, alexithymic individuals have difficulty in appraising their own emotions and cannot communicate how they are feeling with language (Apfel & Sifneos, 1979; Krystal, Giller, & Cicchetti, 1986; Sifneos, 1972, 1973; Taylor, 1984; Thayer-Singer, 1977). Alexithymic individuals are prone to certain psychological problems, which may be linked to their being unable to express how they feel (Salovey et al., 1993). People also differ in the ability to accurately express emotions nonverbally (Buck, 1979, 1984; Friedman, Prince, Riggio, & Dimatteo, 1980).

Perceiving and expressing the emotions of others entails being able to accurately appraise the emotions of other people and communicate those emotions. People's abilities differ in this regard; for example, people differ in terms of being able to accurately appraise emotions from facial expressions (Buck, 1984; Campbell, Kagan, & Krathwohl, 1971).

Knowledge about emotions pertains to having a good and accurate appreciation of the causes and consequences of emotions and moods and their evolution over time (George, 2000). People differ in terms of their knowledge about the wide variety of factors (e.g., situations, contextual factors, events, other people) that can influence their emotions and moods and also in terms of their understanding of how emotions and moods change over time. People also differ in terms of their understanding of the consequences of moods and emotions (George, 2000). For example, some people realize that how they process information and make decisions vary depending upon their mood state.

Importantly, the use of emotions to enhance cognitive processes and decision making suggests that individuals high on emotional intelligence not only possess emotion knowledge and understand their own emotions but are also able to use their feelings to function effectively (George, 2000). For example, emotions can signal pressing concerns and issues (Frijda, 1988; George & Brief, 1996) and can be used to make choices (Damasio, 1994); moods foster different kinds of cognitive processes that may be more or less advantageous for different kinds of tasks (George, 2011). Shifts and alternations in emotions and moods can result in more flexibility, more alternatives being considered, a broader perspective on tasks and issues, and a richer appreciation of complexity and ambiguity (George, 2011; Mayer, 1986; Salovey & Mayer, 1990).

Finally, emotional intelligence also includes the ability to manage emotions of both the self and others. For the self, this is a self-reflective process sometimes referred to as the meta-regulation of mood (Mayer & Salovey, 1997). Being able to manage the emotions and moods of others is an interpersonal skill that can help people exert influence over others (George, 2000; Wasielewski, 1985). Clearly, emotional intelligence has the potential to influence the experience of affect of both the self and those around one.

Although theorizing and research on emotional intelligence is increasing (Côté, DeCelles, McCarthy, Van Kleef, & Hideg, 2011; Mayer et al., 2008; Salovey, Bedell, Detweiler, & Mayer, 2000; Walter, Cole, & Humphrey, 2011; Wranik, Barrett, & Salovey, 2007), as Salovey et al. (2000) indicate: ". . . empirical research on emotional intelligence is still in its infancy" (p. 516). Given this state of affairs and the emotion regulation perspective described earlier, perhaps it is useful at this point to discuss Salovey et al.'s (2000) theorizing concerning how emotional intelligence might contribute to effective self-regulation in terms of coping with the past and the future.

Salovey et al. (2000) suggest that emotional intelligence might influence the approaches people take to cope with negative experiences and the effectiveness of these approaches with subsequent implications for affective experience. That is, more successful coping should lead to less prolonged negative affect following a negative experience. One relatively ineffective means of coping with traumatic experiences is rumination—". . . passively and repetitively focusing on one's symptoms of distress and the circumstances surrounding those symptoms" (Nolen-Hoeksema et al., 1997, p. 855). Studies have found that, when people ruminate in response to stressful experiences and emotions, they tend to experience more distress and negative affect over longer periods of time (Lyubomirsky & Nolen-Hoeksema, 1993, 1995; Nolen-Hoeksema, 1991; Nolen-Hoeksema et al., 1997; Nolen-Hoeksema & Morrow, 1991; Nolen-Hoeksema, Morrow, & Fredrickson, 1993; Nolen-Hoeksema, Parker, & Larson, 1994).

While rumination tends to intensify negative affect, writing about negative emotional experiences tends to lead to more positive outcomes and be an effective means of coping with traumatic events (Pennebaker, 1997; Salovey et al., 2000). As Salovey et al. (2000) suggest, "The outward linguistic expression of traumatic experiences facilitates the coping process, whereas internally ruminating over a negative event makes things worse" (p. 511). Emotional disclosure through writing might help people make sense of traumatic experiences and organize their thoughts and feelings so that the negative experiences are imbued with meaning and integrated in some way in people's lives (Pennebaker, 1997; Salovey et al., 2000). With rumination, people are unable to get out of a focus on their negative feelings and cannot find meaning nor make sense of negative experiences (Salovey et al., 2000).

Salovey et al. (2000) suggest that emotional intelligence might equip individuals with knowledge concerning the benefits of disclosure and the abilities to disclose their emotions (through writing or other means), which might help them organize those feelings, make sense of them, and find meaning in them. Emotional intelligence might also help prevent people from falling into the trap of rumination and, more generally, find ways to alleviate negative feelings that come about from thinking about past negative experiences (Salovey et al., 2000). For example, distraction can help people get out of rumination (Morrow & Nolen-Hoeksema, 1990; Nolen-Hoeksema & Morrow, 1993), and individuals high on emotional intelligence might be especially proficient at using hedonically positive activities and events to halt rumination (Salovey et al., 2000).

In terms of coping with the future, Salovey et al. (2000) describe a number of ways in which emotional intelligence might contribute to effective self-regulation such that individuals high on emotional intelligence engage in mental processes that facilitate long-term goal pursuit and the concurrent enjoyment of that pursuit. On the whole, emotional intelligence likely has direct effects on affective experience and indirect effects via multiple routes (e.g., more effective coping and long-term goal pursuit).

Conclusions

The temperament perspective, the instrumental perspective, and the emotion regulation perspective are complementary perspectives that each shed light on significant ways in which personality influences the experience of affect. Thus, in understanding personality–affect linkages in organizations, it is important to keep in mind that (a) biological, innate, partially genetically determined factors (E/PE and N/NE) influence affect; (b) by virtue of their standing on affective dispositions or traits (E/PE and N/NE), workers may create conditions, events, and circumstances that go on to influence the affective states they experience; and (c) how people regulate or do not regulate their affective states has consequences for the experience of those states and is also partially determined by personality. Moreover, emotional intelligence has the potential to directly influence affective experience (e.g., those high on emotional intelligence are able to effectively manage their emotions) as well as indirectly influence affective experience through its effects on coping and the self-regulation of goal pursuit. With regard to emotional intelligence, it is also important to keep in mind that, while the popularization of the construct has perhaps given it an aura of being related to human goodness, like all abilities, emotional intelligence can be used for good/moral/ethical purposes and for bad/immoral/unethical purposes (Côté et al., 2011).

On the whole, personality has many direct and indirect implications for understanding the experience of affect in organizations. Interesting directions for future research include identifying the ways in which individuals' personalities may result in them creating circumstances and situations in the workplace that subsequently influence their affective experience, understanding how personality influences emotion regulation in the workplace, and gaining a fuller appreciation of the direct and indirect effects of emotional intelligence on affective experience at work.

Moreover, given the fact that many constructs and subareas of organizational behavior are affect-laden, personality likely has interesting implications for these subareas as well. For example, affect has been linked to motivation, leadership, and job stress (e.g., Brief, Burke, George, Robinson, & Webster, 1988; George, 2000; George & Brief, 1996), and personality is likely to play multiple roles in understanding the role and functioning of affect in these domains. As another example, while organizational justice has been linked to a variety of attitudinal and behavioral outcomes (for a review, see Colquitt, Conlon, Wesson, Porter, & Ng, 2001), positive and negative affect are also likely related to justice perceptions, and an appreciation of personality's role in understanding affect–justice linkages may fruitfully advance the field. Consistent with this reasoning, George and Zhou (2007) found that supervisor-referenced interactional justice was significantly associated with E/PE ($r = .21$), positive mood at work ($r = .23$), and negative mood at work ($r = -.23$).

Because personality encompasses "the characteristic manner in which one thinks, feels, behaves, and relates to others" (Widiger, Verheul, & van den Brink, 1999, p. 347), personality and affect, while conceptually and empirically distinct, are inextricably linked. Thus, our understanding of the role of personality in organizational life would be incomplete without consideration of the role of affect. Likewise, our understanding of the role of affect in organizational life would be incomplete without consideration of the role of personality. Indeed affect and personality have the potential to interact in organizational settings in multiple and complex ways.

Practitioner's Window

- Personality influences the moods and emotions people experience at work, their reactivity to affect-inducing events and conditions, and the circumstances and context that give rise to affective experience in organizations.
- Emotions are intense, short-lived feelings that are linked to their causes and which interrupt ongoing thought processes and behaviors.
- Moods are low-intensity, pervasive feelings that provide the affective context for ongoing thoughts and behaviors.
- Naturally occurring positive and negative emotions and moods are functional and adaptive in the workplace.
- Naturally occurring negative emotions experienced at work are important signals of problems in need of focused attention.
- Naturally occurring alternations in the experience of positive and negative moods can help people approach problems and tasks in different ways and from different perspectives.
- Two major personality dimensions or traits underlie the experience of positive and negative affect: extraversion/positive emotionality (E/PE) and neuroticism/negative emotionality (N/NE).
- E/PE and N/NE are innate biological factors that are partially genetically determined.
- Emotion regulation is closely connected to emotion generation.
- How people regulate their moods and emotions influences the nature of their affective experience.
- Personality influences how people regulate their emotions and moods.

- Emotional intelligence may influence how effectively people cope with negative experiences and regulate their moods, emotions, and behaviors.
- Rumination (repeatedly and submissively thinking about how bad one feels and the conditions related to these bad feelings) tends to increase and prolong distress.
- Writing about negative emotional experiences can be an effective means of coping with them.
- While personality and affect are distinct constructs, they are inextricably linked.

References

Allport, G. W. (1937). *Personality: A psychological perspective.* New York: Holt.

Apfel, R. J., & Sifneos, P. E. (1979). Alexithymia: Concept and measurement. *Psychotherapy and Psychosomatics, 32,* 180–190.

Aquino, K., Douglas, S., & Martinko, M. J. (2004). Overt anger in response to victimization: Attributional style and organizational norms as moderators. *Journal of Occupational Health Psychology, 9,* 152–164.

Aquino, K., Tripp, T. M., & Bies, R. J. (2001). How employees respond to personal offense: The effects of blame attribution, victim status, and offender status on revenge and reconciliation in the workplace. *Journal of Applied Psychology, 86,* 52–59.

Bargh, J. A., & Ferguson, M. L. (2000). Beyond behaviorism: On the automaticity of higher mental processes. *Psychological Bulletin, 126,* 925–945.

Barsade, S. G., & Gibson, D. E. (2007). Why does affect matter in organizations? *Academy of Management Perspectives, 21,* 36–59.

Berridge, K. C., & Winkielman, P. (2003). What is an unconscious emotion? (The case for unconscious "liking.") *Cognition & Emotion, 17,* 181–211.

Bies, R. J. (1987). The predicament of injustice: The management of moral outrage. In B. M. Staw & L. L. Cummings (Eds.), *Research in organizational behavior* (pp. 289–319). Greenwich, CT: JAI Press.

Bies, R. J., & Tripp, T. M. (1998). The many faces of revenge: The good, the bad, and the ugly. In R. W. Griffin, A. M. O'Leary-Kelly, & J. Collins (Eds.), *Dysfunctional behavior in organizations* (pp. 49–68). Greenwich, CT: JAI Press.

Bouchard, T. J., Jr., & Loehlin, J. C. (2001). Genes, evolution, and personality. *Behavior Genetics, 31,* 243–273.

Bower, G. H. (1981). Mood and memory. *American Psychologist, 36,* 129–148.

Brackett, M. A., & Mayer, J. D. (2003). Convergent, discriminant, and incremental validity of competing measures of emotional intelligence. *Personality and Social Psychology Bulletin, 29,* 1147–1158.

Brady, J. V. (1970). Emotion: Some conceptual problems and psycho-physiological experiments. In M. B. Arnold (Ed.), *Feelings and emotions: The Loyola Symposium* (pp. 69–100). San Diego, CA: Academic Press.

Brief, A. P., Burke, M. J., George, J. M., Robinson, B., & Webster, J. (1988). Should negative affectivity remain an unmeasured variable in the study of job stress? *Journal of Applied Psychology, 73,* 193–198.

Brief, A. P., & Weiss, H. M. (2002). Organizational behavior: Affect in the workplace. In S. T. Fiske, D. L. Schacter, & C. Zahn-Waxler (Eds.), *Annual review of psychology* (Vol. 53, pp. 279–307). Palo Alto, CA: Annual Reviews.

Brown, K. W., & Moskowitz, D. S. (1997). Does unhappiness make you sick? The role of affect and neuroticism in the experience of common physical symptoms. *Journal of Personality and Social Psychology, 72,* 907–917.

Buck, R. (1979). Individual differences in nonverbal sending accuracy and electrodermal responding: The externalizing–internalizing dimension. In R. Rosenthal (Ed.), *Skill in nonverbal communication: Individual differences* (pp. 140–170). Cambridge, MA: Olegeshlager, Gunn, & Hain.

Buck, R. (1984). *The communication of emotion.* New York: Guilford Press.

Bushman, B. J. (2002). Does venting anger feed or extinguish the flame? Catharsis, rumination, distraction, anger, and aggressive responding. *Personality and Social Psychology Bulletin, 28,* 724–731.

Campbell, R. J., Kagan, N. I., & Krathwohl, D. R. (1971). The development and validation of a scale to measure affective sensitivity (empathy). *Journal of Counseling Psychology, 18,* 407–412.

Campos, J. J., Frankel, C. B., & Camras, L. (2004). On the nature of emotion regulation. *Child Development, 75,* 377–394.

Cherniss, C. (2010). Emotional intelligence: Toward clarification of a concept. *Industrial and Organizational Psychology: Perspectives on Science and Practice, 3,* 110–126.

Clark, L. A., & Watson, D. (2008). Temperament: An organizing paradigm for trait psychology. In O. P. Johns, R. W. Robins, & L. A. Pervin (Eds.), *Handbook of personality: Theory and research* (3rd ed., pp. 265–286). New York: Guilford Press.

Clark, M. S., & Isen, A. M. (1982). Toward understanding the relationship between feeling states and social behavior. In A. H. Hastorf & A. M. Isen (Eds.), *Cognitive social psychology* (pp. 73–108). New York: Elsevier Science.
Colquitt, J. A., Conlon, D. E., Wesson, M. J., Porter, C. O. L. H., & Ng, K.Y. (2001). Justice at the millennium: A meta-analytic review of 25 years of organizational justice research. *Journal of Applied Psychology, 86*, 425–445.
Costa, P. T., & McCrae, R. R. (1992). *Revised NEO Personality Inventory (NEO-PI-R) and NEO Five-Factor Inventory (NEO-FFI) professional manual.* Odessa, FL: Psychological Assessment Resources.
Côté, S. (2010). Taking the "intelligence" in emotional intelligence seriously. *Industrial and Organizational Psychology: Perspectives on Science and Practice, 3*, 127–130.
Côté, S., DeCelles, K. A., McCarthy, J. M., Van Kleef, G. A., & Hideg, I. (2011). The Jekyll and Hyde of emotional intelligence: Emotion regulation knowledge facilitates prosocial and interpersonally deviant behavior. *Psychological Science, 22*, 1073–1080.
Csikszentmihalyi, M. (1975). *Beyond boredom and anxiety: The experience of play in work and games.* San Francisco: Jossey-Bass.
Damasio, A. (1994). *Descartes' error: Emotion, reason, and the human brain.* New York: Putnam.
Damasio, A. (1999). *The feeling of what happens: Body and emotion in the making of consciousness.* New York: Harcourt Brace.
Damasio, A. (2003). *Looking for Spinoza: Joy, sorrow, and the feeling brain.* San Diego, CA: Harcourt.
David, J., & Suls, J. (1999). Coping efforts in daily life: Role of Big Five traits and problem appraisal. *Journal of Personality, 67*, 119–140.
Depue, R. A., & Collins, P. F. (1999). Neurobiology of the structure of personality: Dopamine, facilitation of incentive motivation, and extraversion. *Behavioral and Brain Sciences, 22*, 491–569.
Depue, R. A., Luciana, M., Arbisi, P., Collins, P., & Leon, A. (1994). Dopamine and the structure of personality: Relation of agonist-induced dopamine activity to positive emotionality. *Journal of Personality and Social Psychology, 67*, 485–498.
Diener, E., Smith, H., & Fujita, F. (1995). The personality structure of affect. *Journal of Personality and Social Psychology, 69*, 130–141.
Digman, J. M. (1990). Personality structure: Emergence of the five-factor model. *Annual Review of Psychology, 41*, 417–440.
Digman, J. M. (1997). Higher-order factors of the Big Five. *Journal of Personality and Social Psychology, 73*, 1246–1256.
Eisenberg, N. (2000). Empathy and sympathy. In M. Lewis & J. M. Haviland-Jones (Eds.), *Handbook of emotions* (2nd ed., pp. 677–691). New York: Guilford Press.
Elfenbein, H. A. (2008). Emotion in organizations: A review and theoretical integration. In J. P. Walsh & A. P. Brief (Eds.), *The academy of management annals* (Vol. 1, pp. 315–386). New York: Erlbaum.
Emmons, R. A., & Colby, P. M. (1995). Emotional conflict and well-being: Relation to perceived availability, daily utilization, and observer reports of social support. *Journal of Personality and Social Psychology, 68*, 947–959.
Erber, R., Wegner, D. M., & Therriault, N. (1996). On being cool and collected: Mood regulation in anticipation of social interaction. *Journal of Personality and Social Psychology, 70*, 757–766.
Eysenck, H. J. (1967). *The biological basis of personality.* Baltimore: University Park Press.
Eysenck, H. J. (1992). Four ways five factors are not basic. *Personality and Individual Differences, 13*, 667–673.
Eysenck, H. J. (1997). Personality and experimental psychology: The unification of psychology and the possibility of a paradigm. *Journal of Personality and Social Psychology, 73*, 1224–1237.
Fiedler, K. (1991). On the task, the measures and the mood in research on affect and social cognition. In J. P. Forgas (Ed.), *Emotion and social judgments* (pp. 83–104). Elmsford, NY: Pergamon Press.
Fisher, G. A. (1997). Theoretical and methodological elaborations of the circumplex model of personality traits and emotions. In R. Plutchik & H. R. Conte (Eds.), *Circumplex models of personality and emotions* (pp. 245–269). Washington, DC: American Psychological Association.
Forgas, J. P. (1992). Affect in social judgments and decisions: A multi-process model. In M. Zanna (Ed.), *Advances in experimental and social psychology* (Vol. 25, pp. 227–275). San Diego, CA: Academic Press.
Forgas, J. P. (1995). Mood and judgment: The affect infusion model (AIM). *Psychological Bulletin, 117*, 39–66.
Forgas, J. P. (2007). When sad is better than happy: Negative affect can improve the quality and effectiveness of persuasive messages and social influence strategies. *Journal of Experimental Social Psychology, 43*, 513–528.
Forgas, J. P., & George, J. M. (2001). Affective influences on judgments and behavior in organizations: An information processing perspective. *Organizational Behavior and Human Decision Processes, 86*, 3–34.
Friedman, H. S., Prince, L. M., Riggio, R. E., & Dimatteo, M. R. (1980). Understanding and assessing nonverbal expressiveness: The affective communications test. *Journal of Personality and Social Psychology, 39*, 333–351.
Frijda, N. H. (1986). *The emotions.* Cambridge, UK: Cambridge University Press.
Frijda, N. H. (1988). The laws of emotion. *American Psychologist, 43*, 349–358.

Frijda, N. H. (2007). *The laws of emotion*. Mahwah, NJ: Erlbaum.

Fuller, J. A., Stanton, J. M., Fisher, G. G., Spitzmuller, C., Russell, S. S., & Smith, P. C. (2003). A lengthy look at the daily grind: Time series analyses of events, mood, stress, and satisfaction. *Journal of Applied Psychology, 88*, 1019–1033.

George, J. M. (1989). Mood and absence. *Journal of Applied Psychology, 74*, 317–324.

George, J. M. (1995). Leader positive mood and group performance: The case of customer service. *Journal of Applied Social Psychology, 25*, 778–794.

George, J. M. (1996). Trait and state affect. In K. Murphy (Ed.), *Individual differences and behavior in organizations* (pp. 145–171). San Francisco: Jossey-Bass.

George, J. M. (2000). Emotions and leadership: The role of emotional intelligence. *Human Relations, 53*, 1027–1055.

George, J. M. (2009). The illusion of will in organizational behavior research: Nonconscious processes and job design. *Journal of Management, 35*, 1318–1339.

George, J. M. (2011). Dual tuning: A minimum condition for understanding affect in organizations? *Organizational Psychology Review, 1*, 147–164.

George, J. M., & Brief, A. P. (1992). Feeling good—Doing good: A conceptual analysis of the mood at work–organizational spontaneity relationship. *Psychological Bulletin, 112*, 310–329.

George, J. M., & Brief, A. P. (1996). Motivational agendas in the workplace: The effects of feelings on focus of attention and work motivation. In B. M. Staw & L. L. Cummings (Eds.), *Research in organizational behavior* (Vol. 18, pp. 75–109). Greenwich, CT: JAI Press.

George, J. M., & Jones, G. R. (1996). The experience of work and turnover intentions: Interactive effects of value attainment, job satisfaction, and positive mood. *Journal of Applied Psychology, 81*, 318–325.

George, J. M., & Jones, G. R. (1997). Experiencing work: Values, attitudes, and moods. *Human Relations, 50*, 393–416.

George, J. M., & Zhou, J. (2001). When openness to experience and conscientiousness are related to creative behavior: An interactional approach. *Journal of Applied Psychology, 86*, 513–524.

George, J. M., & Zhou, J. (2002). Understanding when bad moods foster creativity and good ones don't: The role of context and clarity of feelings. *Journal of Applied Psychology, 87*, 687–697.

George, J. M., & Zhou, J. (2007). Dual tuning in a supportive context: Joint contributions of positive mood, negative mood, and supervisory behaviors to employee creativity. *Academy of Management Journal, 50*, 605–622.

Gibson, D. E., & Callister, R. R. (2010). Anger in organizations: Review and integration. *Journal of Management, 36*, 66–93.

Goldberg, L. R. (1992). The development of markers for the Big-Five factor structure. *Psychological Assessment, 4*, 26–42.

Gooty, J., Gavin, M., & Ashkanasy, N. M. (2009). Emotions research in OB: The challenges that lie ahead. *Journal of Organizational Behavior, 30*, 833–838.

Gray, E. K., & Watson, D. (2001). Emotion, mood, and temperament: Similarities, differences, and a synthesis. In R. L. Payne & C. L. Cooper (Eds.), *Emotions at work: Theory, research and applications in management* (pp. 21–43). New York: Wiley.

Gray, J. A. (1981). A critique of Eysenck's theory of personality. In H. J. Eysenck (Ed.), *A model for personality* (pp. 246–276). New York: Springer-Verlag.

Gray, J. A. (1994). Personality dimensions and emotion systems. In P. Ekman & R. J. Davidson (Eds.), *The nature of emotion: Fundamental questions* (pp. 329–331). New York: Oxford University Press.

Gross, J. J. (1998). The emerging field of emotion regulation: An integrative review. *Review of General Psychology, 2*, 271–299.

Gross, J. J. (Ed.). (2007). *Handbook of emotion regulation*. New York: Guilford Press.

Gross, J. J. (2008a). Emotion and emotion regulation: Personality processes and individual differences. In O. P. John, R. W. Robins, & L. A. Pervin (Eds.), *Handbook of personality: Theory and research* (3rd ed., pp. 701–724). New York: Guilford Press.

Gross, J. J. (2008b). Emotion regulation. In M. Lewis, J. M. Haviland-Jones, & L. F. Barrett (Eds.), *Handbook of emotions* (3rd ed., pp. 497–512). New York: Guilford Press.

Gross, J. J., & John, O. P. (1998). Mapping the domain of emotional expressivity: Multi-method evidence for a hierarchical model. *Journal of Personality and Social Psychology, 74*, 170–191.

Gross, J. J., & John, O. P. (2003). Individual differences in two emotion regulation processes: Implications for affect, relationships, and well-being. *Journal of Personality and Social Psychology, 85*, 348–362.

Gross, J. J., Richards, J. M., & John, O. P. (2006). Emotion regulation in everyday life. In D. K. Snyder, J. A. Simpson, & J. N. Hughes (Eds.), *Emotion regulation in couples and families: Pathways to dysfunction and health* (pp. 13–35). Washington, DC: American Psychological Association.

Gross, J. J., Sutton, S. K., & Katelaar, T. (1998). Relations between affect and personality: Support for the affect-level and affect-reactivity views. *Personality and Social Psychology Bulletin, 24*, 279–288.
Gross, J. J., & Thompson, R. A. (2007). Emotion regulation: Conceptual foundations. In J. J. Gross (Ed.), *Handbook of emotion regulation* (pp. 3–24). New York: Guilford Press.
Headey, B., & Wearing, A. (1989). Personality, life events, and subjective well-being: Toward a dynamic equilibrium model. *Journal of Personality and Social Psychology, 57*, 731–739.
Heller, D., Watson, D., & Ilies, R. (2004). The role of person versus situation in life satisfaction: A critical examination. *Psychological Bulletin, 130*, 574–600.
Hogan, J., & Ones, D. S. (1997). Conscientiousness and integrity at work. In R. Hogan, J. Johnson, & S. Briggs (Eds.), *Handbook of personality psychology* (pp. 849–870). San Diego, CA: Academic Press.
Hogan, R., & Blake, R. J. (1996). Vocational interests: Matching self-concept with the work environment. In K. R. Murphy (Ed.), *Individual differences and behavior in organizations* (pp. 89–144). San Francisco: Jossey-Bass.
Hong, R. Y. (2010). Neuroticism, anxiety sensitivity thoughts, and anxiety symptomatology: Insights from an experience-sampling approach. *Cognitive Therapy Research, 34*, 254–262.
Isen, A. M., & Shalker, T. E. (1982). The influence of mood state on evaluation of positive, neutral, and negative stimuli. *Social Psychology Quarterly, 45*, 58–63.
Isen, A. M., Shalker, T. E., Clark, M., & Karp, L. (1978). Affect, accessibility of material in memory, and behavior: A cognitive loop? *Journal of Personality and Social Psychology, 36*, 1–12.
John, O. P., & Gross, J. J. (2007). Individual differences in emotion regulation. In J. J. Gross (Ed.), *Handbook of emotion regulation* (pp. 351–372). New York: Guilford Press.
John, O. P., Naumann, L. P., & Soto, C. J. (2008). Paradigm shift to the integrative Big Five trait taxonomy. In O. P. John, R. W. Robins, & L. A. Pervin (Eds.), *Handbook of personality* (3rd ed., pp. 114–158). New York: Guilford Press.
Johnson-Laird, P. N., & Oatley, K. (2008). Emotions, music, and literature. In M. Lewis, J. M. Haviland-Jones, & L. Feldman Barrett (Eds.), *Handbook of emotions* (3rd ed., pp. 102–113). New York: Guilford Press.
Katz, I. M., & Campbell, J. D. (1994). Ambivalence over emotional expression and well-being: Nomothetic and idiographic tests of the stress-buffering hypothesis. *Journal of Personality and Social Psychology, 67*, 513–524.
King, L. A., & Emmons, R. A. (1990). Conflict over emotional expression: Psychological and physical correlates. *Journal of Personality and Social Psychology, 58*, 864–877.
King, L. A., & Emmons, R. A. (1991). Psychological, physical, and interpersonal correlates of emotional expressiveness, conflict and control. *European Journal of Personality, 5*, 131–150.
Krystal, J. H., Giller, E. L., & Cicchetti, D.V. (1986). Assessment of alexithymia in post-traumatic stress disorder and somatic illness: Introduction of a reliable measure. *Psychosomatic Medicine, 48*, 84–91.
Larsen, R. J. (1992). Neuroticism and selective encoding and recall of symptoms: Evidence from a combined concurrent-retrospective study. *Journal of Personality and Social Psychology, 62*, 480–488.
Larsen, R. J., & Katelaar, T. (1989). Extraversion, neuroticism and susceptibility to positive and negative mood induction procedures. *Personality and Individual Differences, 10*, 1221–1228.
Larsen, R. J., & Katelaar, T. (1991). Personality and susceptibility to positive and negative emotional states. *Journal of Personality and Social Psychology, 61*, 132–140.
Loehlin, J. C., McCrae, R. R., Costa, P. T., Jr., & John, O. P. (1998). Heritabilities of common and measure-specific components of the Big Five personality factors. *Journal of Research in Personality, 32*, 431–453.
Lucas, R. E., Diener, E., Grob, A., Suh, E. M., & Shao, L. (2000). Cross-cultural evidence for the fundamental features of extraversion. *Journal of Personality and Social Psychology, 79*, 452–468.
Lyubomirsky, S., & Nolen-Hoeksema, S. (1993). Self-perpetuating properties of dysphoric rumination. *Journal of Personality and Social Psychology, 65*, 339–349.
Lyubomirsky, S., & Nolen-Hoeksema, S. (1995). Effects of self-focused rumination on negative thinking and interpersonal problem solving. *Journal of Personality and Social Psychology, 69*, 176–190.
Mauss, I. B., Evers, C., Wilhelm, F. H., & Gross, J. J. (2006). How to bite your tongue without blowing your top: Implicit evaluation of emotion regulation predicts affective responding to anger provocation. *Personality and Social Psychology Bulletin, 32*, 589–602.
Mayer, J. D. (1986). How mood influences cognition. In N. E. Sharkey (Ed.), *Advances in cognitive science* (Vol. 1, pp. 290–314). Chichester, UK: Ellis Horwood.
Mayer, J. D., DiPaolo, M., & Salovey, P. (1990). Perceiving affective content in ambiguous visual stimuli: A component of emotional intelligence. *Journal of Personality Assessment, 54*, 772–781.
Mayer, J. D., Roberts, R. D., & Barsade, S. G. (2008). Human abilities: Emotional intelligence. *Annual Review of Psychology, 59*, 507–536.
Mayer, J. D., & Salovey, P. (1993). The intelligence of emotional intelligence. *Intelligence, 17*, 433–442.
Mayer, J. D., & Salovey, P. (1995). Emotional intelligence and the construction and regulation of feelings. *Applied and Preventive Psychology, 4*, 197–208.

Mayer, J. D., & Salovey, P. (1997). What is emotional intelligence? Implications for educators. In P. Salovey & D. Sluyter (Eds.), *Emotional development, emotional literacy, and emotional intelligence* (pp. 3–31). New York: Basic Books.

Mayer, J. D., Salovey, P., & Caruso, D. (2002). *Mayer–Salovey–Caruso Emotional Intelligence Test (MSCEIT), version 2.0.* Toronto, Ontario, Canada: Multi-Health Systems.

McCrae, R. R. (1996). Social consequences of experiential openness. *Psychological Bulletin, 120,* 323–337.

McCrae, R. R., & Costa, P. T., Jr. (1987). Validation of a five-factor model of personality across instruments and observers. *Journal of Personality and Social Psychology, 52,* 81–90.

McCrae, R. R., & Costa, P. T., Jr. (1991). Adding Liebe und Arbeit: The full five-factor model and well-being. *Personality and Social Psychology Bulletin, 17,* 227–232.

McCrae, R. R., & Costa, P. T., Jr. (1997). Personality trait structure as a human universal. *American Psychologist, 52,* 509–516.

Meyer, G. J., & Shack, J. R. (1989). Structural convergence of mood and personality: Evidence for old and new directions. *Journal of Personality and Social Psychology, 57,* 691–706.

Miner, A. G., Glomb, T. M., & Hulin, C. (2005). Experience sampling mood and its correlates at work. *Journal of Occupational and Organizational Psychology, 78,* 171–193.

Morris, W. N. (1989). *Mood: The frame of mind.* New York: Springer-Verlag.

Morrow, J., & Nolen-Hoeksema, S. (1990). Effects of responses to depression on the remediation of depressive affect. *Journal of Personality and Social Psychology, 58,* 519–527.

Muris, P., Roelofs, J., Rassin, E., Franken, I., & Mayer, B. (2005). Mediating effects of rumination and worry on the links between neuroticism, anxiety, and depression. *Personality and Individual Differences, 39,* 1105–1111.

Myllyniemi, R. (1997). The interpersonal circle and the emotional undercurrents of human sociability. In R. Plutchik & H. R. Conte (Eds.), *Circumplex models of personality and emotions* (pp. 271–295). Washington, DC: American Psychological Association.

Nolen-Hoeksema, S. (1991). Responses to depression and their effects on the duration of depressive episodes. *Journal of Abnormal Psychology, 100,* 569–582.

Nolen-Hoeksema, S., McBride, A., & Larson, J. (1997). Rumination and psychological distress among bereaved partners. *Journal of Personality and Social Psychology, 72,* 855–862.

Nolen-Hoeksema, S., & Morrow, J. (1991). A prospective study of depression and posttraumatic stress symptoms after a natural disaster: The 1989 Loma Prieta earthquake. *Journal of Personality and Social Psychology, 61,* 115–121.

Nolen-Hoeksema, S., & Morrow, J. (1993). Effects of rumination and distraction on naturally occurring depressed mood. *Cognition & Emotion,* 7, 561–570.

Nolen-Hoeksema, S., Morrow, J., & Fredrickson, B. L. (1993). Response styles and the duration of episodes of depressed mood. *Journal of Abnormal Psychology, 102,* 20–28.

Nolen-Hoeksema, S., Parker, L., & Larson, J. (1994). Ruminative coping with depressed mood following loss. *Journal of Personality and Social Psychology, 67,* 92–104.

Nolen-Hoeksema, S., Wisco, B. E., & Lyubomirksy, S. (2008). Rethinking rumination. *Perspectives on Psychological Science, 3,* 400–424.

Nowlis, V. (1970). Mood: Behavior and experience. In M. B. Arnold (Ed.), *Feelings and emotions: The Loyola Symposium* (pp. 261–277). San Diego, CA: Academic Press.

Ormel, J., & Wohlfarth, T. (1991). How neuroticism, long-term difficulties, and life situation change influence psychological distress: A longitudinal model. *Journal of Personality and Social Psychology, 60,* 744–755.

Parkinson, B., Totterdell, P., Briner, R. B., & Reynolds, S. (1996). *Changing moods: The psychology of mood and mood regulation.* London: Addison Wesley Longman.

Parrott, W. G. (1993). Beyond hedonism: Motives for inhibiting good moods and maintaining bad moods. In D. M. Wegner & J. W. Pennebaker (Eds.), *Handbook of mental control* (pp. 278–305). Upper Saddle River, NJ: Prentice Hall.

Parrott, W. G. (2002). The functional utility of negative emotions. In L. F. Barrett & P. Salovey (Eds.), *The wisdom in feeling: Psychological processes in emotional intelligence* (pp. 341–359). New York: Guilford Press.

Pennebaker, J. W. (1997). Writing about emotional experiences as a therapeutic process. *Psychological Science, 8,* 162–166.

Ray, R. D., Wilhelm, F. H., & Gross, J. J. (2008). All in the mind's eye? Anger rumination and reappraisal. *Journal of Personality and Social Psychology, 94,* 133–145.

Rusting, C. L., & Larsen, R. J. (1997). Extraversion, neuroticism, and susceptibility to positive and negative affect: A test of two theoretical models. *Personality and Individual Differences, 22,* 607–612.

Ryle, G. (1950). *The concept of mind.* London: Hutchinson.

Salovey, P., Bedell, B. T., Detweiler, J. B., & Mayer, J. D. (2000). Current directions in emotional intelligence research. In M. Lewis & J. M. Haviland-Jones (Eds.), *Handbook of emotions* (2nd ed., pp. 504–520). New York: Guilford Press.

Salovey, P., Hsee, C. K., & Mayer, J. D. (1993). Emotional intelligence and the self-regulation of affect. In D. M. Wegner & J. W. Pennebaker (Eds.), *Handbook of mental control* (pp. 258–277). Englewood Cliffs, NJ: Prentice Hall.
Salovey, P., & Mayer, J. D. (1990). Emotional intelligence. *Imagination, Cognition, and Personality, 9*, 185–211.
Salovey, P., & Mayer, J. D. (1994). Some final thoughts about personality and intelligence. In R. J. Sternberg & P. Ruzgis (Eds.), *Personality and intelligence* (pp. 303–318). Cambridge, UK: Cambridge University Press.
Salovey, P., Mayer, J. D., Goldman, S. L., Turvey, C., & Palfai, T. P. (1995). Emotional attention, clarity, and repair: Exploring emotional intelligence using the trait meta-mood scale. In J. W. Pennebaker (Ed.), *Emotion, disclosure, and health* (pp. 125–154). Washington, DC: American Psychological Association.
Scheier, M. F., & Carver, C. S. (1993). On the power of positive thinking: The benefits of being optimistic. *Current Directions in Psychological Science, 2*, 26–30.
Scherer, K. R. (2005). Unconscious processes in emotion: The bulk of the iceberg. In L. Feldman Barrett, P. Niedenthal, & P. Winkielman (Eds.), *Emotion and consciousness* (pp. 312–334). New York: Guilford Press.
Shiota, M. N., Keltner, D., & John, O. P. (2006). Positive emotion dispositions differentially associated with Big Five personality and attachment style. *The Journal of Positive Psychology, 1*, 61–71.
Sifneos, P. E. (1972). *Short-term psychotherapy and emotional crisis*. Cambridge, MA: Harvard University Press.
Sifneos, P. E. (1973). The presence of "alexithymic" characteristics in psychosomatic patients. *Psychotherapy and Psychosomatics, 22*, 225–262.
Simon, H. A. (1982). Comments. In M. S. Clark & S. T. Fiske (Eds.), *Affect and cognition* (pp. 333–342). Hillsdale, NJ: Erlbaum.
Tafrate, R. C., Kassinove, H., & Dundin, L. (2002). Anger episodes in high- and low-trait anger community adults. *Journal of Clinical Psychology, 58*, 1573–1591.
Tamir, M. (2005). Don't worry, be happy? Neuroticism, trait-consistent affect regulation, and performance. *Journal of Personality and Social Psychology, 89*, 449–461.
Tamir, M. (2009). What do people want to feel and why? Pleasure and utility in emotion regulation. *Current Directions in Psychological Science, 18*, 101–105.
Tamir, M., Chiu, C., & Gross, J. J. (2007). Business or pleasure? Utilitarian versus hedonic considerations in emotion regulation. *Emotion, 7*, 546–554.
Tamir, M., & Ford, B. Q. (2009). Choosing to be afraid: Preferences for fear as a function of goal pursuit. *Emotion, 9*, 488–497.
Tamir, M., Mitchell, C., & Gross, J. J. (2008). Hedonic and instrumental motives in anger regulation. *Psychological Science, 19*, 324–328.
Tamir, M., & Robinson, M. D. (2004). Knowing good from bad: The paradox of neuroticism, negative affect, and evaluative processing. *Journal of Personality and Social Psychology, 87*, 913–925.
Tamir, M., Robinson, M. D., & Clore, G. L. (2002). The epistemic benefits of trait-consistent mood states: An analysis of extraversion and mood. *Journal of Personality and Social Psychology, 83*, 663–677.
Taylor, G. J. (1984). Alexithymia: Concept, measurement, and implications for treatment. *American Journal of Psychiatry, 141*, 725–732.
Tellegen, A. (1982). *Brief manual for the Differential Personality Questionnaire* (Unpublished manuscript). University of Minnesota, Minneapolis.
Tellegen, A. (1985). Structures of mood and personality and their relevance to assessing anxiety, with an emphasis on self-report. In A. H. Tuma & J. D. Maser (Eds.), *Anxiety and the anxiety disorders* (pp. 681–706). Hillsdale, NJ: Erlbaum.
Tellegen, A., Lykken, D. T., Bouchard, T. J., Jr., Wilcox, K. J., Segal, N. L., & Rich, S. (1988). Personality similarity in twins reared apart and together. *Journal of Personality and Social Psychology, 54*, 1031–1039.
Thayer-Singer, M. (1977). Psychological dimensions in psychosomatic patients. *Psychotherapy and Psychosomatics, 28*, 13–27.
Viken, R. J., Rose, R. J., Kaprio, J., & Koskenvuo, M. (1994). A developmental genetic analysis of adult personality: Extraversion and neuroticism from 18 to 59 years of age. *Journal of Personality and Social Psychology, 66*, 722–730.
Walter, F., Cole, M. S., & Humphrey, R. H. (2011). Emotional intelligence: Sine qua non of leadership or folderol? *Academy of Management Perspectives, 25*, 45–59.
Wasielewski, P. L. (1985). The emotional basis of charisma. *Symbolic Interactionism, 8*, 207–222.
Watson, D. (1988). Intraindividual and interindividual analyses of positive and negative affect: Their relation to health complaints, perceived stress, and daily activities. *Journal of Personality and Social Psychology, 54*, 1020–1030.
Watson, D. (2000). *Mood and temperament*. New York: Guilford Press.
Watson, D., & Clark, L. A. (1984). Negative affectivity: The disposition to experience aversive emotional states. *Psychological Bulletin, 96*, 465–490.

Watson, D., & Clark, L. A. (1992). On traits and temperament: General and specific factors of emotional experience and their relation to the five-factor model. *Journal of Personality, 60*, 441–476.
Watson, D., & Clark, L. A. (1993). Behavioral disinhibition versus constraint: A dispositional perspective. In D. M. Wegner & J. W. Pennebaker (Eds.), *Handbook of mental control* (pp. 506–527). New York: Prentice Hall.
Watson, D., & Clark, L. A. (1994). Emotions, moods, traits, and temperaments: Conceptual distinctions and empirical findings. In P. Ekman & R. J. Davidson (Eds.), *The nature of emotion: Fundamental questions* (pp. 89–93). New York: Oxford University Press.
Watson, D., & Clark, L. A. (1997). Extraversion and its positive emotional core. In R. Hogan, J. Johnson, & S. Briggs (Eds.), *Handbook of personality psychology* (pp. 767–793). San Diego, CA: Academic Press.
Watson, D., Clark, L. A., McIntyre, C. W., & Hamaker, S. (1992). Affect, personality, and social activity. *Journal of Personality and Social Psychology, 63*, 1011–1025.
Watson, D., Clark, L. A., & Tellegen, A. (1988). Development and validation of brief measures of positive and negative affect: The PANAS scales. *Journal of Personality and Social Psychology, 54*, 1063–1070.
Watson, D., Kotov, R., & Gamez, W. (2006). Basic dimensions of temperament in relation to personality and psychopathology. In R. F. Krueger & J. L. Tackett (Eds.), *Personality and psychopathology* (pp. 7–38). New York: Guilford Press.
Watson, D., & Pennebaker, J. W. (1989). Health complaints, stress, and distress: Exploring the central role of negative affectivity. *Psychological Review, 96*, 234–254.
Watson, D., Wiese, D., Vaidya, J., & Tellegen, A. (1999). The two general activation systems of affect: Structural findings, evolutionary considerations, and psychological evidence. *Journal of Personality and Social Psychology, 76*, 820–838.
Weiss, H. M., & Cropanzano, R. (1996). Affective events theory: A theoretical discussion of the structure, causes, and consequences of affective experiences at work. In B. M. Staw & L. L. Cummings (Eds.), *Research in organizational behavior* (Vol. 18, pp. 1–74). Greenwich, CT: JAI Press.
Weiss, H. M., Nicholas, J. P., & Daus, C. S. (1999). An examination of the joint effects of affective experiences and job beliefs on job satisfaction and variations in affective experiences over time. *Organizational Behavior and Human Decision Processes, 78*, 1–24.
Widiger, T. A., & Smith, G. T. (2008). Personality and psychopathology. In O. P. Johns, R. W. Robins, & L. A. Pervin (Eds.), *Handbook of personality: Theory and research* (3rd ed., pp. 743–769). New York: Guilford Press.
Widiger, T. A., Verheul, R., & van den Brink, W. (1999). Personality and psychopathology. In L. A. Pervin & O. P. John (Eds.), *Handbook of personality: Theory and research* (2nd ed., pp. 347–366). New York: Guilford Press.
Wilt, J., & Revelle, W. (2009). Extraversion. In M. R. Leary & R. H. Hoyle (Eds.), *Handbook of individual differences in social behavior* (pp. 27–45). New York: Guilford Press.
Winkielman, P., Berridge, K. C., & Wilbarger, J. L. (2005). Emotion, behavior, and conscious experience: Once more without feeling. In L. Feldman Barrett, P. Niedenthal, & P. Winkielman (Eds.), *Emotion and consciousness* (pp. 335–362). New York: Guilford Press.
Wranik, T., Barrett, L. F., & Salovey, P. (2007). Intelligent emotion regulation: Is knowledge power? In J. J. Gross (Ed.), *Handbook of emotion regulation* (pp. 393–407). New York: Guilford Press.
Zelenski, J. M., & Larsen, R. J. (1999). Susceptibility to affect: A comparison of three personality taxonomies. *Journal of Personality, 67*, 761–791.

31

The Role of Personality in Occupational Stress

A Review and Future Research Agenda

Nathan A. Bowling and Steve M. Jex

During the past 30 years, growing scholarly interest has been dedicated to the study of occupational stress. Such interest should not be surprising, given the unfavorable effects of occupational stress on the well-being of individual workers and their employers. Indeed, stressful work situations have been linked to a number of indices of psychological and physical illness (Beehr, 1995; Cooper, Dewe, & O'Driscoll, 2001). Furthermore, because of expenses associated with employee absences and health insurance claims, occupational stress has been estimated to cost U.S. companies US$300 billion annually (Rosch, 2001).

The focus of the current chapter is on the relationship between employee personality and work stressors and strains. This topic has important theoretical and practical implications for a number of reasons. First, personality is theoretically important because its inclusion in occupational stress models recognizes stress as rooted in the unique subjective experience of individual workers. Indeed, two employees exposed to objectively identical working conditions may display very different responses. As a result of differences in personality, two workers assigned to new positions in a foreign country, for example, may view their respective assignments very differently. One worker may perceive the job change as an interesting and exciting opportunity, and thereby view it as a challenge rather than as a threat. The other worker, however, may experience distress at the thought of having to learn a new language and culture and may thus view the new assignment as a stressor. In the preceding example, the first worker is likely to experience positive outcomes as a result of the new assignment, whereas the second worker is likely to experience strain.

The potential effect of employee personality on work stressors and strains also has important practical implications. Much of the occupational stress literature focuses on the applied problem of how to reduce stress, with a number of organizational interventions attempting to combat occupational stress by modifying conditions within the work environment (for a review of these interventions, see Bowling, Beehr, & Grebner, 2012; Richardson & Rothstein, 2008). Such interventions may focus on encouraging effective leader behaviors, on reducing stressors, such as role ambiguity, conflict, or overload, or on increasing employee autonomy. However, to the extent that occupational stress is impacted by employee personality, then the effects of such interventions may be limited. That is, workers may have a "set-point" level of stress that is determined by their personalities, and any efforts to change their stress level may at best have temporary effects. Furthermore, a link between personality and work stress may suggest that employee selection, rather than organizational interventions,

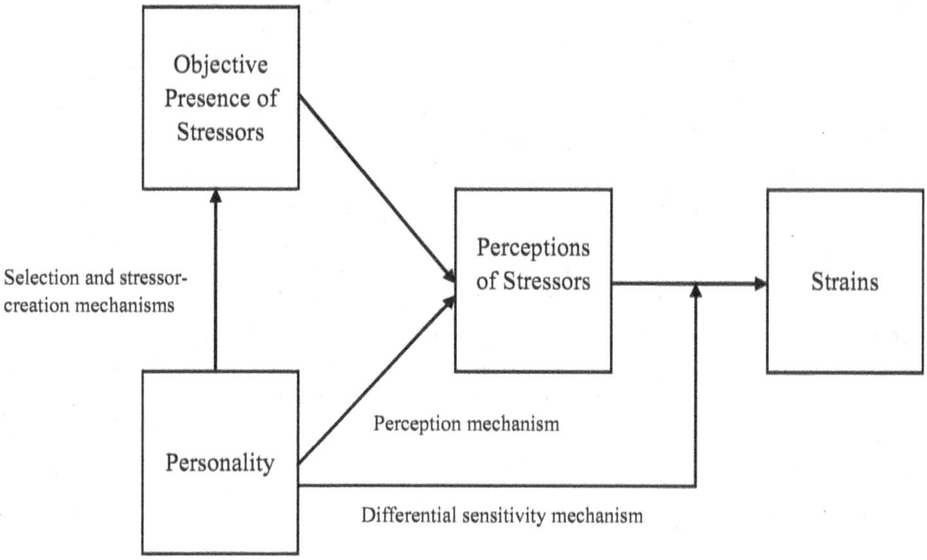

Figure 31.1 Conceptual Model Describing the Mechanisms Linking Personality to Stressors and Strains.

is an effective means of combating occupational stress. In other words, applicants to highly stressful occupations (e.g., firefighter, stockbroker) could be screened based upon how they score on particular personality dimensions.

Our position, however, is that both the person and the work environment must be considered in occupational stress models. Thus, it would be an exaggeration to assume that stress-related variables are *entirely* rooted in one's personality. As is evident in the remainder of the current chapter, stress-related variables are likely the result of main and interaction effects of the person and the work environment. Thus, any comprehensive stress model or intervention should take into account both the situation and employee personality (see Figure 31.1).

We begin the chapter by defining key terms used in the occupational stress literature. We then consider the theoretical mechanisms that potentially link personality to stress-related variables, and discuss research findings involving several different personality traits. The chapter concludes with a discussion of future research directions, as well as the practical implications of personality's link with occupational stress.

Defining Key Variables Used in the Work Stress Literature

Any chapter on occupational stress is incomplete without some discussion of key definitions. Indeed, the occupational stress literature has been stymied by a lack of clarity in terminology (Beehr & Bhagat, 1985; Beehr & Newman, 1978). Two key terms are "stressor" and "strain." A stressor is any aspect of one's environment that requires an adaptive response, and that has the potential to cause physical or psychological illness or maladaptive behaviors (Jex, Beehr, & Roberts, 1992). General life stressors include major life events (e.g., divorce, a serious illness; Holmes & Rahe, 1967), as well as the seemingly less serious but more frequent stressors, such as daily hassles (e.g., misplacing one's house key, being stuck in heavy traffic; Kanner, Coyne, Schaefer, & Lazarus, 1981). Within the workplace, commonly studied stressors include role ambiguity (i.e., having unclear work responsibilities;

Fisher & Gitelson, 1983; Jackson & Schuler, 1985), role conflict (i.e., having work responsibilities that are inconsistent with or compete with each other; Fisher & Gitelson, 1983; Jackson & Schuler, 1985), role overload (i.e., having too much work to do or having work that is too difficult for one's capabilities; Cooper et al., 2001; Ortqvist & Wincent, 2006), interpersonal conflict (i.e., having disagreements with coworkers or supervisors; Spector & Jex, 1998), organizational constraints (i.e., any aspect of one's job that interferes with effective performance, such as not having adequate tools or equipment; Spector & Jex, 1998), work–family conflict (i.e., incompatibility between work and nonwork roles; Greenhaus & Beutell, 1985), and emotional labor (i.e., being required by one's employer to express emotions that one does not genuinely feel, or suppressing emotions that one does indeed feel; Grandey, 2000).

Although stress researchers—as well as members of the general public—usually think of stressors as being negative and undesirable, they can sometimes yield beneficial effects. The idea that stressors can be either "good" or "bad" is explicitly addressed by the distinction between *challenge stressors* and *hindrance stressors* (Lepine, Podsakoff, & Lepine, 2005; Podsakoff, LePine, & LePine, 2007). Challenge stressors, which include high workload, responsibility, and job complexity, are often thought of as "good stressors," because they represent obstacles that provide one with the opportunity for personal growth and learning. Hindrance stressors, on the other hand, are akin to "bad stressors." These stressors are unnecessary nuisances—such as organizational constraints, role ambiguity, and interpersonal mistreatment—that inhibit employees' performance and personal growth. Although the focus of the current chapter is on the undesirable effects of stressors, we consider the importance of studying "good stress" below in the discussion of future research directions.

Strains, on the other hand, are the negative consequences that may result from being exposed to stressors (Jex et al., 1992). A useful categorization introduced by Jex and Beehr (1991) distinguishes between psychological, physical, and behavioral strains. Psychological strains include undesirable emotional and cognitive outcomes produced by stressors, such as anxiety, depression, frustration, and burnout. Physical strains, on the other hand, include such health outcomes as headache, upset stomach, and fever. Finally, behavioral strains include unhealthy behaviors that people engage in as a response to stressors. These behaviors include drug and alcohol abuse, withdrawing from physical activity, overeating, and, in extreme cases, suicide. We should note that, in addition to using the above definitions of "stressors" and "strains," we will occasionally use the term "stress-related variables" to collectively refer to these two categories of variables.

In addition to the terms "stressor" and "strain," researchers also frequently use the term "stress." In most cases, this term is simply used by researchers to refer to the overall process by which exposure to stressors leads to strains (Jex & Beehr, 1991). However, in some cases, researchers have used the term to refer to the immediate, short-term reactions that employees have when they experience stressors (Jex et al., 1992).

Theoretical Mechanisms Linking Employee Personality to Work Stressors and Strains

We now turn to a review of the theoretical mechanisms potentially linking employee personality to work stressors and strains. We should note that much of this section borrows from previous discussions of the processes linking personality to the general social environment (Buss, 1987), as well as from discussions of the processes linking trait negative affectivity (NA; see below) to work stress (Spector, Zapf, Chen, & Frese, 2000). In our review, we consider four substantive processes: perception, selection, stressor-creation, and differential sensitivity (see Figure 31.1). In addition to these substantive processes, we also consider the possibility that personality acts as a methodological "nuisance" variable that produces spurious relationships between work stressors and strains.

Perception

According to the perceptual explanation, employee personality influences stress-related variables by affecting one's subjective interpretation of the work environment (Spector et al., 2000). In other words, workplaces represent inherently ambiguous situations that are open to individual interpretation (Salancik & Pfeffer, 1978). Employee personality traits are hypothesized to "color" one's interpretation of the work environment. This can occur when personality influences which particular aspects of the workplace an individual attends to and remembers (Motowidlo, 1996; Necowitz & Roznowski, 1994). Whereas some workers may be predisposed to interpret ambiguous stimuli in a positive manner, others may be predisposed to interpret the same ambiguous stimuli in a negative manner. A worker high in trait cynicism (W.W. Cook & Medley, 1954; Smith, Pope, Sanders, Allred, & O'Keeffe, 1988), for example, may perceive a supportive action from a coworker as an attempt at interpersonal manipulation, whereas a worker low in trait cynicism may perceive the same supportive action as simply being a selfless act of kindness. Thus, the perceptual hypothesis suggests that workers employed in objectively identical environments may perceive their jobs differently from one another, and these perceptual differences are due to personality.

Evidence for the role of perceptual processes can be seen in research suggesting that employee personality is related to self-reports of one's work environment (e.g., Barsky, Thoresen, Warren, & Kaplan, 2004; Bowling & Eschleman, 2010; Chen & Spector, 1991; Kiffin-Petersen, Jordan, & Soutar, 2011; Michel, Clark, & Jaramillo, 2011). Bowling and Eschleman (2010), for example, found that conscientiousness and agreeableness are negatively correlated with, and that NA is positively correlated with, self-reported work stressors (e.g., interpersonal conflict, organizational constraints). In an effort to provide a more rigorous test of the perceptual hypothesis, future research should examine the relationship between personality and self-reported stressors after objectively measured stressors are controlled.

Selection

According to the selection hypothesis, employees are predisposed to select particular types of work environments as a result of their personalities (Spector et al., 2000). An employee high in type-A personality (Spence, Helmreich, & Pred, 1987), for example, may be predisposed to pursue work in a fast-pace high-stressor occupation, such as a career as a trader on the floor of the New York Stock Exchange. Similarly, the selection mechanism can be seen when organizations either intentionally or unintentionally hire applicants based on their personalities. Intentional selection occurs when organizations formally base hiring decisions on applicants' scores on personality assessments, whereas unintentional selection occurs when personality traits that are not formally used as a basis for selection decisions indirectly influence which employees are hired. As an illustration of this latter form of selection, organizations may indirectly select-out high-NA applicants because they perform more poorly at employment interviews than do low-NA applicants (K.W. Cook, Vance, & Spector, 2000).

The focus of the selection hypothesis is on the link between employee personality and *objectively measured* work stressors, such as stressors assessed using O*NET (Liu, Spector, & Jex, 2005), the Dictionary of Occupational Titles (Spector & Jex, 1991), or the reports of people who are knowledgeable of participants' jobs (Spector, Dwyer, & Jex, 1988). Given the inherent difficulties of assessing the objective work environment, it should be of little surprise that relatively few studies have directly tested the selection mechanism. Those that have examined this mechanism suggest that employee personality has generally weak relationships with the objective work environment. Spector, Jex, and Chen (1995), for example, found that the correlation between trait anxiety and job complexity, as assessed by the Dictionary of Occupational Titles (for more details about the job complexity measures, see Roos & Treiman, 1980), was only −.11.

Stressor-Creation

The stressor-creation mechanism suggests that personality predisposes workers to engage in behaviors that shape the objective nature of one or more aspects of their work environments (Milam, Spitzmueller, & Penney, 2009; Spector et al., 2000). A highly conscientious office worker, for example, may create a heavy workload for herself by volunteering for extra "side projects." Similarly, a worker high in trait anxiety or NA may unwittingly undermine relationships with coworkers as a result of his frequent displays of negative emotion.

The stressor-creation mechanism is similar to the selection mechanism in that both suggest that personality influences the objective nature of one's workplace. They differ, however, in that the selection mechanism assumes that personality influences the particular types of preexisting work environments people either self-select or are selected into, whereas the stressor-creation mechanism suggests that personality influences how workers actively shape their work environments. The two mechanisms are not mutually exclusive, as employees may self-select into a particular type of work environment and subsequently influence that environment once they are there.

The idea that people actively influence the objective nature of their work environments is also consistent with the literature on coping behaviors (see Carver, Scheier, & Weintraub, 1989; Lazarus & Folkman, 1984). A variety of different coping strategies have been described in the literature. Carver et al. (1989), for example, identified 14 types of coping behavior, including active coping, suppression of competing activities, seeking social support, positive reinterpretation, turning to religion, and behavioral and mental disengagement.

Personality is related to several different forms of coping (Costa, Somerfield, & McCrae, 1996; Watson & Hubbard, 1996). Thus, rather than simply predispose workers to create stressful situations, personality may also influence the types of behaviors that workers employ to combat stressors. Much of this research has examined neuroticism's relationship with coping, with lesser attention given to other Five-Factor Model (FFM) traits. Watson and Hubbard (1996), for example, found that neuroticism was generally related to maladaptive coping behaviors (e.g., focusing on and venting emotions, mental disengagement, behavioral disengagement, denial, and substance abuse). Conscientiousness, on the other hand, was generally related to adaptive coping behaviors (e.g., active coping, planning, and suppression of competing activities)—presumably because these behaviors require significant effort and vigilance to enact.

One largely unexplored issue regarding the stressor-creation mechanism is the extent to which workers either intentionally or unintentionally shape their work environments. In some cases, personality may predispose one to intentionally manipulate his or her environment in a particular way. An introverted employee, for example, may intentionally keep her office door closed in order to discourage contact with her coworkers. Alternatively, personality may predispose people to behave in ways that shape their work environment in an unintentional manner. In the pursuit of professional prestige and status, a highly conscientious worker, for example, may engage in behaviors that alienate her coworkers. In this example, the worker may not have intended to undermine her interpersonal relationships at work. Instead, the unfavorable effects on her social environment were an unintended side-effect of her efforts to achieve long-term career goals.

A rigorous testing of the stressor-creation hypothesis requires the objective measurement of specific stressor-creation behaviors. Unfortunately, no such studies are present in the extant literature. As a result, future research should identify the specific behaviors workers engage in to shape their environments and should test these behaviors as mediators of the effects of personality on stress-related variables.

Differential Sensitivity

The differential sensitivity hypothesis suggests that, as a result of personality differences, workers differ in their levels of responsiveness to work stressors (Spector et al., 2000). In other words, personality is hypothesized to moderate the relationship between work stressors and strains. As such, the notion of differential sensitivity fits within the general framework of person–situation interactionism (see Diener, Larsen, & Emmons, 1984; Mischel, 1977; Tett & Burnett, 2003), which is a topic we will discuss in more detail below in the section on "Future Research Directions."

The nature of the differential sensitivity effect, however, is expected to vary across personality traits. First, some traits are expected to exacerbate the effects of work stressors on strains. Such *hypersensitivity effects* are most closely associated with trait NA (Watson & Clark, 1984). Because NA is thought to reflect a fundamental biological tendency to be overly responsive to negative stimuli (Larsen & Ketelaar, 1989, 1991), stronger work stressor–strain relationships are expected to be observed for high-NA workers than for low-NA workers.

Other personality traits are hypothesized to produce a *hyposensitivity effect*, that is, to ameliorate the effects of work stressors on strains. In such cases, personality traits can be viewed as psychological resources that protect workers from stressors (Hobfoll, 1989). The hyposensitivity hypothesis is most closely associated with hardiness (Bartone, 1999), although it has also been applied to other personality traits, including locus of control (Spector, 1982) and trait humor (R. A. Martin & Lefcourt, 1983). As an example of the hyposensitivity effect, emotional labor demands requiring workers to express positive emotions (Grandey, 2000)—a common feature in many customer service jobs—may be relatively less taxing on high-PA workers than on low-PA workers because people who are high in PA are more likely to genuinely experience positive emotions, and thus they can express those emotions with little effort.

Overall, research has found mixed support for the sensitivity hypothesis. Some studies, for example, have found that NA exacerbates the effects of stressors on strains (e.g., Moyle, 1995), whereas other studies have failed to find such a moderator effect (e.g., Jex & Spector, 1996). Similarly, some studies have found that hardiness ameliorates the stressor–strain relationship (e.g., Kobasa, 1979), whereas other studies have failed to find a moderating effect for hardiness (e.g., King, King, Fairbank, Keane, & Adams, 1998). Further research is needed to identify the conditions under which sensitivity effects are most likely to occur.

Personality as a "Nuisance" Variable

In addition to the above substantive mechanisms, personality has also been hypothesized to act as a methodological "nuisance" variable that may produce a spurious relationship between stressors and strains (see Brief, Burke, George, Robinson, & Webster, 1988; Chen & Spector, 1991; Spector et al., 2000). That is, particular personality traits lead people to exhibit consistent response patterns to self-report measures of both work stressors and strains, and, as a result, controlling for the effects of those traits is expected to significantly weaken stressor–strain relationships. This spuriousness hypothesis, which is most closely associated with NA, has received mixed support. Specifically, some studies have found that controlling for NA substantially weakens the work stressor–strain relationships (e.g., Brief et al., 1988), whereas other studies have found that controlling for NA has only trivial effects on work stressor–strain relationships (e.g., Chen & Spector, 1991; Jex & Spector, 1996).

We should note that there may be merit to using other personality traits to test the spuriousness hypothesis. Indeed, any personality trait that is related to both work stressors and strains, including PA (Watson, Clark, & Tellegen, 1988), hardiness (Bartone, 1999), and core self-evaluations (CSEs; Judge, Locke, & Durham, 1997), has the potential to contribute to spurious stressor–strain relationships. As a result, future research on the spuriousness hypothesis should consider the role played by personality traits other than NA.

The Relationships Between Specific Personality Traits and Work Stressors and Strains

Above, we discussed the theoretical mechanisms potentially linking employee personality to stress-related variables. Here, we identify several specific personality traits that are theoretically and/or empirically related to work stressors and strains.

Affective Dispositions

Although psychologists have historically conceptualized affect as a state, a mood, or as a response to a particular stimulus, a growing literature has developed since the 1980s in which affect has been treated as a disposition or trait (Watson et al., 1988). In other words, people are described as displaying characteristic emotional patterns that are relatively stable across time and across situations. Rather than representing transient emotional states, affective dispositions reflect a general tendency to experience particular emotions.

As we discuss in the following subsections, at least three different affective dispositions have been identified in the literature: NA, positive affectivity (PA), and affective disposition as assessed by the *Neutral Objects Satisfaction Questionnaire* (NOSQ; Judge & Bretz, 1993). Important to the current chapter, each disposition is conceptually and empirically associated with stress-related variables. It is of note that the three affective dispositions are largely independent from each other (M. J. Burke, Brief, & George, 1993), suggesting that they should not be regarded as different manifestations of a higher-order "affective disposition" factor. Instead, we use the term "affective dispositions" to refer to a category of heterogeneous traits that are conceptually similar only in that they are emotional in nature (for more coverage of personality and affect see Chapter 30, this volume).

NA

NA (Watson & Clark, 1984; Watson et al., 1988), which represents the extent to which one generally experiences negative emotions (e.g., anxiety, depression, frustration), has received considerable attention within the occupational stress literature (Jex & Yankelevich, 2008). Several of the theoretical processes reviewed above potentially link NA to work stressors and strains (see Spector et al., 2000). Specifically, high-NA employees may be predisposed to perceive the presence of stressors even when they are objectively minimal or absent, and they may have a tendency to be exposed to high levels of objective stressors. This may occur because such individuals either self-select into or are selected by their employers into objectively stressful conditions, or engage in behaviors that create work stressors. Furthermore, when compared with their low-NA counterparts, high-NA workers may display hypersensitivity to work stressors, which is manifested in relatively stronger stressor–strain relationships among high-NA workers (Moyle, 1995).

Consistent with the above theorizing, volumes of research suggest that NA is positively related to work stressors and strains (e.g., Brief et al., 1988; Chen & Spector, 1991; Jex & Spector, 1996). Findings involving work stressors suggest, for example, that NA is positively related to self-reported role stressors, interpersonal conflict, and organizational constraints (Bowling & Eschleman, 2010). Research using strains as criteria has found that NA is positively related to frustration, job dissatisfaction, and physical illness (Chen & Spector, 1991). It is of note that NA has considerable conceptual overlap with neuroticism from the FFM (Digman, 1990). Indeed, aggregating the results of 12 primary studies, Watson, Wiese, Vaidya, and Tellegen (1999) found an average uncorrected correlation of .58 between NA and neuroticism (assuming that NA and neuroticism measures both had Cronbach's alphas of .85—reasonable reliability estimates for these types of measures—the average corrected NA–neuroticism correlation would have been .68).

Finally, NA is often conceptualized as a general tendency to experience various negative emotions. This fact is apparent in the approach employed by the *Positive and Negative Affect Schedule* (PANAS; Watson et al., 1988), the most commonly used measure of NA. The NA subscale of the PANAS provides respondents with 10 negative emotion adjectives (e.g., Watson et al., 1988), and their responses to all items are combined to yield an overall NA score. This approach implies that different negative emotions are interchangeable for each other and may thus obscure the effects of more narrow NA facets. As a result, some researchers have focused on more narrow subfacets of NA rather than on general NA. Both trait anger and trait anxiety, for example, have attracted attention from occupational stress researchers (Bruk-Lee, Khoury, Nixon, Goh, & Spector, 2009). The study of these subfacets, however, may be worthwhile because more narrow conceptualizations of traits can be especially useful for predicting narrow criteria (Ones & Viswesvaran, 1996).

PA

PA is the extent to which one generally experiences positive emotions, such as enthusiasm, excitement, and joy (Watson et al., 1988). Although occupational stress researchers have given considerably less attention to PA than to NA, there are several reasons to expect that PA will be negatively related to work stressors and strains. First, high-PA employees may be predisposed to perceive their work environments favorably, regardless of the objective presence or absence of work stressors (Connolly & Viswesvaran, 2000). In this sense, being high in PA may cause one to see their work through "rose-colored glasses." Furthermore, PA may serve as a psychological resource that protects workers from stress-related variables. The frequent enthusiasm experienced by a high-PA worker, for example, could give him or her the energy needed to deal with a heavy workload, and it may be incompatible with feelings of emotional exhaustion, a key symptom of burnout (Maslach & Jackson, 1986). Being high in PA might also assist one in procuring other resources, such as social support, status, and income.

As predicted by the above theorizing, research has indeed found negative correlations between PA and stress-related variables (Fortunato & Harsh, 2006; Fortunato, LeBourgeois, & Harsh, 2008; Thoresen, Kaplan, Barsky, Warren, & de Chermont, 2003; Zellars, Perrewe, Hochwarter, & Anderson, 2006). Specifically, PA is negatively related to role ambiguity, interpersonal conflict, job tension, depression, health complaints, frustration, and burnout. We should note, however, that PA is generally assumed to be less important for the prediction of stress-related variables than is NA. This is because NA is thought to have a relatively greater influence on one's response to negative stimuli, whereas PA is thought to have a relatively greater influence on one's response to positive stimuli (Fortunato & Stone-Romero, 2001).

Although not examined in the occupational stress literature, many of the benefits of PA may occur because it counteracts the unfavorable effects of NA (for a related discussion of how positive emotion can "undo" the unfavorable effects of negative emotion, see Fredrickson, 2001). Thus, we would expect that PA would "buffer" or ameliorate the unfavorable effects of NA on work stressors and strains. We return to this issue below in discussing interactions among personality traits.

Although one might infer from their names that NA and PA are polar opposites of a single continuum, this is not the case. First, NA and PA are hypothesized as manifestations of two separate biological systems (Gray, 1970, 1981). Whereas NA corresponds to a behavioral inhibition system that governs how sensitive one is to punishment, PA corresponds to a behavioral activation system that governs how sensitive one is to rewards. Furthermore, empirical evidence suggests that NA and PA are largely distinct from each other. A meta-analysis by Connolly and Viswesvaran (1999), for example, found a corrected correlation between NA and PA of only −.30. This suggests that a number of different PA/NA combinations are possible across individuals (e.g., high-PA/high-NA, low-PA/low-NA, high-PA/low-NA, and low-PA/high-NA) and that PA and NA may have unique effects on work stressors and strains.

Affective Disposition as Measured by the NOSQ

Although much of the research on affective disposition has focused on NA and PA, some studies have operationalized affective disposition by the emotional responses one has to ostensibly neutral stimuli. This approach is most closely associated with the NOSQ (Judge & Bretz, 1993). The NOSQ provides respondents with a list of 25 "neutral" everyday objects, such as "modern art," "today's cars," and "8½″ × 11″ paper." Participants are asked to indicate whether they are either satisfied with, feel neutral toward, or are dissatisfied with each object. Given that the objects are intended to be neutral (i.e., not clearly positive or negative), the modal response to each object is assumed to be "feel neutral toward." Thus, respondents who indicate that they are satisfied with the ostensibly neutral items are thought to have a predisposition toward being content. On the other hand, dissatisfied respondents are thought to have a predisposition toward being discontent. Consistent with the assumption that the NOSQ assesses a trait, it has been found to display a higher level of temporal consistency than either the NA or PA subscales of the PANAS (Judge & Bretz, 1993).

Much of the research on the NOSQ has focused on job attitudes, with a recent meta-analysis yielding a mean corrected correlation of .25 between the NOSQ (higher scores reflect greater satisfaction) and global job satisfaction (Eschleman & Bowling, 2011, Study 1). Although few studies have examined the NOSQ as a predictor of stress-related variables, we believe there are strong conceptual bases to expect that it is negatively correlated with work stressors and strains. First, because low scores on the NOSQ may reflect a general tendency to be unhappy and to view neutral situations as unpleasant, we expect that the form of affective disposition assessed by the NOSQ will influence work stressors and strains via the perceptual process described above. In other words, people who score low on the NOSQ are likely to perceive the presence of work stressor and strains despite the objective absence of stressors and strains. Second, the aspect of affective disposition assessed by the NOSQ may influence the extent to which one engages in stressor-creation behaviors. A worker with a low score on the NOSQ, for example, may habitually complain about his or her work, coworkers, and supervisors, thus creating objective social stressors.

We encourage occupational stress researchers to give more attention to the NOSQ. Importantly, the NOSQ has been shown to be largely distinct from both NA and PA. Meta-analytic evidence (Eschleman & Bowling, 2011, Study 1), for example, recently found that the NOSQ yielded a corrected correlation of −.27 with NA and .32 with PA. This finding may surprise many researchers because the NOSQ has sometimes been assumed to be an alternative measure of NA (e.g., Probst, 2003). Given its empirical uniqueness, the NOSQ may be related to work stressors and strains even after the effects of NA and PA have been controlled.

We should note one caveat regarding the NOSQ. Although the objects included in the items are assumed to be "neutral," some appear to be more neutral than others. Whereas items such as "8½″ × 11″ paper" and "modern art" are relatively neutral, "myself" and "my first name" are probably not neutral. Indeed, most people are likely to have favorable responses toward these items, and one could argue that they are contaminated with self-esteem variance. Future research should thus utilize a NOSQ-like measure that excludes self-referent items.

FFM

Since the 1980s, the FFM has emerged as the most popular means of categorizing personality constructs (Costa & McCrae, 1992; Digman, 1990; Goldberg, 1990). According to the FFM, personality can be described along five broad dimensions: neuroticism, extraversion, conscientiousness, agreeableness, and openness to experience. As we discuss below, most of these dimensions are theoretically related to work stressors and strains.

Neuroticism

Neuroticism, which is similar to but broader than NA (see Nemanick & Munz, 1997), is the extent to which one generally displays self-consciousness and immoderation and experiences feelings of anxiety, anger, depression, and vulnerability (Costa & McCrae, 1992; Goldberg, 1990). Compared with their low-neuroticism counterparts, high-neuroticism individuals experience negative emotions more frequently, more intensely, and in a wider range of situations. Both conceptually and empirically, neuroticism plays a more important role in models of occupational stress than do any of the other FFM traits. Because neuroticism and NA display a high degree of conceptual and empirical overlap (Watson & Clark, 1984; Watson et al., 1999), our discussion above regarding the theoretical mechanisms linking NA to work stressors and strains also applies to neuroticism. In short, neuroticism is likely to be related to stress-related variables via perceptual, selection, stressor-creation, and hypersensitivity processes (Spector et al., 2000). Indeed, empirical evidence consistently finds that neuroticism is positively related to both stressors and strains (Grant & Langan-Fox, 2007; Heinisch & Jex, 1997, 1998). Some studies testing the hypersensitivity hypothesis have found that the work stressor–strain relationship is strong for high-neuroticism workers than for low-neuroticism workers (Moyle, 1995), whereas other studies have failed to find such interaction effects.

One of the reasons that some researchers have failed to find evidence of moderator effects is that they have used composite measures of neuroticism, despite the fact that this trait (and all of the other Big Five dimensions) consist of a number of subdimensions (Paunonen & Ashton, 2001). In the case of neuroticism, the subdimensions are anxiety, angry hostility, depression, impulsiveness, and vulnerability. It is quite possible that some of these subdimensions may be more or less likely to moderate certain stressors. We would predict that a person who is high on the vulnerability subdimension would react more strongly to interpersonal mistreatment compared to someone who is low on this subdimension. We would encourage researchers to examine the impact of subdimensions in future research.

Extraversion

Extraversion represents the extent to which one is generally sociable, friendly, talkative, and prone to experience positive emotions, such as excitement and enthusiasm (Costa & McCrae, 1992; Goldberg, 1990). Although not as great as the similarity between neuroticism and NA, the similarity between extraversion and PA should not be overlooked (Watson et al., 1999). This overlap is particularly salient for the "cheerfulness" and "activity level" subdimensions of extraversion (Costa & McCrae, 1992). As a result, the theoretical processes by which PA influences stress-related variables, as discussed above, have relevance for extraversion. Specifically, being high in extraversion may produce perceptual biases that predispose workers to interpret their jobs in favorable ways, and it may serve as a psychological resource that protects workers from stress-related variables.

It is important, however, to consider the explicit social character of extraversion. Extraversion is not simply another label for PA but instead is a relatively broader trait that includes "friendliness," "gregariousness," "assertiveness," and "excitement-seeking" subdimensions (Costa & McCrae, 1992; Goldberg, 1990). These aspects of extraversion have relevance for how workers shape their work environments and how they may facilitate the acquisition of social, psychological, and physical resources. Extraverted workers, for instance, may more easily develop friendships at work, acquire social support, and achieve social status (Bowling, Beehr, & Swader, 2005).

Consistent with the above theorizing, extraversion has been found to be negatively related to several stress-related variables, including role ambiguity, underutilization of skills, physical illness, and job dissatisfaction (Grant & Langan-Fox, 2007; Judge, Heller, & Mount, 2002).

As with neuroticism, it is possible that the subdimensions of extraversion could be related differentially with stress-related variables. According to Paunonen and Ashton (2001), these include warmth, gregariousness, assertiveness, activity, excitement seeking, and positive emotions. One could imagine, for example, that a person who is very high on excitement seeking might find it very stressful with work that is very slow paced or has very low complexity.

Conscientiousness

Conscientiousness is the extent to which a person is responsible, hard working, and detail oriented (Costa & McCrae, 1992; Goldberg, 1990). Because meta-analytic evidence has shown that it is positively related to job performance for nearly all jobs (Barrick & Mount, 1991; Barrick, Mount, & Judge, 2001; see Griffin & Hesketh, 2005, however, for a review of studies finding negative conscientiousness–performance relationships), conscientiousness has attracted considerable attention from industrial and organizational psychologists interested in employee productivity. Conscientiousness, however, has largely been overlooked by occupational stress researchers. Nonetheless, there is good reason to expect it to be negatively associated with work stressors and strains. Indeed, being high in conscientiousness has been found to be associated with many desirable outcomes, such as health-promoting behaviors (Bogg & Roberts, 2004), longevity (L. R. Martin & Friedman, 2000), and life satisfaction (DeNeve & Cooper, 1998). Perhaps similar positive effects will also be observed when conscientiousness is included in occupational stress models. The beneficial effects of this dimension may primarily occur because it represents a psychological resource and because it facilitates the acquisition of other valuable resources (Hobfoll, 1989). Being conscientious, for example, may contribute to career success and income (Judge, Higgins, Thoresen, & Barrick, 1999), both of which could be used as resources to deal with work stressors. A recent study by Grant and Langan-Fox (2007) showed that, indeed, conscientiousness is negatively related to common stressors such as role ambiguity and underutilization of skills, and to strain reactions such as physical illness and behavioral disengagement.

The effects of conscientiousness, however, might not always be favorable. In particular, exceptionally high levels might result in increased levels of stressors and strains. Highly conscientious workers, for example, might experience distress because they take on too many voluntary work tasks or because they set goals for themselves that are unreasonably difficult. Furthermore, highly conscientious workers may alienate their coworkers by setting standards for others that are unreasonable. This may be particularly true among conscientious workers who are also low in agreeableness (Witt, Burke, Barrick, & Mount, 2002), or extremely high on the conscientiousness subdimension of dutifulness (Paunonen & Ashton, 2001). Because conscientiousness might represent a "double-edge sword" for employee well-being, we suggest that future occupational stress studies examine the nonlinear effects of conscientiousness as well as potential interactions between conscientiousness and other personality traits.

Agreeableness

Agreeableness reflects the extent to which an individual is kind, caring, and concerned for other people (Costa & McCrae, 1992; Goldberg, 1990). Given its interpersonal nature, much of the effects of agreeableness on stress-related outcomes may occur via social processes. In some cases, agreeableness may contribute to healthy interpersonal relationships at work. Because they are generally pleasant to interact with, agreeable workers may receive more social support from colleagues (Bowling et al., 2005) and experience fewer instances of interpersonal mistreatment (Milam et al., 2009) than their less agreeable peers. Such processes suggest that agreeableness may contribute to a less stressful working situation.

As with conscientiousness, little research has been done on the relationship between agreeableness and both stressors and strains. Grant and Langan-Fox (2007) did find in their meta-analysis, however, that agreeableness is negatively related to both role ambiguity and behavioral disengagement, suggesting that agreeableness may have a useful role in models of occupational stress.

We should note, though, that being *extremely* agreeable may contribute to a more stressful work environment. An extremely agreeable worker, in an effort to please others and to avoid social conflict, may routinely volunteer to take on too much work or undesirable tasks. This may especially be true if a person were very high on the altruism subdimension of agreeableness. As a result, the employee may become overwhelmed by having an excessive workload. Likewise, highly agreeable employees may often be viewed by others as submissive or weak, leading to their being targets of workplace aggression (see Aquino & Lamertz, 2004). In short, these processes suggest that agreeableness may have nonlinear relationships with work stressors and strains, such that it yields beneficial effects only up to a point, after which negative consequences ensue.

Openness to Experience

Openness to experience, the extent to which a person is curious, creative, and interested in novel ideas and experiences (Costa & McCrae, 1992; Goldberg, 1990), is generally weakly related to organizational criteria, such as job performance (Barrick & Mount, 1991; Barrick et al., 2001) and job satisfaction (Judge, Heller, et al., 2002). We should note that part of the reason for these weak relationships is that openness to experience is positively related to criteria for some jobs but is negatively related to criteria for others (see Barrick et al., 2001). Overall, we see few reasons to expect that openness to experience will be related to work stressors or strains. This assumption has been supported by empirical evidence (Grant & Langan-Fox, 2007). It is also true, however, that there has not been a great deal of research examining the impact of openness to experience in the stress process. It may be possible, for example, that individuals high on openness to experience may be more likely to try different methods of dealing with work-related stressors than individuals low on this trait. This of course needs to be tested in future research.

Additional Personality Traits

In addition to affective disposition and the FFM characteristics, several other personality traits have been examined in the occupational stress literature. Below we consider the role of hardiness, CSEs, proactive personality, type A personality, "dark side" personality traits, and positive personality traits.

Hardiness

Hardiness is a personality trait reflecting the extent to which one is resistant to the effects of stress (Maddi & Kobasa, 1984). In other words, hardy individuals are thought to be able to endure the presence of stressors without experiencing strains. It is unique from other personality characteristics discussed in the current chapter to the extent it is defined by its effects on the stressor–strain relationship. Traditionally, hardiness has been conceptualized as including three constituent subfacets: commitment, control, and challenge. Commitment reflects the extent to which a person has several domains to which he or she is engaged with. Control, on the other hand, is the extent to which one believes that life events are controllable and is synonymous with locus of control (Spector, 1982). Finally, challenge represents the extent to which one generally interprets difficult circumstances as challenges (rather than as threats). This appears to be quite similar to the coping dimension of positive reappraisal (Lazarus & Folkman, 1984).

There are several theoretical processes that potentially link hardiness to work stressors and strains. First, hardiness may influence how one perceives their work environment. This process is particularly salient in the control and challenge dimensions because they explicitly represent a bias toward seeing control and opportunity in a wide range of situations. Hardiness might also be beneficial because it is a psychological resource or is a path to other resources (Bartone, 1999). The commitment facet, for example, implies engagement in a number of nonwork activities (e.g., family life, leisure, religion) that provide a support structure that is useful when work stress is high. Finally, as suggested above, definitions of hardiness often posit it as a factor that ameliorates the effects of stressors on strains (Kobasa, 1979). This is a specific example of the hyposensitivity hypothesis discussed above.

Consistent with the above theorizing about main effects, research consistently finds support for relationships between hardiness and work stressors and strains. A recent meta-analysis by Eschleman, Bowling, and Alarcon (2010), for example, found that a composite of the hardiness facets, as well as commitment, control, and challenge, each generally yielded negative relationships with work stressors (e.g., role conflict, role ambiguity, interpersonal conflict) and strains (e.g., anxiety, depression, burnout). It is of note, however, that hardiness research has found mixed support for the hyposensitivity hypothesis (see Beehr & Bowling, 2005). Whereas early research on hardiness found that exposure to stressors was associated with ill health only in those low in hardiness (e.g., Kobasa, 1979), other research has failed to replicate these moderator effects (e.g., King et al., 1998).

CSEs

Since its introduction in the late 1990s, CSEs (Judge et al., 1997) have emerged as an important dispositional variable in organizational research. The CSE construct is a relatively broad second-order personality construct consisting of four personality traits that have traditionally been studied independently of one another: self-esteem, general self-efficacy, emotional stability, and locus of control (Judge, Locke, Durham, & Kluger, 1998). Accordingly, CSE is described as representing the fundamental conclusions that people draw about their own competence and self-worth (Judge et al., 1997). Factor analyses have shown that the four constituent CSE traits load onto a single latent factor (Judge et al., 1998), thus providing support for the hierarchical nature of the CSE construct. It should be noted, however, that the four CSE traits are not interchangeable with each other (see Judge, Erez, Bono, & Thoresen, 2002), and thus, depending upon one's research objectives, it can be useful to study them separately.

Early theorizing regarding CSE suggests that it represents an alternative and less clinically based conceptualization of emotional stability (Judge & Bono, 2001). Thus, the processes linking CSE to work stressors and strains are likely to be similar to those described above for neuroticism and NA. That is, CSE may produce effects on stress-related variables via perceptual, selection, stressor-creation, and sensitivity mechanisms. Additionally, some of the constituent CSE traits—particularly self-esteem and general self-efficacy—may represent valuable resources that might aid one in dealing with stress-related variables (Hobfoll, 1989). In sum, this theorizing suggests that CSE and its constituent traits will be negatively related to work stressors and strains. This conclusion was supported in a recent meta-analysis by Kammeyer-Mueller, Judge, and Scott (2009), who found that CSE also likely impacts the stress process through its impact on coping: Individuals with high CSE tend to use more problem-focused coping and less emotion-focused coping.

Proactive Personality

Proactive personality reflects the extent to which one generally takes initiative to modify his or her circumstances in a personally advantageous way (Bateman & Crant, 1993). People who are high in proactive personality display a keen awareness for opportunities to improve their environments and are apt to actively respond to and create such opportunities. Furthermore, they are minimally affected by their situations. Proactive personality may influence work stressors and strains primarily via self-selection, stressor-creation, and resource-acquisition mechanisms. First, being high in proactive personality may predispose workers to vigilantly seek out information about unfamiliar work environments, and thus contribute to their ability to avoid environments they are likely to find stressful. When they do select into environments that include high levels of existing stressors, workers high in proactive personality are likely to take initiative to minimize or eliminate the stressors; in essence, those high in proactive personality tend to engage in high levels of active coping (Keoske, Kirk, & Keoske, 1993). This mechanism is likely to be beneficial when the situation allows for opportunities for stressors to be either reduced or removed, but may cause proactive employees to become distressed if they attempt to manipulate stressors that are an inherent part of the job. Finally, the resource-acquisition mechanism suggests that proactive personality may be beneficial because it aids one in acquiring resources needed to deal with work stressors and strains (see Thompson, 2005). Indeed, the behaviors exhibited by proactive people are likely to contribute to their ability to acquire a wide range of resources, such as physical and social resources.

Two recent meta-analyses (Fuller & Marler, 2009; Thomas, Whitman, & Viswesvaran, 2010) summarize the benefits of proactive personality, showing that it is positively related to a number of desirable outcomes, including job satisfaction, organizational commitment, and job performance. More relevant to the above theorizing, proactive personality has been shown to be negatively related to job strain (Parker & Sprigg, 1999). More recently, Cunningham and De La Rosa (2008) found that proactive personality moderated the relation between time-based family-to-work interference and life satisfaction. As expected, interference had less impact on individuals who reported high levels of proactive personality. Given its conceptual relevance to occupational stress, we encourage future studies examining proactive personality's relationship with work stressors and strains.

Type A Personality

The type A personality was a trait developed by Friedman and Rosenman (1959) to describe individuals who were prone to coronary heart disease. In the initial conceptualization of type A, individuals high on this trait were characterized as having a heightened sense of time urgency, high level of competitiveness and desire to achieve, a high activity level, high work involvement, and often a high level of hostility toward others. The approach Friedman and Rosenman used to measure type A was a structured interview that allowed them to classify people as either type A or nontype A.

More recent research on type A has shown that this trait can be broken down into two relatively independent factors: achievement strivings (AS) and impatience–irritability (II) (Spence et al., 1987). The AS dimension of type A reflects an individual's desire to succeed in job- or school-related tasks and has in fact been shown to be positive related to success in these domains (Bluen, Barling, & Burns, 1990; Spence et al., 1987). The II dimension, on the other hand, reflects an individual's propensity to grow impatient in situations that require one to wait (e.g., being in traffic) and become hostile with others in such situations. Spence et al. and others (Bluen et al., 1990) have found that II is positively related to perceptions of stress and reports of psychosomatic symptoms. Interestingly, these two dimensions of type A are not highly related, so it is possible for a person to exhibit a relatively high level of the type A trait, due to high AS, and still not be adversely impacted.

While most occupational stress research has identified type A, particularly the II component, as having a main effect on stressors and strains (e.g., Ganster, 1987; Schaubroeck, Ganster, & Kemmerer, 1994), there is some evidence that type A may moderate an individual's reactions to work. For example, Jex, Adams, Elacqua, and Bachrach (2002) found that mental demands and job complexity were negatively related to job satisfaction among those high on the II component of type A; in contrast, this same relation was positive among those low on II.

"Dark Side" Personality Traits

Recent research attention has been given to socially undesirable or "dark side" personality traits (Paulhaus & Williams, 2002). These traits, the most widely studied of which include narcissism, Machiavellianism, and psychopathy, represent subclinical parallels of various personality disorders. Although few occupational stress studies have examined their effects, we expect these "dark" traits to have undesirable effects on work stressors and strains. First, many of these traits are conceptually and empirically related to NA and neuroticism. Machiavellianism, and psychopathy, for example, correlates in the .30s–.40s with neuroticism (Jakobwitz & Egan, 2006). Given that NA and neuroticism have undesirable effects, these "dark side" personality traits are also likely to have negative consequences. Second, many of the "dark side" traits influence the degree to which people are hypersensitive to social slights. Workers high on narcissism, for example, respond more strongly to perceived injustices than do workers low on narcissism (Alexander, 2011; Penney & Spector, 2005). Given that slights, injustices, and disappointments are inevitable within any work setting, narcissists are likely to experience the workplace as a stressful environment. As a result, perceptual and sensitivity processes may link "dark side" traits with stress-related variables. Finally, "dark side" traits may influence how workers shape their social environments. Machiavellian managers, for example, are likely to objectify and alienate their subordinates. As a result of this behavior, it is likely that they will create a negative social environment for themselves and those around them.

Positive Personality Traits

Positive psychology, which has recently emerged as an influential force within psychology, focuses on the positive aspects of human behavior (Seligman & Csikszentmihalyi, 2000). One of the most important contributions of positive psychology is its promotion of the study of positive personality traits. These traits, which are also referred to as character strengths, constitute a heterogeneous set of personality characteristics that share the common theme of being morally valued and seen as desirable by a large proportion of society (Peterson & Seligman, 2004). Some of these traits include gratitude (McCullough, Emmons, & Tsang, 2002), forgiveness (Emmons, 2000), patience (Schnitker & Emmons, 2007), optimism (Peterson, 2000), humility (Davis, Worthington, & Hook, 2010), and humor (R. A. Martin & Lefcourt, 1983). Given that positivity is not simply the absence of negativity, we expect that these traits may predict unique variance in stress-related variables above and beyond the effects of negative traits, such as neuroticism. We also expect that these positive personality traits, because they are largely independent from existing personality traits, will yield unique relationships with stress-related outcomes after more established positive (e.g., PA) traits are controlled.

Positive personality traits have indeed been found to produce beneficial effects for employees (Avey, Luthans, & Jensen, 2009; Avey, Wernsing, & Mhatre, 2011). Avey et al. (2009), for example, found that psychological capital—a conglomeration of efficacy, hope, optimism, and resilience—was negatively related to psychological strain. The scope of the current section, however, prevents us from describing in detail the processes linking individual positive traits to stress-related variables. In general, we suspect that many of these traits may serve as psychological resources that workers can utilize in response to stressors. Furthermore, because these traits are, by definition, socially respected, and virtuous (Peterson & Seligman, 2004), those who possess them may be held in higher esteem by coworkers and management and, as a result, have strong interpersonal relationships at work. These interpersonal relationships, in turn, may be expected to have favorable effects on stress-related variables. Given their recent introduction, positive personality traits have received very limited research attention from occupational health psychologists and are thus a ripe area for future research.

Future Research Directions

Although recent research has led to many insights regarding the relationship between employee personality and work stressors and strains, there are several unanswered questions that should be addressed by future research. We consider some of these research directions below.

General Versus Domain-Specific Personality Measures

An important principle that has been supported in the personality literature is that predictive validity is maximized when general personality traits are used to predict conceptually relevant general criteria and domain-specific personality traits are used to predict criteria from the same domain. Research has found, for example, that work-specific measures of FFM traits may predict work-related criteria, such as job performance (Hunthausen, Truxillo, Bauer, & Hammer, 2003) and job satisfaction (Bowling & Burns, 2010), better than do general FFM traits. Similar results have been found when comparing work-specific and general measures of self-esteem (Bowling, Eschleman, Wang, Kirkendall, & Alarcon, 2010), locus of control (Wang, Bowling, & Eschleman, 2010), and CSEs (Bowling, Wang, Tang, & Kennedy, 2010). Future research should examine whether work-specific personality is an especially good predictor of work stressors and work-specific strains. Given the findings of past research, we expect that work-specific personality will predict incremental variance in stress-related variables after general personality is controlled, and that it will yield stronger relationships with stress-related variables than will general personality. Correspondingly, we suggest that the effects of general personality on work stressors and strains may be largely mediated via work-specific personality (see Bowling, Eschleman, et al., 2010).

Interactive Effects of Personality Traits

Although several occupational stress studies have examined the main effects of employee personality as well as the moderators of these effects, little attention has been given to the possibility that different personality traits might interact with each other to impact the stress process. Indeed, this argument echoes that of researchers who examine the use of personality to predict job performance (L. A. Burke & Witt, 2002; Judge & Erez, 2007; Witt et al., 2002). One exception to this is Zellars et al. (2006), who found that conscientiousness moderated the relationships between PA and strains.

There are a number of statistical interactions between personality traits that we believe stress researchers should consider. First, it is possible that the effects of undesirable personality traits (e.g., NA, narcissism) could be counteracted by positive personality traits (e.g., PA, hardiness). Indeed, such a prediction is consistent with the notion popular in positive psychology that positive emotions can "cancel-out" the effects of negative emotions (Fredrickson, 2001). Thus, for example, the degree to which negative traits affect perceptions of work stressors may depend on perceivers' standing on positive traits (i.e., stronger negative trait effects when positive trait standing is low). Other personality traits may have either beneficial or detrimental effects depending on how one scores on other traits. Being high in extraversion, for example, might benefit workers who are also high in agreeableness. These particular workers are both sociable and kind, so they likely have many friends at work. As a result of these friendships, those workers are likely to have a dependable stream of social support, which, in turn, has beneficial effects on work stressors and strains (Viswesvaran, Sanchez, & Fisher, 1999). Among workers who are low in agreeableness, on the other hand, scoring high in extraversion may be undesirable. These workers, who could be described as socially dominant and unkind, may have poor social relationships at work, offering little social support and possibly attracting abuse from workplace bullies.

Nonlinear Effects of Personality

Stress researchers have primarily examined the linear effects of employee personality. We expect that, while some personality traits such as NA, hardiness, and CSEs may largely yield linear relationships with work stressors and strains, other traits may produce nonlinear effects. Below a certain threshold, conscientiousness, for example, may be negatively related to stress-related variables. That is, conscientiousness may generally aid in the acquisition of personal resources (Hobfoll, 1989) that are beneficial to employee well-being. Being high in conscientiousness, for example, may facilitate career success, help one acquire tangible resources (e.g., pay and promotions), and facilitate acquisition of social resources (e.g., status and respect from coworkers and supervisors). Being excessively high in conscientiousness, however, may result in distress. Extremely conscientious workers, for example, may experience role overload, disappointment, and frustration because they consistently set overly difficult goals for themselves. Furthermore, by setting unreasonable standards for others, those workers may inadvertently undermine their social relationships with their coworkers.

Similarly, agreeableness may be beneficial to employees, provided it does not surpass a threshold level. That is, moderately high levels of agreeableness may generally result in healthier social experiences at work, such as the receipt of more social support and the experience of less workplace aggression. At extremely high levels, however, it may be associated with distress. That is, workers who score very highly on agreeableness may find it difficult to refuse the request of their coworkers and colleagues, and as a result, they may find themselves chronically overwhelmed by excessive work tasks. Furthermore, excessively agreeable employees may be viewed as submissive or weak and thus easy targets for aggression.

Personality–Situation Interactions

Decades of theorizing suggest that personality traits and environmental factors interact with each other to influence behavior (Diener et al., 1984; Endler & Edwards, 1985, 1986; Mischel, 1977). Trait activation theory (Tett & Burnett, 2003), for example, suggests that situational characteristics can cause a particular trait to be more or less relevant. In the current context, work stressors are likely to activate neuroticism. Having to give an important work presentation to several managers, which is an example of a stressor, is likely to activate trait anxiety. That is, trait anxiety is likely to be relevant for predicting stress-related outcomes (e.g., state anxiety) within this particular situation.

Future research on trait activation should examine whether workers experience strain whenever their jobs suppress the expression of a particular trait. Having to work alone for an extended period of time, for example, may be perceived as a stressor among extraverts, and thus it may have negative effects on their well-being. In a similar way, work situations that require people to engage in behaviors that are incompatible with their personalities may also be experienced as stressors. A heavy workload, for example, may cause low-conscientiousness workers to perceive their jobs as stressful because the behavior prescribed by the situation is inconsistent with their natural predisposition.

Does Personality Influence Stress via Effects on Job Crafting?

Job crafting is the self-initiated activities that workers employ in an effort to improve person–job fit and to increase the meaningfulness of their work (Wrzesniewski & Dutton, 2001). Research has distinguished between three distinct forms of job crafting: (1) activities that change the objective nature of one's work environment, (2) activities that change patterns of interpersonal relationships one participates in while at work, and (3) activities that change one's subjective interpretation of the meaning of one's work. Although occupational stress researchers have yet to incorporate job crafting into their theoretical models, we believe that this would likely prove fruitful. More specifically, job crafting activities may serve as mediators of the effects of personality on work stressors and strains. People high in proactive personality (Bateman & Crant, 1993), for example, may engage in generally high levels of job crafting which in turn could reduce their levels of work stressors and strains. On the other hand, people high in neuroticism may engage in maladaptive forms of job crafting (e.g., avoiding essential job tasks that one considers to be unpleasant), which may result in increased work stressors and strains.

What Role Does Personality Play in Stress Interventions?

Much of the occupational stress literature focuses on whether organizational interventions can effectively reduce problems associated with work stress (for a review, see Bowling et al., 2012; Richardson & Rothstein, 2008). This literature, however, often overlooks the potential effects of employee personality on the effectiveness of stress interventions. That is, it may be important to "match" particular interventions with individual workers because using interventions that are incongruent with a worker's personality may be ineffective or even counterproductive. In other words, the effects of many occupational stress interventions may be moderated by employee personality.

When matching employee personality to particular stress interventions, it is unclear whether practitioners should use interventions that capitalize upon individual strength or instead use interventions that overcome individual weaknesses. Cogent arguments can be made for both positions. Consider, for example, how different employees might respond to a stress intervention designed to produce positive emotion, such as a physical fitness program. On the one hand, high-PA workers may experience considerable benefits from such interventions because they are highly receptive to positive stimuli (Fortunato & Stone-Romero, 2001). Alternatively, low-PA workers may experience the greatest benefits because, unlike their high-PA counterparts who may experience a ceiling effect when it comes to positive emotions, they have more room for improvement. Future research may find that both positions are partially correct. That is, for some traits or interventions, it may be best to take advantage of individual strengths. For other traits or interventions, however, it may be best to target individual weaknesses. Determining which traits might operate in which ways, and under what conditions, is a matter for future research.

Similarly, some traits may predispose workers to be either sensitive or insensitive to any stress intervention. Because they are relatively unresponsive to positive stimuli (Watson & Clark, 1984), high-NA workers, for example, may be minimally affected by any stress intervention, regardless of the content of the intervention. High-conscientious workers, on the other hand, may benefit from most interventions because they are willing to exercise the continued effort required of most interventions.

Distinguishing Between Challenge Stressors and Hindrance Stressors

Above, we briefly discussed the distinction between challenge stressors and hindrance stressors (Lepine et al., 2005; Podsakoff et al., 2007). Although the current chapter has implicitly focused on hindrance stressors and thus has framed stressors as being undesirable, we should note the importance of also studying challenge stressors and their accompanying beneficial effects. In particular, research should examine similarities and differences between how personality influences hindrance stressors and how it influences challenge stressors.

Research Considerations

As with any research area, the occupational stress literature could be advanced via the use of more rigorous research designs. Below, we consider two methodological practices that should be incorporated into future research: within-subject designs and the use of nonself-report measures.

Within-Subject Research Designs

Future occupational stress studies examining the role of employee personality should employ within-subject designs. In such designs, participants may be asked to complete personality measures during an initial session and then provide stressor and strain data multiple times per day over the course of several days. Using this approach, researchers could model whether changes in stressors (or the initial level of stressors) predict changes in strains and whether such relationships are moderated by personality. Furthermore, within-subject designs would allow researchers to examine whether personality predicts changes in stressors (or the initial level of stressors), which, in turn, may impact subsequent strains. Indeed, several of the theoretical mechanisms reviewed above—particularly the selection and stressor-creation mechanisms—imply that the effects of personality on stress-related variables develop over time. Within-subject designs are uniquely suited to tracking such unfolding processes.

Another advantage of within-subject designs is that they allow researchers to capture personality's role in determining how workers respond to a specific stressor event. Whereas the traditional between-subject cross-sectional study can examine the effects of chronic stressors (e.g., the extent to which interpersonal conflict is generally present in one's work environment), within-subject designs can focus on an acute stress event (e.g., a particular instance of interpersonal conflict). This is important because stress-related processes may occur very quickly and disappear before they can be captured by a between-subject design.

An additional advantage of within-subject designs is that, because they employ "real time" assessment, measures are less likely to be biased by participants' faulty memories (Larson & Csikszentmihalyi, 1983). That is, between-subject designs generally ask participants to recall stressors and strains that they have experienced either days or months ago, thus leaving the study vulnerable to participants' forgetting or misremembering. Within-subject designs, on the other hand, typically ask about stressors or strains that just occurred. Thus, the limitations of human memory are less likely to influence participants' responses in within-subject designs.

Nonself-Report Measures

Additional research is needed that examines the relationship between employee personality and stress-related variables using nonself-report measures. Indeed, research examining the personality–stress variable relationship has almost exclusively utilized participants' self-reports. One potential disadvantage of the use of self-reports is that it leaves studies vulnerable to the effects of common-method variance (Crampton & Wagner, 1994). Furthermore, socially desirable responding may threaten the validity of self-report measures used to assess especially socially sensitive constructs, such as undesirable personality traits (e.g., NA, "dark side" traits).

The inclusion of nonself-report measures is also useful because it can aid in testing the mediating processes linking personality to stress-related variables. Specifically, the perceptual mechanism predicts that personality primarily influences stress-related outcomes by influencing one's perceptions of the work environment. Thus, one might expect that personality would predict perceived stressors after objective stressors are controlled. Similarly, the selection and stressor-creation mechanisms predict that personality influences stress-related variables via effects on the objective work environment. Thus, these mechanisms suggest that employee personality would predict objectively measured stressors after perceived stressors are controlled.

Alternatives to self-report measures may involve having significant others (i.e., friends, family members, coworkers, or supervisors) provide reports of participants' personalities or work stressors, which is a practice that has been used occasionally in past research (Judge et al., 1998; Spector et al., 1988). Alternatively, it is possible to assess work stressors using more objective means, such as O*NET (Liu et al., 2005) or expert judges' ratings of job titles (Spector & Jex, 1991). Some strains can be measured objectively using biological assessments, such as blood pressure and cortisol (Ganster, Fox,

& Dwyer, 2001; Kaufmann & Beehr, 1986). Furthermore, recent research on the role of implicit processes within organizations suggests that personality traits (e.g., PA and NA) can be assessed using indirect nonself-report measures (Johnson, Tolentino, Rodopman, & Cho, 2010).

Summary

In the current chapter, we discussed the theoretical processes potentially linking employee personality to work stressors and strains, and we reviewed the links between several specific personality traits and stress-related variables. We also discussed future research directions regarding personality's role in work stress models and considered the practical implications of this research. Given the theoretical and practical implications that the current topic has for employee and organizational well-being, we encourage more research to examine the relationship between employee personality and work stressors and strains.

Practitioner's Window

The link between employee personality and stress-related variables has important practical implications. First, although personality is clearly related to work stressors and strains, the strength of these relationships suggests that stress-related variables are not purely dispositional. Thus, the effects of environmental conditions as well as organizational stress interventions are not likely to be overwhelmed by the effects of employee personality. Second, given the relationships between employee personality and stress-related variables, organizations may find it useful to assess the personalities of both job incumbents and job applicants.

Assessing the personalities of job incumbents could be helpful in the planning of stress interventions. Although the presence of high levels of perceived work stressors and strains could be interpreted as evidence of a dysfunctional work environment calling for organizational intervention, it may instead be indicative of ineffective selection practices. An organization that employs several high-NA job incumbents within objectively stress-free jobs, for example, may experience many of the same stress-related problems (e.g., high levels of perceived work stressors and strains) common in organizations that have objectively unfavorable environments. Thus, the former organization should dedicate its resources to selecting more stress-resistant employees, rather than to making changes to the existing work environment.

As suggested above in the "Future Research Directions" section, incumbent personality assessment may be useful for matching organizational stress interventions to particular employees. That is, it may be important for interventions to fit the personalities of workers. When matching interventions to employee personality, however, it is unclear whether interventions will be most effective when they match the character "strengths" or "weaknesses" of incumbents. Future research should examine personality as a moderator of the effectiveness of stress interventions.

Assessing applicant personality could prove important for selecting employees who are unlikely to experience stress. Efforts to identify stress-resistant job applicants may be especially important when hiring applicants into positions that have high levels of objective stressors. It should be noted, however, that such an application of personality testing could have legal and ethical implications, particularly when personality tests are used that may discriminate against applicants who have mental illness. To help organizations defend themselves in lawsuits regarding adverse impact, it is important that any personality test used in a selection context be job relevant. A test that excludes applicants who have a particular mental illness may be defensible, for example, if it were shown to be essential for protecting public safety.

References

Alexander, K. N. (2011). *Abusive supervision as a predictor of deviance and health outcomes: The exacerbating role of narcissism and social support* (Unpublished doctoral dissertation). Bowling Green State University, Bowling Green, OH.

Aquino, K., & Lamertz, K. (2004). A relational model of workplace victimization: Social roles and patterns of victimization in dyadic relationships. *Journal of Applied Psychology, 89*, 1023–1034.

Avey, J. B., Luthans, F., & Jensen, S. (2009). Psychological capital: A positive resource for combating stress and turnover. *Human Resource Management, 48*, 677–693.

Avey, J. B., Wernsing, T. S., & Mhatre, K. H. (2011). A longitudinal analysis of positive psychological constructs and emotions on stress, anxiety, and well-being. *Journal of Leadership & Organizational Studies, 18*, 216–228.

Barrick, M. R., & Mount, M. K. (1991). The Big Five personality dimensions and job performance: A meta-analysis. *Personnel Psychology, 44*, 1–26.

Barrick, M. R., Mount, M. K., & Judge, T. A. (2001). Personality and performance at the beginning of the new millennium: What do we know and where do we go next? *International Journal of Selection and Assessment, 9*, 9–30.

Barsky, A. P., Thoresen, C. J., Warren, C. R., & Kaplan, S. A. (2004). Modeling negative affectivity and job stress: A contingency-based approach. *Journal of Organizational Behavior, 25*, 915–936.

Bartone, P. T. (1999). Hardiness protects against war-related stress in Army reserve forces. *Consulting Psychology Journal: Practice and Research, 51*, 72–82.

Bateman, T. S., & Crant, J. M. (1993). The proactive component of organizational behavior: A measure and correlates. *Journal of Organizational Behavior, 14*, 103–118.

Beehr, T. A. (1995). *Psychological stress in the workplace*. New York: Routledge.

Beehr, T. A., & Bhagat, R. S. (1985). *Human stress and cognition in organizations: An integrated perspective*. New York: John Wiley & Sons.

Beehr, T. A., & Bowling, N. A. (2005). Hardy personality, stress, and health. In C. L. Cooper (Ed.), *Handbook of stress medicine and health* (2nd ed., pp. 193–211). London: CRC Press.

Beehr, T. A., & Newman, J. E. (1978). Job stress, employee health, and organizational effectiveness: A facet analysis, model, and literature review. *Personnel Psychology, 31*, 665–699.

Bluen, S. D., Barling, J., & Burns, W. (1990). Predicting sales performance, job satisfaction, and depression using the Achievement Strivings and Impatience-Irritability dimensions of Type A behavior. *Journal of Applied Psychology, 75*, 212–216.

Bogg, T., & Roberts, B. W. (2004). Conscientiousness and health-related behaviors: A meta-analysis of the leading behavioral contributors to morality. *Psychological Bulletin, 130*, 887–919.

Bowling, N. A., Beehr, T. A., & Grebner, S. (2012). Practical approaches to managing stress in organizations. In G. P. Hodgkinson & J. K. Ford (Eds.), *International review of industrial and organizational psychology* (Vol. 27, pp. 65–87). Chichester, UK: Wiley-Blackwell.

Bowling, N. A., Beehr, T. A., & Swader, W. M. (2005). Giving and receiving social support at work: The roles of personality and reciprocity. *Journal of Vocational Behavior, 67*, 476–489.

Bowling, N. A., & Burns, G. N. (2010). A comparison of work-specific and general personality measures as predictors of work and non-work criteria. *Personality and Individual Differences, 49*, 95–101.

Bowling, N. A., & Eschleman, K. J. (2010). Employee personality as a moderator of the relationships between work stressors and counterproductive work behavior. *Journal of Occupational Health Psychology, 15*, 91–103.

Bowling, N. A., Eschleman, K. J., Wang, Q., Kirkendall, C., & Alarcon, G. (2010). Meta-analysis of the predictors and consequences of organization-based self-esteem. *Journal of Occupational and Organizational Psychology, 83*, 601–626.

Bowling, N. A., Wang, Q., Tang, H. Y., & Kennedy, K. (2010). A comparison of general and work-specific measures of core self-evaluations. *Journal of Vocational Behavior, 76*, 559–566.

Brief, A. P., Burke, M. J., George, J. M., Robinson, B. S., & Webster, J. (1988). Should negative affectivity remain an unmeasured variable in the study of job stress? *Journal of Applied Psychology, 73*, 193–198.

Bruk-Lee, V., Khoury, H. A., Nixon, A. E., Goh, A., & Spector, P. E. (2009). Replicating and extending past personality/job satisfaction meta-analyses. *Human Performance, 22*, 156–189.

Burke, L. A., & Witt, L. A. (2002). Moderators of the openness to experience–performance relationship. *Journal of Managerial Psychology, 17*, 712–721.

Burke, M. J., Brief, A. P., & George, J. M. (1993). The role of negative affectivity in understanding relations between self-reports of stressors and strain: A comment on the applied psychology literature. *Journal of Applied Psychology, 78*, 402–412.

Buss, D. M. (1987). Selection, evocation, and manipulation. *Journal of Personality and Social Psychology, 53*, 1214–1221.

Carver, C. S., Scheier, M. F., & Weintraub, J. K. (1989). Assessing coping strategies: A theoretically based approach. *Journal of Personality and Social Psychology, 56*, 267–283.

Chen, P.Y., & Spector, P. E. (1991). Negative affectivity as the underlying cause of correlations between stressors and strains. *Journal of Applied Psychology, 76*, 398–407.

Connolly, J. J., & Viswesvaran, C. (1999, April). *The independence of positive and negative affect: A meta-analysis.* Paper presented at the Annual Meeting of the Society for Industrial and Organizational Psychology, Atlanta, GA.

Connolly, J. J., & Viswesvaran, C. (2000). The role of affectivity in job satisfaction: A meta-analysis. *Personality and Individual Differences, 29*, 265–281.

Cook, K. W., Vance, C. A., & Spector, P. E. (2000). The relation of candidate personality with selection-interview outcomes. *Journal of Applied Social Psychology, 30*, 867–885.

Cook, W. W., & Medley, D. M. (1954). Proposed hostility and Pharisaic-Virtue scales for the MMPI. *Journal of Applied Psychology, 38*, 414–418.

Cooper, C. L., Dewe, P. J., & O'Driscoll, M. P. (2001). *Organizational stress: A review and critique of theory, research, and applications.* Thousand Oaks, CA: Sage.

Costa, P. T., Jr., & McCrae, R. R. (1992). *Revised NEO Personality Inventory (NEO-PI-R) and NEO Five Factor Inventory (NEO-FFI) professional manual.* Odessa, FL: Psychological Assessment Resources.

Costa, P. T., Jr., Somerfield, M. R., & McCrae, R. R. (1996). Personality and coping: A reconceptualization. In *Handbook of coping: Theory, research, applications* (pp. 44–61). Oxford, UK: John Wiley & Sons.

Crampton, S. M., & Wagner, J. A. (1994). Percept–percept inflation in microorganizational research: An investigation of prevalence and effect. *Journal of Applied Psychology, 79*, 67–76.

Cunningham, C. J. L., & De La Rosa, G. M. (2008). The interactive effects of proactive personality and work family interference on well-being. *Journal of Occupational Health Psychology, 13*, 271–282.

Davis, D. E., Worthington, E. L., & Hook, J. N. (2010). Humility: Review of measurement strategies and conceptualization as personality judgment. *The Journal of Positive Psychology, 5*, 243–252.

DeNeve, K. M., & Cooper, H. (1998). The happy personality: A meta-analysis of 137 personality traits and subjective well-being. *Psychological Bulletin, 124*, 197–229.

Diener, E., Larsen, R. J., & Emmons, R. A. (1984). Person × Situation interactions: Choice of situations and congruence response models. *Journal of Personality and Social Psychology, 47*, 580–592.

Digman, J. M. (1990). Personality structure: Emergence of the five-factor model. *Annual Review of Psychology, 41*, 417–440.

Emmons, R. A. (2000). Personality and forgiveness. In M. E. McCullough, K. I. Pargament, & C. E. Thoresen (Eds.), *Forgiveness: Theory, research, and practice* (pp. 156–175). New York: Guilford Press.

Endler, N. S., & Edwards, J. M. (1985). Evaluation of the state trait distinction within an interaction model of personality. *Southern Psychologist, 2*, 63–71.

Endler, N. S., & Edwards, J. M. (1986). Interactionism in personality in the twentieth century. *Personality and Individual Differences, 7*, 379–384.

Eschleman, K. J., & Bowling, N. A. (2011). A construct validation of the Neutral Objects Satisfaction Questionnaire. *Journal of Business and Psychology, 26*, 501–515.

Eschleman, K. J., Bowling, N. A., & Alarcon, G. (2010). A meta-analytic examination of hardiness. *International Journal of Stress Management, 17*, 277–307.

Fisher, C. D., & Gitelson, R. (1983). A meta-analysis of the correlates of role conflict and ambiguity. *Journal of Applied Psychology, 68*, 320–333.

Fortunato, V. J., & Harsh, J. (2006). Stress and sleep quality: The moderating role of negative affectivity. *Personality and Individual Differences, 41*, 825–836.

Fortunato, V. J., LeBourgeois, M. K., & Harsh, J. (2008). Development of a five-dimensional measure of adult sleep quality. *Educational and Psychological Measurement, 68*, 488–514.

Fortunato, V. J., & Stone-Romero, E. F. (2001). Positive affectivity as a moderator of the objective-task characteristics/perceived-task characteristics relationship. *Journal of Applied Social Psychology, 31*, 1248–1278.

Fredrickson, B. L. (2001). The role of positive emotions in positive psychology: The broaden-and-build theory of positive emotions. *American Psychologist, 56*, 218–226.

Friedman, M., & Rosenman, R. H. (1959). Association of specific behavior pattern with blood and cardiovascular findings. *Journal of the American Medical Association, 169*, 1286–1296.

Fuller, B., & Marler, L. E. (2009). Change driven by nature: A meta-analytic review of the proactive personality literature. *Journal of Vocational Behavior, 75*, 329–345.

Ganster, D. C. (1987). Type A behavior and occupational stress. In J. M. Ivancevich & D. C. Ganster (Eds.), *Job stress: From theory to suggestion* (pp. 61–89). New York: Haworth Press.

Ganster, D. C., Fox, M. L., & Dwyer, D. J. (2001). Explaining employees' health care costs: A prospective examination of stressful job demands, personal control, and physiological reactivity. *Journal of Applied Psychology, 86*, 954–964.

Goldberg, L. R. (1990). An alternative "description of personality": The Big-Five factor structure. *Journal of Personality and Social Psychology, 59*, 1216–1229.

Grandey, A. A. (2000). Emotion regulation in the workplace: A new way to conceptualize emotional labor. *Journal of Occupational Health Psychology, 5*, 95–110.

Grant, S., & Langan-Fox, J. (2007). Personality and the occupational stressor–strain relationship: The role of the Big Five. *Journal of Occupational Health Psychology, 12*, 20–33.

Gray, J. A. (1970). The psychophysiological basis of introversion–extraversion. *Behavioral Research Therapy, 8*, 249–266.

Gray, J. A. (1981). A critique of Eysenck's theory of personality. In H. J. Eysenck (Ed.), *A model of personality* (pp. 246–276). New York: Springer.

Greenhaus, J., & Beutell, N. (1985). Sources of conflict between work and family roles. *Academy of Management Review, 10*, 76–88.

Griffin, B., & Hesketh, B. (2005). Are conscientious workers adaptable? *Australian Journal of Management, 30*, 245–259.

Heinisch, D. A., & Jex, S. M. (1997). Negative affectivity and gender as moderators of the relationship between work-related stressors and depressed mood at work. *Work & Stress, 11*, 46–57.

Heinisch, D. A., & Jex, S. M. (1998). Measurement of negative affectivity: A comparison of self-reports and observer ratings. *Work & Stress, 12*, 145–160.

Hobfoll, S. E. (1989). Conservation of resources: A new attempt at conceptualizing stress. *American Psychologist, 44*, 513–524.

Holmes, T. H., & Rahe, R. H. (1967). The Social Readjustment Rating Scale. *Journal of Psychosomatic Research, 11*, 213–218.

Hunthausen, J. M., Truxillo, D. M., Bauer, T. B., & Hammer, B. L. (2003). A field study of frame-of-reference effect on Personality Test validity. *Journal of Applied Psychology, 88*, 545–551.

Jackson, S. E., & Schuler, R. S. (1985). A meta-analysis and conceptual critique of research on role ambiguity and role conflict in work settings. *Organizational Behavior and Human Decision Processes, 36*, 16–78.

Jakobwitz, S., & Egan, V. (2006). The dark triad and normal personality traits. *Personality and Individual Differences, 40*, 331–339.

Jex, S. M., Adams, G. A., Elacqua, T. C., & Bachrach, D. G. (2002). Type A as a moderator of stressors and job complexity: A comparison of achievement strivings and impatience-irritability. *Journal of Applied Social Psychology, 32*, 977–996.

Jex, S. M., & Beehr, T. A. (1991). Emerging theoretical and methodological issues in the study of work-related stress. *Research in Personnel and Human Resources Management, 9*, 311–365.

Jex, S. M., Beehr, T. A., & Roberts, C. K. (1992). The meaning of occupational stress items to survey respondents. *Journal of Applied Psychology, 77*, 623–628.

Jex, S. M., & Spector, P. E. (1996). The impact of negative affectivity on stressor–strain relations: A replication and extension. *Work & Stress, 10*, 36–45.

Jex, S. M., & Yankelevich, M. (2008). Work stress. In C. L. Cooper & J. Barling (Eds.), *Handbook of organizational behavior* (pp. 498–518). Thousand Oaks, CA: Sage.

Johnson, R. E., Tolentino, A. L., Rodopman, O. B., & Cho, E. (2010). We (sometimes) know not how we feel: Predicting work behaviors with an implicit measure of trait affectivity. *Personnel Psychology, 63*, 197–219.

Judge, T. A., & Bono, J. E. (2001). A rose by any other name: Are self-esteem, generalized self-efficacy, neuroticism, and locus of control indicators of a common construct? In B. W. Roberts & R. Hogan (Eds.), *Personality psychology in the workplace* (pp. 93–118). Washington, DC: American Psychological Association.

Judge, T. A., & Bretz, R. D. (1993). Report on an alternative measure of affective disposition. *Educational and Psychological Measurement, 53*, 1095–1104.

Judge, T. A., & Erez, A. (2007). Interaction and intersection: The constellation of emotional stability and extraversion in predicting performance. *Personnel Psychology, 60*, 573–596.

Judge, T. A., Erez, A., Bono, J. E., & Thoresen, C. J. (2002). Are measures of self-esteem, neuroticism, locus of control, and generalized self-efficacy indicators of a common core construct? *Journal of Personality and Social Psychology, 83*, 693–710.

Judge, T. A., Heller, D., & Mount, M. K. (2002). Five-factor model of personality and job satisfaction: A meta-analysis. *Journal of Applied Psychology, 87*, 530–541.

Judge, T. A., Higgins, C. A., Thoresen, C. J., & Barrick, M. R. (1999). The Big Five personality traits, general mental ability, and career success across the life span. *Personnel Psychology, 52*, 621–652.

Judge, T. A., Locke, E. A., & Durham, C. C. (1997). The dispositional causes of job satisfaction: A core evaluations approach. *Research in Organizational Behavior, 19*, 151–188.

Judge, T. A., Locke, E. A., Durham, C. C., & Kluger, A. N. (1998). Dispositional effects on job and life satisfaction: The role of core evaluations. *Journal of Applied Psychology, 83*, 17–34.

Kammeyer-Mueller, J. D., Judge, T. A., & Scott, B. A. (2009). The role of core self-evaluations in the coping process. *Journal of Applied Psychology, 94*, 177–195.
Kanner, A. D., Coyne, J. C., Schaefer, C., & Lazarus, R. S. (1981). Comparison of two modes of stress measurement: Daily hassles and uplifts versus major life events. *Journal of Behavioral Medicine, 4*, 1–39.
Kaufmann, G. M., & Beehr, T. A. (1986). Interactions between job stressors and social support: Some counterintuitive results. *Journal of Applied Psychology, 71*, 522–526.
Keoske, G. F., Kirk, S. A., & Keoske, R. D. (1993). Coping with job stress: Which strategies work best? *Journal of Occupational and Organizational Psychology, 66*, 319–335.
Kiffin-Petersen, S., Jordan, C. L., & Soutar, G. N. (2011). The Big Five, emotional exhaustion and citizenship behaviors in service settings: The mediating role of emotional labor. *Personality and Individual Differences, 50*, 43–48.
King, L. A., King, D. W., Fairbank, J. A., Keane, T. M., & Adams, G. A. (1998). Resilience-recovery factors in post-traumatic stress disorder among female and male Vietnam veterans: Hardiness, postwar social support, and additional stressful life events. *Journal of Personality and Social Psychology, 74*, 420–434.
Kobasa, S. C. (1979). Stressful life events, personality, and health: An inquiry into hardiness. *Journal of Personality and Social Psychology, 37*, 1–11.
Larsen, R. J., & Ketelaar, T. (1989). Extraversion, neuroticism, and susceptibility to positive and negative mood induction procedures. *Personality and Individual Differences, 10*, 1221–1228.
Larsen, R. J., & Ketelaar, T. (1991). Personality and susceptibility to positive and negative emotional states. *Journal of Personality and Social Psychology, 61*, 132–140.
Larson, R., & Csikszentmihalyi, M. (1983). The Experience Sampling Method. In H. Reis (Ed.), *New directions for naturalistic methods in the behavioral sciences* (pp. 41–56). San Francisco: Jossey-Bass.
Lazarus, R. S., & Folkman, S. (1984). *Stress, appraisal, and coping*. New York: Springer.
Lepine, J. A., Podsakoff, N. P., & Lepine, M. A. (2005). A meta-analytic test of the challenge stressor–hindrance stressor framework: An explanation for inconsistent relationships among stressors and performance. *Academy of Management Journal, 48*, 764–775.
Liu, C., Spector, P. E., & Jex, S. M. (2005). The relation of job control and complexity with job strains: A comparison of multiple data sources. *Journal of Occupational and Organizational Psychology, 78*, 325–336.
Maddi, S. R., & Kobasa, S. C. (1984). *The hardy executive*. Homewood, IL: Jones Irwin.
Martin, L. R., & Friedman, H. S. (2000). Comparing personality scales across time: An illustrative study of validity and consistency in life-span archival data. *Journal of Personality, 68*, 85–110.
Martin, R. A., & Lefcourt, H. M. (1983). Sense of humor as a moderator of the relation between stressors and mood. *Journal of Personality and Social Psychology, 45*, 1313–1324.
Maslach, C., & Jackson, S. E. (1986). *Maslach Burnout Inventory: Manual* (2nd ed.). Palo Alto, CA: Consulting Psychologists Press.
McCullough, M. E., Emmons, R. A., & Tsang, J. (2002). The grateful disposition: A conceptual and empirical topography. *Journal of Personality and Social Psychology, 82*, 112–127.
Michel, J. S., Clark, M. A., & Jaramillo, D. (2011). The role of the five factor model of personality in the perceptions of negative and positive forms of work–nonwork spillover: A meta-analytic review. *Journal of Vocational Behavior, 79*, 191–203.
Milam, A. C., Spitzmueller, C., & Penney, L. M. (2009). Investigating individual differences among targets of workplace incivility. *Journal of Occupational Health Psychology, 14*, 58–69.
Mischel, W. (1977). The interaction of person and situation. In D. Magnusson & N. S. Endler (Eds.), *Personality at the crossroads: Current issues in interactional psychology* (pp. 333–352). Hillsdale, NJ: Lawrence Erlbaum Associates.
Motowidlo, S. J. (1996). Orientation toward the job and organization. In K. R. Murphy (Ed.), *Individual differences in behavior in organizations* (pp. 175–208). San Francisco: Jossey-Bass.
Moyle, P. (1995). The role of negative affectivity in the stress process: Tests of alternative models. *Journal of Organizational Behavior, 16*, 647–668.
Necowitz, L. B., & Roznowski, M. (1994). Negative affectivity and job satisfaction: Cognitive processes underlying the relationship and effects on employee behaviors. *Journal of Vocational Behavior, 45*, 270–294.
Nemanick, R. C., Jr., & Munz, D. C. (1997). Extraversion and neuroticism, trait mood, and state affect: A hierarchical relationship? *Journal of Social Behavior and Personality, 12*, 1079–1092.
Ones, D. S., & Viswesvaran, C. (1996). Bandwidth–fidelity dilemma in personality measurement for personnel selection. *Journal of Organizational Behavior, 17*, 609–626.
Ortqvist, D., & Wincent, J. (2006). Prominent consequences of role stress: A meta-analytic review. *International Journal of Stress Management, 13*, 399–422.
Parker, S. K., & Sprigg, C. A. (1999). Minimizing strain and maximizing learning: The role of job demands, job control, and proactive personality. *Journal of Applied Psychology, 84*, 925–939.

Paulhaus, D. L., & Williams, K. M. (2002). The Dark Triad of personality: Narcissism, Machiavellianism, and psychopathy. *Journal of Research in Personality, 36*, 556–563.
Paunonen, S.V., & Ashton, M. C. (2001). Big Five factors and the prediction of behavior. *Journal of Personality and Social Psychology, 81*, 524–539.
Penney, L. M., & Spector, P. E. (2005). Job stress, incivility, and counterproductive work behavior (CWB): The moderating role of negative affectivity. *Journal of Organizational Behavior, 26*, 777–796.
Peterson, C. (2000). The future of optimism. *American Psychologist, 55*, 44–55.
Peterson, C., & Seligman, M. E. P. (2004). *Character strengths and virtues: A handbook and classification*. New York: Oxford University Press.
Podsakoff, N. P., LePine, J. A., & LePine, M. A. (2007). Differential challenge stressor–hindrance stressor relationships with job attitudes, turnover intentions, turnover, and withdrawal behavior: A meta-analysis. *Journal of Applied Psychology, 92*, 438–454.
Probst, T. M. (2003). Development and validation of the Job Security Index and the Job Security Satisfaction scale: A classical test theory of the IRT approach. *Journal of Occupational and Organizational Psychology, 76*, 451–467.
Richardson, K. M., & Rothstein, H. R. (2008). Effects of occupational stress management intervention programs: A meta-analysis. *Journal of Occupational Health Psychology, 13*, 69–93.
Roos, P. A., & Treiman, D. J. (1980). DOT scales for the 1970 census classification. In A. R. Miller, D. J. Treiman, P. S. Cain, & P. A. Roos (Eds.), *Work, jobs, and occupations: A critical review of the dictionary of occupational titles* (pp. 336–389). Washington, DC: National Academy Press.
Rosch, P. J. (2001). The quandary of job stress compensation. *Health and Stress, 3*, 1–4.
Salancik, G. R., & Pfeffer, J. (1978). A social information processing approach to job attitudes and task design. *Administrative Science Quarterly, 23*, 224–253.
Schaubroeck, J., Ganster, D. C., & Kemmerer, B. E. (1994). Job complexity, "Type A" behavior, and cardiovascular disorder: A prospective study. *Academy of Management Journal, 37*, 426–439.
Schnitker, S. A., & Emmons, R. A. (2007). Patience as a virtue: Religious and psychological perspectives. *Research in the Social Scientific Study of Religion, 18*, 177–207.
Seligman, M. E. P., & Csikszentmihalyi, M. (2000). Positive psychology: An introduction. *American Psychologist, 55*, 5–14.
Smith, T. W., Pope, M. K., Sanders, J. D., Allred, K. D., & O'Keeffe, J. L. (1988). Cynical hostility at home and work: Psychosocial vulnerability across domains. *Journal of Research in Personality, 22*, 525–548.
Spector, P. E. (1982). Behavior in organizations as a function of employee's locus of control. *Psychological Bulletin, 91*, 482–497.
Spector, P. E., Dwyer, D. J., & Jex, S. M. (1988). Relation of job stressors to affective, health, and performance outcomes: A comparison of multiple data sources. *Journal of Applied Psychology, 73*, 11–19.
Spector, P. E., & Jex, S. M. (1991). Relations of job stressors, job characteristics, and job analysis ratings to affective and health outcomes. *Journal of Applied Psychology, 76*, 46–53.
Spector, P. E., & Jex, S. M. (1998). Development of four self-report measures of job stressors and strain: Interpersonal Conflict at Work Scale, Organizational Constraints Scale, Qualitative Workload Inventory, and Physical Symptoms Inventory. *Journal of Occupational Health Psychology, 3*, 356–367.
Spector, P. E., Jex, S. M., & Chen, P. Y. (1995). Personality traits as predictors of job characteristics. *Journal of Organizational Behavior, 16*, 59–65.
Spector, P. E., Zapf, D., Chen, P. Y., & Frese, M. (2000). Why negative affectivity should not be controlled in job stress research: Don't throw out the baby with the bath water. *Journal of Organizational Behavior, 21*, 79–95.
Spence, J. T., Helmreich, R. L., & Pred, R. S. (1987). Impatience versus achievement strivings in the Type A pattern: Differential effects on students' health and academic achievement. *Journal of Applied Psychology, 72*, 522–528.
Tett, R. P., & Burnett, D. D. (2003). A personality trait-based interactionist model of job performance. *Journal of Applied Psychology, 88*, 500–517.
Thomas, J. P., Whitman, D. S., & Viswesvaran, C. (2010). Employee proactivity in organizations: A comparative meta-analysis of emergent proactive constructs. *Journal of Occupational and Organizational Psychology, 83*, 275–300.
Thompson, J. A. (2005). Proactive personality and job performance: A social capital perspective. *Journal of Applied Psychology, 90*, 1011–1017.
Thoresen, C. J., Kaplan, S. A., Barsky, A. P., Warren, C. R., & de Chermont, K. (2003). The affective underpinnings of job perceptions and attitudes: A meta-analytic review and integration. *Psychological Bulletin, 129*, 914–945.
Viswesvaran, C., Sanchez, J. I., & Fisher, J. (1999). The role of social support in the process of work stress: A meta-analysis. *Journal of Vocational Behavior, 54*, 314–334.

Wang, Q., Bowling, N. A., & Eschleman, K. J. (2010). A meta-analytic examination of work and general locus of control. *Journal of Applied Psychology, 95*, 761–768.
Watson, D., & Clark, L. A. (1984). Negative affectivity: The disposition to experience aversive emotional states. *Psychological Bulletin, 96*, 465–490.
Watson, D., Clark, L. A., & Tellegen, A. (1988). Development and validation of brief measures of positive and negative affectivity: The PANAS scales. *Journal of Personality and Social Psychology, 54*, 1063–1070.
Watson, D., & Hubbard, B. (1996). Adaptational style and dispositional structure: Coping in the context of the five-factor model. *Journal of Personality, 64*, 737–774.
Watson, D., Wiese, D., Vaidya, J., & Tellegen, A. (1999). The two general activation systems of affect: Structural findings, evolutionary considerations, and psychobiological evidence. *Journal of Personality and Social Psychology, 76*, 820–838.
Witt, L. A., Burke, L. A., Barrick, M. R., & Mount, M. K. (2002). The interactive effects of conscientiousness and agreeableness on job performance. *Journal of Applied Psychology, 87*, 164–169.
Wrzesniewski, A., & Dutton, J. E. (2001). Crafting a job: Revisioning employees as active crafters of their work. *Academy of Management Review, 26*, 179–201.
Zellars, K. L., Perrewe, P. L., Hochwarter, W. A., & Anderson, K. S. (2006). The interactive effects of positive affect and conscientiousness on strain. *Journal of Occupational Health Psychology, 11*, 281–289.

32

Personality and Job Attitudes

Bradley J. Brummel and Nathan A. Bowling

Job attitudes and personality traits are two of the most studied predictors of work behavior. Volumes of research have demonstrated that job attitudes (e.g., Harrison, Newman, & Roth, 2006; Judge, Thoresen, Bono, & Patton, 2001) and personality traits (Barrick & Mount, 1991; J. Hogan & Holland, 2003; Tett, Jackson, & Rothstein, 1991) predict workplace behaviors and outcomes such as job performance, organizational citizenship behaviors (OCBs), counterproductive work behaviors (CWBs), and turnover. Furthermore, organizational scholars have argued that an individual's job attitudes are the most important pieces of information an organization can know about an employee (Roznowski & Hulin, 1992). This handbook covers the broad interest and depth of study on personality in the workplace. Research has demonstrated that some personality traits predict some job attitudes (see Table 32.3). However, it is less clear exactly which personality traits influence which job attitudes in what manner and how those relationships ultimately determine workplace behaviors.

In this chapter, we review research on the relationship between personality traits and job attitudes and their joint influence on workplace behaviors and outcomes. First, we define the constructs and describe the theoretical distinctions between them. We then examine how these distinctions are manifested in the measurement of both personality traits and job attitudes. This examination includes a review of some of the most common approaches to measuring job attitudes and personality traits. Second, we review research on the joint influence of job attitudes and personality traits on workplace behaviors and outcomes. We conclude with suggestions for future research areas that will continue to advance our understanding of job attitudes and personality traits in the workplace.

Definitional and Theoretical Distinctions

Attitudes and personality are both foundational constructs in the field of psychology. Job attitudes and personality have also been primary areas of study when psychology has been applied to the workplace. Due to the prominence of these constructs and the diversity of ways in which they have been studied, it is important to clarify corresponding definitions at the outset of this chapter.

An attitude has been defined as "a psychological tendency that is expressed by evaluating a particular entity with some degree of favor or disfavor" (Eagly & Chaiken, 1993, p. 1). This definition includes the three key elements of tendency, entity, and evaluation (Eagly & Chaiken, 2007). Job attitudes include an attitude entity (or target) that is associated with a person's job. Job attitude targets can include a job, the work tasks being done, a supervisor, a work group, or the entire organization, to name a few (Brief, 1998; Spector, 1997). Personality traits can be defined as "... consistent patterns of thoughts, feelings, or actions that distinguish people from one another" (J. A. Johnson, 1997, p. 74). The definition for personality traits—similar to that of attitudes—includes the elements of tendency (consistent patterns) and evaluation (distinguish people from one another in terms of point values on a given trait).

These definitions serve as useful starting points for understanding the relationship between job attitudes and personality. In the following sub-sections, we expand upon the targets, stability, causes, and outcomes of job attitudes and personality traits. Then, we discuss the affective, cognitive, and behavioral aspects of both job attitudes and personality traits. We conclude this section with discussion of mechanisms by which personality traits can influence job attitudes.

Targets

An important distinction between attitudes and personality traits is that attitudes, but not personality traits, have specific targets. The presence of a target makes attitude constructs inherently narrower than personality traits. Job attitudes may, for instance, focus on a coworker or a supervisor, the work that is being done, or the manner in which the work is completed. Personality traits, in contrast, are assumed to influence behavior across situations and targets. However, some research has made a distinction between general and context-specific personality traits (e.g., Bing, Whanger, Davison, & VanHook, 2004; Hunthausen, Truxillo, Bauer, & Hammer, 2003; Lievens, De Corte, & Schollaert, 2008; Schmit, Ryan, Stierwalt, & Powell, 1995). Measures of context-specific personality ask participants to consider their personalities within a specific context, such as at work. Bowling and Burns (2010), for example, assessed work-specific Five-Factor Model (FFM) characteristics by adding an "at work" tag to the end of International Personality Item Pool (IPIP; Goldberg, 1999) items. Because work-specific personality measures share more conceptual overlap with work-related criteria than do general personality measures, they tend to be stronger predictors of other work constructs like job performance and job satisfaction (Bowling & Burns, 2010; Hunthausen et al., 2003). The use of work-specific personality has been extended to measures of locus of control (Spector, 1988; Wang, Bowling, & Eschleman, 2010), self-esteem (Bowling, Eschleman, Wang, Kirkendall, & Alarcon, 2010; Pierce, Gardner, Cummings, & Dunham, 1989), and core self-evaluations (CSE; Bowling, Wang, Tang, & Kennedy, 2010). The addition of the "at work" target to personality traits diminishes one of the primary theoretical differences between the construct, and thereby muddies the distinction between job attitudes and personality traits. However, this contextualization of personality is not the same as an attitude target as it only specifies where the trait is expressed, not necessarily what the trait is about. Also, work-specific personality assesses something about the participant, whereas job attitudes assess the participant's response to a work-specific attitude object. So, one might expect stronger relationships between traits contextualized to the workplace and job attitudes, but the contextualization of the trait does not influence the construct to the level of making the trait fit the definition of an attitude as there are other distinguishing features.

Consistency

Job attitudes and personality traits both contain an element of consistency in their definitions. The nature of this consistency has been the source of much debate in psychology, with some scholars claiming that people show consistency across situations and others claiming that attitudes and personality traits do not exist as they are typically defined. The primary way of determining consistency is to measure the relative scores of individuals within a population over time. This temporal stability is measured using test–retest correlations. Job satisfaction has been found to display significant levels of temporal stability even among workers who have changed jobs (Dormann & Zapf, 2001; Staw & Ross, 1985). A meta-analysis by Dormann and Zapf yielded mean stability coefficients of .50 (k = 60) for samples including both participants who did and did not change jobs and .35 among those who did change jobs (k = 10). Other research has shown similar levels of stability in organizational commitment (r = .58) and job involvement (r = .68) over 5 years (Bowling, Beehr, & Lepisto, 2006). Test–retest stability for FFM personality traits has been reported around .60–.80, even over several decades (Roberts & DelVecchio, 2000), which is noticeably higher than the stability levels that Dormann and Zapf reported for job satisfaction.

These levels of stability should not be taken to mean that job attitudes and personality traits do not change. Mean levels of a construct can change while maintaining high levels of rank-order stability (Roberts, 2006). Also, some personality traits show predictable patterns of change over the lifespan (Roberts & Mroczek, 2008; Roberts, Walton, & Viechtbauer, 2006; for more coverage regarding changes in personality see Chapter 35, this volume). Additionally, organizational scholars have begun to examine the potential influences of personality change on organizational functioning (Roberts, 2006; Slaughter & Feldman, 2009). The main findings about the stability of job attitudes and personality traits are that both are stable enough to predict future workplace behaviors, personality traits tend to be more stable than job attitudes, and change is a potentially important area of study for understanding individual differences in behavior in the workplace.

Causes

Both personality traits and job attitudes have been shown to have environmental and genetic causes. However, the timing and influence of these causes vary. Specifically, personality traits develop earlier in life from a broad range of environmental experiences and genetic factors (Roberts & Jackson, 2008) while job attitudes are necessarily formed after a person begins working. However, earlier experiences and genetic factors also influence job attitudes. Personality is influenced by genetics, with heredity accounting for approximately 40–60% of the variance in most personality characteristics (Tellegen et al., 1988). Perhaps more surprisingly, heredity accounts for about 30% of the variance in job satisfaction (Arvey, Bouchard, Segal, & Abraham, 1989). Hereditary effects on job satisfaction have been suggested to be mediated by associated personality traits (Ilies & Judge, 2003). That is, the hereditability of traits that influence job attitudes account for at least some of the hereditability of job attitudes. However, the dispositional basis for job attitudes does not make organizational interventions targeted at influencing attitudes irrelevant (Gerhart, 2005; Newton & Keenan, 1991). This is because an intervention may increase mean attitude levels while preserving the between-person rank-order of attitude scores.

Multiple models have been developed to understand the environmental causes of job satisfaction. These include the Cornell Model (Hulin, 1991; Smith, Kendall, & Hulin, 1969), Thibaut and Kelley's (1959) comparison level model, Locke's (1976) Value-Percept Model, and Hackman and Oldham's (1975) Job Characteristics Model. In all of these models, job attitudes are predicted by a combination of work role factors, work outcomes, economic and environment factors outside of the work role, frames of reference, individual utility of direct and opportunity costs, and comparators in addition to personality traits (Judge, Hulin, & Dalal, in press). While a full discussion of these factors is beyond the scope of this chapter, it is important to note the complexity of the potential causes of any one individual's job attitudes. A comprehensive summary of the strength of antecedents of many job attitudes can be found in Schleicher, Hansen, and Fox (2010).

Outcomes

Personality traits and job attitudes have both been linked to a variety of workplace outcomes. These outcomes can be organized into two broad classes: individual behaviors and organizational outcomes. Individual behaviors in the workplace are most often measured as performance, defined in keeping with "the total expected value to the organization of the discrete behavioral episodes that an individual carries out over a standard period of time" (Motowidlo, 2003, p. 39). While there are many ways performance behaviors have been grouped, the most common domains include task performance, OCBs (e.g., helping coworkers), CWBs (e.g., theft), and job withdrawal (e.g., absenteeism). Sackett and Lievens (2008) have argued that task performance, OCBs, and CWBs are the three major domains of job performance. Harrison et al. (2006) include task performance, OCBs, and job withdrawal in their behavioral engagement factor. Organizational outcomes include turnover, profitability, unit productivity, and other metrics of success. Individual employees influence these organizational outcomes through their performance behaviors (for more coverage on personality and job performance, citizenship performance, and CWBs, see Chapters 3, 26, and 27, this volume).

Affect, Cognition, and Behavior

Job attitudes and personality traits both theoretically include affective, cognitive, and behavioral components (Brief, 1998; J. A. Johnson, 1997; Schleicher, Watt, & Greguras, 2004). Affective components refer to emotional responses or feelings, cognitive components refer to beliefs or thoughts, and behavioral components refer to actions. Because job attitudes and personality traits are often used to predict behavioral performance outcomes, organizational scholars have questioned whether behavioral components should be included in the definitions and measurement of the constructs. Including behaviors in both the predictors and the criterion should increase the relationship but may contaminate the predictor, making the relationship less meaningful.

Job attitude researchers have argued that removing behaviors from the measurement of attitudes (though not the definition) may be more productive for future research (Judge et al., in press). This issue has also been debated in the general attitude literature, with some researchers advocating for consideration of behavior as a consequence rather than a component of attitudes (Chaiken & Stangor, 1987). This results in a change from the tripartite model that assumes that attitudes have an affective, cognitive, and behavioral component to a two-component affective–cognitive attitude construct. This approach implies different approaches to definitions and measurement of the constructs and the criteria.

Specific job attitude and personality constructs differentially emphasize affect, cognition, and behavior. Among job attitudes, job satisfaction has more of an emphasis on affect than other attitudes, though the degree to which job satisfaction measures actually capture job affect has been debated (Judge et al., in press). Job involvement is primarily a cognitive construct, and some approaches to employee engagement intentionally include behavioral components (Macey & Schneider, 2008). In general, job attitude researchers have tended to downplay the behavioral component of attitudes, considering behavior to be an outcome of the attitude rather than a part of it.

Different personality traits also emphasize affective, cognitive, and behavioral components to varying degrees. Positive affectivity (PA) and negative affectivity (NA) (Watson, Clark, & Tellegen, 1988) primarily emphasize the affective component; some of the FFM characteristics (Digman, 1990; McCrae & Costa, 1987; McCrae & John, 1992), such as conscientiousness, primarily emphasize the behavioral components; and traits such as locus of control (Lefcourt, 1976; Rotter, 1966), general self-efficacy (G. Chen, Gully, & Eden, 2001; Judge, Locke, & Durham, 1997), and need for cognition (Cacioppo & Petty, 1982) primarily emphasize the cognitive component. A general summary of these differences is provided in Table 32.1. Although arguments can be made about how the use of specific operationalizations of each of these constructs influences these designations, this table represents a general reading of the literature on these personality traits. Specifically, the FFM categorizations are derived from Pytlik Zillig, Hemenover, and Dienstbier (2002).

Table 32.1 Affective, Behavioral, and Cognitive Emphases of Traits

Trait	*Affective*	*Behavioral*	*Cognitive*
Openness	X	X	X
Conscientiousness		X	
Extraversion	X	X	
Agreeableness	X	X	X
Neuroticism	X		
PA	X		
NA	X		
Narcissism	X	X	X
Machiavellianism		X	X
Psychopathy	X	X	X
Self-esteem	X		X
Self-efficacy			X
Locus of control			X

Note: X indicates that the trait assesses a significant degree of that component.

Relationship Mechanisms

In the previous subsections, we discussed the nature of job attitudes and personality traits. In the following subsections, we consider the theoretical processes that may explain personality–job attitude relationships. As noted above, personality traits are generally regarded to be a cause of job attitudes. However, personality traits can theoretically influence job attitudes through a number of different mechanisms, including selection, manipulation, perception, and hypersensitivity to cues. These mechanisms each link personality to job attitudes via effects on objective or perceived work environments.

Selection

Personality may predispose people to habitually self-select into particular types of objective work environments (Roberts, 2006; Spector, Zapf, Chen, & Frese, 2000; see Chapter 29, this volume). For example, people who have positive self-concepts might have the confidence to pursue jobs that are complex and thus more satisfying (for a review of the link between job complexity and job satisfaction, see Fried & Ferris, 1987). Research indeed has found a link between positive self-concept and objective work environment (Judge, Bono, & Locke, 2000, Study 1). Other personality traits may influence job attitudes via the same process.

Manipulation

Rather than being passively shaped by their environments, people are active shapers of their environments (Roberts, 2006; Thomas, Whitman, & Viswesvaran, 2010). As a result, personality may predispose people to shape their objective environments in particular ways (Spector et al.,

2000). For example, an employee who is low in emotional stability may engage in behaviors that irritate his or her coworkers, inadvertently creating a work environment with which he or she becomes dissatisfied.

Perception

Two individuals employed in objectively identical work environments can perceive those environments differently due to differences in personality. Research indeed supports the link between personality and perceived work environment (P.Y. Chen & Spector, 1991; Judge, Locke, Durham, & Kluger, 1998; Levin & Stokes, 1989, Study 2). Personality impacts perceptions by influencing what people notice, encode into memory, and are able to recall. A high-NA person, for example, easily notices negative stimuli, is easily able to encode negative information, and easily able to recall it. As a result, they are biased toward perceiving their jobs negatively and are thus likely to have negative job attitudes.

Hypersensitivity to Environmental Cues

Different workers are likely to respond differently to a given set of environmental cues (Spector et al., 2000). That is, a particular workplace condition or event is not likely to produce a uniform attitudinal effect among all employees. Because they are hypersensitive to positive stimuli, workers high in emotional stability, for example, may be expected to display a relatively greater increase in job satisfaction in response to favorable work situations than are workers who are low in emotional stability (Brief, Butcher, & Roberson, 1995).

Summary

Job attitudes differ from personality traits in regards to targets, consistency, and placement within the nomological network of workplace constructs. There are also a number of mechanisms through which personality can influence job attitudes. Figure 32.1 shows how both the work environment and personality traits can influence job attitudes, and how job attitudes and personality traits can combine to influence workplace behaviors and ultimately workplace outcomes that become the new work environment. We further develop this model later in the chapter. First, we discuss how job attitudes and personality traits are most commonly measured within organizational research.

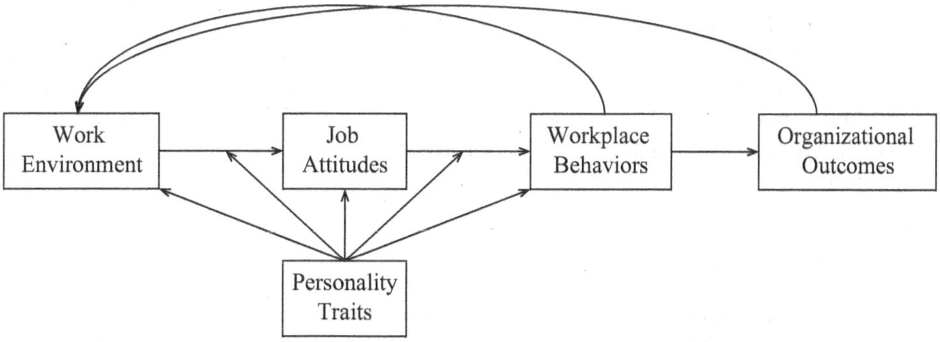

Figure 32.1 A General Model of Personality Traits and Job Attitudes in the Workplace.

Measurement Approaches and Considerations

While there are substantial theoretical differences between job attitudes and personality traits, these differences are not always fully evident in the typical approaches to measuring the constructs in the workplace. In the following subsections, we review the most common measurement approaches used for job attitudes and personality traits in the workplace, discuss the difference between explicit and implicit measurement approaches, examine the importance of examining ratings from different sources, and describe the importance of considering levels of specificity in using both job attitudes and personality traits in the workplace.

Job Attitude Constructs

While a full review of all the job attitude constructs that have been studied is beyond the scope of this chapter, it is useful to describe a few of the most commonly studied attitudes so that their relationships with personality traits can be discussed. We provide short reviews of the most common definitions, structures, and scales for job satisfaction, job involvement, organizational commitment, perceived organizational support, organizational justice perceptions, and employee engagement to facilitate the discussion of the relationships between these constructs and personality. This review is summarized in Table 32.2.

Job Satisfaction

Job satisfaction is the oldest and most researched job attitude construct in industrial/organizational psychology and organizational behavior (Spector, 1997). Brief (1998) defines job satisfaction as "an internal state that is expressed by affectively and/or cognitively evaluating an experienced job with some degree of favor or disfavor" (p. 86). It has been conceptualized both as a single global attitude toward a job and as multiple attitudes. The global approach includes items covering a broad array of workplace targets, while the multiple attitude approach includes sets of items focusing on different satisfaction facets. The *Job Descriptive Index* (JDI; Smith et al., 1969), for example, distinguishes between satisfactions with the work itself, supervision, coworkers, pay, and promotional opportunities.

Many satisfaction scales have been used in the empirical literature and countless scales have been developed by consultants or companies. Commonly used scales include the JDI (Smith et al., 1969), *Minnesota Satisfaction Questionnaire* (MSQ; Weiss, Dawis, England, & Lofquist, 1967), *Job Satisfaction Survey* (JSS; Spector, 1985), *Job Diagnostic Survey* (JDS; Hackman & Oldham, 1975), *Overall Job Satisfaction Scale* (OJS; Brayfield & Rothe, 1951), *Job in General Scale* (JIG; Ironson, Smith, Brannick, Gibson, & Paul, 1989), and the *Michigan Organizational Assessment Questionnaire* (MOAQ; Cammann, Fichman, Jenkins, & Klesh, 1979). These measures differ in length, number of facets, evaluations, targets, and language ability. These differences influence both the conceptual and empirical overlap of the measures. For example, the correlations between the facets of the JDI and the MSQ ranged from .47 to .60 (Kinicki, McKee-Ryan, Schriesheim, & Carson, 2002). The MOAQ global scale correlated with various satisfaction facets between .40 and .74 (Bowling & Hammond, 2008).

Job Involvement

"Job involvement is a generalized cognitive state of psychological identification with the job" (Elloy, Everett, & Flynn, 1991, p. 162). Compared with job satisfaction, job involvement is more focused on the cognitive aspect of job attitudes. Also, as the term suggests, job involvement

Table 32.2 Job Attitude Constructs

Constructs	*Sample Definitions*	*Sample Facets*	*Selected Measures*	*Books*
Job satisfaction	*An internal state that is expressed by affectively and/or cognitively evaluating an experienced job with some degree of favor or disfavor*	Work, pay, promotions, supervisor, and coworkers	JDI, MSQ, JSS, JDS, OJS, JIG, MOAQ	Spector (1997)
Job involvement	*A generalized cognitive state of psychological identification with the job*	Role and setting	Lodahl and Kejner, Kanungo	
Organizational commitment	*Psychological attachment to an organization; the psychological bond linking the individual to the organization*	Affective, normative, and continuance	OCQ, ACS, NCS, CCS	Klein, Becker, and Meyer (2009)
Perceived organizational support	*Global beliefs about the degree to which the organization values an employee's work and cares for the employee*		SPOS	Eisenberger and Stinglhamber (2011)
Organizational justice	*An individual's perception of and reactions to fairness in an organization*	Distributive, procedural, and interactional	Colquitt	Greenberg and Colquitt (2005)
Employee engagement	*An individual's sense of purpose and focused energy, evident to others in the display of personal initiative, adaptability, effort, and persistence toward organizational goals*		UWES, WES, Q12, JES, ES	Albrecht (2010) and Macey, Schneider, Barbera, and Young (2009)

Notes: ACS: Affective Commitment Scale; CCS: Continuance Commitment Scale; ES: Engagement Scale; JDI: Job Descriptive Index; JDS: Job Diagnostic Survey; JES: Job Engagement Scale; JIG: Job in General; JSS: Job Satisfaction Survey; MOAQ: The Michigan Organizational Assessment Questionnaire; MSQ: Minnesota Satisfaction Questionnaire; NCS: Normative Commitment Scale; OCQ: Organizational Commitment Questionnaire; OJS: Overall Job Satisfaction; Q12: Gallup Engagement Measure; SPOS: Survey of Perceived Organizational Support; UWES: Utrecht Work Engagement Scale; WES: Work Engagement Scale.

reflects the degree to which a person is concerned with and preoccupied by a job. This is a different evaluation than job satisfaction's focus on the favorability of various workplace targets. Job involvement is more a matter of the strength of affiliation with a job rather than an evaluation of the job per se.

The most researched measures of job involvement are Lodahl and Kejner's (1965) scale and Kanungo's (1982) measure. Lodahl and Kejner's scale has been used in a 20-item full version and a shorter 6-item version. Kanungo's measure was an attempt to assess the core psychological identification with the job with additional items tapping intrinsic motivation and the link between self-esteem and performance. However, in Brown's (1996) meta-analysis, the scale used to measure job involvement did not generally moderate the relationships between job involvement and other variables.

Organizational Commitment

Organizational commitment is one's "psychological attachment to an organization—the psychological bond linking the individual to the organization" (O'Reilly & Chatman, 1986, p. 492). Although previous researchers described organizational commitment as "attitudinal commitment" (Mowday, Steers, & Porter, 1979), some prominent commitment researchers believe that commitment is better thought of as a psychological bond (Becker, Klein, & Meyer, 2009). Specifically, this commitment bond is different in that it is reflected by volitional dedication and responsibility for a target (Klein, Molloy, & Brinsfield, 2011). While this definition differentiates organizational commitment from job satisfaction and other job attitudes, organizational commitment historically fits within the definition of a job attitude and has been studied as such (Schleicher et al., 2010). Organizational commitment has been conceptualized at both a broad level and as multiple subtypes. Organizational commitment types, as described by Meyer, Allen, and Gellatly (1990), include affective commitment (i.e., one's emotional bond with the organization), normative commitment (i.e., the belief that one ought to be committed because it is the right thing to do), and continuance commitment (i.e., commitment resulting from sunk costs in one's current organization and the belief that alternative job opportunities are scarce).

Organizational commitment has typically been studied using either the *Organizational Commitment Questionnaire* (OCQ; Mowday et al., 1979) or three component scales: the *Affective Commitment Scale* (ACS), *Normative Commitment Scale* (NCS), and the *Continuance Commitment Scale* (CCS), developed by Meyer et al. (1990). Research has shown that the OCQ is most closely aligned with the ACS in the three-component model of organizational commitment (Dunham, Grube, & Castaneda, 1994). A number of researchers have debated the most appropriate approach to measuring organizational commitment because of the substantial overlap between the ACS and the NCS and problems with the CCS (Bergman, 2006; Credé, Baldwin, Brummel, & Thomas, 2005). However, most researchers accept the utility of the three-component model and support research investigating the interactions of the components of commitment in understanding organizational commitment and its outcomes (Becker et al., 2009).

Perceived Organizational Support

Perceived organizational support refers to global beliefs about the degree to which the organization values an employee's contributions and cares for the employee's well-being (Eisenberger, Huntington, Hutchison, & Sowa, 1986). Employees base their perceived organizational support judgments on their perceptions of the favorable or unfavorable treatment received from the organization or its agents (Aselage & Eisnenberger, 2003). Favorable job conditions, such as good pay and supportive actions by supervisors, are thought to contribute directly to perceptions of perceived organizational support, especially when these favorable job conditions are viewed as being the result of voluntary organizational actions (Rhoades & Eisenberger, 2002).

Perceived organizational support is somewhat unique in the field of job attitudes in that it is predominantly measured using only one global scale: the *Survey of Perceived Organizational Support* (SPOS; Eisenberger et al., 1986). Research has been conducted with both the original 36-item scale and shorter forms of this scale including an 8-item version (Eisenberger & Stinglhamber, 2011).

Organizational Justice

Organizational justice is an individual's perception of and reactions to fairness in an organization (Greenberg & Colquitt, 2005). While perceived organizational justice has not typically been conceptualized as a job attitude by justice researchers, the organizational justice construct fits within the broad definition of a job attitude and has been researched in ways similar to those of common job attitudes (Schleicher et al., 2010). Specifically, justice perceptions involve evaluating targets such as organizational outcomes, procedures, and interactions with some degree of favor or disfavor (Colquitt, Conlon, Wesson, Porter, & Ng, 2001). The more formal conceptualization of perceived organizational justice was developed out of prior research on fairness perceptions in the workplace. These perceptions initially focused on the fairness of outcomes (distributive justice) but later expanded to include the processes for making decisions (procedural justice) and the interpersonal treatment one receives during the implementation of organizational decisions (interactional justice) (Greenberg & Colquitt, 2005). Currently, perceived organizational justice is thought to include either three or four dimensions. The four-dimensional structure comes from interactional justice being split into interpersonal and informational justice. Recently, some justice researchers have argued that it is more useful to organize justice according to the foci or sources of the fair or unfair treatment rather than by justice type (Lavelle, Rupp, & Brockner, 2007). That is, studying justice according to whether it comes from a supervisor or a coworker, regardless of whether it is procedural or distributive justice, is more useful in understanding antecedents and outcomes. It remains to be seen whether this approach to the target of justice attitudes will be formally incorporated into the measurement of organizational justice.

The measurement of organizational justice perceptions is less structured than are many other job attitudes. Early justice research tended to be collections of items created for a specific study. In 2001, Colquitt published a paper on the structure of justice that offered a 16-item measure with four items per justice dimension. This scale has been used frequently in subsequent research on organizational justice.

Employee Engagement

Employee engagement is the newest job attitude in the organizational literature. Although numerous definitions of employee engagement have been proposed, the majority have focused on absorption in and enthusiasm for work tasks and roles (Macey & Schneider, 2008). Macey, Schneider, Barbera, and Young (2009) define engagement as "an individual's sense of purpose and focused energy, evident to others in the display of personal initiative, adaptability, effort, and persistence toward organizational goals" (p. 7). Macey and Schneider differentiated between trait, state, and behavioral engagement, with trait engagement being similar to trait positive affect, state engagement being a positive work-related psychological state, and behavioral engagement being discretionary or extra-role contributions such as OCB. State engagement is most similar to other job attitude constructs (Dalal, Brummel, Wee, & Thomas, 2008). Alternatively, others have argued that employee engagement is best conceptualized as a higher-order single factor representing the common variance from other job attitudes (Newman & Harrison, 2008; Newman, Joseph, & Hulin, 2010).

The debate over the most appropriate definition and approach to measuring employee engagement highlights important issues with the measurement of job attitudes more generally. First, it is important to distinguish between the affect, cognition, and the behavior of an attitude when measuring a construct (Dalal et al., 2008). Second, an attitude should be distinguished from personality traits that may contribute to that attitude. Finally, there remains debate over the necessity of additional job attitude constructs to cover the attitudes people feel at work. Empirical research needs to demonstrate that job attitudes with distinct definitions show incremental validity for understanding behavior at work. More information on employee engagement can be found in Macey et al. (2009) and Albrecht (2010), as well as the focal article by Macey and Schneider (2008) and the commentaries in the first issue of *Industrial–Organizational Psychology: Perspectives on Research and Practice.*

A variety of measures have been constructed to measure employee engagement. Perhaps the most well-known proprietary measure is Gallup's Q12 (e.g., Harter, Schmidt, & Hayes, 2002). The academic literature includes the *Utrecht Work Engagement Scale* (UWES; Schaufeli, Salanova, Gonzàlez-Romà, & Bakker, 2002), the *Work Engagement Scale* (WES; Rothbard, 2001), the *Job Engagement Scale* (JES; Saks, 2006), the *Engagement Scale* (May, Gilson, & Harter, 2004), and another JES (Rich, Lepine, & Crawford, 2010).

Personality Constructs

As with the job attitude constructs, a full review of conceptualizations of personality traits is beyond the scope of this chapter, but it is useful to review the major approaches to personality that have been used in research with job attitudes (see Chapter 2, this volume for an overview of the structure of personality traits).

Structural Models

The FFM, currently the dominant approach to categorizing personality traits, was developed using a lexical approach (Digman, 1990; Goldberg, 1990). In this approach, researchers examined several world languages in an effort to categorize adjectives used to describe people. Five categories of adjectives were found to be common across cultures and these are presumed to represent five broad personality traits: extraversion, neuroticism, conscientiousness, agreeableness, and openness. This model has received broad support and acceptance with existing inventories, having been mapped onto the FFM structure (McCrae, Costa, & Piedmont, 1993). However, a variety of researchers have advocated for six- (Ashton & Lee, 2005) and seven- (Saucier, 2003) factor models. These models include evaluative factors like honesty (Ashton & Lee, 2005) or positive and negative evaluation (Saucier, 2003), in addition to constructs covering most of the FFM content (for more coverage on the structures of personality, see Chapter 2, this volume).

Major inventories for measuring personality traits used in research in the workplace include the *Neuroticism–Extraversion–Openness Personality Inventory* (NEO-PI; Costa & McCrae, 1992), the *California Personality Inventory* (CPI; Gough, 1996), the *Sixteen Personality Factor Questionnaire* (16PF; Conn & Rieke, 1994), the *Multidimensional Personality Questionnaire* (MPQ; Tellegen, 1982), the *Jackson Personality Inventory* (JPI; Jackson, 1994), the *Hogan Personality Inventory* (HPI; R. Hogan & Hogan, 2007), and the AB5C scales from the IPIP (Goldberg, 1999). There are also a number of other inventories created by private consulting companies for which peer-reviewed research is scarce (for more coverage on the major personality inventories, see Chapter 10, this volume).

Trait Affect

Individual differences in affect are often assessed as a transient state, but affect can also be conceptualized as a temporally stable trait. This trait approach to affect has distinguished between PA and NA. PA reflects the extent to which a person consistently experiences positive emotions, such as joy, gratitude, and enthusiasm. NA, on the other hand, reflects the extent to which a person consistently experiences negative emotions, such as anxiety, depression, frustration, and anger (Watson et al., 1988). PA has notable overlap with extraversion, and NA, with neuroticism (Watson et al., 1988; Watson, Wiese, Vaidya, & Tellegen, 1999). PA and NA are largely independent of each other (Connolly & Viswesvaran, 2000). Although some researchers (Lucas, Diener, & Suh, 1996) have argued that PA is equivalent to extraversion and NA is equivalent to neuroticism of the FFM, a meta-analysis by Bowling, Hendricks, and Wagner (2008) found that PA predicted facet satisfaction better than did extraversion and NA predicted better than did neuroticism. These findings suggest that extraversion and neuroticism are not entirely redundant with PA and NA (for more coverage of moods and personality, see Chapter 30, this volume).

Trait affect has typically been measured using the *PA/NA Schedule* (PANAS; Watson et al., 1988). The PANAS asks participants to rate the extent to which they have felt a number of adjectives representing positive and negative mood states over a period of time. This time frame can be adjusted from at the moment to over the past year to in general, with the test–retest reliability increasing from around .5 to around .7 with increasing time frames (Watson et al., 1988). Trait affect is measured by asking participants how they feel in general.

The *Neutral Objects Satisfaction Questionnaire* (NOSQ; Judge & Bretz, 1993), which is another trait affect measure, asks participants to indicate whether they are satisfied, feel neutral toward, or dissatisfied with a list of ostensibly neutral everyday objects, such as "8½ × 11 inch paper" and "modern art." Although the NOSQ has been assumed by some researchers to assess NA (e.g., Probst, 2003), it has been shown to be quite independent of NA, as well as other personality traits, including traits from the FFM, locus of control, and general self-efficacy (Eschleman & Bowling, 2011). The high degree of temporal stability of the NOSQ suggests that it assesses trait affect (Judge & Bretz, 1993), but its weak relationships with the PANAS (Eschleman & Bowling, 2011) suggest that it assesses a construct that is largely independent from existing measures of trait affectivity. More research is needed to better understand the construct assessed by the NOSQ.

CSE

CSE are a higher-order construct consisting of four indicators: self-esteem, general self-efficacy, emotional stability, and locus of control (Judge & Bono, 2001a; Judge et al., 1997; Judge et al., 1998). Factor analysis (Judge et al., 2000; Judge et al., 1998), as well as meta-analytic evidence showing that the four constituent CSE traits are related to each other (Judge, Erez, Bono, & Thoresen, 2003), provides support for the CSE construct. A meta-analysis by Judge and Bono (2001b) found that each of the constituent CSE traits was positively related to job satisfaction. Specifically, self-esteem (ρ = .26), general self-efficacy (ρ = .45), emotional stability (ρ = .24), and internal locus of control (ρ = .32) were each positively related to job satisfaction. Although some have suggested that the CSE construct is largely an alternative conceptualization of neuroticism (negatively scored emotional stability; e.g., Judge & Bono, 2001a), meta-analysis has shown that CSE may in fact not be redundant with neuroticism, as the population correlations (ρ) between emotional stability were .40 with locus of control, .64 with self-esteem, and .62 with general self-efficacy (Judge et al., 2003).

Subclinical and Dark Personality

Recent attention has been given to subclinical "dark" personality traits. Researchers have created dimensional models of personality disorders to tap subclinical traits (R. Hogan & Hogan, 2001). Paulhaus and Williams (2002) discussed the Dark Triad, which focuses on narcissism, Machiavellianism, and psychopathy. Narcissism reflects an inflated view of one's own importance and competence. Machiavellianism reflects a manipulative and deceitful personality. Psychopathy is a mixture of low empathy and high levels of impulsivity. Machiavellianism and psychopathy have been shown to have small, predictive relationships with job performance (ρ = −.07 and −.10, respectively). Machiavellianism has a stronger (ρ = .25) relationship with CWBs than psychopathy (ρ = .07). Narcissism predicts CWBs (ρ = .43) but not job performance (ρ = −.03) (O'Boyle, Forsyth, Banks, & McDaniel, 2012). In a recent meta-analysis, Bruk-Lee, Khoury, Nixon, Goh, and Spector (2009) found that both narcissism and Machiavellianism are modestly related to job satisfaction (uncorrected mean correlation = −.07 and −.19, respectively).

Summary

Now that we have discussed a number of different approaches to conceptualizing personality traits and job attitudes, we turn to a discussion of issues related to the measurement of both personality traits and job attitudes.

Measurement Approaches

The most common approaches to measuring both job attitudes and personality traits are explicit self-reports at broad levels of specificity. This approach characterizes most of the measurement tools that have been discussed to this point. However, other approaches to measuring these constructs include implicit tests, other-reports, and more narrow levels of specificity.

Explicit and Implicit Measurement

Although organizational research has typically focused on the assessment of explicit (i.e., conscious) manifestations of employee personality and job attitudes, several recent developments may allow researchers to more easily examine implicit (i.e., unconscious) aspects of these variables. Implicit association tests (IATs), for example, use participant reaction time to assess the strength of association between an attitude object and positive (e.g., health) or negative concepts (e.g., disease). IATs have been developed to assess personality traits, such as the FFM characteristics (Grumm & von Collani, 2007) and self-esteem (Greenwald & Farnham, 2000), and they have been used to assess job satisfaction (Leavitt, Fong, & Greenwald, 2011; for in-depth coverage on implicit personality, see Chapter 7, this volume).

The *Affective Misattribution Procedure* (AMP; Payne, Cheng, Govorun, & Stewart, 2005), another measure of implicit processes, asks participants to view a picture of an attitude object (e.g., George W. Bush) and then to immediately view an ambiguous stimulus (e.g., a nonsense syllable). Participants are asked to ignore the picture of the attitude object and instead provide an evaluation of the ambiguous object. In a series of studies, Payne et al. showed that participants' attitudes toward the attitude object "spill over" into their evaluation of the ambiguous stimulus. A participant who holds a positive attitude toward the attitude object, for example, is likely to positively evaluate the ambiguous stimulus, whereas a participant who holds a negative attitude toward the attitude object is likely to negatively evaluate the ambiguous stimulus. Although organizational researchers have not used the AMP in published research, we believe that it holds much promise for measuring job attitudes.

Another notable method for assessing implicit processes employs word-completing tasks (R. E. Johnson, Tolentino, Rodopman, & Cho, 2010). With this approach, participants are provided with an incomplete word and asked to fill in letters to spell the first word that comes to mind. Consider the following example item:

F E _ _

Spelling the word "FEAR" is coded as being evidence of high NA, whereas spelling words like "FEEL" or "FEED" are coded as being neutral responses. A few studies have used the work completion measure as an indirect approach to measuring employee personality, with particular attention given to the assessment of PA and NA (see R. E. Johnson et al., 2010).

We believe that implicit measures will provide a valuable complement to more traditional explicit measures. Implicit measures, for instance, may be less susceptible to response distortion and they may provide incremental validity beyond the effect of explicit measures (R. E. Johnson et al., 2010; Leavitt et al., 2011).

Nonself-Rating Sources

Both personality traits and job attitudes are typically measured using self-reports. It is also possible to measure both constructs using the perspective of other people as well. This approach has the benefit of avoiding common-method bias and can be useful for assessing sensitive personality traits (Connelly & Ones, 2010). Personality traits have been studied more systematically from the perspective of both the self and others. This research has shown that a number of variables moderate the level of self-other agreement on personality traits, including the observability of the trait, the relationship between the person being rated and the other person, as well as the social desirability of the trait (John & Robins, 1993; Vazire & Carlson, 2011). These differences are reflected in the predictive validity of personality traits. Some outcomes are better predicted by self-ratings, while other outcomes are better predicted by other ratings. Research has also shown that other-reports of the same personality trait provide incremental validity in predicting outcomes about self-ratings (Connelly & Ones, 2010; Vazire, 2010; for in-depth coverage of personality from the perspective of observers, see Chapter 20, this volume).

Job attitudes have almost always been measured using self-reports (Brief, 1998; Spector, 1997). Reliance on such measures seems reasonable, given that job attitudes are an internal state to which only the person who holds the state has direct access. In some cases, however, it may be useful to assess job attitudes using methods that do not involve self-reports, such as implicit measures or reports provided by significant others. These alternative measures may be particularly useful when researchers are concerned that common-method variance will influence the relationship between self-reported job attitudes and self-reported predictor or criterion variables. Additionally, alternatives to self-report can be useful in situations where participants might lie about their job attitudes, such as when one feels pressure from management to provide a favorable response to an organizational questionnaire or when union pressure encourages employees to exaggerate their levels of dissatisfaction (Haines & Sumner, 2006).

Alternatives to self-reported job attitudes have typically used significant others' (e.g., spouses', friends', and parents') reports of the focal person's job attitudes. Judge et al. (1998) found in three independent samples that participants' self-reported job satisfaction yielded strong correlations with significant other-rated job satisfaction (*r*s ranged from .57 to .65 across the samples), thus providing validity evidence for this measurement approach. Others have proposed the use of facial expression to assess job attitudes (Eschleman & Bowling, 2010), but such an approach has not been used in any published studies.

Levels of Specificity

As discussed above, personality traits and job attitudes can be conceptualized at multiple levels of specificity. Job attitude levels are differentiated by target (e.g., pay, coworkers, and the work itself) and/or by type of evaluation (e.g., satisfaction, commitment, and perceived support). Recent work has also suggested that there is a general factor underlying most specific job attitude constructs (Harrison et al., 2006). Job attitudes can be focused on different targets within the organization, ranging from individual level to the organizational level. As an illustration, researchers interested in the job attitude–job performance relationship have assessed attitudes at both the individual level (Judge et al., 2001) and at the organizational or work unit level (Harter et al., 2002; Koys, 2001; Ostroff, 1992; Ryan, Schmit, & Johnson, 1996). Many broad job attitudes can be broken down into multiple subdimensions or facets. Many of the common measures of job satisfaction, such as the JDI (Smith et al., 1969), the MSQ (Weiss et al., 1967), and the JSS (Spector, 1985), for instance, differentiate between different facets of job satisfaction. Recently, scholars have developed the idea that job attitudes and perceptions may exhibit a hierarchical structure. It appears likely that the general structure of the job attitude and job perception domain may be roughly analogous to hierarchical models evident in other areas of psychology (e.g., intelligence, Carroll, 1993; personality, Costa & McCrae, 1992; core self-evaluations, Judge et al., 2003). This finding is in line with theoretical arguments made by Harrison et al. (2006) and Newman and Harrison (2008) and with the general factor (the job attitude "A" factor) proposed and tested by Newman et al. (2010). That is, a model consisting of a general job attitude/job perception factor at the apex or Level 3; justice perceptions, POS, job satisfaction, and commitment as Level 2 group factors; and the various subfacets of each of these constructs arranged at Level 1.

Personality traits have been conceptualized at different levels of specificity, ranging from three to six broad traits to hundreds of single adjectives and many levels in between (for more coverage on the breadth of personality measurement, see Chapter 14, this volume). The FFM can be broken down further into facets. Indeed, there is also a variety of approaches to these subdimensions. In the NEO, Costa and McCrae (1992) posit six subdimensions for each of the five main dimensions. Conscientiousness, for example, is broken into self-efficacy, orderliness, dutifulness, achievement-striving, self-discipline, and cautiousness. Other facet measures of personality include the AB5C (Hofstee, De Raad, & Goldberg, 1992) and the TAPAS (Chernyshenko, Stark, & Drasgow, 2010).

Current Models and Research Findings

Several personality traits have been shown to be correlated with some job attitudes. A summary of meta-analytic findings for these relationships is presented in Table 32.3. However, a larger workplace framework and the causal nature of these relationships cannot be inferred from these bivariate relationships alone. The more interesting questions of how personality traits influence job attitudes and how these relationships fit into a more comprehensive understanding of the workplace are addressed in this section. It is also worth noting that the magnitude and even the direction of these relationships can vary substantially across the studies included in the meta-analyses reported in Table 32.3. This variability can be inferred from the standard deviations of the population correlation estimates, which are quite large for some of the reported relationships, and result in wide criterion intervals. This variability in the relationships between specific personality traits and job attitudes reflects the multitude of pathways by which personality traits and job attitudes influence each other in the workplace. This following review of the current research on personality and job attitude relationships provides the background for our suggestion for future research in the final section of this chapter.

Beside the additive effects of looking at personality traits and job attitudes separately, the most common model for studying the relationship between personality and job attitudes has been to conceptualize job attitudes as a mediator of the relationship between personality traits and workplace behaviors (Figure 32.1). Within this structure, job attitudes may fully mediate, partially mediate, or be irrelevant for understanding the influence of a specific personality trait on a specific workplace behavior. Personality traits may also moderate the relationship between the work environment and job attitudes, and personality and job attitudes may also interact to influence workplace behaviors. The following subsections describe empirical evidence that has been found to support these relationships.

Additive Effects

The most straightforward way to approach the influence of personality and job attitudes on workplace behavior is to consider them as independent predictors. Research on the workplace has a long history of examining the incremental prediction of constructs so that choices can be made about which predictor is most useful, both individually and in conjunction with other predictors (Schmidt

Table 32.3 Meta-Analytic Relationships Between Job Attitudes and Personality Traits

Job Attitude	*Personality Trait*	*r*	ρ	*SD*	*L*	*U*	*k*	*N*	*Meta-Analysis*
Job satisfaction	Openness	.01	.02	.21	−.26	.29	50	15,196	Judge, Heller, and Mount (2002)
	Conscientiousness	.20	.26	.22	−.02	.55	79	21,719	
	Extraversion	.19	.25	.15	.06	.45	75	20,184	
	Agreeableness	.13	.17	.16	−.03	.37	38	11,856	
	Neuroticism	−.24	−.29	.16	−.50	−.08	92	24,527	
	PA	.27	.33	.16	.13	.53	71	22,148	Thoresen, Kaplan, Barsky, Warren, and de Chermont (2003)
	NA	−.27	−.37	.13	−.20	−.54	145	52,120	
	Narcissism	−.07	—	.24[a]	.24[a]	−.38[a]	4	789	Bruk-Lee, Khoury, Nixon, Goh, and Spector (2009)
	Machiavellianism	−.19	—	.25[a]	.11[a]	−.51[a]	7	1,241	
	Self-esteem	.20	.26	.11	.12	.40	56	20,819	Judge and Bono (2001)
	Self-efficacy	.38	.45	.10	.32	.58	12	12,903	
	Locus of control	.24	.32	.16	.12	.52	80	18,491	
Job involvement	Self-esteem	.26	.31	.16	.11	.51	5	1,460	Brown (1996)
	Locus of control	−.12	−.18	.17	.04	−.40	22	5,577	
Organizational commitment	Conscientiousness	.18	.22	.09	.10	.24	7	2,456	Podsakoff, MacKenzie, and Bommer (1996)
	Extraversion	.17	.22	.07	.13	.31	2	492	Thoresen et al. (2003)
	Neuroticism	−.19	−.23	.08	−.13	−.33	3	713	
	PA	.28	.35	.18	.12	.58	15	4,873	
	NA	−.21	−.27	.18	−.04	−.50	27	8,040	
Perceived organizational support	Conscientiousness	.10	.11	.20	−.15	.37	5	817	Rhoades and Eisenberger (2002)
	PA	.31	.34	.07	.25	.43	4	3,363	
	NA	−.39	−.43	.07	−.34	−.52	3	1,481	
Distributive justice	PA	.11	.13	.13	−.04	.30	11	5,088	Ng and Sorensen (2009)
	NA	−.15	−.18	.05	−.12	−.24	19	7,335	
Procedural justice	PA	.44	.47	.00	.47	.47	3	883	
	NA	−.22	−.26	.12	−.11	−.41	12	3,281	
Interactional justice	PA	.19	.22	—	—	—	2	390	Barsky and Kaplan (2007)
	NA	−.16	−.20	.06	−.12	−.28	10	6,818	
Employee engagement	Conscientiousness	.36	.42	.09	.32	.52	12	5,821	Christian, Garza, and Slaughter (2011)
	PA	.37	.43	.16	.23	.64	14	6,715	

Notes: r: mean uncorrected correlation; ρ: mean corrected correlation; *SD*: standard deviation of ρ; *L*: lower bound estimate of 80% criterion interval; *U*: upper bound estimate of 80% criterion interval; *k*: the number of independent effect sizes; *N*: sample size.

[a] Based on *r* because ρ was unavailable.

& Hunter, 1998). Dalal, Baysinger, Brummel, and LeBreton (2012) examined the relative weights of a number of job attitude constructs, trait-positive affect, and trait-negative affect for predicting task performance, OCBs, and CWBs. They found that trait-negative affect, employee engagement, and job satisfaction provided the most unique prediction. While these results may be useful in certain situations, they do not provide much information on *how* personality traits influence job attitudes and work behaviors. Testing theoretical arguments for these relationships requires more than analyzing the relative strength of predictive contributions to outcomes.

Mediation

A number of studies have shown that the relationship between some personality traits and some workplace performance behaviors is mediated by job attitudes. For example, Credé, Chernyshenko, Stark, Dalal, and Bashshur (2007) showed that job satisfaction only partially mediated the relationship between both positive and negative dispositions (PA/extraversion and NA/neuroticism, respectively) and both OCBs and CWBs; however, job satisfaction fully mediated the relationship with withdrawal cognitions. Rich et al. (2010) fit a model with multiple job attitudes (engagement, involvement, and satisfaction) partially mediating the relationship between CSE and both task performance and OCBs. Mount, Ilies, and Johnson (2006) showed that job satisfaction fully mediated the relationship between neuroticism and CWBs, but that job satisfaction only partially mediated the relationship between conscientiousness and organizational CWBs and the relationship between agreeableness and interpersonal CWBs. Depending on the personality trait, job attitude, and outcome, job attitudes can either partially or fully mediate the influence of personality on work behavior.

Moderation

Personality traits can also moderate the relationship between job attitudes and work behaviors. For example, Bowling (2010) found that job satisfaction was more strongly related to OCBs and CWBs among those who were low rather than high in conscientiousness. Wright, Cropanzano, and Bonett (2007) found that employees' positive well-being moderated the relation between job satisfaction and job performance, such that the relationship was stronger for employees higher in positive well-being. For people with some personality traits, the links between certain job attitudes and workplace behaviors may not be as strong.

Perceived Work Environments

To this point, the current chapter has called all evaluations of the work environment job attitudes. However, this approach is not consistent with how some researchers have framed their constructs. Specifically, organizational justice perceptions and perceived organizational support have been placed as perceived work environments rather than job attitudes (e.g., Aselage & Eisenberger, 2003; Burnett, Williamson, & Bartol, 2009). This distinction draws on their evaluative focus on a specific aspect of the organization or event as being objectively true rather than raters' subjective evaluations of their feelings toward the target. Rhoades and Eisenberger (2002) consider organizational justice to be an antecedent of perceived organizational support, and job satisfaction, organizational commitment, and job involvement to be consequences of perceived organizational support. Rich et al. (2010) also specified perceived organizational support as an antecedent of engagement, involvement, and satisfaction. This kind of a framework requires distinguishing between perceptions of the work environment and job attitudes. Also, other measures of the work environment, such as the JDS, measure perceptions of the work environment. Examining the influence of personality on the link between the objective work environment and the perceived work environment requires adding an additional construct to our model (see Figure 32.2). This addition involves another layer of potential additive, mediation, and moderation effects into the

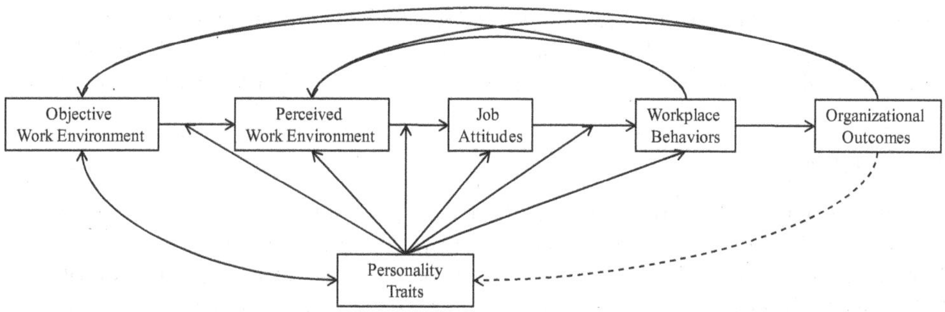

Figure 32.2 Directions in Research on Job Attitudes and Personality at Work.

prediction of workplace behaviors and outcomes from personality traits and job attitudes. For example, Burnett et al. examined the moderating role of extraversion and conscientiousness on the relationship between organizational justice and job satisfaction. This type of research requires the addition of the perceived work environment category that allows for personality to moderate this relationship. It remains to be seen whether this added complexity will enhance or confuse the role of job attitudes in these models.

Summary of Current Models and Research

These approaches to understanding the joint influence of personality traits and job attitudes in the workplace are depicted in the larger model shown in Figure 32.2. The main addition in this model is the perceived work environment as distinct from job attitudes and the objective work environment. This addition opens the door for a variety of studies investigating how various evaluations of the workplace relate to each other and what the role of personality is in these relationships. However, given the potential theoretical and empirical overlap between perceived work environment and job attitudes, these relationships are difficult to disentangle. We discuss some of these issues in the next section of this chapter.

Approaches to Advance Research and Practice

We believe that there are three broad areas in which research can be done to clarify and advance the understanding of the joint influence of job attitudes and personality traits in the workplace. The first area involves further examinations of different approaches to measuring both job attitudes and personality traits. The second involves clarifying the structure and measurement of job attitudes. Finally, longitudinal research designs are needed to show how changes in job attitudes and personality traits occur over time, and what the implications of these changes might be for studying the workplace.

Measurement Approaches

Both job attitudes and personality traits are most commonly measured with explicit self-reports at broad levels of specificity. However, the definitions of these constructs allow for the use of more specific measures, other-reports, and implicit measures. New developments in the influence of personality traits on job attitudes and workplace behavior are most likely to be found as researchers explore the possibilities and limitations of these other approaches to measurement. It may be discovered that implicit measures are useful only for understanding automatic rather than deliberate behaviors in the workplace or that other reports of personality are most useful for predicting other reports of performance. A comprehensive science of how the measurement of job attitudes and personality traits influences the functioning and usefulness of these constructs is far from complete.

Structure of Job Attitudes

Attitudes are differentiated by target and evaluation type. Job attitudes are most often evaluated with some mix of cognition and affect. The target for many global job attitudes is the organization. While job satisfaction, job involvement, organizational commitment, perceived organizational support, organizational justice, and employee engagement have some theoretical differences in their targets, evaluative approach, and measurement, they demonstrate substantial empirical overlap. There is emerging debate on whether it is more useful to consider at least some of these constructs as manifestations of a broad second-order attitude construct (Credé et al., 2005; Harrison et al., 2006; Newman et al., 2010). This approach allows researchers to investigate whether the predictive variance in job attitudes is due to the common variance or the unique variance in each approach to measuring job attitudes.

Dalal et al. (2012) demonstrated some utility in using multiple global attitude constructs in predicting task performance, OCBs, and CWBs, but few researchers use multiple attitude constructs in their research. Further work in this area may also help researchers clarify the utility of conceptualizing some attitude constructs as perceptions of the work environment rather than as job attitudes. Replicable evidence of additive and/or mediation relationships between these constructs will provide evidence for the value of this approach. If personality traits can be shown to reliably influence the relationship between perceived work constructs, like organizational justice and job satisfaction, then there is evidence that the more complex model is important to consider. However, if these relationships cannot be found, it may be better to think of different job attitudes as alternate forms to capture the same information about employees. Longitudinal study designs should be helpful in this work.

Longitudinal Research Designs

Testing causal relationships on the joint influence of personality traits and job attitudes is difficult because personality traits and job attitudes cannot be experimentally manipulated. Longitudinal studies are needed to test causal relationships both among job attitudes and between personality traits and job attitudes.

If perceived work environments are causally prior and different from job attitudes, this could be shown by following the development and change in both across an individual's tenure with an organization or work group. Much of the literature has been satisfied with labeling different job attitudes as correlates of each other (e.g., Schleicher et al., 2010). However, clarity in this field requires more specific efforts to disentangle these approaches to workplace evaluation if possible.

As mentioned previously, organizational researchers are beginning to challenge the notion that personality traits should be studied as unchanging predictors of other workplace variables (Roberts, 2006; Slaughter & Feldman, 2009). The possibility of personality change adds another path through which job attitudes and workplace behaviors could be influenced over time. For example, being placed in a leadership role could make an individual more socially dominant over time. This change in personality could then lead that person to change the work environment to be more positive and thereby influence job attitudes. The possibility of the work environment influencing personality is included in Figure 32.2. These types of relationships can only be studied over time.

Conclusion

This chapter began by noting that job attitudes and personality traits are two of the most studied predictors of important workplace behaviors and outcomes. Given this breadth of research, researchers know a lot about how these differences lead to differences in workplace behavior. However, there remains plenty of work to do as we work to understand all the ways in which personality traits are important for understanding the functioning of job attitudes.

Practitioner's Window

While the relationships between job attitudes and personality traits within the workplace may be interesting to academic researchers, most practitioners use personality traits and job attitudes in very different ways in organizations. Personality traits are most often used in selection or in individual development programs. Job attitudes, on the other hand, are used to understand the opinions of employees, evaluate the success of programs, and predict organizational outcomes. In spite of these differences in use, we believe there are a number of important practical implications for practitioners regarding personnel selection and organizational interventions in this chapter.

1. Personality traits and job attitudes predict a number of important workplace behaviors (e.g., task performance, OCBs, CWBs, and job withdrawal) and organizational outcomes (e.g., turnover and profitability). Within this network, job attitudes provide an explanation for why personality might be related to these behaviors. Personality and job attitudes together predict more variance in these criteria than would either personality or job attitudes alone. So, it is useful to consider both constructs when explaining and predicting these criteria.
2. The presence of a personality trait–job attitude relationship may make it difficult to change employees' job attitudes. So, it may be important to consider who is evaluating a specific aspect of a job before deciding that it needs to be changed. A person high on negative affectivity/neuroticism may never be satisfied with their work, regardless of how it is structured. Beyond performance implications of neuroticism, this inability to be satisfied might be important to consider when selecting employees.
3. Interventions have still been shown to be effective in changing job attitudes in spite of this link with personality traits. Also, researchers are beginning to acknowledge the possibility of changes in personality traits over time. Therefore, organizations should not give up on interventions targeted at improving job attitudes as there is a lot more to these evaluations than trait affect.
4. Finally, it is important to choose appropriate measures of job attitudes, personality traits, and workplace behaviors if you want to get useful information about their relationships in a specific organizational context. Thoughtful consideration to the approach to measurement will yield more useful information about the relationships between these constructs and the best paths for successful interventions.

References

Albrecht, S. L. (Ed.). (2010). *Handbook of employee engagement: Perspectives, issues, research, and practice.* Northampton, MA: Edward Elgar.

Arvey, R. D., Bouchard, T. J., Segal, N. L., & Abraham, L. M. (1989). Job satisfaction: Environmental and genetic components. *Journal of Applied Psychology, 74*, 187–192.

Aselage, J., & Eisenberger, R. (2003). Perceived organizational support and psychological contracts: A theoretical integration. *Journal of Organizational Behavior, 24*, 491–509.

Ashton, A. C., & Lee, K. (2005). The lexical approach to the study of personality structure: Toward the identification of cross-culturally replicable dimensions of personality variation. *Journal of Personality Disorders, 19*, 303–308.

Barrick, M. R., & Mount, M. K. (1991). The Big Five personality dimensions and job performance: A meta-analysis. *Personnel Psychology, 44*, 1–26.

Barsky, A., & Kaplan, S. A. (2007). If you feel bad, it's unfair: A quantitative synthesis of affect and organizational justice perceptions. *Journal of Applied Psychology, 92*, 286–295.

Becker, T. E., Klein, H. J., & Meyer, J. P. (2009). Commitment in organizations: Accumulated wisdom and new directions. In H. J. Klein, T. E. Becker, & J. P. Meyer (Eds.), *Commitment in organizations: Accumulated wisdom and new directions* (pp. 419–452). New York: Routledge, Taylor & Francis Group.

Bergman, M. E. (2006). The relationship between affective and normative commitment: Review and research agenda. *Journal of Organizational Behavior, 27*, 645–663.

Bing, M. N., Whanger, J. C., Davison, H. K., & VanHook, J. B. (2004). Incremental validity of the frame-of-reference effect in Personality Scale scores: A replication and extension. *Journal of Applied Psychology, 89*, 150–157.

Bowling, N. A. (2010). Effects of job satisfaction and conscientiousness on extra-role behaviors. *Journal of Business and Psychology, 25*, 119–130.

Bowling, N. A., Beehr, T. A., & Lepisto, L. R. (2006). Beyond job satisfaction: A five-year prospective analysis of the dispositional approach to work attitudes. *Journal of Vocational Behavior, 69*, 315–330.

Bowling, N. A., & Burns, G. N. (2010). A comparison of work-specific and general personality measures as predictors of work and non-work criteria. *Personality and Individual Differences, 49*, 95–101.

Bowling, N. A., Eschleman, K. J., Wang, Q., Kirkendall, C., & Alarcon, G. (2010). Meta-analysis of the predictors and consequences of organization-based self-esteem. *Journal of Occupational and Organizational Psychology, 83*, 601–626.

Bowling, N. A., & Hammond, G. D. (2008). A meta-analytic examination of the construct validity of the Michigan Organizational Assessment Questionnaire Job Satisfaction Subscale. *Journal of Vocational Behavior, 73*, 63–77.

Bowling, N. A., Hendricks, E. A., & Wagner, S. H. (2008). Positive and negative affectivity and facet satisfaction: A meta-analysis. *Journal of Business and Psychology, 23*, 115–125.

Bowling, N. A., Wang, Q., Tang, H. Y., & Kennedy, K. (2010). A comparison of general and work-specific measures of core self-evaluations. *Journal of Vocational Behavior, 76*, 559–566.

Brayfield, A. H., & Rothe, H. F. (1951). An index of job satisfaction. *Journal of Applied Psychology, 35*, 307–311.

Brief, A. P. (1998). Organizational behavior: Affect in the workplace. *Annual Review of Psychology, 53*, 279–307.

Brief, A. P., Butcher, A. H., & Roberson, L. (1995). Cookies, disposition, and job attitudes: The effects of positive mood-inducing events and negative affectivity on job satisfaction in a field experiment. *Organizational Behavior and Human Decision Processes, 62*, 55–62.

Brown, S. P. (1996). A meta-analysis and review of organizational research on job involvement. *Psychological Bulletin, 120*, 235–255.

Bruk-Lee, V., Khoury, H. A., Nixon, A. E., Goh, A., & Spector, P. (2009). Replicating and extending past personality/job satisfaction meta-analyses. *Human Performance, 22*, 156–189.

Burnett, M. F., Williamson, I. O., & Bartol, K. M. (2009). The moderating effect of personality on employees' reactions to procedural fairness and outcome favorability. *Journal of Business and Psychology, 24*, 469–484.

Cacioppo, J. T., & Petty, R. E. (1982). The need for cognition. *Journal of Personality and Social Psychology, 42*, 116–131.

Cammann, C., Fichman, M., Jenkins, D., & Klesh, J. (1979). *The Michigan Organizational Assessment Questionnaire.* Unpublished manuscript, University of Michigan, Ann Arbor.

Carroll, J. B. (1993). *Human cognitive abilities: A survey of factor-analytic studies.* New York: Cambridge University Press.

Chaiken, S., & Stangor, C. (1987). Attitudes and attitude change. *Annual Review of Psychology, 38*, 575–630.

Chen, G., Gully, S. M., & Eden, D. (2001). Validation of a new general Self-Efficacy Scale. *Organizational Research Methods, 4*, 62–83.

Chen, P. Y., & Spector, P. E. (1991). Negative affectivity as the underlying cause of the correlations between stressors and strains. *Journal of Applied Psychology, 76*, 398–407.

Chernyshenko, O. S., Stark, S., & Drasgow, F. (2010). Individual differences: Their measurement and validity. In S. Zedeck (Ed.), *APA handbook of industrial organizational psychology: Selecting and developing members for the organization* (Vol. 2, pp. 117–151). Washington, DC: American Psychological Association.

Christian, M. S., Garza, A. S., & Slaughter, J. E. (2011). Work engagement: A quantitative review and test of its relations with task and contextual performance. *Personnel Psychology, 64*, 89–136.

Colquitt, J. A. (2001). On the dimensionality of organizational justice: A construct validation of a measure. *Journal of Applied Psychology, 86*, 386–400.
Colquitt, J. A., Conlon, D. E., Wesson, M. J., Porter, C. O. L. H., & Ng, K. Y. (2001). Justice at the millennium: A meta-analytic review of 25 years of organizational justice research. *Journal of Applied Psychology, 86*, 425–445.
Conn, S. R., & Rieke, M. L. (1994). *The 16PF fifth edition technical manual.* Champaign, IL: Institute for Personality and Ability Testing.
Connelly, B. S., & Ones, D. S. (2010). An other perspective on personality: Meta-analytic integration of observers' accuracy and predictive validity. *Psychological Bulletin, 136*, 1092–1122.
Connolly, J. J., & Viswesvaran, C. (2000). The role of affectivity in job satisfaction: A meta-analysis. *Personality and Individual Differences, 29*, 265–281.
Costa, P. T., Jr., & McCrae, R. R. (1992). *Revised NEO Personality Inventory (NEO-PI-R) and NEO Five Factor Inventory (NEO-FFI) professional manual.* Odessa, FL: Psychological Assessment Resources.
Credé, M., Baldwin, A. M., Brummel, B. J., & Thomas, L. L. (2005, April). *The discriminant validity of job satisfaction, commitment, and justice perceptions.* Poster presented at the Twentieth Annual Conference of the Society for Industrial and Organizational Psychology, Los Angeles, CA.
Credé, M., Chernyshenko, O. S., Stark, S., Dalal, R. S., & Bashshur, M. (2007). Job satisfaction as mediator: An assessment of job satisfaction's position within the nomological network. *Journal of Occupational and Organizational Psychology, 80*, 515–553.
Dalal, R. S., Baysinger, M., Brummel, B. J., & LeBreton, J. M. (2012). The relative importance of employee engagement, other job attitudes and trait affect as predictors of overall employee job performance. *Journal of Applied Social Psychology, 42*(Suppl. S1), E295–E325.
Dalal, R. S., Brummel, B. J., Wee, S., & Thomas, L. L. (2008). Defining employee engagement for productive research and practice. *Industrial and Organizational Psychology, 1*, 52–55.
Digman, J. M. (1990). Personality structure: Emergence of the five-factor model. *Annual Review of Psychology, 41*, 417–440.
Dormann, C., & Zapf, D. (2001). Job satisfaction: A meta-analysis of stabilities. *Journal of Organizational Behavior, 22*, 483–504.
Dunham, R. B., Grube, J. A., & Castaneda, M. B. (1994). Organizational commitment: The utility of an integrated definition. *Journal of Applied Psychology, 79*, 370–380.
Eagly, A. H., & Chaiken, S. (1993). *The psychology of attitudes.* New York: Harcourt.
Eagly, A. H., & Chaiken, S. (2007). The advantages of an inclusive definition of attitude. *Social Cognition, 25*, 582–602.
Eisenberger, R., Huntington, R., Hutchison, S., & Sowa, D. (1986). Perceived organizational support. *Journal of Applied Psychology, 71*, 500–507.
Eisenberger, R., & Stinglhamber, F. (2011). *Perceived organizational support: Fostering enthusiastic and productive employees.* Washington, DC: American Psychological Association.
Elloy, D. F., Everett, J. E., & Flynn, W. R. (1991). An examination of the correlates of job involvement. *Group & Organization Management, 16*, 160–177.
Eschleman, K. J., & Bowling, N. A. (2010). Facing the limitations to self-reported strain: Integrating the facial expression and job stress literatures. In P. Perrewé & D. C. Ganster (Eds.), *Research in occupational stress and well-being: New developments in theoretical and conceptual approaches to job stress* (Vol. 8, pp. 199–235). New York: Emerald.
Eschleman, K. J., & Bowling, N. A. (2011). A construct validation of the Neutral Objects Satisfaction Questionnaire (NOSQ). *Journal of Business and Psychology 26*, 501–515.
Fried, Y., & Ferris, G. R. (1987). The validity of the job characteristics model: A review and meta-analysis. *Personnel Psychology, 40*, 287–322.
Gerhart, B. (2005). The (affective) dispositional approach to job satisfaction: Sorting out the policy implications. *Journal of Organizational Behavior, 26*, 79–97.
Goldberg, L. R. (1990). An alternative "description of personality": The Big-Five factor structure. *Journal of Personality and Social Psychology, 59*, 1216–1229.
Goldberg, L. R. (1999). A broad-bandwidth, public domain, Personality Inventory measuring the lower-level facets of several five-factor models. In I. Mervielde, I. Deary, F. De Fruyt, & F. Ostendorf (Eds.), *Personality psychology in Europe* (Vol. 7, pp. 7–28). Tilburg, The Netherlands: Tilburg University Press.
Gough, H. G. (1996). *CPI manual* (3rd ed.). Palo Alto, CA: Consulting Psychologists Press.
Greenberg, J., & Colquitt, J. A. (Eds.). (2005). *Handbook of organizational justice.* Mahwah, NJ: Lawrence Erlbaum Associates.
Greenwald, A. G., & Farnham, S. D. (2000). Using the Implicit Association Test to measure self-esteem and self-concept. *Journal of Personality and Social Psychology, 79*, 1022–1038.

Grumm, M., & von Collani, G. (2007). Measuring the Big-Five personality dimensions with the Implicit Association Test—Implicit personality traits or self-esteem? *Personality and Individual Differences, 43*, 2205–2217.
Hackman, J. R., & Oldham, G. R. (1975). Development of the Job Diagnostic Survey. *Journal of Applied Psychology, 60*, 159–170.
Haines, E. L., & Sumner, K. E. (2006). Implicit measurement of attitudes, stereotypes, and self-concepts in organizations. *Organizational Research Methods, 9*, 536–553.
Harrison, D. A., Newman, D. A., & Roth, P. L. (2006). How important are job attitudes? Meta-analytic comparisons of integrative behavioral outcomes and time sequences. *Academy of Management Journal, 49*, 305–325.
Harter, J. K., Schmidt, F. L., & Hayes, T. L. (2002). Business-unit-level relationship between employee satisfaction, employee engagement, and business outcomes: A meta-analysis. *Journal of Applied Psychology, 87*, 268–279.
Hofstee, W. K., De Raad, B., & Goldberg, L. R. (1992). Integration of the Big Five and circumplex approaches to trait structure. *Journal of Personality and Social Psychology, 63*, 146–163.
Hogan, J., & Holland, B. (2003). Using theory to evaluate personality and job-performance relations: A socio-analytic perspective. *Journal of Applied Psychology, 88*, 100–112.
Hogan, R., & Hogan, J. (2001). Assessing leadership: A view from the dark side. *International Journal of Selection and Assessment, 9*, 40–51.
Hogan, R., & Hogan, J. (2007). *Hogan Personality Inventory manual* (3rd ed.). Tulsa, OK: Hogan Assessment Systems.
Hulin, C. L. (1991). Adaptation, persistence, and commitment in organizations. In M. D. Dunnette & L. M. Hough (Eds.), *Handbook of industrial and organizational psychology* (2nd ed., Vol. 2, pp. 445–505). Palo Alto, CA: Consulting Psychologists Press.
Hunthausen, J. M., Truxillo, D. M., Bauer, T. N., & Hammer, L. B. (2003). A field study of frame-of-reference effects on Personality Test validity. *Journal of Applied Psychology, 88*, 545–551.
Ilies, R., & Judge, T. A. (2003). On the heritability of job satisfaction: The mediating role of personality. *Journal of Applied Psychology, 88*, 750–759.
Ironson, G. H., Smith, P. C., Brannick, M. T., Gibson, W. M., & Paul, K. B. (1989). Construction of a Job In General Scale: A comparison of global, composite, and specific measures. *Journal of Applied Psychology, 74*, 193–200.
Jackson, D. N. (1994). *Manual for the Jackson Personality Inventory—Revised*. Port Huron, MI: Sigma Assessment Systems.
John, O. J., & Robins, R. W. (1993). Determinants of interjudge agreement on personality traits: The Big Five domains, observability, evaluativeness, and the unique perspective of the self. *Journal of Personality, 61*, 521–551.
Johnson, J. A. (1997). Units of analysis for the description and explanation of personality. In R. Hogan, J. Johnson, & S. Briggs (Eds.), *Handbook of personality psychology* (pp. 73–96). San Diego, CA: Academic Press.
Johnson, R. E., Tolentino, A. L., Rodopman, O. B., & Cho, E. (2010). We (sometimes) know not how we feel: Predicting job performance with an implicit measure of trait affectivity. *Personnel Psychology, 63*, 197–219.
Judge, T. A., & Bono, J. E. (2001a). A rose by any other name … are self-esteem, generalized self-efficacy, neuroticism, and locus of control indicators of a common construct? In B. W. Roberts & R. Hogan (Eds.), *Personality psychology in the workplace* (pp. 93–118). Washington, DC: American Psychological Association.
Judge, T. A., & Bono, J. E. (2001b). Relationship of core self-evaluations traits—self-esteem, generalized self-efficacy, locus of control, and emotional stability—with job satisfaction and job performance: A meta-analysis. *Journal of Applied Psychology, 86*, 80–92.
Judge, T. A., Bono, J. E., & Locke, E. A. (2000). Personality and job satisfaction: The mediating role of job characteristics. *Journal of Applied Psychology, 85*, 237–249.
Judge, T. A., & Bretz, R. D. (1993). Report on an alternative measure of affective disposition. *Educational and Psychological Measurement, 53*, 1095–1104.
Judge, T. A., Erez, A., Bono, J. E., & Thoresen, C. J. (2003). The Core Self-Evaluations Scale (CSES): Development of a measure. *Personnel Psychology, 56*, 303–331.
Judge, T. A., Heller, D., & Mount, M. K. (2002). Five-factor model of personality and job satisfaction: A meta-analysis. *Journal of Applied Psychology, 87*, 530–541.
Judge, T. A., Hulin, C. A., & Dalal, R. S. (in press). Job satisfaction and job affect. In S. W. J. Koslowski (Ed.), *The Oxford handbook of industrial and organizational psychology*. New York: Oxford University Press.
Judge, T. A., Locke, E. A., & Durham, C. C. (1997). The dispositional causes of job satisfaction: A core evaluations approach. *Research in Organizational Behavior, 19*, 151–188.
Judge, T. A., Locke, E. A., Durham, C. C., & Kluger, A. N. (1998). Dispositional effects on job and life satisfaction: The role of core evaluations. *Journal of Applied Psychology, 83*, 17–34.
Judge, T. A., Thoresen, C. J., Bono, J. E., & Patton, G. K. (2001). The job satisfaction–job performance relationship: A qualitative and quantitative review. *Psychological Bulletin, 127*, 376–407.

Kanungo, R. N. (1982). Measurement of job and work involvement. *Journal of Applied Psychology, 67*, 341–349.
Kinicki, A. J., McKee-Ryan, F. M., Schriesheim, C. A., & Carson, K. P. (2002). Assessing the construct validity of the Job Descriptive Index: A review and meta-analysis. *Journal of Applied Psychology, 87*, 14–32.
Klein, H. J., Becker, T. E., & Meyer, J. M. (Eds.). (2009). *Commitment in organizations: Accumulated wisdom and new directions*. New York: Routledge, Taylor & Francis Group.
Klein, H. J., Molloy, J. C., & Brinsfield, C. T. (2011). Reconceptualizing workplace commitment to redress a stretched construct: Revisiting assumptions and removing confounds. *Academy of Management Review, 37*, 130–151.
Koys, D. J. (2001). The effects of employee satisfaction, organizational citizenship behavior, and turnover on organizational effectiveness: A unit-level, longitudinal study. *Personnel Psychology, 54*, 101–114.
Lavelle, J. J., Rupp, D. E., & Brockner, J. (2007). Taking a multifoci approach to the study of justice, social exchange, and citizenship behavior: The target similarity model. *Journal of Management, 33*, 841–866.
Leavitt, K., Fong, C. T., & Greenwald, A. G. (2011). Asking about well-being gets you half an answer: Intra-individual processes of implicit and explicit job attitudes. *Journal of Organizational Behavior, 32*, 672–687.
Lefcourt, H. M. (1976). Locus of control and the response to aversive events. *Canadian Psychological Review, 17*, 202–209.
Levin, I., & Stokes, J. P. (1989). Dispositional approach to job satisfaction: Role of negative affectivity. *Journal of Applied Psychology, 74*, 752–758.
Lievens, F., De Corte, W., & Schollaert, E. (2008). A closer look at the frame-of-reference effect in Personality Scale scores and validity. *Journal of Applied Psychology, 93*, 268–279.
Locke, E. A. (1976). The nature and causes of job satisfaction. In M. D. Dunnette (Ed.), *Handbook of industrial and organizational psychology* (pp. 1297–1343). Chicago: Rand McNally.
Lodahl, T. M., & Kejner, M. (1965). The definition and measurement of job involvement. *Journal of Applied Psychology, 49*, 24–33.
Lucas, R. E., Diener, E., & Suh, E. (1996). Discriminant validity of well-being measures. *Journal of Personality and Social Psychology, 71*, 616–628.
Macey, W. H., & Schneider, B. (2008). The meaning of employee engagement. *Industrial and Organizational Psychology, 1*, 3–30.
Macey, W. H., Schneider, B., Barbera, K. M., & Young, S. A. (2009). *Employee engagement: Tools for analysis, practice, and competitive advantage*. West Sussex, UK: Wiley-Blackwell.
May, D., Gilson, R., & Harter, L. (2004). The psychological conditions of meaningfulness, safety, and availability and the engagement of the human spirit at work. *Journal of Occupational and Organizational Psychology, 77*, 11–37.
McCrae, R. R., & Costa, P. T., Jr. (1987). Validation of the five-factor model of personality across instruments and observers. *Journal of Personality and Social Psychology, 52*, 81–90.
McCrae, R. R., Costa, P. T., Jr., & Piedmont, R. L. (1993). Folk concepts, natural language, and psychological constructs: The California Psychological Inventory and the five-factor model. *Journal of Personality, 61*, 1–26.
McCrae, R. R., & John, O. P. (1992). An introduction to the five-factor model and its applications. *Journal of Personality, 60*, 175–215.
Meyer, J. P., Allen, N. J., & Gellatly, I. R. (1990). Affective and continuance commitment to the organization: Evaluation of measures and analysis of concurrent and time-lagged relations. *Journal of Applied Psychology, 75*, 710–720.
Motowidlo, S. J. (2003). Job performance. In W. C. Borman, D. R. Ilgen, & R. J. Klimoski (Eds.), *Comprehensive handbook of psychology: Industrial and organizational psychology* (Vol. 12, pp. 39–53). New York: Wiley.
Mount, M., Ilies, R., & Johnson, E. (2006). Relationship of personality traits and counterproductive work behaviors: The mediating effects of job satisfaction. *Personnel Psychology, 59*, 591–622.
Mowday, R. T., Steers, R. M., & Porter, L. M. (1979). The measurement of organizational commitment. *Journal of Vocational Behavior, 14*, 224–247.
Newman, D. A., & Harrison, D. A. (2008). Been there, bottled that: Are state and behavioral work engagement new and useful construct "wines"? *Industrial and Organizational Psychology, 1*, 31–35.
Newman, D. A., Joseph, D. L., & Hulin, C. L. (2010). Job attitudes and employee engagement: Considering the attitude "A-factor." In S. L. Albrecht (Ed.), *Handbook of employee engagement: Perspectives, issues, research, and practice* (pp. 43–61). Northampton, MA: Edward Elgar.
Newton, T., & Keenan, T. (1991). Further analysis of the dispositional argument in organizational behavior. *Journal of Applied Psychology, 76*, 781–787.
Ng, T. W. H., & Sorensen, K. L. (2009). Dispositional affectivity and work-related outcomes: A meta-analysis. *Journal of Applied Social Psychology, 39*, 1255–1287.
O'Boyle, E. H., Jr., Forsyth, D. R., Banks, G. C., & McDaniel, M. (2012). A meta-analysis of the Dark Triad and work behavior: A social exchange perspective. *Journal of Applied Psychology, 97*, 557–579.

O'Reilly, C. A., & Chatman, J. (1986). Organizational commitment and psychological attachment: The effects of compliance, identification, and internalization on prosocial behavior. *Journal of Applied Psychology, 71*, 492–499.

Ostroff, C. (1992). The relationship between satisfaction, attitudes, and performance: An organizational level analysis. *Journal of Applied Psychology,* 77, 963–974.

Paulhus, D., & Williams, K. (2002). The dark triad of personality: Narcissism, Machiavellianism, and psychopathy. *Journal of Research in Personality, 36*, 556–563.

Payne, K. B., Cheng, C. M., Govorun, O., & Stewart, B. D. (2005). An inkblot for attitudes: Affect misattribution as implicit measurement. *Journal of Personality and Social Psychology, 89*, 277–293.

Pierce, J. L., Gardner, D. G., Cummings, L. L., & Dunham, R. B. (1989). Organization based self-esteem: Construct definition, measurement, and validation. *Academy of Management Journal, 32*, 622–648.

Podsakoff, P. M., MacKenzie, S. B., & Bommer, W. H. (1996). Transformational leader behaviors and substitutes for leadership as determinants of employee satisfaction, commitment, trust, and organizational citizenship behaviors. *Journal of Management, 22*, 259–298.

Probst, T. M. (2003). Exploring employee outcomes of organizational restructuring: A Solomon four-group study. *Group & Organization Management, 28*, 416–439.

Pytlik Zillig, L. M., Hemenover, S. H., & Dienstbier, R. A. (2002). What do we assess when we assess a Big 5 trait? A content analysis of the affective, behavioral, and cognitive processes represented in Big 5 personality inventories. *Personality and Social Psychological Bulletin, 28*, 847–858.

Rhoades, L., & Eisenberger, R. (2002). Perceived organizational support: A review of the literature. *Journal of Applied Psychology, 87*, 698–714.

Rich, B. L., Lepine, J. A., & Crawford, E. R. (2010). Job engagement: Antecedents and effects on job performance. *Academy of Management Journal, 53*, 617–635.

Roberts, B. W. (2006). Personality development and organizational behavior. In B. M. Staw (Ed.), *Research on organizational behavior* (pp. 1–41). San Diego, CA: Elsevier Science/JAI Press.

Roberts, B. W., & DelVecchio, W. F. (2000). The rank-order consistency of personality from childhood to old age: A quantitative review of longitudinal studies. *Psychological Bulletin, 126*, 3–25.

Roberts, B. W., & Jackson, J. J. (2008). Sociogenomic personality psychology. *Journal of Personality, 76*, 1523–1544.

Roberts, B. W., & Mroczek, D. (2008). Personality trait change in adulthood. *Current Directions in Psychological Science, 17*, 31–35.

Roberts, B. W., Walton, K. E., & Viechtbauer, W. (2006). Patterns of mean-level change in personality traits across the life course: A meta-analysis of longitudinal studies. *Psychological Bulletin, 132*, 1–25.

Rothbard, N. P. (2001). Enriching or depleting? The dynamics of engagement in work and family roles. *Administrative Science Quarterly, 46*, 655–684.

Rotter, J. B. (1966). Generalized expectancies for internal versus external control of reinforcement. *Psychological Monographs: General and Applied, 80*, 1–28.

Roznowski, M., & Hulin, C. (1992). The scientific merit of valid measures of general constructs with special reference to job satisfaction and job withdrawal. In C. J. Cranny, P. C. Smith, & E. F. Stone (Eds.), *Job satisfaction: How people feel about their jobs and how it affects their performance* (pp. 123–163). New York: Lexington Books.

Ryan, A. M., Schmit, M. J., & Johnson, R. (1996). Attitudes and effectiveness: Examining relations at an organizational level. *Personnel Psychology, 49*, 853–882.

Sackett, P. R., & Lievens, F. (2008). Personnel selection. *Annual Review of Psychology, 59*, 419–450.

Saks, A. M. (2006). Antecedents and consequences of employee engagement. *Journal of Managerial Psychology, 21*, 600–619.

Saucier, G. (2003). An alternative multi-language structure for personality attributes. *European Journal of Personality, 17*, 179–205.

Schaufeli, W. B., Salanova, M., Gonzàlez-Romà, V., & Bakker, A. B. (2002). The measurement of burnout and engagement: A confirmative analytic approach. *Journal of Happiness Studies, 3*, 71–92.

Schleicher, D. J., Hansen, S. D., & Fox, K. E. (2010). Job attitudes and work values. In S. Zedeck (Ed.), *APA handbook of industrial and organizational psychology: Maintaining, expanding, and contracting the organization* (Vol. 3, pp. 137–190). Washington, DC: American Psychological Association.

Schleicher, D. J., Watt, J. D., & Greguras, G. J. (2004). Reexamining the job satisfaction–performance relationship: The complexity of attitudes. *Journal of Applied Psychology, 89*, 165–177.

Schmidt, F. L., & Hunter, J. E. (1998). The validity and utility of selection methods in personnel psychology: Practical and theoretical implications of 85 years of research findings. *Psychological Bulletin, 124*, 262–274.

Schmit, M. J., Ryan, A. M., Stierwalt, S. L., & Powell, A. B. (1995). Frame-of-reference effects on Personality Scale scores and criterion-related validity. *Journal of Applied Psychology, 80*, 607–620.

Slaughter, J. E., & Feldman, J. (2009, August). *Personality change in organizational settings.* Paper presented at the Sixty-Ninth Annual Conference of the Academy of Management, Chicago.

Smith, P. C., Kendall, L. M., & Hulin, C. L. (1969). *Measurement of satisfaction in work and retirement.* Chicago: Rand McNally.

Spector, P. E. (1985). Method variance as an artifact in self-reported affect and perceptions at work: Myth or significant problem? *Journal of Applied Psychology, 72*, 428–443.

Spector, P. E. (1988). Development of the Work Locus of Control Scale. *Journal of Occupational Psychology, 61*, 335–340.

Spector, P. E. (1997). *Job satisfaction: Application, assessment, causes, and consequences.* Thousand Oaks, CA: Sage.

Spector, P. E., Zapf, D., Chen, P. Y., & Frese, M. (2000). Why negative affectivity should not be controlled in job stress research: Don't throw the baby out with the bath water. *Journal of Organizational Behavior, 21*, 79–95.

Staw, B. M., & Ross, J. (1985). Stability in the midst of change: A dispositional approach to job attitudes. *Journal of Applied Psychology, 70*, 469–480.

Tellegen, A. (1982). *Brief manual for the Multidimensional Personality Questionnaire.* Unpublished manuscript, University of Minnesota, Minneapolis.

Tellegen, A., Lykken, D. T., Bouchard, T. S., Wilcox, K. J., Segal, N. L., & Rich, S. (1988). Personality similarity in twins reared apart and together. *Journal of Personality and Social Psychology, 54*, 1031–1039.

Tett, R. P., Jackson, D. N., & Rothstein, M. (1991). Personality measures as predictors of job performance: A meta-analytic review. *Personnel Psychology, 44*, 703–742.

Thibaut, J. W., & Kelley, H. H. (1959). *The social psychology of groups.* New York: Wiley.

Thomas, J. P., Whitman, D. S., & Viswesvaran, C. (2010). Employee proactivity in organizations: A comparative meta-analysis of emergent proactive constructs. *Journal of Occupational and Organizational Psychology, 83*, 275–300.

Thoresen, C. J., Kaplan, S. A., Barsky, A. P., Warren, C. R., & de Chermont, K. (2003). The affective underpinnings of job perceptions and attitudes: A meta-analytic review and integration. *Psychological Bulletin, 129*, 914–945.

Vazire, S. (2010). Who knows what about a person? The self-other knowledge asymmetry (SOKA) model. *Journal of Personality and Social Psychology, 98*, 281–300.

Vazire, S., & Carlson, E. N. (2011). Others sometimes know us better than we know ourselves. *Current Directions in Psychological Science, 20*, 104–108.

Wang, Q., Bowling, N. A., & Eschleman, K. J. (2010). A meta-analytic examination of work and general locus of control. *Journal of Applied Psychology, 95*, 761–768.

Watson, D., Clark, L. A., & Tellegen, A. (1988). Development and validation of brief measures of positive and negative affect: The PANAS scales. *Journal of Personality and Social Psychology, 54*, 1063–1070.

Watson, D., Wiese, D., Vaidya, J., & Tellegen, A. (1999). The two general activation systems of affect: Structural findings, evolutionary considerations, and psychobiological evidence. *Journal of Personality and Social Psychology, 76*, 820–838.

Weiss, D. J., Dawis, R. V., England, G. W., & Lofquist, L. H. (1967). *Manual for the Minnesota Satisfaction Questionnaire* (Minnesota Studies on Vocational Rehabilitation, 22). Minneapolis: University of Minnesota.

Wright, T. A., Cropanzano, R., & Bonett, D. G. (2007). The moderating role of employee positive well-being on the relation between job satisfaction and job performance. *Journal of Occupational Health Psychology, 12*, 93–104.

33

Personality and Work Teams

James E. Driskell and Eduardo Salas

Every person reading this chapter has experience working in teams of one type or another. This experience may include project teams, committees, study groups, or even sports teams. Moreover, it is probably easy for you to recall teams that you have participated in or that you have observed that performed well and teams that performed poorly. When we think back about these teams, we usually recall the persons who comprised the teams and we often define these persons in trait terms. That is, we may remember effective teams as composed of dependable, hardworking, and cooperative team members, and remember ineffective teams as composed of irresponsible, indolent, and self-oriented team members.

Therefore, our folk wisdom, at least, is that team composition is important in the effective functioning of teams and that the personality of team members is one team composition factor that influences team performance. The objective of this chapter is to examine the relationship between team member personality and team performance—to determine if the "wisdom of the folk" is in fact accurate. This research is important because it is theoretically illuminating to examine how teams function and why some teams are more effective than others. This research is also practically important in that it is of considerable advantage in the workplace if guidelines can be provided on how to compose optimally effective work teams.

Overview

The research literature on personality and team performance is robust and active. One of the earliest investigations of the relationship between personality and team performance was undertaken by Mann (1959), who concluded his review of this literature with the expectation that this work could serve as a take-off point for further research. However, despite some attempts along the way (e.g., Driskell, Hogan, & Salas, 1987), the next steps to examine personality and team performance were taken almost 40 years later by Barrick, Stewart, Neubert, and Mount (1998), Barry and Stewart (1997), Hollenbeck et al. (2002), Judge and Bono (2000), LePine, Hollenbeck, Ilgen, and Hedlund (1997), Neuman and Wright (1999), and others. A more recent wave of research has attempted to integrate this initial research and extend these efforts (see Bell, 2007; Driskell, Goodwin, Salas, & O'Shea, 2006; Halfhill, Sundstrom, Lahner, Calderone, & Nielsen, 2005; Humphrey, Hollenbeck, Meyer, & Ilgen, 2007; O'Neill & Allen, 2011; Peeters, Van Tuijl, Rutte, & Reymen, 2006; Prewett, Walvoord, Stilson, Rossi, & Brannick, 2009).

There are several reasons that account for this sustained research productivity. First, there is a strong intuitive appeal to the proposition that team member personality *should* matter. That is, team inputs such as personality should impact team performance through mediating team processes. In other words, personality reflects characteristic ways of thinking, feeling, and acting that should impact teamwork dimensions such as coordination, team management, performance monitoring and feedback, and interpersonal relations, and subsequently determine how well the team performs. Thus, there is a strong intuitive, as well as theoretical, basis for the belief that personality traits of team members such as conscientiousness, agreeableness, or emotional stability should impact team processes and outcomes.

Second, there has been a growing emphasis on the value of teams for performing work in organizations. Moreover, there is considerable practical value in understanding how to compose or staff teams for optimal performance. From a practical standpoint, if our intuitive assumptions regarding the effects of team member personality on team outcomes are sound, then this information provides one avenue for increasing productivity.

Third, recent research in personality, including the adoption of the Big Five as a common vocabulary for describing and measuring personality, has led to a large body of evidence demonstrating the value of personality for predicting individual performance. As Sackett and Lievens (2008) concluded, "There are sizeable relationships between variables in the personality domain and important work outcomes" (p. 424). Understanding how personality affects performance when several persons combine as a team is a natural, although somewhat more complex, extension of this research.

In the following sections, we examine the relationship of the Big Five personality traits to team performance, and how these individual traits may be aggregated to the team level. We examine how lower-level personality facets drawn from the Big Five may predict lower-level criteria such as teamwork. Finally, we address several issues that are relevant to continuing research in this area.

Relationship of the Big Five Traits to Team Performance

Work teams come in all sizes, from large to small; they work on a variety of types of tasks; they may be short-lived or work together for prolonged periods; and teams may meet face-to-face on a regular basis or, in the case of virtual teams, rarely meet in person at all (see Driskell, Radtke, & Salas, 2003). We note this diversity in how teams perform tasks for two reasons. First, the fact that teams exist in so many different forms reinforces how ubiquitous teams are in the world of work. Second, from a research perspective, it is important to note that almost any overall statement regarding teams must be qualified by factors such as the type of task or the nature of the team. In this chapter, we will attempt to derive some general statements regarding the effects of personality on teams. For example, Bell (2007) concluded that effective teams should be composed of team members high on conscientiousness and agreeableness. However, Bell immediately notes that any such broad guideline must be qualified by the particular team situation. Therefore, the reader is cautioned that, in this chapter, we must walk a tightrope between the desire to offer general guidelines and the realization that almost all general statements regarding personality and teams must be qualified by factors such as the nature of the team or the nature of the task. This reflects both the complexity of understanding personality effects and the fact that situational specificity is a dominant feature of personality–performance relationships (see Tett & Christiansen, 2007; Chapter 5, this volume).

Before we delve too far into this topic, it may be useful to provide a definition of the term *team*. Salas, Dickinson, Converse, and Tannenbaum (1992) define a team as a "set of two or more people who interact, dynamically, interdependently, and adaptively, toward a common and valued goal/objective/mission, who have each been assigned specific roles or functions to perform, and who have a limited life-span of membership" (p. 4). Paulus and Van der Zee (2004) have noted that there are some distinctions between the research on "groups" that is generally found in the social psychology literature and the research on "teams" that is generally published in the organizational literature. We will not distinguish between the two other than to limit our primary focus to work teams—teams embedded in organizations that exist to accomplish tasks. In a typical work team, which Kozlowski, Gully, McHugh, Salas, and Cannon-Bowers (1996) call *action teams*, and Hollenbeck et al. (1995) term *distributed expertise teams*, each team member possesses specific information or expertise to contribute to the team task. Although work teams are often hierarchically structured, we further limit our focus to teams that are unstructured or self-managed (i.e., team members are all of relatively equal status or authority with no established roles of leader, etc.). Thus, our goal is to examine the effect of team member personality on performance in hierarchically unstructured task groups or teams.

Although there is some divergence on how personality traits should be labeled and organized, personality theorists are in general agreement on the nature of the structure of personality. Beginning with Fiske (1949), Tupes and Christal (1961), and Norman (1963), personality researchers have converged on five broad dimensions that constitute normal personality. These factors, often termed the "Big Five" or "Five-Factor" model of personality, include extraversion, emotional stability, agreeableness, conscientiousness, and openness to experience. Most theorists propose a hierarchical model of personality, with these higher-order factors or traits subsuming more specific lower-level facets (cf. Saucier & Ostendorf, 1999). That is, the Big Five model represents a broad set of traits that are themselves a collection of many facets that have something in common. Whereas the broad, higher-level constructs offer an efficient and parsimonious way of describing personality, the more specific facets can offer higher fidelity of trait descriptions and greater predictive validity (Saucier & Ostendorf, 1999; Stewart, 1999).

Thus, at this point, we can pose two broad questions that are at the heart of the research literature on personality and team performance. The first question is, to what extent do the Big Five personality factors predict team performance? This question, seemingly simple, masks a number of qualifications and complexities, such as the type of tasks or types of teams examined as well as the level of specificity in the predictor and the criterion. These issues will be addressed in the latter half of this chapter. For now, broadly speaking, the first question to be addressed is the relationship between the Big Five personality traits and team performance.

It is important to note at this point that there are various ways that one can attempt to examine the relationship of personality and team performance (see Anderson & Tett, 2006). One approach is to examine team member traits that support effective teamwork. We focus on this approach in this chapter, primarily because most of the existing research on personality and teams has addressed this question. Another approach is to examine individual team member compatibility, or how team member personalities interact to influence compatibility and productivity (Anderson & Tett, 2006; Tett & Murphy, 2002). This is a complex question: How do we optimize team member personality compatibility such that Person A works most effectively with Person B and with Person C? Although the question of who prefers to work with whom and who is more productive working with whom has significant implications for team building and selection, there is considerably less existing research that has tackled this problem.

A second question to be addressed is, how do we aggregate individual-level personality scores to the team level? Individual personality scores may be aggregated using several common indices: (a) the *mean* personality score of team members, (b) the *minimum* score or the lowest team member score, (c) the *maximum* score or the highest team member score, and (d) the *variance* or heterogeneity of trait scores in the team. There are two approaches for selecting the appropriate method of aggregating scores, the trait approach and the task approach.

The task approach assumes that the type of aggregation method depends on the type of task being performed. According to Steiner's (1972) task typology, *additive tasks* require each team member's contributions to be summed together to produce the team product. The productivity of the team depends on the sum of each member's contributions and, therefore, the *mean* trait score of the team would be most appropriate. In this case, the more of a certain trait there is in the team as a whole, the better. *Compensatory tasks* are similar to additive tasks in that the team's performance is the average of team member contributions, but, in this case, a higher-performing team member can compensate for a lower-performing team member. Again, the *mean* trait score is appropriate for this type of task. *Disjunctive tasks* require that a "best answer" or best solution is sought from the contributions of team members, and therefore a single team member can determine the team outcome. In this case, the *maximum* trait score is preferable because the team outcome depends on one high-performing member. *Conjunctive tasks* require all team members to complete the task satisfactorily. For this type of task, the *minimum* trait score is preferable, because the team outcome depends on the lowest-performing member. Although the task approach is intuitively appealing, some have argued that it is not easily applied to real-world tasks (see Bell, 2007). For example, tasks in real-world contexts are often a combination of task types.

The trait approach argues that the nature of the personality trait itself is a better guide to aggregation. Humphrey et al. (2007) offer a trait approach that classifies traits as either supplementary or complementary, and argues that the person–team fit is important to determining the type of trait. Supplementary fit occurs when performance is optimized by having team members with similar goals and values. Thus, a supplementary trait is one in which similar levels within the team, or homogeneity, is preferable. For example, conscientiousness is seen as a supplementary trait in that team members who have similarly high levels of this trait are likely to be productive, whereas team member variability in terms of conscientiousness can lead to conflict and poor performance. However, it is important to distinguish similarity per se from similarity at a given pole of a specific trait. Whereas supplementary fit in terms of high conscientiousness may optimize team performance, teams whose members are similarly low on conscientiousness may not perform optimally.

Complementary fit occurs when performance is optimized by a team member who can make a unique contribution. Thus, a complementary trait is one in which heterogeneity is preferable, ensuring greater diversity among team members. According to Humphrey et al. (2007), extraversion is seen as a complementary trait in that higher variance in dominance and sociability will promote role differentiation and leader emergence, whereas a team full of extraverts, or low variance, may lead to role conflict. Complementarity can also be viewed in terms of mutual need at the intertrait level. According to Tett and Murphy (2002), in terms of complementarity, people prefer those who invite the expression of their own traits; thus a high-dominance team member may prefer a low-autonomous (submissive) coworker.

Therefore, Humphrey et al. focus explicitly on trait variability, either minimizing variance for supplementary traits or maximizing variance for complementary traits (however, as Tett & Murphy, 2002, indicated, complementary relationships at the intertrait level require a more complex analysis). Prewett et al. (2009) argue further that, for supplementary traits, the appropriate aggregation methods are those that reflect maximization of trait levels (high *mean* and high *minimum* trait scores) and minimization of variance (i.e., low *variance* scores). They argue that, for complementary traits, the appropriate aggregation methods are those that reflect maximization of variance (i.e., high *variance* scores). However, Prewett et al.'s analysis of these predictions only found limited support.

In summary, the *mean* approach to trait aggregation is appropriate when it is expected that, for a given trait, the more each team member possesses that trait, the more effective team performance will be. *Minimum* and *maximum* trait scores are most appropriate when it is expected that a single individual having a very low trait score or a very high trait score can determine overall team performance. Trait score *variance* or heterogeneity is appropriate when it is expected that a trait operates as a supplementary trait (i.e., similarity among team members promotes effective team performance) or as a complementary trait (i.e., variability among team members promotes effective team performance).

However, further complexity arises in considering the mathematical relationship between mean and variance. For example, a high mean level of a given trait such as emotional stability as well as a low mean level of that trait both entail low variance. As we move from higher (or lower) levels of emotional stability to more moderate mean levels, variance increases. Therefore, one question in such a case is whether similarity (i.e., low variance) per se is the key factor or whether the more important factor is similarity at the high end of the trait scale (which entails a high mean). Teasing apart these issues is a major challenge.

To examine these questions more precisely, we will briefly describe each of the Big Five traits and examine its relationship to team performance. For each trait, we will attempt to specify whether the mean, minimum, maximum, or variance scores will be most predictive of team performance.

Emotional Stability

The trait of emotional stability or adjustment refers to a lack of anxiety and nervous tendencies. Those who are emotionally stable tend to be well adjusted, calm, secure, and self-confident. Viewed from the negative pole of neuroticism, those who score low on this trait tend to be moody, anxious, nervous, insecure, depressed, and high-strung (Barrick & Mount, 2001). Given that those low on adjustment are prone to be distressed, upset, hostile, irritable, and nervous, they are not likely to excel in interpersonal or team settings. In past studies of military teams, Haythorn (1953) and Greer (1955) reported that mean emotional stability was positively related to team effectiveness. Several researchers have claimed that emotional stability is a significant factor in teamwork or any task that requires coordinated behavior (Barrick, Mount, & Judge, 2001; Driskell et al., 1987; Mount, Barrick, & Stewart, 1998). In circumstances in which the organizational structure is out of alignment with environmental requirements, Hollenbeck et al. (2002) found that the mean emotional stability of team members was a critical predictor of performance. Moreover, noting that people's moods are often affected by those around them, Totterdell, Kellett, Teuchmann, and Briner (1998) found that team members reciprocated the mood of other teammates. Thus, not only are poorly adjusted team members displeasing to be around, their negative affect can spread to other team members.

We expect that a higher mean level of emotional stability in the team will lead to more effective performance. Having one team member who is exceptionally low on emotional stability may be disruptive and lead to ineffective performance; thus, minimum trait scores may also be predictive of team performance. Having one team member who is exceptionally high on emotional stability may not have a profound effect on team performance. That is, one highly adjusted team member probably does not have the power to transform the team's performance; thus, maximum trait scores on emotional stability may not be strongly predictive of team performance. Finally, emotional stability should act as a supplementary trait but in a somewhat complex manner. That is, trait variability should be related to team performance in that low variance at the positive pole of emotional stability (team members similarly high on emotional stability) should yield high performance; low variance at the negative pole (team members similarly low on emotional stability) should yield low performance; and high variance (team members mixed on emotional stability) should yield moderate performance.

Predictions

Mean. Emotional stability scores will positively relate to team performance.

Minimum. Emotional stability scores will positively relate to team performance.

Maximum. Emotional stability scores will be unrelated to team performance.

Variance. Emotional stability will be related to team performance in that low variance at the positive pole (high emotional stability) will yield good performance; low variance at the negative pole (low emotional stability) will yield poor performance, and high variance will lead to moderate performance.

Extraversion

The trait of extraversion has been viewed as a combination of assertiveness/dominance and sociability/affiliation (Judge & Bono, 2000; Lucas, Diener, Suh, Shao, & Grob, 2000). Some theorists view dominance as the primary marker of extraversion and some view sociability as the primary component (Hough, 1992; Saucier & Ostendorf, 1999). In other words, there are relevant subfactors underlying the broader extraversion trait: (a) dominance (high scores reflect those who are controlling and assertive) and (b) sociability (high scores reflect those who are sociable and enjoy interacting with others). This distinction produces somewhat conflicting expectations regarding the effect of extraversion on team performance. On the one hand, a team composed of persons who are friendly and socially adept (high sociability) should lead to more effective team interaction and performance. Davis (1969) found that teams composed of members who preferred to work in a group interacted more and solved problems faster than teams composed of members who preferred to work alone. However, some have suggested a curvilinear relationship between sociability and team effectiveness, in that high mean sociability may interfere with instrumental task activities (see Driskell et al., 1987).

On the other hand, a team composed of persons who are dominant and assertive (high dominance) can lead to friction and result in a team composed of all leaders and no followers (see Barrick et al., 1998; Barry & Stewart, 1997). Research suggests that dominant team members tend to engender less positive interpersonal relations (Driskell, Olmstead, & Salas, 1993) and are less likely to attend to the task inputs of other team members in decision making (Driskell & Salas, 1992).

We expect an overall positive relationship between mean levels of extraversion and team performance (see Barrick et al., 1998; Bell, 2007). That is, with some qualifications, we expect that teams composed of members who are sociable and assertive will perform more effectively than teams composed of members who are introverted and withdrawn. However, we expect that extraversion functions as a complementary trait, in that greater variance in extraversion can lead to more effective team performance (i.e., you do not want *everyone* to be relentlessly gregarious or everyone withdrawn). Having one team member high on extraversion can be beneficial because this may promote leadership functions being performed, and thus maximum trait scores may be predictive of team performance. Having one team member low on extraversion may lead to poor team performance, especially for tasks that are dependent on each person's active participation. Accordingly, the minimum score on extraversion may predict team performance on such tasks.

Predictions

Mean. Extraversion scores will positively relate to team performance. We note that there may be a curvilinear relationship between extraversion and team performance in that very high and very low levels of extraversion may degrade performance, whereas intermediate levels of extraversion may result in higher performance.

Minimum. Extraversion scores will positively relate to team performance.

Maximum. Extraversion scores will positively relate to team performance.

Variance. Extraversion will positively relate to team performance.

Openness to Experience

The trait of openness to experience has been described as intellectual curiosity, imaginativeness, and creativity (McCrae & Costa, 1997). In examining the effects of openness on performance in jobs involving interpersonal interaction, Mount et al. (1998) found that openness showed some overall positive effects, although the results were smaller than for the other Big Five predictors.

Other researchers have generally proposed little direct relationship between the trait of openness and team performance (see Driskell et al., 1987; Porter et al., 2003). However, openness is related to adaptability or flexibility, which may impact team performance (LePine, 2003). McCrae and Costa (1997) claimed that the trait of openness is, from the negative pole, related to rigidity in behavior and unwillingness to accept change. Paulhus and Martin (1988) described the interpersonal advantages of flexibility, noting that, in social situations, the flexible person can be either assertive or submissive, or warm or cold, as the situation demands, and Kowslowski, Gully, Nason, and Smith (1999) and others have discussed the importance of adaptability in teams.

We expect that there should be at least a weak positive relationship between mean openness and team performance, given that those high on this trait may be more adaptable as well as more creative. Openness may function as a complementary trait, as teams composed only of team members who are highly creative or intellectually oriented may never get past the point of exploring options (see Humphrey et al., 2007). Thus, variability or heterogeneity in team member openness may lead to higher team performance. In terms of intertrait complementarity and team composition, it may be reasonable to suggest that high openness may be especially beneficial in a team composed of highly conscientious members. Having one team member especially high on openness will probably not impact overall team performance, except in disjunctive tasks in which a single member can determine the team outcome. However, having one team member especially low on openness can disrupt the team if the rigidity of that single person (e.g., one holdout on a jury) stymies team performance.

Predictions

Mean. Openness scores will positively relate to team performance.

Minimum. Openness scores will positively relate to team performance.

Maximum. Openness scores will be unrelated to team performance.

Variance. Openness will positively relate to team performance.

Agreeableness

The trait of agreeableness reflects kindness, trust, and warmth versus selfishness, distrust, and hostility. Persons high on agreeableness are considerate, honest, helpful, and supportive. Persons low on agreeableness are uncaring, intolerant, unsympathetic, and critical. Some researchers have claimed that agreeableness may be the best primary predictor of performance in interpersonal settings (Mount et al., 1998; Neuman & Wright, 1999). Thus, agreeableness seems to have high predictive validity for tasks that involve cooperation and that involve smooth relations with others (Barrick et al., 2001). As Bell (2007) has noted, the extent to which a team is composed of agreeable team members will determine positive interactions and overall team performance, although, as we noted earlier, the nature of the team task is an important qualifier to almost any such generalization.

We expect a positive relationship between mean agreeableness and team performance. We expect that agreeableness functions as a supplemental trait, given that variability in agreeableness, or the presence of several disagreeable team members, can disrupt team performance. However, again, it is likely that low variance at the positive pole of agreeableness (team members similarly high on agreeability) will yield high performance, whereas low variance at the negative pole (team members similarly low on agreeableness) will yield lower performance. It may be reasonable to expect that high variance per se (team members mixed on emotional stability) may be unsupportive of effective team performance. Similar to emotional stability, having one team member who is exceptionally high on agreeableness may not have a profound effect on team performance. However, having one team member who is exceptionally low on agreeableness may be disruptive and lead to ineffective performance.

Predictions

Mean. Agreeableness scores will positively relate to team performance.

Minimum. Agreeableness scores will positively relate to team performance.

Maximum. Agreeableness scores will be unrelated to team performance.

Variance. Agreeableness will be related to team performance in that low variance at the positive pole (high agreeableness) will yield good performance, whereas low variance at the negative pole (low agreeableness) will yield poor performance. High variance will generally be unsupportive of team performance.

Conscientiousness

The trait of conscientiousness has been associated with competence, order, achievement striving, and dutifulness (Costa & McCrae, 1992). Moon (2001) has noted that some researchers have emphasized the responsibility/dependability component of conscientiousness, whereas others have viewed conscientiousness in terms of achievement orientation. Moon (2001) argued that dependability or duty can be viewed as the other-centered component of conscientiousness and that achievement can be seen as the self-centered component. Thus, conscientiousness reflects the tendency to be hardworking, prepared, and organized, to adhere to obligations and duties, to complete tasks thoroughly and on time, and to be reliable. Persons low on conscientiousness are impulsive, irresponsible, and disordered. Whereas some studies have found the general trait of conscientiousness to be related to team effectiveness (Barrick et al., 1998; LePine et al., 1997), others have not (Barry & Stewart, 1997). Hough (1992) found that dependability was related to ratings of teamwork, and Barrick et al. (1998) found that work teams with higher levels of conscientiousness received higher ratings of team performance.

We expect that team member conscientiousness should combine additively such that the higher the mean level of conscientiousness within the team, the more effectively the team will perform. Humphrey et al. (2007) argue that conscientiousness should function as a supplementary trait in that high variance (with some team members working hard and some not working hard) may result in the high-conscientious team members lowering their effort if they observe others "free-riding" or loafing. Again, it is similarity at the positive pole of conscientiousness that may be central to effective team performance, and therefore minimizing conscientiousness variance at the positive pole should result in higher team performance. Minimum conscientiousness scores may affect team performance in that if a single team member is shirking, others may also reduce their effort and team performance may suffer. We believe that, in most cases, having one team member with exceptionally high conscientiousness will not profoundly affect team performance. However, excessive rigidity on the part of one team member may affect tasks such as jury decision making in which consensus must be reached.

Predictions

Mean. Conscientiousness scores will positively relate to team performance.

Minimum. Conscientiousness scores will positively relate to team performance.

Maximum. Conscientiousness scores will be unrelated to team performance.

Variance. Conscientiousness will be related to team performance in that low variance at the positive pole (high conscientiousness) will yield good performance, whereas low variance at the negative pole (low conscientiousness) will yield poor performance. High variance in conscientiousness will generally result in low team performance.

Fortunately, the existing literature allows us to examine these predictions. Recent meta-analyses of the literature on personality and team performance (Bell, 2007; Peeters et al., 2006; Prewett et al., 2009) bring to bear the weight of existing empirical evidence to summarize and integrate these questions. Each of these meta-analyses examined the effects of the Big Five personality traits on team performance outcomes and, when evidence was available, attempted to examine the separate effects of mean, minimum, maximum, and variance methods of aggregation. These results are summarized in Table 33.1.

Table 33.1 Summary of Meta-Analytic Results of Effects of Personality on Team Performance by Aggregation Method

Study	*Bell (2007)*	*Peeters, Van Tuijl, Rutte, and Reymen (2006)*	*Prewett, Walvoord, Stilson, Rossi, and Brannick (2009)*
	Effect Size (r)	*Effect Size (r)*	*Effect Size (r)*
Emotional stability			
Mean	Positive, .18[a]	n.s., .03	Positive, .08
Maximum	n.s., .11	—	Positive, .11
Minimum	Positive, .09[b]	—	n.s., .06
Variance	n.s., .01	n.s., .01	n.s., .03
Extraversion			
Mean	Positive, .14[a]	n.s., .03	Positive, .09
Maximum	n.s., .09	—	Positive, .12
Minimum	n.s., .04	—	n.s., .03
Variance	n.s., .03	n.s., .05	Positive, .06
Conscientiousness			
Mean	Positive, .28[a]	Positive, .15	Positive, .13
Maximum	n.s., .08	—	Positive, .09
Minimum	Positive, .22[a]	—	Positive, .13
Variance	n.s., –.03	Negative, –.17	n.s., –.06
Agreeableness			
Mean	Positive, .28[a]	Positive, .17	Positive, .10
Maximum	n.s., .09	—	n.s., .05
Minimum	Positive, .30[a]	—	Positive, .10
Variance	n.s., –.03	Negative, –.09	Negative, –.07
Openness to experience			
Mean	Positive, .20[a]	n.s., .02	—
Maximum	Positive, .14[a]	—	—
Minimum	n.s., .04	—	—
Variance	n.s., –.02	n.s., –.01	—

Note: *r* is the weighted mean correlation.

[a] Observed for field teams.

[b] Observed for laboratory teams.

In reviewing these results, it is important to note several qualifications. First, one of the advantages of meta-analysis is the precision with which researchers can test specific hypotheses regarding the relationship between independent and dependent variables and moderators such as the type of aggregation method or the type of task. We have attempted in Table 33.1 to abstract summary effects from these meta-analyses on one relationship of interest. However, it is certainly well advised to peruse these meta-analyses directly because they offer a wealth of detailed information integrating and elaborating the personality–team performance relationship that is not captured in Table 33.1. In fact, it is worthwhile to note that our attempt to summarize the results from multiple meta-analyses results in a further glossing-over of details from the separate meta-analyses.

A second point is that, as we scan Table 33.1, there is considerable variation in the results observed from these three sources. However, this is not too surprising, in that each is based on a somewhat different meta-analytic database. For example, the inclusion criteria differed for each study—Bell (2007) specifically excluded studies involving idea generation groups, and Peeters et al. (2006) only included studies in which team performance was assessed by supervisor ratings. Accordingly, for example, Bell's analysis of the conscientiousness–team performance relationship was based on 39 studies, Prewett et al.'s (2009) analysis of this relationship was based on 44 studies, and Peeters et al.'s analysis of this relationship was based on 10 studies. Furthermore, each of the meta-analyses pursued different analytic strategies. For example, Bell conducted separate analyses for field teams and laboratory teams (and found overall stronger effects for field teams). Prewett et al. conducted separate analyses for the effects of personality on team outcome and teamwork behaviors (and tended to find stronger effects of personality on team process than on team outcome). It is also important to note that Peeters et al. calculated "elevation" in trait scores as the mean individual trait scores *or* the proportion of high-scoring individuals on a trait. In brief, comparing results across meta-analyses is not straightforward, and we sacrifice some specificity in order to examine general patterns.

That being said, the next thing that we note regarding Table 33.1 is that there seem to be some general patterns evident in these results. Overall, the effect of mean emotional stability, extraversion, conscientiousness, and agreeableness on team performance is as predicted: The higher the mean levels of these traits are in the team, the higher the overall team performance. Furthermore, there is some evidence that mean openness to experience is related to team performance. Referring to Cohen's (1988) benchmarks for small, medium, and large effect sizes (.10, .30, and .50, respectively), the effects shown are of small-to-medium magnitude. We may note that the magnitude of effects shown in Table 33.1 is not dissimilar to the range of effect sizes obtained from the examination of the effect of personality on individual performance (see Barrick & Mount, 1991). Regarding variance, there is little existing evidence to support the supplementary/complementary distinction, although as we noted earlier, it may not be variability per se that is a critical factor, but variability at one pole of the specific trait. The only modest evidence shown is for agreeableness, in which we find a predicted negative relationship between variance scores and team performance.

Minimum and maximum trait scores offer some interesting patterns. For instance, we argued that having one team member exceptionally low on agreeableness can disrupt team performance. The results for minimum agreeableness scores suggest that this is the case. A similar argument was made for emotional stability, and there is some evidence that having a single team member low on emotional stability can impact team performance. Finally, similar results were found for minimum scores on conscientiousness: It seems that having one team member who is unreliable or not putting forth effort can negatively impact overall team performance.

Regarding maximum scores, there is some weak evidence that having one team member who is highly conscientious supports team performance. As predicted, we find support for the claim that the presence of one team member who scores high on extraversion can benefit the team (perhaps by performing leadership functions in unstructured task groups) and we find unexpected evidence that the presence of one team member who scores high on openness supports team performance (perhaps by performing creative task functions).

It may be useful to note that mean, maximum, and minimum scores are not independent, in that mean scores are calculated using the minimum and maximum scores. Furthermore, Humphrey et al. (2007) and Prewett et al. (2009) have stated that most studies have examined naturally occurring variance in teams, which minimizes the occurrence of very high and very low variance that is required to examine supplementary and complementary fit. Humphrey et al. propose methods for composing teams in order to maximize or minimize variance to better observe these processes.

In brief, for emotional stability, mean trait scores are predictive of team performance. A smaller effect was observed when emotional stability was operationalized as maximum and minimum trait scores. For extraversion, mean trait scores are predictive of team performance, and there is some evidence that maximum trait scores predict team performance. For conscientiousness, mean trait scores and minimum trait scores predict team performance. Weaker evidence exists that maximum trait scores predict performance. For agreeableness, mean trait scores and minimum trait scores predict team performance. Also, results indicate that variability in agreeableness is negatively related to team performance. For openness to experience, some evidence suggests that mean trait scores and maximum trait scores are predictive of team performance.

The purpose of this brief overview of the analyses presented in Table 33.1 is to examine overall mean effects of personality and team performance operationalized as mean, minimum, maximum, and variance scores. However, it is important to note that the mean effects shown in Table 33.1 provide only a partial and potentially misleading summary of the effects of personality on team performance. Meta-analysis can address several important analytic questions (see Mullen, Driskell, & Salas, 1998). The first involves "central tendency": Just as we can determine the mean height in a room full of people, we can seek to determine the typical study outcome, as shown in Table 33.1. However, examining only the overall mean relationship ignores two of the most important analytic questions: variability (what is the variability around the mean study outcome?) and explanation (what factors or moderators are associated with variations in the magnitude of effect sizes?). Thus, when the mean effects are heterogeneous, which is often the case, study attributes such as the type of task performed by the team are examined to explain this inconsistency. As noted previously, such situational specificity is characteristic of personality–performance relations (see Tett & Christiansen, 2007).

Moreover, a weak overall mean effect size does not necessarily indicate that trait is a weak predictor. For example, Peeters et al. (2006) reports considerable variability for the traits of agreeableness and openness, with 80% credibility intervals of (−0.02, 0.50) and (−0.21, 0.27), respectively. Especially in the case of openness in which the upper and lower boundaries are positive and negative around a weak mean, Tett and Christiansen (2007) note that such "bidirectionality" of personality–performance relations may yield a weak mean effect size when aggregated (cf. the mean r for openness of −0.01 in Peeters et al.), but that this may mask the operation of moderators indicating that the effect of the trait may be positive for some situations and negative for others. In brief, Table 33.1 illustrates that, in the studies examined, mean Big Five trait scores are in general positively related to team performance, whereas maximum and minimum trait scores are related in certain instances. However, research indicates that there is often considerable variability around these mean effects, reflecting the situational specificity of the personality–team performance relationship, and further clarification of these relationships can be obtained by examining moderators that are associated with variations in the magnitude of effects.

Increasing Specificity in Personality/Team Performance Relationships

The examination of the relationship of the Big Five traits to team performance represents a strategy in which broad personality traits are related to a broad criterion measure. That is, the Big Five traits are broad factors that represent variance common among a set of lower-level traits or facets. Stewart (1999) has stated that the examination of broad traits is applicable in several circumstances, including when the criterion itself is broad or diffuse (for in-depth coverage on the issue of the breadth of personality measurement, see Chapter 14, this volume). However, Barrick et al. (2001) have noted that sometimes a broad predictor and a broad criterion can mask underlying relationships (see also Rothstein & Goffin, 2006; Tett, Steele, & Beauregard, 2003). For example, we posed the question of whether conscientiousness may be related to team performance in existing research because of the lower-level facet of achievement or because of the lower-level facet of dependability that both comprise conscientiousness in many Big Five models. Moreover, it is unclear whether the overall effect of extraversion on team performance stems from the effect of the assertiveness/dominance component (i.e., extraverts are assertive) or from the sociability/affiliation component (i.e., extraverts are sociable). Thus, research suggests that the examination of lower-level facets may be useful in illuminating relationships, especially when linking lower-level predictors with lower-level criteria (Dudley, Orvis, Lebiecki, & Cortina, 2006; Stewart, 1999; Tett, Guterman, Bleier, & Murphy, 2000). As LePine and Van Dyne (2001) and others have noted, it may be beneficial to consider narrower facets of the Big Five and specific dimensions of contextual performance.

Prewett et al. (2009) found that team process criteria (teamwork behaviors) were more strongly predicted by personality than were team outcome criteria. They argued that team outcome criteria represented a measure of the net outcomes from the task, whereas team process criteria should be more strongly related to personality because they form a more proximal link in the personality → team process → team outcome chain (see Driskell et al., 1987). Moreover, by defining the core teamwork dimensions that underlie team performance, we are able to make more specific predictions regarding the specific personality facets that are predictive of these performance dimensions.

In order to do this, we must have a model or taxonomy of the Big Five facets that we believe are most relevant to teamwork and a taxonomy of teamwork behaviors. Driskell et al. (2006) have presented such an approach, defining lower-level Big Five facets relevant to core teamwork dimensions. They argued that specific facets of team member personality may have differential effects on the activities that underlie effective team performance. For example, a team member that is highly sociable may be quite adept at maintaining good interpersonal relations in teams, but not necessarily adept at task management and planning. Therefore, Driskell et al. attempted to link specific personality facets to the core teamwork dimensions that underlie effective team performance. In the following, we describe the specific personality facets viewed as most relevant to teamwork. We then present a classification of the core teamwork dimensions underlying effective team performance and describe predictions linking team member personality facets to those teamwork requirements.

Lower-Level Big Five Facets Relevant to Teamwork

Figure 33.1 presents a hierarchical model of team member personality, defined by the Big Five trait dimensions of *emotional stability*, *extraversion*, *openness*, *agreeableness*, and *conscientiousness*. These traits are, in turn, composed of more specific facets that are predicted to be relevant to teamwork. In the following subsections, we briefly describe those facets.

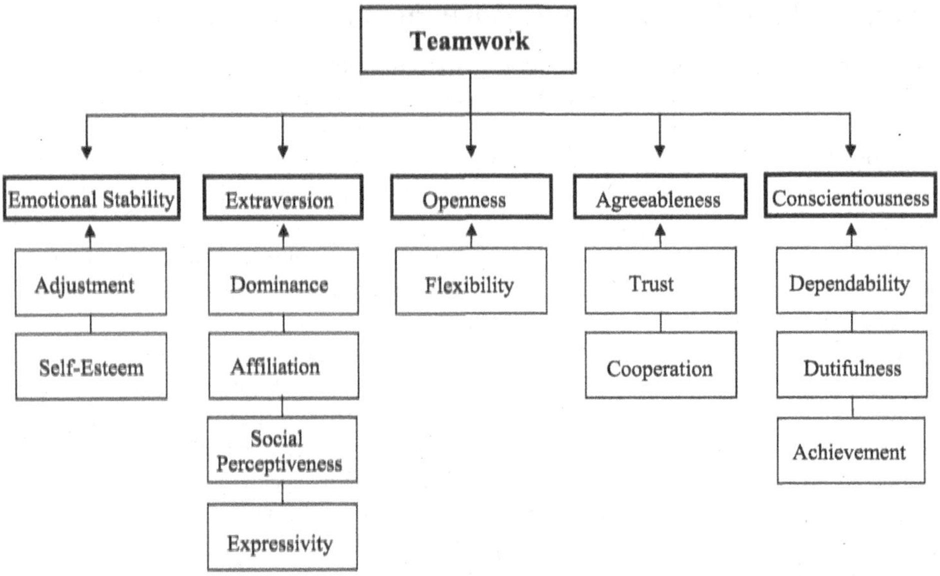

Figure 33.1 Hierarchical Model of Facets Related to Teamwork.
Source: Driskell, Goodwin, Salas, and O'Shea (2006).

Emotional Stability

The facets of emotional stability believed to be most relevant to teamwork are *adjustment* and *self-esteem.*

Adjustment

Adjustment has been defined by Hogan (1986) as freedom from anxiety, depression, and somatic complaints. Watson, Clark, and Tellegen (1988) have viewed lack of adjustment as *negative affect*, a general dimension of subjective distress and unpleasurable engagement. George (1990) found that the positive/negative affectivity of team members was related to the extent to which teams engaged in prosocial behaviors, and Barsade (2002) found that team members' positive affect led to greater cooperation, conflict management, and team performance. According to Barrick et al. (1998) and others, adjustment is critical to any task or teamwork activity that requires coordinated activity.

Self-Esteem

Self-esteem is generally defined as a global assessment of self-worth or of one's value as a person (Crocker & Wolfe, 2001). Those with high self-esteem view themselves in a positive light as good, worthy, and successful, whereas those with low self-esteem view themselves in a more negative light as bad, unworthy, and unlikely to succeed. Judge, Locke, Durham, and Kluger (1998) defined self-esteem as composed of two core components, self-worth and self-efficacy. They further noted that the appraisal of whether one is good and competent versus no good and incompetent has significant implications for how that person will approach and carry out job responsibilities. Baumeister (1997) has noted that those high in self-esteem not only have a favorable opinion of themselves but also see themselves as competent and will work hard to succeed; whereas those low in self-esteem doubt that they will succeed and focus on avoiding failure. Moreover, Murray, Holmes, MacDonald, and Ellsworth (1998) argued that those low in self-esteem are insecure and tend to project their self-doubts onto others.

Extraversion

The specific facets of extraversion believed to be most relevant to teamwork are *dominance, affiliation, social perceptiveness*, and *expressivity*.

Dominance

Dominance reflects striving for superiority, control, and influence over others. This facet has also been referred to as ascendance, assertiveness, or surgency (Costa & McCrae, 1992; Watson & Clark, 1997). Norton (1983) reported three components of dominance: (a) forcefulness (e.g., coming on strong and taking charge), (b) monopolizing (e.g., talking often and not letting others talk), and (c) involvement (e.g., taking precedence in interaction and not waiting for others). Dominant individuals have a desire to direct and influence others. They tend to stand firmly to their own opinions and perspectives and view compromise as a concession. To the extent that interdependent team tasks often require exchange of information among team members who all hold valuable task information, the tendency to be authoritative, controlling, and unreceptive to other team members' opinions can be damaging to team interaction (Driskell & Salas, 1992). Although the dominance component of extraversion may be related to leadership (i.e., leaders need to exert power and control), effective team members need to subjugate the desire for personal ascendancy to work as part of an interdependent, mutually reliant team.

Affiliation

Affiliation refers to the individual's desire to engage in activities with other people versus to be alone. Persons high on affiliation are sociable, friendly, interested in social interaction, and would generally prefer to interact with others than to be alone. Persons low on affiliation are withdrawn, reserved, aloof, and prefer solitary tasks. Lucas et al. (2000) define sociability as the enjoyment of social activities and preference for being with others over being alone. Driskell, Salas, and Hughes (2010) examined differences in *collective orientation* of team members, and found that teams composed of members who were collectively oriented (i.e., who preferred working in a team setting) outperformed teams composed of noncollectively oriented team members on team decision making, negotiation, and executing tasks.

Social Perceptiveness

Zaccaro, Foti, and Kenny (1991) define social perceptiveness as sensitivity to social cues, or the capacity to recognize what others expect in social situations. Social perceptiveness is related to social insight or social understanding, and can be described as the awareness of motives, needs, and intentions of other group members and awareness of relations among group members. Jones and Day (1997) described two related factors of social perception (the capacity to decode others' verbal and nonverbal behaviors) and social insight (the capacity to comprehend and interpret others' behavior in a social context). Marlowe (1986) described social competence as the ability to understand the feelings, thoughts, and behaviors of others in interpersonal situations. Thus, we would expect team members high on social perceptiveness to be more accurate in "reading" others with whom they are interacting, as well as more accurate in comprehending or interpreting relations between other team members.

Expressivity

Individuals high in expressivity are interpersonally expressive and communicative, whereas those low in expressivity are more reserved, taciturn, and impassive. Those who are interpersonally expressive are likely to be viewed as more positive and likeable (Riggio & Friedman, 1986), and are likely to be more energetic and effective communicators (Driskell & Radtke, 2003; Gallaher, 1992). Gross and John (1998) examined one component of expressivity, noting that those high in *expressive confidence* tend to exhibit high levels of expressivity in social situations, but do so in situationally appropriate ways. Moreover, Ambady, Hallahan, and Rosenthal (1995) have noted that some people are more "legible" than others, and that high expressivity is related to accuracy in transmitting nonverbal information to others.

Openness to Experience

The facet of openness believed to be most relevant to teamwork is *flexibility*.

Flexibility

Zaccaro, Gilbert, Thor, and Mumford (1991) defined behavioral flexibility as one component of social intelligence. This conceptualization emphasizes the problem-solving aspects of behavioral flexibility in addition to the interpersonal aspects, defining behavioral flexibility as "the ability and willingness to respond in significantly different ways to correspondingly different situational requirements" (p. 322). Recent research has discussed the importance of adaptability in teams (Kowslowski et al., 1999) and work environments (Pulakos, Arad, Donovan, & Plamondon, 2000). Pulakos et al. identified several critical dimensions of adaptive performance, including flexibility in handling uncertain task conditions, interpersonal flexibility, and flexibility in problem solving.

Agreeableness

The facets of agreeableness believed to be most relevant to teamwork are *trust* and *cooperation*.

Trust

Gurtman (1992) defines trust as the belief that the sincerity, benevolence, and truthfulness of others can generally be relied upon. According to Judge, Erez, and Bono (1998), the opposite of trust is cynicism, the belief that others lack integrity and are "out to get you." Those with dispositionally high trust believe that others are honest and well intentioned, whereas those with low trust are suspicious and doubt the sincerity, motives, or intentions of others. Dirks (1999) noted that interpersonal trust is a hallmark of effective groups, and argued that high trust should lead to greater cooperation and helping behaviors, greater task commitment, and higher effort expended on the task. Dirks found that, in high-trust groups, higher motivation was channeled into more cooperative behavior and better performance. Jarvenpaa and Leidner (1999) also found that lower levels of trust were associated with lower team performance.

Cooperation

Van Lange, De Bruin, Otten, and Joireman (1997) have noted that some people are willing to give others the benefit of the doubt and approach them cooperatively; whereas other people are more inclined to approach others competitively. They distinguished between those who are cooperative or prosocial (who maximize outcomes for both self and others) and those who are competitive (who maximize outcomes for self relative to others). Kelley and Stahelski (1970) found that competitive persons are more likely to expect others to be competitive and to elicit competitive behavior from others. The fact that cooperative persons approach interaction in a cooperative manner, but may be drawn into competitive behavior by a competitive partner, suggests the dual disadvantage of having highly competitive people in an interdependent team—they may not only act in a competitive manner, but draw competitive behavior out in others.

Conscientiousness

The facets of conscientiousness believed to be most relevant to teamwork are *dependability*, *dutifulness*, and *achievement*.

Dependability

Dependability refers to those who are reliable, planful, responsible, and persistent (Stewart, 1999). O'Neill and Allen (2011) examined one facet of conscientiousness that they labeled *endurance* (i.e., willing to work long hours, does not give up easily, and persevering) and found that mean team member endurance predicted overall performance in engineering design teams. Team members high on dependability are likely to be more responsible and can be relied on to back up other team members. They are also likely to be more methodical, to accept responsibilities, set goals, and follow through with them.

Dutifulness

Moon (2001) states that "duty captures differences in individuals' proclivity to do the right thing, not only for themselves, but also, for others" (p. 535). Thus, duty is seen as selfless behavior performed for the betterment of others. Ellemers, de Gilder, and van den Heuvel (1998) have examined a related construct of *team-oriented commitment*, which they defined as a sense of responsibility for team outcomes and motivation to help teammates even if requiring personal sacrifice. Costa and McCrae (1992) define duty as behavior evidenced by individual adherence to ethical principles and moral obligations. Extending this to the team context, duty is viewed as adhering to team principles and team obligations. Thus, those with a high duty orientation are more likely to form an attachment to the team and the team goals (see Aubé & Rosseau, 2005).

Achievement

Achievement is the volitional component of conscientiousness (Stewart, 1999). Those who are achievement-oriented are ambitious and take the initiative in pursuing team goals. In interdependent team tasks, each team member must be motivated to take on those duties that lead to successful accomplishment of the task. This includes not only carrying one's share of the load, but also carrying another team member's share if they are overburdened, as well as performing goal setting, team management, and leadership functions. Zander and Forward (1968) found that achievement-oriented team members were more concerned about team success, and Hough (1992) found achievement to be related to ratings of teamwork.

In summary, Driskell et al. (2006) described 12 lower-level facets of personality that they proposed were descriptive of effective team members. They concluded that

> Good team players are not controlling or domineering (low dominance). They are sociable (affiliation), perceptive and empathic (social perceptiveness), and interpersonally expressive (expressivity). They are emotionally stable (adjustment) and confident (self-esteem). They are adaptive (flexibility), trust other team members (trust) and cooperative (cooperativeness). Finally, good team players are reliable (dependability), have a strong sense of loyalty or duty to the team (dutifulness), and they work hard to achieve team goals (achievement).
>
> *p. 257*

The preceding classification attempts to describe specific lower-level personality facets that are relevant to team effectiveness. However, to specify the relationship between personality and team effectiveness more precisely requires that we not only describe the Big Five traits more precisely, but also provide greater specificity in terms of what we mean by *team effectiveness*. In other words, teams do not just *perform*, they perform certain core tasks, and the extent to which these teamwork activities or requirements are carried out successfully determines overall team effectiveness. In the following section, we attempt to define the core teamwork dimensions or team functions that must be accomplished within a team context.

Teamwork Dimensions

Driven by heightened interest in teams in work settings, recent research has attempted to define the dimensions that underlie effective teamwork (Ilgen, 1999). In a comprehensive review, Salas, Sims, and Burke (2005) identified over 138 models of team effectiveness, which they winnowed down to 20 models focusing on team processes or teamwork. Cannon-Bowers, Tannenbaum, Salas, and Volpe (1995) proposed that the core teamwork functions could be conceptualized as eight broad dimensions (see Table 33.2).

Table 33.2 Teamwork Dimensions

Dimension	*Definition*	*Subskills*
Adaptability	Team members use information from the task environment to adjust strategies through the use of flexibility, compensatory behavior, and reallocation of resources	Flexibility Compensatory or back-up behavior Providing assistance
Shared situational awareness	Team members develop shared knowledge of the team's internal and external environments	Shared orientation Team awareness
Performance monitoring and feedback	Team members give, seek, and receive task-clarifying feedback	Performance monitoring Providing feedback Error correction
Team management	Team members direct and coordinate task activities, assign tasks, plan and organize, and motivate other team members	Resource management Motivation Planning and goal setting
Interpersonal relations	Team members optimize interpersonal interactions by resolving conflicts, use of cooperation, and building morale	Conflict resolution Cooperation Morale building
Coordination	Team members organize team resources, activities, and responses to ensure complete and timely completion of tasks	Task organization Response coordination Timing and activity pacing
Communication	Team members exchange information efficiently	Seeking or requesting information Providing information Acknowledgment and confirmation
Decision making	Team members integrate or pool information, identify alternatives, select solutions, and evaluate consequences	Assessment Evaluation Problem solving

Source: Adapted from Cannon-Bowers, Tannenbaum, Salas, and Volpe (1995).

Although different models specify different dimensions, there is at least a reasonable degree of commonality among teamwork classification approaches, such as Cannon-Bowers et al. (1995), LePine, Piccolo, Jackson, Mathieu, and Saul (2008), Salas et al. (2005), and others. The Cannon-Bowers et al. classification of teamwork behaviors includes the following.

Adaptability

Adaptability refers to adjustment of task strategies or team behaviors in response to changes in the team or task environment. It may include mutual adjustment among team members and reallocation of resources. Because different abilities and procedures are required for different types of tasks, some have suggested that perhaps the only universally effective task strategy may be the capacity to change or adjust to different conditions (Hackman & Morris, 1978; Shiflett, 1972).

Shared Situational Awareness

Team members must develop a shared situational awareness, also referred to as mutual knowledge (Cramton, 2001; Thompson & Coovert, 2003) or common ground (Clark & Brennan, 1991). Team members possess contextual task and team information that must be communicated to and understood by other team members. Some research has shown that the accuracy and similarity of shared mental models among team members predicts the quality of team processes and performance (Marks, Zaccaro, & Mathieu, 2000; Mathieu, Heffner, Goodwin, Salas, & Cannon-Bowers, 2000; Thompson & Coovert, 2003).

Performance Monitoring and Feedback

Performance monitoring and feedback behaviors include monitoring other team members' contributions as well as monitoring team progress, identifying errors, providing constructive feedback, and offering advice for performance improvement. Members of effective teams must be familiar with each other's roles and accept responsibility for providing and accepting feedback (McIntyre & Salas, 1995).

Team Management

Team management behaviors include directing and coordinating the task activities of other team members, assigning tasks, and motivating other team members. These are primarily task behaviors oriented toward instrumental goals. One critical management task, planning, is often overlooked in teams (Hackman & Morris, 1978), although research has clearly demonstrated the value of planning (Janicik & Bartel, 2003; Weingart, 1992) and pretask briefings (Marks et al., 2000) to team performance.

Interpersonal Relations

Team members optimize interpersonal relations by resolving conflicts, encouraging cooperative behavior, and building team morale. These are primarily socioemotional behaviors oriented toward smooth interpersonal relations. Research has shown that cohesive groups report greater satisfaction (Curtis & Miller, 1986), and in general outperform less cohesive groups (Mullen & Copper, 1994).

Coordination

In one of the earliest studies of group performance, Shaw (1932) attributed the effectiveness of groups to the capability of group members to exchange and coordinate information. Janicik and

Bartel (2003) noted that effective coordination, knowing who is going to do what, when, and with whom, is critical to team performance. Behaviors that support effective coordination include matching team member resources to task requirements, regulating the pace of team activities, and coordinating the response and sequencing of team member activities (Fleishman & Zaccaro, 1992).

Communication

Communication is the primary vehicle through which task groups accomplish their goals (Marks et al., 2000). Team members must exchange ideas and information in a clear and timely manner. Research suggests that effective team performance is related to the quantity and quality of communications—effective teams communicate more and better than less effective teams (Foushee, 1982; Kanki, Lozito, & Foushee, 1989; Marks et al., 2000).

Decision Making

Team decision making involves problem identification and assessment, information exchange, generation and evaluation of solutions, implementation, and evaluation of consequences (Hirokawa, 1980; Janis & Mann, 1977). Barriers to effective team decision making may include failure to adequately assess problems (Moreland & Levine, 1992), failure to consider others' input (Driskell & Salas, 1992), failure to disclose uniquely held information (Stasser & Titus, 1995), and undue influence from a single team member (Foushee & Helmreich, 1988).

Predictions

Predicting from specific lower-level Big Five facets to specific teamwork dimensions allows greater specificity and may uncover relationships previously unexamined, but these relationships are speculative as most have been untested. For example, Driskell et al. (2006) propose that those who are more sociable and affiliative are more likely to assist and support other team members (adaptability), share experiences with other team members (shared situational awareness), seek and receive feedback from others (performance monitoring and feedback), engage in socioemotional activities (interpersonal relations), and talk more and exchange information with other team members (communication). However, high affiliation may interfere with instrumental task activities and negatively impact team management, coordination, and decision making.

Table 33.3 (adapted from Driskell et al., 2006) summarizes predictions regarding Big Five facets that are most likely to have positive (+) or negative (–) relationships to specific teamwork dimensions. Note that the facets that are predicted to be critical across all teamwork dimensions are *adjustment* and *flexibility*. Other facets, such as *affiliation* or *dutifulness*, are predicted to affect specific teamwork activities, and these relationships may be positive or negative. This allows us to examine both the "bright side" and the "dark side" of personality—whereas affiliation may have a positive impact on maintaining interpersonal relations in teams, it may have a negative impact on the more instrumental activities involved in team management. However, we note that almost all of the proposed relationships are untested.

Subject to empirical confirmation, the type of model shown in Table 33.3 suggests a number of practical applications. First, it provides greater specificity in prediction from lower-level personality facets to lower-level teamwork behaviors. This increases our understanding of effective team performance and how specific facets of the Big Five traits may impact teamwork. Moreover, it clarifies some incongruencies in Big Five trait–team performance relationships. We noted previously that extraversion is composed of both surgency (dominance) and sociability (affiliation) components. We suggest that dominance may be problematic in hierarchically unstructured task groups (see

Table 33.3 Effects of Team Member Personality Facets on Teamwork Dimensions

Team Member Facets		*Teamwork Dimensions*							
		Adaptability	*Shared Situational Awareness*	*Performance Monitoring and Feedback*	*Team Management*	*Interpersonal Relations*	*Coordination*	*Communication*	*Decision Making*
Emotional stability	Adjustment	+	+	+	+	+	+	+	+
	Self-esteem	+			+	+			
Extraversion	Dominance		–			–		–	–
	Affiliation	+	+	+	–	+	–	+	–
	Social perceptiveness	+	+			+		+	+
	Expressivity	+	+			+		+	+
Openness	Flexibility	+	+	+	+	+	+	+	+
Agreeableness	Trust			+		+		+	+
	Cooperation	+	+			+		+	
Conscientiousness	Dependability	+		+	+		+	+	
	Dutifulness		+	+		+			
	Achievement	+	+	+	+		+	+	+

Driskell et al., 1993). However, it may be the case that a high-dominant team member who is also high on affiliation or cooperation may have different effects on teamwork behaviors. Although this is speculation, the possibility is suggested by the specificity offered by this approach (for a more detailed exploration of personality trait combinations considered from a configural perspective, see Chapter 17, this volume).

In addition to providing potential guidelines for composing teams, the model presented in Table 33.3 suggests an approach to assessing existing team member capabilities and targeting training to support behaviors that may be deficient. For example, if assessment indicates a low score on *trust* for a specific team member, we propose that this will most likely be manifested in activities related to performance monitoring and feedback, interpersonal relations, and decision making (i.e., scanning across the appropriate row of Table 33.3). Efforts to implement training for this team member should focus on these dimensions. Thus, whereas personality brings job-relevant propensities to the workplace to meet job demands, training can compensate for deficiencies in personality propensities.

Discussion

There are several qualifications, limitations, or relevant issues that warrant consideration in thinking about personality in team settings. Although the Big Five trait approach is the most current and influential formulation of individual differences in personality, it is certainly not the only useful model of personality, and it fails to capture the entirety of trait content. We concur with McAdams and Pals (2006), who note that, although the Big Five model is arguably the most recognizable contribution personality psychology has to offer, understanding personality in a more finely grained sense requires going beyond the personality trait concept to include other motivational, social–cognitive, and developmental factors.

Sackett and Lievens (2008) note that a distinction should be made between the construct being measured (i.e., the Big Five) and method of measurement, and that improvements can be made to traditional methods of measuring personality. One suggestion relevant to the examination of personality and team performance is to increase the contextualization of the measurement procedure. For example, traditional self-report Big Five items often take a noncontextualized form (e.g., "It is important to stick to your own decisions") that requires a frame of reference pertaining to situations in general. A contextualized inventory would attempt to lessen this ambiguity by providing a specific frame of reference (e.g., "When I disagree with other team members, I tend to go with my own gut feelings"). Thus, it may be useful to adapt scale items specifically to team contexts (see Schmit, Ryan, Stierwalt, & Powell, 1995).

We have not addressed the more complex question of how personality facets combine or interact with other task or team factors. For example, the impact of expressivity may be considerably different if coupled with high adjustment than if coupled with low adjustment, as inappropriate expressiveness can be problematic (Friedman & Miller-Herringer, 1991). Or, a person who is high on conscientiousness but low on agreeableness may work effectively on an individual-level task, but be a pain in a collaborative environment. Prewett et al. (2009) found that mean team member agreeableness predicted team performance on intensive tasks (requiring complex coordination) but not on pooled tasks (requiring simple pooled contributions). Tasa, Sears, and Schat (2011) found that agreeableness more strongly affected teamwork behavior when collective efficacy was high. These and other studies allow us to examine how individual differences can interact with other individual, group-level, and structural factors to impact performance.

We have focused in this chapter specifically on task-oriented teams—teams in which the primary goal is task accomplishment. That is, the primary goal in task-oriented teams is solving a problem rather than, for example, enjoying each other's company. However, there are other types of groups that are relevant to the workplace that are not primarily task-oriented. These may include study groups (where the primary goal is learning), recreational groups such as yoga groups (where the primary goal is enjoyment or health), and even social groups that form after-hours. Examining these groups requires different measures other than performance outcome, such as perhaps measures of longevity, turnover, or satisfaction. Certainly different theoretical predictions would be made regarding the effects of personality on these types of nontask-oriented groups.

On a related point, it may be useful in the examination of the effects of personality on work teams to expand criterion measures beyond simple performance outcome measures. As Prewett et al. (2009) note, certainly team performance outcome is important, but there is considerable value in examining team process or teamwork measures, in that (a) in an input-process–outcome perspective, personality is theoretically more proximally related to team processes than to team outcomes, and (b) empirically, there seem to be stronger relations between personality and process than between personality and outcome. In a meta-analytic examination of this latter proposition, Prewett et al. found significantly stronger mean effects between personality and process measures than between personality and outcome measures for the traits of extraversion, agreeableness, and emotional stability.

We have not discussed temporal issues or team development over time. For example, our focus has been on initially unstructured teams in which each team member is equal in status or authority. However, initially unstructured task groups develop structure over time, such that some persons assume a higher position in terms of authority or leadership. Differential effects of personality over the course of evolving team interaction are an interesting topic (see Ilgen, Hollenbeck, Johnson, & Jundt, 2005). Moreover, our focus on initially unstructured teams leads us to examine traits that define the effective *team member*, but not necessarily the effective *team leader* (for more coverage on personality and leadership, see Chapter 34, this volume).

Most of the research on personality and team performance either explicitly or implicitly adopts a team composition perspective. That is, how do we compose teams or select team members on the basis of personality to form an effective work team? However, it is useful to consider selection, training, and design approaches to enhancing team effectiveness. For example, Driskell et al. (2010) view *collective orientation* as the preference to work in a collective manner in team settings. This type of construct is less stable than personality traits, but more stable than mere transitory states (see Driskell et al., 2006; Mohammed & Angell, 2004). That is, collective orientation is stable enough to determine how individuals perform in team task settings, but malleable enough to be changed through experience or training. Further research is needed to examine the malleability of lower-level traits and the value of training to develop more effective team members. The success with which well-developed training programs have led to improved teamwork in applied settings (e.g., Smith-Jentsch, Salas, & Brannick, 2001) suggests the utility of this approach. Furthermore, task design is an important but often overlooked factor that may moderate the effect of personality on team performance. For example, conscientiousness may be less relevant to team performance to the extent that back-up or compensatory behaviors are institutionalized in task procedures.

Finally, it is useful to consider how situational context moderates the effect of personality on team performance. Tett and Burnett's (2003) theory of trait activation holds that personality traits are expressed in response to trait-relevant situational cues. For example, team members high on agreeableness are considerate, helpful, and supportive. To assess agreeableness, the situation must be one in which consideration and support are viable responses. In a task in which trait-expressive behavior is depressed, such as a pooled task in which there is little interaction, agreeableness is not relevant (see Prewett et al., 2009). Thus, a specific trait will be related to work team performance to the extent that (a) team members vary in the level of that trait, (b) trait expression is triggered by task, social, or organizational cues, (c) the trait-expressive behavior contributes to team performance, and (d) the situation is not so strong as to override or negate the expression of that trait (i.e., team members will be immediately fired if they do not all express that behavior).

Teams are complex entities, and there are a number of factors that determine how effectively a work team performs. One factor is the composition of the team, and our focus has been on how the personality of team members impacts team performance. Why is the study of personality and team performance useful? First, the idea that the personality of team members affects team performance is strongly intuitive—we can almost *see* the impact of self-centered or moody teammates on team interaction and performance. Second, personality has proven to be a significant predictor of individual job performance, so it stands to reason that we can understand team performance more clearly by examining the role of team member personality. Third, there is an accumulating body of empirical research, some of which we have touched on, that demonstrates the relationship between team member personality and team effectiveness. The consideration of team member personality can add incremental value in composing effective work teams.

Practitioner's Window

Teams are the method of choice in work settings to attack large, complex, or difficult tasks. However, some teams are more effective than others, and we address one factor that determines team effectiveness: the composition of the team in terms of team member personality. Intuitively, we expect that teams composed of well-adjusted, dependable, and cooperative team members will perform more effectively than teams composed of distressed, unreliable, and unaccommodating members. In this chapter, we examine the relationship of the Big Five personality traits to team performance, and how these individual traits may be aggregated to the team level. We examine how lower-level personality facets drawn from the Big Five may predict lower-level criteria such as teamwork behaviors.

Practitioners require clear guidelines for application, yet research results, including those in this chapter, are often couched in complex and conditional terms. This, it seems, is the nature of the scientific enterprise: To paraphrase Vannevar Bush (1945), basic research can provide answers to a large number of important problems, though it may not give a specific answer to any one of them. Nevertheless, we can offer the following broad guidelines for application:

- Mean levels of the Big Five traits of emotional stability, extraversion, conscientiousness, agreeableness, and openness seem to be positively related to effective team performance. In specific instances, minimum trait scores and maximum trait scores may also predict team performance.
- Situational specificity is a feature of almost all personality–team performance relations. That is, trait effects may vary across different types of tasks, teams, and settings.
- Although high mean levels of the Big Five traits are generally conducive to teamwork, there are qualifications to this generalization. Personality–team performance relationships may resemble a curvilinear or inverted U function, in that higher mean trait levels may increase performance to a point, but very high trait levels (e.g., very high sociability) may be counterproductive.
- Mean trait scores and variance are related in that high mean scores entail low variance. For certain traits, similarity or low variance at the positive pole of a trait (i.e., high conscientiousness) may be related to effective team performance, whereas similarity or low variance at the low end of the trait scale (i.e., low conscientiousness) may result in poor performance.
- Attention should also be directed to optimizing team member personality compatibility (i.e., who prefers to work with whom and who is more productive working with whom), although this is a complex issue for which more research is needed.

- It may be beneficial to gain greater specificity in personality–team performance predictions by examining lower-level Big Five facets and lower-level team performance dimensions such as specific teamwork behaviors.
- Researchers have identified core teamwork dimensions or *team functions* that must be accomplished within teams. Teamwork dimensions include activities such as *team management* (i.e., directing and coordinating task activities), *interpersonal relations* (i.e., resolving conflicts and maintaining socioemotional relations), and *adaptability* (i.e., compensatory or back-up behavior). It is likely that specific facets of personality may have differential effects on these activities. For example, a team member who is highly sociable may be quite adept at maintaining good interpersonal relations in teams, but not necessarily adept at task management and planning.

References

Ambady, N., Hallahan, M., & Rosenthal, R. (1995). On judging and being judged accurately in zero-acquaintance situations. *Journal of Personality and Social Psychology, 69*, 518–529.

Anderson, M. G., & Tett, R. P. (2006, May). *Who prefers to work with whom? Trait activation in classroom teams.* Paper presented at the 21st annual conference of the Society for Industrial and Organizational Psychology, Dallas, TX.

Aubé, C., & Rosseau, V. (2005). Team goal commitment and team effectiveness: The role of task interdependence and supportive behaviors. *Group Dynamics, 9*, 189–204.

Barrick, M. R., & Mount, M. K. (1991). The Big Five personality dimensions and job performance: A meta-analysis. *Personnel Psychology, 44*, 1–26.

Barrick, M. R., & Mount, M. K. (2001). Select on conscientiousness and emotional stability. In E. A. Locke (Ed.), *Handbook of principles of organizational behavior* (pp. 15–28). Malden, MA: Blackwell.

Barrick, M. R., Mount, M. K., & Judge, T. A. (2001). Personality and performance at the beginning of the new millennium: What do we know and where do we go next? *International Journal of Selection and Assessment, 9*, 9–30.

Barry, B., & Stewart, G. L. (1997). Composition, process, and performance in self-managed groups: The role of personality. *Journal of Applied Psychology, 82*, 62–78.

Barrick, M. R., Stewart, G. L., Neubert, M. J., & Mount, M. K. (1998). Relating member ability and personality to work–team processes and team effectiveness. *Journal of Applied Psychology, 83*, 377–391.

Barsade, S. G. (2002). The ripple effects: Emotional contagion and its influence on group behavior. *Administrative Science Quarterly, 47*, 644–675.

Baumeister, R. F. (1997). Identify, self-concept, and self-esteem: The self lost and found. In R. Hogan, J. Johnson, & S. Briggs (Eds.), *Handbook of personality psychology* (pp. 681–710). San Diego, CA: Academic Press.

Bell, S. T. (2007). Deep-level composition variables as predictors of team performance: A meta-analysis. *Journal of Applied Psychology, 92*, 595–615.

Bush, V. (1945). *Science: The endless frontier. A report to the President by Vannevar Bush, Director of the Office of Scientific Research and Development.* Washington, DC: U.S. Government Printing Office. Retrieved from http://www.nsf.gov/about/history/vbush1945.htm

Cannon-Bowers, J. A., Tannenbaum, S. I., Salas, E., & Volpe, C. E. (1995). Defining competencies and establishing team training requirements. In R. Guzzo & E. Salas (Eds.), *Team effectiveness and decision making in organizations* (pp. 333–380). San Francisco, CA: Jossey-Bass.

Clark, H. H., & Brennan, S. E. (1991). Grounding in communication. In L. B. Resnick, J. M. Levine, & S. D. Teasley (Eds.), *Perspectives on socially shared cognition* (pp. 127–149). Washington, DC: American Psychological Association.

Cohen, J. (1988). *Statistical power analysis for the behavioral sciences* (2nd ed.). Hillsdale, NJ: Erlbaum.

Costa, P. T., & McCrae, R. R. (1992). *Revised NEO Personality Inventory (NEO-PI-R) and Five Factor Inventory (NEO-FFI) professional manual.* Odessa, FL: Psychological Assessment Resources.

Cramton, C. D. (2001). The mutual knowledge problem and its consequences for dispersed collaboration. *Organizational Science, 12*, 346–371.

Crocker, J., & Wolfe, C. T. (2001). Contingencies of self-worth. *Psychological Review, 108*, 593–623.

Curtis, R. C., & Miller, K. (1986). Believing another likes or dislikes you: Behaviors making the beliefs come true. *Journal of Personality and Social Psychology, 51*, 284–290.

Davis, J. H. (1969). *Group performance.* Reading, MA: Addison-Wesley.

Dirks, K. T. (1999). The effects of interpersonal trust on work group performance. *Journal of Applied Psychology, 84*, 445–455.

Driskell, J. E., Goodwin, G. F., Salas, E., & O'Shea, P. G. (2006). What makes a good team player? Personality and team effectiveness. *Group Dynamics, 10*, 249–271.

Driskell, J. E., Hogan, R., & Salas, E. (1987). Personality and group performance. In C. Hendrick (Ed.), *Review of personality and social psychology* (Vol. 9, pp. 91–112). Newbury Park, CA: Sage.

Driskell, J. E., Olmstead, B., & Salas, E. (1993). Task cues, dominance cues, and influence in task groups. *Journal of Applied Psychology, 78*, 51–60.

Driskell, J. E., & Radtke, P. H. (2003). The effect of gesture on speech production and comprehension. *Human Factors, 45*, 445–454.

Driskell, J. E., Radtke, P. H., & Salas, E. (2003). Virtual teams: Effects of technological mediation on team performance. *Group Dynamics, 7*, 297–323.

Driskell, J. E., & Salas, E. (1992). Collective behavior and team performance. *Human Factors, 34*, 277–288.

Driskell, J. E., Salas, E., & Hughes, S. (2010). Collective orientation and team performance: Development of an individual differences measure. *Human Factors, 52*, 316–328.

Dudley, N. M., Orvis, K. A., Lebiecki, J. E., & Cortina, J. M. (2006). A meta-analytic investigation of conscientiousness in the prediction of job performance: Examining the intercorrelations and the incremental validity of narrow traits. *Journal of Applied Psychology, 91*, 40–57.

Ellemers, N., de Gilder, D., & van den Heuvel, H. (1998). Career-oriented versus team-oriented commitment and behavior at work. *Journal of Applied Psychology, 83*, 717–730.

Fiske, D. W. (1949). Consistency of the factorial structures of personality ratings from different sources. *Journal of Abnormal and Social Psychology, 44*, 329–344.

Fleishman, E. A., & Zaccaro, S. J. (1992). Toward a taxonomy of team performance functions. In R. W. Swezey & E. Salas (Eds.), *Teams: Their training and performance* (pp. 31–56). Norwood, NJ: Ablex.

Foushee, H. C. (1982). The role of communications, socio-psychological, and personality factors in the maintenance of crew coordination. *Aviation, Space, and Environmental Medicine, 53*, 1062–1066.

Foushee, H. C., & Helmreich, R. L. (1988). Group interaction and flight crew performance. In E. L. Weiner & D. C. Nagel (Eds.), *Human factors in aviation* (pp. 189–228). San Diego, CA: Academic Press.

Friedman, H. S., & Miller-Herringer, T. (1991). Nonverbal display of emotion in public and in private: Self-monitoring, personality, and expressive cues. *Journal of Personality and Social Psychology, 61*, 766–775.

Gallaher, P. E. (1992). Individual differences in nonverbal behavior: Dimensions of style. *Journal of Personality and Social Psychology, 63*, 133–145.

George, J. M. (1990). Personality, affect, and behavior in groups. *Journal of Applied Psychology, 75*, 107–116.

Greer, F. L. (1955). *Small group effectiveness* (Institute Report No. 6). Philadelphia, PA: Institute for Research on Human Relations.

Gross, J. J., & John, O. P. (1998). Mapping the domain of expressivity: Multimethod evidence for a hierarchical model. *Journal of Personality and Social Psychology, 74*, 170–191.

Gurtman, M. B. (1992). Trust, distrust, and interpersonal problems: A circumplex analysis. *Journal of Personality and Social Psychology, 62*, 989–1002.

Hackman, J. R., & Morris, C. G. (1978). Group tasks, group interaction process, and group performance effectiveness: A review and proposed integration. In L. Berkowitz (Ed.), *Group processes* (pp. 1–55). New York: Academic Press.

Halfhill, T., Sundstrom, E., Lahner, J., Calderone, W., & Nielsen, T. M. (2005). Group personality composition and group effectiveness: An integrative review of empirical research. *Small Group Research, 36*, 83–105.

Haythorn, W. (1953). The influence of individual members on the characteristics of small groups. *Journal of Abnormal and Social Psychology, 48*, 276–284.

Hirokawa, R. Y. (1980). A comparative analysis of communication patterns within effective and ineffective decision-making groups. *Communication Monographs, 47*, 312–321.

Hogan, R. (1986). *Hogan personality inventory*. Minneapolis, MN: National Computer Systems.

Hollenbeck, J. R., Ilgen, D. R., Sego, D. J., Hedlund, J., Major, D. A., & Phillips, J. (1995). The multilevel theory of team decision making: Decision performance in teams incorporating distributed expertise. *Journal of Applied Psychology, 80*, 292–316.

Hollenbeck, J. R., Moon, H., Ellis, A. P. J., West, B., Ilgen, D., Sheppard, L., . . . Wagner, J. A. (2002). Structural contingency theory and individual differences: Examination of external and internal person–team fit. *Journal of Applied Psychology, 87*, 599–606.

Hough, L. M. (1992). The "Big Five" personality variables: Construct confusion-description versus prediction. *Human Performance, 5*, 139–155.

Humphrey, S. E., Hollenbeck, J. R., Meyer, C. J., & Ilgen, D. R. (2007). Trait configurations in self-managed teams: A conceptual examination of the use of seeding for maximizing and minimizing trait variance in teams. *Journal of Applied Psychology, 92*, 885–892.

Ilgen, D. R. (1999). Teams embedded in organizations. *American Psychologist, 54*, 129–139.

Ilgen, D. R., Hollenbeck, J. R., Johnson, M., & Jundt, D. (2005). Teams in organizations: From input-process-output models to IMOI models. *Annual Review of Psychology, 56*, 517–543.
Janicik, G. A., & Bartel, C. A. (2003). Talking about time: Effects of temporal planning and time awareness norms on group coordination and performance. *Group Dynamics, 7*, 122–134.
Janis, I. L., & Mann, L. (1977). *Decision making: A psychological analysis of conflict, choice, and commitment.* New York: Free Press.
Jarvenpaa, S. L., & Leidner, D. E. (1999). Communication and trust in global virtual teams. *Organizational Science, 10*, 791–815.
Jones, K., & Day, J. D. (1997). Discrimination of two aspects of cognitive–social intelligence from academic intelligence. *Journal of Educational Psychology, 89*, 486–497.
Judge, T. A., & Bono, J. E. (2000). Five-factor model of personality and transformational leadership. *Journal of Applied Psychology, 85*, 751–765.
Judge, T. A., Erez, A., & Bono, J. E. (1998). The power of being positive: The relationship between positive self-concept and job performance. *Human Performance, 11*, 167–187.
Judge, T. A., Locke, E. A., Durham, C. C., & Kluger, A. N. (1998). Dispositional effects on job and life satisfaction: The role of core evaluations. *Journal of Applied Psychology, 83*, 17–34.
Kanki, B. G., Lozito, S. C., & Foushee, H. C. (1989). Communication indices of crew coordination. *Aviation, Space and Environmental Medicine, 60*, 56–60.
Kelley, H., & Stahelski, A. (1970). Social interaction bases of cooperators' and competitors' beliefs about others. *Journal of Personality and Social Psychology, 16*, 66–91.
Kowslowski, S. W. J., Gully, S. M., Nason, E. R., & Smith, E. M. (1999). Developing adaptive teams: A theory of compilation and performance across levels and time. In D. R. Ilgen & E. D. Pulakos (Eds.), *The changing nature of work performance: Implications for staffing, motivation, and development* (pp. 240–294). San Francisco, CA: Jossey-Bass.
Kozlowski, S. W. J., Gully, S. M., McHugh, P. P., Salas, E., & Cannon-Bowers, J. A. (1996). A dynamic theory of leadership and team effectiveness: Developmental and task contingent leader roles. *Research in Personnel and Human Resources Management, 14*, 253–305.
LePine, J. A. (2003). Team adaptation and postchange performance: Effects of team composition in terms of members' cognitive ability and personality. *Journal of Applied Psychology, 88*, 27–39.
LePine, J. A., Hollenbeck, J. R., Ilgen, D., & Hedlund, J. (1997). Effects of individual differences on the performance of hierarchical decision-making teams: Much more than g. *Journal of Applied Psychology, 82*, 803–811.
LePine, J. A., Piccolo, R. F., Jackson, C. L., Mathieu, J. E., & Saul, J. R. (2008). A meta-analysis of teamwork processes: Tests of a multidimensional model and relationships with team effectiveness criteria. *Personnel Psychology, 61*, 273–307.
LePine, J. A., & Van Dyne, L. V. (2001). Voice and cooperative behavior as contrasting forms of contextual performance: Evidence of differential relationships with Big Five personality characteristics and cognitive ability. *Journal of Applied Psychology, 86*, 326–336.
Lucas, R. E., Diener, E., Suh, E. M., Shao, L., & Grob, A. (2000). Cross-cultural evidence for the fundamental features of extraversion. *Journal of Personality and Social Psychology, 79*, 452–468.
Mann, R. D. (1959). A review of the relationships between personality and performance in small groups. *Psychological Bulletin, 56*, 241–270.
Marks, M. A., Zaccaro, S. J., & Mathieu, J. E. (2000). Performance implications of leader briefings and team-interaction training for team adaptation to novel environments. *Journal of Applied Psychology, 85*, 971–986.
Marlowe, H. A. (1986). Social intelligence: Evidence for multidimensionality and construct independence. *Journal of Educational Psychology, 78*, 52–58.
Mathieu, J. E., Heffner, T. S., Goodwin, G. F., Salas, E., & Cannon-Bowers, J. A. (2000). The influence of shared mental models on team process and performance. *Journal of Applied Psychology, 85*, 273–283.
McAdams, D. P., & Pals, J. L. (2006). A new Big Five: Fundamental principles for an integrative science of personality. *American Psychologist, 61*, 204–217.
McCrae, R. R., & Costa, P. T. (1997). Conceptions and correlates of openness to experience. In R. Hogan, J. Johnson, & S. Briggs (Eds.), *Handbook of personality psychology* (pp. 825–847). San Diego, CA: Academic Press.
McIntyre, R. M., & Salas, E. (1995). Measuring and managing for team performance: Lessons from complex environments. In R. A. Guzzo, E. Salas, & Associates (Eds.), *Team effectiveness and decision making in organizations* (pp. 9–45). San Francisco, CA: Jossey-Bass.
Mohammed, S., & Angell, L. C. (2004). Surface- and deep-level diversity in workgroups: Examining the moderating effects of team orientation and team process on relationship conflict. *Journal of Organizational Behavior,* 25, 1015–1039.
Moon, H. (2001). The two faces of conscientiousness: Duty and achievement-striving within escalation of commitment dilemmas. *Journal of Applied Psychology, 86*, 533–540.
Moreland, R. L., & Levine, J. M. (1992). Problem identification by groups. In S. Worchel, W. Wood, & J. A. Simpson (Eds.), *Group process and productivity* (pp. 17–47). Newbury Park, CA: Sage.

Mount, M. K., Barrick, M. R., & Stewart, G. L. (1998). Five-factor model of personality and performance in jobs involving interpersonal interactions. *Human Performance, 11*, 145–165.
Mullen, B., & Copper, C. (1994). The relation between group cohesiveness and performance: An integration. *Psychological Bulletin, 115*, 210–227.
Mullen, B., Driskell, J. E., & Salas, E. (1998). Meta-analysis and the study of group dynamics. *Group Dynamics, 2*, 213–229.
Murray, S. L., Holmes, J. G., MacDonald, G., & Ellsworth, P. C. (1998). Through the looking glass darkly: When self-doubts turn into relationship insecurities. *Journal of Personality and Social Psychology, 75*, 1459–1480.
Neuman, G. A., & Wright, J. (1999). Team effectiveness: Beyond skills and cognitive ability. *Journal of Applied Psychology, 84*, 376–389.
Norman, W. T. (1963). Toward an adequate taxonomy of personality attributes: Replicated factor structure in peer nomination personality ratings. *Journal of Abnormal and Social Psychology, 66*, 574–583.
Norton, R. (1983). *Communicator style: Theory, applications, and measures*. Beverly Hills, CA: Sage.
O'Neill, T. A., & Allen, N. J. (2011). Personality and the prediction of team performance. *European Journal of Personality, 25*, 31–42.
Paulhus, D. L., & Martin, C. L. (1988). Functional flexibility: A new conception of interpersonal flexibility. *Journal of Personality and Social Psychology, 55*, 88–101.
Paulus, P. B., & Van der Zee, K. (2004). Should there be a romance between teams and groups? *Journal of Occupational and Organizational Psychology, 77*, 475–480.
Peeters, M. A., Van Tuijl, H., Rutte, C., & Reymen, I. (2006). Personality and team performance: A meta-analysis. *European Journal of Personality, 20*, 377–396.
Porter, C., Hollenbeck, J. R., Ilgen, D. R., Ellis, A., West, B. J., & Moon, H. (2003). Backing up behaviors in teams: The role of personality and legitimacy of need. *Journal of Applied Psychology, 88*, 391–403.
Prewett, M. S., Walvoord, A. A. G., Stilson, F. R. B., Rossi, M. E., & Brannick, M. T. (2009). The team personality–team performance relationship revisited: The impact of criterion choice, pattern of workflow, and method of aggregation. *Human Performance, 22*, 273–296.
Pulakos, E. D., Arad, S., Donovan, M. A., & Plamondon, K. E. (2000). Adaptability in the workplace: Development of a taxonomy of adaptive performance. *Journal of Applied Psychology, 85*, 612–624.
Riggio, R., & Friedman, H. (1986). Impression formation: The role of expressive behavior. *Journal of Personality and Social Psychology, 50*, 421–427.
Rothstein, M. G., & Goffin, R. D. (2006). The use of personality measures in personnel selection: What does current research support? *Human Resource Management Review, 16*, 155–180.
Sackett, P. R., & Lievens, F. (2008). Personnel selection. *Annual Review of Psychology, 59*, 419–450.
Salas, E., Dickinson, T., Converse, S. A., & Tannenbaum, S. I. (1992). Toward an understanding of team performance and training. In R. W. Swezey & E. Salas (Eds.), *Teams: Their training and performance* (pp. 3–29). Norwood, NJ: Ablex.
Salas, E., Sims, D. A., & Burke, C. S. (2005). Is there a "Big Five" in teamwork? *Small Group Research, 36*, 555–599.
Saucier, G., & Ostendorf, F. (1999). Hierarchical subcomponents of the big five personality factors: A cross-cultural replication. *Journal of Personality and Social Psychology, 76*, 613–627.
Schmit, M. J., Ryan, A. M., Stierwalt, S. L., & Powell, S. L. (1995). Frame-of-reference effects on personality scores and criterion-related validity. *Journal of Applied Psychology, 80*, 607–620.
Shaw, M. E. (1932). A comparison of individuals and small groups in the rational solution of complex problems. *American Journal of Psychology, 44*, 491–504.
Shiflett, S. C. (1972). Group performance as a function of task difficulty and organizational interdependence. *Organizational Behavior and Human Performance, 7*, 442–456.
Smith-Jentsch, K. A., Salas, E., & Brannick, M. T. (2001). To transfer or not to transfer? Investigating the combined effects of trainee characteristics, team leader support, and team climate. *Journal of Applied Psychology, 86*, 279–292.
Stasser, G., & Titus, W. (1995). Effects of information load and percentage of shared information on the dissemination of unshared information during group discussion. *Journal of Personality and Social Psychology, 48*, 1467–1478.
Steiner, I. D. (1972). *Group process and productivity*. New York: Academic Press.
Stewart, G. L. (1999). Trait bandwidth and stages of job performance: Assessing differential effects of conscientiousness and its subtraits. *Journal of Applied Psychology, 84*, 959–968.
Tasa, K., Sears, G. J., & Schat, A. C. H. (2011). Personality and teamwork behavior in context: The cross-level moderating role of collective efficacy. *Journal of Organizational Behavior, 32*, 65–85.
Tett, R. P., & Burnett, D. D. (2003). A personality trait-based interactionist model of job performance. *Journal of Applied Psychology, 88*, 500–517.
Tett, R. P., & Christiansen, N. D. (2007). Personality tests at the crossroads: A response to Morgeson, Campion, Dipboye, Hollenbeck, Murphy, and Schmitt (2007). *Personnel Psychology, 60*, 967–993.

Tett, R. P., Guterman, H. A., Bleier, A., & Murphy, P. J. (2000). Development and content validation of a "hyper-dimensional" taxonomy of managerial competence. *Human Performance, 13*, 205–251.

Tett, R. P., & Murphy, P. J. (2002). Personality and situations in co-worker preference: Similarity and complementarity in worker compatibility. *Journal of Business and Psychology, 17*, 223–243.

Tett, R. P., Steele, J. R., & Beauregard, R. S. (2003). Broad and narrow measures on both sides of the personality–job performance relationship. *Journal of Organizational Behavior, 24*, 335–356.

Thompson, L. F., & Coovert, M. D. (2003). Teamwork online: The effects of computer conferencing on perceived confusion, satisfaction, and postdiscussion accuracy. *Group Dynamics, 7*, 135–151.

Totterdell, P., Kellett, S., Teuchmann, K., & Briner, R. B. (1998). Evidence of mood linkage in work groups. *Journal of Personality and Social Psychology, 74*, 1504–1515.

Tupes, E. C., & Christal, R. E. (1961). *Recurrent personality factors based on trait ratings* (Report No. ASD-TR-61-97). San Antonio, TX: Personnel Laboratory USAF, Lackland Air Force Base.

Van Lange, P., De Bruin, E., Otten, W., & Joireman, J. A. (1997). Development of prosocial, individualistic, and competitive orientations: Theory and preliminary evidence. *Journal of Personality and Social Psychology, 73*, 733–746.

Watson, D., & Clark, L. A. (1997). Extraversion and its positive emotional core. In R. Hogan, J. Johnson, & S. Briggs (Eds.), *Handbook of personality psychology* (pp. 767–793). San Diego, CA: Academic Press.

Watson, D., Clark, L. A., & Tellegen, A. (1988). Development and validation of brief measures of positive and negative affect: The PANAS scales. *Journal of Personality and Social Psychology, 54*, 1063–1070.

Weingart, L. R. (1992). Impact of group goals, task component complexity, effort, and planning on group performance. *Journal of Applied Psychology, 77*, 682–693.

Zaccaro, S. J., Gilbert, J. A., Thor, K. K., & Mumford, M. D. (1991). Leadership and social intelligence: Linking social perceptiveness and behavioral flexibility to leader effectiveness. *Leadership Quarterly, 2*, 317–342.

Zaccaro, S. J., Foti, R. J., & Kenny, D. A. (1991). Self-monitoring and trait-based variance in leadership: An investigation of leader flexibility across multiple group situations. *Journal of Applied Psychology, 76*, 308–315.

Zander, A., & Forward, J. (1968). Position in group, achievement orientation, and group aspirations. *Journal of Personality and Social Psychology, 8*, 282–288.

34

The Personality of Leaders

From Vertical to Shared Leadership

Tiffani R. Chen and Stephen J. Zaccaro

The connections between individual personality attributes and leadership effectiveness and leader role occupancy, respectively, have been a topic of interest to researchers for over 100 years (e.g., Terman, 1904; Zaccaro, LaPort, & Jose, 2013). Despite this long-standing research tradition, however, there remains considerable ambiguity about the relationship between personality and leadership. Early reviews offered bleak assessments of this relationship (Mann, 1959; Stogdill, 1948). However, later meta-analyses offered a brighter, although still mixed, picture (DeRue, Nahrgang, Wellman, & Humphrey, 2011; Hoffman, Woehr, Maldagen-Youngjohn, & Lyons, 2011; Judge, Bono, Ilies, & Gerhart, 2002; Judge, Colbert, & Ilies, 2004; Lord, De Vader, & Alliger, 1986). While corrected correlations tended to be higher than those observed in prior studies, they were still relatively modest, with a fair degree of variability across studies.

Several researchers have argued that studies of leader personality and leadership outcomes need to move beyond simple bivariate approaches and explore more sophisticated models of this relationship (Bass, 1990; DeRue et al., 2011; Lord & Hall, 1992; Van Iddekinge, Ferris, & Heffner, 2009; Zaccaro, Gulick, & Khare, 2008; Zaccaro, Kemp, & Bader, 2004; Zaccaro et al., 2013). Zaccaro et al. (2013; see also Zaccaro, 2012) articulated three such models: (a) multivariate perspectives that include multiple cognitive, social, motivational, and personality variables; (b) multistage models that include personality attributes as one of the several sets of distal predictors of more proximal influences on leadership (e.g., Mumford, Zaccaro, Harding, Jacobs, & Fleishman, 2000; Zaccaro et al., 2004); and (c) pattern approaches, which focus on specific configurations of different personality attributes that influence leadership outcomes (e.g., Foti & Hauenstein, 2007). Studies reflecting such recommendations are now appearing in the extant literature. One set of purposes for this chapter is to (a) provide a brief historical perspective on personality and leadership, and (b) review recent studies that are offering more sophisticated examples of personality and leadership. Our purpose is not to provide a major review of leader trait research, as others have done so (Bass, 2008; Day & Zaccaro, 2007; Zaccaro et al., 2004), but rather to establish the basis for the major focus of our chapter.

Another recent trend in the leadership literature is the increasing focus on shared or team-centric leadership in place of, or in addition to, vertical leadership. While vertical leadership refers to an individual who singularly occupies leadership roles within the collective (Pearce & Sims, 2002), shared leadership has been defined as "a dynamic, interactive influence process among individuals in groups for which the objective is to lead one another to the achievement of group or organizational goals or both" (Pearce & Conger, 2003, p. 1). While such leadership can be defined as an emergent property of team processes (Day, Gronn, & Salas, 2004), its emergence is likely to be grounded in part in the personality composition of the team. However, there has been little or no research that examines personality composition and shared leadership. We ascribe this lack of research to the complexity of the relationship between compositional variables and shared leadership emergence, including varying patterns of personality traits team members can possess, varying ways teams can be composed with respect to personality, and how different configurations of personality composition within the team may affect different processes of shared leadership emergence and activity. Accordingly, a second purpose for this chapter is to (c) describe team members' personality attributes that are likely antecedents to the emergence of shared leadership. Thus, this chapter seeks to review and extend our knowledge of personality characteristics as predictors of both vertical and shared leadership emergence and effectiveness. We seek to stimulate research about the combination of personality traits of a formal leader that will facilitate shared leadership, as well as the personality traits of team members required to engage in shared leadership behaviors. Finally, we aim to extend research on team composition and shared leadership by offering practical suggestions for staffing teams in order to promote the emergence of shared leadership.

Personality and Leadership: A Brief Historical Introduction

Early studies of leadership focused on traits that distinguish leaders from nonleaders (Terman, 1904) and considered leadership as a stable, individual personality characteristic (Gibb, 1947). These studies tended to conflate personality with the larger set of leader traits. For example, while Mann's (1959) review was titled "A Review of the Relationship between *Personality* and Performance in Small Groups" (italics added), he included such attributes as intelligence, interpersonal sensitivity, and masculinity/femininity, the latter defined as "the extent to which an individual's interests or preferences resemble those common to his own or the opposite sex" (p. 243). As suggested by Zaccaro (2007; see also Zaccaro et al., 2004), the set of traits that pertain to leadership processes and outcomes is much broader than personality. For the purposes of this chapter, however, when discussing the "trait" approach, we will refer only to personality attributes.

Early studies of leadership focused primarily on identifying key individual differences including personality that distinguished leaders from nonleaders. Reviews of these studies found little consensus; for example, while Bird (1940) reported 79 traits, he noted that "only a few characteristics, namely, high intelligence, initiative, a sense of humor, and extraversion, are mentioned with sufficient frequency to indicate possible general traits of leadership" (p. 380). Of these, only extraversion would fit within the Big Five or lower-order personality attributes (Costa, 1994). From his review, Stogdill (1948) concluded that "the factors which have been found to be associated with leadership could probably all be classified under the general headings of *capacity, achievement, responsibility, participation,* and *status*" (p. 64). Of these, only "responsibility" included a subset of personality attributes that correspond to one of the Big Five or lower-order personality attributes. Mann (1959) found median correlations of .15, .15, and .20 for extraversion, adjustment (emotional stability), and dominance, respectively. These early reviews indicate that personality attributes were not strongly represented in the list of those traits that were significantly associated with leadership.

In recognition of the lack of consensus regarding the relationship between leader traits and outcomes, researchers studying leadership began to change their focus to the situational characteristics that determined leader behavior and effectiveness. The situational approach to studying leadership dominated the leadership literature into the 1980s, with limited emphasis being placed on the personality characteristics of the leader (Day & Zaccaro, 2007; Zaccaro, Gulick, & Khare, 2008; Zaccaro et al., 2004). In general, situational theories of leadership contend that leader effectiveness is dependent on situational characteristics such as the nature of the organization, the followers, or other contextual elements (Barling, Christie, & Hoption, 2011). One approach, Fiedler's (1967,

1971) contingency model, argued that leadership effectiveness was most likely when the leader's stable personality matched situational requirements. This model outlined eight situations based on leader–follower relations, performance goal clarity, and formal authority or power. Fiedler argued that leaders should be selected to match the situational demands and that optimal leadership would occur when the leader possessed the trait to match the situation. The trait he focused on reflected either a high task or a high social orientation. Thus, through this period of leader situationism, this model was about the only place leader personality mattered in the mainstream literature and only in response to situational factors.

Renewed interest in the relationship between personality and leadership effectiveness came in the 1980s (Barling et al., 2011; Bono & Judge, 2004; Day & Zaccaro, 2007; Judge et al., 2002; Zaccaro et al., 2004), fueled by the rise of more sophisticated statistical techniques and with the solidification of the Five-Factor Model (FFM) of personality as a predictor of job performance (Costa & McCrae, 1988; Digman & Inouye, 1986). These advancements enabled researchers to revisit this relationship. For example, after correcting earlier studies for possible statistical and methodological issues, Lord et al. (1986) meta-analysis found that masculinity, adjustment, and conservatism yielded stronger adjusted correlations with leadership perceptions in this study than in the Mann review. A subsequent meta-analysis by Judge et al. (2002) found medium-sized estimated corrected correlations with each of the Big Five personality variables. They also found a multiple correlation of .48 with leadership criteria. These two studies as well as other contributions (House, 1988; House & Howell, 1992; House, Spangler, & Woycke, 1991) suggested solid support for a significant role in personality explaining leadership.

A more recent meta-analysis, however, yielded lower corrected correlations than those reported by Judge et al. (2002; Hoffman et al., 2011). Table 34.1 indicates comparable correlations across four studies published over a 52-year time period. This comparison shows that the magnitude of observed correlations of personality and leadership has been highly variable and, in several cases, roughly the same as reported by Mann (1959). Indeed, the standard deviations around corrected correlations in recent meta-analyses, and their corresponding 80% credibility intervals (see Table 34.1), indicate

Table 34.1 Magnitude of Correlations Between Personality Characteristics and Leadership

Trait	*Mann (1959)*	*Lord, de Vader, and Alliger (1986)*	*Judge, Bono, Ilies, and Gerhart (2002)*	*Hoffman, Woehr, Maldagen-Youngjohn, and Lyons (2011)*
Dominance	.20	.17	.37; SD_p = .20; 80% CV = .11 to .63	.35; SD_p = .23; 80% CV = .06 to .64
Conscientiousness			.28; SD_p = .17; 80% CV = .06 to .51	.16; SD_p = .07; 80% CV = .08 to .24
Extraversion	.15	.15	.31; SD_p = .17; 80% CV = .09 to .53	.15; SD_p = .08; 80% CV = .05 to .25
Adjustment/ emotional stability[a]	.15	.21	.24; SD_p = .18; 80% CV = .01 to .47	.12; SD_p = .01; 80% CV = –.03 to .28
Flexibility[b]			.24; SD_p = .11; 80% CV = .09 to .38	.19; SD_p = .17; 80% CV = –.03 to .40

Notes:

[a] The sign for these corrected correlations and the 80% *CV* were reversed from those reported in Judge et al. (2002), as they were correlations with neuroticism.

[b] Equated with openness to experience.

considerable variation, suggesting significant differences in the situations in which a single personality attribute can have a higher versus lower influence on leadership. After the early pessimistic reviews, many textbooks of social and organizational psychology dismissed the validity of personality as a predictor of leadership (e.g., Baron & Byrne, 1987; Blum & Naylor, 1956; Ghiselli & Brown, 1955; Muchinsky, 1983; Secord & Backman, 1974); such denigrations mostly disappeared after the resurgence of trait-based approaches in the 1980s. However, the ambiguity in prior findings has prompted at least one recent textbook to conclude that "surprisingly few personality characteristics correlate strongly with leadership effectiveness, and the relationships that have been found tend to be modest" (Aronson, Wilson, & Akert, 2010, p. 273).

Even with stronger theoretical models and data analytic techniques, researchers have still tended to take a bivariate approach to studying the relationship between leader personality and effectiveness (Lord & Hall, 1992; Zaccaro, 2007; Zaccaro et al., 2008), resulting in limited advancement of our conceptual understanding. Further progress is more likely if leadership researchers apply more sophisticated conceptual frames to the relationship between personality and leadership.

The Emergence of More Sophisticated Models of Personality and Leadership

Zaccaro and colleagues (Zaccaro, 2012; Zaccaro et al., 2004; Zaccaro et al., 2013) have argued that research on individual differences, including personality, and leadership, should reflect more multivariate, multistage (process), and pattern/configural approaches to this relationship. In this section, we review their arguments and summarize recent studies that exemplify these approaches with leader personality attributes. Our intent is also to establish a basis for extending these approaches to models of personality and shared leadership.

Multivariate Models of Personality and Leadership

A multivariate approach to individual differences and leadership examines the summative and/or relative contributions of multiple personality variables (i.e., "within set" validity; Zaccaro et al., 2013, p. 28) or the relative contributions of both nonpersonality (e.g., intelligence) and personality attributes (i.e., "between set" validity; Zaccaro et al., 2013). This approach was also labeled by Foti and Hauenstein (2007, p. 347) as the "variable" approach. They noted, "the goal of the variable approach has been to find the individual difference variables with the strongest correlations with leadership emergence and effectiveness" (p. 347).

Of key concern is what variables are to be selected for inclusion in the set of multivariate predictors. Zaccaro et al. (2013, p. 28) argued that such selection should be guided by a "performance requirements" approach that uses the expected work and challenges of leadership to specify necessary attributes (e.g., Coffin, 1944; Jacobs & Jaques, 1987; Zaccaro, 2001). They summarized sets of cognitive (e.g., setting direction, planning), social (e.g., staffing, communication, motivating other, boundary spanning), and self-motivational (e.g., large work scale and scope, accepting and exerting power, handling stress) work requirements. They argued further that several personality characteristics (along with nonpersonality attributes) contributed to the effective accomplishment of each set of performance requirements. Thus, such attributes as openness to experience, emotional stability, tolerance for ambiguity, and consciousness were associated with cognitive leadership requirements; extraversion and agreeableness were associated with social performance requirements; and dominance and emotional stability were associated with self-motivational requirements.

Mumford et al. (2000) provided a similar approach to the selection of personality attributes related to leader effectiveness. They defined leadership in terms of complex problem solving within social and organizational domains, where leaders were required to generate and implement solutions to foster collective goal attainment. They argued that the complexity of organizational environments and the corresponding difficulty in problem solving suggests that leaders need to possess dispositions toward openness, dominance, and tolerance for ambiguity. The need for solution implementation in complex social domains suggested a requirement for leader personality attributes such as sociability, extraversion, and conscientiousness. Thus, the work by Mumford et al. focusing on leadership as problem solving is fully compatible to the performance requirements approach and leads to similar conclusions. The central point is that leadership cannot and should not be predicted by one or two personality attributes but rather a number of them conceptually derived from a model of leadership work.

Several studies have provided evidence for the argument that a summative combination of personality attributes explains significant variance in leadership processes and outcomes. The meta-analysis by Judge et al. (2002) reported multiple correlations of .53 with leader emergence and .39 with leader effectiveness—extraversion, conscientiousness, and openness to experience were the strongest personality predictors of leadership. Zhang and Arvey (2009) found that social potency (related to extraversion) and achievement (related to a facet of conscientiousness) each predicted unique variance in who did or did not occupy a leadership role at work. Personality attribute sets have also been linked to particular leadership styles, including transformational leadership (Bono & Judge, 2004; Judge & Bono, 2000) and ethical leadership (Kalshoven, Den Hartog, & De Hoogh, 2011; Walumbwa & Schaubroeck, 2009; Xu, Yu, & Shi, 2011). Judge and Bono (2000) found a multiple correlation of .40 between Big Five personality factors and transformational leadership. In a meta-analysis of this literature, Bono and Judge (2004) found a modest multiple correlation of .31 with transformational leadership. Zopiatis and Constani (2012) reported a stronger association with a sample of hotel managers, explaining 42% of the variance (i.e., a multiple correlation of .65) in transformational leadership with the FFM. Walumbwa and Schaubroeck (2009) found that agreeableness and conscientiousness explained unique variance in ethical leadership. Xu et al. (2011) also reported significant unique contributions to ethical leadership from agreeableness and conscientiousness, as well as from neuroticism (negative direction). Taken together, these studies support the use of multiple personality attributes in explaining leadership.

What about the relative contribution of personality versus nonpersonality variables to leadership? Several studies have shown that personality retains significant influences on leadership criteria even when included with other sets of nonpersonality predictors. Taggar, Hackett, and Saha (1999) found that conscientiousness, extraversion, and neuroticism (negatively) contributed uniquely beyond cognitive ability to the prediction of individual leadership scores within business student teams. In a meta-analysis of studies that examined leader traits and leader behaviors, DeRue et al. (2011) reported that Big Five personality factors explained significant variance beyond intelligence in leader effectiveness, group performance, follower job satisfaction, and satisfaction with the leader. Other studies have reported significant incremental variance in leadership criteria for one or more personality variables beyond intelligence and motivation to lead (Chan & Drasgow, 2001); intellect, dominance, and hope/fear of power (Harms, Roberts, & Wood, 2007); intelligence and emotional intelligence (Cavazotte, Moreno, & Hickmann, 2011); and sets of cognitive, social, and motivational attributes (Connelly et al., 2000).

Taken together, these studies show that (a) separate personality variables provide unique contributions to the prediction of leadership criteria, and (b) as a set, personality variables still explain significant unique variance in such criteria after controlling a variety of nonpersonality attributes. This body of research attests to the influence of personality on leadership. All of the studies described take a multivariate but additive or summative approach to the prediction of leadership and certainly reflect an improvement on prior bivariate approaches. However, a simple linear combinational approach will still obscure the possibility of discerning how traits relate to one another in the prediction of leadership (Foti & Hauenstein, 2007). Accordingly, recent studies have also explored multistage and pattern or trait profile approaches to leader personality.

Multi-Stage Models of Leader Attributes: Personality as a Distal Attribute

Traditional personality traits such as those incorporated in the FFM represent situationally invariant influences on leadership outcomes (James & Mazerolle, 2002; Michel & LeBreton, 2011). However, research has shown that effective leaders display considerable behavioral flexibility across different situations (Hooijberg, 1996; Zaccaro, Foti, & Kenny, 1991; Zaccaro, Gilbert, Thor, & Mumford, 1991), an observation that is inconsistent with invariant trait influences. Also, the relative immutability of such traits makes leadership development interventions impractical (Day & Zaccaro, 2007). Several researchers, however, argued that these more immutable traits serve as significant influences on the development of skills, knowledge, and abilities that are more sensitive to situational parameters and therefore promote leader flexibility and responsiveness across very different situations (Dinh & Lord, 2012; Mumford et al., 2000; Zaccaro et al., 2004).

Multistage models of leader attributes operate from the basic assumption that certain distal traits predict leadership either through more proximal attributes (e.g., Mumford et al., 2000; Zaccaro et al., 2004) or through direct influences on leadership processes and behaviors (e.g., DeRue et al., 2011; Dinh & Lord, 2012). Distal traits, including personality, influence the growth of these more proximal attributes and/or the display of certain leadership behaviors that, in turn, lead to leadership outcomes (Mumford et al., 2000; Zaccaro et al., 2004). Zaccaro (2007) noted that such distal attributes serve as "foundational or basic qualities that promote core effectiveness across more generic leadership situations" (p. 12).

Zaccaro et al. (2013) specified three types of multistage leader attribute models. The first suggests that the effects of personality on leadership outcomes are mediated by follower, team, and organizational processes. For example, Peterson, Smith, Martorana, and Owens (2003) examined the degree to which top management team (TMT) processes and emergent states mediated the effects of CEO personality on organizational outcomes. They found a canonical correlation of .81 between CEO personality attributes and dimensions of TMT processes/emergent states. Among multiple relationships, they reported associations of CEO conscientiousness with TMT concern for legalities, CEO emotional stability with TMT cohesion and TMT intellectual flexibility, CEO agreeableness with TMT cohesion and TMT decentralization of power, and CEO openness with TMT intellectual flexibility and risk taking. TMT states of flexibility, cohesion, and risk taking were in turn related to organizations' income growth. Nadkarni and Hermann (2010) found that all FFM dimensions of the CEO's personality were related to "the firm's ability to change direction quickly and to reconfigure strategically" (p. 1050), which, in turn, was related to firm performance. CEO emotional stability, extraversion, and openness to experience contributed positively to strategic flexibility, while conscientiousness reduced such adaptability (cf. Griffin & Hesketh, 2005; LePine, 2003). Interestingly, agreeableness displayed a nonlinear relationship with strategic flexibility, such that too little or too much agreeableness had a deleterious effect.

Both of these studies point to significant effects of CEO personality on collective processes and outcomes. An extension of the personality–collective process/emergent state model is one in which leader personality influences one set of team or organizational processes which, in turn, influence other types of processes. For example, some of the TMT team effects that accrued from CEO personality in Peterson et al.'s (2003) study, such as cohesion and intellectual flexibility, may promote the kind of strategic flexibility observed in Nadkarni and Hermann's (2010) study. These kinds of linkages will matter later in this chapter when we explore possible influences of leader personality, team member personality, and shared leadership processes on team and organizational outcomes.

A second type of multistage model noted by Zaccaro et al. (2013) specifies a link between leader traits and leadership behavior, which in turn predicts collective processes and outcomes. The meta-analysis by DeRue et al. (2011) examined whether different leader behavioral styles mediated the influences of intelligence and Big Five personality attributes on a range of outcomes, including leader effectiveness, group performance, follower job satisfaction, and follower satisfaction with the leader. They found that leader behaviors tended to mediate the effects of leader traits on leadership outcomes, with leader conscientiousness exhibiting the most consistent effects. Cavazotte, Moreno, and Hickmann (2011) also found that transformational leadership behavior mediated the effects of intelligence and conscientiousness on managerial performance evaluations in a sample of midlevel managers.

Looking more specifically at leader problem-solving behaviors, Colbert, Judge, Choi, and Wang (2012) examined whether an individual's processes of idea generation, idea integration, and process facilitation mediated the effects of his or her personality on leader emergence scores. They found self-ratings of openness to experience, and observer ratings of extraversion and openness to experience did indeed influence perceptions of leadership through their effects on these problem-solving processes. Walumbwa and Schaubroeck (2009) examined another leader behavioral style—ethical leadership—and found that such behavior partially mediated the effects of agreeableness and conscientiousness on follower perceptions of psychological safety and follower willingness to voice opinions and beliefs.

The third type of multistage model suggested by Zaccaro et al. (2013) is a more complex one, specifying that some leader attributes are precursors to other attributes that in turn influence leader behaviors and collective outcomes (e.g., Mumford et al., 2000; Zaccaro et al., 2004). The more distal attributes, containing leader personality among other attributes, are more invariant than the more proximal ones. For example, Connelly et al. (2000) found that leader problem-solving skills mediated the effects of leader personality and cognitive ability on leader achievement in Army officers. Ng, Ang, and Chan (2008) reported that the effects of leader extraversion, conscientiousness, and neuroticism influenced leader effectiveness through leadership self-efficacy or "the perceived capabilities of the individual to perform functions necessary to accomplish specific leadership roles effectively" (p. 734). They also found that two contextual elements, job demands and job autonomy, moderated the mediated effects of personality, such that they were stronger under conditions of lower job demands and higher job autonomy.

These two studies examined two-stage models of distal and proximal attributes. Other researchers have examined more than one mediating stage between personality and leadership outcomes. Chan and Drasgow (2001) examined the role of leadership self-efficacy as a mediator of the effects of the FFM on motivation to lead. They found that the effects of extraversion and conscientiousness on some dimensions of motivation to lead were partially mediated by leadership self-efficacy. One of these dimensions, affective motivation to lead, was in turn related to ratings of leadership potential. Thus, this study implies a three-stage model of leader personality attributes to a leadership outcome. Hendricks and Payne (2007) added another stage to this model, testing the effects of personality on goal orientation at Stage 1, learning goal orientation on leadership self-efficacy at Stage 2, leadership self-efficacy on two dimensions of motivation to lead at Stage 3, and motivation to lead on measures of leader effectiveness at Stage 4 (they also included some direct effects of performance goal orientation on motivation to lead but found no support for these relationships). They found some support for each of their proposed linkages. Van Iddekinge et al. (2009) also tested a four-stage model, with Big Five personality at Stage 1, motivation to lead and leadership experience at Stage 2, knowledge skills and abilities at Stage 3, and performance at Stage 4. They too found support for these mediating links.

These multistage, multivariate studies of leader personality provide a response to the call by Judge et al. (2002) for leadership researchers to examine how and why Big Five traits are related to leadership. Across the studies reviewed here, each of the Big Five personality attributes influenced leadership outcomes through one or more mediators. Table 34.2 provides a summary of these mediators. While

Table 34.2 Mechanisms Mediating the Effects of Personality on Leadership Outcomes

Trait	*Mediator*
Conscientiousness	• Team climate for legalisms (Peterson, Smith, Martorana, & Owens, 2003) • Adaptability; strategic flexibility (negative effect; Nadkarni & Hermann, 2010) • Leadership self-efficacy (Chan & Drasgow, 2001; Hendricks & Payne, 2007; Ng, Ang, & Chan, 2008) • Motivation to lead (Hendricks & Payne, 2007; Van Iddekinge, Ferris, & Heffner, 2009) • Leadership experiences (Van Iddekinge et al., 2009) • Leader knowledge, skills, and abilities (Van Iddekinge et al., 2009) • Leader learning goal orientation (Hendricks & Payne, 2007) • Ethical leadership (Walumbwa & Schaubroeck, 2009) • Psychological safety (Walumbwa & Schaubroeck, 2009) • Transformational leadership behaviors (Cavazotte, Moreno, & Hickmann, 2011; DeRue, Nahrgang, Wellman, & Humphrey, 2011) • Initiating structure leadership behaviors (DeRue et al., 2011) • Management by exemption behaviors (DeRue et al., 2011) • Contingent reward leadership behaviors (DeRue et al., 2011)
Agreeableness	• Team cohesion (Peterson et al., 2003) • Leadership self-efficacy (Chan & Drasgow, 2001; Hendricks & Payne, 2007) • Motivation to lead (Chan & Drasgow, 2001; Hendricks & Payne, 2007) • Ethical leadership (Walumbwa & Schaubroeck, 2009) • Psychological safety (Walumbwa & Schaubroeck, 2009) • Consideration leadership behaviors (DeRue et al., 2011) • Transformational leadership behaviors (DeRue et al., 2011)
Emotional stability/ neuroticism	• Motivation to lead (Chan & Drasgow, 2001; Hendricks & Payne, 2007; Van Iddekinge et al., 2009) • Leadership self-efficacy (Chan & Drasgow, 2001; Hendricks & Payne, 2007; Ng et al., 2008) • Leadership experiences (Van Iddekinge et al., 2009) • Leader knowledge, skills, and abilities (Van Iddekinge et al., 2009) • Leader prove goal orientation (Hendricks & Payne, 2007) • Leader avoid goal orientation (Hendricks & Payne, 2007) • Initiating structure leadership behaviors (DeRue et al., 2011) • Transformational leadership behaviors (DeRue et al., 2011) • Management by exemption behaviors (DeRue et al., 2011) • Contingent reward leadership behaviors (DeRue et al., 2011)
Openness to experience	• Motivation to lead (Chan & Drasgow, 2001) • Leadership self-efficacy (Chan & Drasgow, 2001) • Social judgment skills (Connelly et al., 2000) • Social construction skills (Connelly et al., 2000) • Problem-solving skills (Connelly et al., 2000) • Leader knowledge structure (Connelly et al., 2000) • Transformational leadership (Cavazotte et al., 2011; DeRue et al., 2011) • Initiating structure leadership behaviors (DeRue et al., 2011) • Management by exemption behaviors (DeRue et al., 2011) • Contingent reward leadership behaviors (DeRue et al., 2011)

(Continued)

Table 34.2 (Continued)

Trait	*Mediator*
Extraversion	• Leadership experiences (Van Iddekinge et al., 2009) • Motivation to lead (Chan & Drasgow, 2001; Hendricks & Payne, 2007; Van Iddekinge et al., 2009) • Leadership self-efficacy (Chan & Drasgow, 2001; Ng et al., 2008) • Leader knowledge, skills, and abilities (Van Iddekinge et al., 2009) • Leader avoid goal orientation (Hendricks & Payne, 2007) • Social judgment skills (Connelly et al., 2000) • Social construction skills (Connelly et al., 2000) • Problem-solving skills (Connelly et al., 2000) • Leader knowledge structure (Connelly et al., 2000) • Leader problem-solving knowledge (Connelly et al., 2000) • Transformational leadership behaviors (Cavazotte et al., 2011; DeRue et al., 2011) • Initiating structure leadership behaviors (DeRue et al., 2011)

the studies summarized here suggest significant advances since Judge et al.'s challenge, research on personality and leadership still remains fragmentary and disconnected. Recently, some researchers have called for more integrated examinations of leadership (Avolio, 2007; DeRue et al., 2011). While we see some improvement (e.g., Dinh & Lord, 2012), we would also echo these calls.

Pattern Approaches to Personality and Leadership

The multistage, multivariate approaches examined in the previous section still reflect mostly linear models of leader personality and outcomes. However, researchers have also called for examinations of more complex configurations of leader personality attributes (Foti & Hauenstein, 2007; Holmes, Sholley, & Walker, 1980; Smith & Foti, 1998; Zaccaro, 2007). Called the "pattern approach" by Foti and Hauenstein (2007, p. 347), this perspective entails defining specific combinations of trait and state-like attributes that leaders must have in order to be effective. For example, research has strongly supported the link between general intelligence and leadership (Judge et al., 2004; Lord et al., 1986). However, a person with high intelligence but no social skills is unlikely to be an effective leader (Moss, 1931; Zaccaro, Gilbert, et al., 1991). Likewise, someone high in both motivation to lead and dominance is not apt to succeed as a leader without also having sufficient levels of intelligence. Note that rather than focusing on additive combinations of leader attributes, this approach examines particular multiplicative combinations of such attributes. A similar approach is offered by Perry, Witt, Penney, and Atwater (2010) in their examination of follower personality configurations and leadership.

We noted earlier how the leader performance requirements approach suggests that sets of cognitive, social, motivational, and personality attributes were necessary for leader effectiveness. The pattern approach would suggest that high leadership performance would depend upon leaders possessing high levels of attributes from each of these sets; the exclusion of any particular set of variables would hinder the leader as much as exclusion of multiple or all sets of attributes. Several studies have provided evidence for such "between-attribute set" patterns (e.g., Foti, Bray, Thompson, & Allgood, 2012; Foti & Hauenstein, 2007; Mumford et al., 2000; O'Shea, Foti, Hauenstein, & Bycio, 2009; Smith & Foti, 1998).

Zaccaro et al. (2008) argued that pattern approaches to leader personality need to combine personality attributes that (a) predispose individuals toward seeking the leader role, (b) predispose individuals' ability to acquire stakeholder endorsement for leader role occupancy, and (c) predispose the development and employment of skills and competencies that foster leader effectiveness. For this chapter, we have expanded their notions into the models illustrated in Figures 34.1 and 34.2. Figure 34.1 shows

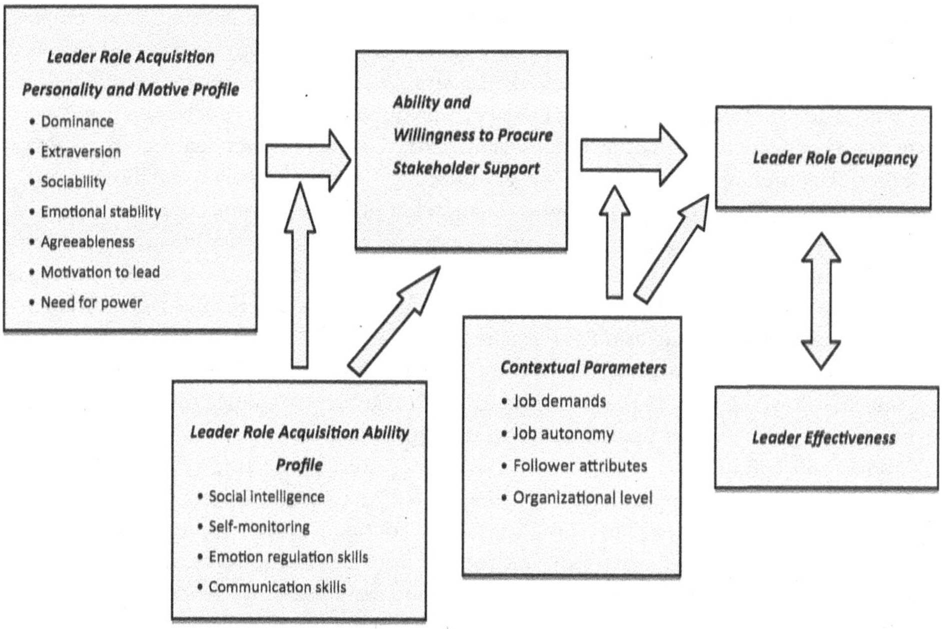

Figure 34.1 Personality Patterns Expected to Predict an Individual's Willingness and Success in Acquiring a Leader Role.

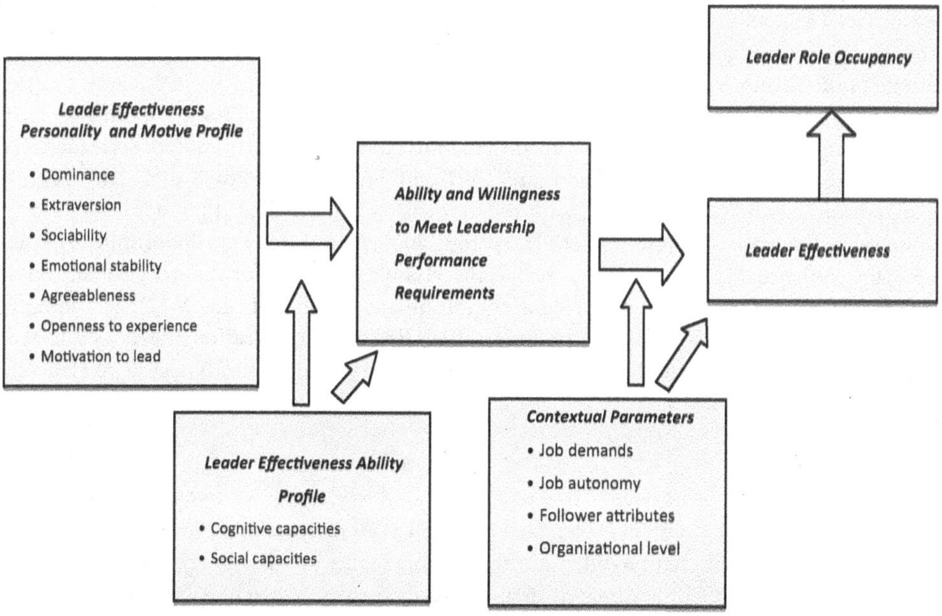

Figure 34.2 Personality Profile That Predisposes an Individual's Ability and Willingness to be Effective in the Leader Role.

the personality patterns that we expect to predict an individual's willingness and success in acquiring a leader role. Figure 34.2 shows the personality profile that predisposes an individual's ability and willingness to be effective in the leader role.

In each figure, the central point is that leader role-seeking and leader role accomplishment each derive from a constellation of personality traits that foster both motivation and ability to accomplish each outcome. For leader role-seeking, this pattern includes such traits as motivation to lead and need for power, which foster the willingness to seek the leader role (Arvey, Rotundo, Johnson, Zhang, & McGue, 2006). The pattern also contains attributes that predispose individuals toward greater social prominence and connectivity with others (dominance, extraversion, sociability, agreeableness, emotional stability). The premise of this pattern is that leader role-seeking is likely to be more strongly linked to high levels of all of these traits—low motivation but high social connectivity, or vice versa, would be insufficient to gain leader status. A similar premise exists for leader effectiveness, that a pattern of motivational and sociability predispositions should foster leader effectiveness. Openness is included here as well because of research showing its link to leadership effectiveness in situations requiring leader adaptability (Nadkarni & Hermann, 2010).

As described earlier in this chapter, there is some evidence linking all of the Big Five personality traits and their lower-order attributes to leadership. However, few studies have examined the efficacy of personality profiles in predicting leadership outcomes. One such study, by Hirschfeld, Jordan, Thomas, and Feild (2008), argued that personality patterns reflecting certain conjunctive combinations of attributes were likely to be more related to leader emergence and leadership potential than other combinations. They noted that, ". . . confidence/assertiveness, self-discipline, and self-control *together* represent a common image of an individual who has attributes conducive to advancing team success and emerging as a leader among teammates" (p. 389, emphasis added). In support, they found that a personality profile of high extraversion, high conscientiousness, and high emotional stability in military team leaders was associated with team cohesion and proactivity, which, in turn, were related to higher leadership potential. They also found that leader agreeableness was positively associated with team cohesion, and openness was similarly associated with proactivity. Thus, while not implicated in their leader personality profile, these other personality traits also influenced leadership outcomes. Hirschfeld et al. did not include any motivational orientations in their study.

Figures 34.1 and 34.2 also capture the premise that personality profiles are insufficient to explain leadership outcomes. Leaders also need the ability and capacity to acquire the leadership role and perform it well. Accordingly, in Figures 34.1 and 34.2, we combined social and cognitive capacities into an ability profile that, with the personality profile, should predict leadership, a premise supported in prior research (Foti & Hauenstein, 2007; Mumford et al., 2000; Smith & Foti, 1998). Finally, contextual influences may change the relative influence of different leader attributes on leader role-seeking and leader role accomplishment (Dinh & Lord, 2012); accordingly, we included job demands, job autonomy, follower attributes, and organizational level as selected examples of such moderating parameters (Ng et al., 2008; Perry et al., 2010; Richards & Hackett, 2012; Zaccaro, 2001).

Summary

While personality was viewed with considerable pessimism as a predictor of leadership in early trait research, more recent research has provided greater support for its validity. As little is to be gained when looking only at individual personality attributes as predictors, researchers have demonstrated success by exploring more complex models of personality and leadership. Thus, we have witnessed the emergence of multivariate, multistage, and pattern or profile models of leader personality and leadership outcomes, with supporting empirical evidence.

All of the studies described above have focused on the emergence and/or success of individual leaders in vertical arrangements with subordinates and followers. These leader-centered approaches have been complemented recently in the leadership literature with more team-centered approaches (Day et al., 2004; Friedrich, Vessey, Schuelke, Ruark, & Mumford, 2009; Gibb, 1954; Hiller, Day, & Vance, 2006; Wolf, Wassenaar, Unterrainer, & Piecha, 2010), in which the leader role is shared among team members, and leadership emerges from the interactions of the team (Boies, Lvina, & Martens, 2010; Gockel & Werth, 2010; Hoch, Pearce, & Welzel, 2010). In team-centered approaches to leadership, personality can still plays an important, albeit different, role in fostering effective leadership. In the remainder of this chapter, we explore this role from two perspectives—from the viewpoint of the external leader who is responsible for shaping and fostering the emergence of shared leadership within the team (Morgeson, DeRue, & Karam, 2010; Zaccaro, Heinen, & Shuffler, 2009) and from the viewpoint of team members who share in leadership responsibilities (Barry & Stewart, 1997; Humphrey, Hollenbeck, Meyer, & Ilgen, 2007; Morgeson, Reider, & Campion, 2005).

In this examination, we will apply the summative, multistage, and pattern models described earlier in this chapter. The linear or summative approach, which has informed our understanding about the role of multiple personality variables in predicting leadership, can serve as a foundation for considering how these individual difference variables may be important for the composition of team members that will lead to shared leadership. For example, multiple team members may need to possess the personality traits that will enable them to engage in leadership on a team, as well as the traits that predispose them to share leadership responsibilities with other team members. Thus, studies of personality and shared leadership would need to consider multiple variables possessed within and across members to explain greater variance in the emergence of shared leadership on teams (for additional coverage of personality and teams, see Chapter 33, this volume). Likewise, in order to extend multistage models to shared leadership, researchers need to determine the distal and proximal personality predictors of team members that will lead to the type of internal team environment which, in turn, will lead to shared leadership emergence. For example, Carson, Tesluk, and Marrone (2007) found that a team environment that encouraged shared purpose, social support, and voice predicted the emergence of shared leadership. This finding raises the question of what personality attributes within and across team members are likely to foster such team climates. Finally, pattern approaches that predict shared leadership can reflect unique configurations of attributes within team members, as well as unique configurations operating across members, residing in the composition of the team as a whole.

Leadership as an Emergent Property of a Group

Some Background on Shared Leadership

During the last half-century, while the prevailing research paradigms of leadership have focused on the individual leader, some note was made of leadership as something to be shared among group members. Gibb (1954) provided one of the first explanations of what it means for group members to share leadership responsibilities, stating "leadership is probably best conceived as a group quality, as a set of functions which must be carried out by the group. This concept of 'distributed leadership' is an important one" (p. 884). Since then, the research on distributed or shared leadership proceeded in a rather haphazard and disjointed manner, although more complex conceptualizations of such leadership have recently begun to emerge. Indeed, Pearce and Conger (2003) recognized 10 different conceptual frameworks offered between 1970 and 2000 to build the research foundation needed to study shared leadership in a more systematic manner.

Although shared leadership has been experiencing a recent surge in research interest, leadership as an emergent group property has been considered using other names for several decades. For example,

Vroom and Yetton's (1973) participative decision-making model specified a process whereby vertical leaders chose the appropriate level of follower involvement in leader decision making. When such leaders use a participative decision-making style, they are encouraging their subordinates to share in leadership responsibilities. Similarly, research during the 1990s on self-managing work teams examined the times at which team members can and do take on the leadership responsibilities of their team (Stewart & Manz, 1995), as well as what type of external leadership a self-managing work team needs (Morgeson, 2005). Shared leadership can emerge in cross-functional teams, as members of such teams likely possess different knowledge about a shared project. Depending on the nature of the task, different group members may be best suited for different leadership tasks from both a skill and a personality perspective (Pearce & Conger, 2003), and accordingly, the leadership role may rotate from member to member (Carson et al., 2007; Erez, Lepine, & Elms, 2002; Friedrich et al., 2009).

Some research has positioned shared leadership against forms of vertical leadership, where a single individual assumes most, if not all, of the responsibilities for leadership (Conger & Pearce, 2003; Zaccaro et al., 2009). However, other researchers have argued that collective leadership more likely emerges from the influences of external leaders (Kozlowski, Gully, Salas, & Cannon-Bowers, 1996; Manz & Sims, 1987; Morgeson et al., 2010; Zaccaro et al., 2009). For example, Morgeson et al. (2010) used a functional leadership perspective to create a taxonomy of leadership behaviors categorized by the type of leader in the best position to engage in the behavior. Morgeson et al. recognized that internal and external leaders have different perspectives and are best suited to provide different types of team leadership. While internal and external leaders were similarly positioned to engage in many leadership behaviors (e.g., define the mission, provide feedback), Morgeson et al. argue that a formal external leader is the primary leader type that can successfully encourage team self-management.

For the purposes of this chapter, and for considering the role of personality as a driver of leadership, we focus on two questions: (a) what personality attributes might support the role of an external leader in fostering shared leadership? and (b) what compositional properties of the team might promote the emergence of collective leadership within the team? Earlier in this chapter, we argued that the specification of personality predictors of leadership should derive from the leader's performance requirements. That raises the question: what are the performance requirements posed by an external leader fostering emergent collective leadership?

Performance Requirements for External Leaders of Team-Centered Leadership

Studies of individual leadership have shown that leader role occupancy and effectiveness were more likely when individuals possess leadership self-efficacy. Such efficacy, defined as "a specific form of efficacy associated with the level of confidence in the knowledge, skills, and abilities associated with leading others" (Hannah, Avolio, Luthans, & Harms, 2008, p. 669), increases one's motivation to lead and overall leadership potential and effectiveness (Chan & Drasgow, 2001; Hendricks & Payne, 2007). This suggests that shared leadership is likely to emerge when the team as a whole has a strong degree of team-level leadership efficacy, creating a collective sense of empowerment in the team. Empowerment refers to

> a multidimensional construct consisting of (a) *impact* (i.e., degree to which employees feel their work affects their organization), (b) *competence* (i.e., perceived ability to accomplish work-related tasks), (c) *meaningfulness* (i.e., intrinsic caring about work tasks), and (d) *choice* (i.e., perceived self-determination or autonomy at work).
>
> *Chen, Kirkman, Kanfer, Allen, & Rosen, 2007, p. 332; See also Kirkman & Rosen, 1997, 1999; Thomas & Velthouse, 1990*

Such empowerment increases the likelihood that team members will be proactive in seeking out and taking on leadership responsibilities (Kirkman & Rosen, 1999; Spreitzer, 1995).

The increased taking on of leadership responsibilities is also likely to raise the sense of felt risk by team members, especially when they are just becoming familiar with the nature of shared leadership. Accordingly, such leadership is also fostered by an emergent state of psychological safety. Edmondson (1999) defined psychological safety as "a shared belief that the team is safe for interpersonal risk taking" (p. 354). She hypothesized and found that psychological safety predicted team learning in field teams because it alleviated team members' concerns about interpersonal embarrassment or other consequences of making mistakes. In a psychologically safe environment, team members can risk leadership actions and bring up mistakes without fear of being belittled or suffering embarrassment. This enables the entire team to learn from the past mistakes of a single team member and fostering mutual trust in the team.

A primary performance requirement of external leadership, at least with respect to fostering shared leadership, then, is to shape and facilitate the emergence of at least two individual states—leadership self-efficacy and personal empowerment—and three collective states—collective leadership efficacy, team empowerment, and psychological safety. A number of conceptual models, with supporting empirical research, have described how external leaders can influence the development of these states. Zaccaro et al. (2009) and Morgeson et al. (2010) included, in their classifications of leadership, behavior such as coaching the team to engage in leadership and supporting attempts at team self-management. Hackman and Wageman (2005) also offered a model of team coaching, which they defined as "direct interaction with a team intended to help members make coordinated and task-appropriate use of their collective resources in accomplishing the team's work" (p. 269) and articulated three types of team coaching—motivational, consultative, and educational. To this mix, Zaccaro et al. (2009) added "leadership coaching" which entailed external leaders helping team members learn and engage in specific leadership functions, including direction setting, boundary spanning, and aligning team goals with environmental dynamics. Finally, models of transformational leadership and leader–member exchange (LMX) quality point to the importance of a leader's individualized consideration behaviors in fostering individual empowerment. Such effects can easily be extended to the team level.

A number of empirical studies have confirmed the effects of these leadership behaviors on team empowerment and shared leadership. For example, Manz and Sims (1987) found that higher levels of team self-management occurred when external leaders encouraged team self-evaluation and reinforcement. Kirkman and Rosen (1999) found that when external leaders engaged in such behaviors as delegating responsibility to the team, soliciting advice from the team, and encouraging team goal setting, teams displayed more collective empowerment and subsequently higher productivity. Edmondson (1999) reported a direct link between team leader coaching behaviors and felt psychological safety. Carson et al. (2007) also found that a team's external leader engagement in supportive coaching behaviors facilitated shared leadership in student project teams. Chen et al. (2007) reported that a leader's display of supportive behaviors and granting of more decision autonomy resulted in higher levels of team empowerment. The results from these studies suggest that the external leader can play a pivotal role in developing a team climate conducive to the emergence of shared leadership.

In a study of self-managing field teams across three organizations, Morgeson (2005) found that members of self-managing teams rated their external team leader as more effective when the leader engaged in supportive coaching behaviors as required by the team. Burke, Stagl, Klein, et al. (2006) conducted a meta-analysis looking at person and task focused team leader behaviors and found that, while both types of leadership behaviors influenced team learning, productivity, and effectiveness, person-oriented leader behaviors had a greater effect than task-oriented leadership behaviors. Relevant to the current discussion, empowerment-oriented leader behaviors accounted for almost 30% of the variance in team learning, a precursor to developing team leadership capacity (Day et al., 2004). Burke et al.'s use of empowerment behaviors included any type of leader behavior that serves to develop team members so that they are capable of self-management. Specifically, they considered team coaching (e.g., Edmondson, 1999; Hackman & Wageman, 2005), monitoring, and feedback (Salas, Sims, & Burke, 2005). Taken together, these studies indicate that leadership behaviors of individualized consideration and team coaching are likely to foster the kinds of team emergent states that support shared leadership. Accordingly, those leader personality attributes that predispose such behaviors should act as distal predictors of shared leadership.

Personality and External Leaders of Team-Centered Leadership

Earlier in this chapter, we made two points about leader personality attributes: (a) leadership is likely to be predicted by more than one set of attributes and (b) leader attributes can be arranged in terms of a multistage model of influence. Figure 34.3 illustrates both of these points as pertaining to external leaders and shared leadership. Shared leadership in teams derives from individual- and team-level states of leadership efficacy, empowerment, and psychological safety. These states, in turn, are driven by leadership behaviors of individualized consideration and team coaching.

The literature is scant in terms of the leader personality attributes that foster effective individual support and team coaching behaviors. However, transformational leadership closely reflects those kinds of behaviors, particularly its subdimension of individualized consideration. Accordingly, studies on personality and such leadership might shed some light on the desired attributes of external leaders. We would argue that leaders can better display individualized consideration when they have a sense of security about themselves and a degree of emotional stability. Allowing greater autonomy in subordinate decision making can pose greater risk to the leader, and being resilient and secure about that risk would encourage such leader behavior. Accordingly, several studies, including two meta-analyses, have reported a negative association between leader neuroticism and transformational leadership (Balthazard, Waldman, & Warren, 2009; Bono & Judge, 2004; DeRue et al., 2011; Popper, Mayseless, & Castelnovo, 2000).

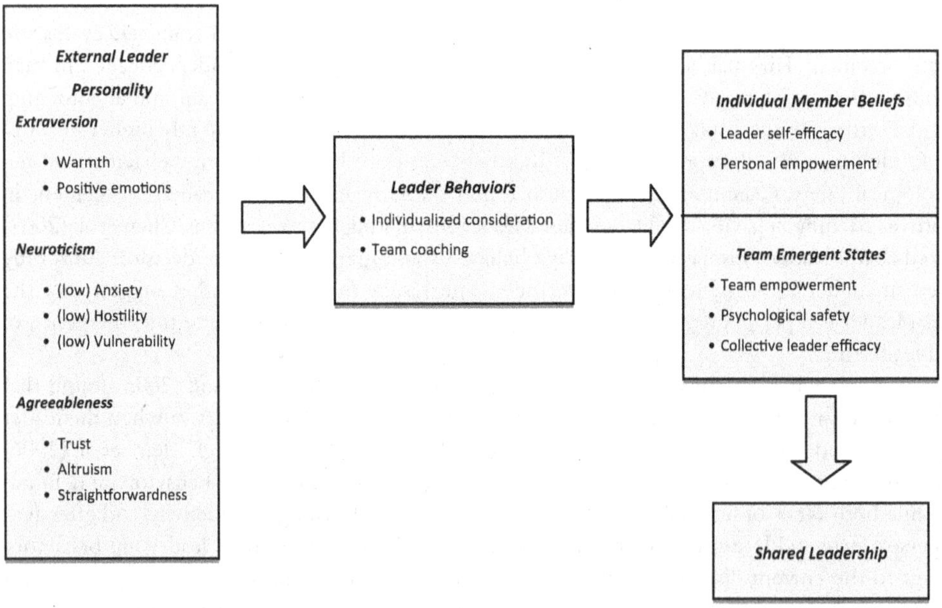

Figure 34.3 External Leader Personality Profile That Facilitates Shared Leadership Emergence.

Providing coaching and support to others is likely to come easier from a leader who (a) is predisposed toward sociability, deriving energy from interactions with others, and (b) possesses a trusting and nurturing orientation. Accordingly, we would expect that external leaders who are "agreeable extraverts" are more likely to display individualized consideration and coaching than "disagreeable introverts." Several studies have reported significant associations between agreeableness and extraversion, respectively, and transformational leadership (Balthazard et al., 2009; DeRue et al., 2011; Zopiaris & Constani, 2012). Two studies also linked these two personality orientations to the individualized consideration component of transformational leadership (DeRue et al., 2011; Judge & Bono, 2000). Other studies have reported significant associations between leader agreeableness and subordinate's reported quality of LMXs, which also reflect leader support and autonomy for the subordinate (Bernerth, Armenakis, Feild, Giles, & Hunter, 2007; Sears & Hackett, 2011). Indeed, Bernerth et al. found that, of the Big Five personality factors, only leader agreeableness was significantly related to LMX (of the remaining factors, only conscientiousness had a marginal effect).

Taken together, these studies support the hypotheses that external leaders' levels of emotional stability, agreeableness, and extraversion should promote the display of leader behaviors fostering the development of shared leadership. We do want to add, however, several key issues at this point. First, in their meta-analysis, Bono and Judge (2004), while reporting significant associations between these three personality factors and transformational leadership, asserted that, while extraversion exhibited a relatively stronger correlation with leadership, the correlations of agreeableness and emotional stability were more modest. They noted that "whereas a broad personality taxonomy, such as the Big Five, can be a useful framework for cumulating research results, it appears that more narrow or specific traits may be relevant in predicting and understanding transformational and transactional leadership" (p. 908). We suspect that certain subdimensions of each personality attribute (see Costa, 1994, for these dimensions; see Chapter 2, this volume, for more on personality trait taxonomies) are likely to be more strongly related to supportive external leadership than others. For example, the neuroticism dimension includes three factors—anxiety, hostility, and vulnerability—that will likely impair an external leader's ability to display consideration and supportive coaching behaviors, more so than other neuroticism subfacets such as depression, self-consciousness, and impulsiveness. For extraversion, we suggest that the warmth and positive emotions subdimensions are likely to be the most efficacious in supporting such behaviors. Finally, we believe external leader consideration and coaching are also likely to be most influenced by the agreeableness dimensions of trust, altruism, and straightforwardness. Accordingly, the multistage model in Figure 34.3 includes these subdimensions as distal predictors of shared leadership through external leader behavior.

Our second note of caution pertains to the attribute pattern arguments we raised earlier in this chapter. Effective leadership does not derive only from a linear combination of multiple attributes; several personality variables in unique configurations with other nonpersonality attributes will be necessary for such leadership. We would suggest the same for the external leadership of teams that are developing shared leadership. Essentially, the emotionally stable, agreeable extravert represents the pattern most likely to support such leadership; these traits alone may not be sufficient to promote shared leadership, akin to personality's role, noted above, in fostering individual leader role occupancy and leadership effectiveness (Zaccaro et al., 2004; Zaccaro et al., 2013).

Personality and Team-Centered Leadership

Our discussion of personality and shared leadership to this point has focused on the external leader of the team who is developing such an emergent state. Once the external leader has established a favorable climate for shared leadership, team members will be in a better position to emerge as leaders. However, in order for shared leadership to emerge, team members also need to be (a) motivated and capable of engaging in individual leadership behaviors and (b) motivated and capable of working with others in collective acts of leadership. Thus, team members need to have not only the requisite pattern of traits to emerge as leaders, but also those personality (and nonpersonality) attributes that foster a willingness to recognize and share leadership responsibilities with other members. Leadership has been recognized as a "claiming and granting" process by which a leader claims leadership and followers grant that individual the recognition of leadership (DeRue & Ashford, 2010, p. 268; Foti, Knee, & Backert, 2008). In a shared leadership situation, team members are engaging in both the granting and claiming of leadership behaviors either simultaneously or reciprocally across different leadership functions. The question becomes what personality composition of the group might contribute to these processes (for more coverage on this issue, refer to Chapter 33, this volume).

To answer this question, we suggest two distinct conceptual directions. First, because shared leadership entails entitativity (Campbell, 1958) around leadership interactions, personality factors that promote teamwork should promote shared leadership. Second, because shared leadership derives from collective leadership capacity, it should also thrive from personality configurations within the team that foster such capacity. Several studies have promoted insight into how the personality composition of the team influences teamwork. For example, in a study of team composition on manufacturing teams, Morgeson et al. (2005) found that team member social skills, extraversion, agreeableness, conscientiousness, emotional stability, and teamwork knowledge were all related to teamwork performance. Quantitative reviews have also revealed significant associations between team personality configurations and team performance across a variety of situations (e.g., Mount, Barrick, & Stewart, 1998; Stewart, 2006). Mount et al. found that emotional stability and agreeableness were associated with team performance, with agreeableness exhibiting the highest relationship of all Big Five personality dimensions.

Supporting this finding, two other meta-analyses again found that agreeableness was positively related to performance, but also reported that variability in agreeableness on a team negatively predicted performance (Peeters, Van Tuijl, Rutte, and Reymen, 2006) and that both minimum and mean levels of agreeableness predicted performance (Bell, 2007). Both meta-analyses also showed that team conscientiousness demonstrated a significant relationship with effective teamwork (Neuman & Wright, 1999). Again, variability in this personality attribute across teammates was found to be negatively associated with the quality of teamwork.

These findings suggest that at least a minimum level of agreeableness and conscientiousness must be present in all team members to have a functioning team, and that to have a few, or perhaps even one, team member low in either attribute can be detrimental to team functioning. Agreeableness promotes a climate of cooperation and collaboration, while conscientiousness fosters a greater sense of responsibility and achievement (Judge et al., 2002; Morgeson et al., 2005); the link between high levels of these attributes across teammates and subsequent team functioning is not surprising.

These personality attributes are presumed to promote teamwork aspects of shared leadership. The attributes that predispose teammates to the leadership aspects of shared leadership likely include a motivational predisposition to dominance and assertiveness in social situations. This suggests that team extraversion, which includes assertiveness as a subfacet (Costa, 1994), should contribute to shared leadership. However, a team consisting of all highly assertive, dominant personalities is not likely to be successful—team members are likely to engage in leader role occupancy battles (cf. Kozlowski, & Ilgen, 2006). We would argue, then, that such personality configurations need to be tempered by other personality attributes fostering willingness to share dominance. Accordingly, we would include agreeableness and psychological collectivism in a compositional profile that would support shared leadership. We have already noted how some facets of agreeableness would foster teamwork. The same predisposition toward cooperation would mitigate tendencies for an individual to assert the leadership role exclusively for himself or herself.

Collectivism refers to the extent to which an individual prefers to work in a team environment. Eby and Dobbins (1997) found that the relationship between collective orientation and team performance was mediated by the quality and degree of cooperation team members perceived in their interaction. High levels of collectivism in a team mean that group members are likely to have the propensity for, as well as an interest in, working together as teammates. This motivation and desire to work together can lead to the development of a strong affective climate in the team, laying the foundation for shared leadership to emerge (Carson et al., 2007), especially when combined with higher levels of extraversion, dominance, and motivation to lead.

We have summarized our suppositions in Figure 34.4 in a multistage model of how team personality composition may influence the emergence of shared leadership through an (a) enhanced capacity for teamwork and (b) enhanced capacity for and orientation toward collective leadership. We assert the proposed personality attributes need to be possessed by all team members at a minimum level; thus, we suggest a pattern or profile of these personality traits within each team member is necessary to contribute to shared leadership.

An interesting question, though, is whether team members can compensate for each other on particular personality attributes. Researchers have described such models of composition as reflecting complementary fit (Cable & Edwards, 2004; Humphrey et al., 2007; Muchinsky & Monahan, 1987). This would suggest models in which members possess different attributes, but together, as a gestalt, they produce the basis for shared leadership. Such compilational models (Kozlowski & Klein, 2000) would be quite complex and may be shaped by the type of shared leadership occurring in the team (i.e., rotated, distributed, or simultaneous; Zaccaro & DeChurch, 2012). However, certain team situations, such as those requiring innovation and adaptation, may demand different configurations of member personalities. LePine (2003; see also Griffin & Hesketh, 2005) reported that some aspects of conscientiousness can hurt adaptability. However, research has shown that conscientiousness does help teamwork (Bell, 2007; Mount et al., 1998). Alternatively, teams whose members exhibit high openness to experience are likely to be more adaptable (Burke, Stagl, Salas, et al., 2006; LePine, Colquitt, & Erez, 2000) but may lack the discipline to reach closure on their work. Thus, in situations where shared leadership is directed toward finding innovative or adaptive solutions to team problems, the most appropriate mix of personality characteristics on the team may include some individuals high in conscientiousness, others high in openness to experience, and everyone high in agreeableness and psychological collectivism. There is little research that has examined personality composition and shared leadership and therefore even fewer studies that take a complementary fit approach to such composition and leadership. This area remains a potentially intriguing and exciting one for future research.

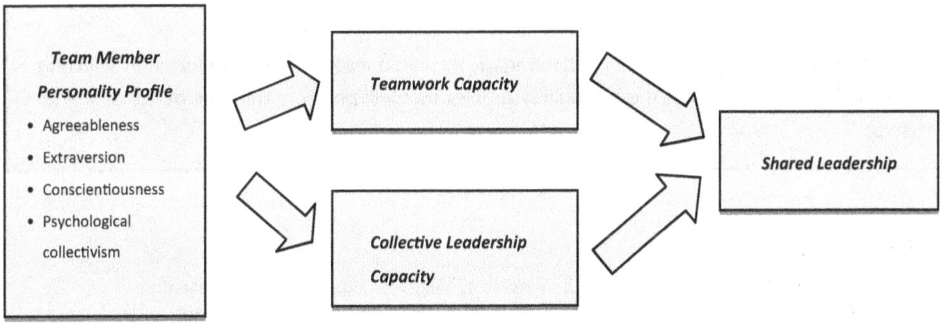

Figure 34.4 Team Member Personal Profile That Facilitates Shared Leadership Emergence.

Conclusion

This chapter had two main purposes: (a) to review multivariate, multistage, and pattern approaches to personality and leadership, and (b) to extend these approaches to understanding personality and shared leadership. Early in its history, the research supporting personality as a driver of leadership was considered rather weak. More recent studies have demonstrated that personality does contribute to leader emergence, leader role occupancy, and leader effectiveness. We summarized research on personality and leadership emphasizing multivariate studies and used this literature to derive and suggest several models of personality and shared leadership. We note that, while we think personality belongs in the mix of attributes that predict leadership, other sets of variables carry equal and perhaps greater weight. Individual leadership is a complex phenomenon, and shared leadership more so. Understanding how personal attributes predict such phenomena will require similar complexity in our explanatory models. This chapter provides what we hope are some starting, or continuing, points in the development of such models.

Practitioner's Window

More research is needed to determine how to select team members who will be willing and able to share in leadership responsibilities. However, there are some practical takeaways from the shared leadership literature that can be applied to the workplace.

- Personality traits are important predictors of leader emergence and effectiveness. Personality traits may also determine the ability of team members to establish shared leadership.
- The personality profile of team members determines their capacity for teamwork and shared leadership. Combining the personality profiles on a team will determine how likely shared leadership is to emerge. Team members need to be (a) motivated and capable of engaging in individual leadership behaviors and (b) motivated and capable of working with team members to engage in collective leadership acts.
- Team members should have a minimum level of agreeableness and conscientiousness as well as a high level of collectivism to be willing and capable of engaging in collective leadership acts.
- External team leaders also play an important role in facilitating shared leadership on a team. Transformational leadership behaviors and coaching by an external leader can empower team members to take on leadership responsibilities.
- External team leaders high in emotional stability, agreeableness, and extraversion are likely to have the personality profile to promote the development of shared leadership by their team members.

Practitioners interested in creating teams that engage in shared leadership should focus on selecting team leaders and members with the personality profiles that will promote the emergence of shared leadership.

References

Aronson, E., Wilson, T. D., & Akert, R. M. (2010). *Social psychology* (7th ed.). New York: Pearson.
Arvey, R. D., Rotundo, M., Johnson, W., Zhang, Z., & McGue, M. (2006). The determinants of leadership role occupancy: Genetic and personality factors. *Leadership Quarterly, 17*, 1–20.

Avolio, B. J. (2007). Promoting more integrative strategies for leadership theory-building. *American Psychologist, 62,* 25–33.

Balthazard, P. A., Waldman, D. A., & Warren, J. E. (2009). Predictors of the emergence of transformational leadership in virtual decision teams. *Leadership Quarterly, 20,* 651–663.

Barling, J., Christie, A., & Hoption, A. (2011). Leadership. In S. Zedeck (Ed.), *APA handbook of industrial and organizational psychology: Building and developing the organization* (Vol. 1, pp. 183–240). Washington, DC: American Psychological Association.

Baron, R. A., & Byrne, D. (1987). *Social psychology: Understanding human interaction* (5th ed.). Needham Heights, MA: Allyn & Bacon.

Barry, B., & Stewart, G. L. (1997). Composition, process, and performance in self-managed groups: The role of personality. *Journal of Applied Psychology, 82,* 62–78.

Bass, B. M. (1990). *Bass & Stogdill's handbook of leadership: Theory, research and managerial applications* (3rd ed.). New York: Free Press.

Bass, B. M. (2008). *The Bass handbook of leadership: Theory, research, and managerial applications* (4th ed.). New York: Free Press.

Bell, S. T. (2007). Deep-level composition variables as predictors of team performance: A meta-analysis. *Journal of Applied Psychology, 92,* 595–615.

Bernerth, J. B., Armenakis, A. A., Field, H. S., Giles, W. F., & Walker, H. J. (2007). Leader–Member Social Exchange (LMSX): Development and validation of a scale. *Journal of Organizational Behavior, 28,* 979–1003.

Bird, C. (1940). *Social psychology.* New York: Appleton-Century.

Blum, M. L., & Naylor, J. C. (1956). *Industrial psychology: Its theoretical and social foundations.* New York: Harper & Row.

Boies, K., Lvina, E., & Martens, M. L. (2010). Shared leadership and team performance in a business strategy simulation. *Journal of Personnel Psychology, 9,* 195–202.

Bono, J. E., & Judge, T. A. (2004). Personality and transformational and transactional leadership: A meta-analysis. *Journal of Applied Psychology, 89,* 901–910.

Burke, C. S., Stagl, K. C., Klein, C., Goodwin, G. F., Salas, E., & Halpin, S. M. (2006). What type of leadership behaviors are functional in teams? A meta-analysis. *Leadership Quarterly, 17,* 288–307.

Burke, C. S., Stagl, K. C., Salas, E., Pierce, L., & Kendall, D. (2006). Understanding team adaptation: A conceptual analysis and model. *Journal of Applied Psychology, 91,* 1189–1207.

Cable, D. M., & Edwards, J. R. (2004). Complementary and supplementary fit: A theoretical and empirical integration. *Journal of Applied Psychology, 89,* 822–834.

Campbell, D. T. (1958). Common fate, similarity, and other indices of the status of aggregates of persons as social entities. *Behavioural Sciences, 3,* 14–25.

Carson, J. B., Tesluk, P. E., & Marrone, J. A. (2007). Shared leadership in teams: An investigation of antecedent conditions and performance. *Academy of Management Journal, 50,* 1217–1234.

Cavazotte, F., Moreno, V., & Hickmann, M. (2011). Effects of leader intelligence, personality and emotional intelligence on transformational leadership and managerial performance. *Leadership Quarterly, 23,* 1–13.

Chan, K., & Drasgow, F. (2001). Toward a theory of individual differences and leadership: Understanding the motivation to lead. *Journal of Applied Psychology, 86,* 481–498.

Chen, G., Kirkman, B. L., Kanfer, R., Allen, D., & Rosen, B. (2007). A multilevel study of leadership, empowerment, and performance in teams. *Journal of Applied Psychology, 92,* 331–346.

Coffin, T. E. (1944). A three-component theory of leadership. *Journal of Abnormal and Social Psychology, 39,* 63–83.

Colbert, A. E., Judge, T. A., Choi, D., & Wang, G. (2012). Assessing the trait theory of leadership using self and observer ratings of personality: The mediating role of contributions to group success. *Leadership Quarterly, 23,* 670–685.

Conger, J. A., & Pearce, C. L. (2003). A landscape of opportunities: Future research in shared leadership. In C. L. Pearce & J. A. Conger (Eds.), *Shared leadership* (pp. 285–303). Thousand Oaks, CA: Sage.

Connelly, M. S., Gilbert, J. A., Zaccaro, S. J., Threlfall, K. V., Marks, M. A., & Mumford, M. D. (2000). Cognitive and temperament predictors of organizational leadership. *Leadership Quarterly, 11,* 65–86.

Costa, P. T., Jr. (1994). Can the SASB bridge personality theory and clinical psychology? A view from the O, C, E, A, N. *Psychological Inquiry, 5,* 319–322.

Costa, P. T., Jr., & McCrae, R. R. (1988). From catalog to classification: Murray's needs and the five-factor model. *Journal of Personality and Social Psychology, 55,* 258–265.

Day, D. V., Gronn, P., & Salas, E. (2004). Leadership capacity in teams. *Leadership Quarterly, 15,* 857–880.

Day, D. V., & Zaccaro, S. J. (2007). Leadership: A critical historical analysis of the influence of leader trait. In L. L. Koppes (Ed.), *The history of industrial-organizational psychology: The first 100 years* (pp. 383–405). Mahwah, NJ: Erlbaum.

DeRue, D. S., & Ashford, S. J. (2010). Who will lead and who will follow? A social process of leadership identity construction in organizations. *Academy of Management Review, 35*, 627–647.
DeRue, D. S., Nahrgang, J. D., Wellman, N., & Humphrey, S. E. (2011). Trait and behavioral theories of leadership: An integration and Meta-Analytic Test of their relative validity. *Personnel Psychology, 64*, 7–52.
Digman, J. M., & Inouye, J. (1986). Further specification of the five robust factors of personality. *Journal of Personality and Social Psychology, 50*, 116–123.
Dinh, J., & Lord, R. G. (2012). Implications of dispositional and process views of traits for individual difference research in leadership. *Leadership Quarterly, 23*, 651–669.
Eby, L., & Dobbins, G. H. (1997). Collectivistic orientation in teams: An individual and group level analysis. *Journal of Organizational Behavior, 18*, 275–295.
Edmondson, A. (1999). Psychological safety and learning behavior in work teams. *Administrative Science Quarterly, 44*, 350–383.
Erez, A., Lepine, J. A., Elms, H. (2002). Effects of rotated leadership and peer evaluation on the functioning and effectiveness of self-managed teams: A quasi-experiment. *Personnel Psychology, 55*, 929–948.
Fiedler, F. E. (1967). *A theory of leadership effectiveness*. New York: McGraw-Hill.
Fiedler, F. E. (1971). Validation and extension of the contingency model of leadership effectiveness: A review of the empirical findings. *Psychological Bulletin, 76*, 128–148.
Foti, R. J., Bray, B. C., Thompson, N. J., & Allgood, S. F. (2012). Know thy self, know thy leader: Contributions of a pattern-oriented approach to examining leader perceptions. *Leadership Quarterly, 23*, 702–717.
Foti, R. J., & Hauenstein, N. M. A. (2007). Pattern and variable approaches in leadership emergence and effectiveness. *Journal of Applied Psychology, 92*, 347–355.
Foti, R. J., Knee, R. E., & Backert, R. S. G. (2008). Multi-level implications of framing leadership perceptions as a dynamic process. *Leadership Quarterly, 19*, 178–194.
Friedrich, T. L., Vessey, W. B., Schuelke, M. J., Ruark, G. A., & Mumford, M. D. (2009). A framework for understanding collective leadership: The selective utilization of leader and team expertise within networks. *Leadership Quarterly, 20*, 933–958.
Ghiselli, E. E., & Brown, C. W. (1955). *Personnel and industrial psychology* (2nd ed.). Columbus, OH: McGraw-Hill.
Gibb, C. A. (1947). The principles and traits of leadership. *Journal of Abnormal and Social Psychology, 42*, 267–284.
Gibb, C. A. (1954). Leadership. In G. Lindzey (Ed.), *Handbook of social psychology* (pp. 877–917). Cambridge, MA: Addison-Wesley.
Gockel, C., & Werth, L. (2010). Measuring and modeling shared leadership. *Journal of Personnel Psychology, 9*, 172–180.
Griffin, B., & Hesketh, B. (2005). Are conscientious workers adaptable? *Australian Journal of Management, 30*, 245–259.
Hackman, J. R., & Wageman, R. (2005). A theory of team coaching. *Academy of Management Review, 30*, 269–287.
Hannah, S. T., Avolio, B. J., Luthans, F., & Harms, P. (2008). Leadership efficacy: Review and future directions. *Leadership Quarterly, 19*, 669–692.
Harms, P. D., Roberts, B. W., & Wood, D. (2007). Who shall lead? An integrative personality approach to the study of the antecedents of status in informal social organizations. *Journal of Research in Personality, 41*, 689–699.
Hendricks, J. W., & Payne, S. C. (2007). Beyond the Big Five: Leader goal orientation as a predictor of leadership effectiveness. *Human Performance, 20*, 317–343.
Hiller, N. J., Day, D. V., & Vance, R. J. (2006). Collective enactment of leadership roles and team effectiveness: A field study. *Leadership Quarterly, 17*, 387–397.
Hirschfeld, R. R., Jordan, M. H., Thomas, C. H., & Feild, H. S. (2008). Observed leadership potential of personnel in a team setting: Big Five traits and proximal factors as predictors. *International Journal of Selection and Assessment, 16*, 385–402.
Hoch, J. E., Pearce, C. L., & Welzel, L. (2010). Is the most effective team leadership shared? The impact of shared leadership, age diversity and coordination on team performance. *Journal of Personnel Psychology, 9*, 105–116.
Hoffman, B. J., Woehr, D. J., Maldagen-Youngjohn, R., & Lyons, B. D. (2011). Great man or great myth? A quantitative review of the relationship between individual differences and leader effectiveness. *Journal of Occupational and Organizational Psychology, 82*, 347–381.
Holmes, C. M., Sholley, B. K., & Walker, W. E. (1980). Leader, follower, and isolate personality patterns in black and white emergent leadership groups. *Journal of Psychology, 105*, 41–46.
Hooijberg, R. (1996). A multidirectional approach toward leadership: An extension of the concept of behavioral complexity. *Human Relations, 49*, 917–947.
House, R. J. (1988). Leadership research: Some forgotten, ignored, or overlooked findings. In J. G. Hunt, B. R. Baliga, H. P. Dachler, & C. A. Schriesheim (Eds.), *Emerging leadership vistas* (pp. 245–260). Lexington, MA: Lexington Books.

House, R. J., & Howell, J. M. (1992). Personality and charismatic leadership. *Leadership Quarterly, 3*, 81–108.
House, R. J., Spangler, W. D., & Woycke, J. (1991). Personality and charisma in the U.S. presidency: A psychological theory of leader effectiveness. *Administrative Science Quarterly, 36*, 364–396.
Humphrey, S. E., Hollenbeck, J. R., Meyer, C. J., & Ilgen, D. R. (2007). Trait configurations in self-managed teams: A conceptual examination of the use of seeding for maximizing and minimizing trait variance in teams. *Journal of Applied Psychology, 92*, 885–892.
Jacobs, T. O., & Jaques, E. (1987). Leadership in complex systems. In J. Zeidner (Ed.), *Human productivity enhancement* (pp. 7–65). New York: Praeger.
James, L. R., & Mazerolle, M. D. (2002). *Personality in work organizations*. Thousand Oaks, CA: Sage.
Judge, T. A., & Bono, J. E. (2000). Five-factor model of personality and transformational leadership. *Journal of Applied Psychology, 85*, 751–765.
Judge, T. A., Bono, J. E., Ilies, R., & Gerhart, M. W. (2002). Personality and leadership: A qualitative and quantitative review. *Journal of Applied Psychology, 87*, 765–780.
Judge, T. A., Colbert, A., & Ilies, R. (2004). Intelligence and leadership: A quantitative review and test of theoretical propositions. *Journal of Applied Psychology, 89*, 542–552.
Kalshoven, K., Den Hartog, D. N., & De Hoogh, A. H. B. (2011). Ethical Leadership at Work Questionnaire (ELW): Development and validation of a multidimensional measure. *Leadership Quarterly, 22*, 51–69.
Kirkman, B. L., & Rosen, B. (1997). A model of work team empowerment. In R. W. Woodman & W. A. Pasmore (Eds.), *Research in organizational change and development* (Vol. 10, pp. 131–167). Greenwich, CT: JAI Press.
Kirkman, B. L., & Rosen, B. (1999). Beyond self-management: Antecedents and consequences of team empowerment. *Academy of Management Journal, 42*, 58–74.
Kozlowski, S. W. J., & Ilgen, D. R. 2006. Enhancing the effectiveness of work groups and teams. *Psychological Science in the Public Interest, 7*, 77–124.
Kozlowski, S. W. J., Gully, S. M., Salas, E., & Cannon-Bowers, J. A. (1996). Team leadership and development: Theory, principles, and guidelines for training leaders and teams. In M. M. Beyerlein, D. Johnson, & S. T. Beyerlein (Eds.), *Interdisciplinary studies of work teams: Team leadership* (Vol. 3, pp. 254–291). Greenwich, CT: JAI Press.
Kozlowski, S. W. J., & Klein, K. J. (2000). A multilevel approach to theory and research in organizations: Contextual, temporal, and emergent processes. In K. J. Klein & S. W. J. Kozlowski (Eds.), *Multilevel theory, research, and methods in organizations: Foundations, extensions and new directions* (pp. 3–90). San Francisco: Jossey-Bass.
LePine, J. A. (2003). Team adaptation and postchange performance: Effects of team composition in terms of members' cognitive ability and personality. *Journal of Applied Psychology, 88*, 27–39.
LePine, J. A., Colquitt, J. A., & Erez, A. (2000). Adaptability to changing task contexts: Effects of general cognitive ability, conscientiousness, and openness to experience. *Personnel Psychology, 53*, 563–593.
Lord, R. G., de Vader, C. L., & Alliger, G. M. (1986). A meta-analysis of the relation between personality traits and leadership perceptions: An application of validity generalization procedures. *Journal of Applied Psychology, 71*, 402–410.
Lord, R. G., & Hall, R. J. (1992). Contemporary views of leadership and individual differences. *Leadership Quarterly, 3*, 137–157.
Mann, R. D. (1959). A review of the relationship between personality and performance in small groups. *Psychological Bulletin, 56*, 241–270.
Manz, C. C., & Sims, H. P., Jr. (1987). Leading workers to lead themselves: The external leadership of self-managed work teams. *Administrative Science Quarterly, 32*, 106–129.
Michel, J. S., & LeBreton, J. M. (2011). Leadership coherence: An application of personality coherence theory to the study of leadership. *Personality and Individual Differences, 50*, 688–694.
Morgeson, F. P. (2005). The external leadership of self-managing teams: Intervening in the context of novel and disruptive events. *Journal of Applied Psychology, 90*, 497–508.
Morgeson, F. P., DeRue, D. S., & Karam, E. P. (2010). Leadership in teams: A functional approach to understanding leadership structures and processes. *Journal of Management, 36*, 5–39.
Morgeson, F. P., Reider, M. H., & Campion, M. A. (2005). Selecting individuals in team settings: The importance of social skills, personality characteristics, and teamwork knowledge. *Personnel Psychology, 58*, 583–611.
Moss, F. A. (1931). Preliminary report of a study of social intelligence and executive ability. *Public Personnel Studies, 9*, 2–9.
Mount, M. K., Barrick, M. R., & Stewart, G. L. (1998). Five factor model of personality and performance in jobs involving interpersonal interactions. *Human Performance, 11*, 145–165.
Muchinsky, P. M. (1983). *Psychology applied to work*. Homewood, IL: Dorsey Press.
Muchinsky, P. M., & Monahan, C. J. (1987). What is person–environment congruence? Supplementary versus complementary models of fit. *Journal of Vocational Behavior, 31*, 268–277.

Mumford, M. D., Zaccaro, S. J., Harding, F. D., Jacobs, T. O., & Fleishman, E. A. (2000). Leadership skills for a changing world: Solving complex social problems. *Leadership Quarterly, 11*, 11–35.

Nadkarni, S., & Hermann, P. (2010). CEO personality, strategic flexibility, and firm performance: The case of the Indian business process outsourcing industry. *Academy of Management Journal, 53*, 1050–1073.

Neuman, G. A., & Wright, J. (1999). Team effectiveness: Beyond skills and cognitive ability. *Journal of Applied Psychology, 84*, 376–389.

Ng, K. Y., Ang, S., & Chan, A. Y. (2008). Personality and leader effectiveness: A moderated mediation model of leadership self-efficacy, job demands, and job autonomy. *Journal of Applied Psychology, 93*, 733–743.

O'Shea, P. G., Foti, R. J., Hauenstein, N. M. A., & Bycio, P. (2009). Are the best leaders both transformational and transactional? A pattern-oriented analysis. *Journal of Leadership, 5*, 237–259.

Pearce, C. L., & Conger, J. A. (2003). All those years ago: The historical underpinnings of shared leadership. In C. L. Pearce & J. A. Conger (Eds.), *Shared leadership: Reframing the hows and whys of leadership* (pp. 1–18). Thousand Oaks, CA: Sage.

Pearce, C. L., & Sims, H. P. (2002). Vertical versus shared leadership as predictors of the effectiveness of change management teams: An examination of aversive, directive, transactional, transformational, and empowering leader behaviors. *Group Dynamics: Theory, Research, and Practice, 6*, 172–197.

Peeters, M. A., Van Tuijl, H. F., Rutte, C. G., & Reymen, I. M. (2006). Personality and team performance: A meta-analysis. *European Journal of Personality, 20*, 377–396.

Perry, S. J., Witt, L. A., Penney, L. M., & Atwater, L. (2010). The downside of goal-focused leadership: The role of personality in subordinate exhaustion. *Journal of Applied Psychology, 95*, 1145–1153.

Peterson, R. S., Smith, D. B., Martorana, P. V., & Owens, P. D. (2003). The impact of chief executive officer personality on top management team dynamics: One mechanism by which leadership affects organizational performance. *Journal of Applied Psychology, 88*, 795–808.

Popper, M., Mayseless, O., & Castelnovo, O. (2000). Transformational leadership and attachment. *Leadership Quarterly, 11*, 267–289.

Richards, D. A., & Hackett, R. D. (2012). Attachment and emotional regulation: Compensatory interactions and leader–member exchange. *Leadership Quarterly, 23*, 686–701.

Salas, E., Sims, D. E., & Burke, C. S. (2005). Is there a "big five" in teamwork? *Small Group Research, 36*, 555–599.

Sears, G. J., & Hackett, R. D. (2011). The influence of role definition and affect in LMX: A process perspective on the personality–LMX relationship. *Journal of Occupational and Organizational Psychology, 84*, 544–564.

Secord, P. E., & Backman, C. W. (1974). *Social psychology*. New York: McGraw-Hill.

Smith, J. A., & Foti, R. J. (1998). A pattern approach to the study of leader emergence. *Leadership Quarterly, 9*, 147–160.

Spreitzer, G. M. (1995). Individual empowerment in the workplace: Dimensions, measurement, and validation. *Academy of Management Journal, 38*, 1442–1465.

Stewart, G. L. (2006). A meta-analytic review of relationships between team design features and team performance. *Journal of Management, 32*, 29–55.

Stewart, G. L., & Manz, C. C. (1995). Leadership for self-managing work teams: A typology and integrative model. *Human Relations, 48*, 347–370.

Stogdill, R. M. (1948). Personal factors associated with leadership: A survey of the literature. *Journal of Psychology, 25*, 35–71.

Taggar, S., Hackett, R., & Saha, S. (1999). Leadership emergence in autonomous work teams: Antecedents and outcomes. *Personnel Psychology, 52*, 899–926.

Terman, L. M. (1904). A preliminary study in the psychology and pedagogy of leadership. *Pedagogical Seminary, 11*, 412–451.

Thomas, K. W., & Velthouse, B. A. (1990). Cognitive elements of empowerment: An "interpretive" model of intrinsic task motivation. *Academy of Management Review, 15*, 666–681.

Van Iddekinge, C. H., Ferris, G. R., & Heffner, T. S. (2009). Test of a multistage model of distal and proximal antecedents of leader performance. *Personnel Psychology, 62*, 463–495.

Vroom, V. H., & Yetton, P. W. (1973). *Leadership and decision making*. Pittsburgh, PA: University of Pittsburgh.

Walumbwa, F. O., & Schaubroeck, J. (2009). Leader personality traits and employee voice behavior: Mediating roles of ethical leadership and work group psychological safety. *Journal of Applied Psychology, 94*, 1275–1286.

Wolf, S., Wassenaar, C. L., Unterrainer, C., & Piecha, A. (2010). Promoting work motivation in organizations. *Journal of Personnel Psychology, 9*, 154–171.

Xu, X., Yu, F., & Shi, J. (2011). Ethical leadership and leaders' personalities. *Social Behavior and Personality, 39*, 361–368.

Zaccaro, S. J. (2001). *The nature of executive leadership: A conceptual and empirical analysis of success*. Washington, DC: APA Books.

Zaccaro, S. J. (2007). Trait-based perspectives in leadership. *American Psychologist, 62*, 6–16.
Zaccaro, S. J. (2012). Individual differences and leadership: Contributions to a third tipping point. *Leadership Quarterly, 23*, 718–728.
Zaccaro, S. J., & DeChurch, L. A. (2012). Leadership forms and functions in multiteam systems. In S. J. Zaccaro, M. A. Marks, & L. A. DeChurch (Eds.), *Multiteam systems: An organization form for dynamic and complex environments* (pp. 253–288). New York: Routledge.
Zaccaro, S. J., Ely, K., & Shuffler, M. (2008). The leader's role in group learning. In V. Sessa & M. London (Eds.), *Work group learning* (pp. 319–360). Mahwah, NJ: Lawrence Erlbaum Associates.
Zaccaro, S. J., Foti, R. J., & Kenny, D. A. (1991). Self-monitoring and trait-based variance in leadership: An investigation of leader flexibility across multiple group situations. *Journal of Applied Psychology, 76*, 308–315.
Zaccaro, S. J., Gilbert, J. A., Thor, K. K., & Mumford, M. (1991). Leadership and social intelligence: Linking social perspectives and behavioral flexibility to leader effectiveness. *Leadership Quarterly, 2*, 317–342.
Zaccaro, S. J., Gulick, L. M. V., & Khare, V. P. (2008). Personality and leadership. In C. L. Hoyt, G. R. Goethals, & D. R. Forsyth (Eds.), *Leadership at the crossroads* (pp. 13–29). New York: Praeger.
Zaccaro, S. J., Heinen, B., & Shuffler, M. (2009). Team leadership and team effectiveness. In E. Salas, G. F. Goodwin, & C. S. Burke (Eds.), *Team effectiveness in complex organizations: Cross-disciplinary perspectives and approaches* (pp. 83–111). New York: Routledge.
Zaccaro, S. J., Kemp, C., & Bader, P. (2004). Leader traits and attributes. In J. Antonakis, R. Sternberg, & A. Ciancola (Eds.), *The nature of leadership* (pp. 101–124). Thousand Oaks, CA: Sage.
Zaccaro, S. J., LaPort, K. A., & Jose, I. J. (2013). The attributes of successful leaders: A performance requirements approach.
Zhang, Z., & Arvey, R. D. (2009). Effects of personality on individual earnings: Leadership role occupancy as a mediator. *Journal of Business and Psychology, 24*, 271–280.
Zopiatis, A., & Constanti, P. (2012). Extraversion, openness and conscientiousness: The route to transformational leadership in the hotel industry. *Leadership & Organization Development Journal, 33*, 86–104.

35

A Developmental Perspective on the Importance of Personality for Understanding Workplace Behavior

Christopher D. Nye and Brent W. Roberts

A commonly used definition of personality traits is that they are the relatively enduring patterns of thoughts, feelings, and behaviors that reflect the tendency to respond in certain ways under certain circumstances (Roberts, 2009). A key component of this definition is that personality traits are "*relatively* enduring." This is often translated to mean that traits are unchanging or unchangeable and personality traits are generally treated as such. However, an increasing amount of research indicates that personality traits do change significantly over an individual's lifetime. Moreover, many of these changes appear to coincide with work-related activities and may be partially a result of an individual's experiences on the job. Thus, work may change personality traits, and this change can have implications for organizational behavior. This chapter describes the evidence for personality trait change, the mutual influences of the organization and the individual, the implications for organizational behavior, and methodological issues with studying this topic.

Continuity and Change in Personality Traits

Research to this point has indicated that personality traits are *relatively* enduring over the life course. In fact, with the exception of cognitive ability (Conley, 1984), vocational interests and personality traits are more stable than most other individual differences (Caspi, Roberts, & Shiner, 2005). Even during childhood, which is a period marked by substantial physical, emotional, and social change (Lewis, 2001), personality remains relatively stable. Test–retest correlations during this time frame are generally above .40 (Roberts & DelVecchio, 2000) and the correlation between childhood temperament and personality in young adulthood is approximately .30 (Moffitt et al., 2011). This level of rank-order stability appears to increase linearly over the life course and peak some time after the age of 50 years. For example, from young adulthood to middle age, test–retest correlations are generally between .40 and .60 over shorter periods of time (e.g., 4–10 years; Ardelt, 2000; Bazana & Stelmack, 2004; Roberts & DelVecchio, 2000). However, between the ages of 50 and 70 years, test–retest correlations are around .70 or .80 after correcting for measurement artifacts (Ferguson, 2010). This increasing stability over the life course has been labeled the *cumulative continuity principle* of personality development (Caspi et al., 2005; Roberts, Wood, & Caspi, 2008).

Despite the relative consistency of personality traits, the potential for change is not precluded by these results. In fact, there is also significant evidence that traits change over the life course. For example, although stability coefficients are moderate to large over shorter periods of time, these correlations approach (but never actually reach) zero as the length of time between measurements increases (Fraley & Roberts, 2005). Other research has shown that there are also mean-level differences in personality traits over time. A meta-analysis of 92 longitudinal studies showed that men and women tend to become more socially dominant (a facet of extraversion), conscientious, and emotionally stable during their lifetime (Roberts, Walton, & Viechtbauer, 2006). In contrast, mean-level changes in social vitality (another facet of extraversion) and openness to experience are nonlinear. Social vitality and openness tend to increase in adolescence and then decrease during old age (Roberts et al., 2008). For all of these traits, the longer the time span of the study, the larger the observed differences. Thus, these results suggest that there is slow but significant change in personality traits over time.

Given this research, the evidence for personality trait change over the life course seems robust and the nature and trajectory of this change is informative. For example, the pattern of change indicates that individuals tend to become more "mature" over time. Roberts and Wood (2006) pointed out that definitions of maturity generally focus on qualities that facilitate functioning in society. Mature people are more liked, respected, and admired in community, social, and interpersonal relationships (R. Hogan & Roberts, 2004). The changes in personality traits over the life course are consistent with these characteristics and may help to facilitate the maturation process. For this reason, the trend toward increased social dominance, conscientiousness, and emotional stability has been labeled the *maturity principle* (Roberts & Wood, 2006).

The timing of these changes during the life course is also informative. For example, meta-analytic evidence indicates that there is little change in conscientiousness during adolescence but substantial changes in young adulthood (Roberts, Walton, & Viechtbauer, 2006). The largest increases in social dominance also occurred during young adulthood (Roberts, Walton, & Viechtbauer, 2006). In contrast, both social vitality and openness to experience increase during adolescence and then decrease again in old age. Overall, results seem to indicate that the largest changes occur between the ages of 20 and 40 years, making young adulthood an important period for understanding personality trait change (Roberts & Mroczek, 2008).

Why do the largest changes in personality occur during this time frame? This period of time coincides with a number of significant life changes. Many people find and marry a mate and begin a family during this time frame. Young adults also begin to get involved in the community through service, activities, and family responsibilities. Finally, many individuals also begin their career during this period. Because work can be a source of identity, reputation, perception of self-worth, and financial security, and because of the amount of time spent at work during one's lifetime, work plays a significant role in an individual's life (Boyce, Ryan, Imus, & Morgeson, 2007; Hulin, 2002). In fact, the importance of work is illustrated by the significant negative mental and emotional consequences of losing one's job (Durkheim, 1897; Feather, 1989; Fryer & Payne, 1986; Jahoda, Lazarsfeld, & Zeisel, 1933; O'Brien, 1986; Warr, Jackson, & Banks, 1988). Given its role in people's lives, it would not be surprising if the expectations, contingencies, and reward structures associated with work do have a significant impact on their personality. The timing of the changes in personality, and the tendency for traits to change in a direction that is consistent with the reward structure of the work environment, suggest that this is the case (Roberts et al., 2008).

Sources of Continuity and Change in the Workplace

A number of studies have focused on identifying the factors that can facilitate change and/or enhance the stability of personality traits over the life course. As a result, both genetic and environmental factors have been proposed. Below, we summarize the empirical evidence on this topic with a particular emphasis on the potential sources of continuity and change in the work environment.

First, evidence from twin studies suggests that genetic factors may contribute to the continuity of personality traits across the life course (e.g., McGue, Bacon, & Lykken, 1993). In the personality literature, it is well established that genetic factors are one potential source of variation in personality traits (Johnson, Vernon, & Feiler, 2008). Although the expression of these genes may change (see Roberts & Jackson, 2008), the genes themselves are unchanging and, therefore, may contribute to stability over time. In fact, research indicates that genetic influences may account for as much as 80% of the consistency observed in twins (McGue et al., 1993). On the other hand, the genetic signature for personality change seems to be lower (Bleidorn, Kandler, Riemann, Angleitner, & Spinath, 2009). Moreover, behavioral genetics studies are quite clear in showing that environmental influences are usually responsible for more than 50% of the variance in either personality stability or change (Krueger, South, Johnson, & Iacono, 2008).

Beyond genetic factors, a broad range of person–environment transactions can also facilitate personality continuity and change. Here, Schneider's (1987) attraction–selection–attrition (ASA) model is informative. This model suggests that the attraction, selection, and attrition processes in an organization will result in homogeneous organizations that comprise individuals with similar personality traits. Although the ASA framework is primarily a model of organizational outcomes (e.g., organizational homogeneity and resistance to change), the same processes can also influence individual personality through person–environment transactions. However, Roberts (2006) has noted that other interactions between the person and the environment can also influence individual behavior. For this reason, Roberts (2006) expanded the ASA model to include *transformation* and *manipulation* processes as additional mechanisms of influence over continuity and change. Thus, in contrast to the ASA framework, this expanded model is focused primarily on the individual outcomes of these five processes and is called the attraction, selection, transformation, manipulation, and attrition (ASTMA) model.

The neo-socioanalytic model of personality (Roberts & Caspi, 2003; Roberts, Harms, Smith, Wood, & Webb, 2006) describes two primary psychological factors that interact with the processes described by the ASTMA model. These factors are the identity and the reputation of the individual. Identity reflects the sum total of opinions that are cognitively available to a person and are based on various individual characteristics (Roberts, 2006). In other words, an individual's identity may include his or her perception that he or she is hard working, friendly, or fun to be around. Moreover, each person will have varying degrees of investment in each aspect of their identity. For example, an individual may consider himself or herself to be hard working, but may be less invested in maintaining this identity than he or she is in maintaining an identity as an outgoing person (Roberts & Wood, 2006). Thus, behaviors will reflect this investment and individuals will find ways to maintain important aspects of their identity when multiple identities are in conflict.

In contrast to identity, reputation refers to others' perceptions of an individual's characteristics. Thus, both self-(identity) and other-perceptions (reputation) of an individual can affect his or her interactions with the environment. However, identity and reputation will also mutually influence each other. For example, an individual's reputation may influence how he or she sees him or herself. If others consistently view a person as outgoing, and treat that person accordingly, then that individual may also begin to see him or herself as outgoing over time. Similarly, self-perceptions will affect how an individual acts around others. In other words, people may try to actively shape their reputation in an effort to maintain their identity.

The differences between identity and reputation are also manifest in the measurement of personality traits. Self- and other-reports of personality are the two primary methods of assessing traits and both measure a slightly different aspect of these individual differences (Roberts, Harms, et al., 2006). Self-reports will be primarily influenced by an individual's identity, whereas other-reports are more indicative of his or her reputation. However, because of their mutual influence on each other, both reputation and identity can interact to influence these assessments as well. In the organizational literature, this interaction is salient in the literature on socially desirable responding. Here, socially desirable responding is viewed as one way that an individual can manage his or her reputation (R. Hogan, Hogan, & Roberts, 1996). However, responses are also influenced by the individual's identity.

Despite their mutual influence, meta-analytic evidence suggests that both self- and other-reports are associated with organizational behaviors even after controlling for the relationship between them (Oh, Wang, & Mount, 2011). Below, we elaborate on the ASTMA model and the distinction between identity and reputation with the neo-socioanalytic model in mind. We also describe how an individual's identity and reputation can influence his or her transactions with the work environment.

Attraction

In Schneider's (1987) ASA model, he proposed that individuals are attracted to organizations that are similar to them on the characteristics that they value. In other words, individuals will only apply to jobs if they perceive that their individual characteristics will fit with that organization. Schneider's claim was based on the theoretical and empirical work of John L. Holland (1959, 1997) who emphasized that individuals choose careers that are compatible with their personality and interests. In fact, the idea that individuals are attracted to similar environments has a long history in person–environment fit research (cf. Parsons, 1909) and a number of studies have supported this hypothesis in the personality development literature (Roberts, Caspi, & Moffitt, 2003; Roberts & Robins, 2004) and in work (Judge & Cable, 1997; Lievens, Decaesteker, Coetsier, & Geirnaert, 2001; Tom, 1971) and academic (Allen, 1998; Boone, van Olffen, & Roijakkers, 2004) settings.

Given that the goal is to maximize fit with the organization, an individual's attraction to an organization or an environment will be influenced by his or her identity and reputation. According to social identity theory (Tajfel & Turner, 1986), individuals seek out roles and/or environments that are consistent with their identity. The consequence of this tendency is that the individual's identity will become strengthened over time. Thus, work can be an important source of identity (Hulin, 2002) and employees often choose careers and organizations that are already consistent with their identities prior to organizational entry. Because personality traits are inseparably linked to identity, this process also suggests that traits should become more stable over time through the process of selecting organizations that are consistent with one's identity (Roberts & Caspi, 2003).

Work is just one potential source of an individual's identity and reputation. In addition to the work environment, people generally encounter different environments related to family and community responsibilities that can influence their identity and reputation as well. However, as with the work environment, individuals self-select into these various situations and contexts based on their identity (Tajfel & Turner, 1986) and this process can increase identity clarity over time (Helson, Stewart, & Ostrove, 1995; Lodi-Smith & Roberts, 2010). In other words, as individuals begin to strengthen their identity, they will also self-select into environments that are consistent with that identity. Over time, the environments that an individual encounters will become more homogeneous and will help to maintain the characteristics that are useful in those situations (Roberts & Caspi, 2003).

Selection

The second component of the ASA model represents an organization's employee selection process. Schneider (1987) suggested that organizations select employees based on perceptions of their fit within the company or group that they will be working in. Again, fit is defined as similarities on important characteristics. Here, an individual's reputation, as indicated by both self- (e.g., responses to personality measures used during the selection process) and other-reports (e.g., recommendation letters and interviewer perceptions) of personality during the hiring process, will be particularly important for determining fit.

From an organizational perspective, these selection processes should result in a workforce with homogeneous personality characteristics (e.g., traits, motives, values). Again, research has supported this prediction of the ASA model (Cable & Judge, 1997; Schneider, Smith, Taylor, & Fleenor, 1998). From the perspective of employees, this process may also facilitate continuity over time. If employees are successful at choosing a career and an organization that fits with their identity, they are likely to remain in that organization for a longer period of time than if they do not fit (see the "Manipulation and Attrition" section).

In contrast to Schneider's perspective, some research suggests that other types of fit are also important to consider. Although fit is typically defined as the similarity between an individual and his or her environment, others have examined the importance of complementary fit as an alternative perspective (Kristof-Brown, Barrick, & Stevens, 2005). Complementary fit occurs when an employee's characteristics fill a gap or weakness within the group. For example, if members of the group are talkative and socially dominant (i.e., high extraversion), selecting a new group member who is more shy and willing to listen may reduce conflict and increase team performance. In fact, empirical studies on the role of extraversion in team performance support this prediction (Hoffman, 1959; Hoffman & Maier, 1961; Kristof-Brown, Barrick, et al., 2005).

Complementary fit may have very different implications for personality trait change. Although selecting employees based on similar characteristics will result in consistency over time, selecting employees that complement existing personalities can lead to personality trait change. As described above, the key to personality development is investment in social roles that are outside of one's identity structure (Roberts et al., 2008). Therefore, employees who invest in work roles that are inconsistent with their own self-perceptions are likely to change due to the influences of their coworkers (we describe the mechanisms for this influence next). However, research suggests that complementary fit may be beneficial for some traits (e.g., extraversion) but not for others (Kristof-Brown, Barrick, et al., 2005). This caveat may explain the contradictory findings that both similarities and dissimilarities can lead to positive work-related outcomes.

Transformation

The attraction and the selection processes described above will facilitate the stability of personality traits over time. Given these forces, why do traits change at all? The transformation component of the ASTMA model identifies the types of experiences at work that presumably promote change (Roberts, 2006). Here, the contingencies in the work environment play an important role in motivating change. As individuals age, maturity (i.e., higher conscientiousness and emotional stability) becomes a valued characteristic and will be increasingly rewarded in social roles. These contingencies are particularly salient in employment settings because organizations typically reward employees for being dependable, industrious (both facets of conscientiousness), and emotionally stable. Consequently, employees may strive to become more conscientious and emotionally stable as a way to keep their jobs and be successful in them. As such, research has shown that personality change is consistent with the reward structure of the work environment.

In one of the first studies, Elder (1969) examined men who were more successful in their jobs than their fathers. Results showed that successful men became more independent, responsible, and motivated to succeed between high school and their mid-30s. Roberts (1997) showed that women who worked became more agentic and those who were successful in their work also increased in norm adherence. In addition, Roberts et al. (2003) showed that individuals in higher status jobs that were more satisfying and provided financial security decreased in negative emotionality quicker than those who were not. In general, it appears that increases in social dominance and conscientiousness are associated with work-related experiences (Clausen & Gilens, 1990; Elder, 1969; Roberts et al., 2003). In addition, positive experiences at work are related to changes in emotional stability (Roberts & Chapman, 2000; Scollon & Diener, 2006). In other words, work-related experiences are associated with the same pattern of change that has been observed in personality traits over the life course.

Interestingly, because individuals are attracted to environments and people that are similar to them on certain personality characteristics, environmental contingencies also frequently result in changes to those traits that led the person to that particular environment in the first place (Roberts et al., 2008). For example, extraverted individuals will be more likely to apply for customer service jobs, and their experiences in these jobs will make them more extraverted. Thus, it is common for environmental experiences to increase the levels of personality traits that are already salient in the individual. Evidence of this effect has been provided in both longitudinal (Roberts & Robins, 2004) and meta-analytic (Roberts & DelVecchio, 2000) studies, and this process has been labeled the *corresponsive principle* in the personality development literature (Roberts & Caspi, 2003; Roberts & Robins, 2004).

The environmental contingencies that influence employees in the workplace may affect them both actively and passively. For example, training interventions are one mechanism through which organizations can actively influence employees' personality traits. Although research on this topic in organizational settings is lacking, evidence that training can successfully change individual characteristics has been provided by intervention studies. Early research showed that cognitive behavioral therapies could change personality traits by more than a standard deviation in relatively short-term intervention studies (Smith, Glass, & Miller, 1980). A more recent study showed that training physicians to become more mindful resulted in changes in conscientiousness, agreeableness, empathy, and emotional stability (Krasner et al., 2009). Likewise, participation in a social skills training program for recovering substance abusers led to increases in agreeableness, conscientiousness, and emotional stability (Piedmont, 2001). Research has also demonstrated that personality traits change in response to a combination of therapy and medication (Costa, Bagby, Herbst, & McCrae, 2005; Santor, Bagby, & Joffe, 1997). For example, De Fruyt, Van Leeuwen, Bagby, Rolland, and Rouillon (2006) found that individuals treated with a combination of either tianeptine or fluoxetine and therapy showed significant changes in all Big Five personality traits. A recent study on the effects of cognitive therapy and medication (SSRIs) on depression found that both treatments were associated with changes in neuroticism and extraversion compared to a control group (Tang et al., 2009). Most importantly, changes in depression were shown to be the result of changes in neuroticism. Specifically, long-term relapses in depression were explained by changes in neuroticism, such that people who decreased the most on neuroticism were the least likely to experience a relapse.

It should be noted that the changes observed in these studies appear to be substantial when compared to the natural development of personality over the life course (Roberts et al., 2008). However, as with other types of training, the employee's willingness to invest time and effort in the training and commit to change are likely to moderate the utility of these interventions. Here, creating contingencies that reinforce the importance of change can impact results, and the literature on the transfer of training may help to identify additional ways of facilitating change (e.g., Baldwin & Ford, 1988).

Within the organizational literature, research on socialization is probably the most salient evidence for the transformative effect. One goal of socialization is for organizations to communicate their expectations (both implicit and explicit) to the employee (Cooper-Thomas & Anderson, 2006). Thus, it is through the socialization process that employees learn their roles in the organization. For this reason, effective socialization processes are associated with higher employee performance, improved job attitudes, and reduced turnover (Bauer, Bodner, Erdogan, Truxillo, & Tucker, 2007). In addition, communicating these role expectations can affect behavior by rewarding desired behaviors and punishing undesired acts (Roberts et al., 2008). In fact, some research suggests that socialization practices have a greater influence on subsequent employee adjustment than the employee's initial personality profile (Chatman, 1991).

Although there are a number of techniques for socializing employees (Bauer et al., 2007), the outcome is that employees become more like others in the organization (Cable & Parsons, 2001; Chatman, 1991). Illustrating this effect, Ostroff and Rothausen (1997) showed that employees' values, attitudes, and interests became more similar to the group's the longer they worked in the organization. In another study, Jordan, Herriot, and Chalmers (1991) demonstrated that organizations can be differentiated based on the personality profiles of the employees within them. Schneider et al.

(1998) found similar results in a larger sample of 12,739 managers and 142 organizations. Although Schneider et al. (1998) were unable to identify the source of the homogeneity that they observed, they hypothesized that selection and socialization processes were potential sources.

Environments, and the people who are in them, also passively influence personality traits through behavioral modeling. Social learning theory (Bandura, 1977) suggests that employees will look to other workers in the organization as models of appropriate behavior. Based on the behaviors that are observed, employees can identify the rewards or punishments that are contingent on behavior. In other words, individuals may look to other group members as a way to determine what is appropriate in that particular environment. Evidence of the effect of group-level behavior on the actions of the individual has been provided in the workplace deviance literature where research suggests that the level of deviance in the group is a predictor of individual-deviant behaviors (Robinson & O'Leary-Kelly, 1998).

Despite the active and passive influences of environments on individual personality change, the *social investment principle* suggests that these effects may be moderated by the individual's investment in the environment (Lodi-Smith & Roberts, 2007). Social investment is defined as occurring when individuals are affectively committed to an adult social role such that they are willing to invest time and mental or physical effort into maintaining it (Roberts & Wood, 2006). Because of the impact that work has on our lives, jobs are an essential element of adulthood and one of the most important roles that people commit to (Hulin, 2002). Thus, role expectations, reward structures, and social norms at work should be influential in employees' lives. However, the extent of this influence will be determined by the employee's commitment to and investment in his or her work role. In an attempt to keep their jobs and be successful in them, invested individuals are more likely to work hard and well with others, show up on time, and be less neurotic. These characteristics will be manifest as the changes in conscientiousness, agreeableness, and neuroticism that are typically observed over the life course (Roberts et al., 2008). For example, in a 3-year longitudinal study of employed adults, those who were more invested in their work or who increased their investment over time also became more agreeable and conscientious (Hudson, Roberts, & Lodi-Smith, 2012). On the other hand, if individuals are not committed to the organization or their role in it, they are likely to withdraw from the work or leave the organization (e.g., Griffeth, Hom, & Gaertner, 2000) and behavioral contingencies are unlikely to motivate personality trait change in the typical way. In fact, Roberts, Walton, Bogg, and Caspi (2006) have shown that this lack of investment (a condition they labeled "de-investment") can lead to decreases in emotional stability and conscientiousness—a finding that contrasts with the normative increases in these traits.

Manipulation and Attrition

Despite the processes described above, individuals often end up in jobs that do not fit their personality. There are several potential reasons why this misfit may occur. In adolescence and the early years of young adulthood, when individuals often choose and begin a career, many people have not yet formed a stable, clearly defined, identity (Erikson, 1963; Sears, 1986). Consequently, some individuals may choose jobs that are not an adequate match for their personality. Alternatively, individuals may have formed inaccurate perceptions of an organization or occupation during the recruitment and selection processes and misfit may not be identified until after the applicant has already started the job. In addition, job applicants may accept offers for less than ideal jobs because of external factors (e.g., poor job market, work–family balance, etc.) that do not reflect ideal patterns of fit. In each of these scenarios, and in a number of others, the employee will enter an organization and/or a role that does not fit with his or her personality.

When poor fit results, employees may choose to leave the job or terminate their employment with the organization (Schaubroeck, Ganster, & Jones, 1998; Schneider, 1987). Although not focused explicitly on personality, a recent meta-analysis showed that the corrected correlation between person–organization fit and intent to quit was −.35 (Kristof-Brown, Zimmerman, & Johnson, 2005). Similarly, other studies have shown that vocational interests are also associated with turnover or turnover intentions (Van Iddekinge, Roth, Putka, & Lanivich, 2011) and that the congruence between the individual and the occupation that they are in is particularly important for predicting attrition (Nye, Su, Rounds, & Drasgow, 2012). Given these results, it is also likely that individuals will leave the organization if their personality does not match their job and/or the organizational environment. In addition, organizations can also choose to terminate an employee when he or she does not fit. These attrition processes will result in a relatively homogeneous workforce in the organization (Schneider et al., 1998) and can facilitate trait continuity by allowing individuals to find work roles that are more appropriate for their personality trait profile. Thus, attrition is the last component of Schneider's (1987) ASA model.

However, despite the homogenizing effect of the processes described above on an organization's workforce, research shows that there is still variability in scores within a company. For example, because the attraction, selection, and attrition processes proposed by the ASA model will result in more homogeneous organizations (Cable & Judge, 1997; Schneider et al., 1998), we would expect the range of personality scores to be restricted within an organizational sample. However, meta-analytic research suggests that the extent of this restriction is relatively small (Schmidt, Shaffer, & Oh, 2008). Thus, although homogeneity does increase, there is still substantial variability within groups, and this variability suggests that some people will continue to work in organizations that do not explicitly fit their personality.

When this is the case, these employees may try to manipulate their environment in ways that are consistent with their personality (Chatman, Wong, & Joyce, 2008; Roberts, 2006). Several influential psychological theories have emphasized the importance of people in constructing the environment. For example, Schneider's original talk (given as the Presidential address at the annual meeting of the Society for Industrial and Organizational Psychology) and the subsequent paper (Schneider, 1987) were titled "The People Make the Place." As implied by the title, Schneider defined the environment as a consequence of the behavior and interactions of the people who are in it. Similarly, Holland (1997) defined the environment by measuring the interests of the people in a particular occupation. Thus, in both of these theories, the environment and the people in it are inseparably connected. Despite these theories, the process by which employees try to shape their work and the environment that they occupy is a relatively understudied topic. Nevertheless, some research has shown that individuals can be successful at shaping and/or changing their environment.

As with transformation processes, individuals can attempt to manipulate their environment both actively and passively. For example, an individual's reputation may passively change how others treat him or her by evoking trait-consistent behaviors from others (Caspi & Roberts, 1999). If an employee develops a reputation for being sociable, coworkers will be more likely to come and talk to him or her and these opportunities will perpetuate the employee's reputation. In addition, these same processes will strengthen the employee's identity as a sociable person when in situations that allow these behaviors (Roberts & Robins, 2004). As another example, aggressive behavior toward others may evoke additional aggressive behavior in retaliation and result in a long-term "spiral of incivility" that enhances aggressive behavior in all who are involved (Andersson & Pearson, 1999). The result is a cycle that starts with employees behaving in ways that are consistent with their personality, which then evokes consistent behaviors from others and effectively changes the environment to better fit their personality. The end result is a continuity of personality traits that increases with age as individuals continue to solidify their identity and reputation and in so doing create environments that support their personality as they age.

Another form of passive manipulation is behavioral modeling. From the observer's perspective, behavioral modeling acts as a transformation process that can indicate the appropriateness of various behaviors at work. However, from the actor's perspective, modeling is one way that he or she can passively manipulate the environment. Through the behaviors that are modeled, employees can influence perceptions of norms and create a "climate" for certain behavior (Robinson & O'Leary-Kelly, 1998; Salancik & Pfeffer, 1978). Moreover, both talking about and doing the behavior can influence others to engage in similar acts (Rice & Grusec, 1975). Social pressure is as much a behavioral contingency as the formal policies and procedures of the organization.

Employees may also try to actively shape their work environment. Here, organizational leaders will be particularly effective because of their formal authority and influence over hiring decisions (Schein, 1992; Schneider, 1987). Consistent with this perspective, research has shown that the personality profile of an organization is correlated with the personality traits of the CEO (Giberson, Resick, & Dickson, 2005). Top management teams and executive leaders may also have a similar influence on the characteristics of the organization (Schneider, 2008).

Organizational leaders can also impact the climate of the organization. Through their influence on policies and procedures, top managers provide behavioral contingencies for employees within the organization (Ostroff, Kinicki, & Tamkins, 2003; Zohar, 2000). However, the extent to which these policies and procedures are enforced will dictate their influence on employee behavior (Williams, Fitzgerald, & Drasgow, 1999), and lower-level supervisors often play an important role in implementing aspects of the climate. For example, Zohar (2000) showed that employees' perceptions of the safety climate in an organization varied across groups with different supervisors. Therefore, through the behavioral contingencies that are enforced, managers can influence employee behavior in ways that are consistent with their own personality.

The climate in various groups and occupations can also be influenced by the lower-level employees that are in them (Holland, 1997). As described above, behavioral modeling and social pressure provide the mechanisms for influencing coworkers. Moreover, because the socialization of new employees will also depend on the rules and norms that are communicated by coworkers, the effects of coworkers on perceptions of the climate may be particularly salient during initial organizational entry.

Because of their unique relationships with other employees, mentors and coaches can also influence others to change. For example, one of the goals of mentoring is to socialize the protégé into the organization and their role in it (Eby, 2011). Through this process, mentors can influence behavior by creating role expectations, modeling behaviors, and providing psychosocial support that focuses on the employee's self- and professional identities (Eby, 2011; Kram, 1985; Noe, 1988). In addition, one potential goal of the coaching process is to facilitate changes in behavior (Kampa & White, 2002). As such, although the effects of coaching on personality traits have yet to be explicitly examined, research has shown that executive coaching does have an effect on behaviors associated with the Big Five traits, including openness to new behaviors (d = .41) and planning (d = 1.05; Finn, 2007).

In contrast to these active and passive mechanisms, other forms of manipulation may not involve an actual change in the environment. In some cases, manipulation of the environment may be more perceptual than actual. For example, one way that employees manipulate their interaction with the environment is through their perceptions of environmental cues. Nishii and Wright (2008) suggested that individual differences will affect how human resource practices are perceived. In other words, personality characteristics will influence whether compensation practices, reward systems, and job structures are perceived favorably or unfavorably. Anecdotal evidence for this effect has been provided by the studies showing that individuals with a high need for achievement are more likely to be attracted to merit-based reward systems and organizations that structure rewards around individual rather than organizational performance (Bretz, Ash, & Dreher, 1989; Turban & Keon, 1993). Other evidence also demonstrates that individuals will change perceptions of the organization over time. In fact, one study showed that students at a large university were more likely to change their perceptions of the university than their self-perceptions (Harms, Roberts, & Winter, 2006).

Given these forms of environment manipulation, it is interesting to consider when an employee might choose to leave the organization versus manipulate the environment to fit his or her needs. Here, models of organizational turnover are informative (e.g., Hulin, Roznowski, & Hachiya, 1985;

Lee & Mitchell, 1994). For example, attempts to manipulate the environment may be the first step in the progression of withdrawal (cf. Hanisch, 2000; Hulin, 1991). If an employee is unsatisfied with the fit between his or her personality and the environment, he or she may first try to manipulate the job or the environment to enhance fit. If this does not work, the employee may then withdraw from the work and eventually leave the organization. However, withdrawal decisions will be affected by other forces that are external to the organization as well (Hulin et al., 1985). For example, alternative job offers will influence decisions to leave as will the overall condition of the labor market and the unemployment rate in similar jobs. It is likely that these factors will be particularly salient as employees choose between leaving the organization and manipulating their environment. More research is needed in this area to understand the role of manipulation in the withdrawal process.

Here, it is important to distinguish between proximal and distal environmental influences. Because an organization is a broad entity, with a number of subgroups and subcultures, it is possible that perceptions of fit, and reactions to them, will be less closely associated with the organization as a whole than with the specific roles that the employee has within the organization. In fact, research has shown that the personality profiles of some occupations are different from that of the broader organization (Ployhart, Weekley, & Baughman, 2006; Schaubroeck et al., 1998). This distinction is widely accepted in the vocational interest literature where Holland (1997) has strongly advocated using occupations rather than broad organizations to operationalize the interest profile of the environment. Other research suggests that friendship networks within the workplace may be another subgroup that can influence perceptions of fit (Newman, Hanges, Duan, & Ramesh, 2008). Thus, understanding employees' reactions to misfit, and the effects on personality traits that can result, may also require an understanding of the interactions and influences of various subgroups.

Overall, the ASTMA model suggests that there are more forces that facilitate consistency than motivate change. In fact, the only process in the ASTMA model that is dedicated to change is the transformation process. For this reason, we would expect the personality change over the life course to be modest. This is exactly what research has shown (Roberts, Walton, & Viechtbauer, 2006). Nevertheless, personality trait change does occur, and work appears to play a role in these changes.

Methodological Challenges for Testing Personality Trait Change

Identifying personality change brings several methodological challenges. In the following paragraphs, we discuss these challenges and potential remedies for them.

Generational Effects

A number of studies have demonstrated that there are generational differences in personality traits. For example, some studies have shown increases in neuroticism (Twenge, 2000), whereas others have found that this trait actually decreases with each generation (Mroczek & Spiro, 2003; Terracciano, McCrae, Brant, & Costa, 2005). Other studies have shown that extraversion (Mroczek & Spiro, 2003) and conscientiousness (Terracciano et al., 2005) have both increased over generations. In a more comprehensive study across successive cohorts, Smits, Dolan, Vorst, Wicherts, and Timmerman (2011) confirmed these findings even after accounting for changes in the response processes over time. In addition, other studies have shown generational effects on non-Big Five personality traits such as narcissism (Twenge & Foster, 2008), self-esteem, and assertiveness (Duncan & Agronick, 1995). Although the majority of these studies focused on mean-level change, Mroczek and Spiro (2003) also found that the rate of change differed across cohorts. The oldest cohort in their sample (born between 1897 and 1919) showed the slowest decline in neuroticism while the younger groups declined much more quickly over time.

These generational differences are important because they have the potential to demonstrate the effects of cultural and environmental changes on personality traits (Roberts, Edmonds, & Grijalva,

2010; Smits et al., 2011). However, these studies can also confound tests of personality change over time. Because of the difficulty of testing personality trait change over a lifetime, many studies examining trait continuity and change have focused on between-person differences across age groups rather than within-person change. When generation differences are present, these between-group tests will confound generational changes with true personality change. For example, there is some evidence that the generational differences in narcissism (e.g., Twenge, 2006) have been misattributed and actually represent the within-person changes in narcissism that result from an investment in age-graded social roles (Roberts et al., 2010).

Although cohort effects can certainly confound tests of personality trait change, these effects cannot explain all of the differences that have been identified in previous research. Despite a general over-reliance on cross-sectional studies, longitudinal research has also replicated the findings on personality trait change. For example, both the continuity of personality traits and their mean-level changes have been supported in meta-analyses of longitudinal studies (Roberts & DelVecchio, 2000; Roberts, Walton, & Viechtbauer, 2006). In addition, evidence for the corresponsive principle was provided in a longitudinal sample of college students (Roberts & Robins, 2004) and evidence for the social investment principle was found in two longitudinal studies of adults (Hudson et al., 2012; Roberts, Walton, Bogg, et al., 2006). Finally, the importance of young adulthood for understanding personality trait change has also been established in longitudinal research (Hopwood et al., 2011). Thus, personality trait changes appear to reflect actual within-person changes. Nevertheless, more longitudinal research is needed, and cohort effects will be a potential concern for future cross-sectional studies of continuity and change.

Broad Versus Narrow Measurement

The appropriate breadth of the personality measure being used to assess trait change is another methodological issue that deserves attention. Although personality traits have generally been examined at the level of the Big Five, recent research has demonstrated the benefits of measuring the narrower facets of these traits for predictive validity (Ashton, Jackson, Paunonen, Helmes, & Rothstein, 1995; Dudley, Orvis, Lebiecki, & Cortina, 2006; Wood, Nye, & Saucier, 2010; also see Chapter 14, this volume). When broad personality factors are measured, facets that are correlated with criteria in the opposite directions may cancel each other out and mitigate the correlation with the criterion (Paunonen, 1998). For example, Wood et al. (2010) showed that the narrow personality characteristics associated with openness to experience were negatively correlated, positively correlated, or not correlated at all with life satisfaction. In addition, Dudley et al. (2006) showed that job performance was positively related to the achievement and dependability facets of conscientiousness and negatively correlated with the cautiousness facet. Clearly, aggregating these characteristics to the broad trait level would obscure information about the relationship between personality and the criterion.

From a developmental perspective, narrow facet measures are also useful for understanding trait change. Again, research has demonstrated that the developmental trajectory of some facets may differ even within the same personality trait. For example, Roberts, Walton, and Viechtbauer (2006) showed that mean levels of the social dominance facet of extraversion increased over the life course while the social vitality facet remained relatively stable. Jackson et al. (2009) also found that the facets of conscientiousness changed at different points in the life course and concluded that "there is a clear need to go beyond the broad Big Five level of analysis to fully understand the development of conscientiousness" (p. 456). More recently, Soto, John, Gosling, and Potter (2011) demonstrated that facet-level differences were common across most of the Big Five traits and were particularly salient for extraversion, conscientiousness, and neuroticism.

Despite these developmental effects, these results do not indicate that all studies of personality in an organizational context should examine facet-level differences. As with all studies relating one construct to another, the best prediction of behavior will be observed when the breadth of the personality measure matches the breadth of the criterion. Roberts (2006) proposed that situations could be viewed hierarchically in the same way that personality traits are. At the broadest level are environmental components like culture in a country and climate in the organization. Next are the role demands and expectations that an individual experiences at work. Finally, specific stimuli, rewards, and punishments represent the narrowest conceptualization of a situation or environment. Thus, when examining the organizational or work-related influences on personality trait change, it is important that the environment is operationalized with the same breadth as the personality measure. When this is not the case, the relationship between environment and personality will be attenuated. For example, if an organization creates a climate for industriousness and rewards hard workers, this situation will likely influence behaviors related to the industriousness facet of conscientiousness. However, this environment may have little effect on the order or dependability facets and, therefore, may have lower correlations with a global conscientiousness measure than with industriousness alone.

One limitation to the use of facets in the study of personality trait change is that systematic empirical studies have not been conducted to identify all of the facets for each of the Big Five traits. For example, the most widely known facet structures, the 45-facet structure of the AB5C model (Hofstee, De Raad, & Goldberg, 1992) and the 30-facet structure of the NEO-PI (Costa, McCrae, & Dye, 1991), were developed primarily using theoretical and rational (rather than empirical) approaches to identify facets. In addition, although several studies have provided rigorous empirical examinations of the Big Five traits (Chernyshenko, Stark, Woo, & Gonz, 2008; Roberts, Chernyshenko, Stark, & Goldberg, 2005), these studies typically focus on only one of the five factors. One exception is the 22-facet structure of the Tailored Adaptive Personality Assessment System (TAPAS; Stark, Drasgow, & Chernyshenko, 2008). This measure is based on a comprehensive set of factor analyses and is currently being examined for use as an Army selection and classification tool (Chernyshenko, Stark, & Drasgow, 2011). At this point, more research is needed to compare these facet structures, identify strengths and weaknesses, and examine their importance for understanding personality trait change.

Measurement and Relational Equivalence

In order to fully understand changes in personality traits over the life course, it is important to differentiate true changes in the latent construct from artifactual changes to the measurement process. Golembiewski, Billingsley, and Yeager (1976) identified three types of change that can occur in self-reports of behavior. Alpha change refers to true differences in the latent construct. When examining personality development over time, this type of change is what researchers are most interested in. In other words, does an individual's level of conscientiousness truly change over time?

A second type of change identified by Golembiewski et al. (1976) is known as gamma change, which reflects changes in the meaning and/or conceptualization of the latent construct. Conceptually, gamma change has occurred if the factor structure, or the nomological network surrounding the latent factor, has changed over the period of examination (Nye, Brummel, & Drasgow, 2010). This type of change is important because comparing personality traits in the presence of gamma change is essentially equivalent to comparing apples and oranges.

A final type of change that can occur is known as beta change, which occurs when the response scale is recalibrated such that some items are more or less closely associated with the latent construct. In confirmatory factor analysis (CFA), the relationship between an item and the latent factor is represented by the factor loading. These loadings indicate how well each item discriminates between individuals with high or low levels of the latent trait. Substantively, the factor loadings also represent the psychological interval between each point on the response scale. Nye et al. (2010) described this type of change using the example of sexual harassment training. Before the training, employees may consider harassment occurring once a month to represent a 3 (*sometimes*) on the response scale of a sexual harassment measure, whereas harassment occurring four times a month represents a 4 (*often*) on the same response scale. After the training, *sometimes* may be defined as harassment occurring once a month and *often* may be defined as occurring twice a month. Thus, the psychological distance between a 3 and a 4 on the response scale has decreased and beta change has occurred.

Beta change may also occur if respondents provide systematically higher or lower responses to a particular item over time. For example, this form of change may occur if a college student fills out a personality inventory before and after they get their first job. When in college, he or she may consider himself/herself hard-working when compared with friends who do not attend class, do not finish assignments, and party instead of working. However, after obtaining a job, this same individual may not consider himself/herself to be hard-working if he or she is surrounded by coworkers who consistently work long hours. In this case, the individual may rate himself/herself consistently lower on a conscientiousness scale than he or she did in college. If similar changes occur at the group level, this phenomenon would result in systematically lower scores on the Time 2 measure of conscientiousness than at Time 1.

As another example, beta change could also occur if individuals try to distort their responses to personality measures (Stark, Chernyshenko, Chan, Lee, & Drasgow, 2001). For example, if employees are rewarded by the organization for personality trait change, workers may try to inflate their scores to obtain these rewards or avoid punishment. In the organizational literature, the most salient form of response distortion occurs in the form of socially desirable responding during the selection process (Birkeland, Manson, Kisamore, Brannick, & Smith, 2006; Mueller-Hanson, Heggestad, & Thornton, 2003). If scores obtained for selection purposes (i.e., contaminated with socially desirable responding) are then compared to scores obtained for developmental purposes (i.e., most likely not contaminated with desirable responding), personality trait levels may appear to change, albeit in the opposite direction of developmental trends (i.e., scores on desirable traits may appear to decrease). Although these forms of response distortion could appear as differences in the latent trait (Zickar & Robie, 1999), research has also shown that this pattern of responding could generate beta change in the measurement process (Stark et al., 2001; Zickar, Gibby, & Robie, 2004).

Because beta or gamma change can affect mean-level differences and confound assessments of alpha change (Nye & Drasgow, 2011), nonequivalence must be evaluated before alpha change can be identified. However, nonequivalence cannot be identified using mean-level tests, exploratory factor analyses (EFA) with target rotation, or correlational results alone (Nye, Roberts, Saucier, & Zhou, 2008). Instead, these questions must be addressed using a combination of measurement and relational equivalence analyses (Nye et al., 2010). Measurement equivalence is concerned with the invariance of the measurement model and can be assessed effectively using CFA or item response theory (IRT) approaches. These methods have been described in detail elsewhere and examined extensively in the organizational literature (Nye & Drasgow, 2011; Stark, Chernyshenko, & Drasgow, 2006; Vandenberg & Lance, 2000). In contrast, relational equivalence is concerned with the equivalence of regression lines (e.g., Cleary, 1968) or correlations with external criteria (Linn, 1978). Whereas measurement nonequivalence may reflect both gamma and beta change (Riordan, Richardson, Schaffer, & Vandenberg, 2001), relational nonequivalence can be considered additional evidence for gamma change (Nye et al., 2010). However, because both forms of equivalence can provide different information about the latent construct, both should be examined before drawing conclusions about changes over time (Nye et al., 2010).

It is important to note that nonequivalence is not necessarily an undesirable feature of the measurement process. In some cases, nonequivalence may reflect the hypothesized effect being studied. Riordan et al. (2001) provided several examples of past research that has explicitly planned for beta and/or gamma change in longitudinal studies of organizational behavior. For example, Ivancevich (1979) showed that rater training could reduce leniency and halo error (i.e., beta change). In addition, Buono, Bowditch, and Lewis (1985) examined whether mergers can change the way that employees viewed their coworkers (i.e., gamma change). Similarly, when examining changes in personality traits over time, changes due to an organizational intervention or increased investment in one's work roles could result in beta or gamma changes (Golembiewski et al., 1976). If this were the case, nonequivalence would reflect an expected change rather than a harmful artifact.

In sum, both measurement and relational equivalence can be either planned and intentional or unplanned and problematic. Consequently, researchers should be careful about attributing nonequivalence to response artifacts rather than substantive sources. For this reason, Ployhart and Oswald (2004) differentiated between the planned and unplanned nonequivalence and suggested different approaches to testing each. In addition, effect-size measures for CFA (Nye & Drasgow, 2011) or IRT (Nye, 2011) studies of measurement equivalence can be used to model the effects of nonequivalence on research results and to differentiate these effects from actual changes in the latent construct.

Measuring the Environment

Finally, the research reviewed above suggests that the environment plays an important role in personality development. However, despite its importance, measurement of the environment is often ignored or poorly operationalized (Roberts, 2007). In order to understand the effects of the environment on individual personality, the environment must be understood more clearly. This idea is certainly not new (cf. Holland, 1959; Parsons, 1909; Roberts, 2007; Schneider, 1987) but has important implications for the future study of personality trait continuity and change.

One way to define and organize situations is around the concept of social roles (Roberts, 2007; Stryker, 2007). In terms of understanding personality development, a benefit of operationalizing situations in this way is that roles are often accompanied by specific expectations and behavioral contingencies. For example, in the work context, one of the goals of socialization is to communicate these expectations and to reduce role ambiguity. In fact, many of the transformational processes described above occur in the context of one's work role. Although we intentionally limited our discussion to the work context, the link between social roles and personality trait change is observed in other life domains as well. Lodi-Smith and Roberts (2012) showed that investing in social roles related to family, religion, and volunteerism was associated with changes in agreeableness, conscientiousness, and emotional stability.

This emphasis on the role of an individual in his or her workplace suggests that an employee's roles within the organization may be more influential than the overall environment in determining fit. In other words, it is possible to be in an organization that does not directly fit with an individual's personality while simultaneously occupying a work role that does (Schaubroeck et al., 1998). Similar distinctions have been made in the vocational interest literature where Holland (1997) has emphasized the importance of examining congruence between the individual and his or her occupation rather than the organization as a whole. The differences between the organization and the expectations and contingencies of work roles may potentially explain the low levels of range restriction that have been observed within organizations on both personality (Schmidt et al., 2008) and vocational interest (Nye et al., 2012) constructs.

There has been some debate about whether the environment of interest comprises the objective characteristics of the environment or the people in it (Schneider, 2001). Both Holland (1997) and Schneider (1987) have suggested that work environments should be based on the people in them. With work roles in mind, this conceptualization of the environment seems appropriate. The importance of social roles for personality development is predicated on the expectations and the behavioral contingencies that are enforced by others. For example, if an individual does not conform to the expectations of his or her supervisor or coworkers (e.g., show up for work on time, stay on task, be a team player), he or she is likely to experience negative job-related (e.g., low performance review or termination) and social (e.g., exclusion, lack of acceptance) consequences. In other words, the people that are associated with a particular role can play a big part in shaping it.

Implications and Conclusions

In general, the research cited above suggests that personality traits are both relatively stable and changing over the life course. But what are the implications of these findings for organizational practices?

Personality measures are widely used for employee selection and have demonstrated validity for predicting performance on the job (Barrick & Mount, 1991; J. Hogan & Holland, 2003; Hurtz & Donovan, 2000). When considering the implications of the personality development literature for these practices, it is important to remember that the rank-order consistency of personality traits is relatively stable over the life course (Roberts & DelVecchio, 2000) and this stability only increases as the individual gets older. In other words, job applicants with the highest scores on a conscientiousness scale are likely to remain conscientious individuals even as they become older incumbents. Thus, selecting job applicants based on their personality scores remains a justified practice.

Despite the rank-order stability of personality traits, there is also evidence of mean-level changes, and research indicates that the rate of personality change may vary across individuals (Mroczek & Spiro, 2003). Therefore, it is possible that selecting individuals based on their intraindividual change trajectory could also benefit organizations. However, we are unaware of any research documenting the benefits or predictive validity of the intraindividual change trajectory in a selection context. Moreover, because an individual's change trajectory is only evident over long periods of time and several measurement occasions, selecting employees based on their propensity for change is dependent on identifying predictors of this individual difference. To date, there has been little or no organizationally relevant research on the predictors of changeability. One obvious implication of the research on personality development is that if people do change, then the next steps should be to identify who is most changeable and what are the best techniques to promote constructive change.

The evidence for personality trait change also indicates that it may be possible to change employees' personality traits with organizational interventions. As discussed above, research in the therapeutic intervention literature (De Fruyt et al., 2006; Piedmont, 2001) suggests that training interventions can successfully change personality. However, research outside of therapeutic settings has yet to demonstrate the utility of training for this purpose. Therapeutic interventions are often more time-intensive than the typical organizational training, are frequently conducted one-on-one with patients, and may require that the patient play a more active role in the intervention. Given that these conditions favor personality trait change, research needs to establish that organizational training interventions can also be successful at inducing personality change when applied in a practical and efficient way.

In this regard, there is some empirical evidence that organizational training efforts can change behavior. For example, Collins and Holton (2004) conducted a meta-analysis of training interventions focused on leadership development. Results showed that there was substantial variation in the effectiveness of training programs but that effect sizes comparing pre- and posttraining behavior generally ranged from .35 to 1.01. Similarly, another meta-analysis (Arthur, Bennet, Edens, & Bell, 2003) found that the overall effect sizes of training interventions on behavioral outcomes and interpersonal skills were .62 and .54, respectively. Primary studies have also demonstrated that training interventions can effectively change personality-related characteristics such as creativity (Barber, 2004) and the ability to cope with stress (Driskell, Johnston, & Salas, 2001).

Other developmental opportunities, including coaching or mentoring programs, are also potentially important influences on employees' personality traits. As described above, many of the environmental influences on personality and individual behavior in the ASTMA model involve interpersonal interactions, observations, and relationships. In particular, mentoring or coaching relationships are one-on-one interactions that emphasize mentors or coaches influencing individual behavior and success. Because these developmental efforts are focused on individual needs and can continue over long time periods, these relationships may be more influential than broadly focused training interventions. In fact, executive coaching is sometimes compared (see Bachkirova

& Cox, 2005) to the type of therapeutic interventions that have successfully changed personality traits in the past (e.g., De Fruyt et al., 2006; Piedmont, 2001).

Although there are few studies that have examined the effectiveness of mentoring or coaching programs (Collins & Holton, 2004; Peterson, 2011), some research has demonstrated their utility for developing individual characteristics. Finn (2007) showed that coaching resulted in improvements in positive affect (d = .23), self-efficacy (d = .31), openness to new behaviors (d = .41), and planning (d = 1.05). In addition, Peterson (1993) found that the average effect size of coaching interventions on employee behavior was d = 1.5 when examining a broad range of behavioral outcomes including leadership, communication, and interpersonal or intrapersonal skills.

The research on training and development programs suggests that employees' developmental experiences can influence personality traits. However, these studies also suggest that the effectiveness of organizational interventions can vary widely (Collins & Holton, 2004). Indeed, Brown and Sitzmann (2011) noted that if "training is ill-conceived, poorly planned, or inadequately executed, then it is likely to waste organizations' and employees' limited resources" (p. 470). As such, it is worth examining how these interventions can be implemented effectively. Again, research on this topic is lacking, and more research is needed to fully understand the association between organizational interventions and personality trait change. However, the ASTMA model and the theoretical mechanisms described above can provide some insight.

In order for training interventions focused on changing personality traits to be effective, it is important to establish contingencies that promote the application of learned behaviors on the job. Because the change processes we describe in this chapter are influenced by the expectations and contingencies associated with work roles, these same factors will also be influential in reinforcing training material. This need for contingencies is not unique to personality training and has been suggested as one way to increase the transfer-of-training more generally (Baldwin & Ford, 1988). Social support is another factor that can facilitate the transfer of training interventions designed to generate personality change. Here, both supervisor support and peer support will be important (Chiaburu & Marinova, 2005; Lim & Johnson, 2002). If other individuals in the work environment do not support these personality changes, interventions are not likely to be effective in the long term. For example, suppose a normally lazy employee completes a training program designed to help him or her to work harder and be more reliable (i.e., to increase conscientiousness). Any behavioral changes that result from this training may not last if coworkers tease him or her for the new behavior.

The employee development literature is also relevant here. This literature is focused on identifying ways to facilitate intraindividual change (Brown & Sitzmann, 2011) and suggests that there are four primary sources of this change—work experiences, interpersonal relationships, education, and assessment and feedback (Noe, Wilk, Mullen, & Wanek, 1997). When used appropriately, education, assessment, and feedback may help to reinforce the behavioral contingencies of an employee's work role. However, as implied by the ASTMA model, an individual's work experiences and interpersonal relationships may be particularly important sources of change. Research on employee development suggests that work assignments must be challenging in order for development to occur (Noe, 2008). Similarly, in order for personality traits to change, employees must be provided with work experiences that challenge their identity structure and reinforce development (Roberts et al., 2008). Obviously, providing these opportunities will require a delicate balance between promoting change and maintaining person–environment fit, particularly because an individual's work roles are so important for determining fit (Roberts, 2007; Stryker, 2007). Nevertheless, research suggests that people's experiences at work are key determinants of their stability and change in personality traits.

Even when organizational interventions are implemented appropriately, questions remain about the long-term effects of these interventions. Job-training interventions, for example, typically target narrow outcomes and tend to ignore broader constructs like personality traits. Thus, it is unclear whether existing knowledge on how to change specific work-related behavior, such as safety behavior, will have any long-lasting effects on clearly related personality traits, such as conscientiousness. However, there is some research suggesting that the changes in behavior that are associated with organizational interventions may remain even months after the intervention itself. For example, Evers, Brouwers, and Tomic (2006) conducted a quasi-experimental study on the effects of coaching and found that the effects of this intervention were still evident 4 months after the program had ended. As such, it is possible that developmental interventions focused on personality traits will also have long-term effects. However, more research is needed to determine whether this is the case and to identify the magnitude of the effects over longer periods of time.

Although past research in the applied psychological literature has viewed personality traits as static individual differences, research in the personality literature has shown that personality traits do change over time. This empirical fact poses challenges and opportunities for organizational researchers. Simply assuming that personality traits are static, hard-wired, and unchanging and thus only to be used as predictors and selection criteria is unfounded. It also poses fascinating possibilities, as now personality traits could become the focus of organizational interventions intended to make employees more capable of performing their current and future jobs. We hope that these findings serve as inspiration to future organizational researchers to take on the mantle of responsibility to study personality change within organizational settings.

Practitioner's Window

The theoretical and empirical findings discussed in this chapter have a number of implications for organizational practices. Below, we summarize several of the key points for those that wish to apply these findings in an organizational setting:

- Because personality traits have high rank-order stability, selecting employees based on their personality characteristics can help to identify successful employees.
- However, personality traits also change over time. The general trend is for individuals to become more mature and to change in ways that are consistent with their work roles.
- Employees' experiences in the workplace can provide incentives for personality trait change. As such, socialization practices, the climate of the organization, and organizational policies and procedures, among other efforts, can play a major role in promoting this change.
- Although more research is needed, it appears that organizational interventions (e.g., training, coaching, and mentoring programs) can also be used to shape employees' personality traits in ways that will help them to be successful on the job.
- Individuals seek out jobs and organizations that they believe are consistent with their personality. As such, individuals who cannot manipulate their job to fit with their personality and/or are not invested enough in their role to adapt are more likely to leave the organization to find work that is consistent with their traits.

In sum, there is robust evidence for personality trait change over time, and understanding these changes, and their antecedents and consequences, can help organizations to build a successful workforce.

References

Allen, G. (1998). Work values in librarianship. *Library & Information Science Research, 20*, 415–424.

Andersson, L. M., & Pearson, C. M. (1999). Tit for tat? The spiraling effect of incivility in the workplace. *Academy of Management Review, 24*, 452–471.

Ardelt, M. (2000). Still stable after all these years? Personality stability theory revisited. *Social Psychology Quarterly, 63*, 392–405.

Arthur, W., Jr., Bennett, W., Jr., Edens, P. S., & Bell, S. T. (2003). Effectiveness of training in organizations: A meta-analysis of design and evaluation features. *Journal of Applied Psychology, 88*, 234–245.

Ashton, M. C., Jackson, D. N., Paunonen, S. V., Helmes, E., & Rothstein, M. G. (1995). The criterion validity of Broad Factor Scales versus specific Facet Scales. *Journal of Research in Personality, 29*, 432–442.

Bachkirova, T., & Cox, E. (2005). A bridge over troubled water: Bringing together coaching and counseling. *Counseling at Work, 48*, 2–9.

Baldwin, T. T., & Ford, J. K. (1988). Transfer of training: A review and directions for future research. *Personnel Psychology, 41*, 63–105.

Bandura, A. (1977). *Social learning theory*. Englewood Cliffs, NJ: Prentice Hall.

Barber, J. (2004). Skill upgrading within informal training: Lessons from the Indian auto mechanic. *International Journal of Training and Development, 8*, 128–139.

Barrick, M. R., & Mount, M. K. (1991). The Big Five personality dimensions and job performance: A meta-analysis. *Personnel Psychology, 44*, 1–26.

Bauer, T. N., Bodner, T., Erdogan, B., Truxillo, D. M., & Tucker, J. S. (2007). Newcomer adjustment during organizational socialization: A meta-analytic review of antecedents, outcomes, and methods. *Journal of Applied Psychology, 92*, 707–721.

Bazana, P. G., & Stelmack, R. M. (2004). Stability of personality across the life span: A meta-analysis. In R. M. Stelmack (Ed.), *On the psychobiology of personality* (pp. 113–144). Oxford, UK: Elsevier.

Birkeland, S. A., Manson, T. M., Kisamore, J. L., Brannick, M. T., & Smith, M. A. (2006). A meta-analytic investigation of job applicant faking on personality measures. *International Journal of Selection and Assessment, 14*, 317–335.

Bleidorn, W., Kandler, C., Riemann, R., Angleitner, A., & Spinath, F. M. (2009). Patterns and sources of adult personality development: Growth curve analyses of the NEO-PI-R scales in a longitudinal twin study. *Journal of Personality and Social Psychology, 97*, 142–155.

Boone, C., van Olffen, W., & Roijakkers, N. (2004). Selection on the road to a career: Evidence of personality sorting in educational choice. *Journal of Career Development, 31*, 61–78.

Boyce, A. S., Ryan, A. M., Imus, A. L., & Morgeson, F. P. (2007). "Temporary worker, permanent loser?" A model of the stigmatization of temporary workers. *Journal of Management, 33*, 5–29.

Bretz, R. D., Ash, R. A., & Dreher, G. F. (1989). Do people make the place? An examination of the attraction–selection–attrition hypothesis. *Personnel Psychology, 42*, 561–581.

Brown, K. G., & Sitzmann, T. (2011). Training and employee development for improved performance. In S. Zedeck (Ed.), *APA handbook of industrial and organizational psychology: Selecting and developing members for the organization* (Vol. 2, pp. 469–503). Washington, DC: American Psychological Association.

Buono, A. F., Bowditch, J. L., & Lewis, J. W. (1985). When cultures collide: The anatomy of a merger. *Human Relations, 38*, 477–500.

Cable, D. M., & Judge, T. A. (1997). Interviewers' perceptions of person–organization fit and organizational selection decisions. *Journal of Applied Psychology, 82*, 546–561.

Cable, D. M., & Parsons, C. K. (2001). Socialization tactics and person–organization fit. *Personnel Psychology, 54*, 1–23.

Caspi, A., & Roberts, B. W. (1999). Personality change and continuity across the life course. In L. A. Pervin & O. P. John (Eds.), *Handbook of personality theory and research* (Vol. 2, pp. 300–326). New York: Guilford Press.

Caspi, A., Roberts, B. W., & Shiner, R. L. (2005). Personality development: Stability and change. *Annual Review of Psychology, 56*, 453–484.

Chatman, J. A. (1991). Matching people and organizations: Selection and socialization in public accounting firms. *Administrative Science Quarterly, 26*, 459–484.

Chatman, J. A., Wong, E., & Joyce, C. K. (2008). When do people make the place? Considering the interactionist foundations of the attraction–selection–attrition model. In D. B. Smith (Ed.), *The people make the place: Dynamic linkages between individuals and organizations* (pp. 65–88). New York: Lawrence Erlbaum Associates.

Chernyshenko, O. S., Stark, S., & Drasgow, F. (2011). Individual differences: Their measurement and validity. In S. Zedeck (Ed.), *APA handbook of industrial and organizational psychology: Selecting and developing members for the organization* (Vol. 2, pp. 117–151). Washington, DC: American Psychological Association.

Chernyshenko, O. S., Stark, S., Woo, S., & Conz, G. (2008, April). *Openness to experience: Its facet structure, measurement and validity*. Paper presented at the 23rd Annual Conference for the Society of Industrial and Organizational Psychologists, New Orleans, LA.

Chiaburu, D. S., & Marinova, S. V. (2005). What predicts skill transfer? An explanatory study of goal orientation, training self-efficacy and organizational supports. *International Journal of Training and Development, 9*, 110–123.

Clausen, J. A., & Gilens, M. (1990). Personality and labor force participation across the life course: A longitudinal study of women's careers. *Sociological Forum, 5*, 595–618.

Cleary, T. A. (1968). Test bias: Prediction of grades of Negro and White students in integrated colleges. *Journal of Educational Measurement, 5*, 115–124.
Collins, D. B., & Holton, E. F., III. (2004). The effectiveness of managerial leadership development programs: A meta-analysis of studies from 1982–2001. *Human Resource Development Quarterly, 15*, 217–248.
Conley, J. J. (1984). Longitudinal consistency of adult personality: Self-reported psychological characteristics across 45 years. *Journal of Personality and Social Psychology, 47*, 1325–1333.
Cooper-Thomas, H. D., & Anderson, N. (2006). Organizational socialization: A new theoretical model and recommendations for future research and HRM practices in organizations. *Journal of Managerial Psychology, 21*, 492–516.
Costa, P. T., Bagby, R. M., Herbst, J. H., & McCrae, R. R. (2005). Personality self-reports are concurrently reliable and valid during acute depressive episodes. *Journal of Affective Disorders, 89*, 45–55.
Costa, P. T., McCrae, R. R., & Dye, D. A. (1991). Facet Scales for agreeableness and conscientiousness: A revision of the NEO Personality Inventory. *Personality and Individual Differences, 12*, 887–898.
De Fruyt, F., Van Leeuwen, K., Bagby, R. M., Rolland, J., & Rouillon, F. (2006). Assessing and interpreting personality change and continuity in patients treated for major depression. *Psychological Assessment, 18*, 71–80.
Driskell, J. E., Johnston, J., & Salas, E. (2001). Does stress training generalize to novel settings? *Human Factors, 42*, 99–110.
Dudley, N. M., Orvis, K. A., Lebiecki, J. E., & Cortina, J. M. (2006). A meta-analytic investigation of conscientiousness in the prediction of job performance: Examining the intercorrelations and the incremental validity of narrow traits. *Journal of Applied Psychology, 91*, 40–57.
Duncan, L. E., & Agronick, G. S. (1995). The intersection of life stage and social events: Personality and life outcomes. *Journal of Personality and Social Psychology, 69*, 558–568.
Durkheim, E. (1897). *Suicide: A study in sociology* [Le Suicide: Etude de sociologie). New York: Free Press.
Eby, L. T. (2011). Mentoring. In S. Zedeck (Ed.), *APA handbook of industrial and organizational psychology: Selecting and developing members for the organization* (Vol. 2, pp. 505–525). Washington, DC: American Psychological Association.
Elder, G. H. (1969). Occupational mobility, life patterns, and personality. *Journal of Health and Social Behavior, 10*, 308–323.
Erikson, E. H. (1963). *Childhood and society* (2nd ed.). New York: W. W. Norton.
Evers, W. J. G., Brouwers, A., & Tomic, W. (2006): A quasi-experimental study on management coaching effectiveness. *Consulting Psychology Journal: Practice and Research, 58*, 174–182.
Feather, N. T. (1989). Reported changes in behavior after job loss in a sample of older unemployed men. *Australian Journal of Psychology, 41*, 175–185.
Ferguson, C. J. (2010). A meta-analysis of normal and disordered personality across the life span. *Journal of Personality and Social Psychology, 98*, 659–667.
Finn, F. A. (2007). *Leadership development through executive coaching: The effects on leaders' psychological states and transformational leadership behavior* (Unpublished doctoral dissertation). Brisbane, Australia: Queensland University of Technology.
Fraley, C., & Roberts, B. W. (2005). Patterns of continuity: A dynamic model for conceptualizing the stability of individual differences in psychological constructs across the life course. *Psychological Review, 112*, 60–74.
Fryer, D. M., & Payne, R. L. (1986). Being unemployed: A review of the literature on the psychological experience of unemployment. In C. L. Cooper & I. Robertson (Eds.), *International review of industrial and organizational psychology* (pp. 235–278). London: Wiley.
Giberson, T. R., Resick, C. J., & Dickson, M. W. (2005). Embedding leader characteristics: An examination of homogeneity of personality and values in organizations. *Journal of Applied Psychology, 90*, 1002–1010.
Golembiewski, R. T., Billingsley, K., & Yeager, S. (1976). Measuring change and persistence in human affairs: Types of change generated by OD designs. *Journal of Applied Behavioral Science, 12*, 133–157.
Griffeth, R. W., Hom, P. W., & Gaertner, S. (2000). A meta-analysis of antecedents and correlates of employee turnover: Update, moderator tests, and research implications for the next millennium. *Journal of Management, 26*, 463–488.
Hanisch, K. A. (2000). The impact of organizational interventions on behaviors: An examination of models of withdrawal. In D. R. Ilgen & C. L. Hulin (Eds.), *Computational modeling of behavior in organizations: The third scientific discipline* (pp. 33–60). Westport, CT: Quorum Books.
Harms, P. D., Roberts, B. W., & Winter, D. (2006). Becoming the Harvard man: Person–environment fit, personality development, and academic success. *Personality and Social Psychology Bulletin, 32*, 851–865.
Helson, R., Stewart, A. J., & Ostrove, J. (1995). Identity in three cohorts of midlife women. *Journal of Personality and Social Psychology, 69*, 544–557.
Hoffman, L. R. (1959). Homogeneity of member personality and its effect on group problem-solving. *Journal of Abnormal and Social Psychology, 58*, 27–32.
Hoffman, L. R., & Maier, N. R. F. (1961). Quality and acceptance of problem solutions by members of homogeneous and heterogeneous groups. *Journal of Abnormal and Social Psychology, 62*, 401–407.

Hofstee, W. K., De Raad, B., & Goldberg, L. R. (1992). Integration of the Big Five and circumplex approaches to trait structure. *Journal of Personality and Social Psychology, 63*, 146–163.
Hogan, J., & Holland, B. (2003). Using theory to evaluate personality and job-performance relations: A socioanalytic perspective. *Journal of Applied Psychology, 88*, 100–112.
Hogan, R., Hogan, J., & Roberts, B. (1996). Personality measurement and employment decisions: Questions and answers. *American Psychologist, 51*, 469–477.
Hogan, R., & Roberts, B. W. (2004). A socioanalytic model of maturity. *Journal of Career Assessment, 12*, 207–217.
Holland, J. L. (1959). A theory of vocational choice. *Journal of Counseling Psychology, 6*, 35–45.
Holland, J. L. (1997). *Making vocational choices: A theory of vocational personalities and work environments* (3rd ed.). Odessa, FL: Psychological Assessment Resources.
Hopwood, C. J., Donnellan, M. B., Blonigen, D. M., Krueger, R. F., McGue, M., Iacono, W. G., & Burt, S. A. (2011). Genetic and environmental influences on personality trait stability and growth during the transition to adulthood: A three-wave longitudinal study. *Journal of Personality and Social Psychology, 100*, 545–556.
Hudson, N. W., Roberts, B. W., & Lodi-Smith, J. (2012). Personality trait development and social investment at work. *Journal of Research in Personality, 46*, 334–344.
Hulin, C. L. (1991). Adaptation, persistence, and commitment in organizations. In M. D. Dunnette & L. M. Hough (Eds.), *Handbook of industrial and organizational psychology* (2nd ed., Vol. 2, pp. 446–505). Palo Alto, CA: Consulting Psychologists Press.
Hulin, C. L. (2002). Lessons from industrial and organizational psychology. In J. M. Brett & F. Drasgow (Eds.), *The psychology of work: Theoretically based empirical research* (pp. 3–22). Mahwah, NJ: Lawrence Erlbaum Associates.
Hulin, C. L., Roznowski, M., & Hachiya, D. (1985). Alternative opportunities and withdrawal decisions: Empirical and theoretical discrepancies and an integration. *Psychological Bulletin, 97*, 233–250.
Hurtz, G. M., & Donovan, J. J. (2000). Personality and job performance: The Big Five revisited. *Journal of Applied Psychology, 85*, 869–879.
Ivancevich, J. M. (1979). Longitudinal study of the effects of rater training on psychometric error in ratings. *Journal of Applied Psychology, 64*, 502–508.
Jackson, J. J., Bogg, T., Walton, K., Wood, D., Harms, P. D., Lodi-Smith, J. L., & Roberts, B. W. (2009). Not all conscientiousness scales change alike: A multi-method, multi-sample study of age differences in the facets of conscientiousness. *Journal of Personality and Social Psychology, 96*, 446–459.
Jahoda, M., Lazarsfeld, P. F., & Zeisel, H. (1933). *Marienthal: The sociography of an unemployed community*. Chicago: Aldine.
Johnson, A. M., Vernon, P. A., & Feiler, A. R. (2008). Behavioral genetic studies of personality: An introduction and review of the results of 50+ years of research. In G. J. Boyle, G. Matthews, & D. H. Saklofske (Eds.), *The Sage handbook of personality theory and assessment: Personality theories and models* (Vol. 1, pp. 145–173). Thousand Oaks, CA: Sage.
Jordan, M., Herriot, P., & Chalmers, C. (1991). Testing Schneider's ASA theory. *Applied Psychology: An International Review, 40*, 47–53.
Judge, T. A., & Cable, D. M. (1997). Applicant personality, organizational culture, and organizational attraction. *Personnel Psychology, 50*, 359–393.
Kampa, S., & White, R. P. (2002). The effectiveness of executive coaching: What we know and what we still need to know. In R. L. Lowman (Ed.), *Handbook of organizational consulting psychology* (pp. 139–158). San Francisco: Jossey-Bass.
Kram, K. E. (1985). *Mentoring at work*. Glenview, IL: Scott Foresman.
Krasner, M. S., Epstein, R. M., Beckman, H., Suchman, A. L., Chapman, B., Mooney, C. J., & Quill, T. E. (2009). Association of an educational program in mindful communication with burnout, empathy, and attitudes among primary care physicians. *Journal of the American Medical Association, 302*, 1284–1293.
Kristof-Brown, A., Barrick, M. R., & Stevens, C. (2005). When opposites attract: A multi-sample demonstration of complementary person–team fit on extraversion. *Journal of Personality, 73*, 935–958.
Kristof-Brown, A., Zimmerman, R., & Johnson, E. (2005). Consequences of individuals' fit at work: A meta-analysis of person–job, person–organization, person–group, and person–supervisor fit. *Personnel Psychology, 58*, 281–342.
Krueger, R. F., South, S., Johnson, W., & Iacono, W. (2008). The heritability of personality is not always 50%: Gene–environment interactions and correlations between personality and parenting. *Journal of Personality, 76*, 1485–1522.
Lee, T. W., & Mitchell, T. R. (1994). An alternative approach: The unfolding model of voluntary employee turnover. *Academy of Management Review, 19*, 51–89.
Lewis, M. (2001). Issues in the study of personality development. *Psychological Inquiry, 12*, 67–83.
Lievens, F., Decaesteker, C., Coetsier, P., & Geirnaert, J. (2001). Organizational attractiveness for prospective applicants: A person–organisation fit perspective. *Applied Psychology: An International Review, 50*, 30–51.
Lim, D. H., & Johnson, S. D. (2002). Trainee perceptions of factors that influence learning transfer. *International Journal of Training and Development, 6*, 36–48.

Linn, R. L. (1978). Single-group validity, differential validity, and differential prediction. *Journal of Applied Psychology, 63*, 507–512.
Lodi-Smith, J., & Roberts, B. W. (2007). Social investment and personality: A meta-analytic analysis of the relationship of personality traits to investment in work, family, religion, and volunteerism. *Personality and Social Psychology Review, 11*, 68–86.
Lodi-Smith, J., & Roberts, B. W. (2010). Getting to know me: Social role experiences and age differences in self-concept clarity during adulthood. *Journal of Personality, 78*, 1383–1410.
Lodi-Smith, J., & Roberts, B. W. (2012). Concurrent and prospective relationships between social engagement and personality traits in older adulthood. *Psychology and Aging, 27*, 720–727.
McGue, M., Bacon, S., & Lykken, D. T. (1993). Personality stability and change in early adulthood: A behavioral genetic analysis. *Developmental Psychology, 29*, 96–109.
Moffitt, T. E., Arseneault, L., Belsky, D., Dickson, N., Hancox, R. J., Harrington, H., & Caspi, A. (2011). A gradient of childhood self-control predicts health, wealth, and public safety. *Proceedings of the National Academy of Sciences, 108*, 2693–2698.
Mroczek, D. K., & Spiro, A. (2003). Modeling intraindividual change in personality traits: Findings from the Normative Aging Study. *Journals of Gerontology, Series B: Psychological Sciences, 58*, 153–165.
Mueller-Hanson, R., Heggestad, E. D., & Thornton, G. C., III. (2003). Faking and selection: Considering the use of personality from select-in and select-out perspectives. *Journal of Applied Psychology, 88*, 348–355.
Newman, D. A., Hanges, P. J., Duan, L., & Ramesh, A. (2008). A network model of organizational climate: Friendship clusters, subgroup agreement, and climate schemas. In D. B. Smith (Ed.), *The people make the place: Dynamic linkages between individuals and organizations* (pp. 101–126). New York: Erlbaum.
Nishii, L. H., & Wright, P. M. (2008). Variability within organizations: Implications for strategic human resource management. In D. B. Smith (Ed.), *The people make the place: Dynamic linkages between individuals and organizations* (pp. 225–248). New York: Lawrence Erlbaum Associates.
Noe, R. A. (1988). An investigation of the determinants of successful assigned mentoring relationships. *Personnel Psychology, 41*, 457–479.
Noe, R. A. (2008). *Employee training and development* (4th ed.). Boston: McGraw-Hill.
Noe, R. A., Wilk, S. L., Mullen, E. J., & Wanek, J. E. (1997). Employee development: Construct validation issues. In J. K. Ford (Ed.), *Improving training effectiveness in work organizations* (pp. 153–189). Mahwah, NJ: Erlbaum.
Nye, C. D. (2011). *The development and validation of effect size measures for IRT and CFA studies of measurement equivalence* (Unpublished doctoral dissertation). Urbana: University of Illinois at Urbana-Champaign.
Nye, C. D., Brummel, B. J., & Drasgow, F. (2010). Too good to be true? Understanding change in organizational outcomes. *Journal of Management, 36*, 1555–1577.
Nye, C. D., & Drasgow, F. (2011). Effect size indices for analyses of measurement equivalence: Understanding the practical importance of differences between groups. *Journal of Applied Psychology, 96*, 966–980.
Nye, C. D., Roberts, B. W., Saucier, G., & Zhou, X. (2008). Testing the measurement equivalence of personality adjective items across cultures. *Journal of Research in Personality, 42*, 1524–1536.
Nye, C. D., Su, R., Rounds, J., & Drasgow, F. (2012). Vocational interests and performance: A quantitative review of over 60 years of research. *Perspectives on Psychological Science, 7*, 384–403.
O'Brien, G. E. (1986). *Psychology of work and unemployment*. New York: Wiley.
Oh, I., Wang, G., & Mount, M. (2011). Validity of observer ratings of the five-factor model of personality traits: A meta-analysis. *Journal of Applied Psychology, 96*, 762–773.
Ostroff, C., Kinicki, A. J., & Tamkins, M. M. (2003). Organizational culture and climate. In W. C. Borman, D. R. Ilgen, & R. J. Klimoski (Eds.), *Handbook of psychology: Industrial and organizational psychology* (Vol. 12, pp. 565–593). Hoboken, NJ: John Wiley & Sons.
Ostroff, C., & Rothausen, T. (1997). The moderating effect of tenure in person–environment fit: A field study in educational organizations. *Journal of Occupational and Organizational Psychology, 70*, 173–188.
Parsons, C. K. (1909). *Choosing a vocation*. Boston: Houghton Mifflin.
Paunonen, S. V. (1998). Hierarchical organization of personality and prediction of behavior. *Journal of Personality and Social Psychology, 74*, 538–556.
Peterson, D. B. (1993). *Skill learning and behavior change in an individually tailored management coaching program* (Unpublished doctoral dissertation). Minneapolis: University of Minnesota.
Peterson, D. B. (2011). Executive coaching: A critical review and recommendations for advancing the practice. In S. Zedeck (Ed.), *APA handbook of industrial and organizational psychology: Selecting and developing members for the organization* (Vol. 2, pp. 527–566). Washington, DC: American Psychological Association.
Piedmont, R. L. (2001). Cracking the plaster cast: Big Five personality change during intensive outpatient counseling. *Journal of Research in Personality, 35*, 500–520.
Ployhart, R. E., & Oswald, F. L. (2004). Applications of mean and covariance structure analysis: Integrating correlational and experimental approaches. *Organizational Research Methods, 7*, 27–65.

Ployhart, R. E., Weekley, J., & Baughman, K. (2006). The structure and function of human capital emergence: A multilevel examination of the attraction–selection–attrition model. *Academy of Management Journal, 49*, 661–677.

Rice, M. E., & Grusec, J. E. (1975). Saying and doing: Effects on observer performance. *Journal of Personality and Social Psychology, 32*, 584–593.

Riordan, C. M., Richardson, H. A., Schaffer, B. S., & Vandenberg, R. J. (2001). Alpha, beta, and gamma change: A review of past research with recommendations for new directions. In C. A. Schriesheim & L. L. Neider (Eds.), *Research in management: Equivalence in measurement* (Vol. 1, pp. 51–98). Greenwich, CT: Information Age.

Roberts, B. W. (1997). Plaster or plasticity: Are work experiences associated with personality change in women? *Journal of Personality, 65*, 205–232.

Roberts, B. W. (2006). Personality development and organizational behavior. In B. M. Staw (Ed.), *Research on organizational behavior* (pp. 1–41). Elsevier Science/JAI Press.

Roberts, B. W. (2007). Contextualizing personality psychology. *Journal of Personality, 75*, 1071–1081.

Roberts, B. W. (2009). Back to the future: Personality and assessment and personality development. *Journal of Research in Personality, 43*, 137–145.

Roberts, B. W., & Caspi, A. (2003). The cumulative continuity model of personality development: Striking a balance between continuity and change in personality traits across the life course. In R. M. Staudinger & U. Lindenberger (Eds.), *Understanding human development: Lifespan psychology in exchange with other disciplines* (pp. 183–214). Dordrecht, Netherlands: Kluwer Academic.

Roberts, B. W., Caspi, A., & Moffitt, T. (2003). Work experiences and personality development in young adulthood. *Journal of Personality and Social Psychology, 84*, 582–593.

Roberts, B. W., & Chapman, C. (2000). Change in dispositional well-being and its relation to role quality: A 30-year longitudinal study. *Journal of Research in Personality, 34*, 26–41.

Roberts, B. W., Chernyshenko, O., Stark, S., & Goldberg, L. (2005). The structure of conscientiousness: An empirical investigation based on seven major Personality Questionnaires. *Personnel Psychology, 58*, 103–139.

Roberts, B. W., & DelVecchio, W. F. (2000). The rank-order consistency of personality from childhood to old age: A quantitative review of longitudinal studies. *Psychological Bulletin, 126*, 3–25.

Roberts, B. W., Edmonds, G., & Grijalva, E. (2010). It is developmental me, not generation me: Developmental changes are more important than generational changes in narcissism—Commentary on Trzesniewski & Donnellan (2010). *Perspectives on Psychological Science, 5*, 97–102.

Roberts, B. W., Harms, P. D., Smith, J., Wood, D., & Webb, M. (2006). Methods in personality psychology. In M. Eid & E. Diener (Eds.), *Handbook of psychological assessment: A multimethod perspective* (pp. 321–335). Washington, DC: American Psychological Association.

Roberts, B. W., & Jackson, J. J. (2008). Sociogenomic personality psychology. *Journal of Personality, 76*, 1523–1544.

Roberts, B. W., & Mroczek, D. (2008). Personality trait change in adulthood. *Current Directions in Psychological Science, 17*, 31–35.

Roberts, B. W., & Robins, R. W. (2004). A longitudinal study of person–environment fit and personality development. *Journal of Personality, 72*, 89–110.

Roberts, B. W., Walton, K., Bogg, T., & Caspi, A. (2006). De-investment in work and non-normative personality trait change in young adulthood. *European Journal of Personality, 20*, 461–474.

Roberts, B. W., Walton, K., & Viechtbauer, W. (2006). Patterns of mean-level change in personality traits across the life course: A meta-analysis of longitudinal studies. *Psychological Bulletin, 132*, 1–25.

Roberts, B. W., & Wood, D. (2006). Personality development in the context of the neo-socioanalytic model of personality. In D. Mroczek & T. Little (Eds.), *Handbook of personality development* (pp. 11–39). Mahwah, NJ: Lawrence Erlbaum Associates.

Roberts, B. W., Wood, D., & Caspi, A. (2008). The development of personality traits in adulthood. In O. P. John, R. W. Robins, & L. A. Pervin (Eds.), *Handbook of personality: Theory and research* (3rd ed., pp. 375–398). New York: Guilford Press.

Robinson, S. L., & O'Leary-Kelly, A. M. (1998). Monkey see, monkey do: The influence of work groups on the antisocial behavior of employees. *Academy of Management Journal, 41*, 658–672.

Salancik, G. R., & Pfeffer, J. (1978). A social information processing approach to job attitudes and task design. *Administrative Science Quarterly, 23*, 224–253.

Santor, D. A., Bagby, R. M., & Joffe, R. T. (1997). Evaluating stability and change in personality and depression. *Journal of Personality and Social Psychology, 73*, 1354–1362.

Schaubroeck, J., Ganster, D. C., & Jones, J. R. (1998). Organization and occupation influences in the attraction–selection–attrition process. *Journal of Applied Psychology, 83*, 869–891.

Schein, E. (1992). *Organizational culture and leadership* (2nd ed.). San Francisco: Jossey-Bass.

Schmidt, F. L., Shaffer, J. A., & Oh, I. (2008). Increased accuracy for range restriction corrections: Implications for the role of personality and general mental ability in job and training performance. *Personnel Psychology, 61*, 827–868.

Schneider, B. (1987). The people make the place. *Personnel Psychology, 40*, 437–453.
Schneider, B. (2001). Fits about fit. *Applied Psychology: An International Review, 50*, 141–152.
Schneider, B. (2008). The people still make the place. In D. B. Smith (Ed.), *The people make the place: Dynamic linkages between individuals and organizations* (pp. 267–290). New York: Lawrence Erlbaum Associates.
Schneider, B., Smith, D. B., Taylor, S., & Fleenor, J. (1998). Personality and organizations: A test of the homogeneity of personality hypothesis. *Journal of Applied Psychology, 83*, 462–470.
Scollon, C. N., & Diener, E. (2006). Love, work, and changes in extraversion and neuroticism over time. *Journal of Personality and Social Psychology, 91*, 1152–1165.
Sears, D. O. (1986). College sophomores in the laboratory: Influences of a narrow data base on social psychology's view of human nature. *Journal of Personality and Social Psychology, 51*, 515–530.
Smith, M. L., Glass, G. V., & Miller, T. I. (1980). *The benefits of psychotherapy*. Baltimore: The Johns Hopkins University Press.
Smits, I. A. M., Dolan, C. V., Vorst, H. C. M., Wicherts, J. M., & Timmerman, M. E. (2011). Cohort differences in Big Five personality factors over a period of 25 years. *Journal of Personality and Social Psychology, 100*, 1124–1138.
Soto, C. J., John, O. P., Gosling, S. D., & Potter, J. (2011). Age differences in personality traits from 10 to 65: Big Five domains and facets in a large cross-sectional sample. *Journal of Personality and Social Psychology, 100*, 330–348.
Stark, S., Chernyshenko, O. S., Chan, K. Y., Lee, W. C., & Drasgow, F. (2001). Effects of the testing situation on item responding: Cause for concern. *Journal of Applied Psychology, 86*, 943–953.
Stark, S., Chernyshenko, O. S., & Drasgow, F. (2006). Detecting differential item functioning with CFA and IRT: Toward a unified strategy. *Journal of Applied Psychology, 91*, 1292–1306.
Stark, S., Drasgow, F., & Chernyshenko, O. S. (2008, October). *Update on the Tailored Adaptive Personality Assessment System (TAPAS): The next generation of personality assessment systems to support personnel selection and classification decisions*. Paper presented at the 50th Annual Conference of the International Military Testing Association, Amsterdam.
Stryker, S. (2007). Identity theory and personality theory: Mutual relevance. *Journal of Personality, 75*, 1083–1102.
Tajfel, H., & Turner, J. C. (1986). The social identity theory of intergroup behavior. In S. Worchel & W. G. Austin (Eds.), *Psychology of intergroup relations* (2nd ed., pp. 7–24). Chicago: NelsonHall.
Tang, T. Z., DeRubeis, R. J., Hollon, S. D., Amsterdam, J., Shelton, R., & Schalet, B. (2009). Personality change during depression treatment: A placebo-controlled trial. *Archives of General Psychiatry, 66*, 1322–1330.
Terracciano, A., McCrae, R. R., Brant, L. J., & Costa, P. T., Jr. (2005). Hierarchical linear modeling analyses of NEO-PI-R scales in the Baltimore Longitudinal Study of Aging. *Psychology and Aging, 20*, 493–506.
Tom, V. R. (1971). The role of personality and organizational images in the recruiting process. *Organizational Behavior and Human Performance, 6*, 573–592.
Turban, D. B., & Keon, T. L. (1993). Organizational attractiveness: An interactionist perspective. *Journal of Applied Psychology, 78*, 184–193.
Twenge, J. M. (2000). The age of anxiety? The birth cohort change in anxiety and neuroticism, 1952–1993. *Journal of Personality and Social Psychology, 50*, 143–151.
Twenge, J. M. (2006). *Generation me: Why today's young Americans are more confident, assertive, entitled—And more miserable than ever before*. New York: Free Press.
Twenge, J. M., & Foster, J. D. (2008). Mapping the scale of the narcissism epidemic: Increases in narcissism 2002–2007 within ethnic groups. *Journal of Research in Personality, 42*, 1619–1622.
Vandenberg, R. J., & Lance, C. E. (2000). A review and synthesis of the measurement invariance literature: Suggestions, practices, and recommendations for organizational research. *Organizational Research Methods, 3*, 4–70.
Van Iddekinge, C., Roth, P., Putka, D., & Lanivich, S. (2011). Are you interested? A meta-analysis of relations between vocational interests and employee performance and turnover. *Journal of Applied Psychology, 96*, 1167–1194.
Warr, P., Jackson, P., & Banks, M. (1988). Unemployment and mental health—Some British studies. *Journal of Social Issues, 44*, 47–68.
Williams, J., Fitzgerald, L. F., & Drasgow, F. (1999). The effects of organizational practices on sexual harassment and individual outcomes in the military. *Military Psychology, 11*, 303–328.
Wood, D., Nye, C. D., & Saucier, G. (2010). Identification and measurement of a more comprehensive set of person-descriptive trait markers from the English lexicon. *Journal of Research in Personality, 44*, 258–272.
Zickar, M. J., Gibby, R. E., & Robie, C. (2004). Uncovering faking samples in applicant, incumbent, and experimental data sets: An application of mixed-model item response theory. *Organizational Research Methods, 7*, 168–190.
Zickar, M. J., & Robie, C. (1999). Modeling faking good on personality items: An item-level analysis. *Journal of Applied Psychology, 84*, 551–563.
Zohar, D. (2000). A group-level model of safety climate: Testing the effect of group climate on microaccidents in manufacturing jobs. *Journal of Applied Psychology, 85*, 587–596.

Conclusions

36

Cultural, Contextual, and Measurement Challenges for the Paradigm of Personality Science

Gerard Saucier and Amber Gayle Thalmayer

The previous chapters in this volume each engage with aspects of personality science. In this chapter, we focus on personality science itself. We advance the position that contemporary personality science presents a dual picture. In part, personality science has accrued a stock of well-accepted knowledge about patterns in human behavior that make for a sort of consensual "paradigm." But there are also major unresolved matters. On these disputed matters, one can delineate opposing views: a received and conservative but probably not entirely correct view, and an alternative and seemingly radical view that is probably just as likely to be correct. Reflecting the lively relevance of industrial–organizational (I/O) psychology for core personality science, numerous chapters in this volume intersect with aspects of this alternative view.

The Consensual Paradigm

There are some things we know about personality. Humans vary psychologically from one another in ways that make different individuals best suited to different social roles (Hogan, 1983; also see Hansen's Chapter 29, this volume). Individual psychological differences have likely been maintained in our species due to trade-offs between costs and benefits for different levels of reactivity and behavioral tendencies (Nettle, 2006). The importance of such individual psychological differences to people and societies everywhere is made clear by the ubiquitous presence of words to describe personality attributes across languages and cultures (Saucier, Thalmayer, & Bel-Bahar, 2012 [unpublished manuscript]). While there are cultural differences in the extent to which individuals are likely to describe themselves using attributes (Heine, 2012), people everywhere describe others with attribute terms indigenous to their native language. This likely speaks to the universal human lifestyle of functioning in groups (Dunbar, 1998), and the ubiquity of differences in individuals' abilities to fulfill specific roles (see Hogan & Blickle's Chapter 4, this volume).

Attempts to make sense of the ways that people differ from one another extend into ancient history, for example, in catalogs of virtues, systems of astrology, or Galen's four humors. Early in the 20th Century, such efforts were framed in clinical terms, for example, in Carl Jung's work on personal growth through the expression of different aspects of typology (see Reynierse's Chapter 16, this volume). For nearly 100 years, there have been attempts to fashion empirically grounded personality inventories to capture broad ranges of attributes (see Prewett, Tett, & Christiansen's Chapter 10, this volume). But the role of experts in determining which content to include inevitably led to some biases, for example, an undue emphasis initially on aspects of abnormal psychology (e.g., the Minnesota Multiphasic Personality Inventory, MMPI).

The lexical rationale, that the most salient differences between persons will be encoded in the natural language, established an empirical procedure that could be deployed across cultures to help identify the most important dimensions of personality attributes (Goldberg, 1981; Saucier, 2009). Lexical studies have helped us to understand the ways that diverse attributes group together into higher-order dimensions. And after evidence from the first handful of languages was available, they led to the establishment of the useful Big Five model (Digman, 1996; see De Fruyt & Wille's Chapter 15, this volume), which is the basis of the popular Revised NEO Personality Inventory (NEO-PI-R; Costa & McCrae, 1992) and other inventories. Lexical studies have also spawned other models, for example, the six-factor structure of the HEXACO Personality Inventory (HEXACO-PI; Lee & Ashton, 2004). Although it is debatable whether these lexicon-inspired structures are sufficient as models of personality (e.g., Block, 1995, 2010), and whether the cross-cultural replicability standard they imply is too strict (e.g., Rolland, 2002), there is little debate that they provide a central reference-point for the field.

We know that personality attributes, operationalized as scores on personality inventories (but likely generalizable to other sources of data), have the capacity to predict career choices and outcomes (see Murphy, Deckert, & Hunter's Chapter 28 this volume). Indeed, personality attributes have predictive ability for virtually every important life outcome studied, including health, longevity, marriage and divorce, social relationships, well-being, and creative expression (Ozer & Benet-Martinez, 2006). They appear to have the same predictive ability as socioeconomic status (SES) or cognitive ability with respect to mortality, divorce, and occupational attainment (Roberts, Kuncel, Shiner, Caspi, & Goldberg, 2007), and they "predict job performance as well as any other procedure, and . . . outperform most other predictors" (Hogan & Blickle's Chapter 4, this volume).

There are widely accepted criteria for evaluating personality measures; many of these consensual criteria are reflected in the review by Prewett et al. (Chapter 10, this volume). Measures built on some combination of empirical and rational (or theoretical) considerations are judged favorably. Assessments are now customarily presented in terms of positions on a continuum rather than in terms of binary "types." Moreover, validity and reliability are consensually regarded as each having some importance.

Personality psychologists would show wide agreement on this point as well: Individual psychological differences can be assessed by more than one method. Drawing on an earlier classification by Cattell, Funder (2010) distinguishes between (S)elf-report, (I)nformant, (L)ife outcome, and (B)ehavioral data. Data gathered in different ways can importantly enrich our understanding of individuals, and might help us make measurement more cross-culturally applicable (Heine, Buchtel, & Norenzayan, 2008).

Contemporary personality science evinces trust in self-report scores on personality variables, even if expert positions range from unconditional trust to a more suspicious "trust but verify" stance. To illustrate this range, the issue of faking on personality tests is mentioned as a concern by several authors in this volume (e.g., McFarland; Prewett et al.), whereas Hogan and Blickle (Chapter 4, this volume) argue that to the extent that people exaggerate or diminish their characteristics, they primarily display their awareness of social expectations and their ability to conform to them. Hogan and Blickle's argument is consistent with findings (Uziel, 2010) that impression management is associated with well-being, job performance, health, and interpersonal adjustment.

Most accept that there will be cultural differences in how personality operates. McCrae (2002), for example, documents that average variances on NEO-PI-R scores are "geographically ordered," with European populations having higher variability than Asian populations. Similarly uncontroversial are findings of cultural differences in the extent to which personality attributes are seen as fixed and enduring, versus malleable and influenced by the situation (Heine, 2012; Kanagawa, Cross, &

Markus, 2001). In individualistic cultures, it is considered desirable to have a consistent identity across situations—in fact, personality consistency is associated with social skills, being well liked, and well-being (Suh, 2002). But in collectivistic cultures, being consistent across situations is not associated with such rewards (Suh, 2002). Instead, people in less individualistic societies appear to value adapting their behavior and identities to the role they play—clinging to a single idea of the self, regardless of context, is viewed as a lack of social skills or maturity. The theoretical framing for these findings of cultural differences is not, however, consensual. Prominently, there is no agreement on whether anything about the cultural environment actually has a *causal* effect on personality tendencies.

As Nye and Roberts (Chapter 35, this volume) point out, current evidence suggests that personality attributes are characterized both by stability and by change over time. The consensus is that people everywhere have *some* consistency in their behavioral tendencies, and that change can also occur. What remains subject to considerable debate and controversy is what the real sources of change in scores over time might be. McCrae (1993) suggests they may be due to little more than measurement error and maturation, whereas Nye and Roberts suggest substantive sources of change.

With these last few points, the reader can see some signs of dispute in the field beginning to creep in about the edges of our account. In the next section, we describe a useful conceptual framework for understanding scientific controversies more broadly. We then turn to deal directly with main lines of dispute within the field.

Paradigms and Anomalies

Kuhn (1970) provided a much-cited account of paradigms in science, and of some processes by which paradigms shift over time. Briefly, a "paradigm" consists of notions shared by scientists in a field about what phenomena should be studied, how they should be studied (with what methods and/or equipment), what questions scientists should be answering, and how results are to be interpreted. It is basic to the shared worldview or mindset of scientists in a field at a particular time. Arguably, in our view, such paradigms are a wider phenomenon within the ideational worlds humans create and inhabit. That is, something like paradigms are not unique to science but might be observed in cultural, political, and religious models of the world as well (as in Wallace, 1961; Westen, 1985). But scientific paradigms differ from such nonscientific models in an important way: Scientific paradigms are explicitly open to revision, and indeed are presented as tentative and potentially imperfect models.

Imperfections within a paradigm are part of the mechanism of change. Certain observations (or findings) do not fit the paradigm, are "anomalies" for it. As awareness of anomalies increases, so will dissatisfaction with the paradigm. When an alternative—or "revised"—paradigm can account for the anomalies, one might then see a paradigm shift, whether this shift be rapid, gradual, or part of a generational shift.

In the Kuhnian approach, then, a fairly typical situation in a scientific field is this: One finds areas of consensus, and a received, popular model that incorporates this consensus but also includes other elements that are more debatable. The ultimate fate of the received model depends on the quantity and importance of the anomalies that build up around it as scientists attempt to apply it.

It can be debated whether personality science has a paradigm in the same sense that physics does. There is less commonly held theory here than one sees in the hard sciences, and arguably the field is a collection of small quasi-paradigms vying for a higher status (a characterization that may fit social psychology even more squarely than personality). We leave that issue aside here, and use the term "paradigm" to cover the consensual as well as the most popularly shared notions in the field (i.e., the received model).

In this chapter, we lay out first what we perceive to be the disputable aspects of the received model and next the major anomalies that arise with respect to them. Then, we suggest what a radically different model might look like, a model opposed to the received model in as many respects as possible, but possibly able to deal better with the anomalies. We stress that, in fact, we do not know of anyone who has proposed *in toto* this exact "negative benchmark" model, knitting together all the elements we suggest it might have. But we identify some proposals found in this volume that go in the direction of doing so. Our aim in organizing views in this way is to stimulate competition between reasonable models, and improve personality science. Obviously, it is possible that the outcome of such competition may be a hybrid that includes the best features of each view, while excluding the least supportable features of each.

The Received View in Personality Science

There are a number of now commonly held assumptions in personality science that may not be entirely justifiable. The popularity of most of these assumptions date back a few decades, to what was arguably a previous era of rapid paradigm shift in the field. This era was associated with the resolution of the personality–situation debate and the widespread adoption of a five-factor model. The following are widely held but debatable assumptions.

1. *Questionnaire responses reflect disinterested, factual descriptions of persons' attributes.* On this assumption, when researchers and assessors present individuals with items describing some range of tendencies or attributes, with a request to describe the self or some other person, respondents oblige by providing the most truthful account they can. That is, they take the opportunity to file a realistic, veridical report (like some journalist or scientist) about how things are, and not about how they ideally wish things to be. Support for this assumption is provided by evidence for *some* accuracy in personality description (Funder, 1995), and for seeing response biases such as social desirability as a sort of "red herring" (Ones, Viswesvaran, & Reiss, 1996). Based on this assumption, we can interpret questionnaire responses as pure indicators of traits, of truly objective basic tendencies of persons, with no need to adjust the method or monitor response protocols to deal with non-veridical responding.
2. *Self-report is the primary data source, and so the main use of informant data is to demonstrate the validity of self-report data.* To support this assumption, one can argue that the self is the best expert on the person's tendencies and attributes, having exposure in all times and situations (except when asleep or perhaps extremely intoxicated). Informants (that is, knowledgeable acquaintances of the person targeted in the description) at best have a far more limited exposure, so should be regarded as secondary sources; informant reports can be (and frequently are) used to establish that self-reports have validity. This assumption, if well founded, would be a tremendous practical boon to personality science, because self-reports are quick and convenient to obtain. It can be linked to a very long tradition in psychology (going back to Wundt and Ebbinghaus) of taking introspection quite seriously; consistent with that tradition, the assumption is that much of the truth of personality can be introspected by the possessor of the traits.
3. *Whatever the target of description, all respondents (no matter the context or culture) compare the target to the same objective standard.* In their initial instructions, some assessment instruments ask the respondent specifically to compare the target (usually self) to some kind of typical person. Therefore, one would be high on a trait if higher than typical or low on a trait if lower than typical. Other instruments leave the reference group implicit—that is, they do not specify what the comparison or reference group should be. This seems more common where the items consist of statements with which one can variously agree or disagree. In either case, the context is usually unspecified, and there is no recommendation to compare oneself to members of other populations and cultures (which would of course pose challenges for those who have not traveled the world). Essentially, it is assumed that trait levels exist in an absolute sense and not mainly in a comparative sense, so that ratings will not shift if the reference group is shifted.

4. *People normally behave consistently across situations, so response instructions regarding contexts are unnecessary.* In instructions for completing personality assessment, respondents are often asked to generalize across the widest range of instances, if they are given any instructions at all on the matter of situations. Evidence that there is some cross-situational consistency might be taken to justify ignoring situations, either in items or instructions. If so, broad and sometimes ambiguous trait-descriptive adjectives applied to someone's behavior across all situations would be an acceptable (in fact, admirable for their efficiency) mode of assessment. As an extension, people might be assumed to behave consistently across time, so that (in a sample being assessed across time) the time of administration of the measure becomes immaterial, as per the next assumption.
5. *The traits emerging from personality assessment are hard-wired and essentially unchangeable "essences of persons" unaffected by culture and context.* Supporting this assumption, at least to a degree, personality attributes measured by contemporary questionnaires are usually found to be substantially heritable and not much affected by variation between environments shared within families (Turkheimer, 2000). They are also routinely found to be relatively stable across time (Caspi, Roberts, & Shiner, 2005). It has been difficult to identify the sources of across-time variation in these attributes, such that it has appeared reasonable to attribute most of the observed across-time variation to measurement error or to generic maturation processes (Costa & McCrae, 2006; McCrae, 1993). Taking all these findings together, it has seemed reasonable to posit that personality traits are basic tendencies influenced by biology but not by culture, context, or other aspects of environment (McCrae & Costa, 1999).
6. *The general nature of these "essences of persons," and their structure/organization, can be identified suitably in European-origin populations, and generalized to the rest of the world.* Many hard-wired psychological processes, like those involved in sensation and psychophysical phenomena, would not be expected to vary much between populations around the world, so it would not matter much which population is sampled to develop a model. More debatable is the extension of this assumption to social behavior and to the personality domain. Some evidence does suggest this to be reasonable. Personality measures developed in the West (e.g., the NEO-PI-R, developed in the American context) do appear to be reasonably translatable and able to function rather well in at least many cultural contexts.
7. *Studies of the natural language of personality in diverse cultural settings have supported a structural model with five factors.* This position is easy to support from literature appearing in the early 1990s, when the "diverse cultural settings" in which studies of personality language (lexical studies) had been conducted included only America, Germany, and the Netherlands. One could add citations to select later studies—a couple of Slavic-language (Polish, Czech) studies and of studies of Italian and Turkish descriptors—to support this view. Certainly, converging results from seven languages must be taken seriously. And perhaps even more seriously because two of those languages—German and English—have been the prime scientific languages of psychology in its (approximately) 130-year history, these being thus "preferred languages" in another way.
8. *If one measures those five factors, one has a sufficient measure of personality.* This assumes, in part, the finality and comprehensiveness of a five-factor model. It assumes that additional factors beyond these five are unnecessary. It might also be taken to assume the unimportance of that specific variance not captured by the broad factors but captured uniquely by facets or subcomponents of these factors (for different views, see O'Neill & Paunonen's Chapter 14, this volume; Wood, Nye, & Saucier, 2010).
9. *A top-tier indicator of measurement quality is coefficient alpha (internal consistency), referencing convergence among indicators.* Reliability is by definition the absence of measurement error, and this is certainly one good index of the quality of a measure. The most convenient (and thus, predictably, the most commonly cited) index of reliability involves measuring how consistent is the scale (or construct) across subsets of its items (or indicators). Of course, reliability is no end in

itself. But the other commonly cited index of measurement quality, validity, is assumed to have reliability as a prerequisite, with higher reliability enabling higher validity. So a central defining quality for any trait measure will be its level of internal consistency (as measured with coefficient alpha). Because internal consistency (like any form of reliability) is often defined in terms of the absence of (measurement) error, one might believe that highly internally consistent measures should give a better approximation to the truth. And, by this reasoning, the prime criterion in scale development should understandably be the maximizing of internal consistency. In scale development, factor analysis gives a guide toward maximizing internal consistency (i.e., select that set of items loading high on a factor, and reject the rest).

10. *In evaluating a personality scale or inventory, it is enough to test against chance rather than making rigorous comparison to competing scales or inventories.* In examining the validity of a scale or inventory, the key things are absolute indices, for example whether self-ratings produce significant correlations with ratings by others, or whether there is significant capacity to predict external outcomes. Once these significant effects are established, the scale/inventory is "validated." If competing scales or inventories are to be studied, they are primarily useful in showing that the present measure measures what it purports to measure (e.g., a scale labeled "sociability" correlates with a previous scale labeled "sociability").

We have presented the foregoing 10 assumptions consecutively and without objection, so as to afford the reader a chance to sense how they fit together. Let us encapsulate them as a linked theoretical narrative. Factual information about persons' traits is available from self-report questionnaire responses, wherein respondents use a common objective standard to reference their various cross-situationally consistent patterns. The factuality of traits scored from these inventories is demonstrated by the correlations of these self-ratings with those by informants, as well as by indications of the traits' genetic heritability. These biologically based traits are relatively impervious to context and culture. So, the nature of these traits as observed in a Western setting (e.g., crucially, in a five-factor array) gives strong indication for how they will be observed anywhere. A key measurement quality is one aided and abetted by factor analysis—internal consistency—although documenting the validity of a scale or inventory (though not necessarily the comparative validity in relation to other scales/inventories) is also important. One can see the phrase "internal consistency" as a hallmark throughout this received view; behavioral patterns are consistent across contexts and cultures, stemming from traits not only internal to the person but internal to the genome, and internal consistency on the psychometric level is also highly valued.

For those well acquainted with contemporary personality science, these assertions are unremarkable. Indeed, despite their debatability, they have the quality of being obvious conventions. As a result, a speech at a scientific meeting that laid out these points would likely induce considerable boredom in the audience. The alternative points of view we describe next, however, go against convention, and may jar the gentle reader out of his or her chair.

A Strong Alternative View

Here, we define an alternative view, by aggregating sensible alternatives to the 10 assumptions just listed. In a sense, we are using the 10 assumptions as a "negative benchmark" and laying out an alternative in systematic contradistinction. Doing so is important because, as pointed out below, the received view has generated anomalies and the sensible alternatives may take better account of evidence, avoid these anomalies, and therefore be building blocks in a better paradigm.

Taken together, these alternatives form a patchwork construction, a loosely strung-together set of potentially viable alternatives to elements in the received view. After delineating them, we discuss the degree to which they form a coherent set.

1. *Personality descriptions are a compound of fact and value, but this tends not to compromise the validity of scores.* If personality ratings were disinterested and factual, reports by different observers would strongly converge, socially desirable responding would not be a concern, and personality language would contain mainly the evaluation-free descriptors necessary for purely objective descriptions. But accuracy in personality ratings is far from perfect; there is a rather surprising degree of divergence between ratings of the same target, between self and various observers (Clifton, Turkheimer, & Oltmanns, 2005). This suggests that value preferences of the respondent influence responses. These value preferences may lead the respondent to enhance the favorability of the description (so as to match an ideal or the way things ought to be), or to diminish its favorability (which may be overall in line with an ideal of modesty). Thus, it is unsurprising that personality descriptors in the natural language form a clearly bimodal distribution with respect to favorability: Most descriptors are either clearly favorable or clearly unfavorable (see, for example, Goldberg, 1978, Figure 1). The same is true of questionnaire items, attributes, or scale names. Personality descriptions as a rule evaluate, that is, invoke a value. Descriptions lie somewhere on a continuum between purely objective description and description in terms of how one ought to be or would ideally be. The fact versus value quotient in personality descriptions clearly depends partly on the assessment situation; where high stakes are involved, responses tend to be different (Levashina & Campion, 2006), as there is more motivation to assert value over fact. Socially desirable responding certainly does occur; however, to competently assert value requires knowledge of the consensual relative value associated with a description. Those individuals who, more than others, choose to assert value over fact and provide a biased description may be cheating (a bad thing) but are also demonstrating their knowledge of social norms (a good thing)—there may be others who attempt to cheat but fail to do so effectively, because they are unable to communicate a fully desirable impression, not fully knowing what one would look like. As a result, the presence of this tendency overall tends not to compromise the validity of scores, and controlling for socially desirable responding does not generally improve predictive validity (consistent with Ones et al., 1996).
2. *The prime source of data for human behavioral patterns, core features of personality, is informants (knowledgeable acquaintances).* If self-reports were the best type of data, they would predict outcomes better than other types of data, in any cultural context. But there are indications (see Connelly's Chapter 20, this volume) that reports by knowledgeable acquaintances (informants and observers) are more predictively valid than self-reports, at least for many kinds of attributes (i.e., excluding those that give particular primacy to a subjective viewpoint, such as affective states, and beliefs and attitudes). Informant data offer some inherent advantages. First, it is possible to aggregate raters and thus improve the reliability of the joint ratings. Second, diverse informant reports about the same individual can be heterogeneous, which would lead to less favorable enhancement than in self-reports. Moreover, informant reports appear to be a more universally generalizable mode of personality assessment; there are parts of the world where self-report is a relatively unnatural activity, whereas talk about others (including gossip) appears to be more universal. Therefore, it is reasonable to give priority to informants, especially those with extensive knowledge of the subjective states and preferences of the target of description, or as Connelly (this volume) puts it, "unique access to internally held information." On this view, for tapping behavioral patterns relevant to work and other settings, self-report data are useful but secondary.
3. *Standards of comparison for self- and informant-ratings vary by culture and context.* If respondents in all settings used the same objective comparison standards, expert ratings of characteristics of various populations should converge with aggregated ratings of laypersons. However, this has not consistently occurred. Experts judge East Asians to be more collectivistic than North Americans, but cross-cultural comparisons failed to reveal this pattern (Heine, Lehman, Peng, & Greenholtz, 2002). Expert views of national characteristics have been found uncorrelated with

means of samples from different nations (McCrae & Terracciano, 2006). And counterintuitively, gender differences in personality have been found to be greater in European than in non-Western populations, despite greater gender equity in the European settings (Costa, Terracciano, & McCrae, 2001). As Heine has pointed out, discrepancies like these can easily arise due to reference-group effects (Heine et al., 2008; Heine et al., 2002). Populations differ in their standards of comparison. A 5-foot-6 male might be considered tall in Malaysia but short in Norway; it may be more difficult to reach the standard of being judged "very hard-working" in a high-pressure achievement-oriented society than in a low-pressure society where there is more focus on enjoying life. Another example comes from Nye and Roberts (Chapter 35, this volume): a college student may see him or herself differently in comparison to peers before and after getting a first job; the peer-group standard changed. Standards of comparison for ratings should be expected to vary by culture and context. Given this hazard, the best approach is to use multiple methods including objective behavior-count data, and to use clearly anchored and easily translated response scales that, as much as possible, require people to count (e.g., how often this happens, if not specifically how many times it has) or make an explicit choice between competing alternatives. These approaches should generally serve to suppress or eliminate reference-group effects (Heine, 2012).

4. *Personality tendencies in part operate across situations and in part are situation-specific.* Although there is evidence for both, the evidence for consistency (stability) across time is more compelling than the evidence for consistency across situations (Mischel & Peake, 1982). There are anomalies for a strict assumption of cross-situational consistency. There are moreover important context-specific traits (e.g., coping and emotion regulation). Indications that self-descriptions are affected by the stakes in the assessment situation are another indicator of situational specificity. Some personality characteristics are best observed and assessed in specific contexts (a key premise of trait activation theory; see Tett et al.'s Chapter 5, this volume); for example, extraversion at parties or purely social events, or conscientiousness from interacting with demands at work or at school. In sum, the premise of cross-situational consistency can easily be taken too far. A better working assumption would allow for both cross-situational consistency and situational specificity in behavioral patterns.
5. *Although personality tendencies are partially genetically based, they represent in part "software" subject to influence by cultural and contextual factors.* If personality traits were hard-wired and unchangeable essences unaffected by culture and context, scientists would be unable to detect coherent sources of personality change in the environment, in the roles individuals adopt, or the belief/value systems that exist in cultures or subcultures. Systematic effects of environments, roles, beliefs, values, and other cultural components are anomalies for a "hard-wired essentialism" view of traits. But such anomalies are observed. For example, personality change can be predicted by individuals engaging and investing in new roles (Lodi-Smith & Roberts, 2012), antecedent variation in attitudinal beliefs (Saucier, 2012), and by the extent to which individuals value specific attributes (Weisberg, De Young, & Simpson, 2012). Moreover, bicultural individuals may answer questionnaires significantly differently according to which of their two cultural identities is made salient (Hong, Morris, Chiu, & Benet-Martinez, 2000). These anomalies indicate systematic patterns in how personality changes.
6. *Models of personality dispositions bear some imprint of the cultural setting in which they were developed.* If the nature and structure of personality dispositions were identified well enough in studies of European-origin populations, then generalizing to the rest of the world would pose no problem. It has been difficult, however, to establish measurement invariance across cultures for personality measures (Allik, Massoudi, Realo, & Rossier, 2012; Poortinga, van de Vijver, & Van Hemert, 2002). Reference-group effects (described above) and differential self-enhancement tendencies (Xie, Roy, & Chen, 2006) make comparisons more difficult. Studies of the natural language of personality indicate that, when the indigenous structure of various lexicons are investigated

independently and then compared, only a core of one or two factors truly arises independently in any language (Saucier et al., in press), the rest being more subject to variation. Personality models embody, almost inevitably, some cultural presuppositions. The best way to eliminate this ethnocentric bias is to develop "culturally decentered" models and measures by anchoring them in investigations that from the beginning involve a culturally, internationally diverse set of populations. This kind of development process is exemplified by the model of "social axioms" (Leung et al., 2002).

7. *Studies of the lexicons of languages do not necessarily support the contemporary five-factor model of personality, although studies of languages having their origins in northern Europe do.* If studies of the natural language of personality in diverse cultural settings supported a structural model with five factors, then studies of the natural language (lexical studies), no matter the language or culture, should lead to the same five factors by an equally direct route. A less demanding, but still relevant, test would involve showing that translated measures of these five factors work about equally well in all populations. Neither of these projected outcomes has materialized. Approximately half of the lexical studies to date have not yielded the full set of five factors where one would expect them, in the five-factor solution (Saucier & Simonds, 2006). And those finding something like a Big Five structure typically diverge in some way from the American template; agreeableness and intellect/openness factors seem especially prone to vary between studies. A factor fully characterizable as "openness to experience" has been difficult to find in most languages (McCrae, 1990), although content related to originality (Saucier, 2009) or unconventionality (Ashton et al., 2004) arises with more frequency. Once one moves to a broader base of languages, beyond those with origins in northern Europe, a six-factor model (Ashton et al., 2004) appears more replicable than the Big Five. Furthermore, when one takes a popular questionnaire measure of the five factors and translates it to numerous languages, one does see some variation across cultural settings in structure, and some attenuated reliability for some scales (Piedmont, Bain, McCrae, & Costa, 2002; Rolland, 2002). Failures to establish full measurement invariance across populations for this questionnaire (Allik et al., 2012; Poortinga et al., 2002) suggest that comparison of means between culturally different populations is hazardous. Given these numerous anomalies, the Big Five structural configuration should be regarded as somewhat culture-specific. Studies of lexicons appear to converge on no more than two large personality factors (Saucier et al., in press) that, given their ubiquity across languages, might be less subject to cross-cultural variation. These "Big Two" factors (social self-regulation and dynamism) map onto well-established higher-order factors of the Big Five (DeYoung, 2006; Digman, 1997). And they yield a more parsimonious and theoretically tractable model than the Big Five; the obvious drawback is that models with five or six factors (not to mention 16 or 30 "facets") should routinely be superior in prediction contexts (Saucier et al., in press). The Big Two cap the structural hierarchy of personality dispositions, but the best practical work is probably done much farther down the hierarchy, indeed perhaps at a level well below any Big Five or Six (see O'Neill & Paunonen's Chapter 14, this volume).

8. *Five factors capture a great deal of the personality-attribute domain, but it takes more than five factors to be comprehensive of this domain.* If the five factors were a sufficiently comprehensive content model for personality attributes, several outcomes would be observed. No characteristics of importance would be found outside the five content domains (i.e., having a low multiple correlation with the five factors). No model with more than five orthogonal factors would be workable (any additional factor would fall apart under tests or scrutiny). And measures of more specific traits would be easily subsumable under one or more of the five factors, with specific subcomponents (or "facets") adding little to prediction beyond what the five factors offer. The reality is otherwise. It is not difficult to detect some important characteristics beyond the Big Five (Paunonen & Jackson, 2000; Saucier & Goldberg, 1998). Six-factor models (Ashton et al., 2004; Hogan &

Hogan, 1997; Jackson, Paunonen, & Tremblay, 2000) appear quite workable. The more specific "facet" level does appear to account for substantial variance beyond the broad factors (O'Neill & Paunonen's Chapter 14, this volume). These outcomes are anomalous for a strong five-factor theory. The alternative view leaves open how many factors *would* be comprehensive. To take account of points 6 and 7 above, we should bear in mind that a comprehensive model for one language and cultural setting may not exactly match the comprehensive model for another. There is likely culture-specific content that is important and necessary in one part of the world, but not in another. As we increase comprehensiveness, we are almost certainly decreasing cross-cultural replicability and compatibility. The value of parsimony (and theoretical clarity) pushes us in one direction toward fewer factors, whereas the value of comprehensiveness pushes us in the other direction, toward more factors. It is not impossible that decades from now scientists will think of personality as more than five types of attributes (perhaps even more than 16 or 30) theoretically organized at the broadest level into less than five major groupings.

9. *Internal consistency is a useful, but not a top-tier, indicator of measurement quality.* If internal consistency (indexed by Cronbach's coefficient alpha) were truly the best standard for evaluating measurement quality, on par with validity, higher internal consistency would guarantee monotonically higher validity. No alternative measure of homogeneity would prove particularly useful. Against this assumption, experts (including Cronbach [Cronbach & Shavelson, 2004] himself) have come to critique an "abusive" overemphasis on internal consistency (Schmitt, 1996). Thorndike (1967, p. 214) commented that "exclusive preoccupation with item internal consistency may lead to an undue narrowing of the scope" of a measure, a decrease of predictive validity consistent with the attenuation paradox identified by Loevinger (1954). In fact, short, content-heterogeneous scales often perform as well as longer, more homogeneous scales, despite much lower internal consistency (Thalmayer, Saucier, & Eigenhuis, 2011). Overemphasis on maximizing alpha easily leads to redundancy or "parallelism" in scales that attenuates rather than enhances predictive capabilities (Loevinger, 1954). Another slight to the cult of internal consistency comes from Item Response Theory, which not only gives importance to heterogeneity in item-difficulty levels (so as to measure effectively at diverse levels of the construct), but sets unidimensionality rather than high internal consistency as a prerequisite for model estimation. Indeed, unidimensionality offers more theoretical clarity: It communicates that a single interpretation can be given to the set of items, as they converge on one thing only. Internal consistency, in contrast, merely tells us the degree to which test variance is attributable to something beyond specific item variance (i.e., item uniqueness, which is treated as measurement error); that "something" could be many things (i.e., multidimensional; Cortina, 1993). Retest stability may be more informative than internal consistency, in that it can be applied even to one-item measures or linear composites. Presented with a choice between a reliable measure and one that lacked reliability but had much stronger validity, most professionals would choose the latter.
10. *The most important test of the value of a measurement instrument comes when it competes against other, partly similar measurement instruments.* Prewett et al. (Chapter 10, this volume) observe that there are many inventories in the marketplace, but few studies comparing them. Goldberg has pointed out that the field of personality assessment has no "consumer's union" to test competing products against each other and make recommendations about which to use and which to avoid. From a commercial standpoint, comparative validity tests might be a hazard to be avoided: Odds are good (at least one in two) that some other instrument(s) will do better than yours, which could have deleterious impacts on future marketing—why take the risk? The current norm, that personality scales and inventories are developed with little testing against other measures, allows each instrument to exist in a little world of its own. Fortunately, some recent studies cut against the grain. Grucza and Goldberg (2007) compared 11 multiscale inventories for their capacity to quantitatively predict diverse outcomes. Thalmayer et al. (2011) and Credé, Harms, Niehorster,

and Gaye-Valentine (2012) each compared brief and medium-length inventories (at least eight in each study). Going beyond comparative prediction, Prewett et al. (Chapter 10, this volume) compare 10 inventories in frequent use in I/O settings with respect to six desiderata (including three approaches to validity). Such comparisons are uniquely informative, and will ultimately strengthen the field by helping to optimize and standardize measurement practices. It becomes easier to decide which is the fastest horse if the horses are actually permitted to run on the same track at the same time.

The Alternative View: Less Coherent Than the Received View?

Let us now summarize the major points in the alternative view (see the right column of Table 36.1). Descriptions of personality patterns are a compound of fact and value. A prime source of data regarding these patterns is knowledgeable acquaintances. Standards of comparison for self- and informant-ratings vary by culture, and may even vary between situations. Although personality

Table 36.1 The Received View in Personality Science Contrasted With an Alternative View

S. No.	*The Received View in Personality Science*	*An Alternative View*
1	Questionnaire responses reflect disinterested, factual descriptions of persons' attributes	Personality descriptions are a compound of fact and value (but this tends not to compromise predictive validity of scores)
2	Self-report is the primary data source (informant data mainly demonstrates the validity of self-report data)	The prime source of data for human behavioral patterns is knowledgeable informants
3	Across contexts and cultures, we compare targets to the same objective standard	Standards of comparison vary by culture and context
4	People behave consistently across situations; instructions regarding context are not needed	Personality tendencies are in part situation-specific
5	Personality traits are hard-wired and essentially unchangeable "essences"	Personality tendencies are based partially in genetics, but also "software" influenced by cultural and contextual factors
6	The most important personality traits, and their structure/organization, can be identified in European-origin populations, and generalized to the rest of the world	Models of personality dispositions bear some imprint of the cultural setting in which they were developed
7	Studies of the natural language of personality in diverse cultures support a structural model with five factors	Studies of the lexicons of northern European languages support the five-factor model, but studies in other languages generally do not
8	The five factors provide a sufficient representation of personality	Five factors capture much of the personality domain, but are not comprehensive
9	Coefficient alpha (internal consistency) is on par with validity as important to evaluations of measurement quality	Unidimensionality and retest stability are as important as internal consistency, and validity is more important
10	In evaluating a personality scale or inventory, it is adequate to test against chance to determine if it has validity	The value of a measurement instrument is best assessed in competition against partly similar instruments

tendencies in part operate across situations, in part they are situation-specific. Although personality tendencies are partially genetically based, they represent in part "software" subject to influence by cultural and contextual factors. Therefore, models of personality dispositions—regarding their structure, their measurement, and their associations—inevitably bear some imprint of the cultural setting in which they were developed. As a prime example, studies of the lexicons of languages do not necessarily support the contemporary five-factor model of personality, although studies of languages having their origins in northern Europe do. Five factors are acknowledged to capture a great deal of the personality-attribute domain, but not all of it. With respect to measurement, unidimensionality and retest stability are as important as internal consistency, and validity is even more important. Rather than evaluating each measure in an isolated way, on its own, the most important test of the value of a measurement instrument comes when a well-controlled study, or rigorous review, forces it to compete against other, partly similar measurement instruments.

What do these pieces have in common? Of what common theoretical narrative might they be a part? There are recurrent key concepts: fluidity, standards, comparisons, complexity, bias reduction, and differentiation of central from peripheral components. In what makes the alternative view distinct from the received view, several kinds of themes can be discerned.

In this alternative view, basic elements of personality are seen as more fluid, subject to variation and "imprints" based on the group and environment in which they occur. Fundamental to this variation are "standards," because different groups and environments have different standards. Human behavioral patterns are seen as partially a product of the cultural and cognitive models that incorporate these standards, a product of their "software" as well as their "hardware." On this view, personality becomes more anchored in the relational world, with less attempt to reduce it to a core set of biological processes. What Hogan and Blickle (Chapter 4, this volume) call "reputation" comes to the fore. By "reputation" here, we mean something of a proposed agreement about how the facts of a person's behavioral history comport with a set of value/evaluative standards, more than the results of "impartial jury deliberations" trying to arrive at the objective truth about someone. Thus, the proposed view of personality and character is more congruent with how it might be observed in traditional societies: the output of convergences in gossip-like processes, in which values are asserted as well as facts, and in which the purported facts exist against a background of asserted or implied values.

In this alternative view, there is an overt attempt to escape from ethnocentric bias in a rapidly globalizing world in which people have more exposure to cultural patterns outside their own, and in which there is no guarantee that the Western way (which has dominated psychology heretofore) will always be pre-eminent. This approach avoids making the personalities of Western, educated, industrialized, rich, and democratic people ("WEIRD" as per Henrich, Heine, & Norenzayan, 2010) the central concern of personality psychology. Instead, there is an attempt to capture patterns operating across a broader variety of contexts. Indeed, the patterns of the "weird" group may turn out to be too atypical to form the optimal template for an optimal model of personality and character.

This view embraces complexity. One moves away from a small set of relatively simple standards (five universal factors, internal consistency, and binary decisions as to scale validity). Both personality and personality measurement are viewed more complexly. What is important about the ways that people vary psychologically from one another cannot be reduced to a few endogenous phenomena that drive all else. And a good measure proves itself by meeting diverse standards, not only those based on classical test theory and factor analysis. Under this approach, it is more challenging to be comprehensive. Scientists need to look beyond a few basic factors, and the assumption of universal cross-situational consistency must be set aside, allowing for context- and culture-specific phenomena.

In this alternative view, personality science becomes more of a science *of* comparisons *about* comparisons. This science compares models and measures of personality patterns, perceptions of which arise as we compare people to one another and to any of various standards. There is more "fluidity": These standards are not necessarily fixed across time and situations; some of the standards are situation-specific. Some of the variation in standards might have to do with facts varying from place to place, but some may be due to evaluative standards varying.

The alternative view is not, however, a wildly relativistic approach in which all possible observations and views are accorded equal importance. Attention is directed to differentiating relatively universal from more culturally and contextually varying aspects of personality. More broadly, an implied overarching meme is the division of phenomena into relatively central and peripheral elements, with the latter not excluded from consideration. Examples of possible "central" phenomena are those established to be more rather than less universal, or the attributes that multiple informants can agree on—broad and parsimonious personality factors, the components of psychological patterns that are cross-situationally consistent, and the components that can be linked to genetic influences or to biological correlates.

Thus, the "patchwork" alternative view is not incoherent. We believe the evidence that has accumulated against the received view need not make the field more chaotic. The anomalies for the received view push us consistently in certain directions, those defined here by the alternative view.

This alternative view does not conform fully to any theoretical framework currently available. But some frameworks proposed in this volume intersect with it. Indeed, in our view, frameworks developed within I/O psychology are currently underappreciated within the science of personality proper; personality psychologists have much to learn from I/O psychologists. Let us review next some key intersections.

In socioanalytic theory (Hogan & Blickle's Chapter 4, this volume), there is a critique of overly "intrapsychic" approaches and an emphasis on reputation (as collective perception), both of which resonate with much of the alternative view (and with a "personality as social perception" view; Srivastava, 2010). In socioanalytic theory, there is also a clear implication that change in roles may be a causal factor in personality change (for more information on personality and change, see also Nye & Roberts' Chapter 35, this volume). Moreover, in socioanalytic theory, acceptance and status are taken to be prime motives underlying personality variation, and these are also key themes in the social self-regulation and dynamism factors that we have described as recurrent across cultural settings. Connelly's (Chapter 20, this volume) review of the observer (in our terminology, "informant") perspective on personality identifies strengths of informant data, and the limits of cross-situational consistency, in a manner consonant with the alternative view. The multilevel constructs identified by Narayan and Ployhart (Chapter 8, this volume) as emergent phenomena include organizational culture, which is defined in terms of "observable norms and values"—which function as standards—that are transmitted between members; we would reframe organizational culture as the context of a specific organization where distinct standards apply. In trait activation theory (Tett et al.'s Chapter 5, this volume), such standards are evident in a "work demands" component, in which constraints and potential consequences are imposed. More broadly, we believe this theory (or a slightly more generalized adaptation of it) has much to offer as a model of how dispositions and situations relate and interact; the received view includes no such model. Finally, we note that the "watershed period" in research on personality and work in the late 1980s and early 1990s, as identified by Christiansen and Tett (Chapter 1, this volume), was simultaneously the period in which what we term "the received view" became consolidated within personality science.

Conclusions

Marking the progress of personality as a science, there are a number of empirically based understandings that are now consensually held. These form the core of an emergent "paradigm of personality science." Going beyond this core, we identify matters of controversy, on which we distinguish the received view and an alternative view.

In contemporary personality science, the received view has tended toward a fairly simple model emphasizing fixed and cross-situationally consistent traits identified in Western populations. The alternative view embraces complexity and attempts to reduce ethnocentric bias; it gives attention to peripheral (relativistic and context-specific) phenomena while differentiating them from central (universal, consistent, etc.) phenomena. The alternative view sees more fluidity in personality attributes, sees them emerging from social comparisons, and attends to the ways in which perception of attributes is influenced by standards that vary across situations and cultural settings. Differing approaches to the creation and evaluation of measures follow in part from some of the same contrasts.

The alternative view delineated here does not correspond exactly to any theoretical framework previously proposed. We see it as emerging organically from anomalies that have arisen within the received view. It brings together various perspectives that seem to help make sense of these anomalies. We suggest the next paradigm shift in personality science will be in the direction of this alternative view, even if all components of this view detailed here are not ultimately retained. When such a shift occurs, it will have important implications for understanding and prediction in the field of "personality at work." Indeed, as chapters in this volume make clear, research on work-relevant personality has vitally participated in and contributed to the current paradigm of personality science. It may likewise participate and contribute to future shifts in that paradigm.

References

Allik, J., Massoudi, K., Realo, A., & Rossier, J. (2012). Personality and culture: Cross-cultural psychology at the next crossroads. *Swiss Journal of Psychology, 71*, 5–12.

Ashton, M. C., Lee, K., Perugini, M., Szarota, P., De Vries, R. E., Di Blas, L., . . . De Raad, B. (2004). A six-factor structure of personality-descriptive adjectives: Solutions from psycholexical studies in seven languages. *Journal of Personality and Social Psychology, 86*, 356–366.

Block, J. (1995). A contrarian view of the five-factor approach to personality description. *Psychological Bulletin, 117*, 187–215.

Block, J. (2010). The five-factor framing of personality and beyond: Some ruminations. *Psychological Inquiry, 21*, 2–25.

Caspi, A., Roberts, B. W., & Shiner, R. L. (2005). Personality development, stability, and change. *Annual Review of Psychology, 56*, 453–484.

Clifton, A., Turkheimer, E., & Oltmanns, T. F. (2005). Self- and peer perspectives on pathological personality traits and interpersonal problems. *Psychological Assessment, 17*, 123–131.

Cortina, J. M. (1993). What is coefficient alpha? An examination of theory and applications. *Journal of Applied Psychology, 78*, 98–104.

Costa, P. T., & McCrae, R. R. (1992). *Revised NEO Personality Inventory (NEO-PI-R) and NEO Five-Factor Inventory (NEO-FFI) professional manual.* Odessa, FL: Psychological Assessment Resources.

Costa, P. T., & McCrae, R. R. (2006). Age changes in personality and their origins: Comment on Roberts, Walton, and Viechtbauer (2006). *Psychological Bulletin, 132*, 26–28.

Costa, P. T., Terracciano, A., & McCrae, R. R. (2001). Gender differences in personality traits across cultures: Robust and surprising findings. *Journal of Personality and Social Psychology, 81*, 322–331.

Credé, M., Harms, P., Niehorster, S., & Gaye-Valentine, A. (2012). An evaluation of the consequences of using short measures of the Big Five personality traits. *Journal of Personality and Social Psychology, 102*, 874–888.

Cronbach, L. J., & Shavelson, R. J. (2004). My current thoughts on coefficient alpha and successor procedures. *Educational and Psychological Measurement, 64*, 391–418.

DeYoung, C. G. (2006). Higher-order factors of the Big Five in a multi-informant sample. *Journal of Personality and Social Psychology, 91*, 1138–1151.

Digman, J. M. (1996). The curious history of the Five Factor model. In J. S. Wiggins (Ed.), *The five factor model of personality: Theoretical perspectives.* New York: Guilford.

Digman, J. M. (1997). Higher order factors of the Big Five. *Journal of Personality and Social Psychology, 73*, 1246–1256.

Dunbar, R. I. M. (1998). The social brain hypothesis. *Evolutionary Anthropology, 6*, 178–190.

Funder, D. C. (1995). On the accuracy of personality judgment: A realistic approach. *Psychological Review, 102*, 652–670.

Funder, D. C. (2010). *The personality puzzle.* New York: Norton & Co.

Goldberg, L. R. (1978). The differential attribution of trait-descriptive terms to oneself as compared to well-liked, neutral, and disliked others: A psychometric analysis. *Journal of Personality and Social Psychology, 36*, 1012–1028.

Goldberg, L. R. (1981). Language and individual differences: The search for universals in personality lexicons. In L. Wheeler (Ed.), *Review of personality and social psychology* (Vol. 2, pp. 141–165). Beverly Hills, CA: Sage.

Grucza, R. A., & Goldberg, L. R. (2007). The comparative validity of 11 modern personality inventories: Predictions of behavioral acts, informant reports, and clinical indicators. *Journal of Personality Assessment, 89*, 167–187.

Heine, S. J. (2012). *Cultural psychology* (2nd ed.). New York: Norton.

Heine, S. J., Buchtel, E. E., & Norenzayan, A. (2008). Research report: What do cross-national comparisons of personality traits tell us? The case of conscientiousness. *Psychological Science, 19*, 309–313.

Heine, S. J., Lehman, D. R., Peng, K., & Greenholtz, J. (2002). What's wrong with cross-cultural comparisons of subjective Likert scales? The reference-group effect. *Journal of Personality and Social Psychology, 82*, 903–918.

Henrich, J., Heine, S. J., & Norenzayan, A. (2010). The weirdest people in the world? *Behavioral and Brain Sciences, 33*, 61–83.

Hogan, R. (1983). A socioanalytic theory of personality. In *Nebraska symposium on motivation* (pp. 55–89). Lincoln, NE: University of Nebraska Press.

Hogan, R., & Hogan, J. (1997). *Hogan Personality Inventory manual*. Tulsa, OK: Hogan Assessment Systems.

Hong, Y., Morris, M. W., Chiu, C., & Benet-Martinez, V. (2000). Multicultural minds: A dynamic constructivist approach to culture and cognition. *American Psychologist, 55*, 709–720.

Jackson, D. N., Paunonen, S., & Tremblay, P. F. (2000). *Six Factor Personality Questionnaire*. Port Huron, MI: Sigma Assessment Systems.

Kanagawa, C., Cross, S. E., & Markus, H. R. (2001). "Who am I?" The cultural psychology of the conceptual self. *Personality and Social Psychology Bulletin, 27*, 90–103.

Kuhn, T. S. (1970). *The structure of scientific revolutions* (2nd ed.). Chicago, IL: University of Chicago Press.

Lee, K., & Ashton, M. C. (2004). Psychometric properties of the HEXACO Personality Inventory. *Multivariate Behavioral Research, 39*, 329–358.

Leung, K., Bond, M. H., de Carrasquel, S. R., Munoz, C., Hernandez, M., & Murakami, F. (2002). Social axioms: The search for universal dimensions of general beliefs about how the world functions. *Journal of Cross-Cultural Psychology, 33*, 286–302.

Levashina, J., & Campion, M. A. (2006). A model of faking likelihood in the employment interview. *International Journal of Selection and Assessment, 14*, 299–316.

Lodi-Smith, J., & Roberts, B. W. (2012). Concurrent and prospective relationships between social engagement and personality traits in older adulthood. *Psychology and Aging, 27*, 720–727.

Loevinger, J. (1954). The attenuation paradox in test theory. *Psychological Bulletin, 51*, 493–504.

McCrae, R. R. (1990). Traits and trait names: How well is openness represented in natural languages? *European Journal of Personality, 4*, 119–129.

McCrae, R. R. (1993). Moderated analyses of longitudinal personality stability. *Journal of Personality and Social Psychology, 65*, 577–585.

McCrae, R. R. (2002). NEO-PI-R data from 36 cultures: Further intercultural comparisons. In R. R. McCrae & J. Allik (Eds.), *The five-factor model of personality across cultures*. New York: Kluwer Academic/Plenum.

McCrae, R. R., & Costa, P. T. (1999). A five-factor theory of personality. In L. A. Pervin & O. P. John (Eds.), *Handbook of personality: Theory and research* (2nd ed., pp. 139–153). New York: Guilford.

McCrae, R. R., & Terracciano, A. (2006). National character and personality. *Current Directions in Psychological Science, 15*, 156–161.

Mischel, W., & Peake, P. K. (1982). Beyond déjà vu in the search for cross-situational consistency. *Psychological Review, 89*, 730–755.

Nettle, D. (2006). The evolution of personality variation in humans and other animals. *American Psychologist, 61*, 622–631.

Ones, D. S., Viswesvaran, C., & Reiss, A. D. (1996). Role of social desirability in personality testing for personnel selection: The red herring. *Journal of Applied Psychology, 81*, 660–679.

Ozer, D. J., & Benet-Martinez, V. (2006). Personality and the prediction of consequential outcomes. *Annual Review of Psychology, 57*, 401–421.

Paunonen, S. V., & Jackson, D. N. (2000). What is beyond the Big Five? Plenty! *Journal of Personality, 68*, 821–835.

Piedmont, R. L., Bain, E., McCrae, R. R., & Costa, P. T. (2002). The applicability of the five-factor model in a sub-Saharan culture: The NEO-PI-R in Shona. In R. R. McCrae & J. Allik (Eds.), *The five-factor model of personality across cultures* (pp. 155–173). New York: Kluwer Academic/Plenum.

Poortinga, Y. H., van de Vijver, F. J. R., & Van Hemert, D. A. (2002). Cross-cultural equivalence of the Big Five: A tentative interpretation of the evidence. In R. R. McCrae & J. Allik (Eds.), *The five-factor model of personality across cultures* (pp. 281–302). New York: Kluwer Academic/Plenum.

Roberts, B. W., Kuncel, N., Shiner, R. N., Caspi, A., & Goldberg, L. R. (2007). The power of personality: The comparative validity of personality traits, socio-economic status, and cognitive ability for predicting important life outcomes. *Perspectives in Psychological Science, 2*, 313–345.

Rolland, J.-P. (2002). The cross-cultural generalizability of the five-factor model of personality. In R. R. McCrae & J. Allik (Eds.), *The five-factor model of personality across cultures* (pp. 7–28). New York: Kluwer Academic/Plenum.

Saucier, G. (2009). Recurrent personality dimensions in inclusive lexical studies: Indications for a Big Six structure. *Journal of Personality, 77*, 1577–1614.

Saucier, G. (2012). *Isms dimensions: Toward a more comprehensive and integrative model of belief-system components.* Manuscript submitted for publication.

Saucier, G., & Goldberg, L. R. (1998). What is beyond the Big Five? *Journal of Personality, 66*, 495–524.

Saucier, G., & Simonds, J. (2006). The structure of personality and temperament. In D. K. Mroczek & T. D. Little (Eds.), *Handbook of personality development* (pp. 109–128). Mahwah, NJ: Erlbaum.

Saucier, G., Thalmayer, A. G., & Bel-Bahar, T. (2012). *Human attribute concepts: Relative ubiquity across twelve mutually isolated languages.* Manuscript submitted for publication.

Saucier, G., Thalmayer, A. G., Payne, D. L., Carlson, R., Sanogo, L., Ole-Kotikash, L., & Zhou, X. (in press). *A basic bivariate structure of personality attributes evident across nine languages.* Manuscript submitted for publication.

Schmitt, N. (1996). Uses and abuses of coefficient alpha. *Psychological Assessment, 8*, 350–353.

Srivastava, S. (2010). The five-factor model describes the structure of social perceptions. *Psychological Inquiry, 21*, 69–75.

Suh, E. M. (2002). Culture, identity consistency, and subjective well-being. *Journal of Personality and Social Psychology, 83*, 1378–1391.

Thalmayer, A. G., Saucier, G., & Eigenhuis, A. (2011). The comparative validity of brief- to medium-length big five and big six personality inventories. *Psychological Assessment, 23*, 995–1009.

Thorndike, R. L. (1967). The analysis and selection of test items. In D. N. Jackson & S. Messick (Eds.), *Problems in human assessment* (pp. 201–216). New York: McGraw-Hill.

Turkheimer, E. (2000). Three laws of behavior genetics and what they mean. *Current Directions in Psychological Science, 9*, 160–164.

Uziel, L. (2010). Rethinking social desirability scales: From impression management to interpersonally oriented self-control. *Perspectives on Psychological Science, 5*, 243–262.

Wallace, A. F. C. (1961). *Culture and personality.* New York: Random House.

Weisberg, Y., De Young, C., & Simpson, J. A. (2012, July). *The influence of ideal personality and significant others on personality change.* Paper presented at the 16th European Conference on Personality, Trieste, Italy.

Westen, D. (1985). *Self and society: Narcissism, collectivism, and the development of morals.* New York: Cambridge University Press.

Wood, D., Nye, C. D., & Saucier, G. (2010). Identification and measurement of a more comprehensive set of person-descriptive trait markers from the English lexicon. *Journal of Research in Personality, 44*, 258–272.

Xie, J. L., Roy, J.-P., & Chen, Z. (2006). Cultural and individual differences in self-rating behavior: An extension and refinement of the cultural relativity hypothesis. *Journal of Organizational Behavior, 27*, 341–364.

37

The Past, Present, and Future of Research Into Personality at Work

Adrian Furnham

The Dream of the Encyclopedists

It became the ambition of Diderot (1713–1789) to bring together every brand of human knowledge into one book that would collect and challenge the thinking of the time. The encyclopedists wanted to be supremely comprehensive: to leave nothing of importance out, and to bring together all knowledge. In some ways, despite the fact that *Encyclopedia Britannica* has gone bankrupt and can now be entirely put on a portable stick, a store of up-to-date knowledge remains a great resource and the symbol of a discipline.

I believe this handbook has similar aims and has, in fact, achieved them. Each of the 34 substantive chapters is, in itself, a clear and concise overview and critique of differential industrial/organizational (I/O) as it stands. Some chapters look back and others forward, as well as discussing current issues in their particular focused area. Many are gems of clarity and critical thinking and will, for sure, be quoted extensively in years to come. It will be a great resource for researchers. It also suggests that this field, at the intersection of I/O (work) and differential/personality psychology, is thriving, and moving forward theoretically as well as empirically.

This chapter will, however, take a "broader brush" to the whole area, from a very personal perspective. It is an attempt to step back and take a view of a rapidly developing and changing field from someone who has been active in it for over a quarter of a century, and one who has taught and consulted in many different countries.

A Personal Memoir

Over twenty years ago, I wrote a book called *Personality and Work*. It was first published (in hardback only) in 1992. It was reviewed well and sold well. I completed a second edition called *Personality and Intelligence at Work* in 2008 (Furnham, 1992, 2008b). In the interim, a number of books have been published with very similar titles like *Personality and Work* edited by Barrick and Ryan (2003) and *Personality in the Workplace* by Fontana (2000).

Up to 10–20 years ago, the relationship between differential/personality and I/O psychologists was distant and cool. So was the relationship between applied, academic psychologists and business consultants. Things have changed a great deal, but not as fast as some would have hoped. The rapprochement between different branches of psychology, or indeed between "applied" and "pure" psychologists, has yet to happen for many.

Three things struck me in the 1980s when I was a full-time academic and "moonlighting" as a management consultant, which led me to write the book on the role of personality traits in the workplace.

The first began as I was hired as an "associate consultant" by various friends who had left academia in the early 1980s because of the recession (in Great Britain) of 1980–1983. Many were using personality tests as part of their assessment and training, but the ones they were using were either long rejected, or unheard of, by the academic psychologists. The dominant tests being used were the MBTI, the FIRO-B, and the very British OPQ. None seemed to have much evidence of construct or predictive validity, particularly when it came to workplace behavior. They seemed to me to be used because of their face validity and the ease of giving feedback to clients who only wanted to hear good news. They were heavily marketed; test publishers pushed them and made lots of money running courses to make one a registered user. The same was true in America, Asia, Australasia and Europe, as far as I could tell.

Surely, I thought, they were aware of all the excitement of the Big Five challenging the Gigantic Three and of the serious developments in personality theory after the tragic and somewhat pointless Person (P) × Situation (S) debate (on which I had done my PhD)? Had they not come across the brilliant and unique Hogan Development Survey (Hogan & Hogan, 1997)? Were they aware that the most popular measures of emotional intelligence were, to put it mildly, psychometrically compromised and that there were now *really* valid measures (Petrides, 2011)? Why were so many hesitant about using ability tests, and why, despite all the talk of integrity, were integrity tests so seldom used? Why so little interest in situational judgment tests that supposedly helped reduce faking, which was an issue that concerned them?

I found no good answers to these questions despite asking them of both academics and practitioners. The consultancy world, happily using and selling personality tests as if they were the great savior for all Human Resources (HR) people, had little or no contact with the academic personality theorists, who rarely ventured into the consultancy world. I later found evidence for this in a study of European HR professionals who seemed to have little experience or knowledge about well-known and validated personality and intelligence tests (Furnham, 2008a), though they tended to be positive about the usefulness of these tests (Furnham & Jackson, 2011).

The second observation was that neither the consultant nor the clients seemed much interested in evidence of predictive validity. The best most of these personality tests could offer was concurrent validity and face validity. In effect, the former meant there is some evidence that (dodgy) Test A agrees with (dodgy) Test B. I would have thought you chose a test on the basis of evidence showing that it could predict work outcomes. Granted, many tests were used more to help the self-awareness process; but I was struck that consultants were very loath to confront issues around neuroticism, poor adjustment, or negative affectivity. They appeared more concerned about giving client feedback than validity. Equally, they rarely used ability tests. It seemed to me then, as the evidence shows now, that intelligence quotient (IQ), neuroticism (N), and conscientiousness (C) are the three best predictors of work success and failure (Furnham, 2008a). There are some important caveats here: The power of N and C do depend on the job itself and the success criteria, but many consultants still remain nervous about testing these dimensions, particularly N.

The consultant philosophy must also never be about things being hard-wired or difficult to change. That, of course, would influence the coaching and the older training "industries," which peddle the idea of growth and change.

Third, it struck me when I looked at the academic literature and the consultancy work on personality at work in the period 1950–2000 that there was, at least in Great Britain, a sudden increase in interest in the topic. In the 1950s and 1960s, few of the major personality theorists (even Eysenck and Cattell) were very interested in the application of, as well as the testing of, personality theory in the workplace. There were exceptions, which I documented in my book, but both were closer to clinical and social psychology than to I/O psychology. But things changed in the 1980s as psychometric test, consultancies grew and discovered a hunger for personality feedback. This, however, may not be the case in the United States (Kanfer, Ackerman, Murtha, & Goff, 1995), where it seems the high point for test use may have been the 1920s and 1930s.

Interestingly, it appeared that it was HR professionals who were the most enthusiastic clients for psychometric tests and I got the impression that it was because it increased their social standing as "scientific" rather than because it made good business sense.

The consultancy world I flirted with seemed very different from my two other worlds. I taught a course on I/O work psychology but spent more and more time researching in the field of individual differences and personality. I also noticed that, when I spoke to clinical and educational psychologists, many were hostile to tests and most were seriously out-of-date with respect to developments in personality research.

The three worlds seemed strangely apart and yet interested in much the same thing. I decided to do something about it. From the mid-1980s to the late 1990s I was in the habit of cycling six miles across London every 3–4 months to go to the quite excellent *Institute of Psychiatry* library that contained some journals I enjoyed reading. Often I would call in for tea with Hans Eysenck. We had got to know each other and I reviewed many papers for *Personality and Individual Differences* (PAID). I told him my story and suggested that we have a special issue of PAID dedicated to work as the dependent variable. As always, Hans was decisive, clear, and bold. Yes, he said, as long as the papers were good enough. We advertised but never got enough submissions of merit to fill an issue. I was disappointed and surprised. Personality psychologists were, it seemed, simply not interested in testing their ideas in the workplace. They were still too attached to clinical and educational psychology.

Why were so few differential psychologists interested in real-world work-related differences; and why were so few applied I/O and work psychologists not very interested in individual differences?

Yet, things were changing. It was, I believe, mainly due to increasingly good meta-analyses. From the late 1980s and throughout the 1990s, there were more and more meta-analyses of the relationship between personality traits and work outcomes (Barrick & Mount, 1991, 2005; Hough, Eaton, Dunnette, Kamp, & McCloy, 1990; Salgado, 1997; Tett, Jackson, & Rothstein, 1991). Hough and Furnham (2003) completed a big review. Others have enthusiastically argued for a personality-at-work research agenda, specifically people like Ones (2005) and Hogan (2005, 2006). Indeed, it has been Bob Hogan who, very unusually for an exceptionally accomplished academic psychologist, has built up a thriving international psychometric company and champions the "marriage" of personality and I/O psychology. He has educated not only practitioners but also academics in the value of understanding personality at work. There are sections of personality conferences on work and work conferences on personality. The great SIOP conference every year is a testament to the rapprochement between these two research areas.

When big handbooks begin to appear, it is a sign of the maturity of the field. Perhaps there will soon be a *Journal of Personality and Organizational Behavior*? The marriage of two (or more) fields often produces a healthy "mixed-blood" infant that thrives. The whole of psychology is moving this way, as new ideas and techniques and theories are developed.

However, there are serious critics and objections to this new field.

The Social Psychological Challenge

The relationship between personality and social psychologists has probably still not fully recovered from Mischel's (1968) attack and the ensuing person–situation debate. Differential/personality and social psychologists want to explain the same phenomena very differently. With some issues like prejudice, the differential psychologists have deferred to the social psychologists, but things may be changing.

The issue came to a head in a series of papers published in *Personnel Psychology* in 2007 led by Morgeson et al. (2007a, 2007b) and challenged by many distinguished differential/personality and I/O psychologists (discussed at length in this volume).

At the heart of the social psychological critique are two issues: first, that personality accounts for too little of the variance in (any, most) work-related behaviors; and second, that personality tests are far too easily faked, so threatening their validity. The faking issue never seems to go away, yet other areas of psychology, from sexology to social psychology, seem much less vulnerable to these attacks although they are very reliant on self-report. It is a common complaint of skeptical managers asked to introduce testing: People fake good, they say, making the data meaningless.

If one examines the many, and increasingly comprehensive, meta-analyses, it seems that two of the Big Five (conscientousness and neuroticism) are the most consistent correlates, being in the range of $.15 < r < .30$. Square this, so the argument goes, and see how *little* variance one is accounting for.

There are various responses to this critique. First, if one considers all traits (i.e., the full profile), rather than one at a time, the variance goes up considerably. Then there are the standard arguments about the range restriction, reliability, and subtlety of the dependent variable (i.e., the work behavior itself). The issue of analysis and moderator and mediator variables is also very common. The response of the personality-at-work psychologists is that, if all efforts are made to measure both variables well, the relationship is clear, important, and meaningful. To account for say 15–30% of the variance by such a cheap and simple method must be very good indeed.

However, the shadow of Mischel's (1968) $r = .30$ (and therefore only 10% of the variance) remains in all this debate. Parenthetically, it seems deeply ironic that Mischel's current fame (on the power of postponement of gratification over time) takes such a dispositional stance. That is, it is now argued that the predictive validity of the Marshmallow test is substantial: Postponement of gratification is a trait. Eysenck (1967) would no doubt have seen this as impulsiveness, which is a subfactor of psychoticism and which would explain all Mischel's (amazing) findings that suggest data collected in one experiment as a young child could predict many important and meaningful life outcomes (marriage, job, health-related) over 40 years later.

Social psychologists like to show the power of situational factors, like the power of priming to shape behavior. It is a form of social behaviorism: not stimulus–response, but situation–response. Social situations influence behavior, and strong situations do so powerfully. Social psychologists rejoice in the old studies on obedience and conformity to provide evidence to reject personality psychological explanations. This can be seen most clearly in the work of Zimbardo (2007) on evil. While there is no doubt that situational variables do affect behavior at work and elsewhere, social psychologists seem unhappy to accept the fact that people choose and change the situations they find themselves in. Furthermore, it is patently obvious from personal observation that *different* people react very *differently* to the *same* situation.

Homosocial pychologicus is a strangely passive individual buffeted by the flotsam and jetsam of social life. They ignore three powerful differential processes that ensure human behavior tends to be consistent over time.

First, personality depends on how people *react* to similar situations. There are dramatic differences, as can be seen most clearly in Milgram's (1964) famous *Obedience to Authority* book. My personal favorite was the Professor of Theology who argued with the experimenter and whose conversation is documented in the book, juxtaposed with others who seemed to react quite differently.

Next, people change situations in the way that *evokes* consistent and specific reactions in others. Third, they *choose* situations *pro-actively*, being drawn to some and avoiding others. People choose their vocations; they change their jobs and offices and colleagues to suit their personalities. All personality psychologists have always acknowledged the interaction of trait and situational variables, but many social psychologists and sociologists who teach "organizational behavior" (OB) on business school courses seem very reticent to ever acknowledge the influence of cognitive and noncognitive individual differences in the workplace.

To a large extent, many differential/personality psychologists have been coy about the variance issue. One may equally take the position that it is deeply impressive that scores generated from a short self-report inventory can account for 10% to 20% of the variance of *many important work behaviors over time.* Perhaps they should be more robust in the face of the social psychological challenge.

How then to respond to the challenge: "How much work variance can you really explain by your personality (and ability) tests?" Assuming there are psychometrically good (valid and reliable) measures of both independent and dependent variables, the question is what other factors have an impact and whether these are all clumsily lumped together as "situational" factors? Work output could be affected by lack of sleep due to a noisy home (neighbor's dog), unreliable equipment or transportation to work, or a difficult and unsupportive boss. Some of these factors are relatively stable, others very transient; some proximal, others distal. Obviously, some can be manipulated to show classic experimental social psychological effects but others cannot. The question also concerns how long the situational effects last.

Another way of doing this would be to ask people (managers, workers) to think of themselves, their colleagues, and their bosses (to avoid more obvious attribution errors). The task is first to list all the factors that influence their work output (productivity). Once an exhaustive list is made and the factors grouped into a coherent and parsimonious list, the judges are then asked to estimate the amount of variance accounted for. Personality and ability factors are always given a reasonably impressive amount of the variance, usually between a quarter and a third, while other factors are always mentioned—not evidence surely, but the perceptions of ordinary people about the role of personality at work.

At the end of the P × S debate, all agreed that the variance question led nowhere. It was not a "how much" but a "how" question. How do traits and situations interact? For how long can situational variables influence work behavior and how do those effects differ for those with different personalities?

Maybe the social psychologists will find more of a home with those researching OB (taught in business schools) rather than organizational psychology (taught in psychology and neuroscience departments). OB seems a curious discipline, half psychology and half sociology, with mostly derivative theories and methodology. However, because, at least in Great Britain, it is taught by those who are trained in sociology and social psychology, and not personality theory, theory there is a preference for studying environmental and situational factors that influence behavior at work and a hostility to intrapersonal, individual difference explanations.

Change at Work

If we are to examine the role of personality at work, it becomes relevant to look at changes in the world of work and to indulge in a little futurology.

There is no shortage in futurological contemplation about the future of work. Donkin (2010) has argued there are specific factors that shape that future:

(a) *Demographics*: In the West, this means fewer young people relative to a larger aging generation who are, very expensively, living longer. This has led to attempts to replace younger people by immigration, which results in a diversified workplace. People will be healthier than ever before and with a significantly increased longevity. This affects the whole concept of retirement: whether it should be mandatory, whether people should be expected to work into their 70s.

(b) *Health*: For obvious reasons, organizations want to encourage a (physically and mentally) healthy workforce. Employers will provide healthcare and fitness facilities, which are a good investment and potentially attractive to many employees.

(c) *The workplace and workforce has been feminized*, which has led to conflict between production and reproduction. This is all about work–life balance, childcare, and related issues, which employers now have to consider particularly when employing large numbers of women with children.
(d) *Technological advances* have been both a scourge and a savior at work. Facebook, Blackberrys, and the Internet in general have changed dramatically how, when, and where we communicate with fellow workers and customers. Thus, it will be the technologically adept, rather than the great orators, who will be particularly influential in the future.
(e) *Social networking* changes contact patterns inside and outside the workplace. It makes secrets much harder to control. The quality and quantity of a person's connections will inevitably influence their work productivity and capability.
(f) *People will seek more meaning, purpose, and authenticity at work.* They will not blindly accept the values and career paths of previous generations; they will ask serious questions about what they have inherited and what they want to pass on to others. In this sense, they will be a lot more skeptical (even cynical) than previous generations.
(g) *Our (business) leaders will be more under the spotlight.* They, in particular, will have to adapt to the demands of the new and ever-changing order.
(h) *There will be changes in how people and their performance are measured at work.* People will be more frequently and subtly evaluated both qualitatively and quantitatively.
(i) *There will be shorter, formal working hours and more discretion for workers for when they should be working.* Work will not be a place you go to, as much as something you do at a place and time that suits you. Thus, all the interest in "working remotely," more specifically working from home.

Gratton (2011), like many other futurologists, believes that, with respect to work, we are in a period of unprecedented change. She argues that these rapid, profound, and uncontrollable changes are profound for people at work. Her strategy was to identify the dispassionate trajectory of *five major forces* of change and then "collect" hard facts around each. They are technology, globalization, demography, social changes, and energy resources.

Gratton (2011), therefore, talks about the importance of intellectual, social, and creative capita. However, the questions for this type of futurology are this: Is there anything new here? Have these forces not been identified by everybody? Are her ideas on shift deeply ethno- and ego-centric: the perspective of an educated, privileged person in the Western world? What implications does this have for theorizing and experimentation on the relationship between personality and work-related behaviors?

Looking at this literature, it seems certain trends are detectable. There are two very different 1984 Orwellian futures that one may well contemplate. The first is where such great advances in biomedical and neuroscience mean that an analysis of a positron emission tomography (PET) scan and a saliva sample will provide all the data one needs to accurately predict work motivation, satisfaction, and productivity. There will be little or no need for personality tests and theories because of advances in cognitive neuroscience. This is clearly naive and simplistic as we will need to have all the situational/job details about individuals to use biological data to make any meaningful and useful predictions. We may have to wait at least a decade if not more to see any results, particularly at the individual level: and then it remains unclear as to how useful they may be.

Second, there is the situation where legal restrictions are so tight and rigorously enforced that it will be impossible to measure any person's ability or personality before or at work, or get records of their behavior at work. Thus, it will become illegal to measure personality lest one detect neuroses, mental illness, or low ability, which are known to relate to productivity at work but which will not be allowed to be measured. Both seriously restrict both the worker and the scientist. This is a world where selection decisions are monitored and prescribed.

One change that is occurring is the "monitored" workplace. The cost, size, and efficiency of electronic equipment allow for the monitoring of every sort of behavior from sitting at one's desk, through computer key depressions, to all aspects of productivity. The surveillance of employees in the workplace is a phenomenon that has always existed. However, in the past several decades, the advent of new technologies has meant that there is an increasing number of novel, cheap, and reliable ways of monitoring employees. Oz, Glass, and Behling (1999) listed eight methods of computer-assisted electronic monitoring: video cameras (such as CCTV), computer sampling, email interception, access codes, expert systems, transaction audits, phone taps, and hidden microphones. Of these, the most technologically advanced are expert systems, which are more commonly referred to as EPM—"electronic performance monitoring." The Office of Technological Assessment (Anon, 1987) described EPM as the "computerized collection, storage, analysis, and reporting of information about employees' activities." In practice, EPM can be used to monitor a variety of mostly quantitative variables, such as the punctuality of employees, the amount of break time taken, the amount of idle time, the number of words written per minute, transactions completed, and number of telephone calls made (time per call, revenue per call), just to name a few. In effect, this now means that there is a potential to monitor employees' specific daily behaviors, which has not been possible through traditional methods.

As these newer methods of surveillance offer continuous control over an employee's time at work, this has unsurprisingly ignited much debate over whether it is morally right or even organizationally wise to implement such control. So far there have been numerous studies looking into the possible effects of EPM, by comparing EPM and non-EPM scenarios and measuring factors such as stress, productivity, job satisfaction, turnover, and so on.

A large-scale questionnaire-based cross-sectional study looking into people's attitudes toward electronic monitoring was done by Oz et al. (1999). The responses of 823 part-time students who were in full-time employment were analyzed, mainly looking for differences between the attitudes of supervisors and their subordinates, but also for any gender differences. Predictably, it found that supervisors were more likely to support the idea of electronic monitoring, while also suggesting that it would be a good tool in reducing theft. Meanwhile, subordinates (nonsupervisors) expressed greater agreement with the idea that electronic monitoring would have a negative impact and create tensions in the workplace, as well as agreeing that employees should be made aware of when monitoring is taking place. It was also found that women were more likely than men to think that monitoring would reduce theft (Oz et al., 1999).

In a more recent study, Samaranayake and Gamage (2011) looked at how electronic monitoring affected employees' satisfaction. They gathered data from 380 employees of a computer software company, using a questionnaire containing 75 questions targeting job satisfaction, task satisfaction, perceived relevance to work, invasion of privacy, level of infringement, rationale of employer, and judgment of effectiveness. This study drew a number of conclusions. It was found that job satisfaction was positively correlated with having a positive opinion of electronic monitoring, supporting the idea that monitoring is fair, unbiased, and provides a fuller image of the employee. However, it also showed that the greater the perception of invasion of privacy, the lower job satisfaction was, and this was also true in those that felt that monitoring made their work more complex. Interestingly, by looking at subgroups, it was found that the effect that monitoring had on job satisfaction was much weaker in those employees with a higher professional experience. This may be a fruitful area of future research.

Technological, economic, and demographic changes will influence how, when, and where we work. Old jobs, industries, and organizations are disappearing and new ones appearing. The criteria for job performance are changing, and I/O psychologists need to be aware of these changes in their research.

The Future of Personality at Work

Glancing in my crystal ball, I see the following.

(a) *Developments in dependent and independent variables.* The independent variable (personality traits) and the dependent variable (work-related behavior) are relatively easy to define in this area, which is at the interface of differential and I/O psychology. To a large extent, the literature in this field has been dominated by the Big Five framework, though there are various other related models, particularly those of Hogan (2006) and Hough and Furnham (2003) who have worked extensively in this area. There is no agreement about which independent measures to use. Quite rightly, journal editors call for multitrait–multimethod designs and an end to self-report measures of work outcomes, and even observer reports, which are also affected by rating errors. Some jobs like sales or call-center work allow for regular, objective measures (like number of calls, sales, revenue, profit), which can be gathered electronically and aggregated over time. One of the main problems that has held I/O psychology back is the measurement of behavior at work: that is, getting aggregated, salient, and sensitive behavioral data on individuals that can be matched to personality test results. Many test developers complain about the difficulty of obtaining behavioral (and even observer) data on individuals by which they can begin to validate their tests. It comes as a shock to many academics that so few organizations even try to measure anything behaviorally, be it negative (i.e., absenteeism) or positive (i.e., productivity). Changes and developments in technology (i.e., uses of electronic media) may, however, make it easier to get various, potentially useful, work-related behavioral measures.

(b) *More interest in the biography of individuals.* While nomothetic psychometricians have always been doubtful about biographical, idiographic, case-study data, books on the personality of very successful business men and women do sell well. Some are hagiographically oriented works that tell the stories of business heroes, whereas others tell of derailed leaders who, despite early success, crashed and burned. Psychohistorians have always been interested in life stories. Indeed, the whole field of biodata continues to thrive, looking at historical markers of business success. Many factors like birth-order have been investigated with little success, but there are many other ideas from this rich but neglected area (Therivel, 1998). We are all products of our past, not necessarily victims of it. Major questions include what role personality plays in shaping life events and life events in shaping personality, and the effect each has on work-related behavior. Biography is popular, and the small world of psychobiography may help enrich some of the ideas and observations of this new area of research.

(c) *The educated consumer.* Among the most prolific users of personality tests are business people and consultants seeking guidance on hiring and training workers (Furnham, 2008a, 2008b). Indeed, psychometric consultancy companies have been an important engine in this whole area and responsible for the development of many tests. Commercial test producers often have to conform to ethical standards and guidelines set by national psychological societies and even the test producers themselves, particularly in the development and sales of tests, but this has not prevented many "start-ups" developing commercially attractive, but psychologically unproven, tests that promise a great deal. In the past, many purchasers of these tests were relatively naive and gullible and not quite sure of which questions to ask a potential sales person. However, things have changed in the developed world and the consumer is much more discriminating. This has had a very beneficial effect on the whole industry and meant that consultancies have been able to provide excellent data for serious analysis (Furnham & Crump, 2005; Furnham & Trickey, 2010; Furnham, Trickey, & Hyde, 2012, in press).

(d) *Meta analyses.* Some observers have never been impressed with meta-analyses. Indeed, Eysenck called them an exercise of meta-silliness. The main objection is that most analyses do not do a very thorough job of filtering papers for research quality and, therefore, what a meta-analysis tells you is what a number of (possibly) mediocre or poor studies find (i.e., garbage-in–garbage-out). Furthermore, if a particular area is very carefully controlled by methodological and theoretical orthodoxy, it is likely the papers will all be highly similar and the analysis not very illuminating. What is needed is a sort of best-evidence synthesis where careful scholarship looks critically at papers and what we really know about an area, topic, or process. This could answer some of the statements made like "Emotional intelligence is a better predictor of work success than cognitive ability"; "Increasing job engagement among employees results in increased output"; and "There is no relationship between job satisfaction and productivity." Both researchers and practitioners desperately want to know what we really know about a topic. They want a succinct, honest, and comprehensive state-of-the-art review they can understand and act upon. Such reviews are surprisingly rare.

(e) *Evidence-based I/O psychology.* We are now used to the evidence-based concept in medicine. Twenty years ago, it was claimed that less than a quarter of regularly applied medical interventions and treatments were supported by "solid scientific evidence." Scientific psychology has always placed considerable importance on achieving systematic evidence and proof of theories, processes, and methodologies through cumulative, quality-controlled research findings and critical analyses.

The question concerns the extent to which work psychologists' practices are (strictly) evidence-based. Is the practice "ahead" of the "science"? There are numerous techniques (i.e., executive coaching; leadership development), which are not fully informed and supported by research findings. Is it a case of a work-in-progress, established findings, or tentative hypotheses? It is time for *a conceptual cleanup* of fuzzy ideas to understand the mechanisms by which psychological interventions in a particular context lead to specific outcomes.

In an important and challenging article, Briner and Rousseau (2011b) consider the issue and the soul-searching by management scholars over the gap/divide between scientific evidence and practice techniques. On the one hand are the fastidious, obsessed academics doing *pedantic science* but far fewer doing *pragmatic science* on real issues and problems arising in work settings. They argue that evidence-based practice is the on-going pursuit of improvements in the acceptance and use of scholarly research and practice-related facts and assessments.

The idea of evidence-based management is that decisions are made and conclusions drawn from a conscientious, explicit, and judicious examination of the data available. The question is, how evidence-based is work psychology? Briner and Rousseau (2011a) suggest seven characteristics to make that judgment.

1. Is the term *evidence-based* used and well known in the area? The answer seems not.
2. Are the latest research findings/summaries/meta-analyses available, and available to all (academics, consultants, managers) concerned? This certainly does not seem the case.
3. Are research articles and critical reviews accessible to practitioners? The answer seems no: at least not without considerable effort and cost.
4. Are new facts, "cutting edge" practices, or panaceas treated with "healthy skepticism" or uncritically embraced? The latter seems to be the norm in work psychology.
5. Do clients and customers ever demand or even ask for the evidence base of recommended theories or practice? Seemingly only on rare occasions.
6. Are practice decisions based on information that integrates external evidence, the perspectives of those affected, local context information, as well as practitioner experience and expertise? The answer is probably sometimes but not often.
7. Does professional training and continuing development adopt evidence-based approaches? Some courses clearly do, but certainly not everywhere.

Their conclusion is that work psychology is *not* strongly evidence-based, though it could be. However, they do make some suggestions. One is to heal the gap between the academic and the practitioner with research being academic-centered and evidence-based but with poor knowledge transfer. The agenda of the academic and the practitioner are different as are the questions, focus, and resources available. To get practice-oriented, scientific knowledge has to mean engaging both academics and researchers.

The necessity of up-to-date, comprehensive, critical, and systematic reviews cannot be overlooked. Those are reviews of all salient studies that allow conclusions to be drawn about what is, and what is not, known about particular phenomena or processes. These are wider than meta-analyses that statistically examine data from studies using similar methodologies. Good reviews can look at phenomena-oriented evidence (i.e., causes of stress) or practice-oriented evidence (i.e., effects of coaching) but need to give guidelines for practice.

Doing good systematic reviews is expensive in terms of research time and effort. All salient studies need to be identified and assessed and the results synthesized in a clear conclusion. More importantly, results need to be disseminated to practitioners. The reviews would do well to meet the usual scientific criteria of making the methods and conclusions open to easy scrutiny for those interested.

Briner and Rousseau (2011a, 2011b) further note at least four barriers to the adoption of evidence-based practices in work psychology. First, clients of work psychology consultancy, rather oddly, rarely demand good dispassionate evidence. Second, many practitioners themselves are not always able to access or evaluate work-based evidence. Third, there is a lack of healthy skepticism with respect to work psychology, believing it undermines the discipline or makes practitioners seem less confident. Fourth, the approach may be particularly difficult in highly political cultures where values and personal interests are seen as more important than evidence. The belief is that the scientist–practitioner gap could be improved if academics did three things: provide briefer and more accessible systematic reviews; help consultants collect and analyze their own data to understand what interventions were and were not working and why; and coach consultants, trainers, and practitioners in evidence-based management. There were various commentaries on Briner and Rousseau's (2011b) paper. Cassell (2011) noted the politics of evidence-based ideas, where one person's evidence is another's dogma or trivia. What constitutes evidence relates to epistemology, which is challenged and clearly value-laden. This approach might crush or at least inhibit methodological diversity, ruling certain techniques like qualitative or projective techniques out-of-order. Third, evidence-based techniques seem to stifle or at least slow down innovation.

(f) *Neuro-cogno-ergo-differential psychology.* When I was a graduate student (30 years ago), psychology was neatly divided into three categories: cognitive, social/applied, and biological/physiological. In Great Britain, the cognitive psychologists were king and, of the few biological/physiological psychologists, many were still running rats, though the more adventurous were doing brain work on higher animals. How things have changed with the advent of PET scanning and related technology. The neuro-psychologists are now top of the food chain, as can be seen by journal development and grant giving. Go to a personality conference and you will see a great increase in those biological and genetic papers with increased excitement about what is just around the corner. Social science seems to be old-fashioned: All the new theories are evolutionary and biological.

Go to an I/O conference and you will hear almost nothing of the biological revolution. It could be a conference 20 years ago except for developments on statistics and other measures. The social psychologists have embraced neuro-psychology with the journal *Social Neuroscience*, which aims to publish studies showing "how the brain mediates social cognition, interpersonal exchanges, affective/cognitive group interactions, and related topics that deal with social/personality psychology." It would be a pity if differential work psychology were to be left behind in these developments.

Conclusion

I recall a question from an exam paper years ago about a famous psychology handbook, probably one of the first of its kind. It went something like, "X's handbook of Y: Milestone, Tombstone, or Millstone." This was rather typical of the academic taste of the time: big questions rather waggishly phrased.

Perhaps it is appropriate to consider the fate and impact of this volume. Handbooks are very useful because they contain critical reviews by experts, that are often more interesting and impactful than meta-analyses because contributors are at liberty to comment more widely on issues. Many chapters in this volume offer a superb, comprehensive, and evaluative review of the area up to this point. Yet, because the field is growing fast, many of these reviews will be out-of-date in 2 to 3 years, no doubt calling for a second edition of this book.

Books are like babies: They take about 9 months to make from conceptions to birth. This is a state-of-the-art book, but all contributors would do well to start working on their revised, second edition, chapter very soon.

Acknowledgments

I am grateful to Phil Ackerman and Robert Hogan for helpful suggestions and criticisms of earlier drafts.

References

Anon. (1987). *The electronic supervisor: New technology, new tensions* (Office of Technology Assessment, Congress of the United States; OTA-CIT-333). Washington, DC: Government Printing Office.

Barrick, M. R., & Mount, M. K. (1991). The "Big 5" personality dimensions and job performance: A meta-analysis. *Personnel Psychology, 44*, 1–25.

Barrick, M. R., & Mount, M. K. (2005). Yes, personality matters: Moving on to more important matters. *Human Performance, 18*, 359–371.

Barrick, M. R., & Ryan, A. (2003). *Personality and work: Reconsidering the role of personality and organizations.* New York: Jossey-Bass.

Briner, R., & Rousseau, D. (2011a). Evidence-based industrial–organizational psychology: Not there yet but now a little nearer. *Industrial and Organizational Psychology, 4*, 76–82.

Briner, R., & Rousseau, D. (2011b). Evidence-based industrial-organizational psychology: Not there yet. *Industrial and Organizational Psychology, 4*, 3–22.

Cassell, C. (2011). Evidence-based industrial–organizational psychology: What did we lose on the way? *Industrial and Organizational Psychology, 4*, 23–26.

Donkin, R. (2010). *The future of work.* Basingstoke, UK: Palgrave Macmillan.

Eysenck, H. (1967). Personality patterns in various groups of businessmen. *Occupational Psychology, 41*, 249–250.

Fontana, D. (2000). *Personality in the workplace.* Basingstoke, UK: Macmillan.

Furnham, A. (1992). *Personality at work.* London: Routledge.

Furnham, A. (2008a). HR professionals' beliefs about, and knowledge of, assessment techniques and psychometric tests. *International Journal of Selection and Assessment, 16*, 301–306.

Furnham, A. (2008b). *Personality and intelligence at work.* London: Routledge.

Furnham, A., & Crump, J. (2005). Personality traits, types and disorders. *European Journal of Personality, 19*, 167–184.

Furnham, A., & Jackson, C. (2011). Practitioner reactions to work-related psychological tests. *Journal of Managerial Psychology, 26*, 549–565.

Furnham, A., & Trickey, G. (2010). Sex differences in dark side traits. *Personality and Individual Differences, 50*, 517–522.

Furnham, A., Trickey, G., & Hyde, G. (2012). Bright aspects to dark side traits: Dark side traits associated with work success. *Personality and Individual Differences, 52*, 908–913.

Furnham, A., Trickey, G., & Hyde, G. (in press). The dark side of career preference. *Journal of Applied Social Psychology.*

Gratton, L. (2011). Workplace 2025—What will it look like? *Organizational Dynamics, 40*, 246–254.

Hogan, R. (2005). In defense of personality measures. *Human Performance, 18*, 331–341.

Hogan, R. (2006). *Personality and the fate of organizations.* Mahwah, NJ: Lawrence Erlbaum.

Hogan, R., & Hogan, J. (1997). *Hogan Personality Inventory manual.* Tulsa, OK: HAS.

Hough, L. M., Eaton, N. K., Dunnette, M. D., Kamp, J. D., & McCloy, R. A. (1990). Criterion-related validities of personality constructs and the effect of response distortion on those validities. *Journal of Applied Psychology, 75*, 581–595.

Hough, L. M., & Furnham, A. (2003). Use of personality variables in work settings. In W. Borman, O. Ilgen, & R. Klimoski (Eds.), *Individual differences and behavior in organizations* (pp. 31–88). San Francisco: Jossey-Bass.

Kanfer, R., Ackerman, P., Murtha, T., & Goff, M. (1995). Personality and intelligence in industrial and organizational psychology. In D. Saklofske & M. Zeidner (Eds.), *International handbook of personality and intelligence* (pp. 577–602). New York: Plenum Press.

Milgram, S. (1964). *Obedience to authority.* New York: Harper & Row.

Mischel, W. (1968). *Personality and assessment.* New York: Wiley.

Morgeson, F. P., Campion, M. A., Dipboye, R. L., Hollenbeck, J. R., Murphy, K., & Schmitt, N. (2007a). Are we getting fooled again? Coming to terms with limitations in the use of personality tests for personnel selection. *Personnel Psychology, 60*, 1029–1049.

Morgeson, F. P., Campion, M. A., Dipboye, R. L., Hollenbeck, J. R., Murphy, K., & Schmitt, N. (2007b). Reconsidering the use of personality tests in personnel selection contexts. *Personnel Psychology, 60*, 683–729.

Ones, D. S. (2005). Personality at work: Raising awareness and correcting misconceptions. *Human Performance, 18*, 389–404.

Oz, E., Glass, R., & Behling, R. (1999). Electronic workplace monitoring: What employees think. *Omega International Journal of Management Science, 27*, 167–177.

Petrides, K. V. (2011). Ability and trait emotional intelligence. In T. Chamorro-Premuzic, S. von Stumm, & A. Furnham (Eds.), *The Wiley-Blackwell handbook of individual differences* (pp. 656–678). Oxford, UK: Wiley-Blackwell.

Salgado, J. (1997). The five factor model of personality and job performance in the European Community. *Journal of Applied Psychology, 82*, 30–43.

Samaranayake, V., & Gamage, C. (2011). Employee perception towards electronic monitoring at work place and its impact on job satisfaction of software professionals in Sri Lanka. *Telematics and Informatics, 29*, 233–244.

Tett, R. D., Jackson, M., & Rothstein, M. (1991). Personality measures as predictors of job performance: A meta-analytic review. *Personnel Psychology, 44*, 703–725.

Therivel, W. (1998). Creative genius and GAM theory of personality. *Journal of Social Behaviour and Personality, 13*, 201–234.

Zimbardo, P. (2007). *The Lucifer effect.* New York: Random House.

38

Personality Psychology in the Workplace

The New Revolution

Robert P. Tett

The middle of the last century bore witness to seminal developments in psychological science, as black-box behaviorism gave way to distinctly cognitive paradigms. Several forces contributed to the cognitive revolution. The first nudge came from learning theorists, like Hebb (1949) and Lashley (1942), who argued that behaviorism, in its purest form, failed to account for unrewarded learning in rats. A second, more pragmatic influence was wartime demands for efficient communication (information theory) and operation of increasingly sophisticated machinery (human engineering). A third major influence was Chomsky's (1957, 1959, 1965) treatises emphasizing linguistic creativity, transformational grammar, and the universal "language organ." The final push came from the advent of computers (e.g., Newell & Simon, 1956), offering not just models for human cognition, but also suitable tools for its investigation. The cognitive revolution took psychology from the science of behavior to the science of the mind, a transformation no other development in psychology is likely to eclipse.

As we contemplate all the contributing chapters to this Handbook, exploring personality's role in diverse work behaviors (e.g., task and contextual performance, counterproductive work behaviors) through assorted mechanisms (e.g., socioanalytic theory, trait activation theory, goal orientation theory) and measurement modes (e.g., assessment centers [ACs] interviews) toward fulfilling a broad array of human resource (HR) functions (e.g., personnel selection, leadership, training), it begs the question whether we may be embarking on a new revolution in psychology—a *personality revolution*—emphasizing stable, predictable individual differences in propensities to behave in characteristic ways in response to situational stimuli. As with its cognitive forerunner, several key forces driving this new revolution are identifiable.

First, personality research is a natural extension of the cognitive revolution, focusing on mental constructs but with an emphasis on individual differences (see below). The cognitive revolution tore the lid off the behaviorists' black box, legitimizing personality as fair game for scientific inquiry. The second influence is the recognition that personality does not operate in a vacuum, but rather unfolds in reaction to relevant situations. Person–situation interactionism has a venerable history in psychology (e.g., Lewin, 1935; Murray, 1938). Its impact was actively suppressed, however, by influential situationist thinkers (e.g., Mischel, 1968; Skinner, 1938) until reemerging in the 1970s (e.g., Bowers, 1973) as a bona fide contender in accounting for behavioral variance. Modern personality psychology is very much an interactionist discipline, and recognizing the importance of situations in understanding personality has been a key factor in the resurgence of personality research. Third, there is the discovery of the Five-Factor Model (FFM; e.g., Tupes & Christal, 1961), without which (or at least without a similarly broad framework) personality trait content would be too disorganized to allow meaningful integration of research findings and, accordingly, to facilitate knowledge growth in this area. The last influence was the advent of meta-analysis, which, starting in the late 1980s and early 1990s, furnished quantitative summaries of empirical literatures on personality at work, offering powerful estimates of personality linkages and a means of identifying situational moderators of those effects.

Personality clearly involves cognitive processes, but its main focus is not how people think, how they store and retrieve information, or how they plan ahead and reason; personality psychology is a science of *individual differences*, seeking principles that can explain how a given situation can lead different people to respond in characteristically different ways. The FFM has cognitive influences (especially with respect to its lexical foundation), but it is not a taxonomy of cognitive processes per se; it is a taxonomy of stable behavioral tendencies combining cognition, affect, and motives to distinguish reliably among individuals. Nothing can supplant cognition's place in psychological science. Personality psychology, however, stands to make its own contributions, perhaps no more so than in the workplace, where individual differences are paramount in hiring and motivating workers, and further play out in training, job design, teamwork, and broader organization-level phenomena. Person–situation fit is central to most HR functions, and managing such fit demands attention to differences among work situations and the people in them. Personality psychology, in this light, has much to contribute to HR practice, beyond that offered by the generalist principles of cognitive science.

Personality psychology bears further comparison to cognitive psychology, specifically in terms of traits. General mental ability (*g*) is widely regarded as the most important individual difference predictor of job performance. Understood as a general capacity to deal with complex information (Gottfredson, 2002), *g* is, somewhat ironically, a lot easier to work with than is personality. Building on points raised in Chapter 1 concerning personality complexities, this is true in several respects.

For one thing, the single factor, *g*, captures the large majority of performance variance attributable to mental ability. Facets of ability are readily identifiable, but they afford very little incremental prediction beyond *g*. Personality traits occupy at least five main factors, each containing more specific facets that can be differentiated conceptually and empirically as unique predictors of job performance. Second, the degree to which *g* predicts performance varies reliably as a function of just one key situational variable: job complexity (Gottfredson, 2002; Hunter, Schmidt, & Judiesch, 1990). The moderating role of job complexity is intuitively obvious, as *g* is defined as the ability to deal effectively with complex information, and so matters more in complex jobs. Situational moderators of personality trait validity are more numerous. A general moderator is job relevance, but what makes one trait job-relevant can be very different from what makes another trait job-relevant. Given numerous personality traits, there are correspondingly numerous factors to consider as possible moderators.

Third, virtually every job demands some degree of information processing, and so *g* is likely to be a valid predictor of performance in most if not all jobs. Demand for any given personality trait varies more widely across jobs. Most traits, in fact, are relevant to relatively few jobs,[1] creating special challenges in identifying particular trait–job pairings. Fourth, *g* contributes positively to performance in every job (albeit the strength of the relationship varies by job complexity), whereas either the high or the low end of a given personality trait can benefit performance, depending on the job. Some leadership roles, for example, call for nurturance in caring for and supporting followers, whereas other leadership roles demand a more tough-minded, directive style. Agreeableness will predict leadership positively in the first job and negatively in the second (cf. Judge, Bono, Ilies, & Gerhardt, 2002). Such bidirectionality is moot in the case of *g* but carries important implications for meta-analysis of personality–outcome linkages, calling for unique aggregation strategies (Tett, Jackson, Rothstein, & Reddon, 1999).

A fifth way in which personality traits are more challenging to deal with than *g* is that *g* relates to performance linearly, such that (possibly with rare exceptions) more is better along the entire *g* continuum. Personality traits generally share this linear pattern but can further relate to performance in a nonlinear fashion, such that there is an optimal trait level. Workers can be too low or too high on conscientiousness, for example, in managerial and leadership roles: Being too low generates sloppy work and being too high can create analysis paralysis. This complicates correlational analyses by the need to consider incremental prediction using polynomial terms (e.g., squares and cubes). Again, *g* requires a much simpler analysis. Sixth, the multiplicity of personality traits affords considerable opportunity for intertrait interactions. Thus, for example, dominance may yield a positive validity estimate in predicting leadership emergence when paired with high nurturance but a negative (or at least weaker) estimate when paired with low nurturance (holding situational demands for dominance constant). Such complexities do not arise when dealing with mental ability: *g* is simply *g*.

A final important point of comparison between personality traits and mental ability is that the former, unlike the latter, carries direct motivational content. Personality traits are often conceptualized as needs or are otherwise identified in terms of emotional (e.g., positive and negative affect) and motivational constructs (e.g., goal orientation). On the other hand, *g* is simply a capacity to process information. Motivation to engage one's *g* (whatever level of ability one has) must come from some other source, either internally (e.g., need for achievement or need for understanding) or externally (e.g., the promise of being paid or the threat of being fired). This raises some complexity in working with *g* as it prompts consideration (implicitly in many cases) of companion motivational constructs to fully elucidate how *g* plays out in work settings; but personality in itself combines behavioral tendencies and motivation (e.g., needs), and also requires companion constructs in the form of abilities and skills to effectively engage the given trait.

All the noted differences in complexity make dealing with personality at work more challenging than dealing with *g* at work. One arena where this has been most evident is in interpretation of meta-analytic output. Most industrial–organizational (I/O) psychologists were introduced to meta-analysis by way of Schmidt and Hunter's (1977) landmark contributions to validity generalization (VG) applied to cognitive ability. The biggest substantive impact of that research was to dispel the common assumption of the day that the validity of ability tests is situationally specific, requiring validation of such measures in every new application. Meta-analysis showed that the lion's share of variability in validity estimates of ability tests across studies was attributable to sampling error and, to lesser but notable extents, differences across studies in measurement reliability and range restriction. Accounting for such artifactual variance in validity left relatively little variance to be explained by other factors. As noted above, what variance remained was mostly attributable to differences in job complexity (Gottfredson, 2002; Hunter et al., 1990).

Despite the relatively sophisticated statistical and measurement principles underpinning meta-analysis, Schmidt and Hunter's findings supporting VG in cognitive ability tests are fairly straightforward. Basically, we have a mean uncorrected correlation of around .30, a corrected population estimate of around .50, and little cross-study variance in *r* that is not due to artifacts. VG is a triumph of simplicity: Cognitive ability tests are (at least minimally) valid in predicting performance in every job. An unfortunate consequence of this simplicity is that researchers have come to expect meta-analysis to champion situational specificity in every domain, to show that cross-study differences in validity estimates are no more than noise generated randomly by sampling error or more systematically by differential measurement artifacts (e.g., reliability). The problem is that few constructs are as uniformly relevant to job performance as cognitive ability. Individual personality traits, in particular, are far more complex as correlates of performance and routinely show evidence of situational specificity in meta-analytic output (Tett & Christiansen, 2007). In particular, artifacts typically account for relatively little observed variance across studies in the strength of personality test validity estimates. Even the direction of those estimates often varies across studies (i.e., bidirectionality), yielding weak overall means through cancellation of positive and negative values (Tett et al., 1999).

Expectations based on watershed applications of meta-analysis to cognitive ability tests have led even highly accomplished researchers (e.g., Morgeson et al., 2007) to overlook meta-analytic evidence for situational specificity in personality test validity, bringing them to conclude, emphasizing weak mean validity estimates, that personality is a generalizably poor predictor of performance (see also Chapter 28, this volume). Closer scrutiny of the evidence, especially that involving variability in r (and corrected r) not accounted for by artifacts, shows that personality tests actually offer substantially valid prediction of job performance when appropriate consideration is given to situational moderators, most notably job relevance. Failing to acknowledge bidirectionality as a special case of situational specificity (i.e., in which validity estimates vary in direction across jobs) leads to serious underestimation of the value of personality traits to predict performance through cancellation of effect sizes. Personality trait validity further doubles in strength when based on estimates from studies in which the researcher has taken steps (through rational and/or empirical preanalysis) to identify traits that are job-relevant, over estimates drawn from randomly selected trait–job pairings (Tett et al., 1999). Added to this is the fact that meta-analytic estimates of personality–performance relations are based on single traits; further increases in validity can thus be expected in light of multivariate prediction afforded by the multidimensionality of personality (i.e., using regression) and associated advantages of using specific over general trait constructs (cf. Rothstein & Goffin, 2006).

The noted challenges involving personality and its measurement mean that predictive gains from reliance on personality in the workplace are harder to realize than are those obtainable from cognitive ability. Such differences have practical implications, for example, on test utility (e.g., lowered utility due to higher costs in identifying job-relevant personality traits); but the challenges also suggest that there is substantial untapped potential in personality to advance prediction and understanding of work behavior. By coming to grips with the complexities, researchers and practitioners can anticipate higher yields from personality-based fit, applied to selection, training, and other fit-promoting strategies. These are promising matters for ongoing research, and the chapters in this Handbook offer generative foundations for such pursuits within specific contexts, applications, and theoretical and assessment paradigms.

Key Issues and Themes Moving Forward

Personality psychology in the workplace faces a number of challenges, each a hurdle to be overcome but offering opportunities for research and advancement of what personality can contribute to understanding work behavior. I focus on four main issues here, which I believe are most likely to yield dividends from personality applications at work.

Job Relevance

Earlier, it was noted that cognitive ability shows positive relations with performance in every job, but that validity estimates tend to be stronger in more complex jobs. In the simplest terms, job complexity is *relevant* to g. Hogan and Holland (2003) refer to this as conceptual "alignment." In more explanatory terms, job complexity is relevant to g to the degree the job places demands on g such that workers higher on g perform better than those lower on g. There is a logic tying job complexity to g (i.e., it makes sense) and research supports the connection (e.g., Hunter et al., 1990).

The general concept of job relevance translates well to personality: Jobs vary in the demands they place on behavior summarized and motivated by a given personality trait; a job that is relevant to trait X is one that demands behaviors expressive of X. Most leadership roles, for example, require directing and motivating followers to pursue a shared goal. Personality traits closely associated with directing and motivating behaviors include dominance, sociability, and exhibition, which combine to form the core of the FFM dimension of extraversion (E). Accordingly, leadership is relevant to E; leadership and E are conceptually aligned.

Job relevance, whether applied to personality, *g*, or any other variable used to aid organizational decision-making, has important legal, ethical, and practical implications. From a legal standpoint, claims of adverse impact are best countered by evidence of job relevance conferred by job analysis and empirical validity. Adverse impact is most often an issue with respect to *g*, but can also arise with personality (e.g., deriving from gender differences in nurturance and emotionality). Job complexity is the only substantive moderator of predictive accuracy based on *g*. Personality has potentially as many moderators as there are personality traits and their combinations. Tracking the impact of differential trait-based selection ratios across races, genders, and other minority-based taxonomies warrants increased attention as personality grows in use for selection and promotion. The job relevance of personality measures, accordingly, should be increasingly important from a legal standpoint.

Ethics are linked to job relevance with respect to fairness. Applicants generally expect to be judged fairly, without bias, on the merits of their qualifications and anticipated fit for the given job opening identified by documented work demands. Most will take as patently unfair the hiring of someone else based on qualities not relevant to performing the job (e.g., having a bubbly disposition in a job involving little interaction with others). This has negative consequences, discussed below; but hiring someone for nonjob-related reasons contradicts societal values favoring merit-based advancement, and warrants scrutiny if for no other reason than it is ethically unjustified.

Closely tied to ethics is the issue of perceived justice. Research shows that applicants tend to prefer personality tests less than other common screening tools (e.g., simulations, interviews, and ability tests; Anderson, Salgado, & Hülsheger, 2010; see Chapter 13, this volume); including assorted personality subscales in the selection battery, regardless of job relevance, feeds this negative reaction. Job relevance is practically important because personality tests are less likely to be used if test-takers and especially test users believe that screening targets behaviors and associated traits not clearly job-relevant, creating negative applicant reactions toward not only the test and screening situation per se but the hiring organization more broadly (e.g., Ni & Hauenstein, 1998).

Arguably the biggest practical concern involving the job relevance of personality tests is the underestimation of personality test validity in meta-analysis due to averaging job-relevant and job-irrelevant validity estimates. As noted earlier, measures of particular personality traits, unlike measures of *g*, are not expected to yield useful and meaningful relations with performance across all jobs. Single-sample studies of personality and job performance often report relations involving all trait measures included in an omnibus personality inventory intended to assess a wide range of traits. Very few of those traits can be expected to be relevant to performance in any given setting. Job-relevant traits, of course, are expected to yield stronger validity estimates (Tett & Christiansen, 2007; Tett, Jackson, & Rothstein, 1991), and so averaging in correlations involving irrelevant traits necessarily underestimates the overall validity estimate applicable to appropriately job-relevant cases.

This underestimation has occurred in most meta-analyses in this area, including highly influential works, such as those of Barrick and Mount (1991) and Salgado (1997). Tett et al. (1991), later replicated by Tett et al. (1999) using refined methods, showed that validity estimates based on confirmatory research strategies are around twice as strong as those based on exploratory strategies. Studies using job analysis explicitly targeting identification of job-relevant traits report validity estimates that tend to be even stronger (p = .056; Tett et al., 1999) than those based on less rigorous confirmatory methods. This is a serious practical matter because researchers look to meta-analysis for powerful answers to big questions, like the overall validity of personality measures in predicting job performance, and underestimation of personality test validity seriously threatens the continued use of such measures (cf. Morgeson et al., 2007).

Job relevance is at the heart of all these legal, ethical, and practical matters involving personality assessment for applicant screening; no other concept is more critical for the future of personality testing at work. The question then becomes how best to identify job-relevant traits out of all those available for assessment in any given job. There are two main approaches to identifying job-relevant traits, one empirical and the other content-based.

Local empirical validation strategies succeed by trial-and-error, examining a broad array of trait measures in relations with valued outcomes (e.g., job performance) and choosing those yielding statistically significant ($p < .05$, two-tailed) and practically useful (usually $r > .10$) results for hiring workers. To protect against random hits due to sampling error, the researcher is urged first to seek replication with a hold-out or some other independent sample. Rigorously conducted empirical methods for identifying job-relevant traits are routinely accepted by the courts. Notably, however, results are often reported for all trait measures included in the search (e.g., in a large correlation table) with no distinction between relevant and irrelevant measures. Reporting all results is generally good practice, except when meta-analysts aggregate all available validity estimates, allowing the more numerous, weaker, irrelevant estimates to wash out the less numerous, stronger, and relevant estimates. As noted above, the resulting underestimation of validity threatens the continued use of personality tests (cf. Morgeson et al., 2007). Accordingly, meta-analysts are urged to aggregate validity estimates for job-relevant traits independently of those for job-irrelevant traits.

Alternative empirical strategies include VG (based on meta-analysis), synthetic, or job-component, validation, and transport validation. The situational specificity of personality test validity (i.e., validity estimates for a particular trait measure vary in strength and often in direction across work settings) greatly constrains the utility of these derivative procedures. With respect to meta-analysis, just because the mean population empirical validity for extraversion in relation to managerial performance is .18 (Barrick & Mount, 1991), for example, it does not follow that the population value is .18 for extraversion in any given managerial position. Using standard meta-analytic methods involving $SD(\rho)$, the 80% credibility interval around the noted .18 mean population value is .01–.35.[2] This means that extraversion is related to managerial performance at or below .01 (including negative relationships) in 10% of job settings represented in the meta-analysis, and falls above .35 in another 10% of represented settings. A similar point applies to synthetic validation, as validity estimates for particular traits and criteria vary considerably across settings, even within similar job titles.

Transport validation, in which validity estimates derived from one job setting are applied to a targeted setting similar to the derivation setting, has potential to capitalize on empirical methods of identifying job-relevant trait measures. Situational specificity, however, again limits the viability of this approach because the targeted (i.e., new) job setting, despite documented similarities to the derivation (i.e., old) setting, may be distinct in ways relevant to the selected traits that are not assessed in the comparison (e.g., organizational or local team culture). All the complexities noted above involving personality at work make it difficult to infer with any certainty whether any two situations are sufficiently similar in trait-relevant ways to warrant generalizability of validity estimates from one to the other. Empirical strategies for identifying job-relevant personality traits are clearly viable when conducted at the local (i.e., job-specific) level; they appear to be less useful when applied across settings due to situational specificity and associated complexities involving personality at work.

The other major approach to identifying job-relevant personality traits is conceptually and theoretically driven, amounting to content validation. In this approach, the researcher carefully analyzes the job to determine a priori which traits are likely to best meet key work demands and otherwise facilitate the fit between the worker and his or her work environment. *Personality-oriented work analysis* (POWA) is covered in some detail by O'Neill, Goffin, and Rothstein in Chapter 11. I underscore their call for research into POWA methods and especially their effects on personality test validity. In light of all the noted complexities involving personality at work, identifying the important situational factors (e.g., work demands) determining which particular traits are relevant in a given setting can be no small undertaking, and developing methods to systematize such identification seems daunting as well. That confirmatory strategies yield validity estimates more than twice as strong as those from empirically driven exploratory strategies (Tett et al., 1991; Tett et al., 1999) argues, however, that this is exactly what is needed to advance personality test usage in the workplace, allowing the full potential of such tests to be realized within a suitably trait–situation interactionist framework.

One can imagine extensive investigations of POWA leading to development of an integrated system akin to O*NET that explicitly targets trait-relevant situational features (e.g., demands) that distinguish among specific work settings. In addition to lists of trait-relevant task features (e.g., serving customers as possibly relevant to dependability, sociability, and nurturance), there might also be lists of traits conceptually linked to teamwork in general, as well as to particular team types, team member roles, and even the specific sorts of individuals with whom a given team member might be expected to work (e.g., as teammates). An even more fully developed POWA could list traits especially relevant to performance and advancement in certain types of organizational, departmental, and broader national cultures. These potentially important levels of personality trait-relevance cut across jobs and industries, calling for a system beyond O*NET, which targets KSAs (knowledge, skills, and abilities) at a relatively broad, cross-organization level.

Organizations looking to use such a system for personality-based hiring would assess the task, interpersonal/team, and broader cultural demands that identify a given job opening, enter that data into an online portal, and receive lists of personality traits (as well as abilities and educational credentials) to key on in hiring best-fit candidates. Possible conflicts would be exposed (e.g., tasks demanding creativity within a rule-oriented culture), perhaps with advice as to how best to navigate those and other complexities (e.g., optimal trait levels and trait-by-trait interactions). Job seekers might just as readily enter their own unique set of traits and qualifications (or complete measures of those factors), and receive lists of jobs and particular hiring organizations where a good fit might be expected. Exploration of such possibilities is ripe for the picking and time will tell which situational features and which methods for identifying them are most helpful in advancing personality testing at work.

Besides serving as a guide to organizations seeking to hire best-fit workers, an important application of any well-developed POWA would be to serve as a framework for aggregating validity estimates across work settings. Meta-analysis of personality–outcome relations in the workplace is hampered by the lack of a unified taxonomy of situational moderators that would permit meaningful aggregation on a grand scale. By focusing on only job-relevant traits (or at least clearly distinguishing relevant from irrelevant traits), researchers could get a much better sense of the generalizable value of personality testing at work and the moderators affecting the accuracy of trait-based predictions of job performance, job satisfaction, turnover, and other indices of person–environment fit. We have reasonable taxonomies of personality traits and organizational outcomes; what is needed most at this point, rounding out the necessary ingredients for understanding personality at work, is an integrated taxonomy of situational moderators of trait–outcome linkages, and POWA research is uniquely suited to generating such a taxonomy.

Job relevance is the most critical issue facing those who seek to exploit stable individual differences in fitting people to their work environments, and POWA, accordingly, should be a key target of research going forward. Three other issues are also important in applying personality data in the workplace.

The Challenge of Applicant Faking

By far the most common way personality is assessed, whether at work or elsewhere, is by self-report questionnaire. Structured surveys offer major conveniences in administration, scoring, and interpretation but suffer from susceptibility to faking and self-deceptive biases challenging the interpretability of test scores and, accordingly, the accuracy of decisions based on those scores.

There is ongoing debate as to how problematic faking is in using self-report personality measures to hire people (see Chapter 12, this volume). Framing the debate are several key findings. Evidence suggests that (a) people *can* fake, when told to, by about one standard deviation, averaging across people, traits, and work situations; (b) people actually *do* fake by about a half standard deviation, averaging across people, traits, and work situations; (c) validity estimates for self-report personality tests are relatively unaffected by faking; but (d) selection decisions are negatively affected by faking; (e) faking is greater on job-relevant traits; (f) smarter people fake better; (g) people truly lower on desirable traits can fake more because they have more room to fake; and (h) people are expected to fake for a variety of internal reasons (e.g., ambition, competitiveness, Machiavellianism, and risk taking) and external reasons (e.g., need for paid employment). Two main implications can be drawn from these points.

First, combining points (e), (f), and (g), faking estimates based on averages across people, traits, and jobs underestimate faking by smart people truly low on job-relevant traits (Tett, Freund, Christiansen, Fox, & Coaster, 2012). Applicants with such qualities pose the biggest challenge to faking researchers. Whether and how self-report measures can be developed to overcome susceptibility to faking by smart and motivated test-takers, especially those at the nondesired pole of job-relevant traits, who pose the greatest risks in hiring, are top questions moving forward in faking research.

The second implication of the points raised above is that faking may be a positive indicator of job performance to the degree it reflects cognitive ability and other desirable qualities (e.g., ambition, social skill). A plausible reconciliation between the seemingly paradoxical points (c) and (d) is that reductions in validity due to faking on targeted job-relevant traits are offset by nontargeted traits that are nonetheless job-relevant (Tett & Simonet, 2011): Smart and ambitious people generally make better performers, and if faking reflects higher standing on such qualities, then faking may be desirable. This argument has been forwarded by influential researchers (e.g., Johnson & Hogan, 2006; Morgeson et al., 2007) and merits careful review. Several critical reasons against this line of reasoning can be identified, as follows.

First, by the logic of stable traits, bright and motivated test-takers who successfully misrepresent themselves when responding to a self-report personality test should be expected to successfully misrepresent themselves on the job, for example, in covering up CWBs such as unexcused lateness and absence. If the test-taker cannot be trusted to be honest in self-description, then why should he or she be trusted to be honest on the job? Second, those scoring lowest on job-relevant traits have the greatest opportunity to fake up, and so the biggest fakers are likely to be least suited to the job in terms of targeted traits (Tett & Christiansen, 2007). This is problematic not only for the organization, but for the faking applicant as well, whose desirable trait scores belie a poor fit to the job. Third, successful fakers will tend to bump better-fit applicants out of the running. Replacing good-fit workers with poor-fit workers is a double-cost of faking. Fourth, faking feeds the sense of injustice felt by many applicants (Gilliland, 1995), undermining reliance on personality testing as a selection tool.

The first four reasons against faking are practical. There are further serious conceptual concerns. Chief among these is the direct affront faking poses to validity. The unitarian approach to validity holds that validity "is the degree to which evidence and theory support the interpretation of test scores proposed by the test user" (American Educational Research Association, 1999; Schmitt, Arnold, & Nieminen, 2010, p. 52). In brief, it is a matter of the degree to which a test measures what it is purported to measure. Various sorts of evidence can be brought to bear in judging validity (e.g., content, criterion, and structural), but it all boils down to how much we can trust a given test to tell us where people fall on the targeted trait. Faking is, by definition, a bias intended to present oneself as better (usually, more job-suitable) than one truly believes to be the case. Thus, a self-report measure of "conscientiousness" on which test-takers fake to varying degrees assesses more than conscientiousness per se: It further assesses the ability and motivation to present oneself as more conscientious than one understands her- or himself to be. This latter ability/proclivity, of course, is not conscientiousness, and so faking is problematic because it directly undermines judgments of validity regarding what a test is truly measuring.

A more practical side of the problem is that test variance will have different independent sources, namely individual differences in the putatively targeted trait (e.g., conscientiousness) and one or more traits underlying faking (e.g., *g*, ambition, Machiavellianism). A test prone to faking is thus essentially a compound scale, severely limiting the clarity with which the test user can infer the test-taker's true standing on any of the component parts (cf. O'Neill & Paunonen's Chapter 14, this volume). If scores on a fakable test predict a valued outcome, it is impossible to know whether this is due to variance on the targeted or nontargeted traits, which, in turn, hampers efforts to refine theory and measurement toward improving prediction.

An argument that might be proposed in defense of faking, despite its undermining descriptive inferences regarding what a test is actually measuring, is that it predicts important outcomes, which is the primary aim of any assessment (cf. Hogan & Blickle's Chapter 4, this volume). This empirically driven perspective fits early conceptualizations of validity in psychological science, borne of positivistic ideals favoring direct behavioral observation and mechanical falsification of hypotheses (e.g., Meehl, 1956). According to this approach, *why* a given measure predicts job performance (for example) matters less than the fact that it *does*. There is considerable practical appeal to this view. Developments in the concept of validity (e.g., Messick, 1995) make room for predictive accuracy as evidence for validity, but they reject it as the sole or even primary basis for validity. The reason is relatively straightforward: An inference of validity is fundamentally tied to a particular defined construct (i.e., as per its nomological network; Cronbach & Meehl, 1955), yet prediction may be served by nontargeted constructs. Showing that a measure correlates in the expected direction with a relevant criterion is evidence favoring validity, but it cannot by itself rule out explanations based on constructs not targeted by the given test. If prediction of job performance based on a measure putatively targeting conscientiousness is in fact due to traits serving faking, then the prediction cannot be taken as evidence favoring the validity of inferences regarding the test as a measure of conscientiousness. The only way to infer validity in this scenario would be to change the definition of the construct (i.e., alter its nomological net): Rather than (or in addition to) conscientiousness per se, the test is measuring the ability and/or propensity to deliberately *appear* to be conscientious. This may solve the immediate problem, but it raises others, not least of which is the need to justify how successfully overstating one's conscientiousness is job-relevant. Some jobs may make this a priority (e.g., sales associate, politician); but the vast majority of jobs will rank honestly perceived conscientiousness ahead of deliberately overstated conscientiousness in the list of relevant attributes.

There is further the issue of what test-takers should be told regarding how to complete the self-report inventory. The assumption promoted by the label "conscientiousness" (even though test-takers are not informed directly of this label) is that test-takers are to answer in a way that reveals his or her honestly held beliefs about how conscientious he or she tends to be. Redefining the construct to denote the ability/propensity to overstate one's conscientiousness suggests, on purely ethical grounds as well as practical considerations of fairness and perceived justice, that respondents might be asked instead to answer the items so as to make the most favorable impression on conscientiousness. This is a fundamentally different request (corresponding directly to the fundamental distinction between the two noted constructs). Whether test users would favor such instructions over traditional honesty assumptions is unclear. In light of such concerns, faking is not easily dismissed as a problem in validation and warrants ongoing investigation regarding its detection and control.

Faking research has paralleled that of personality assessment in terms of its growing popularity and reliance on theory (Griffith & Peterson, 2006). More research is needed to address the apparent paradox that criterion validity estimates for personality tests tend to be relatively immune to faking, and yet selection decisions are negatively affected. An ideal study design, following Griffith, Chmielowski, and Yoshita (2007), is to collect self-report personality data from the same people under true hiring conditions and again under conditions favoring honesty (e.g., posthire with complete assurances of anonymity and safety). Difference scores (hiring minus honesty) could then be used as criterion data in assessing the effects of cognitive ability, need-for-employment, ambition, competitiveness, Machiavellianism, and so forth as individual difference predictors of faking. Adding performance data to the mix would permit direct tests of the value of faking and associated "faking traits" as predictors of performance, with faking serving as a mediating variable. Despite its long research history, faking leaves much to be understood, particularly regarding its causes and its impact on prediction and validity in work settings.

Alternative Personality Assessment Paradigms

Several chapters in this volume present cogent alternatives to self-report, offering at least partial remedies to the fallibility of self-description. ACs (Chapter 21), interviews (Chapter 18), and content analysis (Chapter 22) offer untapped opportunities for assessing job-relevant personality traits and trait-relevant situational moderators.

ACs are particularly well suited to these aims, balancing realism and control of nuisance variables such as cross-job differences in supervisory style, organizational culture, and a host of other factors that can confound interpretations in quasi-experimental field settings (i.e., the real world). ACs show considerable promise as grand venues for personality assessment, allowing separation of trait-expressive behavior per se from its evaluation in meeting (or not meeting) key work demands (Lievens, Tett, & Schleicher, 2009). Faking remains a possibility in ACs, but faking one's way through multiple diverse simulations is far more challenging than responding desirably to a set of self-descriptive statements whose job relevance many test-takers find transparent. Simulations presenting realistic problem scenarios offer rich opportunities to assess not only stability in behavioral propensities but also the ability to override one's behavioral tendencies to meet specific situational demands. Is such adaptability itself a product of personality traits (e.g., need for achievement, need for change)? To what degree is it conferred alternatively by skills and the promise of extrinsic rewards (e.g., a job offer)? ACs permit careful control of situational features varying in trait-relevance, and so could offer valuable data furthering understanding of trait–situation interactions and opportunities for validating traditional self-report trait measures. Given all these advantages, ACs are ideal targets of personality assessment research with special relevance to workplace applications.

Job interviews remain the most common tool for personnel selection decisions. Like ACs, interviews are more resilient to faking attempts by presenting applicants with situations more realistic and engaging than those entailed by self-report personality tests. Also like ACs, interviews permit control of unwanted variability in situational effects by presenting all applicants with the same questions and scenarios and allowing structured scoring by multiple-trained evaluators. Job interviews are much briefer than ACs and are correspondingly less expensive. It is a matter for research to determine the relative utility of interviews and ACs as personality assessment tools. One can readily envision standardized interview questions (e.g., "what-ifs") that target particular traits and combinations of traits, simulating trait-expressive processes assumed to play out on the job. The questions and scoring could be designed purely as trait measures or with evaluation built in with respect to judgments of how well a given response meets targeted work demands. Given the popularity and relatively low cost of interviews, research into their use for assessing job-relevant behavioral propensities seems likely to be accepted by organizations seeking to achieve person–job fit by way of personality.

Content analysis of application materials and behavior more generally opens up broad opportunities for personality assessment outside of specially fabricated scenarios. Assessing behavior as it occurs poses its own challenges, however, including uncontrolled differences between applicants in trait-relevant cues. One applicant, for example, might use a professional resume service, thereby eliminating spelling and grammatical errors, whereas others might rely only on their own writing skills. Choosing to use a professional service may be positively job-relevant (e.g., showing beneficial awareness of one's limitations and astuteness in overcoming them), it may be negatively job-relevant (e.g., in jobs where self-correction in writing is a key demand), or it may be irrelevant. If the latter, then quality of resume writing should properly be ignored in screening; but distinguishing the first two possibilities means having applicants show their writing skills without access to professional services, and submitting resumes typically does not afford this level of control. A further challenge is developing coding rules affording inter-rater agreement at acceptable levels. Such coding can entail considerable detail and nuances in behavioral interpretation, demanding high levels of ability and methodicalness in coding rule development and application. A third challenge is an ethical one: Is it fair to assess people on materials and behavior not deliberately submitted for review on job-relevant traits? This is perhaps no more evident than in social media (e.g., Facebook), where individuals can present themselves (or be presented by other people) in ways that appear ill-suited for a particular job.

Despite these challenges, content analysis offers access to broad swaths of human behavior indicative of true levels of personality traits and, as with ACs and interviews, further permits situational analysis to identify key trait–situation pairings. Taken to plausible extremes, one can readily imagine a world in which individuals' behavior is tracked and coded for personality under natural conditions across prolonged periods of time (e.g., in school, on recreational teams, and in previous jobs), perhaps even across the entire lifespan. The possibility of such a brave new world accentuates concerns regarding privacy and informed consent (like Facebook on steroids); but for those with nothing to hide and/or under real assurances of safety in how extracted personality data are used, content analysis affords a broad expansion of personality assessment serving the maximization of fit aimed at benefiting the individual as well as the hiring organization. Research on content analysis, whether applied to job-specific activities (e.g., resume submission) or more broadly, could have a significant impact on how future applicants are screened and promoted based on personality inferences.

All assessment methods have their strengths and weaknesses. If our goal is to maximize the fit between workers and their jobs, to the benefit of both individuals and organizations, then we need to invest in the use of multiple assessment methods so that method-specific biases can be identified, and scores "triangulated" in zeroing in on individuals' true levels of job-relevant traits. This multimethod strategy is universally recommended for job analysis; there is no reason why it should not apply in equal measure to the assessment of job applicants.

Self-report may be with us for some time to come, owing to its convenience and overall positive track record for use in predicting future work behavior. There may come a time, however, when alternative methods, such as personality-based ACs, job interviews, and content analysis of natural observations, render self-report obsolete. If such a time is on the horizon, then the noted chapters on alternative modalities for personality assessment offer programmatic direction in helping us reach that new and bold reality.

The Need for Theory

Theory is critical for the advancement of any discipline, and this is no more true than in the case of personality at work. Theory is important for knowledge growth because it attempts to explain how things work, and it is only through such understanding that we can efficiently improve the tools that apply that knowledge in practically useful ways. Imagine being in the middle ages and coming across a fully functioning SUV, complete with a key and full tank of fuel. Once figuring out how to drive this mechanical beast, you would enjoy its fantastic utility only as long as the fuel and moving parts hold out. Extended use would require understanding key processes serving internal combustion and associated systems (e.g., cooling and exhaust). One might readily deduce some basic functionality, like that involved in braking and suspension, but operation lacking theory of more complicated components would be short-lived, and efforts to improve functionality (e.g., better fuel economy) would be even more hopelessly out of reach. Personality at work rivals modern automotive technology in its complexity, and theories are accordingly even more critical for productive applications in this area. If we hope to improve our use of personality in fitting people with jobs, we need good theories to guide where best to direct our attention and how best to improve our exploitation of personality as a resource.

Several chapters in this Handbook offer detailed developments in theory pertaining to the role of personality in work settings. Other chapters, targeting applications of personality to predicting specific outcome domains (e.g., CWBs, citizenship) and to understanding key organizational functions (e.g., training, leadership), also raise theoretical issues directly relevant to personality. The theories are notably distinct and it remains to be seen which ones offer the best accounts of observed findings and drive the most productive developments and applications.

That researchers have a growing number of theories from which to choose in designing their studies shows a degree of maturation in the field, moving from raw exploration and basic rationales (e.g., definitional overlap between specific traits and criteria) to generalizable and integrated principles that cut across traits and outcomes (e.g., job relevance and trait–situation interactions), with links to more established paradigms (e.g., developmental psychology and evolutionary theory) and applications (training, motivation, and leadership). This Handbook offers several theoretical routes for making the most of personality data, and it falls to those seeking to improve personality-based fit between individuals and their work settings to continue to build and test those theories in honing our understanding and applications of personality at work.

Conclusions

If we are entering a new personality revolution in psychology—in the workplace if not elsewhere—then this Handbook offers explicit direction to those seeking to carry the revolution forward. It is a gateway to explorations of predictive potentials latent in the noted complexities and their combinations. If the cognitive revolution raised the lid on the scientific study of psychological processes, then applied research over the past 20 years has shown that personality psychology extends that line of investigation, promising especially to advance understanding of work behavior by attending to stable individual differences in behavioral tendencies and associated motivators. If application of meta-analysis to cognitive ability and its relations with job performance drew our attention to the fallacy of situational specificity in that domain, then application of meta-analysis to relations involving personality can build on our understanding of what situational specificity looks like in meta-analytic output (i.e., large $SD(\rho)$ and correspondingly wide credibility intervals around mean ρ), toward identifying plausible moderators that might account for that specificity and offer refined predictions involving particular traits and criteria.

If this volume is to have a legacy in the annals of personality at work, I hope it will be as an impetus for harnessing the potential of personality and its measurement to advance understanding of individuals' tendencies to respond to work situations and the people in them, how they come to attend to different aspects of a given situation and balance intrinsic and extrinsic forces influencing their attention and responses, and how all the moving parts—traits, abilities, skills, knowledge, demands, rewards, goals, intentions, emotions, values, and attitudes—intersect to permit and advance meaningful prediction of valued work behavior. All the chapters, in an important sense, are open chapters: Where they will take us is uncertain, but their being offered here in a single volume should stimulate readers to explore their collective implications for organizational research and practice. This concluding chapter is thus offered as an invitation to the launching of an exciting and challenging new age of exploration into the role of personality at work. This is not so much an end as it is a beginning.

Notes

1 This is not to say that personality, as a set of traits, is relevant to few jobs, but rather any single, specific personality trait. Most if not all jobs are likely to have one or more relevant personality traits, more so at higher levels of trait specificity.
2 The 80% credibility interval is derived very simply as mean $\rho \pm 1.28\ SD(\rho)$.

References

American Educational Research Association, American Psychological Association, & National Council on Measurement in Education. (1999). *Standards for educational and psychological testing*. Washington, DC: American Educational Research Association.

Anderson, N., Salgado, J. F., & Hülsheger, U. R. (2010). Applicant reactions in selection: Comprehensive meta-analysis into reaction generalization versus situational specificity. *International Journal of Selection and Assessment, 18*, 291–304.

Barrick, M. R., & Mount, M. K. (1991). The Big Five personality dimensions and job performance: A meta-analysis. *Personnel Psychology, 44*, 1–26.

Bowers, K. S. (1973). Situationism in psychology: An analysis and a critique. *Psychological Review, 80*, 307–336.

Chomsky, N. (1957). *Synthetic structures*. The Hague: Mouton.

Chomsky, N. (1959). A review of B. F. Skinner's Verbal Behavior. *Language, 35*, 26–58.

Chomsky, N. (1965). *Aspects of the theory of syntax*. Cambridge, MA: MIT Press.

Cronbach, L. J., & Meehl, P. E. (1955). Construct validity in psychological tests. *Psychological Bulletin, 52*, 281–302.

Gilliland, S. W. (1995). Fairness from the applicant's perspective: Reactions to employee selection procedures. *International Journal of Selection and Assessment, 3*, 11–19.

Gottfredson, L. S. (2002). Where and why *g* matters: Not a mystery. *Human Performance, 15*, 25–46.

Griffith, R. L., Chmielowski, T., & Yoshita, Y. (2007). Do applicants fake? An examination of the frequency of applicant faking behavior. *Personnel Review, 36*, 341–355.

Griffith, R. L., & Peterson, M. H. (2006). *A closer examination of applicant faking behavior*. Greenwich, CT: Information Age.

Hebb, D. O. (1949). *The organization of behavior*. New York: Wiley.

Hogan, J., & Holland, B. (2003). Using theory to evaluate personality and job-performance relations: A socio-analytic perspective. *Journal of Applied Psychology, 88*, 100–112.

Hunter, J. E., Schmidt, F. L., & Judiesch, M. K. (1990). Individual differences in output variability as a function of job complexity. *Journal of Applied Psychology, 75*, 28–42.

Johnson, J. A., & Hogan, R. (2006). A socioanalytic view of faking. In R. L. Griffith & M. H. Peterson (Eds.), *A closer examination of applicant faking behavior* (pp. 209–231). Greenwich, CT: Information Age.

Judge, T. A., Bono, J. E., Ilies, R., & Gerhardt, M. W. (2002). Personality and leadership: A qualitative and quantitative review. *Journal of Applied Psychology, 87*, 765–780.

Lashley, K. S. (1942). An examination of the "continuity theory" as applied to discriminative learning. *Journal of General Psychology, 26*, 241–265.

Lewin, K. (1935). *A dynamic theory of personality*. New York: McGraw-Hill.

Lievens, P., Tett, R. P., & Schleicher, D. J. (2009). Assessment centers at the crossroads: Toward a reconceptualization of assessment center exercises. *Research in Personnel and Human Resources Management, 28*, 99–152.

Meehl, P. E. (1956). Wanted—A good cook-book. *American Psychologist, 11*, 263–272.

Messick, S. (1995). Validity of psychological assessment: Validation of inferences from persons' responses and performances as scientific inquiry into score meaning. *American Psychologist, 50*, 741–749.

Mischel, W. (1968). *Personality and assessment*. New York: John Wiley & Sons.

Morgeson, F. P., Campion, M. A., Dipboye, R. L., Hollenbeck, J. R., Murphy, K., & Schmitt, N. (2007). Reconsidering use of personality tests in personnel selection contexts. *Personnel Psychology, 60*, 683–729.

Murray, H. A. (1938). *Explorations in personality*. New York: Oxford University Press.

Newell, A., & Simon, H. A. (1956). The logic theory machine: A complete information processing system. *IRE Transactions on Information Theory, 2*, 61–79.

Ni, Y., & Hauenstein, N. A. (1998). Applicant reactions to personality tests: Effects of item invasiveness and face validity. *Journal of Business and Psychology, 12*, 391–406.

Rothstein, M. G., & Goffin, R. D. (2006). The use of personality measures in personnel selection: What does current research support? *Human Resource Management Review, 16*, 155–180.

Salgado, J. F. (1997). The five factor model of personality and job performance in the European community. *Journal of Applied Psychology, 82*, 30–43.

Schmidt, F. L., & Hunter, J. E. (1977). Development of a general solution to the problem of validity generalization. *Journal of Applied Psychology, 62*, 529–540.

Schmitt, N. W., Arnold, J. D., & Nieminen, L. (2010). Validation strategies for primary studies. In J. L. Farr & N. T. Tippins (Eds.), *Handbook of employee selection* (pp. 51–71). New York: Routledge/Taylor & Francis Group.

Skinner, B. F. (1938). *The behavior of organisms: An experimental analysis*. New York: Appleton-Century.

Tett, R. P., & Christiansen, N. D. (2007). Personality tests at the crossroads: A response to Morgeson, Campion, Dipboye, Hollenbeck, Murphy, and Schmitt (2007). *Personnel Psychology, 60*, 967–993.

Tett, R. P., Freund, K. A., Christiansen, N. D., Fox, K. E., & Coaster, J. (2012). Faking on self-report emotional intelligence and personality tests: Effects of faking opportunity, cognitive ability, and job type. *Personality and Individual Differences, 52*, 195–201.

Tett, R. P., Jackson, D. N., & Rothstein, M. (1991). Personality measures as predictors of job performance: A meta-analytic review. *Personnel Psychology, 44*, 703–742.

Tett, R. P., Jackson, D. N., Rothstein, M., & Reddon, J. R. (1999). Meta-analysis of bi-directional relations in personality–job performance research. *Human Performance, 12*, 1–29.

Tett, R. P., & Simonet, D. (2011). Faking in personality assessment: A "multisaturation" perspective on faking as performance. *Human Performance, 24*, 302–321.

Tupes, E. C., & Christal, R. E. (1961). Recurrent personality factors based on trait ratings. *Journal of Personality, 60*, 225–251.

Author Index

Note: "n. " after a page number indicates the number of a note on that page.

Subject Index

Note: "n. " after a page number indicates the number of a note on that page.